A TREASURY OF
American
Literature

Selected and edited by

JOE LEE DAVIS
University of Michigan

JOHN T. FREDERICK
University of Notre Dame

FRANK LUTHER MOTT
University of Missouri

From the beginning to 1860

VOLUME I

 Grolier
INCORPORATED
NEW YORK

Acknowledgments

Grateful acknowledgment is made to the following publishers and individuals for permission to reprint material which is in copyright or of which they are the authorized publishers:

Barnes and Noble, Inc., publishers, for the selections from ORIGINAL NARRATIVES OF EARLY AMERICAN HISTORY.

Dietz Press, publishers, and Louis B. Wright, editor, for the selections from THE SECRET DIARY OF WILLIAM BYRD OF WESTOVER, 1709-1712.

Houghton Mifflin Company, for the selections from THE HEART OF EMERSON'S JOURNALS, edited by Bliss Perry, and from THE HEART OF THOREAU'S JOURNALS, edited by Odell Shepard.

Princeton University Press, for the selections from THE POETICAL WORKS OF EDWARD TAYLOR, edited by T. H. Johnson.

The United States Catholic Historical Society, for the selection from Waldseemüller's COSMOGRAPHIAE INTRODUCTIO, edited by Charles G. Herbermann.

Yale University Press, for the selections from THE AMERICAN NOTEBOOKS OF NATHANIEL HAWTHORNE, edited by Randall Stewart.

Preface

A NEW COLLEGE ANTHOLOGY of American literature, with which is integrated a comprehensive historical and critical survey, must be designed to meet the needs of students whose perspectives are growing with our complex times. It must offer to their active mentality adequate materials for study of the backgrounds of American thought, of our literary movements, and of the achievement of our best writers. With a review of the building of a national literature, it must also emphasize the internationalism or world-consciousness which has been increasingly prominent in American letters for a hundred years past and is so important today. It must present, moreover, the significant sociological aspects of our literature without neglecting or underrating distinctively esthetic considerations.

These aims have been those of the editors of this work throughout its planning and its making. They have given unusual space and attention to the achievement of the eight American writers now generally recognized to have contributed most conspicuously to the great stream of world literature—Poe, Emerson, Thoreau, Hawthorne, Melville, Whitman, Mark Twain, and Henry James. They have endeavored to present a comprehensive view of the growth of American culture in the development of our literature from the earliest times to the immediate present, but the emphasis has been placed squarely upon the masterpieces and the ideas which these authors, whose work transcends national boundaries, have contributed to the world. Here are the spokesmen whose words are that "something so written to after times" that Americans "should not willingly let it die."

Each of the two volumes is divided into two Books. In Book I of Volume I, the period from the beginnings to 1800 is represented by many selections which are arranged to trace three broad, simple themes: (1) exploration, settlement, and travel; (2) religious thought and experience; and (3) the issues of democracy. It is believed that these generally recognized major themes in Colonial and Early National literature are nowhere else represented so amply or so followed through in orderly arrangement without further distracting groupings. In this section texts are modernized, and translations supplement the English documents to show the polyglot nature of our early culture. Book I is

v

also especially designed to be used as background in the study of the work of our authors with world stature; early writers on religion illuminate the work of Hawthorne and Emerson, and early commentators on democracy are valuable for the understanding of Thoreau, Emerson, and Whitman.

In Book II (Volume I) the period from 1800 to 1860 is approached in terms of cultural patterns—the founding of a national literature, the frontier, humanitarianism and reform, transcendentalism, and humanism. But a large proportion of the selections in Book II consists of leading works by the major writers of the period, each of whom is more fully represented than is usual in general anthologies. Poe, Emerson, Thoreau, Hawthorne, and Melville—five writers of world significance— may here be read in works which should form a part of every American's educational experience. In this section is evident the purpose of the editors to provide a rich context of the writing of the times largely in order to clarify and give point to the great contributions made by the major authors. Thus are included salient writings of Irving, Bryant, Cooper, Simms, Longfellow, Whittier, and Lowell, with briefer selections from minor figures. All these help to define the tendencies which are reflected, but at the same time transcended, by the work of the authors who occupy the central place in this anthology.

In Book III (Volume II) the period from 1860 to 1900 is similarly treated. Here the patterns are four: the reaffirmation of democracy, the new regionalism, the critical reflection of a changing America, and the international theme. The major writers are Whitman, Mark Twain, and Henry James. Their work emerges from a setting formed by selections from Lanier, Holmes, Emily Dickinson, Howells (who is especially well represented), and a considerable number of lesser writers.

In Book IV (Volume II) is found work of the period from 1900 to the present by writers whom the editors believe to have strong claims on our continuing attention. The first group of selections attempts to present adequately and relate significantly the work of recent philosophers and literary critics. This section serves to define both the ideological and the esthetic problems faced by Twentieth Century writers, and thus correlates with the two groups which follow—one devoted to fiction and one to poetry. The selections close with a limited sampling of the work of more recent writers who may be regarded as forerunners of tomorrow.

A leading feature of the present work is the series of historical and critical essays which accompany and interpret the groups of selections. The extensive historical introductions provided for each of the four Books, together with the full critical and biographical essays on each of the major writers and the briefer treatments (varying from short head-notes to rather full discussions) of lesser figures, are designed to form a concise but adequate critical survey of American literature. This material is intended to help the student reader to understand and appreciate the selections. It is intended to be helpful to the teacher because it relieves him from the presentation in lecture form of necessary data. The authors have sought to avoid rash theorizing and innovation for its own sake as earnestly as they have sought to escape empty conventionality, to suggest new approaches, to point out the latest scholarship, and to challenge the thinking of the student.

The critical, historical, biographical, and bibliographical materials are closely integrated with the selections in both arrangement and substance. The annotated bibliographies list the standard authorities and the more recent works of importance and value.

There are many methods of teaching American literature. Any one of them may be successful in the practice of a great teacher. But it is the belief of the editors that the present work, with its unusually copious selections from the greatest writers and its offering of various and stimulating supplementary literature, together with its historical and critical surveys, will lend itself to the most diverse uses in actual teaching. With that conviction they offer it to their fellow teachers.

The editors wish to thank Messrs. Joseph Warren Beach, University of Minnesota, William Charvat, Ohio State University, and Thomas H. Johnson, Lawrenceville School, for aid and advice during the preparation of this anthology.

J. L. D.
J. T. F.
F. L. M.

[Dates inserted following the titles of selections represent the first publication in book form. When a selection was previously published in a periodical, the date of that publication is added in parentheses.]

Contents

⟋

VOLUME ONE

BOOK I: AMERICAN LITERATURE BEFORE 1800

PART II: RELIGIOUS THOUGHT AND EXPERIENCE

PART III: THE ISSUES OF DEMOCRACY

BOOK II: AMERICAN LITERATURE 1800-1860

PART II: THE FRONTIER, WEST AND SOUTH

PART III: HUMANITARIANISM IN NEW ENGLAND

CONTENTS

PART IV: TRANSCENDENTALISM

PART V: HUMANISM AND BEYOND

BOOK I

American Literature Before 1800

I

EXPLORATION, SETTLEMENT, AND TRAVEL

II

RELIGIOUS THOUGHT AND EXPERIENCE

III

THE ISSUES OF DEMOCRACY

I

CREATIVE writers and literary critics are in the habit of using the word "literature" somewhat narrowly to include only *belles-lettres* or writings distinguished by formal aesthetic intention and effect—in other words, poetry, drama, fiction, and the essay. Their exhortations, prophecies, and strictures—from Emerson, Whitman, and Lowell to H. L. Mencken, Branch Cabell, and Van Wyck Brooks—have tended to produce in the average reader the impression that American literature has always been, and still is, comparatively "young," that its real beginnings should be dated after 1800, that only in the 19th Century or our own day has it come of age, that its full maturity yet lies ahead.

Historians and bibliographers have an altogether different conception of the word "literature." They apply it loosely to embrace every kind of written document which yields information as to how men have lived or what they have thought or felt in a given period. The labors of such scholars—of Moses Coit Tyler in his *A History of American Literature During the Colonial Time* and *The Literary History of the American Revolution,* of Charles Evans in his *American Bibliography,* and of Joseph Sabin and Wilberforce Eames in their *Bibliotheca Americana*—have shown that American literature before 1800 consists of a vast body of documents representing the printing presses of two hemispheres and recording two centuries and more of experience and reflection.

Of these two seemingly antithetical views, the second is an indispensable corrective for the first. There is little doubt, of course, that the literature which "matters" for the average reader is "the literature of power" rather than "the literature of knowledge," to employ Thomas De Quincey's famous distinction. We should read to add to our stature, not as antiquarians, but as men and women. For this reason it is entirely valid to chart the history of American literature in terms of the emergence of the aesthetically first-rate, whatever one may consider this to be. But such charting is bound to be an arbitrary and capricious falsification unless it is based on a more than superficial acquaintance with the kind of writing Americans did in what may be called the pre-aesthetic centuries of their expression. In some of this writing the aesthetic motive is to be found in its germinal state alongside the practical motive. Much of this writing actually provided subject-matter for later belletristic achievements. Most of it helps us to understand some phase of the many-sided American spirit that inspired our best 19th Century writers and still inspires our best 20th Century ones—its adventurous self-reliance, its faith in divinely establ lished moral law, its animus against all forms of tyranny, including that of the people themselves when under the influence of unscrupulous demagogues. Finally, it must not be forgotten that the first American "literature of power," our earliest poetry, fiction, essay-writing, and drama, makes its appearance before 1800, and that some of it is far better than mere apprentice work,—is, indeed, pure gold amidst the quartz.

II

The growth of American colonial literature is intimately connected with the fortunes of American colonial printing. J. Dumbleton, a forgotten versifier of the 18th Century, had this relationship in mind when, to celebrate the establishment of a paper mill by the printer, William Parks, he contributed the following verses to the *Virginia Gazette*:

> The sage Philosophers have said
> Of nothing, can be nothing made;
> Yet much thy will, O Parks, brings forth
> From what we reckon nothing worth.
>
> . . . .
>
> The Bards, be sure, their Aids will lend;
> The Printer is the Poet's Friend;
> Both cram the News, and stuff the Mills,
> For Bards have rags, and—little else.

The earliest books written about America or by Americans either remained in manuscript or were published in Europe. Probably the first printing press to be set up in the New World came from the shop of one of the leading printers of Spain in the 16th Century, Juan Cromberger, of Seville, and its operation was begun under the direction of Juan Pablos in Tenochtitlán, Mexico, sometime in the early 1540's. Four books produced by this press in 1543 and 1544 are in the possession of the New York Public Library. All are theological or devotional in content. The first printing press in English-speaking America arrived at Cambridge, Massachusetts, almost a century later, in September, 1638, and was in operation sometime before October 10 of that same year. It had been sent from England as a result of the efforts of the Reverend Josse Glover, the original publicity man for Harvard College. The twelve overseers of the College provided living quarters for the inaugurator of the printing-house, Stephen Daye, and his family. It was probably his son, Matthew Day, already an experienced printer at the age of eighteen, who printed the first English books in America. After the death of Matthew Day, Samuel Green was appointed printer for the Harvard College press. Between 1649 and 1692, the years of his active connection with it, 190 items were issued, including the first American printing of the Bible, translated into the language of the Natick Indians by the Reverend John Eliot. The New and Old Testaments of the *Up-Biblum God,* the title Eliot coined for "Holy Bible," ran to a total of 1,088 pages. So monumental was this project that Green, on the strength of undertaking it, acquired a new press and other equipment from England. Marmaduke Johnson, who was added to Green's staff to produce the Indian Bible, became the third Massachusetts printer and the first American to found a printing-house as a private business enterprise. He founded it at Boston in 1674, and on his death that same year the house passed into the control of John Foster. Among later Boston printers should be mentioned Thomas Fleet, Samuel Kneeland, Gamaliel Rogers and Daniel Fowle, Benjamin Edes and John Gill. Isaiah Thomas, who started in the printing business in Boston and later moved to Worcester, wrote the still standard work, *The History of Printing in America,* which he published in 1810.

Printing in the Southern Colonies was begun in the 1680's by William Nuthead, at first in Virginia and then in Maryland. He was followed by William Parks, who established a press at Annapolis, Maryland, in the middle 1720's, and at Williamsburg, Virginia, in 1730. William Bradford, not to be confused with the historian of Plymouth Plantation, was the first printer in the Middle Colonies. A member of William Penn's colonizing expedition in 1682, he began to print either near or in Philadelphia in 1685, with a press he had just brought from London. In 1693 he moved to New York City, where he had as an apprentice John Peter Zenger, later famous as a champion of liberty of the press. Among 18th Century printers, the Franklin family, including James, Ann, and the great Benjamin himself, deserve special citation. Beginning at Boston, James moved on to Newport, Rhode Island, and was succeeded by his widow, Ann, while Benjamin became a prosperous printer in Philadelphia. The name of William Goddard should also be remembered. Founder of the United States postal system, he operated printing presses in New Haven, Connecticut; in Providence, Rhode Island; and in New York City, Philadelphia, and Baltimore. It was not until the late 18th Century that printing moved into the Middle West. Extant Cincinnati imprints date from 1793; extant Detroit imprints from 1797.

Accounts of exploration and descriptions of the fauna and flora of the New World served often as excellent propaganda for colonization. Furthermore they were always in demand to satisfy the Old World's widespread popular interest in overseas adventure. Hence their publication proved profitable for European printers; and many such works, which must be regarded as a part of American literature, had appeared abroad in several languages before printing in the Americas amounted to very much. Political and religious controversy in early New England vented itself in pamphlets and books published in London.

Not only were the disputants seeking a foreign jury; the issues with which they were belligerently concerned were the same ones that were being debated in the mother country. American printers, however, had plenty of work to do as they set up their presses. Either at their own risk or at the expense of the authors, they issued a great number of sermons in pamphlet form and eventually attempted such tomes as Samuel Willard's 988-page *A Compleat Body of Divinity*, Boston, 1726. Booksellers placed orders with them for psalters and psalm-books. Laws and ordinances of provincial governments were routine jobs.

Perhaps the three most important ventures undertaken by these printers were, in chronological sequence, almanacs, newspapers, and magazines. Matthew Day inaugurated the vogue of the almanac when he issued that of Captain William Pierce in 1638, no copy of which is extant, and that of Samuel Danforth "for the year of our Lord 1646," the oldest existing specimen of printing in the English-speaking colonies. Of the many almanacs that followed, those compiled by Daniel Leeds and his sons and printed by William Bradford and those both written and published by the brothers Franklin are the most interesting for their verse and essays. Preceded by a broadside entitled *The Present State of New English Affairs*, issued by Samuel Green in 1689, and a promptly suppressed news-sheet entitled *Publick Occurrences, Both Forreign and Domestick*, Boston, September 25, 1690, the first regularly published American newspaper was a weekly, the *Boston News-Letter*, started by John Campbell. Its initial number was dated "From Monday, April 17, to Monday, April 24, 1704." James Franklin's *New-England Courant*, which was the fourth weekly newspaper to be printed in the colonies, started the vogue of essay-writing in the style of the *Spectator* when it featured the "Silence Dogood" papers of Benjamin Franklin and other contributions intended to "expose the Vices and Follies of Persons of all Ranks and Degrees, under feign'd Names . . ." The first daily newspaper in America was the *Pennsylvania Evening Post, and Daily Advertiser*, which made its appearance in Philadelphia, June 17, 1783, and was published by Benjamin Towne, formerly a partner of William Goddard. In January, 1741, the first two American magazines were established, both in Philadelphia. Andrew Bradford, son of the printer William Bradford, brought out his *American Magazine, or a monthly view of the Political State of the Colonies*, three days ahead of Benjamin Franklin's *General Magazine, and Historical Chronicle, for all the British Plantations in America*. The first of these lasted for only three numbers, the second for only six, but they were forerunners of many more before 1800, some of which, such as the *American Museum*, the *Massachusetts Magazine*, and the *New York Magazine*, were of relatively long life. During the last three decades of the 18th Century, from the onset of the Revolution to the triumph of Jefferson at the polls, American printers issued a vast literature of political pamphlets, as well as important travel-books, histories, plays, novels, and volumes of poetry.

III

So much for the printing record. As for the literature itself, it is so extensive, heterogeneous, and inchoate that the schemes of presentation and frames of order commonly used by the literary historian cannot be applied to it without seeming somewhat inappropriate and futile. To treat of it according to periods, each with its *zeit-geist* or prevailing climate of opinion and taste, is to read into it patterns that only the literature of a full-fledged nation and a settled culture actually reflects. To discuss it in terms of literary types is to attribute to many of its writers a self-conscious concern with form which they in all likelihood did not possess and to lose oneself in attempts to define precisely the scope and limits of "the pamphlet of newes," frequently written to lure new colonists across the Atlantic, or of "the scientific essay," as this was developed by the almanac-makers, or of other genres still more indeterminable. A less misleading approach, even though it involves oversimplification and considerable omission, is to select the main themes or motifs, the broad obvious emphases and directions, of this literature, and to follow each one through from its beginnings to whatever point it had reached by 1800.

The earliest, the most persistent, the most fascinating of these themes was the mastering of the new physical environment, of the whole vast strange continent abounding with peril and promise, with infinite surprises of beauty and evil. This mastering had three main stages. First was the stage of exploration from European ports. It began long before Columbus, during the Norse revival that sent Viking swaggerers and brawlers eastward into Russia, southward into Normandy and England, and also westward to make important geographical discoveries. These discoveries were a kind of wild overture to the incredible sustained opera of bold enterprise that was to begin with the voyages of Columbus. The age of feudalism was passing. In the cities of mediaeval Europe had arisen a new capitalism, far more expansive than that of ancient Rome or of contemporaneous Byzantium. Baronial localism and ecclesiastical universalism, which between them had constituted the temporal and spiritual "order" of the Middle Ages, were yielding to powerful integrated national states, competing with each other for commercial supremacy. Developments in science, including the wide use and perfection of such instruments of navigation as the compass and the astrolabe and the rise of a new cosmography, a new astronomy, a new mathematics, affected the course which this competition was to take. Portugal, Spain, France, England, and the Netherlands sent explorers westward. The aim of finding a new and better passage to India yielded to the aim of exploiting the New World, which had been so inappropriately named "America" by an obscure pedantical cosmographer.

The second stage was that of settlement or colonization. The competition between the great states of Europe continued. Religious conflict and persecution, economic depression and insecurity, were European evils that now became added incentives to colonization. One of the last states of Europe to enter the competition for a place in the western sun—England—began to win out in North America, partly because, of all these states, she had the largest number of dissatisfied and exploited "good citizens." These "good citizens" swarmed overseas to establish the Southern, the New England, and the Middle Colonies of the Atlantic seaboard. Each settlement had its individual problems, political, economic, religious, and all had to deal in one way or another with the Indians. As these individual problems were solved, as the Indians were Christianized or counter-massacred or driven farther inland, the seaboard settlements became true outposts of European civilization, and the frontier was created—a line of straggling, turbulent settlements moving ever westward.

At this point began the third stage of mastering the new environment— the stage of American travel, either from one part of the seaboard to another or into the still mysterious, the ever-beckoning West. These three great stages— exploration, settlement, and travel—were "matters" which the first poets, dramatists, and novelists of the new nation had at their disposal and which they did not neglect. The literature recording these three stages—from *The Flat Island Book* and Columbus' Letter through the histories of Bradford and Winthrop to the travels of Jonathan Carver and William Bartram, and the historical fiction of Mrs. Rowson—exhibits all gradations of narrative art or the lack of it and reveals fully the kinds of personalities in which the polyglot national character of the early 19th Century had its roots.

IV

Another central theme in American literature before 1800 was religion. Although most of the colonists risked the tremendous hazards of the overseas voyage because they thought the New World would afford them a chance to make a better living, many of them put alongside this motive the need of worshipping God in their own way. What they encountered on the voyage and after they arrived confirmed them in their supernaturalism: Only a power greater than themselves had enabled them to surmount the malice of circumstance. Without belief in such a power, they could not confront intrepidly or calmly the hardships, the violence, the loneliness that they knew lay ahead.

Religion meant two things to them—a corpus of thought and a mode of experience. In treatises and sermons, they formulated their ideas about general and particular providence, grace and revelation, sin and repentance and judgment. In intimate prose narratives or ventures into verse, they recorded the ebb and flow of their spiritual feelings. Sometimes the ideas and the feelings curiously commingled to produce versified doctrine, as in the case of Wigglesworth or Freneau, or philosophical rhapsody, as in the case of Jonathan Edwards.

Puritanism, Quaker and Methodist Enthusiasm, Deism—these were the three great religious forces that had most impact upon the literature of the English-speaking colonies. Each originated in Europe and had there a long and complicated history. Yet each developed peculiar nuances and distinctive spokesmen in the American environment. Puritanism, which in 17th Century England was rapidly transformed in the crucible of the Civil War and the laboratory of the Commonwealth, achieved in New England an orthodoxy that opposed all forms of sectarian and individualistic worship and that provided dogmatic patterns and limits for the guidance and advancement of scientific learning. This orthodoxy was gradually undermined from within as its leading concepts were subtly affected by the 18th Century climate of opinion. From without, this orthodoxy was formidably challenged by the rise of Enthusiasm and Deism, both of which appeared to some extent in New England itself but had their fullest growth and widest spread in the Middle and the Southern Colonies. Enthusiasm, whether Quaker or Methodist or of a more outlandish type, tended to exaggerate and democratize the emotive elements held in solution in the Puritan synthesis. In Deism, the Reason and Nature which Puritan thought regarded as among the sources of insight into God's plan were turned against the Scripture, which Puritan thought had asserted to be the supreme and final arbiter, at least when interpreted by a properly educated clergy.

Puritanism had the distinction of producing in Edward Taylor one of the finest poets, and in Jonathan Edwards one of the greatest philosophers, of America before 1800. Deism, although it did not *produce* writers as great as these, had the distinction of serving as the religion of a Freneau, a Paine, a Jefferson. Enthusiasm was responsible for a considerable amount of writing, but most of it was of indifferent literary merit. William Penn and John Woolman were the best prose stylists and thinkers that any Enthusiastic sect could boast of. Yet it was Enthusiasm that provided material for *Wieland,* one of the most readable books by the father of the American novel, Charles Brockden Brown.

V

Puritanism, Enthusiasm, Deism, and the unclassifiable individualistic credo of a Roger Williams, no matter what their differences, had one tenet in common —that there exists a fundamental moral law of divine origin. The belief in such a law was necessary for the full development of two ideas: (1) that the individual is free, in the sense that he can attain to understanding of the fundamental law and can conduct himself in obedience to it; and (2) that hence, with the growth of a proper individualism, the external controls established by the state can be gradually minimized and even dispensed with. With the clear emergence of these ideas in the 19th Century, the American Dream was full-blown, and democracy became a world-shaking faith. But it still had its pros and cons, of long standing, and these may be said to have constituted a third main theme of American literature before 1800.

The importance of the state, and of the obligations which the individual owed to it, was a ruling concept of Renaissance political thought. Puritans had suffered persecution in England as a result of the hold which this concept had on the administrative mind. When they themselves faced the task of administering a state in the New World, they adopted the same concept, with a canny insensitivity to the contradiction, and were for a while as crustily disregardful of the rights of the individual as any high-church authoritarian back home. When they carried their policy too far, Roger Williams and others amongst their number challenged them. The challenge was significant because it eventually led to the establishment of one of the Four Freedoms—freedom of religion—as a Constitutional right. In the 17th Century the fight for this freedom was waged, not only in New England, but in the Southern Colonies as well. It was in New England, however, that its pros and cons found most adequate literary expression—in the writings of John Winthrop, John Cotton, Nathaniel Ward, and Roger Williams.

The next series of colonial documents setting forth the controversies of democracy was the offspring of conflicts during the 17th and early 18th Century between the colonists and their royal governors. These conflicts were not confined to any one colony or group of colonies. The three most significant involved Governors Berkeley of Virginia, Andros of New England, and Cosby of New York. Freedom from fear was one of the several rights for which the colonists were struggling; freedom of speech and the press was the real issue at the trial of the printer, John Peter Zenger. Already, however, conservative or Tory polemics were taking shape. Against the spirit of insurgency was advanced the view that the great foes of orderly rule were the demagogue and the mob. The profoundest expression of the spirit of insurgency during this period was the work of John Wise.

Most revolutions begin, not on the plane of action, but on the plane of the spoken and written word. The American Revolution was no exception. Such clergymen as Jonathan Mayhew and such publicists as John Adams prepared the way for it when they drew arguments for the rights of the colonists from the great tradition of England's own revolutionary apologetics, best represented perhaps by Milton and Locke. The Loyalist clergyman, Jonathan Boucher, tried to reanimate the tradition of England's anti-revolutionary propaganda, but to no avail. The three major writers of the Revolution were the radical democrats, Paine, Jefferson, and Freneau. One of the works of Paine, *Agrarian Justice*, which was inspired by the French rather than by the American Revolution, outdistanced most of the political and economic writing of its time in visionary democracy by expounding a plan to promote freedom from want.

Democracy may be defined as that form of government in which the majority rules with constant respect for individual and minority rights. Among minority rights may be included: (1) the rights of defeated political parties; (2) the rights of the states or of each section or region of which the nation is composed; (3) the rights of each of the socio-economic classes—workingmen, bourgeoisie, capitalists, and the like; (4) the rights of foreign, colored, and "racial" groups; (5) the rights of religious sects. It is arguable that the Four Freedoms are primarily individual and minority rights. Freedom of speech has meaning chiefly with reference to members of political parties out of power and to the intelligentsia as a class. Freedom of religion applies most to religious sects. Freedom from want has meaning largely for exploited working-class groups. Freedom from fear, save when interpreted as freedom from the threat of aggressive war, relates most closely to the status and treatment of foreign, colored and "racial" groups.

This definition of democracy is, of course, but one of many. Among its merits is the emphasis that democracy at its best is a precarious equilibrium of forces, a constantly threatened compromise between extremes, a dynamic resolution of paradoxical values. When the majority rules without proper respect for individual and minority rights, one form of tyranny insinuates itself. When majority rule is directly or indirectly usurped, and individual and minority rights are flaunted, by any one minority, such as a combination of states, or vested economic interests, or a bureaucracy of office-holders, democracy is negated or obstructed. And of course any form of legal slavery means that democracy is quite incomplete.

In the post-Revolutionary period, the discussion of the new Constitution, the strife between Federalists and anti-Federalists, with their very different concepts of the centralized and the decentralized state, and the excitement produced by the French Revolution and its refugees—all created a tremendous popular interest in the meaning of democracy. A soberer critical spirit may be said to have replaced revolutionary fervor. The Hamilton of *The Federalist,* the Franklin of the Constitutional Convention, the Jefferson of the 1801 Inaugural, the John Adams who now exchanged letters with Samuel Adams were more mature political thinkers than the John Adams of the *Dissertation on the Canon and the Feudal Law,* the Paine of *Common Sense,* the Jefferson of the Declaration of Independence. One of the literary monuments of this period of constructive criticism of the democratic ethos was the satire of Brackenridge. Even though the Federalists went down in defeat in the first year of the new century, suspicion of the demagogue and of the mob persisted, and Jefferson himself was to propose a plan of education that had among its objectives, not only the raising of the general electorate's mental level, but also the creation of an aristocracy of talent to provide humane and rational political and other kinds of leadership.

VI

American literature before 1800 can be related in many ways to that of the 19th and 20th Centuries. Of the eight major American writers of the 19th Century, Melville and Mark Twain have an adventurous self-reliance and a narrative gusto that far surpass, but at least suggest, the spirit and style of some of the early explorers and travelers. The religious thought and experience of Puritans, Enthusiasts, and Deists involved concepts—of God, of the Inner Light, of Nature—that received a new formulation and synthesis in the essays and poems of Emerson. Hawthorne and Thoreau actually steeped themselves in colonial narratives of exploration, settlement, travel, and religious experience. The subject-matter of some of Hawthorne's best fiction, Thoreau's view of nature—these owe a good deal to such reading. Some of the poems of Freneau and the best novels of Charles Brockden Brown mark the beginnings of that concern for aesthetic effect that is so pronounced in the poetry and fiction of Poe. Whitman, in "Passage to India," celebrates the great explorers; in "Chanting the Square Deific," he adds Satan to the Trinity and so conceives the Holy Ghost that it might easily square the circle; in his *Democratic Vistas,* there is scathing criticism of the realities of democracy in the early Gilded Age and yet the most rhapsodic rhetoric about democracy's ideals and future. As for 20th Century American writers, the re-evaluation of democracy has been for them a constantly more important concern, as unprecedented national and international crises have produced cumulative repercussions in their creative consciousness. So necessary for this re-evaluation did John Dos Passos consider Roger Williams and several of the publicists of the Revolution that he wrote a book about them, *The Ground We Stand On* (1941), with an introductory chapter entitled "The Use of the Past." If such recognition seems somewhat belated, one should remember that on July 4, 1945, the city of New Rochelle, New York, officially conferred on Thomas Paine the American citizenship it had denied him 139 years before.

The best short histories of America before 1800 are Curtis Nettels' *The Roots of American Civilization* (New York, 1938) and Max Savelle's *The Foundations of American Civilization* (New York, 1942). John Clyde Oswald's *Printing in the Americas* (New York, 1938), Frank Luther Mott's *A History of American Magazines 1741-1850* (New York, 1930), the first volume of his three-volume work, and *American Journalism* (New York, 1941), and W. W. Sweet's *Religion in Colonial America* (New York, 1942) are standard treatments of their subjects. Moses Coit Tyler's *A History of American*

Literature During the Colonial Time in two volumes (revised edition, New York, 1897, of a work originally published in 1879) and *The Literary History of the American Revolution, 1763-1783,* also in two volumes (New York, 1897), have never been superseded. Among important contributions to American intellectual history before 1800 are V. L. Parrington's *The Colonial Mind* (New York, 1927), the first volume in his *Main Currents in American Thought;* B. F. Wright's *American Interpretations of Natural Law* (Cambridge, Mass., 1931); Joseph Haroutunian's *Piety Versus Moralism: the Passing of the New England Theology* (New York, 1932); E. A. J. Johnson's *American Economic Thought in the Seventeenth Century* (London, 1932); G. A. Koch's *Republican Religion: the American Revolution and the Cult of Reason* (New York, 1933); Perry Miller's *The New England Mind* (New York, 1939); Leon Howard's *The Connecticut Wits* (Chicago, 1943); Merle Curti's *The Growth of American Thought* (New York, 1943); Ralph Barton Perry's *Puritanism and Democracy* (New York, 1944); and Herbert W. Schneider's *A History of American Philosophy* (New York, 1947).

Among the more readable biographical studies devoted to early American worthies and men of letters may be listed the following: S. E. Morison's *Builders of the Bay Colony* (Boston, 1930); George F. Willison's *Saints and Strangers* (New York, 1945); S. H. Brokunier's *The Irrepressible Democrat, Roger Williams* (New York, 1945); Kenneth B. Murdock's *Increase Mather* (Cambridge, 1925); Ola Elizabeth Winslow's *Jonathan Edwards* (New York, 1940); Carl Van Doren's *Benjamin Franklin* (New York, 1938); Frank Smith's *Thomas Paine, Liberator* (New York, 1938); Claude G. Bowers' series, *Young Jefferson* (Boston, 1945), *Jefferson and Hamilton* (Boston, 1925), and *Jefferson in Power* (Boston, 1936); C. M. Newlin's *The Life and Writings of Hugh Henry Brackenridge* (Princeton, 1932); and Lewis Leary's *That Rascal Freneau* (New Brunswick, N. J., 1941).

Important essays on various aspects of American literature before 1800 are to be found in Perry Miller and T. H. Johnson's *The Puritans* (New York, 1938) and in F. L. Mott and C. E. Jorgenson's *Franklin* (New York, 1936), C. H. Faust and T. H. Johnson's *Edwards* (New York, 1935), H. H. Clark's *Paine* (New York, 1944), and F. C. Prescott's *Hamilton and Jefferson* (New York, 1934), all in American Writers Series.

American Literature Before 1800

I

EXPLORATION, SETTLEMENT, AND TRAVEL

From

The Vinland History of the Flat Island Book

c. 1380 (MS.)

NOT LONG before the year 985, the Norseman, Eric the Red, discovered Greenland and later attempted to colonize it. The best account of Eric is contained in one of the Icelandic sagas or prose narratives known as *The Saga of Eric the Red*. It remained for Eric the Red's son, Leif, to discover Vinland about the year 1000. Having sailed from Greenland to Norway, where he was baptized at the court of King Olaf, he returned to Greenland, where he visited another explorer, Biarni Heriulfsson, also recently arrived from Norway and full of news of lands he had seen. The most circumstantial account of Leif's discovery of Vinland is contained in one of the Icelandic sagas or prose narratives in that vellum manuscript known as *The Flat Island Book* because it was long owned by a family that lived on Flat Island in Broad Firth on the north-western coast of Iceland. Most of the material contained in *The Flat Island Book* was transcribed about 1380 by two priests from originals of which nothing is known. [The following selection is taken from a translation of "The Vinland History" of *The Flat Island Book* included in *The Northmen, Columbus, and Cabot 985-1503*, New York, 1906, one of the volumes in the series, *Original Narratives of Early American History*.]

THERE was now much talk about voyages of discovery. Leif, the son of Eric the Red, of Brattahlid [Eric's home in the Eastern Settlement of Greenland], visited Biarni Heriulfsson and bought a ship of him, and collected a crew, until they formed altogether a company of thirty-five men. Leif invited his father, Eric, to become the leader of the expedition, but Eric declined, saying that he was then stricken in years, and adding that he was less able to endure the exposure of sea-life than he had been. Leif replied that he would nevertheless be the one who would be most apt to bring good luck, and Eric yielded to Leif's solicitation, and rode from home when they were ready to sail. When he was but a short distance from the ship, the horse which Eric was riding stumbled, and he was thrown from his back and wounded his foot, whereupon he exclaimed, "It is not designed for me to discover more lands than the one in which we are now living, nor can we now continue longer together." Eric returned home to Brattahlid, and Leif pursued his way to the ship with his companions, thirty-five men; one of the company was a German named Tyrker. They put the ship in order, and when they were ready, they sailed out to sea, and found first that land which Biarni and his ship-mates found last. They sailed up to the land and cast anchor, and launched a boat and went ashore, and saw no grass there; great ice mountains lay inland back from the sea, and it was as a flat rock all the way from the sea to the ice mountains, and the country seemed to them to be entirely devoid of good qualities. Then said Leif, "It has not come to pass with us in regard to this land as with Biarni, that we have not gone upon it. To this country I will now give a name, and call it Helluland." They returned to the ship, put out to sea, and found a second land. They sailed again to the land, and came to anchor, and launched the boat, and went ashore. This was a level wooded land, and there were broad stretches of white sand, where they went, and the land was level by the sea. Then said Leif, "The land shall have a name after its nature, and we will call it Markland." They returned to the ship forthwith, and sailed away upon the main with north-east winds, and were out two "doegr" [1] before they sighted land. They sailed toward this land, and came to an island which lay to the northward off the land. There they went ashore and looked about them, the weather being fine, and they observed that there was dew upon the grass, and it so happened that they touched the dew with their hands, and touched their hands to their mouths, and it seemed to them that they had never before tasted anything so sweet as this. They went aboard their ship again and sailed into a certain sound, which lay between the island and a cape, which jutted out from the land on the north, and they stood in westering past the cape. At ebb-tide there were broad reaches of shallow water there, and they ran their ship aground there, and it was a long distance from the ship to the ocean; yet were they so anxious to go ashore that they could not wait until the tide should rise under their ship, but hastened to the land, where a certain river flows out from a lake. As

soon as the tide rose beneath their ship, however, they took the boat and rowed to the ship, which they conveyed up the river, and so into the lake, where they cast anchor and carried their hammocks ashore from the ship, and built themselves booths there. They afterwards determined to establish themselves there for the winter, and they accordingly built a large house. There was no lack of salmon there either in the river or in the lake, and larger salmon than they had ever seen before. The country thereabouts seemed to be possessed of such good qualities that cattle would need no fodder there during the winters. There was no frost there in the winters, and the grass withered but little. The days and nights there were of more nearly equal length than in Greenland or Iceland. On the shortest day of winter the sun was up between "eyktarstad" and "dagmalastad." [2] When they had completed their house Leif said to his companions, "I propose now to divide our company into two groups, and to set about an exploration of the country; one half of our party shall remain at home at the house, while the other half shall investigate the land, and they must not go beyond a point from which they can return home the same evening, and are now to separate." Thus they did for a time; Leif himself, by turns, joined the exploring party or remained behind at the house. Leif was a large and powerful man, and of a most imposing bearing, a man of sagacity, and a very just man in all things.

It was discovered one evening that one of their company was missing, and this proved to be Tyrker, the German. Leif was sorely troubled by this, for Tyrker had lived with Leif and his father for a long time, and had been very devoted to Leif, when he was a child. Leif severely reprimanded his companions, and prepared to

---

[1] Doegr was a period of twelve hours. A doegr's sailing is estimated to have been about one hundred miles.

[2] These two words designate positions of the sun at two points of time.

go in search of him, taking twelve men with him. They had proceeded but a short distance from the house, when they were met by Tyrker, whom they received most cordially. Leif observed at once that his foster-father was in lively spirits. Tyrker had a prominent forehead, restless eyes, small features, was diminutive in stature, and rather a sorry-looking individual withal, but was, nevertheless, a most capable handicraftsman. Leif addressed him, and asked: "Wherefore art thou so belated, foster-father mine, and astray from the others?" In the beginning Tyrker spoke for some time in German, rolling his eyes, and grinning, and they could not understand him; but after a time he addressed them in the Northern tongue: "I did not go much further, and yet I have something of novelty to relate. I have found vines and grapes." "Is this indeed true, foster-father?" said Leif. "Of a certainty it is true," quoth he, "for I was born where there is no lack of either grapes or vines." They slept the night through, and on the morrow Leif said to his shipmates: "We will now divide our labors, and each day will either gather grapes or cut vines and fell trees, so as to obtain a cargo of these for my ship." They acted upon this advice, and it is said, that their after-boat was filled with grapes. A cargo sufficient for the ship was cut, and when the spring came, they made their ship ready, and sailed away; and from its products Leif gave the land a name, and called it Wineland. They sailed out to sea, and had fair winds until they sighted Greenland, and the fells below the glaciers; then one of the men spoke up, and said, "Why do you steer the ship so much into the wind?" Leif answers: "I have my mind upon my steering, but on other matters as well. Do ye not see anything out of the common?" They replied, that they saw nothing strange. "I do not know," says Leif, "whether it is a ship or a skerry that I

see." Now they saw it, and said, that it must be a skerry; but he was so much keener of sight than they, that he was able to discern men upon the skerry. "I think it best to tack," says Leif, "so that we may draw near to them, that we may be able to render them assistance, if they should stand in need of it; and if they should not be peaceably disposed, we shall still have better command of the situation than they." They approached the skerry, and lowering their sail, cast anchor, and launched a second small boat, which they had brought with them. Tyrker inquired who was the leader of the party. He replied that his name was Thori, and that he was a Norseman; "but what is thy name?" Leif gave his name. "Art thou a son of Eric the Red of Brattahlid?" says he. Leif responded that he was. "It is now my wish," says Leif, "to take you all into my ship, and likewise so much of your possessions as the ship will hold." This offer was accepted, and thus laden, they held away to Ericsfirth, and sailed until they arrived at Brattahlid. Having discharged the cargo, Leif invited Thori, with his wife, Gudrid, and three others, to make their home with him, and procured quarters for the other members of the crew, both of his own and Thori's men. Leif rescued fifteen persons from the skerry. He was afterward called Leif the Lucky. Leif had now goodly store both of property and honor. There was serious illness that winter in Thori's party, and Thori and a great number of his people died. Eric the Red also died that winter. There was now much talk about Leif's Wineland journey, and his brother, Thorvald, held that the country had not been sufficiently explored. Thereupon Leif said to Thorvald: "If it be thy will, brother, thou mayest go to Wineland with my ship, but I wish the ship first to fetch the wood, which Thori had upon the skerry." And so it was done.

1446(?) ∽ *Christopher Columbus* ∽ 1506

HOMEWARD bound from his first voyage, Columbus wrote an account of it in a Spanish letter addressed to no particular person but intended for the public at large. Of this letter, inclosed in one to Ferdinand and Isabella that has been lost, several manuscript copies were made for various court officials. One of these copies—endorsed to Luis de Santangel, *Escrivano de Racien* or high steward or controller of the expenditures of the royal houshold in the kingdom of Aragon—was printed in Barcelona, April, 1493, shortly before Columbus was received in state by the King and Queen. From another copy, a Latin version was made by Leander de Cosco, printed in Rome probably in May, 1493, and reprinted in Rome, Basel, Paris, Antwerp. Thus it was through this letter, rather than from the more extensive journal which Columbus kept of his first voyage, that the public first learned of his discoveries.

Samuel Eliot Morison, in his biography of Columbus, *Admiral of the Ocean Sea*, Boston, 1942, suggests that Columbus, in dating the letter as composed "off the Canary Islands," should have written the "Azores," of which he was within sight on the date given. [The translation reprinted here is that included in *The Northmen, Columbus, and Cabot 985-1503*, New York, 1906, one of the volumes in the series, *Original Narratives of Early American History*.]

THE FIRST VOYAGE
[1493]

SIR: As I know that you will have pleasure from the great victory which our Lord hath given me in my voyage, I write you this, by which you shall know that in thirty-three days I passed over to the Indies with the fleet which the most illustrious King and Queen, our Lords, gave me; where I found very many islands peopled with inhabitants beyond number. And, of them all, I have taken possession for their Highnesses, with proclamation and the royal standard displayed; and I was not gainsaid. To the first which I found, I gave the name San Salvador, in commemoration of His High Majesty, who marvellously hath given all this: the Indians call it Guanaham. The second I named the Island of Santa Maria de Conception, the third Fernandina, the fourth Isla bella,[1] the fifth La Isla Juana; and so for each one a new name. When I reached Juana,

I followed its coast westwardly, and found it so large that I thought it might be mainland, the province of Cathay. And as I did not thus find any towns and villages on the sea-coast, save small hamlets with the people whereof I could not get speech, because they all fled away forthwith, I went on further in the same direction, thinking I should not miss of great cities or towns. And at the end of many leagues, seeing that there was no change, and that the coast was bearing me northwards, whereunto my desire was contrary, since the winter was already confronting us, I formed the purpose of making from thence to the South, and as the wind also blew

[1] In the Journal for October 20, Columbus says that he named this island Isabella. This was either Fortune Island or Great Inaqua. San Salvador was probably Watling's Island; Santa Maria was either Crooked Island or North Caico; Fernandina was either Long Island or Little Inaqua; Juana was Cuba; Spañola was Hayti.

against me, I determined not to wait for other weather and turned back as far as a port agreed upon; from which I sent two men into the country to learn if there were a king, or any great cities. They travelled for three days, and found innumerable small villages and a numberless population, but nought of ruling authority; wherefore they returned. I understood sufficiently from other Indians whom I had already taken, that this land, in its continuousness, was an island; and so I followed its coast eastwardly for a hundred and seven leagues as far as where it terminated; from which headland I saw another island to the east, eighteen leagues distant from this, to which I at once gave the name La Spañola. And I proceeded thither, and followed the northern coast, as with La Juana, eastwardly for a hundred and eighty-eight great leagues in a direct easterly course, as with La Juana. The which, and all the others, are most fertile to an excessive degree, and this extremely so. In it, there are many havens on the sea-coast, incomparable with any others that I know in Christendom, and plenty of rivers so good and great that it is a marvel. The lands thereof are high, and in it are very many ranges of hills, and most lofty mountains incomparably beyond the island of Tenerife,[2] all most beautiful in a thousand shapes, and all accessible, and full of trees of a thousand kinds, so lofty that they seem to reach the sky. And I am assured that they never lose their foliage; as may be imagined, since I saw them as green and as beautiful as they are in Spain during May. And some of them were in flower, some in fruit, some in another stage according to their kind. And the nightingale was singing, and other birds of a thousand sorts, in the month of November, there where I was going. There are palm-trees of six or eight species, wondrous to see for their beautiful variety; but so are the other trees, and fruits, and plants therein. There are wonderful pine-groves, and very large plains of verdure, and there is honey, and many kinds of birds, and many various

fruits. In the earth there are many mines of metals; and there is a population of incalculable number. Española is a marvel; the mountains and hills, and plains, and fields, and the soil, so beautiful and rich for planting and sowing, for breeding cattle of all sorts, for building of towns and villages. There could be no believing, without seeing, such harbors as are here, as well as the many and great rivers, and excellent waters, most of which contain gold. In the trees and fruits and plants, there are great diversities from those of Juana. In this, there are many spiceries, and great mines of gold and other metals. The people of this island, and of all the others that I have found and seen, or not seen, all go naked, men and women, just as their mothers bring them forth; although some women cover a single place with the leaf of a plant, or a cotton something which they make for that purpose. They have no iron or steel, nor any weapons; nor are they fit thereunto; not because they be not a well-formed people and of fair stature, but that they are most wondrously timorous. They have no other weapons than the stems of reeds in their seeding state, on the end of which they fix little sharpened stakes. Even these, they dare not use; for many times has it happened that I sent two or three men ashore to some village to parley, and countless numbers of them sallied forth, but as soon as they saw those approach, they fled away in such wise that even a father would not wait for his son. And this was not because any hurt had ever been done to any of them:— on the contrary, at every headland where I have gone and been able to hold speech with them, I gave them of everything which I had, as well cloth as many other things, without accepting aught therefor;—but such they are, incurably timid. It is true that since they have become more assured,

---

[2] The Peak of Teneriffe in the Canaries is over 12,000 feet high, while Mt. Tina, the highest elevation in Santo Domingo, is only 10,300 feet. Thus Columbus' wonder misled him.

and are losing that terror, they are artless and generous with what they have, to such a degree as no one would believe but him who had seen it. Of anything they have, if it be asked for, they never say no, but do rather invite the person to accept it, and show as much lovingness as though they would give their hearts. And whether it be a thing of value, or one of little worth, they are straightways content with whatsoever trifle of whatsoever kind may be given them in return for it. I forbade that anything so worthless as fragments of broken platters, and pieces of broken glass, and strap buckles, should be given them; although when they were able to get such things, they seemed to think they had the best jewel in the world, for it was the hap of a sailor to get, in exchange for a strap, gold to the weight of two and a half castellanos,[3] and others much more for other things of less value; while for new blancas they gave everything they had, even though it were [the worth of] two or three gold castellanos, or one or two arrobas of spun cotton.[4] They took even pieces of broken barrel-hoops, and gave whatever they had, like senseless brutes; insomuch that it seemed to me bad. I forbade it, and I gave gratuitously a thousand useful things that I carried, in order that they may conceive affection, and furthermore may become Christians; for they are inclined to the love and service of their Highnesses and of all the Castilian nation, and they strive to combine in giving us things which they have in abundance, and of which we are in need. And they knew no sect, nor idolatry; save that they all believe that power and goodness are in the sky, and they believed very firmly that I, with these ships and crews, came from the sky; and in such opinion, they received me at every place where I landed, after they had lost their terror. And this comes not because they are ignorant: on the contrary, they are men of very subtle wit, who navigate all those seas, and who give a marvellously good account of everything, but because they never saw men wearing clothes nor the like of our ships. And as soon as I arrived in the Indies, in the first island that I found, I took some of them by force, to the intent that they should learn [our speech] and give me information of what there was in those parts. And so it was, that very soon they understood [us] and we them, what by speech or what by signs; and those [Indians] have been of much service. To this day I carry them [with me] who are still of the opinion that I come from Heaven [as appears] from much conversation which they have had with me. And they were the first to proclam it wherever I arrived; and the others went running from house to house and to the neighboring villages, with loud cries of "Come! come to see the people from Heaven!" Then, as soon as their minds were reassured about us, every one came, men as well as women, so that there remained none behind, big or little; and they all brought something to eat and drink, which they gave with wondrous lovingness. They have in all the islands very many *canoas*,[5] after the manner of rowing-galleys, some larger, some smaller; and a good many are larger than a galley of eighteen benches. They are not so wide, because they are made of a single log of timber, but a galley could not keep up with them in rowing, for their motion is a thing beyond belief. And with these, they navigate through all those islands, which are numberless, and ply their traffic. I have seen some of those *canoas* with seventy and eighty men in them, each one with his oar. In all those islands, I saw not much diversity in the looks of the people, nor in their manners and language; but they all understand each other, which is a thing of singular advantage for what I hope their Highnesses will decide upon

---

[3] The *castellano* was one-sixth of an ounce of gold.

[4] The *blanca* was a coin worth about one-third of a cent. The *arroba* was 25 pounds.

[5] Canoes: the first appearance of this West Indian word in Europe.

for converting them to our holy faith, unto which they are well disposed. I have already told how I had gone a hundred and seven leagues, in a straight line from West to East, along the sea-coast of the Island of Juana; according to which itinerary, I can declare that that island is larger than England and Scotland combined; as, over and above those hundred and seven leagues, there remain for me, on the western side, two provinces whereto I did not go—one of which they call Avan, where the people are born with tails—which provinces cannot be less in length than fifty or sixty leagues, according to what may be understood from the Indians with me, who know all the islands. This other, Española, has a greater circumference than the whole of Spain from Col[ibre in Catal]unya, by the sea-coast, as far as Fuente Ravia in Biscay; since, along one of its four sides, I went for a hundred and eighty-eight great leagues in a straight line from west to east.[6] This is [a land] to be desired,—and once seen, never to be relinquished—in which (although, indeed, I have taken possession of them all for their Highnesses, and all are more richly endowed than I have skill and power to say, and I hold them all in the name of their Highnesses who can dispose thereof as much and as completely as of the kingdoms of Castile) in this Española, in the place most suitable and best for its proximity to the gold mines, and for traffic with the mainland both on this side and with that over there belonging to the Great Can,[7] where there will be great commerce and profit, I took possession of a large town which I named the city of Navidad [Nativity]. And I have made fortification there, and a fort (which by this time will have been completely finished) and I have left therein men enough for such a purpose, with arms and artillery, and provisions for more than a year, and a boat, and a master of all sea-craft for making others; and great friendship with the king of that land, to such a degree that he prided himself on calling and holding me as his brother. And even

though his mind might change towards attacking those men, neither he nor his people know what arms are, and go naked. As I have already said, they are the most timorous creatures there are in the world, so that the men who remain there are alone sufficient to destroy all that land, and the island is without personal danger for them if they know how to behave themselves. It seems to me that in all those islands, the men are all content with a single wife; and to their chief or king they give as many as twenty. The women, it appears to me, do more work than the men. Nor have I been able to learn whether they held personal property, for it seemed to me that whatever one had, they all took share of, especially of eatable things. Down to the present, I have not found in those islands any monstrous men, as many expected, but on the contrary all the people are very comely; nor are they black like those in Guinea, but have flowing hair; and they are not begotten where there is an excessive violence of the rays of the sun. It is true that the sun is there very strong, although it is twenty-six degrees distant from the equinoctial line. In those islands, where there are lofty mountains, the cold was very keen there, this winter; but they endure it by being accustomed thereto, and by the help of the meats which they eat with many and inordinately hot spices. Thus I have not found, nor had any information of monsters, except of an island which is here the second in the approach to the Indies, which is inhabited by a people whom, in all the islands, they regard as very ferocious, who eat human flesh. These have many *canoas* with which they run through all the islands of India, and plunder and take as much as they can. They are no more ill-shapen than the

[6] The area of Spain is about 191,000 square miles; that of Española or Hayti is 28,000. The extreme length of Hayti is 407 miles.
[7] That is, with the mainland of Europe on this side of the Atlantic and with the mainland on that side of the ocean belonging to the Great Can, i. e., China.

others, but have the custom of wearing their hair long, like women; and they use bows and arrows of the same reed stems, with a point of wood at the top, for lack of iron which they have not. Amongst those other tribes who are excessively cowardly, these are ferocious; but I hold them as nothing more than the others. These are they who have to do with the women of Matinino [Martinique]—which is the first island that is encountered in the passage from Spain to the Indies—in which there are no men. Those women practice no female usages, but have bows and arrows of reed such as above mentioned; and they arm and cover themselves with plates of copper of which they have much. In another island, which they assure me is larger than Española, the people have no hair. In this there is incalculable gold; and concerning these and the rest I bring Indians with me as witnesses. And in conclusion, to speak only of what has been done in this voyage, which has been so hastily performed, their Highnesses may see that I shall give them as much gold as they may need, with very little aid which their Highnesses will give me; spices and cotton at once, as much as their Highnesses will order to be shipped, and as much as they shall order to be shipped of mastic,—which till now has never been found except in Greece, in the island of Xio, and the Seignory sells it for what it likes; [8] and aloe-wood as much as they shall order to be shipped,—and these shall be from idolators. And I believe that I have discovered rhubarb and cinnamon, and I shall find that the men whom I am leaving there will have discovered a thousand other things of value; as I made no delay at any point, so long as the wind gave me an opportunity of sailing, except only in the town of Navidad till I had left things safely arranged and well established. And in truth I should have done much more if the ships had served me as well as might reasonably have been expected. This is enough; and [thanks to] Eternal God our Lord who gives to all those who walk His

way, victory over things which seem impossible; and this was signally one such, for although men have talked or written of those lands, it was all by conjecture, without confirmation from eyesight, amounting only to this much that the hearers for the most part listened and judged that there was more fable in it than anything actual, however trifling. Since thus our Redeemer has given to our most illustrious King and Queen, and to their famous kingdoms, this victory in so high a matter, Christendom should have rejoicing therein and make great festivals, and give solemn thanks to the Holy Trinity for the great exaltation they shall have by the conversion of so many peoples to our holy faith; and next for the temporal benefit which will bring hither refreshment and profit, not only to Spain, but to all Christians. This briefly, in accordance with the facts. Dated, on the caravel, off the Canary Islands, the 15 February of the year 1493.

At your command,

The Admiral.

Postscript which came within the Letter.

After having written this letter, and being in the sea of Castile, there rose upon me so much wind, South and Southeast, that it has caused me to lighten the vessels; however, I ran hither to-day into this port of Lisbon, which was the greatest wonder in the world; where I decided to write to their Highnesses. I have always found the seasons like May in all the Indies, whither I passed in thirty-three days, and returned in twenty-eight, but that these storms have delayed me twenty-three days running about this sea. All the seamen say here that there never has been so bad a winter, nor so many shipwrecks.

Dated the 14th of March.

Colom sent this letter to the Escrivano de Racion. Of the islands found in the Indies. Received with another for their Highnesses.

[8] The Seignory was the government of Genoa to which Chios [Scio] belonged at this time.

1475(?) ∽ *Martin Waldseemüller* ∽ 1522(?)

IN THE literature of exploration of the Western Hemisphere, the works
of Renaissance cosmographers, usually composed in Latin, the esperanto or
universal language of learned men, occupy an important place. The *Cosmographiae Introductio* or *Introduction to Cosmography* of Martin Waldseemüller, a cleric born probably at Radolfszell on Lake Constance sometime between 1470 and 1475 and dying while Canon at St. Dié, a small Vosges village
in Lorraine, may be taken as representative of this kind of writing, which
profoundly affected European conceptions of the New World.

Published at St. Dié with a preface dedicated to Maximilian I, Emperor
of the Holy Roman Empire from 1493 to 1519, this work has the distinction
of having misnamed two great continents in honor of Amerigo Vespucci rather
than Columbus. When Waldseemüller was later convinced that he had made
an error, he sought to withdraw the name "America," but so influential had
his cosmographical writings become that it was too late.

[The following selections are reprinted from the translation by Edmund
Burke contained in C. G. Hebermann's edition of the *Cosmographiae Introductio,* Monograph IV, United States Catholic Historical Society, New York,
1907.]

From
COSMOGRAPHIAE INTRODUCTIO
[1507]

From the Preface

IF it is not only pleasant but also profitable in life to visit many lands and to see
the most distant races (a fact that is made
clear in Plato, Apollonius of Tyana, and
many other philosophers, who went to the
most remote regions for the purpose of exploration), who, I ask, most invincible
Maximilian Caesar, will deny that it is
pleasant and profitable to learn from
books the location of lands and cities and
of foreign peoples,

Which Phoebus sees when he buries his
    rays beneath the waves,
Which he sees as he comes from the
    farthest east,
Which the cold northern stars distress,
Which the south wind parches with its
    torrid heat,
Baking again the burning sands?
                        (Boethius)

Who, I repeat, will deny that it is pleasant and profitable to learn from books
the manners and customs of all these peoples? Surely—to express my own opinion
—just as it is worthy of praise to travel
far, so it can not be foolish for one who
knows the world, even from maps alone,
to repeat again and again that passage of
the Odyssey which Homer, the most learned
of poets, wrote abut Ulysses:

Tell me, O Muse, of the man who after
    the capture of Troy
Saw the customs and the cities of many
    men.

Therefore, studying, to the best of my
ability and with the aid of several persons,
the books of Ptolemy from a Greek copy,
and adding the relations of the four voyages of Amerigo Vespucci, I have prepared for the general use of scholars a
map of the whole world—like an introduction, so to speak, both in the solid and
projected on the plane. This work I have

determined to dedicate to your most sacred Majesty, since you are the lord of the world, feeling certain that I shall accomplish my end and shall be safe from the intrigues of my enemies under your protecting shield, as though under that of Achilles, if I know that I have satisfied, to some extent at least, your Majesty's keen judgment in such matters. Farewell, most illustrious Caesar. . . .

ORDER OF TREATMENT

Since no one can obtain a thorough knowledge of Cosmography without some previous understanding of astronomy, nor even of astronomy itself without the principles of geometry, we shall in this brief outline say a few words:

(1) Of the elements of geometry that will be helpful to a better understanding of the material sphere;

(2) Of the meaning of *sphere, axis, poles,* etc.;

(3) Of the circles of the heavens;

(4) Of a certain theory, which we shall propose, of the sphere itself according to the system of degrees;

(5) Of the five celestial zones, and the application of these and of the degrees of the heavens to the earth;

(6) Of parallels;

(7) Of the climates [1] of the earth;

(8) Of winds, with a general diagram of these and other things;

(9) Of the divisions of the earth, of the various seas, of islands, and of the distances of places from one another. There will be added also a quadrant useful to the cosmographer.

Lastly, we shall add the four voyages of Amerigo Vespucci. Thus we shall describe the cosmography, both in the solid and projected on the plane.

OF THE WINDS

. . . A wind . . ., as defined by the philosophers, is an exaltation, warm and dry, moving laterally around the earth.

Now, inasmuch as the sun has a triple rising and setting, the summer rising and setting, the equinoctial rising and setting, and the winter rising and setting, according to its relation to the two tropics and the equator, and inasmuch as there are also two sides—to the north and to the south, all of which have winds peculiar to them; therefore it follows that there are twelve winds in all, three eastern, three western, three northern, and three southern. . . .

The poets, however, by poetic license, according to their custom, instead of the principal winds use their secondary winds, which are also called side winds. Thus Ovid says:

> Far to the east
> Where Persian mountains greet the rising sun
> Eurus withdrew. Where sinking Phoebus' rays
> Glow on the western shores mild Zephyr fled.
> Terrific Boreas frozen Scythia seiz'd,
> Beneath the icy bear. On southern climes
> From constant clouds the showery Auster rains.
> —[*Metamorphoses*, i, 61-66.]

. . . Although the north winds are naturally cold, they are softened because they pass through the torrid zone. This has been found to be true of the south wind, which passes through the torrid zone before it reaches us. . . .

Wherever the cold south wind goes, it rages and binds the waters with tight fetters. But . . . it comes welcome to our shores and hurls back the merciless shafts of the north wind. The latter wind on the contrary, which deals harshly with us, slackening its flight, becomes in like manner gentler in the lowest part of the globe. The other winds, where they direct their various courses, soon change, as they go,

---

[1] The word *climate* is here used in its ancient sense of a zone of the earth's surface comprised between two specified parallels of latitude.

the natures which are proper to their homes.

We have said enough about winds . . .

OF CERTAIN ELEMENTS OF COSMOGRAPHY

It is clear from astronomical demonstrations that the whole earth is a point in comparison with the entire extent of the heavens; so that if the earth's circumference be compared to the size of the celestial globe, it may be considered to have absolutely no extent. There is about a fourth part of this small region in the world which was known to Ptolemy and is inhabited by living beings like ourselves. Hitherto it has been divided into three parts, Europe, Africa, and Asia.

. . . Europe is so called after Europa, the daughter of King Agenor. While with a girl's enthusiasm she was playing on the sea-shore accompanied by her Tyrian maidens and was gathering flowers in baskets, she is believed to have been carried off by Jupiter, who assumed the form of a snow-white bull, and after being brought over the seas to Crete seated upon his back to have given her name to the land lying opposite.

. . . Asia is so called after a queen of that name.

Now, these parts of the earth have been more extensively explored and a fourth part has been discovered by Amerigo Vespucci (as will be set forth in what follows). Inasmuch as both Europe and Asia received their names from women, I see no reason why any one should justly object to calling this part Amerige, i.e., the land of Amerigo, or America, after Amerigo, its discoverer, a man of great ability. Its position and the customs of its inhabitants may be clearly understood from the four voyages of Amerigo, which are subjoined.[2]

Thus the earth is now known to be divided into four parts. The first three parts are continents, while the fourth is an island, inasmuch as it is found to be surrounded on all sides by the ocean. Although there is only one ocean, just as there is only one earth, yet, being marked by many seas and filled with numberless islands, it takes various names. . . .

---

[2] A Portuguese expedition of 1501 sailed hundreds of miles along the coast of South America. Amerigo Vespucci, a Florentine merchant, was a member of this expedition and later claimed that he had made four western voyages between 1497 and 1503. His account of these voyages, sent to a friend, came to the attention of Waldseemüller and so impressed him that he made his unfortunate suggestion.

Alvar Nuñez Cabeza de Vaca
1490(?) ∾ 1557(?)

AMONG Spanish explorations of the American mainland in the 16th century, that undertaken by Pámfilo de Narvaez, who sailed in five vessels with 600 colonists and soldiers from Sanlúcar de Barrameda, June 17, 1527, was one of the most remarkable from the point of view of adventure, privation, and suffering. After losses in a hurricane on the southern coast of Cuba, the expedition landed April, 1528, near what is now Tampa, Florida, and a part of it struck inland in a northerly direction. After arriving at a place called Aute near what is now St. Marks Bay, Florida, the inland expedition turned back to the sea, built five makeshift boats, and ventured to brave the tropical storms of the Gulf of Mexico. At the mouth of the Mississippi, strong currents and winds dispersed the boats and carried them all beyond sight of land.

The boat containing Alvar Nuñez Cabeza de Vaca and his party was cast ashore on an island which was probably somewhere off the coast of what is now Texas and to which they gave the name of Malhado or "Misfortune." Of the twelve survivors who ultimately left the island, Cabeza and three companions, after many adventures, reached by 1536 a point on the Sonoro River in what is now Mexico where they fell in with Spanish slave-hunters who conducted them southward to the city of Compostela near the Pacific coast.

Returning to civilization, Cabeza de Vaca wrote a matter-of-fact account of the unsuccessful Narvaez expedition and the adventures of himself and his companions. This *Relacion* was first printed at Zamora, Spain, fifteen years before the death of its author.

[The following selection is composed of parts of Chapter 8, a section of Chapter 10, and all of Chapters 11 and 12, and tells how the makeshift boats were made at St. Marks Bay and how Cabeza's party was given an unusual reception by the savages on the island of Malhado. The translation used is that reprinted in *Spanish Explorers in the Southern United States 1528-1543*, ed. F. W. Hodge and T. H. Lewis, New York, 1907, one of the volumes in the series, *Original Narratives of Early American History*.]

From
RELACION
[1542]

THE next morning we left Aute, and travelled all day before coming to the place I had visited. The journey was extremely arduous. There were not horses enough to carry the sick, who went on increasing in numbers day by day, and we knew of no cure. It was piteous and painful to witness our perplexity and distress. We saw on our arrival how small were the means for advancing farther. There was not anywhere to go; and if there had been, the people were unable to move forward, the greater part being ill, and those were few who could be on duty. I cease here to relate more of this, because any one may suppose what would occur in a country so remote and malign, so destitute of all resource, whereby either to live in it or go out of it; but most certain assistance is in God, our Lord, on whom we never failed to place reliance.

One thing occurred, more afflicting to us than all the rest, which was, that of the persons mounted, the greater part commenced secretly to plot, hoping to secure a better fate for themselves by abandoning the Governor and the sick, who were in a state of weakness and prostration. But, as among them were many hidalgos and persons of gentle condition, they would not permit this to go on, without informing the Governor and the officers of your Majesty;[1] and as we showed them the deformity of their purpose, and placed before them the moment when they should desert their captain, and those who were ill and feeble, and above all the disobedience to the orders of your Majesty, they determined to remain, and that whatever might happen to one should be the lot of all, without any forsaking the rest.

After the accomplishment of this, the Governor called them all to him, and of

---

[1] The *Relacion* is addressed to his "Sacred Caesarian Catholic Majesty," the Emperor Charles V.

each apart he asked advice as to what he should do to get out of a country so miserable, and seek that assistance elsewhere which could not here be found, a third part of the people being very sick, and the number increasing every hour; for we regarded it as certain that we should all become so, and could pass out of it only through death, which from its coming in such a place was to us all the more terrible. These, with many other embarrassments being considered, and entertaining many plans, we coincided in one great project extremely difficult to put in operation, and that was to build vessels in which we might go away. This appeared impossible to every one; we knew not how to construct, nor were there tools, nor iron, nor forge, nor tow, nor resin, nor rigging; finally, no one thing of so many that are necessary, nor any man who had a knowledge of their manufacture; and, above all, there was nothing to eat, while building, for those who should labor. Reflecting on all this, we agreed to think of the subject with more deliberation, and the conversation dropped from that day, each going his way, commending our course to God, our Lord, that he should direct it as should best serve Him.

The next day it was His will that one of the company should come saying that he could make some pipes out of wood, which with deer-skins might be made into bellows; and, as we lived in a time when anything that had the semblance of relief appeared well, we told him to set himself to work. We assented to the making of nails, saws, axes, and other tools of which there was such need, from the stirrups, spurs, crossbows, and the other things of iron there were; and we laid out for support, while the work was going on, that we should make four entries into Aute, with all the horses and men that were able to go, and that on every third day a horse should be killed to be divided among those who labored in the work of the boats and the sick. The incursions were made with the people and horses that were available,

and in them were brought back as many as four hundred fanegas [2] of maize; but these were not got without quarrels and contentions with the Indians. We caused many palmitos to be collected for the woof or covering, twisting and preparing it for use in the place of tow for the boats.

We commenced to build on the fourth, with the only carpenter in the company, and we proceeded with so great diligence that on the twentieth day of September five boats were finished, twenty-two cubits in length, each caulked with the fibre of the palmito. We pitched them with a certain resin, made from pine trees by a Greek, named Don Theodoro; from the same husk of the palmito, and from the tails and manes of the horses we made ropes and rigging, from our shirts, sails, and from the savins growing there we made the oars that appeared to us requisite. Such was the country into which our sins had cast us, that only by very great search could we find stone for ballast and anchors, since in it all we had not seen one. We flayed the horses, taking the skin from their legs entire, and tanning them to make bottles wherein to carry water.

During this time some went gathering shell-fish in the coves and creeks of the sea, at which employment the Indians twice attacked them and killed ten men in sight of the camp, without our being able to afford succor. We found their corpses traversed from side to side with arrows; and for all some had on good armor, it did not give adequate protection or security against the nice and powerful archery of which I have spoken. . . .

Before we embarked there died more than forty men of disease and hunger, without enumerating those destroyed by the Indians. By the twenty-second of the month of September, the horses had been consumed, one only remaining; and on that day we embarked in the following order: In the boat of the Governor went

[2] A Spanish measure somewhat in excess of the bushel.

forty-nine men; in another, which he gave
to the comptroller and the commissary,
went as many others; the third, he gave
to Captain Alonzo del Castillo and An-
drés Dorantes, with forty-eight men; and
another he gave to two captains, Tellez
and Penalosa, with forty-seven men. The
last was given to the assessor and myself,
with forty-nine men. After the provisions
and clothes had been taken in, not over a
span of the gunwales remained above
water; and more than this, the boats were
so crowded that we could not move: so
much can necessity do, which drove us to
hazard our lives in this manner, running
into a turbulent sea, not a single one who
went having a knowledge of navigation.

．　　．　　．　　．　　．　　．

. . . Because of winter and its inclem-
ency, the many days we had suffered hunger, and the heavy beating of the waves,
the people began next day to despair in
such a manner that when the sun sank, all
who were in my boat were fallen one on
another, so near to death that there were
few among them in a state of sensibility.
Of the whole number at this time not five
men were on their feet; and when night
came, only the master and myself were
left, who could work the boat. Two hours
after dark, he said to me that I must take
charge of her as he was in such condition
he believed he should die that night. So I
took the paddle, and going after midnight
to see if the master was alive he said to
me he was rather better, and would take
the charge until day. I declare in that
hour I would more willingly have died
than seen so many people before me in
such condition. After the master took the
direction of the boat, I lay down a little
while; but without repose, for nothing at
that time was farther from me than sleep.

Near the dawn of day, it seemed to me
I heard the tumbling of the sea; for as the
coast was low, it roared loudly. Surprised
at this, I called to the master, who answered me that he believed we were near
the land. We sounded and found ourselves
in seven fathoms. He advised that we
should keep to sea until sunrise; accordingly I took an oar and pulled on the land
side, until we were a league distant, when
we gave her stern to the sea. Near the
shore a wave took us, that knocked the
boat out of water the distance of the
throw of a crowbar, and from the violence
with which she struck, nearly all the people who were in her like dead, were roused
to consciousness. Finding themselves near
the shore, they began to move on hands
and feet, crawling to land into some ravines. There we made fire, parched some
of the maize we brought, and found rain
water. From the warmth of the fire the
people recovered their faculties, and began
somewhat to exert themselves. The day on
which we arrived was the sixth of November [1528].

After the people had eaten, I ordered
Lope de Oviedo, who had more strength
and was stouter than any of the rest, to
go to some trees that were near by, and
climbing into one of them to look about
and try to gain knowledge of the country.
He did as I bade, and made out that we
were on an island. He saw that the land
was pawed up in the manner that
ground is wont to be where cattle range,
whence it appeared to him that this
should be a country of Christians; and
thus he reported to us. I ordered him to
return and examine much more particularly, and see if there were any roads
that were worn, but without going far,
because there might be danger.

He went, and coming to a path, took
it for the distance of half a league, and
found some huts, without tenants, they
having gone into the field. He took from
these an earthen pot, a little dog, some few
mullets, and returned. As it appeared to us
he was gone a long time, we sent two men
that they should look to see what might
have happened. They met him near by,
and saw that three Indians with bows and
arrows followed and were calling to him,
while he, in the same way, was beckoning
them on. Thus he arrived where we were,
the natives remaining a little way back,

seated on the shore. Half an hour after, they were supported by one hundred other Indian bowmen, who if they were not large, our fears made giants of them. They stopped near us with the first three. It were idle to think that any among us could make defence, for it would have been difficult to find six that could rise from the ground. The assessor and I went out and called to them, and they came to us. We endeavored the best we could to encourage them and secure their favor. We gave them beads and hawk-bells, and each of them gave me an arrow, which is a pledge of friendship. They told us by signs that they would return in the morning and bring us something to eat, as at that time they had nothing.

At sunrise the next day, the time the Indians appointed, they came according to their promise, and brought us a large quantity of fish with certain roots, some a little larger than walnuts, others a trifle smaller, the greater part got from under the water and with much labor. In the evening they returned and brought us more fish and roots. They sent their women and children to look at us, who went back rich with the hawk-bells and beads given them, and they came afterwards on other days, returning as before. Finding that we had provision, fish, roots, water, and other things we asked for, we determined to embark again and pursue our course. Having dug out our boat from the sand in which it was buried, it became necessary that we should strip, and go through great exertion to launch her, we being in such a state that things very much lighter sufficed to make us great labor.

Thus embarked, at the distance of two crossbow shots in the sea we shipped a wave that entirely wet us. As we were naked, and the cold was very great, the oars loosened in our hands, and the next blow the sea struck us, capsized the boat. The assessor and two others held fast to her for preservation, but it happened to be far otherwise; the boat carried them over, and they were drowned under her.

As the surf near the shore was very high, a single roll of the sea threw the rest into the waves and half drowned upon the shore of the island, without our losing any more than those the boat took down. The survivors escaped naked as they were born, with the loss of all they had; and although the whole was of little value, at that time it was worth much, as we were then in November, the cold was severe, and our bodies were so emaciated the bones might be counted with little difficulty, having become the perfect figures of death. For myself I can say that from the month of May passed, I had eaten no other thing than maize, and sometimes I found myself obliged to eat it unparched; for although the beasts were slaughtered while the boats were building, I could never eat their flesh, and I did not eat fish ten times. I state this to avoid giving excuses, and that every one may judge in what condition we were. Besides all these misfortunes, came a north wind upon us, from which we were nearer to death than life. Thanks be to our Lord that, looking among the brands we had used there, we found sparks from which we made great fires. And thus were we asking mercy of Him and pardon for our transgressions, shedding many tears, and each regretting not his own fate alone, but that of his comrades about him.

At sunset, the Indians thinking we had not gone, came to seek us and bring us food; but when they saw us thus, in a plight so different from what it was before, and so extraordinary, they were alarmed and turned back. I went toward them and called, when they returned much frightened. I gave them to understand by signs that our boat had sunk and three of our number had been drowned. There, before them, they saw two of the departed, and we who remained were near joining them. The Indians, at sight of what had befallen us, and our state of suffering and melancholy destitution, sat down among us, and from the sorrow and pity they felt, they all began to lament so earnestly that they might have been heard at a distance, and continued so doing more than half an hour. It was strange to see these men, wild and untaught, howling like brutes over our misfortunes. It caused in me as in others, an increase of feeling and a livelier sense of our calamity.

The cries having ceased, I talked with the Christians, and said that if it appeared well to them, I would beg these Indians to take us to their houses. Some, who had been in New Spain, replied that we ought not to think of it; for if they should do so, they would sacrifice us to their idols. But seeing no better course, and that any other led to a nearer and more certain death, I disregarded what was said, and besought the Indians to take us to their dwellings. They signified that it would give them delight, and that we should tarry a little, that they might do what we asked. Presently thirty men loaded themselves with wood and started for their houses,

which were far off, and we remained with the others until near night, when, holding us up, they carried us with all haste. Because of the extreme coldness of the weather, lest any one should die or fail by the way, they caused four or five very large fires to be placed at intervals, and at each they warmed us; and when they saw that we had regained some heat and strength, they took us to the next so swiftly that they hardly let us touch our feet to the ground. In this manner we went as far as their habitations, where we found that they had made a house for us with many fires in it. An hour after our arrival, they began to dance and hold great rejoicing, which lasted all night, although for us there was no joy, festivity nor sleep, awaiting the hour they should make us victims. In the morning they again gave us fish and roots, showing us such hospitality that we were reassured, and lost somewhat the fear of sacrifice. . . .

1494(?) ∞ *Jacques Cartier* ∞ 1555(?)

ON THE strength of a voyage made by Giovanni Verrazano in 1523-24, Francis I, King of France, felt that his country had a claim to North America and financed further voyages by Jacques Cartier, a Breton pilot of the port of St. Malo, who desired at first to discover a passage to the Orient and later to find gold and silver, establish a settlement on the St. Lawrence River, and Christianize the Indians. A report of Cartier's first voyage of 1534 was preserved in an Italian translation by Ramusio in the third volume of his *Navigationi* published at Venice, 1556. An account of Cartier's second voyage of 1535-36 was printed in France under the title *Brief Récit et Succincte Narration*. The account of his third voyage of 1541-42 has survived only in fragmentary form in a translation made by Richard Hakluyt from the official French report. The following selection is from the account of Cartier's second voyage, during which he sailed up the St. Lawrence River past the site of Quebec to the Indian village of Hochelaga, lying at the foot of a mountain which the French named Mount Royal or Montreal. From this mountain Cartier was able to get a fine view of the country that was later to become New France.

[The translation used here is that made from Ramusio's version of the

Brief Récit et Succincte Narration and printed in the 1600 edition of Hakluyt's *Voyages*. This translation has been reprinted in *Early English and French Voyages*, ed. H. S. Burrage, New York, 1906, one of the volumes in the series, *Original Narratives of Early American History*. In the present selection, spelling and punctuation have been modernized.]

From
BRIEF RÉCIT
[1545]

SO soon as we were come near the town [Hochelaga], a great number of the inhabitants thereof came to present themselves before us after their fashion, making very much of us; we were by our guides brought into the midst of the town. They have in the middlemost part of their houses a large square place, being from side to side a good stone's cast, whither we were brought, and there with signs were commanded to stay; then suddenly all the women and maidens of the town gathered themselves together, part of which had their arms full of young children, and as many as could came to rub our faces, our arms, and what part of the body soever they could touch, weeping for very joy that they saw us, showing us the best countenance that possibly they could, desiring us with their signs that it would please us to touch their children. That done, the men caused the women to withdraw themselves back, then they every one sat down on the ground round about us, as if they would have shown and rehearsed some comedy or other show; then presently came the women again, every one bringing a four-square mat in manner of carpets, and spreading them abroad on the ground in that place, they caused us to sit upon them. That done, the Lord and King of the country was brought upon 9 or 10 men's shoulders (whom in their tongue they call Agouhanna) sitting upon a great stag's skin, and they laid him down upon the foresaid mats near to the Captain [Cartier], every one beckoning unto us that he was their Lord and King. This Agouhanna was a man about fifty years old: he was

no whit better apparelled than any of the rest, only excepted, that he had a certain thing made of the skins of hedgehogs like a red wreath, and that was instead of his crown. He was full of the palsy, and his members shrunk together. After he had with certain signs saluted our Captain and all his company, and by manifest tokens bid all welcome, he showed his legs and arms to our Captain, and with signs desired him to touch them, and so he did, rubbing them with his own hands; then did Agouhanna take the wreath or crown he had about his head, and gave it unto our Captain; that done, they brought before him divers diseased men, some blind, some cripple, some lame and impotent, and some so old that the hair of their eyelids came down and covered their cheeks, and laid them all along before our Captain, to the end they might of him be touched: for it seemed unto them that God was descended and come down from heaven to heal them. Our Captain seeing the misery and devotion of this poor people recited the Gospel of St. John, that is to say, "In the Beginning was the Word"; touching every one that were diseased, praying to God that it would please him to open the hearts of this poor people, and to make them know his holy word, and that they might receive baptism and Christendom: that done, he took a service-book in his hand, and with a loud voice read all the passion of Christ, word by word that all the standers by might hear him: all which while this poor people kept silence, and were marvellously attentive, looking up to heaven and imitating us in gestures. Then he caused the men all orderly to be set on one side, the women on another, and likewise the children on another, and to the chiefest of them he gave hatchets, to the other knives, and to the women beads and such other small trifles. Then where the children were he cast rings, counters, and brooches made of tin, whereat they seemed to be very glad. That done, our Captain commanded trumpets and other musical instruments to be sounded, which when they heard, they were very merry. Then we took our leave and went to our boat: the women seeing that, put themselves before to stay us, and brought us out of their meats that they had made ready for us, as fish, pottage beans, and such other things, thinking to make us eat and dine in that place: but because the meats had no savor at all of salt, we liked them not, but thanked them, and with signs gave them to understand that we had no need to eat. When we were out of the town, diverse of the men and women followed us, and brought us to the top of the foresaid mountain, which we named Mount Royal; it is about a league from the town. When as we were on the top of it, we might discern and plainly see thirty leagues about. On the north side of it there are many hills to be seen running west and east, and as many more on the south, amongst and between the which the country is as fair and as pleasant as possibly can be seen, being level, smooth, and very plain, fit to be husbanded and tilled: and in the midst of those fields we saw the river further up a great way than where we had left our boats, where was the greatest and the swiftest fall of water that anywhere hath been seen, and as great, wide, and large as our sight might discern, going southwest along three fair and round mountains that we saw, as we judged about fifteen leagues from us. Those which brought us thither told and showed us, that in the said river there were three such falls of water more, as that was where we had left our boats: but because we could not understand their language, we could not know how far they were from one another. Moreover they showed us with signs, that the said three falls being past, a man might sail the space of three months more alongst that river, and that along the hills that are on the north side there is a great river, which (even as the other) cometh from the West. . . .

1560 ∽ *Thomas Hariot* ∽ 1621

BEFORE the first settlement of the English at Jamestown in 1607, Sir Walter Raleigh attempted to plant colonies at Roanoke in Pimlico Sound. He sponsored the voyage of discovery led by Philip Amadas and Arthur Barlowe in 1584, a voyage reported by Barlowe to Raleigh in one of the classic accounts included in Richard Hakluyt's monumental *Principall Navigations*. Raleigh likewise sponsored the colony led by Richard Grenville and Ralph Lane in 1585 and the famous "lost colony," of 1587.

Among those in the unsuccessful Grenville-Lane expedition, most of which was brought back to England by Sir Francis Drake, were the English astronomer and mathematician, Thomas Hariot or Harriot, who acted as chronicler, and John White, a painter, who made sketches of the Indians and of the fauna and flora. Hariot's *A briefe and true report of the new found land of Virginia* was privately printed in London with a foreword by Ralph Lane and without the White illustrations.

In 1590 the great continental publisher of travel literature, Theodore de Bry, at Frankfurt-am-Main, reprinted, after a visit to London, the Hariot text with twenty-three realistic engravings, twenty made from the White sketches of Indian life and, for comparison, an appendix of five engravings of ancient Picts of early Britain from "pictures" provided him by John White "fownd as he did assure me in a oolld English cronicle." Each of the plates is accompanied by a carefully written descriptive commentary in English prose. These commentaries are said to be translated by Richard Hakluyt "out of Latin." The Latin had probably been written out from John White's oral explanations, possibly by de Bry himself. De Bry's edition was later issued in both Latin and German.

Hariot's *Virginia*, included later in Hakluyt's *Principall Navigations*, may thus be regarded as the main source of Europeans' first detailed and systematically arranged information concerning what is now Virginia, a name originally applied to a vast territory lying north of Florida as the possession of Elizabeth, the Virgin Queen.

[The first five of the following selections have been taken from the copy of the excessively rare 1588 Hariot "quarto" at the William L. Clements Library of Americana at the University of Michigan; the last two are examples of the descriptive commentary accompanying White's illustrations from the 1590 de Bry Hariot; all selections have been modernized in spelling, etc.; the titles for the first five have been supplied by the present editors.]

From
BRIEFE AND TRUE REPORT
[1588]

Ralph Lane's Foreword

ALBEIT (gentle reader) the credit of the reports in this treatise contained can little be furthered by the testimony of one as myself, through affection judged partial, though without desert: nevertheless, for so much as I have been requested by some, my particular friends, who conceive more rightly of me, to deliver freely my knowledge of the same, not only for the satisfying of them, but also for the true information of any other whatsoever, that comes not with a prejudicate mind to the reading thereof: thus much upon my credit I am to affirm: that things universally are so truly set down in this treatise by the author thereof, an actor in the colony and a man no less for his honesty than learning

commendable: as that I dare boldly avouch it may very well pass with the credit of truth even amongst the most true relations of this age. Which as for mine own part I am ready any way with my word to acknowledge, so also (of the certainty thereof assured by mine own experience) with this my public assertion, I do affirm the same. Farewell in the Lord.

From
HARIOT'S INTRODUCTION

Since the first undertaking by Sir Walter Raleigh to deal in the action of discovering of that country which is now called and known by the name of Virginia, many voyages having been thither made at sundry times to his great charge, as first in the year 1584, and afterwards in the years 1585, 1586, and now of late this last year of 1587: there have been divers and variable reports with some slanderous and shameful speeches bruited abroad by many that returned from thence. Especially of that discovery which was made by the colony transported by Sir Richard Grenville in the year 1585, being of all the others the most principal and as yet of most effect, the time of their abode in the country being a whole year, when as in the other voyage before they stayed but six weeks and the others after were only for supply and transportation, nothing more being discovered than had been before. Which reports have not done a little wrong to many that otherwise would have also favored and adventured in the action, to the honor and benefit of our nation, besides the particular profit and credit which would redound to themselves, the dealers therein . . .

I have therefore thought it good, being one that have been in the discovery and in dealing with the natural inhabitants specially employed, and having therefore seen and known more than the ordinary, to impart so much unto you of the fruits of our labors as that you may know how injuriously the enterprise is slandered. . . .

The treatise whereof for your more ready view and easier understanding I will divide into three special parts. In the first I will make declaration of such commodities there already found or to be raised, which will not only serve the ordinary turns of you which are and shall be the planters and inhabitants, but such an overplus sufficiently to be yielded, or by men of skill to be provided, as by way of traffic and exchange with our own nation of England, will enrich yourselves the providers, those that shall deal with you, the enterprisers in general, and greatly profit our own countrymen, to supply them with most things which heretofore they have been fain to provide either of strangers or of our enemies: which commodities, for distinction sake, I call *Merchantable.*

In the second, I will set down all the commodities which we know the country by our experience doth yield of itself for victual and sustenance of man's life; such

as is usually fed upon by the inhabitants of the country, as also by us during the time we were there.

In the last part I will make mention generally of such other commodities besides as I am able to remember and as I shall think behooveful for those that shall inhabit and plant there to know of; which especially concern building, as also some other necessary uses: with a brief description of the nature and manners of the people of the country.

From the
FIRST PART

Silk of grass or grass silk. There is a kind of grass in the country upon the blades whereof there groweth very good silk in form of a thin glittering skin to be stripped off. It groweth two foot and a half high or better: the blades are about two foot in length and half inch broad. The like groweth in Persia, which is in the self-same climate as Virginia, of which very many of the silk works that come from thence into Europe are made. Hereof if it be planted and ordered as in Persia, it cannot in reason be otherwise but that there will rise in short time great profit to the dealers therein, seeing there is so great use and vent thereof as well in our country as elsewhere. And by the means of sowing and planting it in good ground, it will be far greater, better, and more plentiful than it is. Although notwithstanding there is great store thereof in many places of the country growing naturally and wild. Which also by proof here in England in making a piece of silk grogram we found to be excellent good.

From the
SECOND PART

Of fowl: turkey cocks and turkey hens, stockdoves, partridges, cranes, hernes, and in winter great store of swans and geese. Of all sorts of fowl I have the names in the country language of forescore and six, of which number besides those that be named we have taken, eaten, and have the pictures as they were there drawn with the names of the inhabitants of several strange sorts of water fowl eight, and seventeen kinds more of land fowl, although we have seen and eaten of many more, which for want of leisure there for the purpose could not be pictured; and after we are better furnished and stored upon further discovery, with their strange beasts, fish, trees, plants, and herbs, they shall be also published.

There are also parrots, falcons, and marlin hawks, which although with us they be not used for meat, yet for other causes I thought good to mention.

From the
THIRD PART

It resteth I speak a word or two of the natural inhabitants, their natures and manners, leaving large discourse thereof until time more convenient hereafter . . .

For mankind, they say a woman was made first, which, by the working of one of the gods, conceived and brought forth children: and in such sort they say they had their beginning. . . .

They think that all the gods are of human shape and therefore they represent them by images in the forms of men. . . .

They believe also the immortality of the soul, that after this life as soon as the soul is departed from the body according to the works it hath done, it is either carried to heaven, the habitacle of gods, there to enjoy perpetual bliss and happiness, or else to a great pit or hole, which they think to be in the furthest parts of their part of the world toward the sunset, there to burn continually: the place they call *Popogusso*. . . .

Many times and in every town where I came, according as I was able, I made declaration of the contents of the Bible, that therein was set forth the true and only God and his mighty works, that therein was contained the true doctrine of salvation through Christ, with many particularities of miracles and chief points of religion, as I was able then to utter and thought fit for the time. And although I told them the book materially and of itself was not of any such virtue as I thought they did conceive, but only the doctrine therein contained, yet would many be glad to touch it, to embrace it, to kiss it, to hold it to their breasts and heads, and stroke over all their body with it, to shew their hungry desire of that knowledge which was spoken of.

The *Werowance* [1] with whom we dwelt called *Wingina* and many of his people would be glad many times to be with us at our prayers and many times call upon us both in his own town, as also in others whither he sometimes accompanied us, to pray and sing psalms, hoping thereby to be partaker of the same effects which we by that means also expected.

Twice this *Werowance* was so grievously sick that he was like to die, and as he lay languishing, doubting of any help by his own priests, and thinking he was in such danger for offending us and thereby our god, sent for some of us to pray and be a means to our god that it would please him either that he might live or after death dwell with him in bliss, so likewise were the requests of many others in the like case.

On a time also when their corn began to wither by reason of a drouth which happened extraordinarily, fearing that it had come to pass by reason that in something they had displeased us, many would come to us and desire us to pray to our God of England that he would preserve their corn, promising that when it was ripe we also should be partakers of the fruit.

A CHIEF LADY OF POMEIOOC

About 20 miles from that island, near the lake of Paquippe, there is another town called Pomeiooek hard by the sea. The ap-

---

[1] Hariot spells it "Wiroans": the word for chieftain.

parel of the chief ladies of that town dif-
fereth but little from the attire of those
which live in Roanoac. For they wear their
hair trussed up in a knot, as the maidens do
which we spake of before, and have their
skins pounced in the same manner, yet
they wear a chain of great pearls or beads
of copper or smooth bones 5 or 6 fold about
their necks, bearing one arm in the same;
in the other hand they carry a gourd full
of some kind of pleasant liquor. They tie
deer's skin doubled about them crotching
higher about their breasts, which hang down
before almost to their knees, and are almost altogether naked behind. Commonly
their young daughters of 7 or 8 years old
do wait upon them wearing about them a
girdle of skin, which hangeth down behind,
and is drawn underneath between their
thighs and bound above their navel with
moss of trees between that and their skins
to cover their privities withal. After they
be once past 10 years of age, they wear deer
skins as the older sort do. They are greatly
delighted with puppets and babes [dolls]
which were brought out of England.

THEIR DANCES WHICH THEY USE AT THEIR HIGH FEASTS

At a certain time of the year they make
a great and solemn feast whereunto their
neighbors of the towns adjoining repair
from all parts, every man attired in the
most strange fashion they can devise, having certain marks on the backs to declare
of what place they be. The place where they
meet is a broad plain, about the which are
planted in the ground certain posts carved
with heads like to the faces of nuns covered with their veils. Then, being set in
order, they dance, sing, and use the strangest gestures that they can possibly devise.
Three of the fairest virgins of the company
are in the midst, which, embracing one
another, do as it were turn about in their
dancing. All this is done after the sun is
set for avoiding of heat. When they are
weary of dancing, they go out out of the
circle and come in until their dances be
ended and they go to make merry. . . .

1580 ∾ *Captain John Smith* ∾ 1631

FROM his fifteenth to his twenty-fourth year, Captain John Smith, born
in 1580, led a life of swashbuckling adventure on the European continent,
serving in the French, Dutch, and Transylvanian armies. Having survived,
according to his own account, such experiences as being robbed and beaten
by outlaws, thrown into the sea as a heretic, captured by the Turks and sold
into slavery to a Pasha, he managed to make his way back to England in 1604
by a route that led him through Russia and Africa.

Late in 1606, when an expedition financed by the Virginia Company of
London to colonize Virginia sailed from England in three ships, Smith was one
of the few shareholders to go with it. The expedition founded Jamestown,
but would not have been able to maintain itself for long had not Smith, by
his courageous leadership, forced even the disaffected to work and dealt diplo-
matically with the Indians. He likewise interested England in the new colony
by writing such a "pamphlet of newes" as his *A True Relation*, published in
London in 1608.

Leaving his ill-assorted and quarrelsome fellow colonists to work out their own destiny, Smith returned to England in 1609, became a colonization promoter for New England, and explored its coast in 1614. From 1615 to his death in 1631, he lived quietly in England devoting his time to writing, his best known works being *The Generall Historie of Virginia, New-England, and the Summer Isles*, London, 1624, and *The True Travels, Adventures, and Observations of Captaine John Smith*, London, 1630.

Of the three selections printed here, the first is the concluding section of his *A Map of Virginia, with a Description of the Countrey, the Commodities, People, Government and Religion*, and contains an account of Powhatan, the father of Pocahontas, and a succinct review of the difficulties of the first Jamestown colonists; the second is an exhortation to planters from his *A Description of New England*, an important document in the extensive literature of colonization promotion;. and the third is an exposition of his hopes for the Massachusetts Bay Colony from *Advertisements For the unexperienced Planters* of *New England, or any where*.

[In all three selections, the texts of the original editions have been modernized in spelling and to some extent in punctuation. Bracketed interpolations are editorial. *Travels and Works of Captain John Smith*, ed. E. Arber (Edinburgh, 1910), contains complete texts.]

From
A MAP OF VIRGINIA
[1612]

ALTHOUGH the country people be very barbarous, yet have they amongst them such government as that their Magistrates for good commanding, and their people for due subjection and obeying, excel many places that would be counted very civil.

The form of their commonwealth is a monarchical government. One as Emperor ruleth over many kings or governors. Their chief ruler is called Powhatan, and taketh his name of the principal place of dwelling called Powhatan. But his proper name is Wahunsonacock.

Some countries he hath, which have been his ancestors', and came unto him by inheritance, as the country called Powhatan, Arrohateck, Appamatuke, Pamaunke, Youghtanund, and Mattapanient. All the rest of his Territories expressed in the Map, they report have been his several conquests.

In all his ancient inheritances, he hath houses built after their manner like arbors; some 30, some 40 yards long; and at every house provision for his entertainment according to the time. At Werowcomoco he was seated upon the north side of the river Pamaunke, some 14 miles from James Town; where for the most part he was resident, but he took so little pleasure in our near neighborhood, that were able to visit him against his will in 6 or 7 hours, that he retired himself to a place in the deserts at the top of the river Chichahamania between Youghtanund and Powhatan. His habitation there is called Orapakes, where he ordinarily now resideth.

He is of personage a tall, well-proportioned man, with a sour look; his head somewhat gray, his beard so thin that it seemeth none at all. His age near 60; of a very able and hardy body to endure any labor. About his person ordinarily attendeth a guard of 40 or 50 of the tallest men his country doth afford. Every night upon the 4 quarters of his house are 4 sentinels, each standing from other a flight shoot: and at every half hour one from the *corps du guard* doth holloa, unto whom every sentinel doth answer round from his stand. If any fail, they presently send forth an officer that beateth him extremely.

A mile from Orapakes in a thicket of wood he hath a house in which he keepeth his kind of treasure, as skins, copper, pearl, and beads, which he storeth up against the time of his death and burial. Here also is his store of red paint for ointment, and bows and arrows. This house is 50 or 60 yards in length, frequented only by priests. At the 4 corners of this house stand 4 images as sentinels: one of a dragon, another a bear, the 3 like a leopard, and the fourth like a giant-like man: all made evil-favoredly, according to their best workmanship.

He hath as many women as he will: whereof when he lieth on his bed, one sitteth at his head, and another at his feet; but when he sitteth, one sitteth on his right hand and another on his left. As he is weary of his women, he bestoweth them on those that best deserve them at his hands.

When he dineth or suppeth, one of his women, before and after meat, bringeth him water in a wooden platter to wash his hands. Another waiteth with a bunch of feathers to wipe them instead of a towel, and the feathers when he hath wiped are dried again.

His kingdom descendeth not to his sons nor children, but first to his brethren, whereof he hath 3, namely Opitchapan, Opechancanough, and Catataugh, and after their decease to his sisters. First to the eldest sister, then to the rest: and after them to the heirs male and female of the eldest sister; but never to the heirs of the males.

[Neither] he nor any of his people understand any letters whereby to write or read; the only laws whereby he ruleth is custom. Yet when he listeth, his will is a law and must be obeyed: not only as a king, but as half a God they esteem him.

His inferior kings whom they call *werowances* are tied to rule by customs and have

power of life and death as their command in that nature. But this word *werowance* which we call and conster [construe] for a king is a common word whereby they call all commanders: for they have but few words in their language and but few occasions to use any officers more than one commander, which commonly they call *werowances*.

They all know their several lands and habitations and limits to fish, fowl, or hunt in; but they hold all of their great *Werowance*, Powhatan, unto whom they pay tribute of skins, beads, copper, pearl, deer, turkeys, wild beasts, and corn. What he commandeth they dare not disobey in the least thing. It is strange to see with what great fear and adoration all these people do obey this Powhatan. For at his feet they present whatsoever he commandeth, and at the least frown of his brow, their greatest spirits will tremble with fear: and no marvel, for he is very terrible and tryannous in punishing such as offend him.

For example, he caused certain malefactors to be bound hand and foot; then, having of many fires gathered great store of burning coals, they rake these coals round in the form of a cockpit, and in the midst they cast the offenders to broil to death. Sometimes he causeth the heads of them that offend him to be laid upon the altar of sacrificing stone, and one with clubs beats out their brains. When he would punish any notorious enemy or malefactor, he causeth him to be tied to a tree, and, with mussel shells or reeds, the executioner cutteth off his joints one after another, ever casting what they cut off into the fire; then doth he proceed with shells and reeds to case the skin from his head and face; then do they rip his belly, and so burn him with the tree and all. Thus themselves reported they executed George Cassen.[1]

Their ordinary correction is to beat them with cudgels. We have seen a man kneeling on his knees; and at Powhatan's command,

---

[1] Among the first planters of Jamestown, George Cassen is listed as a laborer.

two men have beat him on the bare skin till he hath fallen senseless in a swoon and yet never cry [cried] nor complained.

In the year 1608 he surprised the people of Payankatank, his near neighbors and subjects. The occasion was to us unknown, but the manner was thus. First he sent divers of his men as to lodge amongst them that night, then the *Ambuscadoes* environed all their houses, and at the hour appointed they all fell to the spoil: 24 men they slew; the long hair of the one side of their heads with the skin cased off with shells or reeds, they brought away. They surprised also the women and the children and the *Werowance*. All these they present [ed] to Powhatan. The *Werowance,* women and children became his prisoners and do him service.

The locks of hair with their skins he hanged on a line unto two trees. And thus he made ostentation as of a great triumph at Werowocomoco, shewing them to the Englishmen that then came unto him, at his appointment: they expecting provision; he, to betray them, supposed to half conquer them by this spectacle of his terrible cruelty. [2]

And this is as much as my memory can call to mind worthy of note; which I have purposely collected to satisfy my friends of the true worth and quality of Virginia. Yet some bad natures will not stick to slander the country, that will slovenly spit at all things, especially in company where they can find none to contradict them. Who though they were scarce ever 10 miles from James Town, or at the most but at the falls; yet holding it a great disgrace that amongst so much action their actions were nothing, exclaim of all things, though they never adventured to know anything, nor ever did anything but devour the fruits of other men's labors. Being for most part of such tender educations and small experience in martial accidents: because they found not English cities, nor such fair houses, nor at their own wishes any of their accustomed dainties, with feather beds and down pillows, taverns and alehouses in every breathing place, neither such plenty of gold and silver and dissolute liberty as they expected, had little or no care of anything, but to pamper their bellies, to fly away with our pinnaces, or procure their means to return for England. For the country was to them a misery, a ruin, a death, a hell; and their reports here and their own actions there according.

Some other there were that had yearly stipends to pass to and again for transportation: who to keep the mystery of the business in themselves, though they had neither time nor means to know much of themselves; yet all men's actions or relations they so formally tuned to the temporizing time's simplicity, as they could make their ignorances seem much more than all the true actors could by their experience. And those with their great words deluded the world with such strange promises as abused the business much worse than the rest. For the business being builded upon the foundation of their feigned experience, the planters, the money, time, and means have still miscarried: yet they ever returning, and the planters so far absent, who could contradict their excuses? which, still to maintain their vainglory and estimation, from time to time they have used such diligence as made them pass for truths, though nothing more false. And that the adventurers might be thus abused, let no man wonder, for the wisest living is soonest abused by him that hath a fair tongue and a dissembling heart.

There were many in Virginia merely projecting verbal and idle contemplators, and those so devoted to pure idleness that though they had lived two or three years in Virginia lordly, necessity itself could not compel them to pass the Peninsula or *Pallisadoes* of James Town; and those witty spirits, what would they not affirm in the behalf of our transporters, to get victual from their ships, or obtain their good words in England to get their passes?

---

[2] Smith probably refers here to a visit which he and a party of his men made to Powhatan January 12, 1609.

Thus from the clamors and the ignorance of false informers are sprung those disasters that spring in Virginia, and our ingenious verbalists were no less plague to us in Virginia than the locusts to the Egyptians. For the labor of 30 of the best only, preserved in Christianity, by their industry, the idle livers of near 200 of the rest: who lived near 10 months of such natural means as the country naturally of itself afforded.

Notwithstanding all this and the worst fury of the savages, the extremity of sickness, mutinies, faction, ignorances, and want of victual; in all that time I lost but 7 or 8 men: yet subjected the savages to our desired obedience and received contribution from 35 of their kings to protect and assist them against any that should assault them; in which order they continued true and faithful and as subjects to his Majesty so long after as I did govern there, until I left the country.

Since, how they have revolted, the country lost, and again replanted, and the businesses hath succeeded from time to time, I refer you to the relations of them returned from Virginia, that have been more diligent in such observations.

From
A DESCRIPTION OF NEW ENGLAND
[1616]

Who can desire more content that hath small means or but only his merit to advance his fortune than to tread and plant that ground he hath purchased by the hazard of his life? If he have but the taste of virtue and magnanimity, what to such a mind can be more pleasant than planting and building a foundation for his posterity, got from the rude earth by God's blessing and his own industry, without prejudice to any? If he have any grain of faith or zeal in religion, what can he do less hurtful to any or more agreeable to God than to seek to convert those poor savages to know Christ and humanity, whose labors with discretion will triply requite thy charge and pains? What so truly suits

with honor and honesty as the discovering things unknown? erecting towns, peopling countries, informing the ignorant, reforming things unjust, teaching virtue, and gain to our native mother-country a kingdom to attend her: find employment for those that are idle because they know not what to do: so far from wronging any, as to cause posterity to remember thee; and remembering thee, ever honor that remembrance with praise?

Consider: what were the beginnings and endings of the monarchies of the Chaldeans, the Syrians, the Grecians, and Romans, but this one rule; what was it they would not do, for the good of the commonwealth or their mother-city? For example: Rome, what made her such a monarchess, but only the adventures of her youth, not in riots at home, but in dangers abroad? and the justice and judgment out of their experience when they grew aged. What was their ruin and hurt but this: the excess of idleness, the fondness of parents, the want of experience in magistrates, the admiration of their undeserved honors, the contempt of true merit, their unjust jealousies, their politic incredulities, their hypocritical seeming goodness, and their deeds of secret lewdness? finally, in fine, growing only formal temporists, all that their predecessors got in many years, they lost in few days. Those by their pain and virtues became lords of the world; they by their ease and vices became slaves to their servants. This is the difference betwixt the use of arms in the field and on the monuments of stones, the golden age and the leaden age, prosperity and misery, justice and corruption, substance and shadows, words and deeds, experience and imagination, making commonwealths and marring commonwealths, the fruits of virtue and the conclusions of vice.

Then, who would live at home idly (or think in himself any worth to live) only to eat, drink, and sleep, and so die? Or by consuming that carelessly, his friends got worthily? Or by using that miserably, that maintained virtue honestly? Or for being descended nobly, pine with the vain vaunt of great kindred, in penury? Or (to maintain a silly show of bravery) toil out thy heart, soul, and time basely, by shifts, tricks, cards, and dice? Or by relating news of others' actions shark here or there for a dinner or supper; deceive thy friends, by fair promises and dissimulation, in borrowing where thou never intendest to pay; offend the laws, surfeit with excess, burden thy country, abuse thyself, despair in want, and then couzen thy kindred, yea even thine own brother, and wish thy parents' death (I will not say damnation) to have their estates? though thou seest what honors and rewards the world yet hath for them [who] will seek them and worthily deserve them.

I would be sorry to offend or that any should mistake my honest meaning: for I wish good to all, hurt to none. But rich men for the most part are grown to that dotage, through their pride in their wealth, as though there were no accident could end it or their life.

And what hellish care do such take to make it their own misery and their country's spoil, especially when there is most need of their employment? drawing by all manner of inventions, from the prince and his honest subjects, even the vital spirits of their powers and estates: as if their bags or brags were so powerful a defence, the malicious could not assault them; when they are the only bait, to cause us not to be only assaulted, but betrayed and murdered in our own security, ere we well perceive it.

May not the miserable ruin of Constantinople, their impregnable walls, riches, and pleasures [at] last taken by the Turk (which are but a bit, in comparison of their now mightiness) remember us of the effects of private covetousness? at which time the good emperor held himself rich enough, to have such rich subjects, so formal in all excess of vanity, all kind of delicacy and prodigality. His poverty when the Turk besieged, the citizens (whose merchandizing thoughts were only to get wealth, little conceiving the desperate resolution of a valiant expert enemy) left the emperor so long to his conclusions, having spent all he had to pay his young, raw, discontented soldiers, that suddenly he, they, and their city were all a prey to the devouring Turk. And what they would not spare for the maintenance of them who adventured their lives to defend them did serve only their enemies to torment them, their friends and country, and all Christendom to this present day. Let this lamentable example remember you that are rich (seeing there are such great thieves in the world to rob you) not to grudge to lend some proportion to breed them that have little, yet are willing to learn how to defend you: for it is too late when the deed is a-doing.

The Romans' estate hath been worse than this: for the mere covetousness and extortion of a few of them so moved the rest that, not having any employment but contemplation, their great judgments grew to so great malice as themselves were sufficient to destroy themselves by faction: let this move you to embrace employment for those whose educations, spirits, and judgments want but your purses, not only to prevent such accustomed dangers, but also to gain more thereby than you have. . . .

My purpose is not to persuade children from their parents, men from their wives, nor servants from their masters: only such as with free consent may be spared: but that each parish or village, in city or country, that will but apparel their fatherless children, of thirteen or fourteen years of age, or young married people, that have small wealth to live on: here by their labor may live exceeding well: provided always that first there be a sufficient power to command them, houses to receive them, means to defend them, and meet provisions for them. . . .

Who seeth not what is the greatest good of the Spaniard but these new conclusions in searching those unknown parts of the unknown world? By which means he dives even into the very secrets of all his neighbors and the most part of the world: and when the Portugal [Portuguese] and Spaniard had found the East and West Indies, how many did condemn themselves, that did not accept of that honest offer of noble Columbus? who, upon our neglect, brought them to it, persuading ourselves the world had no such places as they had found: and yet ever since we find they still (from time to time) have found new lands, new nations, and trades, and still daily do find both in Asia, Africa, Terra Incognita, and America; so that there is neither soldier nor mechanic, from the lord to the beggar, but those parts afford them all employment: and discharge their native soil of so many thousands of all sorts that else, by their sloth, pride, and imperfections, would long ere this have troubled their neighbors or have eaten the pride of Spain itself.

Now he knows little that knows not England may well spare many more people than Spain and is as well able to furnish them with all manner of necessaries. And seeing, for all they have, they cease not still to search that they have not and know not, it is strange we should be so dull as not [to] maintain that which we have and pursue that we know.

From
ADVERTISEMENTS
[1631]

The wars in Europe, Asia, and Africa taught me how to subdue the wild savages in Virginia and New England in America; which now after many a stormy blast of ignorant contradictors, projectors, and undertakers, both they and I have been so tossed and tortured into so many extremities, as despair was the next we both expected, till it pleased God now at last to stir up some good minds, that I hope will produce glory to God, honor to his Majesty, and profit to his kingdoms; although all our plantations have been so foiled and abused, their best good willers have

been for the most part discouraged, and their good intents disgraced, as the general history of them will at large truly relate [to] you.

Pardon me if I offend in loving that I have cherished truly by the loss of my prime fortunes, means, and youth: if it over-glad me to see industry herself adventure now to make use of my aged endeavors, not by such (I hope) as rumour doth report, a many of discontented Brownists, Anabaptists, Papists, Puritans, Separatists, and such factious Humorists: for no such they will suffer among them, if known, as many of the chief of them [John Winthrop, etc.] have assured me; and the much conferences I have had with many of them doth confidently persuade me to write thus much in their behalf.

I mean not the Brownists of Leyden and Amsterdam at New Plymouth, who although by accident, ignorance, and wilfulness have endured, with a wonderful patience, many losses and extremities; yet they subsist and prosper so well, not any of them will abandon the country, but to the utmost of their powers increase their numbers. But of those which are gone within this eighteen months [April, 1629—October, 1630] for Cape Anne and the Bay of Massachusetts. Those which are their chief undertakers are gentlemen of good estate, some of 500, some a thousand pound land a year, all which they say they will sell for the advancing this harmless and pious work; men of good credit and well-beloved in their country, not such as fly for debt or any scandal at home; and are good Catholic Protestants according to the reformed Church of England; if not, it is well they are gone. The rest of them men of good means, or arts, occupations, and qualities, much more fit for such a business and better furnished of all necessaries if they arrive well than was ever any plantation went out of England.

I will not say but some of them may be more precise than needs, nor that they all be so good as they should be; for Christ had but twelve apostles, and one was a traitor: and if there be no dissemblers among them, it is more than a wonder; therefore do not condemn all for some. But however they have as good authority from his Majesty as they could desire: if they do ill, the loss is but their own; if well, a great glory and exceeding good to this kingdom, to make good at last what all our former conclusions have disgraced. Now they take not that course the Virginia Company did for the planters there; their purses and lives were subject to some few here in London who were never there, that consumed all in arguments, projects, and their own conceits: every year trying new conclusions, altering everything yearly as they altered opinions, till they had consumed more than two hundred thousand pounds and near eight thousand men's lives.

Walam Olum

[Date uncertain]

CONSTANTINE SAMUEL RAFINESQUE, of French-German descent, born in Galata, a suburb of Constantinople, Oct. 22, 1783, visited the United States in 1802, then went to Sicily, where he carried on business under the name of his mother's family, "Schmaltz," returned to the United States in 1815, served as "Professor of Historical and Natural Sciences" at Transylvania University, Lexington, Kentucky, from 1819 to 1826, and died in Philadelphia, Sept. 18, 1840. A prolific writer of scientific and antiquarian essays, Rafinesque copied in 1820 a collection of bark or board plates incised and painted with the picture writings of the Lenape or Delaware Indians and in 1822 the verses in Lenape dialect that were supposed to accompany each ideograph.

Rafinesque published a translation of this Walam Olum or "Red Score" in 1836. This translation was once thought to be a forgery, but the manuscript of Rafinesque's copy of the original is now regarded as a fairly accurate rendering of some later copy of a very early oral culture-saga of the Lenape, "the earliest American book," as it has been called. [The following translation of the entire *Walam Olum* is reprinted from *Library of Aboriginal American Literature,* ed. D. G. Brinton, Vol. V, Philadelphia, 1885, pp. 171-217. Brackets and parentheses are Brinton's to indicate interpolations or problematical renderings.

I

At first, in that place, at all times, above the earth,
On the earth, [was] an extended fog, and there the great Manito was.
At first, forever, lost in space, everywhere, the great Manito was.
He made the extended land and the sky.
He made the sun, the moon, the stars.
He made them all to move evenly.
Then the wind blew violently, and it cleared, and the water flowed off far and strong.

5

And groups of islands grew newly, and there remained.
Anew spoke the great Manito, a manito to manitos,
To beings, mortals, souls and all,   10
And ever after he was a manito to men, and their grandfather.
He gave the first mother, the mother of beings.
He gave the fish, he gave the turtles, he gave the beasts, he gave the birds.
But an evil Manito made evil beings only, monsters . . .
He made the flies, he made the gnats.   15
All beings were then friendly.
Truly the manitos were active and kindly
To those very first men, and to those first mothers; fetched them wives,
And fetched them food, when first they desired it.
All had cheerful knowledge, all had leisure, all thought in gladness.   20
But very secretly an evil being, a mighty magician, came on earth,
And with him brought badness, quarreling, unhappiness,
Brought bad weather, brought sickness, brought death.
All this took place of old on the earth, beyond the great tide-water, at the first.

II

Long ago there was a mighty snake and beings evil to men.   25
This mighty snake hated those who were there (and) greatly disquieted those whom
    he hated.
They both did harm, they both injured each other, both were not in peace.
Driven from their homes they fought with this murderer.
The mighty snake firmly resolved to harm the men.
He brought three persons, he brought a monster, he brought a rushing water.   30
Between the hills the water rushed and rushed, dashing through and through, destroying
    much.
Nanabush, the Strong White One, grandfather of beings, grandfather of men, was on
    the Turtle Island.
There he was walking and creating, as he passed by and created the turtle.
Beings and men all go forth, they walk in the floods and shallow waters, down stream
    thither to the Turtle Island.
There were many fishes, which ate some of them.   35
The Manito daughter, coming, helped with her canoe, helped all, as they came and came.
[And also] Nanabush, Nanabush, the grandfather of all, the grandfather of beings, the
    grandfather of men, the grandfather of the turtle.
The men then were together on the turtle, like to turtles.
Frightened on the turtle, they prayed on the turtle that what was spoiled should be
    restored.   40
The water ran off, the earth dried, the lakes were at rest, all was silent, and the mighty
    snake departed.

III

After the rushing waters (had subsided) the Lenape of the turtle were close together, in
    hollow houses, living together there.
It freezes where they abode, it snows where they abode, it storms where they abode, it is
    cold where they abode.

At this northern place they speak favorably of mild, cool (lands), with many deer
and buffaloes.

As they journeyed, some being strong, some rich, they separated into house-builders
and hunters;   45

The strongest, the most united, the purest, were the hunters.

The hunters showed themselves at the north, at the east, at the south, at the west.

In that ancient country, in that northern country, in that turtle country, the best of the
Lenape were the Turtle men.

All the cabin fires of that land were disquieted, and all said to their priest, "Let us go."

To the Snake land to the east they went forth, going away, earnestly grieving.   50

Split asunder, weak, trembling, their land burned, they went, torn and broken, to the
Snake Island.

Those from the north being free, without care, went forth from the land of snow, in
different directions.

The fathers of the Bald Eagle and the White Wolf remain along the sea, rich in fish
and mussels.

Floating up the streams in their canoes, our fathers were rich, they were in the light,
when they were at those islands.   55

Head Beaver and Big Bird said,

"Let us go to Snake Island," they said.

All say they will go along to destroy all the land.

Those of the north agreed,

Those of the east agreed.

Over the water, the frozen sea,   60

They went to enjoy it.

On the wonderful, slippery water,

On the stone-hard water all went,

On the great Tidal Sea, the mussel-bearing sea.

Ten thousand at night,   65

All in one night,

To the Snake Island, to the east, at night,

They walk and walk, all of them.

The men from the north, the east, the south,

The Eagle clan, the Beaver clan, the Wolf clan,   70

The best men, the rich men, the head men,

Those with wives, those with daughters, those with dogs,

They all come, they tarry at the land of the spruce pines;

Those from the west come with hesitation,

Esteeming highly their old home at the Turtle land.   75

IV

Long ago the fathers of the Lenape were at the land of spruce pines.

Hitherto the Bald Eagle band had been the pipe bearer,

While they were searching for the Snake Island, that great and fine land.

They having died, the hunters, about to depart, met together.

All say to Beautiful Head, "Be thou chief."   80

"Coming to the Snakes, slaughter at that Snake hill, that they leave it."

All of the Snake tribe were weak, and hid themselves in the Swampy Vales.

After Beautiful Head, White Owl was chief at Spruce Pine land.
After him, Keeping-Guard was chief of that people.
After him, Snow Bird was chief; he spoke of the south,   85
That our fathers should possess it by scattering abroad.
Snow Bird went south, White Beaver went east.
The Snake land was at the south, the great Spruce Pine land was toward the shore;
To the east was the Fish land, toward the lakes was the buffalo land.
After Snow Bird, the Seizer was chief, and all were killed,   90
The robbers, the snakes, the evil men, the stone men.
After the Seizer there were ten chiefs, and there was much warfare south and east.
After them, the Peaceable was chief at Snake land.
After him, Not-Black was chief, who was a straight man.
After him, Much-Loved was chief, a good man.   95
After him, No-Blood was chief, who walked in cleanliness.
After him, Snow-Father was chief, he of the big teeth.
After him, Tally-Maker was chief, who made records.
After him, Shiverer-with-Cold was chief, who went south to the corn land.
After him, Corn-Breaker was chief, who brought about the planting of corn.   100
After him, the Strong-Man was chief, who was useful to the chieftains.
After him, the Salt-Man was chief; after him the Little-One was chief.
There was no rain, and no corn, so they moved further seaward.
At the place of caves, in the buffalo land, they at last had food, on a pleasant plain.
After the Little-One (came) the Fatigued; after him, the Stiff-One.   105
After him, the Reprover; disliking him, and unwilling (to remain),
Being angry, some went off secretly, moving east.
The wise ones who remained made the Loving-One chief.
They settled again on the Yellow river, and had much corn on stoneless soil.
All being friendly, the Affable was chief, the first of that name.   110
He was very good, this Affable, and came as a friend to all the Lenape.
After this good one, Strong-Buffalo was chief and pipe-bearer.
Big-Owl was chief; White Bird was chief.
The Willing-One was chief and priest; he made festivals.
Rich-Again was chief; the Painted-One was chief.   115
White-Fowl was chief; again there was war, north and south.
The Wolf-wise-in-Counsel was chief.
He knew how to make war on all; he slew Strong-Stone.
The Always-Ready-One was chief; he fought against the Snakes.
The Strong-Good-One was chief; he fought against the northerners.   120
The Lean-One was chief; he fought against the Tawa people.
The Opossum-Like was chief; he fought in sadness,
And said, "They are many; let us go together to the east, to the sunrise."
They separated at Fish river; the lazy ones remained there.
Cabin-Man was chief; the Talligewi possessed the east.   125
Strong-Friend was chief; he desired the eastern land.
Some passed on east; the Talega ruler killed some of them.
All say, in unison, "War, war."
The Talamatan, friends from the north, come, and all go together.
The Sharp-One was chief; he was the pipe-bearer beyond the river.   130
They rejoiced greatly that they should fight and slay the Talega towns.

The Stirrer was chief; the Talega towns were too strong.
The Fire-Builder was chief; they all gave to him many towns.
The Breaker-in-Pieces was chief; all the Talega go south.
He-has-Pleasure was chief; all the people rejoice.   135
They stay south of the lakes; the Talamatan friends north of the lakes.
When Long-and-Mild was chief, those who were not his friends conspired.
Truthful-Man was chief; the Talamatans made war.
Just-and-True was chief; the Talamatans trembled.

V

All were peaceful, long ago, there at the Talega land.   140
The Pipe-Bearer was chief at the White river.
White-Lynx was chief; much corn was planted.
Good-and-Strong was chief; the people were many.
The Recorder was chief; he painted the records.
Pretty-Blue-Bird was chief; there was much fruit.   145
Always-There was chief; the towns were many.
Paddler-up-Stream was chief; he was much on the rivers.
Little Cloud was chief; many departed,
The Nanticokes and the Shawnees going to the south.
Big-Beaver was chief, at the White Salt Lick.   150
The Seer, the praised one, went to the west.
He went to the west, to the southwest, to the western villages.
The Rich-Down-River-Man was chief, at Talega river.
The Walker was chief; there was much war.
Again with the Tawa people, again with the Stone people, again with the northern
    people.   155
Grandfather-of-Boats was chief; he went to lands in boats.
Snow-Hunter was chief; he went to the north land.
Look-About was chief; he went to the Talega mountains.
East-Villager was chief; he was east of Talega.
A great land and a wide land was the east land,   160
A land without snakes, a rich land, a pleasant land.
Great Fighter was chief, toward the north.
At the Straight river, River-Loving was chief.
Becoming-Fat was chief at Sassafras land.
All the hunters made wampum again at the great sea.   165
Red-Arrow was chief at the stream again.
The Painted-Man was chief at the Mighty Water.
The Easterners and the Wolves go northeast.
Good-Fighter was chief, and went to the north.
The Mengwe, the Lynxes, all trembled.   170
Again an Affable was chief, and made peace with all,
All were friends, all were united, under this great chief.
Great-Beaver was chief, remaining in Sassafras land.
White-Body was chief on the sea shore.
Peace-Maker was chief, friendly to all.   175
He-Makes-Mistakes was chief, hurriedly coming.

At this time whites came on the Eastern sea.
Much-Honored was chief; he was prosperous.
Well-Praised was chief; he fought at the south.
He fought in the land of the Talega and Koweta.   180
White-Otter was chief; a friend of the Talamatans.
White-Horn was chief; he went to the Talega,
To the Hilini, to the Shawnees, to the Kanawhas.
Coming-as-a-Friend was chief; he went to the Great Lakes,
Visiting all his children, all his friends.   185
Cranberry-Eater was chief, friend of the Ottawas.
North-Walker was chief; he made festivals.
Slow-Gatherer was chief at the shore.
As three were desired, three those were who grew forth,
The Unami, the Minsi, the Chikini.   190
Man-Who-Fails was chief; he fought the Mengwe.
He-is-Friendly was chief; he scared the Mengwe.
Saluted was chief; thither,
Over there, on the Scioto, he had foes.
White-Crab was chief; a friend of the shore.   195
Watcher was chief; he looked toward the sea.
At this time, from north and south, the whites came.
They are peaceful; they have great things; who are they?

SYNOPSIS OF THE *WALAM OLUM*

(Reprinted, with some omissions, from Brinton, *op. cit.*, pp. 166-168)

I

The formation of the universe by the Great Manito is described. In the primal fog and watery waste he formed land and sky, and the heavens cleared. He then created men and animals. These lived in peace and joy until a certain evil manito came, and sowed discord and misery. . . . The notion of the earth rising from the primal waters is strictly a part of the earliest Algonkin mythology. . . .

II

The Evil Manito, who now appears under the guise of a gigantic serpent, determines to destroy the human race, and for that purpose brings upon them a flood of water. Many perish, but a certain number escape to the turtle, that is, to solid land, and are there protected by Nanabush (Manibozho or Michabo). They pray to him for assistance, and he caused the water to disappear, and the great serpent to depart.

This canto is a brief reference to the conflict between the Algonkin hero god and the serpent of the waters, originally, doubtless, a meteorological myth. It is an ancient and authentic aboriginal legend, shared both by Iroquois and Algonkins, under slightly different forms. In one aspect, it is the Flood or Deluge Myth.

III

The waters having disappeared, the home of the tribe is described as in a cold northern clime. This they concluded to leave in search of warmer lands. Having divided their people into a warrior and a peaceful class, they journeyed southward, toward what is called the "Snake land." They approached this land in winter, over a frozen river. Their number was large, but all had not joined in the expedition with equal willingness, their members at the west preferring their ancient seats in the north to the uncertainty of southern conquests. They, however, finally united with the other bands, and they all moved south to the land of spruce pines.

IV

The first sixteen verses record the gradual conquest of most of the Snake land. It seems to have required the successive efforts of six or seven head chiefs, one after another, to bring this about, probably but a small portion at a time yielding to the attacks of these enemies. Its position is described as being to the southwest, and in the interior of the country. Here they first learned to cultivate maize.

The remainder of the canto is taken up with a long list of chiefs, and with the removal of the tribe, in separate bands and at different times, to the east. In this journey from the Snake land to the east, they encountered and had long wars with the Talega. These lived in strong towns, but by the aid of the Hurons (Talamatans), they overcame them and drove them to the south.

V

Having conquered the Talegas, the Lenape possessed their land and that of the Snake people, and for a certain time enjoyed peace and abundance. Then occurred a division of their people, some, as Nantocokes and Shawnees, going to the south, others to the west, and later, the majority toward the east, arriving finally at the Salt sea, the Atlantic ocean. Thence a portion turned north and east, and encountered the Iroquois. Still later, the three sub-tribes of the Lenape settled themselves definitely along the Delaware river, and received the geographical names by which they were known, as Minsi, Unami and Unalachtgo. They were often at war with the Iroquois, generally successfully. Rumors of the whites had reached them, and finally these strangers approached the river, both from the north (New York Bay) and the south. Here the song closes.

1590 ∾ *William Bradford* ∾ 1657

BORN in 1590 in Austerfield, England, of Yorkshire farming folk, William Bradford became an ardent student of the Scriptures at the age of twelve, joined a dissenting group that met at the house of William Brewster in Scrooby, and left England with them when, organized into a Separatist Church, they decided to remove to the Low Countries to escape persecution by intolerant Anglicans. After living first at Amsterdam and then at Leyden, they pondered emigration to America, but only a part of the Leyden congregation resolved to go. Through the good offices of Sir Edward Sandys they gained permission to found an independent settlement on land granted to the Virginia Company of London. From London promoters they obtained capital for their venture and from James I. the promise that they would not be molested in their new home if they stirred up no strife.

Led by Brewster and Bradford, they sailed in 1620 from Delft Haven via Southampton and Plymouth, England, arrived early in November at Cape Cod in the *Mayflower* after much buffeting by adverse weather, and founded Plymouth, Massachusetts, which was in territory under the jurisdiction of the Council for New England rather than the Virginia Company of London. Their backers in England secured a patent in 1621 from the Council, and their leaders purchased this patent in 1629-30; but the colony was never the recipient of a royal charter. In 1691 the Plymouth colony was merged with that of Massachusetts Bay. Whereas the settlers of the latter were moderate Puritans or congregationalists who preferred not to think of themselves as separated from the Church of England, those of Plymouth, by their insistence on Separatism, were nearer the left-wing or radical fringe of the complex Puritan movement.

Bradford became second governor of Plymouth Colony in 1621 and held that office during thirty of the remaining thirty-six years of his life. He began writing his *History* in 1630 and probably brought it to completion about 1650, seven years before his death. The *History* remained in manuscript form for more than 200 years. Used freely by early New England historians, it was finally believed to be lost irrecoverably. By good luck and shrewd literary detective work, it was located in the Fulham Library, England, by Charles Deane in 1855 and first published, under his editorship and the auspices of the Massachusetts Historical Society, in 1856. The edition of William T. Davis, New York, 1908, is one of the volumes in the series, *Original Narratives of Early American History.*

[The present selections are modernized in spelling, punctuation, and, to some extent, in paragraphing. Titles have been supplied by the present editors.]

From
HISTORY OF PLYMOUTH PLANTATION
[1856 (written 1630-1650)]

The Decision to Leave England

THE one side labored to have the right worship of God and discipline of Christ established in the church, according to the simplicity of the gospel, without the mixture of men's inventions, and to have and be ruled by the laws of God's word dispensed in those offices and by those officers of pastors, teachers, and elders, etc., according to the Scriptures. The other party, though under many colors and pretences, endeavored to have the episcopal dignity (after the popish manner) with their large power and jurisdiction still retained; with all those courts, canons, and ceremonies, together with all such livings, revenues, and subordinate officers, with other such means as formerly upheld their anti-Christian greatness, and enabled them with lordly and tyrannous power to persecute the poor servants of God. This contention was so great as neither the honor of God, the common persecution, nor the mediation of Mr. Calvin and other worthies of the Lord in those places, could prevail with those thus episcopally minded, but they proceeded by all means to disturb the peace of this poor persecuted church, even so far as to charge (very unjustly and ungodlily, yet prelate-like) some of their chief opposers with rebellion and high treason against the Emperor and other such crimes.

And this contention died not with Queen Mary, nor was left beyond the seas, but at her death these people returning into England under gracious Queen Elizabeth, many of them were preferred to bishoprics and other promotions, according to their aims and desires, that inveterate hatred against the holy discipline of Christ in his church hath continued to this day. In so much that for fear it should prevail, all plots and devices have been used to keep it out, incensing the queen and state against it as dangerous for the commonwealth; and that it was most needful that the fundamental points of religion should be preached in those ignorant and superstitious times; and to win the weak and ignorant, they might retain divers harmless ceremonies; and though it were to be wished that divers things were reformed, yet this was not a season for it. And many the like, to stop the mouths of the more godly, to bring them over to yield to one ceremony after another and one corruption after another; by these wiles beguiling some and corrupting others till at length they began to persecute all the zealous professors in the land (though they knew little what this discipline meant) both by word and deed, if they would not submit to their ceremonies and become slaves to them and their popish trash, which have no ground in the word of God but are relics of that man of sin. And the more the light of the gospel grew, the more they urged their subscriptions to these corruptions. So as (notwithstanding all their former pretences and fair colors) they whose eyes God had not justly blinded might easily see whereto these things tended. And to cast contempt the more upon the sincere servants of God, they opprobriously and most injuriously gave unto and imposed upon them that name of Puritans, which it is said the

Novatians[1] out of pride did assume and take unto themselves. And lamentable it is to see the effects which have followed. Religion hath been disgraced, the godly grieved, afflicted, persecuted, and many exiled, sundry have lost their lives in prisons and other ways. On the other hand, sin hath been countenanced, ignorance, profaneness, and atheism increased, and the papists encouraged to hope again for a day. . . .

So many therefore of these professors as saw the evil of these things in these parts, and whose hearts the Lord had touched with heavenly zeal for his truth, they shook off this yoke of anti-Christian bondage, and as the Lord's free people joined themselves (by a covenant of the Lord) into a church estate, in the fellowship of the gospel, to walk in all his ways, made known or to be made known unto them, according to their best endeavors, whatsoever it should cost them, the Lord assisting them. And that it cost them something this ensuing history will declare.

These people became two distinct bodies or churches and in regard of distance of place did congregate severally, for they were of sundry towns and villages, some in Nottinghamshire, some of Lincolnshire, and some of Yorkshire, where they border nearest together. In one of these churches (besides others of note) was Mr. John Smith, a man of able gifts and a good preacher, who afterwards was chosen their pastor. But these afterwards falling into some errors in the Low Countries, there (for the most part) buried themselves and their names.

But in this other church (which must be the subject of our discourse) besides other worthy men, was Mr. Richard Clifton, a grave and reverend preacher, who by his pains and diligence had done much good, and under God had been a means of the

---

[1] A sect of Roman Christians who in 251, under the leadership of L. Noviatianus, caused a schism which lasted for several centuries.

conversion of many. And also that famous and worthy man Mr. John Robinson, who afterwards was their pastor for many years until the Lord took him away by death. Also Mr. William Brewster, a reverent man, who afterwards was chosen an elder of the church and lived with them till old age.

But after these things they could not long continue in any peaceable condition, but were hunted and persecuted on every side, so as their former afflictions were but as flea-bitings in comparison of these which now came upon them. For some were taken and clapped up in prison, others had their houses beset and watched night and day, and hardly escaped their hands; and the most were fain to fly and leave their houses and habitations and the means of their livelihood. Yet these and many other sharper things which afterwards befell them were no other than they looked for, and therefore were the better prepared to bear them by the assistance of God's grace and spirit. Yet seeing themselves thus molested and that there was no hope of their continuance there, by a joint consent they resolved to go into the Low Countries, where they heard was freedom of religion for all men; as also how sundry from London and other parts of the land had been exiled and persecuted for the same cause, and were gone thither, and lived at Amsterdam and in other places of the land. So, after they had continued together about a year and kept their meetings every Sabbath in one place or other, exercising the worship of God amongst themselves, notwithstanding all the diligence and malice of their adversaries, they seeing they could no longer continue in that condition, they resolved to get over into Holland as they could, which was in the year 1607 and 1608, of which more at large in the next chapter.

THE DECISION TO LEAVE LEYDEN

. . . After they had lived in this city about some 11 or 12 years (which is the more observable being the whole time of

that famous truce between that state and the Spaniards) and sundry of them were taken away by death and many others began to be well stricken in years (the grave mistress, Experience, having taught them many things), those prudent governors, with sundry of the sagest members, began both deeply to apprehend their present dangers and wisely to foresee the future and think of timely remedy. In the agitation of their thoughts, and much discourse of things hereabout, at length they began to incline to this conclusion—of removal to some other place. Not out of any newfangledness or other such like giddy humor, by which men are oftentimes transported to their great hurt and danger, but for sundry weighty and solid reasons, some of the chief of which I will here briefly touch.

And first, they saw and found by experience the hardness of the place and country to be such, as few in comparison would come to them and fewer that would bide it out and continue with them. For many that came to them and many more that desired to be with them could not endure that great labor and hard fare, with other inconveniences, which they underwent and were contented with. But though they loved their persons, approved their cause, and honored their sufferings, yet they left them, as it were, weeping, as Orpah did her mother-in-law, Naomi, or as those Romans did Cato in Utica, who desired to be excused and borne with, though they could not all be Catos. [2] For many, though they desired to enjoy the ordinances of God in their purity and the liberty of the gospel with them, yet, alas, they admitted of bondage, with danger of conscience, rather than to endure those hardships; yea, some preferred and chose the prisons in England rather than this liberty in Holland, with these afflictions. But it was thought that if

---

[2] These allusions to the Book of Ruth in the Bible and to Plutarch's Life of Cato the Younger illustrate Bradford's fusion of Christian and classical learning, so typical of the Renaissance man of letters.

a better and easier place of living could be had, it would draw many and take away these discouragements. Yea, their pastor would often say that many of those who both wrote and preached now against them, if they were in a place where they might have liberty and live comfortably, they would then practice as they did.

Secondly, they saw that though the people generally bore all these difficulties very cheerfully and with a resolute courage, being in the best and strength of their years, yet old age began to steal on many of them (and their great and continual labors, with other crosses and sorrows, hastened it before the time) so as it was not only probably thought, but apparently seen, that within a few years more they would be in danger to scatter, by necessity's pressing them, or sink under their burdens, or both. And therefore, according to the divine proverb that a wise man seeth the plague when it cometh and hideth himself (Pro.-22.3.), so they, like skillful and beaten soldiers, were fearful either to be entrapped or surrounded by their enemies, so as they should neither be able to fight nor fly; and therefore thought it better to dislodge betimes to some place of better advantage and less danger, if any such could be found.

Thirdly, as necessity was a taskmaster over them, so they were forced to be such, not only to their servants, but in a sort to their dearest children; the which, as it did not a little wound the tender hearts of many a loving father and mother, so it produced likewise sundry sad and sorrowful effects. For many of their children, that were of best dispositions and gracious inclinations, having learned to bear the yoke in their youth and willing to bear part of their parents' burden, were oftentimes so oppressed with their heavy labors that, though their minds were free and willing, yet their bodies bowed under the weight of the same and became decrepit in their early youth, the vigor of nature being consumed in the very bud, as it were. But that which was most lamentable, and of all sorrows to be borne, was that many of their children, by

these occasions and the great licentiousness of youth in that country and the manifold temptations of the place, were drawn away by evil examples into extravagant and dangerous courses, getting the reins off their necks and departing from their parents. Some became soldiers, others took upon them far voyages by sea, and others some worse courses tending to dissoluteness and the danger of their souls, to the great grief of their parents and dishonor of God. So that they saw their posterity would be in danger to degenerate and be corrupted.

Lastly (and which was not least), a great hope and inward zeal they had of laying some good foundation, or at least to make some way thereunto, for the propagating and advancing the gospel of the kingdom of Christ in those remote parts of the world; yea, though they should be but even as stepping-stones unto others for the performing of so great a work.

These and some other like reasons moved them to undertake this resolution of their removal; the which they afterward prosecuted with so great difficulties, as by the sequel will appear.

The place they had thoughts on was some of those vast and unpeopled countries of America, which are fruitful and fit for habitation, being devoid of all civil inhabitants, where there are only savage and brutish men, which range up and down little otherwise than the wild beasts of the same. This proposition being made public and coming to the scanning of all, it raised many variable opinions amongst men and caused many fears and doubts among themselves. Some, from their reasons and hopes conceived, labored to stir up and encourage the rest to undertake and prosecute the same; others, again, out of their fears, objected against it and sought to divert from it, alleging many things, and those neither unreasonable nor unprobable; as that it was a great design and subject to many unconceivable perils and dangers; as, besides the casualties of the seas (which none can be freed from), the length of the voyage was such, as the weak bodies of women and other persons worn out with age and travail (as many of them were) could never be able to endure. And yet, if they should, the miseries of the land which they should be exposed to would be too hard to be borne, and likely, some or all of them together, to consume and utterly to ruinate them. For there they should be liable to famine and nakedness and the want, in a manner, of all things. The change of air, diet, and drinking of water would infect their bodies with sore sicknesses and grievous diseases. And also those which should escape or overcome these difficulties should yet be in continual danger of the savage people, who are cruel, barbarous, and most treacherous, being most furious in their rage and merciless where they overcome; not being content only to kill and take away life, but delight to torment men in the most bloody manner that may be, flaying some alive with the shells of fishes, cutting off the members and joints of others by piecemeal, and, broiling on the coals, eat the collops of their flesh in their sight whilst they live, with other cruelties horrible to be related. And surely it could not be thought but the very hearing of these things could not but move the very bowels of men to grate within them and make the weak to quake and tremble. It was further objected that it would require greater sums of money to furnish such a voyage and to fit them with necessaries than their consumed estates would amount to; and yet they must as well look to be seconded with supplies as presently to be transported. Also many precedents of ill success and lamentable miseries befallen others in the like designs were easy to be found, and not forgotten to be alleged; besides their own experience, in their former troubles and hardships in their removal into Holland, and how hard a thing it was for them to live in that strange place, though it was a neighbor country and a civil and rich commonwealth.

It was answered that all great and honorable actions are accompanied with great difficulties and must be both enterprised and overcome with answerable courages. It was granted the dangers were great, but not desperate; the difficulties were many, but not invincible. For though there were many of them likely, yet they were not certain; it might be sundry of the things feared might never befall; others, by provident care and the use of good means, might in a great measure be prevented; and all of them, through the help of God, by fortitude and patience, might either be borne or overcome. True it was that such attempts were not to be made and undertaken without good ground and reason, not rashly or lightly as many have done for curiosity or hope of gain, etc. But their condition was not ordinary; their ends were good and honorable; their calling lawful and urgent; and therefore they might expect the blessing of God in their proceeding. Yea, though they should lose their lives in this action, yet might they have comfort in the same, and their endeavors would be honorable. They lived here but as men in exile and in poor condition; and as great miseries might possibly befall them in this place, for the twelve years of truce were now out and there was nothing but beating of drums and preparing for war, the events whereof are always uncertain. The Spaniard might prove as cruel as the savages of America, and the famine and pestilence as sore here as there, and their liberty less to look out for remedy.

After many other particular things answered and alleged on both sides, it was fully concluded, by the major part, to put this design in execution and to prosecute it by the best means they could.

ARRIVAL AT CAPE COD

. . . After they had enjoyed fair winds and weather for a season, they were encounted many times with cross winds and met with many fierce storms. . . . In sundry of these storms the winds were so fierce and the seas so high, as they could not bear a knot of sail, but were forced to hull for divers days together. And in one of them, as they thus lay at hull, in a mighty storm, a lusty young man (called John Howland) coming upon some occasion above the gratings, was, with a seel[3] of the ship, thrown into the sea, but it pleased God that he caught hold of the topsail hallyards, which hung overboard and ran out at length; yet he held his hold, though he was sundry fathoms under water, till he was hauled up by the same rope to the brim of the water, and then with a boat hook and other means got into the ship again, and his life saved; and though he was something ill with it, yet he lived many years after, and became a profitable member both in church and commonwealth. In all this voyage there died but one of the passengers, which was William Butten, a youth, servant to Samuel Fuller, when they drew near the coast.

But, to omit other things (that I may be brief), after long beating at sea they fell with that land which is called Cape Cod; the which being made and certainly known to be it, they were not a little joyful. After some deliberation had amongst themselves and with the master of the ship, they tacked about and resolved to stand for the southward (the wind and water being fair) to find some place about Hudson's river for their habitation. But after they had sailed that course about half the day, they fell amongst dangerous shoals and roaring breakers, and they were so far entangled therewith as they conceived themselves in great danger; and the wind shrinking upon them withal, they resolved to bear up again for the Cape, and thought themselves happy to get out of those dangers before night overtook them, as by God's providence they did. And the next day they got into the Cape harbor, where they rid in safety . . .

Being thus arrived in a good harbor and brought safe to land, they fell upon their knees and blessed the God of heaven, who had brought them over the vast and furious ocean and delivered them from all the perils and miseries thereof, again to set their feet on the firm and stable earth,

their proper element. And no marvel if they were thus joyful, seeing wise Seneca was so affected with sailing a few miles on the coast of his own Italy, as he affirmed that he had rather remain twenty years on his way by land than pass by sea to any place in a short time, so tedious and dreadful was the same unto him.

But here I cannot but stay and make a pause, and stand half amazed at this poor people's present condition; and so I think will the reader too, when he well considers the same. Being thus passed the vast ocean, and a sea of troubles before in their preparation . . ., they had now no friends to welcome them, nor inns to entertain or refresh their weather-beaten bodies, no houses or much less towns to repair to, to seek for succor. It is recorded in Scripture, as a mercy to the apostle and his ship-racked company, that the barbarians showed them no small kindness in refreshing them, but these savage barbarians, when they met them (as after will appear), were readier to fill their sides full of arrows than otherwise. And for the season, it was winter; and they that know the winters of that country know them to be sharp and violent and subject to cruel storms, dangerous to travel to known places, much more to search an unknown coast. Besides, what could they see but a hideous and desolate wilderness, full of wild beasts and wild men? and what multitudes there might be of them they knew not. Neither could they, as it were, go up to the top of Pisgah to view from this wilderness a more goodly country to feed their hopes; for which way soever they turned their eyes (save upward to the heavens), they could have little solace or content in respect of any outward objects. For summer being done, all things stand upon them with a weather-beaten face, and the whole country, full of woods and thickets, represented a wild and savage view. If they looked behind them, there was the mighty ocean which they had

---

[3] A lurch of a ship under the impact of breakers.

passed and was now as a main bar and gulf to separate them from all the civil parts of the world. If it be said they had a ship to succor them, it is true; but what heard they daily from the master and company but that with speed they should look out a place with their shallop, where they would be at some near distance, for the season was such as he would not stir from thence till a safe harbor was discovered by them where they would be, and he might go without danger; and that victuals consumed apace, but he must and would keep sufficient for themselves and their return. Yea, it was muttered by some that, if they got not a place in time, they would turn them and their goods ashore and leave them. Let it also be considered what weak hopes of supply and succor they left behind them, that might bear up their minds in this sad condition and trials they were under; and they could not but be very small. It is true, indeed, the affections and love of their brethren at Leyden was cordial and entire towards them, but they had little power to help them or themselves; and how the case stood between them and the merchants at their coming away hath already been declared. What could now sustain them but the spirit of God and his grace? May not and ought not the children of these fathers rightly say: *Our fathers were Englishmen which came over this great ocean, and were ready to perish in this wilderness; but they cried unto the Lord, and he heard their voice, and looked on their adversity, etc. Let them therefore praise the Lord, because he is good, and his mercies endure forever. Yea, let them which have been redeemed of the Lord show how he hath delivered them from the hand of the oppressor. When they wandered in the desert wilderness out of the way, and found no city to dwell in, both hungry and thirsty, their soul was overwhelmed in them. Let them confess before the Lord his loving kindness, and his wonderful works before the sons of men.*

. . . I shall a little return back and begin with a combination made by them before they came ashore, being the first foundation of their government in this place; occasioned partly by the discontented and mutinous speeches that some of the strangers amongst them had let fall from them in the ship—that when they came ashore they would use their own liberty, for none had power to command them, the patent they had being for Virginia, and not for New-England, which belonged to another government, with which the Virginia Company had nothing to do. And partly that such an act by them done (this their condition considered) might be as firm as any patent and in some respects more sure.

The form was as followeth:

In the name of God, Amen. We whose names are under-written, the loyal subjects of our dread sovereign Lord, King James, by the grace of God, of Great Britain, France, and Ireland king, defender of the faith, etc., having undertaken, for the glory of God, and advancement of the Christian faith, and honor of our king and country, a voyage to plant the first colony in the northern parts of Virginia, do by these presents solemnly and mutually in the presence of God, and one of another, covenant and combine ourselves together into a civil body politic, for our better ordering and preservation and furtherance of the ends aforesaid; and by virtue hereof to enact, constitute, and frame such just and equal laws, ordinances, acts, constitutions, and offices, from time to time, as shall be thought most meet and convenient for the general good of the Colony, unto which we promise all due submission and obedience. In witness whereof we have hereunder subscribed our names at Cape Cod the 11 of November, in the year of the reign of our sovereign lord, King James, of England, France, and Ireland the eighteenth, and of Scotland the fifty-fourth. An°. Dom. 1620.

After this they chose, or rather confirmed, Mr. John Carver (a man godly and well-approved amongst them) their Governor for that year. And after they had provided a place for their goods or common store (which were long in unlading for want of boats, foulness of winter weather, and sickness of divers) and begun some small cottages for their habitation, as time would admit, they met and consulted of laws and orders, both for their civil and military government, as the necessity of their condition did require, still adding thereunto as urgent occasion in several times and as cases did require. . . .

COMMUNISM TRIED AND FOUND WANTING

[1623] They began to think how they might raise as much corn as they could and obtain a better crop than they had done, that they might not still thus languish in misery. At length, after much debate of things, the Governor (with the advice of the chiefest amongst them) gave way that they should set corn every man for his own particular and in that regard trust to themselves; in all other things to go on in the general way as before. And so assigned to every family a parcel of land, according to the proportion of their number for that end, only for present use (but made no division for inheritance), and ranged all boys and youth under some family. This had very good success, for it made all hands very industrious, so as much more corn was planted than otherwise would have been by any means the Governor or any other could use, and saved him a great deal of trouble and gave far better content. The women now went willingly into the field and took their little ones with them to set corn, which before would allege weakness and inability; whom to have compelled would have been thought great tyranny and oppression.

The experience that was had in this common course and condition, tried sundry years, and that amongst godly and sober men, may well evince the vanity of that conceit of Plato's and other ancients, applauded by some of later times;—that the taking away of property and bringing in community into a commonwealth would make them happy and flourishing, as if they were wiser than God. For this community (so far as it was) was found to breed much confusion and discontent and retard much employment that would have been to their benefit and comfort. For the young men that were most able and fit for labor and service did repine that they should spend their time and strength to work for other men's wives and children without any recompense. The strong or man of parts had no more in division of victuals and clothes than he that was weak and not able to do a quarter the other could: this was thought injustice. The aged and graver men to be ranked and equalized in labors and victuals, clothes, etc., with the meaner and younger sort, thought it some indignity and disrespect unto them. And for men's wives to be commanded to do service for other men, as dressing their meat, washing their clothes, etc., they deemed it a kind of slavery; neither could many husbands well brook it. Upon the point all being to have alike and all to do alike, they thought themselves in the like condition and one as good as another; and so, if it did not cut off those relations that God hath set amongst men, yet it did at least much diminish and take off the mutual respects that should be preserved amongst them. And would have been worse if they had been men of another condition. Let none object this is men's corruption and nothing to the course itself. I answer, seeing all men have this corruption in them, God in his wisdom saw another course fitter for them. . . .

STRIFE WITH THOMAS MORTON

[1628] About some 3 or 4 years before this time, there came over one Captain Wollaston, a man of pretty parts, and with him 3 or 4 more of some eminency, who brought with them a great many servants, with provisions and other implements for to begin a plantation, and pitched themselves in a place within the Massachusetts, which they called, after their captain's name, Mount-Wollaston. Amongst whom was one Mr. Morton, who, it should seem, had some small adventure (of his own or other men's) amongst them, but had little respect amongst them and was slighted by the meanest servants. Having continued there some time and not finding things to answer their expectations nor profit to arise as they looked for, Captain Wollaston takes a great part of the servants and transports them to Virginia, where he puts them off at good rates, selling their time to other men, and writes back to one Mr. Rasdall, one of his chief partners and accounted their merchant, to bring another part of them to Virginia likewise, intending to put them off there as he had done the rest. And he, with the consent of the said Rasdall, appointed one Fitcher to be his lieutenant and govern the remains of the plantation, till he or Rasdall returned to take further order thereabout. But this Morton abovesaid, having more craft than honesty (who had been a kind of pettifogger of Furnival's Inn [4]), in the others' absence watches an opportunity (commons being but hard amongst them) and got some strong drink and other junkets and made them a feast; and after they were merry, he began to tell them he would give them good counsel. You see (saith he) that many of your fellows are carried to Virginia; and if you stay till this Rasdall return, you will also be carried away and sold for slaves with the rest. Therefore I would advise you to thrust out this Lieutenant Fitcher, and I, having a part in the plantation, will receive you as my partners and consociates; so may you be free from service and we will converse, trade, plant, and live together as equals and support and protect one another, or to like effect. This counsel was easily received; so they took opportunity and thrust Lieutenant Fitcher out-a-doors and would suffer him to come no more amongst them, but forced him to seek bread to eat and other relief from his neighbors, till he could get passage for England. After this they fell to great licentiousness and led a dissolute life, pouring out themselves into all profaneness. And Morton became lord of misrule and maintained (as it were) a school of Atheism. And after they had got some goods into their hands and got much by trading with the Indians, they spent it as vainly, in quaffing and drinking both wine and strong waters in great excess, and, as some reported, 10 *li.* worth in a morning. They also set up a maypole, drinking and dancing about it many days together, inviting the Indian women for their consorts, dancing and frisking together (like so many fairies, or furies rather) and worse practices. As if they had anew revived and celebrated the feasts of the Roman goddess Flora or the beastly practices of the mad Bacchanalians. Morton likewise (to show his poetry) composed sundry rimes and verses, some tending to lasciviousness and others to the detraction and scandal of some persons, which he affixed to this idle or idol maypole. They changed also the name of their place and instead of calling it Mount Wollaston, they call it Merry-mount, as if this jollity would have lasted ever. But this continued not long, for after Morton was sent for England (as follows to be declared), shortly after came over that worthy gentleman, Mr. John Endecott, who brought over a patent under the broad seal for the government of the Massachusetts, who, visiting those parts, caused that maypole to be cut down and rebuked them for their profaneness and admonished them to look there should be better walking; so they now, or others, changed the name of their place again and called it Mount-Dagon.

Now to maintain this riotous prodigality and profuse excess, Morton, thinking himself lawless and hearing what gain the French and fishermen made by trading of pieces, powder, and shot to the Indians, he, as the head of this consortship, began

---

[4] One of the four Inns of Court in London where attorneys lodged and studied and maintained their fraternal groups

the practice of the same in these parts; and first he taught them how to use them, to charge and discharge and what proportion of powder to give the piece, according to the size or bigness of the same, and what shot to use for fowl and what for deer. And having thus instructed them, he employed some of them to hunt and fowl for him, so as they became far more active in that employment than any of the English, by reason of their swiftness of foot and nimbleness of body, being also quick-sighted and by continual exercise well knowing the haunts of all sorts of game. So as when they saw the execution that a piece would do and the benefit that might come by the same, they became mad, as it were, after them and would not stick to give any price they could attain to for them, accounting their bows and arrows but baubles in comparison of them. . . . O the horribleness of this villainy! how many both Dutch and English have been lately slain by those Indians, thus furnished; and no remedy provided, nay, the evil more increased and the blood of their brethren sold for gain, as is to be feared; and in what danger all those colonies are in is too well known. Oh! that princes and parliaments would take some timely order to prevent this mischief and at length to suppress it by some exemplary punishment upon some of these gainthirsty murderers (for they deserve no better title) before their colonies in these parts be overthrown by these barbarous savages, thus armed with their own weapons by these evil instruments and traitors to their neighbors and country. . . .

This Morton having thus taught them the use of pieces, he sold them all he could spare; and he and his consorts determined to send for many out of England and had by some of the ships sent for above a score. The which being known and his neighbors meeting the Indians in the woods armed with guns in this sort, it was a terror unto them who lived stragglingly and were of no strength in any place. And other places (though more remote) saw this

mischief would quickly spread over all, if not prevented. Besides, they saw they should keep no servants, for Morton would entertain any, how vile soever, and all the scum of the country or any discontents would flock to him from all places, if this nest was not broken; and they should stand in more fear of their lives and goods (in short time) from this wicked and debauched crew than from the savages themselves.

So sundry of the chief of the straggling plantations, meeting together, agreed by mutual consent to solicit those of Plymouth (who were then of more strength than them all) to join with them to prevent the further growth of this mischief and suppress Morton and his consorts before they grew to further head and strength. Those that joined in this action (and after contributed to the charge of sending him for England) were from Pascataway, Mankeake, Winisimett, Weesagascusett, Natasco, and other places where any English were seated.

Those of Plymouth, being thus sought to by their messengers and letters and weighing both their reasons and the common danger, were willing to afford them their help, though themselves had least cause of fear or hurt. So, to be short, they first resolved jointly to write to him and in a friendly and neighborly way to admonish him to forbear these courses and sent a messenger with their letters to bring his answer. But he was so high as he scorned all advice and asked who had to do with him; he had and would trade pieces with the Indians in despite of all, with many other scurrilous terms full of disdain. They sent to him a second time and bade him be better advised and more temperate in his terms, for the country could not bear the injury he did; it was against their common safety and against the king's proclamation. He answered in high terms as before and that the king's proclamation was no law, demanding what penalty was upon it. It was answered, more than he could bear, his majesty's displeasure. But insolently he persisted and said the king was dead and his displeasure with him and many the like things, and threatened withal that, if any came to molest him, let them look to themselves, for he would prepare for them.

Upon which, they saw there was no way but to take him by force; and having so far proceeded, now to give over would make him far more haughty and insolent. So they mutually resolved to proceed and obtained of the Governor of Plymouth to send Captain Standish and some other aid with him to take Morton by force. The which accordingly was done, but they found him to stand stiffly in his defence, having made fast his doors, armed his consorts, set divers dishes of powder and bullets ready on the table; and if they had not been over-armed with drink, more hurt might have been done. They summoned him to yield, but he kept his house, and they could get nothing but scoffs and scorns from him; but at length, fearing they would do some violence to the house, he and some of his crew came out, but not to yield, but to shoot; but they were so steeled with drink as their pieces were too heavy for them; himself with a car-

bine (over-charged and almost half-filled with powder and shot, as was after found) had thought to have shot Captain Standish; but he stepped to him, and put by his piece, and took him. Neither was there any hurt done to any of either side, save that one was so drunk that he ran his own nose upon the point of a sword that one held before him as he entered the house, but he lost but a little of his hot blood.

Morton they brought away to Plymouth, where he was kept till a ship went from the Isle of Shoals for England, with which he was sent to the Council of New England and letters written to give them information of his course and carriage, and also one was sent at their common charge to inform their Honors more particularly and to prosecute against him. But he fooled off the messenger, after he was gone from hence, and though he went for England, yet nothing was done to him, not so much as rebuked, for aught was heard, but returned the next year. Some of the worst of the company were dispersed and some of the more modest kept the house till he should be heard from. But I have been too long about so unworthy a person and bad a cause . . .

1588 ∽ *John Winthrop* ∽ 1649

JOHN WINTHROP belonged to a prosperous middle-class family of Suffolk, England. His grandfather had been a clothier; his father was a lawyer who served for fifteen years as auditor for St. John's and Trinity Colleges, Cambridge. While his father held the latter position, John Winthrop attended Trinity College for a year and some months and then, at the age of seventeen, abandoned his university career to get married. He became a justice of the peace, proprietor of the family estate of Groton Manor, and a prominent attorney. At the age of forty-two, having been married thrice, blessed with a numerous brood of children and grandchildren, and enjoying a sizeable annual income, he decided to risk "a hazard of new fortunes" as co-leader with Thomas Dudley of an expedition sponsored by the Massachusetts Bay Company to strengthen the settlement it supported at Salem in New England.

The Winthrop-Dudley expedition left England in March, 1630, took with it the government and charter of the Massachusetts Bay Company, landed at Salem, and eventually founded Boston and several of its adjacent towns. Sailing on the flag-ship of the small fleet, the *Arbella*—so named for the Lady Arbella Johnson, who was one of its passengers and who died two months after the arrival at Salem—Winthrop began his *Journal* at Southampton as the ship was preparing to embark; he continued it, as a repository for occasional jottings, until his death. Because Winthrop played so important a part in the Massachusetts Bay Colony, serving as governor or deputy-governor so frequently, this *Journal,* contained in three notebooks difficult to decipher, is one of the most valuable source-books for early New England history and was drawn upon by such early New England historians as William Hubbard, Cotton Mather, and Thomas Prince. Two of the notebooks were published in 1790; the third, regarded as lost, was found in 1816; the *Journal* in its entirety was not published until 1825-6, its editor, James Savage, having made a careful modernized transcript from the originals.

[For the present selections titles have been supplied by the editors of this anthology. A convenient edition is that of J. K. Hosmer (New York, 1908), comprising two volumes in the series *Original Narratives of Early American History.* The most authoritative version of the original text of the *Journal* is that in the *Winthrop Papers,* Vol. II, Massachusetts Historical Society, 1939 ——. See Book I, Part 3, for further selections from Winthrop.]

From
JOURNAL
[1790, 1825-26 (written 1630-1649)]

Voyage and Arrival

[Thursday, April 8, Yarmouth] About six in the morning (the wind being E. and N. and fair weather) we weighed anchor and set sail, and before ten we gat through the Needles,[1] having so little wind as we had much to do to stem the tide, so as the rest of our fleet (we being nine in all, whereof some were small ships, which were bound for Newfoundland) could not get out all then till the ebb. In the afternoon the wind came S. and W. and we were becalmed, so as being not able to get above three or four leagues from the Needles, our captain tacked about, and putting his four-sheets aback stays, he stayed for the rest of the fleet, and as they came by us we spake to them, and about eight in the evening we let fall an anchor, intending to stop till the ebb. But before ten at night the wind came about to the N. a good gale; so we put up a light in the poop, and weighed and set sail, and by daylight, Friday 9, we were come to Portland; but the other ships being not able to hold up with us, we were forced to spare our mainsail, and went on with a merry gale. In the morning we descried from the top eight sail astern of us, (whom Capt. Lowe told us he had seen at Dunnose in the evening). We supposing they might be Dunkirkers,[2] our captain caused the gun-room and gundeck to be cleared; all the hammocks were taken down, our ordnance loaded, and our powder-chests and fireworks made ready, and our landmen quartered among the seamen, and twenty-five of them appointed for muskets, and

---

[1] Three pointed rocks, English Channel, west of Isle of Wight.

[2] Dunkirk was then a possession of Spain, at that time at war with England.

every man written down for his quarter.

The wind continued N. with fair weather, and afternoon it calmed, and we still saw those eight ships to stand towards us; having more wind than we, they came up apace, so as our captain and the masters of our consorts were more occasioned to think they might be Dunkirkers, (for we were told at Yarmouth, that there were ten sail of them waiting for us;) whereupon we all prepared to fight with them, and took down some cabins which were in the way of our ordnance, and out of every ship were thrown such bed matters as were subject to take fire, and we heaved out our long boats, and put up our waste cloths, and drew forth our men, and armed them with muskets and other weapons, and instruments for fireworks; and for an experiment our captain shot a ball of wild-fire fastened to an arrow out of a cross-bow, which burnt in the water a good time. The lady Arbella and the other women and children were removed into the lower deck, that they might be out of danger. All things being thus fitted, we went to prayer upon the upper deck. It was much to see how cheerful and comfortable all the company appeared; not a woman or child that showed fear, though all did apprehend the danger to have been great, if things had proved as might well be expected, for there had been eight against four, and the least of the enemy's ships were reported to carry thirty brass pieces; but our trust was in the Lord of Hosts; and the courage of our captain, and his care and diligence, did much encourage us. It was now about one of the clock, and the fleet seemed to be within a league of us; therefore our captain, because he would show he was not afraid of them, and that he might see the issue before night should overtake us, tacked about and stood to meet them, and when we came near we perceived them to be our friends,—the *Little Neptune,* a ship of some twenty pieces of ordnance, and her two consorts, bound for the Straits; a ship of Flushing, and a Frenchman, and three other English ships bound for Canada and

Newfoundland. So when we drew near, every ship (as they met) saluted each other, and the musketeers discharged their small shot; and so (god be praised) our fear and danger was turned into mirth and friendly entertainment. Our danger being thus over, we espied two boats on fishing in the channel; so every of our four ships manned out a skiff, and we bought of them great store of excellent fresh fish of divers sorts. . . .

[Saturday, May 1] All the night much wind at S.S.W. and rain. In the morning the wind still strong, so as we could bear little sail, and so it continued a growing storm all the day, and towards night so much wind as we bore no more sail but so much as should keep the ship stiff. Then it grew a very great tempest all the night with fierce showers of rain intermixed, and very cold.

[Lord's day, 2] The tempest continued all day, with the wind W. and by N., and the sea raged and tossed us exceedingly; yet, through God's mercy, we were very comfortable, and few or none sick, but had opportunity to keep the Sabbath, and Mr. Phillips preached twice that day. The *Ambrose* and *Jewel* were separated far from us the first night, but this day we saw them again, but Capt. Kirk's ships we saw not since.

[Monday, 3] In the night the wind abated, and by morning the sea was well assuaged, so as we bare our foresail again, and stood W.S.W.; but all the time of the tempest we could make no way, but were driven to the leeward, and the *Ambrose* struck all her sails but her mizzen, and lay a hull. She brake her main yard. This day we made observation, and found we were in forty-three and a half north latitude. We set two fighters in the bolts till night, with their hands bound behind them. A maid-servant in the ship, being stomach-sick, drank so much strong water, that she was senseless, and had near killed herself. We observed it a common fault in our young people, that they gave themselves to drink hot waters very immoderately. . . .

[Saturday, June 12, 1630, Salem] About four in the morning we were near our port. We shot off two pieces of ordnance, and sent our skiff to Mr. Peirce[3] his ship (which lay in the harbor, and had been there —— days before). About an hour later, Mr. Allerton[4] came aboard us in a shallop as he was sailing to Pemaquid. As we stood towards the harbor, we saw another shallop coming to us; so we stood in to meet her, and passed through the narrow strait between Baker's Isle and Little Isle, and came to an anchor a little within the islands.

After Mr. Peirce came aboard us, and returned to fetch Mr. Endecott,[5] who came to us about two of the clock, and with him Mr. Skelton[6] and Capt. Levett. We that were of the assistants,[7] and some other gentlemen, and some of the women, and our captain, returned with them to Nahumkeck, where we supped with a good venison pasty and good beer, and at night we returned to our ship, but some of the women stayed behind.

In the mean time most of our people went on shore upon the land of Cape Ann, which lay very near us, and gathered store of fine strawberries.

An Indian came aboard us and lay there all night.

ROGER WILLIAMS ESCAPES ARREST

[January 11, 1636] The governor[8] and assistants met at Boston to consider about Mr. Williams, for that they were credibly informed, that, notwithstanding the injunction laid upon him (upon the liberty granted him to stay till the spring) not to go about to draw others to his opinions, he did use to entertain company in his house, and to preach to them, even of such points as he had been censured for; and it was agreed to send him into England by ship then ready to depart. The reason was, because he had drawn above twenty persons to his opinion, and they were intended to erect a plantation about the Narragansett Bay, from whence the infec-

tion would easily spread into these churches, (the people being, many of them, much taken with the apprehension of his godliness). Whereupon a warrant was sent to him to come presently to Boston, to be shipped, etc. He returned answer, (and divers of Salem came with it,) that he could not come without hazard of his life, etc. Whereupon a pinnace was sent with commission to Capt. Underhill, etc., to apprehend him, and carry him aboard the ship, (which then rode at Natascutt;) but, when they came at his house, they found he had been gone three days before; but whither they could not learn.

He had so far prevailed at Salem, as many there (especially of devout women) did embrace his opinions, and separated from the churches, for this cause, that some of their members, going into England, did hear the ministers there, and when they came home the churches here held communion with them.

THE ANTINOMIAN CRISIS

[October 21, 1636] One Mrs. Hutchinson, a member of the church of Boston, a woman of a ready wit and bold spirit, brought over with her two dangerous errors: 1. That the person of the Holy Ghost dwells in a justified person. 2. That no sanctification can help to evidence to us our justification.[9]—From these two grew

---

[3] William Peirce, a sailor in the service of the Plymouth colony.

[4] Isaac Allerton, a leading financier of the Plymouth colony.

[5] John Endecott (1589-1665) had come to Salem two years before and was its governor.

[6] Pastor of the church at Salem.

[7] Magistrates, who were elected by the church members and composed the main governing body.

[8] John Haynes, who later went to Connecticut, was governor of the Bay Colony at this time.

[9] Sanctification referred to the good works and behavior of a person who had presumably received God's grace; justification was the inward experience of this grace.

many branches; as, 1. Our union with the Holy Ghost, so as a Christian remains dead to every spiritual action, and hath no gifts nor graces, other than such as are in hypocrites, nor any other sanctification but the Holy Ghost himself.

There joined with her in these opinions a brother of hers, one Mr. Wheelwright, a silenced minister sometimes in England.

[October 25] The other ministers in the bay, hearing of these things, came to Boston at the time of a general court, and entered conference in private with them, to the end they might know the certainty of these things; that if need were, they might write to the church of Boston about them, to prevent (if it were possible) the dangers, which seemed hereby to hang over that and the rest of the churches. At this conference, Mr. Cotton was present, and gave satisfaction to them, so as he agreed with them all in the point of sanctification, and so did Mr. Wheelwright; so as they all did hold, that sanctification did help to evidence justification. The same he had delivered plainly in public, divers times; but, for the indwelling of the person of the Holy Ghost, he held that still, as some others of the ministers did, but not union with the person of the Holy Ghost, (as Mrs. Hutchinson and others did,) so as to amount to a personal union . . .

[November 17] The governor, Mr. Vane, a wise and godly gentleman, held, with Mr. Cotton and many others, the indwelling of the person of the Holy Ghost in a believer, and went so far beyond the rest, as to maintain a personal union with the Holy Ghost; but the deputy, with the pastor and divers others,[10] denied both; and the question proceeded so far by disputation, (in writing, for the peace sake of the church, which all were tender of,) as at length they could not find the person of the Holy Ghost in scripture, nor in the primitive churches three hundred years after Christ. So that, all agreeing in the chief matter of substance, viz. that the Holy Ghost is God, and that he doth dwell in the believers, (as the Father and Son both are

said also to do,) but whether by his gifts and power only, or by any other manner of presence, seeing the scripture doth not declare it,—it was earnestly desired, that the word person might be forborn, being a term of human invention, and tending to doubtful disputation in this case. . . .

[January 20, 1637] The differences in the said points of religion increased more and more, and the ministers of both sides (there being only Mr. Cotton of one party) did publicly declare their judgments in some of them, so as all men's mouths were full of them.

[February 3] And there being . . . a ship ready to go for England, and many passengers in it, Mr. Cotton took occasion to speak to them about the differences, etc., and willed them to tell our countrymen, that all the strife amongst us was about magnifying the grace of God; one party seeking to advance the grace of God within us, and the other to advance the grace of God towards us, (meaning by the one justification, and by the other sanctification;) and so bade them tell them, that, if there were any among them that would strive for grace, they should come hither; and so declared some particulars. Mr. Wilson spake after him, and declared, that he knew none of the elders or brethren of the churches, but did labor to advance the free grace of God in justification, so far as the word of God required; and spake also about the doctrine of sanctification, and the use and necessity, etc., of it; by occasion whereof no man could tell (except some few, who knew the bottom of the matter) where any difference was: which speech, though it offended those of Mr. Cotton's party, yet it was very seasonable to clear the rest, who otherwise should have been reputed to have opposed free grace. Thus every occasion increased the contention, and caused great alienation of minds; and the members of Boston (frequenting the lectures of other ministers) did make much disturb-

---

[10] The "deputy" was Winthrop, deputy-governor; the pastor was John Wilson.

ance by public questions, and objections to their doctrines, which did any way disagree from their opinions; and it began to be as common here to distinguish between men, by being under a covenant of grace or a covenant of works, as in other countries between Protestants and papists. . . .

[March 9] Mr. Wheelwright, one of the members of Boston, preaching at the last fast, inveighed against all that walked in a covenant of works, as he described it to be, viz., such as maintain sanctification as an evidence of justification, etc., and called them antichrists, and stirred up the people against them with much bitterness and vehemency. For this he was called into the court, and his sermon being produced, he justified it, and confessed he did mean all that walk in such a way. Whereupon the elders of the rest of the churches were called, and asked whether they, in their ministry, did walk in such a way. They all acknowledged they did. So, after much debate, the court adjudged him guilty of sedition, and also of contempt, for that the court had appointed the fast as a means of reconciliation of the differences, etc., and he purposely set himself to kindle and increase them. The governor and some few more (who dissented) tendered a protestation, which, because it wholly justified Mr. Wheelwright, and condemned the proceedings of the court, was rejected. The church of Boston also tendered a petition in his behalf, justifying Mr. Wheelwright's sermon. The court deferred sentence till the next court, and advised with the ministers, etc., whether they might enjoin his silence, etc. They answered, that they were not clear in that point, but desired rather, that he might be commended to the church of Boston to take care of him, etc., which accordingly was done, and he enjoined to appear at the next court. Much heat of contention was this court between the opposite parties; so as it was moved, that the next court might be kept at Newtown. . . .

[May 17] Our court of elections was at Newtown. So soon as the court was set, being about one of the clock, a petition was preferred by those of Boston. The governor would have read it, but the deputy said it was out of order; it was a court for elections, and those must first be dispatched, and then their petitions should be heard. Divers others also opposed that course, as an ill precedent, etc.; and the petition, being about pretence of liberty, etc., (though intended chiefly for revoking the sentence given against Mr. Wheelwright), would have spent all the day in debate, etc.; but yet the governor and those of that party would not proceed to election, except the petition was read. Much time was already spent about this debate, and the people crying out for election, it was moved by the deputy, that the people should divide themselves, and the greater number must carry it. And so it was done, and the greater number by many were for election. But the governor and that side kept their place still, and would not proceed. Whereupon the deputy told him, that, if he would not go to election, he and the rest of that side would proceed. Upon that, he came from his company, and they went to election; and Mr. Winthrop was chosen governor, Mr. Dudley deputy and Mr. Endecott of the standing council; and Mr. Israel Stoughton and Mr. Richard Saltonstall were called in to be assistants; and Mr. Vane, Mr. Coddington, and Mr. Dummer, (being all of that faction,) were left quite out.

There was great danger of a tumult that day; for those of that side grew into fierce speeches, and some laid hands on others; but seeing themselves too weak, they grew quiet. They expected a great advantage that day, because remote towns were allowed to come in by proxy; but it fell out, that there were enough beside . . .

[August 30] The synod, called the assembly, began at Newtown. There were all the teaching elders through the country, and some new come out of England, not yet called to any place here, as Mr. Davenport, etc.

The assembly began with prayer, made by Mr. Shepherd, the pastor of Newtown.

Then the erroneous opinions, which were spread in the country, were read, (being eighty in all:) next the unwholesome expressions; then the scriptures abused. Then they chose two moderators for the next day, viz., Mr. Buckly and Mr. Hooker, and these were continued in that place all the time of the assembly. There were about eighty opinions, some blasphemous, others erroneous, and all unsafe, condemned by the whole assembly; whereto near all the elders, and others sent by the churches, subscribed their names; but some few liked not subscription, though they consented to the condemning of them. . . .

[November 1] There was great hope that the late general assembly would have had some good effect in pacifying the troubles and dissensions about matters of religion; but it fell out otherwise. For though Mr. Wheelwright and those of his party had been clearly confuted and confounded in the assembly, yet they persisted in their opinions, and were as busy in nourishing contentions (the principal of them) as before. Whereupon the general court, being assembled in the 2 of the 9th month,[11] and finding, upon consultation, that two so opposite parties could not contain in the same body, without apparent hazard of ruin to the whole, agreed to send away some of the principal; . . . Then the court sent for Mr. Wheelwright, and, he persisting to justify his sermon, and his whole practice and opinions, and refusing to leave either the place or his public exercisings, he was disfranchised and banished. Upon which he appealed to the king, but neither called witnesses, nor desired any act to be made of it. The court told him, that an appeal did not lie; for by the king's grant we had power to hear and determine without any reservation, etc. So he relinquished his appeal, and the court gave him leave to go to his house, upon his promise, that, if he were not gone out of our jurisdiction within fourteen days, he would render himself to one of the magistrates.

The court also sent for Mrs. Hutchinson, and charged her with divers matters, as her keeping two public lectures every week in her house, whereto sixty or eighty persons did usually resort, and for reproaching most of the ministers (viz., all except Mr. Cotton) for not preaching a covenant of free grace, and that they had not the seal of the spirit, nor were able ministers of the New Testament; which were clearly proved against her, though she sought to shift it off. And, after many speeches to and fro, at last she was so full as she could not contain, but vented her revelations; amongst which this was one, that she had it revealed to her, that she should come into New England, and should here be persecuted, and that God would ruin us and our posterity, and the whole state, for the same. So the court proceeded and banished her; but, because it was winter, they committed her to a private house, where she was well provided, and her own friends and the elders permitted to go to her, but none else. . . .

After this, many of the church of Boston, being highly offended with the governor for this proceeding, were earnest with the elders to have him called to account for it; but they were not forward in it, and himself, understanding their intent, thought fit to prevent such a public disorder, and so took occasion to speak to the congregation to this effect:—

. . . He did nothing in the cases of the brethren, but by the advice and direction of our teacher and other of the elders. . . .

He would give them one reason, which was a ground for his judgment, and that was, for that he saw, that those brethren, etc., were so divided from the rest of the country in their judgment and practice, as it could not stand with the public peace, that they should continue amongst us. So, by the example of Lot in Abraham's family, and after Hagar and Ishmael, he saw they must be sent away. . . .

---

[11] November, according to Winthrop's calendar.

[March 1, 1638] While Mrs. Hutchinson continued at Roxbury, divers of the elders and others resorted to her, and finding her to persist in maintaining those gross errors beforementioned, and many others, to the number of thirty or thereabout, some of them wrote to the church at Boston, offering to make proof of the same before the church, etc., [March] 15; whereupon she was called, (the magistrates being desired to give her license to come,) and the lecture was appointed to begin at ten. . . . When she appeared, the errors were read to her. . . . These were also clearly confuted, but yet she held her own; so as the church (all but two of her sons) agreed she should be admonished, and because her sons would not agree to it, they were admonished also.

Mr. Cotton pronounced the sentence of admonition with great solemnity, and with much zeal and detestation of her errors and pride of spirit. The assembly continued till eight at night, and all did acknowledge the special presence of God's spirit therein; and she was appointed to appear again the next lecture day. . . .

[March 22] Mrs. Hutchinson appeared again; (she had been licensed by the court, in regard she had given hope of her repentance, to be at Mr. Cotton's house, that both he and Mr. Davenport might have the more opportunity to deal with her); and the articles being again read to her, and her answer required, she delivered it in writing, wherein she made a retraction of near all, but with such explanations and circumstances as gave no satisfaction to the church; so as she was required to speak further to them. Then she declared, that it was just with God to leave her to herself, as he had done, for her slighting his ordinances, both magistracy and ministry; and confessed that what she had spoken against the magistrates at the court (by way of revelation) was rash and ungrounded; and desired the church to pray for her. This gave the church good hope of her repentance; but when she was examined about some particulars, as that she had

denied inherent righteousness, etc., she affirmed that it was never her judgment; and though it was proved by many testimonies, that she had been of that judgment, and so had persisted, and maintained it by argument against divers, yet she impudently persisted in her affirmation, to the astonishment of all the assembly. So that, after much time and many arguments had been spent to bring her to see her sin, but all in vain, the church, with one consent, cast her out. Some moved to have her admonished once more; but, it being for manifest evil in matter of conversation, it was agreed otherwise; and for that reason also the sentence was denounced by the pastor, matter of manners belonging properly to his place.

After she was excommunicated, her spirits, which seemed before to be somewhat dejected, revived again, and she gloried in her sufferings, saying, that it was the greatest happiness, next to Christ, that ever befel her. Indeed, it was a happy day to the churches of Christ here, and to many poor souls, who had been seduced by her, who, by what they heard and saw that day, were (through the grace of God) brought off quite from her errors, and settled again in the truth. . . .

After two or three days, the governor sent a warrant to Mrs. Hutchinson to depart this jurisdiction before the last of this month, according to the order of court, and for that end set her at liberty from her former constraint, so as she was not to go forth of her own house till her departure; and upon the 28th she went by water to her farm at the Mount, where she was to take water, with Mr. Wheelwright's wife and family, to go to Pascataquack; but she changed her mind, and went by land to Providence, and so to the island in the Narragansett Bay, which her husband and the rest of that sect had purchased of the Indians, and prepared with all speed to remove unto. For the court had ordered, that, except they were gone with their families by such a time, they should be summoned to the general court. . . .

NOTES ON EDUCATION

(October 5, 1642) Nine bachelors commenced at Cambridge; they were young men of good hope, and performed their acts, so as gave good proof of their proficiency in the tongues and arts. The general court had settled a government or superintendency over the college, viz., all the magistrates and elders over the six nearest churches and the president, or the greatest part of these. Most of them were now present at this first commencement,[12] and dined at the college with the scholars' ordinary commons, which was done of purpose for the students' encouragement, etc., and it gave good content to all.

At this commencement, complaint was made to the governors of two young men, of good quality, lately come out of England, for foul misbehavior, in swearing and ribaldry speeches, etc., for which, though they were adulti, they were corrected in the college, and sequestered, etc., for a time.

(July 3, 1645) Divers free schools were erected, as at Roxbury [13] (for maintenance whereof every inhabitant bound some house or land for a yearly allowance forever) and at Boston (where they made an order to allow forever 50 pounds to the master and an house, and 30 pounds to an usher, who should also teach to read and write and cipher, and Indians' children were to be taught freely, and the charge to be by yearly contribution, either by voluntary allowance, or by rate of such as refused, etc., and this order was confirmed by the general court [blank]). Other towns did the like, providing maintenance by several means.

By agreement of the commissioners, and the motions of the elders in their several churches, every family in each colony gave one peck of corn or twelve pence to the college at Cambridge.

(April 13, 1645) Mr. Hopkins, the governor of Hartford upon Connecticut, came to Boston, and brought his wife with him, (a godly young woman, and of special parts,) who was fallen into sad infirmity, the loss of her understanding and reason, which had been growing upon her divers years, by occasion of her giving herself wholly to reading and writing, and had written many books. Her husband, being very loving and tender of her, was loath to grieve her; but he saw his error, when it was too late. For if she had attended her household affairs, and such things as belong to women, and not gone out of her way and calling to meddle in such things as are proper for men, whose minds are stronger, etc., she had kept her wits, and might have improved them usefully and honorably in the place God had sent her. He brought her to Boston, and left her with her brother, one Mr. Yale, a merchant, to try what means might be had for her. But no help could be had.[14]

PROVED AND SUSPECTED ADULTERY

[March 7, 1644] . . . At this court of assistants, one James Britton, a man ill affected both to our church discipline and civil government, and one Mary Latham, a proper young woman about 18 years of age, whose father was a godly man and had brought her up well, was condemned to die for adultery, upon a law formerly made and published in print. It was thus occasioned and discovered. This woman, being rejected by a young man whom she had an affection unto, vowed she would marry the next that came to her, and accordingly, against her friends' minds, she matched with an ancient man who had neither honesty nor ability, and one whom she had no affection unto. Whereupon, soon after she was married, divers young men solicited her chastity, and drawing her into bad company, and giving her wine and other gifts, easily prevailed with her, and among others this Britton. But God smiting him with a deadly palsy and fearful horror of conscience withal, he could not keep secret,

---

[12] Harvard College was founded in 1636.

[13] The first common school in New England was established in Boston 1635-6.

[14] Mrs. Hopkins was aunt of Elihu Yale, founder of Yale University.

but discovered this, and other the like with other women, and was forced to acknowledge the justice of God in that having often called others fools, etc., for confessing against themselves, he was now forced to do the like. The woman dwelt now in Plymouth patent, and one of the magistrates there, hearing she was detected, etc., sent her to us. Upon her examination, she confessed he did attempt the fact, but did not commit it, and witness was produced that testified (which they both confessed) that in the evening of a day of humiliation through the country for England, etc., a company met at Britton's and there continued drinking sack, etc., till late in the night, and then Britton and the woman were seen upon the ground together, a little from the house. It was reported also that she did frequently abuse her husband, setting a knife to his breast and threatening to kill him, calling him old rogue and cuckold, and said she would make him wear horns as big as a bull. And yet some of the magistrates thought the evidence not sufficient against her, because there were not two direct witnesses; but the jury cast her, and then she confessed the fact, and accused twelve others, whereof two were married men. Five of these were apprehended and committed, (the rest were gone,) but denying it, and there being no other witness against them than the testimony of a condemned person, there could be no proceeding against them. The woman proved very penitent, and had deep apprehension of the foulness of her sin, and at length attained to hope of pardon by the blood of Christ, and was willing to die in satisfaction to justice. The man also was very much cast down for his sins, but was loth to die, and petitioned the general court for his life, but they would not grant it, though some of the magistrates spake much for it, and questioned the letter, whether adultery was death by God's law now. This Britton had been a professor in England, but coming hither he opposed our church government, etc., and grew dissolute, losing both power and profession of godliness.

[March 21] They were both executed, they both died very penitently, especially the woman, who had some comfortable hope of pardon of her sin, and gave good exhortation to all young maids to be obedient to their parents, and to take heed of evil company, etc. . . .

[March 5, 1645] A sad business fell out this year in Boston. One of the brethren of the church there, being in England in the parliament service about two years, had committed the care of his family and business to another of the same church, (a young man of good esteem for piety and sincerity, but his wife was in England,) who in time grew over familiar with his master's wife, (a young woman no member of the church,) so as she would be with him oft in his chamber, etc., and one night two of the servants, being up, perceived him to go up into their dame's chamber, which coming to the magistrates' knowledge, they were both sent for and examined, (but it was not discovered till about a quarter of a year after, her husband being then come home,) and confessed not only that he was in the chamber with her in such a suspicious manner, but also that he was in bed with her, but both denied any carnal knowledge; and being tried by a jury upon their lives by our law, which makes adultery death, the jury acquitted them of the adultery, but found them guilty of adulterous behavior. This was much against the minds of many, both of the magistrates and elders, who judged them worthy of death; but the jury attending what was spoken by others of the magistrates, 1. that seeing the main evidence against them was their own confession of being in bed together, their whole confession must be taken, and not a part of it; 2. the law requires two witnesses, but here was no witness at all, for although circumstances may amount to a testimony against the person, where the fact is evident, yet it is otherwise where no fact is apparent; 3. all that the evidence could evince was but suspicion of adultery, but neither God's law nor ours doth make suspicion of adultery (though never so strong) to be death; whereupon the case seeming doubtful to the jury, they judged it safest in case of life to find as they did. So the court adjudged them to stand upon the ladder at the place of execution with halters about their necks one hour, and then to be whipped, or each of them to pay 20 pounds. The husband (although he condemned his wife's immodest behavior, yet) was so confident of her innocency in point of adultery, as he would have paid 20 pounds rather than she should have been whipped; but their estate being but mean, she chose rather to submit to the rest of this punishment than that her husband should suffer so much for her folly. So he received her again, and they lived lovingly together. All that she had to say for herself upon her trial was the same which she had revealed to her husband as soon as he came home, before the matter had been discovered, viz. that he did indeed come into bed to her, which so soon as she perceived, she used the best arguments she could to dissuade him from so foul a sin, so as he lay still, and did not touch her, but went away again as he came; and the reason why she did not cry out, was because he had been very faithful and helpful to her in her husband's absence, which made her very unwilling to bring him to punishment or disgrace.

This punishment of standing upon the gallows was not so well approved by some of the magistrates; because the law of God appoints in case of whipping, that they should not exceed forty stripes, and the reason given is, lest thy brother should seem despised in thine eyes, and why this reason should not hold in all cases and punishments not capital doth not appear.

(?) ∾ *Thomas Morton* ∾ 1647

LITTLE is known of the early life and antecedents of the Jacobean attorney, Thomas Morton. Of gentle birth, probably from a Catholic family, he was living in Somerset, England, in 1619, where he had a none too savory reputation, and in 1622, the date he alleged that he first came to New England, he was defendant in a lawsuit in the Star Chamber Court in England. First appearing in New England in June, 1624, he established himself on Mount Wollaston, a hill in what is now Quincy, Mass., and proceeded to conduct himself in a fashion offensive to the Plymouth Colony. In 1628 he was seized by Captain Miles Standish and sent for punishment to England, as Bradford relates. Although he returned a year and a half later, he was not allowed to continue at his plantation of Merry-mount. A party of Salem Puritans led by John Endecott destroyed his famous maypole and banished him.

In 1637 Morton published at Amsterdam his *New English Canaan*, wherein he sought to satisfy the taste for "pamphlets of newes" from the New World, to justify himself, to display his gifts as a scoffing humorist and libertine wit, and to satirize New England Puritanism, plastering the leaders of both the Plymouth and Massachusetts Bay Colony with derogatory names worthy of the cast of characters in a comedy by Ben Jonson or one of his Puritan-baiting Caroline "Sons." Another motive that probably actuated Morton in the writing of his "curiosity of literature" was to ingratiate himself further with his patron, Sir Ferdinando Gorges, who had a claim on the territory where the Puritans had settled, but Gorges did not apparently approve of the book. In 1643 Morton once more came to Massachusetts, but was forced to leave. After going to Maine and Rhode Island, he came still again to Massachusetts. This time he was imprisoned for a year; he died in 1647, two years after his release.

[The following selections from Morton have been modernized in both spelling and punctuation and are, respectively, from Book I, Chapters II, XIX, XX, and Book III, Chapters XIV, XV, XXI, XXIII, XXVIII of *New English Canaan*, with their original titles.]

From
NEW ENGLISH CANAAN
[1637]

Of the Original of the Natives

IN the year since the incarnation of Christ, 1622, it was my chance to be landed in the parts of New England, where I found two sorts of people, the one Christians, the other infidels; these I found most full of humanity and more friendly than the other, as shall hereafter be made apparent in due course by their several actions from time to time whilst I lived among them. After my arrival in those parts, I endeavored by all the ways and means that I could to find out from what people or nation the natives of New England might be conjectured originally to proceed; and by continuance and conversation amongst them, I attained to so much of their language as by all probable conjecture may make the same manifest: for it hath been found by divers, and those of good judgment, that the natives of this country do use very many words, both of Greek and Latin, to the same signification that the Latin and Greeks have done . . .

And whereas it hath been the opinion of some men, which shall be nameless, that the natives of New England may proceed from the race of the Tartars and come from Tartaria into those parts over the frozen sea, I see no probability for any such conjecture . . .

But it may perhaps be granted that the natives of this country might originally come of the scattered Trojans, for after that Brutus, who was the fourth from Aeneas, left Latium . . ., this people were dispersed: there is no question but the people that lived with him, by reason of their conversation with the Grecians and Latins, had a mixed language that participated of both, . . . for this is commonly seen where 2 nations traffic together; the one endeavoring to understand the others' meaning makes them both many times speak a mixed language, as is approved by the natives of New England, through the covetous desire they have to commerce with our nation and we with them . . .

Therefore . . . now I am bold to conclude that the original of the natives of New England may be well conjectured to be from the scattered Trojans, after such time as Brutus departed from Latium.[1]

---

[1] It must be remembered that Morton's fantastic theory of Indian origins was no more fantastic than that set forth by Roger Williams in a letter to Thomas Thorowgood in England dated October 20, 1640, giving three reasons for believing that Indians were Jews, descendants of the lost tribes of Israel. This letter is quoted in Thorowgood's *Jewes in America, or, Probabilities That the Americans are of that Race*, London, 1650, p. 6. Williams, author of *A key into the language of America*, London, 1643, based his theory, partly at least, on linguistic observation, as did Morton. Williams adds to his three other reasons in the Thorowgood letter: ". . . and some tast of affinity with the Hebrew I have found."

OF THEIR INCLINATION TO DRUNKENNESS

Although drunkenness be justly termed a vice which the savages are ignorant of, yet the benefit is very great that comes to the planters by the sale of strong liquor to the savages, who are much taken with the delight of it, for they will pawn their wits to purchase the acquaintance of it. Yet in all the commerce that I had with them, I never proffered them any such thing; nay, I would hardly let any of them have a dram unless he were a sachem, or a *Winnaytue,* that is, a rich man of estimation next in degree to a sachem or sagamore. I always told them it was amongst us the sachems drink . . .

THAT THE SAVAGES LIVE A CONTENTED LIFE

I cannot deny but a civilized nation hath the preeminence of an uncivilized by means of those instruments that are found to be common amongst civil people, and the uncivil want the use of, to make themselves masters of those ornaments that make such a glorious show, that will give a man occasion to cry, *sic transit gloria mundi.*

Now since it is but food and raiment that men that live needeth (though not all alike), why should not the natives of New England be said to live richly, having no want of either? Clothes are the badge of sin, and the more variety of fashions is but the greater abuse of the creature: the beasts of the forest there do serve to furnish them at any time when they please: fish and flesh they have in great abundance, which they both roast and boil.

They are indeed not served in dishes of plate with variety of sauces to procure appetite; that needs not there. The rarity of the air, begot by the medicinable quality of the sweet herbs of the country, always procures good stomachs to the inhabitants.

I must needs commend them in this particular, that, though they buy many commodities of our nation, yet they keep but few and those of special use.

They love not to be cumbered with many utensils, and although every proprietor knows his own, yet all things (so long as they will last) are used in common amongst them: a biscuit cake given to one, that one breaks it equally into so many parts as there be persons in his company and distributes it. Plato's commonwealth is so much practiced by these people.

According to human reason, guided only by the light of nature, these people leads [lead] the more happy and freer life, being void of care, which torments the minds of so many Christians. . . .

OF THE REVELS OF NEW CANAAN

The inhabitants of Pasonagessit, having translated the name of their habitation from that ancient savage name to Ma-re Mount,[2] and being resolved to have the new name confirmed for a memorial to after-ages, did devise amongst themselves to have it performed in a solemn manner with revels and merriment after the old English custom; [they] prepared to set up a Maypole upon the festival day of Philip and Jacob, and therefore brewed a barrel of excellent beer and provided a case of bottles, to be spent, with other good cheer, for all comers of that day. And because they would have it in a complete form, they had prepared a song fitting to the time and present occasion. And upon May Day they brought the Maypole to the place appointed, with drums, guns, pistols, and other fitting instruments for that purpose, and there erected it with the help of savages that came thither of purpose to see the manner of our revels. A goodly pine tree of eighty foot long was reared up, with a pair of buck's horns nailed on somewhat near unto the top of it; where it stood as a fair sea-mark for directions how to find out the way to mine host of Ma-re Mount.

---

[2] Morton's insistence throughout *New English Canaan* on this name, meaning a hill on the sea, was probably a pun on the name "Merie-mounte," as Bradford spells it, being designed to confound Separatists and their kind.

And because it should more fully appear to what end it was placed there, they had a poem in readiness made, which was fixed to the Maypole, to show the new name confirmed upon the plantation; which, although it were made according to the occurrences of the time, it being enigmatically composed, puzzled the Separatists most pitifully to expound it . . .

The setting up of this Maypole was a lamentable spectacle to the precise Separatists that lived at New Plymouth. They termed it an idol; yea, they called it the calf of Horeb, and stood at defiance with the place, naming it Mount Dagon, threatening to make it a woeful mount and not a merry mount . . .

There was likewise a merry song made, which, to make their revels more fashionable, was sung with a chorus, every man bearing his part; which they performed in a dance, hand in hand about the Maypole, while one of the company sung and filled out the good liquor, like Ganymede and Jupiter.

The Song

Chorus

Drink and be merry, merry, merry boys;
Let all your delight be in the Hymen's
    joys;
Iô [i.e., Joy] to Hymen! now the day
    is come,
About the merry Maypole take a room.
Make green garlands, bring bottles out,
And fill sweet nectar freely about;
Uncover thy head and fear no harm,
For here's good liquor to keep it warm.
Then drink and be merry, etc.
Iô to Hymen, etc.
Nectar is a thing assigned
By the deity's own mind
To cure the heart oppressed with grief,
And of good liquors is the chief.
Then drink, etc.
Iô to Hymen, etc.
Give to the melancholy man
A cup or two of't now and then;
This physic will soon revive his blood,

And make him to be of a merrier mood.
Then drink, etc.
Iô to Hymen, etc.
Give to the nymph that's free from
    scorn
No Irish stuff nor Scotch overworn.
Lasses in beaver coats, come away,
Ye shall be welcome to us night and day.
To drink and be merry, etc.
Iô to Hymen, etc.

This harmless mirth made by young men (that lived in hope to have wives brought over to them, that would save them a labor to make a voyage to fetch any over) was much distasted of the precise Separatists . . .

OF A GREAT MONSTER SUPPOSED TO BE AT
MA-RE MOUNT AND THE PREPARATION
    MADE TO DESTROY IT

The Separatists, envying the prosperity and hope of the plantation at Ma-re Mount, which they perceived began to come forward and to be in a good way for gain in the beaver trade, conspired together against mine host especially, who was the owner of that plantation, and made up a party against him; and mustered up what aid they could, accounting of him as of a great monster.

Many threatening speeches were given out both against his person and his habitation, which they divulged should be consumed with fire; and taking advantage of the time when his company, which seemed little to regard their threats, were gone up into the islands to trade with the savages for beaver, they set upon my honest host at a place called Wessaguscus, where by accident they found him. The inhabitants there were in good hope of the subversion of the plantation at Ma-re Mount, which they principally aimed at; and the rather because mine host was a man that endeavored to advance the dignity of the Church of England, which they, on the contrary part, would labor to vilify with uncivil terms, inveighing against the sacred Book of Common Prayer and mine host, that used it in a laudable manner amongst his family as a practice of piety . . .

Much rejoicing was made that they had gotten their capital enemy, as they concluded him, whom they purposed to hamper in such sort that he should not be able to uphold his plantation at Ma-re Mount.

The conspirators sported themselves at my honest host, that meant them no hurt, and were so jocund that they feasted their bodies and fell to tippling as if they had obtained a great prize, like the Trojans when they had the custody of Hippeus' pine-tree horse.

Mine host feigned grief and could not be persuaded either to eat or drink, because he knew emptiness would be a means to make him as watchful as the geese kept in the Roman capitol: whereon the contrary part, the conspirators, would be so drowsy that he might have an opportunity to give them a slip instead of a tester.[3] Six persons of the conspiracy were set to watch him at Wessaguscus. But he kept waking, and in the dead of night (one lying on the bed for further surety) up gets mine host and got to the second door that he was to pass, which, notwithstanding the lock, he got open, and shut it after him with such violence that it affrighted some of the conspirators.

The word, which was given with an alarm, was: "Oh, he's gone, he's gone! What shall we do? He's gone!" The rest, half asleep, start up in amaze, and like rams ran their heads one at another full butt in the dark.

Their grand leader, Captain Shrimp,[4] took on most furiously and tore his clothes for anger to see the empty nest, and their bird gone.

The rest were eager to have torn their hair from their heads; but it was so short that it would give them no hold. Now Captain Shrimp thought in the loss of this prize, which he accounted his masterpiece, all his honor would be lost forever.

In the meantime mine host was got home

to Ma-re Mount through the woods, eight miles round about the head of the river Monatoquit that parted the two plantations, finding his way by the help of the lightning (for it thundered as he went, terribly); and there he prepared powder, three pounds dried, for his present employment, and four good guns for him and the two assistants left at his house, with bullets of several sizes, three hundred or thereabouts, to be used if the conspirators should pursue him thither; and these two persons promised their aids in the quarrel and confirmed that promise with health in good rosa solis.

Now Captain Shrimp, the first captain in the land (as he supposed) must do some new act to repair this loss and to vindicate his reputation, who had sustained blemish by this oversight; begins now to study how to repair or survive his honor. In this manner, calling of council, they conclude.

He takes eight persons more to him, and like the nine worthies of New Canaan they embark with preparation against Ma-re Mount, where this monster of a man, as their phrase was, had his den; the whole number, had the rest not been from home, being but seven, would have given Captain Shrimp (a quondam drummer) such a welcome as would have made him wish for a drum as big as Diogenes' tub, that he might have crept into it out of sight.

Now the nine worthies are approached, and mine host prepared, having intelligence by a savage that hastened in love from Wessaguscus to give him notice of their intent.

One of mine host's men proved a craven; the other had proved his wits to purchase a little valor before mine host had observed his posture.

The nine worthies coming before the den of this supposed monster (this seven-

---

[3] Morton here puns on the meanings of these words. "Slip" was a counterfeit coin; "tester" was slang for sixpence.

[4] Morton's name for Captain Miles Standish.

headed Hydra, as they termed him), and began, like Don Quixote against the windmill, to beat a parley and to offer quarter if mine host would yield, for they resolved to send him for England and bade him lay by his arms.

But he, who was the son of a soldier, having taken up arms in his just defense, replied that he would not lay by those arms, because they were so needful at sea if he should be sent over. Yet, to save the effusion of so much worthy blood as would have issued out of the veins of these nine worthies of New Canaan if mine host should have played upon them out at his portholes (for they came within danger like a flock of wild geese, as if they had been tailed one to another, as colts to be sold at a fair), mine host was content to yield upon quarter, and did capitulate with them in what manner it should be, for more certainty, because he knew what Captain Shrimp was.

He expressed that no violence should be offered to his person, none to his goods nor any of his household, but that he should have his arms and what else was requisite for the voyage; which, their herald returns, it was agreed upon and should be performed.

But mine host no sooner had set open the door and issued out, but instantly Captain Shrimp and the rest of the worthies stepped to him, laid hold of his arms, and had him down; and so eagerly was every man bent against him (not regarding any agreement made with such a carnal man) that they fell upon him as if they would have eaten him. Some of them were so violent that they would have a slice with scabbard, and all for haste; until an old soldier ("of the Queen's," as the proverb is) that was there by accident, clapped his gun under the weapons and sharply rebuked these worthies for their unworthy practices. So the matter was taken into more deliberate consideration.

Captain Shrimp and the rest of the nine worthies made themselves, by this outrageous riot, masters of mine host of

Ma-re Mount and disposed of what he had at his plantation.

This they knew, in the eye of the savages, would add to their glory and diminish the reputation of mine honest host, whom they practiced to be rid of upon any terms, as willingly as if he had been the very Hydra of the time.

OF CAPTAIN LITTLEWORTH . . .

In the meantime . . . there was a great swelling fellow, of Littleworth,[5] crept over to Salem (by the help of Master Charterparty, the Treasurer, and Master Ananias Increase, the Collector for the Company of Separatists) to take upon him their employments for a time.

He, resolving to make hay while the sun did shine, first pretended himself to be sent over as Chief Justice of the Massachusetts Bay and Salem, forsooth, and took upon him a council; and a worthy one, no doubt, for the Cowkeeper of Salem was a prime man in those employments; and to add a majesty, as he thought, to his new-assumed dignity, he caused the patent of the Massachusetts, new brought into the land, to be carried where he went in his progress to and fro, as an emblem of his authority: which the vulgar people, not acquainted with, thought it to be some instrument of music locked up in that covered case, and thought (for so some said) this man of littleworth had been a fiddler, and the rather because he had put into the mouths of poor silly things, that were sent along with him, what skill he had in engines, and in things of quaint device: all which proved in conclusion to be but imposture.

OF A GREAT BONFIRE MADE FOR JOY OF THE ARRIVAL OF GREAT JOSUA, SURNAMED TEMPERWELL . . .

Seven ships set forth at once, and altogether arrived in the Land of Canaan, to take a full possession thereof . . .

[5] Morton's name for John Endecott.

And here comes their Josua [6] too among them; and they make it a more miraculous thing for these seven ships to set forth together and arrive at New Canaan together than it was for the Israelites to go over Jordan dry-shod . . .

These are the men that come prepared to rid the land of all pollution . . . These men have brought a very snare indeed; and now mine host must suffer . . .

A court is called of purpose for mine host: he there convented and must hear his doom before he go . . .

There they all with one assent put him to silence, crying out, "Hear the Governor! Hear the Governor!"—who gave this sentence against mine host at first sight: that he should be put in the bilboes, his goods should be all confiscated, his plantation should be burned down to the ground, because the habitation of the wicked should no more appear in Israel, and his person banished from those territories; and this put in execution with all speed.

The harmless savages, his neighbors, came the while (grieved, poor silly lambs, to see what they went about) and did reprove these Eliphants [7] of wit for their inhuman deed: the Lord above did open their mouths like Balaam's Ass and make them speak in his behalf unexpected divinity, besides morality, and told them that God would not love them that burned this good man's house and plainly said that they who were new come would find the want of such a house in the winter: so much themselves to him confessed.

The smoke that did ascend appeared to be the very sacrifice of Cain. Mine host (that a far off aboard a ship did there behold this woeful spectacle) knew not what he should do in this extremity but bear and forbear, as Epictetus says: it was bootless to exclaim.

He did consider then these transitory things are but *ludibria fortunae* [8], as Cicero calls them. All was burnt down to the ground and nothing did remain but the bare ashes as an emblem of their cruelty:

and unless it could (like to the Phoenix) rise out of these ashes and be new again (to the immortal glory and renown of this fertile Canaan the new), the stumps and posts in their black liveries will mourn, and piety itself will add a voice to the bare remnant of that monument and make it cry for recompense, or else revenge, against the sect of cruel schismatics . . .

OF THEIR POLICY IN PUBLIC JUSTICE

Now that I have anatomized the two extreme parts of this politic commonwealth, the head and the inferior members, I will show you the heart and read a short lecture over that too: which is Justice.

I have a petition to exhibit to the high and mighty Mr. Temperwell, and I have my choice whether I shall make my plaint in a case of conscience or bring it within the compass of a point in law. And because I will go the surest way to work, at first I will see how others are answered in the like kind, whether it be hab or nab, as the judge did the countryman. [9]

Here comes Mr. Hopewell: his petition is in a case of conscience, as he says. But, see, great Josua allows conscience to be of his side, yet cuts him off with this answer: law is flat against him. Well, let me see another. Aye, marry! here comes one Master Doubtnot: his matter depends, I am sure, upon a point in law: alas, what will it not do, look ye it is affirmed that law is on his side, but conscience, like a blanket, overspreads it. This passage is like to the Procustes of Rome,

[6] Joshua Temperwell is Morton's name for John Winthrop.

[7] A pun on the word "elephants" and "Eliphants", i.e., high priests of Eli or of Israel.

[8] Jests of the Goddess Fortuna or Fortune. The reference is to Cicero's *Paradoxa*, I, i.

[9] "Hab or nab" means "hit or miss." Morton is probably alluding to an incident in Act IV, sc. i of Ben Jonson's *Tale of a Tub*.

methinks; and therefore I may very well say of them:

Even so, by racking out the joints and chopping off the head, Procustes fitted all his guests into his iron bed.

And if these speed no better, with whom they are friends, that neither find law nor conscience to help them, I do not wonder to see mine host of Ma-re Mount speed so ill, that has been proclaimed an enemy so many years in New Canaan to their church and state.

1602 ∾ *Peter Stuyvesant* ∾ 1672

PETER STUYVESANT was sent by the Dutch West India Company in 1647 to be director of New Netherland, which had been settled in 1624 and which was inefficiently administered by the Company and inadequately supported by the Estates-General. Contemptuous of popular elections, harassed by the state of affairs resulting from unwise remote control, Stuyvesant subjected the colonists to irascible dictatorship and high-handed exploitation, provoking from his council of nine—consisting of merchants, artisans, petty tradesmen, and landowners—a remonstrance against his rule to the Estates-General.

When Stuyvesant was forced to yield the colony to English conquest in 1664, the Estates-General summoned him home to give an account of himself. He arrived in Holland in October, 1665, and presented his report, the original of which was committed to the National Archives at the Hague. After the English were granted New York by the treaty of Breda in 1667, Stuyvesant returned there to spend the rest of his life on his farm, Great Bouwery.

[The following selection is from the English translation of this report, printed in *Narratives of New Netherland, 1609-1664*, ed. J. F. Jameson, New York, 1909, one of the volumes in the series, *Original Narratives of Early American History*.]

From the
REPORT
[1858 (1665)]

ILLUSTRIOUS, High and Mighty Lords: Whilst I, your Illustrious High Mightinesses' humble servant, was still in New Netherland I was informed, verbally and in writing, that the unfortunate loss and reduction of New Netherland were, in consequence of ignorance of the facts, spoken of and judged in this country by many variously, and by most people not consistently with the truth according to the appetite and learning of each. Therefore your Illustrious High Mightinesses' servant, sustained by the tranquillity of an upright and loyal heart, was moved to abandon all, even his most beloved wife, to inform you, Illustrious, High and Mighty, of the true state of the case, that you, when so informed, may decide according to your profound wisdom . . .

I dare not interrupt your Illustrious High Mightinesses' most important business by a lengthy narrative of the poor condition in which I found New Netherland on my assuming its government. The open country was stripped of inhabitants to such a degree that, with the exception of the three English villages of Heemstede, New Flushing and Gravesend, there were not fifty bouweries and plantations on it, and the whole province could not muster 250, at most 300 men capable of bearing arms.

Which was caused, first, (in default of a settlement of the boundary so repeatedly requested) by the troublesome neighbors of New England, who numbered full fifty to our one,[1] continually encroaching on lands within established bounds, possessed and cultivated in fact by your Illustrious High Mightinesses' subjects.

Secondly, by the exceedingly detrimental, land-destroying and people-expelling wars with the cruel barbarians, which endured two years before my arrival there, whereby many subjects who possessed means were necessitated to depart, others to retreat under the crumbling fortress of New Amsterdam, which, on my arrival, I found resembling more a molehill than a fortress, without gates, the walls and bastions trodden under foot by men and cattle.

Less dare I, to avoid self-glorification, encumber your weighty occupations, Illustrious, High and Mighty, with the trouble, care, solicitude and continual zeal with which I have endeavored to promote the increase of population, agriculture and commerce; the flourishing condition whereunto they were brought, not through any wisdom of mine, but through God's special blessing, and which might have been more flourishing if your formerly dutiful, but now afflicted, inhabitants of that conquest had been, Illustrious, High and Mighty, protected and remained protected by a suitable garrison, as necessity demanded, against the deplorable and tragical massacres by the barbarians,

whereby (in addition to ten private murders) we were plunged three times into perilous wars, through want of sufficient garrisons; especially had they, on the supplicatory remonstrances of the people and our own so iterated entreaties, which must be considered almost innumerable, been helped with the long sought for settlement of boundary, or in default thereof had they been seconded with the oft besought reinforcement of men and ships against the continual troubles, threats, encroachments and invasions of the English neighbors and government of Hartford Colony, our too powerful enemies.

That assistance, nevertheless, appears to have been retarded so long (wherefore and by what unpropitious circumstances the Honorable Directors best know) that our above-mentioned too powerful neighbors and enemies found themselves reinforced by four royal ships, crammed full with an extraordinary amount of men and warlike stores. Our ancient enemies throughout the whole of Long Island, both from the east end and from the villages belonging to us united with them, hemmed us by water and by land, and cut off all supplies. Powder and provisions failing, and no relief nor reinforcement being expected, we were necessitated to come to terms with the enemy, not through neglect of duty or cowardice, as many, more from passion than knowledge of the facts, have decided, but in consequence of an absolute impossibility to defend the fort, much less the city of New Amsterdam, and still less the country . . .

[1] A considerable exaggeration. In 1647 New Netherland had probably a population of about 1,500, New England of about 25,000.

1603(?) ∾ *Roger Williams* ∾ 1683

BORN in London, his father a merchant tailor, Roger Williams was assisted by the famous jurist, Sir Edward Coke, in completing his education. Receiving a B. A. degree from Pembroke College, Cambridge, in 1627, he came to New England in 1631, served as pastor of the church in Salem, later functioned as an unordained minister at Plymouth, and then returned to his Salem pastorate, but not for long. He clashed with the Massachusetts Bay authorities on a number of issues, including his advocacy of complete separation from the Church of England and his insistence that the state had no right to persecute anyone for holding any kind of religious opinion, and was banished from the colony in October, 1635, as a radical comparable to some of the more extreme sectarians who were bringing Puritanism into discredit in England.

Early in 1636 he had to flee to the Narragansett country to escape arrest. Here, by founding Providence, he established the colony of Rhode Island, in whose government and affairs he played a major role until his death in 1683. To orthodox Puritans 17th Century Rhode Island seemed a bedlam anarchy of heretics. Later Americans have hymned it as the very cradle of our democracy, where all those, such as the Quakers, who were hounded and imprisoned and even put to death for their beliefs by Puritans and other tyrants, were able to find haven and to worship undisturbed. The truth lies somewhere between these extreme views. The Quakers, for example, who had received incredibly harsh treatment in Massachusetts, were permitted to settle in Rhode Island; they were not left entirely undisturbed, however, but were challenged to justify their heresies in open and free debate by Roger Williams himself.

Williams' challenge, setting forth the numerous "positions" or points on which he desired them to give him satisfaction, was directed to the great English Quaker leader, George Fox, who had come on a missionary expedition to Newport. Fox either chose deliberately to evade Williams' challenge, as the latter seemed to believe, or, as the Quakers insisted, left before he received it, but other Quakers were willing to meet and argue with Williams. After the debate, part of which was held at the Quaker stronghold of Newport on August 9, 10, and 12, 1672, and part of which took place in Williams' home town of Providence on August 17 of the same year, Williams published his account of the proceedings under the punning title, *George Fox Digg'd out of his Burrowes,* the reference being to Edward Burroughs, another Quaker, who had asked for debate in his preliminary epistle to one of Fox's controversial works, *The Great Mystery of the Great Whore unfolded,* London,

1659. Fox and one of the Quaker participants in the Williams debate, John Burnyeat, drew up an answer to Williams' tome in another entitled, *A New England Firebrand Quenched*, London, 1678.

[The following modernized selection from Williams' account, relating how the Quakers finally took up his gage and how he made the trip to Newport and began the first round of the prolonged theological bout, reveals much of the spirit of early Rhode Island and of the character of its founder. For further selections from Williams' works, see Book I, Parts 2 and 3.]

From
GEORGE FOX DIGG'D OUT OF HIS
BURROWES
[1676]

WITHIN some few days after that our Deputy Governor had delivered my paper to them, the strange Quakers (as was agreed with G. Fox) came to Providence— John Stubs [Stubbs], John Burnet [Burnyeat], and others—and came to my house six or seven together; their salutations were (like the meetings of their dumb spirit) in silence. I bid them welcome, etc. John Stubs began and said they had received a paper from me, and they came to me to tell me that they accepted my offer, and that they had appointed (according to the liberty given them by myself in my paper) the 9th of the present August to be the day at Newport. I told them they were welcome and the more welcome because they brought me tidings of their resolution, for I longed for opportunities of such exercises, to which I thought the most High invited us by our precious liberties, etc. I added that my paper was in the first place directed to G. Fox, but they suddenly catched at my word, and John Burnet told me that G. Fox was departed before my letters were opened, and that G. Fox never saw my paper (and probably as afterward in the dispute he spake honestly, not knowing the mystery); John Stubs added that my paper gave liberty to G. Fox or his friends. I said therefore I would not fail (if God pleased) to meet them at the place, and by nine in the morning, on the day they had appointed.

They departed (after drink offered and accepted by some), but the next morning, being the first of the week, I sent them word in writing that divers of our neighbors were grieved that the conference should be carried away from Providence to Newport wholly; (as some of them had also spoken) I told them that the accepting of my proffer necessarily included the conference about the latter seven [points of debate] at Providence; I told them their consciences and credits lay on it and therefore desired them to fix on a day for the dispute of the latter seven at Providence before their departure hence. This paper was delivered to one of their company in the room where they were together, but, whether on purpose or (as 'tis possible) by mistake, they say the paper was lost; so, receiving no answer from them, I late in the evening sent them another writing, signifying that I could not hold myself engaged to meet them at Newport about the first seven without their promise of discussing the latter seven at Providence. Then they wrote to me that I had seemed willing and that they had given notice and the country would come in; therefore they challenged me to appear and prove my malicious and bitter charges against them, and withal promised that upon the finishing of the first seven at Newport, some of them would give me a meeting at Providence, etc. Upon the receipt of this, I sent them a third writing signifying that I rested in their promise, and therefore (if God pleased) I would not fail to be with them at the time and place appointed. And God graciously assisted me in rowing all day with my old bones so that I got to Newport toward the midnight before the morning appointed.

Then I sent them a fourth paper (with a copy of my first that miscarried as they said) and signified to them that it would be convenient to agree about some order of transition or passing from one position to another, as also, since they were many and I but one, I presumed their reason told them that I expected but one at once, and that, if another desired to speak, the first should hold his peace; as also I signified that some were scrupulous of going into the Quakers' meeting-house, and therefore I desired some thoughts about it; they thought it convenient to send H. Bull to request me to go to his house to them; I went; they urged the capaciousness and conveniency of their house, and I told such as scrupled that it was one thing to go into a Jewish synagogue or a Popish chapel to worship or countenance their worships, another thing to profess and contest against them, in which respect Paul disputed many days in the Jews' synagogues against them, and I could freely go into the Pope's chapel to dispute against the Pope and his worship.

I knew our aged Governor, Mr. Nich. Easton and other magistrates (of their judgment) would be there, and so the civil peace maintained, and I had a strange assurance given in to my spirit from God in answer to my poor requests, etc., viz., that by moderation and patience I should conquer their immoderations and impatiencies; I therefore thought it in vain to spend time about a moderator. 'Tis true they gave me no answer either by speech or writing concerning their coming on me one at once, but to their seeming great advantage they constantly fell on me all at once and one of them, William Edmundson, with grievous language and insulting.

When I came into the place aforesaid I found three able and noted preachers amongst them, viz. John Stubs, John Burnet, William Edmundson sitting together on a high bench with some of the magis

trates of their judgment with them. I had heard that John Stubs was learned in the Hebrew and the Greek (and I found him so); as for John Burnet, I found him to be of a moderate spirit and a very able speaker. The third, W. Edmundson, was newly come (as was said) from Virginia, and he proved the chief speaker, a man not so able nor so moderate as the other two. For the two first would speak argument and discuss and produce Scripture, but William Edmundson was very ignorant in the Scripture or any other learning. He had been a soldier in the late wars, a stout portly man of a great voice, and fit to make a Bragadocia [1] (as he did) and a constant exercise merely of my patience: he would often vapour and preach long, and, when I had patiently waited till the gust was over, and began to speak, then would he stop my mouth with a very unhandsome clout of a grievous interruption, so that sometimes I was forced to play the moderator and to protest that such practices were against the sober rules of civility and humanity. It pleased God to help me with such patience to weather them that John Stubs openly confessed twice that, though some others had given them some interruptions, yet that I had not done it.

I took my seat at the other end of the house opposite to them, and began telling them that the most High was my witness that not out of any prejudice against or disrespect to the persons of the Quakers (many of whom I knew and did love and honor) nor any foolish passion or pride or boldness (for I desired to be sensible of my many decays of my house of clay, and other ways) nor any earthly or worldly ends I had that occasioned this trouble to myself and them.

I was first commanded this work from Heaven. Why should not this argument be good for me and for others as well as the Quakers? They say their commands are immediate (for interpretations are immediate), but I say they herein suffer

<hr/>

[1] An allusion to Braggadocio, a swaggering boaster in Spenser's *Faerie Queene*.

Satan to cheat them, for they say they pray, they fast, they wait, they listen, they judge of the motions that arise within them, and so have I done. The great maker and searcher of all hearts knows that none but his holy Majesty was privy to the conception of this business.

1. My end was the vindicating his most holy name, which my soul saw was trodden in the dirt by Satan clothed with Samuel's mantle and the bright garment of an angel of light, which once he was, but pride deceived him.

2. I had in mine eye the vindicating this colony for receiving of such persons whom others would not; we suffer for their sakes and are accounted their abettors; that therefore, together with the improvement of our liberties which the God of Heaven and our King's Majesty have graciously given us, I might give a public testimony against their opinions in such a way and exercise, I judged it incumbent upon my spirit and conscience to do it (in some regards) more than most in the colony. I may also truly say that

3. I had also in mine eye that this exercise might occasion some soul consideration in many. I told them that we had a doleful alarum and instruction lately, we were taught what salvation and saving was, in the late death and drowning of a person so known to us (and all N. England)— Nicholas Davis. I told them our case and the case of all mankind is his (in spiritual and soul matters)—Oh, a world for an oar, a rope, a plank! Only it must be to all of us our work, to try whether our savior, our salvation be real and not failing in so great a straight.

Some of these blessed ends it hath pleased God to propagate by this occasion all this colony over, and all of us round about have put forth ourselves in disquisitions and searchings after the true grounds of the Christian religion and worship.

I had many thoughts of beginning such an exercise with prayer unto God for his presence, but I knew I could not join with them nor would they own my pray-

ers; I had thoughts (as Eliah among the Baalites) to have prayed in the singular number. But some considerations made my spirit content with this kind of petition unto God. For not only in my closet and my heart, but publicly before them all I said: "I do humbly hope and beg of God, the father of spirits, so to order and direct our spirits in these our agitations that his holy name may receive glory and the souls of all of us some soul-profit and advantage."

I began with the first position, which I think W. Edmundson also read out of the paper, viz.—

"That the people called Quakers are not true Quakers according to the Scriptures."

I said I knew they did not own that name Quakers as imposed on them by God or taken up by themselves, but given them in scorn and derision, as G. Fox, Ed. Burrowes (and I had heard John Stubs who joined with them) declared, and that one Gervace Bennet, a justice in Derby, first so called them in the year 1650.[2] And yet I had cause to judge that the name was given by Justice Bennet and others to them from that strange and uncouth possessing of their bodies, with quaking and shaking of their bodies even in public assemblies and congregations, which extraordinary motions I judged to come upon them, not from the holy spirit and power of God, but from the spirit and power of Satan for divers reasons . . .

To this purpose I told them at the first coming of this spirit to London and Westminster, some parliament men told me that themselves went to one of the Quakers' meeting about Charing Cross, but were so affrighted with the shaking of their own bodies and of their chairs and stools under them that they could never again be got into their assemblies.

I added that such shakings, motions,

---

[2] George Fox records in his *Journal* that Bennet applied this name to the zealots brought before him for trial with the following explanation, "I bid them tremble at the word of the Lord."

ecstasies, etc., were known to be the frequent workings of Satan upon his servants in all ages. Such were the furious motions of Baal's priests, the motions of the possessed mentioned in the Gospels, and other histories, and known to be amongst the Barbarians, our neighbors about this time. John Burnet and William Edmundson rose up and said that I had laid many deep and heavy charges upon the people of the Lord, which I should never be able to prove: I had denied them to be Christians and so had wronged the good spirit of God in them and their profession of worshipping God in the spirit. Yea, I had taken away

their being (as men) out of the world as a dangerous people to nations and kingdoms and commonweals, yea to kings and princes, and so not fit to live amongst men in the world. These speeches were often uttered and enlarged by one or other of them and that with zeal (and passion in W. Edmundson).

I waited patiently till these gusts of their angry spirit was [were] over, and then I told them I had not wronged them in a tittle, but by the help of the most High I would make all good against them and then leave it to every man's and woman's soul to judge at their own peril . . .

1619(?) ∼ *Claude Dablon* ∼ 1697

AMONG the Jesuit missionaries of New France in the 17th Century, Jacques Marquette, 1637-1675, distinguished himself as an explorer of the Mississippi and a bearer of the gospel to far-flung Indian tribes. The following account of his last voyage, his death, and his final obsequies is part of a document written by Claude Dablon, Marquette's superior at Quebec. From manuscripts in the possession of St. Mary's College, Montreal, this and other Marquette documents were published in several collections after 1850; the best texts, with translations, are in *The Jesuit Relations*. This great series, in seventy-three volumes, was published between 1896 and 1901 under the editorship of the American historian, Reuben Gold Thwaites, and contains the French, Latin, and Italian texts with English translations.

[The present selection, with a few revisions in punctuation, capitalization, and spelling, is reproduced from Vol. LIX, 185-205. The title has been supplied by the present editors.]

THE LAST VOYAGE, THE DEATH, AND THE FINAL OBSEQUIES OF FATHER MARQUETTE
[Written 1677]

I

FATHER Jacques Marquette, having promised the Illinois on his first voyage to them, in 1673, that he would return to them the following year, to teach them the mysteries of our religion, had much difficulty in keeping his word. The great hard-

ships of his first voyage had brought upon him a bloody flux, and had so weakened him that he was giving up the hope of undertaking a second. However, his sickness decreased; and, as it had almost entirely abated by the close of the summer of the following year, he obtained the permission of his superiors to return to the Illinois and there begin that fair mission.

He set out for that purpose, in the month of November of the year 1674, from the Bay des Puants, with two men, one of whom had made the former voyage with him. During a month of navigation on the lake of the Illinois, he was tolerably well; but, as soon as the snow began to fall, he was again seized with his bloody flux, which compelled him to halt in the river which leads to the Illinois. It was there that they constructed a cabin in which to pass the winter, amid such inconveniences that, his malady increasing more and more, he saw clearly that God was granting to him the favor which he had so many times besought from him; and he even told his two companions very plainly that he would certainly die of that malady, and during that voyage. Duly to prepare his soul, despite the severe indisposition of his body, he began this so severe winter sojourn by the retreat of St. Ignatius, which he performed with every feeling of devotion, and many celestial consolations; and then he passed the whole of the remaining time in holding communion with all Heaven—having, in these deserts, no intercourse with the earth except with his two companions. He confessed them and administered communion to them twice in the week, and exhorted them as much as his strength permitted him. A short time after Christmas, that he might obtain the favor of not dying without having taken possession of his dear mission, he invited his companions to make a novena[1] in honor of the immaculate conception of the blessed virgin. His prayer was answered, against all human probability; and, his health improving, he prepared himself to go to the village of the Illinois as soon as navigation should open—which he did with much joy, setting out for that place on the 29th of March. He spent eleven days on the way, during which time he had occasion to suffer much, both from his own illness, from which he had not entirely recovered, and from the very severe and unfavorable weather.

On at last arriving at the village, he was received as an angel from Heaven. After he had assembled at various times the chiefs of the nation, with all the old men, that he might sow in their minds the first seeds of the gospel, and after having given instruction in the cabins, which were always filled with a great crowd of people, he resolved to address all in public, in a general assembly which he called together in the open air, the cabins being too small to contain all the people. It was a beautiful prairie, close to a village, which was selected for the great council; this was adorned, after the fashion of the country, by covering it with mats and bearskins. Then the father, having directed them to stretch out upon lines several pieces of Chinese taffeta, attached to these four large pictures of the blessed virgin, which were visible on all sides. The audience was composed of 500 chiefs and elders, seated in a circle around the father, and of all the young men, who remained standing. They numbered more than 1,500 men, without counting the women and children, who are always numerous—the village being composed of 5 or 600 fires. The father addressed the whole body of people, and conveyed to them 10 messages, by means of ten presents which he gave them. He explained to them the principal mysteries of our religion, and the purpose that had brought him to their country. Above all, he preached to them Jesus Christ, on the very eve (of that great day) on which he had died upon the cross for them, as well as for all the rest of mankind; then he said holy mass. On the third day after, which was Easter Sunday, things being prepared in the same manner as on Thursday, he celebrated the holy mysteries for the 2nd time; and by these two, the only sacrifices ever offered there to God, he took possession of that land in the name of Jesus Christ, and gave to that mission the name of the Immaculate Conception of the blessed virgin.

He was listened to by all those peoples with universal joy; and they prayed him with most earnest entreaty to come back to them as soon as possible, since his sick-

[1] A nine days' devotion.

ness obliged him to return. The father, on his side, expressed to them the affection which he felt for them, and the satisfaction that they had given him; and pledged them his word that he, or some other of our fathers, would return to carry on that mission so happily inaugurated. This promise he repeated several times, while parting with them to go upon his way; and he set out with so many tokens of regard on the part of those good peoples that, as a mark of honor, they chose to escort him for more than 30 leagues on the road, vying with each other in taking charge of his slender baggage.

II

After the Illinois, filled with great esteem for the gospel, had taken leave of the father, he continued his journey, and shortly after reached the lake of the Illinois, upon whose waters he had to journey nearly a hundred leagues, by an unknown route, whereon he had never before traveled; for he was obliged to coast along the southern shore of the lake, having come by the northern. But his strength was so rapidly diminishing that his two men despaired of being able to bring him alive to the end of their journey. Indeed, he became so feeble and exhausted that he was unable to assist or even to move himself, and had to be handled and carried about like a child.

Meanwhile, he preserved in that condition an admirable equanimity, resignation, joy, and gentleness, consoling his dear companions and encouraging them to suffer patiently all the hardships of that voyage, in the assurance that God would not abandon them after his death. It was during this voyage that he began to make more special preparation for death. He held communion, sometimes with our Lord, sometimes with his holy mother, or with his guardian angel, or with all paradise. He was often overheard repeating these words, *Credo quod redemptor meus vivit;* or, *maria, mater gratiae, mater dei, memento mei.*[2] In addition to the spiritual

exercise, which was read to him every day, he requested toward the close that they would read to him his meditation preparatory for death, which he carried about with him. He recited every day his breviary; and although he was so low that his sight and strength were greatly enfeebled, he continued to do so to the last day of his life, despite the remonstrance of his companions.

Eight days before his death, he was thoughtful enough to prepare the holy water for use during the rest of his illness, in his agony, and at his burial, and he instructed his companions how it should be used.

The evening before his death, which was a Friday, he told them, very joyously, that it would take place on the morrow. He conversed with them during the whole day as to what would need to be done for his burial: about the manner in which they should inter him; of the spot that should be chosen for his grave; how his feet, his hands, and his face should be arranged; how they should erect a cross over his grave. He even went so far as to counsel them, 3 hours before he expired, that as soon as he was dead they should take the little hand-bell of his chapel, and sound it while he was being put under ground. He spoke of all these things with so great tranquillity and presence of mind that one might have supposed that he was concerned with the death and funeral of some other person, and not with his own.

Thus did he converse with them as they made their way upon the lake—until, having perceived a river, on the shore of which stood an eminence that he deemed well suited to be the place of his interment, he told them that that was the place of his last repose. They wished, however, to proceed farther, as the weather was favorable, and the day was not far advanced; but God raised a contrary wind, which compelled them to return, and enter

---

[2] "I believe that my redeemer lives" and "Mary, mother of grace, mother of God, remember me."

the river which the father had pointed out. They accordingly brought him to the land, lighted a little fire for him, and prepared for him a wretched cabin of bark. They laid him down therein, in the least uncomfortable way that they could; but they were so stricken with sorrow that, as they have since said, they hardly knew what they were doing.

The father, being thus stretched on the ground in much the same way as was St. Francis Xavier, as he had always so passionately desired, and finding himself alone in the midst of these forests, for his companions were occupied with the disembarkation, he had leisure to repeat all the acts in which he had continued during these last days.

His dear companions having afterward rejoined him, all disconsolate, he comforted them, and inspired them with the confidence that God would take care of them after his death, in these new and unknown countries. He gave them the last instructions, thanked them for all the charities which they had exercised in his behalf during the whole journey, and entreated pardon for the trouble that he had given them. He charged them to ask pardon for him also, from all our fathers and brethren who live in the country of the Outaouacs. Then he undertook to prepare them for the sacrament of penance, which he administered to them for the last time. He gave them also a paper on which he had written all his faults since his own last confession, that they might place it in the hands of the father superior, that the latter might be enabled to pray to God for him in a more special manner. Finally, he promised not to forget them in paradise. And, as he was very considerate, knowing that they were much fatigued with the hardships of the preceding days, he bade them go and take a little repose. He assured them that his hour was not yet so very near, and that he would awaken them when the time should come—as, in fact, 2 or 3 hours afterward he did summon them, being ready to enter into the agony.

They drew near to him, and he embraced them once again, while they burst into tears at his feet. Then he asked for holy water and his reliquary; and having himself removed his crucifix, which he carried always suspended round his neck, he placed it in the hands of one of his companions, begging him to hold it before his eyes. Then, feeling that he had but a short time to live, he made a last effort, clasped his hands, and, with a steady and fond look upon his crucifix, he uttered aloud his profession of faith, and gave thanks to the divine majesty for the great favor which he had accorded him of dying in the Society, of dying in it as a missionary of Jesus Christ—and, above all, of dying in it, as he had always prayed, in a wretched cabin in the midst of the forests and bereft of all human succor.

After that, he was silent, communing within himself with God. Nevertheless, he let escape from time to time these words, *Sustinuit anima mea in verbo ejus;* or these, *mater dei, memento mei—*[3] which were the last words that he uttered before entering his agony, which was, however, very mild and peaceful.

He had prayed his companions to put him in mind, when they should see him about to expire, to repeat frequently the names of Jesus and Mary, if he could not himself do so. They did as they were bidden; and, when they believed him to be near his end, one of them called aloud, "Jesus, Mary!" The dying man repeated the words distinctly, several times; and as if, at these sacred names, something presented itself to him, he suddenly raised his eyes above his crucifix, holding them riveted on that object, which he appeared to regard with pleasure. And so, with a countenance beaming and all aglow, he expired without any struggle, and so gently that it might have been regarded as a pleasant sleep.

His two poor companions, shedding many tears over him, composed his body

[3] "My soul sustains itself in his word" and "mother of God, remember me."

in the manner which he had prescribed to them. Then they carried him devoutly to burial, ringing the while the little bell as he had bidden them, and planted a large cross near to his grave, as a sign to passers-by.

When it became a question of embarking, to proceed on their journey, one of the two, who for some days had been so heartsick with sorrow, and so greatly prostrated with an internal malady, that he could no longer eat or breathe except with difficulty, bethought himself, while the other was making all preparations for embarking, to visit the grave of his good father, and ask his intercession with the glorious virgin, as he had promised, not doubting in the least that he was in Heaven. He fell, then, upon his knees, made a short prayer, and having reverently taken some earth from the tomb, he pressed it to his breast. Immediately his sickness abated, and his sorrow was changed into a joy which did not forsake him during the remainder of his journey.

III

God did not permit that a deposit so precious should remain in the midst of the forest, unhonored and forgotten. The savages named Kiskakons, who have been making public profession of Christianity for nearly ten years, and who were instructed by Father Marquette when he lived at the point of St. Esprit, at the extremity of Lake Superior, carried on their last winter's hunting in the vicinity of the lake of the Illinois. As they were returning in the Spring, they were greatly pleased to pass near the grave of their good father, whom they tenderly loved; and God also put it into their hearts to remove his bones and bring them to our church at the mission of St. Ignace at Missilimakinac, where those savages make their abode.

They repaired, then, to the spot, and resolved among themselves to act in regard to the father as they are wont to do toward those for whom they profess great respect. Accordingly, they opened the grave, and uncovered the body; and, although the flesh and internal organs were all dried up, they found it entire, so that not even the skin was in any way injured. This did not prevent them from proceeding to dissect it, as is their custom. They cleansed the bones and exposed them to the sun to dry; then, carefully laying them in a box of birch-bark, they set out to bring them to our mission of St. Ignace.

There were nearly 30 canoes which formed, in excellent order, that funeral procession. There were also a goodly number of Iroquois, who united with our Algonquin savages to lend more honor to the ceremonial. When they drew near our house, Father Nouvel, who is its superior, with Father Piercon, went out to meet them, accompanied by the Frenchmen and savages who were there; and, having halted the procession, he put the usual questions to them, to make sure that it was really the father's body which they were bringing. Before conveying it to land, they intoned the *de profundis* in the presence of the 30 canoes, which were still on the water, and of the people who were on the shore. After that, the body was carried to the church, care being taken to observe all that the ritual appoints in such ceremonies. It remained exposed under the pall, all that day, which was Whitsun Monday, the 8th of June; and on the morrow, after having rendered to it all the funeral rites, it was lowered into a small vault in the middle of the church, where it rests as the guardian angel of our Outaouac missions. The savages often come to pray over his tomb. Not to mention more than this instance, a young girl, aged 19 or 20 years, whom the late father had instructed, and who had been baptized in the past year, fell sick, and applied to Father Nouvel to be bled and to take certain remedies. The father prescribed to her, as sole medicine, to come for 3 days and say a *pater* and three *ave's* at the tomb of Father Marquette. She did so, and before the 3rd day was cured, without bleeding or any other remedies . . .

1635(?) ∾ *Mrs. Mary Rowlandson* ∾ *1678(?)*

ONE OF the most stirring periods of New England colonial history was that of King Philip's War. Philip, son of the Wampanoag chieftain, Massasoit, began to make raids on the settlements in 1675, partly in protest against what he considered an unjust treaty imposed upon his tribesmen in 1671. Other tribes, such as the Narragansets and Nipmucks, became his allies. New England, surprised and unprepared, suffered numerous defeats, but by the end of 1675 had taken the offensive. Although peace was made in 1676 with some of the tribes, the war dragged on until 1678, involving New Hampshire and Maine.

Perhaps the most vivid piece of narrative writing produced by the war was the account by Mrs. Mary Rowlandson of her experiences as a captive among Philip's Indians. She was the wife of a minister of Lancaster, Mass., and had three children living at the time she was taken captive. Her account, published in Cambridge, Mass., under the title, *The Sovereignty & Goodness of God, Together with the Faithfulness of His Promises Displayed; Being a Narrative of the Captivity and Restoration of Mrs. Mary Rowlandson,* was a best seller in both America and England. After describing the attack, which took place while her husband was in Boston, Mrs. Rowlandson develops her story by detailing the events which occurred on each of the twenty removes she made with the Indians, to one of whom, a sagamore, named Quannopin, she was sold as a slave by her Narraganset captor.

[For the first and last of the following selections, titles have been supplied by the present editors. The text has been modernized. *Narratives of the Indian Wars 1675-1699,* ed. C. H. Lincoln, New York, 1913, one of the volumes in the series, *Original Narratives of Early American History,* contains a complete text.]

From
THE CAPTIVITY AND RESTORATION
[1682]

The Attack

ON THE 10th of February, 1676, came the Indians with great numbers upon Lancaster. Their first coming was about sun-rising. Hearing the noise of some guns, we looked out; several houses were burning, and the smoke ascending to Heaven.

There were five persons taken in one house; the father and the mother and a sucking child, they knocked on the head; the other two they took and carried away alive. There were two others, who, being out of their garrison upon some occasion, were set upon; one was knocked on the head, the other escaped. Another there was, who, running along, was shot and wounded, and fell down; he begged of them his life, promising them money, as they told me, but they would not hearken to him, but knocked him in head, and stripped him naked, and split open his bowels. Another, seeing many of the Indians about his barn, ventured and went out, but was quickly shot down. There were three others belonging to the same garrison who were killed; the Indians, getting up upon the roof of the barn, had advantage to shoot down upon them over their fortification. Thus these murderous wretches went on, burning and destroying before them.

At length they came and beset our own house, and quickly it was the dolefulest day that ever mine eyes saw. The house stood upon the edge of a hill; some of the Indians got behind the hill, others into the barn, and others behind anything that could shelter them; from all which places they shot against the house, so that the bullets seemed to fly like hail, and quickly they wounded one man among us, then another, and then a third.

About two hours, according to my observation in that amazing time, they had been about the house before they prevailed to fire it, which they did with flax and hemp which they brought out of the barn, and there being no defense about the house, only two flankers [1] at two opposite corners and one of them not finished, they fired it once, and one ventured out and quenched it, but they quickly fired it again, and that took.

Now is the dreadful hour come that I have often heard of in time of war, as it was in the case of others, but now mine eyes see it. Some in our house were fighting for their lives, others wallowing in their blood, the house on fire over our heads, and the bloody heathen ready to knock us on the head, if we stirred out. Now might we hear mothers and children crying out for themselves and one another, "Lord, what shall we do?" Then I took my children (and one of my sisters, hers) to go forth and leave the house, but as soon as we came to the door and appeared, the Indians shot so thick that the bullets rattled against the house as if one had taken a handful of stones and threw them, so that we were fain to give back. We had six stout dogs belonging to our garrison,

but none of them would stir, though another time, if any Indian had come to the door, they were ready to fly upon him and tear him down. The Lord hereby would make us the more to acknowledge his hand, and to see that our help is always in him. But out we must go, the fire increasing and coming along behind us roaring and the Indians gaping before us with their guns, spears, and hatchets to devour us.

No sooner were we out of the house but my brother-in-law (being before wounded, in defending the house, in or near the throat) fell down dead, whereat the Indians scornfully shouted and hallooed, and were presently upon him, stripping off his clothes. The bullets flying thick, one went through my side, and the same, as would seem, through the bowels and hand of my dear child in my arms. One of my elder sister's children, named William, had then his leg broken, which the Indians perceiving, they knocked him on the head. Thus were we butchered by those merciless heathen, standing amazed, with the blood running down to our heels.

My eldest sister being yet in the house and seeing those woeful sights, the infidels haling mothers one way and children another, and some wallowing in their blood, and her elder son telling her that her son William was dead and myself was wounded, she said, "And, Lord, let me die with them," which was no sooner said but she was struck with a bullet and fell down dead over the threshold. . . . The Indians laid hold of us, pulling me one way and the children another, and said, "Come, go along with us." I told them they would kill me; they answered, if I were willing to go along with them, they would not hurt me . . .

There were twelve killed, some shot, some stabbed with their spears, some knocked down with their hatchets. When we are in prosperity, oh, the little that we think of such dreadful sights and to see

---

[1] Projections behind which defenders could operate.

our dear friends and relations lie bleeding out their heart-blood upon the ground. There was one who was chopped into the head with a hatchet, and stripped naked, and yet was crawling up and down. It is a solemn sight to see so many Christians lying in their blood, some here and some there, like a company of sheep torn by wolves, all of them stripped naked by a company of hell-hounds, roaring, singing, ranting, and insulting, as if they would have torn our very hearts out; yet the Lord by his almighty power preserved a number of us from death, for there were twenty-four of us taken alive and carried captive.

I had often before this said that, if the Indians should come, I should choose rather to be killed by them than taken alive, but, when it came to the trial, my mind changed; their glittering weapons so daunted my spirit that I chose rather to go along with those (as I may say) ravenous beasts than that moment to end my days. And that I may the better declare what happened to me during that grievous captivity, I shall particularly speak of the several removes we had up and down the wilderness. . . . .

The Eighth Remove

On the morrow morning we must go over the river, i.e., Connecticut, to meet with King Philip. Two canoes full they had carried over; the next turn I myself was to go; but, as my foot was upon the canoe to step in, there was a sudden outcry among them, and I must step back; and instead of going over the river, I must go four or five miles up the river farther northward. Some of the Indians ran one way, and some another. The cause of this rout was, as I thought, their espying some English scouts who were thereabout. In this travel up the river, about noon the company made a stop and sat down, some to eat and others to rest them. As I sat amongst them, musings of things past, my son Joseph unexpectedly came to me: we

asked of each other's welfare, bemoaning our doleful condition and the change that had come upon us . . . .

We traveled on till night, and in the morning we must go over the river to Philip's crew. When I was in the canoe, I could not but be amazed at the numerous crew of pagans that were on the bank on the other side. When I came ashore, they gathered all about me, I sitting alone in the midst: I observed they asked one another questions, and laughed, and rejoiced over their gains and victories.

Then my heart began to fail, and I fell a-weeping, which was the first time to my remembrance that I wept before them. . . . There one of them asked me why I wept; I could hardly tell what to say, yet I answered, they would kill me. "No," said he, "none will hurt you." Then came one of them and gave me two spoonfuls of meal to comfort me, and another gave me half a pint of peas, which was worth more than many bushels at another time.

Then I went to see King Philip. He bade me come in and sit down and asked me whether I would smoke it (a usual compliment nowadays amongst saints and sinners), but this no way suited me, for though I had formerly used tobacco, yet I had left it ever since I was first taken. It seems to be a bait the devil lays to make men lose their precious time; I remember with shame how, formerly, when I had taken two or three pipes, I was presently ready for another, such a bewitching thing it is; but I thank God he has now given me power over it; surely there are many who may be better employed than to lie sucking a stinking tobacco-pipe.

Now the Indians gather their forces to go against Northampton. Over night one went about yelling and hooting to give notice of the design. Whereupon they fell to boiling of ground-nuts and parching of corn (as many as had it) for their provision; and in the morning away they went. During my abode in this place, Philip spake to me to make a shirt for his boy, which I did, for which he gave me a shilling. I offered the money to my master, but he bade me keep it, and with it I bought a piece of horseflesh.

Afterward he asked me to make a cap for his boy, for which he invited me to dinner. I went, and he gave me a pancake, about as big as two fingers; it was made of parched wheat, beaten and fried in bear's grease, but I thought I never tasted pleasanter meat in my life. There was a squaw who spake to me to make a shirt for her *sannup* [husband], for which she gave me a piece of bear. Another asked me to knit a pair of stockings, for which she gave me a quart of peas. I boiled my peas and bear together and invited my master and mistress to dinner, but the proud gossip, because I served them both in one dish, would eat nothing except one bit that he gave her upon the point of his knife.

Hearing that my son was come to this place, I went to see him and found him lying flat upon the ground. I asked him how he could sleep so. He answered me that he was not asleep, but at prayer, and lay so that they might not observe what he was doing. I pray God he may remember these things now he is returned in safety.

At this place (the sun now getting higher), what with the beams and heat of the sun and the smoke of the wigwams, I thought I should have been blind. I could scarce discern one wigwam from another. There was here one Mary Thurston of Medfield who, seeing how it was with me, lent me a hat to wear; but as soon as I was gone, the squaw (who owned that Mary Thurston) came running after me and got it away again. Here was the squaw that gave me one spoonful of meal. I put it in my pocket to keep it safe, yet notwithstanding somebody stole it, but put five Indian corns in the room of it, which corns were the greatest provisions I had in my travel for one day.

The Indians, returning from Northampton, brought with them some horses and sheep and other things which they had taken. I desired them that they would carry me to Albany upon one of those horses and sell me for powder, for so they had sometimes discoursed. I was utterly hopeless of getting home on foot the way that I came. I could hardly bear to think of the many weary steps I had taken to come to this place.

THE THIRTEENTH REMOVE

Instead of going toward the Bay, which was that I desired, I must go with them five or six miles down the river into a mighty thicket of brush, where we abode almost a fortnight. Here one asked me to make a shirt for her papoose, for which she gave me a mess of broth, which was thickened with meal made of the bark of a tree; and to make it the better, she had put into it about a handful of peas and a few roasted ground-nuts.

I had not seen my son a pretty while, and here was an Indian of whom I made inquiry after him, and asked him when he saw him. He answered me that such a time his master roasted him and that himself did eat a piece of him as big as his two fingers and that he was very good meat. But the Lord upheld my spirit under this discouragement, and I considered their horrible addictedness to lying and that there is not one of them that makes the least conscience of speaking of truth.

In this place, on a cold night, as I lay by the fire, I removed a stick that kept the heat from me; a squaw moved it down again, at which I looked up, and she threw a handful of ashes in mine eyes. I thought I should have been quite blinded, and have never seen more; but, lying down, the water run out of my eyes, and carried the dirt with it, that by the morning I recovered my sight again. . . .

About this time they came yelping from Hadley, where they had killed three Englishmen and brought one captive with them, viz., Thomas Read. They all gathered about the poor man, asking him many questions. I desired also to go and see him; and when I came, he was crying bitterly, supposing they would quickly kill him. Whereupon I asked one of them whether they intended to kill him; he answered me they would not. He, being a little cheered with that, I asked him about the welfare of my husband; he told me he saw him such a time in the Bay and he was well but very melancholy. By which I certainly understood (though I suspected it before) that whatsoever the Indians told me respecting him was vanity and lies. Some of them told me he was dead and they had killed him; some said he was married again and that the Governor wished him to marry, and told him he should have his choice, and that all persuaded I was dead. So like were these barbarous creatures to him who was a liar from the beginning.

As I was sitting once in the wigwam here, Philip's maid came in with the child in her arms and asked me to give her a piece of my apron to make a flap for it; I told her I would not; then my mistress bade me give it, but still I said no; the maid told me if I would not give her a piece, she would tear a piece off it; I told her I would tear her coat then. With that, my mistress rises up and takes up a stick big enough to have killed me and struck at me with it, but I stepped out and she struck the stick into the mat of the wigwam. But while she was pulling it out, I ran to the maid and gave her all my apron, and so that storm went over.

Hearing that my son was come to this place, I went to see him and told him his father was well but very melancholy. He told me he was as much grieved for his father as for himself. I wondered at his speech, for I thought I had enough upon my spirit in reference to myself to make me mindless of my husband and everyone else, they being safe among their friends. He told me also that, a while before, his master, together with other Indians, were going to the French for powder; but by the way the Mohawks met with them and killed four of their company, which made the rest turn back again, for which I desire that myself and he may bless the Lord, for it might have been worse with him had he been sold to the French than it proved to be in his remaining with the Indians. . . .

I asked his master to let him stay a while with me that I might comb his head and look over him, for he was almost overcome with lice. He told me, when I had done, that he was very hungry, but I had nothing to relieve him, but bid him go into the wigwams as he went along and see if he could get anything among them. Which he did, and it seems tarried a little too long, for his master was angry with him, and beat him, and then sold him. Then he came running to tell me he had a new master and that he had given him some ground-nuts already. Then I went along with him to his new master, who told me he loved him and he should not want. So his master carried him away, and I never saw him afterward, till I saw him at Pascataqua in Portsmouth.

That night they bade me go out of the wigwam again; my mistress's papoose was sick, and it died that night, and there was one benefit in it, that there was more room. I went to a wigwam, and they bade me come in, and gave me a skin to lie upon and a mess of venison and ground-nuts, which was a choice dish among them. On the morrow they buried the papoose; and afterward, both morning and evening, there came a company to mourn and howl with her, though I confess I could not much condole with them. . . .

THE TWENTIETH REMOVE

It was their usual manner to remove when they had done any mischief, lest they should be found out; and so they did at this time. We went about three or four miles, and there they built a great wigwam, big enough to hold an hundred Indians, which they did in preparation to a great day of dancing. They would say now amongst themselves that the Governor would be so angry for his loss at Sudbury that he would send no more about the captives, which made me grieve and tremble.

My sister being not far from the place where we now were, and hearing that I was here, desired her master to let her come and see me, and he was willing to it and would go with her, but she, being ready before him, told him she would go before and was come within a mile or two of the place. Then he overtook her and began to rant as if he had been mad and made her go back again in the rain, so that I never saw her till I saw her in Charlestown. But the Lord requited many of their ill doings, for this Indian, her master, was hanged afterward in Boston. The Indians now began to come from all quarters, against their merry dancing day. Among some of them came one Goodwife Kettle. I told her my heart was so heavy that it was ready to break. "So is mine too," said she, but yet said, "I hope we will hear some good news shortly." I could hear how earnestly my sister desired to see me, and I as earnestly desired to see her; and yet neither of us could get an opportunity. My daughter was also now about a mile off, and I had not seen her in nine or ten weeks, as I had not seen my sister since our first taking. I earnestly desired them to let me go and see them; yea, I entreated, begged, and persuaded them but to let me see my daughter, and yet so hard-hearted were they that they would not suffer it. They made use of their tyrannical power whilst they had it, but through the Lord's wonderful mercy, their time was now but short.

On a Sabbath day, the sun being about an hour high in the afternoon, came Mr. John Hoar (the Council permitting him and his own forward spirit inclining him) . . . When they had talked their fill with him, they suffered me to go to him. We asked each other of our welfare and how my husband did and all my friends. He told me they were all well and would be glad to see me. Amongst other things which my husband sent me, there came a pound of tobacco, which I sold for nine shillings in money, for many of the Indians for want of tobacco, smoked hemlock and ground-ivy. It was a great mistake in any who thought I sent for tobacco, for through the favor of God that desire was overcome.

I now asked them whether I should go home with Mr. Hoar. They answered no, one and another of them; and, it being night, we lay down with that answer. In the morning Mr. Hoar invited the sagamores to dinner, but, when we went to get it ready, we found that they had stolen the greatest part of the provision Mr. Hoar had brought, out of his bags, in the night. And we may see the wonderful power of God in that one passage, in that when there was such a great number of the Indians together and so greedy of a little good food and no English there, but Mr. Hoar and myself, that there they did not knock us in the head and take what we had, there being not only some provision, but also trading cloth, a part of the twenty pounds agreed upon. But, instead of doing us any mischief, they seemed to be ashamed of the fact and said it were some *matchit* [wicked] Indian that did it. Oh, that we could believe that there is no thing too hard for God! God showed his power over the heathen in this, as he did over the hungry lions when Daniel was cast into the den.

Mr. Hoar called them betime to dinner, but they ate very little, they being so busy in dressing themselves and getting ready for their dance, which was carried on by eight of them, four men and four squaws, my master and mistress being two. He was dressed in his Holland shirt, with great laces sewed at the tail of it; he had his silver buttons, his white stockings, his garters were hung round with shillings; and he had girdles of wampum upon his head and shoulders. She had a kersey coat and covered with girdles of wampum from the loins upward; her arms, from her elbows to her hands, were covered with bracelets; there were handfuls of necklaces about her neck and several sorts of jewels in her ears. She had fine red stockings and white shoes, her hair powdered and face painted red, that was always before black. And all the dancers were after the same manner.

There were two others singing and knocking on a kettle for their music. They kept hopping up and down one after another, with a kettle of water in the midst, standing warm upon some embers, to drink of when they were dry. They held on till it was almost night, throwing out wampum to the standers by. At night I asked them again if I should go home. They all as one said no, except my husband would come for me. When we were lain down, my master went out of the wigwam and by and by sent in an Indian called James the Printer, who told Mr. Hoar that my master would let me go home tomorrow, if he would let him have one pint of liquors. Then Mr. Hoar called his own Indians, Tom and Peter, and bid them go and see whether he would promise it before them three, and if he would, he should have it; which he did, and he had it. Then Philip, smelling the business, called me to him and asked me what I would give him to tell me some good news and speak a good word for me. I told him I could not tell what to give him; I would anything I had and asked him what he would have. He said, "Two coats and twenty shillings in money, and half a bushel of seed corn, and some tobacco." I thanked him for his love, but I knew the good news as well as the crafty fox. My master, after he had had his drink, quickly came ranting into the wigwam again and called for Mr. Hoar, drinking to him, and saying he was a good man, and then again he would say, "Hang him, Rogue!" Being almost drunk, he would drink to him, and yet presently say he should be hanged. Then he called for me. I trembled to hear him, yet I was fain to go to him, and he drank to me, showing no incivility. He was the first Indian I saw drunk all the while that I was amongst them. At last his squaw ran out, and he after her, round the wigwam, with his money jingling at his knees. But she escaped him. But having an old squaw, he ran to her; and so, through the Lord's mercy, we were no more troubled that night. . . .

On Tuesday morning they called their General Court (as they call it) to consult and determine whether I should go home or no. And they all as one man did seemingly consent to it, that I should go home, except Philip, who would not come among them. . . .

At first they were all against it, except my husband would come for me; but afterwards they assented to it and seemed much to rejoice in it; some asked me to send them some bread, others some tobacco, others shaking me by the hand, offering me a hood and scarf to ride in, not one moving hand or tongue against it. Thus hath the Lord answered my poor desire and the many earnest requests of others put up unto God for me. In my travels an Indian came to me and told me, if I were willing, he and his squaw would run away and go home along with me. I told him no, I was not willing to run away, but desired to wait God's time, that I might go home quietly and without fear. And now God hath granted me my desire.

The Return and Reunion

Oh, the wonderful power of God that I have seen and the experience that I have had. I have been in the midst of these roaring lions and savage bears, that feared neither God nor man nor the devil, by night and day, alone and in company, sleeping all sorts together, and yet not one of them ever offered me the least abuse of unchastity to me, in word or action. Though some are ready to say I speak it for my own credit, but I speak it in the presence of God and to his glory. God's power is as great now, and as sufficient to save, as when he preserved Daniel in the lions' den or the three children in the fiery furnace. . . . Let the redeemed of the Lord say so, whom he hath redeemed from the hand of the enemy, especially that I should come away in the midst of so many hundreds of enemies quietly and peaceably and not a dog moving his tongue.

So I took my leave of them, and, in coming along, my heart melted into tears, more than all the while I was with them, and I was almost swallowed up with the thoughts that ever I should go home again. About the sun going down, Mr. Hoar and myself and the two Indians came to Lancaster, and a solemn sight it was to me. There had I lived many comfortable years amongst my relations and neighbors, and now not one Christian to be seen nor one house left standing. We went on to a farmhouse that was yet standing, where we lay all night, and a comfortable lodging we had, though nothing but straw to lie on. The Lord preserved us in safety that night, and raised us up again in the morning, and carried us along, that before noon we came to Concord. Now was I full of joy, and yet not without sorrow: joy to see such a lovely sight, so many Christians together, and some of them my neighbors . . .

Being recruited with food and raiment, we went to Boston that day, where I met with my dear husband, but the thoughts of our dear children, one being dead and the other we could not tell where, abated our comfort each to other. I was not before so much hemmed in with the merciless and cruel heathen, but now as much with pitiful, tender-hearted, and compassionate Christians. In that poor and distressed and beggarly condition I was received in, I was kindly entertained in several houses. . . . The twenty pounds, the price of my redemption, was raised by some Boston gentlemen and Mrs. Usher, whose bounty and religious charity I would not forget to make mention of. Then Mr. Thomas Shepard of Charlestown [2] received us into his house, where we continued eleven weeks, and a father and mother they were to us. And many more tender-hearted friends we met with in that place. We were now in the midst of love, yet not

without much and frequent heaviness of heart for our poor children and other relations, who were still in affliction.

The week following, after my coming in, the Governor and Council sent forth to the Indians again, and that not without success; for they brought in my sister and Goodwife Kettle . . .

About this time the Council had ordered a day of public thanksgiving,[3] though I thought I had still cause of mourning, and being unsettled in our minds, we thought we would ride toward the eastward, to see if we could hear anything concerning our children. And as we were riding along (God is the wise disposer of all things) between Ipswich and Rowley we met with Mr. William Hubbard,[4] who told us that our son Joseph was come in to Major Waldron's, and another with him, which was my sister's son. I asked him how he knew it. He said the Major himself told him so. So along we went till we came to Newbury; and their minister being absent, they desired my husband to preach the thanksgiving for them; but he was not willing to stay there that night, but would go over to Salisbury to hear farther, and come again in the morning, which he did, and preached there that day.

At night, when he had done, one came and told him that his daughter was come in at Providence. Here was mercy on both hands . . . Now we were between them, the one on the east and the other on the west. Our son being nearest, we went to him first, to Portsmouth, where we met with him, and with the Major also, who told us he had done what he could, but could not redeem him under seven pounds, which the good people thereabouts were pleased to pay. . . . On Monday we came

---

[2] Son of the more famous Rev. Thomas Shepard of Cambridge.

[3] This was the Thanksgiving of June 29, 1676.

[4] Minister of Ipswich whose *A Narrative of the Troubles with the Indians in New-England*, Boston, 1677, is the best history of Philip's War.

to Charlestown, where we heard that the Governor of Rhode Island had sent over for our daughter, to take care of her, being now within his jurisdiction; which should not pass without our acknowledgments. But she being nearer Rehoboth than Rhode Island, Mr. Newman went over and took care of her, and brought her to his own house. And the goodness of God was admirable to us in our low estate, in that he raised up passionate [i.e. compassionate] friends on every side to us, when we had nothing to recompense any for their love. . . .

Our family being now gathered together (those of us that were living), the South Church in Boston hired an house for us. Then we removed from Mr. Shepard's (those cordial friends) and went to Boston, where we continued about three quarters of a year. . . .

I can remember the time when I used to sleep quietly without workings in my thoughts whole nights together, but now it is other ways with me. When all are fast about me and no eye open, but his who ever waketh, my thoughts are upon things past, upon the awful dispensation of the Lord towards us, upon his wonderful power and might in carrying of us through so many difficulties, in returning us in safety, and suffering none to hurt us. I remember in the night season how the other day I was in the midst of thousands of enemies and nothing but death before me. It is then hard work to persuade myself that ever I should be satisfied with bread again. But now we are fed with the finest of the wheat, and, as I may say, with honey out of the rock: instead of the husk we have the fatted calf . . .

I have seen the extreme vanity of this world: one hour I have been in health and wealth, wanting nothing: but the next hour in sickness and wounds and death, having nothing but sorrow and affliction.

Before I knew what affliction meant, I was ready sometimes to wish for it. When I lived in prosperity, having the comforts of the world about me, my relations by me, my heart cheerful, and taking little care for anything, and yet seeing many, whom I preferred before myself, under many trials and afflictions, in sickness, weakness, poverty, losses, crosses, and cares of the world, I should be sometimes jealous lest I should have my portion in this life, and that scripture would come to my mind, Heb. 16. 6: "For whom the Lord loveth he chasteneth and scourgeth every son whom he receiveth." But now I see the Lord had his time to scourge and chasten me. The portion of some is to have their afflictions by drops, now one drop and then another, but the dregs of the cup, the wine of astonishment, like a sweeping rain that leaveth no food, did the Lord prepare to be my portion. Affliction I wanted, and affliction I had, full measure (I thought) pressed down and running over; yet I see, when God calls a person to anything and through never so many difficulties, yet he is fully able to carry them through and make them see and say they have been gainers thereby. And I hope I can say in some measure, as David did, "It is good for me that I have been afflicted." The Lord hath showed me the vanity of these outward things, that they are the vanity of vanities, and vexation of spirit, that they are but a shadow, a blast, a bubble, and things of no continuance. . . .

1612 ∾ *Daniel Gookin* ∾ 1687

EFFORTS in 17th Century Massachusetts to Christianize the Indians were considerably successful because of the "apostleship" of the Rev. John Eliot, 1604-1690, who preached to them in their own language and translated the entire Bible into Indian dialect, his New Testament being printed at Cambridge in 1661 and his complete text in 1663.

One of Eliot's most ardent supporters was Daniel Gookin. Born in England, probably in Kent, Gookin came to Virginia with his father in 1621. Because of persecution of those who would not conform to the established Episcopal Church in Virginia, Gookin emigrated to Massachusetts in 1644, residing first at Boston and later at Cambridge. He held several offices of public trust, including the Major-Generalship of the colony, and in 1656 was appointed Superintendent of the Indians within the jurisdiction of Massachusetts. His experience in the latter position provided him with materials for two unusual works, *Historical Collections of the Indians in New England,* with dedicatory epistles dated 1674, and *An Historical Account of the Doings and Sufferings of the Christian Indians in New England, in the Years 1675, 1676, 1677,* with dedicatory epistle dated 1677. He also wrote a history of New England, the manuscript of which was lost when fire destroyed the home of his son at Sherburne, Mass. The two extant works on the Christian Indians remained in manuscript and were first published, respectively, in 1792 and 1836.

The first of the following selections, slightly modernized from the text of *Historical Collections* in *Collections of the Massachusetts Historical Society,* I (1792), 141-227, reveals to what an extent the unconverted Indians were inclined to commit atrocities on the Christian Indians before the outbreak of King Philip's War. The second and third of the following selections have been slightly modernized from the text of *An Historical Account of the Doings and Sufferings of the Christian Indians* or *History of the Christian Indians* in *Transactions and Collections of the American Antiquarian Society,* II (1836), 423-534. One shows how precarious was the lot of the Christian Indians during King Philip's War, when, looked upon as Fifth Columnists by many of the colonists, they were routed out of such superintended villages as that of Nashobah and consigned to Deer Island, which seems to have been a kind of concentration camp for "red aliens." The other selection enables us to realize what an important role the Christian Indians played in making negotiations for the return of such captives of the unregenerate Indians as Mrs. Rowlandson, her children, and friends.

Gookin died at Cambridge, having never swerved in his zeal to see that the large minority of Christian Indians should receive just treatment, especially in a time of dire emergency. This zeal may partly be ascribed to his memories of another kind of intolerance in Virginia.

[The titles have been supplied by the present editors.]

AN INCIDENT IN THE WARFARE BETWEEN THE UNCHRISTIAN AND THE CHRISTIAN INDIANS

[1792 (written 1674)]

IN the year 1670, a party of Mauqas [Mohawks], being looking after their prey, met with some Indians in the woods, belonging to Naamkeek, or Wamesit, upon the north side of Merrimac River, not far from some English houses; where, falling upon these Indians, that were travelling in a path, they killed some, and took others, whom they also killed; and, among the rest, a young maid of about fourteen years old was taken, and the scalp of her head taken off, and her skull broken, and left for dead with others. Some of the Indians escaping, came to their fellows; and with a party of men, they went forth to bring off the dead bodies, where they found this maid with life in her. So they brought her home, and got Lieutenant Thomas Henchman, a good man, and one that hath inspection over them by my order, to use means for her recovery; and though he had little hope thereof, yet he took the best care he could about it; and as soon as conveniently he could, sent the girl to an ancient and skillful woman living at Woburn, about ten miles distant, called Goodwife Brooks, to get her to use her best endeavors to recover the maid: which, by the blessing of God, she did, though she were about two years or more in curing her. I was at Goodwife Brooks' house in May, 1673, when she was in cure; and she showed me a piece or two of the skull, that she had taken out. And in May last, 1674, the second day, I being among the Indians at Pawtuckett, to keep court, and Mr. Elliot, and Mr. Richard Daniel, and others, with me, I saw the maid alive and in health; and looked upon her head, which was whole, except a little spot as big as a sixpence might cover, and the maid fat and lusty; but there was no hair come again upon the head, where the scalp was flayed off. This cure, as some skillful in chirurgery apprehend, is extraordinary and wonderful; and hence the glory and praise is to be ascribed to God, that worketh wonders without number. . . .

THE PLIGHT OF THE CHRISTIAN INDIANS OF NASHOBAH
[1836 (1677)]

ABOUT this time [February, 1676] there befell another great trouble and exercise to the Christian Indians of Nashobah, who sojourned in Concord by order; the matter was this. The Council had, by several orders, empowered a committee, who, with the consent of the selectmen of Concord, settled those Indians at that town, under the government and tuition of Mr. John Hoare; the number of those Indians were about fifty-eight of all sorts, whereof were not above twelve able men, the rest were women and children. These Indians lived very soberly, and quietly, and industriously, and were all unarmed; neither could any of them be charged with any unfaithfulness to the English interest. In pursuance of this settlement, Mr. Hoare had begun to build a large and convenient work-house for the Indians, near his own dwelling, which stood about the midst of the town, and very nigh the town watch-house. This house was made, not only to secure those Indians under lock and key by night, but to employ them and set them to work by day, whereby they earned their own bread, and in an ordinary way (with God's blessing) would have lived well in a short time. But some of the inhabitants of the town, being influenced with a spirit of animosity and distaste against all Indians, disrelished this settlement; and therefore privately sent to a Captain of the army, [1] that quartered his company not far off at that time, of whom they had experience that he would not be backward to put in execution anything that tended to distress the praying Indians; for this was the same man that had formerly, without order, seized upon divers of the praying Indians at Marlborough, which brought much trouble and disquiet to the country of the Indians, and was a great occasion of their defection. . . . This Captain accordingly came to Concord with a party of his men, upon the Sabbath day, into the meeting-house, where the people were convened in the worship of God. And after the exercise was ended, he spake openly to the congregation to this effect: "That he understood there were some heathen in the town, committed to one Hoare, which he was informed were a trouble and disquiet to them; therefore if they desired it, he would remove them to Boston;" to which speech of his, most of the people being silent, except two or three that encouraged him, he took, as it seems, the silence of the rest for consent; and immediately after the assembly were dismissed, he went with three or four files of men, and a hundred or two of the people, men, women, and children, at his heels, and marched away to Mr. Hoare's house, and there demanded of him to see the Indians under his care. Hoare opened the door and showed them to him, and they were all numbered and found there; the Captain then said to Mr. Hoare that he would leave a corporal and soldiers to secure them; but Mr. Hoare answered, there was no need of that, for they were already secured, and were committed to him by order of the Council, and he would keep and secure them. But yet the Captain left his corporal and soldiers there, who were abusive enough to the poor Indians by ill language. The next morning the Captain came again, to take the Indians and send them to Boston. But Mr. Hoare refused to deliver them unless he showed him an order of the Council; but the Captain could

show him no other but his commission to kill and destroy the enemy; but Mr. Hoare said, these were friends and under order. But the Captain would not be satisfied with his answer, but commanded his corporal forthwith to break open the door and take the Indians all away, which was done accordingly; and some of the soldiers plundered the poor creatures of their shirts, shoes, dishes, and such other things as they could lay their hands upon, though the Captain commanded the contrary. They were all brought to Charlestown with a guard of twenty men. And the Captain wrote a letter to the General Court, then sitting, giving them an account of his action. This thing was very offensive to the Council, that a private captain should (without commission or some express order) do an act so contradictory to their former orders; and the Governor and several others spake of it at a conference with the Deputies [2] at the General Court, manifesting their dissatisfaction at this great irregularity, in setting up a military power in opposition to the chief authority of the country; declaring of what evil consequence such a precedent was; instancing the ill effects of the like practices in England in latter times; urging that due testimony might be borne against the same, by the whole Court. The Deputies seemed generally to agree to the reason of the magistrates in this matter; yet, notwithstanding, the Captain (who appeared in the Court shortly after, upon another occasion) met with no rebuke for this high irregularity and arbitrary action. To conclude this matter, those poor Indians, about fifty-eight of them of all sorts, were sent down to Deer Island, there to pass into the furnace of affliction with their brethren and countrymen. But all their corn and other provision, sufficient to maintain them for six months, was lost at Concord; and all their

[1] Captain Mosely.

[2] Representing the towns and elected by popular vote, the deputies were to the magistrates or assistants a kind of lower house or subordinate governing body.

other necessaries, except what the soldiers had plundered. And the poor Indians got very little or nothing of what they lost, but it was squandered away, lost by the removal of Mr. Hoare and other means, so that they were necessitated to live upon clams as the others did, with some little corn provided at the charge of the Honorable Corporation for the Indians, residing in London. Besides, Mr. Hoare lost all his building, and other cost, which he had provided for the entertainment and employment of those Indians, which was considerable . . .

THE CHRISTIAN INDIANS AND THE ROWLANDSONS
[1836 (1677)]

MR. ROWLANDSON, minister of Lancaster, a pious and good man, having his wife, children, and several friends in captivity among the enemy, being surprised at Lancaster . . ., himself, and several other ministers in his behalf, had some time since petitioned the Council to use what means they could for the redemption of his wife, etc.; which the Council consented to, and, in pursuance thereof, ordered Major Gookin to endeavor to procure at Deer Island one or two Indians that for a reward might adventure to go with a message to the enemy, to offer for the redemption of our captives, particularly Mrs. Rowlandson. But, although the Major went to the Island, and did his utmost endeavors to procure an Indian to adventure upon this service at that time, yet could not prevail with any; so the matter lay dormant a good space of time.

But, on the 23rd of March, some friends advised Mr. Rowlandson to make another petition to revive the former motion; which he did that day. The Council declared themselves ready to promote it, and send a messenger, if any could be procured. Major Gookin, who stirred up Mr. Rowlandson hereunto, was informed that one of the Indians lately brought down from Concord, named Tom Dublot, *alias* Nep-

ponit, had some inclination to run that adventure; of which the Major informing the Council, they ordered Capt. Henchman to treat and agree with him, which he accordingly did, and brought him up from Deer Island some few days after; and he was sent to Major Gookin's, at Cambridge, where he was, according to the order of the Council, fitted and furnished for this enterprise; and had a letter from the Council to the enemy, concerning the redemption of the captives; and upon Monday, April 3rd, he was sent away from Cambridge upon his journey; and he did effect it with care and prudence, and returned again upon the 12th of April, with this answer in writing, from the enemy:—

"To Governor and Council in Boston, and people that are in war with us:

"We now give answer by this one man; but if you like my answer, send one more man besides this Tom Neppanit, and send with all true heart, and with all your mind, by two men. Because you know, and we know, you have great sorrowful with crying; for you lost many, many hundred men, and all your house, all your land, and woman, child, and cattle, and all your things that you have lost." Moreover they add that Mrs. Rowlandson and other captives are alive. This was signed by Sam and Kutquen Quanohit, sagamores, and Peter Jethro, scribe. To this letter the Council gave answer, tending to abate their pride and insolence; and sent again Tom Neppanit, and another Indian named Peter Conway, to move further about the redemption of Mrs. Rowlandson and her friends, which the enemy inclined unto. Those two Indians were sent a second, third, and fourth time, and some English with them; and at last prevailed so far, that Mrs. Rowlandson and some others were redeemed, and brought home about the Election time following. This treaty about the captives, and the consequences thereof, had no small influence into the abatement of the enemy's violence and our troubles, and had a tendency to dividing them and break their union, and consequently their strength; for Philip, and some others of the enemy's chief men, were utterly against treating with the English or surrendering the captives. But some other of their principal sachems, that were more inclinable to a reconciliation with the English, thought that their compliance with the English about surrendering the captives (especially being well paid for their redemption) would mollify the Englishmen's minds in order to a peace. This contest about the treaty caused them to fall out and divide. Philip and most of the Narraganset Indians separated from the inland Indians, and went down into their own country, and the inland Indians stayed about Wachuset mountain, which was a means under God to weaken and destroy them. . . . This was another piece of service done by our praying Indians; at least they broke the ice and made way for it, by their first adventuring to treat with the enemy . . .

1644 ∾ *William Penn* ∾ *1718*

WILLIAM PENN, son of an English baronet and admiral, dreamed, while he was still a student at Oxford, of an ideal colony governed in accord with Quaker principles. In seeking satisfaction for a claim of 16,000 pounds his father had held against the crown, Penn petitioned Charles II in June, 1680, for a tract of land contiguous to the New Jersey settlements, in the management of whose affairs he had had some experience since 1675. On March 4, 1681, the King signed Penn's charter for a domain as extensive as England itself.

Shortly thereafter, Penn wrote a pamphlet from which the following selections are taken. Published in London in 1681, it is one of the most lucidly written and unswervingly truthful documents in the literature of colonization promotion. On October 28, 1682, Penn first came to Pennsylvania, where his cousin, William Markham, acting as his Deputy Governor, had already made considerable progress toward putting the new plantation upon a lasting basis and where the flow of immigration had been steady since the spring of that year, partly, no doubt, as a result of Penn's pamphlet.

[The text has been modernized. *Narratives of Early Pennsylvania, West New Jersey, and Delaware 1630-1707*, ed. A.C. Myers, New York, 1912, one of the volumes in the series, *Original Narratives of Early American History*, contains a complete text.]

From

SOME ACCOUNT OF THE PROVINCE OF PENNSYLVANIA
[1681]

SINCE (by the good providence of God) a country in America is fallen to my lot, I thought it not less my duty than my honest interest to give some public notice of it to the world that those of our own or other nations, that are inclined to transport themselves or families beyond the seas, may find another country added to their choice, that, if they shall happen to like the place, conditions, and constitutions (so far as the present infancy of things will allow us any prospect), they may, if they please, fix with me in the province hereafter described . . .

The place lies 600 miles nearer the sun than England, for England begins at the 50th degree and ten minutes of north latitude, and this place begins at forty, which is about the latitude of Naples in Italy or Montpellier in France. I shall say little in its praise to excite desires in any, whatever I could truly write as to the soil, air, and water. This shall satisfy me, that by the blessing of God and the honesty and industry of man, it may be a good and fruitful land.

For navigation it is said to have two conveniences; the one by lying ninescore miles upon Delaware River; that is to say, about threescore and ten miles before we come to the falls, where a vessel of two hundred tons may sail (and some creeks and small harbors in that distance, where ships may come nearer than the river into the country) and above the falls, for sloops and boats, as I am informed, to the extent of the patent. The other convenience is through Chesapeake Bay.

For timber and other wood, there is variety for the use of man.

For fowl, fish and wild deer, they are reported to be plentiful in those parts. Our English provision is likewise now to be had there at reasonable rates. The commodities that the country is thought capable of are silk, flax, hemp, wine, cider, woad, madder,[1] liquorish, tobacco, potashes, and iron, and it does actually produce hides, tallow, pipe-staves, beef, pork, sheep, wool, corn, as wheat, barley, rye, and also furs, as your peltry, minks, raccoons, martins, and such like—store of furs which is to be found among the Indians, that are profitable commodities in Europe.

The way of trading in those countries is thus: they send to the Southern plantations corn, beef, pork, fish, and pipe-staves, and take their growth and bring for England, and return with English goods to their own country. Their furs they bring for England, and either sell them here or carry them out again to other parts of Europe, where they will yield a better price. And for those that will follow merchandize and navigation, there is conveniency and timber sufficient for shipping.

For the constitutions of the country, the patent shows, first, that the people and governor have a legislative power, so that no law can be made nor money raised but by the people's consent.

2dly. That the rights and freedoms of England (the best and largest in Europe) shall be in force there.

3dly. That making no law against allegiance (which, should we, 'twere by the law of England void of itself that moment), we may enact what laws we please for the good prosperity and security of the said province.

4thly. That so soon as any are engaged with me, we shall begin a scheme or draught together such as shall give ample testimony of my sincere inclinations to encourage planters and settle a free, just, and industrious colony there.

My conditions will relate to three sorts of people: 1st, those that will buy; 2dly, those that take up land upon rent; 3dly, servants. To the first, the shares I sell shall be certain as to number of acres; that is to say, every one shall contain five thousand acres, free from any Indian incumbrance, the price a hundred pounds, and for the quit-rent but one English shilling or the value of it yearly for a hundred acres; and the said quit-rent not to begin to be paid till 1684. To the second sort, that take up land upon rent, they shall have liberty so to do, paying yearly one penny per acre, not exceeding two hundred acres. To the third sort, to wit, servants that are carried over, fifty acres shall be allowed to the master for every head and fifty acres to every servant when their time is expired. And because some engage with me that may not be disposed to go, it were

---

[1] Woad and madder were dyes made from herbs.

very advisable for every three adventurers to send an overseer with their servants, which would well pay the cost.

The divident may be thus: if the persons concerned please, a tract of land shall be surveyed, say fifty thousand acres to a hundred adventurers; in which some of the best shall be set out for towns or cities; and there shall be so much ground allotted to each in those towns as may maintain some cattle and produce some corn; then the remainder of the fifty thousand acres shall be shared among the said adventurers (casting up the barren for commons and allowing for the same) whereby every adventurer will have a considerable quantity of land together; likewise every one a proportion by a navigable river and then backward into the country. The manner of divident I shall not be strict in; we can but speak roughly of the matter here; but let men skillful in plantations be consulted, and I shall leave it to the majority of votes among the adventurers, when it shall please God we come there, how to fix it to their own content.

These persons that providence seems to have most fitted for plantations are:

1st. Industrious husbandmen and day-laborers that are hardly able (with extreme labor) to maintain their families and portion their children.

2dly. Laborious handicrafts, especially carpenters, masons, smiths, weavers, tailors, tanners, shoemakers, shipwrights, etc., where they may be spared or are low in the world: and as they shall want no encouragement, so their labor is worth more there than here, and there provision cheaper.

3dly. A plantation seems a fit place for those ingenious spirits that, being low in the world, are much clogged and oppressed about a livelihood, for the means of subsisting being easy there, they may have time and opportunity to gratify their inclinations and thereby improve science and help nurseries of people.

4thly. A fourth sort of men to whom a plantation would be proper takes in those that are younger brothers of small inheritances, yet, because they would live in sight of their kindred in some proportion to their quality and can't do it without a labor that looks like farming, their condition is too strait for them; and, if married, their children are often too numerous for the estate and are frequently bred up to no trades, but are a kind of hangers on or retainers to the elder brother's table and charity: which is a mischief, as in itself to be lamented, so here to be remedied. For land they have for next to nothing, which with moderate labor produces plenty of all things necessary for life, and such an increase as by traffic may supply them with all conveniences.

Lastly, there are another sort of persons, not only fit for but necessary in plantations, and that is, men of universal spirits, that have an eye to the good of posterity and that both understand and delight to promote good discipline and just government among a plain and well-intending people; such persons may find room in colonies for their good counsel and contrivance, who are shut out from being of much use or service to great nations under settled customs. These men deserve much esteem and would be harkened to. Doubtless 'twas this . . . that put some of the famous Greeks and Romans upon transplanting and regulating colonies of people in divers parts of the world; whose names, for giving so great proof of their wisdom, virtue, labor, and constancy, are with justice honorably delivered down by story to the praise of our own times, though the world, after all its higher pretences of religion, barbarously errs from their excellent example . . .

Selections from the New England Witchcraft Papers

MODERN spiritualists, among whom have been men of considerable intellectual distinction, have believed in the existence of individuals with the power of extra-sensory perception that enables them to hold converse with, and in a certain measure control, the spirits of the dead. In the 17th Century, when the premise that a supernatural world impinges on the domain of the natural was accepted without question by most men, it was inevitable that, in continental Europe, in England, and in America, there should be widespread belief in witchcraft, i.e., the existence of individuals with special powers to hold converse with evil spirits, to harbor them as parasites upon their persons, and to control them in such a way as to produce mysterious afflictions in their enemies. It was inevitable, too, that scholars and intellectuals should regard the investigation of the phenomena of witchcraft as a legitimate field of scientific curiosity and that laws should be enacted to punish witches for their alleged nefarious practices.

In New England, during the last two decades of the 17th Century, the question of witchcraft became one of vital social importance when Increase Mather, 1629-1723, and his son, Cotton Mather, 1663-1728, two of the leading Puritan intellectuals and learned men of letters, grew interested in its manifestations, from a scientific as well as a theological point of view. Their writings and sermons on the subject led to the apprehension, trial, and execution of a number of suspected witches, proceedings that had long been common in old England. At the time when the persecution of suspected witches was at its height, the New England legal mind, with scientific training in the criteria of testimony—a mind best represented by Thomas Brattle, 1658-1716—entertained doubts as to the validity of the evidence by which convictions of witches were obtained. It was this mind that soon prevailed to bring to a close the witch-hunting frenzy, although at the time no attempt was made to challenge the fundamental assumptions on which belief in witches rested.

[The following selections, designed to bring into contrast the theological-scientific and the legal-scientific attitudes toward witchcraft, are taken, respectively, from Cotton Mather's *Memorable Providences, Relating to Witchcrafts and Possessions,* and a private letter written by Thomas Brattle in 1692 and widely circulated in manuscript, but not published until 1798. The texts have been modernized and titles supplied. Both documents are reprinted in *Narratives of the Witchcraft Cases 1648-1706,* ed. G.L. Burr, New York, 1914, one of the volumes in the series, *Original Narratives of Early American History.*]

MATHER'S ACCOUNT OF THE GOOD-WIN CASE
[1689]

THERE dwells at this time, in the south part of Boston, a sober and pious man, whose name is John Goodwin, whose trade is that of a mason, and whose wife (to which a good report gives a share with him in all the characters of virtue) has made him the father of six (now living) children. Of these children, all but the eldest, who works with his father at his calling, and the youngest, who lives yet upon the breast of its mother, have labored under the direful effects of a (no less palpable than) stupendous witchcraft. Indeed that exempted son had also, as was thought, some lighter touches of it, in unaccountable stabs and pains now and then upon him, as indeed every person in the family at some time or other had, except the godly father and the sucking infant, who never felt any impressions of it. But these four children mentioned were handled in so sad and strange a manner as has given matter of discourse and wonderment to all the country and of history not unworthy to be considered by more than all the serious or the curious readers in this New-English world.

The four children (whereof the eldest was about thirteen and the youngest was perhaps about a third part so many years of age) had enjoyed a religious education and answered it with a very towardly ingenuity. They had an observable affection unto divine and sacred things, and those of them that were capable of it seemed to have such a resentment [realization] of their eternal concernments as is not altogether usual. Their parents also kept them to a continual employment, which did more than deliver them from the temptations of idleness, and as young as they were, they took a delight in it, it may be as much as they should have done. In a word, such was the whole temper and carriage of the children that there cannot easily be anything more unreasonable than to imagine that a design to dissemble could cause them to fall into any of their odd fits . . .

About midsummer, in the year 1688, the eldest of these children, who is a daughter, saw cause to examine their washerwoman upon their missing of some linen, which 'twas feared she had stolen from them; and of what use this linen might be to serve the witchcraft intended, the thief's tempter knows! This laundress was the daughter of an ignorant and a scandalous old woman in the neighborhood, whose miserable husband before he died had sometimes complained of her that she was undoubtedly a witch and that, whenever his head was laid, she would quickly arrive unto the punishments due to such an one. This woman, in her daughter's defence, bestowed very bad language upon the girl that put her to the question; immediately upon which, the poor child became variously indisposed in her health and visited with strange fits, beyond those that attend an epilepsy or a catalepsy or those that they call the diseases of astonishment.

It was not long before one of her sisters and two of her brothers were seized, in order one after another, with effects like those that molested her. Within a few weeks, they were all four tortured everywhere in a manner so very grievous that it would have broke an heart of stone to have seen their agonies. Skilful physicians were consulted for their help and particularly our worthy and prudent friend, Dr. Thomas Oakes, who found himself so affronted [nonplussed] by the distempers of the children that he concluded nothing but an hellish witchcraft could be the original of these maladies. And that which yet more confirmed such apprehension was that, for one good while, the children were tormented just in the same part of their bodies all at the same time together; and though they saw and heard not one another's complaints, though likewise their pains and sprains were swift like lightning, yet when (suppose) the neck or the hand or the back of one was racked, so it was at that instant with t'other too.

The variety of their tortures increased continually; and though about nine or ten at night they always had a release from their miseries and ate and slept all night for the most part indifferently well, yet in the day time they were handled with so many sorts of ails that it would require of us almost as much time to relate them all as it did of them to endure them. Sometimes they would be deaf, sometimes dumb, and sometimes blind, and often all this at once. One while their tongues would be drawn down their throats; another while they would be pulled out upon their chins to a prodigious length. They would have their mouths opened unto such a wideness that their jaws went out of joint and anon they would clap together again with a force like that of a strong spring-lock. The same would happen to their shoulder-blades and their elbows and hand-wrists and several of their joints. They would at times lie in a benumbed condition and be drawn together as those that are tied neck and heels, and presently be stretched out, yea, drawn backwards, to such a degree that it was feared the very skin of their bellies would have cracked. They would make most piteous outcries that they were cut with knives and struck with blows that they could not bear. Their necks would be broken, so that their neck-bone would seem dissolved unto them that felt after it; and yet on the sudden it would become again so stiff that there was no stirring of their heads; yea, their heads would be twisted almost round; and if main force at any time obstructed a dangerous motion which they seemed to be upon, they would roar exceedingly. Thus they lay some weeks most pitiful spectacles; and this while, as a further demonstration of witchcraft in these horrid effects, when I went to prayer by one of them that was very desirous to hear what I said, the child utterly lost her hearing till our prayer was over . . .

The report of the calamities of the family for which we were thus concerned arrived now unto the ears of the magistrates, who presently and prudently applied themselves with a just vigor to enquire into the story. The father of the children complained of his neighbor, the suspected ill woman, whose name was Glover; and she, being sent for by the justices, gave such a wretched account of herself that they saw cause to commit her unto the jailer's custody. Goodwin had no proof that could have done her any hurt, but the hag had not power to deny her interest in the enchantment of the children and when she was asked whether she believed there was a God, her answer was too blasphemous and horrible for any pen of mine to mention. An experiment was made whether she could recite the Lord's Prayer; and it was found that, though clause after clause was most carefully repeated unto her, yet when she said it after them that prompted her, she could not possibly avoid making nonsense of it, with some ridiculous depravations. This experiment I had the curiosity since to see made upon two more, and it had the same event. Upon the commitment of this extraordinary woman, all the children had some present ease, until one (related unto her), accidentally meeting one or two of them, entertained them with her blessing, that is, railing, upon which three of them fell ill again, as they were before.

It was not long before the witch thus in the trap was brought upon her trial; at which, through the efficacy of a charm, I suppose, used upon her by one or some of her crew, the court could receive answers from her in none but the Irish, which was her native language, although she understood the English very well and had accustomed her whole family to none but that language in her former conversation; and therefore the communication between the bench and the bar was now chiefly conveyed by two honest and faithful men that were interpreters. It was long before she could with any direct answers plead unto her indictment; and when she did plead, it was with confession rather than denial of her guilt. Order was given to search the old woman's house, from whence there were brought into the court several small images or puppets or babies made of rags and stuffed with goat's hair and other such ingredients. When these were produced, the vile woman acknowledged that her way to torment the objects of her malice was by wetting of her finger with her spittle and stroking of those little images. The abused children were then present, and the woman still kept stooping and shrinking as one that was almost pressed to death with a mighty weight upon her. But one of the images being brought unto her, immediately she started up after an odd manner and took it into her hand, but she had no sooner taken it than one of the children fell into sad fits before the whole assembly. This the judges had their just apprehensions at and, carefully causing the repetition of the experiment, found again the same event of it. They asked her whether she had any to stand by her. She replied she had and, looking very pertly in the air, she added, "No, he's gone." And she then confessed that she had one who was her prince, with whom she maintained I know not what communion. For which cause, the night after, she was heard expostulating with a devil for his thus deserting her, telling him that because he had served her so basely and falsely, she had confessed all. However, to make all clear, the court appointed five or six physicians one evening to examine her very strictly whether she were not crazed in her intellectuals and had not procured to herself by folly and madness the reputation of a witch. Divers hours did they spend with her, and in all that while no discourse came from her but what was pertinent and agreeable, particularly when they asked her what she thought would become of her soul. She replied, "You ask me a very solemn question and I cannot well tell what to say to it." She owned herself a Roman Catholic and could recite her Pater Noster in Latin very readily, but there was one clause or two always too hard for her, whereof she said she could

not repeat it if she might have all the world. In the upshot the doctors returned her *compos mentis* [of sound mind] and sentence of death was passed upon her. . . .

While the miserable old woman was under condemnation, I did myself twice give a visit unto her. She never denied the guilt of the witchcraft charged upon her, but she confessed very little about the circumstances of her confederacies with the devils; only she said that she used to be at meetings which her prince and four more were present at. As for those four, she told who they were, and, for her prince, her account plainly was that he was the devil. She entertained me with nothing but Irish, which language I had not learning enough to understand without an interpreter. . . .

However, against her will I prayed with her, which, if it were a fault, it was in excess of pity. When I had done, she thanked me with many good words, but I was no sooner out of her sight than she took a stone, a long and slender stone, and with her finger and spittle fell to tormenting it, though whom or what she meant, I had the mercy never to understand.

When this witch was going to her execution, she said the children should not be relieved by her death, for others had a hand in it as well as she, and she named one among the rest, whom it might have been thought natural affection would have advised the concealing of. It came to pass accordingly that the three children continued in their furnace as before, and it grew rather seven times hotter than it was. All their former ails pursued them still, with an addition of ('tis not easy to tell how many) more, but such as gave more sensible demonstrations of an enchantment growing very far towards a possession by evil spirits. . . .

My employments were such that I could not visit this afflicted family so often as I would; wherefore, that I might show them what kindness I could, as also that I might have a full opportunity to observe the extraordinary circumstances of the children and that I might be furnished with evidence and argument as a critical eye-witness to confute the Sadducism [i.e., skepticism] of this debauched age, I took the eldest of them home to my house. The young woman continued well at our house for divers days and applied herself to such actions not only of industry but of piety as she had been no stranger to. But on the twentieth of November in the forenoon she cried out, "Ah, *They* have found me out! I thought it would be so!" and immediately she fell into her fits again . . .

In her ludicrous fits, one while she would be for flying; and she would be carried hither and thither, though not long from the ground, yet so long as to exceed the ordinary power of nature in our opinion of it; another while she would be for diving and use the actions of it towards the floor, on which, if we had not held her, she would have thrown herself. Being at this exercise, she told us that They said she must go down to the bottom of our well, for there was plate there, and They said They would bring her safely up again. This did she tell us, though she had never heard of any plate there! and we ourselves, who had newly bought the house, hardly knew of any, but the former owner of the house, just then coming in, told us there had been plate for many years at the bottom of the well.

She had once a great mind to have eaten a roasted apple, but whenever she attempted to eat it, her teeth would be set, and sometimes, if she went to take it up, her arm would be made so stiff that she could not possibly bring her hand to her mouth; at last she said, "Now They say I shall eat it, if I eat it quickly," and she nimbly eat it all up . . .

While she was in her frolics, I was willing to try whether she could read or no; and I found, not only that if she went to read the Bible her eyes would be strangely twisted and blinded and her neck presently broken, but also that if anyone else did read the Bible in the room, though it were wholly out of her sight and without the least voice or noise of it, she would be cast into very terrible agonies. . . . But when I showed her a Jest-book, as *The Oxford Jests* or the *Cambridge Jests,* she could read them without any disturbance and have witty descants upon them too. . . . When I read in the room the story of Ann Cole in my father's *Remarkable Providences* and came to the exclamation which the narrative says the daemons made upon her, "Ah, she runs to the rock!" it cast her into inexpressible agonies. . . . A Popish book also she could endure very well, but it would kill her to look into any book that (in my opinion) it might have been profitable and edifying for her to be reading of. . . . The good books that were found so mortal to her were chiefly such as lay ever at hand in the room. One was the *Guide to Heaven from the Word,* which I had given her. Another of them was Mr. Willard's little (but precious) *Treatise of Justification.* Divers books published by my father I also tried upon her, particularly his *Mystery of Christ,* and another small book of his about faith and repentance and the day of judgment.

Once being very merrily talking by a table that had this last book upon it, she just opened the book and was immediately struck backwards as dead upon the floor. I hope I have not spoiled the credit of the books by telling how much the devils hated them. I shall therefore add that my grandfather Cotton's catechism, called *Milk for Babes,* and *The Assembly's Catechism* would bring hideous convulsions on the child if she looked into them, though she had once learned them with all the love that could be . . .

There was another most unaccountable circumstance which now attended her; and until she came to our house, I think, she never had experience of it. Ever now and then an invisible horse would be brought unto her, by those whom she only called "them" and "her company," upon the approach of which her eyes would be still closed up, for (said she) "They say I am a telltale and therefore they will not let me see them." Upon this would she give a spring as one mounting an horse and, settling herself in a riding posture, she would in her chair be agitated as one sometimes ambling, sometimes trotting, and sometimes galloping very furiously. . . .

. . . Mr. Morton of Charlestown and Mr. Allen, Mr. Moody, Mr. Willard, and myself, of Boston, with some devout neighbors, kept another day of prayer at John Goodwin's house, and we had all the children present with us there. The children were miserably tortured while we labored in our prayers, but our good God was nigh unto us in what we called upon Him for. From this day the power of the enemy was broken, and the children, though assaults after this were made upon them, yet were not so cruelly handled as before. The liberty of the children increased daily more and more, and their vexation abated by degrees, till within a little while they arrived to perfect ease, which for some weeks or months they cheerfully enjoyed. Thus good it is for us to draw near to God.

Within a day or two after the Fast, the young woman had two remarkable attempts made upon her by her invisible adversaries. Once they were dragging her into the oven that was then heating while there was none in the room to help her. She clapped her hands on the mantletree to save herself, but they were beaten off, and she had been burned if at her outcries one had not come in from abroad for her relief. Another time they put an unseen rope with a cruel noose about her neck, whereby she was choked until she was black in the face, and, though it was taken off before it had killed her, yet there were the red marks of it and of a finger and a thumb near it, remaining to be seen for a while afterwards.

This was the last molestation that they gave her for a while, and she dwelt at my house the rest of the winter, having by an obliging and virtuous conversation made herself enough welcome to the family. But within about a fortnight she was visited with two days of as extraordinary obsessions as any we had been the spectators of. I thought it convenient for me to entertain my congregation with a sermon upon the memorable providences which these children had been concerned in. When I had begun to study my sermon, her tormentors again seized upon her, and all Friday and Saturday did they manage her with a special design, as was plain, to disturb me in what I was about. In the worst of her extravagancies formerly, she was more dutiful to myself than I had reason to expect, but now her whole carriage to me was with a sauciness that I had not been used to be treated with. She would knock at my study door, affirming that some below would be glad to see me when there was none that asked for me. She would call to me with multiplied impertinencies and throw small things at me wherewith she could not give me any hurt. She'd hector me at a strange rate for the work I was at and threaten me with I know not what mischief for it. She got a history that I had written of this witchcraft, and, though she had before this read it over and over, yet now she could not read (I believe) one entire sentence of it, but she made of it the most ridiculous travesty in the world, with such a patness and excess of fancy to supply the sense that she put upon it as I was amazed at. And she particularly told me that I should quickly come to disgrace by that history . . .

BRATTLE'S CRITIQUE OF THE SALEM JUSTICES
[1798 (written 1692)]

October 8, 1692.

Reverend Sir: Yours I received the other day and am very ready to serve you to my utmost. I should be very loath to bring myself into any snare by my freedom with you, and therefore hope that you will put the best construction on what I write and secure me from such as would interpret my lines otherwise than they are designed. Obedience to lawful authority I evermore accounted a great duty and willingly I would not practice anything that might thwart and contradict such a principle. Too many are ready to despise dominions and speak evil of dignities, and I am sure the mischiefs which arise from a factious and rebellious spirit are very sad and notorious, insomuch that I would sooner bite my finger's ends than willingly cast dirt on authority or any way offer reproach to it. . . . But I shall no longer detain you with my preface, but pass to some things you look for, and whether you expect such freedom from me, yea or no, yet shall you find that I am very open to communicate my thoughts unto you and in plain terms to tell you what my opinion is of the Salem proceedings.

First, as to the method which the Salem Justices do take in their examinations, it is truly this: a warrant being issued out to apprehend the persons that are charged and complained of by the afflicted children (as they are called), said persons are brought before the Justices (the afflicted being present). The Justices ask the apprehended why they afflict those poor children, to which the apprehended answer they do not afflict them. The Justices order the apprehended to look upon the said children, which accordingly they do; and at the time of that look (I dare not say by that look, as the Salem Gentlemen do), the afflicted are cast into a fit. The apprehended are then blinded and ordered to touch the afflicted, and at that touch (though not by the touch, as above), the afflicted ordinarily do come out of their fits. The afflicted persons then declare and affirm that the apprehended have afflicted them, upon which the apprehended persons, though of never so good repute, are forthwith committed to prison on suspicion of witchcraft. . . .

I would fain know of these Salem Gentlemen, but as yet could never know, how it comes about that, if these apprehended persons are witches, and, by a look of the eye, do cast the afflicted into their fits by poisoning them, how it comes about, I say, that, by a look of their eye, they do not cast others into fits and poison others by their looks, and, in particular, tender, fearful women who often are beheld by them and as likely as any in the whole world to receive an ill impression from them. This Salem philosophy some men may call the new philosophy; but I think it rather deserves the name of Salem superstition and sorcery, and it is not fit to be named in a land of such light as New-England is. I think the matter might be better solved another way, but I shall not make any attempt that way further than to say that these afflicted children, as they are called, do hold correspondence with the devil even in the esteem and account of the S [alem] G [entlemen], for when the black man, i.e., say these gentlemen, the devil, does appear to them, they ask him many questions and accordingly give information to the inquirer; and if this is not holding correspondence with the devil and something worse, I know not what is.

But furthermore, I would fain know of these Salem Justices what need there is of further proof and evidence to convict and condemn these apprehended persons than this look and touch, if so be they are so certain that this falling down and arising up, when there is a look and a touch, are natural effects of the said look and touch, and so a perfect demonstration and proof of witchcraft in those persons. What can the jury or judges desire more to convict any man of witchcraft than a plain demonstration that the said man is a witch? Now if this look and touch, circumstanced as before, be a plain demonstration, as their philosophy teaches, what need they seek for further evidences when, after all, it can be but a demonstration?

But let this pass with the S.G. for never so plain and natural a demonstration, yet certain it is that the reasonable part of the world, when acquainted herewith, will laugh at the demonstration and conclude that the said S.G. are actually possessed, at least, with ignorance and folly.

I most admire that Mr. N[icholas] N[oyes], the Reverend Teacher at Salem, who was educated at the school of knowledge and is certainly a learned, a charitable, and a good man, though all the devils in Hell and all the possessed girls in Salem should say to the contrary; at him, I say, I do most admire that he should cry up the above-mentioned philosophy after the manner that he does. I can assure you that I can bring you more than two, or twice two (very credible persons), that will affirm that they have heard him vindicate the above-mentioned demonstration as very reasonable.

Secondly, with respect to the confessors, as they are improperly called, or such as confess themselves to be witches (the second thing you inquire into in your letter), there are now about fifty of them in prison, many of which I have again and again seen and heard; and I cannot but tell you that my faith is strong concerning them that they are deluded, imposed upon, and under the influence of some evil spirit, and therefore unfit to be evidences either against themselves or anyone else. . . .

The great cry of many of our neighbors now is, What, will you not believe the confessors? Will you not believe men and women who confess that they have signed to the devil's book? that they were baptized by the devil and that they were at the mock-sacrament once and again? What! will you not believe that this is witchcraft and that such and such men are witches, although the confessors do own and assert it?

Thus, I say, many of our good neighbors do argue, but methinks they might soon be convinced that there is nothing at all in all these their arguings, if they would but duly consider of the premises . . .

Now for the proof of the said sorcery and witchcraft, the prisoner at the bar pleading not guilty.

1. The afflicted persons are brought into court and, after much patience and pains taken with them, do take their oaths that the prisoner at the bar did afflict them: And here I think it very observable that often, when the afflicted do mean and intend only the appearance and shape of such an one (say G. Proctor), yet they positively swear that G. Proctor did afflict them; and they have been allowed so to do; as though there was no real difference between G. Proctor and the shape of G. Proctor. This, methinks, may readily prove a stumbling block to the jury, lead them into a very fundamental error, and occasion innocent blood, yea the innocentest blood imaginable, to be in great danger. Whom it belongs unto to be eyes unto the blind and to remove such stumbling blocks, I know full well, and yet you and everyone else do know as well as I who do not.

2. The confessors do declare what they know of the said prisoner, and some of the confessors are allowed to give their oaths, a thing which I believe was never heard of in this world, that such as confess themselves to be witches, to have renounced God and Christ and all that is sacred, should yet be allowed and ordered to swear by the name of the great God! This indeed seemeth to me to be a gross taking of God's name in vain. I know the S.G. do say that there is hope that the said confessors have repented: I shall only say that, if they have repented, it is well for themselves; but if they have not, it is very ill for you know who. But then,

3. Whoever can be an evidence against the prisoner at the bar is ordered to come into the court, and here it scarce ever fails but that evidences of one nature and another are brought in, though, I think, all of them altogether alien to the matter of indictment; for they none of them do respect witchcraft upon the bodies of the afflicted, which is the alone matter of charge in the indictment.

4. They are searched by a jury; and as to some of them, the jury brought in that on such or such a place there was a preternatural excrescence. And I wonder what person there is, whether man or woman,

of whom it cannot be said but that, in some part of their body or other, there is a preternatural excrescence. The term is a very general and inclusive term.

Some of the S.G. are very forward to censure and condemn the poor prisoner at the bar because he sheds no tears, but such betray great ignorance in the nature of passion and as great heedlessness as to common passages of a man's life. Some there are who never shed tears; others there are that ordinarily shed tears upon light occasions, and yet for their lives cannot shed a tear when the deepest sorrow is upon their hearts; and who is there that knows not these things? Who knows not that an ecstasy of joy will sometimes fetch tears whenas the quite contrary passion will shut them close up? Why then should any be so silly and foolish as to take an argument from this appearance? But this is by the by. In short, the prisoner at the bar is indicted for sorcery and witchcraft acted upon the bodies of the afflicted. Now, for the proof of this, I reckon that the only pertinent evidences brought in are the evidences of the said afflicted . . .

I cannot but admire that the Justices, whom I think to be well-meaning men, should so far give ear to the devil as merely upon his authority to issue out their warrants and apprehend people. Liberty was evermore accounted the great privilege of an Englishman, but certainly, if the devil will be heard against us and his testimony taken, to the seizing and apprehending of us, our liberty vanishes, and we are fools if we boast of our liberty. Now that the Justices have thus far given ear to the devil I think may be mathematically demonstrated to any man of common sense: And for the demonstration and proof hereof, I desire only that these

two things may be duly considered, viz.,

1. That several persons have been apprehended purely upon the complaints of these afflicted, to whom the afflicted were perfect strangers and had not the least knowledge of imaginable, before they were apprehended.

2. That the afflicted do own and assert, and the Justices do grant, that the devil does inform and tell the afflicted the names of those persons that are thus unknown unto them. Now these two things being duly considered, I think it will appear evident to anyone that the devil's information is the fundamental testimony that is gone upon in the apprehending of the aforesaid people.

If I believe such or such an assertion as comes immediately from the minister of God in the pulpit, because it is the word of the ever-living God, I build my faith on God's testimony; and, if I practice upon it, this my practice is properly built on the word of God: even so in the case before us,

If I believe the afflicted persons as informed by the devil and act thereupon, this my act may properly be said to be grounded upon the testimony or information of the devil. And now, if things are thus, I think it ought to be for a lamentation to you and me and all such as would be accounted good Christians . . .

What will be the issue of these troubles, God only knows; I am afraid that ages will not wear off that reproach and those stains which these things will leave behind them upon our land. I pray God pity us, humble us, forgive us, and appear mercifully for us in this our mount of distress: herewith I conclude and subscribe myself,

Reverend sir, your real friend and humble servant,

T.B.

1662 ∾ *Sarah Kemble Knight* ∾ 1727

DAUGHTER of a Boston merchant, Sarah Kemble Knight was left a widow by her shipmaster husband and had a family to support. She kept a school where Benjamin Franklin was probably at one time her pupil, acted as a minor public official, and attended to her own business affairs. She died in New Haven, where she removed after having spent most of her life in Boston.

On October 2, 1704, she left Boston on a business trip which eventually took her to New York. She rode on horseback with no other company than what she picked up on the way. She passed through Rhode Island and New Haven and came home by the same route, arriving in March, 1705. Her *Journal* of this trip, first published in 1825, is one of the sprightliest accounts in American colonial literature of the life of the Eastern seaboard settlements and the fortunes of the road.

[The following selection has been supplied with a title by the present editors. The text has been to some extent modernized, but not so as to destroy the flow of her distinctly "feminine prose," which suggests the stopless patter of Dickens' Flora Finching in *Little Dorrit* and James Joyce's Molly Bloom in *Ulysses*. Dorothy Richardson remarks in the introduction to her novel, *Pilgrimage*: "Feminine prose, as Charles Dickens and James Joyce have delightfully shown themselves to be aware, should properly be unpunctuated, moving from point to point without formal obstructions."]

NEW HAVEN TO NEW YORK
[1825 (written 1704-1705)]

DEC. 6TH. Being by this time well recruited and rested after my journey, my business lying unfinished by some concerns at New York depending thereupon, my kinsman, Mr. Thomas Trowbridge, of New Haven, must needs take a journey there before it could be accomplished. I resolved to go there in company with him and a man of the town which I engaged to wait on me there. Accordingly, Dec. 6th we set out from New Haven and about 11 same morning came to Stratford ferry; which crossing, about two miles on the other side baited our horses and would have eat a morsel ourselves, but the pumpkin and Indian mixed bread had such an aspect and the bare-legged punch so awkward or rather awful a sound that we left both and proceeded forward and about seven at night came to Fairfield, where we met with good entertainment and lodged; and early next morning set forward to Norowalk, from its half-Indian name, Northwalk, when about 12 noon we arrived, and had a dinner of fried venison, very savory. Landlady wanting some pepper in the seasoning bid the girl hand her the spice in the little gay cup on the shelf. From hence we hasted towards Rye, walking and leading our horses near a mile together up a prodigious high hill, and so riding till about nine at night, and there arrived and took up our lodgings at an ordinary which a French family kept. Here, being very hungry, I desired a fricasse, which the Frenchman undertaking managed so contrary to my notion of cookery that I hastened to bed supperless, and being showed the way up a pair of stairs which had such a narrow passage that I had almost stopped by the bulk of my body, but arriving at my apartment found it to be a little lean-to chamber furnished amongst other rubbish with a high bed and a low one, a long table, a bench, and a bottomless chair. Little Miss went to scratch up my kennel, which rustled as if she'd been in the barn amongst the husks, and suppose such was the contents of the ticking; nevertheless, being exceeding weary, down I laid my poor carcass (never more tired) and found my covering as scanty as my bed was hard. Anon I heard another rustling noise in the room —called to know the matter. Little Miss said she was making a bed for the men, who, when they were in bed, complained their legs lay out of it by reason of its shortness. My poor bones complained bitterly, not being used to such lodgings, and so did the man who was with us; and poor I made but one groan, which was from the time I went to bed to the time I riss [rose], which was about three in the morning, setting up by the fire till light; and having discharged our ordinary, which was as dear as if we had had far better fare, we took our leave of Monsieur, and about seven in the morn come to New Rochelle, a French town, where we had a good breakfast. And in the strength of that, about an hour before sunset got to New York. Here I applied myself to Mr. Burroughs, a merchant to whom I was recommended by my kinsman, Capt. Prout, and received great civilities from him and his spouse, who were now both deaf but very agreeable in their conversation, diverting me with pleasant stories of their knowledge of Britain, from whence they both come, one of which was above the rest very pleasant to me, viz., my Lord Darcy had a very extravagant brother who had mortgaged what estate he could not sell, and in good time died, leaving only one son. Him his lordship (having none of his own) took and made him heir of his whole estate, which he was to re-

ceive at the death of his aunt. He and his aunt in her widowhood held a right understanding and lived as become such relations, she being a discreet gentlewoman and he an ingenious young man. One day he fell into some company though far his inferiors, very freely told him of the ill circumstances his father's estate lay under, and the many debts he left unpaid to the wrong of poor people with whom he had dealt. The young gentleman was put out of countenance—no way he could think of to redress himself—his whole dependence being on the lady his aunt, and how to speak to her he knew not—he went home, sat down to dinner and as usual sometimes with her when the chaplain was absent, she desired him to say grace, which he did after this manner:

Pray God in mercy take my Lady Darcy
    Unto his heavenly throne,
That little John may live like a man,
    And pay every man his own.

The prudent lady took no present notice, but finished dinner, after which having sat and talked awhile (as customary), he riss, took his hat, and going out she desired him to give her leave to speak to him in her closet, where being come she desired to know why he prayed for her death in the manner aforesaid, and what part of her deportment towards him merited such desires. He replied, none at all, but he was under such disadvantages that nothing but that could do him service, and told her how he had been affronted as above, and what impressions it had made upon him. The lady made him a gentle reprimand that he had not informed her after another manner, bid him see what his father owed and he should have money to pay it to a penny, and always to let her know his wants and he should have a ready supply. The young gentleman, charmed with his aunt's discreet management, begged her pardon and accepted her kind offer and retrieved his father's estate, etc., and said he hoped his aunt would never die, for she had done better by him than he could have done for himself.—Mr. Burroughs went with me to vendue,[1] where I bought about 100 ream of paper which was retaken in a flyboat from Holland and sold very reasonably here—some ten, some eight shillings per ream by the lot, which was ten ream in a lot. And at the vendue I made a great many acquaintances amongst the good women of the town, who courteously invited me to their houses and generously entertained me.

The city of New York is a pleasant, well-compacted place, situated on a commodious river which is a fine harbor for shipping. The buildings brick generally, very stately and high, though not altogether like ours in Boston. The bricks in some of the houses are of divers colors and laid in checkers, being glazed to look very agreeable. The inside of them are neat to admiration, the wooden work, for only the walls are plastered, and the sumers and gist[2] are planed and kept very white scoured, as so is all the partitions, if made of boards. The fire places have no jambs (as ours have), but the backs run flush with the walls, and the hearth is of tiles and is as far out into the room at the ends as before the fire, which is generally five foot in the lower rooms, and the piece over where the mantletree should be is made as ours with joiner's work, and, as I suppose, is fastened to iron rods inside. The house where the vendue was had chimney corners like ours, and they and the hearths were laid with the finest tile that I ever see, and the staircases laid all with white tile which is ever clean, and so are the walls of the kitchen, which had a brick floor. They were making great preparations to receive their governor, Lord Cornbury,[3] from the Jerseys, and for that end raised the militia to guard him on shore to the fort.

They are generally of the Church of England and have a New England gentleman for their minister, and a very fine church set out with all customary requisites. There are also a Dutch and divers conventicles, as they call them, viz. Baptist, Quakers, etc. They are not strict in keeping the sabbath as in Boston and other places where I had been, but seem to deal with great exactness as far as I see or deal with. They are sociable to one another and courteous and civil to strangers and fare well in their houses. The English go very fashionable in their dress. But the Dutch, especially the middling sort, differ from our women, in their habit go loose, wear French mouches which are like a cap and a head-band in one, leaving their ears bare, which are set out with jewels of a large size and many in number. And their fingers hooped with rings, some with large stones in them of many colors as were their pendants in their ears, which you should see very old women wear as well as young.

They have vendues very frequently and make their earnings very well by them, for they treat with good liquor liberally, and the customers drink as liberally and generally pay for't as well, by paying for that which they bid up briskly for, after the sack has gone plentifully about, though sometimes good penny worths are got there. Their diversions in the winter is riding sleighs about three or four miles out of town, where they have houses of entertainment at a place called the Bowery, and some go to friends' houses who handsomely treat them. Mr. Burroughs carried his spouse and daughter and myself out to one Madame Dowes', a gentlewoman that lived at a farm house, who gave us a handsome entertainment of five or six dishes and choice beer and metheglin,[4] cider, etc., all which she said was the produce of her farm. I believe we met 50 or 60 sleighs that day—they fly with great swiftness and some are so furious that they'll turn out of the path for none except a loaden cart. Nor do they spare for any diversion the place affords, and sociable to a degree, their tables being as free to their neighbors as to themselves.

[1] A public sale or auction.
[2] Beams and joints.
[3] Edward Hyde, Lord Cornbury, governor of New York, 1702-1708.
[4] Fermented honey and water.

Having here transacted the affair I went upon and some other that fell in the way, after about a fortnight's stay there I left New York with no little regret, and Thursday, Dec. 21, set out for New Haven with my kinsman Trowbridge, and the man that waited on me about one afternoon, and about three come to half-way house about ten miles out of town, where we baited and went forward, and about 5 come to Spiting Devil, else Kingsbridge,[5] where they pay three pence for passing over with a horse, which the man that keeps the gate set up at the end of the bridge receives. . . .

1652 ∽ *Samuel Sewall* ∽ 1730

THE CAREER and personality of Samuel Sewall reflect New England Puritanism in transition from an era of stern piety to one of more canny and humane this-worldliness. His father first came to New England in 1634 but returned to England. Born in England in 1652, Samuel accompanied his family to New England in 1661. Graduated from Harvard in 1671, he was ready to enter the ministry, but marriage to the wealthy Hannah Hull caused him to pursue the more worldly "callings" of printing, politics, and the law. During the Salem witchcraft trials he was one of the judges who sentenced nineteen suspects to be hanged, for which error he was later man enough to do public penance in the Old South Church. His liberalism was also expressed in a pamphlet, *The Selling of Joseph,* 1700, the first antislavery tract published in America. He was chief justice of the Bay Colony from 1718 to 1728, two years before his death. Between December 3, 1673, and October 13, 1729, he kept a diary that is not only one of the most valuable sources for New England's history, but also has delightful moments of self-revelation that make Sewall comparable to Pepys, although he wrote considerably less in fifty-seven years than Pepys did in nine.

[The following selections from the *Diary* concern one of Judge Sewall's clients at a time when he was a somewhat restive widower. The text has been modernized and the title supplied by the present editors.]

A PROPOSITION TO MRS. DENISON
[1878 (written 1718)]

MARCH 19. Col. Townsend, Mr. Leverett, Fitch, Oliver meet at my house to speak with the trespassers on Hopkinston. I write Mr. William Denison's will, being desired by a messenger from Roxbury . . .

March 22. Stormy day. Mr. Pierpont comes in and tells me that Mr. Denison of Roxbury was dead. I think March 21. Mr. John Eyre brings me a letter that came from Newbury.

March 23. Next Friday is agreed on for a church meeting to adjust matters relating to the ordination. Wednesday was mentioned, but Mr. Bromfield said he supposed Mr. Denison's funeral would be on that day. . . .

March 26. Mr. Simeon Stoddard carried me, Mr. Bromfield, and Anthony Stoddard esqr., in his coach to Mr. Denison's funeral. Mr. Walter prayed very well, said

---

[5] Spuyten Duyvil Creek, near Kingsbridge.

Mr. Denison was a man of truth and of trust, a man of prayer, integrity, and piety. Bearers, Mr. Danforth of Dorchester, Mr. John White, Anthony Stoddard esqr., Col. William Dudley, Major Bowls, Mr. Ebenezer Thayer. Major Denison led the widow. Gov. Dudley and I went next the mourners. Went back to the house in a coach; at coming away, I prayed God to keep house with the widow. . . .

April 4. I had thoughts of going to Charlestown lecture, but was prevented by the great snow. In the evening I married Chasling Warrick and Esther Bate. Oh! that they and I might be married to CHRIST, and that our marriage might be known to ourselves and others! Now there is a great man. . . .

April 7. I prove Mr. William Denison's will. Her brother, Edmund [Weld], brought the widow to town and gave me notice before hand. I asked her how old Mr. Denison was. She told me he was born in September, was 53 years old last September. I gave her 10 shillings to give her sister Weld for her Indian Bible. Asked me whether 'twas necessary to bring in an inventory. Inclined to think she ought, but I would speak with her again. Mr. Door took occasion in her absence to say she was one of the most dutiful wives in the world. Her cousin, the widow Hayden, accidentally came in with her.

April 8. Mr. Boydell, when I was at his office and signed the papers, smiling said Mr. Denison's will looked as if it was written by me. I told him yes, but there was not a tittle of it mine but the form. . . .

[April] 17. Mr. Cooper preaches. Dr. Clark and his bride appear at lecture. Mrs. Denison comes to our house. I give her a widow's book bound, having writ her name in it. Mr. D. Oliver calls me to take Col. Byfield and Mrs. Sarah Leverett the acknowledgement of their deeds in order to marriage. And they were married presently after. . . .

[April] 24. I visit Dr. Clark and his new wife. They seem to take it kindly. . . .

June 3. Go to Roxbury in my son's calash and with him visit Gov. Dudley, Mr. Walter. Talk with him about Mrs. D——n. He advises me not to see her then, lest should surprise her undressed. Told him I came on purpose, yet finally submitted to his advice. He spake of her coming to town on Thursday.

June 5. Nobody came. I writ to Mr. Walter.

June 9. Mr. Corwin dies about 9. m. Col. Brown sent me word of it by Chapman. Note. Mrs. D——n came in the morning about 9 o'clock, and I took her up into my chamber and discoursed thoroughly with her. She desired me to provide another and better nurse. I gave her the two last news-letters—told her I intended to visit her at her own house next lecture day. She said, 'twould be talked of. I answered, in such cases persons must run the gantlet. Gave her Mr. Whiting's Oration for Abijah Walter, who brought her on horseback to town. I think little or no notice was taken of it . . .

June 17. Went to Roxbury lecture, visited Mr. Walter. Mr. Webb preached. Visited Gov. Dudley, Mrs. Denison, gave her Dr. Mather's sermons very well bound, told her we were in it invited to a wedding. She gave me very good curds . . .

July 7. I give Mrs. Denison her oath to the inventory, gave her a catalogue subscribed to her. Her brother brought her. Mr. Shelden of Northampton dines with me. At night, when all were gone to bed, Cousin Moodey went with me into the new hall, read the history of Rebekah's courtship and prayed with me respecting my widowed condition. . . .

July 16. Went to Mr. Gee's to dinner. Dr. Cotton Mather and his lady, Deacon Barnard, Procter, Mr. Gee, wife, son sat down, Mr. Wadsworth, who returned thanks excellently, as Dr. Mather had craved a blessing. Viewed my lot at the north burying place. Went to Woodell's and rode in his coach to Meers's, from thence went and visited Mrs. Denison. Gave her K. George's effigies in copper and an English crown of K. Charles II, 1677. Eat curds with her; I craved a blessing and returned thanks; came home after it. . . .

July 25. I go in the hackney coach to Roxbury. Call at Mr. Walter's, who is not at home, nor Gov. Dudley nor his lady. Visit Mrs. Denison: she invites me to eat. I give her two cases with a knife and fork in each; one turtle shell tackling; the other long, with ivory handles, squared, cost, 4 shillings, 6 pence; pound of raisins with proportionable almonds. Visited her brother and sister Weld. Came home by daylight in the coach, which stayed for me at the Gray-Hound. . . .

Aug. 1. Court rises; gave Mr. Appleton 20 shillings, who had prayed 4 times. This was the longest court that I remember at Cambridge. Rode home round with Stedmand, visit Mrs. Denison. Madam Rogers and Leverett much congratulated me upon my courting her.

Aug. 6. Visited Mrs. Denison, carried her, her sister Weld the widow, and Mrs. Weld to her brother, Mr. Samuel Weld, where we were courteously entertained. Brought Mr. Edmund Weld's wife home with me in the coach; she is in much darkness. Gave Mrs. Denison a psalm-book neatly bound in England with Turkey-leather. . . .

[Aug.] 15. I, with my son and daughter, J. Sewall, dine at Gov. Dudley's; Mr. Walter and his wife and son, son and daughter Sewall of Brooklin and their daughter there, and Col. Dudley: Mrs. Denison, I suppose, was the principal guest. I waited on her home . . .

[Aug.] 27. I ride and visit Mrs. Denison, leave my horse at the Gray-Hound. She mentions her discouragements by reason of discourses she heard. I prayed God to direct her and me.

[Aug.] 28. None in the fore-seat at lecture. Gov. I think was at Mr. Nelson's. Mr. Stephens and Capt. Burnap dine with us. Mr. Bromfield, J. Sewall and I go to the funeral of Mrs. Peck, Mr. Williams of Deerfield's mother. 4 ministers there: Mr. Walter, Danforth, Sewall, Thair, besides

young Mr. Walter. Mr. Walter in his prayer made a very honorable mention of her. Is about 82 years old, born at Roxbury. Called at Mrs. Denison's before the funeral. . . .

[Sept.] 4. Set out for Bristol with Scipio [his servant] after lecture and dinner. Called at Mrs. Denison's . . .

[Sept.] 26. A council is called, Capt. Moodey's men dismissed. One that came from New York is taken with the small pox at his house in Charlestown. Visit Mrs. Denison, bring the widow Weld to town in the coach, in her way to her cousin Carter. . . .

Oct. 3 or 4. Visit Mrs. Denison . . .

Oct. 11. Visit Mrs. Denison. Bring Dr. Cotton Mather's youngest daughter home with me in the coach, at Mr. Walter's desire.

Oct. 15. Visit Mrs. Denison on horseback; present her with a pair of shoebuckles, cost 5 shillings, 3 pence. . . .

[Oct.] 24. Brother Sewall visits me. While he was here, Mrs. Elisabeth Byles, Dr. Mather's daughter, tells me of Col. Thomas' death, whereby he is freed from his solicitude as to a judge of the supreme court at Salem next November. Mr. Dwight of Woodstock dines with us. Visit Mrs. Denison. The private meeting was at her house, which I was not aware of. I went to Mr. Walter's to condole him and, knocking at the door, was called to and told they were all gone to the meeting. I asked where. They said at Mrs. Denison's. I went thither and found Mr. Walter at prayer. Mr. Thomas Walter made a very good sermon from John, 17.7. Showing the duty of submitting to God's sovereignty, the great sin of doing contrarily. Prayed. Sung part of the 145 Psalm, which he set to Low Dutch very well. Prayed. The room was full. Gov Dudley and his lady, widow Ruggles, etc., there. Rained hard. I supped with Mrs. Denison, got home about 8 at night. *Laus Deo.* . . .

Oct. 29. Mr. Thomas Walter was ordained. Dr. Cotton Mather prayed, Dr. Increase Mather preached from Hebr. 13.

18. Pray for us. Mr. Danforth of Dorchester prayed. Dr. Increase Mather ordained, Mr. Neh. Walter, Mr. Danforth and Dr. Cotton Mather laying on hands with him. Dr. Cotton Mather gave the right hand of fellowship after a considerable discourse . . . Mr. Thomas Walter gave the blessing. Entertainment was at Mr. Walter's and Major Bowls's. Supped with the Gov. Dudley, His Excellency Gov. Shute. Visited Mrs. Denison. Sam Hirst and Hall supped at her house. Went and came home in Mr. Stoddard's coach. . . .

[Nov.] 1. His Excellency comes not into council. My son from Brooklin being here, I took his horse and visited Mrs. Denison. Sat in the chamber next Major Bowls. I told her 'twas time now to finish our business: asked her what I should allow her. She not speaking, I told her I was willing to give her two [hundred] and fifty pounds per annum during her life, if it should please God to take me out of the world before her. She answered she had better keep as she was than give a certainty for an uncertainty; she should pay dear for dwelling at Boston. I desired her to make proposals, but she made none. I had thoughts of publishment next Thursday the 6th. But I now seem to be far from it. May God, who has the pity of a father, direct and help me! . . .

[Nov.] 28. Having consulted with Mr. Walter after lecture, he advised me to go and speak with Mrs. Denison. I went this day in the coach, had a fire made in the chamber where I spake with her before, Nov. 1: I inquired how she had done these 3 or 4 weeks. Afterwards I told her our conversation had been such when I was with her last that it seemed to be a direction in providence not to proceed any further. She said it must be what I pleased, or to that purpose. Afterward she seemed to blame that I had not told her so Nov. 1. Because the man had been there several times to take the living and she knew not what answer to give. I said I knew not, but that intended to let the living although she lived single. I repeated her words of

Nov. 1. She seemed at first to start at the words of her paying dear, as if she had not spoken them. But she said she thought 'twas hard to part with all and have nothing to bestow on her kindred. I said, I did not intend anything of the movables, I intended all the personal estate to be to her. She said I seemed to be in a hurry on Saturday, Nov. 1, which was the reason she gave me no proposals. Whereas I had asked her long before to give me proposals in writing, and she upbraided me that I who had never written her a letter should ask her to write. She asked me if I would drink. I told her yes. She gave me cider, apples and a glass of wine, gathered together the little things I had given her, and offered them to me, but I would take none of them. Told her I wished her well, should be glad to hear of her welfare. She seemed to say she should not again take in hand a thing of this nature. Thanked me for what I had given her and desired my prayers. I gave Abijah Weld an Angel.[1] Mr. Stoddard and his wife came in their coach to see their sister, which broke off my visit. Upon their asking me, I dismissed my coach and went with them to see Mr. Danforth and came home by moonshine. Got home about 9 at night. *Laus Deo.*

My bowels yearn towards Mrs. Denison, but I think God directs me in his providence to desist. . . .

Nov. 30. Lord's-day. In the evening I sung the 120 Psalm in the family. About 7 o'clock Mrs. Dorothy Denison comes in, her cousin Weld coming first, saying she desired to speak with me in private. I had a fire in the new hall and was at prayer; was very much startled that she should come so far a-foot in that exceeding cold season; she entered into discourse of what passed between us at Roxbury last Friday; I seemed to be altered in my affection; asked pardon if she had affronted me. Seemed to incline the match should not break off, since I had kept her company so long. Said Mr. Denison spake to her after

---

[1] An English gold coin.

his signing the will that he would not make her put all out of her hand and power, but reserve somewhat to bestow on his friends that might want. I told her she might keep all. She excused, and said 'twas not such an all. I commended the estate. I could not observe that she made me any offer of any part all this while. She mentioned two glass bottles she had. I told her they were hers, and the other small things I had given her, only now they had not the same signification as before. I was much concerned for her being in the cold, would fetch her in a plate of something warm (for I had not supped). She refused.

However, I fetched a tankard of cider and drank to her. She desired that no body might know of her being here. I told her they should not . . . She went away in the bitter cold, no moon being up, to my great pain. I saluted her at parting . . .

Dec. 22. Mrs. Dorothy Denison brings an additional inventory. I give her her oath, asked her brother, Brewer, and her to dine with me. She said she needed not to eat. Caused her to sit by the fire and went with her to the door at her going away. She said nothing to me, nor her brother, Brewer.

1674 ~ *William Byrd* ~ 1744

BELONGING to the second generation of his family in Virginia, William Byrd was educated in England. A member of the Middle Temple and the Royal Society, he settled down in Virginia in 1705 at his estate of Westover and played a brillant rôle in both politics and society. In 1706 he married Lucy Parke, who died in London in 1716. In 1724 Byrd married Maria Taylor. He built up at Westover one of the finest private libraries in the colonies and went far toward realizing his long-cherished desire to be a writer by producing three stylistically impressive manuscripts dealing with his experiences as a surveyor and traveler, *History of the Dividing Line Run in the Year 1728*, *A Progress to the Mines in the Year 1732*, and *A Journey to the Land of Eden in the Year 1733*, all published for the first time in 1841.

[The first of the following selections is taken from *The Secret Diary of William Byrd of Westover, 1709-1712*, ed. L. B. Wright and M. Tinling, Richmond, 1941, a transcription from a shorthand manuscript which Byrd kept for his own pleasure and which is unique among personal records in American colonial literature for its quaintly scabrous intimacies. The second selection is from *A Progress to the Mines*. Both selections reveal much of Byrd's unusual personality, so different from that of the New England diarist, Samuel Sewall, and at the same time convey vivid impressions of the life of 18th Century Virginia. Titles have been supplied by the present editors. For the second selection, the modernized text of 1841 has been followed with few changes.]

A WEEK AT WESTOVER IN JUNE
[1941 (written 1710)]

[JUNE] 15. I rose at 5 o'clock and read a chapter in Hebrew and some Greek in Thucydides. I said my prayers and ate milk for breakfast. The weather was very hot. I wrote a letter to England. I ate some broiled pork for dinner. In the afternoon my gripes returned on me and continued till the evening with some violence. Hot things did it no good but in the evening I drank some warm milk from the cow which eased me immediately. It rained this afternoon very hard with a little wind and thunder. This hindered my walking anywhere but in the garden. I foretold by my cellar stinking that it would rain. I impute my gripes to cherry wine, or else pulling my coat off about noon. I said my prayers and had good thoughts, good humor, but indifferent good health, thank God Almighty.

16. I rose at 5 o'clock and drank some milk warm from the cow. I read a chapter in Hebrew and some Greek in Thucydides. I said my prayers and danced my dance.[1] About 10 o'clock Captain Drury Stith and his wife came to make us a visit, notwithstanding it was very hot. I was glad to see them because I think them excellent people. We played at billiards till dinner. I ate boiled pork. In the afternoon we passed away the time pleasantly till about 6 o'clock and then they went home. In the evening I took a walk with my wife. We made a little cider of the G-n-t-n [2] apples, which yielded but little juice. I was better of my gripes, thank God. I neglected to say my prayers but had good health, good thoughts, and good humor, thank God Almighty.

17. I rose at 5 o'clock and drank some milk hot from the cow. I read a chapter in Hebrew and some Greek in Thucydides. I said my prayers and danced my dance. About 8 o'clock Mr. Anderson came on his way over the river. He told me the quarrel was made up between Parson Slater and his vestry without coming to trial. He stayed about half an hour. Colonel Hill sent his man with a basket of apricots, of which my wife ate twelve immediately and I ate eight which however did not make my gripes return. I set my closet right. I ate tongue and chicken for dinner. In the afternoon I caused L-s-n to be whipped for beating his wife and Jenny was whipped for being his whore.[3] In the evening the sloop came from Appomatox with tobacco. I took a walk about the plantation. I said my prayers and drank some new milk from the cow. I had good health, good thoughts, and good humor, thanks be to God Almighty.

18. I rose at 5 o'clock and drank some new milk from the cow. I read a chapter in Hebrew and some Greek in Thucydides. I said my prayers. It was extremely hot. I read a sermon in Dr. Tillotson about angels.[4] I wrote a letter to Williamsburg to send by my sloop which I sent for rum, wine, and sugar from thence and that this might come safely I resolved to send Bannister with the sloop. I ate chicken for dinner but very little because I had no appetite. In the afternoon my wife told me a dream she had two nights. She thought she saw a scroll in the sky in form of a light cloud with writing on it. It ran extremely fast from west to east with great swiftness. The writing she could not read but there was a woman before her that told her there would be a great dearth because of want of rain and after that a pestilence for that the seasons were changed and time inverted. Mr. James Burwell and Charles Doyley came and in the evening I took a walk with them. Our nurse went away in the sloop. I said my prayers and had good health, good thoughts, and good humor, thanks be to God Almighty.

19. I rose at 5 o'clock and read a chapter

---

[1] Fond of dancing, Byrd kept himself limber by constant practice.

[2] Only these letters can be deciphered from Byrd's shorthand.

[3] L-s-n was one of Byrd's servants and Jenny was the family maid.

[4] Tillotson was one of the great Anglican divines of Restoration England.

in Hebrew and some Greek in Thucydides. I drank some warm milk from the cow. I said my prayers and danced my dance. About 10 o'clock came Isham Randolph and Mr. Finney to see us. They told me Colonel Randolph was very ill and very melancholy. We played at billiards till dinner. I ate fish for dinner. In the afternoon Mr. Stith came over with my cousin Berkeley, who all stayed here till the evening and then they all went away but Mr. Finney. In the evening we took a walk. Mr. Finney is a sensible man and good natured. He told me that Major Allen died on Thursday last. In our walk we met Mr. C—s who came home with us. I neglected to say my prayers but had good health, good thoughts, and good humor, thank God Almighty.

20. I rose at 5 o'clock and drank milk from the cow. I read a chapter in Hebrew and some Greek in Thucydides. I said my prayers and danced my dance. Mr. Finney returned home without any breakfast but I gave him some strong water. Colonel Hill sent us another present of apricots. I wrote a letter to England. I ate five apricots which put my belly out of order. I ate roast mutton for dinner. In the afternoon my belly was griped. I played with my wife at piquet and then I ordered the boat to carry us to my cousin Harrison's where we found my cousin Berkeley and Jimmy Burwell. I was out of order in my belly. About 8 o'clock we returned home where we found all well, thank God. I said my prayers and had good health, good thoughts, and good humor, thanks be to God Almighty.

21. I rose at 5 o'clock and drank milk from the cow. I read a chapter in Hebrew and some Greek in Thucydides. I said my prayers and danced my dance. My wife was indisposed. I sent Tom to Appomattox to desire Mr. Mumford to go to the outcry [5] of my uncle's estate. About five nights since I dreamed I saw a flaming star in the air at which I was much frightened and called some others to see it but when they came it disappeared. I fear this portends some judgment to this country or at least

to myself. I ate roast mutton for dinner. In the afternoon I settled the closet. About 5 o'clock I received an express from Mr. Clayton that the Governor, Colonel Spotswood, with two men-of-war arrived last night at Kiquotan with several other ships. I sent word of this to Mrs. Harrison and then prepared to go to Williamsburg tomorrow. In the evening I took a walk about the plantation. I said my prayers and had good thoughts, good humor, and good health, thank God Almighty. . . .

A VISIT TO NEIGHBORING GENTRY IN SEPTEMBER
[1841 (1732)]

20TH. I continued the bark,[6] and then tossed down my poached eggs, with as much ease as some good breeders slip children into the world. About nine I left the prudentest orders I could think of with my vizier, and then crossed the river to Shacco's. I made a running visit to three of my quarters, where, besides finding all the people well, I had the pleasure to see better crops than usual both of corn and tobacco. I parted there with my intendant, and pursued my journey to Mr. Randolph's, at Tuckahoe, without meeting any adventure by the way. Here I found Mrs. Fleming, who was packing up her baggage with design to follow her husband the next day, who had gone to a new settlement in Goochland. Both he and she have been about seven years persuading themselves to remove to that retired part of the country, though they had the two strong arguments of health and interest for so doing. The widow smiled graciously upon me, and entertained me very handsomely. Here I learned all the tragical story of her daughter's humble marriage with her uncle's overseer. Besides the meanness of this mortal's aspect, the man has not one visible qualification, except impudence, to recommend him to a female's inclinations.

---

[5] Public auction.
[6] Medicine prescribed by Byrd's physician.

But there is sometimes such a charm in that Hibernian endowment, that frail woman cannot withstand it, though it stand alone without any other recommendation. Had she run away with a gentleman or a pretty fellow, there might have been some excuse for her, though he were of inferior fortune: but to stoop to a dirty plebeian, without any kind of merit, is the lowest prostitution. I found the family justly enraged at it; and though I had more good nature than to join in her condemnation, yet I could devise no excuse for so senseless a prank as this young gentlewoman had played. Here good drink was more scarce than good victuals, the family being reduced to the last bottle of wine, which was therefore husbanded very carefully. But the water was excellent. The heir of the family did not come home till late in the evening. He is a pretty young man, but had the misfortune to become his own master too soon. This puts young fellows upon wrong pursuits, before they have sense to judge rightly for themselves. Though at the same time they have a strange conceit of their own sufficiency, when they grow near twenty years old, especially if they happen to have a small smattering of learning. It is then they fancy themselves wiser than all their tutors and governors, which makes them headstrong to all advice, and above all reproof and admonition.

21st. I was sorry in the morning to find myself stopped in my career by bad weather brought upon us by a northeast wind. This drives a world of raw unkindly vapors upon us from Newfoundland, laden with blight, coughs, and pleurisies. However, I complained not, lest I might be suspected to be tired of the good company. Though Mrs. Fleming was not so much upon her guard, but mutinied strongly at the rain, that hindered her from pursuing her dear husband. I said what I could to comfort a gentlewoman under so sad a disappointment. I told her a husband, that stayed so much at home as hers did, could be no such violent rarity, as for a woman to venture her precious health, to go daggling through the rain after him, or to be miserable if she happened to be prevented. That it was prudent for married people to fast sometimes from one another, that they might come together again with the better stomach. That the best things in this world, if constantly used, are apt to be cloying, which a little absence and fortitude would prevent. This was strange doctrine to a fond female, who fancies people should love with as little reason after marriage as before. In the afternoon Monsieur Marij, the minister of the parish, came to make me a visit. He had been a Romish priest, but found reasons, either spiritual or temporal, to quit that gay religion. The fault of this new convert is, that he looks for as much respect from his protestant flock, as is paid to the popish clergy, which our ill-bred Huguenots do not understand. Madam Marij had so much curiosity as to want to come too; but another horse was wanting, and she believed it would have too vulgar an air to ride behind her husband. This woman was of the true exchange breed, full of discourse, but void of discretion, and married a parson, with the idle hopes he might some time or other come to be his grace of Canterbury. The gray mare is the better horse in that family, and the poor man submits to her wild vagaries for peace sake. She has just enough of the fine lady to run in debt, and be of no signification in her household. And the only thing that can prevent her from undoing her loving husband will be, that nobody will trust them beyond the sixteen thousand,[7] which is soon run out in a Goochland store. The way of dealing there is for some small merchant or peddler to buy a Scots pennyworth of goods, and clap one hundred and fifty per cent. upon that. At this rate the parson cannot be paid much more for his preaching than it is worth. No sooner was our visitor retired, but the facetious widow was so kind

---

[7] The reference is to the salary of a minister, which was legally set at 16,000 pounds of tobacco.

as to let me into all this secret history, but was at the same time exceedingly sorry that the woman should be so indiscreet, and the man so tame as to be governed by an unprofitable and fantastical wife.

22d. We had another wet day, to try both Mrs. Fleming's patience and my good breeding. The northeast wind commonly sticks by us three or four days, filling the atmosphere with damps, injurious both to man and beast. The worst of it was, we had no good liquor to warm our blood, and fortify our spirits against so strong a malignity. However, I was cheerful under all these misfortunes, and expressed no concern but a decent fear lest my long visit might be troublesome. Since I was like to have thus much leisure, I endeavored to find out what subject a dull married man could introduce that might best bring the widow to the use of her tongue. At length I discovered she was a notable quack, and therefore paid that regard to her knowledge, as to put some questions to her about the bad distemper that raged then in the country. I mean the bloody flux, that was brought us in the negro-ship consigned to Col. Braxton. She told me she made use of very simple remedies in that case, with very good success. She did the business either with hartshorn drink, that had plantain leaves boiled in it, or else with a strong decoction of St. Andrew's cross, in new milk instead of water. I agreed with her that those remedies might be very good, but

would be more effectual after a dose or two of Indian physic. But for fear this conversation might be too grave for a widow, I turned the discourse, and began to talk of plays, and finding her taste lay most towards comedy, I offered my service to read one to her, which she kindly accepted. She produced the second part of *The Beggar's Opera,* which had diverted the town for forty nights successively, and gained four thousand pounds to the author. This was not owing altogether to the wit or humor that sparkled in it, but to some political reflections, that seemed to hit the ministry. But the great advantage was, that his interest was solicited by the Duchess of Queensbury, which no man could refuse who had but half an eye in his head, or half a guinea in his pocket. Her grace, like death, spared nobody, but even took my Lord Selkirk in for two guineas, to repair which extravagance he lived upon Scots herrings two months afterwards. But the best story was, she made a very smart officer in his majesty's guards give her a guinea, who swearing at the same time it was all he had in the world, she sent him fifty for it the next day, to reward his obedience. After having acquainted my company with the history of the play, I read three acts of it, and left Mrs. Fleming and Mr. Randolph to finish it, who read as well as most actors do at a rehearsal. Thus we killed the time, and triumphed over the bad weather. . . .

c. 1730 ∾ *Jonathan Carver* ∾ 1780

LITTLE is known for certain of the early life of Jonathan Carver. The probabilities are that he was born of a poor family in Canterbury, Connecticut, shortly after 1730. He married in 1746, had seven children, and was wounded in battle with the French in 1757 while a captain in a regiment of rangers. After the cessation of hostilities, he set out to explore the country west of what is now Michigan. How far his travels actually extended is a matter of some controversy, but at least he is granted to have explored northern Wisconsin.

Returning to Boston, he went to England to get further assistance in

Western exploration, received some money as a needy servant of the government, and enlisted the sympathy of Dr. John Coakley Lettsom, who apparently helped him to write an account of his wanderings which was first published in London in 1778 under the title, *Travels Through the Interior Parts of North America in the Years 1766, 1767 and 1768.* Despite Carver's insistence on his unimpeachable veracity, the book was padded with Munchausen-like anecdotes of strange sights and encounters, with rhetorical descriptions highly colored by a facile imagination, and with unacknowledged pilferings from previous travel literature. None the less, it was enormously popular, helped stimulate interest on two continents in the exploration of the West, and now and then launched into far-flung speculations that time has proved strikingly prophetic.

Carver, however, never realized his ambitions to undertake further western exploration, and died in misery at the age of fifty. He may be called Dr. Lettsom's Trader Horn.

[The titles for the following selections have been supplied by the present editors; the text has been modernized in punctuation and to some extent in spelling.]

From
TRAVELS
[1778]

Northwest Passage

NO SOONER was the late war with France concluded and peace established by the Treaty of Versailles in the year 1763 than I began to consider (having rendered my country some services during the war) how I might continue still serviceable and contribute, as much as lay in my power, to make that vast acquisition of territory gained by Great Britain in North America advantageous to it. It appeared to me indispensably needful that government should be acquainted in the first place with the true state of the dominions they were now become possessed of. To this purpose, I determined, as the next proof of my zeal, to explore the most unknown parts of them and to spare no trouble or expense in acquiring a knowledge that promised to be so useful to my countrymen. I knew that many obstructions would arise to my scheme from the want of good maps and charts, for the French, whilst they retained their power in North America, had taken every artful method to keep all other nations, particularly the English, in ignorance of the concerns of the interior parts of it: and to accomplish this design with the greater certainty, they had published inaccurate maps and false accounts, calling the different nations of the Indians by nicknames they had given them and not by those really appertaining to them. Whether the intention of the French in doing this was to prevent these nations from being discovered and traded with, or to conceal their discourse when they talked to each other of the Indian concerns in their presence, I will not determine; but whatsoever was the cause from which it arose, it tended to mislead.

As a proof that the English had been greatly deceived by these accounts and that their knowledge relative to Canada had usually been very confined, before the conquest of Crown Point in 1759, it had been esteemed an impregnable fortress; but no sooner was it taken than we were convinced that it had acquired its greatest security from false reports given out by its possessors and might have been battered down with a few four pounders. Even its situation, which was represented to be so very advantageous, was found to owe its advantages to the same source. It cannot be denied but that some maps of these countries have been published by the French with an appearance of accuracy, but these are of so small a size and drawn on so minute a scale that they are nearly inexplicable. The sources of the Mississippi, I can assert from my own experience, are greatly misplaced; for, when I had explored them and compared their situation with the French charts, I found them very erroneously represented, and am satisfied that these were only copied from the rude sketches of the Indians.

Even so lately as their evacuation of Canada they continued their schemes to deceive, leaving no traces by which any knowledge might accrue to their conquerors; for though they were well acquainted with all the lakes, particularly with Lake Superior, having constantly a vessel of considerable burden thereon, yet their plans of them are very incorrect. I discovered many errors in the descriptions given therein of its islands and bays, during a progress of eleven hundred miles that I coasted it in canoes. They likewise, on giving up the possession of them, took care to leave the places they had occupied in the same uncultivated state they had found them, at the same time destroying all their naval force. I observed myself part of the hulk of a very large vessel, burnt to the water's edge, just at the opening from the Straits of St. Marie's into the lake.

These difficulties, however, were not sufficient to deter me from the undertaking, and I made preparations for setting out. What I chiefly had in view, after gaining a knowledge of the manners, customs, languages, soil, and natural productions of the different nations that inhabit the back of the Mississippi, was to ascertain the breadth of that vast continent which extends from the Atlantic to the Pacific Ocean, in its broadest part between 43 and 46 degrees northern latitude. Had I been able to accomplish this, I intended to have proposed to government to establish a post in some of those parts about the Straits of Annian, which, having been first discovered by Sir Francis Drake, of course belong to the English. This, I am convinced, would greatly facilitate the discovery of a Northwest Passage or a communication between Hudson's Bay and the Pacific Ocean. An event so desirable, and which has been so often sought for, but without success. Besides this important end, a settlement on that extremity of America would answer many good purposes and repay every expense the establishment of it might occasion. For it would not only disclose new sources of trade and promote many useful discoveries, but would open a passage for conveying intelligence to China and the English settlements in the East Indies with greater expedition than a tedious voyage by the Cape of Good Hope or the Straits of Magellan will allow of.

How far the advantages arising from such an enterprise may extend can only be ascertained by the favorable concurrence of future events. But that the completion of the scheme I have had the honor of first planning and attempting will some time or other be effected, I make no doubt. From the unhappy divisions that at present subsist between Great Britain and America, it will probably be some years before the attempt is repeated; but, whenever it is and the execution of it carried on with propriety, those who are so fortunate as to succeed will reap, exclusive of the national advantages that must ensue, emoluments beyond their most sanguine expectations. And whilst their spirits are elated by their success, perhaps they may bestow some commendations and blessings on the person that first pointed out to them the way. These, though but a shadowy recompense for all my toil, I shall receive with pleasure.

To what power of authority this new world will become dependent, after it has arisen from its present uncultivated state, time alone can discover. But as the seat of empire from time immemorial has been gradually progressive towards the West, there is no doubt but that at some future period mighty kingdoms will emerge from these wildernesses, and stately palaces and solemn temples, with gilded spires reaching the skies, supplant the Indian huts, whose only decorations are the barbarous trophies of their vanquished enemies. . . .

A RUIN OF TIME

One day, having landed on the shore of the Mississippi some miles below Lake Pepin,[1] whilst my attendants were preparing my dinner, I walked out to take a view of the adjacent country. I had not proceeded far before I came to a fine, level, open plain, on which I perceived at a little distance a partial elevation that had the appearance of an entrenchment. On a nearer inspection I had greater reason to suppose that it had really been intended for this many centuries ago. Notwithstanding it was now covered with grass, I could plainly discern that it had once been a breastwork of about four feet in height, extending the best part of a mile and sufficiently capacious to cover five thousand men. Its form was somewhat circular, and its flanks reached to the river. Though much defaced by time, every angle was distinguishable and appeared as regular, and fashioned with as much military skill, as if planned by Vauban himself.[2] The ditch was not visible, but I thought on examining more curiously that I could perceive there certainly had been one. From its situation also I am convinced that it must have been designed for this purpose. It fronted the river, and the rear was covered by the river; nor was there any rising ground for a considerable way that commanded it; a few straggling oaks were alone to be seen near it. In many places small tracks were worn across it

by the feet of the elks and deer, and from the depth of the bed of earth by which it was covered, I was able to draw certain conclusions of its great antiquity. I examined all the angles and every part with great attention and have often blamed myself since for not encamping on the spot and drawing an exact plan of it. To show that this description is not the offspring of a heated imagination or the chimerical tale of a mistaken traveler, I find on inquiry since my return that Mon. St. Pierre[3] and several traders have, at different times, taken notice of similar appearances, on which they have formed the same conjectures but without examining them so minutely as I did. How a work of this kind could exist in a country that has hitherto (according to the general received opinion) been the seat of war to untutored Indians alone, whose whole stock of military knowledge has only till within two centuries amounted to drawing the bow and whose only breastwork even at present is the thicket, I know not. I have given as exact an account as possible of this singular appearance and leave to future explorers of these distant regions to discover whether it is a production of nature or art. Perhaps the hints I have here given might lead to a more perfect investigation of it and give us very different ideas of the ancient state of realms that we at present believe to have been from the earliest period only the habitations of savages. . . .

[1] Extension of Mississippi in Wisconsin and Minnesota 24 miles long and from 2 to 4 miles wide.

[2] Marquis Sébastien le Prestre de Vauban, 1633-1707, was a French military engineer and marshal.

[3] It is uncertain whether Carver refers to Jacques Legardeur, Sieur de Saint-Pierre, 1701-1755, commandant at Fort Beauharnois on Lake Pepin, or to the early Milwaukee fur trader, Mon. St. Pierre, active at the time of Carver's travels and mentioned in contemporary documents, for which cf. *Wisconsin Hist. Coll.*, XI, 210f and XVIII, 267f.

THE SHINING MOUNTAINS

That range of mountains of which the Shining Mountains are a part begin at Mexico, and, continuing northward on the back or to the east of California, separate the waters of those numerous rivers that fall either into the Gulf of Mexico or the Gulf of California. From thence, continuing their course still northward, between the sources of the Mississippi and the rivers that run into the South Sea, they appear to end in about forty-seven or forty-eight degrees of north latitude, where a number of rivers arise and empty themselves either into the South Sea, into Hudson's Bay, or into the waters that communicate between these two seas.

Among these mountains, those that lie to the west of the river St. Pierre are called the Shining Mountains, from an infinite number of crystal stones, of an amazing size, with which they are covered and which, when the sun shines full upon them, sparkle so as to be seen at a very great distance.

This extraordinary range of mountains is calculated to be more than three thousand miles in length, without any very considerable intervals, which I believe surpasses anything of the kind in the other quarters of the globe. Probably in future ages they may be found to contain more riches in their bowels than those of Indostan and Malabar or that are produced on the golden coast of Guinea, nor will I except even the Peruvian mines. To the west of these mountains, when explored by future Columbuses or Raleighs, may be found other lakes, rivers, and countries, full fraught with all the necessaries or luxuries of life; and where future generations may find an asylum, whether driven from their country by the ravages of lawless tyrants, or by religious persecutions, or reluctantly leaving it to remedy the inconveniences arising from a superabundant increase of inhabitants; whether, I say, impelled by these or allured by hopes of commercial advantages, there is little doubt but their expectations will be fully gratified in these rich and unexhausted climes. . . .

Michel-Guillaume Jean de Crèvecoeur
1735 ∾ 1813

CRÈVECOEUR, who assumed the name of "John Hector St. John" when he became a citizen of New York province in 1765, was born near Caen, in Normandy. After attending the Jesuit Collège du Mont in Caen, he completed his education in England, where he lived with relatives near Salisbury. In 1754 he migrated to Canada, where he served with the forces of Montcalm. In 1769, after working as an explorer and surveyor, he married Mehitable Tippet of Yonkers and purchased a large estate in Orange County, New York. Here he thought he had achieved one of the most enviable of human situations, when the Revolution broke.

Assuming toward either side the attitude of a half-cosmopolitan, half-frontier Mercutio—"A plague o' both your houses!"—he incurred his neighbors' suspicion and was imprisoned by the British. Upon his release, he had to sail to Europe without his family. His farmhouse was destroyed; his children, after suffering captivity by the Indians, were scattered; his wife died. On his return to America after the war, Crèvecoeur became French consul at New York and busied himself with problems of scientific farming, botany, and transatlantic transportation. He returned to France in 1790, lived for some years in Munich, and died in his native Normandy in 1813. Some of his best writing is found in the work published from his manuscripts in 1925, *Sketches of Eighteenth Century America*.

[The following selections are from the final letter in his *Letters from an American Farmer*, first published in London in 1782, the first American edition appearing in Philadelphia, 1793. Unlike the earlier letters of this volume, which have so much to say of the serenity he had found in America, this letter, as the title indicates, sets forth his state of mind after all serenity had been shaken by the onset of the war. Although he never carried out the project he here describes, these selections from the letter—which is somewhat prolix in its entirety—reveal much of his character and thought and one phase at least of the frontier and pioneer spirit—the urge to solve impossibly complex dilemmas by courageous escape into some Shangri-la or Islandia beyond the horizon, over trackless wilds or difficult water.]

DISTRESSES OF A FRONTIER MAN
[1782]

I

AS A member of a large society which extends to many parts of the world, my connection with it is too distant to be as strong as that which binds me to the inferior division in the midst of which I live. I am told that the great nation, of which we are a part, is just, wise, and free, beyond any other on earth, within its own insular boundaries; but not always so to its distant conquests: I shall not repeat all I have heard, because I cannot believe half of it. As a citizen of a smaller society, I find that any kind of opposition to its now prevailing sentiments, immediately begets hatred: how easily do men pass from loving, to hating and cursing one another! I am a lover of peace, what must I do? I am divided between the respect I feel for the ancient connection, and the fear of innovations, with the consequence of which I am not well acquaint-

ed; as they are embraced by my own countrymen. I am conscious that I was happy before this unfortunate Revolution. I feel that I am no longer so; therefore I regret the change. This is the only mode of reasoning adapted to persons in my situation. If I attach myself to the Mother Country, which is 3000 miles from me, I become what is called an enemy to my own region; if I follow the rest of my countrymen, I become opposed to our ancient masters: both extremes appear equally dangerous to a person of so little weight and consequence as I am, whose energy and example are of no avail. As to the argument on which the dispute is founded, I know little about it. Much has been said and written on both sides, but who has a judgment capacious and clear enough to decide? The great moving principles which actuate both parties are much hid from vulgar eyes, like mine; nothing but the plausible and the probable are offered to our contemplation. The innocent class are always the victim of the few; they are in all countries and at all times the inferior agents, on which the popular phantom is erected; they clamour, and must toil, and bleed, and are always sure of meeting with oppression and rebuke. It is for the sake of the great leaders on both sides, that so much blood must be spilt; that of the people is counted as nothing. Great events are not achieved for us, though it is *by* us that they are principally accomplished; by the arms, the sweat, the lives of the people. Books tell me so much that they inform me of nothing. Sophistry, the bane of freemen, launches forth in all her deceiving attire! After all, most men reason from passions; and shall such an ignorant individual as I am decide, and say this side is right, that side is wrong? Sentiment and feeling are the only guides I know. Alas, how should I unravel an argument, in which reason herself hath given way to brutality and bloodshed! What then must I do? I ask the wisest lawyers, the ablest casuists, the warmest patriots; for I mean honestly. Great Source of wisdom! inspire me with light sufficient to guide my benighted steps out of this intricate maze! Shall I discard all my ancient principles, shall I renounce that name, that nation which I held once so respectable? I feel the powerful attraction; the sentiments they inspired grew with my earliest knowledge, and were grafted upon the first rudiments of my education. On the other hand, shall I arm myself against that country where I first drew breath, against the playmates of my youth, my bosom friends, my acquaintance?—the idea makes me shudder! Must I be called a parricide, a traitor, a villain, lose the esteem of all those whom I love, to preserve my own; be shunned like a rattlesnake, or be pointed at like a bear? I have neither heroism nor magnanimity enough to make so great a sacrifice. Here I am tied, I am fastened by numerous strings, nor do I repine at the pressure they cause; ignorant as I am, I can pervade the utmost extent of the calamities which have already overtaken our poor afflicted country. I can see the great and accumulated ruin yet extending itself as far as the theatre of war has reached; I hear the groans of thousands of families now ruined and desolated by our aggressors. I cannot count the multitude of orphans this war has made; nor ascertain the immensity of blood we have lost. Some have asked, whether it was a crime to resist; to repel some parts of this evil. Others have asserted, that a resistance so general makes pardon unattainable, and repentance useless; and dividing the crime among so many, renders it imperceptible. What one party calls meritorious, the other denominates flagitious. These opinions vary, contract, or expand, like the events of the war on which they are founded. What can an insignificant man do in the midst of these jarring contradictory parties, equally hostile to persons situated as I am? And after all who will be the really guilty?—Those must certainly who fail of success. Our fate, the fate of thousands, is then necessarily involved in the dark wheel of fortune. . . .

II

. . . Self-preservation is above all political precepts and rules, and even superior to the dearest opinions of our minds; a reasonable accommodation of ourselves to the various exigencies of the time in which we live, is the most irresistible precept. To this great evil I must seek some sort of remedy adapted to remove or to palliate it; situated as I am, what steps should I take that will neither injure nor insult any of the parties, and at the same time save my family from that certain destruction which awaits it, if I remain here much longer? Could I insure them bread, safety, and subsistence, not the bread of idleness, but that earned by proper labour as heretofore; could this be accomplished by the sacrifice of my life, I would willingly give it up. I attest before heaven, that it is only for these I would wish to live and to toil: for these whom I have brought into this miserable existence. I resemble, methinks, one of the stones of a ruined arch, still retaining that pristine form that anciently fitted the place I occupied, but the centre is tumbled down; I can be nothing until I am replaced, either in the former circle, or in some stronger one. I see one on a smaller scale, and at a considerable distance, but it is within my power to reach it: and since I have ceased to consider myself as a member of the ancient state now convulsed, I willingly descend into an inferior one. I will revert into a state approaching nearer to that of nature, unencumbered either with voluminous laws, or contradictory codes, often galling the very necks of those whom they protect; and at the same time sufficiently remote from the brutality of unconnected savage nature. Do you, my friend, perceive the path I have found out? it is that which leads to the tenants of the great ――――― village of ―――――, where, far removed from the accursed neighbourhood of Europeans, its inhabitants live with more ease, decency, and peace, than you imagine: where, though governed by no laws, yet find in uncontaminated simple manners all that laws can afford. Their system is sufficiently complete to answer all the primary wants of man, and to constitute him a social being, such as he ought to be in the great forest of nature. There it is that I have resolved at any rate to transport myself and family: an eccentric thought, you may say, thus to cut asunder all former connections, and to form new ones with a people whom nature has stamped with such different characteristics! But as the happiness of my family is the only object of my wishes, I care very little where we be, or where we go, provided that we are safe, and all united together. Our new calamities being shared equally by all, will become lighter; our mutual affection for each other, will in this great transmutation become the strongest link of our new society, will afford us every joy we can receive on a foreign soil, and preserve us in unity, as the gravity and coherency of matter prevents the

world dissolution. Blame me not, it would be cruel in you, it would beside be entirely useless; for when you receive this we shall be on the wing . . .

III

. . . I will either die in the attempt or succeed; better perish all together in one fatal hour, than to suffer what we daily endure. I do not expect to enjoy in the village of ――――― an uninterrupted happiness; it cannot be our lot, let us live where we will; I am not founding my future prosperity on golden dreams. Place mankind where you will, they must always have adverse circumstances to struggle with; from nature, accidents, constitution; from seasons, from that great combination of mischances which perpetually lead us to new diseases, to poverty, etc. Who knows but I may meet in this new situation, some accident from whence may spring up new sources of unexpected prosperity? Who can be presumptuous enough to predict all the good? Who can forsee all the evils, which strew the paths of our lives? But after all, I cannot but recollect what sacrifice I am going to make, what amputation I am going to suffer, what transition I am going to experience. Pardon my repetitions, my wild, my trifling reflections, they proceed from the agitations of my mind, and the fulness of my heart; the action of thus retracing them seems to lighten the burden, and to exhilarate my spirits; this is besides the last letter you will receive from me; I would fain tell you all, though I hardly know how. Oh! in the hours, in the moments of my greatest anguish, could I intuitively represent to you that variety of thought which crowds on my mind, you would have reason to be surprised, and to doubt of their possibility. Shall we ever meet again? If we should, where will it be? On the wild shores of ―――――. If it be my doom to end my days there, I will greatly improve them; and perhaps make room for a few more families, who will choose to retire from the fury of a storm, the agitated billows of which will yet roar for many years on our extended shores. Perhaps I may repossess my house, if it be not burnt down; but how will my improvements look? why, half defaced, bearing the strong marks of abandonment, and of the ravages of war. However, at present I give everything over for lost; I will bid a long farewell to what I leave behind. If ever I repossess it, I shall receive it as a gift, as a reward for my conduct and fortitude. Do not imagine, however, that I am a stoic—by no means: I must, on the contrary, confess to you, that I feel the keenest regret, at abandoning an house which I have in some measure reared with my own hands. Yes, perhaps I may never revisit those fields which I have cleared, those trees which I have planted, those meadows which, in my youth, were a hideous wilderness, now converted by my industry into rich pastures and pleasant lawns. If in Europe it is praiseworthy to be attached to paternal inheritances, how much more natural, how much more powerful must the tie be with us, who, if I may be permitted the expression, are the founders, the creators of our own farms! When I see my table surrounded with my blooming offspring, all united in the bonds of the strongest affection, it kindles in my paternal heart a variety of tumultuous sentiments, which none but a father and a husband in my situation can feel or describe. Perhaps I may see my wife, my children, often distressed, involuntarily recalling to their minds the ease and abundance which they enjoyed under the paternal roof. Perhaps I may see them want that bread which I now leave behind; overtaken by diseases and penury, rendered more bitter by the recollection of former days of opulence and plenty. Perhaps I may be assailed on every side by unforeseen accidents, which I shall not be able to prevent or to alleviate. Can I contemplate such images without the most unutterable emotions? My fate is determined; but I have not determined it, you may assure yourself, with-

out having undergone the most painful conflicts of a variety of passions;—interest, love of ease, disappointed views, and pleasing expectations frustrated;—I shuddered at the review! Would to God I was master of the stoical tranquillity of that magnanimous sect; oh, that I were possessed of those sublime lessons which Appollonius of Chalcis gave to the Emperor Antoninus! I could then with much more propriety guide the helm of my little bark, which is soon to be freighted with all that I possess most dear on earth, through this stormy passage to a safe harbour; and when there, become to my fellow passengers, a surer guide, a brighter example, a pattern more worthy of imitation, throughout all the new scenes they must pass, and the new career they must traverse. I have observed notwithstanding, the means hitherto made use of, to arm the principal nations against our frontiers. Yet they have not, they will not take up the hatchet against a people who have done them no harm. The passions necessary to urge these people to war, cannot be roused, they cannot feel the stings of vengeance, the thirst of which alone can compel them to shed blood: far superior in their motives of action to the Europeans, who for sixpence a day, may be engaged to shed that of any people on earth. They know nothing of the nature of our disputes, they have no ideas of such revolutions as this: a civil division of a village or tribe, are events which have never been recorded in their traditions: many of them know very well that they have too long been the dupes and the victims of both parties; foolishly arming for our sakes, sometimes against each other, sometimes against our white enemies. They consider us as born on the same land, and, though they have no reasons to love us, yet they seem carefully to avoid entering into this quarrel, from whatever motives. I am speaking of those nations with which I am best acquainted, a few hundreds of the worst kind mixed with whites, worse than themselves, are now hired by Great Britain, to perpetuate those dreadful incursions. In my youth I traded with the ————, under the conduct of my uncle, and always traded justly and equitably; some of them remember it to this day. Happily their village is far removed from the dangerous neighbourhood of the whites; I sent a man last spring to it, who understands the woods extremely well, and who speaks their language; he is just returned, after several weeks absence, and has brought me, as I had flattered myself, a string of thirty purple wampum, as a token that their honest chief will spare us half of his wigwam until we have time to erect one. He has sent me word that they have land in plenty, of which they are not so covetous as the whites; that we may plant for ourselves, and that in the meantime he will procure for us some corn and some meat; that fish is plenty in the waters of ————, and that the village to which he had laid open my proposals, have no objection to our becoming dwellers with them. I have not yet communicated these glad tidings to my wife, nor do I know how to do it; I tremble lest she refuse to follow me; lest the sudden idea of this removal rushing on her mind, might be too powerful. I flatter myself I shall be able to accomplish it, and to prevail on her; I fear nothing but the effects of her strong attachment to her relations. I will willingly let you know how I purpose to remove my family to so great a distance, but it would become unintelligible to you, because you are not acquainted with the geographical situation of this part of the country. Suffice it for you to know, that with about twenty-three miles land carriage, I am enabled to perform the rest by water; and when once afloat, I care not whether it be two or three hundred miles. I propose to send all our provisions, furniture, and clothes to my wife's father, who approves of the scheme, and to reserve nothing but a few necessary articles of covering; trusting to the furs of the chase for our future apparel. Were we imprudently to encumber ourselves too much

with baggage, we should never reach to the waters of ————, which is the most dangerous as well as the most difficult part of our journey; and yet but a trifle in point of distance. I intend to say to my negroes—In the name of God, be free, my honest lads, I thank you for your past services; go, from henceforth, and work for yourselves; look on me as your friend, and fellow labourer; be sober, frugal, and industrious, and you need not fear earning a comfortable subsistence.—Lest my countrymen should think that I am gone to join the incendiaries of our frontiers, I intend to write a letter to Mr. ————, to inform him of our retreat, and of the reasons that have urged me to it. The man whom I sent to ———— village, is to accompany us also, and a very useful companion he will be on every account.

You may therefore, by means of anticipation, behold me under the Wigwam; I am so well acquainted with the principal manners of these people, that I entertain not the least apprehension from them. I rely more securely on their strong hospitality, than on the witnessed compacts of many Europeans. As soon as possible after my arrival, I design to build myself a wigwam, after the same manner and size with the rest, in order to avoid being thought singular, or giving occasion for any railleries; though these people are seldom guilty of such European follies. I shall erect it hard by the lands which they propose to allot me, and will endeavour that my wife, my children, and myself may be adopted soon after our arrival. Thus becoming truly inhabitants of their village, we shall immediately occupy that rank within the pale of their society, which will afford us all the amends we can possibly expect for the loss we have met with by the convulsions of our own. According to their customs we shall likewise receive names from them, by which we shall always be known. My youngest children shall learn to swim, and to shoot with the bow, that they may acquire such talents as will necessarily raise them into some degree of esteem among the Indian lads of their own age; the rest of us must hunt with the hunters. I have been for several years an expert marksman; but I dread lest the imperceptible charm of Indian education, may seize my younger children, and give them such a propensity to that mode of life, as may preclude their returning to the manners and customs of their parents. I have but one remedy to prevent this great evil; and that is, to employ them in the labour of the fields as much as I can; I am even resolved to make their daily subsistence depend altogether on it. As long as we keep ourselves busy in tilling the earth, there is no fear of any of us becoming wild; it is the chase and food it procures, that have this strange effect. Excuse a simile—those hogs which range in the woods, and to whom grain is given once a week, preserve their former degree of tameness; but if, on the contrary, they are reduced to live on ground nuts, and on what they can get, they soon become wild and fierce. For my part, I can plough, sow, and hunt, as occasion may require; but my wife, deprived of wool and flax, will have no room for industry; what is she then to do? Like the other squaws, she must cook for us the nasaump, the ninchickè, and such other preparations of corn as are customary among these people. She must learn to bake squashes and pumpkins under the ashes; to slice and smoke the meat of our own killing, in order to preserve it; she must cheerfully adopt the manners and customs of her neighbours, in their dress, deportment, conduct, and internal economy, in all respects. Surely if we can have fortitude enough to quit all we have, to remove so far, and to associate with people so different from us; these necessary compliances are but part of the scheme. The change of garments, when those they

carry with them are worn out, will not be the least of my wife's and daughter's concerns: though I am in hopes that self-love will invent some sort of reparation. Perhaps you would not believe that there are in the woods looking-glasses, and paint of every colour; and that the inhabitants take as much pains to adorn their faces and their bodies, to fix their bracelets of silver, and plait their hair, as our forefathers the Picts used to do in the time of the Romans. Not that I would wish to see either my wife or daughter adopt those savage customs; we can live in great peace and harmony with them without descending to every article; the interruption of trade hath, I hope, suspended this mode of dress. My wife understands inoculation perfectly well, she inoculated all our children one after another, and has successfully performed the operation on several scores of people, who, scattered here and there through our woods, were too far removed from all medical assistance. If we can persuade but one family to submit to it, and it succeeds, we shall then be as happy as our situation will admit of; it will raise her into some degree of consideration, for whoever is useful in any society will always be respected. If we are so fortunate as to carry one family through a disorder, which is the plague among these people, I trust to the force of example, we shall then become truly necessary, valued, and beloved; we indeed owe every kind office to a society of men who so readily offer to assist us into their social partnership, and to extend to my family the shelter of their village, the strength of their adoption, and even the dignity of their names. God grant us a prosperous beginning, we may then hope to be of more service to them than even missionaries who have been sent to preach to them a Gospel they cannot understand . . .

1752 ∾ *Philip Freneau* ∾ 1832

OF FRENCH Huguenot parentage, Philip Freneau was born in New York, January 2, 1752. When he was ten years old, his family moved to his grandfather's thousand-acre estate in New Jersey. Before his graduation at Princeton in 1771, he had already achieved distinction as a poet and with H. H. Brackenridge composed the commencement poem, "The Rising Glory of America." After teaching school for a while on Long Island, Freneau wrote voluminously as a propagandist for the Revolution and was at various times a sea-captain, a postal employee, a newspaper editor in New York and Philadelphia, and a translator in Jefferson's Department of State. Returning to the family's New Jersey estate in 1793, he devoted his time to writing for American periodicals. Between 1797 and 1798 he was editor of one of the most interesting literary magazines of the period, *The Time-Piece and Literary Companion*, published in New York. Because of poverty he had to return to work as a master of coast-line freight ships between 1803 and 1807. In 1815 his home burned and, without adequate resources, he moved to the adjacent town in Freehold, New Jersey. He was frozen to death December 18, 1832, in a snowstorm.

[During his lifetime, collections of his poetry were published in 1786, 1788, 1795, 1809, and 1815. For both of the following poems, the text of the 1809 edition has been used. See other poems by Freneau in Book I, Parts 1 and 2.]

DISCOVERY
[1786 (written 1772)]

SIX thousand years in these dull regions pass'd
'Tis time, you'll say, we knew their bounds at last,
Knew to what skies our setting suns retire,
And where the wintry suns expend their fire;
What land to land protracts the varied scene,   5
And what extended oceans roll between;
What worlds exist beneath *antarctic* skies,
And from *Pacific* waves what verdant islands rise.
  In vain did Nature shore from shore divide:
Art formed a passage and her waves defied: 10
When his bold plan the master pilot drew

Dissevered worlds stept forward at the view,
And lessening still the intervening space,
Disclosed new millions of the human race.
Proud even of toil, succeeding ages joined   15
New seas to vanquish, and new worlds to find;
Age following age still farther from the shore,
Found some new wonder that was hid before,
'Till launched at length, with avarice doubly bold,
Their hearts expanding as the world grew old,   20
Some to be rich, and some to be renowned,
The earth they rifled, and explored it round.
  Ambitious Europe! polished in thy pride,
Thine was the art that toil to toil allied,

Thine was the gift, to trace each heavenly
    sphere,   25
And seize its beams, to serve ambition
    here:
Hence, fierce *Pizarro* stock'd a world with
    graves,
Hence *Montezuma* left a race of slaves—
Which project suited best with heaven's
    decree
To force new doctrines, or to leave them
    free?—   30
Religion only feigned to claim a share,
Their riches, not their souls, employed
    your care—
  Alas! how few of all that daring train
That seek new worlds embosomed in the
    main,
How few have sailed on virtue's nobler
    plan,   35
How few with motives worthy of a man!—
While through the deep-sea waves we saw
    them go
Where'er they found a *man* they made a
    foe;
Superior only by superior art,
Forgot the social virtues of the heart,   40
Forgetting still, where'er they madly ran,
That sacred friendship binds mankind to
    man,
Fond of exerting power untimely shewn,
The momentary triumph all their own!
Met on the wrecks and ravages of time, 45
They left no native master of their clime,
His trees, his towns, with hardened front
    they claimed,
Seized every region that a despot named
And forced the oath that bound him to
    obey
Some prince unknown, ten thousand miles
    away.   50
  Slaves to their passions, man's imperious
    race,
Born for contention, find no resting place,
And the vain mind, bewildered and per-
    plext,
Makes this world wretched to enjoy the
    next.
Tired of the scenes that Nature made
    their own,   55

They rove to conquer what remains un-
    known:
Avarice, undaunted, claims whate'er she
    sees,
Surmounts earth's circle, and foregoes all
    ease;
Religion, bolder, sends some *sacred* chief
To bend the nations to her own belief.   60
To their vain standard Europe's sons
    invite,
Who hold no other *world* can think aright.
Behold their varied tribes, with self ap-
    plause,
First in religion, liberty, and laws,
And while they bow to cruelty and blood, 65
Condemn the Indian with his milder god—
Ah, race to justice, truth, and honour blind,
Are thy convictions to convert mankind—!
Vain pride—convince them that your own
    are just,
Or leave them happy, as you found them
    first.   70
  What charm is seen through Europe's
    realms of strife
That adds new blessings to the savage
    life?—
On them warm suns with equal splendour
    shine,
Their each domestic pleasure equals thine,
Their native groves as soft a bloom dis-
    play,   75
As self-contented roll their lives away,
And the gay soul, in fancy's visions blest,
Leaves to the care of chance her heaven
    of rest.—
  What are the arts that rise on Europe's
    plan
But arts destructive to the bliss of man? 80
What are all wars, wher'er the marks you
    trace,
But the sad records of our world's dis-
    grace?
Reason degraded from her tottering throne,
And precepts, called divine, observed by
    none.
  Blest in their distance from that bloody
    scene,   85
Why spread the sail to pass the gulphs
    between?—

If winds can waft to ocean's utmost verge,
And there new islands and new worlds
    emerge—
If wealth, or war, or science bid thee
    roam,
Ah, leave religion and thy laws at home, 90
Leave the free native to enjoy his store,
Nor teach destructive arts, unknown be-
    fore—
Woes of their own those new found worlds
    invade,
There, too, fierce passions the weak soul
    degrade,
Invention there has winged the unerring
    dart,   95
There the swift arrow vibrates to the
    heart,
Revenge and death contending bosoms
    share,
And pining envy claims her subjects
    there.—
Are these too few?—then see despotic
    power
Spends on a throne of logs her busy
    hour.   100
Hard by, and half ambitious to ascend,
Priests, interceding with the gods, attend—
Atoning victims at their shrines they lay,
Their crimson knives tremendous rites dis-
    play,
Or the proud despot's gore remorseless
    shed,   105
Through life detested, or adored when dead.
  Born to be wretched, search this globe
    around,
Dupes to a few the race of man is found!
Seek some new world in some new climate
    plac'd,
Some gay *Ta-ia* [1] on the watery waste, 110
Though Nature clothes in all her bright
    array,
Some proud tormentor steals her charms
    away:
Howe'er she smiles beneath those milder
    skies,
Though men decay the monarch never dies!
Howe'er the groves, howe'er the gardens
    bloom,   115
A *monarch* and a *priest* is still their doom!

THE INDIAN BURYING GROUND
[1788]

In spite of all the learned have said,
I still my old opinion keep;
The *posture,* that *we* give the dead,
Points out the soul's eternal sleep.

Not so the ancients of these lands—   5
The Indian, when from life released,
Again is seated with his friends,
And shares again the joyous feast. [2]

His imaged birds, and painted bowl,
And venison, for a journey dressed,   10
Bespeak the nature of the soul,
Activity, that knows no rest.

His bow, for action ready bent,
And arrows, with a head of stone,
Can only mean that life is spent,   15
And not the old ideas gone.

Thou, stranger, that shalt come this way,
No fraud upon the dead commit—
Observe the swelling turf, and say
They do not *lie,* but here they *sit.*   20

Here still a lofty rock remains,
On which the curious eye may trace
(Now wasted, half, by wearing rains)
The fancies of a ruder race.

Here still an aged elm aspires,   25
Beneath whose far-projecting shade
(And which the shepherd still admires)
The children of the forest played!

There oft a restless Indian queen
(Pale *Shebah,* with her braided hair)   30
And many a barbarous form is seen
To chide the man that lingers there.

---

[1] A reference to Otaheite, an island in
the Southern Pacific.

[2] A reference to some Indians' custom of
burying their dead in a sitting posture.

By midnight moons, o'er moistening dews,
In habit for the chase arrayed,
The hunter still the deer pursues,   35
The hunter and the deer, a shade!

And long shall timorous fancy see
The painted chief, and pointed spear,
And Reason's self shall bow the knee
To shadows and delusions here.   40

1739 ∽ *William Bartram* ∽ 1823

WILLIAM BARTRAM was a Philadelphia Quaker and the son of the botanist, John Bartram. Accompanying his father upon scientific explorations, he became intensely interested in all forms of natural history, traveled extensively on his own account, and kept a journal, which was first published in Philadelphia in 1791 under the title, *Travels through North and South Carolina, Georgia, East and West Florida.* This book had a wide European circulation, attracting the excited attention of Coleridge, Wordsworth, Lamb, Southey, and Chateaubriand. Among American travelers of the 18th Century, Bartram most strikingly combined the artist's interest in colorful descriptive detail, the humanitarian's love for all phases of God's creation, and the scientist's flair for factual accuracy and orderly classification in recording his impressions of plants, animals, Indians, and landscape.

[The title of the following selection has been supplied by the present editors.]

OF SNAKES
[1791]

BUT LET us again resume the subject of the rattle snake; a wonderful creature, when we consider his form, nature, and disposition. It is certain that he is capable by a puncture or scratch of one of his fangs, not only to kill the largest animal in America, and that in a few minutes time, but to turn the whole body into corruption; but such is the nature of this dreadful reptile, that he is never known to strike until he is first assaulted or fears himself in danger, and even then always gives the earliest warning by the rattles at the extremity of the tail. I have in the course of my travels in the Southern states (where they are the largest, most numerous and supposed to be the most venomous and vindictive) stept unknowingly so close as almost to touch one of them with my

feet, and when I perceived him he was already drawn up in circular coils ready for a blow. But, however incredible it may appear, the generous, I may say magnanimous creature lay as still and motionless as if inanimate, his head crouched in, his eyes almost shut. I precipitately withdrew, unless when I have been so shocked with surprise and horror as to be in a manner riveted to the spot, for a short time not having strength to go away; when he often slowly extends himself and quietly moves off in a direct line, unless pursued, when he erects his tail as far as the rattles extend, and gives the warning alarm by intervals. But if you pursue and overtake him with a shew of enmity, he instantly throws himself into the spiral coil; his tail by the rapidity of its motion appears like a vapour, making a quick tremulous sound; his whole body swells through rage, continually rising and falling as a bellows; his beautiful parti-coloured skin becomes speckled and rough by dilatation; his head and neck are flattened, his cheeks swollen and his lips constricted, discovering his mortal fangs; his eyes red as burning coals, and his brandishing forked tongue of the colour of the hottest flame, continually menaces death and destruction, yet never strikes unless sure of his mark.

The rattle snake is the largest serpent yet known to exist in North America. I have heard of their having been seen formerly, at the first settling of Georgia, seven, eight, and even ten feet in length, and six or eight inches diameter; but there are none of that size now to be seen; yet I have seen them above six feet in length, and above six inches in thickness, or as large as a man's leg; but their general size is four, five, and six feet in length. They are supposed to have the power of fascination in an eminent degree, so as to inthral their prey. It is generally believed that they charm birds, rabbits, squirrels and other animals, and by steadfastly looking at them possess them with infatuation: be the cause what it may, the miserable creatures undoubtedly strive by every possible means to escape, but alas! their endeavours are in vain, they at last lose the power of resistance, and flutter or move slowly, but reluctantly, towards the yawning jaws of their devourers, and creep into their mouths, or lie down and suffer themselves to be taken and swallowed.

Since, within the circle of my acquaintance, I am known to be an advocate or vindicator of the benevolent and peaceable disposition of animal creation in general, not only towards mankind, whom they seem to venerate, but always towards one another, except where hunger or the rational and necessary provocations of the sensual appetite interfere, I shall mention a few instances, amongst many, which I have had an opportunity of remarking during my travels, particularly with regard to the animal I have been treating of. I shall strictly confine myself to facts.

When on the sea coast of Georgia, I consented, with a few friends, to make a party of amusement at fishing and fowling on the Sapello, one of the sea coast islands. We accordingly descended the Alatamaha, crossed the sound and landed on the North end of the island, near the inlet, fixing our encampment at a pleasant situation, under the shade of a grove of Live Oaks, and Laurels,[1] on the high banks of a creek which we ascended, winding through a salt marsh, which had its source from a swamp and savanna in the island: our situation elevated and open, commanded a comprehensive landscape; the great ocean, the foaming surf breaking on the sandy beach, the snowy breakers on the bar, the endless chain of islands, checkered sound and high continent all appearing before us. The diverting toils of the day were not fruitless, affording us opportunities of furnishing ourselves plentifully with a variety of game, fish and oysters for our supper.

About two hundred yards from our camp was a cool spring, amidst a grove of the odoriferous Myrica: the winding path to this salubrious fountain led through a grassy savanna. I visited the spring several times in the night, but little did I know, or any of my careless drowsy companions, that every time we visited the fountain we were in imminent danger, as I am going to relate. Early in the morning, excited by unconquerable thirst, I arose and went to the spring; and having, thoughtless of harm or danger, nearly half past the dewy vale, along the serpentine foot-path, my hasty steps were suddenly stopped by the sight of a hideous serpent, the formidable rattle snake, in a high spiral coil, forming a circular mound half the height of my knees, within six inches of the narrow path. As soon as I recovered my senses and strength from so sudden a surprise, I started back out of his reach, where I stood to view him: he lay quiet

[1] Magnolia grandiflora, called by the inhabitants the Laurel—Bartram's note.

whilst I surveyed him, appearing no way surprised or disturbed, but kept his half-shut eyes fixed on me. My imagination and spirits were in a tumult, almost equally divided betwixt thanksgiving to the supreme Creator and Preserver, and the dignified nature of the generous though terrible creature, who had suffered us all to pass many times by him during the night, without injuring us in the least, although we must have touched him, or our steps guided therefrom by a supreme guardian spirit. I hastened back to acquaint my associates, but with a determination to protect the life of the generous serpent. I presently brought my companions to the place, who were, beyond expression, surprised and terrified at the sight of the animal, and in a moment acknowledged their escape from destruction to be miraculous; and I am proud to assert, that all of us, except one person, agreed to let him lie undisturbed, and that person was at length prevailed upon to suffer him to escape.

Again, when in my youth, attending my father on a journey to the Catskill Mountains, in the government of New-York; having nearly ascended the peak of Giliad, being youthful and vigorous in the pursuit of botanical and novel objects, I had gained the summit of a steep rocky precipice, ahead of our guide; when just entering a shady vale, I saw, at the root of a small shrub, a singular and beautiful appearance, which I remember to have instantly apprehended to be a large kind of Fungus which we call Jews ears, and was just drawing back my foot to kick it over; when at the instant, my father being near, cried out, "A rattle snake, my son!" and jerked me back, which probably saved my life. I had never before seen one. This was of the kind which our guide called a yellow one, it was very beautiful, speckled and clouded. My father pleaded for his life, but our guide was inexorable, saying he never spared the life of a rattle snake, and killed him; my father took his skin and fangs.

Some years after this, when again in company with my father on a journey into East Florida, on the banks of St. Juan, at Fort Picolata, attending the congress at a treaty between that government and the Creek Nation, for obtaining a territory from that people to annex to the new government; after the Indians and a detachment from the garrison of St. Augustine had arrived and encamped separately, near the fort, some days elapsed before the business of the treaty came on, waiting the arrival of a vessel from St. Augustine, on board of which were the presents for the Indians. My father employed this time of leisure in little excursions round about the fort; and one morning, being the day the treaty commenced, I attended him on a botanical excursion. Some time after we had been rambling in a swamp about a quarter of a mile from the camp, I being ahead a few paces, my father bid me observe the rattle snake before and just at my feet. I stopped and saw the monster formed in a high spiral coil, not half his length from my feet: another step forward would have put my life in his power, as I must have touched if not stumbled over him. The fright and perturbation of my spirits at once excited resentment; at that time I was entirely insensible to gratitude or mercy. I instantly cut off a little sapling, and soon dispatched him: this serpent was about six feet in length, and as thick as an ordinary man's leg. The encounter deterred us from proceeding on our researches for that day. So I cut off a long tough withe or vine, which fastening round the neck of the slain serpent, I dragged him after me, his scaly body sounding over the ground, and entering the camp with him in triumph, was soon surrounded by the amazed multitude, both Indians and my countrymen. The adventure soon reached the ears of the commander, who sent an officer to request that, if the snake had not bit himself, he might have him served up for his dinner. I readily delivered up the body of the snake to the cooks, and being that day invited to dine at the governor's table, saw the snake served up in several dishes; governor Grant being fond of the flesh of the rattle snake. I tasted of it, but could not swallow it. I, however, was sorry after killing the serpent, when coolly recollecting every circumstance. He certainly had it in his power to kill me almost instantly, and I make no doubt but that he was conscious of it. I promised myself that I would never again be accessory to the death of a rattle snake, which promise I have invariably kept to. This dreaded animal is easily killed; a stick no thicker than a man's thumb is sufficient to kill the largest at one stroke, if well directed, either on the head or across the back; nor can they make their escape by running off, nor indeed do they attempt it when attacked.

The moccasin snake is a large and horrid serpent to all appearance, and there are very terrifying stories related of him by the inhabitants of the Southern states, where they greatly abound, particularly in East Florida; that their bite is always incurable, the flesh for a considerable space about the wound rotting to the bone, which then becomes carious and a general mortification ensues, which infallibly destroys the patient; the members of the body rotting and dying by piecemeal: and that there is no remedy to prevent a lingering miserable death but by immediately cutting away the flesh to the bone, for some distance around about the wound. In shape and proportion of parts they much resemble the rattle snake, and are marked or clouded much after the same manner, but the colours more dull and obscure; and in their disposition seem to agree with that dreadful reptile, being slow of progression, and throwing themselves in a spiral coil ready for a blow when attacked. They have one peculiar quality, which is this, when discovered, and observing their enemy to take notice of them, after throwing themselves in a coil, they gradually raise their upper mandible or jaw until it falls back nearly touching

their neck, at the same time slowly vibrating their long purple forked tongue, their crooked poisonous fangs directed right at you, which gives the creature a most terrifying appearance. They are from three to four and even five feet in length, and as thick as a man's leg; they are not numerous, yet too common, and a sufficient terror to the miserable naked slaves, who are compelled to labour in the swamps and low lands where only they abound.

I never could find any that knew an instance of any person's losing their life from the bite of them only by hearsay. Yet I am convinced it is highly prudent for every person to be on their guard against them. They appear to be of the viper tribe, from their swelling of their body, and flattening their neck when provoked, and from their large poisonous fangs: their head, mouth and eyes are remarkably large.

There is another snake in Carolina and Florida called the moccasin, very different from this; which is a very beautiful creature, and I believe not of a destructive or vindictive nature. These when grown to their greatest size are about five feet in length, and near as thick as a man's arm; their skin scaly but smooth and shining, of a pale grey and sky colour ground, uniformly marked with transverse undulatory ringlets or blotches of a deep nut brown, edged with red or bright Spanish brown. They appear innocent, very active and swift, endeavouring to escape from one; they have no poisonous fangs. These are seen in high forest lands, about rotten logs or decayed fallen limbs of trees, and they harbour about old log buildings. They seem to be a species, if not the very same snake, which in Pennsylvania and Virginia is called the wampum snake; but here in warmer Southern climes they grow to a much larger size, and from the same accident their colour may be more variable and deeper. They are by the inhabitants asserted to be dangerously venomous, their bite incurable, &c. But as I could never learn an instance of their bite being mortal, or attended with any dangerous consequence, and have had frequent opportunities of observing their nature and disposition, I am inclined to pronounce them an innocent creature, with respect to mankind.

The bastard rattle snake, by some called ground rattle snake, is a dangerous little creature: their bite is certainly mortal if present medical relief is not administered: they seem to be much of the nature of the asp or adder of the old world.

This little viper is in form and colour much like the rattle snake, but not so bright and uniformly marked; their head is broader and shorter in proportion to the other parts of their body: their nose prominent and turned upwards: their tail becomes suddenly small from the vent to the extremity, which terminates with three minute articulations, resembling rattles: when irritated they turn up their tail, which vibrates so quick as to appear like a mist or vapour, but causes little or no sound or noise; yet it is the common report of the inhabitants, that they cause that remarkable vehement noise, so frequently observed in forests in the heat of summer and autumn, very terrifying to strangers, which is, probably, caused by a very sable small insect of the genus cicadae, or which are called locusts in America; yet it is possible I may be mistaken in this conjecture. This dangerous viper is from eight to ten inches in length, and of proportionable thickness. They are spiteful, snippish creatures; and throwing themselves into a little coil, they swell and flatten themselves, continually darting out their head; and they seem capable of springing beyond their length. They seem destitute of the pacific disposition and magnanimity of the rattle snake, and are unworthy of an alliance with him. No man ever saves their lives, yet they remain too numerous, even in the oldest settled parts of the country.

The green snake is a beautiful innocent creature: they are from two to three feet in length, but not so thick as a person's little finger; of the finest green colour. They are very abundant, commonly seen on the limbs of trees and shrubs; they prey upon insects and reptiles, particularly the little green chameleon: and the forked tailed hawk or kite feeds on both of them, snatching them off the boughs of the trees.

The ribband snake is another very beautiful innocent serpent: they are eighteen inches in length, and about the thickness of a man's little finger; the head is very small; the ground colour of a full, clear vermilion, variegated with transverse bars or zones of a dark brown, which people fancy represents a ribband wound round the creature's body: they are altogether inoffensive to man, and are in a manner domestic, frequenting old wooden buildings, open grounds and plantations.

The chicken snake is a large, strong and swift serpent, six or seven feet in length, but scarcely so thick as a man's wrist; they are of a cinereous, earthy colour, and striped longitudinally with broad lines or lists, of a dusky or blackish colour. They are a domestic snake, haunting about houses and plantations; and would be useful to man if tamed and properly tutored, being great devourers of rats, but they are apt to disturb hen-roosts and prey upon chickens. They are as innocent as a worm with respect to venom, are easily tamed, and soon become very familiar.

The pine or bull snake is very large and inoffensive with respect to mankind, but devours squirrels, birds, rabbits, and every other creature it can take as food. They are the largest snake yet known in North America, except the rattle snake, and perhaps exceed him in length: they are pied black and white: they utter a terrible loud hissing noise, sounding very hollow and like distant thunder, when irritated, or at the time of incubation, when the males contend with each other for the desired female. These serpents are also called horn snakes, from their tail terminating with a hard, horny spur, which they vibrate very quick when disturbed, but they never attempt to strike with it; they have dens in the earth, whither they retreat precipitately when apprehensive of danger.

There are many other species of snakes in the regions of Florida and Carolina; as the water snake, black snake, garter snake, copper belly, ring neck, and two or three varieties of vipers, besides those already noticed in my journal.

1762 ∽ *Mrs. Susanna Haswell Rowson* ∽ 1824

WHEN the belletristic impulse manifested itself markedly in American writing, themes which had been recurrent in the earlier literature of exploration, settlement, and travel persisted in poetry, fiction, and drama, especially the theme of the relations between the colonists and the Indians. Mrs. Susanna Haswell Rowson's *Reuben and Rachel; or, Tales of Old Times,* Boston, 1798, which helped prepare the way for the vogue of historical romance in the time of Cooper, Simms, and John Neal, is a "novel" which sweeps through ten generations from the period of Columbus to the early 18th Century and displays a disregard for historical accuracy that outdoes that of the most fancy-free cloak-and-sword or cut-and-thrust romancers of a later day. Mrs. Rowson's right to be called an American novelist may be fairly disputed, but must ultimately be allowed.

She was born in Portsmouth, England, in 1762; accompanied her father, Lieutenent Haswell of the British Army, to Boston in 1769; lived for some time at Nantasket; after the Haswells were deported in 1777, returned to her native country, married William Rowson, and became a novelist and an actress. Her career as actress brought her to Philadelphia in 1793 and later to Boston, where, after retiring from the stage in 1798, she was mistress of a girls' school of long and reputable standing. She died in Boston in 1824.

Most of Mrs. Rowson's novels—both those written in England and those written in America—are of the school of sensibility, such as *Charlotte; a Tale of Truth,* London, 1791, later an American best seller under the title of *Charlotte Temple; Trials of the Human Heart,* Philadelphia, 1795; *Sarah; or, The Exemplary Wife,* first appearing under the title of *Sincerity* in the *Boston Weekly Magazine* during 1803-1804; and *Charlotte's Daughter; or, The Three Orphans,* Boston, 1828, a sequel to *Charlotte Temple.*

[The following selections from *Reuben and Rachel* are all from Vol. I and consist of a part of Chap. XVI, all of Chap. XVIII, and a part of Chap. XIX. The text has been modernized from that of the first edition; the title has been supplied by the present editors to suggest that these selections form a complete and unified short-story in themselves. The elder Dudley, father of the family that suffers a fate in some respects comparable to but far more romantic than that of the Rowlandsons during King Philip's War, is represented as a grandson of the important historical figure, Sir Ferdinando Gorges, colonization promoter, who is elaborately characterized in an earlier chapter of the novel. These selections are particularly remarkable for their humanization of the Indian.]

THE WHITE SACHEM

[1798]

I

THE morning was fine. Cheerful had Arabella arose, and, surrounded by her little family, joined with their father in their morning adorations to the Giver of all good. This indispensable duty performed, Dudley went to superintend his mowers; and his wife, calling her girls, to the number of five, together, began the usual task of instruction. But the little Rachel was not inclined to be quiet; she was more inclined for play than sitting still. She climbed up in her mother's lap, kissed her, and in childish sport threw the book on the floor.

"It is impossible to attend seriously to anything," said her mother, "whilst this little mad-cap is here. Do, William, take her into the garden." William obeyed, and from the garden strayed into an adjoining wood, where, intent on a book which his father had desired him to peruse with attention, he suffered the little prattler to play round, pluck flowers, and catch grasshoppers.

Arabella was pursuing her employment, with all the delight a fond mother can feel, who marks the daily improvement of her children, and sees them eagerly striving who should foremost reach the goal of perfection, when an old servant, the only male then about the house, rushed into the apartment, exclaiming, with looks of horror, "The natives! The natives!" Starting from her seat with precipitation, she turned towards the window, and saw a band of savages crossing through a field of corn, not very far from the house. "Fly! fly! my children," she cried, taking the two youngest by the hand; and followed by the eldest, they rushed out of a door that led a con-

trary way to the road the savages were coming.

There was in the very wood where William had wandered with his infant sister a cavern formed by the cunning hand of nature, the recesses of which Arabella had in days of happiness frequently explored. Her presence of mind in this terrifying exigence did not forsake her. With hasty, yet trembling steps, she led her children thither; nor was it till resting on the ground in its remotest winding, when she felt her five children hanging about her, that she recollected William and Rachel.

"Oh, my children, my children!" exclaimed she, suddenly starting up. "We are all here, mother," they answered with united voices.

"But where! Oh where!" cried she franticly, "is your brother William, and your sister Rachel?" "Oh! my poor brother, my dear, sweet little sister," said the children severally; "Let us go back, mother, let us go back and look for them."

"No, my darlings, no!" she replied, sinking again on the ground, and drawing them closer towards her; "that would indeed be to suffer you to run into the very claws of the destroyer. The great God of heaven and earth inspired me with the thought of bringing you here for safety; he will, I trust, protect us; and his power to protect and save, even from the jaws of death, is equal throughout this wide-extended universe. He can guard all your brothers, your sister, and your father too. Let us kneel, my children, and implore his mercy."

At the mention of their father, and the recollection of their brothers, Charles, James, and Christopher, who were in the field with him, the girls wept aloud. Arabella poured forth her soul in fervent prayer, and the kneeling innocents, in broken accents, sobbed *amen*.

The female servants, terrified at the approach of the savages, in their eagerness to elude them ran directly into their power, and instantly became victims to their fury. They dispatched them with their tomahawks, and, stripping off their scalps, kept them as proofs of their endeavors to extirpate the English from amongst them. The man who had alarmed his mistress ran out of the house by the same way she had taken; but thinking it would be right to alarm his master, instead of following her, made the best of his way to the field where the mowers were at work.

The savages, having rifled the house of provisions, wearing apparel, and everything which they conceived would be any ways serviceable to themselves, set fire to it, and then departed, with horrid yells of exultation at having done all the mischief in their power to an English family. William was, at the moment the flames burst forth, just returning with his little sister. His father's house on fire, and a band of Indians in frantic rage hastening towards them, was a sight that filled with the most horrid presages the breast of William. He saw there would be no way to escape them; so, clasping the infant Rachel in his arms, he knelt on the ground, fear almost suspending every faculty.

One of the foremost of the savage troop had raised his tomahawk to dispatch the boy; but the child, with one arm clinging to her brother's neck, extended the other little innocent hand as if to ward off the blow, and screaming, cried, "Don'tee, don'tee." At that moment a squaw, who held a papoose at her breast, threw herself before the suppliant children, and said in their own language, "You shall not kill the infant."

The attempt seemed to have been the impulse of the moment, for it required but little persuasion to turn the Indian from his purpose; he dropped the instrument of death; William started from the ground, ran to the kind-hearted woman, kissed her hands, bathed them with his tears, and pointing to the sky, gave her to understand that the Power who dwelt above that azure firmament would reward her. Her own infant being returned to her back (the mode in which the Indian women in general carry their children), she took Rachel in her arms; and William being made to assist in carrying their plunder, they proceeded on their march; a weary march it was to the poor little captives.

Otawee, for that was the name of their protectress, did all she could to make little Rachel easy, but she continued at intervals to cry for her mother; and William, his feet lacerated by the sharp flints and thorns he encountered in the rugged paths through which he was obliged to pass, his heart bleeding for what he thought must have been the fate of his beloved parents, brothers, and sisters, proceeded as well as he could till towards the evening of the second day, when, overcome with fatigue, grief, and long fasting (for he could not eat the food they offered him), he fell fainting to the earth. Fortunately they were now near the end of their march, or it is more than probable the unfortunate boy would have been left to perish in the woods. As it was, two young Indians bore him between them to the water-side, put him in a canoe, and Otawee sitting down beside him, threw water on his face, raised his head on her knee, and forcing him to swallow a little spirits, he by degrees recovered.

This party of plunderers were natives of Narhaganset. Two or three unprincipled and licentious Europeans having made incursions amongst them, plundering their little settlements, burning their wigwams, and practicing other enormities, as must certainly awaken a spirit of revenge in the bosom of persons better regulated than those of untutored savages, several families who had been particularly injured formed themselves into a party, and, embarking in their canoes, proceeded up Connecticut river, landing wherever they thought there was no fear of opposition to them, and wreaking their vengeance on the unguarded and innocent inhabitants.

Dudley had, from his first settlement,

been a man of *peace;* happy in his family, fully employed in cultivating and improving his little domain, he stepped not out of his own domestic concerns, except it was to assist a neighbor (for any European family, settled within twenty miles, was at that early period termed a neighbor) or to instruct a new settler in the best mode of clearing his lands; to which instructions he ever readily added any help his servants, horses, oxen, or even himself could give.

Such a man could hardly be supposed an object of enmity to any; but his habitation had been marked by an Indian who had strayed from his companions. Its lonely situation, its flourishing appearance, which promised plenty of plunder without fear of opposition, determined them to attack it; but when they had committed this outrage on a quiet, inoffensive family, they well knew it would not be long before they were pursued. They accordingly made all the haste they could to the place where they had left their canoes, and, embarking with the plunder they had obtained, proceeded immediately home. On their way thither, meeting with a party who came from the more eastern parts, and, fearful that the young captives they had, might, if seen, betray them to the English, they sold them, and William and Rachel were carried to a greater distance than it could hardly be believed possible for the Indians to proceed in their little birch canoes. When being landed on a very wild and totally uncultivated place, they were marched three days journey from the sea-shore, and presented to the squaw of their sachem for servants.

Otooganoo was a man naturally gentle, fond of peace, and eager in his endeavors to promote the welfare of his people. He had ever recommended to them to treat the strangers who were come to settle amongst them with hospitality; but it was not in his power to restrain the impetuosity of youth, or to curb the licentious hand of the rapacious. When the young captives were brought to his wigwam, he rebuked those who brought them, and bade William

to banish all his fears; for he would be a father to him, and, if ever opportunity offered, restore him to his natural parent. His wife was particularly pleased with little Rachel, and the kindness of these two good Indians rendered the lives of the brother and sister as comfortable as the nature of their situation would admit of . . .

II

In the year 1674 the war between the native Americans and the European settlers raged with uncommon fury. William Dudley, who had, with his little sister, been carried into captivity in 1661, had now become a personage of great consequence amongst them. Otooganoo, the sachem to whom he had been presented, possessing talents naturally good, and thirsting for knowledge, yet unable to attain it, soon learnt, from his conversations with William, that he could in some measure gratify this very laudable desire to be instructed. William, though young, had, by attention to the documents of his father and the milder instructions of his mother, obtained a very decent knowledge of reading, writing, arithmetic, geography, and history.

Otooganoo no sooner made this discovery than William became to him the most valuable thing he possessed. "I will certainly restore him to his European friends," said he, "but he shall first teach me all he knows. In the meantime, I will be kind to him, nor shall his little sister ever want a friend or protector; as soon as he has imparted to me his stock of knowledge, I will certainly send him to his friends."

Thus argued Otooganoo. But, alas! human nature will be human nature; and when the period arrived that he had gleaned all the knowledge poor William had to impart, his heart was so attached to him, his society had afforded him so many days, months, years of real felicity that he made to his own conscience daily fresh excuses for not sending him from him.

William himself, though he frequently

spoke of them, and expressed a wish to see his parents, no longer felt that ardent desire to return to them, which he experienced in the early days of his captivity. He had become insensibly attached to Otooganoo; and as, from the effects of his instructions, his protector had made rapid advances towards civilization, had entirely lost his natural ferocity, and attained such a degree of rational information as made him a pleasant companion, William felt that attachment daily increase.

Otooganoo had a daughter. Oberea was full five years younger than William; she was tall, straight, and finely formed. She was, at the time of his arrival amongst them, a lively girl of ten years old, wild as the reindeer, that with fleet steps bounds over the frozen plains of Lapland, and untutored as it is possible for a human being to be. Her looks, her words, her actions, were the genuine impulses of nature.

As the little Rachel increased in years, it was the employment of her brother's leisure hours to instruct her in the English language in the best manner possible. The book he had with him, on the morning of his capture, was of infinite assistance to him, as by looking at that, he was enabled to form a very tolerable alphabet upon bark, using some of their strong dye instead of ink; and this alphabet served alike Otooganoo, Rachel, and Oberea, who delighted in partaking their lessons and profited daily by his instructions.

Educated under the immediate eye of a woman like Arrabella, it may naturally be supposed William, though young, had imbibed very strong and just ideas of female delicacy and decorum, and these ideas he labored incessantly to impress on the mind of his sister. Oberea listened attentively and treasured every sentence he uttered in her heart. She had heard him tell his sister that his country-women were the most charming women in the world, and Oberea early formed the wish of being thought charming in the eyes of William. This wish was a powerful talisman to correct the bad effects of habit, and at the age of seventeen, she was so much superior in manner to her uncivilized associates, that William, without being aware of it, adored the lively statue his art had animated.

He was not sensible of the excess of his tenderness for the charming Indian, till an accident, by nearly depriving him of her, convinced him at once how necessary she was to his happiness. Some Indians, who dwelt in the town with them, having by traffic with the Europeans, who inhabited the sea-coasts, procured two or three muskets, one was brought and presented to Otooganoo, who, being mightily pleased with the present, loaded it, with a design of going out in pursuit of game; but not putting his design in immediate execution, it was left standing in one corner of the wigwam. A young savage, particularly attached to Oberea, took it up to examine it, and, not understanding how to handle it properly, touched the trigger. It went off, and the contents were lodged in the right side of Oberea.

William heard the report, and the instant cries of his sister; he flew to them, and, entering, saw both his sister and her he now found he loved equal with her, lying on the ground, which was covered with blood. The young man, frantic at what had happened, told what he had done, and that he feared he had killed both the girls; but Rachel's fall was the effect of sudden surprise, and it was soon discovered she was not in the least hurt. But Oberea wounded, to all appearance dying, was an object distracting to William. He raised her in his arms, called aloud for help, and, having assisted his sister and an old squaw to staunch the blood and bind up the wounds, which were chiefly in the fleshy part of the arm, and having seen her open her eyes and sign to him that she knew him, he walked backwards and forwards, watching her as she dozed, sometimes applying a feather to her mouth to be satisfied she still breathed, and often kneeling down to kiss her hand, which lay motionless on the outside of the bed.

Otooganoo, during the time she was

thought in danger, observed the extreme solicitude of William and, when she was perfectly recovered, thus addressed him: "You have been to me, young Englishman, a friend, a companion, an instructor, now above eight years. I love you with sincerity, and I believe you love me."

"Do you doubt?" asked William eagerly.

"No, I do not for a moment doubt your sincerity. But I have also discovered that you love my daughter. Your counsels and instructions have rendered her unfit to match with any of her own countrymen; you are now almost become one of us; take her, then, to wife; and when age, infirmity, or death shall occasion me to cease from the cares of life, supply my place, govern my people, direct them by your wisdom, teach them the real value of well-constructed laws, encourage them in studying the arts of war; yet lead them, by your example and forbearance, to cultivate a social and commercial intercourse, and to preserve peace with your countrymen, who are become their neighbors, as long as they can preserve it with honor."

William, weaned from his natural friends, tenderly attached to Oberea, perhaps not altogether insensible to the charms of power, and harboring a fond hope that by this union with the family of a sachem he might promote the interests of his countrymen in general, and be the cement to bind them in bonds of lasting amity, listened with delighted attention, plighted his vows of love and constancy to Otooganoo, and in a few days ratified those vows by binding himself, by the most sacred of all ties, to protect and love through life his charming Oberea.

Otooganoo lived to see his son-in-law equally beloved and respected with himself, to embrace a grandson whom William called Reuben: "For," said he, "I have been a bondman and a servant unto my wife's father, and this my first-born shall pay my ransom."

As the old sachem felt his hour approaching, he called his chiefs, and the oldest men of his tribe, about him; and,

taking the little Reuben in his arms, whilst Oberea, William, and Rachel stood on his right hand, thus addressed them:

"Warriors and chiefs, natives and undoubted lords of this vast country, listen to your departing father. I have ruled over you now above forty years; I have ever found you obedient to my commands, and affectionate to my family. But the great Spirit whose throne is on the loftiest mountain and whose breath, passing over the great lake, can make it rage even as the wild tiger, when, suddenly springing from his secret hiding place, he tears and mangles his defenceless prey, or, softly moving over its broad surface, renders it smooth, beautiful, and enticing as is the siren, who charms but to destroy—this wondrous, incomprehensible Spirit, who gave me life and motion, recalls the precious gift, and in a short time I shall be dust."

Otooganoo paused; his whole soul was filled with the sublimity of the Being of whom he had been speaking, and a moment was given to feelings beyond expression exquisite. Recovering the firmness of his voice, he thus proceeded:

"Friends, countrymen, children, had I a son, I well know your unanimous consent would nominate him my successor. Behold, then, the son of my choice, the friend of my soul, the husband of my daughter. He is brave, he is wise, he is humane! alike competent to prosecute war with vigor or preserve peace with honor. He is, you will say, a son of our invaders, of our common enemy. But consider them as enemies no longer. Bury the war-hatchet twenty feet under ground, and smoke the great pipe of peace, whose fragrance may ascend even to the heaven of heavens. Hail these Europeans as brethren, and follow henceforth their precept of doing as you would be done by."

"We will! we will!" they all exclaimed; when Otooganoo thus continued:

"Chiefs, elders, and brother warriors, in recommending to your choice this young man, I mean not to relinquish the affection you have ever shown my family. No. Behold this child, the son of my daughter; in him you see your rightful sachem. But I am passing from this world to the land of spirits, and this infant is incompetent to supply my place. Who then so able, who so worthy as his father, to govern and direct you, and instruct the young sachem how to guard your liberties, and preserve your love inviolate?"

Otooganoo ceased, and an old warrior thus replied: "The offspring of Otooganoo, the son of Oberea, will ever be honored and respected. We are content to receive, during his childhood, the Englishman William, and to adopt the new faith thou hast lately taught and practiced. As the Europeans deal by us, so deal we by them, and the great Spirit judge us both."

Otooganoo survived this conference but a few days; he passed (to use his own expression) to the land of spirits, and William Dudley was chosen sachem in his stead, by the unanimous voice of the whole tribe.

"As the Europeans deal by us, so deal we by them, and the great Spirit judge us both." This was the oath they took, and most religiously did they keep it. But if the professors of Christianity practice not themselves what they would teach to others, who can blame the savage, who (in seeking his own gratification, or promoting his own interest, regards not the happiness or interest of a fellow creature) follows but the example set him?

The new settlers made daily encroachments on the native inhabitants, drove them from their lands, robbed them of their wives, and made their children prisoners. Was it in human nature to bear these injuries tamely? No; they resented them. And even William himself, though his heart bled at what must be the consequence, could not attempt to repel the spirit of just vengeance that actuated the minds of all. War was declared on both sides, and pursued with unremitting fury.

Amongst the young warriors that lived under the government of William was Yankoo. He was intrepid, bold, and daring. He hated the Europeans; yet, spite of that hate

which seemed inherent in his nature, his heart was susceptible of tenderness for one of the race. The beauty of Rachel had penetrated his soul. He loved, revealed his love, and found it was returned.

The war continuing to rage, it became necessary for the sachem in person to quit his home and head his warriors. The undaunted Oberea would follow her husband to the field, and Rachel, though naturally more timid, yet having her nerves newstrung by affection, accompanied her. They encamped near the sea-shore. By the morning's dawn they expected the enemy.

Yankoo passed a few hours the preceding evening in the wigwam of Oberea. "Oh! my friend," said Rachel, as she was parting from him, "be careful of your own life for my sake; and if at any time your tomahawk should be raised against an ancient Englishman, pause for a moment, and think, perhaps it may be the father of Rachel, and let the idea disarm your rage."

"It would do so," replied Yankoo, "did I not at the same time remember that every Englishman is the enemy of my country."

"Would you not spare my father then?" said Rachel.

"No! not even my own father in such a cause," answered the warrior, and broke from her embrace. Rachel retired to her bed and passed the night in tears.

III

The situation or feelings of William Dudley were at this period by no means enviable. Ruler over a nation of savages, who by their attachment and fidelity had conciliated his affection, his principles would by no means suffer him to desert their cause in the hour of danger; yet, remembering that his natural parents were Europeans, and the tenderness he once experienced for them not being extinct in his bosom, he felt his heart divided between two separate interests; and if at any time a skirmish took place, he would think that, perhaps, amongst the killed or wounded of the enemy he might have to lament a father or a brother. And whilst he was publicly obliged to appear rejoiced at the success of the Indians, he would privately lament the defeat of his own countrymen.

The soul of Rachel was equally agitated. Alas! who can describe the feelings of a heart thus divided? She dared not pray, for to which party could she wish success? "Oh! save, protect, and support my father," she would cry; then in a moment recollecting, she would wring her hands and cry, "Oh! poor Yankoo." It is anguish only to be felt, it is impossible to convey the smallest idea of its excruciating tortures, to any who have not experienced the agonizing effects of divided affection.

The English had been driven to the very borders of the sea; the Indians had pursued them with unremitting fury, ravaging the habitations and giving the unoffending inmates a quick passport to eternal rest with their tomahawks, nor command nor entreaty could restrain their impetuosity.

William had followed a party led by Yankoo to a house situated in a deep wood. As they approached, a cry of terror issued from the dwelling. The heart of William throbbed with anxiety; he quickened his steps and arrived at the door just as Yankoo had dragged forth by his venerable locks a man whom he no sooner beheld than he recognized the features of his father. The arm was raised that was meant to destroy him.

"Hold, monster! barbarian!" exclaimed William, and, throwing himself on the body of his father, received the falling weapon on his own shoulder. It fell heavy, it sunk deep, and the blood issued in a torrent from the wound.

Yankoo recoiled with horror; he beheld his ruler, his friend, and more than those, the brother of Rachel, weltering in gore, wounded even unto death, and by his hand. He knelt upon the ground, he took his hand. "Oh! brave warrior," said he, "why did you throw yourself in my way?" William raised himself and, pointing to old Mr. Dudley, cried, "To save a father."

The old gentleman, in some measure relieved from his fright, endeavored to rise from the earth; but, hearing the expression of father from the lips of one whom he supposed an Indian chief, the truth began to dawn upon his mind. He knelt beside the dying sachem and, taking his hand, looked earnestly in his face, and cried, "Is it indeed possible? are you my son?"

"Your own son William," replied the bleeding warrior.

"But alas!" said the old man, "you are, I fear, mortally wounded."

"And if I am," replied the heroic William, "it is a glorious wound; for I give my life to preserve the life of him from whom I received it."

As he finished these words, he fell back and his eyes closed. The whole party were now assembled round their wounded chief; they raised him from the earth and bore him into his father's cottage, where, confined by infirmity, was the unfortunate, patient Arrabella. She had heard the exclamations of her husband; her heart had not yet become callous to misery. The beholding her long-lost son was double agony, since she but beheld his closing scene. He recovered a moment after they had laid him on the bed, gazed on the countenance of his mother, faintly articulated her name, and his last breath passed in imploring a blessing on her.

The news of their sachem's death, and by whom, soon reached the tribe William had governed, and they repaired to the place of his decease, vowing revenge on his murderer; for in that light they looked upon Yankoo. But when they rushed furiously into the house, intending to wreak their vengeance on him, the mute sorrow depicted on his face, as with his arms folded on his bosom he stood contemplating the mangled form of his departed friend, for a moment disarmed their rage. He saw them enter, and advancing intrepidly towards them,

"Friends, countrymen, and brother warriors," said he, with a firm voice, "that I have incurred your hatred, that your rage is justly excited, is a truth I pretend not to evade or deny. I have deserved death at your hands, and behold, here I stand prepared to meet it. Strike; I will not flinch; or lead me forth and let me experience the most cruel tortures, I will not complain; nor sigh nor groan shall escape my lips. Alas! if torture could wring them from me, how loud would my lamentations now be! The chief whom we all loved, the man we all revered, is gone to the land of spirits; is gone to that Father, that great First Cause, of whom we have so often heard him speak. He is passed from us, and my hand gave the passport, signing it with his blood."

He paused, and his untamed spirit swelled even to his eyes; but he repelled the tokens of his sensibility, that were almost bursting from the glistening orbits, and struggling for a moment to recover the firmness of his voice, proceeded:

"Thou art gone, brave chief!" (turning as he spoke towards the body of his friend), "thou art gone; and where shall thy equal be found to supply thy place? Thou wert bold and daring as the young lion, and like him, generous and noble, exerted not thy power against the feeble and defenceless. Firm and unshaken in asserting the rights of innocence, as the mountain whose foundation is in the center of the earth and whose top reacheth unto the clouds; yet gentle as the southwest breeze on an evening in the blossom season, and complying as the willow, that inclines its head as the breeze passes. Thy voice was the voice of wisdom. Thy words taught lessons which thy example enforced. But thou art gone! and where shall thy equal be found to supply thy place? Thou wert glorious as the sun at his uprising, mild and beautiful as the beams of the moon, when it dances on the bosom of the lake which the wind gently agitates. In the chase, fleet as the young stag, and the arrow from thy bow never missed its aim. Thou didst speak, and none could refuse to believe; thou didst command, and none but were eager to obey. The bad loved, whilst they feared thee; the good adored, and endeavored to

imitate thee. Under thy wise government we rested in peace, on mats made of osiers; our wigwams were improved, our bows better strung, our corn was multiplied an hundredfold, and our skins dried with more care. In peace thou wert as the dew of the evening, refreshing and invigorating all who lived beneath thy influence; and in war terrible as the tempest that breaks the tall pine, roots up the stubborn oak, and makes the forest tremble, as it rushes with tremendous fury through it. Thy enemies beheld thee, and fear shook their souls; thou wert the father of thy people, Oh! valiant sachem. But thou art gone—by my hand gone! and where shall thy equal be found to supply thy place?"

The numerous affecting images he had called together, whilst speaking the eulogium of the deceased, had now awakened feelings too powerful to be repressed. The afflictions of his heart burst forth in loud lamentations. The rage of his countrymen was totally subdued. They dropped their tomahawks and joined him in piercing cries and groans, repeating at intervals, "Our chief, our warrior, our friend is gone, and who can supply his place?"

Arrabella had not lived so many years in the very bosom of America, at different times obliged to have some kind of intercourse with the natives, without attaining a considerable knowledge of their language. She listened whilst Yankoo was speaking, and, as he enumerated the virtues of her son, she felt that, amongst the tears of regret that fell for his death, were some of exultation that he had deserved such an eulogium, and her heart was consoled.

But who can paint the anguish, the distress of Rachel, or the distraction of Oberea? When they heard the fatal tidings, they sought the body of their husband, brother, chief. But here nor tears nor cries declared their sorrow. When the soul is too full, language is of little use. There are no words capable of expressing real affliction.

Oberea led her son Reuben (now nearly six years old) to the bed on which lay the corpse of his father, and, pointing to the body, pronounced in a tone deeply mournful, "Behold!"

"My father!" said the boy, and, terrified at his ghastly appearance, clasped his arms round his mother and hid his face in her bosom. She seated herself on the side of the bed, folded her arms round her child, and, resting her head on his shoulder, appeared the mute image of despair.

The feelings of Rachel would have been equally poignant, had they not been directed to another channel. She had, as she entered the apartment, faintly articulated the word *brother*. Arrabella caught the sound, and, calling her daughter by name, Rachel was folded in a moment to her bosom, and in the embrace of a new-found mother felt a relief from her sorrows. Dudley kissed his daughter with tenderness, but the lively affection he had once experienced towards his children was now almost extinct. It had indeed for a moment revived when he heard the voice of William, but the icy finger of death had silenced that voice forever, and the heart of Dudley could no more vibrate with the exquisite delights springing from paternal love.

By the united efforts of Rachel and Arrabella, Oberea was at last aroused from that state of apparent insensibility into which she had fallen. Rachel released her arms from the neck of her child, and drew her gently towards her mother, who soothed, caressed, and called her her dear daughter, the relic of her beloved William.

At the name of William, she started. Arrabella perceived she had awakened her attention, and from her own son made a quick transition to the son of Oberea. She begged her to call forth her fortitude, to exert the faculties of her mind, and as she loved her husband, for his sake, live, to protect and instruct his son.

"I am his mother," said she; "have I not reason to lament the loss of a son so worthy? But that he was worthy is my comfort. Had he not a thousand virtues? and will you not strive to live, to teach his son to emulate his father, to be as good, as great, as wise as he was?"

Oberea cast her eyes on her child, then suddenly covering her face with part of her garments, she wept aloud. The desired end was now attained. Acute sensibility being relieved by the effusion, Arrabella was silent, and, leaving nature to its course, waited till the first rude shock was past before she attempted, by reasoning, to convince her of the inutility of grieving. Alas! it was a lesson (hard as it was) which Arrabella had long since learnt; but it is what the children of sorrow all learn. Repeated disappointment first blunts the keenness of our feelings; corroding sorrow, from overstraining, weakens the chords of sensibility, and at length age and infirmity, creeping by chilling yet almost imperceptible degrees through the whole system, totally relaxes every fibre, whilst the heart becomes cold and impenetrable as the ice on the highest summit of the Andes.

The Indians mourned with sincerity for their departed sachem. The chiefs and elders assembled, declared that Reuben, when of a proper age, should fill the seat of government, till when they entreated Dudley to take the charge of his education. In the meantime, they prepared to inter the remains of their chief, with every mark of respect and honor. But on the very day when the solemnity was to be performed, the Europeans made an unexpected sally on them, routed the main body, killed many, and took the remainder prisoners. Amongst those who fell was Yankoo. He fought, defending the house where lay the body of William, and died exhorting his companions to conquer or die.

Dudley, his wife and daughter, with Oberea and Reuben, were conducted to an English settlement, where the former sunk into a state of debility nearly approaching second childhood, and in a few months rested from all his sorrows. When this event took place, Arrabella determined to return to England, partly from the hope of her native air acting as a restorative to her health, and partly in the wish of securing to Reuben the estates of his great-grandfather Sir Ferdinando Gorges; besides which, she knew that in Europe she could procure him to be properly educated, which the very imperfect state of literature in America, at that early period, would not allow her to hope, should she continue there. Rachel of consequence accompanied her mother; and Oberea, attached to them by every tender tie, would not be left behind. "The mother and the son of my William," said she, "I will follow to the furthermost part of the earth."

It was early in the spring of 1680 when the widow Arrabella Dudley, her daughter, daughter-in-law, and grandson arrived in England, from which she had been absent about thirty-four years. . . .

American Literature Before 1800

II
RELIGIOUS THOUGHT AND EXPERIENCE

1584 ∾ *John Cotton* ∾ 1652

SON of a prosperous barrister, John Cotton was born in 1584 in Derby, Derbyshire; received his B.A. in 1603 from Trinity College, Cambridge, and his M.A. from Emmanuel College in 1606; served as fellow and lecturer at the college; was ordained in 1610; became vicar of St. Botolph's in Boston, Lincolnshire, in 1612; and was made B.D. in 1613. During the following twenty years he was a leading Anglican churchman and won enviable repute both for the quality of his preaching and the profundity of his learning in "divinity." In 1633 he resigned under pressure because of his nonconformist views, came to New England, was chosen teacher of the Boston church, and was prominent thereafter in the councils of the colony.

One crucial moment in his New England career was the "Antinomian Crisis" of 1636-38, during which Anne Hutchinson claimed sanction for her religious "Enthusiasm" from his mystically-tinged expositions of the doctrine of grace. Another such moment was his controversy with Roger Williams over religious toleration in a series of publications between 1644 and 1648. At once flattered and embarrassed by Anne Hutchinson's discipleship, by turns tender-hearted toward her sincerity and intensity and apprehensive of her capacity for heresy, he teetered precariously between the opposing factions, but in the outcome proved adamant in his orthodoxy, denouncing her errors and acquiescing in her exile. He managed to hold his own with the redoubtable Williams in logical rigor, scriptural citation, and polemic rhetoric. Author of a small library of works expounding Puritan divinity and polity, he died in 1652.

As a theologian Cotton was most notable, as Anne Hutchinson discerned, for his emphasis on grace as one of the most essential of God's several "operations." It was the mysterious means by which God raised one from the category of the damned to that of the elect. To receive it, the individual must prepare himself carefully by taking advantage of all legitimate avenues to it, including meditation, the study of Scripture, church-attendance; whether one received it depended ultimately on God's incalculable will alone; reception of it was not sudden and complete, not an unheralded inspirational seizure by the Holy Ghost, but an elaborately gradual process, a mystical life's pilgrimage toward beatitude, a step-by-step immersion in the boundless, laving waters of supernal goodness.

[This view of grace is conveyed in part by the following selections, modernized from the first edition of his *The Way of Life,* a volume of sermons which Cotton most probably preached in England, where Anne Hutchinson first heard and doted on his eloquence. The titles have been supplied by the present editors. For further selections from Cotton's works, see Book I, Part 3.]

RECEIVING GRACE
[1641]

. . . NOW the spirit of grace which God
bestows upon his people is partly a spirit
of adoption and partly a spirit of regeneration, both one spirit, only having divers
manner of workings. . . . We receive the
adoption of sons by our redemption by the
Lord Jesus, and then we receive the spirit
of the Son into our hearts, whereby we are
not only adopted, but regenerated and
made the sons of God, and thereby come
to cry Abba,[1] Father. . . .

But how shall I get a spirit of grace?
First, if God be pleased to open thine eyes
to see what a dry soul thou hast and art
sensible of the dryness of thine own heart
wanting sap and moisture and art therefore athirst for want of grace, then it is
very hopeful God will give thee a spirit of
grace, *Esau* [Isaiah] 44.3. To whom will
God give the spirit of grace? To those that
are dry and thirsty, that feel themselves
athirst for want of grace. Though thou
canst not yet call God Father, nor look at
him as thy friend, yet if thou hast but a
thirsty soul and longest for grace, under
sense of thine own droughtiness, then God
will not deny the Holy Ghost to them that
ask him, *Luk.* 11.9, 13. And suppose God
will not give you a spirit of grace for any
love's sake you discern in God towards you
and any neighborly and fatherly care he
hath over you, yet if God give thee but an
heart to feel thine own want and thirst
after it, when you ask such bread for your
souls, he will not give you a stone, but he
will give you a spirit of grace.

Secondly, by a diligent hearing the
Word of God, *Gal.* 3.2., implying that he
doth usually breathe the spirit by the
breath of his Word; he breathes indeed
where he lists, *Joh.* 3.8. But yet as it is
with material churches, if there be any
wind anywhere, it will gather about them;
so doth the spirit of grace most gather to
the congregation of God's people; if there
be any breath of the spirit stirring, usually
it is there.

Thirdly, another means is that, *Prov.*
1. 22, 23, "How long will ye love scorning?
turn ye at my reproof, and I will pour out
my spirit upon you," implying that if God
give a man but so much honesty of heart
as to leave his folly and scorning and turn
from his evil ways, then God will pour out
his spirit upon him: implying, that which
hinders the spirit from being poured out
upon us is because we will not part with
some or other beastly sin, as pride, hypocrisy, etc. The spirit of grace will not
come but into an heart in some measure
prepared; the spirit of grace will not
come into a cage of unclean lusts; but if
God give a man a heart to lend a patient
ear to a reproof and lay down all scorning
and turn from his loose and unprofitable
courses, then the promise is evident, *I
will pour out my spirit upon you.*

WADING IN GRACE
[1641]

For further encouragements hereunto,
consider that place, *Ezech.* 47.3, 4, 5. It
shows you the marvelous efficacy of the
spirit of grace in the days of the Gospel.
First a Christian wades in the rivers of
God his grace up to the ankles with some
good frame of spirit, yet but weakly, for
a man hath strength in his ankle bones,
Acts 3., and yet may have but feeble knees,
Heb. 12. 12. So far as you walk in the
waters, so far are you healed; why then
in the next place he must wade till he
come to the knees, go a thousand cubits,
a mile further, and get more strength to
pray and to walk on in your callings with
more power and strength.

Secondly, but yet a man that wades but
to the knees, his loins are not drenched, for
nothing is healed but what is in the water.
Now the affections of a man are placed in
his loins, God tries the reins; a man may
have many unruly affections, though he be

---

[1] Aramaic for father: used by Jesus and
his contemporaries and by Greek-speaking
Christian Jews to refer to the Deity.

paddling in the ways of grace; he may walk on in some evenness and yet have many distempered passions and may have just cause to complain of the rottenness of his heart in the sight of God; why then, thou hast waded but to the knees, and it is a mercy that thou art come so far; but yet the loins want healing, why, wade a mile further then; the grace of God yet comes too shallow in us, our passions are yet unmortified, so as we know not how to grieve in measure, our wrath is vehement and immoderate; you must therefore wade until the loins be girt with a golden girdle; wade an-end and think all is not well until you be so deep, and by this you may take a scantling what measure of grace is poured out upon you. And if thou hast gone so far that God hath in some measure healed thy affections, that thou canst be angry and sin not, etc., it is well, and this we must attain to. But suppose the loins should be in a good measure healed, yet there is more goes to it than all this; and yet when a man is come thus far, he may laugh at all temptations and bless God in all changes. But yet go another thousand cubits, and then you shall swim; there is such a measure of grace in which a man may swim as fish in the water, with all readiness and dexterity, gliding an-end, as if he had water enough to swim in; such a Christian doth not creep or walk but he runs the ways of God's commandments; whatever he is to do or to suffer he is ready for all, so every way drenched in grace as let God turn him any way, he is never drawn dry.

c. 1590 ∾ *Anne Hutchinson* ∾ 1643

ANNE HUTCHINSON has been made the heroine of Theda Kenyon's epic poem, *Scarlet Anne*, New York, 1939, and of several earlier novelized biographies—one of which claims for her the distinction of having founded the first Woman's Club in America. She was born in England about 1590, a daughter of the Rev. Francis Marbury, who was imprisoned and unfrocked for his criticism of Anglican episcopacy, and a niece of such gentry as Sir Edward Marbury, of the manor of Girsby, and of Sir Erasmus Dryden, of Canons Ashby, ancestor of the great John Dryden. In 1612 she married young William Hutchinson, a rising draper of Alford, in Lincolnshire, and fell under the spell of John Cotton's preaching at St. Botolph's, near Alford. When Cotton left for New England, she and her family followed him in 1634.

Gaining popularity among the women of Boston because of her knowledge of midwifery, Anne held at her home weekly meetings, during which matters of doctrine raised in sermons were discussed with unwontedly frank and pointed criticism of specific ministers. These meetings and a debate between her and a group of ministers at the home of John Cotton brought down upon Anne the bitter disapprobation of the orthodox. Anne and her followers, her brother-in-law, the Rev. John Wheelwright, who came to Boston in 1636 and was given a church at Wollaston, and the new governor of the colony, the aristocratic young Harry Vane, constituted a group which, in the eyes of John Winthrop and his followers, were encouraging an heretical religious Enthusiasm as a means to bulwark themselves in political power. Winthrop succeeded in unseat-

ing Vane and in passing a kind of immigration law to keep out potential
Hutchinsonians. After Vane was called back to England to attend to urgent
family concerns, Wheelwright, previously arraigned for an allegedly seditious
fast-day sermon, was excommunicated and banished.

Then the Winthrop faction instituted official proceedings to determine
Anne's orthodoxy. Finally, as a result of her claim to special revelations from
God in a speech in her own defense in 1637, she was denounced as a dangerous
heretic and sent into sequestration while pregnant. When she persisted in
denying the charges drawn up against her, and showed a disposition to recant
her presumed recantations of error, she was formally exiled from the precincts of the Bay in March, 1638, in the last month of her pregnancy.
Although she found sanctuary at Roger Williams' Providence, she suffered a
miscarriage. After the death of her unswervingly loyal husband, she moved with
her numerous family to a tract of land near Pelham Bay, in New Netherland.
In 1643 the family was massacred by Indians whom the Dutch had not paid
for the land. A daughter, Susan, taken captive by the Indians, survived; a son,
Edward, was ancestor of Thomas Hutchinson, perhaps the greatest of the
colonial historians of New England, and, ironically enough, the Tory governor
of Massachusetts just before the outbreak of the Revolution.

[Although Anne was not a writer, her 1637 speech on her revelations was
recorded, as a part of her trial testimony, by John Winthrop and Thomas
Weld in their incontinently partisan and obviously self-justifying *A Short
Story of the Rise, reign, and ruine of the Antinomians, Familists & Libertines,
that infected the Churches of New England*, London, 1644. From the first
edition of this work, Anne's speech is here reprinted in a modernized text. It
reveals that her conception of grace was close to that of the early Quakers,
with their "Inner Light." She thought of herself as coached and prompted by
the voice of God, as having his intimate, privately vouchsafed warrant for her
decisions, actions, feelings, and opinions. Since most orthodox Protestants in
England regarded such a claim as evidence of traffic with Satan, it is little
wonder that Winthrop and his followers looked on her as dangerous, for such
traffic, if condoned, might bring down the wrath of God on the entire colony.
Their conviction on this point was doubtless sincere, but was somewhat complicated by their other probable motives—fear of her as a threat to their
political supremacy, apprehension that her demagogic appeal to her revelations
might eventually undermine the institution of a learned ministry upon which
public order rested.]

SPEECH ON THE REVELATIONS
[1644]

WHEN I was in Old England, I was
much troubled at the constitution of the

churches there, so far as I was ready to
have joined to the separation, whereupon
I set apart a day for humiliation by myself, to seek direction from God, and then
did God discover unto me the unfaithful-

ness of the churches and the danger of them, and that none of those ministers could preach the Lord Jesus aright, for he had brought to my mind that in the 1 *John* 4.3, every spirit that confesseth not that Jesus Christ is come in the flesh is the spirit of Anti-Christ; I marvelled what this should mean, for I knew that neither Protestants nor Papists did deny that Christ was come in the flesh; and are the Turks then the only Anti-Christs? Now I had none to open the Scripture to me but the Lord: he must be the prophet. Then he brought to my mind another Scripture, he that denies the Testament denies the death of the Testator, from whence the Lord did let me see that everyone that did not preach the new covenant denies the death of the Testator. Then it was revealed to me that the ministers of England were these Anti-Christs, but I knew not how to bear this. I did in my heart rise up against it; then I begged of the Lord that this Atheism might not be in my heart. After I had begged this light, a twelve-month together, at last he let me see how I did oppose Christ Jesus, and he revealed to me that place in *Esau* [Isaiah] 46. 12, 13, and from thence showed me the Atheism of my own heart, and how I did turn in upon a covenant of works, and did oppose Christ Jesus; from which time the Lord did discover to me all sorts of ministers and how they taught and to know which voice I heard, which was the voice of Moses, which of John Baptist, and which of Christ; the voice of my beloved from the voice of strangers; and thenceforth I was the more careful whom I heard, for after our teacher, Mr. Cotton, and my brother, Wheelwright, were put down, there was none in England that I durst hear. Then it pleased God to reveal himself to me in that of *Esau* 30. 20, though the Lord give thee the bread of adversity, etc., yet thine eyes shall see thy teachers.

After this the Lord carrying Mr. Cotton to New England (at which I was much troubled), it was revealed to me that I must go thither also and that there I should be persecuted and suffer much trouble. I will give you another Scripture, *Jer.* 46, fear not, Jacob, my servant, for I am with thee, I will make a full end of all the nations, etc. Then the Lord did reveal himself to me sitting upon a throne of justice and all the world appearing before him, and, though I must come to New England, yet I must not fear nor be dismayed. The Lord brought another Scripture to me, *Esau* [Isaiah] 8.9. The Lord spake this to me with a strong hand and instructed me that I should not walk in the way of this people, etc. I will give you one place more which the Lord brought to me by immediate revelations, and that doth concern you all; it is in *Dan.* 6, when the presidents and princes could find nothing against him, because he was faithful, they sought matter against him concerning the law of his God to cast him into the lions' den; so it was revealed to me that they should plot against me, but the Lord bid me not to fear, for he that delivered Daniel and the three children, his hand was not shortened. And see this Scripture fulfilled this day in mine eyes; therefore take heed what you go about to do unto me, for you have no power over my body, neither can you do me any harm, for I am in the hands of the eternal Jehovah, my savior; I am at his appointment; the bounds of my habitation are cast in Heaven; no further do I esteem of any mortal man than creatures in his hand; I fear none but the great Jehovah, which hath foretold me of these things, and I do verily believe that he will deliver me out of our [your?] hands; therefore take heed how you proceed against me, for I know that for this you go about to do to me, God will ruin you and your posterity and this whole state.

c. 1612 ∽ *Anne Bradstreet* ∽ 1672

DAUGHTER of Thomas Dudley, who later became governor of the Massachusetts Bay Colony, Anne Bradstreet was born in England, probably in Northampton, in 1612-1613. At the age of sixteen, she married Simon Bradstreet, of Lincolnshire, who, as an adopted member of the family of the Earl of Lincoln, had been under the care of Dudley, the Earl's steward. Simon succeeded Dudley in this position and was also steward for the Countess of Warwick. The Bradstreets migrated to New England in 1630 and established a farm near the Merrimac River. Simon, still following in the footsteps of his father-in-law, also became governor of the colony.

Mother of a large family, Anne, in her spare moments, composed poetry, the manuscripts of which John Woodbridge, husband of her sister Mercy, took to England in 1647 and had published at London in 1650, without Anne's knowledge, under the title, *The Tenth Muse Lately sprung up in America, or Severall Poems, compiled with great variety of Wit and Learning, full of delight*. The Rev. Nathaniel Ward of Ipswich, one of Anne's ex-neighbors and author of *The Simple Cobler of Aggawam*, London, 1647, was apparently a party to the publishing conspiracy, for in the Bradstreet volume are his commendatory verses entitled "On Mrs. Bradstreet's Tenth Muse." There he refers to her as "a right *Du Bartas* Girle" and indulges in the following quippish couplet, characteristic of him, since in his own book—primarily a tract against religious toleration—he had taken time out to satirize women for their outlandish fashions in dress:

"It half revives my chil frost-bitten blood,
    To see a Woman once, do ought that's good." . . .

His allusion to Du Bartas is apt, since one of Anne's inspirations was the work of the French Protestant poet, William de Salluste Du Bartas, whose *Semaines* had appeared in 1605-1606 in an English translation by Josuah Sylvester entitled *Divine Weekes and Workes*.

Until shortly before her death in 1672, Anne continued to write poetry as well as prose meditations and admonitions. The posthumous second edition of her poems, Boston, 1678, contains some of her finest, including "Contemplations," which one modern critic has cited as worthy of comparison and contrast with three later important philosophical poems by Americans—William Cullen Bryant's "Thanatopsis," Sidney Lanier's "The Marshes of Glynn," and Edna St. Vincent Millay's "Renascence." Anne's most ambitious compositions, "The Four Elements," "Of the Four Humours in Mans Constitution," "Of the four Ages of Man," "The four Seasons of the Year," and "The four Monarchyes," are versified summaries of Renaissance learning. After her death, a book written expressly for her children was found among her papers.

[The opening piece, known as "Religious Experiences," was a letter to her children. This letter in its entirety—save for its verse epigraph, which has been omitted—and the whole of "Contemplations" are here modernized from the texts in *The Works of Anne Bradstreet*, ed. J. H. Ellis, Charlestown, Mass., 1867, reprinted New York, 1932. Both selections show that Anne, in her religious experience and expression, represented what may be called the mystical strain in Puritan orthodoxy. The letter provides an interesting contrast with Anne Hutchinson's speech on her revelations; the poem is comparable in thought and feeling, although not in form, to some of the best of Edward Taylor.]

RELIGIOUS EXPERIENCES
[1867 (written c. 1672)]

MY dear Children: I, knowing by experience that the exhortations of parents take most effect when the speakers leave to speak, and those especially sink deepest which are spoke latest—and being ignorant whether on my death bed I shall have opportunity to speak to any of you, much less to all—thought it the best, whilst I was able to compose some short matters (for what else to call them I know not) and bequeath to you, that when I am no more with you, yet I may be in your remembrance—although that is the least in my aim in what I now do, but that you may gain some spiritual advantage by my experience. I have not studied in this you read to show my skill, but to declare the truth—not to set forth myself, but the glory of God. If I had minded the former, it had been perhaps better pleasing to you,—but, seeing the last is the best, let it be best pleasing to you.

The method I will observe shall be this—I will begin with God's dealing with me from my childhood to this day. In my young years, about 6 or 7 as I take it, I began to make conscience of my ways, and what I knew was sinful, as lying, disobedience to parents, etc., I avoided it. If at any time I was overtaken with the like evils, it was a great trouble. I could not be at rest till by prayer I had confessed it unto God. I was also troubled at the neglect of private

duties, though too often tardy that way. I also found much comfort in reading the Scriptures, especially those places I thought most concerned my condition, and, as I grew to have more understanding, so the more solace I took in them.

In a long fit of sickness which I had on my bed I often communed with my heart and made my supplication to the most High, who set me free from that affliction.

But as I grew up to be about 14 or 15 I found my heart more carnal, and sitting loose from God, vanity and the follies of youth take hold of me.

About 16, the Lord laid his hand sore upon me and smote me with the small pox. When I was in my affliction, I besought the Lord and confessed my pride and vanity and he was entreated of me and again restored me. But I rendered not to him according to the benefit received.

After a short time I changed my condition and was married, and came into this country, where I found a new world and new manners, at which my heart rose. But after I was convinced it was the way of God, I submitted to it and joined to the church at Boston.

After some time I fell into a lingering sickness like a consumption, together with a lameness, which correction I saw the Lord sent to humble and try me and do me good, and it was not altogether ineffectual.

It pleased God to keep me a long time without a child, which was a great grief to me and cost me many prayers and tears before I obtained one, and after him gave me many more, of whom I now take the care, that as I have brought you into the world, and with great pains, weakness, cares, and fears brought you to this, I now travail in birth again of you till Christ be formed in you.

Among all my experiences of God's gracious dealings with me I have constantly observed this, that he hath never suffered me long to sit loose from him, but by one affliction or other hath made me look home and search what was amiss—so usually thus it hath been with me, that I have no sooner felt my heart out of order but I have expected correction for it, which most commonly hath been upon my own person, in sickness, weakness, pains, sometimes on my soul, in doubts and fears of God's displeasure, and my sincerity toward him; sometimes he hath smote a child with sickness, sometimes chastened by losses in estate,—and these times (through his great mercy) have been the times of my greatest getting and advantage; yea, I have found them the times when the Lord hath manifested the most love to me. Then have I gone to searching and have said with David, Lord search me and try me, see what ways of wickedness are in me, and lead me in the way everlasting; and seldom or never but I have found either some sin I lay under which God would have reformed or some duty neglected which he would have performed. And by his help I have laid vows and bonds upon my soul to perform his righteous commands.

If at any time you are chastened of God, take it as thankfully and joyfully as in greatest mercies, for, if ye be his, ye shall reap the greatest benefit by it. It hath been no small support to me in times of darkness when the Almighty hath hid his face from me that yet I have had abundance of sweetness and refreshment after affliction and more circumspection in my walking after I have been afflicted. I have been with God like an untoward child that no longer than the rod has been on my back (or at least in sight) but I have been apt to for-get him and myself too. Before I was afflicted I went astray, but now I keep thy statutes.

I have had great experience of God's hearing my prayers and returning comfortable answers to me, either in granting the thing I prayed for or else in satisfying my mind without it, and I have been confident it hath been from him, because I have found my heart through his goodness enlarged in thankfulness to him.

I have often been perplexed that I have not found that constant joy in my pilgrimage and refreshing which I supposed most of the servants of God have; although he hath not left me altogether without the witness of his holy spirit, who hath oft given me his word and set to his seal that it shall be well with me. I have sometimes tasted of that hidden manna that the world knows not, and have set up my Ebenezer,[1] and have resolved with myself that against such a promise, such tastes of sweetness, the gates of Hell shall never prevail. Yet have I many times sinkings and droopings and not enjoyed that felicity that sometimes I have done. But when I have been in darkness and seen no light, yet have I desired to stay myself upon the Lord.

And, when I have been in sickness and pain, I have thought if the Lord would but lift up the light of his countenance upon me, although he ground me to powder, it would be but light to me; yea, oft have I thought were it hell itself and could there find the love of God toward me, it would be a heaven. And, could I have been in heaven without the love of God, it would have been a hell to me; for, in truth, it is the absence and presence of God that makes heaven or hell.

Many times hath Satan troubled me concerning the verity of the Scriptures, many times by Atheism how I could know whether there was a God; I never saw any miracles to confirm me, and those which I read of, how did I know but they were feigned?

[1] A memorial stone or any commemoration of divine assistance; also a house of worship; see 1 Sam. 7:12.

That there is a God my reason would soon tell me by the wondrous works that I see, the vast frame of the heaven and the earth, the order of all things, night and day, summer and winter, spring and autumn, the daily providing for this great household upon the earth, the preserving and directing of all to its proper end. The consideration of these things would with amazement certainly resolve me that there is an eternal being.

But how should I know he is such a God as I worship in trinity and such a savior as I rely upon?—though this hath thousands of times been suggested to me, yet God hath helped me over. I have urged thus with myself. That there is a God I see. If ever this God hath revealed himself, it must be in his word, and this must be it or none. Have I not found that operation by it that no human invention can work upon the soul? hath not judgments befallen divers who have scorned and contemned it? hath it not been preserved through all ages maugre all the heathen tyrants and all of the enemies who have opposed it? Is there any story but that which shows the beginnings of times and how the world came to be as we see? Do we not know the prophecies in it fulfilled which could not have been so long foretold by any but God himself?

When I have got over this block, then have I another put in my way: that, admit this be the true God whom we worship and that be his word, yet why may not the Popish religion be the right? They have the same God, the same Christ, the same word: they only interpret it one way, we another.

This hath sometimes stuck with me, and more it would but the vain fooleries that are in their religion, together with their lying miracles and cruel persecutions of the saints, which admit were they as they term them, yet not so to be dealt withal.

The consideration of these things and many the like would soon turn me to my own religion again.

But some new troubles I have had since the world has been filled with blasphemy

and sectaries, and some who have been accounted sincere Christians have been carried away with them, that sometimes I have said, "Is there faith upon the earth?" and I have not known what to think. But then I have remembered the words of Christ that so it must be and that, if it were possible, the very elect should be deceived. Behold, saith our savior, I have told you before. That hath stayed my heart, and I can now say, "Return, O my soul, to thy rest; upon this rock, Christ Jesus, will I build my faith; and, if I perish, I perish." But I know all the powers of hell shall never prevail against it. I know whom I have trusted and whom I have believed and that he is able to keep that I have committed to his charge.

Now to the King, immortal, eternal, and invisible, the only wise God, be honor and glory for ever and ever! Amen.

This was written in much sickness and weakness and is very weakly and imperfectly done, but, if you can pick any benefit out of it, it is the mark which I aimed at.

CONTEMPLATIONS
[1678]

1

Some time now past in the autumnal tide,
When Phoebus wanted but one hour to bed,
The trees all richly clad, yet void of pride,
Were gilded o'er by his rich golden head;
Their leaves and fruits seemed painted,
    but was true,
Of green, of red, of yellow, mixèd hue;
Rapt were my senses at this delectable
    view.

2

I wist not what to wish. Yet sure, thought I,
If so much excellence abide below,
How excellent is He that dwells on high?
Whose power and beauty by His works we
    know!
Sure He is goodness, wisdom, glory, light,
That hath this under-world so richly dight.
More heaven than earth was here, no winter
    and no night.

3

Then on a stately oak I cast mine eye,
Whose ruffling top the clouds seemed to
    aspire;
How long since thou wast in thine infancy?
Thy strength and stature, more thy years
    admire.
Hath hundred winters passed since thou
    wast born,
Or thousand since thou brakest thy shell
    of horn?
If so, all these as nought eternity doth
    scorn.

4

Then higher on the glistering sun I gazed,
Whose beams was shaded by the leafy
    tree;
The more I looked the more I grew amazed,
And softly said, what glory's like to thee?
Soul of this world, this universe's eye,
No wonder some made thee a deity;
Had I not better known, alas, the same
    had I.

5

Thou as a bridegroom from thy chamber
    rushes,
And as a strong man joys to run a race,
The morn doth usher thee, with smiles and
    blushes,
The earth reflects her glances in thy face.
Birds, insects, animals, with vegative,
Thy heart from death and dulness doth re-
    vive,
And in the darksome womb of fruitful na-
    ture dive.

6

Thy swift annual and diurnal course,
Thy daily straight and yearly oblique path,
Thy pleasing fervor and thy scorching
    force,
All mortals here the feeling knowledge
    hath.

Thy presence makes it day, thy absence
    night,
Quaternal seasons caused by thy might.
Hail, creature, full of sweetness, beauty,
    and delight!

7

Art thou so full of glory that no eye
Hath strength thy shining rays once to
    behold?
And is thy splendid throne erect so high
As to approach it can no earthly mould?
How full of glory then must thy Creator
    be,
Who gave this bright light luster unto
    thee!
Admired, adored forever be that majesty!

8

Silent, alone, where none or saw or heard,
In pathless paths I led my wand'ring feet,
My humble eyes to lofty skies I reared
To sing some song my mazèd muse thought
    meet;
My great Creator I would magnify
That nature had thus deckèd liberally:
But ah, and ah, again, my imbecility!

9

I heard the merry grasshopper then sing,
The black-clad cricket bear a second part;
They kept one tune and played on the same
    string,
Seeming to glory in their little art.
Shall creatures abject thus their voices
    raise,
And in their kind resound their Maker's
    praise,
Whilst I, as mute, can warble forth no
    higher lays?

10

When present times look back to ages past,
And men in being fancy those are dead,
It makes things gone perpetually to last
And calls back months and years that long
    since fled;

It makes a man more agèd in conceit
Than was Methuselah or's grandsire great
While of their persons and their acts his
    mind doth treat.

11

Sometimes in Eden fair he seems to be,
Sees glorious Adam there made lord of all,
Fancies the apple dangle on the tree
That turned his sovereign to a naked thrall,
Who like a miscreant's driven from that
    place
To get his bread with pain and sweat of
    face:
A penalty imposed on his backsliding race.

12

Here sits our grandame in retirèd place,
And in her lap her bloody Cain new-born;
The weeping imp oft looks her in the face,
Bewails his unknown hap, and fate for-
    lorn;
His mother sighs to think of paradise,
And how she lost her bliss to be more wise,
Believing him that was, and is, father of
    lies.

13

Here Cain and Abel come to sacrifice;
Fruits of the earth and fatlings each do
    bring;
On Abel's gift the fire descends from skies,
But no such sign on false Cain's offering;
With sullen hateful looks he goes his ways,
Hath thousand thoughts to end his brother's
    days,
Upon whose blood his future good he hopes
    to raise.

14

There Abel keeps his sheep, no ill he thinks;
His brother comes, then acts his fratricide;
The virgin earth of blood her first draught
    drinks,
But since that time she often hath been
    cloyed.

The wretch with ghastly face and dreadful
    mind
Thinks each he sees will serve him in his
    kind,
Though none on earth but kindred near
    then could he find.

15

Who fancies not his looks now at the bar,
His face like death, his heart with horror
    fraught?
Nor malefactor ever felt like war
When deep despair with wish of life hath
    fought.
Branded with guilt and crushed with treble
    woes,
A vagabond to land of Nod he goes;
A city builds that walls might him secure
    from foes.

16

Who thinks not oft upon the father's ages?
Their long descent, how nephews' sons they
    saw, [1]
The starry observations of those sages,
And how their precepts to their sons were
    law,
How Adam sighed to see his progeny
Clothed all in his black sinful livery,
Who neither guilt nor yet the punishment
    could fly?

17

Our life compare we with their length of
    days,
Who to the tenth of theirs doth now ar-
    rive?
And though thus short, we shorten many
    ways,
Living so little while we are alive,
In eating, drinking, sleeping, vain delight.
So unawares comes on perpetual night,
And puts all pleasures vain unto eternal
    flight.

---

[1] Nephew is here used in the obsolete
sense of grandson.

18

When I behold the heavens as in their
          prime,
And then the earth, though old, still clad
          in green,
The stones and trees, insensible of time,
Nor age nor wrinkle on their front are
          seen;
If winter come and greenness then do fade,
A spring returns, and they more youthful
          made.
But man grows old, lies down, remains
          where once he's laid.

19

By birth more noble than those creatures
          all,
Yet seems by nature and by custom cursed,
No sooner born but grief and care makes
          fall
That state obliterate he had at first:
No youth nor strength nor wisdom spring
          again,
Nor habitations long their names retain,
But in oblivion to the final day remain.

20

Shall I then praise the heavens, the trees,
          the earth
Because their beauty and their strength
          last longer?
Shall I wish there or never to had birth,
Because they're bigger and their bodies
          stronger?
Nay, they shall darken, perish, fade, and
          die,
And when unmade so ever shall they lie,
But man was made for endless immortality.

21

Under the cooling shadow of a stately elm
Close sat I by a goodly river's side,
Where gliding streams the rocks did over-
          whelm,
A lonely place with pleasures dignified.

I once that loved the shady woods so well
Now thought the rivers did the trees excel,
And if the sun would ever shine, there
          would I dwell.

22

While on the stealing stream I fixed mine
          eye,
Which to the long'd-for ocean held its
          course,
I marked nor crooks nor rubs that there did
          lie
Could hinder aught but still augment its
          force.
O happy flood, quoth I, that holds thy
          race
Till thou arrive at thy belovèd place,
Nor is it rocks or shoals that can obstruct
          thy pace!

23

Nor is't enough that thou alone mayst slide,
But hundred brooks in thy clear waves do
          meet,
So hand in hand along with thee they
          glide
To Thetis' house, where all embrace and
          greet.
Thou emblem true of what I count the
          best,
O could I lead my rivulets to rest!
So may we press to that vast mansion ever
          blest.

24

Ye fish which in this liquid region bide,
That for each season have your habitation,
Now salt, now fresh, where you think best
          to glide,
To unknown coasts to give a visitation,
In lakes and ponds you leave your nu-
          merous fry;
So nature taught, and yet you know not
          why,
You wat'ry folk that know not your felic-
          ity.

25

Look how the wantons frisk to taste the
     air,
Then to the colder bottom straight they
     dive,
Eftsoon to Neptune's glassy hall repair
To see what trade they, great ones, there
     do drive,
Who forage o'er the spacious sea-green field
And take the trembling prey before it
     yield,
Whose armor is their scales, their spreading
     fins their shield.

26

While musing thus with contemplation fed,
And thousand fancies buzzing in my brain,
The sweet-tongued Philomel perched o'er
     my head
And chanted forth a most melodious strain,
Which rapt me so with wonder and delight,
I judged my hearing better than my sight,
And wished me wings with her awhile to
     take my flight.

27

O merry bird, said I, that fears no snares,
That neither toils nor hoards up in thy
     barn,
Feels no sad thoughts nor cruciating cares
To gain more good or shun what might thee
     harm,
Thy clothes ne'er wear, thy meat is every-
     where,
Thy bed a bough, thy drink the water
     clear,
Reminds not what is past, nor what's to
     come dost fear.

28

The dawning morn with songs thou dost
     prevent,
Sets hundred notes unto thy feathered
     crew,

So each one tunes his pretty instrument
And warbling out the old, begin anew.
And thus they pass their youth in summer
     season,
Then follow thee into a better region,
Where winter's never felt by that sweet
     airy legion.

29

Man at the best a creature frail and vain,
In knowledge ignorant, in strength but
     weak,
Subject to sorrows, losses, sickness, pain,
Each storm his state, his mind, his body
     break,
From some of these he never finds ces-
     sation,
But day or night, within, without, vexa-
     tion,
Troubles from foes, from friends, from
     dearest, near'st relation.

30

And yet this sinful creature, frail and
     vain,
This lump of wretchedness, of sin and sor-
     row,
This weather-beaten vessel wracked with
     pain,
Joys not in hope of an eternal morrow,
Nor all his losses, crosses, and vexation,
In weight, in frequency and long duration,
Can make him deeply groan for that divine
     translation.

31

The mariner that on smooth waves doth
     glide
Sings merrily and steers his bark with ease,
As if he had command of wind and tide,
And now become great master of the seas;
But suddenly a storm spoils all the sport
And makes him long for a more quiet port
Which 'gainst all adverse winds may serve
     for fort.

32

So he that saileth in this world of pleasure,
Feeding on sweets, that never bit of th'
   sour,
That's full of friends, of honor, and of
   treasure,
Fond fool, he takes this earth ev'n for
   heaven's bower.
But sad affliction comes and makes him
   see
Here's neither honor, wealth, nor safety;
Only above is found all with security.

33

O time, the fatal wrack of mortal things,
That draws oblivion's curtains over kings!

Their sumptuous monuments, men know
   them not,
Their names without a record are forgot,
Their parts, their ports, their pomp's all
   laid in th' dust;
Nor wit nor gold nor buildings scape time's
   rust.
But he whose name is graved in the white
   stone [2]
Shall last and shine when all of these are
   gone.

---

[2] A reference to *Rev.* 2:17: "He that hath an ear let him hear what the Spirit saith unto the churches; To him that overcometh will I give to eat of the hidden manna, and will give him a white stone, and in the stone a new name written, which no man knoweth saving he that receiveth it."

1631 ∾ *Michael Wigglesworth* ∾ 1705

MICHAEL WIGGLESWORTH, born in England, accompanied his parents, when he was seven years old, to Connecticut. A graduate of Harvard in 1651, he served as fellow and tutor from 1652 to 1654. Leaving this position because of poor health, he became a minister at Malden, Mass., but preached only on infrequent occasions.

The "Little Feeble Shadow of a Man," as Cotton Mather called him, became, to quote Paul Elmer More's characterization, the "doggerel Dante of the New England meeting-house" when he produced the macabre didactic ballad-epic of the last judgment, *The Day of Doom*, Cambridge, 1662. This strange poetic *tour de force* of a gnarled but powerful imagination dramatizes Calvinistic doctrine for both the young and the adult with some of the metrical effects and emotive overtones achieved later by Coleridge in "The Rime of the Ancient Mariner" and Oscar Wilde in "The Ballad of Reading Gaol." Becoming almost as much of a best seller in 17th Century America as Franklin's *The Way to Wealth* was in the America of the next century—a fact which one scholar has cited as replete with significance for the cultural historian—Wigglesworth's sing-song saga of damnation and reprieve ran through numerous editions in its author's lifetime and was apparently read with such tense excitement that no copy of its original edition has survived. As a curiosity of literature, it will probably be read, to paraphrase a remark of one of Wigglesworth's friends in 1705, until the coming of the day which it describes. It represents the dogmatic rather than the mystical side of Puritan orthodoxy, and few

other poems have ever succeeded in combining in such equalized doses the
seemingly disparate aims—to teach, to delight, and to horrify. Joseph Morgan's
The History of the Kingdom of Basaruah, Boston, 1715, ed. by Richard
Schlatter, Harvard University Press, 1946, an attempt to expound Calvinistic
doctrine in allegorical prose fiction, provides good parallel reading with *The
Day of Doom.*

[The selections included here have been to some extent modernized in text,
and the titles have been supplied by the present editors.]

From
THE DAY OF DOOM
[1662]

CHRIST COMES TO JUDGE

1

Still was the night, serene and bright, when
    all men sleeping lay;
Calm was the season, and carnal reason
    thought so 'twould last for ay.
Soul, take thine ease, let sorrow cease,
    much good thou hast in store:
This was their song, their cups among, the
    evening before.

2

Wallowing in all kind of sin, vile wretches
    lay secure:
The best of men had scarcely then their
    lamps kept in good ure.
Virgins unwise who through disguise
    amongst the best were numbered,
Had closed their eyes; yea, and the wise
    through sloth and frailty slumbered.

3

Like as of old, when men grow bold God's
    threat'nings to contemn,
Who stopped their ear and would not hear
    when Mercy warnèd them:
But took their course, without remorse, till
    God began to pour
Destruction the world upon in a tem-
    pestuous shower.

4

They put away the evil day and drowned
    their care and fears,

Till drowned were they and swept away
    by vengeance unawares;
So at the last, whilst men sleep fast in
    their security,
Surprised they are in such a snare as
    cometh suddenly.

5

For at midnight brake forth a light which
    turned the night to day,
And speedily an hideous cry did all the
    world dismay.
Sinners awake, their hearts do ache, trem-
    bling their loins surpriseth;
Amazed with fear by what they hear, each
    one of them ariseth.

6

They rush from beds with giddy heads and
    to their windows run,
Viewing this light which shines more
    bright than doth the noon-day sun.
Straightway appears (they see't with tears)
    the Son of God most dread,
Who with his train comes on amain to
    judge both quick and dead.

7

Before his face the heav'ns gave place, and
    skies are rent asunder,
With mighty voice and hideous noise more
    terrible than thunder.
His brightness damps heav'n's glorious
    lamps and makes them hide their
    heads,
As if afraid and quite dismayed, they quit
    their wonted steads.

8

Ye sons of men that durst contemn the
    threat'nings of God's word,
How cheer you now? your hearts, I trow,
    are thrilled as with a sword.
Now, atheist blind, whose brutish mind a
    God could never see,
Dost thou perceive, dost now believe, that
    Christ thy judge shall be?

9

Stout courages (whose hardiness could
    death and hell out-face),
Are you as bold now you behold your judge
    draw near apace?
They cry, "No, no: Alas! and wo! our
    courage all is gone,
Our hardiness, fool hardiness, hath us un-
    done, undone."

10

No heart so bold but now grows cold and
    almost dead with fear,
No eye so dry but now can cry and pour
    out many a tear.
Earth's potentates and pow'rful states, cap-
    tains and men of might,
Are quite abashed, their courage dashed,
    at this most dreadful sight.

11

Mean men lament, great men do rent their
    robes and tear their hair,
They do not spare their flesh to tear
    through horrible despair.
All kindreds wail, all hearts do fail, horror
    the world doth fill
With weeping eyes and loud outcries, yet
    knows not how to kill.

12

Some hide themselves in caves and delves,
    in places underground,
Some rashly leap into the deep to scape
    by being drowned;

Some to the rocks (O senseless blocks!)
    and woody mountains run,
That there they might this fearful sight
    and dreaded presence shun.

13

In vain do they to mountains say, "Fall on
    us, and us hide
From Judge's ire more hot than fire, for
    who may it abide?"
No hiding place can from his face sinners
    at all conceal,
Whose flaming eye hid things doth 'spy
    and darkest things reveal.

14

The Judge draws nigh, exalted high upon
    a lofty throne,
Amidst the throng of angels strong, lo,
    Israel's Holy One!
The excellence of whose presènce and aw-
    ful majesty
Amazeth nature, and every creature doth
    more than terrify.

15

The mountains smoke, the hills are shook,
    the earth is rent and torn,
As if she should be clean dissolved or from
    the center borne.
The sea doth roar, forsakes the shore, and
    shrinks away for fear;
The wild beasts flee into the sea as soon
    as he draws near.

16

Whose glory bright, whose wondrous might,
    whose power imperial,
So far surpass whatever was in realms ter-
    restrial,
That tongues of men nor angels' pen can-
    not the same express,
And therefore I must pass it by, lest speak-
    ing should transgress.

17

Before his throne a trump is blown, proclaiming th' Day of Doom;
Forthwith he cries, "Ye dead, arise, and
unto judgment come!"
No sooner said but 'tis obeyed; sepulchres
opened are;
Dead bodies all rise at his call and's mighty
power declare.

18

Both sea and land, at his command, their
dead at once surrender;
The fire and air constrainèd are also their
dead to tender.
The mighty word of this great Lord links
body and soul together,
Both of the just and the unjust, to part no
more forever.

19

The same translates from mortal states to
immortality
All that survive and be alive i' th' twinkling of an eye,
That so they may abide for ay to endless
weal or woe;
Both the renate and reprobate are made to
die no more.

20

His wingèd hosts fly through all coasts together gathering
Both good and bad, both quick and dead,
and all to judgment bring.
Out of their holes those creeping moles
that hid themselves for fear,
By force they take and quickly make before the Judge appear.

21

Thus every one before the throne of Christ
the Judge is brought,
Both righteoùs and impious that good or
ill had wrought.

A separation and diff'ring station by Christ
appointed is
To sinners sad, 'twixt good and bad, 'twixt
heirs of woe and bliss.

22

At Christ's right hand the sheep do stand,
his holy martyrs who
For his dear name suffering shame, calamity
and woe,
Like champions stood and with their blood
their testimony sealed,
Whose innocence without offence to Christ
their Judge appealed.

23

Next unto whom there find a room all
Christ's afflicted ones,
Who, being chastised, neither despised nor
sank amidst their groans,
Who by the rod were turned to God and
lovèd him the more,
Not murmuring nor quarreling when they
were chastened sore.

24

Moreover, such as lovèd much, that had
not such a trial,
As might constrain to so great pain and
such deep self-denial,
Yet ready were the cross to bear when
Christ them called thereto,
And did rejoice to hear his voice—they're
counted sheep also.

25

Christ's flock of lambs there also stands,
whose faith was weak yet true,
All sound believers, Gospel-receivers, whose
grace was small, but grew:
And them among an infant throng of
babes for whom Christ died,
Whom for his own, by ways unknown to
men, he sanctified.

26

All stand before their Savior in long white
    robes y-clad,
Their countenànce full of pleasance, ap-
    pearing wondrous glad.
O glorious sight! Behold how bright dust
    heaps are made to shine,
Conformèd so their Lord unto, whose glory
    is divine.

27

At Christ's left hand the goats do stand,
    all whining hypocrites,
Who for self-ends did seem Christ's friends
    but fostered guileful sprites,
Who sheep resembled, but they dissembled
    (their hearts were not sincere),
Who once did throng Christ's lambs among,
    but now must not come near.

28

Apostatès and run-aways such as have
    Christ forsaken,
Of whom the devil, with seven more evil
    hath fresh possession taken,
Sinners in grain, reserved to pain and
    torments most severe,
Because 'gainst light they sinned with spite,
    are also placèd here.

29

There also stand a num'rous band that no
    profession made
Of godliness, nor to redress their ways at
    all essayed,
Who better knew, but (sinful crew!)
    Gospel and law despised,
Who all Christ's knocks withstood like
    blocks and would not be advised.

30

Morever, there with them appear a num-
    ber, numberless,
Of great and small, vile wretches all, that
    did God's law transgress,

Idolaters, false worshippers, prophaners of
    God's name,
Who not at all thereon did call or took
    in vain the same.

31

Blasphemers lewd and swearers shrewd,
    scoffers at purity,
That hated God, contemned his rod, and
    loved security,
Sabbath-polluters, saints' persecutors, pre-
    sumptuous men and proud,
Who never loved those that reproved—all
    stand amongst this crowd.

32

Adulterèrs and whoremongèrs were there,
    with all unchaste,
There covetous and ravenous that riches
    got too fast,
Who used vile ways themselves to raise
    t'estates and worldly wealth,
Oppression by, or knavery, by force, or
    fraud, or stealth.

33

Moreover, there together were children fla-
    gitious,
And parents who did them undo by nurture
    viciòus,
False-witness-bearers and self-forswearers,
    murd'rers and men of blood
Witches, enchanters, and ale-house-haun-
    ters, beyond account there stood.

34

Their place there find all heathen blind that
    nature's light abused,
Although they had no tidings glad of Gos-
    pel-grace refused.
There stands all nations and generations of
    Adam's progeny
Whom Christ redeemed not, who Christ
    esteemed not, through infidelity.

35

Who no peace-maker, no undertaker, to
   shroud them from God's ire
Ever obtained; they must be pained with
   everlasting fire.
These num'rous bands, wringing their hands
   and weeping, all stand there,
Filled with anguish, whose hearts do languish through self-tormenting fear.

36

Fast by them stand at Christ's left hand
   the lion fierce and fell,
The dragon bold, that serpent old, that
   hurried souls to Hell.
There also stand, under command, Legions
   of sprites unclean,
And hellish fiends, that are no friends to
   God nor unto men.

37

With dismal chains and strongest reins,
   like prisoners of Hell,
They're held in place before Christ's face,
   till he their doom shall tell.
These void of tears but filled with fears and
   dreadful expectation
Of endless pains and scalding flames stand
   waiting for damnation. . . .

CHRIST DEBATES WITH THE REPROBATE
INFANTS

166

Then to the bar all they drew near who
   died in infancy
And never had or good or bad effected
   pers'nally,
But from the womb unto the tomb were
   straightway carrièd
(Or at the least ere they transgressed),
   who thus began to plead:

167

"If for our own transgressiòn, or disobedience,
We here did stand at thy left-hand, just
   were the recompence;
But Adam's guilt our souls hath spilt, his
   fault is charged on us,
And that alone hath overthrown and utterly undone us.

168

"Not we, but he, ate of the tree whose
   fruit was interdicted,
Yet on us all, of his sad fall, the punishment's inflicted.
How could we sin that had not been, or
   how is his sin our,
Without consent, which to prevent, we
   never had a power?

169

"O great Creator, why was our nature de-
   pravèd and forlorn?
Who so defiled and made so vild whilst we
   were yet unborn?
If it be just, and needs we must transgressors reckoned be,
Thy mercy, Lord, to us afford, which sinners hath set free.

170

"Behold we see Adam set free and saved
   from his trespass,
Whose sinful fall hath split us all and
   brought us to this pass.
Canst thou deny us once to try, or grace
   to us to tender,
When he finds grace before thy face, that
   was the chief offender?"

171

Then answerèd the Judge most dread,
   "God doth such doom forbid,
That men should die eternally for what they
   never did.

But what you call old Adam's fall, and
  only his trespass,
You call amiss to call it his, both his and
  yours it was.

172

"He was designed of all mankind to be a
  public head,
A common root, whence all should shoot,
  and stood in all their stead.
He stood and fell, did ill or well, not for
  himself alone,
But for you all, who now his fall and
  trespass would disown.

173

"If he had stood, then all his brood had
  been establishèd
In God's true love, never to move, nor
  once awry to tread;
Then all his race my father's grace should
  have enjoyed forever,
And wicked sprites by subtle sleights could
  them have harmèd never.

174

"Would you have grieved to have received
  through Adam so much good,
As had been your forevermore, if he at
  first had stood?
Would you have said, we ne'er obeyed,
  nor did thy laws regard;
It ill befits with benefits us, Lord, so to
  reward?

175

"Since then to share in his welfare you
  could have been content,
You may with reason share in his treason
  and in the punishment.
Hence you were born in state forlorn with
  natures so depraved:
Death was your due, because that you had
  thus yourselves behaved."

176

"You think, 'if we had been as he whom
  God did so betrust
We to our cost would ne'er have lost all
  for a paltry Lust?'
Had you been made in Adam's stead, you
  would like things have wrought,
And so into the self-same woe yourselves
  and yours have brought.

177

"I may deny you once to try, or grace
  to you to tender,
Though he finds grace before my face, who
  was the chief offender:
Else should my grace cease to be grace,
  for it should not be free,
If to release whom I should please, I have
  no liberty!

178

"If upon one what's due to none I frankly
  shall bestow,
And on the rest shall not think best compassion's skirt to throw,
Whom injure I? will you envý and grudge
  at others' weal?
Or me accuse, who do refuse yourselves to
  help and heal?

179

"Am I alone of what's my own, no master
  or no Lord?
Or if I am, how can you claim what I to
  some afford?
Will you demand grace at my hand, and
  challenge what is mine?
Will you teach me whom to set free, and
  thus my grace confine?

180

"You sinners are, and such a share as
  sinners may expect,
Such you shall have, for I do save none but
  mine own elect.

Yet to compare your sin with their who
    lived a longer time,
I do confess yours is much less though every
    sin's a crime.

181

"A crime it is, therefore in bliss you may
    not hope to dwell;

But unto you I shall allow the easiest room
    in Hell."
The glorious King thus answering, they
    cease and plead no longer:
Their consciences must needs confess his
    reasons are the stronger. . . .

1645(?) ∽ *Edward Taylor* ∽ 1729

SUPREME among the poets of 17th Century American Puritanism stands
Edward Taylor. He was born in or near Coventry, England, probably in 1645.
Arriving at Boston in 1668, he entered Harvard, from which he was graduated
in 1671. Both a minister and a physician, he lived at Westfield, Mass., for
fifty-eight years, married twice, was the father of a large family, and collected
one of the most unusual libraries in the colonies, especially strong in expensive
editions of the best European scholarship in "divinity." In 1720 Harvard
conferred upon him an honorary M.A. degree. Ezra Stiles, 18th Century
worthy, was his grandson.

Of the abundant poetry which Taylor wrote, it has so far been found that
only one poem was published during his lifetime. Like Emily Dickinson, he
apparently regarded publication as "the auction of the mind of man." *The
Poetical Works of Edward Taylor* was published for the first time in 1939,
edited from his manuscripts by Thomas H. Johnson; the three poems included
here have been taken from this volume, with some modernization of the texts.

A master of "metaphysical conceits," Taylor had, in Austin Warren's
phrase, the "baroque sensibility" characteristic of such English poets as Donne
and Crashaw and Herbert. So creative was this sensibility that it was able to
seize and express the essence of both the dogmatic and mystical phases of
Puritan orthodoxy. Dogmatic or doctrinal Puritanism permeates that sequence
of his poems that bears the title "Gods Determinations," but the doctrine
is transmuted beyond mere didacticism. From this sequence is taken the first
of the following poems, its full title being "The Soule Bemoning Sorrow rowling
upon a resolution to Seek Advice of Gods people." Mysticism predominates in
his "Sacramental Meditations," which are here represented by "The Experience"
and "Meditation Eighty-Two."

[From the short "Diary of Edward Taylor," published in *Proceedings of
the Massachusetts Historical Society,* XVIII (1881), 4-18, the following prose
selection has been reprinted with some modernization of the text. His impres-

sions of his Atlantic voyage show a remarkable feeling for language and sensuous detail. The final incident of the "dove pigeon" entering the chamber window as Poe imagined that his raven did is one of the most memorable bits in any personal record of the colonial period. For to young Taylor the pigeon's visitation was obviously fraught with symbolic meaning. "It was ominous surely"—not only of God's grace bestowed, or in process of bestowal, but of something more—perhaps the "calling" of a sacred poet.]

From
DIARY
[1881 (written 1668)]

THURSDAY, June 18. Morning foggy and misty; the wind southeast, but low. Many whales were heard in the morning about three o'clock, but not seen for the fog. About eight, I being between decks at study against Lord's Day, was called to see one, for they heard one coming toward the ship, and when I got above deck I only heard his voice (which was a rough, hoarse noise, blothering in the water), but could not see him by reason of the misty fog. The fog being of continuance from Lord's Day, we could not well see any further than we went; but it pleased the Lord so far to answer our prayers as to clear the air in the afternoon, and to give us a fresh, gentle gale that made us slide on a great pace. We had a tide now again, which, when we came to it, they called a rippling, because the water by the running of the stream curled and rippled the top of the waves. . . .

Wednesday, July 1. Day dark and drizzly; wind fresh and northeasterly. We sailed west and northerly. There was a blue pigeon came and settled on the main-topsail yard, which the boatswain shot, but as it fell it hit against the mainsail yard, and so was struck overboard. We saw a gannet, and after, some New England rockweed on the water, which was like yellow mareblobs.[1] The wind was very high toward night, insomuch that we took down all our sails and lay by, lest we should be drove upon the shore before we were aware, and so suffer damage. About sunset we saw a fish rise, spouting water out and leaping out of the water, as big as a huge horse. Some took it for a young whale, some for a grampus; our master, a thresher. . . .

Saturday, July 4. Wind east by south; the day thick with fogs. We saw our consort on the head of us, and spake with him in the afternoon. We sailed faintly on, because the day was so foggy. We sounded, and had some forty-five or forty fathoms water, and we saw many whale spouts. After the day clearing up, we saw land on both hands—Plymouth on the left, and Salem on the right—toward sunsetting. About five o'clock we saw the islands in our passage up to Boston. About eight I saw a flying creature like a spark of red fire (about the bigness of an humble-bee) fly by the side of the ship; and presently after, there flew another by. The men said they were fire-flies. About eleven or twelve o'clock I went to lie down to sleep on my cabin (for none went to bed because we were nigh our harbor, and waited to go ashore as soon as we cast anchor). But when I was dropped in a slumber there was a sad outcry made, insomuch that I was wakened with it in a fright, thinking the ship had been cast upon some rock; but the cause was this: there was a ketch at anchor, and coming to it, our men did so *hoe* the ship (for that is their word when they call to any in another ship), and there being a horse aboard, he leaped overboard into the sea. [It was] that they hooted at so. . . .

July 7. I delivered a letter from Mr.

[1] Marsh marigolds.

Clarke, and another from his brother, Meadwel, to their kinsman, Mr. Hull, who invited me to his house till I had despatched my business and was settled in the college, and also to bring my chest to his warehouse. This gentleman would not be said nay,—therefore I was with him, and received much kindness from him. I continued with him till I settled at Cambridge.

About July 14, I went to Cambridge to speak with the President, who gave me encouragement. At night it thundered and lightened very dreadfully, insomuch that I had little rest for the flashes of lightning. . . .

About July 22 I went to Cambridge and lay at the President's. At night it thundered, lightened, and rained very much; and as his son, Elnathan, and I were going to bed about ten or eleven o'clock in the night, as it rained there came a white peckled [2] dove pigeon, and flew against the casement of our chamber window, and there sat. I only being in bed, when I heard it was a pigeon got up, and so we opened the casement upon the dove so far as that we took him in, and when he was in, we would have caught him, and he ran from us and cooed and bristled at us. In the morning he was let out again. The President, when he heard it, said he would not (of any good) he should be hurt, for one should not hear of the like; it was ominous surely.

July 23. I was admitted into the college.

THE SOUL BEMOANING . . .
[1939]

Alas! my soul, product of breath divine
For to illuminate a lump of slime.
Sad providence! Must thou below thus tent
In such a cote as strangles with ill scent?
Or in such sensual organs make thy
    stay,   5
Which from thy noble end do make thee
    stray?
My nobler part, why dost thou lackey to
The carnal whinings of my senses so?
What? thou become a page, a peasant! nay.

A slave unto a dirty clod of clay!   10
Why should the kernel bring such cankers
    forth
To please the shell as will devour them
    both?
Why didst thou thus thy milkwhite robes
    defile
With crimson spots of scarlet sins most
    vile?

My muddy tent, why hast thou done so
    ill   15
To court and kiss my soul, yet kissing
    kill?
Why didst thou, whining, egg her thus
    away,
Thy sensual appetite to satisfy?
Art thou so safe and firm a cabinet
As though thou soaking lie in nasty
    wet   20
And in all filthy puddles, yet the thin
Can ne'er drench through to stain the
    pearl therein?
It's no such thing! Thou'rt but a cawl-
    wrought case,
And when thou fallst, thou foulst its shin-
    ing face;
Or but her mudwalled lid which, wet by
    sin,   25
Diffuseth all in her that enters in.
One stain stains both, when both in one
    combine:
A musty cask doth mar rich Malmsey wine

Woe's me! my mouldering heart! What
    must I do?
When is my moulting time to shed my
    woe?   30
Oh! Woeful fall! what, fall from heavenly
    bliss
To th' bottom of the bottomless abyss?
Above, an angry God! Below, black-blue
Brimstony flames of hell where sinners rue!
Behind, a trail of sins! Before appear   35
An host of mercies that abusèd were!
Without, a raging devil! and within,
A wracking conscience galling home for
    sin!

---

[2] Old form for "speckled."

What! Canst not find one remedy, my soul,
On mercy's file for me? Oh, search the
    roll.   40
What! Freeze to death under such melting
    means
Of grace's golden, life-enliv'ning beams?
What? Not one hope? Alas! I hope there's
    some,
Although I know not in what way it come.
Although there is no hope within my
    mind,   45
I'll force hope's faculty till hope I find.
Some glimmerings of hope I hope to spy
In mercy's golden stacks, or remedy.
I therefore am resolved a search to make
And of the pious wise some counsel
    take.   50
I'll then in pensiveness myself apply
To them in hope, but yet half hopelessly.
Perhaps these thoughts are blessèd motions,
    though
From whence they are, as yet I do not
    know.
And if from Christ, oh, then, thrice
    happy me!   55
If not, I'st not be worser than I be.

THE EXPERIENCE
[1939]

Oh! that I always breathed in such an air
As I sucked in, feeding on sweet content!
Dished up unto my soul ev'n in that prayer
    Poured out to God over last sacrament.
What beam of light rapt up my sight
    to find   5
    Me nearer God than ere came in my
    mind?

Most strange it was! But yet more strange
    that shine
Which filled my soul then to the brim
    to spy
My nature with thy nature all divine
    Together joined in him that's thou
    and I.   10
Flesh of my flesh, bone of my bone:
    there's run
    Thy godhead and my manhood in thy
    son.

Oh! that that flame which thou didst on me
    cast
    Might me inflame and lighten ev'rywhere.
Then Heaven to me would be less at last,
    So much of heaven I should have while
    here.   15
Oh! Sweet though short! I'll not forget
    the same.
    My nearness, Lord, to thee did me in-
    flame.

I'll claim my right: give place, ye angels
    bright,
    Ye further from the godhead stand
    than I,
My nature is your Lord and doth unite   20
    Better than yours unto the Deity.
    God's throne is first and mine is next;
    to you
    Only the place of waiting-men is due.

Oh, that my heart thy golden harp might
    be,
    Well-tuned by glorious grace, that ev'ry
    string   25
Screwed to the highest pitch might unto
    thee
    All praises wrapped in sweetest music
    bring.
I praise thee, Lord, and better praise
    thee would,
    If what I had, my heart might ever hold.

MEDITATION EIGHTY-TWO
[1939]

My tattered fancy and my ragged rhymes
    Teem leaden metaphors, which yet might
    serve
To hum a little touching terrene shines.
    But spiritual life doth better fare
    deserve.
This, thought on, sets my heart upon the
    rack,   5
    I fain would have this life but han't its
    knack.

Reason stands for it, moving to pursue't
    But flesh and blood are elemental things

That sink me down, dulling my spirit's
  fruit.
Life animal a spiritual spark ne'er
  springs.   10
But if thy altar's coal enfire my heart,
With this blessed life my soul will be
  thy spark.

I'm common matter: Lord, thine altar make
  me,
Then sanctify thine altar with thy blood.
I'll offer on't my heart to thee. Oh! take
  me   15
And let thy fire calcine mine altar's wood,
Then let thy spirit's breath, as bellows
  blow,
That this new-kindled life may flame and
  glow.

Some life with spoon or trencher do maintain
Or suck its food through a small quill
  or straw,   20
But make me, Lord, this life thou giv'st,
  sustain
With thy sweet flesh and blood, by Gospel law.
Feed it on Zion's pasty plate-delights,
I'd suck it from her candlestick's sweet
  pipes.

Need makes the oldwife trot; Necessity 25
Saith I must eat this flesh and drink
  this blood,
If not, no life's in me that's worth a fly;
This mortal life, while here, eats mortal
  food

That sends out influences to maintain
A little while, and then holds back the
  same.   30
But soul sweet bread is in God's bakehouse
  made
On Heaven's high dresser-board and
  thoroughly baked,
On Zion's gridiron sapped in'ts dripping
  trade,
That all do live that on it do partake,
It's flesh and blood even of the
  Deity;   35
None that do eat and drink it ever die!

Have I a vital spark even of this fire?
How dull am I? Lord, let thy spirit blow
Upon my coal until its heart is higher
  And I be quickened by the same, and
    glow.   40
Here's manna, angel food, to fatten them
That I must eat or be a withered stem.

Lord, make my faith thy golden quill where-
  through
I vital spirits from thy blood may suck,
Make faith my grinders, thy choice flesh
  to chew,   45
My withered stock shall with frim[1]
  fruits be stuck.
My soul shall then in lively notes forth
  ring
Upon her virginals[2] praise for this thing.

[1] Provincial phrase meaning "flourishing."
[2] A 16th and 17th Century musical instrument.

1603(?) ∾ *Roger Williams* ∾ 1683

ON THE OCCASION of a boundary dispute between Connecticut and
Rhode Island in 1670—in the course of which men from Connecticut invaded a
Rhode Island town, and Rhode Island officially incarcerated some of them—
Roger Williams wrote a letter, dated Providence, June 22, 1670, to Major
Mason, a Connecticut magistrate. The present selection from this letter is

reprinted in a modernized text from *Collections of the Massachusetts Historical Society*, I (1792), 279-280. Williams here implies that New England Puritanism, despite its doctrinal professions, was actually too much of this world in its acquisitive propensities. He reveals, furthermore, the nature of his own Puritanism, still colored by the intransigeance of his "Seeker" days. It was not an Enthusiasm like that of Anne Hutchinson. Nor was it, although a form of mysticism, the sort that found adequate expression for itself in the symbols of orthodoxy. Rather it was an uncompromising renunciant idealism, an extreme ascetic otherworldliness, surprising in a man of Williams' administrative abilities. Primitively Christian and neo-mediaeval was its radical and simplistic reduction of Christianity to the ethics of complete unselfishness and an attitude of total non-attachment toward any of the shadows on the wall of Plato's cave.

[For other selections from the writings of Roger Williams, see Book I, Parts 1 and 3.]

LETTER TO MAJOR MASON
[1792 (1670)]

HOWEVER you satisfy yourselves with the Pequot conquest; with the sealing of your charter some few weeks before ours; with the complaints of particular men to your colony, yet upon due and serious examination of [the] matter, in the sight of God, you will find the business at bottom to be . . . a depraved appetite after the great vanities, dreams, and shadows of this vanishing life, great portions of land, land in this wilderness, as if men were in as great necessity and danger for want of great portions of land, as poor, hungry, thirsty seamen have after a sick and stormy, a long and starving passage. This is one of the gods of New England which the living and most high eternal will destroy and famish. . . . Only this I must crave leave to say, that it looks like a prodigy or monster that countrymen among savages in a wilderness, that professors of God and one mediator, of an eternal life, and that this is like a dream, should not be content with those vast and large tracts which all the other colonies have (like platters and tables full of dainties) but pull and snatch away their poor neighbors' bit or crust: and a crust it is, and a dry hard one too, because of the natives' continual troubles, trials, and vexations.

Alas, Sir, in calm midnight thoughts, what are these leaves and flowers, and smoke, and shadows, and dreams of earthly nothings, about which we poor fools and children, as David saith, disquiet ourselves in vain? Alas, what is all the scuffling of this world for but, *come will you smoke it?* What are all the contentions and wars of this world about, generally, but for greater dishes and bowls of porridge, of which, if we believe God's spirit in scripture, Esau and Jacob were types? Esau will part with the heavenly birthright for his supping, after his hunting, for god belly: and Jacob will part with his porridge for an eternal inheritance: O Lord, give me to make Jacob's and Marie's choice, which shall never be taken from me.

How much sweeter is the counsel of the son of God, to mind first the matters of his kingdom: to take no care for tomorrow; to pluck out, cut off, and fling away right eyes, hands, and feet rather than to be cast whole into hell fire: to consider the ravens and the lilies whom an heavenly father so clothes and feeds: and the counsel of his servant Paul, to roll our cares, for this life also, upon the most high lord, steward of his people, the eternal God: to be content with food and raiment: to mind not our own but every man the things of another; yea and to suffer wrong and part with what we judge is right, yea our lives, and, as poor women martyrs have said, as many as there be hairs upon our heads for the name of God and the son of God his sake. This is humanity, yea this is Christianity. The rest is but formality and picture, courteous idolatry and Jewish and Popish blasphemy against the Christian religion, the Father of spirits, and his son the Lord Jesus. Besides, Sir, the matter with us is not about these children's toys of land, meadows, cattle, government, etc. But here, all over this colony, a great number of weak and distressed souls scattered are flying hither from Old and New England; the Most High and only wise hath in his infinite wisdom provided this country and this corner as a shelter for the poor and persecuted, according to their several persuasions. . . .

1639 ∽ *Increase Mather* ∽ 1723

IN MOST OF the kinds of writing done by American Puritans, one constantly encounters references to Divine Providence. No other concept played so important a rôle in their daily experience and in their religious musings. In factual narratives such as those of Bradford, Winthrop, and Mrs. Rowlandson, in the "witchcraft papers," in sermons, letters, and poetry, it crops up again and again to designate what to the Puritan was an omnipresent reality, both indispensable and indisputable. A heritage from European religious tradition, the concept of Providence, as it was interpreted in New England, embraced two different "operations" of God—one general, and the other particular or special. By his general providence, which was roughly synonymous with creation, God had brought into being the universe and all the agents—supernatural, natural, and human—by which its processes were kept going. He had also determined upon the covenant of Scripture and the sacrificial mediatory "passion" of his son as means by which his foreordained ends for mankind might eventually be realized. So complex, however, was the enterprise of his created cosmos that he had to supplement his general providence and original determinations by a more specific superintendence. And this superintendence demonstrated, more than any other of his "operations," his absolute sovereignty. By an act of special or particular providence, he might suspend the normal workings of things as carried on by his created agents, and interfere personally and miraculously to right some anomaly in human concerns or natural economy, or to hasten the occurrence of any event he desired, or to visit his wrath or grace or his forewarnings upon this or that individual. This special providence, which one American Puritan writer, Edward Johnson, preferred to call "wonder-working providence," was so emphasized by the Puritans that they may be said, as Moses Coit Tyler has suggested, to have reduced God's dealings with man to the category of the picayune and the microscopic.

Despite the interest of many Puritans in studying nature scientifically to arrive at a better understanding of God's intentions in his works, their belief in "special providences" became ultimately an obstacle to the progress of science. It postulated suspension of natural cause and effect and supplied for certain phenomena a facile type of explanation which it was impious to bring into question or to inquire beyond. Long after intelligent New Englanders had greatly modified or even abandoned the concept of special providence, it flourished throughout America as one of the doctrinal "stand-bys" of evangelical sectarian Christianity. Of the numerous attempts made by American Puritans to expound Providence, Increase Mather's treatise, *The Doctrine of Divine Providence,* is one of the most comprehensive.

Born in Dorchester, Mass., Increase Mather, the father of Cotton Mather, was one of the most distinguished Puritan intellectuals of the second generation. Receiving his B.A. from Harvard in 1656 and his M.A. from Trinity College, Dublin, in 1658, he served as a minister in England, returned to Boston and married Maria Cotton, daughter of John Cotton, and thereafter entered on a career which, among its many honors, included a diplomatic mission to England, leadership in New England politics, and the presidency of Harvard College. A prolific writer, Increase published books on a wide variety of subjects. Although a considerable time before his death his power and influence as a pillar of orthodoxy had begun to decline, he had enough flexibility of character to meet, in part at least, the challenge of changing mores and new opinions.

[The following selections, which have been modernized in text, separated by Roman numerals, and arranged in the order of their appearance in different portions of the treatise, are taken from the original edition.]

From
THE DOCTRINE OF DIVINE PROVIDENCE
[1684]

I

THE PROVIDENCE of God is extended to the least and most inconsiderable things that happen in the world. Heathen philosophers acknowledged that the God of heaven has an over-ruling providence in the great affairs and concernments of this lower world, but not in lesser matters. They could say, *Non vacat exiguis rebus adesse Jovi,* [i.e.], the great God had something else to do than to mind little matters, but they know not the Lord aught; he would not be God if the least thing in the world should happen without him. The Scripture teacheth us to believe that the least as well as the greatest matters are ordered by him whose understanding is infinite. His wisdom does extend to fowls of the air, and to the grass of the field, *Mat.* 6. 26, 39; to the sparrows, and to every single sparrow; not one of them is killed without the ordering hand of divine providence. Yea, it reacheth to the very hair upon the heads of men, *Mat.* 10. 29, 30, which showeth that there is not the least thing happening in the world without the knowledge and providence of the most High. . . .

II

For as the world could not give itself a being at first, so neither can it continue itself in being. If the same hand which made all creatures should not preserve them, they would all presently return to their first nothing, *Heb.* 1. 3. Now that is Providence. Creation giveth *primo esse,* but providence giveth *porro esse,* as the schools express it.[1] The frame of nature would be dissolved the next moment, if there were not an hand of providence to uphold and govern all. To preserve and govern the world is too high a work for any mere creature to undertake. Inasmuch, then, as all creatures are preserved and kept in their order, it is because he that sitteth in heaven ruleth over all. A wheel must have a hand to guide it or it will presently turn out of the way and fall to the ground; so, if there were not a divine hand to manage the wheel of providence, all things would run into confusion, and the world would come to ruin in one day. . . .

III

Sometimes there is a seeming contradiction in divine providence. Hence, in *Ezek.* 11. 16, 'tis said *their appearance and their*

work was as it were a wheel in the middle of a wheel. The providences of God seem to interfere with one another sometimes. One providence seems to look this way, another providence seems to look that way, quite contrary one to another. Hence these works are marvelous. Yea, and that which adds to the wonderment is in that the works of God sometimes seem to run counter to his Word: so that there is dark and amazing intricacy in the ways of providence. There is a wheel within a wheel. Not only wise but good men have sometimes been put to a non-plus here. The God of Truth hath in his Word said it shall go well with the righteous and ill with the wicked, and yet he so orders things by his providence, as that the righteous see nothing but miserable days in this world and the vilest of men are at the same time in the highest prosperity, *Jer.* 12. 1. The penman of the seventy-third psalm was sadly puzzled and had like to have lost himself with amazement at this thing. . . .

[1] The distinction is between *original existence* and *continuing existence.*

1663 ∽ *Cotton Mather* ∽ 1728

INCREASE MATHER'S son, Cotton, born in Boston, was so precocious that at the age of twelve he could read, write, and speak Latin and had gone a good way toward mastering Greek and Hebrew. He overcame, like Demosthenes, a serious speech defect—stammering. With two degrees from Harvard, he was a minister at eighteen and soon rose to be his father's colleague at the Second Church in Boston, one of the largest in the colonies. He served its congregation until his death. He was thrice married, had numerous children, and wrote so many books, tracts, and pamphlets—some five hundred in all—that he has proved a major problem to the modern bibliographer. Taking all knowledge for his province, he corresponded with learned men in many parts of Europe. A *locus classicus* of Puritan literary criticism, "Of Poetry and Style," is to be found in his *Manuductio ad Ministerium,* a handbook for students of divinity, first printed in Boston in 1726 and reprinted in London in 1781 and 1789.

Family difficulties, including the insanity of his third wife and the profligacy of a son, gave his later intellectual activity certain curious nuances, but did not materially inhibit its prodigiousness. Becoming a member of the Royal Society in 1713, he contributed scientific papers to its *Transactions*. Although his scientific interests helped launch the witchcraft mania of the early 1690's, they also led him to carry on a fight in 1721, with the help of his father, to promote smallpox inoculation.

The mind of Cotton Mather was an omnivorous, inexhaustible receptacle of heterogeneous erudition; hence many of his books have the motley, crochety, digressive, and encylopedic quality that distinguishes the writing of such English polymaths as Robert Burton and Sir Thomas Browne.

[Two of his most remarkable productions are *Magnalia Christi Americana*, London, 1702, a vast ecclesiastical history of New England, and *The Christian Philosopher,* London, 1721, from which the following selections have been modernized in text by the present editors and supplied with a title indicative of Cotton's unpredictable range of discourse even in brief compass. These selections, which occur in Essay XXXII, "Of Man," illuminate the orthodox Puritans' concept of revelation. For evidences of God's will in creation, they looked not only to scripture, but also to nature and to human reason. In discussing the trinity, Cotton Mather becomes involved in a notion of correspondence between the planes of the human and the supernatural that anticipates one of the central doctrines of later Transcendentalism—the correspondence between man's inner life and the whole of nature.]

OBSERVATIONS ON ATHEISM, NATURE, REASON, AND THE GOSPEL OF CHRIST
[1721]

ATHEISM is now for ever chased and hissed out of the world; everything in the world concurs to a sentence of banishment upon it. Fly, thou monster, and hide, and let not the darkest recesses of Africa itself be able to cherish thee; never dare to show thyself in a world where everything stands ready to overwhelm thee! A Being that must be superior to matter, even the creator and governor of all matter, is everywhere so conspicuous that there can be nothing more monstrous than to deny the God that is above. No system of Atheism has ever yet been offered among the children of men but what may presently be convinced of such inconsistencies that a man must ridiculously believe nothing certain before he can imagine them; it must be a system of

things which cannot stand together! A bundle of contradictions to themselves and to all common sense. I doubt it has been an inconsiderate thing to pay so much of a compliment to Atheism as to bestow solemn treatises full of learned arguments for the refutation of a delirious frenzy which ought rather to be put out of countenance with the most contemptuous indignation. And I fear such writers as have been at the pains to put the objections of Atheism into the most plausible terms, that they may have the honor of laying a devil when they have raised him, have therein done too unadvisedly. However, to so much notice of the raving Atheist we may condescend while we go along, as to tell him that for a man to question the Being of a God, who requires from us an homage of affection and wonderment and obedience to himself and a perpetual concern for the welfare of the human society for which he has in our formation evidently suited us, would be an exalted folly, which undergoes especially two condemnations: it is first condemned by this, that every part of the universe is continually pouring in something for the confuting of it; there is not a corner of the whole world but what supplies a stone towards the infliction of such a death upon the blasphemy as justly belongs to it: and it has also this condemning of it, that men would soon become cannibals to one another by embracing it; men being utterly destitute of any principle to keep them honest in the dark, there would be no integrity left in the world, but they would be as the fishes of the sea to one another, and worse than the creeping things, that have no ruler over them. Indeed from everything in the world there is this voice more audible than the loudest thunder to us: *God hath spoken, and these two things have I heard!* First, *believe and adore a glorious God, who has made all these things, and know thou that he will bring thee into judgment!* And then *be careful to do nothing but what shall be for the good of the community which the glorious God has made thee a member of.* Were what God hath spoken duly regarded and were these two things duly complied with, the world would be soon revived into a desirable garden of God and mankind would be fetched up into very comfortable circumstances; till then the world continues in a wretched condition, full of doleful creatures, with wild beasts crying in its desolate houses, dragons in its most pleasant palaces. And now declare, O everything that is reasonable, declare and pronounce upon it whether it be possible that maxims absolutely necessary to the subsistence and happiness of mankind can be falsities! There is no possibility for this, that cheats and lies must be so necessary that the ends which alone are worthy of a glorious God cannot be attained without having them imposed upon us!

Having dispatched the Atheist with bestowing on him not many thoughts, yet more than could be deserved by such an idiot, I will proceed now to propose two general strokes of piety, which appear to a Christian Philosopher as unexceptionable as any proposals that ever were made to him.

First, the works of the glorious God exhibited to our view, 'tis most certain they do bespeak, and they should excite our acknowledgment of, his glories appearing in them: the great God is infinitely gratified in beholding the displays of his own infinite power and wisdom and goodness in the works which he has made; but it is also a most acceptable gratification to him when such of his works as are the rational beholders of themselves and of the rest shall with devout minds acknowledge his perfections, which they see shining there. Never does one endued with Reason do anything more evidently reasonable than when he makes everything that occurs to him in the vast fabric of the world an incentive to some agreeable efforts and sallies of religion. . . .

And then, secondly, the Christ of God must not be forgotten, who is the Lord of all. I am not ashamed of the Gospel of Christ, of which I will affirm constantly, that if the philosopher do not call it in, he paganizes and leaves the finest and brightest part of his work unfinished. . . .

We will add one thing more: though the one God in his three subsistences be the governor as well as the creator of the world, and so the son of God ever had what we call the natural government of the world, yet upon the fall of mankind there is a mediatory kingdom that becomes expedient, that so guilty man and that which was lost may be brought to God; and the singular honor of this mediatory kingdom is more immediately and most agreeably assigned to the Son of God, who assumes the man Jesus into his own person and has all power in heaven and earth given to him; all things are now commanded and ordered by the Son of God in the man upon the throne and this to the glory of the Father, by whom the mediatory kingdom is erected and so conferred. This peculiar kingdom, thus managed by the Son of God in our Jesus, will cease when the illustrious ends of it are all accomplished, and then the Son of God, no longer having such a distinct kingdom of his own, shall return to those eternal circumstances, wherein he shall reign with the Father and the Holy Spirit, one God, blessed for ever. In the mean time, what creatures can we behold without being obliged to some such doxology as this: *O son of God, incarnate and enthroned in my Jesus, this is part of thy dominion! What a great king art thou, and what a name hast thou above every name, and how vastly extended is thy dominion! Dominion and fear is with thee, and there is no number of thine armies! All the inhabitants of the earth, and their most puissant emperors, are to be reputed as nothing before thee!* . . .

I will finish with a speculation which my most valuable Dr. Cheyne[1] has a little more largely prosecuted and cultivated.

All intelligent compound beings have their whole entertainment in these three principles, the *desire,* the *object,* and the *sensation* arising from the congruity between them; this analogy is preserved full and clear through the spiritual world, yea, and through the material also; so universal and perpetual an analogy can arise from nothing but its pattern and archetype in the infinite God or Maker; and could we carry it up to the source of it, we should find the trinity of persons in the eternal Godhead admirably exhibited to us. In the Godhead we may first apprehend a desire, an infinitely active, ardent, powerful thought, proposing of satisfaction; let this represent God the Father: but it is not possible for any object but God Himself to satisfy Himself and fill His desire of happiness; therefore He Himself reflected in

upon himself, and contemplating His own infinite perfections, even the brightness of His glory and the express image of His person, must answer this glorious intention; and this may represent to us God the Son. Upon this contemplation, wherein God Himself does behold and possess and enjoy Himself, there cannot but arise a love, a joy, an acquiescence of God Himself within Himself and worthy of a God; this may shadow out to us the third and the last of the principles in this mysterious ternary, that is to say, the Holy Spirit. Though these three relations of the Godhead in itself, when derived analogically down to creatures, may appear but modifications of a real subsistence, yet in the supreme infinitude of the Divine Nature they must be infinitely real and living principles. Those which are but relations when transferred to created beings are glorious realities in the infinite God. And in this view of the Holy Trinity, low as it is, it is impossible the Son should be without the Father, or the Father without the Son, or both without the Holy Spirit; it is impossible the Son should not be necessarily and eternally begotten of the Father or that the Holy Spirit should not necessarily and eternally proceed both from Him and from the Son. Thus from what occurs throughout the whole creation, Reason forms an imperfect idea of this incomprehensible mystery.

But it is time to stop here, and indeed how can we go any further!

---

[1] Dr. George Cheyne's *Philosophical Principles of Religion, Natural and Revealed* (London, 1715) is the source of this "speculation."

1703 ∾ ***Jonathan Edwards*** ∾ *1758*

THREE OF the most complex and interesting minds among American men of letters before 1800 were those of Jonathan Edwards, Benjamin Franklin, and Thomas Paine, although they were minds of an entirely different cast. Son of the Rev. Timothy Edwards and grandson of the Rev. Solomon Stoddard, Edwards was born at East Windsor, Connecticut. His precocious interest in both science and philosophy was soon supplemented by a desire to excel in theology. After his graduation from Yale in 1720, he spent two more years mastering the intricacies of the latter study. In 1723, a convert to Calvinism, he was minister of a Presbyterian church in New York City, and in 1724 returned to Yale as a tutor. When his academic career was interrupted by illness, he became the colleague of his grandfather in the pastorate at Northampton, Mass. He married Sarah Pierrepont in July, 1727.

In the 1730's and the early 1740's Edwards' fervid and sometimes brimstony preaching was one of the stimuli to a revival of religion throughout New England known as "the Great Awakening" and destined to have its counterparts in other sections of the country as the century advanced. Thereafter his reputation as a theologian steadily increased, bulwarked by his series of publications. Dissension, however, eventually broke out in his pastorate over minutiae of doctrine and polity, and reached a climax when Edwards sought to curb among the young in his congregation the reading of allegedly indecent books dealing with the secrets of the midwife's art. Dismissed in 1750 from his Northampton church, Edwards became virtually an exile in the Western Massachusetts frontier settlement of Stockbridge, where he served as pastor of the church and missionary to the Indians. In 1757 he was chosen president of the College of New Jersey, now Princeton, to succeed his son-in-law, the Rev. Aaron Burr, father of the Aaron Burr of later historical notoriety. Assuming his new duties in January, 1758, President Edwards died in March of that year after an inoculation against smallpox, leaving among the unwritten masterpieces of literature his projected *History of the Work of Redemption*, which he planned to be the crowning achievement of his career as theologian.

Without this unwritten all-embracing *Summa*, Edwards' published work remains of immense significance in the development of American religious thought. In seeking to reestablish the main doctrines of Calvinism on a philosophic basis that would make them acceptable to the 18th Century, he was perhaps most successful in his closely reasoned *A Careful and Strict Enquiry, into the Modern Prevailing Notions of that Freedom of Will which is supposed to be Essential to Moral Agency, Vertue and Vice, Reward and*

Punishment, Praise and Blame, Boston, 1754. Yet, in his hands, the tradition of Puritanism was subtly transformed.

[For one thing, its mystical strain appealed strongly to his sensibility. This is strikingly apparent in a brief tribute to his wife-to-be, Sarah Pierrepont, written in 1723 upon a blank leaf in a book and first printed in S. E. Dwight's *Life* in Edwards' *Works,* 1829, Vol. I. It is also apparent in his "Personal Narrative," written some time after January, 1739, and first printed in Samuel Hopkins' *Life and Character,* Boston, 1765. Of his numerous writings that grew out of his experience in "the Great Awakening," the most mature is *A Treatise Concerning Religious Affections,* Boston, 1746; here his mysticism leads him to exalt a religion of the heart above a mere religion of the head, as is shown by the third of the following selections, which is taken from this treatise and supplied with a title by the present editors. Finally, Edwards' metaphysical bent caused him to conceive of God as a kind of supreme creative artist producing the universe out of that "obscure inner necessity" to express himself which, according to Joseph Conrad, is the source of all works of art. This bizarre phase of Edwards' thinking emerges in his posthumous *Concerning the End for which God Created the World,* published with his *The Nature of True Virtue* under the title *Two Dissertations,* Boston, 1765. The last of the following selections is from this work, with a title supplied by the present editors.]

SARAH PIERREPONT
[1829 (written 1723)]

THEY SAY there is a young lady in [New Haven] who is beloved of that Great Being, who made and rules the world, and that there are certain seasons in which this Great Being, in some way or other invisible, comes to her and fills her mind with exceeding sweet delight, and that she hardly cares for anything, except to meditate on him—that she expects after a while to be received up where he is, to be raised up out of the world and caught up into heaven; being assured that he loves her too well to let her remain at a distance from him always. There she is to dwell with him, and to be ravished with his love and delight forever. Therefore, if you present all the world before her, wth the richest of its treasures, she disregards it and cares not for it, and is unmindful of any pain or affliction. She has a strange sweetness in her mind, and singular purity in her af-

fections; is most just and conscientious in all her conduct; and you could not persuade her to do any thing wrong or sinful, if you would give her all the world, lest she should offend this Great Being. She is of a wonderful sweetness, calmness and universal benevolence of mind; especially after this Great God has manifested himself to her mind. She will sometimes go about from place to place, singing sweetly; and seems to be always full of joy and pleasure; and no one knows for what. She loves to be alone, walking in the fields and groves, and seems to have some one invisible always conversing with her.

From
PERSONAL NARRATIVE
[1765]

I HAD a variety of concerns and exercises about my soul from my childhood; but had two more remarkable seasons of awakening, before I met with that change by whick

I was brought to those new dispositions, and that new sense of things, that I have since had. The first time was when I was a boy, some years before I went to college, at a time of remarkable awakening in my father's congregation. I was then very much affected for many months, and concerned about the things of religion, and my soul's salvation; and was abundant in duties. I used to pray five times a day in secret, and to spend much time in religious talk with other boys, and used to meet with them to pray together. I experienced I know not what kind of delight in religion. My mind was much engaged in it, and had much self-righteous pleasure; and it was my delight to abound in religious duties. I with some of my school-mates joined together, and built a booth in a swamp, in a very retired spot, for a place of prayer. And besides, I had particular secret places of my own in the woods, where I used to retire by myself; and was from time to time much affected. My affections seemed to be lively and easily moved, and I seemed to be in my element when engaged in religious duties. And I am ready to think, many are deceived with such affections, and such a kind of delight as I then had in religion, and mistake it for grace.

But in process of time, my convictions and affections wore off; and I entirely lost all those affections and delights and left off secret prayer, at least as to any constant performance of it; and returned like a dog to his vomit, and went on in the ways of sin. Indeed I was at times very uneasy, especially towards the latter part of my time at college; when it pleased God, to seize me with the pleurisy; in which he brought me nigh to the grave, and shook me over the pit of hell. And yet, it was not long after my recovery, before I fell again into my old ways of sin. But God would not suffer me to go on with my quietness; I had great and violent inward struggles, till, after many conflicts, with wicked inclinations, repeated resolutions, and bonds that I laid myself under by a kind of vows to God, I was brought wholly to break off all former wicked ways, and all ways of known outward sin; and to apply myself to seek salvation, and practice many religious duties; but without that kind of affection and delight which I had formerly experienced. My concern now wrought more by inward struggles and conflicts, and self-reflections. I made seeking my salvation the main business of my life. But yet, it seems to me, I sought after a miserable manner; which has made me sometimes since to question, whether ever it issued in that which was saving; being ready to doubt, whether such miserable seeking ever succeeded. I was indeed brought to seek salvation in a manner that I never was before; I felt a spirit to part with all things in the world, for an interest in Christ.—My concern continued and prevailed, with many exercising thoughts and inward struggles; but yet it never seemed to be proper to express that concern by the name of terror.

From my childhood up, my mind had been full of objections against the doctrine of God's sovereignty, in choosing whom he would to eternal life, and rejecting whom he pleased; leaving them eternally to perish, and be everlastingly tormented in hell. It used to appear like a horrible doctrine to me. But I remember the time very well, when I seemed to be convinced, and fully satisfied, as to this sovereignty of God, and his justice in thus eternally disposing of men, according to his sovereign pleasure. But never could give an account, how, or by what means, I was thus convinced, not in the least imagining at the time, nor a long time after, that there was any extraordinary influence of God's Spirit in it; but only that now I saw further, and my reason apprehended the justice and reasonableness of it. However, my mind rested in it; and it put an end to all those cavils and objections. And there has been a wonderful alteration in my mind, with respect to the doctrine of God's sovereignty, from that day to this; so that I scarce ever have found so much as the rising of an objection against it, in the most absolute sense, in God's shewing mercy to whom he will shew mercy, and hardening whom he will. God's absolute sovereignty and justice, with respect to salvation and damnation, is what my mind seems to rest assured of, as much as of any thing that I see with my eyes; at least it is so at times. But I have often, since that first conviction, had quite another kind of sense of God's sovereignty than I had then. I have often since had not only a conviction, but a delightful conviction. The doctrine has very often appeared exceeding pleasant, bright, and sweet.

Absolute sovereignty is what I love to ascribe to God. But my first conviction was not so.

The first instance that I remember of that sort of inward, sweet delight in God and divine things that I have lived much in since, was on reading those words, 1 Tim. i :17. *Now unto the King eternal, immortal, invisible, the only wise God, be honor and glory forever and ever, Amen.* As I read the words, there came into my soul, and was as it were diffused through it, a sense of the glory of the Divine Being; a new sense, quite different from any thing I ever experienced before. Never any words of scripture seemed to me as these words did. I thought within myself, how excellent a being that was, and how happy I should be, if I might enjoy that God, and be wrapt up in heaven, and be as it were swallowed up in him forever! I kept saying, and as it were singing over these words of scripture to myself; and went to pray to God that I might enjoy him, and prayed in a manner quite different from what I used to do; with a new sort of affection. But it never came into my thought, that there was any thing spiritual, or of a saving nature in this.

From about that time, I began to have a new kind of apprehensions and ideas of Christ, and the work of redemption, and the glorious way of salvation by him. An inward, sweet sense of these things, at times, came into my heart; and my soul was led away in pleasant views and contemplations of them. And my mind was greatly engaged to spend my time in read-

ing and meditating on Christ, on the beauty and excellency of his person, and the lovely way of salvation by free grace in him. I found no books so delightful to me, as those that treated of these subjects. Those words, Cant. ii : 1, used to be abundantly with me, *I am the Rose of Sharon, and the Lily of the valleys.* The words seemed to me, sweetly to represent the loveliness and beauty of Jesus Christ. The whole book of Canticles used to be pleasant to me, and I used to be much in reading it, about that time; and found, from time to time, an inward sweetness, that would carry me away, in my contemplations. This I know not how to express otherwise, than by a calm, sweet abstraction of soul from all the concerns of this world; and sometimes a kind of vision, or fixed ideas and imaginations, of being alone in the mountains, or some solitary wilderness, far from all mankind, sweetly conversing with Christ, and wrapt and swallowed up in God. The sense I had of divine things, would often of a sudden kindle up, as it were, sweet burning in my heart; an ardor of soul, that I know not how to express.

Not long after I began to experience these things, I gave an account to my father of some things that had passed in my mind. I was pretty much affected by the discourse we had together; and when the discourse was ended, I walked abroad alone, in a solitary place in my father's pasture for contemplation. And as I was walking there and looking up on the sky and clouds, there came into my mind so sweet a sense of the glorious *majesty* and *grace* of God, that I know not how to express. I seemed to see them both in a sweet conjunction; majesty and meekness joined together; it was a gentle, and holy majesty; and also a majestic meekness; a high, great, and holy gentleness.

After this my sense of divine things gradually increased, and became more and more lively, and had more of that inward sweetness. The appearance of every thing was altered; there seemed to be, as it were, a calm, sweet cast, or appearance of divine glory, in almost every thing. God's excellency, his wisdom, his purity and love, seemed to appear in every thing; in the sun, moon, and stars; in the clouds, and blue sky; in the grass, flowers, trees; in the water, and all nature; which used greatly to fix my mind. I often used to sit and view the moon for continuance; and in the day, spent much time in viewing the clouds and sky, to behold the sweet glory of God in these things; in the mean time, singing forth, with a low voice, my contemplations of the Creator and Redeemer. And scarce any thing, among all the works of nature, was so delightful to me as thunder and lightning; formerly, nothing had been so terrible to me. Before, I used to be uncommonly terrified with thunder, and to be struck with terror when I saw a thunder storm rising; but now, on the contrary, it rejoiced me. I felt God, so to speak, at the first appearance of a thunder storm; and used to take the opportunity, at such times, to fix myself in order to view the clouds, and see the lightnings play, and hear the majestic and awful voice of God's thunder, which oftentimes was exceedingly entertaining, leading me to sweet contemplations of my great and glorious God. While thus engaged, it always seemed natural to me to sing, or chant for my meditations; or, to speak my thoughts in soliloquies with a singing voice.

I felt then great satisfaction, as to my good state; but that did not content me. I had vehement longings of soul after God and Christ, and after more holiness, wherewith my heart seemed to be full, and ready to break; which often brought to my mind the words of the Psalmist, Psal. cxix. 28: *My soul breaketh for the longing it hath.* I often felt a mourning and lamenting in my heart, that I had not turned to God sooner, that I might have had more time to grow in grace. My mind was greatly fixed on divine things; almost perpetually in the contemplation of them. I spent most of my time in thinking of divine things, year after year; often walking alone in the woods, and solitary places, for meditation, solilo-

quy, and prayer, and converse with God; and it was always my manner, at such times, to sing forth my contemplations. I was almost constantly in ejaculatory prayer wherever I was. Prayer seemed to be natural to me, as the breath by which the inward burnings of my heart had vent. The delights which I now felt in the things of religion, were of an exceedingly different kind from those before mentioned, that I had when a boy; and what I then had no more notion of, than one born blind has of pleasant and beautiful colors. They were of a more inward, pure, soul-animating and refreshing nature. Those former delights never reached the heart; and did not arise from any sight of the divine excellency of the things of God; or any taste of the soul-satisfying and life-giving good there is in them.

My sense of divine things seemed gradually to increase, until I went to preach at New York, which was about a year and a half after they began; and while I was there, I felt them, very sensibly, in a higher degree than I had done before. My longings after God and holiness, were much increased. Pure and humble, holy and heavenly Christianity, appeared exceedingly amiable to me. I felt a burning desire to be in every thing a complete Christian; and conform to the blessed image of Christ; and that I might live, in all things, according to the pure and blessed rules of the gospel. I had an eager thirsting after progress in these things; which put me upon pursuing and pressing after them. It was my continual strife day and night, and constant inquiry, how I should *be* more holy, and *live* more holily, and more becoming a child of God, and a disciple of Christ. I now sought an increase of grace and holiness, and a holy life, with much more earnestness, than ever I sought grace before I had it. I used to be continually examining myself, and studying and contriving for likely ways and means, how I should live holily, with far greater diligence and earnestness, than ever I pursued any thing in my life; but yet with too great a dependence on my own strength; which afterwards proved a great damage to me. My experience had not then taught me, as it has done since, my extreme feebleness and impotence, every manner of way; and the bottomless depths of secret corruption and deceit there was in my heart. However, I went on with my eager pursuit after more holiness, and conformity to Christ.

The heaven I desired was a heaven of holiness; to be with God, and to spend my eternity in divine love, and holy communion with Christ. My mind was very much taken up with contemplations on heaven, and the enjoyments there; and living there in perfect holiness, humility and love. And it used at that time to appear a great part of the happiness of heaven, that there the saints could express their love to Christ. It appeared to me a great clog and burden, that what I felt within, I could not express as I desired. The inward ardor of my soul, seemed to be hindered and pent up, and could not freely flame out as it would. I used often to think, how in heaven this principle should freely and fully vent and express itself. Heaven appeared exceedingly delightful, as a world of love; and that all happiness consisted in living in pure, humble, heavenly, divine love.

I remember the thoughts I used then to have of holiness; and said sometimes to myself, "I do certainly know that I love holiness, such as the gospel prescribes." It appeared to me, that there was nothing in it but what was ravishingly lovely; the highest beauty and amiableness—a *divine* beauty; far purer than any thing here upon earth; and that every thing else was like mire and defilement, in comparison of it.

Holiness, as I then wrote down some of my contemplations on it, appeared to me to be of a sweet, pleasant, charming, serene, calm nature; which brought an inexpressible purity, brightness, peacefulness and ravishment to the soul. In other words, that it made the soul like a field or garden of God, with all manner of pleasant flowers; all pleasant, delightful, and undisturbed; enjoying a sweet calm, and the gently

vivifying beams of the sun. The soul of a true Christian, as I then wrote my meditations, appeared like such a little white flower as we see in the spring of the year; low and humble on the ground, opening its bosom to receive the pleasant beams of the sun's glory; rejoicing as it were in a calm rapture; diffusing around a sweet fragrancy; standing peacefully and lovingly, in the midst of other flowers round about; all in like manner opening their bosoms, to drink in the light of the sun. There was no part of creature holiness, that I had so great a sense of its loveliness, as humility, brokenness of heart and poverty of spirit; and there was nothing that I so earnestly longed for. My heart panted after this, to lie low before God, as in the dust; that I might be nothing, and that God might be ALL, that I might become as a little child.

While at New York, I was sometimes much affected with reflections on my past life, considering how late it was before I began to be truly religious; and how wickedly I had lived till then; and once so as to weep abundantly, and for a considerable time together.

On *January* 12, 1723, I made a solemn dedication of myself to God, and wrote it down; giving up myself, and all that I had to God; to be for the future in no respect my own; to act as one that had no right to himself, in any respect. And solemnly vowed to take God for my whole portion and felicity; looking on nothing else as any part of my happiness, nor acting as if it were; and his law for the constant rule of my obedience; engaging to fight with all my might, against the world, the flesh and the devil, to the end of my life. But I have reason to be infinitely humbled, when I consider how much I have failed of answering my obligation.

I had then abundance of sweet religious conversation in the family where I lived, with Mr. John Smith and his pious mother. My heart was knit in affection to those in whom were appearances of true piety; and I could bear the thoughts of no other companions, but such as were holy, and the disciples of the blessed Jesus. I had great longings for the advancement of Christ's kingdom in the world; and my secret prayer used to be, in great part, taken up in praying for it. If I heard the least hint of any thing that happened, in any part of the world, that appeared, in some respect or other, to have a favorable aspect on the interest of Christ's kingdom, my soul eagerly catched at it; and it would much animate and refresh me. I used to be eager to read public news letters, mainly for that end; to see if I could not find some news favorable to the interest of religion in the world.

I very frequently used to retire into a solitary place, on the banks of Hudson's river, at some distance from the city, for contemplation on divine things, and secret converse with God; and had many sweet hours there. Sometimes Mr. Smith and I walked there together, to converse on the things of God; and our conversation used to turn much on the advancement of Christ's kingdom in the world, and the glorious things that God would accomplish for his church in the latter days. I had then, and at other times the greatest delight in the holy scriptures, of any book whatsoever. Oftentimes in reading it, every word seemed to touch my heart. I felt a harmony between something in my heart, and those sweet and powerful words. I seemed often to see so much light exhibited by every sentence, and such a refreshing food communicated, that I could not get along in reading; often dwelling long on one sentence, to see the wonders contained in it; and yet almost every sentence seemed to be full of wonders.

I came away from New York in the month of April, 1723, and had a most bitter parting with Madam Smith and her son. My heart seemed to sink within me at leaving the family and city, where I had enjoyed so many sweet and pleasant days. I went from New York to Weathersfield, by water, and as I sailed away, I kept sight of the city as long as I could.

However, that night, after this sorrowful parting, I was greatly comforted in God at Westchester, where we went ashore to lodge; and had a pleasant time of it all the voyage to Saybrook. It was sweet to me to think of meeting dear Christians in heaven, where we should never part more. At Saybrook we went ashore to lodge, on Saturday, and there kept the Sabbath; where I had a sweet and refreshing season, walking alone in the fields.

After I came home to Windsor, I remained much in a like frame of mind, as when at New York; only sometimes I felt my heart ready to sink with the thoughts of my friends at New York. My support was in contemplations on the heavenly state; as I find in my Diary of May 1, 1723. It was a comfort to think of that state, where there is fulness of joy; where reigns heavenly, calm, and delightful love, without alloy; where there are continually the dearest expressions of this love; where is the enjoyment of the persons loved, without ever parting; where those persons who appear so lovely in this world, will really be inexpressibly more lovely and full of love to us. And how sweetly will the mutual lovers join together to sing the praises of God and the Lamb! How will it fill us with joy to think, that this enjoyment, these sweet exercises will never cease, but will last to all eternity! I continued much in the same frame, in the general, as when at New York, till I went to New Haven as tutor to the college; particularly once at Bolton, on a journey from Boston, while walking out alone in the fields. After I went to New Haven I sunk in religion; my mind being diverted from my eager pursuits after holiness, by some affairs that greatly perplexed and distracted my thoughts.

In September, 1725, I was taken ill at New Haven, and while endeavoring to go home to Windsor, was so ill at the North Village, that I could go no further; where I lay sick for about a quarter of a year. In this sickness God was pleased to visit me again with the sweet influences of his

Spirit. My mind was greatly engaged there in divine, pleasant contemplations, and longings of soul. I observed that those who watched with me, would often be looking out wishfully for the morning; which brought to my mind those words of the Psalmist, and which my soul with delight made its own language, *My soul waiteth for the Lord, more than they that watch for the morning, I say, more than they that watch for the morning;* and when the light of day came in at the windows, it refreshed my soul from one morning to another. It seemed to be some image of the light of God's glory.

I remember, about that time, I used greatly to long for the conversion of some that I was concerned with; I could gladly honor them, and with delight be a servant to them, and lie at their feet, if they were but truly holy. But, some time after this, I was again greatly diverted in my mind with some temporal concerns that exceedingly took up my thoughts, greatly to the wounding of my soul; and went on through various exercises, that it would be tedious to relate, which gave me much more experience of my own heart, than ever I had before.

Since I came to this town, I have often had sweet complacency in God, in views of his glorious perfections and the excellency of Jesus Christ. God has appeared to me a glorious and lovely being, chiefly on the account of his holiness. The holiness of God has always appeared to me the most lovely of all his attributes. The doctrines of God's absolute sovereignty, and free grace, in shewing mercy to whom he would shew mercy; and man's absolute dependence on the operations of God's Holy Spirit, have very often appeared to me as sweet and glorious doctrines. . . .

Once as I rode out into the woods for my health, in 1737, having alighted from my horse in a retired place, as my manner commonly has been, to walk for divine contemplation and prayer, I had a view that for me was extraordinary, of the glory of the Son of God, as Mediator between

God and man, and his wonderful, great, full, pure and sweet grace and love, and meek and gentle condescension. This grace that appeared so calm and sweet, appeared also great above the heavens. The person of Christ appeared ineffably excellent with an excellency great enough to swallow up all thought and conception—which continued as near as I can judge, about an hour; which kept me the greater part of the time in a flood of tears, and weeping aloud. I felt an ardency of soul to be, what I know not otherwise how to express, emptied and annihilated; to lie in the dust, and to be full of Christ alone; to love him with a holy and pure love; to trust in him; to live upon him; to serve and follow him; and to be perfectly sanctified and made pure, with a divine and heavenly purity. I have, several other times, had views very much of the same nature, and which have had the same effects.

I have many times had a sense of the glory of the third person in the Trinity, in his office of Sanctifier; in his holy operations, communicating divine light and life to the soul. God, in the communications of his Holy Spirit, has appeared as an infinite fountain of divine glory and sweetness; being full, and sufficient to fill and satisfy the soul; pouring forth itself in sweet communications; like the sun in its glory, sweetly and pleasantly diffusing light and life. And I have sometimes had an affecting sense of the excellency of the word of God, as a word of life; as the light of life; a sweet, excellent, life-giving word; accompanied with a thirsting after that word, that it might dwell richly in my heart.

Often, since I lived in this town, I have had very affecting views of my own sinfulness and vileness; very frequently to such a degree as to hold me in a kind of loud weeping, sometimes for a considerable time together; so that I have often been forced to shut myself up. I have had a vastly greater sense of my own wickedness, and the badness of my own heart, than ever I had before my conversion. It has often appeared to me, that if God should mark iniquity against me, I should appear the very worst of all mankind; of all that have been, since the beginning of the world to this time; and that I should have by far the lowest place in hell. When others, that have come to talk with me about their soul concerns, have expressed the sense they have had of their own wickedness, by saying that it seemed to them, that they were as bad as the devil himself; I thought their expression seemed exceedingly faint and feeble, to represent my wickedness.

My wickedness, as I am in myself, has long appeared to me perfectly ineffable, and swallowing up all thought and imagination; like an infinite deluge, or mountains over my head. I know not how to express better what my sins appear to me to be, than by heaping infinite upon infinite, and multiplying infinite by infinite. Very often, for these many years, these expressions are in my mind, and in my mouth, "Infinite upon infinite—Infinite upon infinite!" When I look into my heart, and take a view of my wickedness, it looks like an abyss infinitely deeper than hell. And it appears to me, that were it not for free grace, exalted and raised up to the infinite height of all the fulness and glory of the great Jehovah, and the arm of his power and grace stretched forth in all the majesty of his power, and in all the glory of his sovereignty, I should appear sunk down in my sins below hell itself; far beyond the sight of every thing, but the eye of sovereign grace, that can pierce even down to such a depth. And yet, it seems to me, that my conviction of sin is exceedingly small, and faint; it is enough to amaze me, that I have no more sense of my sin. I know certainly, that I have very little sense of my sinfulness. When I have had turns of weeping and crying for my sins, I thought I knew at the time, that my repentance was nothing to my sin.

I have greatly longed of late, for a broken heart, and to lie low before God;

and, when I ask for humility, I cannot bear the thoughts of being no more humble than other Christians. It seems to me, that though their degrees of humility may be suitable for them, yet it would be a vile self-exaltation to me, not to be the lowest in humility of all mankind. Others speak of their longing to be "humbled to the dust"; that may be a proper expression for them, but I always think of myself, that I ought, and it is an expression that has long been natural for me to use in prayer, "to lie infinitely low before God." And it is affecting to think, how ignorant I was, when a young Christian, of the bottomless, infinite depths of wickedness, pride, hypocrisy and deceit, left in my heart.

I have a much greater sense of my universal, exceeding dependence on God's grace and strength, and mere good pleasure, of late, than I used formerly to have; and have experienced more of an abhorrence of my own righteousness. The very thought of any joy arising in me, on any consideration of my own amiableness, performances, or experiences, or any goodness of heart or life, is nauseous and detestable to me. And yet I am greatly afflicted with a proud and self-righteous spirit, much more sensibly than I used to be formerly. I see that serpent rising and putting forth its head continually, every where, all around me.

Though it seems to me, that, in some respects, I was a far better Christian, for two or three years after my first conversion, than I am now; and lived in a more constant delight and pleasure; yet, of late years, I have had a more full and constant sense of the absolute sovereignty of God, and a delight in that sovereignty; and have had more of a sense of the glory of Christ, as a Mediator revealed in the gospel. On one Saturday night, in particular, I had such a discovery of the excellency of the gospel above all other doctrines, that I could not but say to myself, "This is my chosen light, my chosen doctrine"; and of Christ, "This is my chosen Prophet." It appeared sweet, beyond all expression, to follow Christ, and to be taught, and enlightened, and instructed by him; to learn of him, and live to him. Another Saturday night, (*January*, 1739) I had such a sense, how sweet and blessed a thing it was to walk in the way of duty; to do that which was right and meet to be done, and agreeable to the holy mind of God; that it caused me to break forth into a kind of loud weeping, which held me some time, so that I was forced to shut myself up, and fasten the doors. I could not but, as it were, cry out, "How happy are they which do that which is right in the sight of God! They are blessed indeed, they are the happy ones!" I had, at the same time, a very affecting sense, how meet and suitable it was that God should govern the world, and order all things according to his own pleasure; and I rejoiced in it, that God reigned, and that his will was done.

AFFECTIVE VERSUS MERELY DOCTRINAL RELIGION
[1746]

THE AFFECTIONS and passions are frequently spoken of as the same; and yet in the more common use of speech, there is in some respect a difference; and affection is a word that in its ordinary signification seems to be something more extensive than passion, being used for all vigorous lively actings of the will or inclination; but passion for those that are more sudden and whose effects on the animal spirits are more violent, and the mind more overpowered, and less in its own command.

As all the exercises of the inclination and will are either in approving and liking, or disapproving and rejecting, so the affections are of two sorts: they are those by which the soul is carried out to what is in view, cleaving to it, or seeking it; or those by which it is averse from it, and opposes it.

Of the former sort are love, desire, hope, joy, gratitude, complacence. Of the latter kind are hatred, fear, anger, grief, and such like; which it is needless now to stand particularly to define. . . .

The Author of the human nature has not only given affections to men, but has made them very much the spring of men's actions. As the affections do not only necessarily belong to the human nature, but are a very great part of it; so (inasmuch as by regeneration persons are renewed in the whole man and sanctified throughout) holy affections do not only necessarily belong to true religion, but are a very great part of it. And as true religion is of a practical nature, and God hath so constituted the human nature that the affections are very much the spring of men's actions, this also shows that true religion must consist very much in the affections.

Such is man's nature that he is very inactive any otherwise than he is influenced by some affection, either love or hatred, desire, hope, fear, or some other. These affections we see to be the springs that set men a-going, in all the affairs of life, and engage them in all their pursuits: these are the things that put men forward, and carry them along, in all their worldly business; and especially are men excited and animated by these, in all affairs wherein they are earnestly engaged, and which they pursue with vigor. We see the world of mankind to be exceeding busy and active; and the affections of men are the springs of the motion: take away all love and hatred, all hope and fear, all anger, zeal, and affectionate desire, and the world would be in a great measure motionless and dead; there would be no such thing as activity amongst mankind or any earnest pursuit whatsover. It is affection that engages the covetous man, and him that is greedy of worldly profits, in his pursuits; and it is by the affections that the ambitious man is put forward in his pursuit of worldly glory; and it is the affections also that actuate the voluptuous man in his pursuit of pleasure and sensual delights:

the world continues, from age to age, in a continual commotion and agitation in a pursuit of these things; but take away all affection, and the spring of all this motion would be gone, and the motion itself would cease. And as in worldly things worldly affections are very much the spring of men's motion and action, so in religious matters the spring of their actions is very much religious affection: he that has doctrinal knowledge and speculation only, without affection, never is engaged in the business of religion.

Nothing is more manifest, in fact, than that the things of religion take hold of men's souls no further than they affect them. There are multitudes that often hear the word of God, and therein hear of those things that are infinitely great and important, and that most nearly concern them, and all that is heard seems to be wholly ineffectual upon them, and to make no alteration in their disposition or behavior; and the reason is, they are not affected with what they hear. There are many that often hear of the glorious perfections of God, his almighty power and boundless wisdom, his infinite majesty, and that holiness of God by which he is of purer eyes than to behold evil, and cannot look on iniquity, and the heavens are not pure in his sight, and of God's infinite goodness and mercy, and hear of the great works of God's wisdom, power, and goodness, wherein there appear the admirable manifestations of these perfections; they hear particularly of the unspeakable love of God and Christ, and of the great things that Christ has done and suffered, and of the great things of another world, of eternal misery in bearing the fierceness and wrath of Almighty God, and of endless blessedness and glory in the presence of God, and the enjoyment of his dear love; they also hear the peremptory commands of God, and his gracious counsels and warnings, and the sweet invitations of the gospel; I say they often hear these things and yet remain as they were before, with no sensible alteration in them, either in heart or practice, because they are not affected with what they hear; and ever will be so till they are affected.—I am bold to assert that there never was any considerable change wrought in the mind or conversation of any person by anything of a religious nature that ever he read, heard, or saw, that had not his affections moved. Never was a natural man engaged earnestly to seek his salvation; never were any such brought to cry after wisdom, and lift up their voice for understanding, and to wrestle with God in prayer for mercy; and never was one humbled and brought to the foot of God from anything that ever he heard or imagined of his own unworthiness and deserving of God's displeasure; nor was ever one induced to fly for refuge unto Christ, while his heart remained unaffected. Nor was there ever a saint awakened out of a cold, lifeless frame, or recovered from a declining state in religion, and brought back from a lamentable departure from God, without having his heart affected. And in a word, there never was anything considerable brought to pass in the heart or life of any man living, by the things of religion, that had not his heart deeply affected by those things. . . .

THE AESTHETICS OF PLENITUDE
[1765]

IT SEEMS a thing in itself proper and desirable that the glorious attributes of God, which consist in a *sufficiency* to certain acts and effects, should be *exerted* in the production of such effects as might manifest his infinite power, wisdom, righteousness, goodness, etc. If the world had not been created, these attributes never would have had any *exercise*. The *power* of God, which is a sufficiency in him to produce great effects, must forever have been dormant and useless as to any effect. The divine *wisdom* and prudence would have had no exercise in any wise contrivance, any prudent proceeding of disposal of things, for there would have been no objects of contrivance or disposal. The same might be observed of God's *justice*, *goodness*, and *truth*. Indeed God might have *known* as perfectly that he possessed these attributes, if they never had been exerted or expressed in any effect. But then, if the attributes which consist in a *sufficiency* for correspondent effects are in themselves excellent, the *exercises* of them must likewise be excellent. If it be an excellent thing that there should be a sufficiency for a certain kind of action or operation, the excellency of such a sufficiency must consist in its *relation* to this kind of operation or effect; but that could not be unless the *operation itself* were excellent. A sufficiency for any work is no farther valuable than the work itself is valuable. As God therefore esteems these attributes *themselves* valuable and delights in them, so it is natural to suppose that he delights in their proper *exercise* and expression. For the same reason that he esteems his own sufficiency wisely to *contrive* and dispose effects, he also will esteem the wise *contrivance* and disposition itself. And for the same reason, as he delights in his own disposition to do justly and to dispose of things according to truth and just proportion, so he must delight in such a righteous disposal itself.

It seems to be a thing in itself fit and desirable that the glorious perfections of God should be *known,* and the operations and expressions of them *seen,* by *other beings* besides himself. If it be fit that God's power and wisdom, etc., should be exercised and *expressed* in some effects, and not lie eternally dormant, then it seems proper that these exercises should *appear,* and not be totally hidden and unknown. For if they are, it will be just the same, as to the above purpose, as if they were not. God as perfectly knew himself and his perfections, had as perfect an idea of the exercises and effects they were sufficient for, *antecedently* to any such actual operations of them. and since. If therefore it be nevertheless a thing in itself valuable and worthy to be desired that these glorious

perfections be actually *exhibited* in their correspondent effects, then it seems also that the *knowledge* of these perfections and discoveries is valuable in itself absolutely considered, and that it is *desirable* that this knowledge should exist. It is a thing infinitely good in itself that God's glory should be *known* by a glorious society of created beings. And that there should be in them an *increasing* knowledge of God to all eternity is worthy to be regarded by him, to whom it belongs to order what is fittest and best. If *existence* is more worthy than defect and nonenity, and if any *created* existence is in itself worthy to be, then *knowledge* is; and if any knowledge, then the most *excellent sort* of knowledge, *viz.* that of God and his glory. This knowledge is one of the highest, most real, and substantial parts of all created existence, most remote from nonentity and defect.

As it is desirable in itself that God's glory should be known, so when known it seems equally reasonable it should be esteemed and delighted in, answerably to its dignity. There is no more reason to esteem it a suitable thing that there should be an idea in the *understanding* corresponding unto the glorious object than that there should be a corresponding *affection* in the will. If the perfection itself be excellent, the knowledge of it is excellent, and so is the esteem and love of it excellent. And as it is fit that God should love and esteem his own *excellence,* it is also fit that he should value and esteem the love of his excellency. And if it becomes a being highly to *value* himself, it is fit that he should love to have himself *valued* and esteemed. If the idea of God's perfection in the understanding be valuable, then the love of the heart seems to be more especially valuable, as moral beauty especially consists in the disposition and affection of the heart.

As there is an infinite fulness of all possible good in God—a fulness of every perfection, of all excellency and beauty, and of infinite happiness—and as this fulness is capable of communication, or emanation *ad extra;* so it seems a thing amiable and valuable in *itself* that this infinite fountain of good should send forth abundant streams. And as this is in itself excellent, so a *disposition* to this in the divine being must be looked upon as an *excellent* disposition. Such an emanation of good is, in some sense, a *multiplication* of it. So far as the stream may be looked upon as anything besides the fountain, so far it may be looked on as an *increase* of good. And if the fulness of good that is in the fountain is in itself excellent, then the emanation, which is as it were an increase, repetition, or multiplication of it, is excellent. Thus it is fit, since there is an infinite fountain of light and knowledge, that this light should shine forth in beams of communicated knowledge and understanding; and as there is an infinite fountain of holiness, moral excellence and beauty, that so it should flow out in communicated holiness. And that, as there is an infinite fulness of joy and happiness, so these should have an emanation, and become a fountain flowing out in abundant streams, as beams from the sun.

Thus it appears reasonable to suppose that it was God's last end that there might be a glorious and abundant emanation of his infinite fulness of good *ad extra*, or without himself; and that the disposition to communicate himself, or diffuse his own FULNESS, [1] was what moved him to create the world. But here I observe that there would be some impropriety in saying that a disposition in God to communicate himself *to the creature* moved him to create the world. For an inclination in God to communicate himself to an *object* seems to presuppose the *existence* of the object, at least in idea. But the diffusive disposition that excited God to give creatures existence was rather a communicative *disposition* in general, or a disposition in the fulness of the divinity to flow out and diffuse itself. Thus the disposition there is in the root and stock of a tree to diffuse sap and life is doubtless the reason of their communication to its buds, leaves, and fruits, *after* these exist. But a disposition to communicate of its life and sap to its *fruits* is not so properly the cause of its *producing* those fruits as is its disposition to diffuse its sap and life in general. Therefore, to speak strictly according to truth, we may suppose *that a disposition in God, as an original property of his nature, to an emanation of his own infinite fulness, was what excited him to create the world; and so, that the emanation itself was aimed at by him as a last end of the creation.*

[1] I shall often use the phrase *God's fulness* as signifying and comprehending all the good which is in God natural and moral, either excellence or happiness; partly because I know of no better phrase to be used in this general meaning; and partly because I am led hereto by some of the inspired writers, particularly the apostle Paul, who often useth the phrase in this sense.—Edwards' note.

1706 ∾ *Benjamin Franklin* ∾ 1790

IN HIS many-sided life and writings, Benjamin Franklin sums up the American 18th Century. Born at Boston, he learned printing and embarked in journalism at an early age. He moved to Philadelphia in 1723, spent eighteen months in England, and returned to Philadelphia to become a prosperous printer and newspaper editor, a leading man of affairs, and a devoted student of science. He was instrumental in founding the American Philosophical Society, the Philadelphia Academy—which became the University of Pennsylvania—and the Philadelphia City Hospital. In 1741 he issued one of the two earliest colonial magazines, *The General Magazine and Historical Chronicle*. He won several honorary degrees, including one from Oxford.

After holding various posts as a colonial statesman, he served as agent for the Pennsylvania Assembly in England from 1757 to 1762 and moved in the most cultivated circles. After a brief visit to America, he returned to England in 1764, represented not only Pennsylvania, but several other colonies, and traveled extensively. Returning to America in 1775 as he saw that the Revolution was inevitable, he was a member of many history-making committees, including that which drafted the Declaration of Independence. In 1776 he went to France as one of three American emissaries entrusted with the delicate mission of effecting an alliance. His personal popularity in France as a representative American intellectual was immense; the mission was crowned with success in 1778; in 1779 he became a minister plenipotentiary to the French court. After a distinguished diplomatic career, he returned to Philadelphia in 1785, continued to take part in Pennsylvania affairs, and carried on an extensive correspondence as a member of scientific, philosophical, and literary societies. In 1787 he became president of the Pennsylvania Society for the Abolition of Slavery and sat as delegate from Pennsylvania in the Constitutional Convention. He died at Philadelphia in 1790.

Although Franklin's contributions to science, to educational, economic, and political theory, and to the development of belles-lettres in America must be regarded as more substantial than his contribution to religious thought, his interest in the latter developed early and is discoverable in his writings to the very end of his career. What he has to say on the subject reveals both the liberalism and the moderation of the age of the Enlightenment. Attracted to Deism, always something of a skeptic, he was yet fully aware of the importance of more orthodox belief as a beneficent social force. To him the essence of religion lay not in mystical piety or doctrinal subtleties, but in philanthropic moralism. The rapport which religion might effect in the relations of men with men took precedence in his thinking over the rapport which each individual should establish with his God or with the dogma of his church.

[The first of the selections reprinted here is from a credo which Franklin drew up for his own use in 1728 and which he apparently adhered to throughout his life; the second is from his *Autobiography*, which he began writing in 1771 and which was first published in a French translation appearing in Paris in 1791; the third is from a letter to the great Methodist missionary to America, George Whitefield, with whom his friendship began in 1739; the fourth reproduces the complete text of a letter which some scholars think was written to Thomas Paine; the fifth is from a letter to the Rev. Ezra Stiles, president of Yale from 1778 to 1795. In each case, the text has been modernized by the present editors. For the original texts, consult *The Writings of Benjamin Franklin*, ed. with a Life and Introduction by Albert Henry Smyth, 10 volumes, 1905-1907. For other selections from Franklin, see Book I, Part 3.]

From
ARTICLES OF BELIEF AND ACTS
OF RELIGION
[1818 (written 1728)]

I BELIEVE that there is one supreme, most perfect Being, author and father of the Gods themselves. For I believe that man is not the most perfect being but one, rather that as there are many degrees of beings his inferiors, so there are many degrees of beings superior to him.

Also, when I stretch my imagination through and beyond our system of planets, beyond the visible fixed stars themselves, into that space that is every way infinite, and conceive it filled with suns like ours, each with a chorus of worlds forever moving round him, then this little ball on which we move seems, even in my narrow imagination, to be almost nothing, and myself less than nothing, and of no sort of consequence.

When I think thus, I imagine it great vanity in me to suppose that the *Supremely Perfect* does in the least regard such an inconsiderable nothing as man. More especially, since it is impossible for me to have any positive clear idea of that which is infinite and incomprehensible, I cannot conceive otherwise than that he, *the Infinite Father,* expects or requires no worship or praise from us, but that he is even infinitely above it.

But, since there is in all men something like a natural principle, which inclines them to devotion, or the worship of some unseen power;

And since men are endued with reason superior to all other animals that we are in our world acquainted with;

Therefore I think it seems required of me, and my duty as a man, to pay divine regards to Something.

I conceive, then, that the Infinite has created many beings or Gods, vastly superior to man, who can better conceive his perfections than we, and return him a more rational and glorious praise.

As, among men, the praise of the ig-norant or of children is not regarded by the ingenious painter or architect, who is rather honored and pleased with the approbation of wise men and artists.

It may be that these created Gods are immortal; or it may be that after many ages, they are changed, and others supply their places.

Howbeit, I conceive that each of these is exceeding wise and good, and very powerful; and that each has made for himself one glorious sun, attended with a beautiful and admirable system of planets.

It is that particular wise and good God, who is the author and owner of our system, that I propose for the object of my praise and adoration.

For I conceive that he has in himself some of those passions he has planted in us, and that, since he has given us reason whereby we are capable of observing his wisdom in the creation, he is not above caring for us, being pleased with our praise and offended when we slight him or neglect his glory.

I conceive for many reasons that he is a *good Being;* and as I should be happy to have so wise, good, and powerful a Being my friend, let me consider in what manner I shall make myself most acceptable to him.

Next to the praise resulting from and due to his wisdom, I believe he is pleased and delights in the happiness of those he has created; and since without virtue man can have no happiness in this world, I firmly believe he delights to see me virtuous, because he is pleased when he sees me happy.

And since he has created many things which seem purely designed for the delight of man, I believe he is not offended when he sees his children solace themselves in any manner of pleasant exercises and innocent delights; and I think no pleasure innocent that is to man hurtful.

I *love* him therefore for his goodness, and I *adore* him for his wisdom.

Let me then not fail to praise my God continually, for it is his due, and it is all I can return for his many favors and great goodness to me; and let me resolve to be virtuous, that I may be happy, that I may please him, who is delighted to see me happy. Amen!

From
AUTOBIOGRAPHY
[1791 (written 1771)]

BEFORE I enter upon my public appearance in business, it may be well to let you know the then state of my mind with regard to my principles and morals, that you may see how far those influenced the future events of my life. My parents had early given me religious impressions and brought me through my childhood piously in the Dissenting way. But I was scarce 15 when, after doubting by turns of several points as I found them disputed in the different books I read, I began to doubt of revelation itself. Some books against Deism fell into my hands; they were said to be the substance of sermons preached at Boyle's Lectures. [1] It happened that they wrought an effect on me quite contrary to what was intended by them. For the arguments of the Deists which were quoted to be refuted, appeared to me much stronger than the refutations. In short I soon became a thorough Deist. [2] My arguments perverted some others, particularly Collins and Ralph: but each of them having afterwards wronged me greatly without the least compunction and recollecting Keith's conduct toward me (who was another Freethinker) and my own towards Vernon and Miss Read, [3] which at times gave me great trouble, I began to suspect that this doctrine, though it might be true, was not very useful. My London pamphlet, which had for its motto these lines of Dryden—

Whatever is, is right. Tho' purblind man
Sees but a part of the chain, the nearest
  link,
His eyes not carrying to the equal beam,
That poises all, above.—

and from the attributes of God, his infinite wisdom, goodness, and power, concluded that nothing could possibly be wrong in the world, and that vice and virtue were empty distinctions, no such things existing—appeared now not so clever a performance as I once thought it; and I doubted whether some error had not insinuated itself unperceived into my argument, so as to infect all that followed, as is common in metaphysical reasonings. [4] I grew convinced that *truth, sincerity,* and *integrity* in dealings between man and man were of the utmost importance to the felicity of life, and I formed written resolutions (which still remain in my Journal Book) to practice them ever while I lived.

---

[1] Robert Boyle, 1627-1691, one of the leading members of the Royal Society, whose lectures were first published in 1660 under the title, *New Experiments Physico-Mechanical,* and who wrote voluminously thereafter on scientific and philosophical subjects.

[2] Between 1718-1723, Franklin was reading the works of Anthony Collins, Shaftesbury, Locke, Addison and Steele, Cotton Mather, Bunyan, Defoe, etc.

[3] John Collins, a boyhood friend of Franklin, accompanied him to New York and Philadelphia and parted company with him after a quarrel. James Ralph, another friend whom Franklin met in New York, accompanied him to London, where they went under the unreliable patronage of Sir William Keith, Governor of Pennsylvania, became stranded, and broke off their friendship. Vernon was a friend of Franklin's brother, John; after collecting money owed Vernon, Franklin and Collins borrowed from it, and the debt haunted Franklin until he was able to pay it off in 1732. Although Franklin met Deborah Read shortly after his arrival in Philadelphia in 1723 and courted her in the summer of 1724, he did not marry her until 1730, after she had been Mrs. Rogers.

[4] The "London pamphlet" to which Franklin refers is *A Dissertation on Liberty and Necessity, Pleasure and Pain* (London, 1725). Based on his thinking about Wollaston's *The Religion of Nature Delineated,* it was dedicated to his friend, James Ralph, and had as its motto a misquotation from Dryden and Lee's *Oedipus.*

Revelation had indeed no weight with me as such; but I entertained an opinion that, though certain actions might not be bad *because* they were forbidden by it, or good *because* it commanded them; yet probably those actions might be forbidden *because* they were bad for us, or commanded *because* they were beneficial to us, in their own natures, all the circumstances of things considered. And this persuasion, with the kind hand of Providence, or some guardian angel, or accidental favorable circumstances and situations, or all together, preserved me (through this dangerous time of youth and the hazardous situations I was sometimes in among strangers, remote from the eye and advice of my father) without any *wilful* gross immorality or injustice that might have been expected from my want of religion. I say *wilful,* because the instances I have mentioned had something of *necessity* in them, from my youth, inexperience, and the knavery of others. I had therefore a tolerable character to begin the world with, I valued it properly, and determined to preserve it. . . .

I had been religiously educated as a Presbyterian; and though some of the dogmas of that persuasion, such as *the eternal decrees of God, election, reprobation, etc.,* appeared to me unintelligible, others doubtful, and I early absented myself from the public assemblies of the sect, Sunday being my studying day, I never was without some religious principles. I never doubted, for instance, the existence of the Deity; that he made the world and governed it by his Providence; that the most acceptable service of God was the doing good to man; that our souls are immortal; and that all crime will be punished, and virtue rewarded, either here or hereafter. These I esteemed the essentials of every religion; and, being to be found in all the religions we had in our country, I respected them all, though with different degrees of respect, as I found them more or less mixed with other articles, which, without any tendency to inspire, promote, or confirm morality, served principally to divide us and make us un-friendly to one another. This respect to all, with the opinion that the worst had some good effects, induced me to avoid all discourse that might tend to lessen the good opinion another might have of his own religion; and as our province increased in people, and new places of worship were continually wanted, and generally erected by voluntary contribution, my mite for such purpose, whatever might be the sect, was never refused.

Though I seldom attended any public worship, I had still an opinion of its propriety, and of its utility when rightly conducted, and I regularly paid my annual subscription for the support of the only Presbyterian minister or meeting house we had in Philadelphia. He used to visit me sometimes as a friend, and admonish me to attend his administrations, and I was now and then prevailed on to do so, once for five Sundays successively. Had he been in my opinion a good preacher, perhaps I might have continued, notwithstanding the occasion I had for the Sunday's leisure in my course of study; but his discourses were chiefly either polemic arguments, or explications of the peculiar doctrines of our sect, and were all to me very dry, uninteresting, and unedifying, since not a single moral principle was inculcated or enforced, their aim seeming to be rather to make us Presbyterians than good citizens.

At length he took for his text that verse of the fourth chapter of Philippians, *"Finally, brethren, whatsoever things are true, honest, just, pure, lovely, or of good report, if there be any virtue, or any praise, think on these things."* And I imagined, in a sermon on such a text, we could not miss of having some morality. But he confined himself to five points only, as meant by the apostle, viz.: 1. Keeping holy the Sabbath day. 2. Being diligent in reading the holy Scriptures. 3. Attending duly the public worship. 4. Partaking of the Sacrament. 5. Paying a due respect to God's ministers. These might be all good things; but, as they were not the kind of good things that I expected from that text, I despaired of ever meeting with them from any other, was disgusted, and attended his preaching no more. I had some years before composed a little liturgy, or form of prayer, for my own private use (viz., in 1728), entitled *Articles of Belief and Acts of Religion.* I returned to the use of this, and went no more to the public assemblies. My conduct might be blameable, but I leave it, without attempting further to excuse it; my present purpose being to relate facts, and not to make apologies for them. . . .

From
A LETTER TO GEORGE WHITEFIELD
[1887]

Philadelphia, July 6, 1749.

DEAR SIR—Since your being in England, I have received two of your favors and a box of books to be disposed of. It gives me great pleasure to hear of your welfare and that you purpose soon to return to America. . . .

I am glad to hear that you have frequent opportunities of preaching among the great. If you can gain them to a good and exemplary life, wonderful changes will follow in the manners of the lower ranks; for *ad exemplum regis,* etc. On this principle, Confucius, the famous Eastern reformer, proceeded. When he saw his country sunk in vice, and wickedness of all kinds triumphant, he applied himself first to the grandees; and having, by his doctrine, won *them* to the cause of virtue, the commons followed in multitudes. The mode has a wonderful influence on mankind; and there are numbers who, perhaps, fear less the being in hell, than out of the fashion. Our most western reformations began with the ignorant mob; and when numbers of them were gained, interest and party views drew in the wise and great. Where both methods can be used, reformations are likely to be more speedy. O that some method could be found to make them lasting! He who discovers that will, in my

opinion, deserve more, ten thousand times, than the inventor of the longitude. . . .

LETTER TO AN UNNAMED CORRESPONDENT
[1817]

Philadelphia, July 3, 1786 [?]

DEAR SIR—I have read your manuscript with some attention. By the argument it contains against the doctrines of a particular providence, though you allow a general providence, you strike at the foundation of all religion. For without the belief of a providence, that takes cognizance of, guards, and guides, and may favor particular persons, there is no motive to worship a deity, to fear its displeasure, or to pray for its protection. I will not enter into any discussion of your principles, though you seem to desire it. At present I shall only give you my opinion, that, though your reasonings are subtle, and may prevail with some readers, you will not succeed so as to change the general sentiments of mankind on that subject, and the consequence of printing this piece will be, a great deal of odium drawn upon yourself, mischief to you, and no benefit to others. He that spits against the wind spits in his own face.

But, were you to succeed, do you imagine any good would be done by it? You yourself may find it easy to live a virtuous life, without the assistance afforded by religion; you having a clear perception of the advantages of virtue, and the disadvantages of vice, and possessing a strength of resolution sufficient to enable you to resist common temptations. But think how great a proportion of mankind consists of weak and ignorant men and women, and of inexperienced and inconsiderate youth of both sexes, who have need of the motives of religion to restrain them from vice, to support their virtue, and retain them in the practice of it till it becomes *habitual,* which is the great point for its security. And perhaps you are indebted to her originally, that is, to your religious education, for the habits of virtue upon which you now justly value yourself. You might easily display your excellent talents of reasoning upon a less hazardous subject, and thereby obtain a rank with our most distinguished authors. For among us it is not necessary, as among the Hottentots, that a youth, to be received into the company of men, should prove his manhood by beating his mother.

I would advise you, therefore, not to attempt unchaining the tiger, but to burn this piece before it is seen by any other person; whereby you will save yourself a great deal of mortification from the enemies it may raise against you, and perhaps a good deal of regret and repentance. If men are so wicked as we now see them *with religion,* what would they be *if without it?* I intend this letter itself as a *proof* of my friendship, and therefore add no *professions* to it; but subscribe simply yours,

B.F.

From
A LETTER TO EZRA STILES
[1840]

Philadelphia, March 9, 1790.

REVEREND and Dear Sir—I received your kind letter of Jan'y 28, and am glad you have at length received the portrait of Gov'r Yale from his family, and deposited it in the College Library. He was a great and good man, and had the merit of doing infinite service to your country by his munificence to that institution. The honor you propose doing me by placing mine in the same room with his is much too great for my deserts; but you always had a partiality for me, and to that it must be ascribed. I am however too much obliged to Yale College, the first learned society that took notice of me and adorned me with its honors, to refuse a request that comes from it through so esteemed a friend. But I do not think any one of the portraits you mention, as in my possession, worthy of the place and company you propose to place it in.

You have an excellent artist lately arrived. If he will undertake to make one for you, I shall cheerfully pay the expense; but he must not delay setting about it, or I may slip through his fingers, for I am now in my eighty-fifth year, and very infirm.

I send with this a very learned work, as it seems to me, on the ancient Samaritan coins, lately printed in Spain, and at least curious for the beauty of the impression. Please to accept it for your College Library. I have subscribed for the Encyclopaedia now printing here, with the intention of presenting it to the College. I shall probably depart before the work is finished, but shall leave directions for its continuance to the end. With this you will receive some of the first numbers.

You desire to know something of my religion. It is the first time I have been questioned upon it. But I cannot take your curiosity amiss, and shall endeavor in a few words to gratify it. Here is my creed. I believe in one God, creator of the universe. That he governs it by his Providence. That he ought to be worshipped. That the most acceptable service we render to him is doing good to his other children. That the soul of man is immortal, and will be treated with justice in another life respecting its conduct in this. These I take to be the fundamental principles of all sound religion, and I regard them as you do in whatever sect I meet with them.

As to Jesus of Nazareth, my opinion of whom you particularly desire, I think the system of morals and his religion, as he left them to us, the best the world ever saw or is likely to see; but I apprehend it has received various corrupting changes, and I have, with most of the present Dissenters in England, some doubts as to his divinity; though it is a question I do not dogmatize upon, having never studied it, and think it needless to busy myself with it now, when I expect soon an opportunity of knowing the truth with less trouble. I see no harm, however, in its being believed, if that belief has the good consequence, as probably it has, of making his doctrines more respected and better observed; especially as I do not perceive that the Supreme takes it amiss by distinguishing the unbelievers in his government of the world with any peculiar marks of his displeasure.

I shall only add, respecting myself, that, having experienced the goodness of that Being in conducting me prosperously through a long life, I have no doubt of its continuance in the next, though without the smallest conceit of meriting such goodness. . . .

1705 ∾ *Charles Chauncy* ∾ 1787

GREAT-GRANDSON of an earlier Charles Chauncy, 1592-1672, who was the second president of Harvard, and son of a Boston merchant who was also named Charles, the most distinguished of the Charles Chauncys was born in 1705. Receiving two degrees from Harvard in 1721 and 1724, he was ordained minister of the First Church in Boston in 1727 and spent sixty years in its service. He was thrice married. Next to Jonathan Edwards and Jonathan Mayhew, he was one of the most influential clergymen in the colonies during the 18th Century. A close friend of Mayhew, he supported him in opposing the establishment of an Anglican episcopate in America and wrote a series of brilliant controversial discourses on this subject between 1762 and 1771.

During the first "Great Awakening" that was stimulated by Edwards and given its main impetus by Whitefield, Chauncy proved its most powerfully equipped theological critic, comparing its "Enthusiasm" to that of the Antinomian followers of Anne Hutchinson in the previous century in his *Seasonable Thoughts on the State of Religion in New-England*, Boston, 1743.

[Of his several writings against all forms of revivalistic religion, his sermon, *Enthusiasm Described and Caution'd Against,* from which the following selection has been printed in a modernized text, best reveals his rationalism, his refusal to identify true grace with the kind of inspiration or special revelations claimed by Quakers and Methodists, and his reverence for the authority of Scripture as interpreted by a learned ministry. He played an important rôle as critic of Calvinist doctrines preached by some of Edwards' successors.]

From
ENTHUSIASM DESCRIBED AND CAUTION'D AGAINST
[1742]

THE WORD, from its etymology, carries in it a good meaning, as signifying *inspiration from God:* in which sense the prophets under the old testament, and the apostles under the new, might properly be called *Enthusiasts.* For they were under a divine influence, spoke as moved by the Holy Ghost, and did such things as can be accounted for in no way but by recurring to an immediate power, present with him.

But the word is more commonly used in a bad sense, as intending an *imaginary,* not a *real* inspiration: according to which sense, the Enthusiast is one who has a conceit of himself as a person favored with the extraordinary presence of the Deity. He mistakes the workings of his own passions for divine communications, and fancies himself immediately inspired by the Spirit of God when all the while he is under no other influence than that of an over-heated imagination.

The cause of this Enthusiasm is a bad temperament of the blood and spirits; 'tis properly a disease, a sort of madness: and there are few, perhaps none at all, but are subject to it; though none are so much in danger of it as those in whom *melancholy* is the prevailing ingredient in their constitution. In these it often reigns; and sometimes to so great a degree that they are really beside themselves, acting as truly by the blind impetus of a wild fancy as though they had neither reason nor understanding.

And various are the ways in which their Enthusiasm discovers itself.

Sometimes it may be seen in their countenance. A certain wildness is discernible in their general look and air, especially when their imaginations are moved and stirred.

Sometimes it strangely loosens their tongues and gives them such an energy, as well as fluency and volubility in speaking, as they themselves, by their utmost efforts, can't so much as imitate when they are not under the Enthusiastic influence.

Sometimes it affects their bodies, throws them into convulsions and distortions, into quakings and tremblings. This was formerly common among the people called Quakers. I was myself, when a lad, an eyewitness to such violent agitations and foamings, in a boisterous female speaker, as I could not behold but with surprise and wonder.

Sometimes it will unaccountably mix itself with their conduct and give it such a tincture of that which is freakish or furious as none can have an idea of but those who have seen the behavior of a person in a frenzy.

Sometimes it appears in their imaginary peculiar intimacy with heaven. They are, in their own opinion, the special favorites of God, have more familiar converse with him than other good men, and receive immediate, extraordinary communications from him. The thoughts which suddenly rise up in their minds they take for suggestions of the Spirit; their very fancies are divine illuminations; nor are they strongly inclined to anything but 'tis an impulse from God, a plain revelation of his will.

And what extravagances, in this temper of mind, are they not capable of, and under the specious pretext too of paying obedience to the authority of God! Many have fancied themselves acting by immediate warrant from heaven while they have been committing the most undoubted wickedness. There is indeed scarce anything so wild, either in speculation or practice, but they have given in to it. They have, in many instances, been blasphemers of God and open disturbers of the peace of the world.

But in nothing does the Enthusiasm of these persons discover itself more than in the disregard they express to the dictates of reason. They are above the force of argument, beyond conviction from a calm and sober address to their understanding. As for them, they are distinguished persons; God himself speaks inwardly and immediately to their souls. . . . And in vain will you endeavor to convince such persons of any mistakes they are fallen into. They are certainly in the right and know themselves to be so. They have the Spirit opening their understandings and revealing the truth to them. They believe only as he has taught them, and to suspect they are in the wrong is to do dishonor to the Spirit; 'tis to oppose his dictates, to set up their own wisdom in opposition to his, and shut their eyes against that light with which he has shined into their souls. They are not therefore capable of being argued with; you had as good reason with the wind.

And as the natural consequence of their being thus sure of everything, they are not only infinitely stiff and tenacious, but impatient of contradiction, censorious, and uncharitable: they encourage a good opinion of none but such as are in their way of thinking and speaking. Those, to be sure, who venture to debate with them about their errors and mistakes, their weaknesses and indiscretions, run the risk of being stigmatized by them as poor unconverted wretches, without the Spirit, under the government of carnal reason, enemies to God and religion, and in the broad way to hell.

They are likewise positive and dogmatical, vainly fond of their own imaginations, and invincibly set upon propagating them: and in the doing of this, their powers being awakened and put as it were upon the stretch from the strong impressions they are under that they are authorized by the immediate command of God himself, they sometimes exert themselves with a sort of *ecstatic* violence. And 'tis this that gives them the advantage, among the less knowing and judicious, of those who are modest, suspicious of themselves, and not too assuming in matters of conscience and salvation. The extraordinary fervor of their minds, accompanied with uncommon bodily motions and an excessive confidence and assurance, gains them great reputation among the populace, who speak of them as *men of God* in distinction from all others, and too commonly harken to and revere their dictates, as though they really were, as they pretend, immediately communicated to them from the Divine Spirit.

This is the nature of Enthusiasm, and this its operation, in a less or greater degree, in all who are under the influence of it. 'Tis a kind of religious frenzy and evidently discovers itself to be so whenever it rises to any great height.

And much to be pitied are the persons who are seized with it. Our compassion commonly works towards those who, while under distraction, fondly imagine themselves to be Kings and Emperors: and the like pity is really due to those who, under the power of Enthusiasm, fancy themselves to be *prophets, inspired of God,* and *immediately called* and *commissioned by him to deliver his messages to the world.* And though they should run into disorders, and act in a manner that cannot but be condemned, they should notwithstanding be treated with tenderness and lenity, and the rather because they don't commonly act so much under the influence of a *bad mind* as a *deluded imagination.* And who more worthy of Christian pity than those who, under the notion of serving God and the interest of religion, are filled with zeal and exert themselves to the utmost, while all the while they are hurting and wounding the very cause they take so much pains to advance? 'Tis really a pitiable case: and though the honesty of their intentions won't legitimate their bad actions, yet it very much alleviates their guilt. We should think as favorably of them as may be, and be disposed to judge with mercy, as we would hope to obtain mercy. . . .

'Tis true it won't certainly follow that a man pretending to be a *prophet,* or *spiritual,* really is so if he owns the Bible and receives the truths therein revealed as the mind of God. But the conclusion, on the other hand, is clear and certain: if he pretends to be conducted by the Spirit, and disregards the scripture, pays no due reverence to *the things there delivered as the commandments of God,* he is a mere pretender, be his pretences ever so bold and confident or made with ever so much seeming seriousness, gravity, or solemnity.

And the reason of this is obvious, viz., that the things contained in the scripture were wrote by holy men as they were moved by the Holy Ghost: they were received from God and committed to writing under his immediate, extraordinary influence and guidance. And the divine, ever-blessed Spirit is consistent with himself. He cannot be supposed to be the author of any *private* revelations that are contradictory to the *public standing* ones which he has preserved in the world to this day. This would be to set the Spirit of Truth at variance with himself, than which a greater reproach can't be cast upon him. 'Tis therefore as true that those are Enthusiastical who pretend to the Spirit, and at the same time express a disregard to the scripture, as that the Spirit is a great revealer of the things therein declared to us. . . .

Get a true understanding of the *proper work of the Spirit* and don't place it in those things wherein the gospel does not make it consist. The work of the Spirit is

different now from what it was in the first days of Christianity. Men were then favored with the extraordinary presence of the Spirit. He came upon them in miraculous gifts and powers, as a spirit of prophecy, of knowledge, of revelation, of tongues, of miracles. But the Spirit is not now to be expected in these ways. His great business lies in preparing men's minds for the grace of God . . . this he does by the *word* and *prayer.* . . .

1720 ∽ *John Woolman* ∽ 1772

BELIEVING in the divine guide of the "Inner Light," the Quakers were regarded as "Enthusiasts" by more orthodox Protestant groups and suffered much persecution and martyrdom both in England and America, especially in the 17th Century. In the 18th Century, Quakerism was a more respectable heresy, well-established in several of the American colonies.

John Woolman, born at Northampton, New Jersey, was one of the most distinguished of American Quaker missionaries. He chose tailoring as a career, married Sarah Ellis in 1749, and became a prosperous shopkeeper at Mount Holly. His first journey to spread the gospel of the Friends was made to East Jersey in 1743, and from that time on he traveled extensively—to Virginia, North Carolina, and Maryland, in New England, to Philadelphia and Long Island, and among the Indians. In 1772 he made a voyage to England as a delegate from the Friends of Pennsylvania and died of smallpox in York.

His *Essay on Some Considerations on the Treatment of Negroes,* one of the important documents in the early literature of anti-slavery agitation, was issued in two parts, the first in 1753 or 1754 and the second in 1762. His *Journal,* begun in 1756 and first published in 1774, is a classic among Quaker personal records.

[The first of the following selections, which has been given a title by the present editors, is modernized from the *Journal,* the best text of which is found in *The Journal and Essays of John Woolman,* ed. A. M. Gummere, New York, 1922. The other selections, also modernized and supplied with appropriate titles, are from short essays which Woolman wrote in 1772 during his mission to England and which were published in London in 1773 by the Quaker publisher, Mary Hinde. They provide insight into the Quakers' humanitarianism and their conception of the "Inner Light."]

PORTRAIT OF THE QUAKER AS A
YOUNG MAN
[1774]

I HAVE often felt a motion of love to leave some hints of my experience of the goodness of God; and pursuant thereto, in the thirty-sixth year of my age, I begin this work.

I was born in Northampton, in Burlington county, in West Jersey, in the year of our Lord 1720; and before I was seven years old I began to be acquainted with the operations of Divine love. Through the care of my parents, I was taught to read near as soon as I was capable of it; and as I went from school one seventh-day, I remember, while my companions went to play by the way, I went forward out of sight, and sitting down, I read the twenty-second chapter of the Revelation: "He showed me a pure river of water of life, clear as crystal, proceeding out of the throne of God and of the lamb," etc.; and in the reading of it, my mind was drawn to seek after that pure habitation, which, I then believed, God had prepared for his servants. The place where I sat, and the sweetness that attended my mind, remain fresh in my memory.

This, and the like gracious visitations, had that effect upon me, that when boys used ill language, it troubled me, and through the continued mercies of God, I was preserved from it. The pious instructions of my parents were often fresh in my mind when I happened to be among wicked children, and were of use to me.

My parents having a large family of children, used frequently, on first-days after meeting, to put us to read in the Holy Scriptures, or some religious books, one after another, the rest sitting by without much conversation; which I have since often thought was a good practice. From what I had read and heard, I believed there had been, in past ages, people who walked in uprightness before God, in a degree exceeding any that I knew or heard of, now living; and the apprehension of there being

less steadiness and firmness amongst people in this age than in past ages, often troubled me while I was still young.

I had a dream about the ninth year of my age as follows. I saw the moon rise near the west, and run a regular course eastward, so swift that in about a quarter of an hour she reached our meridian; when there descended from her a small cloud on a direct line to the earth, which lighted on a pleasant green about twenty yards from the door of my father's house (in which I thought I stood) and was immediately turned into a beautiful green tree. The moon appeared to run on with equal swiftness, and soon set in the east, at which time the sun arose at the place where it commonly doth in the summer, and shining with full radiance in a serene air, it appeared as pleasant a morning as ever I saw.

All this time I stood still in the door, in an awful frame of mind, and observed that as heat increased by the rising sun, it wrought so powerfully on the little green tree, that the leaves gradually withered, and before noon it appeared dry and dead. There then appeared a being, small of size, moving swift from the north southward, called a *"Sun Worm."* Though I was a child, this dream was instructive to me.

Another thing remarkable in my childhood was, that once, as I went to a neighbor's house, I saw, on the way, a robin sitting on her nest; and as I came near she went off, but having young ones, flew about, and with many cries expressed her concern for them. I stood and threw stones at her, till one striking her, she fell down dead. At first I was pleased with the exploit; but after a few minutes was seized with horror, as having, in a sportive way, killed an innocent creature while she was careful for her young. I beheld her lying dead, and thought those young ones, for which she was so careful, must now perish for want of their dam to nourish them; and after some painful considerations on the subject, I climbed up the tree, took all the young birds, and killed them—supposing that better than to leave them to pine away and die miserably; and believed, in this case, that Scripture proverb was fulfilled, "The tender mercies of the wicked are cruel." I then went on my errand, but, for some hours, could think of little else but the cruelties I had committed, and was much troubled. Thus He, whose tender mercies are over all his works, hath placed that in the human mind, which incites to exercise goodness towards every living creature, and this being singly attended to, people become tender-hearted and sympathizing; but being frequently and totally rejected, the mind shuts itself up in a contrary disposition.

About the twelfth year of my age, my father being abroad, my mother reproved me for some misconduct, to which I made an undutiful reply; and the next first-day, as I was with my father returning from meeting, he told me he understood I had behaved amiss to my mother, and advised me to be more careful in future. I knew myself blamable, and in shame and confusion remained silent. Being thus awakened to a sense of my wickedness, I felt remorse in my mind, and getting home, I retired and prayed to the Lord to forgive me; and do not remember that I ever, after that, spoke unhandsomely to either of my parents, however foolish in some other things.

Having attained the age of sixteen, I began to love wanton company; and though I was preserved from profane language or scandalous conduct, still I perceived a plant in me which produced much wild grapes. Yet my merciful Father forsook me not utterly, but at times, through his grace, I was brought seriously to consider my ways; and the sight of my backsliding affected me with sorrow; but for want of rightly attending to the reproofs of instruction, vanity was added to vanity, and repentance. Upon the whole, my mind was more and more alienated from the Truth, and I hastened towards destruction. While I meditate on the gulf towards which I travelled, and reflect on my youthful disobedience, my heart is affected with sorrow.

Advancing in age, the number of my ac-quaintance increased, and thereby my way grew more difficult. Though I had heretofore found comfort in reading the Holy Scriptures, and thinking on heavenly things, I was now estranged therefrom. I knew I was going from the flock of Christ, and had no resolution to return; hence serious reflections were uneasy to me, and youthful vanities and diversions my greatest pleasure. Running in this road I found many like myself; and we associated in that which is reverse to true friendship. But in this swift race it pleased God to visit me with sickness, so that I doubted of recovering; and then did darkness, horror, and amazement, with full force seize me, even when my pain and distress of body was very great. I thought it would have been better for me never to have had a being, than to see the day which I now saw. I was filled with confusion; and in great affliction, both of mind and body, I lay and bewailed myself. I had not confidence to lift up my cries to God, whom I had thus offended; but in a deep sense of my great folly, I was humbled before him: and at length, that Word which is as a fire and a hammer, broke and dissolved my rebellious heart, and then my cries were put up in contrition; and in the multitude of his mercies I found inward relief, and felt a close engagement, that if he was pleased to restore my health, I might walk humbly before him.

After my recovery, this exercise remained with me a considerable time; but by degrees, giving way to youthful vanities, they gained strength, and getting with wanton young people I lost ground. The Lord had been very gracious, and spoke peace to me in the time of my distress; and I now most ungratefully turned again to folly; on which account, at times, I felt sharp reproof, but did not get low enough to cry for help. I was not so hardy as to commit things scandalous; but to exceed in vanity and promote mirth, was my chief study. Still I retained a love and esteem for pious people; and their company brought an awe upon me. My dear parents several times admonished me in the fear of the Lord, and their admonition entered into my heart, and had a good effect for a season; but not getting deep enough to pray rightly, the tempter, when he came, found entrance. I remember once, having spent a part of a day in wantonness, as I went to bed at night, there lay in a window near my bed a Bible, which I opened, and first cast my eye on the text, "we lie down in our shame, and our confusion covers us"; this I knew to be my case; and meeting with so unexpected a reproof, I was somewhat affected with it, and went to bed under remorse of conscience; which I soon cast off again.

Thus time passed on: my heart was replenished with mirth and wantonness, while pleasing scenes of vanity were presented to my imagination, till I attained the age of eighteen years, near which time I felt the judgments of God in my soul like a consuming fire, and looking over my past life, the prospect was moving. I was often sad, and longed to be delivered from those vanities; then, again, my heart was strongly inclined to them, and there was in me a sore conflict. At times I turned to folly; and then again, sorrow and confusion took hold of me. In a while, I resolved totally to leave off some of my vanities; but there was a secret reserve in my heart, of the more refined part of them, and I was not low enough to find true peace. Thus for some months, I had great troubles and disquiet, there remaining in me an unsubjected will, which rendered my labors fruitless, till at length, through the merciful continuance of heavenly visitations, I was made to bow down in spirit before the Lord. I remember one evening I had spent some time in reading a pious author; and walking out alone, I humbly prayed to the Lord for his help, that I might be delivered from those vanities which so ensnared me. Thus, being brought low, he helped me, and as I learned to bear the Cross, I felt refreshment to come from his presence, but not keeping in that strength which gave victory, I lost ground again, the sense of which

greatly afflicted me; and I sought deserts and lonely places, and there with tears did confess my sins to God, and humbly craved help of him. And I may say with reverence, he was near to me in my troubles, and in those times of humiliation opened my ear to discipline. I was now led to look seriously at the means by which I was drawn from the pure truth, and learned this, that if I would live in the life which the faithful servants of God lived in, I must not go into company as heretofore, in my own will; but all the cravings of sense must be governed by a Divine principle. In times of sorrow and abasement, these instructions were sealed upon me, and I felt the power of Christ prevail over all selfish desires, so that I was preserved in a good degree of steadiness; and being young, and believing, at that time, that a single life was best for me, I was strengthened to keep from such company as had often been a snare to me.

I kept steady to meetings; spent firstdays in the afternoon chiefly in reading the Scriptures, and other good books; and was early convinced in my mind that true religion consisted in an inward life, wherein the heart doth love and reverence God the Creator, and learn to exercise true justice and goodness, not only toward all men, but also toward the brute creatures. That as the mind was moved by an inward principle to love God as an invisible, incomprehensible Being, by the same principle it was moved to love him in all his manifestations in the visible world. That, as by his breath the flame of life was kindled in all animal and sensible creatures, to say we love God as unseen, and, at the same time, exercise cruelty toward the least creature moving by his life, or by life derived from him, was a contradiction in itself.

I found no narrowness respecting sects and opinions; but believed that sincere, upright-hearted people, in every society, who truly love God, were accepted of him.

As I lived under the cross, and simply followed the openings of Truth, my mind, from day to day, was more enlightened; my former acquaintance were left to judge of me as they would, for I found it safest for me to live in private, and to keep these things sealed up in my own breast. While I silently ponder on that change which was wrought in me, I find no language equal to it, nor any means to convey to another a clear idea of it. I looked upon the works of God in this visible creation, and an awfulness covered me; my heart was tender, and often contrite, and a universal love to my fellow-creatures increased in me. This will be understood by such who have trodden in the same path.

Some glances of real beauty is perceivable in their faces who dwell in true meekness, some tincture of true harmony in the sound of that voice to which divine love gives utterance, and some appearance of right order in their temper and conduct whose passions are fully regulated; yet all these do not fully show forth that inward life to such who have not felt it; but this white stone and new name is known rightly to such only who have it. . . .

THE SLAVE TRADE
[1773]

MANY are the vanities and luxuries of the present age, and in laboring to support a way of living comfortable to the present world, the departure from that wisdom that is pure and peaceable hath been great.

Under the sense of a deep revolt and an overflowing stream of unrighteousness, my life has been often a life of mourning, and tender desires are raised in me that the nature of this practice may be laid to heart.

I have read some books wrote by people who were acquainted with the manner of getting slaves in Africa.

I have had verbal relations of this nature from several Negroes brought from Africa who have learned to talk English.

I have sundry times heard Englishmen speak on this subject, who have been at Africa on this business; and from all these accounts it appears evident that great violence is committed and much blood shed in Africa in getting slaves.

When three or four hundred slaves are put in the hold of a vessel in a hot climate, their breathing soon affects the air. Were that number of free people to go passengers with all things proper for their voyage, there would inconvenience arise from their number, but slaves are taken by violence, and frequently endeavor to kill the white people that they may return to their native land. Hence they are frequently kept under some sort of confinement by means of which a scent ariseth in the hold of a ship and distempers often break out amongst them, of which many die. Of this tainted air in the hold of ships freighted with slaves I have had several accounts, some in print, and some verbal, and all agree that the scent is grievous. When these people are sold in America and in the Islands, they are made to labor in a manner more servile and constant than that which they were used to at home, that with grief, with different diet from what has been common with them, and with hard labor, some thousands are computed to die every year in what is called the "seasoning."

Thus it appears evident that great numbers of these people are brought every year to an untimely end, many of them being such who never injured us.

When the innocent suffer under hardhearted men even unto death and the channels of equity are so obstructed that the cause of the sufferers is not judged in righteousness, *the land is polluted with blood: Numb.* xxxv. 33.

When blood hath been shed unrighteously and remains unatoned for, the cry thereof is very piercing.

Under the humbling dispensations of divine providence, this cry hath deeply affected my heart, and I feel a concern to open, as I may be enabled, that which lieth heavy on my mind . . .

Now in a revolt so deep as this, when much blood has been shed unrighteously in

carrying on the slave trade and in supporting the practice of keeping slaves, which at
this day is unatoned for, and crieth from
the earth, and from the seas against the
oppressor!—while this practice is continued, and under a great load of guilt there
is more unrighteousness committed, the
state of things is very moving!

There is a love which stands in nature,
and a parent beholding his child in misery
hath a feeling of the affliction, but in divine love the heart is enlarged towards mankind universally and prepared to sympathize with strangers, though in the lowest
station of life. . . .

THE POOR
[1773]

THERE is a proportion between labor
and the necessaries of life, and in true
brotherly love the mind is open to feel after
the necessities of the poor.

Amongst the poor there are some that
are weak through age, and others of a
weakly nature, who pass through straights
in very private life without asking relief
from the public.

Such who are strong and healthy may do
that business which to the weakly may be
oppressive; and in performing that in a
day which is esteemed a day's labor by
weakly persons in the field and in the shops
and by weakly women who spin and knit
in the manufactories, they often pass
through weariness, and many sighs I believe are uttered in secret, unheard by some
who might ease their burdens.

Labor in the right medium is healthy,
but in too much of it there is a painful
weariness, and the hardships of the poor
are sometimes increased through want of a
more agreeable nourishment, more plentiful fuel for the fire, and warmer clothing
in the winter than their wages will answer.

When I have beheld plenty in some
houses to a degree of luxury, the condition
of poor children brought up without learning and the condition of the weakly and
aged who strive to live by their labor have
often revived in my mind as cases of which
some who live in fulness need to be put
in remembrance. . . .

SILENT WORSHIP
[1773]

AS I have traveled at times where those
of other societies have attended our meetings and have perceived how little some of
them knew of the nature of silent worship,
I have felt tender desires in my heart that
we who often sit silent in our meetings
may live answerable to the nature of an
inward fellowship with God that no stum-
bling-block through us may be laid in
their way.

Such is the load of unnecessary expense
which lieth on that which is called divine
service in many places, and so much are
the minds of many people employed in
outward forms and ceremonies, that the
opening of an inward silent worship in
this nation to me hath appeared to be a
precious opening. . . .

In real silent worship the soul feeds on
that which is divine, but we cannot partake of the table of the Lord and that table
which is prepared by the god of this world.

If Christ is our shepherd and feedeth
us and we are faithful in following him,
our lives will have an inviting language,
and the table of the Lord will not be polluted.

1738 ∾ *Thomas Rankin* ∾ 1810

THOMAS RANKIN was born in England. As a young man, he disregarded the religious precepts which he had been taught as a child and led a somewhat dissipated life. He began to think seriously about religion when he attended Methodist meetings held by a troop of converted dragoons quartered at his home town of Dunbar, in Haddingtonshire. He was further drawn toward Methodism by hearing the great George Whitefield preach. After a several months' stay in South Carolina as agent for a firm of Edinburgh merchants, he returned to England, began to preach himself at Methodist gatherings, and was soon a regular on the Sussex circuit and one held in high esteem by John Wesley, who addressed him in letters as "My dear Tommy." Rankin left England as Wesley's special missionary to America to breathe new life into the Methodist movement. It was Rankin who called the first conference of American Methodist societies in Philadelphia on July 4, 1773. One of his most successful tours while in America was in Virginia and North Carolina. The Virginian Episcopal clergyman, Devereux Jarratt, 1733-1801, welcomed to his parish such Methodist evangelists as Rankin and the much more eloquent George Shadford. Because of the feeling against Englishmen after the outbreak of the Revolution, Rankin returned permanently to his native land in 1777 and died in London.

[The following selection from a letter Rankin wrote to John Wesley concerning his Virginia tour is modernized from Devereux Jarratt's *A brief narrative of the revival of religion in Virginia,* London, 1778. In brief compass, this selection conveys vividly the impact of the Methodist movement in the Southern colonies and the conception of religion cherished by a Methodist leader who may be regarded as an American for the period of his colonial mission.]

LETTER TO JOHN WESLEY
[1778 (written 1776)]

MONDAY, June 24. I left Leesburg in company with Wright Brickell (a truly devout man, who now rests from his labors) and came to Petersburg on Saturday the 29th, where I preached about three in the afternoon, and then rode on to Mr. Bosheua's about ten miles further. A little company was waiting for me, and God was with them of a truth.

Sunday, 30. I was comforted by the sight of my dear Brother Shadford. But I was weak in body through riding so far in extreme heat and much exercised in mind and did not know how I should be able to go through the labor of the day. We went to the Chapel at ten, where I had liberty of mind and strength of body beyond my expectation. After preaching I met the Society and was more relieved both in body and mind. At four in the afternoon I preached again, from *I set before thee an open door, and none can shut it.* I had gone through about two-thirds of my discourse and was bringing the words home to the present Now when such power descended that hundreds fell to the ground and the house seemed to shake with the presence of God. The Chapel was full of white and black, and many were without that could not get in. Look wherever we would, we saw nothing but streaming eyes and faces bathed in tears, and heard nothing but groans and strong cries after God and the Lord Jesus Christ. My voice was drowned amidst the groans and prayers of the congregation. I then sat down in the pulpit, and both Mr. Shadford and I were so filled with the divine presence that we could only say, "This is none other than the house of God! This is the gate of Heaven!" Husbands were inviting their wives to go to Heaven, wives their husbands, parents their children and children their parents, brothers their sisters and sisters their brothers. In short, those who were happy in God themselves were for bringing all their friends to him in their arms. This mighty effusion of the spirit continued for above an hour, in which time many were awakened, some found peace with God and others his pure love. We attempted to speak or sing again and again, but no sooner we began than our voices were drowned. It was with much difficulty that we at last persuaded the people, as night drew on, to retire to their own homes.

Tuesday, July 2. I rode with Mr. Shadford to Mr. Jarratt's, who with Mrs. Jarratt received us with open arms. I preached the next day not far from his house to a deeply attentive congregation. Many were much affected at the preaching, but far more at the meeting at the Society. Mr. Jarratt himself was constrained to praise God aloud for his great love to him and to his people.

Sunday, 7. I preached at White's Chapel, about twenty miles from Mr. Jarratt's. I intended to preach near the house under the shade of some large trees. But the rain made it impracticable. The house was greatly crowded, and four or five hundred stood at the doors and windows and listened with unabated attention. I preached from Ezekiel's vision of the dry bones: *And there was a great shaking.* I was obliged to stop again and again and beg of the people to compose themselves. But they could not: some on their knees and some on their faces were crying mightily to God all the time I was preaching. Hundreds of Negroes were among them, with the tears streaming down their black faces. The same power we found in meeting the Society, and many were enabled to rejoice with joy unspeakable. In the cool of the evening I preached out of doors, and many found an uncommon blessing.

Every day in the ensuing week I preached to large and attentive congregations. Indeed, the weather was violently hot, and the fatigue of riding and preaching so often was great. But God made up all this to me by his comfortable presence. Thursday, 11, I preached to a large congregation at the preaching-house near Mr. Jarratt's. After preaching at several places on Friday and Saturday, on Sunday, 14, I came to Mr. Bosheua's, where I preached and met the Society. The congregation was, as before, abundantly larger than the Chapel could contain. And we had almost such a day as fourteen days ago: only attended with a more deep and solemn work. What a work is God working in this corner of Mr. Jarratt's parish! It seemed as if all the country, for nine or ten miles round, were ready to turn to God.

In the evening I rode to Mr. Smith's and found a whole family fearing and loving God. Mr. Smith, a sensible and judicious man, had been for many years a Justice of the Peace. By hearing the truth as it is in Jesus, he and his wife first, and then all his children, had attained that peace that passeth all understanding. He observed, "How amazing the change was which had been lately wrought in the place where he lived! That before the Methodists came into these parts, when he was called by his office to attend the court, there was nothing but drunkenness, cursing, swearing, and fighting most of the time the court sat: whereas now nothing is heard but prayer and praise and conversing about God and the things of God."

Monday, 15. I rode towards North Carolina. In every place the congregations were large and received the word with all readiness of mind. I know not that I have spent such a week since I came to America. I saw everywhere such a simplicity in the people, with such a vehement thirst after the word of God, that I frequently preached and continued in prayer till I was hardly able to stand. Indeed, there was no getting away from them while I was able to speak one sentence for God.

Sunday, 21. I preached at Ronoaky Chapel to more than double of what the house would contain. In general, the white people were within the Chapel and the black people without. The windows being all open, every one could hear, and hundreds felt the word of God. Many were bathed in tears and others rejoicing with joy unspeakable. When the Society met, many could not refrain from praising God aloud. I preached to a large company in the afternoon and concluded the day with prayer and thanksgiving.

Tuesday, 23. I crossed the Ronoaky River and preached at a Chapel in North Carolina. And I preached every day to very large and deeply attentive congregations, although not without much labor and pain, through the extreme heat of the weather.

On Tuesday, 30, was our Quarterly Meeting. I scarce ever remember such a season. No Chapel or preaching-house in Virginia would have contained one-third of the congregation. Our friends, knowing this, had contrived to shade with boughs of trees a space that would contain two or three thousand persons. Under this, wholly screened from the rays of the sun, we held our general love-feast. It began between eight and nine on Wednesday morning and continued till noon. Many testified that they had redemption in the blood of Jesus, even the forgiveness of sins. And many were enabled to declare that it had cleansed them from all sin. So clear, so full, so strong was their testimony that while some were speaking their experience, hundreds were in tears and others vehemently crying to God for pardon or holiness.

About eight our watch-night began. Mr. Jarratt preached an excellent sermon; the rest of the preachers exhorted and prayed with divine energy. Surely, for the work wrought on these two days, many will praise God to all eternity!

1738 ∽ *Ethan Allen* ∽ 1789

DEISM, the religion of nature and reason, which had interested the young Benjamin Franklin, was opposed to all forms of Christian orthodoxy and to any variety of evangelical "Enthusiasm." The history of Deism in 17th and 18th Century England and in the France of the Enlightenment is a long and interesting one; in America before, during, and for several decades after the Revolution, Deism had the status of a "Republican religion," a creed for those who abjured every type of tyranny.

Dr. Thomas Young, an M.D. from Yale practising at Salisbury, Conn., and possessing a well-stocked philosophical library, struck up a friendship in the 1760's with Ethan Allen, a hulking, brawling, picturesquely profane, and tavern-haunting young backwoodsman, loaned him books, and converted him to Deism. An ancestor of the Allens had followed the great Puritan clergyman, Thomas Hooker, from Massachusetts into Connecticut; in the period of religious ferment provoked by the "Great Awakening" Ethan's father had turned to Arminian doctrines; Ethan, himself, born in 1738 in Litchfield, Conn., had a restless native originality of mind that was fruitful soil for a vigorous anti-clericalism. After enlisting as a soldier but missing any action in the French and Indian War, Ethan organized his fellow settlers of the New-Hampshire Grants—now Vermont—into a kind of outlaw militia known as the Green Mountain Boys to resist any attempt on the part of New York to confiscate their lands. At the outbreak of the Revolution he led his liberty-loving hellions in a surprise foray upon Fort Ticonderoga, a strategical British post on Lake Champlain, and took possession of it and all its supplies, including the Captain's ninety gallons of rum, "in the name of the Great Jehovah and the Continental Congress," although there is some controversy as to whether these were his exact words. It was the first successful American offensive of the war. Captured by the British in a reckless attempt to surprise Montreal, Allen was held prisoner for two years.

In 1779, the year following his exchange, he published at Boston *A Narrative of Colonel Ethan Allen's Captivity,* which became very popular. Later, as a general of the local militia and as a trouble-making and intriguing politician, he helped shape the destinies of the future State of Vermont. Keeping in touch with his old friend, Dr. Young, Allen had long planned to write a book on Deism in collaboration with him. After Dr. Young's death, Allen acquired, on a visit to Philadelphia, a sheaf of notes among the doctor's papers, and, using them as a basis and with the assistance of an amanuensis, completed at his Sunderland home early in July of 1782 the manuscript of *Reason the Only Oracle of Man, or a Compenduous System of Natural Religion,* which was published at Bennington, Vt., in 1784. Shortly before the publication of this work, Allen, on a visit to New York, made the acquaintance of Hector St. John de Crèvecoeur, then serving as French consul, and the two became firm friends. Happy with his second wife and enjoying the stir produced throughout New England by his book on Deism, Allen showed signs of mellowing when he refused to aid Daniel Shays in his rebellion. After too much carousing with old cronies at a party given by his cousin Ebenezer, the retired "Green Mountain Boy" died at his home in Burlington.

[The following selections from *Reason the Only Oracle of Man,* a neglected classic of the American Enlightenment, are from Section V of Chapter I and Section III of Chapter XIV. The original title of the first of these sections has been retained in full, but that of the other section has been shortened. The text has been modernized.]

THE CAUSE OF IDOLATRY AND THE
REMEDY OF IT
[1784]

INASMUCH as God is not corporeal and
consequently does not and cannot come
within the notice of our bodily sensations,
we are therefore obliged to deduce inferences from his providence and particularly
from our own rational nature in order to
form our conceptions of the divine character, which through inattention, want of
learning, or through the natural imbecility
of mankind, or through the artifice of designing men, or all together, they have been
greatly divided and subdivided in their
notions of a God. Many have so groped in
the dark as wholly to mistake the proper
object of divine worship and, not distinguishing the creator from his creation, have paid adoration to "four-footed
beasts and creeping things." And some
have ascribed divine honors to the sun,
moon, or stars, while others have been infatuated to worship dumb, senseless, and
unintelligent idols, which derived their existence as Gods partly from mechanics, who
gave them their figure, proportion, and
beauty, and partly from their priests,
who gave them their attributes; whose believers, it appears, were so wrought upon
that they cried out in the ecstasy of their
deluded zeal, "Great is Diana!" Whatever
delusions have taken place in the world relative to the object of divine worship or
respecting the indecencies or immoralities
of the respective superstitions themselves,
or by what means soever introduced or perpetuated, whether by designing men whose
interest it has always been to impose on
the weakness of the great mass of the vulgar
or, as it is probable that part of those delusions took place in consequence of the
weakness of uncultivated reason, in deducing a visible instead of an invisible
God from the works of nature—be that
as it will, mankind are generally possessed
of an idea that there is a God, however
they may have been mistaken or misled
as to the object. This notion of a God, as

has been before observed, must have originated from a universal sense of dependence which mankind have on something that
is more wise, powerful, and beneficent than
themselves, or they could have had no apprehensions of any superintending principle in the universe, and consequently would
never have sought after a God, or have
had any conceptions of his existence, nor
could designing men have imposed on their
credulity by obtruding false Gods upon
them; but, taking advantage of the common
belief that there is a God, they artfully
deceive their adherents with regard to the
object to be adored. There are other sorts
of idols which have no existence but in the
mere imagination of the human mind; and
these are vastly the most numerous, and
universally (either in a greater or lesser
degree) interspersed over the world; the
wisest of mankind are not and cannot be
wholly exempt from them, inasmuch as
every wrong conception of God is (as far
as the error takes place in the mind) idolatrous. To give a sample, an idea of a
jealous God is of this sort. Jealousy is
the offspring of finite minds, proceeding
from the want of knowledge which in
dubious matters makes us suspicious and
distrustful; but in matters which we clearly
understand there can be no jealousy, for
knowledge excludes it, so that to ascribe
it to God is a manifest infringement of his
omniscience.

The idea of a revengeful God is likewise
one of that sort, but this idea of divinity,
being borrowed from a savage nature,
needs no further consideration. The representation of a God who (as we are told
by certain divines) from all eternity elected
an inconsiderable part of mankind to eternal life and reprobated the rest to eternal
damnation, merely from his own sovereignty, adds another to the number. This representation of the Deity undoubtedly took its
rise from that which we discover in great,
powerful, and wicked tyrants among men,
however tradition may since have contributed to its support, though I am apprehensive that a belief in those who adhere to

that doctrine that they themselves constitute that blessed elect number has been a greater inducement to them to close with it than all other motives added together. It is a selfish and inferior notion of a God void of justice, goodness, and truth, and has a natural tendency to impede the cause of true religion and morality in the world, and diametrically repugnant to the truth of the divine character, and which, if admitted to be true, overturns all religion, wholly precluding the agency of mankind in either their salvation or damnation, resolving the whole into the sovereign disposal of a tyrannical and unjust being, which is offensive to reason and common sense and subversive of moral rectitude in general. But as it was not my design so much to confute the multiplicity of false representations of a God, as to represent just and consistent ideas of the true God, I shall therefore omit any further observations on them in this place with this remark, that all unjust representations or ideas of God are so many detractions from his character among mankind. To remedy these idolatrous notions of a God, it is requisite to form right and consistent ideas in their stead.

The discovery of truth necessarily excludes error from the mind, which nothing else can possibly do; for some sort of God or other will crowd itself into the conceptions of dependent creatures, and if they are not so happy as to form just ones, they will substitute erroneous and delusive ones in their stead; so that it serves no valuable purpose to mankind to confute their idolatrous opinions concerning God without communicating to them just notions concerning the true one, for if this is not effected, nothing is done to purpose. For, as has been before observed, mankind will form to themselves, or receive from others, an idea of Divinity either right or wrong: this is the universal voice of intelligent nature, from whence a weighty and conclusive argument may be drawn of the reality of a God, however inconsistent most of their conceptions of him may be. The

fact is, mankind readily perceive that there is a God by feeling their dependence on him, and as they explore his works, and observe his providence, which is too sublime for finite capacities to understand but in part, they have been more or less confounded in their discoveries of a just idea of a God, and of his moral government. Therefore we should exercise great application and care, whenever we assay to speculate upon the Divine character, accompanied with a sincere desire after truth, and not ascribe anything to his perfections or government which is inconsistent with reason or the best information which we are able to apprehend of moral rectitude, and be at least wise enough not to charge God with injustice and contradictions which we should scorn to be charged with ourselves. . . .

OF THE IMPORTANCE OF THE EXERCISE OF REASON
[1784]

THE PERIOD of life is very uncertain, and at the longest is but short: a few years bring us from infancy to manhood, a few more to a dissolution; pain, sickness, and death are the necessary consequences of animal life. Through life we struggle with physical evils, which eventually are certain to destroy our earthly composition; and well would it be for us did evils end here; but alas! moral evil has been more or less predominant in our agency, and though natural evil is unavoidable, yet moral evil may be prevented or remedied by the exercise of virtue. Morality is therefore of more importance to us than any or all other attainments; as it is a habit of mind which, from a retrospective consciousness of our agency in this life, we should carry with us into our succeeding state of existence, as an acquired appendage of our rational nature and as the necessary means of our mental happiness. Virtue and vice are the only things in this world which, with our souls, are capable of surviving death; the former is the rational and only procuring cause of all intellectual happiness, and the latter of conscious guilt and misery; and therefore, our indispensable duty and ultimate interest is to love, cultivate, and improve the one, as the means of our greatest good, and to hate and abstain from the other, as productive of our greatest evil. And in order thereto, we should so far divest ourselves of the incumbrances of this world (which are too apt to engross our attention) as to enquire a consistent system of the knowledge of religious duty and make it our constant endeavor in life to act conformably to it. The knowledge of the being, perfections, creation and providence of God, and of the immortality of our souls, is the foundation of religion. . . . And as the Pagan, Jewish, Christian, and Mahometan countries of the world have been overwhelmed with a multiplicity of revelations diverse from each other, and which, by their respective promulgators, are said to have been immediately inspired into their souls by the spirit of God, or immediately communicated to them by the intervening agency of angels (as in the instance of the invisible Gabriel to Mahomet) and as those revelations have been received and credited by far the greater part of the inhabitants of the several countries of the world (on whom they have been obtruded) as supernaturally revealed by God or Angels, and which, in doctrine and discipline, are in most respects repugnant to each other, it fully evinces their imposture, and authorizes us, without a lengthy course of arguing, to determine with certainty that not more than one, if any one of them, had their original from God, as they clash with each other, which is ground of high probability against the authenticity of each of them.

A revelation that may be supposed to be really of the institution of God must also be supposed to be perfectly consistent or uniform and to be able to stand the test of truth: therefore such pretended revelations, as are tended to us as the contrivance of heaven, which do not bear that test, we may be morally certain was [were] either originally a deception, or has [have] since, by adulteration, become spurious. Furthermore, should we admit, that among the numerous revelations on which the respective priests have given the stamp of divinity, some one of them was in reality of divine authority, yet we could not otherwise, as rational beings, distinguish it from others, but by reason.

Reason therefore must be the standard by which we determine the respective claims of revelation; for otherwise we may as well subscribe to the divinity of the one as of the other, or to the whole of them, or to none at all. So likewise on this thesis, if reason rejects the whole of those revelations, we ought to return to the religion of nature and reason.

Undoubtedly it is our duty, and for our best good, that we occupy and improve the faculties with which our Creator has endowed us, but so far as prejudice, or prepossession of opinion, prevails over our minds, in the same proportion reason is excluded from our theory or practice. Therefore, if we would acquire useful knowledge, we must first divest ourselves of those impediments, and sincerely endeavor to search out the truth, and draw our conclusions from reason and just argument, which will never conform to our inclination, interest, or fancy; but we must conform to that if we would judge rightly. As certain as we determine contrary to reason, we make a wrong conclusion; therefore, our wisdom is to conform to the nature and reason of things, as well in religious matters as in other sciences. Preposterously absurd would it be to negative the exercise of reason in religious concerns, and yet be actuated by it in all other and less occurrences of life. All our knowledge of things is derived from God, in and by the order of nature, out of which we cannot perceive, reflect, or understand anything whatsoever; our external senses are natural and so are our souls; by the instrumentality of the former we perceive the objects of sense, and with the latter we reflect on them. And those objects are also natural; so that ourselves, and all things about us, and our knowledge collected therefrom, is natural, and not supernatural. . . .

We may and often do connect or arrange our ideas together in a wrong or improper manner, for the want of skill or judgment, or through mistake or the want of application, or through the influence of prejudice; but in all such cases the error does not originate from the ideas themselves, but from the composer; for a system or an arrangement of ideas justly composed always contain the truth; but an unjust composition never fails to contain error and falsehood. Therefore an unjust connection of ideas is not derived from nature, but from the imperfect composition of man. Misconnection of ideas is the same as misjudging, and has no positive existence, being merely a creature of the imagination; but nature and truth are real and uniform; and the rational mind by reasoning discerns the uniformity and is thereby enabled to make a just composition of ideas, which will stand the test of truth. But the fantastical illuminations of the credulous and superstitious part of mankind proceed from weakness, and as far as they take place in the world, subvert the religion of REASON and TRUTH.

1737 ∽ *Thomas Paine* ∽ 1809

ALTHOUGH Ethan Allen and Elihu Palmer, 1764-1806, did pioneer work in spreading the gospel of Deism in America, the most widely read and discussed exposition of Deism by an American was Thomas Paine's *The Age of Reason.* Born at Thetford, England, Paine was trained in his father's creed of Quakerism and in his father's trade of stay-making. After going to sea on a privateer, he returned to London to become a journeyman stay-maker. While living there, he attended scientific lectures at the Royal Society and developed his interest in astronomy. In 1759, while a master stay-maker in Sandwich, Kent, he married Mary Lambert, a serving-girl, who died in 1760. During the next ten years Paine supported himself in one job after another. From stay-making he turned to collecting taxes as an excise officer; next he became a teacher of English at an academy in London; and then he was an excise officer again. While teaching, he occasionally served as a Methodist lay-preacher in the open fields about London. In 1771, after his second appointment to the excise, he married Elizabeth Ollive, of Lewes, Sussex, the daughter of a tobacconist. On the death of her father, he succeeded to the business. His first extended piece of writing, *The Case of the Officers of the Excise,* done in 1772 as an appeal to Parliament, was distinguished for its vigorous social protest against the ill effects of poverty on the honesty and efficiency of the typical excise collector.

Two years later, bankrupt, separated from his wife, and dismissed from the excise, Paine, at the suggestion of his friend, Benjamin Franklin, became an emigrant to Philadelphia. Here, on the eve of the Revolution, he edited *The Pennsylvania Magazine or American Museum* and contributed to the *Pennsylvania Journal.* When the Revolutionary crisis broke, his brilliant pamphlet, *Common Sense,* published early in 1776, convinced Americans that their struggle must be a war of independence. Serving as an aide-de-camp to General Greene, Paine wrote the first number of his *The American Crisis,* the successive installments of which were hard-hitting, sure-fire propaganda for the American cause.

After devoting himself to this cause in numerous capacities, Paine became, between 1787 and 1802, a true "citizen of the world," pursuing scientific invention and championing political innovation in both England and France. He perfected models for an iron bridge, obtained a patent for it from the British government, had his bridge built and set up in a field in the village of Paddington, near London. He sought to combat English conservative reaction to the French Revolution by replying, in his *The Rights of Man,* 1791 and 1792, to Edmund Burke's *Reflections on the Late Revolution in France,* 1790. Elected to a seat in the French National Convention, appointed to the committee on drafting a constitution, and outlawed from England, he was yet too moderate in his views on regicide to please the more radical French revolutionaries. When the Girondin party was overthrown, Paine was arrested and imprisoned in the Luxembourg.

It was here, in 1793, that he wrote the first part of *The Age of Reason* to combat the tendency of the extreme radicals to go too far in nihilism and atheism. Paine regarded this work, published early in 1794, as "exceedingly necessary, lest in the general wreck of superstition, of false systems of government, and false theology, we lose sight of morality, of humanity, and of the theology that is true." Ironically enough, America did not receive *The Age of Reason* in the spirit in which Paine wrote it. Released from prison in 1794 through the help of James Monroe, Paine, after a period of convalescence with the Monroe family in 1795, the year in which the second part of *The Age of Reason* was published, remained for some time in France and continued writing in support of a sane French democracy, although he lived in virtual retirement.

Urged by Jefferson to return to America, Paine finally accepted the invitation, landed at Baltimore in 1802, and went on to Washington, where he was for a while the President's honored guest. But he was soon to find that post-Revolutionary America, despite the ascendency of Jefferson's democratic Republicanism, was not the America of his dreams, and his old age was anything but happy. Living in Bordentown, New York City, and New Rochelle, he was anathema to orthodox Christians of all creeds and doubly so if they happened to be Federalists. At New Rochelle an attempt was made to assassinate him and he was denied the right to vote on the ground that he was not technically a citizen. Despite ill health, poverty, and ostracism, he kept writing in behalf of just government and the advancement of science and against both political and religious reaction.

Although religious opposition to Paine's Deism has long tended to obscure his reputation, he has exerted a profound influence on free-thought in America through such disciples as Robert G. Ingersoll, and within recent years has steadily gained recognition as a major writer and as a germinal *ideologue* of American democracy.

[The first of the following selections is from Part I of *The Age of Reason;* the second is the conclusion of Part II. They have been modernized and supplied with titles by the editors. For other selections from Paine's work, see Book I, Part 3.]

PERSONAL NARRATIVE
[1794]

MY FATHER being of the Quaker profession, it was my good fortune to have an exceedingly good moral education and a tolerable stock of useful learning. Though I went to the grammar school, I did not learn Latin, not only because I had no inclination to learn languages, but because of the objection the Quakers have against the books in which the language is taught. But this did not prevent me from being acquainted with the subject of all the Latin books used in the school.

The natural bent of my mind was to science. I had some turn, and I believe some talent, for poetry; but this I rather repressed than encouraged, as leading too much into the field of imagination. As soon as I was able I purchased a pair of globes, and attended the philosophical lectures of Martin and Ferguson, and became afterward acquainted with Dr. Bevis, of the society called the Royal Society, then living in the Temple, and an excellent astronomer.

I had no disposition for what is called politics. It presented to my mind no other idea than as contained in the word Jockeyship. When, therefore, I turned my thoughts toward matters of government, I had to form a system for myself that accorded with the moral and philosophic principles in which I have been educated. I saw, or at least I thought I saw, a vast

scene opening itself to the world in the affairs of America, and it appeared to me that unless the Americans changed the plan they were pursuing with respect to the government of England, and declared themselves independent, they would not only involve themselves in a multiplicity of new difficulties, but shut out the prospect that was then offering itself to mankind through their means. It was from these motives that I published the work known by the name of "Common Sense," which was the first work I ever did publish; and so far as I can judge of myself, I believe I should never have been known in the world as an author, on any subject whatever, had it not been for the affairs of America. I wrote "Common Sense" the latter end of the year 1775, and published it the first of January, 1776. Independence was declared the fourth of July following.

Any person who has made observations on the state and progress of the human mind, by observing his own, cannot but have observed that there are two distinct classes of what are called thoughts—those that we produce in ourselves by reflection and the act of thinking, and those that bolt into the mind of their own accord. I have always made it a rule to treat these voluntary visitors with civility, taking care to examine, as well as I was able, if they were worth entertaining, and it is from them I have acquired almost all the knowledge that I have. As to the learning that any person gains from school education, it serves only, like a small capital, to put him in a way of beginning learning for himself afterward.

Every person of learning is finally his own teacher, the reason of which is that principles, being a distinct quality to circumstances, cannot be impressed upon the memory; their place of mental residence is the understanding and they are never so lasting as when they begin by conception. Thus much for the introductory part.

From the time I was capable of conceiving an idea and acting upon it by reflection, I either doubted the truth of the Christian system or thought it to be a strange affair; I scarcely knew which it was, but I well remember, when about seven or eight years of age, hearing a sermon read by a relation of mine, who was a great devotee of the Church, upon the subject of what is called *redemption by the death of the Son of God.*

After the sermon was ended, I went into the garden, and as I was going down the garden steps (for I perfectly recollect the spot) I revolted at the recollection of what I had heard, and thought to myself that it was making God Almighty act like a passionate man, that killed His son when He could not revenge Himself in any other way, and as I was sure a man would be hanged that did such a thing, I could not see for what purpose they preached such sermons.

This was not one of that kind of thoughts that had anything in it of childish levity; it was to me a serious reflection, arising from the idea I had that God was too good to do such an action, and also too almighty to be under any necessity of doing it. I believe in the same manner at this moment; and I moreover believe that any system of religion that has anything in it that shocks the mind of a child cannot be a true system.

It seems as if parents of the Christian profession were ashamed to tell their children anything about the principles of their religion. They sometimes instruct them in

morals, and talk to them of the goodness of what they call Providence, for the Christian mythology has five deities—there is God the Father, God the Son, God the Holy Ghost, the God Providence, and the Goddess Nature. But the Christian story of God the Father putting His son to death, or employing people to do it (for that is the plain language of the story) cannot be told by a parent to a child; and to tell him that it was done to make mankind happier and better is making the story still worse—as if mankind could be improved by the example of murder; and to tell him that all this is a mystery is only making an excuse for the incredibility of it.

How different is this to the pure and simple profession of Deism! The true Deist has but one Deity, and his religion consists in contemplating the power, wisdom, and benignity of the Deity in His works, and in endeavoring to imitate Him in everything moral, scientifical and mechanical.

The religion that approaches the nearest of all others to true Deism, in the moral and benign part thereof, is that professed by the Quakers; but they have contracted themselves too much, by leaving the works of God out of their system. Though I reverence their philanthropy, I cannot help smiling at the conceit that if the taste of a Quaker could have been consulted at the creation, what a silent and drab-colored creation it would have been! Not a flower would have blossomed its gayeties, nor a bird been permitted to sing. . . .

DEISM AND SCIENCE
[1795]

IF WE consider the nature of our condition here, we must see there is no occasion for such a thing as *revealed religion.* What is it we want to know? Does not the creation, the universe we behold, preach to us the existence of an Almighty Power that governs and regulates the whole? And is not the evidence that this creation holds out to our senses infinitely stronger than anything we can read in a book that any impostor might make and call the Word of God? As for morality, the knowledge of it exists in every man's conscience.

Here we are. The existence of an Almighty Power is sufficiently demonstrated to us, though we cannot conceive, as it is impossible we should, the nature and manner of its existence. We cannot conceive how we came here ourselves, and yet we know for a fact that we are here.

We must know also that the Power that called us into being, can, if He pleases, and when He pleases, call us to account for the manner in which we have lived here; and, therefore, without seeking any other motive for the belief, it is rational to believe that He will, for we know beforehand that He can. The probability or even possibility of the thing is all that we ought to know; for if we knew it as a fact, we should be the mere slaves of terror; our belief would have no merit, and our best actions no virtue.

Deism, then, teaches us, without the possibility of being deceived, all that is necessary or proper to be known. The creation is the Bible of the Deist. He there reads, in the handwriting of the Creator himself, the certainty of His existence and the immutability of His power, and all other Bibles and Testaments are to him forgeries.

The probability that we may be called to account hereafter will, to a reflecting mind, have the influence of belief; for it is not our belief or disbelief that can make or unmake the fact. As this is the state we are in, and which it is proper we should be in, as free agents, it is the fool only, and not the philosopher, or even the prudent man, that would live as if there were no God.

But the belief of a God is so weakened by being mixed with the strange fable of the Christian creed, and with the wild adventures related in the Bible, and with the obscurity and obscene nonsense of the Testament, that the mind of man is bewildered as in a fog. Viewing all these things in a confused mass, he confounds fact with fable; and as he cannot believe all, he feels a disposition to reject all.

But the belief of a God is a belief distinct from all other things, and ought not to be confounded with any. The notion of a Trinity of Gods has enfeebled the belief of one God. A multiplication of beliefs acts as a division of belief; and in proportion as anything is divided it is weakened.

Religion, by such means, becomes a thing of form, instead of fact—of notion, instead of principles; morality is banished to make room for an imaginary thing called faith, and this faith has its origin in a supposed debauchery; a man is preached instead of God; an execution is an object for gratitude; the preachers daub themselves with blood, like a troop of assassins, and pretend to admire the brilliancy it gives them; they preach a humdrum sermon on the merits of the execution; then praise Jesus Christ for being executed, and condemn the Jews for doing it. A man, by hearing all this nonsense lumped and preached together, confounds the God of the Creation with the imagined God of the Christians, and lives as if there were none.

Of all the systems of religion that ever were invented, there is none more derogatory to the Almighty, more unedifying to man, more repugnant to reason, and more contradictory in itself, than this thing called Christianity. Too absurd for belief, too impossible to convince, and too inconsistent for practice, it renders the heart torpid, or produces only atheists and fanatics. As an engine of power, it serves the purpose of despotism; and as a means of wealth, the avarice of priests; but so far as respects the good of man in general, it leads to nothing here or hereafter.

The only religion that has not been invented, and that has in it every evidence of divine originality, is pure and simple Deism. It must have been the first, and will probably be the last, that man believes. But pure and simple Deism does not answer the purpose of despotic governments. They cannot lay hold of religion as an engine, but by mixing it with human inventions, and making their own authority a part; neither does it answer the avarice of priests, but by incorporating themselves and their functions with it, and becoming, like the government, a party in the system. It is this that forms the otherwise mysterious connection of Church and State; the Church humane, and the State tyrannic.

Were man impressed as fully and as strongly as he ought to be with the belief of a God, his moral life would be regulated by the force of that belief; he would stand in awe of God and of himself, and would not do the thing that could not be concealed from either. To give this belief the full opportunity of force, it is necessary that it acts alone. This is Deism. But when, according to the Christian Trinitarian scheme, one part of God is represented by a dying man, and another part called the Holy Ghost, by a flying pigeon,[1] it is impossible that belief can attach itself to such wild conceits.

It has been the scheme of the Christian Church, and of all the other invented systems of religion, to hold man in ignorance of the Creator, as it is of Government to hold man in ignorance of his rights. The systems of the one are as false as those of the other, and are calculated for mutual support.

The study of theology, as it stands in Christian churches, is the study of nothing; it is founded on nothing; it rests on no principles; it proceeds by no authorities; it has no data; it can demonstrate nothing; and it admits of no conclusion. Not any thing can be studied as a science, without our being in possession of the principles upon which it is founded; and as this is not the case with Christian theology, it is therefore the study of nothing.

Instead, then, of studying theology, as is now done, out of the Bible and Testa-ment, the meanings of which books are always contraverted and the authenticity of which is disproved, it is necessary that we refer to the Bible of the Creation. The principles we discover there are eternal and of divine origin; they are the foundation of all the science that exists in the world, and must be the foundation of theology.

We can know God only through His works. We cannot have a conception of any one attribute but by following some principle that leads to it. We have only a confused idea of His power, if we have not the means of comprehending something of its immensity. We can have no idea of His wisdom, but by knowing the order and manner in which it acts. The principles of science lead to this knowledge; for the Creator of man is the Creator of science, and it is through that medium that man can see God, as it were, face to face.

Could a man be placed in a situation, and endowed with the power of vision, to behold at one view, and to contemplate deliberately, the structure of the universe; to mark the movements of the several planets, the cause of their varying appearances, the unerring order in which they revolve, even to the remotest comet; their connection and dependence on each other, and to know the system of laws established by the Creator, that governs and regulates the whole, he would then conceive, far beyond what any church theology can teach him, the power, the wisdom, the vastness, the munificence of the Creator; he would then see, that all the knowledge man has

---

[1] The book called the book of Matthew says, chap. iii, verse 16, that *the Holy Ghost descended in the shape of a dove.* It might as well have said a goose; the creatures are equally harmless, and the one is as much of a nonsensical lie as the other. The second of Acts, ver. 2, 3, says that it descended in a mighty *rushing wind,* in the shape of *cloven tongues,* perhaps it was cloven feet. Such absurd stuff is only fit for tales of witches and wizards.— Paine's note.

of science, and that all mechanical arts by which he renders his situation comfortable here, are derived from that source; his mind, exalted by the scene, and convinced by the fact, would increase in gratitude as it increased in knowledge; his religion or his worship would become united with his improvement as a man; any employment he followed, that had any connection with the principles of the creation, as everything of agriculture, of science and of the mechanical arts has, would teach him more of God, and of the gratitude he owes to Him, than any theological Christian sermon he now hears.

Great objects inspire great thoughts; great munificence excites great gratitude; but the groveling tales and doctrines of the Bible and the Testament are fit only to excite contempt.

Though man cannot arrive, at least in this life, at the actual scene I have described, he can demonstrate it, because he has a knowledge of the principles upon which the creation is constructed.[2] We know that the greatest works can be represented in model and that the universe can be represented by the same means.

The same principles by which we measure an inch, or an acre of ground, will measure to millions in extent. A circle of an inch diameter has the same geometrical properties as a circle that would circumscribe the universe.

The same properties of a triangle that will demonstrate upon paper the course of a ship will do it on the ocean; and when applied to what are called the heavenly bodies, will ascertain to a minute the time of an eclipse, though these bodies are millions of miles from us. This knowledge is of divine origin, and it is from the Bible of the creation that man has learned it, and not from the stupid Bible of the Church, that teacheth man nothing.

All the knowledge man has of science and of machinery, by the aid of which his existence is rendered comfortable upon earth, and without which he would be scarcely distinguishable in appearance and condition from a common animal, comes from the great machine and structure of the universe.

The constant and unwearied observations of our ancestors upon the movements and revolutions of the heavenly bodies, in what are supposed to have been the early ages of the world, have brought this knowledge upon earth. It is not Moses and the prophets, nor Jesus Christ, nor his apostles, that have done it. The Almighty is the great mechanic of the creation; the first philosopher and original teacher of all science. Let us, then, learn to reverence our master, and let us not forget the labors of our ancestors.

Had we, at this day, no knowledge of machinery, and were it possible that man could have a view, as I have before described, of the structure and machinery of the universe, he would soon conceive the idea of constructing some at least of the mechanical works we now have; and the idea so conceived would progressively

---

[2] The Bible-makers have undertaken to give us, in the first chapter of Genesis, an account of the Creation; and in doing this, they have demonstrated nothing but their ignorance. They make there to have been three days and three nights, evenings and mornings, before there was a sun; when it is the presence or absence of the sun that is the cause of day and night, and what is called his rising and setting that of morning and evening. Besides, it is a puerile and pitiful idea to suppose the Almighty to say, Let there be light. It is the imperative manner of speaking that a conjuror uses when he says to his cups and balls, Presto, begone, and most probably has been taken from it; as Moses and his rod are a conjuror and his wand. Longinus calls this expression the sublime; and, by the same rule, the conjuror is sublime, for the manner of speaking is expressively and grammatically the same. When authors and critics talk of the sublime, they see not how nearly it borders on the ridiculous. The sublime of the critics, like some parts of Edmund Burke's "Sublime and Beautiful," is like a wind-mill just visible in a fog, which imagination might distort into a flying mountain, or an archangel, or a flock of wild geese.—Paine's note.

advance in practice. Or could a model of the universe, such as is called an orrery, be presented before him and put in motion, his mind would arrive at the same idea.

Such an object and such a subject would, while it improved him in knowledge useful to himself as a man and a member of society, as well as entertaining, afford far better matter for impressing him with a knowledge of, and a belief in, the Creator, and of the reverence and gratitude that man owes to Him, than the stupid texts of the Bible and of the Testament, from which, be the talents of the preacher what they may, only stupid sermons can be preached.

If man must preach, let him preach something that is edifying, and from texts that are known to be true.

The Bible of the Creation is inexhaustible in texts. Every part of science, whether connected with the geometry of the universe, with the systems of animal and vegetable life, or with the properties of inanimate matter, is a text as well for devotion as for philosophy—for gratitude as for human improvement. It will perhaps be said, that if such a revolution in the system of religion takes place, every preacher ought to be a philosopher. *Most certainly;* and every house of devotion a school of science.

It has been by wandering from the immutable laws of science, and the right use of reason, and setting up an invented thing called revealed religion, that so many wild and blasphemous conceits have been formed of the Almighty.

The Jews have made Him the assassin of the human species to make room for the religion of the Jews. The Christians have made Him the murderer of Himself and the founder of a new religion to supersede and expel the Jewish religion. And to find pretense and admission for these things, they must have supposed His power or His wisdom imperfect, or His will changeable; and the changeableness of the will is imperfection of the judgment.

The philosopher knows that the laws of the Creator have never changed with respect either to the principles of science, or the properties of matter. Why, then, is it supposed they have changed with respect to man?

I here close the subject. I have shown in all the foregoing parts of this work, that the Bible and Testament are impositions and forgeries; and I leave the evidence I have produced in proof of it, to be refuted, if any one can do it; and I leave the ideas that are suggested in the conclusion of the work, to rest on the mind of the reader; certain as I am, that when opinions are free, either in matters of government or religion, truth will finally and powerfully prevail.

1771 ∽ *Charles Brockden Brown* ∽ *1810*

OF A PROMINENT Quaker family, Charles Brockden Brown was born in Philadelphia. He attended the select Quaker school kept by Robert Proud. Frail in health, bookish in habit, and morbidly introspective in temperament, young Brown aspired to be an epic poet and became passionately interested in the more radical ideologies of his generation, including Deism. Yielding to the wishes of his family, he studied law with the Philadelphia barrister, Alexander Wilcox, and was an active member of a legal students' club. Literature, however, proved more attractive to him than the law; he became leader of the Belles Letters Club and in August, 1789, a series of his literary essays began to appear in the *Columbian Magazine* under the title, "The Rhapsodist." He gave up the law altogether when he was ready to enter upon its practice. When Elihu Hubbard Smith, of Litchfield, Conn., was studying medicine in Philadelphia, Brown found him a congenial friend because of his literary interests. Smith took up the practice of his profession near Yale and later in New York. Brown visited him at both places and met his literary friends, among whom, at New York, was William Dunlap, the dramatist.

Brown became a member of the Friendly Club, the city's most active intellectual circle, began to write prolifically for magazine publication, and edited *The Monthly Magazine and American Review.* When this magazine failed late in 1800, Brown returned to Philadelphia, where he continued to do magazine work, starting in 1803 the *Literary Magazine and American Register.* In 1804 he married the brilliant Elizabeth Linn, of New York, sister of the poet, John Blair Linn, and proved an exemplary husband and father. Having won an international reputation as a novelist with such productions as *Wieland,* 1798, *Ormond,* 1799, *Arthur Merwyn,* 1799-1800, *Edgar Huntly,* 1799, *Jane Talbot,* 1801, and *Clara Howard,* 1801, Brown preoccupied himself, in his last years, with historical surveys and political tracts. He died of tuberculosis.

Brown's fiction reflects all the tendencies which had been developed for several decades in the short stories published in 18th Century American magazines. He provided his readers with Gothic thrills in native settings; themes and characters that had become the stock in trade of both English and American "sentimental" fiction play an important rôle in his stories; on occasion, he was capable of a graphic, Defoe-like realism based on his own experiences and observations during plague years in both Philadelphia and New York; above all, he was a novelist of ideas, a kind of Aldous Huxley of his time, dramatizing post-revolutionary conflicts in American thought, creating characters memorable as spokesmen or representatives of this or that current attitude in religion or politics. *Wieland,* for example, although replete with Gothic thrills, is also a psychological study of religious Enthusiasm.

[The following selection from this novel includes most of Chapter I and all of Chapter II and has been modernized in text and given a title by the present editors. These chapters tell the story of Wieland's father, whose religious Enthusiasm was transmitted to his son. It should be noted that Brown does not attempt to clear up entirely the mystery of the elder Wieland's death, but leaves the reader to choose between two quite different explanations, one of which is calculated to appeal to the deistically inclined with their belief in natural causes and the other of which is for those who retain faith in a special providence. The selection thus illustrates the impact of contemporary religious discussion upon early American *belles lettres.*]

THE FATE OF WIELAND'S FATHER
[1798]

(As narrated by his daughter, Clara, the sister of the hero, Wieland)

I

MY FATHER'S ancestry was noble on the paternal side; but his mother was the daughter of a merchant. My grandfather was a younger brother, and a native of Saxony. He was placed, when he had reached the suitable age, at a German college. During the vacations, he employed himself in traversing the neighboring territory. On one occasion it was his fortune to visit Hamburg. He formed an acquaintance with Leonard Weise, a merchant of that city, and was a frequent guest at his house. The merchant had an only daughter, for whom his guest speedily contracted an affection; and, in spite of parental menaces and prohibitions, he, in due season, became her husband.

By this act he mortally offended his relations. Thenceforward he was entirely disowned and rejected by them. They refused to contribute anything to his support. All intercourse ceased, and he received from them merely that treatment to which an absolute stranger, or detested enemy, would be entitled.

He found an asylum in the house of his new father, whose temper was kind, and whose pride was flattered by this alliance. The nobility of his birth was put in the balance against his poverty. Weise conceived himself, on the whole, to have acted with the highest discretion in thus disposing of his child. My grandfather found it incumbent on him to search out some mode of independent subsistence. His youth had been eagerly devoted to literature and music. These had hitherto been cultivated merely as sources of amusement. They were now converted into the means of gain. At this period there were few works of taste in the Saxon dialect. My ancestor **may** be considered as the founder of the German Theater. The modern poet of the same name is sprung from the same family, and, perhaps, surpasses but little, in the fruitfulness of his invention, or the soundness of his taste, the elder Wieland.[1] His life was spent in the composition of sonatas and dramatic pieces. They were not unpopular, but merely afforded him a scanty subsistence. He died in the bloom of his life, and was quickly followed to the grave by his wife. Their only child was taken under the protection of the merchant. At an early age he was apprenticed to a London trader, and passed seven years of mercantile servitude.

My father was not fortunate in the character of him under whose care he was now placed. He was treated with rigor, and full employment was provided for every hour of his time. His duties were laborious and mechanical. He had been educated with a view to this profession, and, therefore, was not tormented with unsatisfied desires. He did not hold his present occupations in abhorrence, because they withheld him from paths more flowery and more smooth, but he found in unintermitted labor, and in the sternness of his master, sufficient occasions for discontent. No opportunities of recreation were allowed him. He spent all his time pent up in a gloomy apartment, or traversing narrow and crowded streets. His food was coarse, and his lodging humble.

His heart gradually contracted a habit of morose and gloomy reflection. He could not accurately define what was wanting to his happiness. He was not tortured by comparisons drawn between his own situation and that of others. His state was such as suited his age and his views as to fortune. He did not imagine himself treated with extraordinary or unjustifiable rigor. In this respect he supposed the condition of others, bound like himself to mercantile service, to resemble his own; yet every

---

[1] The reference is to the German classical poet, Christoph Martin Wieland, 1733-1813.

engagement was irksome, and every hour tedious in its lapse.

In this state of mind he chanced to light upon a book written by one of the teachers of the Albigenses, or French Protestants. He entertained no relish for books, and was wholly unconscious of any power they possessed to delight or instruct. The volume had lain for years in a corner of his garret, half buried in dust and rubbish. He had marked it as it lay; had thrown it, as his occasions required, from one spot to another; but had felt no inclination to examine its contents, or even to inquire what was the subject of which it treated. One Sunday afternoon, being induced to retire for a few minutes to his garret, his eye was attracted by a page of this book, which, by some accident, had been opened and placed full in his view. He was seated on the edge of his bed, and was employed in repairing a rent in some part of his clothes. His eyes were not confined to his work, but occasionally wandering, lighted at length upon the page. The words "Seek and ye shall find" were those that first offered themselves to his notice. His curiosity was roused by these so far as to prompt him to proceed. As soon as he finished his work, he took up the book and turned to the first page. The further he read, the more inducement he found to continue, and he regretted the decline of the light which obliged him for the present to close it.

The book contained an exposition of the doctrine of the sect of Camissards,[2] and an historical account of its origin. His mind was in a state peculiarly fitted for the reception of devotional sentiments. The craving which had haunted him was now supplied with an object. His mind was at no loss for a theme of meditation. On days of business, he rose at the dawn, and retired to his chamber not till late at night. He now supplied himself with candles, and employed his nocturnal and Sunday hours in studying this book. It, of course, abounded with allusions to the Bible. All its conclusions were deduced from the

sacred text. This was the fountain, beyond which it was unnecessary to trace the stream of religious truth; but it was his duty to trace it thus far.

A Bible was easily procured, and he ardently entered on the study of it. His understanding had received a particular direction. All his reveries were fashioned in the same mould. His progress toward the formation of his creed was rapid. Every fact and sentiment in this book were viewed through a medium which the writings of the Camissard apostle had suggested. His constructions of the text were hasty, and formed on a narrow scale. Everything was viewed in a disconnected position. One action and one precept were not employed to illustrate and restrict the meaning of another. Hence arose a thousand scruples to which he had hitherto been a stranger. He was alternately agitated by fear and by ecstasy. He imagined himself beset by the snares of a spiritual foe, and that his security lay in ceaseless watchfulness and prayer.

His morals, which had never been loose, were now modelled by a stricter standard. The empire of religious duty extended itself to his looks, gestures, and phrases. All levities of speech, and negligences of behavior, were proscribed. His air was mournful and contemplative. He labored to keep alive a sentiment of fear, and a belief of the awe-creating presence of the Deity. Ideas foreign to this were sedulously excluded. To suffer their intrusion was a crime against the Divine Majesty inexpiable but by days and weeks of the keenest agonies.

No material variation had occurred in the lapse of two years. Every day confirmed him in his present modes of thinking and acting. It was to be expected that the tide of his emotions would sometimes recede, that intervals of despondency and doubt would occur; but these gradually were more rare, and of shorter duration;

---

[2] An early 18th Century French Huguenot sect.

and he, at last, arrived at a state considerably uniform in this respect.

His apprenticeship was now almost expired. On his arrival of age he became entitled, by the will of my grandfather, to a small sum. This sum would hardly suffice to set him afloat as a trader in his present situation, and he had nothing to expect from the generosity of his master. Residence in England had, besides, become almost impossible, on account of his religious tenets. In addition to these motives for seeking a new habitation, there was another of the most imperious and irresistible necessity. He had imbibed an opinion that it was his duty to disseminate the truths of the gospel among the unbelieving nations. He was terrified at first by the perils and hardships to which the life of a missionary is exposed. This cowardice made him diligent in the invention of objections and excuses; but he found it impossible wholly to shake off the belief that such was the injunction of his duty. The belief, after every new conflict with his passions, acquired new strength; and, at length, he formed a resolution of complying with what he deemed the will of heaven.

The North American Indians naturally presented themselves as the first objects for this species of benevolence. As soon as his servitude expired, he converted his little fortune into money, and embarked for Philadelphia. Here his fears were revived, and a nearer survey of savage manners once more shook his resolution. For a while he relinquished his purpose, and, purchasing a farm on the Schuylkill, within a few miles of the city, set himself down to the cultivation of it. The cheapness of land, and the service of African slaves, which were then in general use, gave him who was poor in Europe all the advantages of wealth. He passed fourteen years in a thrifty and laborious manner. In this time new objects, new employments, and new associates appeared to have nearly obliterated the devout impressions of his youth. He now became acquainted with a woman of a meek and quiet disposition, and of slender acquirements like himself. He proffered his hand and was accepted.

His previous industry had now enabled him to dispense with personal labor, and direct attention to his own concerns. He enjoyed leisure, and was visited afresh by devotional contemplation. The reading of the scriptures, and other religious books, became once more his favorite employment. His ancient belief relative to the conversion of the savage tribes was revived with uncommon energy. To the former obstacles were now added the pleadings of parental and conjugal love. The struggle was long and vehement; but his sense of duty would not be stifled or enfeebled, and finally triumphed over every impediment.

His efforts were attended with no permanent success. His exhortations had sometimes a temporary power, but more frequently were repelled with insult and derision. In pursuit of this object he encountered the most imminent perils, and underwent incredible fatigues, hunger, sickness, and solitude. The license of savage passion, and the artifices of his depraved countrymen, all opposed themselves to his progress. His courage did not forsake him till there appeared no reasonable ground to hope for success. He desisted not till his heart was relieved from the supposed obligation to persevere. With his constitution somewhat decayed, he at length returned to his family. An interval of tranquillity succeeded. He was frugal, regular, and strict in the performance of domestic duties. He allied himself with no sect, because he perfectly agreed with none. Social worship is that by which they are all distinguished; but this article found no place in his creed. He rigidly interpreted that precept which enjoins us, when we worship, to retire into solitude, and shut out every species of society. According to him, devotion was not only a silent office, but must be performed alone. An hour at noon, and an hour at midnight were thus appropriated.

At the distance of three hundred yards

from his house, on the top of a rock whose sides were steep, rugged, and encumbered with dwarf cedars and stony asperities, he built what to a common eye would have seemed a summer-house. The eastern verge of this precipice was sixty feet above the river which flowed at its foot. The view before it consisted of a transparent current, fluctuating and rippling in a rocky channel, and bounded by a rising scene of corn-fields and orchards. The edifice was slight and airy. It was no more than a circular area, twelve feet in diameter, whose flooring was the rock, cleared of moss and shrubs, and exactly levelled, edged by twelve Tuscan columns, and covered by an undulating dome. My father furnished the dimensions and outlines, but allowed the artist whom he employed to complete the structure on his own plan. It was without seat, table, or ornament of any kind.

This was the temple of his Deity. Twice in twenty-four hours he repaired hither, unaccompanied by any human being. Nothing but physical inability to move was allowed to obstruct or postpone this visit. He did not exact from his family compliance with his example. Few men, equally sincere in their faith, were as sparing in their censures and restrictions, with respect to the conduct of others, as my father. The character of my mother was no less devout; but education had habituated her to a different mode of worship. The loneliness of their dwelling prevented her from joining any established congregation; but she was punctual in the offices of prayer, and in the performance of hymns to her Saviour, after the manner of the disciples of Zinzendorf.[3] My father refused to interfere in her arrangements. His own system was embraced not, accurately speaking, because it was the best, but because it had been expressly prescribed to him. Other modes, if practiced by other persons, might be equally acceptable.

His deportment to others was full of charity and mildness. A sadness perpetually overspread his features, but was un-mingled with sternness or discontent. The tones of his voice, his gestures, his steps, were all in tranquil unison. His conduct was characterized by a certain forbearance and humility, which secured the esteem of those to whom his tenets were most obnoxious. They might call him a fanatic and a dreamer, but they could not deny their veneration to his invincible candor and invariable integrity. His own belief of rectitude was the foundation of his happiness. This, however, was destined to find an end.

Suddenly the sadness that constantly attended him was deepened. Sighs, and even tears, sometimes escaped him. To the expostulations of his wife he seldom answered anything. When he designed to be communicative, he hinted that his peace of mind was flown, in consequence of deviation from his duty. A command had been laid upon him, which he had delayed to perform. He felt as if a certain period of hesitation and reluctance had been allowed him, but that this period was passed. He was no longer permitted to obey. The duty assigned to him was transferred in consequence of his disobedience, to another, and all that remained was to endure the penalty.

He did not describe this penalty. It appeared to be nothing more for some time than a sense of wrong. This was sufficiently acute, and was aggravated by the belief that his offence was incapable of expiation. No one could contemplate the agonies which he seemed to suffer, without the deepest compassion. Time, instead of lengthening the burden, appeared to add to it. At length he hinted to his wife that his end was near. His imagination did not prefigure the mode or the time of his decease, but was fraught with an incurable persuasion that his death was at hand. He was likewise haunted by the belief that the kind of death that awaited him was strange and

---

[3] Count von Zinzendorf, 1700-1760, founded the reorganized Moravian Church or United Brethren, an "Enthusiastic" sect.

terrible. His anticipations were thus far vague and indefinite; but they sufficed to poison every moment of his being, and devote him to ceaseless anguish.

II

Early in the morning of a sultry day in August, he left Mettingen, to go to the city. He had seldom passed a day from home since his return from the shores of the Ohio. Some urgent engagements at this time existed, which would not admit of further delay. He returned in the evening, but appeared to be greatly oppressed with fatigue. His silence and dejection were likewise in more than ordinary degree conspicuous. My mother's brother, whose profession was that of a surgeon, chanced to spend this night at our house. It was from him that I have frequently received an exact account of the mournful catastrophe that followed.

As the evening advanced, my father's inquietudes increased. He sat with his family as usual, but took no part in their conversation. He appeared fully engrossed by his own reflections. Occasionally his countenance exhibited tokens of alarm; he gazed steadfastly and wildly at the ceiling; and the exertions of his companions were scarcely sufficient to interrupt his reverie. On recovering from these fits he expressed no surprise; but pressing his hand to his head, complained, in a tremulous and terrified tone, that his brain was scorched to cinders. He would then betray marks of insupportable anxiety.

My uncle perceived, by his pulse, that he was indisposed, but in no alarming degree, and ascribed appearances chiefly to the workings of his mind. He exhorted him to recollection and composure, but in vain. At the hour of repose he readily retired to his chamber. At the persuasion of mother he even undressed and went to bed. Nothing could abate his restlessness. He checked her tender expostulations with some sternness. "Be silent," said he, "For that which I feel there is but one cure, and that will shortly come. You can help me nothing. Look to your own condition and pray to God to strengthen you under the calamities that await you." "What am I to fear?" she answered, "What terrible disaster is it that you think of?" "Peace—as yet I know it not myself, but come it will, and shortly." She repeated her inquiries and doubts; but he suddenly put an end to the discourse, by a stern command to be silent.

She had never before known him in this mood. Hitherto all was benign in his deportment. Her heart was pierced with sorrow at the contemplation of his change. She was utterly unable to account for it, or to figure to herself the species of disaster that was menaced.

Contrary to custom, the lamp, instead of being placed on the hearth, was left upon the table. Over it against the wall there hung a small clock, so contrived as to strike a very hard stroke at the end of every sixth hour. That which was now approaching was the signal for retiring to the fane at which he addressed his devotions. Long habit had occasioned him to be always awake at this hour, and the toll was instantly obeyed.

Now frequent and anxious glances were cast at the clock. Not a single movement of the index appeared to escape his notice. As the hour verged toward twelve his anxiety visibly augmented. The trepidations of my mother kept pace with those of her husband; but she was intimidated into silence. All that was left to her was to watch every change of his features, and give vent to her sympathy in tears.

At length the hour was spent, and the clock tolled. The sound appeared to communicate a shock to every part of my father's frame. He rose immediately, and threw over himself a loose gown. Even this office was performed with difficulty, for his joints trembled, and his teeth chattered with dismay. At this hour his duty called him to the rock, and my mother naturally concluded that it was thither he intended to repair. Yet these incidents were so uncommon, as to fill her with astonishment and foreboding. She saw him leave the room, and heard his steps as they hastily descended the stairs. She half resolved to rise and pursue him, but the wildness of the scheme quickly suggested itself. He was going to a place whither no power on earth could induce him to suffer an attendant.

The window of her chamber looked toward the rock. The atmosphere was clear and calm, but the edifice could not be discovered at that distance through the dusk. My mother's anxiety would not allow her to remain where she was. She rose, and seated herself at the window. She strained her sight to get a view of the dome, and of the path that led to it. The first painted itself with sufficient distinctness on her fancy, but was undistinguishable by the eye from the rocky mass on which it was erected. The second could be imperfectly seen; but her husband had already passed, or had taken a different direction.

What was it she feared? Some disaster impended over her husband or herself. He had predicted evils, but professed himself ignorant of what nature they were. When were they to come? Was this night, or this hour, to witness the accomplishment? She was tortured with impatience, and uncertainty. All her fears were at present linked to his person, and she gazed at the clock, with nearly as much eagerness as my father had done, in expectation of the next hour.

An half hour passed away in this state of suspense. Her eyes were fixed upon the rock; suddenly it was illuminated. A light proceeding from the edifice made every part of the scene visible. A gleam diffused itself over the intermediate space, and instantly a loud report, like the explosion of a mine, followed. She uttered an involuntary shriek, but the new sounds that greeted her ear, quickly conquered her surprise. They were piercing shrieks, and uttered without intermission. The gleams which had diffused themselves far and wide were in a moment withdrawn, but the interior of the edifice was filled with rays.

The first suggestion was that a pistol was discharged, and that the structure was on fire. She did not allow herself time to meditate a second thought, but rushed into the entry and knocked loudly at the door of her brother's chamber. My uncle had been previously roused by the noise, and instantly flew to the window. He also imagined what he saw to be fire. The loud and vehement shrieks which succeeded the first explosion, seemed to be an invocation of succor. The incident was inexplicable; but he could not fail to perceive the propriety of hastening to the spot. He was unbolting the door, when his sister's voice was heard on the outside conjuring him to come forth.

He obeyed the summons with all the speed in his power. He stopped not to question her, but hurried down stairs and across the meadow which lay between the house and the rock. The shrieks were no longer to be heard; but a blazing light was clearly discernible between the columns of the temple. Irregular steps, hewn in the stone, led him to the summit. On three sides, this edifice touched the very verge of the cliff. On the fourth side, which might be regarded as the front, there was an area of small extent, to which the rude staircase conducted you. My uncle speedily gained this spot. His strength was for a moment exhausted by his haste. He paused to rest himself. Meanwhile he bent the most vigilant attention toward the object before him.

Within the columns he beheld what he could not better describe than by saying that it resembled a cloud impregnated with light. It had the brightness of flame, but was without its upward motion. It did not occupy the whole area, and rose but a few feet above the floor. No part of the building was on fire. This appearance was astonishing. He approached the temple. As he went forward the light retired, and, when he put his feet within the apartment, utterly vanished. The suddenness of this transition increased the darkness that succeeded in a tenfold degree. Fear and wonder rendered him powerless. An occurrence like this, in a place assigned to devotion, was adapted to intimidate the stoutest heart.

His wandering thoughts were recalled by the groans of one near him. His sight gradually recovered its power, and he was able to discern my father stretched on the floor. At that moment, my mother and servants arrived with a lanthorn, and enabled my uncle to examine more closely this scene. My father, when he left the house, besides a loose upper vest and slippers, wore a shirt and drawers. Now he was naked, his skin throughout the greater part of his body was scorched and bruised. His right arm exhibited marks as of having been struck by some heavy body. His clothes had been removed, and it was not immediately perceived that they were reduced to ashes. His slippers and his hair were untouched.

He was removed to his chamber, and the requisite attention paid to his wounds, which gradually became more painful. A mortification speedily showed itself in the arm, which had been most hurt. Soon after, the other wounded parts exhibited the like appearance.

Immediately subsequent to this disaster, my father seemed nearly in a state of insensibility. He was passive under every operation. He scarcely opened his eyes, and was with difficulty prevailed upon to answer the questions that were put to him. By his imperfect account it appeared that, while engaged in silent orisons, with thoughts full of confusion and anxiety, a faint gleam suddenly shot athwart the apartment. His fancy immediately pictured to itself a person bearing a lamp. It seemed to come from behind. He was in the act of turning to examine the visitant, when his right arm received a blow from a heavy club. At the same instant, a very bright spark was seen to light upon his clothes. In a moment, the whole was reduced to ashes. This was the sum of the information which he chose to give. There was somewhat in his manner that indicated an imperfect tale. My uncle was inclined

to believe that half the truth had been suppressed.

Meanwhile, the disease thus wonderfully generated betrayed more terrible symptoms. Fever and delirium terminated in lethargic slumber, which, in the course of two hours, gave place to death. Yet not till insupportable exhalations and crawling putrefaction had driven from his chamber and the house everyone whom their duty did not detain.

Such was the end of my father. None surely was ever more mysterious. When we recollect his gloomy anticipations and unconquerable anxiety, the security from human malice which his character, the place, and the condition of the times might be supposed to confer; the purity and cloudlessness of the atmosphere, which rendered it impossible that lightning was the cause; what are the conclusions that we must form?

The prelusive gleam, the blow upon his arm, the fatal spark, the explosion heard so far, the fiery cloud that environed him, without detriment to the structure, though composed of combustible materials, the sudden vanishing of this cloud at my uncle's approach—what is the inference to be drawn from these facts? Their truth cannot be doubted. My uncle's testimony is peculiarly worthy of credit, because no man's temper is more skeptical, and his belief is unalterably attached to natural causes.[4]

I was at this time a child of six years of age. The impressions that were then made upon me can never be effaced. I was ill qualified to judge respecting what was then passing; but as I advanced in age, and became more fully acquainted with these facts, they oftener became the subject of my thoughts. Their resemblance to

---

[4] A case, in its symptoms exactly parallel to this, is published in one of the Journals of Florence. See, likewise, similar cases reported by Messrs. Merrille and Mureure, in the "Journal de Medicine" for February and May, 1783. The researches of Maffei and Fontana have thrown some light upon this subject.—Brown's note.

recent events revived them with new force in my memory, and made me more anxious to explain them.[5] Was this the penalty of disobedience? this the stroke of a vindictive and invisible hand? Is it a fresh proof that the Divine Ruler interferes in human affairs, meditates an end, selects and commissions his agents, and enforces, by unequivocal sanctions, submission to his will? Or, was it merely the irregular expansion of the fluid that imparts warmth to our heart and our blood, caused by the fatigue of the preceding day, or flowing, by established laws, from the condition of his thoughts?[6]

1752 ∾ *Philip Freneau* ∾ 1832

DEISM was such a militantly rationalistic religion that it did not provide so effective a basis for moving poetry as had been provided by earlier Puritanism. This may be seen by comparing the following deistic poems written by Philip Freneau with Anne Bradstreet's "Contemplations" or the selections from the poetry of Edward Taylor.

[See other selections from the poetry of Freneau in Book I, Parts 1 and 3.]

REFLECTIONS ON THE CONSTITUTION OR FRAME OF NATURE
[1809]

From what high source of being came
This system, Nature's aweful frame;
This sun, that motion gives to all,
The planets, and this earthly ball:

This sun, who life and heat conveys,   5
And comforts with his cheering rays;
This image of the God, whose beam
Enlivens like the GREAT SUPREME,

We see, with most exact design,
The WORLD revolve, the planets shine,   10
The nicest order all things meet,
A structure in ITSELF complete.

Beyond our proper solar sphere
Unnumbered orbs again appear,
Which, sunk into the depths of space,   15
Unvarying keep their destined place.

Great Frame! what wonders we survey,
In part alone, from day to day!
And hence the reasoning, human soul
Infers an author of the whole: 20

A power, that every blessing gives,
Who through eternal ages lives,
All space inhabits, space his throne,
Spreads through all worlds, confin'd to none;

Infers, through skies, o'er seas, o'er lands   25
A power throughout the whole commands;
In all extent its dwelling place,
Whose mansion is unbounded space.

---

[5] Clara refers to mysterious events in the story of her brother, to which the rest of *Wieland* is devoted.

[6] Brown's note, previously cited, refers to cases of "spontaneous combustion" in human beings, a possibility in which medical science at one time believed, especially in the case of alcoholics. Characters are disposed of by "spontaneous combustion" in Dickens' *Bleak House,* Marryat's *Jacob Faithful,* and Melville's *Redburn.* Was the fate of Wieland's father the result of supernatural intervention by a special providence or "spontaneous combustion" caused by religious Enthusiasm? The unsolved mystery establishes the "atmosphere" for the portrayal of religious Enthusiasm and its effects in the case of the hero, Clara's brother.

Where ends this world, or when began
This spheric point displayed to man?— 30
No limit has the work divine,
Nor owns a circumscribing line.

Beyond what mind or thought conceives,
Our efforts it in darkness leaves;
Existing in the eternal scheme,   35
Vast, undivided, and supreme.

Here beauty, order, power behold
Exact, all perfect, uncontrolled;
All in its proper place arranged,
Immortal, endless, and unchanged.   40

Its powers, still active, never rest,
From motions, by THAT GOD impressed,
Who life through all creation spread,
Nor left the meanest atom dead.

SCIENCE, FAVOURABLE TO
VIRTUE
[1809]

This mind, in this uncertain state,
Is anxious to investigate
All knowledge through creation sown,
And would no atom leave unknown.

So warm, so ardent in research,   5
To wisdom's *source* she fain would march;
And find by study, toil, and care
The secrets of all nature *there*.

Vain wish, to fathom all we see,
For nature is all mystery;   10
The mind, though perch'd on eagle's wings,
With pain surmounts the scum of things.

Her knowledge on the surface floats,
Of things supreme she dreams or dotes;
Fluttering awhile, she soon descends,   15
And all in disappointment ends.

And yet this proud, this strong desire,
Such ardent longings to aspire,
Prove that this weakness in the mind
For some wise purpose was designed.   20

From efforts and attempts, like these,
Virtue is gained by slow degrees;
And science, which from truth she draws,
Stands firm on Reason and her cause.

However small, its use we find   25
To tame and civilize mankind,
To throw the brutal instinct by,
To honour Reason, ere we die.

The lovely philanthropic scheme
(Great image of the power supreme),   30
On growth of science must depend;
With this all human duties end.

ON THE
UNIFORMITY AND PERFECTION
OF NATURE
[1815]

On one fix'd point all nature moves,
Nor deviates from the track she loves;
Her system, drawn from reason's source,
She scorns to change her wonted course.

Could she descend from that great plan   5
To work unusual things for man,
To suit the insect of an hour—
This would betray a want of power,

Unsettled in its first design
And erring, when it did combine   10
The parts that form the vast machine,
The figures sketch'd on nature's scene.

Perfections of the great first cause
Submit to no contracted laws,
But all-sufficient, all-supreme,   15
Include no trivial views in them.

Who looks through nature with an eye
That would the scheme of heaven descry,
Observes her constant, still the same,
In all her laws, through all her frame.   20

No imperfection can be found
In all that is, above, around,—
All, nature made, in reason's sight
Is order all, and *all is right*.

ON THE RELIGION OF NATURE

[1815]

The power, that gives with liberal hand
  The blessings man enjoys, while here,
And scatters through a smiling land
  Abundant products of the year;
    That power of nature, ever bless'd, 5
    Bestow'd religion with the rest.

Born with ourselves, her early sway
  Inclines the tender mind to take
The path of right, fair virtue's way
  Its own felicity to make. 10
    This universally extends
    And leads to no mysterious ends.

Religion, such as nature taught,
  With all divine perfection suits;

Had all mankind this system sought 15
Sophists would cease their vain disputes,
  And from this source would nations know
  All that can make their heaven below.

This deals not curses on mankind,
  Or dooms them to perpetual grief, 20
If from its aid no joys they find,
  It damns them not for unbelief;
    Upon a more exalted plan
    Creatress nature dealt with man—

Joy to the day, when all agree 25
  On such grand systems to proceed,
From fraud, design, and error free,
  And which to truth and goodness lead:
    Then persecution will retreat
    And man's religon be complete. 30

American Literature Before 1800

III
THE ISSUES OF DEMOCRACY

1588 ∾ *John Winthrop* ∾ *1649*

THE GENERAL Court of the Massachusetts Bay Colony was in session during May and July, 1645, to consider charges that John Winthrop, then deputy governor, and other magistrates had exceeded their authority in refusing to approve as captain of militia for the town of Hingham a Mr. Allen chosen by a majority of the townspeople to replace their previous choice, a Mr. Emes. By threats of an appeal to a ministerial board of arbitration, the magistrates persuaded the General Court to vote an acquittal for Winthrop and a fine for those who had petitioned against his exercise of authority.

At the conclusion of these proceedings, on July 3, Winthrop requested and was permitted to deliver "a little speech," in which he distinguished between two kinds of liberty—that which he deemed possible only when authority was respected and that which led to disrespect for any authority that ran counter to the demands of the mob. This speech is a good statement of the premises that lay behind the attempt of Puritan leadership in New England to restrain the development of the democratic spirit by imposing rigorous checks upon majority rule.

[A portion of Winthrop's speech, with title supplied by the present editors, is here reprinted from his *Journal*. A convenient edition is that of J. K. Hosmer, New York, 1908. The most authoritative version of the original text of the *Journal* is that in the *Winthrop Papers*, Vol. II, Massachusetts Historical Society, 1931. The last published volume, Vol. IV, 1944, carries the *Journal* through 1644. Other selections from the *Journal* will be found in Book I, Part 1.]

TWO KINDS OF LIBERTY
[1790 (written 1645)]

. . . THERE is a twofold liberty, natural (I mean as our nature is now corrupt) and civil or federal. The first is common to man with beasts and other creatures. By this, man, as he stands in relation to man simply, hath liberty to do what he lists; it is a liberty to evil as well as to good. This liberty is incompatible and inconsistent with authority and cannot endure the least restraint of the most just authority. The exercise and maintaining of this liberty makes men grow more evil, and in time to be worse than brute beasts. . . . This is that great enemy of truth and peace, that wild beast, which all the ordinances of God are bent against, to restrain and subdue it. The other kind of liberty I call civil or federal, it may also be termed moral, in reference to the covenant between God and man, in the moral law, and the politic covenants and constitutions, amongst men themselves. This liberty is the proper end and object of authority, and cannot subsist without it; and it is a liberty to that only which is good, just, and honest. This liberty you are to stand for, with the hazard (not only of your goods, but) of your lives, if need be. Whatsoever crosseth this, is not authority, but a distemper thereof. This liberty is maintained and exercised in a way of subjection to authority; it is of the same kind of liberty wherewith Christ hath made us free. The woman's own choice makes such a man her husband; yet being so chosen, he is her lord, and she is to be subject to him, yet in a way of liberty, not of bondage; and a true wife accounts her subjection her honor and freedom, and would not think her condition safe and free, but in her subjection to her husband's authority. Such is the liberty of the church under the authority of Christ, her king and husband; his yoke is so easy and sweet to her as a bride's ornaments; and if through frowardness or wantonness, etc., she shake it off, at any time, she is at no rest in her spirit, until she take it up again; and whether her lord smiles upon her, and embraceth her in his arms, or whether he frowns, or rebukes, or smites her, she apprehends the sweetness of his love in all, and is refreshed, supported, and instructed by every such dispensation of his authority over her. On the other side, ye know who they are that complain of this yoke and say, let us break their bands, etc., we will not have this man to rule over us. Even so, brethren, it will be between you and your magistrates. If you stand for your natural corrupt liberties, and will do what is good in your own eyes, you will not endure the least weight of authority, but will murmur, and oppose, and be always striving to shake off that yoke; but if you will be satisfied to enjoy such civil and lawful liberties, such as Christ allows you, then will you quietly and cheerfully submit unto that authority which is set over you, in all the administrations of it, for your good. Wherein, if we fail at any time, we hope we shall be willing (by God's assistance) to hearken to good advice from any of you, or in any other way of God; so shall your liberties be preserved, in upholding the honor and power of authority amongst you.

1584 ∾ *John Cotton* ∾ *1652*

A GROUP of English Puritan nobles, under the leadership of Lord Say and Seale, contemplated migration to New England, but first desired assurance that the government there was ordered according to their liking. To this end they sent an emissary to the Bay Colony with a series of formal demands defining their conception of the principles that should prevail in a commonwealth acceptable to them as a place of refuge. To make clear to his lordship what the nobles should expect if they chose to come to New England and to allay his lordship's own doubts about the theocratic tendencies in the government of the Bay Colony, John Cotton wrote a personal letter to him dated 1636. Along with this letter went a document drawn up at a special meeting of the Bay Colony leaders. This document contained formal answers to each of the nobles' demands or proposals. Neither Cotton's letter nor the document containing the formal answers satisfied Lord Say and Seale and his followers.

[Cotton's personal letter is here reprinted in its entirety. The text has been modernized from Thomas Hutchinson's *History of the Colony of Massachusetts-Bay*, London, 1760, I, 496-501. See other selections from Cotton's writings in Book I, Part 2.]

LETTER TO LORD SAY AND SEALE

[1760 (written 1636)]

RIGHT honorable: What your Lordship writeth of Dr. Twisse his works—*de scientia media* and of the sabbath—it did refresh me to read that his labors of such arguments were like to come to light [1]; and it would refresh me much more to see them here: though (for my own particular) till I get some release from some constant labors here (which the church is desirous to procure) I can get little or no opportunity to read anything, or attend to anything, but the daily occurrences which press in upon me continually, much beyond my strength either of body or mind. Your Lordship's advertisement touching the civil state of this colony, as they do breathe forth your singular wisdom and faithfulness and tender care of the peace, so we have no reason to misinterpret or undervalue your Lordship's either directions or intentions therein. I know no man under heaven (I speak in God's fear without flattery) whose counsel I should rather depend upon for the wise administration of a civil state according to God than upon your Lordship, and such confidence have I (not in you) but in the Lord's presence in Christ with you that I should never fear to betrust a greater commonwealth than this (as much as in us lieth) under such a *perpetua dictatura* as your Lordship should prescribe. For I nothing doubt that either your Lordship would prescribe all things according to the rule or be willing to examine again and again all things according to it. I am very apt to believe what Mr. Perkins hath, in one of his prefatory pages to his *Golden Chain*,[2] that the word and scriptures of God do contain a short *upoluposis* or platform, not only of theology, but also of other sacred sciences (as he calleth them), attendants and handmaids thereunto, which he maketh ethics, economics, politics, church-government, prophecy, academy. It is very suitable to God's all-sufficient wisdom and

to the fulness and perfection of Holy Scriptures, not only to prescribe perfect rules for the right ordering of a private man's soul to everlasting blessedness with himself, but also for the right ordering of a man's family, yea, of the commonwealth too, so far as both of them are subordinate to spiritual ends, and yet avoid both the church's usurpation upon civil jurisdictions, *in ordine ad spiritualia*,[3] and the commonwealth's invasion upon ecclesiastical administrations, *in ordine* to civil peace and conformity to the civil state. God's institutions (such as the government of church and of commonwealth be) may be close and compact and coordinate one to another and yet not confounded. God hath so framed the state of church government and ordinances that they may be compatible to any commonwealth, though never so much disordered in his frame. But yet when a commonwealth hath liberty to mold his own frame (*scripturae plenitudinem adoro*) [4] I conceive the scripture hath given full direction for the right ordering of the same and that in such sort as may best maintain the *euexia* [5] of the church. Mr. Hooker [6] doth often quote a saying of our Mr. Cartwright [7] (though I have not

---

[1] The *Dissertatio de scientia media tribus libris absoluta* of Dr. William Twisse, Puritan theologian of England, was published at Arnheim, 1639.

[2] *Armilla Aurea*, 1590, by one of the leaders of English Puritanism, William Perkins, was published in English as *A Golden Chain*, 1600, and went through numerous editions both in Latin and English.

[3] In order towards things spiritual.

[4] I speak with reverence for the plenitude of scripture.

[5] Vigor.

[6] Thomas Hooker, 1586-1647, was pastor of Newtown, founder of Connecticut, and author of *Survey of the Summe of Church Discipline*, 1648, the best formulation of the New England Congregational church polity.

[7] Thomas Cartwright, 1535-1603, was one of the foremost spokesmen of Elizabethan Puritanism.

read it in him) that no man fashioneth his house to his hangings, but his hangings to his house. It is better that the commonwealth be fashioned to the setting forth of God's house, which is his church, than to accommodate the church frame to the civil state. Democracy I do not conceive that ever God did ordaine as a fit government either for church or commonwealth. If the people be governors, who shall be governed? As for monarchy and aristocracy, they are both of them clearly approved and directed in scripture, yet so as referreth the sovereignty to himself and setteth up theocracy in both as the best form of government in the commonwealth as well as in the church.

The law which your Lordship instanceth in (that none shall be chosen to magistracy among us but a church member) was made and enacted before I came into the country, but I have hitherto wanted sufficient light to plead against it. 1st. The rule that directeth the choice of supreme governors is of like equity and weight in all magistrates, that one of their brethren (not a stranger) should be set over them, *Deut*. 17.15., and Jethro's counsel to Moses was approved of God, that the judges and officers to be set over the people should be men fearing God, *Exod*. 18.21., and Solomon maketh it the joy of a commonwealth when the righteous are in authority and their mourning when the wicked rule, *Prov*. 29.21., *Job* 34.30. Your Lordship's fear that this will bring in papal excommunication is just and pious, but let your Lordship be pleased again to consider whether the consequence is necessary. *Turpius ejicitur quam non admittitur:* nonmembership may be a just cause of nonadmission to the place of magistracy, but yet ejection out of his membership will not be a just cause of ejecting him out of his magistracy. A godly woman, being to make choice of an husband, may justly refuse a man that is either cast out of church fellowship, or is not yet received into it, but yet, when she is once given to him, she may not reject him then for such

defect. Mr. Humfrey was chosen for an assistant (as I hear) before the colony came over hither; and, though he be not as yet joined into church fellowship (by reason of the unsettledness of the congregation where he liveth) yet the commonwealth do still continue his magistracy to him as knowing he waiteth for opportunity of enjoying church fellowship shortly.

When your Lordship doubteth, that this course will draw all things under the determination of the church, *in ordine ad spiritualia* (seeing the church is to determine who shall be members, and none but a member may have to do in the government of a commonwealth) be pleased (I pray you) to conceive that magistrates are neither chosen to office in the church nor do govern by directions from the church, but by civil laws, and those enacted in general courts and executed in courts of justice by the governors and assistants. In all which the church (as the church) hath nothing to do; only, it prepareth fit instruments both to rule and to choose rulers, which is no ambition in the church nor dishonor to the commonwealth; the apostle, on the contrary, thought it a great dishonor and reproach to the Church of Christ if it were not able to yield able judges to hear and determine all causes amongst their brethren, I *Cor.* 6 1. to 5., which place alone seemeth to me fully to decide this question, for it plainly holdeth forth this argument: it is a shame to the church to want able judges of civil matters (as v. 5.) and an audacious act in any church member voluntarily to go for judgment otherwise than before the saints (as v. 1.); then it will be no arrogance nor folly in church members nor prejudice to the commonwealth if voluntarily they never choose any civil judges but from amongst the saints, such as church members are called to be. But the former is clear: and how then can the latter be avoided? If this therefore be (as your Lordship rightly conceiveth one of the main objections, if not the only one) which hindereth this commonwealth from the entertainment of the propositions of those worthy gentlemen, we entreat them, in the name of the Lord Jesus, to consider, in meekness of wisdom, it is not any conceit or will of ours, but the holy counsel and will of the Lord Jesus (whom they seek to serve as well as we) that overruleth us in this case: and we trust will overrule them also, that the Lord only may be exalted amongst all his servants. What pity and grief were it that the observance of the will of Christ should hinder good things from us!

But your Lordship doubteth, that if such a rule were necessary, then the church estate and the best ordered commonwealth in the world were not compatible. But let not your Lordship so conceive. For the church submitteth itself to all the laws and ordinances of men, in what commonwealth soever they come to dwell. But it is one thing to submit unto what they have no calling to reform: another thing, voluntarily to ordain a form of government which to the best discerning of many of us (for I speak not of myself) is expressly contrary to rule. Nor need your Lordship fear (which yet I speak with submission to your Lordship's better judgment) that this course will lay such a foundation as nothing but a mere democracy can be built upon it. Bodin [8] confesseth that, though it be *status popularis* where a people choose their own governors, yet the government is not a democracy if it be administered, not by the people, but by the governors, whether one (for then it is a monarchy, though elective) or by many, for then (as you know) it is aristocracy. In which respect it is that church government is justly denied (even by Mr. Robinson) [9] to be democratical, though the people choose their own officers and rulers.

Nor need we fear that this course will in time cast the commonwealth into distractions and popular confusions. For (under correction) these three things do not undermine, but do mutually and strongly maintain one another (even those three which we principally aim at)—authority in magistrates, liberty in people, purity in the church. Purity, preserved in the church, will preserve well-ordered liberty in the people, and both of them establish well-balanced authority in the magistrates. God is the author of all these three, and neither is himself the God of confusion, nor are his ways the ways of confusion, but of peace.

What our brethren (magistrates or ministers, or leading freeholders) will answer to the rest of the propositions, I shall better understand before the gentleman's return from Connecticut who brought them over. Meanwhile, two of the principal of them the general court hath already condescended unto: 1. In establishing a standing council, who, during their lives, should assist the governor in managing the chiefest affairs of this little estate. They have chosen for the present only two (Mr. Winthrop and Mr. Dudley), not willing to choose more till they see what further better choice the Lord will send over to them that so they may keep an open door for such desirable gentlemen as your Lordship mentioneth. 2. They have granted the governor and assistants a negative voice and reserved to the freemen the like liberty also. Touching other things, I hope to give your Lordship further account when the gentleman returneth.

He being now returned, I have delivered to him an answer to the rest of your demands, according to the minds of such leading men amongst us as I thought meet to consult withal, concealing your name from any except 2 or 3 who alike do concur in a joint desire of yielding to any such propositions as your Lordship demandeth, so far as with allowance from the word they may, beyond which I know your Lordship would not require anything.

Now the Lord Jesus Christ (the prince of peace) keep and bless your Lordship and dispose of all your times and talents to

---

[8] Jean Bodin, 1530-1596, French political philosopher.

[9] John Robinson, pastor of the Scrooby congregation, members of which founded "Plymouth Plantation."

his best advantage: and let the covenant of his grace and peace rest upon your honorable family and posterity throughout all generations.

Thus, humbly craving pardon for my boldness and length, I take leave and rest,

Yours Honours to serve in Christ Jesus
J.C.

1578 ∽ *Nathaniel Ward* ∽ 1652

THE CONTROVERSY over religious toleration in early New England was merely a minor reflection of the controversy that agitated England in the period of conservative Puritan dominance from 1640 to 1648 and that was to continue to agitate it during the period of sectarian dominance from 1648 to 1660. The New England Puritans were not only opposed to sectarian diversity of creeds within the confines of the Bay, but also feared that toleration of sects would cause the English Puritan revolution to degenerate into chaos. Roger Williams, in his advocacy of liberty of conscience, was writing not only against the attitude of the Bay leaders but also in behalf of the movement for toleration in England. John Cotton, in answering him, had the English situation and an English audience in mind.

This may likewise be said of Nathaniel Ward when he wrote *The Simple Cobler of Aggawam* in Massachusetts in 1645 and had it published in London in 1647. Combining a tirade against religious toleration with ridicule of women's fondness for newfangledness in dress and written in a picturesque rhetoric reminiscent of Elizabethan and early Jacobean prose satire, Ward's pamphlet is one of the curiosities of early New England literature. His resort to unorthodox wit to bolster orthodoxy is not unlike the strategy of C. S. Lewis in our own day in such works as *The Screwtape Letters* and *Miracles*.

Ward spent only a slight part of his long career in New England. Born in Essex, he took his B.A. at Cambridge in 1596 and his M.A. in 1603. He then prepared himself for the law, practiced it for a while, traveled extensively on the continent, and returned to England to become a curate. He helped form the Massachusetts Bay Colony and came to New England in 1634 after having been silenced by Laud. Until 1636 he was minister at Ipswich, the Indian name of which was Aggawam. He was prominent in New England affairs until 1646, when he went back to England. There he preached a sermon before the House of Commons and in 1648 returned to his native Essex to become a minister. As a spokesman for New England's opposition to religious toleration he surpasses John Cotton in verbal, although not in logical, power.

[The following selection from *The Simple Cobler* has been modernized by the present editors and supplied with an appropriate title.]

THE FOLLY OF RELIGIOUS TOLERATION

[1647]

SATAN is now in his passions, he feels his passion approaching; he loves to fish in roiled waters. Though that Dragon cannot sting the vitals of the elect mortally, yet that Beelzebub can fly-blow their intellectuals miserably. The finer religion grows, the finer he spins his cobwebs, he will hold pace with Christ so long as his wits will serve him. He sees himself beaten out of gross idolatries, heresies, ceremonies, where the light breaks forth with power; he will therefore bestir him to prevaricate evangelical truths and ordinances. . . .

Nor shall he need to stretch his strength overmuch in this work: too many men, having not laid their foundation sure nor ballasted their spirits deep with humility and fear, are pressed enough of themselves to evaporate their own apprehensions. Those that are acquainted with story know it hath ever been so in new editions of churches: such as are least able are most busy to putter in the rubbish and raise dust in the eyes of more steady repairers. Civil commotions make room for uncivil practices; religious mutations, for irreligious opinions; change of air discovers corrupt bodies; reformation of religion, unsound minds. He that hath any well-faced fancy in his crown and doth not vent it now fears the pride of his own heart will dub him dunce forever. Such a one will trouble the whole Israel of God with his most untimely births, though he makes the bones of his vanity stick up to the view and grief of all that are godly wise. The devil desires no better sport than to see light heads handle their heels and fetch their careers in a time when the roof of liberty stands open.

The next perplexed question with pious and ponderous men will be: what should be done for the healing of these comfortless exulcerations? I am the unablest adviser of a thousand, the unworthiest of ten thousand; yet I hope I may presume to assert what follows without just offence.

First, such as have given or taken any unfriendly reports of us New-English should do well to recollect themselves. We have been reputed a colluvies [1] of wild opinionists swarmed into a remote wilderness to find elbow-room for our fanatic doctrines and practices: I trust our diligence past and constant sedulity [2] against such persons and courses will plead better things for us. I dare take upon me to be the herald of New England so far as to proclaim to the world in the name of our colony that all Familists, Antinomians, Anabaptists, and other Enthusiasts shall have free liberty to keep away from us, and such as will come to be gone as fast as they can, the sooner the better.

Secondly, I dare aver that God doth nowhere in his word tolerate Christian states to give tolerations to such adversaries of his truth if they have power in their hands to suppress them. . . .

If the devil might have his free option, I believe he would ask nothing else but liberty to enfranchise all other religions and to embondage the true; nor should he need: it is to be feared that lax tolerations upon state pretences and planting necessities will be the next subtle stratagem he will spread to disstate the truth of God and supplant the peace of the churches. Tolerations in things tolerable, exquisitely drawn out by the lines of the Scripture and pencil of the spirit, are the sacred favors of truth, the due latitudes of love, the fair compartments of Christian fraternity, but irregular dispensations, dealt forth by the facilities of men, are the frontiers of error, the redoubts of schism, the perilous irritaments of carnal enmity.

My heart hath naturally detested four things: the standing of the Apocrypha in the Bible; foreigners dwelling in my country to crowd out native subjects into the corners of the earth; alchemized coins;

---

[1] Collection or gathering.

[2] Sedulousness or zealous care.

tolerations of divers religions or of one religion in segregant shapes: he that willingly assents to the last, if he examines his heart by daylight, his conscience will tell him he is either an atheist or an heretic or an hypocrite or at best a captive to some lust: polchpiety [3] is the greatest impiety in the world. . . .

Not to tolerate things merely indifferent to weak consciences argues a conscience too strong; pressed conformity in these causes much disunity. To tolerate more than indifference is not to deal indifferently with God; he that doth it takes His sceptre out of His hand and bids Him stand by. The power of all religion and ordinances lies in their purity: their purity in their simplicity: then are mixtures pernicious. I lived in a city where a Papist preached in one church, a Lutheran in another, a Calvinist in a third; a Lutheran one part of the day, a Calvinist the other, in the same pulpit: the religion of that place was but motley and meager, their affections leopard-like.

If the whole creature should conspire to do the creator a mischief or offer him an insolency, it would be in nothing more than in erecting untruths against his truth or by sophisticating his truths with human medleys: the removing of some one iota in Scripture may draw out all the life and traverse [4] all the truth of the whole Bible: but to authorize an untruth by a toleration of state is to build a sconce against the walls of heaven, to batter God out of his chair. To tell a practical lie is a great sin but yet transient; but to set up a theorical [5] untruth is to warrant every lie that lies from its root to the top of every branch it hath.

I would willingly hope that no member of the Parliament hath skillfully ingratiated himself into the hearts of the House that he might watch a time to midwife out some ungracious toleration for his own

turn and, for the sake of that, some others. I would also hope that a word of general caution should not be particularly misapplied. Yet, good gentlemen, look well about you and remember how Tiberius played the fox with the senate of Rome and how Fabius Maximus cropped his ears for his cunning.

That state is wise that will improve all pains and patience rather to compose than tolerate differences in religion. There is no divine truth but hath much celestial fire in it from the spirit of truth: nor no irreligious untruth without its proportion of anti-fire from the spirit of error to contradict it: the zeal of the one, the virulency of the other, must necessarily kindle combustions. Fiery diseases seated in the spirit embroil the whole frame of the body; others more external and cool are less dangerous. They which divide in religion divide in God; they who divide in him divide beyond *Genus Generalissimum*,[6] where there is no reconciliation without atonement; that is, without uniting in Him, who is One, and in his truth, which is also one.

Wise are those men who will be persuaded rather to live within the pale of truth where they may be quiet than in the purlieus where they are sure to be hunted ever and anon, do authority what it can. Every singular opinion hath a singular opinion of itself; and he that holds it a singular opinion of himself and a simple opinion of all contra-sentients: he that confutes them must confute all three at once or else he does nothing; which will not be done without more stir than the peace of the state or church can endure. . . .

---

[3] Palchpiety or a religious belief of shreds and patches. Palch means mended or patched, an English dialect word.

[4] Thwart or subvert.

[5] Theoretical.

[6] The most generic genus.

1603(?) ∞ *Roger Williams* ∞ *1683*

ROGER WILLIAMS was the foremost American advocate in the 17th Century of democratic ideas held widely by sectarian Puritans in England. Some of the works in which he most ably set forth these ideas to embarrass the Bay Colony conservatives who had forced him to become the founder of Rhode Island were written under the direct stimulus of the struggle going on in England between the right and left wings of the Puritan revolution.

The first two of the following selections are modernized from *The Bloudy Tenent of Persecution, for cause of Conscience, discussed in a Conference between Truth and Peace,* London, 1644. This work is a lengthy expository dialogue, with the allegorical figures of Truth and Peace as its mouthpieces. It was written in England, where Williams went as agent for Rhode Island in 1643. It was during this visit that he became a friend of John Milton. Parliament ordered *The Bloudy Tenent* burned by the common hangman, and John Cotton replied to it with *The Bloudy Tenent, washed, And made white in the bloud of the Lambe,* London, 1647. When Williams was again in England in 1651 he published a reply to Cotton's reply entitled *The Bloody Tenent yet More Bloody: by Mr. Cottons endevour to wash it white in the Blood of the Lambe.* The third of the following selections is modernized from this work, which also employs Truth and Peace as mouthpieces.

When Williams came home from England in 1654, he found his beloved Providence in a turmoil and immediately took steps to quell the troublemakers. When a paper was circulated arguing that it was against Scripture to use the power of a state to force individuals to conform to its laws, Williams wrote a letter to the town, dated 1655, to make clear that his democratic views on church and state, on the sources of civil authority, and on the infamy of religious persecution, as expressed in his published writings, should not be construed to mean that he sanctioned a lawless liberty on the part of members of a commonwealth.

[This letter is here reprinted in its entirety as the fourth selection. The text may be found in *Publications of the Narragansett Club,* Vol. VI, Providence, 1874, pp. 278-279. Titles for all the following selections have been supplied by the editors. See other selections from Williams' works in Book I, Parts 1 and 2.]

CHURCH AND STATE

[1644]

. . . THE CHURCH, or company of worshippers, whether true or false, is like unto a body or college of physicians in a city, like unto a corporation, society, or company of East India or Turkey merchants, or any other society or company in London; which companies may hold their courts, keep their records, hold disputations, and in matters concerning their society may dissent, divide, break into schisms and factions, sue and implead each other at the law, yea, wholly break up and dissolve into pieces and nothing, and yet the peace of the city not be in the least measure impaired or disturbed; because the essence or being of the city, and so the well-being and peace thereof, is essentially distinct from those particular societies; the city courts, city laws, city punishments, distinct from theirs. The city was before them, and stands absolute and entire when such a corporation or society is taken down. . . .

THE SOURCES OF CIVIL AUTHORITY

[1644]

. . . AS IT is most true that magistracy in general is of God, *Rom.* 13, for the preservation of mankind in civil order and peace—the world otherwise would be like the sea wherein men, like fishes, would hunt and devour each other, and the greater devour the less—so also it is true that magistracy in special, for the several kinds of it, is of man, 1 *Pet.* 2. 13. Now what kind of magistrate soever the people shall agree to set up, whether he receive Christianity before he be set in office, or whether he receive Christianity after, he receives no more power of magistracy than a magistrate that hath received no Christianity. For neither of them both can receive more than the commonweal, the body of people and civil state, as men, communicate unto them and betrust with them. All lawful magistrates in the world, both before the coming of Christ Jesus and since, excepting those unparalleled typical magistrates of the church of Israel, are but derivatives and agents, immediately derived and employed as eyes and hands, serving for the good of the whole. Hence they have and can have no more power than fundamentally lies in the bodies or

fountains themselves, which power, might or authority is not religious, Christian, etc., but natural, human, and civil. . . .

THE INFAMY OF RELIGIOUS PERSECUTION

[1651]

TRUTH: . . . and for myself I must proclaim before the Most Holy God, angels, and men that whatever other white and heavenly tenents Mr. Cotton holds, yet this is a foul, a black, and a bloody tenent.

A tenent of high blasphemy against the God of Peace, the God of Order, who hath of one blood made all mankind, to dwell upon the face of the earth, now all confounded and destroyed in their civil beings and subsistences by mutual flames of war from their several respective religions and consciences.

A tenent warring against the Prince of Peace, Christ Jesus, denying his appearance and coming in the flesh to put an end to and abolish the shadows of that ceremonial and typical land of Canaan.

A tenent fighting against the sweet end of his coming, which was not to destroy men's lives for their religions, but to save them by the meek and peaceable invitations and persuasions of his peaceable wisdom's maidens.

A tenent foully charging his wisdom, faithfulness, and love, in so poorly providing such magistrates and civil powers all the world over as might effect so great a charge pretended to be committed to them.

A tenent lamentably guilty of his most precious blood, shed in the blood of so many hundred thousand of his poor servants by the civil powers of the world, pretending to suppress blasphemies, heresies, idolatries, superstition, etc.

A tenent fighting with the spirit of love, holiness, and meekness, by kindling fiery spirits of false zeal and fury, when yet such spirits know not of what spirit they are.

A tenent fighting with those mighty angels who stand up for the peace of the saints against Persia, Greece, etc., and so consequently all other nations who, fighting for their several religions and against the truth, leave no room for such as fear and love the Lord on the earth.

A tenent against which the blessed souls under the altar cry aloud for vengeance, this tenent having cut their throats, torn out their hearts, and poured forth their blood in all ages, as the only heretics and blasphemers in the world.

A tenent which no uncleanness, no adultery, incest, sodomy, or bestiality can equal, this ravishing and forcing (explicitly or implicitly) the very souls and consciences of all the nations and inhabitants of the world.

A tenent that puts out the very eye of all true faith, which cannot but be as free and voluntary as any virgin in the world, in refusing or embracing any spiritual offer or object.

A tenent loathsome and ugly (in the eyes of the God of Heaven, and serious sons of men) I say, loathsome with the palpable filths of gross dissimulation and hypocrisy; thousands of peoples and whole nations compelled by this tenent to put on the foul vizard of religious hypocrisy for fear of laws, losses, and punishments, and for the keeping and hoping for of favor, liberty, worldly commodity, etc.

A tenent woefully guilty of hardening all false and deluded consciences (of whatsoever sect, faction, heresy, or idolatry, though never so horrid and blasphemous) by cruelties and violences practiced against them, all false teachers and their followers (ordinarily) contracting a brawny and steely hardness from their sufferings for their consciences.

A tenent that shuts and bars out the gracious prophecies and promises and discoveries of the most glorious Sun of Righteousness, Christ Jesus; that burns up the Holy Scriptures, and forbids them, upon the point, to be read in English, or that any trial or search or truly free disquisi-tion be made by them; when the most able, diligent, and conscionable readers must pluck forth their own eyes and be forced to read by the (whichsoever predominant) clergy's spectacles.

A tenent that seals up the spiritual graces of all men, Jews and Gentiles, and consequently stands guilty of the damnation of all men, since no preachers nor trumpets of Christ himself may call them out but such as the several and respective nations of the world themselves allow of.

A tenent that fights against the common principles of all civility, and in the very civil being and combinations of men in nations, cities, etc., by commixing (explicitly or implicitly) a spiritual and civil state together, and so confounding and overthrowing the purity and strength of both.

A tenent that kindles the devouring flames of combustions and wars in most nations of the world, and (if God were not infinitely gracious) had almost ruined the English, French, and Scotch and Irish, and many other nations, German, Polish, Hungarian, Bohemian, etc.

A tenent that bows down the backs and necks of all civil states and magistrates, kings and emperors, under the proud feet of that man and monster of sin and pride, the pope, and all popish and proud clergymen, rendering such laics and seculars (as they call them) but slavish executioners (upon the point) of their most imperious synodical decrees and sentences.

A tenent that renders the highest civil magistrates and ministers of justice (the fathers and gods of their countries) either odious or lamentably grievous unto the very best subjects by either clapping or keeping on the iron yokes of cruelest oppression. No yoke or bondage comparably so grievous as that upon the soul's neck of men's religion and consciences.

A tenent all besprinkled with the bloody murders, stabs, poisonings, pistolings, powder-plots, etc., against many famous kings, princes, and states, either actually performed or attempted, in France, England,

Scotland, Low Countries, and other nations.

A tenent all red and bloody with those most barbarous and tiger-like massacres of so many thousand and ten thousands formerly in France and other parts, and so lately and so horribly in Ireland; of which, whatever causes be assigned, this chiefly will be found the true; and while this continues (to wit, violence against conscience), this bloody issue sooner or later must break forth again (except God wonderfully stop it) in Ireland and other places too.

A tenent that stunts the growth and flourishing of the most likely and hopefulest commonweals and countries, while consciences the best and the best-deserving subjects are forced to fly (by enforced or voluntary banishment) from their native countries; the lamentable proof whereof England hath felt in the flight of so many worthy English into the Low Countries and New England, and from New England into Old again and other foreign parts.

A tenent whose gross partiality denies the principles of common justice, while men weigh out to the consciences of all others that which they judge not fit nor right to be weighed out to their own, since the persecutor's rule is to take and persecute all consciences, only himself must not be touched.

A tenent that is but Machiavellism, and makes a religion but a cloak or stalking-horse to policy and private ends of Jeroboam's crown,[1] and the priest's benefice, etc.

A tenent that corrupts and spoils the very civil honesty and natural conscience of a nation, since conscience to God, violated, proves (without repentance) ever after a very jade, a drug, loose and unconscionable in all converse with men.

Lastly, a tenent in England most unseasonable, as pouring oil upon those flames which the high wisdom of the Parliament (by easing the yokes on men's consciences) had begun to quench.

In the sad consideration of all which, dear Peace, let heaven and earth judge of the washing and color of this tenent. For thee, sweet heavenly guest, go lodge thee in the breasts of the peaceable and humble witnesses of Jesus, that love the truth in peace! Hide thee from the world's tumults and combustions, in the breasts of thy truly noble children, who profess and endeavor to break the irony and insupportable yokes upon the souls and consciences of any of the sons of men.

Peace: Methinks, dear Truth, if any of the least of these deep charges be found against this tenent, you do not wrong it when you style it bloody; but since, in the woeful proof of all ages past since Nimrod (the hunter or persecutor before the Lord), these and more are lamentably evident and undeniable, it gives me wonder that so many and so excellent eyes of God's servants should not espy so foul a monster, especially considering the universal opposition this tenent makes against God's glory, and the good of all mankind. . . .

THE LIMITS OF LIBERTY
[1655]

THAT ever I should speak or write a tittle that tends to such an infinite liberty of conscience is a mistake, and which I have ever disclaimed and abhorred. To prevent such mistakes, I shall at present only propose this case: there goes many a ship to sea, with many hundred souls in one ship, whose weal and woe is common, and is a true picture of a commonwealth or a human combination or society. It hath fallen out sometimes that both Papists and Protestants, Jews and Turks may be embarked in one ship; upon which supposal I affirm that all the liberty of conscience that ever I pleaded for turns upon these two hinges —that none of the Papists, Protestants, Jews, or Turks be forced to come to the ship's prayers or worship, nor compelled from their own particular prayers and

---

[1] A reference to the first King of Israel in 1 *Kings* 12-14.

worship, if they practice any. I further add that I never denied that, notwithstanding this liberty, the commander of this ship ought to command the ship's course, yea, and also command that justice, peace, and sobriety be kept and practiced, both among the seamen and all the passengers. If any of the seamen refuse to perform their services, or passengers to pay their freight; if any refuse to help, in person or purse, towards the common charges or defence; if any refuse to obey the common laws and orders of the ship concerning their common peace or preservation; if any shall mutiny and rise up against their commanders and officers; if any should preach or write that there ought to be no commanders or officers, because all are equal in Christ, therefore no masters nor officers, no laws nor orders, nor corrections nor punishments—I say, I never denied but in such cases, whatever is pretended, the commander or commanders may judge, resist, compel, and punish such transgressors, according to their deserts and merits. This, if seriously and honestly minded, may, if it so please the Father of Lights, let in some light to such as willingly shut not their eyes.

I remain studious of your common peace and liberty.

Documents of Bacon's Rebellion

THE DEMOCRATIC spirit that was eventually to flare forth in the American Revolution was kindled in early popular insurrections against colonial governors. In 1676, Nathaniel Bacon, a young Englishman who had lived in Virginia for two years and had been a member of the council of the governor, Sir William Berkeley, undertook to correct the governor's lax defense policy against Indian outrages by organizing a militia of his own. Declared a rebel, Bacon led his followers against Berkeley's anti-insurrection forces, routed them, took charge of the government, and made ready to resist any royal troops that might be sent to the governor's aid. When Bacon died of a fever, his leaderless army, now containing escaped servants and slaves who engaged in plundering the rich, was easily overcome by Berkeley's better organized supporters, and numerous hangings followed. Berkeley got into disputes with commissioners of Charles II sent to quell the revolt and make an official report. As a consequence he was relieved of his governorship and recalled to England, where he died in 1677 in disgrace. Extant documents that tell the story of Bacon's rebellion either exalt him as a hero battling for the rights of the people of Virginia against tyranny and incompetence or deride him as an ambitious demagogue seeking to gain power by manipulation of the "rascal many's" passions and credulity.

The first of the following selections is a characterization of Bacon from *A True Narrative of the Late Rebellion in Virginia, By the Royal Commissioners*, drawn up in 1677 after two of the commissioners, Captain Sir John Berry and Francis Moryson, had returned to England, leaving their colleague, Colonel

Herbert Jeffreys, in Virginia as Berkeley's successor. The second selection, taken from the same source, is Bacon's speech to his followers before leading them against Berkeley's anti-insurrection forces. The third selection, also from the commissioners' *True Narrative,* is the oath which Bacon is said to have imposed upon the people in various parts of Virginia after he had routed Berkeley's army and captured and burned Jamestown.

The last two selections are from *The History of Bacon's and Ingram's Rebellion,* a work apparently composed by a Virginian contemporary of Bacon. The original manuscript is now among the Burwell Papers in the custody of the Virginia Historical Society. "Bacon's Epitaph, made by his Man" and "Upon the Death of G.B.," quoted in the *History,* are anonymous poems, the latter apparently written in answer to the former. The historian refers to them as "a relish taken from both appetites." In other words, they reflect, respectively, the two extreme attitudes taken by Bacon's contemporaries toward his character and exploits—one the attitude of democratic myth-making and the other that of aristocratic debunking.

[All the selections have been modernized. Complete texts are contained in *Narratives of the Insurrections 1675-1690,* ed. C. M. Andrews, New York, 1915, one of the volumes in the series, *Original Narratives of Early American History.* Titles of the first three selections have been supplied by the present editors.]

ONE VIEW OF THE CHARACTER OF BACON

[1677]

HE WAS a person whose erratic fortune had carried and shown him many foreign parts, and of no obscure family. Upon his first coming into Virginia, he was made one of the Council, the reason of that advancement (all on a sudden) being best known to the Governor, which honor made him the more considerable in the eye of the vulgar and gave some advantage to his pernicious designs. He was said to be about four or five and thirty years of age, indifferent tall but slender, black-haired, and of an ominous, pensive, melancholy aspect, of a pestilent and prevalent logical discourse tending to atheism in most companies, not given to much talk, or to make sudden replies, of a most imperious and dangerous hidden pride of heart, despising the wisest of his neighbors for their ignorance, and very ambitious and arrogant. But all these things lay hid in him till after he was a councillor, and until he became powerful and popular.

Now this man being in company with one Crews, Isham, and Bird, who, growing to a height of drinking and making the sadness of the times their discourse, and the fear they all lived in, because of the Susquahanocks who had settled a little above the falls of James River and committed many murders upon them, among whom Bacon's overseer happened to be one, Crews and the rest persuaded Mr. Bacon to go over and see the soldiers on the other side James River and to take a quantity of rum with them to give the men to drink, which they did, and (as Crews, etc., had before laid the plot with the soldiers) they all at once in field shouted and cried out, "A Bacon! A Bacon! A Bacon!" which, taking fire with his ambition and spirit of faction and popularity, easily prevailed on him to resolve to head them, his friends endeavoring to fix him the faster to his resolves by telling him that they would also go along with him to take revenge upon the Indians and drink damnation to their souls to be true to him, and if he could not obtain a commission, they would assist him as well and as much as if he had one; to which Bacon agreed.

This forwardness of Bacon's greatly cheered and animated the people, who looked upon him as the only patron of the country and preserver of their lives and fortunes.

For he pretended and boasted what great service he would do for the country in destroying the common enemy, securing their lives and estates, liberties, and such like fair frauds he subtly and secretly insinuated by his own instruments over all the country, which he seduced the vulgar and most ignorant people to believe (two thirds of each county being of that sort) so that their whole hearts and hopes were set now upon Bacon. Next he charges the Governor as negligent and wicked, treacherous and incapable, the laws and taxes as unjust and oppressive, and cries up absolute necessity of redress.

Thus Bacon encouraged the tumult, and, as the unquiet crowd follow and adhere to him, he listeth them as they come in upon a large paper, writing their name circularwise, that their ring-leaders might not be found out.

Having conjured them into this circle, given them brandy to wind up the charm, and enjoined them by an oath to stick fast together and to him, and the oath being administered, he went and infected New Kent County ripe for rebellion.

Bacon having got about 300 men together in arms prepared to go out against the Indians, the Governor and his friends endeavor to divert his designs, but cannot.

He proclaims Bacon and his followers rebels and mutineers for going forth against the Indians without a commission, and (getting a company of gentlemen together) the Governor marcheth up to the falls of James River to pursue and take Bacon or to seize him at his return. . . .

A SPEECH OF BACON'S TO HIS FOLLOWERS

[1677]

GENTLEMEN and Fellow Soldiers: The news just now brought me may not a little startle you as well as myself. But seeing it is not altogether unexpected, we may the better bear it and provide our remedies. The Governor is now in Gloster County endeavoring to raise forces against us, having declared us rebels and traitors: if true, crimes indeed too great for pardon; our consciences herein are our best witnesses, and theirs so conscious as like cowards therefore they will not have the courage to face us. It is revenge that hurries them on without regard to the people's safety, and had rather we should be murdered and our ghosts sent to our slaughtered countrymen by their actings than we live to hinder them of their interest with the heathen, and preserve the remaining part of our fellow subjects from their cruelties. Now then we must be forced to our own defence, or expose ourselves to their mercies, or fortune of the woods, whilst His Majesty's country here lies in blood, and wasting (like a candle) at both ends. How incapable we may be made (if we should proceed) through sickness, want of provisions, slaughter, wounds less or more, none of us is void of the sense hereof.

Therefore, while we are sound at heart, unwearied, and not receiving damage by the fate of war, let us descend to know the reasons why such proceedings are used against us, that those whom they have raised for their defence to preserve them against the fury of the heathen they should thus seek to destroy, and to betray our lives whom they raised to preserve theirs; if ever such treachery was heard of, such wickedness and inhumanity (and call all the former ages to witness), and if any, that they suffered in like nature as we are like by the sword and ruins of war.

But they are all damned cowards, and you shall see they will not dare to meet us in the field to try the justness of our cause, and so we will down to them, etc.

ONE OF THE OATHS ADMINISTERED BY BACON TO HIS FOLLOWERS
[1677]

WHEREAS Sir William Berkeley, Knight, late Governor of Virginia, hath in a most barbarous and abominable manner exposed and betrayed our lives, and for greediness of sordid gain did defer our just defence and hinder all the loyal endeavors of His Majesty's faithful subjects; and, further, when the country did raise a sufficient force for the effectual proceeding against the Indian enemy, he did, contrary to all equity and justice and the tenors of his commission, endeavor to oppose the said forces by himself and the Assembly set forth: of which attempts being several times defeated by the people's abhorrence of so bloody design he left the country in a small vessel, it being unknown to all people to what parts of the world he did repair, and whereas as our army upon his departure betaking themselves to the care of the frontiers did march out against the Indians and obtain so great a victory, as hath in a manner finished all the disaster and almost resettled the country in a happy peace, yet notwithstanding Sir Wm. Berkeley, with forces raised in Accomac, did invade the country with acts of hostility, with all intentions to persecute the said army with these aforesaid reasons, as also having betrayed his trust to the king by flying from his seat of judicature, and acting wholly contrary to his commission, we protest against him unanimously as a traitor and most pernicious enemy to the public, and further we swear that in all places of His Majesty's Colony of Virginia we will oppose and prosecute him with all our endeavors by all acts of hostility as occasion shall present, and further whereas plotting and wishing in his heart a total ruin and destruction of this poor colony he hath endeavored to set the heart of our sovereign against us by false information and lies, requesting forces of His Majesty wherewith to compel and subdue us, hindering, intercepting, and preventing all our remonstrances for peace, which might have gone home in our justification, as also hindering of our sending home of agents in the people's behalf, which was the most humble and earnest request of the people at first, we do further declare and swear that we think it absolutely consisting with our allegiance and loyalty to treat with and discourse with the said forces and commissioners with all submission to His Majesty. But otherwise, if it shall so prove that notwithstanding all entreaties and offers we shall make, they shall offer to land by force, in our own defence to fly together as in a common calamity and jointly with the present army now under the command of General Bacon, to stand or fall in the defense of him and the country in so just a cause, and in all places to oppose their proceedings (only until such time as His Majesty by our agents shall fully understand the miserable case of the country, and the justice of our proceedings) which most just request if they shall refuse and by force endeavor to enter the country, we are resolved to uphold the country as long as we can and never to absent and join with any such army whatever, and lastly in case of utmost extremity rather than submit to any so miserable a slavery (when none can longer defend ourselves, our lives and liberties) to acquit the colony rather than submit to so unheard of injustice, and this we all swear in the presence of Almighty God as unfeignedly and freely as ever we desire of him for happiness to come.

By the General.

BACON'S EPITAPH, MADE BY HIS MAN
[1814 (Written c. 1677)]

Death, why so cruel? What! No other way
To manifest thy spleen, but thus to slay
Our hopes of safety, liberty, our all,

Which, through thy tyranny, with him must
    fall
To its late chaos? Had thy rigid force 5
Been dealt by retail, and not thus in gross,
Grief had been silent. Now we must com-
    plain,
Since thou, in him, hast more than thou-
    sand slain,
Whose lives and safeties did so much
    depend
On him their life, with him their lives
    must end.   10
  If't be a sin to think Death bribed can
    be,
We must be guilty; say it was bribery
Guided the fatal shaft, Virginia's foes,
To whom for secret crimes just vengeance
    owes
Deservèd plagues, dreading their just de-
    sert,   15
Corrupted death by Paracelsian art,
Him to destroy, whose well tried courage
    such,
Their heartless hearts, nor arms nor
    strength could touch.
  Who now must heal those wounds or stop
    that blood
The Heathen made, and drew into a
    flood?   20
Who is it must plead our cause? Nor
    trump nor drum
Nor deputations; these, alas! are dumb
And cannot speak. Our arms (though ne'er
    so strong)
Will want the aid of his commanding
    tongue,
Which conquered more than Caesar. He
    o'erthrew   25
Only the outward frame; this could sub-
    due
The rugged works of nature. Souls re-
    plete
With dull chill cold, he'd animate with
    heat
Drawn forth of reason's limbec. In a word,
Mars and Minerva both in him con-
    curred   30
For arts, for arms, whose pen and sword
    alike
As Cato's did, may admiration strike

Into his foes; while they confess withal
It was their guilt styled him a criminal.
Only this difference does from truth pro-
    ceed: 35
They in the guilt, he in the name must
    bleed.
While none shall dare his obsequies to
    sing
In deserved measures: until time shall bring
Truth crowned with freedom, and from
    danger free
To sound his praises to posterity.   40
  Here let him rest; while we this truth
    report
He's gone from hence unto a higher court
To plead his cause, where he by this doth
    know
Whether to Caesar he was friend, or foe.

UPON THE DEATH OF G[ENERAL] B[ACON]

[1814 (written c. 1677)]

  Whether to Caesar he was friend or
    foe?
Pox take such ignorance, do you not know?
Can he be friend to Caesar that shall bring
The arms of Hell to fight against the King?
(Treason, Rebellion)—Then what reason
    have   5
We for to wait upon him to his grave,
There to express our passions? Wilt not be
Worse than his crimes, to sing his elegy
In well-tuned numbers, where each Ella
    bears
(To his flagitious name) a flood of tears? 10
A name that hath more souls with sorrow
    fed
Than wretched Niobe single tears ere shed;
A name that filled all hearts, all ears, with
    pain,
Until blest Fate proclaimed, Death had
    him slain.
Then how can it be counted for a sin, 15
Though Death (nay, though myself) had
    bribèd been
To guide the fatal shaft? We honor all

That lends a hand unto a traitor's fall.
What though the well-paid rochet[1] soundly
    ply
And box the pulpit in to flattery,   20
Urging his rhetoric and strained eloquence,
T'adorn incoffined filth and excrements;
Though the defunct (like ours) ne'er
    tried
A well-intended deed until he died?
'Twill be nor sin, nor shame, for us to
    say   25
A two-fold passion checker-works this
    day—
Of joy and sorrow; yet the last doth move
On foot impotent, waiting strength to
    prove
(Nor can the art of logic yield relief)
How joy should be surmounted by our
    grief.   30
Yet that we grieve it cannot be denied,
But 'tis because he was, not 'cause he died.
So wept the poor distressèd Ilium dames,

Hearing those named their city put in
    flames
And country ruined; if we thus lament 35
It is against our present joy's consent.
For if the rule in physic true doth prove,
Remove the cause, th'effects will after
    move,
We have outlived our sorrows, since we
    see
The causes shifting, of our misery.   40
  Nor is't a single cause that's slipped
    away,
That made us warble out a well-a-day.
The brains to plot, the hands to execute
Projected ills, Death jointly did non-suit
At his black bar. And what no bail could
    save   45
He hath committed prisoner to the grave,
From whence there's no reprieve. Death
    keep him close!
We have too many devils still go loose.

[1] An obsolete word meaning "bishop."

Documents of the Andros Administration

AFTER the restoration of the Stuarts in 1660, there were numerous signs that the British government desired to bring its American colonies under a more centralized administration in accordance with its traditional mercantilist policy. A royal commission sifted complaints against Massachusetts' violation of imperial laws and disregard for the provisions of her charter. The Revenue Act of 1673 and the creation of the Lords of Trade in 1675 were other straws in the wind. In 1684 Charles II revoked Massachusetts' charter. Finally, in 1686, James I sent over Sir Edmund Andros, 1637-1714, as governor of the Dominion of New England. Arriving in Massachusetts December, 1686, Andros assumed autocratic powers. The colonial legislatures were abolished; a colonial council appointed by the king was to assist the governor; all New England, including Connecticut and Rhode Island, which alone retained their charters, submitted to this rule, as well as the middle colonies, New Jersey and New York.

The Andros administration lasted only three years. Its collapse was due to three main causes. First, Andros was too conscientious an aristocratic absolutist: he went so far as to try to establish the Anglican Church in Puritan Boston; he did his best to enforce the Navigation Acts against New England trade; he acted on his authorization to investigate existing land grants, impose quit-rents to validate titles, and levy taxes. Secondly, the spirit of independence from Britain was so strong in New England that the opposition against Andros became too ominous for the British government to ignore. Finally, the "Glorious Revolution" of 1688 removed Andros' sponsor, James II, from the throne and precipitated an uprising against Andros in Boston, as a result of which he was imprisoned in Boston harbor and later sent back to England. The destruction of his rule did not bring any immediate change in British mercantilist policy, but did lead to important modifications in the Dominion government.

[The first of the following selections is taken from the report which Andros made in 1690 to the Lords of Trade after his return home. On the basis of this report, he was acquitted of all guilt. The second selection is from an account drawn up in Boston in 1690 by five members of his council who were critical of the manner in which he executed the duties of his office. These were William Stoughton, Thomas Hinckley, Wait Winthrop, Bartholomew Gedney, and Samuel Shrimpton. Their account was printed in 1691. Both selections have been modernized. Complete texts may be found in *Narratives of the Insurrections 1675-1690*, New York, 1915.]

From
ANDROS' REPORT OF HIS
ADMINISTRATION
[1690]

ON THE 18th of April, 1689, several of His Majesty's council in New England having combined and conspired together with those who were magistrates and officers in the late charter government annually chosen by the people, and several other persons, to subvert and overthrow the government, and in stead thereof to introduce their former commonwealth; and having by their false reports and aspersions got to their assistance the greatest part of the people, whereof appeared in arms at Boston under the command of those who were officers in the said former popular government, to the number of about two thousand horse and foot; which strange and sudden appearance being wholly a surprise to Sir Edmund Andros, as knowing no cause or occasion for the same, but understanding that several of the council were at the council chamber where (it being the ordinary council day) they were

to meet, and some particularly by him sent from distant parts also there, he and those with him went thither. And though (as he passed) the streets were full of armed men, yet none offered him or those that were with him the least rudeness or incivility, but on the contrary usual respect; but when he came to the council chamber, he found several of the said former popular magistrates and other chief persons then present, with those of the council, who had no suitable regard to him, nor the peace and quiet of the country, but instead of giving any assistance to support the government, made him a prisoner and also imprisoned some members of the council and other officers, who in pursuance of their respective duties and stations attended on him, and kept them for the space of ten months under severe and close confinement until by His Majesty's command they were sent for England to answer what might be objected them, where, after summons given to the pretended agents of New England and their twice appearance at the council board, nothing being objected by them or others, they

were discharged. In the time of his confinement being denied the liberty of discourse or conversation with any person, his
own servants to attend him, or any communication or correspondence with any by
letters, he hath no particular knowledge of
their further proceedings, but hath heard
and understand:

That soon after the confinement of his
person, the confederates took the fort and
castle from the officers that had the
command of them, whom they also imprisoned. . . .

By the encouragement and persuasion of
the Massachusetts, the several other provinces and colonies in New England as far
as New York have disunited themselves, and
set up their former separate charter, or
popular governments without charter, and
by that means the whole revenue of the
crown continued and settled in the several
parts for the support of the government
is lost and destroyed.

The usual time for election of new magistrates at Boston coming on in the beginning
of May, 1689, great controversy arose
about the settling of civil government, some
being for a new election, and others that
the magistrates chosen and sworn in 1686
before the alteration should reassume; the
latter of which was concluded on by them
and the pretended representatives of the
several towns of the Massachusetts, and
assumed by the said magistrates accordingly, and thereupon the old charter
government, though vacated in Westminster
Hall, was reassumed without any regard to
the crown of England, and they revived
and confirmed their former laws contrary
and repugnant to the laws and statutes
of England, settled their courts of judicature, and appointed new officers, and have
presumed to try and judge all cases civil
and criminal, and to pass sentence of death
on several of Their Majesties' subjects,
some of whom they have caused to be
executed. . . .

Since this insurrection and alteration in
New England, they do tolerate an unlimited
irregular trade, contrary to the several

acts of plantations, trade, and navigation,
now as little regarded as in the time of
their former charter government, they esteeming no laws to be binding on them but
what are made by themselves, nor admit
English laws to be pleaded there, or appeals to His Majesty. And many ships and
vessels have since arrived from Scotland,
Holland, Newfoundland, and other places
prohibited, they having imprisoned his Majesty's collector, surveyor and searcher, and
displaced other customhouse officers. . . .

From
A NARRATIVE OF THE PROCEED-
INGS OF SIR EDMOND ANDROSSE
AND HIS COMPLICES
[1691]

HAVING received from Mr. Addington,[1]
by order of the council and representatives
of the Massachusetts colony, a signification
of their desire, that whereas we were members of the late council in the time of Sir
Edmund Andros' government, we would
give some information of the grievances and
maladministrations under the same, upon
consideration had thereof and in answer
thereunto, we cannot but own and declare
that not only ourselves but many others in
the same station (not now present to join
with us) were of a long time much dissatisfied and discouraged with very many of
the proceedings and administrations in the
said government, and had little reason to
wonder that so great a number of the
people were so too. It might well have been
expected that the Governor, not so successful heretofore, notwithstanding the ex-
traordinariness (to say no more) of many
clauses and powers in his commission, yea,
the rather and the more because thereof,
would have cautioned and moderated the
execution of the same. But to our great
trouble we found it very much otherwise.
Many were the things that were accounted
irregular and grievous therein, far from

---

[1] Isaac Addington, secretary of the colony.

conducing to the public weal of the territory, and not a little to the disservice of the crown, as tending rather to the disturbing and disaffecting of the subjects here, than to the furtherance of that cheerful obedience, loyalty, love, and duty in them which ought by all means to have been nourished and promoted. And of all this unhappiness, we must reckon the first step and in-let to be that the Governor did so quickly neglect the great number of the council, and chiefly adhere unto and govern by the advice only of a few others, the principal of them strangers to the country, without estates or interest therein to oblige them, persons of known and declared prejudices against us, and that had plainly laid their chiefest designs and hopes to make unreasonable profit of this poor people. Innumerable were the evil effects that from hence were continually growing up amongst us. The debates in council were not so free as ought to have been, but too much over-ruled, and a great deal of harshness continually expressed against persons and opinions that did not please. The greatest rigor and severity was too often used towards the soberest sort of people, when anything could be found or pretended against them; their humble submissions were little regarded, and inexorable persecutions ordered against them, whilst in the mean time the notorious viciousness and profaneness of others met not with the like discountenance, but persons of such a character were put into places of business and trust. The long-settled maintenance of the public ministry, even from those that applied themselves to no other way of worship, but continued ordinary hearers, could not be upheld by any act of authority providing for the same, and schools of learning, so well taken care of formerly, were in most places fallen to decay, and many more such like might be reckoned up. . . .

These are the chief matters which upon this occasion (without any undue prejudice against any man, or design to justify the defects of ourselves in the performance of our own shares of duty, but in answer to the desire signified to us as above) we have to set forth, professing truly that by such a state of things as we had the experience and feeling of, the places that we held were rendered exceeding uneasy to us, and that out of a sincere respect to the prosperity of Their Majesties' plantations, we could not but be very desirous that, through the favor of God and our superiors, all due redress might in a good happy season be obtained, and the way of governing English subjects in Their Majesties' dominions without an assembly of the people's representatives banished out of a world forever.

1652 ∾ *John Wise* ∾ 1725

JOHN WISE had a background that predetermined him to become one of the first colonial spokesman of truly democratic ideas. He was the son of an indentured servant, became a Congregational minister at Ipswich in 1680, seven years after his graduation from Harvard, owned a farm of ten acres, and was jailed and fined by Sir Edmund Andros for speaking to his fellow Ipswichians against the governor's tax policies. He continued to be a "come-outer" of liberal views, as is shown by his signing of a petition in 1703 to clear those condemned for witchcraft and by his advocacy in his last years of both inoculation and paper money. His *Vindication of the Government of New-England Churches* is a defense of the Congregational church polity. He wrote it after several years of thought and study. In 1705 a group of Boston and Cambridge ministers had issued a proposal suggesting that the autonomy of the individual minister had been carried too far. Wise assailed them in his pamphlet, *The Churches Quarrel Espoused,* in 1710, which led him to undertake the more sober and systematic *Vindication.*

In expounding the basis of Congregational church polity, Wise sets forth some of the fundamental principles of democracy, drawing heavily on *De Jure Nature et Gentium,* a treatise by Samuel von Pufendorf, 1632-1694, the German philosopher and theologian. This treatise had been translated into English in 1703 and became one of the main sources for conceptions of natural law advanced by 18th Century philosophers.

[The present selections have been modernized and provided with titles by the editors.]

THE NATURAL AND THE CIVIL STATES
[1717]

I SHALL disclose several principles of natural knowledge, plainly discovering the law of nature, or the true sentiments of natural reason, with respect to man's being and government. And in this essay, I shall peculiarly confine the discourse to two heads, viz.,

1. Of the natural (in distinction to the civil) and then,

2. Of the civil being of man. And I shall principally take Baron Pufendorf as my chief guide and spokesman.

1. I shall consider man in a state of natural being, as a free-born subject under the crown of heaven and owing homage to none but God himself. It is certain civil government in general is a very admirable result of providence and an incomparable benefit to mankind, yet must needs be acknowledged to be the effect of human free compacts and not of divine institution; it is the produce of man's reason, of human and rational combinations, and not from any direct orders of infinite wisdom, in any positive law wherein is drawn up this or that scheme of civil government. Government (says the Lord Warrington) [1] is necessary—in that no society of men can

subsist without it; and that particular form of government is necessary which best suits the temper and inclination of a people. Nothing can be God's ordinance but what he has particularly declared to be such; there is no particular form of civil government described in God's word, neither does nature prompt it. . . .

1. The prime immunity in man's state is that he is most properly the subject of the law of nature. He is the favorite animal on earth in that this part of God's image, viz., reason, is congenate with his nature, wherein by a law immutable, instamped upon his frame, God has provided a rule for men in all their actions, obliging each one to the performance of that which is right, not only as to justice, but likewise as to all other moral virtues, the which is nothing but the dictate of right reason founded in the soul of man. . . .

(2) The second great immunity of man is an original liberty instamped upon his rational nature. He that intrudes upon this liberty violates the law of nature. In this discourse I shall waive the consideration of man's moral turpitude, but shall view him physically as a creature which God has made and furnished essentially with many ennobling immunities, which render him

---

[1] Archibald Johnson, Lord Warrington, Scottish judge, may be referred to here.

the most august animal in the world, and still, whatever has happened since his creation, he remains at the upper-end of nature, and as such is a creature of a very noble character. . . .

(3) The third capital immunity belonging to man's nature is an equality amongst men, which is not to be denied by the law of nature till man has resigned himself with all his rights for the sake of a civil state; and then his personal liberty and equality is to be cherished, and preserved to the highest degree, as will consist with all just distinctions amongst men of honor, and shall be agreeable with the public good. . . . And thus we come,

2. To consider man in a civil state of being, wherein we shall observe the great difference between a natural and political state; for in the latter state many great disproportions appear, or at least many obvious distinctions are soon made amongst men; which doctrine is to be laid open under a few heads.

(1) Every man considered in a natural state must be allowed to be free, and at his own dispose; yet to suit man's inclinations to society, and in a peculiar manner to gratify the necessity he is in of public rule and order, he is impelled to enter into a civil community, and divests himself of his natural freedom, and puts himself under government; which, amongst other things, comprehends the power of life and death over him, together with authority to enjoin him some things to which he has an utter aversion and to prohibit him other things for which he may have as strong an inclination; so that he may be often under this authority obliged to sacrifice his private for the public good. So that though man is inclined to society, yet he is driven to a combination by great necessity. For that the true and leading cause of forming governments, and yielding up natural liberty, and throwing man's equality into a common pile to be new cast by the rules of fellowship, was really and truly to guard themselves against the injuries men were liable to interchangeably; for none so good

to man as man, and yet none a greater enemy. So that,

(2) The first human subject and original of civil power is the people. For as they have a power every man over himself in a natural state, so upon a combination they can and do bequeath this power unto others, and settle it according as their united discretion shall determine. For that this is very plain, that when the subject of sovereign power is quite extinct, that power returns to the people again. And when they are free, they may set up what species of government they please; or if they rather incline to it, they may subside into a state of natural being, if it be plainly for the best. . . .

(3) The formal reason of government is the will of a community, yielded up and surrendered to some other subject, either of one particular person, or more, conveyed in the following manner.

Let us conceive in our mind a multitude of men, all naturally free and equal, going about voluntarily to erect themselves into a new commonwealth. Now their condition being such, to bring themselves into a politic body they must needs enter into divers covenants.

1. They must interchangeably each man covenant to join in one lasting society, that they may be capable to concern the measures of their safety, by a public vote.

2. A vote or decree must then nextly pass to set up some particular species of government over them. And if they are joined in their first compact upon absolute terms to stand to the decision of the first vote concerning the species of government, then all are bound by the majority to acquiesce in that particular form thereby settled, though their own private opinion incline them to some other model.

3. After a decree has specified the particular form of government, then there will be need of a new covenant, whereby those on whom sovereignty is conferred engage to take care of the common peace and welfare, and the subjects on the other hand to yield them faithful obedience. In

which covenant is included that submission and union of wills by which a state may be conceived to be but one person. So that the most proper definition of a civil state is this, viz., a civil state is a compound moral person whose will (united by those covenants before passed) is the will of all; to the end it may use and apply the strength and riches of private persons toward maintaining the common peace, security, and well-being of all. Which may be conceived as though the whole state was now become but one man; in which the aforesaid covenants may be supposed under God's providence to be the divine fiat, pronounced by God, let us make man. . . .

THE NATURE OF A DEMOCRACY
[1717]

A DEMOCRACY is then erected when a number of free persons do assemble together in order to enter into a covenant for uniting themselves in a body: and such a preparative assembly hath some appearance already of a democracy; it is a democracy in embryo properly in this respect, that every man hath the privilege freely to deliver his opinion concerning the common affairs. Yet he who dissents from the vote of the majority is not in the least obliged by what they determine till by a second covenant a popular form be actually established; for not before then can we call it a democratical government, viz., till the right of determining all matters relating to the public safety is actually placed in a general assembly of the whole people, or, by their own compact and mutual agreement, determine themselves the proper subject for the exercise of sovereign power. And to complete this state and render it capable to exert its power to answer the end of a civil state, these conditions are necessary:

1. That a certain time and place be assigned for assembling.

2. That when the assembly be orderly met, as to time and place, that then the vote of the majority must pass for the vote of the whole body.

3. That magistrates be appointed to exercise the authority of the whole for the better dispatch of business, of every day's occurrence; who also may with more mature diligence search into more important affairs; and if in case anything happens of greater consequence may report it to the assembly; and be peculiarly serviceable in putting all public decrees into execution. Because a large body of people is almost useless in respect of the last service, and of many others, as to the more particular application and exercise of power, therefore it is most agreeable with the law of nature that they institute their officers to act in their name and stead. . . .

This [a democracy] is a form of government which the light of nature does highly value and often directs to as most agreeable to the just and natural prerogatives of human beings. This was of great account in the early times of the world. And not only so, but upon the experience of several thousand years, after the world had been tumbled and tossed from one species of government to another, at a great expense of blood and treasure, many of the wise nations of the world have sheltered themselves under it again, or at least have blendished and balanced their governments with it.

It is certainly a great truth, *scil.*, that man's original liberty after it is resigned (yet under due restrictions) ought to be cherished in all wise governments; or otherwise a man, in making himself a subject, he alters himself from a freeman into a slave, which to do is repugnant to the law of nature. Also the natural equality of men amongst men must be duly favored, in that government was never established by God or nature to give one man a prerogative to insult over another; therefore in a civil, as well as in a natural state of being, a just equality is to be indulged so far as that every man is bound to honor every man, which is agreeable both with nature and religion, I *Pet.* 2.17. *Honour all men.—*

The end of all good government is to cultivate humanity, and promote the happiness of all, and the good of every man in all his rights, his life, liberty, estate, honor, etc., without injury or abuse done to any. Then certainly it cannot easily be thought that a company of men that shall enter into a voluntary compact to hold all power in their own hands, thereby to use and improve their united force, wisdom, riches, and strength for the common and particular good of every member, as is the nature of a democracy—I say, it cannot be that this sort of constitution will so readily furnish those in government with an appetite or disposition to prey upon each other or embezzle the common stock; as some particular persons may be apt to do when set off and entrusted with the same power. And moreover this appears very natural, that when the aforesaid government or power, settled in all, when they have elected certain capable persons to minister in their affairs, and the said ministers remain accountable to the assembly, these officers must needs be under the influence of many wise cautions from their own thoughts (as well as under confinement by their commission) in their whole administration: and from thence it must needs follow that they will be more apt and inclined to steer right for the main point, viz., the peculiar good and benefit of the whole, and every particular member fairly and sincerely. And why may not these stand for very rational pleas in church order?

For certainly, if Christ has settled any form of power in his church, he has done it for his church's safety, and for the benefit of every member: then he must needs be presumed to have made choice of that government as should least expose his people to hazard, either from the fraud or arbitrary measures of particular men. And it is as plain as daylight there is no species of government like a democracy to attain this end. There is but about two steps from an aristocracy to a monarchy, and from thence but one to a tyranny; an able standing force and an ill-nature, *ipso facto,* turns an absolute monarch into a tyrant; this is obvious among the Roman Caesars and through the world. And all these direful transformations are easier in church affairs (from the different qualities of things) than in civil states. For what is it that cunning and learned men can't make the world swallow as an article of their creed, if they are once invested with an uncontrollable power, and are to be the standing orators to mankind in matters of faith and obedience?

1656 ∽ *Andrew Hamilton* ∽ 1741

ONE EPISODE in the struggle between colonial liberalism and the conservatism of royal governors was the case of John Peter Zenger, a German printer of New York City. In 1733 Zenger's *The New York Weekly Journal* carried a series of articles in defense of Lewis Morris, deposed chief justice of the province. These articles attacked William Cosby, the royal governor. On a charge of libel, Zenger was arrested, held in prison, and brought finally to trial in 1735. In Zenger's defense, the Morris faction retained one of the greatest of American lawyers, Andrew Hamilton, of Philadelphia, then nearing his eightieth year.

Born in Scotland in 1656, Hamilton had been Attorney General of Pennsylvania between 1717 and 1726 and Recorder of Philadelphia in 1727. He served as Vice Admiralty Judge in 1737 and was Speaker of the Assembly from 1729 to 1739. Although suffering from gout at the time of his retention for the Zenger trial, he delivered so powerful a defense that the jury decided the articles in Zenger's paper were not libelous. The trial was an important victory for freedom of the press in America.

[*A brief Narrative of the Case and Tryal of John Peter Zenger,* containing Hamilton's defense, was first printed in 1736. That it was widely read both in the colonies and in England is shown by a number of reprintings between 1737 and 1799. The following selection from Hamilton's defense has been modernized by the editors.]

SPEECH AT THE TRIAL OF JOHN PETER ZENGER
[1736]

... I BEG leave to insist that the right of complaining or remonstrating is natural; and the restraint upon this natural right is the law only, and that those restraints can only extend to what is *false*: for as it is truth alone which can excuse or justify any man for complaining of a bad administration, I as frankly agree that nothing ought to excuse a man who raises a false charge or accusation, even against a private person, and that no manner of allowance ought to be made to him who does so against a public magistrate. *Truth* ought to govern the whole affair of libels, and yet the party accused runs risk enough even then; for if he fails in proving every tittle of what he has wrote, and to the satisfaction of the court and jury too, he may find to his cost that, when the prosecution is set on foot by men in power, it seldom wants friends to favor it. And from thence (it is said) has arisen the great diversity of opinions among judges about what words were or were not scandalous or libellous. . . .

If then upon the whole there is so great an uncertainty among judges (learned and great men) in matters of this kind, if power has so great an influence on judges, how cautious ought we to be in determining by their judgments, especially in the

plantations and in the case of libels! There is heresy in law as well as in religion, and both have changed very much; and we well know that it is not two centuries ago that a man would have been burnt as a heretic for owning such opinions in matters of religion as are publicly wrote and printed at this day. They were fallible men, it seems, and we take the liberty not only to differ from them in religious opinions, but to condemn them and their opinions too; and I must presume that, in taking these freedoms in thinking and speaking about matters of faith or religion, we are in the right. For though it is said there are very great liberties of this kind taken in New York, yet I have heard of no information preferred by Mr. Attorney General for any offences of this sort. From which I think it is pretty clear that in New York a man may make very free with his God, but he must take special care what he says of his Governor. It is agreed upon by all men that this is a reign of liberty; and while men keep within the bounds of truth, I hope they may with safety speak and write their sentiments of the conduct of men in power—I mean of that part of their conduct only which affects the liberty or property of the people under their administration; were this to be denied, then the next step may make them slaves. For what notions can be entertained of slavery beyond that of suffering the greatest injuries and oppressions without the liberty of complaining; or, if they do, to be destroyed, body and estate, for so doing?

It is said and insisted on by Mr. Attorney General, *that government is a sacred thing; that it is to be supported and reverenced; it is government that protects our persons and estates; that prevents treasons, murders, robberies, riots, and all the train of evils that overturns kingdoms and states, and ruins particular persons; and if those in the administration, especially the supreme magistrate, must have all their conduct censured by private men, government cannot subsist.* This is called *a licentiousness not to be tolerated.* It is said, *that it brings the rulers of the people into contempt, and their authority not to be regarded, and so in the end the laws cannot be put in execution.* These I say, and such as these, are the general topics insisted upon by men in power and their advocates. But I wish it might be considered at the same time how often it has happened that the abuse of power has been the primary cause of these evils, and that it was the injustice and oppression of these great men which has commonly brought them into contempt with the people. The craft and art of such men is great, and who that is the least acquainted with history or law can be ignorant of the specious pretences which have often been made use of by men in power to introduce arbitrary rule and destroy the liberties of a free people? . . .

The loss of liberty to a generous mind is worse than death; and yet we know there have been those in all ages who for the sake of preferment, or some imaginary honor, have freely lent a helping hand to oppress, nay to destroy, their country. This brings to my mind that saying of the immortal Brutus, when he looked upon the creatures of Caesar, who were very great men, but by no means good men. "You Romans," said Brutus, "if yet I may call you so, consider what you are doing; remember that you are assisting Caesar to forge those very chains which one day he will make yourselves wear." This is

what every man (that values freedom) ought to consider: he should act by judgment and not by affection or self-interest; for, where those prevail, no ties of either country or kindred are regarded; as upon the other hand, the man who loves his country prefers its liberty to all other considerations, well knowing that without liberty, life is a misery.

A famous instance of this you will find in the history of another brave Roman of the same name, I mean Lucius Junius Brutus, whose story is well known and therefore I shall mention no more of it than only to show the value he put upon the freedom of his country. After this great man, with his fellow citizens whom he had engaged in the cause, had banished Tarquin the Proud, the last king of Rome, from a throne which he ascended by inhuman murders and possessed by the most dreadful tyranny and proscriptions, and had by this means amassed incredible riches, even sufficient to bribe to his interest many of the young nobility of Rome to assist him in recovering the crown; but the plot being discovered, the principal conspirators were apprehended, among whom were two of the sons of Junius Brutus. It was absolutely necessary that some should be made examples of, to deter others from attempting the restoring of Tarquin and destroying the liberty of Rome. And to effect this it was that Lucius Junius Brutus, one of the consuls of Rome, in the presence of the Roman people, sat judge and condemned his own sons as traitors to their country. And to give the last proof of his exalted virtue, and his love of liberty, he, with a firmness of mind (only becoming so great a man) caused their heads to be struck off in his own presence; and when he observed that his rigid virtue caused a sort of horror among the people, it is observed he only said, "My fellow citizens, do not think that this proceeds from any want of natural affection: no, the death of the sons of Brutus can affect Brutus only; but the loss of liberty will affect my country."

Thus highly was liberty esteemed in those days that a father could sacrifice his sons to save his country. But why do I go to heathen Rome to bring instances of the love of liberty? The best blood in Britain has been shed in the cause of liberty, and the freedom we enjoy at this day may be said to be (in a great measure) owing to the glorious stand the famous Hampden, and other of our countrymen, made against the arbitrary demands and illegal impositions of the times in which they lived; who rather than give up the rights of Englishmen, and submit to pay an illegal tax, of no more, I think, than 3 shillings, resolved to undergo, and for the liberty of their country did undergo, the greatest extremities, in that arbitrary and terrible Court of Star Chamber, to whose arbitrary proceedings (it being composed of the principal men of the realm and calculated to support arbitrary government) no bounds or limits could be set, nor could any other hand remove the evil but a parliament.

Power may justly be compared to a great river; while kept within its due bounds, it is both beautiful and useful; but when it overflows its banks, it is then too impetuous to be stemmed, it bears down all before it, and brings destruction and desolation wherever it comes. If, then, this is the nature of power, let us at least do our duty, and like wise men (who value freedom) use our utmost care to support liberty, the only bulwark against lawless power, which in all ages has sacrificed to its wild lust and boundless ambition the blood of the best men that ever lived.

I hope to be pardoned, Sir, for my zeal upon this occasion; it is an old and wise caution: that when our neighbor's house is on fire, we ought to take care of our own. For though, blessed be God, I live in a government where liberty is well understood and freely enjoyed, yet experience has shown us all (I'm sure it has to me) that a bad precedent in one government is soon set up for an authority in another; and therefore I cannot but think it mine,

and every honest man's duty, that (while we pay all due obedience to men in authority) we ought at the same time to be upon our guard against power, wherever we apprehend that it may affect ourselves or our fellow-subjects.

I am truly very unequal to such an undertaking on many accounts. And you see I labor under the weight of many years, and am borne down with great infirmities of body; yet old and weak as I am, I should think it my duty, if required, to go to the utmost part of the land where my service could be of any use in assisting to quench the flame of prosecutions upon informations, set on foot by the government, to deprive a people of the right of remonstrating (and complaining too) of the arbitrary attempts of men in power. Men who injure and oppress the people under their administration provoke them to cry out and complain, and then make that very complaint the foundation for new oppressions and prosecutions. I wish I could say there were no instances of this kind. But to conclude: the question before the court and you gentlemen of the jury is not of small nor private concern; it is not the cause of the poor printer, nor of New York alone, which you are now trying: No! It may in its consequence affect every freeman that lives under a British government on the main of America. It is the best cause. It is the cause of liberty; and I make no doubt but your upright conduct, this day, will not only entitle you to the love and esteem of your fellow-citizens; but every man who prefers freedom to a life of slavery will bless and honor you, as men who have baffled the attempt of tyranny; and by an impartial and uncorrupt verdict have laid a noble foundation for securing to ourselves, our posterity, and our neighbors, that to which nature and the laws of our country have given us a right—the liberty both of exposing and opposing arbitrary power (in these parts of the world, at least) by speaking and writing truth.

1720 ∾ *Jonathan Mayhew* ∾ 1766

AMONG the most liberal of 18th Century American clergymen was Jonathan Mayhew, born on Martha's Vineyard, where his father, Experience Mayhew, had distinguished himself as an Indian missionary. Jonathan was graduated from Harvard in 1744 and was ordained minister at the West Church in Boston in 1747. Prominent conservative ministers, in protest against his ordination, did not attend. A pioneer Unitarian, he attacked the five cardinal points of Calvinism, opposed equally the Great Awakening and the establishment of an Anglican episcopate in the colonies, defended the right of revolution, and fomented feeling against the Stamp Act. Between 1749 and 1766, the year of his death, he published a long series of sermons. One of the most influential on later revolutionary thought and sentiment was the *Discourse Concerning Unlimited Submission and Non-Resistance to the Higher Powers,* delivered January 30, 1750, the anniversary day of the execution of Charles I, and printed at Boston in that same year.

[The following selection from this sermon has been modernized by the editors.]

From
DISCOURSE CONCERNING UNLIMITED SUBMISSION
[1750]

IF WE calmly consider the nature of the thing itself, nothing can well be imagined more directly contrary to common sense than to suppose that millions of people should be subjected to the arbitrary, precarious pleasure of one single man—who has naturally no superiority over them in point of authority—so that their estates, and everything that is valuable in life, and even their lives also, shall be absolutely at his disposal, if he happens to be wanton and capricious enough to demand them. What unprejudiced man can think that God made *all* to be thus subservient to the lawless pleasure and frenzy of *one*, so that it shall always be a sin to resist him? Nothing but the most plain and express revelation from heaven could make a sober, impartial man believe such a monstrous, unaccountable doctrine; and, indeed, the thing itself appears so shocking, so out of all proportion, that it may be questioned whether all the miracles that ever were wrought could make it credible that this doctrine really came from God. At present there is not the least syllable in Scripture which gives any countenance to it. The hereditary, indefeasible, divine right of kings, and the doctrine of non-resistance, which is built upon the supposition of such a right, are altogether as fabulous and chimerical as transubstantiation, or any of the most absurd reveries of ancient or modern visionaries. These notions are fetched neither from divine revelation nor human reason; and, if they are derived from neither of those sources, it is not much matter from whence they come or whither they go. Only it is a pity that such doctrines should be propagated in society, to raise factions and rebellions, as we see they have, in fact, been, both in the last and in the present reign.

But, then, if unlimited submission and passive obedience to the higher powers, in all possible cases, be not a duty, it will be asked, "How far are we obliged to submit?

If we may innocently disobey and resist in some cases, why not in all? Where shall we stop? What is the measure of our duty? This doctrine tends to the total dissolution of civil government, and to introduce such scenes of wild anarchy and confusion as are more fatal to society than the worst of tyranny."

After this manner some men object; and, indeed, this is the most plausible thing that can be said in favor of such an absolute submission as they plead for. But the worst, or, rather, the best of it is, that there is very little strength or solidity in it; for similar difficulties may be raised with respect to almost every duty of natural and revealed religion. To instance only in two, both of which are near akin, and indeed exactly parallel to the case before us: it is unquestionably the duty of children to submit to their parents, and of servants to their masters; but no one asserts that it is their duty to obey and submit to them in all supposable cases, or universally a sin to resist them. Now, does this tend to subvert the just authority of parents and masters, or to introduce confusion and anarchy into private families? No. How, then, does the same principle tend to unhinge the government of that larger family and body politic? We know, in general, that children and servants are obliged to obey their parents and masters respectively; we know also, with equal certainty, that they are not obliged to submit to them in all things without exception, but may, in some cases, reasonably, and therefore innocently, resist them. These principles are acknowledged upon all hands, whatever difficulty there may be in fixing the exact limits of submission. Now, there is at least as much difficulty in stating the measure of duty in these two cases as in the case of rulers and subjects; so that this is really no objection—at least, no reasonable one—against resistance to the higher powers. Or, if it is one, it will hold equally against resistance in the other cases mentioned. It is indeed true, that turbulent, vicious-minded men may take occasion,

from this principle that their rulers may in some cases be lawfully resisted, to raise factions and disturbances in the state, and to make resistance where resistance is needless, and therefore sinful. But is it not equally true that children and servants, of turbulent, vicious minds, may take occasion, from this principle that parents and masters may in some cases be lawfully resisted, to resist when resistance is unnecessary, and therefore criminal? Is the principle, in either case, false in itself merely because it may be abused, and applied to legitimate disobedience and resistance in those instances to which it ought not to be applied? According to this way of arguing, there will be no true principles in the world; for there are none but what may be wrested and perverted to serve bad purposes, either through the weakness or wickedness of men.

A people, really oppressed in a great degree by their sovereign, cannot well be insensible when they are so oppressed; and such a people—if I may allude to an ancient fable—have, like the hesperian fruit, a dragon for their protector and guardian.[1] Nor would they have any reason to mourn if some Hercules should appear to dispatch him. For a nation thus abused to arise unanimously and resist their prince, even to the dethroning him, is not criminal, but a reasonable way of vindicating their liberties and just rights: it is making use of the means, and the only means, which God has put into their power for mutual and self defence. And it would be highly criminal in them not to make use of this means. It would be stupid tameness and unaccountable folly for whole nations to suffer *one* unreasonable, ambitious, and cruel man to wanton and riot in their misery. And in such a case, it would,

---

[1] In Greek mythology, the golden apples which Juno had received as a wedding present from the goddess of Earth were given for safekeeping to the daughters of Hesperis and guarded by a dragon. One of the labors of Hercules was to get these apples by slaying the dragon.

of the two, be more rational to suppose that they that did not resist, than that they who did, would receive to themselves damnation.

And this naturally brings us to make some reflections upon the resistance which was made, about a century since, to that unhappy King Charles I., and upon the anniversary of his death. This is a point which I should not have concerned myself about, were it not that some men continue to speak of it, even to this day, with a great deal of warmth and zeal, and in such a manner as to undermine all the principles of liberty, whether civil or religious, and to introduce the most abject slavery both in church and state—so that it is become a matter of universal concern. . . .

For what reason, then, was the resistance to King Charles made? The general answer to this inquiry is, that it was on account of the tyranny and oppression of his reign. Not a great while after his accession to the throne, he married a French Catholic, and with her seemed to have wedded the politics, if not the religion of France, also. For afterwards, during a reign, or, rather, a tyranny of many years, he governed in a perfectly wild and arbitrary manner, paying no regard to the constitution and the laws of the kingdom, by which the power of the crown was limited, or to the solemn oath which he had taken at his coronation. It would be endless, as well as needless, to give a particular account of all the illegal and despotic measures which he took in his administration—partly from his own natural lust of power, and partly from the influence of wicked counsellors and ministers. He committed many illustrious members of both Houses of Parliament to the Tower for opposing his arbitrary schemes. He levied many taxes upon the people without consent of Parliament, and then imprisoned great numbers of the principal merchants and gentry for not paying them. He erected, or at least revived, several arbitrary courts, in which the most unheard-of

barbarities were committed with his knowledge and approbation. He supported that more than fiend, Archbishop Laud, and the clergy of his stamp, in all their church-tyranny and hellish cruelties. He authorized a book in favor of sports upon the Lord's day; and several clergymen were persecuted by him and the mentioned *pious* bishop for not reading it to the people after divine service. When the Parliament complained to him of the arbitrary proceedings of his corrupt ministers, he told that august body, in a rough, domineering, unprincely manner, that he wondered why any one should be so foolish and insolent as to think that he would part with the meanest of his servants upon their account. He refused to call any Parliament at all for the space of twelve years together, during all which time he governed in an absolute, lawless, and despotic manner. He took all opportunities to encourage the Papists, and to promote them to the highest offices of honor and trust. He (probably) abetted the horrid massacre in Ireland, in which two hundred thousand Protestants were butchered by the Roman Catholics. He sent a large sum of money, which he had raised by his arbitrary taxes, into Germany, to raise foreign troops, in order to force more arbitrary taxes upon his subjects. He not only, by a long series of actions, but also in plain terms, asserted an absolute, uncontrollable power —saying, even, in one of his speeches to Parliament, that, as it was blasphemy to dispute what God might do, so it was sedition in subjects to dispute what the king might do! Towards the end of his tyranny he came to the House of Commons, with an armed force, and demanded five of its principal members to be delivered up to him; and this was a prelude to that unnatural war which he soon after levied against his own dutiful subjects, whom he was bound, by all the laws of honor, humanity, piety, and, I might add, of interest also, to defend and cherish with a paternal affection. I have only time to hint at these facts in a general way, all which, and many more of the same tenor, may be proved by good authorities. So that the figurative language which St. John uses concerning the just and beneficent deeds of our blessed Saviour may be applied to the unrighteous and execrable deeds of this prince, viz.: "And there are also many other things which 'King Charles' did, the which, if they should be written every one, I suppose that even the world itself would not contain the books that should be written." Now, it was on account of King Charles' thus assuming a power above the laws, in direct contradiction to his coronation oath, and governing, the greatest part of his time, in the most arbitrary, oppressive manner—it was upon this account that resistance was made to him, which at length issued in the loss of his crown, and of that head which was unworthy to wear it.

But by whom was this resistance made? Not by a private junto, not by a small seditious party, not by a few desperadoes, who to mend their fortunes would embroil the state; but by the Lords and Commons of England. It was they that almost unanimously opposed the king's measures for overturning the constitution, and changing that free and happy government into a wretched, absolute monarchy. It was they that, when the king was about levying forces against his subjects in order to make himself absolute, commissioned officers, and raised an army to defend themselves and the public; and it was they that maintained the war against him all along, till he was made a prisoner. This is indisputable; though it was not, properly speaking, the Parliament, but the army, which put him to death afterwards. And it ought to be freely acknowledged that most of their proceeding, in order to get this matter effected, and particularly the court by which the king was at last tried and condemned, was little better than a mere mockery of justice.

The next question which naturally arises is, whether this resistance which was made to the king by the Parliament was properly rebellion or not? The answer to which is plain—that it was not, but a most righteous and glorious stand, made in defence of the natural and legal rights of the people, against the unnatural and illegal encroachments of arbitrary power. Nor was this a rash and too sudden opposition. The nation had been patient under the oppressions of the crown, even to long-suffering, for a course of many years, and there was no rational hope of redress in any other way. Resistance was absolutely necessary, in order to preserve the nation from slavery, misery, and ruin. And who so proper to make this resistance as the Lords and Commons—the whole representative body of the people—guardians of the public welfare; and each of which was, in point of legislation, vested with an equal, coördinate power with that of the crown? Here were two branches of the legislature against one; two, which had law and equity and the constitution on their side, against one which was impiously attempting to overturn law and equity and the constitution, and to exercise a wanton, licentious sovereignty over the properties, consciences, and lives of all the people—such a sovereignty as some inconsiderately ascribe to the Supreme Governor of the world. I say, inconsiderately, because God himself does not govern in an absolutely arbitrary and despotic manner. The power of this almighty King—I speak it not without caution and reverence—the power of this almighty King is limited by law; not indeed by acts of Parliament, but by the eternal laws of truth, wisdom, and equity, and the everlasting tables of right reason —tables that cannot be repealed, or thrown down and broken like those of Moses. But King Charles set himself up above all these, as much as he did above the written laws of the realm, and made mere humor and caprice, which are no rule at all, the only rule and measure of his administration. And now is it not perfectly ridiculous to call resistance to such a tyrant by the name of *rebellion?*—the grand rebellion? . . .

1735 ∾ *John Adams* ∾ 1826

JOHN ADAMS, born at Braintree, Massachusetts, was graduated from Harvard in 1755, taught school for a while, then became a lawyer, practicing first in Braintree, later in Boston. He was the author of Braintree's protest against the Stamp Act; this document served as a model for other Massachusetts towns to follow. He served in the State Assembly and the Executive Council, belonged to the first and second Continental Congresses, and was one of the signers of the Declaration of Independence, having been on the committee charged with its preparation. He rendered diplomatic service in Paris, in the Netherlands, in the peace negotiations with England, and as minister to England from 1785 to 1788. Becoming the first Vice-president of the United States in 1789, he succeeded Washington as President in 1797. Defeated for re-election in the Federalist débacle of 1800, he lived in retirement at Braintree, taking some part in the politics of Massachusetts, reading widely, and writing to a host of correspondents. He died at Quincy, Massachusetts.

[One of the most profound and lucid of early American political philosophers, he published extensively, some of his most important books being the *Defence of the Constitutions of Government of the United States* in three volumes, 1787-88, and *Discourses of Davila,* 1805. In August, 1765, he published in the *Boston Gazette* four essays protesting against the Stamp Act; these were also published in the *London Chronicle.* They appeared as a single article entitled "Dissertation on the Canon and Feudal Law" in the collection, *The True Sentiments of America,* London, 1768. The text of the present selection is from his *Works,* Boston, 1851.]

From

DISSERTATION ON THE CANON AND THE FEUDAL LAW

[1768 (written 1765)]

"IGNORANCE and inconsideration are the two great causes of the ruin of mankind." This is an observation of Dr. Tillotson, with relation to the interest of his fellow men in a future and immortal state. But it is of equal truth and importance if applied to the happiness of men in society, on this side the grave. In the earliest ages of the world, absolute monarchy seems to have been the universal form of government. Kings, and a few of their great counsellors and captains, exercised a cruel tyranny over the people, who held a rank in the scale of intelligence, in those days, but little higher than the camels and elephants that carried them and their engines to war.

By what causes it was brought to pass that the people in the middle ages became more intelligent in general would not, perhaps, be possible in these days to discover. But the fact is certain; and wherever a general knowledge and sensibility have prevailed among the people, arbitrary government and every kind of oppression have lessened and disappeared in proportion. Man has certainly an exalted soul; and the same principle in human nature—that aspiring, noble principle founded in benevolence, and cherished by knowledge; I mean the love of power, which has been so often the cause of slavery—has, whenever freedom has existed, been the cause of freedom. If it is this principle that has always prompted the princes and nobles of the earth, by every species of fraud and violence to shake off all the limitations of their power, it is the same that has always stimulated the common people to aspire at independency, and to endeavor at confining the power of the great within the limits of equity and reason.

The poor people, it is true, have been much less successful than the great. They have seldom found either leisure or opportunity to form a union and exert their strength; ignorant as they were of arts and letters, they have seldom been able to frame and support a regular opposition. This, however, has been known by the great to be the tempter of mankind; and they have accordingly labored, in all ages, to wrest from the populace, as they are contemptuously called, the knowledge of their rights and wrongs, and the power to assert the former or redress the latter. I say RIGHTS, for such they have, undoubtedly, antecedent to all earthly government—*Rights,* that cannot be repealed or restrained by human laws—*Rights,* derived from the great Legislator of the universe.

Since the promulgation of Christianity, the two greatest systems of tyranny that have sprung from this original are the canon and the feudal law. The desire of dominion, that great principle by which we have attempted to account for so much good and so much evil, is, when properly restrained, a very useful and noble movement in the human mind. But when such restraints are taken off, it becomes an encroaching, grasping, restless, and ungovernable power. Numberless have been the systems of iniquity contrived by the

great for the gratification of this passion in themselves; but in none of them were they ever more successful than in the invention and establishment of the canon and the feudal law.

By the former of these, the most refined, sublime, extensive, and astonishing constitution of policy that ever was conceived by the mind of man was framed by the Romanish clergy for the aggrandisement of their own order. All the epithets I have here given to the Romish policy are just, and will be allowed to be so when it is considered, that they even persuaded mankind to believe, faithfully and undoubtingly, that God Almighty had entrusted them with the keys of heaven, whose gates they might open and close at pleasure; with a power of dispensation over all the rules and obligations of morality; with authority to license all sorts of sins and crimes; with a power of procuring or withholding the rain of heaven and the beams of the sun; with the management of earthquakes, pestilence, and famine; nay, with the mysterious, awful, incomprehensible power of creating out of bread and wine the flesh and blood of God himself. All these opinions they were enabled to spread and rivet among the people by reducing their minds to a state of sordid ignorance and staring timidity, and by infusing into them a religious horror of letters and knowledge. Thus was human nature chained fast for ages in a cruel, shameful, and deplorable servitude to him, and his subordinate tyrants, who, it was foretold, would exalt himself above all that was called God, and that was worshipped.

In the latter we find another system, similar in many respects to the former; which, although it was originally formed, perhaps, for the necessary defence of a barbarous people against the inroads and invasions of her neighboring nations, yet for the same purposes of tyranny, cruelty, and lust, which had dictated the canon law, it was soon adopted by almost all the princes of Europe, and wrought into the constitutions of their government. It was originally a code of laws for a vast army in a perpetual encampment. The general was invested with the sovereign propriety of all the lands within the territory. Of him, as his servants and vassals, the first rank of his great officers held the lands; and in the same manner the other subordinate officers held of them; and all ranks and degrees held their lands by a variety of duties and services, all tending to bind the chains the faster on every order of mankind. In this manner the common people were held together in herds and clans in a state of servile dependence on their lords, bound, even by the tenure of their lands, to follow them, whenever they commanded, to their wars, and in a state of total ignorance of everything divine and human, excepting the use of arms and the culture of their lands.

But another event still more calamitous to human liberty was a wicked confederacy between the two systems of tyranny above described. It seems to have been even stipulated between them, that the temporal grandees should contribute everything in their power to maintain the ascendency of the priesthood, and that the spiritual grandees in their turn, should employ their ascendency over the consciences of the people, in impressing on their minds a blind, implicit obedience to civil magistracy.

Thus, as long as this confederacy lasted, and the people were held in ignorance, liberty, and with her, knowledge and virtue too, seem to have deserted the earth, and one age of darkness succeeded another, till God in his benign providence raised up the champions who began and conducted the Reformation. From the time of the Reformation to the first settlement of America, knowledge gradually spread in Europe, but especially in England; and in proportion as that increased and spread among the people, ecclesiastical and civil tyranny, which I use as synonymous expressions for the canon and feudal laws, seem to have lost their strength and weight. The people grew more and more sensible of

the wrong that was done them by these systems, more and more impatient under it, and determined at all hazards to rid themselves of it; till at last, under the execrable race of the Stuarts, the struggle between the people and the confederacy aforesaid of temporal and spiritual tyranny, became formidable, violent, and bloody.

It was this great struggle that peopled America. It was not religion alone, as is commonly supposed; but it was a love of universal liberty, and a hatred, a dread, a horror, of the infernal confederacy before described, that projected, conducted, and accomplished the settlement of America....

We have been afraid to think. We have felt a reluctance to examining into the grounds of our privileges, and the extent to which we have an indisputable right to demand them, against all the power and authority on earth. And many who have not scrupled to examine for themselves have yet for certain prudent reasons been cautious and diffident of declaring the result of their inquiries.

The cause of this timidity is perhaps hereditary, and to be traced back in history as far as the cruel treatment the first settlers of this country received, before their embarkation for America, from the government at home. Everybody knows how dangerous it was to speak or write in favor of anything, in those days, but the triumphant system of religion and politics. And our fathers were particularly the objects of the persecutions and proscriptions of the times. It is not unlikely, therefore, that although they were inflexibly steady in refusing their positive assent to anything against their principles, they might have contracted habits of reserve, and a cautious diffidence of asserting their opinions publicly. These habits they probably brought with them to America, and have transmitted down to us. Or we may possibly account for this appearance by the great affection and veneration Americans have always entertained for the country from whence they sprang; or by the quiet temper for which they have been remarkable, no country having been less disposed to discontent than this; or by a sense they have that it is their duty to acquiesce under the administration of government, even when in many smaller matters grievous to them, and until the essentials of the great compact are destroyed or invaded. These peculiar causes might operate upon them; but without these, we all know that human nature itself, from indolence, modesty, humanity, or fear, has always too much reluctance to a manly assertion of its rights. Hence, perhaps, it has happened that nine tenths of the species are groaning and gasping in misery and servitude.

But whatever the cause has been, the fact is certain, we have been excessively cautious of giving offence by complaining of grievances. And it is as certain, that American governors, and their friends, and all the crown officers, have availed themselves of this disposition in the people. They have prevailed on us to consent to many things which were grossly injurious to us, and to surrender many others, with voluntary tameness, to which we had the clearest right. Have we not been treated, formerly, with abominable insolence, by officers of the navy? I mean no insinuation against any gentleman now on this station, having heard no complaint of any one of them to his dishonor. Have not some generals from England treated us like servants, nay, more like slaves than like Britons? Have we not been under the most ignominious contribution, the most abject submission, the most supercilious insults, of some custom-house officers? Have we not been trifled with, brow-beaten, and trampled on, by former governors, in a manner which no king of England since James the Second has dared to indulge towards his subjects? . . .

Let us take it for granted that the same great spirit which once gave Caesar so warm a reception, which denounced hostilities against John till Magna Charta was signed, which severed the head of Charles the First from his body, and drove James the Second from his kingdom, the same

great spirit (may heaven preserve it till the earth shall be no more) which first seated the great grandfather of his present most gracious majesty on the throne of Britain,—is still alive and active and warm in England; and that the same spirit in America, instead of provoking the inhabitants of that country, will endear us to them for ever, and secure their good-will.

This spirit, however, without knowledge, would be little better than a brutal rage. Let us tenderly and kindly cherish, therefore, the means of knowledge. Let us dare to read, think, speak, and write. Let every order and degree among the people rouse their attention and animate their resolution. Let them all become attentive to the grounds and principles of government, ecclesiastical and civil. Let us study the law of nature; search into the spirit of the British constitution; read the histories of ancient ages; contemplate the great examples of Greece and Rome; set before us the conduct of our British ancestors, who have defended for us the inherent rights of mankind against foreign and domestic tyrants and usurpers, against arbitrary kings and cruel priests, in short, against the gates of earth and hell. Let us read and recollect and impress upon our souls the views and ends of our more immediate forefathers, in exchanging their native country for a dreary, inhospitable wilderness. Let us examine into the nature of that power, and the cruelty of that oppression, which drove them from their homes. Recollect their amazing fortitude, their bitter sufferings—the hunger, the nakedness, the cold, which they patiently endured —the severe labors of clearing their grounds, building their houses, raising their provisions, amidst dangers from wild beasts and savage men, before they had time or money or materials for commerce. Recollect the civil and religious principles and hopes and expectations which constantly supported and carried them through all hardships with patience and resignation. Let us recollect it was liberty, the hope of liberty for themselves and us and ours, which conquered all discouragements, dangers, and trials. In such researches as these, let us all in our several departments cheerfully engage — but especially the proper patrons and supporters of law, learning, and religion!

Let the pulpit resound with the doctrines and sentiments of religious liberty. Let us hear the danger of thraldom to our consciences from ignorance, extreme poverty, and dependence, in short, from civil and political slavery. Let us see delineated before us the true map of man. Let us hear the dignity of his nature, and the noble rank he holds among the works of God— that consenting to slavery is a sacrilegious breach of trust, as offensive in the sight of God as it is derogatory from our own honor or interest or happiness—and that God Almighty has promulgated from heaven, liberty, peace, and good-will to man!

Let the bar proclaim "the laws, the rights, the generous plan of power" delivered down from remote antiquity—inform the world of the mighty struggles and numberless sacrifices made by our ancestors in defence of freedom. Let it be known that British liberties are not the grants of princes or parliaments, but original rights, conditions of original contracts, coequal with prerogative and coeval with government; that many of our rights are inherent and essential, agreed on as maxims, and established as preliminaries, even before a parliament existed. Let them search for the foundations of British laws and government in the frame of human nature, in the constitution of the intellectual and moral world. There let us see that truth, liberty, justice, and benevolence are its everlasting basis; and if these could be removed, the superstructure is overthrown of course.

Let the colleges join their harmony in the same delightful concert. Let every declamation turn upon the beauty of liberty and virtue, and the deformity, turpitude, and malignity of slavery and vice. Let the public disputations become researches into the grounds and nature and ends of government, and the means of preserving the good and demolishing the evil. Let the dialogues, and all the exercises, become the instruments of impressing on the tender mind, and of spreading and distributing far and wide, the ideas of right and the sensations of freedom.

In a word, let every sluice of knowledge be opened and set a-flowing. The encroachments upon liberty in the reigns of the first James and the first Charles, by turning the general attention of learned men to government, are said to have produced the greatest number of consummate statesmen which has ever been seen in any age or nation. The Brookes, Hampdens, Vanes, Seldens, Miltons, Nedhams, Harringtons, Nevilles, Sidneys, Lockes, are all said to have owed their eminence in political knowledge to the tyrannies of those reigns.[1] The prospect now before us in America ought in the same manner to engage the attention of every man of learning to matters of power and of right, that we may be neither led nor driven blindfolded to irretrievable destruction. Nothing less than this seems to have been meditated for us, by somebody or other in Great Britain. There seems to be a direct and formal design on foot, to enslave all America. This, however, must be done by degrees. The first step that is intended seems to be an entire subversion of the whole system of our fathers by the introduction of the canon and feudal law into America. The canon and feudal systems, though greatly mutilated in England, are not yet destroyed. Like the temples and palaces in which the great contrivers of them once worshipped and inhabited, they exist in

---

[1] Robert Greville, Lord Brooke (1608-1643); John Hampden (1594-1643); Sir Henry Vane the elder (1589-1655) and Sir Henry Vane the younger (1613-1662); John Selden (1584-1654); John Milton (1608-1674); Marchamont Nedham (1620-1678); James Harrington (1611-1677); Sir Henry Neville (1564?-1615) and his grandson, Henry Neville (1620-1694); Algernon Sidney (1622-1683); John Locke (1632-1704).

ruins; and much of the domineering spirit of them still remains. The designs and labors of a certain society, to introduce the former of them into America, have been well exposed to the public by a writer of great abilities;[2] and the further attempts to the same purpose, that may be made by that society, or by the ministry or parliament, I leave to the conjectures of the thoughtful. But it seems very manifest from the Stamp Act itself that a design is formed to strip us in a great measure of the means of knowledge, by loading the press, the colleges, and even an almanac and a newspaper, with restraints and duties; and to introduce the inequalities and dependencies of the feudal system, by taking from the poorer sort of people all their little subsistence, and conferring it on a set of stamp officers, distributors, and their deputies. But I must proceed no further at present. The sequel, whenever I shall find health and leisure to pursue it, will be a "disquisition of the policy of the stamp act." In the meantime, however, let me add—these are not the vapors of a melancholy mind, nor the effusions of envy, disappointed ambition, nor of a spirit of opposition to government, but the emanations of a heart that burns for its country's welfare. No one of any feeling, born and educated in this once happy country, can consider the numerous distresses, the gross indignities, the barbarous ignorance, the haughty usurpations, that we have reason to fear are meditating for ourselves, our children, our neighbors, in short, for all our countrymen and all their posterity, without the utmost agonies of heart and many tears.

[2] The reference is to Jonathan Mayhew's opposition to the attempt to establish an Anglican Episcopate in the colonies.

1738 ∾ *Jonathan Boucher* ∾ 1804

THE LOYALISTS were those Americans who, in the face of revolutionary sentiment and feeling, insisted that the colonies' obligations to England were more important than their rights. The label "Tories" was also applied to them in derogation. Kenneth Roberts' *Oliver Wiswell*, 1940, is a brilliant historical novel sympathetically treating the Loyalists.

Among the clergymen representing the Loyalist point of view, none was more learned and eloquent than Jonathan Boucher. He was thus the antithesis of Jonathan Mayhew. Boucher was born in England and came to America in 1759. Ordained priest by the Bishop of London in 1762, he served as an Anglican rector in Virginia and Maryland. His sermons were so anti-revolutionary in spirit that a body of armed men forbade him on one occasion to enter his pulpit; thereafter he preached with a pair of loaded pistols on the cushion before him. He was burned in effigy and had to leave for England in September, 1775. He remained there the rest of his life, serving as vicar of Epsom.

Thirteen of the sermons he preached in America between 1763 and 1775 were published in a volume entitled *A View of the Causes and Consequences of the American Revolution*, London, 1797. No more thorough an attack on the natural rights philosophy of the American Revolution appeared in English during the 18th Century. The sermons read as if they were the work of some 17th Century aristocrat brought up on the doctrines of Sir Robert Filmer's *Patriarcha* and the great Anglo-Catholic Caroline divines. Boucher had his sermons published at this late date because he hoped that, with the Revolution an accomplished fact, his philosophy would be pondered with more objectivity and might provide the American Federalists with arguments to combat the rising tide of Jeffersonian Republicanism.

It is significant that he dedicated the work to George Washington, who had at one time been his neighbor and friend and with whom he had exchanged numerous letters. Thackeray read these letters with some profit when he wrote his novel, *The Virginians*. Boucher also left a highly interesting *Autobiography* and compiled a *Glossary of Archaic and Provincial Words*.

[The following selections have been modernized and provided with titles by the editors.]

RELIGIOUS AND POLITICAL ENTHUSIASM

[1797 (written 1775?)]

... ENTHUSIASTS conceive it to be the commencement of a millennium: whilst others, of a less sanguine temperament, though they cannot so far give up their common sense as to imagine that these blind guides can possibly lead their still blinder followers to anything that is really good, yet plead for their being let alone and suffered to pursue their own projects in their own way, from a persuasion that they are too insignificant to do any harm; and that the taking any public notice of them is giving them too much consequence, and pursuing that plan which of all others is best calculated to render them still more popular. To this common and trite argument it may be answered that this is not a case in which there can be any neutrality: those who are not for the Church are against it; and if Micah of old was guilty of a great crime,[1] these men cannot be innocent. Nor is there more real weight in the suggestions of cautious discretion, that it is best not to notice erroneous opinions and mischievous persons, lest censure should raise them into consequence. Neither moralists, nor preachers, nor legislators, in denouncing vices, regard who the persons are that are guilty of them: were the case otherwise, and were it true that vice, by being prohibited, becomes popular, moralists and preachers, and even legislators, might be charged with being the authors, rather than the correctors, of immorality and impiety.

What evils this prevalence of sectarianism, so sudden, so extraordinary, and so general, may portend to the State, I care not to think, recollecting with horror, that just such were the *signs of the times* previous to the grand rebellion in the last century. There is no denying that such disorders indicate a distempered government, just as blotches and boils indicate a bad habit of body. For it has been observed that sects in religion, and parties in politics, generally prevail together. By a sort of mutual action and reaction they produce one another, both, in their turns, becoming causes and effects. Whenever (to use Scripture phraseology) *there is no king in Israel*, that is to say, whenever, through any cause, the reins of government are relaxed, or its energies impeded,

---

[1] Micah, Hebrew prophet of the 8th Century B.C.; cf. Old Testament Book of Micah.

then are mankind tempted to act the part of Micah, that is, to run into parties, and to frame new schemes of religion for themselves. Indeed, sects in Religion and parties in the State originate, in general, from similar principles. A sect is, in fact, a revolt against the authority of the Church, just as a faction is against the authority of the State; or, in other words, a sect is a faction in the Church, as a faction is a sect in the State; and the spirit which refuses obedience to the one is equally ready to resist the other. . . .

POLITICAL PARTIES AND THE DECAY OF EMPIRE

[1797 (written 1775?)]

I AM not conscious that I am of a temper to rail indiscriminately against my own times. In many respects they merit much commendation, perhaps beyond all that have preceded them. Through a deference to public opinion, which abhors everything that is monstrous in manners; through the influence of fashion and habit, our character as a people is not marked by any prevailing propensity to commit great and flagrant crimes: but, I own, I hardly know how far such negative kind of merit is entitled to praise; at most, it seems to be but the virtues of that particular class of bees which in autumn are called drones, and which are innoxious only because they are impotent. However commendable it is in the character of a people that they are not marked by any great and flagrant vices, we are entitled to this commendation, if at all, by accident rather than by design, that is to say, because, fortunately for us, it is not fashionable to be eminently vicious; whilst our equal deficiency in any great virtues is in no slight degree studied and deliberate. There never was a time when a whole people were so little governed by settled good principles. Nor is this unconcern about good principles confined to matters which relate to government. By

a natural gradation in error, it pervades the whole compass of our conduct. Wise and observing persons see with sorrow that it has gained a footing in, and materially injured, every department of society. Parents complain, and not without reason, that children are no longer so respectful and dutiful as they ought to be, and as they used to be; whilst children might, with not less reason, object to their parents still more culpable instances of a failure of duty. Both employers and the employed, much to their mutual shame and inconvenience, no longer live together with anything like attachment and cordiality on either side: and the laboring classes, instead of regarding the rich as their guardians, patrons, and benefactors, now look on them as so many over-grown colossuses whom it is no demerit in them to wrong. A still more general (and it is to be feared not less just) topic of complaint is that the lower classes, instead of being industrious, frugal, and orderly, (virtues so peculiarly becoming their station in life) are become idle, improvident, and dissolute. And, however much it is to be regretted by all ranks, it does not admit of a doubt that this dissoluteness in the inferior members of the community may be traced to some corresponding profligacy in the higher orders. The manners of a community may be regarded as one great chain, of which persons in superior spheres are but the upper links. The same causes which, in the upper walks of life, lead men of active minds to engage in seditious and factious conspiracies and rebellions, lead those in lower spheres (when not attached as satellites to powerful revolters) to become either drunkards, and unmannerly, and abusive; or else, smugglers, gamblers, and cheats.

But these deviations from rectitude, though by no means inconsiderable in themselves, yet, when comprehensibly considered, are but small parts of a great whole. It is in our character, as subjects, that our loss of good principles, and consequent errors in practice, are most manifest and most mischievous. The doctrine of *obedience for conscience sake* is (as has just been observed) the great *cornerstone* of all good government; which, whenever any *builder* of constitutions shall be so unwise as to *refuse,* or, not refusing, shall afterwards suffer to be *destroyed,* what can he expect but that the whole fabric should be overturned; and that *on whomsoever it may fall it will grind them to powder?* . . .

Mal-administration, corruption, and tyranny, in those who govern, sap the foundations of all good government, if with less show, yet with hardly less reality, than they are sapped by sedition and rebellion in those who are governed. That it is of great moment carefully to watch the conduct of all administrations is readily admitted; but it is of equal moment to attend with equal care to everything else which relates to legislation and government. Such vigilance, however, is the particular and exclusive duty of no individual member or members of the community, whether in a public or private capacity: it is the common duty of every man in his sphere, and the especial duty of our constitutional guardians, whom we elect for that purpose, though not for that only. This duty they equally discharge, when, in cases where the executive power requires and is entitled to support, they give it support; as when, on a contrary supposition, they oppose and endeavour to counteract measures of which they cannot conscientiously approve. But this neither supposes nor justifies a distinct and united body of systematic opponents, nor indiscriminate opposition: yet, both in the British Parliament, and in our Colonial Assemblies, ever since the system began, there has never wanted a regular corps of members in opposition; as well known and as clearly designated as any of the officers of State. This body of men has far too often opposed, not only particular measures (as every individual member is supposed to do when schemes are patronized either by those entrusted with the administration or others, which such members conceive to be unwise or unjust) but in general all measures whatever which are supported by the executive power, or by a minister: and what is most alarming is that, in this thwarting and opposing the immediate supporters of government, many instances might be mentioned, in which the Members in Opposition, as they are regularly denominated, have, indirectly at least, taken part with, encouraged, and assisted the avowed enemies of their country: one also of its more certain and constant effects is that, in common with its ministers, government in the abstract is vilified and traduced.

That some good has occasionally been effected by oppositions (which now seem to be as regular appendages to our legislatures, as if they actually were a constitutional and essential part of them) I am far from denying; but I much fear the good that is thus done bears no proportion to the evil: the former at best is uncertain, but not so the latter. As, however, it is no part of my purpose to go into a full discussion of this important question, suffice it for the present to observe (what perfectly corresponds with the sum of this discourse) that one of its certain effects is (as has just been observed) its giving rise to a low and unworthy opinion of government. Hence men of ill-informed or misdirected minds are naturally led, instead of reverencing government, to do all they can to dishonor it. It was this general habit of *speaking evil of dignities, and despising dominion,* which in the last century, more than anything else, engendered and fostered infinite *confusion and every evil work* in the State; and at length produced those *secret conspiracies and open attempts* against the laws, the liberties, and the religion of the land; such as now once more fill the minds of all observing and thinking men with apprehension and awe.

The low opinion of government naturally produces another false and dangerous estimate of things: in proportion as government is degraded, those who depress it exalt themselves. Hence, to be the friend of government, subjects a man to the mortifying suspicion of being an abject and servile mind; whilst popularity is sure to attach to those who oppose government, or rather perhaps the ministers of government. And hence, too, as flimsy oratory is always most in vogue when sound principles and sound learning are least so, our forest committees, aping the members of our conventions and congresses in their volubility of speech, as well as in their patriotism, harangue not less vehemently on these unvarying topics, the abuses of government, the vileness of those whom they call the tools of government, the disinterestedness of opposition, and the genuine love of liberty which actuates those who conduct opposition. These seem always to have been the favorite topics of that "swollen and turgid elocution," which a Roman writer, distinguished for his elegance, mentions as characteristical of his countrymen in the decline of their empire.[2]

FICTIONS OF THE REVOLUTIONARY MIND

[1797 (written 1775?)]

THIS popular notion, that government was originally formed by the consent or by a compact of the people, rests on, and is supported by, another similar notion, not less popular, nor better founded. This other notion is that the whole human race is born equal; and that no man is naturally inferior, or, in any respect, subjected to another; and that he can be made subject to another only by his own consent. The position is equally ill-founded and false both in its premises and conclusions. In hardly any sense that can be imagined is the position strictly true; but, as applied to the case under consideration, it is demonstrably not true. Man differs from man in everything that can be supposed to lead to supremacy and subjection, *as one star differs from another star in glory*. It was the purpose of the Creator that man should be social: but, without government, there can be no society; nor, without some relative inferiority and superiority, can there be any government. A musical instrument composed of chords, keys, or pipes, all perfectly equal in size and power, might as well be expected to produce harmony, as a society composed of members all perfectly equal to be productive of order and peace. If (according to the idea of the advocates of this chimerical scheme of authority) no man could rightfully *be compelled to come in* and be a member even of a government to be formed by a regular compact, but by his own individual consent; it clearly follows, from the same principles, that neither could he rightfully be made or compelled to submit to the ordinances of any government already formed, to which he has not individually or actually consented. On the principle of equality, neither his parents, nor even the vote of a majority of society (however virtuously and honorably that vote might be obtained) can have any such authority over any man. Neither can it be maintained that acquiescence implies consent, because acquiescence may have been extorted from impotence or incapacity. Even an explicit consent can bind a man no longer than he chooses to be bound. The same principle of equality that exempts him from being governed without his own consent, clearly entitles him to recall and resume that consent whenever he sees fit; and he alone has a right to judge when and for what reasons it may be resumed.

Any attempt, therefore, to introduce this fantastic system into practice would reduce the whole business of social life to the wearisome, confused, and useless task of mankind's first expressing, and then withdrawing, their consent to an endless succession of schemes of government. Governments, though always forming, would never be completely formed: for the majority today might be the minority tomorrow;

---

[2] As Boucher indicates in his notes, the quotation is from Petronius' *The Satyricon*, but the "Roman writer" referred to is Tacitus, in his *Dialogus de Oratoribus*.

and, of course, that which is now fixed might and would be soon unfixed. Mr. Locke indeed says that "by consenting with others to make one body-politic under government, a man puts himself under an obligation to every one of that society to submit to the determination of the majority, and to be concluded by it." [3] For the sake of the peace of society, it is undoubtedly reasonable and necessary that this should be the case: but, on the principles of the system now under consideration, before Mr. Locke or any of his followers can have authority to say that it actually is the case, it must be stated and proved that every individual man, on entering into the social compact, did first consent, and declare his consent, to be concluded and bound in all cases by the vote of the majority. In making such a declaration, he would certainly consult both his interest and his duty; but at the same time he would also completely relinquish the principle of equality, and eventually subject himself to the possibility of being governed by ignorant and corrupt tyrants. Mr. Locke himself afterwards disproves his own position respecting this supposed obligation to submit to the "determination of the majority," when he argues that a right of resistance still exists in the governed; for what is resistance but a recalling and resuming the consent heretofore supposed to have been given, and in fact refusing to submit to the "determination of the majority?" It does not clearly appear what Mr. Locke exactly meant by what he calls "the determination of the majority": but the only rational and practical public manner of declaring "the determination of the majority" is by law: the laws, therefore, in all countries, even in those that are despotically governed, are to be regarded as the declared "determination of a majority" of the members of that community; because, in such cases, even acquiescence only must be looked upon as equivalent to a declaration. A right of resistance, therefore, for which Mr. Locke contends, is incompatible with the duty of submitting

to the determination of "the majority," for which he also contends.

It is indeed impossible to carry into effect any government which, even by compact, might be framed with this reserved right of resistance. Accordingly there is no record that any such government ever was so formed. If there had, it must have carried the seeds of its decay in its very constitution. For, as those men who make a government (certain that they have the power) can have no hesitation to vote that they also have the right to unmake it; and as the people, in all circumstances, but more especially when trained to make and unmake governments, are at least as well disposed to do the latter as the former, it is morally impossible that there should be anything like permanency or stability in a government so formed. Such a system, therefore, can produce only perpetual dissensions and contests, and bring back mankind to a supposed state of nature; arming every man's hand, like Ishmael's, against every man, and rendering the world an *aceldama*,[4] or field of blood.—Such theories of government seem to give something like plausibility to the notions of those other modern theorists who regard all governments as invasions of the natural rights of men, usurpations, and tyranny. On this principle it would follow, and could not be denied, that government was indeed fundamentally, as our people are sedulously taught it still is, an evil. Yet it is to government that mankind owe their having, after their fall and corruption, been again reclaimed, from a state of barbarity and war, to the conveniency and the safety of the social state: and it is by means of government that society is still preserved, the weak protected from the strong, and the artless and innocent from the wrongs of proud oppressors. It was not without

---

[3] John Locke's *Two Treatises of Government* were published in 1690.

[4] Field purchased with the thirty pieces of silver which were Judas' reward for the betrayal of Christ. According to *Acts* 1.18, Aceldama was the scene of Judas' suicide.

reason, then, that Mr. Locke asserted that a greater wrong cannot be done to prince and people than is done by "propagating wrong notions concerning government."

Ashamed of this shallow device, that government originated in superior strength and violence, another party, hardly less numerous, and certainly not less confident than the former, fondly deduce it from some imaginary compact. They suppose that, in the decline perhaps of some fabulous age of gold, a multitude of human beings, who, like their brother beasts, had hitherto ranged the forests, *without guide, overseer, or ruler*—at length convinced, by experience, of the impossibility of living either alone with any degree of comfort or security, or together in society, with peace, without government, had (in some lucid interval of reason and reflection) met together in a spacious plain, for the express purpose of framing a government. Their first step must have been the transferring to some individual, or individuals, some of those rights which are supposed to have been inherent in each of them: of these it is essential to government that they should be divested: yet can they not, rightfully, be deprived of them otherwise than by their own consent. Now admitting this whole supposed assembly to be perfectly equal as to rights, yet all agreed as to the propriety of ceding some of them, on what principles of equality is it possible to determine, either who shall relinquish such a portion of his rights, or who shall be invested with such new accessory rights? By asking another to exercise jurisdiction over me, I clearly confess that I do not think myself his equal; and by his consenting to exercise such authority, he also virtually declares that he thinks himself superior. And, to establish this hypothesis of a compact, it is farther necessary that the whole assembly should concur in this opinion—a concurrence so extremely improbable that it seems to be barely possible. The supposition that a large concourse of people, in a rude and imperfect state of society, or even a majority of them, should thus

rationally and unanimously concur to subject themselves to various restrictions, many of them irksome and unpleasant, and all of them contrary to all their former habits, is to suppose them possessed of more wisdom and virtue than multitudes in any instance in real life have ever shown. Another difficulty respecting this notion may yet be mentioned. Without a power of life and death, it will, I presume, be readily admitted that there could be no government. Now, admitting it to be possible that men, from motives of public and private utility, may be induced to submit to many heavy penalties, and even to corporal punishment, inflicted by the sentence of the law, there is an insuperable objection to any man's giving to another a power over his life: this objection is that no man has such a power over his own life; and cannot therefore transfer to another, or to others, be they few or many, on any conditions, a right which he does not himself possess. He only who gave life can give the authority to take it away: and as such authority is essential to government, this argument seems very decidedly to prove, not only that government did not originate in any compact, but also that it was originally from God.

This visionary idea of a government by compact was, as Filmer says, "first hatched in the schools; and hath, ever since, been fostered by Papists for good divinity."[5] For some time, the world seemed to regard it merely as another Utopian fiction; and it was long confined to the disciples of Rome and Geneva, who, agreeing in nothing else, yet agreed in this. In an evil hour it gained admittance into the Church of England, being patronized by her during the civil wars, by "a few miscreants, who were as far from being true Protestants as true subjects." Mankind have listened, and continue to listen to it with a predilection

---

[5] Sir Robert Filmer (d. 1653) was the author of *Patriarcha, or the Natural Power of Kings,* first published in 1680. The first of Locke's *Two Treatises* is a reply to Filmer's *Patriarcha.*

and partiality, just as they do to various other exceptionable notions, which are unfavorable to true religion and sound morals; merely from imagining that, if such doctrines be true, they shall no longer be subjected to sundry restraints, which, however wholesome and proper, are too often unpalatable to our corrupt natures. What we wish to be true, we easily persuade ourselves is true. On this principle it is not difficult to account for our thus eagerly following these *ignes fatui* of our own fancies or "feelings," rather than the sober steady light of the word of God; which (in this instance as well as in others) lies under this single disadvantage, that it proposes no doctrines which may conciliate our regards by flattering our pride.

If, however, we can ever resolve no longer to be bewildered by these vain imaginations, still the interesting question presses on us, "Where," in the words of Plato, "where shall we look for the origin of government?" [6] Let Plato himself instruct us. Taught then by this oracle of Heathen wisdom, "we will take our stations there, where the prospect of it is most easy and beautiful." Of all the theories respecting the origin of government with which the world has ever been either puzzled, amused, or instructed, that of the Scriptures alone is accompanied by no insuperable difficulties.

It was not to be expected from an all-wise and all-merciful Creator that, having formed creatures capable of order and rule, he should turn them loose into the world under the guidance only of their own unruly wills; that, like so many wild beasts, they might tear and worry one another in their mad contests for preëminence. His purpose from the first, no doubt, was that men should *live godly and sober lives*. But such is the sad estate of our corrupted nature that, ever since the Fall, we have been averse from good, and prone to evil. We are, indeed, so disorderly and unmanageable that, were it not for the restraints and terrors of human laws, it would not be possible for us to dwell together. But as men were clearly formed for society and to dwell together, which yet they cannot do without the restraints of law, or, in other words, without government, it is fair to infer that government was also the original intention of God, who never decrees the end, without also decreeing the means. Accordingly, when man was made, his Maker did not turn him adrift into a shoreless ocean, without star or compass to steer by. As soon as there were some to be governed, there were also some to govern: and the first man, by virtue of that paternal claim, on which all subsequent governments have been founded, was first invested with the power of government. For we are not to judge of the Scriptures of God as we do of some other writings; and so, where no express precept appears, hastily to conclude that none was given. On the contrary, in commenting on the Scriptures, we are frequently called upon to find out the precept from the practice. Taking this rule, then, for our direction in the present instance, we find that, copying after the fair model of heaven itself, wherein there was government even among the angels, the families of the earth were subjected to rulers, at first set over them by God: *for, there is no power, but of God; the powers that be are ordained of God.* The first father was the first king: and if (according to the rule just laid down) the law may be inferred from the practice, it was thus that all government originated, and monarchy is its most ancient form. . . .

---

[6] *Laws*, Book III—Boucher's note.

1750 ∾ *John Trumbull* ∾ *1831*

THE TERM "Connecticut Wits" has been applied to a miscellaneous group of writers of that State who came to prominence before, during, and after the American Revolution. The four older members of the group were John Trumbull, Timothy Dwight, David Humphreys, and Joel Barlow. Their juniors were Theodore Dwight, Richard Alsop, Elihu H. Smith, Mason W. Cogswell, and Nathaniel Dwight. Between the "oldsters" and the "youngsters," Lemuel Hopkins, an "oldster" himself, was a kind of connecting link.

Son of a Congregational minister, Trumbull was born at Waterbury, Connecticut, and was graduated from Yale in 1767. He returned in the fall of that year to study for his M.A., which he received in 1770. He was for a while a tutor at Yale and then went to Boston to study law with John Adams. He rose to such eminence in this profession that he became State Attorney for the County of Hartford and a judge of the Superior Court of the State and of its Supreme Court of Errors. He was also Treasurer of Yale, which bestowed upon him the degree of LL.D. in 1818. He removed to Detroit in 1825 to live with his daughter, and died there.

Trumbull's friend, Samuel G. Goodrich, published his *Poetical Works* in two volumes in 1820, but by that time Trumbull's popularity had declined sharply. His two important poems, *The Progress of Dullness,* published in three parts at New Haven in 1772 and 1773, and *M'Fingal,* the first canto of which appeared in 1775 and the complete version of which was issued in four cantos at Hartford in 1782, continued the traditions of English satire, with most obvious indebtedness to Charles Churchill, Swift, Prior, and Butler's *Hudibras.* One of the distinctions of *M'Fingal,* both in its earlier and its later form, is that it adopts an attitude of burlesque detachment toward both the "Whigs" and "Tories" in the Revolutionary struggle. Trumbull himself was a middle-of-the-road "Whig," reserving his keenest thrusts for the "Tories," but being no lover of the kind of radicalism that was associated with Paine, Jefferson, and Freneau.

[The present selection is slightly modernized from the 1820 edition: the title has been supplied by the editors.]

PORTRAIT OF A TORY
[1775]

When Yankees, skilled in martial rule,
First put the British troops to school;
Instructed them in warlike trade,
And new manoeuvres of parade;

The true war-dance of Yankee-reels,   5
And manual exercise of heels;
Made them give up, like saints complete,
The arm of flesh and trust the feet,
And work, like Christians undissembling,
Salvation out, by fear and trembling;   10
Taught Percy fashionable races,

And modern modes of Chevy-Chases: [1]
From Boston, in his best array,
Great 'Squire M'Fingal took his way,
And graced with ensigns of renown,   15
Steered homeward to his native town.

His high descent our heralds trace
To Ossian's famed Fingalian race:
For though their name some part may lack,
Old Fingal spelt it with a Mac;   20
Which great M'Pherson, with submission
We hope will add, the next edition. [2]
His fathers flourished in the Highlands
Of Scotia's fog-benighted islands;
Whence gained our 'Squire two gifts by
      right,   25
Rebellion and the second-sight.
Of these the first, in ancient days,
Had gained the noblest palms of praise,
'Gainst kings stood forth and many a
      crown'd head
With terror of its might confounded;   30
Till rose a king with potent charm
His foes by goodness to disarm,
Whom ev'ry Scot and Jacobite
Straight fell in love with, at first sight;
Whose gracious speech, with aid of pen-
      sions,   35
Hushed down all murmurs of dissensions,
And with the sound of potent metal,
Brought all their blust'ring swarms to
      settle; [3]
Who rained his ministerial mannas,
Till loud Sedition sung hosannas;   40
The good Lords-Bishops and the Kirk
United in the public work; [4]
Rebellion from the Northern regions,
With Bute and Mansfield swore alle-
      giance; [5]
And all combined to raze as nuisance,   45
Of church and state, the constitutions;
Pull down the empire, on whose ruins
They meant to edify their new ones;
Enslave th' American wildernesses
And tear the provinces in pieces: 50
For these our 'Squire among the valiant'st,
Employed his time and tools and talents;
And in their cause with manly zeal
Used his first virtue, to rebel;

And found this new rebellion pleasing   55
As his old king-destroying treason.

Nor less availed his optic sleight,
And Scottish gift of second-sight.
No ancient sybil famed in rhyme
Saw deeper in the womb of time;   60
No block in old Dodona's grove, [6]
Could ever more orac'lar prove.
Not only saw he all that was,
But much that never came to pass;
Whereby all prophets far outwent he,   65
Though former days produced a plenty;
For any man with half an eye,
What stands before him may espy;
But optics sharp it needs I ween,
To see what is not to be seen.   70
As in the days of ancient fame
Prophets and poets were the same,
And all the praise that poets gain
Is but for what th' invent and feign:
So gained our 'Squire his fame by seeing   75
Such things as never would have being.
Whence he for oracles was grown
The very tripod of his town.
Gazettes no sooner rose a lie in,

---

[1] Lord Percy commanded the party that was first opposed to the Americans at Lexington. This allusion to the family renown of Chevy-Chase arose from the precipitate manner of his Lordship's quitting the field of battle and returning to Boston —Trumbull's note.

[2] To Ossian, Gaelic hero of the 3rd century, son of Finn Mac Cool, James Mac-Pherson, the Scottish poet, ascribed his *The Poems of Ossian*, published 1760 and 1762 and including *Fingal, an Epic Poem in Six Books* and *Temora, an Epic Poem in Eight Books*.

[3] An allusion to the fact that swarming bees may be brought to "settle" by loud beating of tin pans, kettles, or some other sounding metal.

[4] Here Trumbull alludes to the influence in favor of the crown exerted by the established churches of England and Scotland.

[5] John, Earl of Bute, and Lord Mansfield were supporters and officials of George the Third.

[6] Abode of ancient Grecian oracle.

But straight he fell to prophesying;   80
Made dreadful slaughter in his course,
O'erthrew provincials, foot and horse;
Brought armies o'er by sudden pressings
Of Hanoverians, Swiss, and Hessians;
Feasted with blood his Scottish clan,   85
And hanged all rebels, to a man;
Divided their estates and pelf,
And took a goodly share himself.
All this with spirit energetic,
He did by second-sight prophetic.   90

   Thus stored with intellectual riches,
Skilled was our 'Squire in making speeches,
Where strength of brain united centers
With strength of lungs surpassing Sten-
    tor's.
But as some muskets so contrive it,   95
As oft to miss the mark they drive at,
And though well aimed at duck or plover,
Bear wide and kick their owners over:
So fared our 'Squire, whose reas'ning toil
Would often on himself recoil,   100
And so much injured more his side,
The stronger arg'ments he applied:
As old war-elephants dismayed
Trod down the troops that came to aid,
And hurt their own side more in battle 105
Than less and ordinary cattle.
Yet at town-meetings ev'ry chief
Pinned faith on great M'Fingal's sleeve,

And as he motioned, all by rote
Raised sympathetic hands to vote.   110

   The town, our hero's scene of action,
Had long been torn by feuds of faction,
And as each party's strength prevails,
It turned up diff'rent, heads or tails;
With constant rattling in a trice   115
Showed various sides as oft as dice:
As that famed weaver, wife t'Ulysses,
By night each day's work picked in pieces,
And though she stoutly did bestir her,
Its finishing was ne'er the nearer: [7]   120
So did this town with steadfast zeal
Weave cob-webs for the public weal,
Which when completed, or before,
A second vote in pieces tore.
They met, made speeches full long wind-
    ed,   125
Resolved, protested, and rescinded;
Addresses signed, then chose committees,
To stop all drinking of Bohea-teas;
With winds of doctrine veered about,
And turned all Whig-committees out. 130
Meanwhile our hero, as their head,
In pomp the Tory faction led,
Still following, as the 'Squire should please,
Successive on, like files of geese.

---

[7] The reference is to Penelope's strategy against her suitors, as set forth in Homer's *Odyssey*.

1737 ∾ *Thomas Paine* ∾ 1809

   AS HAS BEEN pointed out in the headnote to the selections from *The Age of Reason* (Book I, Part 2), Paine ranks high as a spokesman for the "pros" of democracy. His major political and economic writings were the product of both the American and the French Revolution.

   The first of these revolutions was already well under way when he wrote and issued *Common Sense*. When it appeared on January 10, 1776, almost a year after the battle of Lexington, which was fought on April 19, 1775, most of the arguments which he advanced for independence of the colonies from England were familiar to intelligent Americans, but he summed them up so cogently and invested them with such emotive appeal that the result was a *tour de force* of propaganda. He was heavily indebted to William Burgh's *Political Disquisitions,* 1773-75, a three-volume English anthology of political thought from the Greeks to Paine's own day.

Signed "Common Sense," *The Crisis* papers were a series of pamphlets in which Paine sought to bolster American morale at successive critical moments of the Revolution. There were sixteen pamphlets in all, thirteen of which were numbered, and they appeared between 1776 and 1783, printed on many kinds of paper and read widely. The selection included here is from *Crisis I;* this number came out at a very dark moment in the early stages of the war. At the battle of Long Island the American army had been turned back in retreat toward Philadelphia, the capital city; Congress fled to Baltimore. In Philadelphia, at the height of this chaos, Paine wrote and issued *Crisis I.*

In 1782 appeared Paine's *Letter to the Abbé Raynal,* on which he had been working at intervals for about a year. One of the French Encyclopedists, the Abbé Guillaume Raynal had written a pamphlet translated as *Observations on the Revolution in America* and read widely in England and America. Paine, while admiring the Abbé's genius for ideas and rhetoric, sought to correct some of his misapprehensions as to the broader rationale behind the American Revolution.

Paine was so intimate a friend of Edmund Burke that he lived at his home for a while after going to England in 1787. In 1790 he wrote to Burke from Paris to inform him on French affairs, and was naturally shocked at Burke's arraignment of France both in his parliamentary speech of February 9, 1790, and in his *Reflections on the Late Revolution in France* of the same year. Part I of *The Rights of Man,* Paine's answer to Burke's *Reflections,* was written in England; Part II in France.

[The following two excerpts from *The Rights of Man* are taken respectively from Part I, 1791, and Part II, 1792.]

Agrarian Justice, here given in its entirety save for a brief appendix, was written in the winter of 1795-96 while Paine was in Paris, and was intended to influence French thought concerning the problem of what should be done about the property of aristocratic *emigrés.* This property was subject to confiscation as the result of laws passed during the Revolution. One radical faction was pressing for a "share-the-land" program; a reactionary or royalist faction had been conspiring to protect the property of the rich and to insure the continuance of inheritance rights. Paine's pamphlet, proposing a middle-of-the-road course, anticipated some of the ideas of English Chartism in the next century and of the American "single tax" reformer, Henry George. [*Agrarian Justice* appeared in both French and English in 1797. See Book I, Part 2, for other selections from Paine's work.]

From
COMMON SENSE

[1776]

SOME writers have so confounded society with government, as to leave little or no distinction between them; whereas they are not only different, but have different origins. Society is produced by our wants, and government by our wickedness; the former promotes our happiness *positively*, by uniting our affections; the latter *negatively*, by restraining our vices. The one encourages intercourse, the other creates distinctions. The first is a patron, the last a punisher.

Society in every state is a blessing, but government, even in its best state, is but a necessary evil; in its worst state, an intolerable one; for when we suffer, or are exposed to the same miseries *by a government*, which we might expect in a country *without government*, our calamity is heightened by reflecting that we furnish the means by which we suffer.

Government, like dress, is the badge of lost innocence: the palaces of kings are built on the ruins of the bowers of paradise. For, were the impulses of conscience clear, uniform, and irresistibly obeyed, man would need no other law-giver; but that not being the case, he finds it necessary to surrender up a part of his property to furnish means for the protection of the rest; and this he is induced to do by the same prudence which in every other case, advises him out of two evils to choose the least.

Wherefore, security being the true design and end of government, it unanswerably follows, that whatever *form* thereof appears most likely to ensure it to us with the least expense and greatest benefit, is preferable to all others.

In order to give a clear and just idea of the design and end of government, let us suppose a small number of persons set-tled in some sequestered part of the earth, unconnected with the rest; they will then represent the first peopling of any country, or of the world. In this state of natural liberty, society will be their first thought. A thousand motives will excite them thereto; the strength of one man is so unequal to his wants, and his mind so unfitted for perpetual solitude, that he is soon obliged to seek assistance and relief of another, who in his turn requires the same.

Four or five united would be able to raise a tolerable dwelling in the midst of a wilderness; but *one* man might labor out the common period of life without accomplishing anything: when he had felled his timber he could not remove it, nor erect it after it was removed; hunger in the meantime would urge him from his work, and every different want call him a different way. Disease, nay even misfortune, would be death; for though neither might be mortal, yet either would disable him from living, and reduce him to a state in which he might rather be said to perish than to die.

Thus necessity, like a gravitating power, would soon form our newly-arrived emigrants into society, the reciprocal blessings of which would supersede and render the obligations of law and government unnecessary while they remained perfectly just to each other; but as nothing but heaven is impregnable to vice, it will unavoidably happen, that in proportion as they surmount the first difficulties of emigration, which bound them together in a common cause, they will begin to relax in their duty and attachment to each other; and this remissness will point out the necessity of establishing some form of government to supply the defect of moral virtue.

Some convenient tree will afford them a state-house, under the branches of which the whole colony may assemble to deliberate on public matters. It is more than probable that their first laws will have the title only of *Regulations,* and be enforced by no other penalty than public disesteem. In this first parliament every man, by natural right, will have a seat.

But as the colony increases, the public concerns will increase likewise, and the distance at which the members may be separated, will render it too inconvenient for all of them to meet on every occasion as at first, when their number was small, their habitations near, and the public concerns few and trifling. This will point out the convenience of their consenting to leave the legislative part to be managed by a select number chosen from the whole body, who are supposed to have the same concerns at stake which those have who appointed them, and who will act in the same manner as the whole body would were they present.

If the colony continue increasing, it will become necessary to augment the number of representatives, and that the interest of every part of the colony may be attended to, it will be found best to divide the whole into convenient parts, each part sending its proper number; and that the *elected* might never form to themselves an interest separate from the *electors*, prudence will point out the propriety of having elections often; because as the *elected* might by that means return and mix again with the general body of the *electors* in a few months, their fidelity to the public will be secured by the prudent reflection of not making a rod for themselves. And as this frequent interchange will establish a common interest with every part of the community, they will mutually and naturally support each other, and on this (not on the unmeaning name of king) depends the *strength of government and the happiness of the governed.*

Here, then, is the origin and rise of government; namely, a mode rendered necessary by the inability of moral virtue to govern the world; here, too, is the design and end of government, viz., freedom and security. And however our eyes may be dazzled with show, or our ears deceived by sound; however prejudice may warp our wills, or interest darken our under-

standing; the simple voice of nature and reason will say, it is right. . . .

Most wise men in their private sentiments have ever treated hereditary right with contempt; yet it is one of those evils, which when once established is not easily removed; many submit from fear, others from superstition, and the more powerful part shares with the king the plunder of the rest.

This is supposing the present race of kings in the world to have had an honorable origin; whereas it is more than probable, that, could we take off the dark covering of antiquity and trace them to their first rise, we should find the first of them nothing better than the principal ruffian of some restless gang, whose savage manners or preëminence in subtility obtained him the title of chief among plunderers; and who by increasing in power, and extending his depredations, overawed the quiet and defenseless to purchase their safety by frequent contributions. Yet his electors could have no idea of giving hereditary right to his descendants, because such a perpetual exclusion of themselves was incompatible with the free and unrestrained principles they professed to live by.

Wherefore, hereditary succession in the early ages of monarchy could not take place as a matter of claim, but as something casual or complemental; but as few or no records were extant in those days, and traditionary history is stuffed with fables, it was very easy after the lapse of a few generations, to trump up some superstitious tale, conveniently timed, Mahomet like, to cram hereditary rights down the throats of the vulgar.

Perhaps the disorders which threatened, or seemed to threaten, on the decease of a leader, and the choice of a new one (for elections among ruffians could not be very orderly) induced many at first to favor hereditary pretensions; by which means it happened, as it hath happened since, that what at first was submitted to as a convenience, was afterwards claimed as a right.

England, since the Conquest, hath known

some good monarchs, but groaned beneath a much larger number of bad ones; yet no man in his senses can say that their claim under William the Conqueror is a very honorable one.

A French bastard, landing with an armed banditti, and establishing himself King of England against the consent of the natives, is in plain terms a very paltry, rascally original. It certainly hath no divinity in it.

However, it is needless to spend much time in exposing the folly of hereditary right. If there are any so weak as to believe it, let them promiscuously worship the ass and the lion, and welcome. I shall neither copy their humility nor disturb their devotion.

Yet I should be glad to ask, how they suppose kings came at first? The question admits but of three answers, viz., either by lot, by election, or by usurpation. If the first king was taken by lot, it establishes a precedent for the next, which excludes hereditary succession. Saul was, by lot, yet the succession was not hereditary, neither does it appear from that transaction that there was any intention it ever should be.

If the first king of any country was by election, that likewise establishes a precedent for the next; for to say that the right of all future generations is taken away, by the act of the first electors, in their choice not only of a king, but of a family of kings forever, hath no parallel in or out of Scripture but the doctrine of original sin, which supposes the free will of all men lost in Adam; and from such comparison, and it will admit of no other, hereditary succession can derive no glory.

For as in Adam all sinned, and as in the first electors all men obeyed; as in the one all mankind were subjected to Satan, and in the other to sovereignty; as our innocence was lost in the first, and our authority in the last; and as both disable us from reassuming some former state and privilege, it unanswerably follows that original sin and hereditary succession are parallels.

Dishonorable rank! Inglorious connection! Yet the most subtile sophist cannot produce a juster simile.

As to usurpation, no man can be so hardy as to defend it; and that William the Conqueror was an usurper is a fact not to be contradicted.

The plain truth is, that the antiquity of English monarchy will not bear looking into. . . .

As to government matters, it is not in the power of Britain to do this continent justice: the business of it will soon be too weighty and intricate to be managed with any tolerable degree of convenience by a power so distant from us, and so very ignorant of us; for if they cannot conquer us, they cannot govern us. To be always running three or four thousand miles with a tale or a petition; waiting four or five months for an answer, which, when obtained, requires five or six more to explain it in, will in a few years be looked upon as folly and childishness—there was a time when it was proper, and there is a proper time for it to cease.

Small islands, not capable of protecting themselves, are the proper objects for kingdoms to take under their care; but there is something very absurd in supposing a continent to be perpetually governed by an island. In no instance hath nature made the satellite larger than its primary planet; and as England and America, with respect to each other, reverse the common order of nature, it is evident that they belong to different systems: England to Europe—America to itself.

I am not induced by motives of pride, party, or resentment to espouse the doctrine of separation and independence; I am clearly, positively, and conscientiously persuaded that it is the true interest of this continent to do so; that everything short of *that* is mere patchwork; that it can afford no lasting felicity—that it is leaving the sword to our children, and shrinking back at a time when a little more, a little further, would have rendered this continent the glory of the earth. . . .

From
THE AMERICAN CRISIS
[1776]

THESE are the times that try men's souls: The summer soldier and the sunshine patriot will, in this crisis, shrink from the service of his country; but he that stands it NOW, deserves the love and thanks of man and woman. Tyranny, like hell, is not easily conquered; yet we have this consolation with us, that the harder the conflict, the more glorious the triumph. What we obtain too cheap, we esteem too lightly:—'Tis dearness only that gives everything its value. Heaven knows how to set a proper price upon its goods; and it would be strange indeed, if so celestial an article as FREEDOM should not be highly rated. . . .

We did not make a proper use of last winter, neither could we, while we were in a dependent state. However, the fault, if it were one, was all our own; we have none to blame but ourselves. . . .

I have as little superstition in me as any man living, but my secret opinion has ever been, and still is, that God Almighty will not give up a people to military destruction, or leave them unsupportedly to perish, who have so earnestly and so repeatedly sought to avoid the calamities of war, by every decent method which wisdom could invent. Neither have I so much of the infidel in me, as to suppose that HE has relinquished the government of the world, and given us up to the care of devils. . . .

'Tis surprising to see how rapidly a panic will sometimes run through a country. . . . Yet panics, in some cases, have their uses; they produce as much good as hurt. Their duration is always short; the mind soon grows through them, and acquires a firmer habit than before. But their peculiar advantage is, that they are the touchstones of sincerity and hypocrisy, and bring things and men to light, which might otherwise have laid forever undiscovered. In fact, they have the same effect on secret traitors, which an imaginary apparition would have upon a private murderer. They sift out the hidden thoughts of man, and hold them up in public to the world. . . .

I once felt that kind of anger, which a man ought to feel, against the mean principles that are held by the Tories: A noted one, who kept a tavern at Amboy, was standing at his door, with as pretty a child in his hand, about eight or nine years old, as most I ever saw, and after speaking his mind as freely as he thought was prudent, finished with this unfatherly expression, *"Well! give me peace in my day."* Not a man lives on the continent but fully believes that a separation must some time or other finally take place, and a generous parent would have said, *"If there must be trouble, let it be in my day, that my child may have peace;"* and this single reflection, well applied, is sufficient to awaken every man to duty. . . .

America did not, nor does not, want force; but she wanted a proper application of that force. Wisdom is not the purchase of a day, and it is no wonder that we should err at first setting off. From an excess of tenderness, we were unwilling to raise an army, and trusted our cause to the temporary defence of a well-meaning militia. . . . I have always considered a militia as the best troops in the world for a sudden exertion, but they will not do for a long campaign. . . .

. . . I turn with the warm ardour of a friend to those who have nobly stood, and are yet determined to stand the matter out: I call not upon a few, but upon all; not on THIS State or THAT State, but on EVERY State; up and help us; lay your shoulders to the wheel; better have too much force than too little, when so great an object is at stake. Let it be told to the future world, that in the depth of winter, when nothing but hope and virtue could survive, that the city and the country, alarmed at one common danger, came forth to meet and to repulse it. Say not, that thousands are gone, turn out your tens of thousands; throw not the burden of the day upon Providence, but "show your faith by your works," that GOD may bless you. It matters not where you live, or what rank of life you hold, the evil or the blessing will reach you all. The far and the near, the home counties and the back, the rich and the poor, shall suffer or rejoice alike. The heart that feels not now, is dead: The blood of his children shall curse his cowardice, who shrinks back at a time when a little might have saved the whole, and made *them* happy. I love the man that can smile in trouble, that can gather strength from distress, and grow brave by reflection. 'Tis the business of little minds to shrink; but he whose heart is firm, and whose conscience approves his conduct, will pursue his principles unto death. My own line of reasoning is to myself as straight and clear as a ray of light. Not all the treasures of the world, so far as I believe, could have induced me to support an offensive war, for I think it murder; but if a thief break into my house, burn and destroy my property, and kill or threaten to kill me, or those that are in it, and to *"bind me in all cases whatsoever,"* to his absolute will, am I to suffer it? . . .

There are cases which cannot be overdone by language, and this is one. There are persons too who see not the full extent of the evil that threatens them; they solace themselves with hopes that the enemy, if they succeed, will be merciful. It is the madness of folly to expect mercy from those who have refused to do justice; and even mercy, where conquest is the object, is only a trick of war: The cunning of the fox is as murderous as the violence of the wolf; and we ought to guard equally against both. . . . I dwell not upon the vapors of imagination; I bring reason to your ears; and in language as plain as A, B, C hold up truth to your eyes.

I thank GOD that I fear not. I see no real cause for fear. I know our situation well, and can see the way out of it. . . . Once more we are again collected and

collecting; our new army at both ends of the continent is recruiting fast, and we shall be able to open the next campaign with sixty thousand men, well armed and clothed. This is our situation, and who will may know it. By perseverance and fortitude we have the prospect of a glorious issue; by cowardice and submission, the sad choice of a variety of evils—a ravaged country—a depopulated city— habitations without safety, and slavery without hope—our homes turned into barracks and baudy-houses for Hessians, and a future race to provide for whose fathers we shall doubt of. Look on this picture, and weep over it!—and if there yet remains one thoughtless wretch who believes it not, let him suffer it unlamented.

From
LETTER TO THE ABBÉ RAYNAL
[1782]

IT IS an observation I have already made in some former publications, that the circle of civilization is yet incomplete. Mutual wants have formed the individuals of each country into a kind of national society, and here the progress of civilization has stopped. For it is easy to see, that nations with regard to each other (notwithstanding the ideal civil law, which every one explains as it suits him) are like individuals in a state of nature. They are regulated by no fixed principle, governed by no compulsive law, and each does independently what it pleases or what it can.

Were it possible we could have known the world when in a state of barbarism, we might have concluded that it never could be brought into the order we now see it. The untamed mind was then as hard, if not harder, to work upon in its individual state, than the national mind is in its present one. Yet we have seen the accomplishment of one, why then should we doubt that of the other?

There is a greater fitness in mankind to extend and complete the civilization of nations with each other at this day, than there was to begin it with the unconnected individuals at first; in the same manner that it is somewhat easier to put together the materials of a machine after they are formed, than it was to form them from original matter. The present condition of the world, differing so exceedingly from what it formerly was, has given a new cast to the mind of man, more than what he appears to be sensible of. The wants of the individual, which first produced the idea of society, are now augmented into the wants of the nation, and he is obliged to seek from another country what before he sought from the next person.

Letters, the tongue of the world, have in some measure brought all mankind acquainted, and by an extension of their uses are every day promoting some new friendship. Through them distant nations become capable of conversation, and losing by degrees the awkwardness of strangers, and the moroseness of suspicion, they learn to know and understand each other. Science, the partisan of no country, but the beneficent patroness of all, has liberally opened a temple where all may meet. Her influence on the mind, like the sun on the chilled earth, has long been preparing it for higher cultivation and further improvement. The philosopher of one country sees not an enemy in the philosopher of another: he takes his seat in the temple of science, and asks not who sits beside him.

This was not the condition of the barbarian world. Then the wants of men were few and the objects within his reach. While he could acquire these, he lived in a state of individual independence; the consequence of which was, there were as many nations as persons, each contending with the other, to secure something which he had, or to obtain something which he had not. The world had then no business to follow, no studies to exercise the mind. Their time was divided between sloth and fatigue. Hunting and war were their chief occupations; sleep and food their principal enjoyments.

Now it is otherwise. A change in the mode of life has made it necessary to be busy; and man finds a thousand things to do now which before he did not. Instead of placing his ideas of greatness in the rude achievements of the savage, he studies arts, sciences, agriculture and commerce, the refinements of the gentleman, the principles of society, and the knowledge of the philosopher.

There are many things which in themselves are neither morally good nor bad, but they are productive of consequences, which are strongly marked with one or other of these characters. Thus commerce, though in itself a moral nullity, has had a considerable influence in tempering the human mind. It was the want of objects in the ancient world, which occasioned in them such a rude and perpetual turn for war. Their time hung on their hands without the means of employment. The indolence they lived in afforded leisure for mischief, and being all idle at once, and equal in their circumstances, they were easily provoked or induced to action.

But the introduction of commerce furnished the world with objects, which, in their extent, reach every man, and give him something to think about and something to do; by these his attention is mechanically drawn from the pursuits which a state of indolence and an unemployed mind occasioned, and he trades with the same countries which, in former ages, tempted by their productions, and too indolent to purchase them, he would have gone to war with.

Thus, as I have already observed, the condition of the world being materially changed by the influence of science and commerce, it is put into a fitness not only to admit of, but to desire, an extension of civilization. . . .

The true idea of a great nation, is that which extends and promotes the principles of universal society; whose mind rises above the atmosphere of local thoughts, and considers mankind, of whatever nation or profession they may be, as the work of one Creator. The rage for conquest has had its fashion, and its day. Why may not the amiable virtues have the same? The Alexanders and Caesars of antiquity have left behind them their monuments of destruction, and are remembered with hatred; while those more exalted characters, who first taught society and science, are blessed with the gratitude of every age and country. Of more use was *one* philosopher, though a heathen, to the world, than all the heathen conquerors that ever existed.

Should the present Revolution be distinguished by opening a new system of extended civilization, it will receive from heaven the highest evidence of approbation; and as this is a subject to which the Abbé's powers are so eminently suited, I recommend it to his attention with the affection of a friend, and the ardor of a universal citizen.

From

THE RIGHTS OF MAN
[1791, 1792]

THERE never did, there never will, and there never can exist a parliament, or any description of men, or any generation of men, in any country, possessed of the right or the power of binding and controlling posterity to the *"end of time,"* or of commanding forever how the world shall be governed, or who shall govern it; and therefore, all such clauses, acts or declarations, by which the makers of them attempt to do what they have neither the right nor the power to do, nor the power to execute, are in themselves null and void.

Every age and generation must be as free to act for itself, *in all cases,* as the ages and generation which preceded it. The vanity and presumption of governing beyond the grave, is the most ridiculous and insolent of all tyrannies.

Man has no property in man; neither

has any generation a property in the generations which are to follow. The Parliament or the people of 1688, or of any other period, had no more right to dispose of the people of the present day, or to bind or to control them *in any shape whatever,* than the Parliament or the people of the present day have to dispose of, bind, or control those who are to live a hundred or a thousand years hence.

Every generation is, and must be, competent to all the purposes which its occasions require. It is the living, and not the dead, that are to be accommodated. When man ceases to be, his power and his wants cease with him; and having no longer any participation in the concerns of this world, he has no longer any authority in directing who shall be its governors, or how its government shall be organized, or how administered.

I am not contending for nor against any form of government, nor for nor against any party here or elsewhere. That which a whole nation chooses to do, it has a right to do. Mr. Burke says, No. Where then *does* the right exist? I am contending for the rights of the *living,* and against their being willed away, and controlled and contracted for, by the manuscript assumed authority of the dead; and Mr. Burke is contending for the authority of the dead over the rights and freedom of the living. . . .

All the European governments (France now excepted) are constructed not on the principle of universal civilization, but on the reverse of it. So far as those governments relate to each other, they are in the same condition as we conceive of savage, uncivilized life; they put themselves beyond the law as well of God as of man, and are, with respect to principle and reciprocal conduct, like so many individuals in a state of nature.

The inhabitants of every country, under the civilization of laws, easily associate together, but governments being yet in an uncivilized state, and almost continually at war, they pervert the abundance which civilized life produces to carry on the uncivilized part to a greater extent.

By thus ingrafting the barbarism of government upon the internal civilization of a country, it draws from the latter, and more especially from the poor, a great portion of those earnings which should be applied to their own subsistence and comfort. Apart from all reflections of morality and philosophy it is a melancholy fact, that more than one-fourth of the labor of mankind is annually consumed by this barbarous system. What has served to continue this evil, is the pecuniary advantage which all the governments of Europe have found in keeping up this state of uncivilization. It affords to them pretenses for power and revenue, for which there would be neither occasion nor apology, if the circle of civilization were rendered complete.

Civil government alone, or the government of laws, is not productive of pretenses for many taxes; it operates at home, directly under the eye of the country, and precludes the possibility of much imposition. But when the scene is laid in the uncivilized contention of governments, the field of pretenses is enlarged, and the country, being no longer a judge, is open to every imposition, which governments please to act.

Not a thirtieth, scarcely a fortieth, part of the taxes which are raised in England are either occasioned by, or applied, to the purposes of civil government. It is not difficult to see, that the whole which the actual government does in this respect, is to enact laws, and that the country administers and executes them, at its own expense, by means of magistrates, juries, sessions, and assize, over and above the taxes which it pays.

In this view of the case, we have two distinct characters of government; the one, the civil government, or the government of laws, which operates at home; the other, the court or cabinet government, which operates abroad, on the rude plan of uncivilized life; the one attended with little

charge, the other with boundless extravagance; and so distinct are the two, that if the latter were to sink, as it were, by a sudden opening of the earth, and totally disappear, the former would not be deranged. It would still proceed, because it is the common interest of the nation that it should, and all the means are in practise.

Revolutions, then, have for their object, a change in the moral condition of governments, and with this change the burden of public taxes will lessen, and civilization will be left to the enjoyment of that abundance, of which it is now deprived. . . .

AGRARIAN JUSTICE
[1797]

TO PRESERVE the benefits of what is called civilized life, and to remedy at the same time the evil which it has produced, ought to be considered as one of the first objects of reformed legislation.

Whether that state that is proudly, perhaps erroneously, called civilization, has most promoted or most injured the general happiness of man, is a question that may be strongly contested. On one side, the spectator is dazzled by splendid appearances; on the other, he is shocked by extremes of wretchedness; both of which it has erected. The most affluent and the most miserable of the human race are to be found in the countries that are called civilized.

To understand what the state of society ought to be, it is necessary to have some idea of the natural and primitive state of man; such as it is at this day among the Indians of North America. There is not, in that state, any of those spectacles of human misery which poverty and want present to our eyes in all the towns and streets of Europe.

Poverty, therefore, is a thing created by that which is called civilized life. It exists not in the natural state. On the other hand, the natural state is without those advantages which flow from agriculture, arts, science, and manufactures.

The life of an Indian is a continual holiday, compared with the poor of Europe; and, on the other hand, it appears to be abject when compared to the rich. Civilization, therefore, or that which is so called, has operated two ways: to make one part of society more affluent, and the other more wretched, than would have been the lot of either in a natural state.

It is always possible to go from the natural to the civilized state, but it is never possible to go from the civilized to the natural state. The reason is, that man in a natural state, subsisting by hunting, requires ten times the quantity of land to range over to procure himself sustenance, than would support him in a civilized state, where the earth is cultivated.

When, therefore, a country becomes populous by the additional aids of cultivation, art, and science, there is a necessity of preserving things in that state; because without it there cannot be sustenance for more, perhaps, than a tenth part of its inhabitants. The thing, therefore, now to be done is to remedy the evils and preserve the benefits that have arisen to society by passing from the natural to that which is called the civilized state.

In taking the matter upon this ground, the first principle of civilization ought to have been, and ought still to be, that the condition of every person born into the world, after a state of civilization commences, ought not to be worse than if he had been born before that period.

But the fact is, that the condition of millions, in every country in Europe, is far worse than if they had been born before civilization began, or had been born among the Indians of North America at the present day. I will show how this fact has happened.

It is a position not to be contraverted that the earth, in its natural, uncultivated state was, and ever would have continued to be, *the common property of the human race*. In that state every man would have been born to property. He would have been a joint life proprietor with the rest in the property of the soil, and in all its natural productions, vegetable and animal.

But the earth in its natural state, as before said, is capable of supporting but a small number of inhabitants compared with what it is capable of doing in a cultivated state. And as it is impossible to separate the improvement made by cultivation from the earth itself, upon which that improvement is made, the idea of landed property arose from that inseparable connection; but it is nevertheless true, that it is the value of the improvement, only, and not the earth itself, that is individual property.

Every proprietor, therefore, of cultivated lands, owes to the community a *ground-rent* (for I know of no better term to express the idea) for the land which he holds; and it is from this ground-rent that the fund proposed in this plan is to issue.

It is deducible, as well from the nature of the thing as from all the histories transmitted to us, that the idea of landed property commenced with cultivation, and that there was no such thing as landed property before that time. It could not exist in the first state of man, that of hunters. It did not exist in the second state, that of shepherds: neither Abraham, Isaac, Jacob, nor Job, so far as the history of the Bible may be credited in probable things, were owners of land.

Their property consisted, as is always enumerated, in flocks and herds, and they traveled with them from place to place. The frequent contentions at that time, about the use of a well in the dry country of Arabia, where those people lived, also show that there was no landed property. It was not admitted that land could be claimed as property.

There could be no such thing as landed property originally. Man did not make the earth, and, though he had a natural right to *occupy* it, he had no right to *locate as his property* in perpetuity any part of it; neither did the Creator of the earth open a land-office, from whence the first title-deeds should issue. Whence, then, arose the idea of landed property? I answer as before, that when cultivation began, the idea of landed property began with it, from the impossibility of separating the improvement made by cultivation from the earth itself, upon which that improvement was made.

The value of the improvement so far exceeded the value of the natural earth, at that time, as to absorb it; till, in the end, the common right of all became confounded into the cultivated right of the individual. But there are, nevertheless, distinct species of rights, and will continue to be, so long as the earth endures.

It is only by tracing things to their origin that we can gain rightful ideas of them, and it is by gaining such ideas that we discover the boundary that divides right from wrong, and teaches every man to know his own. I have entitled this tract "Agrarian Justice" to distinguish it from "Agrarian Law."

Nothing could be more unjust than agrarian law in a country improved by cultivation; for though every man, as an inhabitant of the earth, is a joint proprietor of it in its natural state, it does not follow that he is a joint proprietor of cultivated earth. The additional value made by cultivation, after the system was admitted, became the property of those who did it, or who inherited it from them, or who purchased it. It had originally no owner. While, therefore, I advocate the right, and interest myself in the hard case of all those who have been thrown out of their natural inheritance by the introduction of the system of landed property, I equally defend the right of the possessor to the part which is his.

Cultivation is at least one of the greatest natural improvements ever made by human invention. It has given to created earth a tenfold value. But the landed monopoly that began with it has produced the greatest evil. It has dispossessed more than half the inhabitants of every nation of their natural inheritance, without providing for them, as ought to have been done, an indemnification for that loss, and has thereby created a species of poverty and wretchedness that did not exist before.

In advocating the case of the persons thus dispossessed, it is a right, and not a charity, that I am pleading for. But it is that kind of right which, being neglected at first, could not be brought forward afterwards till heaven had opened the way by a revolution in the system of government. Let us then do honor to revolutions by justice, and give currency to their principles by blessings.

Having thus, in a few words, opened the merits of the case, I shall now proceed to the plan I have to propose, which is,

To create a national fund, out of which there shall be paid to every person, when arrived at the age of twenty-one years, the sum of fifteen pounds sterling, as a compensation in part, for the loss of his or her natural inheritance, by the introduction of the system of landed property:

And also, the sum of ten pounds per annum, during life, to every person now living, of the age of fifty years, and to all others as they shall arrive at that age.

MEANS BY WHICH THE FUND IS TO BE CREATED

I have already established the principle, namely, that the earth, in its natural uncultivated state was, and ever would have continued to be, the *common property of the human race;* that in that state, every person would have been born to property; and that the system of landed property, by its inseparable connection with cultivation, and with what is called civilized life, has absorbed the property of all those whom it dispossessed, without providing, as ought to have been done, an indemnification for that loss.

The fault, however, is not in the present possessors. No complaint is intended, or ought to be alleged against them, unless they adopt the crime by opposing justice. The fault is in the system, and it has stolen imperceptibly upon the world, aided afterwards by the agrarian law of the sword.

But the fault can be made to reform itself by successive generations; and without diminishing or deranging the property of any of the present possessors, the operation of the fund can yet commence, and be in full activity, the first year of its establishment, or soon after, as I shall show.

It is proposed that the payments, as already stated, be made to every person, rich or poor. It is best to make it so, to prevent invidious distinctions. It is also right it should be so, because it is in lieu of the natural inheritance, which, as a right, belongs to every man, over and above the property he may have created, or inherited from those who did. Such persons as do not choose to receive it can throw it into the common fund.

Taking it then for granted that no person ought to be in a worse condition when born under what is called a state of civilization, than he would have been had he been born in a state of nature, and that civilization ought to have made, and ought still to make, provision for that purpose, it can only be done by subtracting from property a portion equal in value to the natural inheritance it has absorbed.

Various methods may be proposed for this purpose, but that which appears to be the best (not only because it will operate without deranging any present possessors, or without interfering with the collection of taxes or *emprunts* necessary for the purposes of government and the Revolution, but because it will be the least troublesome and the most effectual, and also because the subtraction will be made at a time that best admits it) is at the moment that property is passing by the death of one person to the possession of another. In this case, the bequeather gives nothing: the receiver pays nothing. The only matter to him is, that the monopoly of natural inheritance, to which there never was a right, begins to cease in his person. A generous man would not wish it to continue, and a just man will rejoice to see it abolished.

My state of health prevents my making sufficient inquiries with respect to the doctrine of probabilities, whereon to found calculations with such degrees of certainty as they are capable of. What, therefore, I offer on this head is more the result of observation and reflection than of received information; but I believe it will be found to agree sufficiently with fact.

In the first place, taking twenty-one years as the epoch of maturity, all the property of a nation, real and personal, is always in the possession of persons above that age. It is then necessary to know, as a datum of calculation, the average of years which persons above that age will live. I take this average to be about thirty years, for though many persons will live forty, fifty, or sixty years after the age of twenty-one years, others will die much sooner, and some in every year of that time.

Taking, then, thirty years as the average of time, it will give, without any material variation one way or other, the average of time in which the whole property or capital of a nation, or a sum equal thereto, will have passed through one entire revolution in descent, that is, will have gone by deaths to new possessors; for though, in many instances, some parts of this capital will remain forty, fifty, or sixty years in the possession of one person, other parts will have revolved two or three times before those thirty years expire, which will bring it to that average; for were one-half the capital of a nation to revolve twice in thirty years, it would produce the same fund as if the whole revolved once.

Taking, then, thirty years as the average of time in which the whole capital of a nation, or a sum equal thereto, will revolve once, the thirtieth part thereof will be the sum that will revolve every year, that is, will go by deaths to new possessors; and this last sum being thus known, and the ratio per cent to be subtracted from it determined, it will give the annual amount or income of the proposed fund, to be applied as already mentioned.

In looking over the discourse of the English Minister, Pitt, in his opening of what is called in England the budget (the scheme of finance for the year 1796), I find an estimate of the national capital of that country. As this estimate of a national capital is prepared ready to my hand, I take it as a datum to act upon. When a calculation is made upon the known capital of any nation, combined with its population, it will serve as a scale for any other nation, in proportion as its capital and population be more or less.

I am the more disposed to take this estimate of Mr. Pitt, for the purpose of showing to that minister, upon his own calculation, how much better money may be employed than in wasting it, as he has done, on the wild project of setting up Bourbon kings.[1] What, in the name of heaven, are Bourbon kings to the people of England? It is better that the people have bread.

Mr. Pitt states the national capital of England, real and personal, to be one thousand three hundred millions sterling, which is about one-fourth part of the national capital of France, including Belgia. The event of the last harvest in each country proves that the soil of France is more productive than that of England, and that it can better support twenty-four or twenty-five millions of inhabitants than that of England can seven or seven and a half millions.

The thirtieth part of this capital of £1,300,000,000 is £43,333,333, which is the part that will revolve every year by deaths in that country to new possessors; and the sum that will annually revolve in France in the proportion of four to one, will be about one hundred and seventy-three millions sterling. From this sum of £43,333,333 annually revolving, is to be subtracted the value of the natural inheritance absorbed in it, which, perhaps, in fair justice, cannot be taken at less, and ought not to be taken for more, than a tenth part.

It will always happen, that of the property thus revolving by deaths every year a part will descend in a direct line to sons and daughters, and the other part col-

laterally, and the proportion will be found to be about three to one; that is, about thirty millions of the above sum will descend to direct heirs, and the remaining sum of £13,333,333 to more distant relations, and in part to strangers.

Considering, then, that man is always related to society, that relationship will become comparatively greater in proportion as the next of kin is more distant; it is therefore consistent with civilization to say that where there are no direct heirs society shall be heir to a part over and above the tenth part *due* to society.

If this additional part be from five to ten or twelve per cent, in proportion as the next of kin be nearer or more remote, so as to average with the escheats that may fall, which ought always to go to society and not to the government (an addition of ten per cent more), the produce from the annual sum of £43,333,333 will be:

From
£30,000,000 at ten per cent......£3,000,000
From
£13,333,333 at ten per cent with
      the addition of ten
      per cent more...... 2,666,666

£43,333,333   £5,666,666

Having thus arrived at the annual amount of the proposed fund, I come, in the next place, to speak of the population proportioned to this fund and to compare it with the uses to which the fund is to be applied.

The population (I mean that of England) does not exceed seven millions and a half, and the number of persons above the age of fifty will in that case be about four hundred thousand. There would not, how-

---

[1] The second William Pitt, 1759-1806, prime minister of Britain during her crucial struggle with revolutionary France, supported the unsuccessful attempt of the French Royalists to gain a foothold in France in the summer of 1795 and to set up as king Comte d'Artois, the Bourbon heir presumptive.

ever, be more than that number that would
accept the proposed ten pounds sterling
per annum, though they would be entitled
to it. I have no idea it would be accepted
by many persons who had a yearly income
of two or three hundred pounds sterling.
But as we often see instances of rich
people falling into sudden poverty, even
at the age of sixty, they would always
have the right of drawing all the arrears
due to them. Four millions, therefore, of
the above annual sum of £5,666,666 will
be required for four hundred thousand
aged persons, at ten pounds sterling each.

I come now to speak of the persons
annually arriving at twenty-one years of
age. If all the persons who died were above
the age of twenty-one years, the number of
persons annually arriving at that age,
must be equal to the annual number of
deaths, to keep the population stationary.
But the greater part die under the age of
twenty-one, and therefore the number of
persons annually arriving at twenty-one
will be less than half the number of deaths.

The whole number of deaths upon a
population of seven millions and an half
will be about 220,000 annually. The number
arriving at twenty-one years of age will be
about 100,000. The whole number of these
will not receive the proposed fifteen
pounds, for the reasons already mentioned,
though, as in the former case, they would
be entitled to it. Admitting then that a
tenth part declined receiving it, the amount
would stand thus:

Fund annually................ £5,666,666
To 400,000 aged persons at
    £10 each......£4,000,000
To 90,000 per-
    sons of 21 yrs.,
    £15 ster. each. 1,350,000
                            5,350,000
                            ─────────
Remains .... £ 316,666

There are, in every country, a number
of blind and lame persons, totally incapable of earning a livelihood. But as it will

always happen that the greater number
of blind persons will be among those who
are above the age of fifty years, they will
be provided for in that class. The remaining sum of £316,666 will provide for the
lame and blind under that age, at the same
rate of £10 annually for each person.

Having now gone through all the necessary calculations and stated the particulars
of the plan, I shall conclude with some
observations.

It is not charity but a right, not bounty
but justice, that I am pleading for. The
present state of civilization is as odious as
it is unjust. It is absolutely the opposite
of what it should be, and it is necessary
that a revolution should be made in it. The
contrast of affluence and wretchedness continually meeting and offending the eye, is
like dead and living bodies chained together. Though I care as little about riches
as any man, I am a friend to riches because
they are capable of good.

I care not how affluent some may be,
provided that none be miserable in consequence of it. But it is impossible to
enjoy affluence with the felicity it is capable of being enjoyed, while so much
misery is mingled in the scene. The sight
of the misery, and the unpleasant sensations it suggests, which, though they may
be suffocated, cannot be extinguished, are
a greater drawback upon the felicity of
affluence than the proposed ten per cent
upon property is worth. He that would
not give the one to get rid of the other
has no charity, even for himself.

There are, in every country, some magnificent charities established by individuals.
It is, however, but little that any individual
can do, when the whole extent of the
misery to be relieved is considered. He may
satisfy his conscience, but not his heart. He
may give all that he has, and that all
will relieve but little. It is only by organizing civilization upon such principles
as to act like a system of pulleys, that the
whole weight of misery can be removed.

The plan here proposed will reach the
whole. It will immediately relieve and take

out of view three classes of wretchedness —the blind, the lame, and the aged poor; and it will furnish the rising generation with means to prevent their becoming poor; and it will do this without deranging or interfering with any national measures.

To show that this will be the case, it is sufficient to observe that the operation and effect of the plan will, in all cases, be the same as if every individual were *voluntarily* to make his will and dispose of his property in the manner here proposed.

But it is justice, and not charity, that is the principle of the plan. In all great cases it is necessary to have a principle more universally active than charity; and, with respect to justice, it ought not to be left to the choice of detached individuals whether they will do justice or not. Considering, then, the plan on the ground of justice, it ought to be the act of the whole, growing spontaneously out of the principles of the revolution, and the reputation of it ought to be national and not individual.

A plan upon this principle would benefit the revolution by the energy that springs from the consciousness of justice. It would multiply also the national resources; for property, like vegetation, increases by offsets. When a young couple begin the world, the difference is exceedingly great whether they begin with nothing or with fifteen pounds apiece. With this aid they could buy a cow, and implements to cultivate a few acres of land; and instead of becoming burdens upon society, which is always the case where children are produced faster than they can be fed, would be put in the way of becoming useful and profitable citizens. The national domains also would sell the better if pecuniary aids were provided to cultivate them in small lots.

It is the practice of what has unjustly obtained the name of civilization (and the practice merits not to be called either charity or policy) to make some provision for persons becoming poor and wretched only at the time they become so. Would it not, even as a matter of economy, be far better to adopt means to prevent their becoming poor? This can best be done by making every person when arrived at the age of twenty-one years an inheritor of something to begin with.

The rugged face of society, checkered with the extremes of affluence and want, proves that some extraordinary violence has been committed upon it, and calls on justice for redress. The great mass of the poor in all countries are become an hereditary race, and it is next to impossible for them to get out of that state of themselves. It ought also to be observed that this mass increases in all countries that are called civilized. More persons fall annually into it than get out of it.

Though in a plan of which justice and humanity are the foundation-principles, interest ought not to be admitted into the calculation, yet it is always of advantage to the establishment of any plan to show that it is beneficial as a matter of interest. The success of any proposed plan submitted to public consideration must finally depend on the numbers interested in supporting it, united with the justice of its principles.

The plan here proposed will benefit all, without injuring any. It will consolidate the interest of the republic with that of the individual. To the numerous class dispossessed of their natural inheritance by the system of landed property it will be an act of national justice. To persons dying possessed of moderate fortunes it will operate as a tontine to their children, more beneficial than the sum of money paid into the fund: and it will give to the accumulation of riches a degree of security that none of the old governments of Europe, now tottering on their foundations, can give.

I do not suppose that more than one family in ten, in any of the countries of Europe, has, when the head of the family dies, a clear property left of five hundred pounds sterling. To all such the plan is advantageous. That property would pay fifty pounds into the fund, and if there were only two children under age they would receive fifteen pounds each (thirty pounds), on coming of age, and be entitled to ten pounds a year after fifty.

It is from the overgrown acquisition of property that the fund will support itself; and I know that the possessors of such property in England, though they would eventually be benefited by the protection of nine-tenths of it, will exclaim against the plan. But without entering into any inquiry how they came by that property, let them recollect that they have been the advocates of this war, and that Mr. Pitt has already laid on more new taxes to be raised annually upon the people of England, and that for supporting the despotism of Austria and the Bourbons against the liberties of France, than would pay annually all the sums proposed in this plan.

I have made the calculations stated in this plan, upon what is called personal, as well as upon landed property. The reason for making it upon land is already explained; and the reason for taking personal property into the calculation is equally well founded though on a different principle. Land, as before said, is the free gift of the Creator in common to the human race. Personal property is the *effect of society;* and it is as impossible for an individual to acquire personal property without the aid of society, as it is for him to make land originally.

Separate an individual from society, and give him an island or a continent to possess, and he cannot acquire personal property. He cannot be rich. So inseparably are the means connected with the end, in all cases, that where the former do not exist the latter cannot be obtained. All accumulation, therefore, of personal property, beyond what a man's own hands produce, is derived to him by living in society; and he owes on every principle of justice, of gratitude, and of civilization, a part of that accumulation back again to society from whence the whole came.

This is putting the matter on a general principle, and perhaps it is best to do so; for if we examine the case minutely it will

be found that the accumulation of personal property is, in many instances, the effect of paying too little for the labor that produced it; the consequence of which is, that the working hand perishes in old age, and the employer abounds in affluence.

It is, perhaps, impossible to proportion exactly the price of labor to the profits it produces; and it will also be said, as an apology for the injustice, that were a workman to receive an increase of wages daily he would not save it against old age, nor be much better for it in the interim. Make, then, society the treasurer to guard it for him in a common fund; for it is no reason, that because he might not make a good use of it for himself, another should take it.

The state of civilization that has prevailed throughout Europe, is as unjust in its principle, as it is horrid in its effects; and it is the consciousness of this, and the apprehension that such a state cannot continue when once investigation begins in any country, that makes the possessors of property dread every idea of a revolution. It is the hazard and not the principle of revolutions that retards their progress. This being the case, it is necessary as well for the protection of property, as for the sake of justice and humanity, to form a system that, while it preserves one part of society from wretchedness, shall secure the other from depredation.

The superstitious awe, the enslaving reverence, that formerly surrounded affluence, is passing away in all countries, and leaving the possessor of property to the convulsion of accidents. When wealth and splendor, instead of fascinating the multitude, excite emotions of disgust; when, instead of drawing forth admiration, it is beheld as an insult upon wretchedness; when the ostentatious appearance it makes serves to call the right of it in question, the case of property becomes critical, and it is only in a system of justice that the possessor can contemplate security.

To remove the danger, it is necessary to remove the antipathies, and this can only be done by making property productive of a national blessing, extending to every individual. When the riches of one man above another shall increase the national fund in the same proportion; when it shall be seen that the prosperity of that fund depends on the prosperity of individuals; when the more riches a man acquires, the better it shall be for the general mass; it is then that antipathies will cease, and property be placed on the permanent basis of national interest and protection.

I have no property in France to become subject to the plan I propose. What I have, which is not much, is in the United States of America. But I will pay one hundred pounds sterling toward this fund in France, the instant it shall be established; and I will pay the same sum in England, whenever a similar establishment shall take place in that country.

A revolution in the state of civilization is the necessary companion of revolutions in the system of government. If a revolution in any country be from bad to good, or from good to bad, the state of what is called civilization in that country, must be made conformable thereto, to give that revolution effect.

Despotic government supports itself by abject civilization, in which debasement of the human mind, and wretchedness in the mass of the people, are the chief criterions.

Such governments consider man merely as an animal; that the exercise of intellectual faculty is not his privilege; *that he has nothing to do with the laws but to obey them;* and they politically depend more upon breaking the spirit of the people by poverty, than they fear enraging it by desperation.

It is a revolution in the state of civilization that will give perfection to the Revolution of France. Already the conviction that government by representation is the true system of government is spreading itself fast in the world. The reasonableness of it can be seen by all. The justice of it makes itself felt even by its opposers. But when a system of civilization, growing out of that system of government, shall be so organized that not a man or woman born in the Republic but shall inherit some means of beginning the world, and see before them the certainty of escaping the miseries that under other governments accompany old age, the Revolution of France will have an advocate and an ally in the heart of all nations.

An army of principles will penetrate where an army of soldiers cannot; it will succeed where diplomatic management would fail: it is neither the Rhine, the Channel, nor the ocean that can arrest its progress: it will march on the horizon of the world, and it will conquer.

1743 ∾ *Thomas Jefferson* ∾ 1826

THE EPITAPH on the shaft above Jefferson's grave at Monticello, Virginia—"Here was buried Thomas Jefferson, author of the Declaration of Independence, of the statute of Virginia for religious freedom, and father of the University of Virginia"—was his own composition and thus may be said to sum up the three achievements of which he was most proud.

Born at Shadwell, Albemarle County, Virginia, April 13, 1743, he came, on his father's side, from prosperous yeomanry, and, on his mother's side, from one of the first families of Virginia—the Randolphs. Graduated from William and Mary College in 1762, he successfully practiced law and was elected in

1769 to the House of Burgesses. He married Martha Wayles Skelton in 1772. Through this marriage and through his own inheritance, he was owner of about 10,000 acres of land and over 100 slaves. From an early age he showed an amazing versatility. He became a linguist, a student of history and literature, a collector of books and art objects, an inventor, and an amateur architect. He was president of the American Philosophical Society from 1797 to 1815 and belonged to several European scientific societies. A delegate to the Continental Congress in 1775, he was appointed on the committee charged with drafting the Declaration of Independence and composed this document. He became a member of the Virginia Assembly in 1776, served one term as Governor of Virginia, and resigned this office shortly after being elected to a second term in 1780. He was a member of Congress, minister to France 1785-1789, first Secretary of State of the United States 1790-1793, and Vice-president 1797-1801.

As leader of the so-called "Republican" party, he was the foe of Hamilton and the Federalists, who regarded him as a dangerous democratic radical under French revolutionary influence. He was elected to the Presidency in the bitter campaign of 1800 and was re-elected in 1804. In 1803 he negotiated the Louisiana Purchase. Retiring to Monticello in 1809, he brought about the establishment of the University of Virginia, which was chartered in 1819. He died at Monticello July 4, 1826.

Although Jefferson was the author of but one complete book, *Notes on Virginia*, 1781-82, he was one of the most influential of early American publicists and political thinkers, greatly in advance of his day in his attitudes toward a host of problems, from Negro slavery to education. Many of his ideas received their best formulation in letters.

[The second and fourth of the following selections are from letters, respectively, to James Madison, January 30, 1787, and Gideon Granger, August 13, 1800. The third selection is from a series of memoranda which he left at his death and which were first published under the title "Anas" in Vol. IV of T. J. Randolph's *Memoirs*, 1829. The editors have provided two of these selections with titles.]

DECLARATION OF INDEPENDENCE
[1776]

A DECLARATION by the Representatives of the United States of America in General Congress assembled.

When in the course of human events it becomes necessary for one people to dissolve the political bands which have connected them with another and to assume among the powers of the earth the separate and equal station to which the laws of nature and of nature's God entitle them, a decent respect to the opinions of mankind requires that they should declare the causes which impel them to the separation.

We hold these truths to be self-evident: that all men are created equal; that they are endowed by their Creator with inherent and inalienable rights; that among these are life, liberty, and the pursuit of happiness; that to secure these rights governments are instituted among men, deriving their just powers from the consent of the governed; that whenever any form of government becomes destructive of these ends, it is the right of the people to alter or to abolish it, and to institute new government, laying its foundation on such principles and organizing its powers in such form as to them shall seem most likely to effect their happiness. Prudence indeed will dictate that governments long established should not be changed for light and transient causes; and accordingly all experience hath shown that mankind are more disposed to suffer while evils are sufferable than to right themselves by abolishing the forms to which they are accustomed. But when a long train of abuses and usurpations, begun at a distinguished period and pursuing invariably the same object, evinces a design to reduce them under absolute despotism, it is their right, it is their duty, to throw off such government and to provide new guards for their future security. Such has been the patient sufferance of these colonies, and such is now the necessity which constrains them to expunge their former systems of government. The history of the present King of Great Britain is a history of unremitting injuries and usurpations, among which appears no solitary fact to contradict the uniform tenor of the rest; but all having in direct object the establishment of an absolute tyranny over these states. To prove this let facts be submitted to a candid world, for the truth of which we pledge a faith yet unsullied by falsehood.

He has refused his assent to laws the most wholesome and necessary for the public good.

He has forbidden his governors to pass laws of immediate and pressing importance, unless suspended in their operation till his assent should be obtained, and when so suspended, he has utterly neglected to attend to them.

He has refused to pass other laws for the accommodation of large districts of people unless those people would relinquish the right of representation in the legislature, a right inestimable to them, and formidable to tyrants only.

He has called together legislative bodies at places unusual, uncomfortable, and distant from the depository of the public records, for the sole purpose of fatiguing them into compliance with his measures.

He has dissolved representative houses repeatedly and continually for opposing with manly firmness his invasions on the right of the people.

He has refused for a long time after such dissolutions to cause others to be elected whereby the legislative powers incapable of annihilation have returned to the people at large for their exercise, the state remaining in the meantime exposed to all the dangers of invasion from without and convulsions within.

He has endeavored to prevent the population of these states, for that purpose obstructing the laws for naturalization of foreigners, refusing to pass others to encourage their migrations hither, and raising the conditions of new appropriations of lands.

He has suffered the administration of justice totally to cease in some of these states, refusing his assent to laws for establishing judiciary powers.

He has made judges dependent on his will alone, for the tenure of their offices and the amount and payment of their salaries.

He has erected a multitude of new offices by a self-assumed power and sent hither swarms of officers to harass our people and eat out their substance.

He has kept among us, in times of peace, standing armies and ships of war without the consent of our legislatures.

He has affected to render the military independent of and superior to the civil power.

He has combined with others to subject us to a jurisdiction foreign to our constitutions and unacknowledged by our laws, giving his assent to their acts of pretended legislation, for quartering large bodies of armed troops among us; for protecting them by a mock trial from punishment for any murders which they should commit on the inhabitants of these states; for cutting off our trade with all parts of the world; for imposing taxes on us without our consent; for depriving us in many cases of the benefits of trial by jury; for transporting us beyond seas to be tried for pretended offenses; for abolishing the free system of English laws in a neighboring province, establishing therein an arbitrary government and enlarging its boundaries so as to render it at once an example and fit instrument for introducing the same absolute rule into these colonies; for taking away our charters, abolishing our most valuable laws, and fundamentally the forms of our governments; for suspending our own legislatures and declaring themselves invested with power to legislate for us in all cases whatsoever.

He has abdicated government here, withdrawing his governors, and declaring us out of his allegiance and protection.

He has plundered our seas, ravaged our coasts, burnt our towns, and destroyed the lives of our people.

He is at this time transporting large armies of foreign mercenaries to complete the works of death, desolation, and tyranny already begun, with circumstances of cruelty and perfidy unworthy the head of a civilized nation.

He has endeavored to bring on the inhabitants of our frontiers the merciless Indian savages, whose known rule of warfare is an undistinguished destruction of all ages, sexes, and conditions of existence.

He has incited treasonable insurrections of our fellow citizens, with the allurements of forfeiture and confiscation of our property.

He has constrained others, taken captive on the high seas, to bear arms against their country, to become the executioners of their friends and brethren, or to fall themselves by their hands.

He has waged cruel war against human nature itself, violating its most sacred rights of life and liberty in the persons of distant people, who never offended him, captivating and carrying them into slavery in another hemisphere, or to incur miserable death in their transportation thither. This piratical warfare, the opprobrium of infidel powers, is the warfare of the Christian King of Great Britain. Determined to keep open a market where men should be bought and sold, he has prostituted his negative for suppressing every legislative attempt to prohibit or to restrain this execrable commerce; and that this assemblage of horrors might want no fact of distinguished dye, he is now exciting those very people to rise in arms among us, and to purchase that liberty of which he has deprived them by murdering the people upon whom he also obtruded them; thus paying off former crimes committed against the liberties of one people with crimes which he urged them to commit against the lives of another.

In every stage of these oppressions we have petitioned for redress in the most humble terms; our repeated petitions have been answered only by repeated injuries. A prince whose character is thus marked by every act which may define a tyrant is unfit to be the ruler of a people who mean to be free. Future ages will scarce believe that the hardiness of one man adventures, within the short compass of twelve years only, to build a foundation so broad and undisguised for tyranny over a people fostered and fixed in principles of freedom.

Nor have we been wanting in attentions to our British brethren. We have warned them from time to time of attempts by their legislature to extend an unwarrantable jurisdiction over these our states. We have reminded them of the circumstances of our emigration and settlement here, no one of which could warrant so strange a pretension: that these were effected at the expense of our own blood and treasure, unassisted by the wealth or strength of Great Britain; that in constituting indeed our several forms of government, we had adopted a common king, thereby laying a foundation for perpetual league and amity with them; but that submission to their Parliament was no part of our constitution nor ever in idea, if history be credited; and we have appealed to their native justice and magnanimity, as well as to the ties of our common kindred, to disavow these usurpations which were likely to interrupt our connection and correspondence. They too have been deaf to the voice of justice and of consanguinity, and when occasions have been given them, by the regular course of their laws, of removing from their councils the disturbers of our harmony, they have by their free elections re-established them in power. At this very time they are permitting their chief magistrate to send over not only soldiers of our own blood, but Scotch and other foreign mercenaries, to invade and destroy us. These facts have given the last stab to agonizing affections, and manly spirit bids us to renounce forever these unfeeling brethren. We must endeavor to forget our former love for them, to hold them as we hold the rest of mankind enemies in war, in peace friends.

We might have been a free and a great people together; but a communication of grandeur and freedom, it seems, is below their dignity. Be it so, since they will have it: the road to happiness and to glory is open to us too; we will climb it apart from them, and acquiesce in the necessity which denounces our eternal separation!

We therefore, the representatives of the United States in General Congress assembled in the name and by authority of the good people of these states, reject and renounce all allegiance and subjection to the kings of Great Britain and all others who may hereafter claim by, through, or under them; we utterly dissolve all political connection which may heretofore have subsisted between us and the people or Parliament of Great Britain; and finally we do assert and declare these colonies to be free and independent, and that as free and independent states they have full power to levy war, conclude peace, contract

alliances, establish commerce, and to do all other acts and things which independent states may of right do. And for the support of this declaration we mutually pledge to each other our lives, our fortunes, and our sacred honor.

DEMOCRACY AND INSURGENCY

[1829 (written 1787)]

. . . I AM impatient to learn your sentiments on the late troubles in the Eastern States.[1] So far as I have yet seen, they do not appear to threaten serious consequences. Those States have suffered by the stoppage of the channels of their commerce, which have not yet found other issues. This must render money scarce, and make the people uneasy. This uneasiness has produced acts absolutely unjustifiable; but I hope they will provoke no severities from their governments. A consciousness of those in power that their administration of the public affairs has been honest, may, perhaps, produce too great a degree of indignation; and those characters, wherein fear predominates over hope, may apprehend too much from these instances of irregularity. They may conclude too hastily that nature has formed man insusceptible of any other government but that of force, a conclusion not founded in truth nor experience. Societies exist under three forms, sufficiently distinguishable. 1. Without government, as among our Indians. 2. Under governments, wherein the will of every one has a just influence; as is the case in England, in a slight degree, and in our States, in a great one. 3. Under governments of force; as is the case in all other monarchies, and in most of the other republics. To have an idea of the curse of existence under these last, they must be seen. It is a government of wolves over sheep. It is a problem, not clear in

[1] The reference is to Shays' Rebellion against the Massachusetts state government in 1786-7.

my mind, that the first condition is not the best. But I believe it to be inconsistent with any great degree of population. The second state has a great deal of good in it. The mass of mankind under that enjoys a precious degree of liberty and happiness. It has its evils, too; the principal of which is the turbulence to which it is subject. But weigh this against the oppressions of monarchy, and it becomes nothing. *Malo periculosam libertatem quam quietam servitutem.*[2] Even this evil is productive of good. It prevents the degeneracy of government, and nourishes a general attention to the public affairs. I hold it that a little rebellion, now and then, is a good thing, and as necessary in the political world as storms in the physical. Unsuccessful rebellions, indeed, generally establish the encroachments on the rights of the people, which have produced them. An observation of this truth should render honest republican governors so mild in their punishment of rebellions, as not to discourage them too much. It is a medicine necessary for the sound health of government. . . .

DEMOCRACY AND LEADERSHIP
[1829 (written 1818)]

. . . THE ALLIANCE between the States under the old Articles of Confederation, for the purpose of joint defence against the aggression of Great Britain, was found insufficient, as treaties of alliance generally are, to enforce compliance with their mutual stipulations; and these, once fulfilled, that bond was to expire of itself, and each State to become sovereign and independent in all things. Yet it could not but occur to every one that these separate independencies, like the petty states of Greece, would be eternally at war with each other, and would become at length the mere partisans and satellites of the leading powers of Europe. All then must have looked forward to some further bond of union, which would insure eternal peace, and a political system of our own, independent of that of Europe. Whether all should be

consolidated into a single government, or each remain independent as to internal matters, and the whole form a single nation as to what was foreign only, and whether that national government should be a monarchy or republic, would of course divide opinions, according to the constitutions, the habits, and the circumstances of each individual. Some officers of the army, as it has always been said and believed (and Steuben and Knox have been named as the leading agents),[3] trained to monarchy by military habits, are understood to have proposed to General Washington to decide this great question by the army before its disbandment, and to assume himself the crown on the assurance of their support. The indignation with which he is said to have scouted this parricide proposition was equally worthy of his virtue and wisdom.

The next effort was (on suggestion of the same individuals, in the moment of their separation) the establishment of an hereditary order, under the name of the Cincinnati, ready prepared by that distinction to be ingrafted into the future frame of government, and placing General Washington still at their head. The General wrote to me on this subject, while I was in Congress at Annapolis, and an extract from my letter is inserted in 5th Marshall's history, page 28.[4] He afterwards called on me at that place, on his way to a meeting of the society, and after a whole evening of consultation, he left that place fully determined to use all his endeavors for its total suppression. But he found it so

---

[2] Better hazardous liberty than peaceful servitude.

[3] Frederick William, Baron von Steuben, 1730-1794, was a Prussian-American general; Henry Knox, 1750-1806, was a major general and served as secretary of war 1785-1795.

[4] Jefferson refers to John Marshall's *The Life of George Washington . . . to which is prefixed an Introduction containing a Compendious View of the Colonies Planted by the English in the Continent of North America*, which appeared in five volumes between 1804 and 1807.

firmly riveted in the affections of the members that, strengthened as they happened to be by an adventitious occurrence of the moment, he could effect no more than the abolition of its hereditary principle. He called again on his return, and explained to me fully the opposition which had been made, the effect of the occurrence from France, and the difficulty with which its duration had been limited to the lives of the present members. Further details will be found among my papers, in his and my letters, and some in the *Encyclopédie Méthodique et Dictionnaire d'Economie Politique,* communicated by myself to M. Meunier, its author, who had made the establishment of this society the ground, in that work, of a libel on our country.

The want of some authority which should procure justice to the public creditors, and an observance of treaties with foreign nations, produced, some time after, the call of a convention of the States at Annapolis. Although, at this meeting, a difference of opinion was evident on the question of a republican or kingly government, yet, so general through the States was the sentiment in favor of the former, that the friends of the latter confined themselves to a course of obstruction only, and delay, to everything proposed; they hoped that nothing being done, and all things going from bad to worse, a kingly government might be usurped, and submitted to by the people, as better than anarchy and wars internal and external, the certain consequences of the present want of a general government. The effect of their manoeuvres, with the defective attendance of deputies from the States, resulted in the measure of calling a more general convention, to be held at Philadelphia. At this, the same party exhibited the same practices, and with the same views of preventing a government of concord, which they foresaw would be republican, and of forcing through anarchy their way to monarchy. But the mass of that convention was too honest, too wise, and too steady, to be baffled and misled by their manoeuvres.

One of these was a form of government proposed by Colonel Hamilton, which would have been in fact a compromise between the two parties of royalism and republicanism. According to this, the executive and one branch of the legislature were to be during good behavior, *i.e.* for life, and the governors of the States were to be named by these two permanent organs. This, however, was rejected; on which Hamilton left the Convention, as desperate, and never returned again until near its final conclusion. These opinions and efforts, secret or avowed, of the advocates for monarchy, had begotten great jealousy through the States generally; and this jealousy it was which excited the strong opposition to the conventional constitution; a jealousy which yielded at last only to a general determination to establish certain amendments as barriers against a government either monarchical or consolidated. In what passed through the whole period of these conventions, I have gone on the information of those who were members of them, being absent myself on my mission to France.

I returned from that mission in the first year of the new government, having landed in Virginia in December, 1789, and proceeded to New York in March, 1790, to enter on the office of Secretary of State. Here, certainly, I found a state of things which, of all I had ever contemplated, I the least expected. I had left France in the first year of its revolution, in the fervor of natural rights, and zeal for reformation. My conscientious devotion to these rights could not be heightened, but it had been aroused and excited by daily exercise. The President received me cordially, and my colleagues and the circle of principal citizens apparently with welcome. The courtesies of dinner parties given me, as a stranger newly arrived among them, placed me at once in their familiar society. But I cannot describe the wonder and mortification with which the table conversations filled me. Politics were the chief topic, and a preference of kingly over republican government was evidently the favorite sentiment. An apostate I could not be, nor yet a hypocrite; and I found myself, for the most part, the only advocate on the republican side of the question, unless among the guests there chanced to be some member of that party from the legislative Houses. Hamilton's financial system had then passed. It had two objects: 1st, as a puzzle, to exclude popular understanding and inquiry; 2nd, as a machine for the corruption of the legislature; for he avowed the opinion that man could be governed by one of two motives only, force or interest; force, he observed, in this country was out of the question; and the interests, therefore, of the members must be laid hold of, to keep the legislative in unison with the executive. And with grief and shame it must be acknowledged that his machine was not without effect; that even in this, the birth of our government, some members were found sordid enough to bend their duty to their interests, and to look after personal rather than public good....

FROM A LETTER TO
GIDEON GRANGER
[1829]

Monticello, August 13, 1800.

DEAR SIR—I received with great pleasure your favor of June 4th, and am much comforted by the appearance of a change of opinion in your State; for though we may obtain, and I believe shall obtain, a majority in the Legislature of the United States, attached to the preservation of the federal Constitution according to its obvious principles, and those on which it was known to be received; attached equally to the preservation to the States of those rights unquestionably remaining with them; friends to the freedom of religion, freedom of the press, trial by jury and to economical government; opposed to standing armies, paper systems, war, and all connection, other than commerce, with any foreign

nation; in short, a majority firm in all those principles which we have espoused and the federalists have opposed uniformly; still, should the whole body of New England continue in opposition to these principles of government, either knowingly or through delusion, our government will be a very uneasy one. It can never be harmonious and solid, while so respectable a portion of its citizens support principles which go directly to a change of the federal Constitution, to sink the State governments, consolidate them into one, and to monarchize that. Our country is too large to have all its affairs directed by a single government. Public servants at such a distance, and from under the eye of their constituents, must, from the circumstance of distance, be unable to administer and overlook all the details necessary for the good government of the citizens, and the same circumstance, by rendering detection impossible to their constituents, will invite the public agents to corruption, plunder, and waste. And I do verily believe that if the principle were to prevail of a common law being in force in the United States (which principle possesses the General Government at once of all the powers of the State governments, and reduces us to a single consolidated government), it would become the most corrupt government on the earth. You have seen the practises by which the public servants have been able to cover their conduct, or, where that could not be done, delusions by which they have varnished it for the eye of their constituents. What an augmentation of the field for jobbing, speculating, plundering, office-building and office-hunting would be produced by an assumption of all the State powers into the hands of the General Government! The true theory of our Constitution is surely the wisest and best, that the States are independent as to everything within themselves, and united as to everything respecting foreign nations. Let the General Government be reduced to foreign concerns only, and let our affairs be disentangled from those of all other nations, except as to commerce, which the merchants will manage the better, the more they are left free to manage for themselves, and our General Government may be reduced to a very simple organization, and a very unexpensive one; a few plain duties to be performed by a few servants. But I repeat, that this simple and economical mode of government can never be secured, if the New England States continue to support the contrary system. I rejoice, therefore, in every appearance of their returning to those principles which I had always imagined to be almost innate in them. . . .

INAUGURATION ADDRESS
[1801]

FRIENDS and Fellow Citizens: Called upon to undertake the duties of the first executive office of our country, I avail myself of the presence of that portion of my fellow citizens which is here assembled, to express my grateful thanks for the favor with which they have been pleased to look towards me, to declare a sincere consciousness that the task is above my talents, and that I approach it with those anxious and awful presentiments which the greatness of the charge and the weakness of my powers so justly inspire. A rising nation, spread over a wide and fruitful land, traversing all the seas with the rich productions of their industry, engaged in commerce with nations who feel power and forget right, advancing rapidly to destinies beyond the reach of mortal eye—when I contemplate these transcendent objects, and see the honor, the happiness, and the hopes of this beloved country committed to the issue and the auspices of this day, I shrink from the contemplation, and humble myself before the magnitude of the undertaking. Utterly indeed should I despair, did not the presence of many whom I here see remind me, that in the other high authorities provided by our Constitution, I shall find resources of wisdom, of virtue, and of zeal, on which to rely under all diffi-

culties. To you, then, gentlemen, who are charged with the sovereign functions of legislation, and to those associated with you, I look with encouragement for that guidance and support which may enable us to steer with safety the vessel in which we are all embarked amidst the conflicting elements of a troubled world.

During the contest of opinion through which we have passed, the animation of discussions and of exertions has sometimes worn an aspect which might impose on strangers unused to think freely and to speak and to write what they think; but this being now decided by the voice of the nation, enounced according to the rules of the Constitution, all will, of course, arrange themselves under the will of the law, and unite in common efforts for the common good. All, too, will bear in mind this sacred principle, that though the will of the majority is in all cases to prevail, that will, to be rightful, must be reasonable; that the minority possess their equal rights, which equal laws must protect, and to violate would be oppression. Let us, then, fellow citizens, unite with one heart and one mind. Let us restore to social intercourse that harmony and affection without which liberty and even life itself are but dreary things. And let us reflect that having banished from our land that religious intolerance under which mankind so long bled and suffered, we have yet gained little if we countenance a political intolerance as despotic, as wicked, and capable of as bitter and bloody persecutions. During the throes and convulsions of the ancient world, during the agonizing spasms of infuriated man, seeking through blood and slaughter his long-lost liberty, it was not wonderful that the agitation of the billows should reach even this distant and peaceful shore, that this should be more felt and feared by some and less by others; that this should divide opinions as to measures of safety. But every difference of opinion is not a difference of principle. We have called by different names brethren of the same principle. We are all republicans; we are all federalists. If there be any among us who would wish to dissolve this Union or to change its republican form, let them stand undisturbed as monuments of the safety with which error or opinion may be tolerated where reason is left free to combat it. I know, indeed, that some honest men fear that a republican government cannot be strong; that this government is not strong enough. But would the honest patriot, in the full tide of successful experiment, abandon a government which has so far kept us free and firm, on the theoretic and visionary fear that this government, the world's best hope, may by possibility want energy to preserve itself? I trust not. I believe this, on the contrary, the strongest government on earth. I believe it the only one where every man, at the call of the law, would fly to the standard of the law, and would meet invasions of the public order as his own personal concern. Sometimes it is said that man cannot be trusted with the government of himself. Can he, then, be trusted with the government of others? Or have we found angels in the form of kings to govern him? Let history answer this question.

Let us, then, with courage and confidence pursue our own federal and republican principles, our attachment to our union and representative government. Kindly separated by nature and a wide ocean from the exterminating havoc of one quarter of the globe; too high-minded to endure the degradations of the others; possessing a chosen country, with room enough for our descendants to the hundredth and thousandth generation; entertaining a due sense of our equal right to the use of our own faculties, to the acquisitions of our own industry, to honor and confidence from our fellow citizens, resulting not from birth but from our actions and their sense of them; enlightened by a benign religion, professed, indeed, and practiced in various forms, yet all of them inculcating honesty, truth, temperance, gratitude, and the love of man; acknowledging and adoring an overruling Providence, which by all its

dispensations proves that it delights in the happiness of man here and his greater happiness hereafter; with all these blessings, what more is necessary to make us a happy and a prosperous people? Still one thing more, fellow citizens—a wise and frugal government, which shall restrain men from injuring one another, shall leave them otherwise free to regulate their own pursuits of industry and improvement, and shall not take from the mouth of labor the bread it has earned. This is the sum of good government, and this is necessary to close the circle of our felicities.

About to enter, fellow citizens, on the exercise of duties which comprehend everything dear and valuable to you, it is proper you should understand what I deem the essential principles of our government, and consequently those which ought to shape its administration. I will compress them within the narrowest compass they will bear, stating the general principle, but not all its limitations. Equal and exact justice to all men, of whatever state or persuasion, religious or political; peace, commerce, and honest friendship, with all nations; entangling alliances with none; the support of the state governments in all their rights, as the most competent administrations for our domestic concerns and the surest bulwarks against anti-republican tendencies; the preservation of the General Government in its whole constitutional vigor, as the sheet anchor of our peace at home and safety abroad; a jealous care of the right of election by the people—a mild and safe corrective of abuses which are lopped by the sword of revolution where peaceable remedies are unprovided; absolute acquiescence in the decisions of the majority— the vital principle of republics, from which is no appeal but to force, the vital principle and immediate parent of despotism; a well-disciplined militia—our best reliance in peace and for the first moments of war, till regulars may relieve them; the supremacy of the civil over the military authority; economy in the public expense, that labor may be lightly burdened; the honest payment of our debts and sacred preservation of the public faith; encouragement of agriculture, and of commerce as its handmaid; the diffusion of information and arraignment of all abuses at the bar of public reason; freedom of religion; freedom of the press; and freedom of person under the protection of the *habeas corpus;* and trial by juries impartially selected—these principles form the bright constellation which has gone before us, and guided our steps through an age of revolution and reformation. The wisdom of our sages and blood of our heroes have been devoted to their attainment. They should be the creed of our political faith, the text of civil instruction, the touchstone by which to try the services of those we trust; and should we wander from them in moments of error or alarm, let us hasten to retrace our steps and to regain the road which alone leads to peace, liberty, and safety.

I repair, then, fellow citizens, to the post you have assigned me. With experience enough in subordinate offices to have seen the difficulties of this, the greatest of all, I have learned to expect that it will rarely fall to the lot of imperfect man to retire from this station with the reputation and the favor which bring him into it. Without pretensions to that high confidence you reposed in our first and great revolutionary character, whose preëminent services had entitled him to the first place in his country's love, and destined for him the fairest page in the volume of faithful history, I ask so much confidence only as may give firmness and effect to the legal administration of your affairs. I shall often go wrong through defect of judgment. When right, I shall often be thought wrong by those whose positions will not command a view of the whole ground. I ask your indulgence for my own errors, which will never be intentional; and your support against the errors of others who may condemn what they would not if seen in all its parts. The approbation implied by your suffrage is a great consolation to me for the past; and my future solicitude will be to retain the good opinion of those who have bestowed it in advance, to conciliate that of others by doing them all the good in my power, and to be instrumental to the happiness and freedom of all.

Relying, then, on the patronage of your good will, I advance with obedience to the work, ready to retire from it whenever you become sensible how much better choice it is in your power to make. And may that Infinite Power which rules the destinies of the universe lead our councils to what is best, and give them a favorable issue for your peace and prosperity.

1752 ∾ *Philip Freneau* ∾ 1832

THESE SELECTIONS represent different phases of Freneau as a political poet. In "A Political Litany," he is a fiery propagandist of the American Revolution. His devotion to the "radicalism" of Paine and Jefferson in the 1790's is shown in the other pieces.

[The selections are taken, respectively, from the editions of 1809, 1795, and 1815. Other selections from Freneau will be found in Book I, Parts 1 and 2.]

A POLITICAL LITANY
[1786(1775)]

Libera Nos, Domine.—Deliver Us, O Lord,
not only from British Dependence,
but also,

From a junto that labour with absolute
power,
Whose schemes disappointed have made
them look sour,
From the lords of the council, who fight
against freedom,
Who still follow on where delusion shall
lead them.

From the group at St. James's, who slight
our petitions,   5
And fools that are waiting for further
submissions—
From a nation whose manners are rough
and severe,
From scoundrels and rascals,—do keep us
all clear.

From pirates sent out by command of the
king
To murder and plunder, but never to
swing;   10
From *Wallace* and *Greaves,* and *Vipers*
and *Roses,*[1]
Who, if heaven pleases, we'll give bloody
noses.

From the valiant *Dunmore,* with his crew
of banditti,
Who plunder Virginians at *Williamsburg*
city,
From hot-headed *Montague,* mighty to
swear,   15
The little fat man, with his pretty white
hair. [2]

From bishops in Britain, who butchers are
grown,
From slaves, that would die for a smile
from the throne,
From assemblies that vote against *Congress*
proceedings,
(Who now see the fruit of their stupid
misleadings.)   20

From *Tryon* the mighty, who flies from our
city,
And swelled with importance disdains the
committee:
(But since he is pleased to proclaim us his
foes,
What the devil care we where the devil he
goes.) [3]

From the caitiff, Lord *North,* who would
bind us in chains,   25
From a royal King Log, with his tooth-
full of brains,
Who dreams, and is certain (when taking a
nap)
He has conquered our lands, as they lay
on his map. [4]

From a kingdom that bullies, and hectors,
and swears,
We send up to heaven our wishes and
prayers   30
That we, disunited, may freemen be still,
And Britain go on—to be damned if she
will.

ON MR. PAINE'S *RIGHTS OF MAN*
[1795]

Thus briefly sketched the sacred RIGHTS
OF MAN,
How inconsistent with the ROYAL PLAN!
Which for itself exclusive honour craves,

---

[1] These are references to captains and ships in the British navy on the American coast.

[2] Lord Dunmore, 1732-1809, was governor of Virginia; John Montagu, 4th Earl of Sandwich, 1718-1792, was a British statesman active in American affairs.

[3] William Tryon, governor of North Carolina, whose harsh treatment of his rebellious subjects was sanctioned by the British government.

[4] Lord North, 1732-1792, was prime minister 1770-1782; King Log was made king of the frogs in one of Aesop's fables by an act of Jupiter; when the frogs discovered his true nature, Jupiter had to send them another king; thus Freneau stigmatizes George the Third.

Where some are masters born, and millions
    slaves.
With what contempt must every eye look
    down   5
On that base, childish bauble called a
    crown,
The gilded bait, that lures the crowd, to
    come,
Bow down their necks, and meet a slavish
    doom;
The source of half the miseries men en-
    dure.
The quack that kills them, while it seems
    to cure.   10
  Roused by the REASON of his manly
    page,
Once more shall PAINE a listening world
    engage:
From Reason's source, a bold reform he
    brings,
In raising up *mankind,* he pulls down
    kings,
Who, source of discord, patrons of all
    wrong,   15
On blood and murder have been fed too
    long:
Hid from the world, and tutored to be
    base,
The curse, the scourge, the ruin of our
    race,
Their's was the task, a dull designing few,
To shackle beings that they scarcely
    knew,   20
Who made this globe the residence of
    slaves,
And built their thrones on systems formed
    by knaves.
—Advance, bright years, to work their
    final fall,
And haste the period that shall crush them
    all.
  Who, that has read and scann'd the
    historic page   25
But glows, at every line, with kindling
    rage,
To see by them the rights of men aspersed,
Freedom restrain'd, and Nature's law re-
    versed,
Men, ranked with beasts, by monarchs
    will'd away,

And bound young fools, or madmen to
    obey: 30
Now driven to wars, and now oppressed
    at home,
Compelled in crowds o'er distant seas to
    roam,
From India's climes the plundered prize
    to bring
To glad the strumpet, or to glut the king.
  COLUMBIA, hail! immortal be thy
    reign: 35
Without a king, we till the smiling plain;
Without a king, we trace the unbounded
    sea,
And traffic round the globe, through each
    degree;
Each foreign clime our honour'd flag re-
    veres,
Which asks no monarch, to support the
    STARS: 40
Without a *king,* the laws maintain their
    sway,
While honour bids each generous heart
    obey.
Be ours the task the ambitious to restrain,
And this great lesson teach—that kings are
    vain;
That warring realms to certain ruin
    haste,   45
That kings subsist by war, and wars are
    waste:
So shall our nation, form'd on Virtue's
    plan,
Remain the guardian of the Rights of
    Man,
A vast Republic, famed through every
    clime,
Without a king, to see the end of time. 50

REFLECTIONS ON THE MUTABILITY
OF THINGS
[1809 (1798)]

The time is approaching, deny it who may,
  The days are not very remote,
When the pageant that glitter'd for many
    a day,
  On the stream of oblivion will float.

The times are advancing when matters
    will turn,   5
And some, who are now in the shade,
And pelted by malice, or treated with
    scorn,
Will pay, in coin that was paid:

The time it will be, when the people
    aroused,
For better arrangements prepare, 10
And firm to the cause, that of old they
    espoused,
Their steady attachment declare:

When tyrants will shrink from the face of
    the day,
Or, if they presume to remain,
To the tune of *peccavi*, a solo will play, 15
And lower the royalty strain:

When government favors to flattery's press
Will halt on their way from afar,

And people will laugh at the comical dress
    Of the knights of the garter and
    star: 20

When a *monarch*, new fangled, with law-
    yer and scribe,
In junto will cease to convene,
Or take from old England a pitiful bribe,
    To pamper his "highness serene;"

When virtue and merit will have a fair
    chance   25
The loaves and the fishes to share,
And *Jefferson*, you to your station advance,
    The man from the president's chair:

When honesty, honor, experience, ap-
    proved,
No more in disgrace will retire; 30
When fops from the places of trust are
    removed
    And the leaders of faction retire.

1786 ∽ *The Anarchiad* ∽ 1787

SUGGESTED by *The Rolliad*, an English satiric poem directed at the Tories, *The Anarchiad*, a mock-heroic castigation of demagoguery in America, was printed between October 26, 1786, and September 13, 1787, in twelve installments in *The New Haven Gazette, and the Connecticut Magazine*. It was the work of four of the famous "Connecticut Wits," David Humphreys, 1752-1818, Lemuel Hopkins, 1750-1801, Joel Barlow, 1754-1812, and John Trumbull.

[The authorship of the following selection, taken from the fourth installment, is uncertain. The title has been supplied by the present editors. The text is based on that of the 1861 reprint of *The Anarchiad*, edited by Luther G. Riggs.]

INTERREGNUM
[1787]

Bow low, ye heavens, and all ye lands,
    draw near,
The voice prophetic of great Anarch hear!
From Eastern climes, by light and order
    driven,

To me, by fate, this Western world was
    giv'n;
My standard rear'd, the realm imperial
    rules,   5
The last asylum for my knaves and fools.
Here shall my best and brightest empire
    rise,
Wild riot reign, and discord greet the skies.

Awake, my chosen sons, in folly brave,
Stab Independence! dance o'er Freedom's
    grave!   10
Sing choral songs, while conq'ring mobs
    advance,
And blot the debts to Holland, Spain, and
    France—
Till ruin come, with fire, and sword, and
    blood,
And men shall ask where your republic
    stood.

Thrice happy race! how blest are discord's
    heirs!   15
Blest while they know what anarchy is
    theirs;
Blest while they feel to them alone 'tis
    given
To know no sovereign, neither law nor
    Heaven.
From all mankind, by traits peculiar
    known,
By frauds and lies distinguish'd for mine
    own,   20
Wonder of worlds! like whom, to mortal
    eyes,
None e'er have risen, and none e'er shall
    rise!

Lo, the poor Briton, who, corrupted, sold,
Sees God in courts, or hears him chink in
    gold:
Whose soul, proud empire oft has taught
    to stray   25
Far as the Western world, and gates of
    day;
Though plagu'd with debts, with rage of
    conquest curst,
In rags and tender-acts he puts no trust;
But in the public weal his own forgets,
Finds heaven for him who pays the na-
    tion's debts;   30
A heaven like London, his fond fancy
    makes,
Of nectar'd porter and ambrosial steaks.

Not so, Columbia, shall thy sons be known
To prize the public weal above their own;

In faith and justice least, as last in
    birth,   35
Their race shall grow, a by-word through
    the earth.
Long skill'd to act the hypocritic part,
Grace on the brow, and knav'ry at the
    heart,
Perform their frauds with sanctimonious
    air,
Despise good works, and balance sins by
    pray'r—   40
Forswear the public debt, the public cause;
Cheat heaven with forms, and earth with
    tender-laws,
And leave the empire, at its latest groan,
To work salvation out by *faith alone*.

Behold the reign of anarchy, begun,   45
And half the business of confusion done.
From hell's dark caverns discord sounds
    alarms,
Blows her loud trump, and calls my *Shays*
    to arms,
O'er half the land the desperate riot runs,
And maddening mobs assume their rusty
    guns.   50
From councils feeble, bolder faction grows,
The daring corsairs, and the savage foes;
O'er Western wilds, the tawny bands allied,
Insult the States of weakness and of pride;
Once friendly realms, unpaid each gen-
    erous loan,   55
Wait to divide and share them for their
    own.

Now sinks the public mind; a death-like
    sleep
O'er all the torpid limbs begins to creep;
By dull degrees decays the vital heat,
The blood forgets to flow, the pulse to
    beat;   60
The powers of life, in mimic death with-
    drawn,
Closed the fixed eyes with one expiring
    yawn;
Exposed in state, to wait the funeral hour,
Lie the pale relics of departed power;
While conscience, harrowing up their souls,
    with dread,   65

Their ghost of empire stalks without a
    head.

No more stands forth to check the rising
    feud,
Their great DEFENDER of the public
    good;
Retired, in vain his sighs their fate deplore,
He hears, unmoved, the distant tempest
    roar;   70
No more to save a realm, dread GREENE
    appears,
Their second hope, prime object of my
    fears;
Far in the south, from his pale body
    riven,
The deathful angel wings his soul to
    heaven.[1]

Here shall I reign, unbounded and
    alone,   75
Nor men, nor demons, shake my baseless
    throne;
Till comes the day—but late, oh, may it
    spring—
When their tumultuous mobs shall ask a
    king;
A king, in wrath, shall heaven, vindictive
    send,
And my confusion and my empire end. 80

---

[1] The reference is to Nathanael Greene,
American Revolutionary major general,
1742-1786, prevented by death from assuming the leadership which the authors
assume Washington had permanently relinquished when he retired to private life
at the close of the Revolution.

1757 ∞ *Alexander Hamilton* ∞ 1804

BORN in the island of Nevis January 11, 1757, Hamilton came to New
York in 1772 and entered King's College, now Columbia University, the following year. His aristocratic manner and precocious intellect won him friends
easily. He achieved even wider influence by writing two pamphlets against
a critic of Congress, now known to be Samuel Seabury, who signed himself
"A Westchester Farmer." Hamilton's pamphlets were *A Full Vindication of the
Measures of Congress,* 1774, and *The Farmer Refuted,* 1775. During the Revolution, Hamilton served as an artillery captain and as secretary on Washington's
staff.

Hamilton married Elizabeth Schuyler in 1780. Becoming a lawyer and a
member of Congress, he was soon regarded as a great political leader. He
was a delegate to the Constitutional Convention of 1787 and, when it completed its work, joined with James Madison and John Jay in writing *The
Federalist* papers. The three collaborators produced a total of eighty-five of
these papers or short essays, which appeared in the *New York Independent
Journal* for seven months beginning with the October 27, 1787, issue. They
occupy an important place in American political literature as the earliest
extensive exposition of the Constitution.

Appointed Secretary of the Treasury in September, 1789, Hamilton shaped
the destinies of the new nation with his *Report on Public Credit* and *Report
on a National Bank,* both 1790, and *Report on Manufactures,* 1791. Advocate
of a strong centralized government which would foster trade and industry

and achieve national order and power, Hamilton was a foe of the decentralization dear to agrarians as well as to insurgency in the name of the common man and an international policy concerned more with ideological consistency than with what was best for the United States. Resigning as Secretary of the Treasury in 1795, Hamilton devoted himself to the law and to political intrigue in behalf of the Federalist Party. He was shot by Aaron Burr in a duel, July 11, 1804, and died in New York the following day. Of the historical novels based on his career, one of the best is Gertrude Atherton's *The Conqueror,* 1902.

[The first of the following selections is from *The Federalist,* No. VI, and the second is from a letter to Edward Carrington, May 26, 1792. Titles have been supplied by the editors.]

TOWARD A CONFEDERATIVE REPUBLIC
[1787]

A MAN must be far gone in Utopian speculations who can seriously doubt that, if these States should either be wholly disunited, or only united in partial confederacies, the subdivisions into which they might be thrown would have frequent and violent contests with each other. To presume a want of motives for such contests as an argument against their existence, would be to forget that men are ambitious, vindictive, and rapacious. To look for a continuation of harmony between a number of independent, unconnected sovereignties in the same neighborhood, would be to disregard the uniform course of human events, and to set at defiance the accumulated experience of ages.

The causes of hostility among nations are innumerable. There are some which have a general and almost constant operation upon the collective bodies of society. Of this description are the love of power or the desire of pre-eminence and dominion—the jealousy of power, or the desire of equality and safety. There are others which have a more circumscribed though an equally operative influence within their spheres. Such are the rivalships and competitions of commerce between commercial nations. And there are others,

not less numerous than either of the former, which take their origin entirely in private passions; in the attachments, enmities, interests, hopes, and fears of leading individuals in the communities of which they are members. Men of this class, whether the favorites of a king or of a people, have in too many instances abused the confidence they possessed; and assuming the pretext of some public motive, have not scrupled to sacrifice the national tranquillity to personal advantage or personal gratification.

The celebrated Pericles, in compliance with the resentment of a prostitute,[1] at the expense of much of the blood and treasure of his countrymen, attacked, vanquished, and destroyed the city of the Samnians. The same man, stimulated by private pique against the Megarensians, another nation of Greece, or to avoid a prosecution with which he was threatened as an accomplice in a supposed theft of the statuary of Phidias,[2] or to get rid of the accusations prepared to be brought against him for dissipating the funds of the state in the purchase of popularity, or from a combination of all these

[1] Aspasia, vide Plutarch's Life of Pericles —Hamilton's note.

[2] Phidias was supposed to have stolen some public gold, with the connivance of Pericles, for the embellishment of the statue of Minerva—Hamilton's note. Statuary here means sculptor.

causes, was the primitive author of that famous and fatal war, distinguished in the Grecian annals by the name of the Peloponnesian War; which, after various vicissitudes, intermissions, and renewals, terminated in the ruin of the Athenian commonwealth.

The ambitious cardinal, who was prime minister to Henry VIII, permitting his vanity to aspire to the triple crown, entertained hopes of succeeding in the acquisition of that splendid prize by the influence of the Emperor Charles V. To secure the favor and interest of this enterprising and powerful monarch, he precipitated England into a war with France, contrary to the plainest dictates of policy, and at the hazard of the safety and independence, as well of the kingdom over which he presided by his counsels, as of Europe in general. For if there ever was a sovereign who bid fair to realize the project of universal monarchy, it was the Emperor Charles V, of whose intrigues Wolsey was at once the instrument and the dupe.

The influence which the bigotry of one female, the petulance of another, and the cabals of a third,[3] had in the contemporary policy, ferments, and pacifications, of a considerable part of Europe, are topics that have been too often descanted upon not to be generally known.

To multiply examples of the agency of personal considerations in the production of great national events, either foreign or domestic, according to their direction, would be an unnecessary waste of time. Those who have but a superficial acquaintance with the sources from which they are to be drawn, will themselves recollect a variety of instances; and those who have a tolerable knowledge of human nature will not stand in need of such lights, to form their opinion either of the reality or extent of that agency. Perhaps, however, a reference, tending to illustrate the general principle, may with propriety be made to a case which has lately happened among ourselves. If Shays had not been a *desperate debtor,* it is much to be doubted

whether Massachusetts would have been plunged into a civil war.[4]

But notwithstanding the concurring testimony of experience, in this particular, there are still to be found visionary or designing men, who stand ready to advocate the paradox of perpetual peace between the States, though dismembered and alienated from each other. The genius of republics (say they) is pacific; the spirit of commerce has a tendency to soften the manners of men, and to extinguish those inflammable humors which have so often kindled into wars. Commercial republics, like ours, will never be disposed to waste themselves in ruinous contentions with each other. They will be governed by mutual interest, and will cultivate a spirit of mutual amity and concord.

Is it not (we may ask these projectors in politics) the true interest of all nations to cultivate the same benevolent and philosophic spirit? If this be their true interest, have they in fact pursued it? Has it not, on the contrary, invariably been found that momentary passions, and immediate interests, have a more active and imperious control over human conduct than general and remote considerations of policy, utility, or justice? Have republics in practice been less addicted to war than monarchies? Are not the former administered by *men* as well as the latter? Are there not aversions, predilections, rivalships, and desires of unjust acquisitions, that affect nations as well as kings? Are not popular assemblies frequently subject to the impulses of rage, resentment, jealousy, avarice, and of other irregular and violent propensities? Is it not well known that their determinations are often governed by a few individuals in whom they place confidence, and are, of course, liable to be tinctured by the

[3] Hamilton refers respectively to Madame de Maintenon, the Duchess of Marlborough, and Madame de Pompadour, as he indicates in his notes.

[4] Daniel Shays of Massachusetts, 1747-1825, was the leader of an uprising in 1786-87.

passions and views of those individuals? Has commerce hitherto done anything more than change the object of war? Is not the love of wealth as domineering and enterprising a passion as that of power or glory? Have there not been as many wars founded upon commercial motives since that has become the prevailing system of nations, as were before occasioned by the cupidity of territory or dominion? Has not the spirit of commerce, in many instances, administered new incentives to the appetite, both for the one and for the other? Let experience, the least fallible guide of human opinions, be appealed to for an answer to these inquiries.

Sparta, Athens, Rome, and Carthage were all republics; two of them, Athens and Carthage, of the commercial kind. Yet were they as often engaged in wars, offensive and defensive, as the neighboring monarchies of the same times. Sparta was little better than a well-regulated camp; and Rome was never sated of carnage and conquest.

Carthage, though a commercial republic, was the aggressor in the very war that ended in her destruction. Hannibal had carried her arms into the heart of Italy, and to the gates of Rome, before Scipio, in turn, gave him an overthrow in the territories of Carthage, and made a conquest of the commonwealth.

Venice, in later times, figured more than once in wars of ambition, till, becoming an object to the other Italian states, Pope Julius II found means to accomplish that formidable league,[5] which gave a deadly blow to the power and pride of this haughty republic.

The provinces of Holland, till they were overwhelmed in debts and taxes, took a leading and conspicuous part in the wars of Europe. They had furious contests with England for the dominion of the sea, and were among the most persevering and most implacable of the opponents of Louis XIV.

In the government of Britain the representatives of the people compose one branch of the national legislature. Commerce has been for ages the predominant pursuit of that country. Few nations, nevertheless, have been more frequently engaged in war; and the wars in which that kingdom has been engaged have, in numerous instances, proceeded from the people.

There have been, if I may so express it, almost as many popular as royal wars. The cries of the nation and the importunities of their representatives have, upon various occasions, dragged their monarchs into war, or continued them in it, contrary to their inclinations, and sometimes contrary to the real interests of the state. In that memorable struggle for superiority between the rival houses of Austria and Bourbon, which so long kept Europe in a flame, it is well known that the antipathies of the English against the French, seconding the ambition, or rather the avarice, of a favorite leader,[6] protracted the war beyond the limits marked out by sound policy, and for a considerable time in opposition to the views of the court.

The wars of these two last-mentioned nations have in a great measure grown out of commercial considerations—the desire of supplanting and the fear of being supplanted, either in particular branches of traffic or in the general advantages of trade and navigation.

From this summary of what has taken place in other countries, whose situations have borne the nearest resemblance to our own, what reason can we have to confide in those reveries which would seduce us into an expectation of peace and cordiality between the members of the present confederacy, in a state of separation? Have we not already seen enough of the fallacy and extravagance of those idle theories which have amused us with prom-

---

[5] The League of Cambray, comprehending the Emperor, the King of France, the King of Aragon, and most of the Italian princes and states—Hamilton's note.

[6] The Duke of Marlborough—Hamilton's note.

ises of an exemption from the imperfections, weaknesses, and evils incident to society in every shape? Is it not time to awake from the deceitful dream of a golden age, and to adopt as a practical maxim for the direction of our political conduct that we, as well as the other inhabitants of the globe, are yet remote from the happy empire of perfect wisdom and perfect virtue?

Let the point of extreme depression to which our national dignity and credit have sunk, let the inconveniencies felt everywhere from a lax and ill administration of government, let the revolt of a part of the State of North Carolina, the late menacing disturbances in Pennsylvania, and the actual insurrections and rebellions in Massachusetts, declare——!

So far is the general sense of mankind from corresponding with the tenets of those who endeavor to lull asleep our apprehensions of discord and hostility between the States, in event of disunion, that it has from long observation of the progress of society become a sort of axiom in politics, that vicinity, or nearness of situation, constitutes nations natural enemies. An intelligent writer expresses himself on this subject to this effect: "NEIGHBORING NATIONS (says he) are naturally enemies of each other, unless their common weakness forces them to league in a CONFEDERATIVE REPUBLIC, and their constitution prevents the differences that neighborhood occasions, extinguishing that secret jealousy which disposes all states to aggrandize themselves at the expense of their neighbors."[7] This passage, at the same time, points out the EVIL and suggests the REMEDY.

TWO FOES OF FEDERAL
AUTHORITY
[1879 (written 1792)]

IN ALMOST all the questions, great and small, which have arisen since the first session of Congress, Mr. Jefferson and

Mr. Madison have been found among those who are disposed to narrow the federal authority. The question of a national bank is one example. The question of bounties to the fisheries is another. Mr. Madison resisted it on the ground of constitutionality, till it was evident, by the intermediate questions taken, that the bill would pass; and he then, under the wretched subterfuge of a change of a single word, "bounty" for "allowance," went over to the majority, and voted for the bill. On the militia bill, and in a variety of minor cases, he has leaned as much as possible to the States; and he lost no opportunity of sounding the alarm, with great affected solemnity, at encroachments, meditated on the rights of the States, and of holding up the bugbear of a faction in the government having designs unfriendly to liberty.

This kind of conduct has appeared to me the more extraordinary on the part of Mr. Madison, as I know for a certainty, it was a primary article in his creed, that the real danger in our system was the subversion of the national authority by the preponderancy of the State governments. All his measures have proceeded on an opposite supposition. I recur again to the instance of Freneau's paper.[8] In matters of this kind one cannot have direct proof of men's latent views; they must be inferred from circumstances. As coadjutor of Mr. Jefferson in the establishment of this paper, I include Mr. Madison in the consequences imputable to it. In respect to foreign politics, the views of these gentlemen are, in my judgment, equally unsound and dangerous. They have a womanish attachment to France and a womanish resentment against Great Britain. They would draw us into the closest embrace of the former, and involve us in all the consequences of her politics; and they would risk the peace of the country in their endeavors to keep us at the greatest possible distance from the

---

[7] Vide *Principes des Négociations*, par l'Abbé de Mably—Hamilton's note.

[8] A reference to the *National Gazette*.

latter. This disposition goes to a length, particularly in Mr. Jefferson, of which, till lately, I had no adequate idea. Various circumstances prove to me that if these gentlemen were left to pursue their own course, there would be, in less than six months, an open war between the United States and Great Britain. I trust I have a due sense of the conduct of France towards this country in the late revolution; and that I shall always be among the foremost in making her every suitable return; but there is a wide difference between this and implicating ourselves in all her politics; between bearing good will to her and hating and wrangling with all those whom she hates. The neutral and the pacific policy appears to me to mark the true path to the United States.

Having delineated to you what I conceive to be the true complexion of the politics of these gentlemen, I will now attempt a solution of these strange appearances. Mr. Jefferson, it is known, did not in the first instance cordially acquiesce in the new Constitution for the United States; he had many doubts and reserves. He left this country before we had experienced the imbecilities of the former.[9]

In France, he saw government only on the side of its abuses. He drank freely of the French philosophy, in religion, in science, in politics. He came from France in the moment of a fermentation, which he had a share in exciting, and in the passions and feelings of which he shared both from temperament and situation. He came here probably with a too partial idea of his own powers; and with the expectation of a greater share in the direction of our councils than he has in reality enjoyed. I am not sure that he had not peculiarly marked out for himself the department of the finances.

He came, electrified with attachment to France, and with the project of knitting together the two countries in the closest political bands.

Mr. Madison had always entertained an exalted opinion of the talents, knowledge, and virtues of Mr. Jefferson. The sentiment was probably reciprocal. A close correspondence subsisted between them during the time of Mr. Jefferson's absence from the country. A close intimacy arose upon his return.

Whether any peculiar opinions of Mr. Jefferson's concerning the public debt wrought a change in the sentiments of Mr. Madison (for it is certain that the former is more radically wrong than the latter), or whether Mr. Madison, seduced by the expectation of popularity, and possibly by the calculation of advantage to the State of Virginia, was led to change his own opinion, certain it is that a very material change took place, and that the two gentlemen were united in the new ideas. Mr. Jefferson was indiscreetly open in his approbation of Mr. Madison's principles, upon his first coming to the seat of government. I say indiscreetly, because a gentleman in the administration, in one department, ought not to have taken sides against another, in another department. The course of this business and a variety of circumstances which took place left Mr. Madison a very discontented and chagrined man, and begot some degree of ill-humor in Mr. Jefferson. Attempts were made by these gentlemen, in different ways, to produce a commercial warfare with Great Britain. In this, too, they were disappointed. And, as they had the liveliest wishes on the subject, their dissatisfaction has been proportionably great; and, as I had not favored the project, I was comprehended in their displeasure.

These causes, and perhaps same others, created, much sooner than I was aware of it, a systematic opposition to me, on the part of these gentlemen. My subversion, I am now satisfied, has been long an object with them. . . .

---

[9] By "former" Hamilton refers to the former "constitution" or union based on the Articles of Confederation.

1706 ∾ *Benjamin Franklin* ∾ *1790*

THE CONSTITUTIONAL Convention which opened at Philadelphia May 25, 1787, and completed its deliberations September 17 of the same year, needed a harmonizing and moderating influence. Precisely such an influence was provided by Benjamin Franklin, who, nearing his eighty-second birthday, was the oldest delegate.

Two of his Convention speeches, which he wrote out and which were read by James Wilson, are included here. The first, delivered June 2, was in opposition to proposed executive salaries. Although it had little effect on the action of the Convention, it was listened to with respect and is interesting for its incidental reflections of Franklin's political philosophy. The second speech, delivered at the very close of the Convention, reveals strikingly the spirit of this philosophy and was widely circulated afterwards as the most brilliant literary achievement of four months of speechifying. The third of the following selections was a letter to the *Federal Gazette.* Probably written in 1788, it shows to what an extent Franklin desired to influence public opinion to accept the new Constitution, despite its imperfections, which he recognized. The last selection is one of his addresses as president of the society which was to exercise considerable influence on later Abolitionism. This address was delivered Nov. 9, 1789.

[The texts of these selections have been modernized; for original texts, consult the Smyth edition of Franklin's *Writings.* Other selections from Franklin's works will be found in Book I, Part 2.]

SPEECH IN THE CONSTITUTIONAL
CONVENTION ON THE SUBJECT
OF SALARIES
[1818 (written 1787)]

SIR: It is with reluctance that I rise to express a disapprobation of any one article of the plan, for which we are so much obliged to the honorable gentleman who laid it before us. From its first reading, I have borne a good will to it, and, in general, wished it success. In this particular of salaries to the executive branch, I happen to differ; and, as my opinion may appear new and chimerical, it is only from a persuasion that it is right, and from a sense of duty, that I hazard it. The Committee will judge of my reasons when they have heard them, and their judgment may

possibly change mine. I think I see inconveniences in the appointment of salaries; I see none in refusing them, but on the contrary great advantages.

Sir, there are two passions which have a powerful influence in the affairs of men. These are *ambition* and *avarice;* the love of power and the love of money. Separately, each of these has great force in prompting men to action; but when united in view of the same object, they have in many minds the most violent effects. Place before the eyes of such men a post of *honor,* that will at the same time be a place of *profit,* and they will move heaven and earth to obtain it. The vast number of such places it is that renders the British Government so tempestuous. The struggles for them are the true source of all those factions which are perpetually dividing the nation, distracting its councils, hurrying it sometimes into fruitless and mischievous wars, and often compelling a submission to dishonorable terms of peace.

And of what kind are the men that will strive for this profitable preëminence, through all the bustle of cabal, the heat of contention, the infinite mutual abuse of parties, tearing to pieces the best of characters? It will not be the wise and moderate, the lovers of peace and good order, the men fittest for the trust. It will be the bold and the violent, the men of strong passions and indefatigable activity in their selfish pursuits. These will thrust themselves into your government, and be your rulers. And these, too, will be mistaken in the expected happiness of their situation; for their vanquished competitors, of the same spirit, and from the same motives, will perpetually be endeavoring to distress their administration, thwart their measures, and render them odious to the people.

Besides these evils, Sir, though we may set out in the beginning with moderate salaries, we will find that such will not be of long continuance. Reasons will never be wanting for proposed augmentations, and there will always be a party for giving more to the rulers, that the rulers may be able in return to give more to them. Hence, as all history informs us, there has been in every state and kingdom a constant kind of warfare between the governing and the governed; the one striving to obtain more for its support, and the other to pay less. And this has alone occasioned great convulsions, actual civil wars, ending either in dethroning of the princes or enslaving of the people. Generally, indeed, the ruling power carries its point, and we see the revenues of princes constantly increasing, and we see that they are never satisfied, but always in want of more. The more the people are discontented with the oppression of taxes, the greater need the prince has of money to distribute among his partisans, and pay the troops that are

to suppress all resistance, and enable him to plunder at pleasure. There is scarce a king in a hundred who would not, if he could, follow the example of Pharaoh— get first all the people's money, then all their lands, and then make them and their children servants forever. It will be said that we do not propose to establish kings. I know it. But there is a natural inclination in mankind to kingly government. It sometimes relieves them from aristocratic domination. They had rather have one tyrant than 500. It gives more of the appearance of equality among citizens; and that they like. I am apprehensive, therefore—perhaps too apprehensive—that the government of these States may in future times end in a monarchy. But this catastrophe, I think, may be long delayed, if in our proposed system we do not sow the seeds of contention, faction, and tumult, by making our posts of honor places of profit. If we do, I fear that, though we employ at first a number and not a single person, the number will in time be set aside; it will only nourish the foetus of a king (as the honorable gentleman from Virginia very aptly expressed it), and a king will the sooner be set over us.

It may be imagined by some that this is an Utopian idea, and that we can never find men to serve us in the executive department without paying them well for their services. I conceive this to be a mistake. Some existing facts present themselves to me, which incline me to a contrary opinion. The high sheriff of a county in England is an honorable office, but it is not a profitable one. It is rather expensive, and therefore not sought for. But yet it is executed, and well executed, and usually by some of the principal gentlemen of the county. In France, the office of counsellor, or member of their judiciary parliaments, is more honorable. It is therefore purchased at a high price; there are indeed fees on the law proceedings, which are divided among them, but these fees do not amount to more than three per cent on the sum paid for the place. Therefore, as legal interest is there at five per cent, they in fact pay two per cent for being allowed to do the judiciary business of the nation, which is at the same time entirely exempt from the burden of paying them any salaries for their services. I do not, however, mean to recommend this as an eligible mode for our judiciary department. I only bring the instance to show that the pleasure of doing good and serving their country, and the respect such conduct entitles them to, are sufficient motives with some minds to give up a great portion of their time to the public, without the mean inducement of pecuniary satisfaction.

Another instance is that of a respectable society who have made the experiment and practiced it with success, now more than a hundred years. I mean the Quakers. It is an established rule with them that they are not to go to law, but in their controversies they must apply to their monthly, quarterly, and yearly meetings. Committees of these sit with patience to hear the parties, and spend much time in composing their differences. In doing this, they are supported by a sense of duty, and the respect paid to usefulness. It is honorable to be so employed, but it was never made profitable by salaries, fees, or perquisites. And indeed, in all cases of public service, the less the profit the greater the honor.

To bring the matter nearer home, have we not seen the greatest and most important of our offices, that of General of our armies, executed for eight years together, without the smallest salary, by a patriot whom I will not now offend by any other praise; and this, through fatigues and distresses, in common with the other brave men, his military friends and companions, and the constant anxieties peculiar to his station? And shall we doubt finding three or four men in all the United States with public spirit enough to bear sitting in peaceful council for perhaps an equal term, merely to preside over our civil concerns, and see that our laws are duly executed? Sir, I have a better opinion of our country. I think we shall never be

without a sufficient number of wise and good men to undertake, and execute well and faithfully, the office in question.

Sir, the saving of the salaries, that may at first be proposed, is not an object with me. The subsequent mischiefs of proposing them are what I apprehend. And therefore it is that I move the amendment. If it is not seconded or accepted, I must be contented with the satisfaction of having delivered my opinion frankly, and done my duty.

SPEECH IN THE CONVENTION AT THE CONCLUSION OF ITS DELIBERATIONS
[1787 and 1793 (written 1787)]

MR. PRESIDENT: I confess that I do not entirely approve of this Constitution at present; but, Sir, I am not sure I shall never approve it; for, having lived long, I have experienced many instances of being obliged, by better information or fuller consideration, to change my opinions even on important subjects, which I once thought right, but found to be otherwise. It is therefore that, the older I grow, the more apt I am to doubt my own judgment of others. Most men, indeed, as well as most sects in religion, think themselves in possession of all truth, and that wherever others differ from them, it is so far error. Steele, a Protestant, in a dedication, tells the Pope that the only difference between our two churches in their opinions of the certainty of their doctrine is the Romish Church is *infallible* and the Church of England is *never in the wrong*. But, though many private persons think almost as highly of their own infallibility as of that of their sect, few express it so naturally as a certain French lady who, in a little dispute with her sister, said, "But I meet with nobody but myself that is *always* in the right." *"Je ne trouve que moi qui aie toujours raison."*

In these sentiments, Sir, I agree to this Constitution, with all its faults—if they are such; because I think a general government necessary for us, and there is no *form* of government but what may be a blessing to the people, if well administered; and I believe, farther, that this is likely to be well administered for a course of years, and can only end in despotism, as other forms have done before it, when the people shall become so corrupted as to need despotic government, being incapable of any other. I doubt, too, whether any other convention we can obtain may be able to make a better constitution; for, when you assemble a number of men, to have the advantage of their joint wisdom, you inevitably assemble with those men all their prejudices, their passions, their errors of opinion, their local interests, and their selfish views. From such an assembly can a *perfect* production be expected? It therefore astonishes me, Sir, to find this system approaching so near to perfection as it does; and I think it will astonish our enemies, who are waiting with confidence to hear that our councils are confounded like those of the builders of Babel, and that our States are on the point of separation, only to meet hereafter for the purpose of cutting one another's throats. Thus I consent, Sir, to this Constitution, because I expect no better, and because I am not sure that it is not the best. The opinions I have had of its *errors* I sacrifice to the public good. I have never whispered a syllable of them abroad. Within these walls they were born, and here they shall die. If every one of us, in returning to our constituents, were to report the objections he has had to it, and endeavor to gain partisans in support of them, we might prevent its being generally received, and thereby lose all the salutary effects and great advantages resulting naturally in our favor among foreign nations, as well as among ourselves, from our real or apparent unanimity. Much of the strength and efficiency of any government, in procuring and securing happiness to the people, depends on *opinion*, on the general opinion of the goodness of that government, as

well as of the wisdom and integrity of its governors. I hope, therefore, for our own sakes, as a part of the people, and for the sake of our posterity, that we shall act heartily and unanimously in recommending this Constitution, wherever our influence may extend, and turn our future thoughts and endeavors to the means of having it *well administered.*

On the whole, Sir, I cannot help expressing a wish, that every member of the Convention who may still have objections to it, would with me on this occasion doubt a little of his own infallibility, and, to make *manifest* our *unanimity,* put his name to this instrument.

A COMPARISON OF THE CONDUCT OF THE ANCIENT JEWS AND OF THE ANTI-FEDERALISTS IN THE UNITED STATES OF AMERICA
[1788 and 1793 (written 1788?)]

A ZEALOUS advocate for the proposed Federal Constitution, in a certain public assembly, said that "the repugnance of a great part of mankind to good government was such that he believed that, if an angel from heaven was to bring down a constitution formed there for our use, it would nevertheless meet with violent opposition." He was reproved for the supposed extravagance of the sentiment; and he did not justify it. Probably it might not have immediately occurred to him that the experiment had been tried and that the event was recorded in the most faithful of all histories, the Holy Bible; otherwise he might, as it seems to me, have supported his opinion by that unexceptionable authority.

The Supreme Being had been pleased to nourish up a single family by continued acts of his attentive Providence till it became a great people; and, having rescued them from bondage, by many miracles performed by his servant Moses, he personally delivered to that chosen servant, in the presence of the whole nation, a constitution and code of laws for their observance, accompanied and sanctioned with promises of great rewards, and threats of severe punishments, as the consequence of their obedience or disobedience.

This constitution, though the Deity himself was to be at its head (and it is therefore called by political writers a *theocracy*), could not be carried into execution but by the means of his ministers; Aaron and his sons were therefore commissioned to be, with Moses, the first established ministry of the new government.

One would have thought that this appointment of men who had distinguished themselves by procuring the liberty of their nation and had hazarded their lives in openly opposing the will of a powerful monarch, who would have retained that nation in slavery, might have been an appointment acceptable to a grateful people; and that a constitution framed for them by the Deity himself might, on that account, have been secure of a universal welcome reception. Yet there were in every one of the *thirteen tribes* some discontented, restless spirits, who were continually exciting them to reject the proposed new government, and this from various motives.

Many still retained an affection for Egypt, the land of their nativity; and these, whenever they felt any inconvenience or hardship, though the natural and unavoidable effect of their change of situation, exclaimed against their leaders as the authors of their trouble; and were not only for returning into Egypt, but for stoning their deliverers. Those inclined to idolatry were displeased that their *Gold Calf* was destroyed. Many of the chiefs thought the new constitution might be injurious to their particular interests, that the *profitable places* would be *engrossed by the families and friends of Moses and Aaron,* and others equally well-born excluded. In Josephus and the Talmud, we learn some particulars, not so fully narrated in the

Scripture. We are there told, "That Corah was ambitious of the priesthood, and offended that it was conferred on Aaron; and this, as he said, by the authority of Moses only, *without the consent of the people.* He accused Moses of having, by various artifices, fraudulently obtained the government, and deprived the people of their liberties; and of *conspiring* with Aaron to perpetuate the tyranny in their family. Thus, though Corah's real motive was the supplanting of Aaron, he persuaded the people that he meant only the public good; and they, moved by his insinuations, began to cry out, 'Let us maintain the common liberty of our *respective* tribes; we have freed ourselves from the slavery imposed on us by the Egyptians, and shall we now suffer ourselves to be made slaves by Moses? If we must have a master, it were better to return to Pharaoh, who at least fed us with bread and onions, than to serve this new tyrant, who by his operations has brought us into danger of famine.' Then they called in question the *reality of his conference* with God; and objected the *privacy of the meetings,* and the *preventing any of the people from being present* at the colloquies, or even approaching the place, as grounds of great suspicion. They accused Moses also of peculation; as embezzling part of the golden spoons and the silver chargers, that the princes had offered at the dedication of the altar, and the offerings of gold by the common people, as well as most of the poll-tax; and Aaron they accused of pocketing much of the gold of which he pretended to have made a molten calf. Besides *peculation,* they charged Moses with *ambition*; to gratify which passion he had, they said, deceived the people, by promising to bring them *to* a land flowing with milk and honey; instead of doing which, he had brought them *from* such a land; and that he thought light of all this mischief, provided he could make himself an *absolute prince.* That, to support the new dignity with splendor in his family, the partial poll-tax already levied and given to Aaron was to be followed by a general one, which would probably be augmented from time to time, if he were suffered to go on promulgating new laws, on pretence of new occasional revelations of the divine will, till their whole fortunes were devoured by that aristocracy."

Moses denied the charge of peculation; and his accusers were destitute of proofs to support it; though *facts*, if real, are in their nature capable of proof. "I have not," said he (with holy confidence in the presence of his God), "I have not taken from this people the value of an ass, nor done them any other injury." But his enemies had made the charge, and with some success among the populace; for no kind of accusation is so readily made, or easily believed, by knaves as the accusation of knavery.

In fine, no less than two hundred and fifty of the principal men, "famous in the congregation, men of renown," heading and exciting the mob, worked them up to such a pitch of frenzy that they called out, "Stone 'em, stone 'em, and thereby *secure our liberties*; and let us choose other captains, that may lead us back into Egypt, in case we do not succeed in reducing the Canaanites!"

On the whole, it appears that the Israelites were a people jealous of their newly-acquired liberty, which jealousy was in itself no fault; but, when they suffered it to be worked upon by artful men, pretending public good, with nothing really in view but private interest, they were led to oppose the establishment of the *new constitution*, whereby they brought upon themselves much inconvenience and misfortune. It appears further, from the same inestimable history, that, when after many ages that constitution was become old and much abused, and an amendment of it was proposed, the populace, as they had accused Moses of the ambition of making himself a *prince*, and cried out, "Stone him, stone him;" so, excited by their high priests and *scribes*, they exclaimed against the Messiah, that he aimed at becoming

King of the Jews, and cried out, "Crucify him, Crucify him." From all which we may gather that popular opposition to a public measure is no proof of its impropriety, even though the opposition be excited and headed by men of distinction.

To conclude, I beg I may not be understood to infer that our General Convention was divinely inspired, when it formed the new Federal Constitution, merely because that Constitution has been unreasonably and vehemently opposed; yet I must own I have so much faith in the general government of the world by *Providence*, that I can hardly conceive a transaction of such momentous importance to the welfare of millions now existing, and to exist in the posterity of a great nation, should be suffered to pass without being in some degree influenced, guided, and governed by that omnipotent, omnipresent, and beneficent Ruler, in whom all inferior spirits live, and move, and have their being.

AN ADDRESS TO THE PUBLIC FROM THE PENNSYLVANIA SOCIETY FOR PROMOTING THE ABOLITION OF SLAVERY AND THE RELIEF OF FREE NEGROES UNLAWFULLY HELD IN BONDAGE
[1789 and 1806 (written 1789)]

IT IS with peculiar satisfaction we assure the friends of humanity that, in prosecuting the design of our association, our endeavors have proved successful, far beyond our most sanguine expectations.

Encouraged by this success and by the daily progress of that luminous and benign spirit of liberty, which is diffusing itself throughout the world, and humbly hoping for the continuance of the divine blessing on our labors, we have ventured to make an important addition to our original plan, and do therefore earnestly solicit the support and assistance of all who can feel the tender emotions of sympathy and compassion, or relish the exalted pleasure of beneficence.

Slavery is such an atrocious debasement of human nature that its very extirpation, if not performed with solicitous care, may sometimes open a source of serious evils.

The unhappy man who has long been treated as a brute animal too frequently sinks beneath the common standard of the human species. The galling chains that bind his body do also fetter his intellectual faculties and impair the social affections of his heart. Accustomed to move like a mere machine, by the will of a master, reflection is suspended; he has not the power of choice; and reason and conscience have but little influence over his conduct, because he is chiefly governed by the passion of fear. He is poor and friendless; perhaps worn out by extreme labor, age, and disease.

Under such circumstances, freedom may often prove a misfortune to himself, and prejudicial to society.

Attention to emancipated black people, it is therefore to be hoped, will become a branch of our national policy; but, as far as we contribute to promote this emancipation, so far that attention is evidently a serious duty incumbent on us, and which we mean to discharge to the best of our judgment and abilities.

To instruct, to advise, to qualify those, who have been restored to freedom, for the exercise and enjoyment of civil liberty, to promote in them habits of industry, to furnish them with employments suited to their age, sex, talents, and other circumstances, and to procure their children an education calculated for their future situation in life; these are the great outlines of the annexed plan, which we have adopted, and which we conceive will essentially promote the public good, and the happiness of these our hitherto too much neglected fellow-creatures.

A plan so extensive cannot be carried into execution without considerable pecuniary resources, beyond the present ordinary funds of the Society. We hope much from the generosity of enlightened and benevolent freemen, and will gratefully receive any donations or subscriptions for this purpose, which may be made to our treasurer, James Starr, or to James Pemberton, chairman of our committee of correspondence.

Signed, by order of the Society,

B. Franklin, President.

An Exchange of Letters Between John Adams and Samuel Adams

1802

WHILE John Adams was vice-president of the United States, he exchanged letters with Samuel Adams, then lieutenant-governor of Massachusetts, on one of the fundamental issues confronting the new nation—the rôle of the people, of the common man, versus the rôle of a civilized minority, of the uncommon man, in preserving liberty. The exchange, including two letters from each, was published in Boston in 1802 in a pamphlet of thirty-two pages. The John Adams selection is taken from the third letter in the series, dated New York, October 18, 1790; the Samuel Adams selection is part of his reply, the fourth letter, dated November 20 of the same year.

Samuel Adams, a second cousin of John, was born in Boston in 1722. A graduate of Harvard, he proved unsuccessful as a lawyer, a petty official, and a business man, but became one of the most effective organizers of various forms of opposition to Britain, such as non-importation associations, the "Sons of Liberty," the "Boston Tea Party," and the "committees of correspondence," which were propaganda agencies. He was also the author of several of the more influential documents stating the grievances of the colonies, such as the "Resolves" adopted October 29, 1765, by the Massachusetts House of Representatives, and "The Rights of the Colonists," which anticipated the Declaration of Independence and was officially approved by the Town of Boston at a public meeting, November 20, 1772. His later public life was a long and distinguished one. He belonged to the Continental Congresses, signed the Declaration of Independence, was a delegate to the Massachusetts constitutional convention of 1779-80, and held various posts in the government of that State. After serving as lieutenant-governor, he was governor from 1794 to 1797. He died in 1803. [For other selections from the writings of John Adams, see pp. 277-82.]

JOHN ADAMS TO SAMUEL ADAMS
[1802 (written 1790)]

I AM very willing to agree with you in fancying that in the greatest improvements of society government will be in the republican form. It is a fixed principle with me that all good government is and must be republican. But, at the same time, your candor will agree with me that there is not in lexicography a more fraudulent word. Whenever I use the word *republic* with approbation, I mean a government in which the people have collectively, or by representation, an essential share in the sovereignty. . . .

With you I have also the honor most perfectly to harmonize in your sentiments of the humanity and wisdom of promoting education in knowledge, virtue, and benevolence. But I think that these will confirm mankind in the opinion of the necessity of preserving and strengthening the dikes against the ocean, its tides and storms. Human appetites, passions, prejudices, and self-love will never be conquered by benevolence and knowledge alone, introduced by human means. The millennium itself neither supposes nor implies it. All civil government is then to cease, and the Mes-

siah is to reign. That happy and holy state is therefore wholly out of this question. You and I agree in the utility of universal education; but will nations agree in it as fully and extensively as we do, and be at the expense of it? We know, with as much certainty as attends any human knowledge, that they will not. We cannot, therefore, advise the people to depend for their safety, liberty, and security upon hopes and blessings which we know will not fall to their lot. If we do our duty then to the people, we shall not deceive them, but advise them to depend upon what is in their power and will to relieve them.

Philosophers, ancient and modern, do not appear to me to have studied nature, the whole of nature, and nothing but nature. Lycurgus' principle was war and family pride; Solon's was what the people would bear, etc. The best writings of antiquity upon government, those, I mean, of Aristotle, Zeno, and Cicero, are lost. We have human nature, society, and universal history to observe and study, and from these we may draw all the real principles which ought to be regarded. Disciples will follow their masters, and interested partisans their chieftans; let us like it or not, we cannot help it. But if the true principles can be discovered, and fairly, fully, and impartially laid before the people, the more light increases, the more the reason of them will be seen, and the more disciples they will have. Prejudice, passion, and private interest, which will always mingle in human inquiries, one would think might be enlisted on the side of truth, at least in the greatest number; for certainly the majority are interested in the truth, if they could see to the end of all its consequences. "Kings have been deposed by aspiring nobles." True, and never by any other. "These" (the nobles, I suppose) "have waged everlasting war against the common rights of men." True, when they have been possessed of the *summa imperii* [1] in one body, without a check. So have the plebeians; so have the people; so have kings; so has human nature, in every shape and combination, and so it ever will. But, on the other hand, the nobles have been essential parties in the preservation of liberty, whenever and wherever it has existed. In Europe, they alone have preserved it against kings and people, wherever it has been preserved; or, at least, with very little assistance from the people. One hideous despotism, as horrid as that of Turkey, would have been the lot of every nation of Europe, if the nobles had not made stands. By nobles, I mean not peculiarly an hereditary nobility, or any particular modification, but the natural and actual aristocracy among mankind. The existence of this you will not deny. You and I have seen four noble families rise up in Boston—the Crafts, Gores, Dawes, and Austins. These are as really a nobility in our town as the Howards, Somersets, Berties, etc., in England. Blind, undistinguishing reproaches against the aristocratical part of mankind, a division which nature has made and we cannot abolish, are neither pious nor benevolent. They are as pernicious as they are false. They serve only to foment prejudice, jealousy, envy, animosity, and malevolence. They serve no ends but those of sophistry,

fraud, and the spirit of party. It would not be true, but it would not be more egregiously false, to say that the people have waged everlasting war against the rights of men.

"The love of liberty," you say, "is interwoven in the soul of man." So it is, according to La Fontaine, in that of a wolf; [2] and I doubt whether it be much more rational, generous, or social, in one than in the other, until in man it is enlightened by experience, reflection, education, and civil and political institutions, which are at first produced and constantly supported and improved by a few; that is, by the nobility. The wolf in the fable, who preferred running in the forest, lean and hungry, to the sleek, plump, and round sides of the dog, because he found the latter was sometimes restrained, had more love of liberty than most men. The numbers of men in all ages have preferred ease, slumber, and good cheer to liberty, when they have been in competition. We must not then depend alone upon the love of liberty in the soul of man for its preservation. Some political institutions must be prepared to assist this love against its enemies. Without these, the struggle will ever end only in a change of impostors. When the people, who have no property, feel the power in their own hands to determine all questions by a majority, they ever attack those who have property, till the injured men of property lose all patience, and recur to finesse, trick, and stratagem, to outwit those who have too much strength, because they have too many hands to be resisted any other way. Let us be impartial, then, and speak the whole truth. Till we do, we shall never discover all the true principles that are necessary. The multitude, therefore, as well as the nobles, must have a check. . . .

---

[1] Highest powers.

[2] The *Fables* of the French poet, Jean de La Fontaine, 1621-1695, were published 1668-1694.

SAMUEL ADAMS TO JOHN ADAMS
[1802 (written 1790)]

A REPUBLIC, you tell me, is a government in which "the people have an essential *share* in the sovereignty." Is not the *whole* sovereignty, my friend, essentially in the people? Is not government designed for the welfare and happiness of all the people? And is it not the uncontrollable, essential right of the people to amend and alter, or annul their constitution and frame a new one, whenever they shall think it will better promote their own welfare and happiness to do it? That the sovereignty resides in the people is a political doctrine which I have never heard an American politician seriously deny. The constitutions of the American States reserve to the people the exercise of the rights of sovereignty, by the annual or biennial elections of their governors, senators, and representatives; and by empowering their own representatives to impeach the greatest officers of the state before the senators, who are also chosen by themselves. *We, the people* is the style of the federal Constitution. They adopted it; and, conformably to it, they delegate the exercise of the powers of government to particular persons who, after short intervals, resign their powers to the people, and they will reëlect them, or appoint others, as they think fit. . . .

We agree in the utility of universal education, but "will nations agree in it as fully and extensively as we do?" Why should they not? It would not be fair to conclude that, because they have not yet been disposed to agree in it, they never will. It is allowed that the present age is more enlightened than former ones. Freedom of inquiry is certainly more encouraged; the feelings of humanity have softened the heart; the true principles of civil and religious liberty are better understood; tyranny in all its shapes is more detested; and bigotry, if not still blind, must be mortified to see that she is despised. Such an age may afford at least a

flattering expectation that nations, as well as individuals, will view the utility of *universal education* in so strong a light as to induce sufficient national patronage and support. Future ages will probably be more enlightened than this.

The love of liberty is interwoven in the soul of man. "So is it in that of a wolf." However irrational, ungenerous, and unsocial the love of liberty may be in a rude savage, he is capable of being enlightened by experience, reflection, education, and civil and political institutions. But the nature of the wolf is, and ever will be, confined to running in the forest to satisfy his hunger and his brutal appetites; the dog is inclined, in a very easy way, to seek his living, and fattens his sides from what comes from his master's kitchen. The comparison of La Fontaine is, in my opinion, ungenerous, unnatural, and unjust.

Among the numbers of men, my friend, are to be found not only those who have "preferred ease, slumber, and good cheer, to liberty;" but others, who have eagerly sought after thrones and sceptres, hereditary shares in sovereignty, riches and splendor, titles, stars, garters, crosses, eagles, and many other childish playthings, at the expense of real nobility, without one thought or care for the liberty and happiness of the rest of mankind.

"The people, who have no property, feel the power of government by a majority, and ever attack those who have property." "The injured men of property recur to finesse, trick, and stratagem to outwit them." True. These may proceed from a lust of domination in *some* of both parties. Be this as it may, it has been known that such deceitful tricks have been practiced by some of the rich upon their unsuspecting fellow-citizens, to turn the determination of questions so as to answer their own selfish purposes. To plunder or filch the rights of men are crimes equally immoral and nefarious, though committed in different manners. Neither of them is confined to the rich or the poor; they are too common among both. The lords, as well as the commons, of Great Britain, by continued large majorities, endeavored by finesse, tricks, and stratagems, as well as threats, to prevail on the American colonies to surrender their liberty and property to their disposal. These failing, they attempted to *plunder* our rights by force of arms. We feared their arts more than their arms. Did the members of that hereditary house of lords, who constituted those repeated majorities, then possess the spirit of nobility? Not so, I think. That spirit resided in the *illustrious* minorities in both houses.

But, "by nobles," who have prevented "one hideous despotism, as horrid as that of Turkey, from falling to the lot of every nation of Europe," you mean, "not peculiarly an hereditary nobility, or any particular modification, but the natural and actual aristocracy among mankind;" the existence of which I am not disposed to deny. Where is this aristocracy found? Among men of all ranks and conditions. The cottager may beget a wise son; the noble, a fool. The one is capable of great improvement; the other, not. Education is within the power of man and societies of men. Wise and judicious modes of education, patronized and supported by communities, will draw together the sons of

the rich and the poor, among whom it makes no distinction; it will cultivate the natural genius, elevate the soul, excite laudable emulation to excel in knowledge, piety, and benevolence; and, finally, it will reward its patrons and benefactors, by shedding its benign influence on the public mind. Education inures men to thinking and reflection, to reasoning and demonstration. It discovers to them the moral and religious duties they owe to God, their country, and to all mankind. Even savages might, by the means of education, be instructed to frame the best civil and political institutions, with as much skill and ingenuity as they now shape their arrows. Education leads youth to "the study of human nature, society, and universal history," from whence they may "draw all the principles" of political architecture which ought to be regarded. All men are "interested in the truth." Education, by showing them "the end of all its consequences," would induce at least the greatest numbers to enlist on its side. The man of good understanding, who has been well-educated, and improves these advantages, as far as his circumstances will allow, in promoting the happiness of mankind, in my opinion, and I am inclined to think in yours, is indeed "well-born". . . .

1765 ∽ *William Hill Brown* ∽ 1793

DURING the post-Revolutionary flowering of *belles-lettres*, a great deal of sentimental fiction appeared in American magazines and in book form. Strongly influenced by the work of Richardson, much of this fiction was intended to warn its bourgeois female readers against the libertinism of men still behaving according to the aristocratic double standard of morality. It was intended, further, to improve the character of these readers by emptying their tear ducts over the plight of virtue. Actually, it often increased their frivolity by making them more sexually conscious and emotionally vulnerable. Yet this trend in fiction had a definite relationship to the ideology of democracy. Social and educational notions tending to undermine the prejudices derived from a more feudal or stratified order of things were introduced into the love story.

The Power of Sympathy, published anonymously in Boston in 1789 in two volumes, was dedicated "To the Young Ladies of United Columbia" as "Intended to represent the specious Causes, and to Expose the fatal Consequences of SEDUCTION; To inspire the Female Mind With a Principle of Self Complacency, and to Promote the Economy of Human Life." The seduction is mostly in the past and in interpolated stories. The hero, Harrington, is virtuously in love with Harriot and writes of his love to his friend, Worthy. Harriot's confidante, Myra, is advised by a cultivated mentor, Mrs. Holmes. Poor Harrington and Harriot are foredoomed to tragedy because Harrington's father was guilty of a libertine lapse.

This first American sentimental novel was for a long time erroneously attributed to the poetess, Mrs. Sarah Wentworth Morton, but is now known to have been the work of William Hill Brown, of Boston. He also wrote verse, essays, two plays, and another short novel, *Ira and Isabella,* published in 1807, which has a plot somewhat similar to that of *The Power of Sympathy* with the exception that the ending is happy.

From
THE POWER OF SYMPATHY
[1789]

HARRINGTON TO WORTHY
Boston

AM I to believe my eyes—my ears—my heart!—and yet I cannot be deceived.— We are generally most stupid and incredulous in what most materially concerns us. We find the greatest difficulty, in persuading ourselves of the attainment of what we most ardently desire—She loves!—I say to myself, Harriot loves me, and I reverence myself.

I think I may now take upon me some share of happiness—I may say I have not lived in vain—for all my heart holds dear is mine—joy and love encompass me— peace and tranquillity are before me; the prospect is fair and promising as the gilded dawn of a summer's day—There is none to supplant me in her affection—I dread no rival, for our tempers are similar, and our hearts beat in unison together.
Adieu!

HARRINGTON TO WORTHY
Boston

LOVE softens and refines the manners—

polishes the asperities of awkwardness, and fits us for the society of gentle beings. It goes further, it mends the heart, and makes us better men—it gives the faint-hearted an extraordinary strength of soul, and renders them equal and frequently superior to danger and distress.

My passions you know are quick, my prejudices sometimes obstinate—She tells me these things are wrong—This gentle reprimand is so tempered with love that I think she commends me. I however promise a reform, and am much pleased with the improvement. Harriot moulds my heart into what form she chooses.

A little party is proposed tomorrow evening, and I shall attend Harriot. These elegant relaxations prevent the degeneracy of human nature, exhilarate the spirits, and wind up this machine of ours for another revolution of business.

HARRINGTON TO WORTHY
Boston

OUR little party was overthrown by a strange piece of folly. A Miss P—— was introduced, a young lady of beauty and elegant accomplishments. The whole company were beginning to be cheerful— business and care were disgusted at the sight of so many happy countenances, and had gone out from among us. Jollity and good humour bade us prepare for the dance—unhappily at this juncture a lady and gentleman were engaged in a conversation concerning Miss P——, and one of them repeated the words "a mechanic's daughter"—it is supposed the word "mechanic" was repeated scornfully —She heard it—thought herself insulted— and indignantly retired—Disorder and confusion immediately took place, and the amusement was put an end to for the evening.

I wish people would consider how little time they have to frolic here—that they would improve it to more advantage, and not dispute for any precedence or superiority but in good nature and sociability —"a mechanic"—and pray whence this distinction!

Inequality among mankind is a foe to our happiness—it even affects our little parties of pleasure—Such is the fate of the human race, one order of men lords it over another; but upon what grounds its right is founded I could never be satisfied.

For this reason, I like a democratical better than any other kind of government; and were I a Lycurgus no distinction of rank should be found in my commonwealth.

In my tour through the United States, I had an opportunity of examining and comparing the different manners and dispositions of the inhabitants of the several republics. Those of the southern states, accustomed to a habit of domineering over their slaves, are haughtier, more tenacious of honour, and indeed possess more of an aristocratic temper than their sisters of the confederacy. As we travel to the northward, the nature of the constitution seems to operate on the minds of the people— slavery is abolished—all men are declared free and equal, and their tempers are open, generous and communicative. It is the same in all those countries where the people enjoy independence and equal liberty. Why then should those distinctions arise which are inimical to domestic quietude? Or why should the noisy voice of those

who seek distinction, so loudly reëcho in the ears of peace and jollity, as to deafen the sound of the music? For while we are disputing who shall lead off the dance, behold! the instrument gets out of tune— a string snaps—and where is our chance for dancing?

Adieu!

MRS. HOLMES TO MYRA

Belleview

I AM sometimes mortified to find the books which I recommend to your perusal are not always applicable to the situation of an American lady. The general observations of some English books are the most useful things contained in them; the principal parts being chiefly filled with local descriptions, which a young woman here is frequently at a loss to understand.

I send you a little work entitled, "A Lady of Quality's Advice to her Children," which, though not altogether free from this exception, is highly worthy of your attention. A parent who is represented struggling with the distress of a lingering illness bequeaths a system of education to her offspring. I do not recommend it to you as a novel, but as a work that speaks the language of the heart and that inculcates the duty we owe to ourselves, to society and the Deity.

Didactic essays are not always capable of engaging the attention of young ladies. We fly from the labored precepts of the essayist to the sprightly narrative of the novelist. Habituate your mind to remark the difference between truth and fiction. You will then always be enabled to judge of the propriety and justness of a thought; and never be misled to form wrong opinions, by the meretricious *dress* of a pleasing tale. You will then be capable of deducing the most profitable lessons of instruction, and the design of your reading will be fully accomplished.—

Hence you will be provided with a key to the characters of men: To unlock these curious cabinets is a very useful as well as entertaining employment. Of those insidious gentlemen, who plan their advances towards us on the Chesterfieldian system, let me advise you to beware. A prudent commander would place a double watch, if he apprehended the enemy were more disposed to take the fort by secrecy and undermining than by an open assault.

I cannot but smile sometimes to observe the ridiculous figure of some of our young gentlemen, who affect to square their conduct by his Lordship's principles of politeness—they never tell a story unless it be very short—they talk of decorum and the *etiquette*—they detest everything vulgar or common—they are on the rack if an old man should let fall a proverb—and a thousand more trifling affectations, the ridicule of which arises, not so much from their putting on this foreign dress, as from their ignorance or vanity in pretending to imitate those rules which were designed for an English nobleman—Unless, therefore, they have a prospect of being called by Congress to execute some foreign negotiation, they ought certainly to be minding their business.

This affectation of fine breeding is destructive to morals. Dissimulation and insincerity are connected with its tenets; and are mutually inculcated with the art of pleasing.

A person of this character grounds his motives for pleasing on the most selfish principle—He is polite, not for the honor of obliging you, as he endeavors to make you believe, but that he himself might be obliged. Suspect him, therefore, of insincerity and treachery, who sacrifices truth to complaisance, and advises you to the pursuit of an object, which would tend to his advantage.

Always distinguish the man of sense from the coxcomb. Mr. Worthy is possessed of a good understanding and an exact judgment. If you are united with him, let it be the study of your life to preserve his love and esteem. His amiable character is adorned with modesty and a disposition to virtue and sobriety. I never anticipate your future happiness, but I contemplate this part of his character with pleasure. But remember the fidelity of a wife alone will not always secure the esteem of a husband; when her personal attractions do not continue to delight his eye, she will flatter his judgment. I think you are enabled to perform this, because you are solicitous to supply your mind with those amiable qualities which are more durable than beauty. When you are no longer surrounded with a flattering circle of young men, and the world shall cease to call you beautiful, your company will be courted by men of sense, who know the value of your conversation.

I am pleased with the conduct of some agreeable girls and the return of civility and attention they often make to the conceited compliments of a certain class of beaux. These ladies wisely consider them as the butterflies of a day, and therefore generally scorn *to break them on a wheel!*

When you are in company, where the vain and thoughtless endeavor to show their ingenuity by ridiculing particular orders of men, your prudence will dictate to you not to countenance their abuse—The book I have just mentioned intimates that "there are a great many things done and said in company which a woman of virtue will neither see nor hear."—To discountenance levity is a sure way to guard against the encroachment of temptation; to participate in the mirth of a buffoon is to render yourself equally ridiculous. We owe to ourselves a detestation of folly, and to the world, the appearance of it. I would have you avoid coquetry and affectation, and the observance of my maxims will never make you a prude—Pretend, therefore, should a vain youth throw out illiberal sarcasms against mechanics, lawyers, ministers, virtue, religion, or any serious subject, not to comprehend the point of his wit.

I have seldom spoken to you on the importance of religion, and the veneration due to the characters of the clergy. I always supposed your good sense capable of suggesting their necessity and eligibility. The ministers of no nation are more remarkable for learning and piety than those of this country. The fool may pretend to scorn, and the irreligious to contemn, but every person of sense and reflection must admire that sacred order, whose business is to inform the understanding, and regulate the passions of mankind. Surely, therefore, that class of men will continue to merit our esteem and affection, while virtue remains upon earth.

I am always pleased with the reasonable and amiable light in which the clergy are placed by the author of the *Guardian*—"The light," says he, "in which these points should be exposed to the view of one who is prejudiced against the names, *Religion, Church, Priest,* or the like, is to consider the clergy as so many philosophers, the churches as schools, and their sermons as lectures for the improvement and information of the audience. How would the heart of Tully or Socrates have rejoiced, had they lived in a nation where the law had made provision for philosophers to read lectures of philosophy, every seventh day, in several thousands of schools, erected at the public charge, throughout the whole country, at which lectures, all ranks and sexes, without distinction, were obliged to be present, for their general improvement!"

You may, perhaps, think this letter too serious, but remember that virtue and religion are the foundation of education.

Adieu!

MRS. HOLMES TO MYRA
Belleview

YOU will observe, my dear friend, that most of the letters I have written to you of late, on female education, are confined to the subject of study. I am sensible of the ridicule sometimes levelled at those who are called learned ladies. Either these ladies must be uncommonly pedantic, or those who ridicule them, uncommonly ignorant—Do not be apprehensive of acquiring that

title, or sharing the ridicule, but remember that the knowledge which I wish you to acquire is necessary to adorn your many virtues and amiable qualifications. This ridicule is evidently a transatlantic idea, and must have been imbibed from the source of some English novel or magazine—The American ladies of this class, who come within our knowledge, we know to be justly celebrated as ornaments to society, and an honor to the sex. When it is considered how many of our countrywomen are capable of the task, it is a matter of regret that American literature boasts so few productions from the pens of the ladies.

Self-complacency is a most necessary acquirement—for the value of a woman will always be commensurate to the opinion she entertains of herself. A celebrated European wit, in a letter to a lady, concenters much good advice in one short rule of conduct, "Reverence Thyself."

I was this morning reading Swift's letter to a very young lady on her marriage. Although this famous writer is not celebrated for delicacy or respect towards us, yet I wish some of his observations contained less truth—If you are in company, says this writer, when the conversation turns on the manners and customs of remote nations, or on books in verse or prose, or on the nature and limits of virtue and vice, it is a shame for a lady not to relish such discourses, not to improve by them, and endeavor by reading and information to have her share in those entertainments, rather than turn aside, as is the usual custom, and consult with the woman who sits next her about a new cargo of fans.

He then descends to particulars and insists on the necessity of orthography. Is it not a little hard, continues he, that not one gentleman's daughter in a thousand should be brought to read or understand her own natural tongue, or be judge of the easiest books that are written in it; as any one may find, who can have the patience to hear them mangle a play or a novel?

If there be any of your acquaintance to whom this passage is applicable, I hope you will recommend the study of Mr. Webster's *Grammatical Institute,* as the best work in our language to facilitate the knowledge of grammar. I cannot but think Mr. Webster intended his valuable book for the benefit of his countrywomen: For while he delivers his rules in a pure, precise, and elegant style, he explains his meaning by examples which are calculated to inspire the female mind with a thirst for emulation and a desire of virtue.

No subject has been more exhausted than that of education. Many Utopian schemes have been delineated, and much speculation employed. When I peruse these labors, and am persuaded the intention of their authors is to promote our welfare, I feel myself prompted to a prudent and amiable demeanour; and I suppose every woman of reason and reflection feels the same inclination to virtue, and the same sensations of gratitude in reading the works of those writers, the characteristics of whom are sentiment, morality and benevolence.

What books do you read, my dear? We are now finishing Barlow's *Vision of Columbus,* and shall begin upon Dwight's *Conquest of Canaan* in a few days.[1] It is very agreeable to read with one who points out the beauties of the author as we proceed. Such an one is Worthy.—Sometimes Mr. Holmes makes one of our party, and his notes and references to the ancient poets are very entertaining. Worthy is delighted with the ease and freedom with which we live here. We have little concerts, we walk, we ride, we read, we have good company—this is Belleview in all its glory!

Adieu, Adieu, my dear—I shall continue this subject no longer, though I flatter myself you would receive my hints with satisfaction, because you must be persuaded I love you, and so interest myself in your welfare—I need not add that I think your conduct worthy of you. You are such a good girl that I know not in what to direct you; for you leave me no room for advice—continue to anticipate the desires of my heart, and to secure the high opinion you have there obtained.

Your friend forever!

[1] *The Vision of Columbus* by Joel Barlow, 1754-1812, was published 1787. A patriotic poem in nine books, it is superior to his later epic, *The Columbrad* (1807). *The Conquest of Canaan* by Timothy Dwight, 1752-1817, was published in 1785. Both Barlow and Dwight were "Connecticut Wits."

1748 ∽ *Hugh Henry Brackenridge* ∽ 1816

THE SENTIMENTAL spirit in fiction found its counterbalance in the satiric spirit. Fielding and Smollett did not keep pace in America with Richardson and Sterne, but they were not absent, and of course Cervantes was found with them. Where the sentimental spirit had dispensed democratic ideology with a free hand and without critical reservations, the satiric spirit tended to subject some of this ideology to a more rigorously realistic view.

At least this is the case in the lone satiric masterpiece of early American fiction, *Modern Chivalry; or, The Adventures of Captain Farrago and Teague O'Regan,* which was issued in installments from 1792 to 1815. Chaotically episodic in structure and mixed in style, with short essays interrupting the narrative, *Modern Chivalry* has a zest and power that rarely flag. Hugh Henry Brackenridge, its author, was born in Scotland. His father, a poor farmer, brought the family to frontier Pennsylvania when Hugh was five. Despite an environment not likely to lead to intellectual distinction, Hugh knew a great deal of Latin and some Greek by the time he was thirteen, and two years later was teaching school in Gunpowder Falls, Maryland. His five years there made him realize the need of more education, with the consequence that he was graduated in 1771 from the College of New Jersey, now Princeton University. There he had Philip Freneau and James Madison as classmates, belonged to the Whig Literary Society, and made his début as a writer when he and Freneau collaborated on a prose tale entitled *Father Bombo's Pilgrimage to Mecca* and on the commencement poem, *The Rising Glory of America.*

After returning for his M.A., Brackenridge continued to teach, even during the first years of the Revolution, but eventually he entered Washington's army as chaplain. Leaving the army in 1778, he invested capital and energy at Philadelphia in the *United States Magazine,* the first number of which appeared January, 1779. When it succumbed at the end of that year, Brackenridge turned to the study of the law. He was admitted to the bar in 1780 at Philadelphia and then went on to less crowded Pittsburgh to practice, remaining there for twenty years. He bought land, built a house, married, had a son, helped start the *Pittsburgh Gazette,* and ran successfully for the State Assembly. Changing his mind concerning his campaign promises, he was accused of being a traitor, despite his attempt to give his reasons fully. The experience made him severely critical of the democratic electorate. With his political ambitions frustrated and his first wife dead, Brackenridge married again. Politics continued to interest him, but the course he steered was sometimes an uncertain one. Getting involved in the Whisky Insurrection of western Pennsylvania because he was in demand for legal advice, he was questioned by Alexander Hamilton and absolved of treason.

At first an ardent advocate of the French Revolution, Brackenridge had a revulsion of feeling toward it. Although he founded the Republican party in western Pennsylvania, he was defeated in a bitter campaign for the State Assembly. The party rewarded him, however, for his activity in its behalf: he was appointed a justice of the Supreme Court of Pennsylvania. Establishing the newspaper, *Tree of Liberty,* he gave further support to Jefferson's cause. Yet he was to differ with Jefferson on the importance and integrity of law and lawyers. His collection of legal papers, *Law Miscellanies,* 1814, was a real contribution to his profession. He died at Carlisle, Pennsylvania.

The story of Brackenridge's life is that of a true democrat who yet had his reservations about democracy. This is the point of view of *Modern Chivalry,* which utilizes all his rich knowledge of the frontier, of men and manners, of local and world politics.

[The following selections, taken from the opening chapters, have been supplied with titles by the editors.]

From
MODERN CHIVALRY
[1792]

HORSES AND MEN

JOHN FARRAGO was a man of about fifty-three years of age, of good natural sense, and considerable reading; but in some things whimsical, owing perhaps to his greater knowledge of books than of the world; but, in some degree also, to his having never married, being what they call an old bachelor, a characteristic of which is, usually, singularity and whim. He had the advantage of having had in early life an academic education; but having never applied himself to any of the learned professions, he had lived the greater part of his life on a small farm, which he cultivated with servants or hired hands, as he could conveniently supply himself with either. The servant that he had at this time was an Irishman, whose name was Teague Oregan [O'Regan]. I shall say nothing of the character of this man, because the very name imports what he was.

A strange idea came into the head of Captain Farrago about this time; for, by the bye, I had forgot to mention that having been chosen captain of a company of militia in the neighborhood, he had gone by the name of Captain ever since; for the rule is, once a captain, and always a captain; but, as I was observing, the idea had come into his head, to saddle an old horse that he had, and ride about the world a little, with his man Teague at his heels, to see how things were going on here and there, and to observe human nature. For it is a mistake to suppose that a man cannot learn man by reading him in a corner as well as on the widest space of transaction. At any rate, it may yield amusement.

It was about a score of miles from his own house that he fell in with what we call races. The jockeys, seeing him advance, with Teague by his side, whom they took for his groom, conceived him to be some person who had brought his horse to enter for the purse. Coming up and accosting him, said they, "You seem to be for the races, Sir, and have a horse to enter." "Not at all," said the Captain; "this is but a common palfrey, and by no means remarkable for speed or bottom; he is a common plough horse which I have used on my farm for several years, and can scarce go beyond a trot; much less match himself with your blooded horses that are going to take the field on this occasion."

The jockeys were of opinion, from the speech, that the horse was what they call a bite, and that under the appearance of leanness and stiffness, there was concealed some hidden quality of swiftness uncommon. For they had heard of instances, where the most knowing had been taken in by mean looking horses; so that having laid two, or more, to one, they were nevertheless bit by the bet; and the mean looking nags proved to be horses of a more than common speed and bottom. So that there is no trusting appearances. Such was the reasoning of the jockeys. For they could have no idea that a man could come there in so singular a manner, with a groom at his foot, unless he had some great object of making money by the adventure. Under this idea, they began to interrogate him with respect to the blood and pedigree of his horse: whether he was of the Dove, or the bay mare that took the purse; and was imported by such a one at such a time? whether his sire was Tamerlane or Bajazet?

The Captain was irritated at the questions and could not avoid answering.— "Gentlemen," said he, "it is a strange thing that you should suppose that it is of any consequence what may be the pedigree of a horse. For even in men it is of no avail. Do we not find that sages have had blockheads for their sons; and that blockheads have had sages? It is remarkable that, as estates have seldom lasted three generations, so understanding and ability have seldom been transmitted to the second. There never was a greater man, take him as an orator and philosopher, than Cicero: and never was there a person who had greater opportunities than his son Marcus; and yet he proved of no account or reputation. This is an old instance, but there are a thousand others. Chesterfield and his son are mentioned. It is true, Philip and Alexander may be said to be exceptions: Philip of the strongest possible mind; capable of almost everything we can conceive; the deepest policy and the most determined valor; his son Alexander not deficient in the first, and before him in the last; if it is possible to be before a man than whom you can suppose nothing greater. It is possible, in modern times, that Tippo Saib may be equal to his father Hyder Ali.[1] Some talk of the two Pitts. I have no idea that the son is, in any respect, equal to old Sir William. The one is a labored artificial minister; the other spoke with the thunder and acted with the lightning of the gods. I will venture to say that when the present John Adamses, and Lees, and Jeffersons, and Jays, and Henrys, and other great men, who figure upon the stage at this time, have gone to sleep with their fathers, it is an hundred to one if there is any of their descendants who can fill their places. Was I to lay a bet for a great man, I would sooner pick up the brat of a tinker than go into the great houses to choose a piece of stuff for a man of genius. Even with respect to personal appearance, which is more in the power of natural production, we do not see that beauty always produces beauty; but, on the contrary, the homeliest persons have oftentimes the best favored offspring; so that there is no rule or reason in these things. With respect to this horse, therefore, it can be of no moment whether he is blooded or studded, or what he is. He is a good old horse, used to the plough, and carries my weight very well; and I have never yet made enquiry with respect to his ancestors, or affronted him so much as to cast up to him the defect of parentage. I bought him some years ago from Neil Thomas, who had him from a colt. As far as I can understand, he was of a brown mare that John M'Neis had; but of what horse I know no more than the horse himself. His gaits are good enough, as to riding a short journey or seven or eight miles, or the like; but he is rather a pacer than a trotter; and though his bottom may be good enough in carrying a bag to the mill, or going in the plough, or the sled, or the harrow, etc., yet his wind is not so good, nor his speed, as to be fit for the heats."

The jockeys thought the man a fool and gave themselves no more trouble about him. . . .

AN ELECTION

THE CAPTAIN, rising early next morning and setting out on his way, had now arrived at a place where a number of people were convened, for the purpose of electing persons to represent them in the legislature of the state. There was a weaver who was a candidate for this appointment and seemed to have a good deal of interest among the people. But another, who was a man of education, was his competitor. Relying on some talent of speaking which he thought he possessed, he addressed the multitude.

Said he, "Fellow citizens, I pretend not to any great abilities; but am conscious to myself that I have the best good will to serve you. But it is very astonishing to me that this weaver should conceive himself qualified for the trust. For though my acquirements are not great, yet his are still less. The mechanical business which he pursues must necessarily take up so much of his time that he cannot apply himself to political studies. I should therefore think it would be more answerable to your dignity, and conducive to your interest, to be represented by a man at least of some letters than by an illiterate handi-

---

[1] Tippo Sahib, 1749-1799, was sultan of Mysore, India, and son of Haidar Ali, or Hyder Ali, who died 1782 and was sultan before him.

craftsman like this. It will be more honorable for himself to remain at his loom and knot threads than to come forward in a legislative capacity: because, in the one case, he is in the sphere where God and nature has placed him; in the other, he is like a fish out of water, and must struggle for breath in a new element.

"Is it possible he can understand the affairs of government, whose mind has been concentered to the small object of weaving webs; to the price by the yard, the grist of the thread, and such like matters as concern a manufacturer of cloths? The feet of him who weaves are more occupied than the head, or at least as much; and therefore the whole man must be, at least, but in half accustomed to exercise his mental powers. For these reasons, all other things set aside, the chance is in my favor, with respect to information. However, you will decide, and give your suffrages to him or to me, as you shall judge expedient."

The Captain, hearing these observations and looking at the weaver, could not help advancing, and undertaking to subjoin something in support of what had been just said. Said he, "I have no prejudice against a weaver more than another man. Nor do I know any harm in the trade; save that from the sedentary life in a damp place, there is usually a paleness of the countenance: but this is a physical, not a moral evil. Such usually occupy subterranean apartments; not for the purpose, like Demosthenes, of shaving their heads, and writing over eight times the history of Thucydides, and perfecting a style of oratory; but rather to keep the thread moist; or because this is considered but as an inglorious sort of trade, and is frequently thrust away into cellars, and damp outhouses, which are not occupied for a better use.

"But to rise from the cellar to the senate house would be an unnatural hoist. To come from counting threads, and adjusting them to the splits of a reed, to regulate the finances of a government, would be preposterous; there being no congruity in the case. There is no analogy between knotting threads and framing laws. It would be a reversion of the order of things. Not that a manufacturer of linen or woolen, or other stuff, is an inferior character, but a different one from that which ought to be employed in affairs of state. It is unnecessary to enlarge on this subject; for you must all be convinced of the truth and propriety of what I say. But if you will give me leave to take the manufacturer aside a little, I think I can explain to him my ideas on the subject; and very probably prevail with him to withdraw his pretensions." The people, seeming to acquiesce, and beckoning to the weaver, they drew aside, and the Captain addressed him in the following words:

"Mr. Traddle," said he, for that was the name of the manufacturer. "I have not the smallest idea of wounding your sensibility; but it would seem to me it would be more your interest to pursue your occupation than to launch out into that of which you have no knowledge. When you go to the senate house, the application to you will not be to warp a web, but to make laws for the commonwealth. Now, suppose that the making of these laws requires a knowledge of commerce, or of the interests of agriculture, or those principles on which the different manufactures depend, what service could you render? It is possible you might think justly enough, but could you speak? You are not in the habit of public speaking. You are not furnished with those commonplace ideas with which even very ignorant men can pass for knowing something. There is nothing makes a man so ridiculous as to attempt what is above his sphere. You are no tumbler, for instance; yet should you give out that you could vault upon a man's back, or turn head over heels, like the wheels of a cart, the stiffness of your joints would encumber you; and you would fall upon your backside to the ground. Such a squash as that would do you damage. The getting up to ride on the state is an unsafe thing to those who are not accustomed to such horseman-ship. It is a disagreeable thing for a man to be laughed at, and there is no way of keeping oneself from it but by avoiding all affectation."

While they were thus discoursing, a bustle had taken place among the crowd. Teague, hearing so much about elections and serving the government, took it into his head that he could be a legislator him-self. The thing was not displeasing to the people, who seemed to favor his preten-sions; owing, in some degree, to there being several of his countrymen among the crowd; but more especially to the fluctua-tion of the popular mind, and a disposi-tion to what is new and ignoble. For though the weaver was not the most ele-vated object of choice, yet he was still pref-erable to this tatterdemalion, who was but a menial servant, and had so much of what is called a brogue on his tongue as to fall far short of an elegant speaker.

The Captain, coming up and finding what was on the carpet, was greatly chagrined at not having been able to give the mul-titude a better idea of the importance of a legislative trust; alarmed, also, from an apprehension of the loss of his servant. Under these impressions, he resumed his address to the multitude. Said he, "This is making the matter still worse, gentlemen: this servant of mine is but a bog-trotter; who can scarcely speak the dialect in which your laws ought to be written; but cer-tainly has never read a single treatise on any political subject; for the truth is, he cannot read at all. The young people of the lower class, in Ireland, have seldom the advantage of a good education; especially the descendants of the ancient Irish, who have most of them a great assurance of countenance, but little information, or liter-ature. This young man, whose family name is Oregan, has been my servant for several years. And, except a too great fondness for women, which now and then brings him into scrapes, he has demeaned himself in a manner tolerable enough. But he is totally ignorant of the great principles of legislation; and more especially, the partic-ular interests of the government. A free government is a noble possession to a people: and this freedom consists in an equal right to make laws, and to have the benefit of the laws when made. Though doubtless, in such a government, the lowest citizen may become chief magistrate, yet it is sufficient to possess the right, not absolutely necessary to exercise it. Or even if you should think proper, now and then, to show your privilege, and exert, in a signal manner, the democratic prerogative, yet is it not descending too low to filch away from me a hireling, which I cannot well spare, to serve your purpose? You are surely carrying the matter too far, in thinking to make a senator of this hostler; to take him away from an employment to which he has been bred, and put him to another, to which he has served no ap-prenticeship: to set those hands which have been lately employed in currying my horse, to the draughting bills, and preparing busi-ness for the house."

The people were tenacious of their choice and insisted on giving Teague their suf-frages; and by the frown upon their brows seemed to indicate resentment at what had been said; as indirectly charging them with want of judgment, or calling in question their privilege to do what they thought proper. "It is a very strange thing," said one of them, who was a speaker for the rest, "that after having conquered Burgoyne and Cornwallis, and got a government of our own, we cannot put in it whom we please. This young man may be your serv-ant, or another man's servant; but if we choose to make him a delegate, what is that to you? He may not be yet skilled in the matter, but there is a good day a-coming. We will impower him; and it is better to trust a plain man like him than one of your high flyers, that will make laws to suit their own purposes."

Said the Captain, "I had much rather you would send the weaver, though I thought that improper, than to invade my house-hold, and thus detract from me the very person that I have about me to brush my boots and clean my spurs." The prolocutor of the people gave him to understand that his surmises were useless, for the people had determined on the choice, and Teague they would have for a representative.

Finding it answered no end to expostulate with the multitude, he requested to speak a word with Teague by himself. Stepping aside, he said to him, composing his voice and addressing him in a soft manner, "Teague, you are quite wrong in this matter they have put into your head. Do you know what it is to be a member of a deliberate body? What qualifications are necessary? Do you understand anything of geography? If a question should be, to make a law to dig a canal in some part of the state, can you describe the bearing of the mountains, and the course of the rivers? Or if commerce is to be pushed to some new quarter, by the force of regulations, are you competent to decide in such a case? There will be questions of law and astronomy on the carpet. How you must gape and stare like a fool, when you come to be asked your opinion on these subjects? Are you acquainted with the abstract principles of finance; with the funding public securities; the ways and means of raising the revenue; providing for the discharge of the public debts, and all other things which respect the economy of the government? Even if you had knowledge, have you a facility of speaking? I would suppose you would have too much pride to go to the house just to say, Ay, or No. This is not the fault of your nature, but of your education; having been accustomed to dig turf in your early years, rather than instructing yourself in the classics, or common school books.

"When a man becomes a member of a public body, he is like a racoon, or other beast that climbs up the fork of a tree; the boys pushing at him with pitch-forks, or throwing stones, or shooting at him with an arrow, the dogs barking in the meantime. One will find fault with your not speaking; another with your speaking, if you speak at all. They will have you in the newspapers, and ridicule you as a perfect beast. There is what they call the caricatura; that is, representing you with a dog's head, or a cat's claw. As you have a red head, they will very probably make a fox of you, or a sorrel horse, or a brindled cow. It is the devil in hell to be exposed to the squibs and crackers of the gazette wits and publications. You know no more about these matters than a goose; and yet you would undertake rashly, without advice, to enter on the office; nay, contrary to advice. For I would not for a thousand guineas, though I have not the half of it to spare, that the breed of the Oregans should come to this; bringing on them a worse stain than stealing sheep, to which they are addicted. You have nothing but your character, Teague, in a new country to depend upon. Let it never be said that you quitted an honest livelihood, the taking care of my horse, to follow the new-fangled whims of the times, and to be a statesman."

Teague was moved chiefly with the last part of the address, and consented to give up the object.

The Captain, glad of this, took him back to the people, and announced his disposition to decline the honor which they had intended him.

Teague acknowledged that he had changed his mind, and was willing to remain in a private station.

The people did not seem well pleased with the Captain; but as nothing more could be said about the matter, they turned their attention to the weaver, and gave him their suffrages.

BOOK II

American Literature 1800-1860

GENERAL INTRODUCTION 1800-1860

I

GRADUATING at 18 in the Bowdoin College class of 1825, Henry Wadsworth Longfellow wrote the required commencement oration on the subject "Our Native Writers." He voiced an almost religious devotion to the ideal of a national literature, and expressed his confidence that "palms are to be won by our native writers!—by those, that have been nursed and brought up . . . in the civil and religious freedom of our country."

The young Longfellow spoke for a generation. The creation of a worthy national literature was consciously recognized as a present and imperative duty by many young men and women who came to maturity in the first half-century of the nation's life. They were stimulated by earlier American writers. As a sophomore, Longfellow had read *"Arthur Mervyn, a novel—an American novel—from the elegant pen of C. B. Brown,"* as he reported to his mother in a letter gushing with enthusiastic appreciation of Brown and regret that "the author . . . as an American has never received from his countrymen that praise and renown, which was his due." The work of Franklin and Freneau, the "Connecticut Wits" and Brackenridge; the narratives of settlers, explorers, Indian fighters; the great political documents of the revolutionary period: all these gave ground on which to build. Divided as they were by political and sectional differences in the first years of the new nation, Americans were united in the feeling that "the eyes of the world were upon them," as one editor put it; and the expression of the already varied life of America in literature seemed to many an essential part of what was expected of them. The new West, powerful as a symbol in the American mind and swiftly gaining importance in practical affairs, contributed mightily to the conception of a national literature. As the century advanced, economic and social conflicts, religious and philosophical problems, shared in its shaping.

For the building of an American literature, however, there must be American readers, and the facilities for bringing American writers and readers into fruitful relationship: literary periodicals and book publishers. The young Longfellow stated the problem bluntly in his commencement address: "If we would ever have a national literature, our native writers must be patronized." Provision of the channels for that patronage was a mandatory first step in the early decades of the new century. Though a few important literary magazines had been established before 1800, none of these survived into the new century. American book publishing was similarly undeveloped.

Colonial publishing had not been a specialized industry, but had been undertaken by booksellers and job-printers working together. Indeed the local printer, whether in city or village, was often also a newspaper editor, a bookseller, and a publisher of pamphlets, textbooks, and even works of general literature. Up until the middle of the nineteenth century, small-town printers continued occasionally to issue books, thus providing work for their typesetters in dull seasons.

Isaiah Thomas, of Worcester, editor of the famous *Massachusetts Spy*, attempted two magazines at different times, and by 1800 had built up, with the aid of his partner Andrews, one of the largest book publishing houses in the United States. From the by-product of a country shop to the output of a large and profitable business with its main office in Boston, the Thomas & Andrews books exemplify the growth of early American publishing. Mathew Carey, of Philadelphia, who had edited one of the best of the American magazines shortly before the turn of the century, was by 1800 devoting his energies to the founding of a publishing concern which was later famous as Carey & Lea. In the first few decades of the new century, specialized book publishing firms sprang up in all the leading American cities.

Many of these houses found their prosperity in pirating English books and thus seemed to some observers to be doing a disservice to American literature. Carey & Lea, invading New York bookstores, strained every resource to get new Scott and Dickens romances to an avid public before the Harpers could do it. But the Carey firm also published Freneau, Irving, and Cooper, and later some of the early work of Poe and Simms. About the middle of the century the works of both Irving and Cooper were taken over by G. P. Putnam, whose publishing business had grown out of the Wiley Bookshop established in New York in 1807. Up in Boston, William D. Ticknor bought the Old Corner Bookstore in 1832; from that beginning there later emerged the firm of Ticknor & Fields, which eventually became the publisher of the great New England poets and essayists.

Several of the important literary periodicals before 1850 were published by their editors or by supporting literary clubs. The *Port Folio* (1801-27), of Philadelphia, was both edited and published during its early and best years by the brilliant Joseph Dennie. The *North American Review* (1815-1940) was owned for many years by a Boston literary coterie and edited by Harvard professors. Heavy though it was, its criticism was often distinguished and it was generally conceded to be the best of American reviews. More popular in tone was *Graham's Magazine* (1841-58), of Philadelphia, edited and published by George R. Graham, who had Edgar Allan Poe as an assistant for a short time. Poe was editor for a little more than two years of the *Southern Literary Messenger* (1834-64), of Richmond, but for the most part this magazine was edited by its publishers. The *Knickerbocker, or New York Monthly Magazine* (1833-65) was edited and published in its best years by Lewis Gaylord Clark. And the inimitable *Godey's Lady's Book* (1830-98), of Philadelphia, was owned and published by Louis A. Godey & Company until 1877.

Graham's and *Godey's* did no small service to American literature in the forties and fifties by paying good writers well. Poe, Lowell, Bryant, Cooper, Longfellow, and Simms, as well as many who were vastly inferior, enjoyed the largess of these princes of the magazine world.

Encouraged and supported by American publishers and periodicals, the "native writers" envisioned by the young Longfellow fulfilled their obligation, realized their dream: in the period between 1825 and the Civil War, they created a great national literature.

II

Definition of the problem was another necessary part of the job. What were to be the purposes and the distinguishing characteristics of American literature—what should the American writer try to do? How far should American literature build on that of Britain and of Europe, how far be militantly independent? Was a real American literature as yet practicable at all? On this last as on all these questions there was the widest disagreement, ranging from the assertion that significant literary production is impossible in a raw and crude society, that only the cultural silt of many centuries can feed the fine flower of letters (an attitude still sometimes encountered after one hundred and fifty years), to the confident vision of an American literature that should surpass all the literary achievements of earlier ages and other lands.

These were properly questions for critical analysis; and the need for "confident and independent criticism of American books," voiced by the elder Richard Henry Dana in *The Idle Man* (1821-22), was generally recognized. Many critics and reviewers helped to state the issues. Joseph Dennie of the *Port Folio,* firm in the Federalist tradition, held for the most part to the view that little could be expected of American writers and that few American books deserved attention. Edward Everett, as editor of the *North American Review,* defended himself against the charge of neglecting his own country by declaring that "the American books are too poor to praise." On the other hand, Robert Walsh in his *American Quarterly Review* rebuked "the prevalence of a certain colonial spirit." The editor of the Philadelphia *Literary Gazette* recommended, as the best method to create a national literature, "to make our poetry national and peculiar, to hang its flowers around our history, to interweave it with our local attachments, to dye it deeply in the grain of our prejudices and passions." John Knapp, writing on "National Poetry" in the *North American Review* in 1818, exhorted poets to find subjects in Indian antiquities. More substantial contributions to American criticism were such discriminating discussions of current books, both British and American, as those of F. W. P. Greenwood, also in the *North American Review.*

But by far the most important contributions to the definition of the problem of a national literature were made by those who combined the force of creative example with their critical analysis. First among these was Washington Irving. His *A History of New York . . . by Diedrich Knickerbocker* was an already existing answer to Sydney Smith's derisive question, in the *Edinburgh Review* for January, 1820, "Who reads an American book?" Popular on both sides of the Atlantic, it demonstrated the ability of at least one American writer to deal entertainingly and effectively, in the modes of satire and burlesque, with both historical and contemporary American materials. It was in the *Sketch Book,* however, that Irving made his greatest contribution. One of its essays, "English Writers on America," deals directly with one of the crucial issues in the definition of our national literature—that of the relation of American writers to British writers, of America to Britain. It is an attempt at mediation in the literary warfare in which Irving's friend, James Kirke Paulding, was notably belligerent. Irving did not hesitate to speak plainly of the unworthy motives and evil effects of many British books which he thought unfairly critical of America; but he was equally candid in pointing out the disservice to their own country of American writers who wrote in the same temper.

It was in other parts of the *Sketch Book,* however, that Irving did most to establish and clarify the conception of a national literature. In "Philip of Pokanoket" and "Traits of Indian Character" he laid foundations for all subsequent significant treatments of the American Indian. In the great Hudson Valley tales, "Rip Van Winkle" and the rest, he showed conclusively that American life could be made the substance of enduringly satisfying literary expression.

William Cullen Bryant was one of the early makers of our national literature who participated most substantially in the conscious definition of its purposes and the establishment of its standards. In "An Essay on American Poetry," published in the *North American Review* for July, 1818, he examined candidly and fairly the work of a large number of American writers of verse, and then proceeded to an eminently sensible and constructive statement of the whole problem of the American poet in his time, and a discriminating appraisal of current trends. This article is one of the major early documents in the definition of a national literature. Bryant's later critical articles in the *North American Review* and elsewhere are of similar quality. The impact of his own creative work, however, was far greater than that of his criticism. Such pieces as "The Hunter of the Prairies," "To the Fringed Gentian," and "To a Waterfowl" are as unmistakably American as they are indisputably poetry. To Bryant's contemporaries, they had the force of living examples.

Like Irving, James Fenimore Cooper practised American literature before he preached it. Cooper's failure with British materials in *Precaution,* his success when he turned to American scenes and characters in *The Spy,* was adduced as evidence by Robert Walsh in his argument for the use of native materials by American writers, in an article in the *American Quarterly Review* for June, 1827. Certainly Cooper's example was stimulating. As he struck out in rapid succession, within four years, the broad fields of his major achievement in fiction—the American past in *The Spy,* the frontier with its typical figure, Natty Bumppo, in *The Pioneers,* the sea in *The Pilot,* the conflict between red and white in *The Last of the Mohicans*—the structure of the national literature grew swiftly.

But Cooper was not content to teach by example. When in 1828, from the vantage point of Paris, he undertook to write a British traveler's account of America as it should be written, in *Notions of the Americans,* he devoted one of his hypothetical "traveling bachelor's" letters to the subject, "American Literature." His analysis was clear and firm, though some of his findings were inconsistent with his own previously published successful work. Cooper's definition of American literature was part of his general view of American life, explicitly set forth in *A Letter to His Countrymen* (1834) and *The American Democrat* (1838). Cooper held a high ideal for the American citizen, as for the American writer. His rebuke of whatever seemed to him inconsistent with or inimical to the attainment of that ideal was always caustic, sometimes contentious. The American temper in the 1830's was scarcely amenable to influence by adverse criticism, and Cooper's expository writing had little practical effect beyond the exasperation of his enemies. His very great contribution to the development of a national literature was made almost wholly by his continuing production as a novelist.

Edgar Allan Poe shared largely in the shaping of the conception of a national literature, both by precept and by example. His contribution was to create more interest in artistic standards, to emphasize the writer's conscience. He did this not only in his criticism, but also through the widely influential example of his stories and his poems. Though Poe used American scenes in "The Gold Bug" and a few other stories, that use was merely incidental. His theory of poetry precluded the introduction of details derived directly from external experience. Hence his creative work served as a salutary and timely demonstration of the truth that the American writer need not be narrowly limited in his choice of subject matter, while at the same time it provided the stimulus of the attainment of high literary standards by a native writer. Poe's criticism was the most effective of his generation. As a practicing reviewer he was fearless in appraisal, merciless in castigation; he was also forthright in recognition of merit where he saw it. He went beyond mere reviewing to the formulation of critical theory and the examination of literary problems, including those peculiar to the American writer. His work as a whole was a major contribution to the development of the national literature.

Yet it remained for a writer whose greatness Poe failed to recognize, Ralph Waldo Emerson, to make the definitive statement of the whole matter. The great sentences of "The American Scholar," his Harvard Phi Beta Kappa address of 1837—clearly meant for the writer as well as the teacher and student—held for Emerson's contemporaries, and still hold in large degree, the essence of what it is that must make American literature American.

Emerson's disciple, Margaret Fuller, applied his teachings in her practical work as reviewer and editor. Henry David Thoreau, in parts of *Walden* and *A Week on the Concord and Merrimac Rivers,* developed and clarified Emerson's principles—with added elements from his own thinking—in some of the most illuminating discussion of fundamental literary problems to be found anywhere in American literature.

William Gilmore Simms, appraising Cooper's work as American historical novelist from the vantage point of his own interest and experience in historical fiction, displayed broad critical vision of American literary problems as well as his personal capacity for justice and generosity. Herman Melville likewise made his chief critical contribution to contemporary understanding of the national literature in his comment on a fellow novelist. In his essay, "Hawthorne and His Mosses," which appeared in the New York *Literary World* in August, 1850, he not only pointed out in Hawthorne's choice and use of materials depths of significance which other contemporaries had missed, but made both for Hawthorne and for the national literature as a whole bold claims of positive greatness.

The mature Longfellow gently satirized in his novel *Kavanagh* (1849) the more blatant and bumptious varieties of literary nationalism. He had already achieved, in the popularity of *Evangeline* (1847), all that his youthful vision had promised for the "native writers" of America—even to the patronage which he had demanded as necessary "if we are ever to have a national literature." By the mid-century that national literature was accomplished fact. The facilities for bringing writers and readers together had been created and had been used. The definition of the purposes and character of such a literature had been largely achieved. Meanwhile other motives had gained primary importance in its development and direction.

III

From the very beginning of this period, and gaining force with every decade, a new factor had naturally and spontaneously aided in the development of a truly national literature. The successive development of the trans-Appalachian region, the Middle West, the great plains, and the Far West brought great rivers and valleys and deserts and plains and mountains within the grand over-view of the American scene. Land and opportunity in the West drew men and money steadily from the older seaboard states throughout the first two generations of our national history. Pioneer ideals, manners and ways of life affected the East as well as the West and helped to form the conception and shape the expression of Americanism. Products of the West modified the national economy and motivated national politics, from the whisky of Pennsylvania to the gold of California. Perhaps most significantly, the national thinking was affected by the West, both as fact and as symbol.

It was inevitable, then, that the West should have a place in the national literature. Most of the major writers of these generations saw the West, if only briefly, at first hand: Irving, Cooper, Simms, Bryant, Emerson, Thoreau, Whitman; and for each his western experience was significant and stimulating, finding expression in his writing. No doubt the popular conception of the West was more largely shaped, however, by the books of such romancers as Robert Montgomery Bird of Philadelphia, whose *Nick of the Woods* (1837) is a lurid tale of Indian fighting in frontier Kentucky, and Judge James Hall, of Illinois and Ohio, whose stories in *Legends of the West* (1832) and other volumes follow conventional patterns but are based on direct observation.

For the reader of today the best understanding of the westward movement is to be found in the writings of actual participants in the life of the frontier. Often crude in form, these documents of first-hand experience have force and flavor exceeding anything transient visitors to the frontier could produce. From the first groups of settlers who crossed the mountains into Tennessee and Kentucky came back letters and journals, records of things seen and done; and this autobiographical record of the frontier continued for a century, forming a great body of writing marked by richness of detail and vitality of incident, and often possessing true literary distinction.

Explorers, traders, naturalists, missionaries, and first settlers of the wilderness were the makers of this literature. For example, the *Journals* of the Lewis and Clark expedition of 1804-6 have positive literary interest. Timothy Flint's *Recollections of the Last Ten Years* (1826) give vivid pictures of life on the Mississippi and in Missouri and Arkansas in 1815, when Flint traveled those frontiers as a missionary. John J. Audubon's study of the birds and animals of the West yielded incidental portrayals of the region and the life of the frontier. The *Narrative of the Life of David Crockett, of the State of Tennessee* (1834), is one of the liveliest and most enjoyable of all books of the frontier. Peter Cartwright's *Autobiography* (1857) and *The Backwoods Preacher* (1858) narrate with gusto the exploits of a redoubtable Methodist evangelist in the Ohio River valley during the period of settlement.

Though not a bona-fide settler, Francis Parkman participated in the westward migration in such fashion as to make *The California and Oregon Trail* (1849) a classic of the westward movement. Lewis G. Garrard's *Wah-to'-yah and the Taos Trail* (1850) is a less widely known but equally valuable book of the same period. The Gold Rush and the settlement of California brought forth a great body of writing about that new frontier and the journey thither.

Originating as autobiographical record of personal observation and later assuming fictional elaboration, one specialized type of writing about the frontier deserves emphasis both for its historical importance and for its intrinsic interest. This is the humorous tale of frontier incidents and characters. Flourishing especially in what was then the Southwest, in the years from 1835 to 1855, frontier humor developed into a body of writing which afforded the background for the regional writing of Mark Twain and possesses marked interest and value today.

Most of the makers of this literature were professional men—lawyers, physicians, journalists—who saw and shared the rough life of the border settlements. Their humorous intention freed these writers from many of the constraints to which serious fiction of the time was subjected. The result is that we find in these stories a degree of realism unparalleled elsewhere in their literary generation—a realism which makes them of first importance as documents of social history and at the same time relates them closely to fiction of much later date. Elements of folklore, of fantasy and exaggeration, give these stories added value as revelations of the mind of the frontier and of the America of a century ago.

Augustus Baldwin Longstreet, a Georgia lawyer and judge, teacher and editor, was a pioneer in this field. His *Georgia Scenes,* a collection of sketches previously published in local newspapers, appeared in 1835. Nearly all of the books of frontier humor were similarly collections of tales first written for local newspapers. Many found their way to ultimate book publication through the columns of *The Spirit of the Times,* a New York periodical of the world of sport —especially horse racing—edited by William T. Porter.

Another Georgian for a time associated with Longstreet, William Tappan Thompson, wrote some of the most pleasing examples of frontier humor in the collections called *Major Jones' Courtship* (1843), *Chronicles of Pineville* (1845), and *Major Jones' Sketches of Travel* (1847). *The Adventures of Simon Suggs* (1845), by Johnson J. Hooper, an Alabama lawyer, legislator and editor, is an episodic novel portraying with brilliant realism the career of a frontier swindler and minor criminal. Thomas Bangs Thorpe, painter and editor, wrote some of the most finished examples of the humorous tale of frontier life for his volumes *The Mysteries of the Back-woods* (1846) and *The Hive of the Bee Hunter* (1854). Joseph G. Baldwin put his own experience as a young lawyer in the old Southwest into the flavorful pages of *The Flush Times of Alabama and Mississippi* (1853). Perhaps most gifted of all these humorists of the frontier was George W. Harris, of Tennessee, postmaster and hunter, silversmith and river boat captain, and creator of Sut Lovingood, a frontier yarn-spinner, practical joker, and poet. Coarse and elemental in their humorous elements, Harris's stories are memorable in their figurative language and in their frank pictures of the life of the border settlements. They were seemingly not collected in book form until 1867, under the title *Sut Lovingood*.

In these two types of writing, the autobiographical record of frontier experience and the humorous fictional elaboration of that experience, the contribution of the westward movement to American literature is of high importance, increasingly recognized both as the source of a powerful impulse toward the native and the authentic in our national literature, and for its own lasting interest and meaning.

IV

But the West of the decades from 1800 to 1850 was more than a rich mine for students of nature and of human nature, far more than a nursery for bizarre characters and the humorists who wrote of them. It was a fateful reality in the practical affairs of the whole nation, politically, economically, socially. By the mid-century the lines had been drawn, the stage set, for what had already been called "the irrepressible conflict" between North and South. Sectionalism threatened nationalism. And in the genesis of the conflict, as in its ultimate solution, the part played by the West was decisive.

Sectional differentiation had begun in the colonies and was reflected in colonial literature. The South had early adopted—though not wholly, either then or later—the plantation system, dependent on slave labor. The middle colonies and New England had developed a system of small farming based on individual ownership and operation. The pre-eminence of New England in commerce was early established.

Political independence and the two wars with Britain made domestic industry necessary if that commerce was to survive. But the industrial revolution came slowly to America: Hamilton's dream of great native manufacturing enterprises had to wait almost a generation for fulfilment. It was hard to overcome the ingrained predilections and prejudices of an agrarian society. The West played a part in this retardation: why should a man stay in a factory in Rhode Island or Connecticut when he could buy a rich farm in the West for a few months' wages? But what the exhortations of economists and the persuasions of traders could not accomplish, the development of this same West eventually achieved. Its cheap grains and meats broke the back of New England's agriculture; its boundless market for manufactured goods made industrialization the inescapable alternative.

The maintenance of a labor force was exceedingly difficult in the days of industrial pioneering—again because of the land of opportunity beyond the mountains. But a rising flood of immigration from Europe—systematically cultivated as a part of New England's commerce, just as the slave trade had been earlier—solved that problem. Between 1820 and 1860 over five million immigrants came to America—roughly one-sixth of the nation's population at the latter date. Economic necessity kept most of these immigrants at least temporarily in the seaboard states. Irish immigrant women replaced the Massachusetts farm girls in the mills of Lowell. Before that shift had been accomplished, industrialism had begun to display all the ugly by-products which had become familiar in England a generation earlier. The speculative character of both the rapid industrial expansion and the exploitation of the resources of the West kept the economy of the whole nation unstable, and panics—that of 1837 was especially severe—brought recurring unemployment and fluctuation in wages. Labor organization followed, at first local and largely impotent; strikes, lockouts, the blacklist and the speed-up, became well known phenomena. It was in 1837 that Horace Greeley, New England farm boy making his way in New York, saw with incredulous horror able-bodied men and women begging for a chance to work: that, in America! George Ripley found thirty human beings, diseased and starving, living in one cellar room in a Boston slum.

It was against this background of expanding industrialism that the writers of New England and the middle states in the 1830's and 40's lived their lives and did their work. Some of them were almost wholly untouched by it, seemingly unaware of it—Longfellow most notably. Perhaps Poe's private tragedies insulated him against the woes of the world. Others were affected only narrowly, as Whittier; or briefly, as Lowell.

For some of the greatest the problem presented to their minds by the life about them was at once complicated and intensified by the religious dilemma of the times. The traditional Calvinism had largely lost its authority in the centres in which men thought and wrote; its hold upon the more active minds of the new generation was weak indeed. The Unitarianism which had succeeded it in parts of New England had grown so tepid, so hollow, as to make its ministry intolerable to men of such diverse backgrounds as Emerson and Orestes A. Brownson—the Harvard graduate and descendant of a long line of clergymen and scholars, the Vermont farm boy who had never entered a college door. Brownson became a minister to the people of Boston without denominational ties, a social reformer and agitator like George Ripley. Before he reached the goal of his pilgrimage, he startlingly anticipated the findings of Marx and Engels in his study of "The Laboring Classes," published in the *Boston Quarterly Review* in July and October, 1840. He resolved the dilemma at last by becoming a Roman Catholic, to continue his editing and writing for thirty years as the most influential lay spokesman of Catholicism in the United States. Emerson left the Unitarian ministry to write *Nature* (1836) and to become the prophet of American transcendentalism.

V

Transcendentalism must be viewed in its social matrix, in relation to the political instability of the young democracy which so vexed and alarmed Cooper, to the economic tensions attendant on the adolescence of American industrialism, to the humanitarian impulses which found their most substantial expression in abolitionism, to the rapid advance of American science in this period, and especially to the religious dilemma already noted. But transcendentalism was primarily an intellectual attitude, a philosophical position, and its interest to the student of American thought far exceeds the measure of its influence on the practical affairs of the nation. To its contemporaries, it is true, transcendentalism assumed the character of a movement, with social and political reformers numbered among its leaders as well as writers and philosophers, with its dissident religious groups and its experimental socialistic or communistic communities, with its lectures, magazines, and books. The term "transcendental nonsense" came to be widely applied to whatever seemed radical, revolutionary, or merely unconventional.

Emerson recognized this popular attitude in his lecture "The Transcendentalist," one of a series of eight on "The Times" which he delivered in Boston in 1841-42. In this lecture he defined transcendentalism simply as "Idealism; Idealism as it appears in 1842." The name, he explained, had been derived from "Immanuel Kant, of Königsberg, who replied to the skeptical philosophy of Locke, which insisted that there was nothing in the intellect which was not previously in the experience of the senses, by showing that there was a very important class of ideas or imperative forms which did not come by experience, but through which experience was acquired; that these were intuitions of the mind itself; and he denominated them *Transcendental* forms." Major contributions to Emerson's thinking came directly from Coleridge, whose *Aids to Reflection* was published in the United States in 1829, and from Carlyle, Emerson's friend and correspondent. *Sartor Resartus* was published in book form in the United States earlier than in England, and became a kind of bible to many American readers. Behind Coleridge and Carlyle lay the work of the German idealistic philosophers, not Kant alone but also notably Fichte and Schelling, read in their own language by William Ellery Channing the elder and other Americans. To the thinking of Emerson and of Thoreau Oriental philosophy and religion contributed materially. The transcendentalists read also with definite effect British poets and prose writers of the seventeenth century. Emerson quoted Herbert at length in *Nature,* and Melville declared that "had not Sir Thomas Browne lived, Emerson would not have mystified." Emerson went beyond all these sources to give much study to Swedenborg. Finally, transcendentalism owed more than has been often recognized to native American religious and philosophical influences—the God and "grace" of Puritan mysticism, the "inner light" of the Quakers, the "Bible of creation" of the Deists.

Transcendentalism had direct relation to the philosophical foundations of democracy in its emphasis on the perfectibility of the individual. Emerson asked in *Nature*, "Who can set bounds to the possibilities of man?" In his assertion of intuition as the supreme source of truth the transcendentalist found sanction for unconventional and even for revolutionary conduct. As Emerson put it, "In action he easily incurs the charge of antinomianism by his avowal that he, who has the Law-giver, may with safety not only neglect, but even contravene every written commandment." It was not hard for a sincere transcendentalist to defy the Fugitive Slave Law.

"Build therefore your own world," Emerson instructed his reader in the final paragraph of *Nature*. "As fast as you conform your life to the pure idea in your mind, that will unfold its great proportions. A correspondent revolution in things will attend the influx of the spirit. So fast will disagreeable appearances, swine, spiders, snakes, pests, mad-houses, prisons, enemies, vanish; they are temporary and shall be no more seen." Thus did transcendentalism dispose of the problem of evil.

For Herman Melville, as for Nathaniel Hawthorne, neither Brownson's solution of the dilemma of the times nor Emerson's proved possible. The "darkness" that Melville heralded in Hawthorne, in "Hawthorne and His Mosses," was in his own heart as well: both men found it inescapable in the world around them. Neither could find in transcendentalism's assertion of absolute good an answer to the problems of human suffering, to the ultimate question of the nature of evil. Hawthorne was in some degree content to embody his vision of life's unreconciled conflicts in allegory and legend. Melville came to grips with the problem, profoundly and desperately, almost to the point of his own destruction, and attained only late in his life a partial resolution.

Perhaps of them all Thoreau came closest to a durable integration. What Emerson taught he tested in the fire of intense actual experience. In all American literature there is no clearer vision of the meanness and ugliness of life as it was (and is) lived than in *Walden,* or a surer grasp of life's potential wholeness and ultimate meaning.

VI

The humanitarian concern which was a striking characteristic of New England society in this period, finding its most significant manifestation in abolitionism, may well have had its roots in the religious dilemma of the times. Perhaps the Puritan conscience, denied the sanctions of a vigorous creed but far from dead, had a share in driving New Englanders to the evangel of reforms in diet, dress and recreation as well as in more fundamental things.

From New England the gospels spread to the middle states and—largely through the efforts of transplanted New Englanders—throughout the West.

Some of the efforts toward reform were primarily economic in intention. George Ripley's observation of the life of the poor in Boston's congested slums fired him with radical enthusiasm. The experiment in communal living which he inaugurated at Brook Farm—with Hawthorne as a temporary participant, and Emerson and Margaret Fuller as interested observers—was the most famous of many attempts to demonstrate the reconstruction of society in the image of widely varying utopias. Brook Farm was soon reorganized along the lines proposed by Fourier, the French socialistic thinker whose ideas were propagated in America by Albert Brisbane and, in somewhat modified form, by Horace Greeley. Fourierism attained for a time the prominence of national organization, and many experiments in its application were undertaken. But all the Fourierist communities were short-lived—as were, indeed, all the other experiments of the kind except those which possessed definite religious elements.

More substantial in its ultimate effect was the agitation for a liberalized land policy on the part of the federal government. Sustained and concerted demand that the still undeveloped lands of the West should be withheld from speculation and opened to actual settlers on liberal terms finally resulted in the Homestead Act which Abraham Lincoln signed in 1862, with its profound influence on the character of subsequent western settlement.

Also of great practical effectiveness was the effort for educational reform which, like so many other reform movements, originated in Massachusetts in the 1830's. The experiments of Bronson Alcott in teaching little children should be better known by educators today. Horace Mann, as commissioner of education for Massachusetts, was the prime mover in the gradual achievement of better training for teachers, in the general improvement of both elementary and secondary schools, and indirectly in the tardy enactment of laws restricting the paid labor of children.

Paralleling the agitation for educational reform was that for improved legal status for women, and later for equal suffrage. Lucretia Mott was an early leader in this movement, and Margaret Fuller, in her *Woman in the Nineteenth Century* (1845), its chief literary exponent. Women played leading parts in many of the humanitarian crusades. Dorothea Dix, for example, almost single-handed brought about nation-wide improvement in the care of the feeble-minded and insane. Increasingly during this period women demanded and obtained admission to college and professional training. Oberlin, the first co-educational college in America, was founded in 1833 and gave its first degrees to women in 1841. Elizabeth Blackwell, graduating at the Geneva Medical School of Western New York in 1849, became America's first woman to be licensed as a doctor of medicine.

Women were leaders, too, in the most spectacular of the crusades marked by moral purpose, that against intemperance. This movement attained great prominence in the 1830's and 40's, with its bannered parades of the boys and girls of the "cold water army," its Washingtonian Society of reformed drunkards—who found emotional lectures on their past experiences highly remunerative—and its enormous and flamboyant literature. Timothy Shay Arthur was one of the most popular of the writers who used fiction in the cause of temperance, and his *Ten Nights in a Bar-Room and What I Saw There* (1855) may properly be called a classic of the movement.

VII

But the movement which dwarfed all the others both in the quality of its literary expression and in its effect on American history was that for the abolition of Negro slavery. Abolitionism had deeper roots, for some of its leaders, than any of the other movements. Members of the Society of Friends had been agitating against slavery in America for almost a century. Such a Friend as John Greenleaf Whittier, devout by inheritance and by conviction, came naturally to his abolitionism. Yet there is something like escapism in his complaisant comment on New England's industrialism—as in "The Lighting Up"—while devoting his full energy to the condemnation of human wrong in another part of the country. Orestes Brownson indicted, in "The Laboring Classes," the New Englander who "in these times . . . is shedding crocodile tears over the deplorable condition of the poor laborer, while he docks his wages twenty-five per cent . . . shouts for liberty, stickles for equality, and is horrified at a Southern planter who keeps slaves." He was not alone, even in New England, in seeing something of inconsistency in the fierceness of such abolitionists as Wendell Phillips and William Lloyd Garrison toward the South, while they gave but small attention to the faults of the social system of their own section.

The South saw changes during the first half of the century, too. The opening of the rich black lands along the Mississippi after the Creek War gave great impetus to the plantation system, and made the labor of black men profitable again after a generation in which it seemed that the problem of slavery might solve itself peacefully through economic causes. The South experienced an industrial revolution, also, but in reverse. It possessed natural facilities for extensive industry and commerce—water power, fine harbors, inland waterways. But the plantation system which involved ownership of the labor force soaked up the South's fluid capital, and her industries dwindled and died early in the century. Thereafter the development of the "cotton kingdom" and of the industrial oligarchy of New England's textile factories was reciprocal.

The intellectual life of the South remained largely static through the earlier decades of the century, its small minority of readers comfortably addicted to the Roman classics and Walter Scott. It quickened in response to the attacks of the abolitionists. Such rejoinders as W. J. Grayson's *The Hireling and the Slave,* a long poem which compared the sufferings of New England's factory workers with an idyllic picture of the comfort and security of Southern slaves, may have caused some Northerners to see more clearly the faults of their own society, but probably had little practical effect except in the sharpening of sectional animosity. Almost universally the abolitionist attack identified the individual Southerner with the institution of slavery, and the section with both. Even Whittier, Lowell, Thoreau came to voice an intemperate hatred of the people and the region. Southern writers replied in kind and in full measure. The war between the states began on the printing presses of Boston and Charleston.

The enactment of the new Fugitive Slave Law in 1850 and subsequent attempts to enforce it in the North brought the controversy to its bitterest extremities of word and deed. The South had long maintained the doctrine of states' rights, had appealed to the principle of self-determination. Yet Southern control of the administration and the Congress resulted in this law, which meant the use of the federal power to compel citizens of Northern states to violate their ideas of freedom and humanity. The Burns case at Boston, the Dred Scott decision, and John Brown's raid at Harper's Ferry marked stages in the intensification of the conflict.

As the pressure of sectional antagonisms had increased, the South had felt compelled to look to the developing West for its only hope of retaining a balance in political power. The contest for control of the West was crucial. Successive measures of compromise proved ineffective. In the end sectionalism became the greatest force in American life. Literature had played a great part in creating it, and was decisively affected by it. Even before 1850 the conflict was called inevitable. When it came it shattered the structure of national literature which the half-century had built, affected profoundly the life and work of every important American writer of a generation, and made necessary after 1865 a new beginning.

Economic, political, social, and intellectual backgrounds for American literature from 1800 to 1861 may most conveniently be reviewed in Charles and Mary Beard's *The Rise of American Civilization,* Vol. I (New York, 1927) and in Vols. V, VI, and VII of *A History of American Life,* edited by A. M. Schlesinger and D. R. Fox: these are, respectively, J. A. Krout and D. R. Fox's *The Completion of Independence 1790-1830* (New York, 1944); Carl R. Fish's *The Rise of the Common Man 1830-1850* (New York, 1935); and A. C. Cole's *The Irrepressible Conflict 1850-1865* (New York, 1934). E. D. Branch's *The Sentimental Years* (New York, 1936) is a valuable general study of the 1840's. H. W. Schneider's *A History of American Philosophy* (New York, 1946), Merle Curti's *The Growth of American Thought* (New York, 1943), V. L. Parrington's *The Romantic Revolution in America 1800-1860* (New York, 1927), which is Vol. II in his *Main Currents in American Thought,* R. H. Gabriel's *The Course of American Democratic Thought* (New York, 1940), Charles and Mary Beard's *The American Spirit* (New York, 1942), H. M. Jones' *Ideas in America* (Cambridge, 1944), and H. A. Myers' *Are Men Equal?* (New York, 1945) are stimulating contributions to the history of ideas. H. M. Jones' *America and French Culture 1750-1848* (Chapel Hill, 1927) and O. W. Long's *Literary Pioneers* (New York, 1935) treat the impact of Europe on the shaping of a national literature; for the impact of the West, consult Lucy Hazard's *The Frontier in American Literature* (New York, 1927), R. L. Rusk's *The Literature of the Middle Western Frontier,* in two volumes (New York, 1925), Constance Rourke's *American Humor* (New York, 1931), and Walter Blair's *Horse Sense in American Humor* (Chicago, 1942). Useful studies of transcendentalism are O. B. Frothingham's *Transcendentalism in New England* (New York, 1876); H. C. Goddard's *Studies in New England Transcendentalism* (New York, 1908); Clarence Gohdes' *Periodicals of American Transcendentalism* (Durham, 1931); and Arthur Christy's *The Orient in American Transcendentalism* (New York, 1932). Van Wyck Brooks' *The World of Washington Irving* (New York, 1944), *The Flowering of New England 1815-1865* (New York, 1936), and *The Times of Melville and Whitman* (New York, 1947), are readable impressionistic cultural histories, with a tendency to create a literary mythology. F. O. Matthiessen's *American Renaissance* (New York, 1941) is a penetrating if sometimes prolix commentary on the work of major writers. A. H. Quinn's *A History of the American Drama from the Beginning to the Civil War* (New York, 1923, revised 1943) and *American Fiction* (New York, 1936), F. L. Pattee's *The Development of the American Short Story* (New York, 1923), H. R. Brown's *The Sentimental Novel In America 1789-1860* (New York, 1940), E. C. Stedman's *Poets of America* (Boston, 1885), Alfred Kreymborg's *A History of American Poetry: Our Singing Strength* (New York, 1929), G. W. Allen's *American Prosody* (New York, 1935), and Bernard Smith's *Forces in American Criticism* (New York, 1939) are stimulating surveys of literary genres. G. H. Orians' *A Short History of American Literature* (New York, 1940) offers synoptic analyses of literary decades; F. L. Pattee's *The Feminine Fifties* (New York, 1940) is an entertaining excursion into every phase of the literary production of one of these decades. Standard literary histories are *The Cambridge History of American Literature* (New York, 1917-1921), W. F. Taylor's *A History of American Letters* (Boston and New York, 1936), P. H. Boynton's *Literature and American Life* (Boston and New York, 1936); and F. L. Pattee's *The First Century of American Literature 1770-1870* (New York, 1935). F. L. Mott's *A History of American Magazines,* Vols. I and II, and *American Journalism,* both previously listed, are the best treatments of their subjects.

American Literature 1800-1860

I

THE FOUNDING OF A NATIONAL LITERATURE

American Literature 1800-1860

I

THE FOUNDING OF A NATIONAL LITERATURE

1783 ∾ *Washington Irving* ∾ *1859*

WITH the possible exception of Benjamin Franklin, Washington Irving was the first American to achieve real literary fame on both sides of the Atlantic; also he was probably the first American to enjoy adequate income from literary work. He was one of the chief shapers and builders of our national literature. The best of his books are still widely read and enjoyed today.

The youngest child in a large New York family, he had little formal education, none at the collegiate level. He studied law in desultory fashion for some years, "reading" as was the custom of the time in the offices of established lawyers, but giving much more serious attention to the business of being a young man about town—dancing and theater-going, dining and talking with congenial groups of friends—and to writing. He was only nineteen when his brother Peter began publishing in the newspaper he edited a series of Washington's juvenile essays in the *Spectator* vein, over the signature "Jonathan Oldstyle, Gent."

When he was twenty-three, Washington Irving finally gained admission to the bar; but the event was completely overshadowed in his personal interest by a project which matured just two months later—the launching of the satirical magazine *Salmagundi* on Jan. 24, 1807. It was a joint enterprise of Washington and his brother William Irving, and their friend James Kirke Paulding, whose sister William had married. Current fashions and fashionable people, plays and actors, periodicals and editors, politicians and militia officers, were sharply and saucily satirized in the pocket-size numbers. This not unworthy prototype of today's *New Yorker* was a great success in the already cosmopolitan city of 68,000. The sophisticated and the intellectuals bought it, discussed it, speculated as to the identities thinly concealed in such "profiles" as those of Ichabod Fungus, Timothy Giblet, and Dr. Christopher Costive.

The young editors (or their publisher) soon tired of *Salmagundi*, but within its twenty varied and experimental numbers Washington Irving had measured his talent, and had struck out the field of his further development. Barely two years later—on Dec. 6, 1809—appeared *A History of New York*, by "Diedrich Knickerbocker"—Irving's first important work and the foundation of his later success and fame.

Washington Irving's first book sold amazingly well. It was condemned in certain quarters as an irreverent caricature of the founding fathers; but there is much more sound history in the book than its primary purpose of entertainment would suggest. Irving had done no little real research, and presented a clearer and more complete account of New York's colonial history—in spite of emphasis on burlesque elements—than had previously appeared. More largely responsible for the immediate popularity of *A History of New York* was the considerable element of satire directed toward contemporary figures and affairs. Irving was a fashionable New Yorker in politics as in other things— a Federalist, though never a violent partisan. Jefferson and the Democrats were targets of "Knickerbocker's" pen. The sketch of the New Amsterdam governor "William the Testy" is a satirical portrait of Jefferson in physiognomy, dress, personal interests and habits, and public policies.

Ten years elapsed before the publication of Irving's next book. In the interval he had read widely, especially in the private library of his friend Henry Brevoort; had edited for two years one of the short-lived magazines of the period, the *Analectic* of Philadelphia, writing for it memorable essays demanding greater justice in the national attitude toward the Indians; had worked for his brothers' importing firm, at first only desultorily, later earnestly and gallantly in the period of economic disorder following the War of 1812. It was the failure of this business, with resulting loss of income to himself and his brothers' need for help, which brought the easy-going Irving to the writing of *The Sketch Book of Geoffrey Crayon, Gent.*, published serially in 1819-20 and immediately successful in both England and America.

A new Irving appeared in *The Sketch Book*—a writer not only more mature, more sure in his craft, but different in his essential purpose. The focus of his work had shifted, in those ten years, from satire to sentiment. It is precisely this change in Irving which gives him peculiar interest to the literary historian. *Salmagundi* and *A History of New York* belonged to the 18th century in spirit, in method, and in purpose. *The Sketch Book* belonged to the 19th. Irving had become a Romantic.

Few books of the Romantic period are so readable today as Irving's *Sketch Book*. It is good reading straight through; the universal fame of such school book favorites as "Rip Van Winkle" and "The Legend of Sleepy Hollow" should not be permitted to obscure its other widely varied delights. Irving included in it the temperate but forceful essays in defense of the American Indian which he had written for the *Analectic*, "Traits of Indian Character" and "Philip of Pokanoket"; these are consistent with the general Romantic attitude toward primitive peoples, but unmistakably personal and genuine in feeling. Similarly American in details and Romantic in source and attitude are the stories of the Hudson Valley which have done most to make the *Sketch Book* immortal. But more than half its material is British—a cordial sharing of Irving's experience in visiting Westminster Abbey and Stratford-on-Avon, of English Christmas festivities and village stories. In "English Writers on America" he expressed his regret at "the literary animosity daily growing up between England and America," and at once announced and exemplified his determination to combat it.

That determination he put into effect in *Bracebridge Hall*, published in

1822. More unified than Irving's other books of this period, this idyllic record of experience in a rural England untouched by industrial revolution and social conflict is still pleasant reading. "I had always a great facility at receiving pleasurable impressions," Irving testified in an "Autobiographical Fragment" which is the most revealing document of his life. This characteristic is peculiarly evident to the reader of *The Sketch Book* and *Bracebridge Hall*.

For most of the materials of *Tales of a Traveller* (1824) Irving went to Germany. But the best things in it were results of returns to American folk materials—notably one of Irving's finest short stories, "The Devil and Tom Walker."

The remaining 33 years of Irving's long life were divided between Europe and America, between diplomatic service and arduous and productive literary labor. There were three years in Spain, 1826-29, and two in England, 1830-31; a triumphal return to America and an extensive tour in the South and West in 1832; then ten years in New York. Irving returned to Spain in 1842 as American Minister, remaining for three years. Back in America once more, he resumed his residence at "Sunnyside," a comfortable country home at Tarrytown-on-the-Hudson, and remained there, except for a period of research at Washington, until his death in 1859.

None of the books of these later years hold for modern readers the appeal of Irving's earlier work. From his residence and study in Spain came *The Alhambra* (1832), a readable volume of descriptive sketches and traditional tales, and four works in Spanish history. From his western expedition he drew the material of *A Tour on the Prairies* (1835) and the inspiration for *Astoria* (1836) and *Adventures of Captain Bonneville* (1837). *Wolfert's Roost* (1855) is the best of three volumes of later gleanings from *Sketch Book* fields. Of his four biographies, the five-volume *Life of Washington* (1855-59) was the consuming and triumphant labor of Irving's last years. Though there is much good reading in the many pages of these later books, much of lively narrative and colorful detail, Irving's permanent place in our literature is secured primarily by the *Sketch Book* and his other earlier work.

"It is with delight we share the world with you." So wrote one of his older brothers to young Washington Irving in 1804. The words express the experience of millions of readers through five generations. There is little depth in Irving's work, either intellectual or emotional, little outright power or striking beauty. Yet one need look no further for an explanation of its durable appeal than to the personality it reveals. Irving was a man of lively and kindly curiosity about a multitude of things, sensitive and generous, unfailingly sincere, both a regionalist and a cosmopolitan. Not only his brothers, but literally hundreds of friends through his long life, found it a delight to share the world with him. And so does the reader even today, in the writing which is so warm and full an expression of a very likable man.

[S. T. Williams' *The Life of Washington Irving,* 2 vols. (New York, 1934) is the standard biography. H. A. Pochmann's *Irving* (New York, 1934) in the American Writers Series and Van Wyck Brooks' *The World of Washington Irving* (New York, 1934) provide good critical material. The authorized biography is Pierre M. Irving's *The Life and Letters of Washington Irving* (New York, 1862-63).

The text of the selections from *A History of New York* has been abridged from that of the first edition, 1809, as reprinted in *Diedrich Knickerbocker's A History of New York,* edited by Stanley Williams and Tremaine McDowell, American Authors series, 1927. The text of the other selections is that of *The Works of Washington Irving,* Spuyten Duyvil edition, 1881. Most of Irving's notes have been omitted.]

From

A HISTORY OF NEW YORK

[1809]

How THE FORT GOED HOOP WAS FEARFULLY BELEAGUERED—HOW THE RENOWNED WOUTER FELL INTO A PROFOUND DOUBT, AND HOW HE FINALLY EVAPORATED.

BY THIS time my readers must fully perceive what an arduous task I have undertaken—collecting and collating, with painful minuteness, the chronicles of past times, whose events almost defy the powers of research—raking in a little kind of Herculaneum of history, which had lain nearly for ages buried under the rubbish of years, and almost totally forgotten—raking up the limbs and fragments of disjointed facts, and endeavouring to put them scrupulously together, so as to restore them to their original form and connexion—now lugging forth the character of an almost forgotten hero, like a mutilated statue—now deciphering a half-defaced inscription, and now lighting upon a mouldering manuscript, which, after painful study, scarce repays the trouble of perusal.

In such case, how much has the reader to depend upon the honour and probity of his author, lest, like a cunning antiquarian, he either impose upon him some spurious fabrication of his own, for a precious relic from antiquity—or else

dress up the dismembered fragment with such false trappings, that it is scarcely possible to distinguish the truth from the fiction with which it is enveloped. This is a grievance which I have more than once had to lament, in the course of my wearisome researches among the works of my fellow-historians, who have strangely disguised and distorted the facts respecting this country; and particularly respecting the great province of New Netherlands; as will be perceived by any who will take the trouble to compare their romantic effusions, tricked out in the meretricious gauds of fable, with this excellent little history—universally to be renowned for its severe simplicity and unerring truth.

I have had more vexations of the kind to encounter, in those parts of my history which treat of the transactions on the eastern border, than in any other, in consequence of the troops of historians who have infested those quarters, and have shewn the honest people of New Nederlandt no mercy in their works. Among the rest, Mr. Benjamin Trumbull [1] arrogantly declares, that "the Dutch were always mere intruders." Now to this I shall make no other reply than to proceed in the steady narration of my history, which will contain

---

[1] Clergyman and historian (1735-1820), native and life-long resident of Connecticut, author of *A General History of the United States of America,* 3 vols. (Boston, 1765-1810).

not only proofs that the Dutch had clear title and possession in the fair valleys of the Connecticut, and that they were wrongfully dispossessed thereof—but likewise, that they have been scandalously maltreated ever since by the misrepresentations of the crafty historians of New England. And in this I shall be guided by a spirit of truth and impartiality, and a regard to my immortal fame—for I would not wittingly dishonour my work by a single falsehood, misrepresentation, or prejudice, though it should gain our forefathers the whole country of New England.

It was at an early period of the province, and previous to the arrival of the renowned Wouter, that the cabinet of Nieuw Nederlandts purchased the lands about the Connecticut, and established, for their superintendence and protection, a fortified post on the banks of the river, which was called Fort Goed Hoop, and was situated hard by the present fair city of Hartford. The command of this important post, together with the rank, title, and appointment of commissary, were given in charge to the gallant Jacobus Van Curlet, or, as some historians will have it, Van Curlis—a most doughty soldier, of that stomachful class of which we have such numbers on parade days—who are famous for eating all they kill. He was of a very soldierlike appearance, and would have been an exceeding tall man had his legs been in proportion to his body; but the latter being long, and the former uncommonly short, it gave him the uncouth appearance of a tall man's body mounted upon a little man's legs. He made up for this turnspit construction of body by throwing his legs to such an extent when he marched, that you would have sworn he had on the identical seven-league boots of the far-famed Jack the giant-killer; and so astonishingly high did he tread, on any great military occasion, that his soldiers were oftimes alarmed, lest the little man should trample himself underfoot.

But notwithstanding the erection of this fort, and the appointment of this ugly little man of war as a commander, the intrepid Yankees continued those daring interlopings, which I have hinted at in my last chapter; and taking advantage of the character which the cabinet of Wouter Van Twiller soon acquired, for profound and phlegmatic tranquillity—did audaciously invade the territories of the Nieuw Nederlandts, and *squat* themselves down within the very jurisdiction of Fort Goed Hoop.

On beholding this outrage, the longbodied Van Curlet proceeded as became a prompt and valiant officer. He immediately protested against these unwarrantable encroachments, in Low Dutch, by way of inspiring more terror, and forthwith despatched a copy of the protest to the governor at New Amsterdam, together with a long and bitter account of the aggressions of the enemy. This done, he ordered his men, one and all, to be of good cheer— shut the gate of the fort, smoked three pipes, went to bed, and awaited the result with a resolute and intrepid tranquillity that greatly animated his adherents, and no doubt struck sore dismay and affright into the hearts of the enemy.

Now it came to pass, that about this time the renowned Wouter Van Twiller, full of years and honours, and council dinners, had reached that period of life and faculty which, according to the great Gulliver, entitles a man to admission into the ancient order of Struldbruggs. He employed his time in smoking his Turkish pipe, amid an assembly of sages equally enlightened and nearly as venerable as himself, and who, for their silence, their gravity, their wisdom, and their cautious averseness to coming to any conclusion in business, are only to be equalled by certain profound corporations which I have known in my time. Upon reading the protest of the gallant Jacobus Van Curlet, therefore, his excellency fell straightway into one of the deepest doubts that ever he was known to encounter; his capacious head gradually drooped on his chest, he closed his eyes, and inclined his ear to one side, as if listening with great attention to the discussion that was going on in his belly; which all who knew him declared to be the huge court-house or council chamber of his thoughts; forming to his head what the House of Representatives does to the Senate. An articulate sound, very much resembling a snore, occasionally escaped him— but the nature of this internal cogitation was never known, as he never opened his lips on the subject to man, woman, or child. In the meantime, the protest of Van Curlet lay quietly on the table, where it served to light the pipes of the venerable sages assembled in council; and in the great smoke which they raised, the gallant Jacobus, his protest, and his mighty Fort Goed Hoop, were soon as completely beclouded and forgotten as is a question of emergency swallowed up in the speeches and resolution of a modern session of Congress.

There are certain emergencies when your profound legislators and sage deliberative councils are mightily in the way of a nation; and when an ounce of hare-brained decision is worth a pound of sage doubt and cautious discussion. Such, at least, was the case at present; for while the renowned Wouter Van Twiller was daily battling with his doubts, and his resolution growing weaker and weaker in the contest, the enemy pushed further and further into his territories, and assumed a most formidable appearance in the neighbourhood of Fort Goed Hoop. Here they founded the mighty town of *Piquag*, or, as it has since been called, *Weathersfield*, a place which, if we may credit the assertion of that worthy historian, John Josselyn, Gent.,[2] "hath been infamous by reason of the witches therein." And so daring did these men of Piquag become, that they extended those plantations of onions, for which their town is illustrious, under the very noses of the garrison of Fort Goed Hoop—insomuch that the honest Dutchmen could not look toward that quarter without tears in their eyes.

This crying injustice was regarded with proper indignation by the gallant Jacobus Van Curlet. He absolutely trembled with the amazing violence of his choler, and the exacerbations of his valour; which seemed to be the more turbulent in their workings, from the length of the body in which they were agitated. He forthwith proceeded to strengthen his redoubts, heighten his breastworks, deepen his fosse, and fortify his position with a double row of abattis; after which valiant precautions, he with unexampled intrepidity despatched a fresh courier with tremendous accounts of his perilous situation. Never did the modern hero, who immortalized himself at the second Sabine war, show greater valour in the art of letter writing, or distinguish himself more gloriously upon paper, than the heroic Van Curlet.

The courier chosen to bear these alarming despatches was a fat, oily little man, as being least liable to be worn out, or to lose leather on the journey; and to insure his speed, he was mounted on the fleetest waggon horse in the garrison, remarkable for his length of limb, largeness of bone, and hardness of trot; and so tall, that the little messenger was obliged to climb on his back by means of his tail and crupper. Such extraordinary speed did he make, that he arrived at Fort Amsterdam in little less than a month, though the distance was full two hundred pipes, or about a hundred and twenty miles.

The extraordinary appearance of this portentous stranger would have thrown the whole town of New Amsterdam into a quandary, had the good people troubled themselves about any thing more than their domestic affairs. With an appearance of great hurry and business, and smoking a short travelling pipe, he proceeded on a long swing trot through the muddy lanes of the metropolis, demolishing whole batches of dirt pies, which the little Dutch

---

[2] Author of *New England Rarities* (London, 1672) and *Two Voyages to New England* (London, 1674).

children were making in the road; and for which kind of pastry the children of this city have ever been famous. On arriving at the governor's house, he climbed down from his steed in great trepidation; roused the gray-headed door-keeper, old Skaats, who, like his lineal descendant and faithful representative, the venerable crier of our court, was nodding at his post—rattled at the door of the council chamber, and startled the members as they were dozing over a plan for establishing a public market.

At that very moment a gentle grunt, or rather a deep-drawn snore, was heard from the chair of the governor; a whiff of smoke was at the same instant observed to escape from his lips, and a slight cloud to ascend from the bowl of his pipe. The council of course supposed him engaged in deep sleep for the good of the community, and, according to custom in all such cases established, every man bawled out silence, in order to maintain tranquillity; when, of a sudden, the door flew open, and the little courier straddled into the apartment, cased to the middle in a pair of Hessian boots, which he had got into for the sake of expedition. In his right hand he held forth the ominous despatches, and with his left he grasped firmly the waistband of his galligaskins, which had unfortunately given way, in the exertion of descending from his horse. He stumped resolutely up to the governor, and with more hurry than perspicuity, delivered his message. But fortunately his ill tidings came too late to ruffle the tranquillity of this most tranquil of rulers. His venerable excellency had just breathed and smoked his last—his lungs and his pipe having been exhausted together, and his peaceful soul, as Dan Homer would have said, having escaped in the last whiff that curled from his tobacco pipe. In a word, the renowned Wouter Van Twiller, alias Walter the Doubter, who had so often slumbered with his contemporaries, now slept with his fathers, and Wilhelmus Kieft governed in his stead.

CONTAINING THE CHRONICLES OF THE REIGN OF WILLIAM THE TESTY

HE WAS a brisk, waspish, little old gentleman, who had dried and wilted away, partly through the natural process of years, and partly from being parched and burnt up by his fiery soul; which blazed like a vehement rush light in his bosom, constantly inciting him to most valorous broils, altercations and misadventures. I have heard it observed by a profound and philosophical judge of human nature, that if a woman waxes fat as she grows old, the tenure of her life is very precarious, but if haply she wilts, she lives forever—such likewise was the case with William the Testy, who grew tougher in proportion as he dried. He was some such a little dutchman as we may now and then see, stumping briskly about the streets of our city, in a broad skirted coat, with buttons nearly as large as the shield of Ajax, which makes such a figure in Dan Homer, an old fashioned cocked hat stuck on the back of his head, and a cane as high as his chin. His visage was broad, but his features sharp, his nose turned up with a most petulant curl; his cheeks, like the region of Terra del Fuego, were scorched into a dusky red—doubtless in consequence of the neighborhood of two fierce little grey eyes, through which his torrid soul beamed as fervently, as a tropical sun blazing through a pair of burning glasses. The corners of his mouth were curiously modeled into a kind of fret work, not a little resembling the wrinkled proboscis of an irritable pug dog—in a word he was one of the most positive, restless, ugly little men, that ever put himself in a passion about nothing. . . .

No sooner had this bustling little man been blown by a whiff of fortune into the seat of government, than he called together his council and delivered a very animated speech on the affairs of the province. As everybody knows what a glorious opportunity a governor, a president, or even an emperor has, of drubbing his enemies in his speeches, messages and bulletins, where he has the talk all on his own side, they may be sure the high mettled William Kieft did not suffer so favorable an occasion to escape him, of evincing that gallantry of tongue, common to all able legislators. . . . .

The council remained for some time silent, after he had finished; whether struck dumb with admiration at the brilliancy of his project, or put to sleep by the length of his harangue, the history of the times doth not mention. Suffice it to say, they at length gave a universal grunt of acquiescence. . . . Governor Kieft having thus vented his indignation, felt greatly relieved —adjourned the council *sine die*—put on his cocked hat and corduroy small clothes, and mounting a tall raw boned charger, trotted out to his country seat, which was situated in a sweet, sequestered swamp, now called Dutch street, but more commonly known by the name of Dog's Misery. . . .

Now it happened that at this time there sojourned in New Amsterdam one Anthony Van Corlear, a jolly fat Dutch trumpeter, of a pleasant burley visage—famous for his long wind and his huge whiskers, and who as the story goes, could twang so potently upon his instrument, as to produce an effect upon all within hearing, as though ten thousand bag-pipes were singing most lustily i' the nose. Him did the illustrious Kieft pick out as the man of all the world, most fitted to be the champion of New Amsterdam, and to garrison its fort; making little doubt but that his instrument would be as effectual and offensive in war as was that of the Paladin Astolpho,[3] or the more classic horn of Alecto.[4] It would have done one's heart good to have seen the governor snapping his fingers and fidgeting with delight, while his sturdy trumpeter strutted up and down the ramparts, fearlessly twanging his trumpet in the face of the whole world, like a thrice valorous editor daringly in-

sulting all the principalities and powers on the other side of the Atlantic.

Nor was he content with thus strongly garrisoning the fort, but he likewise added exceedingly to its strength by furnishing it with a formidable battery of Quaker guns—rearing a stupendous flagstaff in the centre which overtopped the whole city —and moreover by building a great windmill on one of the bastions. This last to be sure, was somewhat of a novelty in the art of fortification, but as I have already observed William Kieft was notorious for innovations and experiments, and traditions do affirm that he was much given to mechanical inventions—constructing patent smoke-jacks—carts that went before the horses, and especially erecting windmills, for which machines he had acquired a singular predilection in his native town of Saardam.

All these scientific vagaries of the little governor were cried up with ecstasy by his adherents as proofs of his universal genius—but there were not wanting illnatured grumblers who railed at him as employing his mind in frivolous pursuits, and devoting that time to smoke-jacks and windmills, which should have been occupied in the more important concerns of the province. Nay they even went so far as to hint once or twice, that his head was turned by his experiments, and that he really thought to manage his government, as he did his mills—by mere wind!—such is the illiberality and slander to which your enlightened rulers are ever subject. . . . .

The great defect of Wilhelmus Kieft's policy was, that though no man could be more ready to stand forth in an hour of emergency, yet he was so intent upon guarding the national pocket, that he suffered the enemy to break its head—in other words, whatever precaution for public safety he adopted, he was so intent upon rendering it cheap, that he invariably

---

[3] A character in the Charlemagne romances, who possessed a horn which, when sounded, brought terror to hearers.

[4] One of the three Erinnyes or Furies.

rendered it ineffectual. All this was a remote consequence of his profound education at the Hague—where having acquired a smattering of knowledge, he was ever after a great conner of indexes, continually dipping into books, without ever studying to the bottom of any subject; so that he had the scum of all kinds of authors fermenting in his pericranium. In some of these title page researches he unluckily stumbled over a grand political *cabalistic word*, which, with his customary facility he immediately incorporated into his great scheme of government, to the irretrievable injury and delusion of the honest province of Nieuw Nederlandts, and the eternal misleading, of all experimental rulers. . . .

Not to keep my reader in any suspense, the word which had so wonderfully arrested the attention of William the Testy and which in German characters, had a particularly black and ominous aspect, on being fairly translated into the English is no other than *economy*—a talismanic term, which by constant use and frequent mention, has ceased to be formidable in our eyes, but which has as terrible potency as any in the arcana of necromancy.

When pronounced in a national assembly it has an immediate effect in closing the hearts, beclouding the intellects, drawing the purse strings and buttoning the breeches pockets of all philosophic legislators. Nor are its effects on the eye less wonderful. It produces a contraction of the retina, an obscurity of the crystalline lens, a viscidity of the vitreous and an inspiration of the aqueous humours, an induration of the tunica sclerotica and a convexity of the cornea; insomuch that the organ of vision loses its strength and perspicuity, and the unfortunate patient becomes *myopes* or in plain English, purblind; perceiving only the amount of immediate expense without being able to look further, and regard it in connexion with the ultimate object to be effected. "So that," to quote the words of the eloquent Burke, "a briar at his nose is of greater magnitude than an oak at five hundred

yards distance." Such are its instantaneous operations, and the results are still more astonishing. By its magic influence seventy-fours shrink into frigates—frigates into sloops, and sloops into gunboats. As the defenceless fleet of Eneas, at the command of the protecting Venus, changed into sea nymphs and protected itself by diving;[5] so the mighty navy of America, by the cabalistic word economy, dwindles into small craft, and shelters itself in a mill-pond!

ENGLISH WRITERS ON AMERICA
[1820 (1819)]

"Methinks I see in my mind a noble and puissant nation, rousing herself like a strong man after sleep, and shaking her invincible locks; methinks I see her as an eagle, mewing her mighty youth, and kindling her undazzled eyes at the full midday beam."—*Milton on the Liberty of the Press.*[1]

IT IS with feelings of deep regret that I observe the literary animosity daily growing up between England and America. Great curiosity has been awakened of late with respect to the United States, and the London press has teemed with volumes of travels through the Republic; but they seem intended to diffuse error rather than knowledge; and so successful have they been, that, notwithstanding the constant intercourse between the nations, there is no people concerning whom the great mass of the British public have less pure information, or entertain more numerous prejudices.

English travellers are the best and the worst in the world. Where no motives of pride or interest intervene, none can equal them for profound and philosophical views of society, or faithful and graphical descriptions of external objects; but when either the interest or reputation of their

---

[5] A reference to Virgil's *Aeneid.*
[1] *Areopagitica: A Defense of Unlicensed Printing.*

own country comes in collision with that of another, they go to the opposite extreme, and forget their usual probity and candor, in the indulgence of splenetic remark, and an illiberal spirit of ridicule.

Hence, their travels are more honest and accurate, the more remote the country described. I would place implicit confidence in an Englishman's descriptions of the regions beyond the cataracts of the Nile; of unknown islands in the Yellow Sea; of the interior of India; or of any other tract which other travellers might be apt to picture out with the illusions of their fancies. But I would cautiously receive his account of his immediate neighbors, and of those nations with which he is in habits of most frequent intercourse. However I might be disposed to trust his probity, I dare not trust his prejudices.

It has also been the particular lot of our country to be visited by the worst kind of English travellers. While men of philosophical spirit and cultivated minds have been sent from England to ransack the poles, to penetrate the deserts, and to study the manners and customs of barbarous nations, with which she can have no permanent intercourse of profit or pleasure; it has been left to the broken-down tradesman, the scheming adventurer, the wandering mechanic, the Manchester and Birmingham agent, to be her oracles respecting America. From such sources she is content to receive her information respecting a country in a singular state of moral and physical development; a country in which one of the greatest political experiments in the history of the world is now performing; and which presents the most profound and momentous studies to the statesman and the philosopher.[2]

That such men should give prejudicial accounts of America is not a matter of surprise. The themes it offers for contemplation are too vast and elevated for their capacities. The national character is yet in a state of fermentation; it may have its frothiness and sediment, but its ingredients are sound and wholesome; it has already given proofs of powerful and generous qualities; and the whole promises to settle down into something substantially excellent. But the causes which are operating to strengthen and ennoble it, and its daily indications of admirable properties, are all lost upon these purblind observers; who are only affected by the little asperities incident to its present situation. They are capable of judging only of the surface of things; of those matters which come in contact with their private interests and personal gratifications. They miss some of the snug conveniences and petty comforts which belong to an old, highly-finished, and over-populous state of society; where the ranks of useful labor are crowded, and many earn a painful and servile subsistence by studying the very caprices of appetite and self-indulgence. These minor comforts, however, are all-important in the estimation of narrow minds; which either do not perceive, or will not acknowledge, that they are more than counterbalanced among us, by great and generally diffused blessings.

They may, perhaps, have been disappointed in some unreasonable expectation of sudden gain. They may have pictured America to themselves an El Dorado, where gold and silver abounded, and the natives were lacking in sagacity; and where they were to become strangely and suddenly rich, in some unforeseen but easy manner. The same weakness of mind that indulges absurd expectations produces petulance in disappointment. Such persons become embittered against the country on finding that there, as everywhere else, a man must sow before he can reap; must win wealth by industry and talent; and must contend with the common difficulties of nature and the shrewdness of an intelligent and enterprising people.

Perhaps, through mistaken or ill-directed hospitality, or from the prompt disposition

---

[2] Channing and Hart's *Guide to the Study of American History* (Boston, 1896), pp. 78-86, presents an extensive list of books recording the travels of Englishmen in America.

to cheer and countenance the stranger prevalent among my countrymen, they may have been treated with unwonted respect in America; and, having been accustomed all their lives to consider themselves below the surface of good society, and brought up in a servile feeling of inferiority, they become arrogant on the common boon of civility; they attribute to the lowliness of others their own elevation; and underrate a society where there are no artificial distinctions, and where, by any chance, such individuals as themselves can rise to consequence.

One would suppose, however, that information coming from such sources, on a subject where the truth is so desirable, would be received with caution by the censors of the press; that the motives of these men, their veracity, their opportunities of inquiry and observation, and their capacities for judging correctly, would be rigorously scrutinized before their evidence was admitted, in such sweeping extent, against a kindred nation. The very reverse, however, is the case, and it furnishes a striking instance of human inconsistency. Nothing can surpass the vigilance with which English critics will examine the credibility of the traveller who publishes an account of some distant and comparatively unimportant country. How warily will they compare the measurements of a pyramid, or the descriptions of a ruin; and how sternly will they censure any inaccuracy in these contributions of merely curious knowledge: while they will receive, with eagerness and unhesitating faith, the gross misrepresentations of coarse and obscure writers, concerning a country with which their own is placed in the most important and delicate relations. Nay, they will even make these apocryphal volumes text-books, on which to enlarge, with a zeal and an ability worthy of a more generous cause.

I shall not, however, dwell on this irksome and hackneyed topic; nor should I have adverted to it, but for the undue interest apparently taken in it by my countrymen, and certain injurious effects which

I apprehend it might produce upon the national feeling. We attach too much consequence to these attacks. They cannot do us any essential injury. The tissue of misrepresentations attempted to be woven round us are like cobwebs woven round the limbs of an infant giant. Our country continually outgrows them. One falsehood after another falls off of itself. We have but to live on, and every day we live a whole volume of refutation.

All the writers of England united, if we could for a moment suppose their great minds stooping to so unworthy a combination, could not conceal our rapidly-growing importance and matchless prosperity. They could not conceal that these are owing, not merely to physical and local, but also to moral causes—to the political liberty, the general diffusion of knowledge, the prevalence of sound moral and religious principles, which give force and sustained energy to the character of a people; and which, in fact, have been the acknowledged and wonderful supporters of their own national power and glory.

But why are we so exquisitely alive to the aspersions of England? Why do we suffer ourselves to be so affected by the contumely she has endeavored to cast upon us? It is not in the opinion of England alone that honor lives and reputation has its being. The world at large is the arbiter of a nation's fame; with its thousand eyes it witnesses a nation's deeds, and from their collective testimony is national glory or national disgrace established.

For ourselves, therefore, it is comparatively of but little importance whether England does us justice or not; it is, perhaps, of far more importance to herself. She is instilling anger and resentment into the bosom of a youthful nation, to grow with its growth, and strengthen with its strength. If in America, as some of her writers are laboring to convince her, she is hereafter to find an invidious rival and a gigantic foe, she may thank those very writers for having provoked rivalship and irritated hostility. Every one knows the all-pervading influence of literature at the present day, and how much the opinions and passions of mankind are under its control. The mere contests of the sword are temporary; their wounds are but in the flesh, and it is the pride of the generous to forgive and forget them; but the slanders of the pen pierce to the heart; they rankle longest in the noblest spirits; they dwell ever present in the mind, and render it morbidly sensitive to the most trifling collision. It is but seldom that any one overt act produces hostilities between two nations; there exists, most commonly, a previous jealousy and ill-will, a predisposition to take offence. Trace these to their cause, and how often will they be found to originate in the mischievous effusions of mercenary writers, who, secure in their closets, and for ignominious bread, concoct and circulate the venom that is to inflame the generous and the brave.

I am not laying too much stress upon this point; for it applies most emphatically to our particular case. Over no nation does the press hold a more absolute control than over the people of America; for the universal education of the poorest classes makes every individual a reader. There is nothing published in England on the subject of our country that does not circulate through every part of it. There is not a calumny dropped from an English pen, nor an unworthy sarcasm uttered by an English statesman, that does not go to blight good-will, and add to the mass of latent resentment. Possessing, then, as England does, the fountain-head whence the literature of the language flows, how completely is it in her power, and how truly is it her duty, to make it the medium of amiable and magnanimous feeling—a stream where the two nations might meet together and drink in peace and kindness. Should she, however, persist in turning it to waters of bitterness, the time may come when she may repent her folly. The present friendship of America may be of but little moment to her; but the future destinies of that country do not admit of a doubt;

over those of England there lower some shadows of uncertainty. Should, then, a day of gloom arrive—should those reverses overtake her, from which the proudest empires have not been exempt—she may look back with regret at her infatuation, in repulsing from her side a nation she might have grappled to her bosom, and thus destroying her only chance for real friendship beyond the boundaries of her own dominions.

There is a general impression in England, that the people of the United States are inimical to the parent country. It is one of the errors which have been diligently propagated by designing writers. There is, doubtless, considerable political hostility, and a general soreness at the illiberality of the English press; but, generally speaking, the prepossessions of the people are strongly in favor of England. Indeed, at one time they amounted, in many parts of the Union, to an absurd degree of bigotry. The bare name of Englishman was a passport to the confidence and hospitality of every family, and too often gave a transient currency to the worthless and the ungrateful. Throughout the country there was something of enthusiasm connected with the idea of England. We looked to it with a hallowed feeling of tenderness and veneration, as the land of our forefathers —the august repository of the monuments and antiquities of our race—the birthplace and mausoleum of the sages and heroes of our paternal history. After our own country, there was none in whose glory we more delighted—none whose good opinion we were more anxious to possess—none toward which our hearts yearned with such throbbings of warm consanguinity. Even during the late war,[2] whenever there was the least opportunity for kind feelings to spring forth, it was the delight of the generous spirits of our country to show that, in the midst of hostilities, they still kept alive the sparks of future friendship.

Is all this to be at an end? Is this

---

[2] The War of 1812-14.

golden band of kindred sympathies, so rare between nations, to be broken forever? Perhaps it is for the best—it may dispel an illusion which might have kept us in mental vassalage; which might have interfered occasionally with our true interests, and prevented the growth of proper national pride. But it is hard to give up the kindred tie! and there are feelings dearer than interest—closer to the heart than pride—that will still make us cast back a look of regret as we wander farther and farther from the paternal roof, and lament the waywardness of the parent that would repel the affections of the child.

Short-sighted and injudicious, however, as the conduct of England may be in this system of aspersion, recrimination on our part would be equally ill-judged. I speak not of a prompt and spirited vindication of our country, nor the keenest castigation of her slanderers—but I allude to a disposition to retaliate in kind, to retort sarcasm and inspire prejudice, which seems to be spreading widely among our writers. Let us guard particularly against such a temper; for it would double the evil, instead of redressing the wrong. Nothing is so easy and inviting as the retort of abuse and sarcasm; but it is a paltry and an unprofitable contest. It is the alternative of a morbid mind, fretted into petulance, rather than warmed into indignation. If England is willing to permit the mean jealousies of trade, or the rancorous animosities of politics, to deprave the integrity of her press, and poison the fountain of public opinion, let us beware of her example. She may deem it her interest to diffuse error and engender antipathy, for the purpose of checking emigration; we have no purpose of the kind to serve. Neither have we any spirit of national jealousy to gratify; for as yet, in all our rivalships with England, we are the rising and the gaining party. There can be no end to answer, therefore, but the gratification of resentment—a mere spirit of retaliation; and even that is impotent. Our retorts are never republished in England; they fall

short, therefore, of their aim; but they foster a querulous and peevish temper among our writers; they sour the sweet flow of our early literature, and sow thorns and brambles among its blossoms. What is still worse, they circulate through our own country, and, as far as they have effect, excite virulent national prejudices. This last is the evil most especially to be deprecated. Governed, as we are, entirely by public opinion, the utmost care should be taken to preserve the purity of the public mind. Knowledge is power, and truth is knowledge; whoever, therefore, knowingly propagates a prejudice, wilfully saps the foundation of his country's strength.

The members of a republic, above all other men, should be candid and dispassionate. They are, individually, portions of the sovereign mind and sovereign will, and should be enabled to come to all questions of national concern with calm and unbiased judgments. From the peculiar nature of our relations with England, we must have more frequent questions of a difficult and delicate character with her, than with any other nation; questions that affect the most acute and excitable feelings; and as, in the adjustment of these, our national measures must ultimately be determined by popular sentiment, we cannot be too anxiously attentive to purify it from all latent passion or prepossession.

Opening, too, as we do, an asylum for strangers from every portion of the earth, we should receive all with impartiality. It should be our pride to exhibit an example of one nation, at least, destitute of national antipathies, and exercising, not merely the overt acts of hospitality, but those more rare and noble courtesies which spring from liberality of opinion.

What have we to do with national prejudices? They are the inveterate diseases of old countries, contracted in rude and ignorant ages, when nations knew but little of each other, and looked beyond their own boundaries with distrust and hostility. We, on the contrary, have sprung into national existence in an enlightened and philosophic age, when the different parts of the habitable world, and the various branches of the human family, have been indefatigably studied and made known to each other; and we forego the advantages of our birth, if we do not shake off the national prejudices, as we would the local superstitions, of the old world.

But above all let us not be influenced by any angry feelings, so far as to shut our eyes to the perception of what is really excellent and amiable in the English character. We are a young people, necessarily an imitative one, and must take our examples and models, in a great degree, from the existing nations of Europe. There is no country more worthy of our study than England. The spirit of her constitution is most analogous to ours. The manners of her people—their intellectual activity, their freedom of opinion, their habits of thinking on those subjects which concern the dearest interests and most sacred charities of private life—are all congenial to the American character; and, in fact, are all intrinsically excellent; for it is in the moral feeling of the people that the deep foundations of British prosperity are laid; and however the superstructure may be timeworn or overrun by abuses, there must be something solid in the basis, admirable in the materials, and stable in the structure of an edifice that so long has towered unshaken amidst the tempests of the world.

Let it be the pride of our writers, therefore, discarding all feelings of irritation, and disdaining to retaliate the illiberality of British authors, to speak of the English nation without prejudice, and with determined candor. While they rebuke the indiscriminating bigotry with which some of our countrymen admire and imitate everything English, merely because it is English, let them frankly point out what is really worthy of approbation. We may thus place England before us as a perpetual volume of reference, wherein are recorded sound deductions from ages of experience; and while we avoid the errors and absurdities which may have crept into the page, we may draw thence golden maxims of practical wisdom, wherewith to strengthen and to embellish our national character.

PHILIP OF POKANOKET

An Indian Memoir

[1820 (1813)]

As monumental bronze unchanged his look;
A soul that pity touch'd, but never shook;
Train'd from his tree-rock'd cradle to his
  bier
The fierce extremes of good and ill to
  brook,
Impassive—fearing but the shame of fear—
A stoic of the woods—a man without a
  tear.—Campbell.

IT IS to be regretted that those early writers who treated of the discovery and settlement of America have not given us more particular and candid accounts of the remarkable characters that flourished in savage life. The scanty anecdotes which have reached us are full of peculiarity and interest; they furnish us with nearer glimpses of human nature, and show what man is in a comparatively primitive state and what he owes to civilization. There is something of the charm of discovery in lighting upon these wild and unexplored tracts of human nature; in witnessing, as it were, the native growth of moral sentiment, and perceiving those generous and romantic qualities which have been artificially cultivated by society vegetating in spontaneous hardihood and rude magnificence.

In civilized life, where the happiness, and indeed almost the existence, of man depends so much upon the opinion of his fellow-men, he is constantly acting a studied part. The bold and peculiar traits of native character are refined away or softened down by the levelling influence of what is termed good-breeding; and he practises so many petty deceptions and affects so many generous sentiments for the purposes of popularity that it is difficult to distinguish his real from his artificial character. The Indian, on the contrary, free from the restraints and refinements of polished life, and in a great degree a solitary and independent being, obeys the impulses of his inclination or the dictates of his judgment; and thus the attributes of his nature, being freely indulged, grow singly great and striking. Society is like a lawn, where every roughness is smoothed, every bramble eradicated, and where the eye is delighted by the smiling verdure of a velvet surface; he, however, who would study Nature in its wildness and variety must plunge into the forest, must explore the glen, must stem the torrent, and dare the precipice.

These reflections arose on casually looking through a volume of early colonial history wherein are recorded, with great bitterness, the outrages of the Indians and their wars with the settlers of New England. It is painful to perceive, even from these partial narratives, how the footsteps of civilization may be traced in the blood of the aborigines; how easily the colonists were moved to hostility by the lust of conquest; how merciless and exterminating was their warfare. The imagination shrinks at the idea how many intellectual beings were hunted from the earth, how many brave and noble hearts, of Nature's sterling coinage, were broken down and trampled in the dust.

Such was the fate of Philip of Pokanoket, an Indian warrior whose name was once a terror throughout Massachusetts and Connecticut. He was the most distinguished of a number of contemporary sachems who reigned over the Pequods, the Narragansetts, the Wampanoags, and the other eastern tribes at the time of the first settlement of New England; a band of native untaught heroes who made the most generous struggle of which human nature is capable, fighting to the last gasp in the cause of their country, without a hope of victory or a thought of renown. Worthy of an age of poetry and fit subjects for

local story and romantic fiction, they have left scarcely any authentic traces on the page of history, but stalk like gigantic shadows in the dim twilight of tradition.

When the Pilgrims, as the Plymouth settlers are called by their descendants, first took refuge on the shores of the New World from the religious persecutions of the Old, their situation was to the last degree gloomy and disheartening. Few in number, and that number rapidly perishing away through sickness and hardships, surrounded by a howling wilderness and savage tribes, exposed to the rigors of an almost arctic winter and the vicissitudes of an ever-shifting climate, their minds were filled with doleful forebodings, and nothing preserved them from sinking into despondency but the strong excitement of religious enthusiasm. In this forlorn situation they were visited by Massasoit, chief sagamore of the Wampanoags, a powerful chief who reigned over a great extent of country. Instead of taking advantage of the scanty number of the strangers and expelling them from his territories, into which they had intruded, he seemed at once to conceive for them a generous friendship, and extended towards them the rites of primitive hospitality. He came early in the spring to their settlement of New Plymouth, attended by a mere handful of followers, entered into a solemn league of peace and amity, sold them a portion of the soil, and promised to secure for them the good-will of his savage allies. Whatever may be said of Indian perfidy, it is certain that the integrity and good faith of Massasoit have never been impeached. He continued a firm and magnanimous friend of the white men, suffering them to extend their possessions and to strengthen themselves in the land, and betraying no jealousy of their increasing power and prosperity. Shortly before his death he came once more to New Plymouth with his son Alexander, for the purpose of renewing the covenant of peace and of securing it to his posterity.

At this conference he endeavored to protect the religion of his forefathers from the encroaching zeal of the missionaries, and stipulated that no further attempt should be made to draw off his people from their ancient faith; but, finding the English obstinately opposed to any such condition, he mildly relinquished the demand. Almost the last act of his life was to bring his two sons, Alexander and Philip (as they had been named by the English), to the residence of a principal settler, recommending mutual kindness and confidence, and entreating that the same love and amity which had existed between the white men and himself might be continued afterwards with his children. The good old sachem died in peace, and was happily gathered to his fathers before sorrow came upon his tribe; his children remained behind to experience the ingratitude of white men.

His eldest son, Alexander, succeeded him. He was of a quick and impetuous temper, and proudly tenacious of his hereditary rights and dignity. The intrusive policy and dictatorial conduct of the strangers excited his indignation, and he beheld with uneasiness their exterminating wars with the neighboring tribes. He was doomed soon to incur their hostility, being accused of plotting with the Narragansetts to rise against the English and drive them from the land. It is impossible to say whether this accusation was warranted by facts or was grounded on mere suspicions. It is evident, however, by the violent and overbearing measures of the settlers that they had by this time begun to feel conscious of the rapid increase of their power, and to grow harsh and inconsiderate in their treatment of the natives. They despatched an armed force to seize upon Alexander and to bring him before their courts. He was traced to his woodland haunts, and surprised at a hunting-house where he was reposing with a band of his followers, unarmed, after the toils of the chase. The suddenness of his arrest and the outrage offered to his sovereign dignity so preyed upon the irascible feelings of this proud

savage as to throw him into a raging fever. He was permitted to return home on condition of sending his son as a pledge for his reappearance; but the blow he had received was fatal, and before he reached his home he fell a victim to the agonies of a wounded spirit.

The successor of Alexander was Metacomet, or King Philip, as he was called by the settlers on account of his lofty spirit and ambitious temper. These, together with his well-known energy and enterprise, had rendered him an object of great jealousy and apprehension, and he was accused of having always cherished a secret and implacable hostility towards the whites. Such may very probably and very naturally have been the case. He considered them as originally but mere intruders into the country, who had presumed upon indulgence and were extending an influence baneful to savage life. He saw the whole race of his countrymen melting before them from the face of the earth, their territories slipping from their hands, and their tribes becoming feeble, scattered, and dependent. It may be said that the soil was originally purchased by the settlers; but who does not know the nature of Indian purchases in the early periods of colonization? The Europeans always made thrifty bargains through their superior adroitness in traffic, and they gained vast accessions of territory by easily-provoked hostilities. An uncultivated savage is never a nice inquirer into the refinements of law by which an injury may be gradually and legally inflicted. Leading facts are all by which he judges; and it was enough for Philip to know that before the intrusion of the Europeans his countrymen were lords of the soil, and that now they were becoming vagabonds in the land of their fathers.

But whatever may have been his feelings of general hostility and his particular indignation at the treatment of his brother, he suppressed them for the present, renewed the contract with the settlers, and resided peaceably for many years at Pokanoket, or, as it was called by the English,

Mount Hope,[1] the ancient seat of dominion of his tribe. Suspicions, however, which were at first but vague and indefinite, began to acquire form and substance, and he was at length charged with attempting to instigate the various eastern tribes to rise at once, and by a simultaneous effort to throw off the yoke of their oppressors. It is difficult at this distant period to assign the proper credit due to these early accusations against the Indians. There was a proneness to suspicion and an aptness to acts of violence on the part of the whites that gave weight and importance to every idle tale. Informers abounded where talebearing met with countenance and reward, and the sword was readily unsheathed when its success was certain and it carved out empire.

The only positive evidence on record against Philip is the accusation of one Sausaman, a renegado Indian, whose natural cunning had been quickened by a partial education which he had received among the settlers. He changed his faith and his allegiance two or three times with a facility that evinced the looseness of his principles. He had acted for some time as Philip's confidential secretary and counsellor, and had enjoyed his bounty and protection. Finding, however, that the clouds of adversity were gathering round his patron, he abandoned his service and went over to the whites, and in order to gain their favor charged his former benefactor with plotting against their safety. A rigorous investigation took place. Philip and several of his subjects submitted to be examined, but nothing was proved against them. The settlers, however, had now gone too far to retract; they had previously determined that Philip was a dangerous neighbor; they had publicly evinced their distrust, and had done enough to insure his hostility; according, therefore, to the usual mode of reasoning in these cases, his destruction had become necessary to their security. Sausaman, the treacherous informer, was shortly afterwards found dead in a pond, having fallen a victim to the vengeance of his tribe. Three Indians, one of whom was a friend and counsellor of Philip, were apprehended and tried, and on the testimony of one very questionable witness were condemned and executed as murderers.

This treatment of his subjects and ignominious punishment of his friend outraged the pride and exasperated the passions of Philip. The bolt which had fallen thus at his very feet awakened him to the gathering storm, and he determined to trust himself no longer in the power of the white men. The fate of his insulted and broken-hearted brother still rankled in his mind; and he had a further warning in the tragical story of Miantonimo, a great sachem of the Narragansetts, who, after manfully facing his accusers before a tribunal of the colonists, exculpating himself from a charge of conspiracy and receiving assurances of amity, had been perfidiously despatched at their instigation. Philip therefore gathered his fighting-men about him, persuaded all strangers that he could to join his cause, sent the women and children to the Narragansetts for safety, and wherever he appeared was continually surrounded by armed warriors.

When the two parties were thus in a state of distrust and irritation, the least spark was sufficient to set them in a flame. The Indians, having weapons in their hands, grew mischievous and committed various petty depredations. In one of their maraudings a warrior was fired on and killed by a settler. This was the signal for open hostilities; the Indians pressed to revenge the death of their comrade, and the alarm of war resounded through the Plymouth colony.

In the early chronicles of these dark and melancholy times we meet with many indications of the diseased state of the public mind. The gloom of religious abstraction and the wildness of their situation among trackless forests and savage tribes had

[1] New Bristol, Rhode Island.—Irving's note.

disposed the colonists to superstitious fancies, and had filled their imaginations with the frightful chimeras of witchcraft and spectrology. They were much given also to a belief in omens. The troubles with Philip and his Indians were preceded, we are told, by a variety of those awful warnings which forerun great and public calamities. The perfect form of an Indian bow appeared in the air at New Plymouth, which was looked upon by the inhabitants as a "prodigious apparition." At Hadley, Northampton, and other towns in their neighborhood "was heard the report of a great piece of ordnance, with a shaking of the earth and a considerable echo." [2] Others were alarmed on a still sunshiny morning by the discharge of guns and muskets; bullets seemed to whistle past them, and the noise of drums resounded in the air, seeming to pass away to the westward; others fancied that they heard the galloping of horses over their heads; and certain monstrous births which took place about the time filled the superstitious in some towns with doleful forebodings. Many of these portentous sights and sounds may be ascribed to natural phenomena—to the northern lights which occur vividly in those latitudes, the meteors which explode in the air, the casual rushing of a blast through the top branches of the forest, the crash of fallen trees or disrupted rocks, and to those other uncouth sounds and echoes which will sometimes strike the ear so strangely amidst the profound stillness of woodland solitudes. These may have startled some melancholy imaginations, may have been exaggerated by the love for the marvellous, and listened to with that avidity with which we devour whatever is fearful and mysterious. The universal currency of these superstitious fancies and the grave record made of them by one of the learned men of the day are strongly characteristic of the times.

The nature of the contest that ensued was such as too often distinguishes the warfare between civilized men and savages. On the part of the whites it was con-

ducted with superior skill and success, but with a wastefulness of the blood and a disregard of the natural rights of their antagonists; on the part of the Indians it was waged with the desperation of men fearless of death, and who had nothing to expect from peace but humiliation, dependence, and decay.

The events of the war are transmitted to us by a worthy clergyman of the time, who dwells with horror and indignation on every hostile act of the Indians, however justifiable, whilst he mentions with applause the most sanguinary atrocities of the whites. Philip is reviled as a murderer and a traitor, without considering that he was a true-born prince gallantly fighting at the head of his subjects to avenge the wrongs of his family, to retrieve the tottering power of his line, and to deliver his native land from the oppression of usurping strangers.

The project of a wide and simultaneous revolt, if such had really been formed, was worthy of a capacious mind, and had it not been prematurely discovered might have been overwhelming in its consequences. The war that actually broke out was but a war of detail, a mere succession of casual exploits and unconnected enterprises. Still, it sets forth the military genius and daring prowess of Philip, and wherever, in the prejudiced and passionate narrations that have been given of it, we can arrive at simple facts, we find him displaying a vigorous mind, a fertility of expedients, a contempt of suffering and hardship, and an unconquerable resolution that command our sympathy and applause.

Driven from his paternal domains at Mount Hope, he threw himself into the depths of those vast and trackless forests that skirted the settlements and were almost impervious to anything but a wild beast or an Indian. Here he gathered together his forces, like the storm accumulating its stores of mischief in the bosom of

[2] The Rev. Increase Mather's history.—Irving's note.

the thundercloud, and would suddenly emerge at a time and place least expected, carrying havoc and dismay into the villages. There were now and then indications of these impending ravages that filled the minds of the colonists with awe and apprehension. The report of a distant gun would perhaps be heard from the solitary woodland, where there was known to be no white man; the cattle which had been wandering in the woods would sometimes return home wounded; or an Indian or two would be seen lurking about the skirts of the forests and suddenly disappearing, as the lightning will sometimes be seen playing silently about the edge of the cloud that is brewing up the tempest.

Though sometimes pursued and even surrounded by the settlers, yet Philip as often escaped almost miraculously from their toils, and, plunging into the wilderness, would be lost to all search or inquiry until he again emerged at some far distant quarter, laying the country desolate. Among his strongholds were the great swamps or morasses which extend in some parts of New England, composed of loose bogs of deep black mud, perplexed with thickets, brambles, rank weeds, the shattered and mouldering trunks of fallen trees, overshadowed by lugubrious hemlocks. The uncertain footing and the tangled mazes of these shaggy wilds rendered them almost impracticable to the white man, though the Indian could thread their labyrinths with the agility of a deer. Into one of these, the great swamp of Pocasset Neck, was Philip once driven with a band of his followers. The English did not dare to pursue him, fearing to venture into these dark and frightful recesses, where they might perish in fens and miry pits or be shot down by lurking foes. They therefore invested the entrance to the Neck, and began to build a fort with the thought of starving out the foe; but Philip and his warriors wafted themselves on a raft over an arm of the sea in the dead of night, leaving the women and children behind, and escaped away to the westward, kindling the flames of war among the tribes of Massachusetts and the Nipmuck country and threatening the colony of Connecticut.

In this way Philip became a theme of universal apprehension. The mystery in which he was enveloped exaggerated his real terrors. He was an evil that walked in darkness, whose coming none could foresee and against which none knew when to be on the alert. The whole country abounded with rumors and alarms. Philip seemed almost possessed of ubiquity, for in whatever part of the widely-extended frontier an irruption from the forest took place, Philip was said to be its leader. Many superstitious notions also were circulated concerning him. He was said to deal in necromancy, and to be attended by an old Indian witch or prophetess, whom he consulted and who assisted him by her charms and incantations. This, indeed, was frequently the case with Indian chiefs, either through their own credulity or to act upon that of their followers; and the influence of the prophet and the dreamer over Indian superstition has been fully evidenced in recent instances of savage warfare.

At the time that Philip effected his escape from Pocasset his fortunes were in a desperate condition. His forces had been thinned by repeated fights and he had lost almost the whole of his resources. In this time of adversity he found a faithful friend in Canonchet, chief sachem of all the Narragansetts. He was the son and heir of Miantonimo, the great sachem who, as already mentioned, after an honorable acquittal of the charge of conspiracy, had been privately put to death at the perfidious instigations of the settlers. "He was the heir," says the old chronicler, "of all his father's pride and insolence, as well as of his malice towards the English;" he certainly was the heir of his insults and injuries and the legitimate avenger of his murder. Though he had forborne to take an active part in this hopeless war, yet he received Philip and his broken forces with open arms and gave them the most generous countenance and support. This at once drew upon him the hostility of the English, and it was determined to strike a signal blow that should involve both the sachems in one common ruin. A great force was therefore gathered together from Massachusetts, Plymouth, and Connecticut, and was sent into the Narragansett country in the depth of winter, when the swamps, being frozen and leafless, could be traversed with comparative facility and would no longer afford dark and impenetrable fastnesses to the Indians.

Apprehensive of attack, Canonchet had conveyed the greater part of his stores, together with the old, the infirm, the women and children of his tribe, to a strong fortress, where he and Philip had likewise drawn up the flower of their forces. This fortress, deemed by the Indians impregnable, was situated upon a rising mound or kind of island of five or six acres in the midst of a swamp; it was constructed with a degree of judgment and skill vastly superior to what is usually displayed in Indian fortification, and indicative of the martial genius of these two chieftains.

Guided by a renegado Indian, the English penetrated, through December snows, to this stronghold and came upon the garrison by surprise. The fight was fierce and tumultuous. The assailants were repulsed in their first attack, and several of their bravest officers were shot down in the act of storming the fortress, sword in hand. The assault was renewed with greater success. A lodgment was effected. The Indians were driven from one post to another. They disputed their ground inch by inch, fighting with the fury of despair. Most of their veterans were cut to pieces, and after a long and bloody battle, Philip and Canonchet, with a handful of surviving warriors, retreated from the fort and took refuge in the thickets of the surrounding forest.

The victors set fire to the wigwams and the fort; the whole was soon in a blaze;

many of the old men, the women, and the children perished in the flames. This last outrage overcame even the stoicism of the savage. The neighboring woods resounded with the yells of rage and despair uttered by the fugitive warriors, as they beheld the destruction of their dwellings and heard the agonizing cries of their wives and offspring. "The burning of the wigwams," says a contemporary writer, "the shrieks and cries of the women and children, and the yelling of the warriors, exhibited a most horrible and affecting scene, so that it greatly moved some of the soldiers." The same writer cautiously adds, "They were in *much doubt* then, and afterwards seriously inquired, whether burning their enemies alive could be consistent with humanity, and the benevolent principles of the gospel." [3]

The fate of the brave and generous Canonchet is worthy of particular mention: the last scene of his life is one of the noblest instances on record of Indian magnanimity.

Broken down in his power and resources by this signal defeat, yet faithful to his ally and to the hapless cause which he had espoused, he rejected all overtures of peace offered on condition of betraying Philip and his followers, and declared that "he would fight it out to the last man, rather than become a servant to the English." His home being destroyed, his country harassed and laid waste by the incursions of the conquerors, he was obliged to wander away to the banks of the Connecticut, where he formed a rallying-point to the whole body of western Indians and laid waste several of the English settlements.

Early in the spring he departed on a hazardous expedition, with only thirty chosen men, to penetrate to Seaconck, in the vicinity of Mount Hope, and to procure seed corn to plant for the sustenance of his troops. This little band of adventurers

[3] MS. of the Rev. W. Ruggles.—Irving's note.

had passed safely through the Pequod country, and were in the centre of the Narragansett, resting at some wigwams near Pautucket River, when an alarm was given of an approaching enemy. Having but seven men by him at the time, Canonchet despatched two of them to the top of a neighboring hill to bring intelligence of the foe.

Panic-struck by the appearance of a troop of English and Indians rapidly advancing, they fled in breathless terror past their chieftain, without stopping to inform him of the danger. Canonchet sent another scout, who did the same. He then sent two more, one of whom, hurrying back in confusion and affright, told him that the whole British army was at hand. Canonchet saw there was no choice but immediate flight. He attempted to escape round the hill, but was perceived and hotly pursued by the hostile Indians and a few of the fleetest of the English. Finding the swiftest pursuer close upon his heels, he threw off, first his blanket, then his silver-laced coat and belt of peag, by which his enemies knew him to be Canonchet, and redoubled the eagerness of pursuit.

At length, in dashing through the river, his foot slipped upon a stone, and he fell so deep as to wet his gun. This accident so struck him with despair that, as he afterwards confessed, "his heart and his bowels turned within him, and he became like a rotten stick, void of strength."

To such a degree was he unnerved that, being seized by a Pequod Indian within a short distance of the river, he made no resistance, though a man of great vigor of body and boldness of heart. But on being made prisoner the whole pride of his spirit arose within him, and from that moment we find, in the anecdotes given by his enemies, nothing but repeated flashes of elevated and prince-like heroism. Being questioned by one of the English who first came up with him, and who had not attained his twenty-second year, the proud-hearted warrior, looking with lofty contempt upon his youthful countenance, replied, "You are a child—you cannot understand matters of war; let your brother or your chief come: him will I answer."

Though repeated offers were made to him of his life on condition of submitting with his nation to the English, yet he rejected them with disdain, and refused to send any proposals of the kind to the great body of his subjects, saying that he knew none of them would comply. Being reproached with his breach of faith towards the whites, his boast that he would not deliver up a Wampanoag nor the paring of a Wampanoag's nail, and his threat that he would burn the English alive in their houses, he disdained to justify himself, haughtily answering that others were as forward for the war as himself, and "he desired to hear no more thereof."

So noble and unshaken a spirit, so true a fidelity to his cause and his friend, might have touched the feelings of the generous and the brave; but Canonchet was an Indian, a being towards whom war had no courtesy, humanity no law, religion no compassion: he was condemned to die. The last words of his that are recorded are worthy the greatness of his soul. When sentence of death was passed upon him, he observed "that he liked it well, for he should die before his heart was soft or he had spoken anything unworthy of himself." His enemies gave him the death of a soldier, for he was shot at Stoningham by three young sachems of his own rank.

The defeat at the Narragansett fortress and the death of Canonchet were fatal blows to the fortunes of King Philip. He made an ineffectual attempt to raise a head of war by stirring up the Mohawks to take arms; but, though possessed of the native talents of a statesman, his arts were counteracted by the superior arts of his enlightened enemies, and the terror of their warlike skill began to subdue the resolution of the neighboring tribes. The unfortunate chieftain saw himself daily stripped of power, and his ranks rapidly thinning around him. Some were suborned by the whites; others fell victims to hunger **and** fatigue and to the frequent attacks by which they were harassed. His stores were all captured; his chosen friends were swept away from before his eyes; his uncle was shot down by his side; his sister was carried into captivity; and in one of his narrow escapes he was compelled to leave his beloved wife and only son to the mercy of the enemy. "His ruin," says the historian, "being thus gradually carried on, his misery was not prevented, but augmented thereby; being himself made acquainted with the sense and experimental feeling of the captivity of his children, loss of friends, slaughter of his subjects, bereavement of all family relations, and being stripped of all outward comforts before his own life should be taken away."

To fill up the measure of his misfortunes, his own followers began to plot against his life, that by sacrificing him they might purchase dishonorable safety. Through treachery a number of his faithful adherents, the subjects of Wetamoe, an Indian princess of Pocasset, a near kinswoman and confederate of Philip, were betrayed into the hands of the enemy. Wetamoe was among them at the time, and attempted to make her escape by crossing a neighboring river; either exhausted by swimming or starved with cold and hunger, she was found dead and naked near the water-side. But persecution ceased not at the grave. Even death, the refuge of the wretched, where the wicked commonly cease from troubling, was no protection to this outcast female, whose great crime was affectionate fidelity to her kinsman and her friend. Her corpse was the object of unmanly and dastardly vengeance; the head was severed from the body and set upon a pole, and was thus exposed at Taunton to the view of her captive subjects. They immediately recognized the features of their unfortunate queen, and were so affected at this barbarous spectacle that we are told they broke forth into the "most horrid and diabolical lamentations."

However Philip had borne up against the complicated miseries and misfortunes that surrounded him, the treachery of his followers seemed to wring his heart and reduce him to despondency. It is said that "he never rejoiced afterwards, nor had success in any of his designs." The spring of hope was broken—the ardor of enterprise was extinguished; he looked around, and all was danger and darkness; there was no eye to pity nor any arm that could bring deliverance. With a scanty band of followers, who still remained true to his desperate fortunes, the unhappy Philip wandered back to the vicinity of Mount Hope, the ancient dwelling of his fathers. Here he lurked about like a spectre among the scenes of former power and prosperity, now bereft of home, of family, and of friend. There needs no better picture of his destitute and piteous situation than that furnished by the homely pen of the chronicler, who is unwarily enlisting the feelings of the reader in favor of the hapless warrior whom he reviles. "Philip," he says, "like a savage wild beast, having been hunted by the English forces through the woods above a hundred miles backward and forward, at last was driven to his own den upon Mount Hope, where he retired, with a few of his best friends, into a swamp, which proved but a prison to keep him fast till the messengers of death came by divine permission to execute vengeance upon him."

Even in this last refuge of desperation and despair a sullen grandeur gathers round his memory. We picture him to ourselves seated among his care-worn followers, brooding in silence over his blasted fortunes, and acquiring a savage sublimity from the wildness and dreariness of his lurking-place. Defeated, but not dismayed—crushed to the earth, but not humiliated—he seemed to grow more haughty beneath disaster, and to experience a fierce satisfaction in draining the last dregs of bitterness. Little minds are tamed and subdued by misfortune, but great minds rise above it. The very idea of submission awakened the fury of Philip, and he smote to death one of his followers who proposed an expedient of peace. The brother of the victim made his escape, and in revenge betrayed the retreat of his chieftain. A body of white men and Indians were immediately despatched to the swamp where Philip lay crouched, glaring with fury and despair. Before he was aware of their approach they had begun to surround him. In a little while he saw five of his trustiest followers laid dead at his feet; all resistance was vain; he rushed forth from his covert, and made a headlong attempt to escape, but was shot through the heart by a renegado Indian of his own nation.

Such is the scanty story of the brave but unfortunate King Philip, persecuted while living, slandered and dishonored when dead. If, however, we consider even the prejudiced anecdotes furnished us by his enemies, we may perceive in them traces of amiable and lofty character sufficient to awaken sympathy for his fate and respect for his memory. We find that amidst all the harassing cares and ferocious passions of constant warfare he was alive to the softer feelings of connubial love and paternal tenderness and to the generous sentiment of friendship. The captivity of his "beloved wife and only son" are mentioned with exultation as causing him poignant misery; the death of any near friend is triumphantly recorded as a new blow on his sensibilities; but the treachery and desertion of many of his followers, in whose affections he had confided, is said to have desolated his heart and to have bereaved him of all further comfort. He was a patriot attached to his native soil— a prince true to his subjects and indignant of their wrongs—a soldier daring in battle, firm in adversity, patient of fatigue, of hunger, of every variety of bodily suffering, and ready to perish in the cause he had espoused. Proud of heart and with an untamable love of natural liberty, he preferred to enjoy it among the beasts of the forests or in the dismal and famished recesses of swamps and morasses, rather than bow his haughty spirit to submission and live dependent and despised in the ease and luxury of the settlements. With heroic qualities and bold achievements that would have graced a civilized warrior, and have rendered him the theme of the poet and the historian, he lived a wanderer and a fugitive in his native land, and went down, like a lonely bark foundering amid darkness and tempest, without a pitying eye to weep his fall or a friendly hand to record his struggle.

THE DEVIL AND TOM WALKER
[1824]

A FEW miles from Boston in Massachusetts, there is a deep inlet, winding several miles into the interior of the country from Charles Bay, and terminating in a thickly-wooded swamp or morass. On one side of this inlet is a beautiful dark grove; on the opposite side the land rises abruptly from the water's edge into a high ridge, on which grow a few scattered oaks of great age and immense size. Under one of these gigantic trees, according to old stories, there was a great amount of treasure buried by Kidd the pirate. The inlet allowed a facility to bring the money in a boat secretly and at night to the very foot of the hill; the elevation of the place permitted a good lookout to be kept that no one was at hand; while the remarkable trees formed good landmarks by which the place might easily be found again. The old stories add, moreover, that the devil presided at the hiding of the money, and took it under his guardianship; but this, it is well known, he always does with buried treasure, particularly when it has been ill-gotten. Be that as it may, Kidd never returned to recover his wealth; being shortly after seized at Boston, sent out to England, and there hanged for a pirate.

About the year 1727, just at the time that earthquakes were prevalent in New England, and shook many tall sinners down upon their knees, there lived near this place a meagre, miserly fellow, of the name of Tom Walker. He had a wife as miserly as himself: they were so miserly that they even conspired to cheat each other. Whatever the woman could lay hands on, she hid away; a hen could not cackle but she was on the alert to secure the new-laid egg. Her husband was continually prying about to detect her secret hoards, and many and fierce were the conflicts that took place about what ought to have been common property. They lived in a forlorn-looking house that stood alone, and had an air of starvation. A few straggling savin-trees, emblems of sterility, grew near it; no smoke ever curled from its chimney; no traveller stopped at its door. A miserable horse, whose ribs were as articulate as the bars of a gridiron, stalked about a field, where a thin carpet of moss, scarcely covering the ragged beds of pudding-stone, tantalized and balked his hunger; and sometimes he would lean his head over the fence, look piteously at the passer-by, and seem to petition deliverance from this land of famine.

The house and its inmates had altogether a bad name. Tom's wife was a tall termagant, fierce of temper, loud of tongue, and strong of arm. Her voice was often heard in wordy warfare with her husband; and his face sometimes showed signs that their conflicts were not confined to words. No one ventured, however, to interfere between them. The lonely wayfarer shrunk within himself at the horrid clamor and clapper-clawing; eyed the den of discord askance; and hurried on his way, rejoicing, if a bachelor, in his celibacy.

One day that Tom Walker had been to a distant part of the neighborhood, he took what he considered a short cut homeward, through the swamp. Like most short cuts, it was an ill-chosen route. The swamp was thickly grown with great gloomy pines and hemlocks, some of them ninety feet high, which made it dark at noonday, and a retreat for all the owls of the neighborhood. It was full of pits and quagmires, partly covered with weeds and mosses, where the green surface often betrayed the traveller into a gulf of black, smothering mud: there were also dark and stagnant pools, the abodes of the tadpole, the bullfrog, and the water-snake; where the trunks of pines and hemlocks lay half-drowned, half-rotting, looking like alligators sleeping in the mire.

Tom had long been picking his way cautiously through this treacherous forest; stepping from tuft to tuft of rushes and roots, which afforded precarious footholds among deep sloughs; or pacing carefully, like a cat, along the prostrate trunks of trees; startled now and then by the sudden screaming of the bittern, or the quacking of a wild duck rising on the wing from some solitary pool. At length he arrived at a firm piece of ground, which ran out like a peninsula into the deep bosom of the swamp. It had been one of the strongholds of the Indians during their wars with the first colonists. Here they had thrown up a kind of fort, which they had looked upon as almost impregnable, and had used as a place of refuge for their squaws and children. Nothing remained of the old Indian fort but a few embankments, gradually sinking to the level of the surrounding earth, and already overgrown in part by oaks and other forest trees, the foliage of which formed a contrast to the dark pines and hemlocks of the swamp.

It was late in the dusk of evening when Tom Walker reached the old fort, and he paused there awhile to rest himself. Any one but he would have felt unwilling to linger in this lonely, melancholy place, for the common people had a bad opinion of it, from the stories handed down from the time of the Indian wars; when it was asserted that the savages held incantations here, and made sacrifices to the evil spirit.

Tom Walker, however, was not a man to be troubled with any fears of the kind. He reposed himself for some time on the trunk of a fallen hemlock, listening to the boding cry of the tree-toad, and delving with his walking-staff into a mound of black mould at his feet. As he turned up the soil unconsciously, his staff struck against something hard. He raked it out of the vegetable mould, and lo! a cloven skull, with an Indian tomahawk buried deep in it, lay before him. The rust on the weapon showed the time that had elapsed since this deathblow had been given. It was a dreary memento of the fierce struggle that had taken place in this last foothold of the Indian warriors.

"Humph!" said Tom Walker, as he gave it a kick to shake the dirt from it.

"Let that skull alone!" said a gruff voice. Tom lifted up his eyes, and beheld a great black man seated directly opposite him, on the stump of a tree. He was exceedingly surprised, having neither heard nor seen any one approach; and he was still more perplexed on observing, as well as the gathering gloom would permit, that the stranger was neither negro nor Indian. It is true he was dressed in a rude half-Indian garb, and had a red belt or sash swathed round his body; but his face was neither black nor copper-color, but swarthy and dingy, and begrimed with soot, as if he had been accustomed to toil among fires and forges. He had a shock of coarse black hair, that stood out from his head in all directions, and bore an axe on his shoulder.

He scowled for a moment at Tom with a pair of great red eyes.

"What are you doing on my grounds?" said the black man, with a hoarse growling voice.

"Your grounds!" said Tom, with a sneer, "no more your grounds than mine; they belong to Deacon Peabody."

"Deacon Peabody be d——d," said the stranger, "as I flatter myself he will be, if he does not look more to his own sins and less to those of his neighbors. Look yonder, and see how Deacon Peabody is faring."

Tom looked in the direction that the stranger pointed, and beheld one of the great trees, fair and flourishing without, but rotten at the core, and saw that it had been nearly hewn through, so that the first high wind was likely to blow it down. On the bark of the tree was scored the name

of Deacon Peabody, an eminent man, who had waxed wealthy by driving shrewd bargains with the Indians. He now looked around, and found most of the tall trees marked with the name of some great man of the colony, and all more or less scored by the axe. The one on which he had been seated, and which had evidently just been hewn down, bore the name of Crowninshield; and he recollected a mighty rich man of that name, who made a vulgar display of wealth, which it was whispered he had acquired by buccaneering.

"He's just ready for burning!" said the black man, with a growl of triumph. "You see I am likely to have a good stock of firewood for winter."

"But what right have you," said Tom, "to cut down Deacon Peabody's timber?"

"The right of a prior claim," said the other. "This woodland belonged to me long before one of your white-faced race put foot upon the soil."

"And pray, who are you, if I may be so bold?" said Tom.

"Oh, I go by various names. I am the wild huntsman in some countries; the black miner in others. In this neighborhood I am known by the name of the black woodsman. I am he to whom the red men consecrated this spot, and in honor of whom they now and then roasted a white man, by way of sweet-smelling sacrifice. Since the red men have been exterminated by you white savages, I amuse myself by presiding at the persecutions of Quakers and Anabaptists; I am the great patron and prompter of slave-dealers, and the grand-master of the Salem witches."

"The upshot of all which is, that, if I mistake not," said Tom, sturdily, "you are he commonly called Old Scratch."

"The same, at your service!" replied the black man, with a half civil nod.

Such was the opening of this interview, according to the old story; though it has almost too familiar an air to be credited. One would think that to meet with such a singular personage, in this wild, lonely place, would have shaken any man's nerves;

but Tom was a hard-minded fellow, not easily daunted, and he had lived so long with a termagant wife, that he did not even fear the devil.

It is said that after this commencement they had a long and earnest conversation together, as Tom returned homeward. The black man told him of great sums of money buried by Kidd the pirate, under the oak-trees on the high ridge, not far from the morass. All these were under his command, and protected by his power, so that none could find them but such as propitiated his favor. These he offered to place within Tom Walker's reach, having conceived an especial kindness for him; but they were to be had only on certain conditions. What these conditions were may be easily surmised, though Tom never disclosed them publicly. They must have been very hard, for he required time to think of them, and he was not a man to stick at trifles when money was in view. When they had reached the edge of the swamp, the stranger paused. "What proof have I that all you have been telling me is true?" said Tom. "There's my signature," said the black man, pressing his finger on Tom's forehead. So saying, he turned off among the thickets of the swamp, and seemed, as Tom said, to go down, down, down, into the earth, until nothing but his head and shoulders could be seen, and so on, until he totally disappeared.

When Tom reached home, he found the black print of a finger burnt, as it were, into his forehead, which nothing could obliterate.

The first news his wife had to tell him was the sudden death of Absalom Crowninshield, the rich buccaneer. It was announced in the papers, with the usual flourish, that "A great man had fallen in Israel."

Tom recollected the tree which his black friend had just hewn down, and which was ready for burning. "Let the freebooter roast," said Tom, "who cares!" He now felt convinced that all he had heard and seen was no illusion.

He was not prone to let his wife into his confidence; but as this was an uneasy secret, he willingly shared it with her. All her avarice was awakened at the mention of hidden gold, and she urged her husband to comply with the black man's terms, and secure what would make them wealthy for life. However Tom might have felt disposed to sell himself to the Devil, he was determined not to do so to oblige his wife; so he flatly refused, out of the mere spirit of contradiction. Many and bitter were the quarrels they had on the subject; but the more she talked, the more resolute was Tom not to be damned to please her.

At length she determined to drive the bargain on her own account, and if she succeeded, to keep all the gain to herself. Being of the same fearless temper as her husband, she set off for the old Indian fort towards the close of a summer's day. She was many hours absent. When she came back, she was reserved and sullen in her replies. She spoke something of a black man, whom she had met about twilight hewing at the root of a tall tree. He was sulky, however, and would not come to terms: she was to go again with a propitiatory offering, but what it was she forebore to say.

The next evening she set off again for the swamp, with her apron heavily laden. Tom waited and waited for her, but in vain; midnight came, but she did not make her appearance: morning, noon, night returned, but still she did not come. Tom now grew uneasy for her safety, especially as he found she had carried off in her apron the silver tea-pot and spoons, and every portable article of value. Another night elapsed, another morning came; but no wife. In a word, she was never heard of more.

What was her real fate nobody knows, in consequence of so many pretending to know. It is one of those facts which have become confounded by a variety of historians. Some asserted that she lost her way among the tangled mazes of the swamp, and sank into some pit or slough; others, more uncharitable, hinted that she had eloped with the household booty, and made off to some other province; while others surmised that the tempter had decoyed her into a dismal quagmire, on the top of which her hat was found lying. In confirmation of this, it was said a great black man, with an axe on his shoulder, was seen late that very evening coming out of the swamp, carrying a bundle tied in a check apron, with an air of surly triumph.

The most current and probable story, however, observes, that Tom Walker grew so anxious about the fate of his wife and his property, that he set out at length to seek them both at the Indian fort. During a long summer's afternoon he searched about the gloomy place, but no wife was to be seen. He called her name repeatedly, but she was nowhere to be heard. The bittern alone responded to his voice, as he flew screaming by: or the bull-frog croaked dolefully from a neighboring pool. At length, it is said, just in the brown hour of twilight, when the owls began to hoot, and the bats to flit about, his attention was attracted by the clamor of carrion crows hovering about a cypress-tree. He looked up, and beheld a bundle tied in a check apron, and hanging in the branches of the tree, with a great vulture perched hard by, as if keeping watch upon it. He leaped with joy; for he recognized his wife's apron, and supposed it to contain the household valuables.

"Let us get hold of the property," said he, consolingly to himself, "and we will endeavor to do without the woman."

As he scrambled up the tree, the vulture spread its wide wings, and sailed off, screaming, into the deep shadows of the forest. Tom seized the checked apron, but, woeful sight! found nothing but a heart and liver tied up in it!

Such, according to this most authentic old story, was all that was to be found of Tom's wife. She had probably attempted to deal with the black man as she had been accustomed to deal with her husband; but though a female scold is generally considered a match for the devil, yet in this instance she appears to have had the worse of it. She must have died game, however; for it is said Tom noticed many prints of cloven feet deeply stamped about the tree, and found handfuls of hair, that looked as if they had been plucked from the coarse black shock of the woodman. Tom knew his wife's prowess by experience. He shrugged his shoulders, as he looked at the signs of a fierce clapper-clawing. "Egad," said he to himself, "Old Scratch must have had a tough time of it!"

Tom consoled himself for the loss of his property, with the loss of his wife, for he was a man of fortitude. He even felt something like gratitude towards the black woodman, who, he considered, had done him a kindness. He sought, therefore, to cultivate a further acquaintance with him, but for some time without success; the old blacklegs played shy, for whatever people may think, he is not always to be had for calling for: he knows how to play his cards when pretty sure of his game.

At length, it is said, when delay had whetted Tom's eagerness to the quick, and prepared him to agree to anything rather than not gain the promised treasure, he met the black man one evening in his usual woodman's dress, with his axe on his shoulder, sauntering along the swamp, and humming a tune. He affected to receive Tom's advances with great indifference, made brief replies, and went on humming his tune.

By degrees, however, Tom brought him to business, and they began to haggle about the terms on which the former was to have the pirate's treasure. There was one condition which need not be mentioned, being generally understood in all cases where the devil grants favors; but there were others about which, though of less importance, he was inflexibly obstinate. He insisted that the money found through his means should be employed in his service. He proposed, therefore, that Tom should employ it in the black traffic; that is to say, that he should fit out a slave-ship. This, however, Tom resolutely refused: he was bad enough in all conscience; but the devil himself could not tempt him to turn slave-trader.

Finding Tom so squeamish on this point, he did not insist upon it, but proposed, instead, that he should turn usurer; the devil being extremely anxious for the increase of usurers, looking upon them as his peculiar people.

To this no objections were made, for it was just to Tom's taste.

"You shall open a broker's shop in Boston next month," said the black man.

"I'll do it to-morrow, if you wish," said Tom Walker.

"You shall lend money at two per cent a month."

"Egad, I'll charge four!" replied Tom Walker.

"You shall extort bonds, foreclose mortgages, drive the merchants to bankruptcy"——

"I'll drive them to the d——," cried Tom Walker.

"You are the usurer for my money!" said black-legs with delight. "When will you want the rhino?"

"This very night."

"Done!" said the devil.

"Done!" said Tom Walker.—So they shook hands and struck a bargain.

A few days' time saw Tom Walker seated behind his desk in a counting-house in Boston.

His reputation for a ready-moneyed man, who would lend money out for a good consideration, soon spread abroad. Everybody remembers the time of Governor Belcher, when money was particularly scarce. It was a time of paper credit. The country had been deluged with government bills, the famous Land Bank had been established; there had been a rage for speculating; the people had run mad with schemes for new settlements; for building cities in the wilderness; land-jobbers went about with maps of grants, and townships, and Eldorados, lying nobody knew where, but which everybody was ready to purchase. In a word, the great speculating fever which breaks out every now and then in the country, had raged to an alarming degree, and everybody was dreaming of making sudden fortunes from nothing. As usual the fever had subsided; the dream had gone off, and the imaginary fortunes with it; the patients were left in doleful plight, and the whole country resounded with the consequent cry of "hard times."

At this propitious time of public distress did Tom Walker set up as usurer in Boston. His door was soon thronged by customers. The needy and adventurous; the gambling speculator; the dreaming land-jobber; the thriftless tradesman; the merchant with cracked credit; in short, everyone driven to raise money by desperate means and desperate sacrifices, hurried to Tom Walker.

Thus Tom was the universal friend of the needy, and acted like a "friend in need"; that is to say, he always exacted good pay and good security. In proportion to the distress of the applicant was the highness of his terms. He accumulated bonds and mortgages; gradually squeezed his customers closer and closer: and sent them at length, dry as a sponge, from his door.

In this way he made money hand over hand; became a rich and mighty man, and exalted his cocked hat upon 'Change. He built himself, as usual, a vast house, out of ostentation; but left the greater part of it unfinished and unfurnished, out of parsimony. He even set up a carriage in the fulness of his vainglory, though he nearly starved the horses which drew it; and as the ungreased wheels groaned and screeched on the axle-trees, you would have thought you heard the souls of the poor debtors he was squeezing.

As Tom waxed old, however, he grew thoughtful. Having secured the good things of this world, he began to feel anxious about those of the next. He thought with regret on the bargain he had made with his black friend, and set his wits to work to cheat him out of the conditions. He became, therefore, all of a sudden, a violent

church-goer. He prayed loudly and strenuously, as if heaven were to be taken by
force of lungs. Indeed, one might always
tell when he had sinned most during the
week, by the clamor of his Sunday devotion.
The quiet Christians who had been modestly
and steadfastly travelling Zionward, were
struck with self-reproach at seeing themselves so suddenly outstripped in their career by this new-made convert. Tom was
as rigid in religious as in money matters; he
was a stern supervisor and censurer of his
neighbors, and seemed to think every sin
entered up to their account became a credit
on his own side of the page. He even talked
of the expediency of reviving the persecution of Quakers and Anabaptists. In a
word, Tom's zeal became as notorious as
his riches.

Still, in spite of all this strenuous attention to forms, Tom had a lurking dread
that the devil, after all, would have his
due. That he might not be taken unawares,
therefore, it is said he always carried a
small Bible in his coat-pocket. He had
also a great folio Bible on his counting-
house desk, and would frequently be found
reading it when people called on business;
on such occasions he would lay his green
spectacles in the book, to mark the place,
while he turned round to drive some
usurious bargain.

Some say that Tom grew a little crack-
brained in his old days, and that, fancying
his end approaching, he had his horse new
shod, saddled and bridled, and buried with
his feet uppermost; because he supposed
that at the last day the world would be
turned upside down; in which case he
should find his horse standing ready for
mounting, and he was determined at the
worst to give his old friend a run for it.
This, however, is probably a mere old
wives' fable. If he really did take such a
precaution, it was totally superfluous; at
least so says the authentic old legend; which
closes his story in the following manner.

One hot summer afternoon in the dog-
days, just as a terrible black thunder-gust
was coming up, Tom sat in his counting-
house, in his white linen cap and India
silk morning-gown. He was on the point
of foreclosing a mortgage, by which he
would complete the ruin of an unlucky
land-speculator for whom he had professed
the greatest friendship. The poor land-
jobber begged him to grant a few months'
indulgence. Tom had grown testy and irritated, and refused another day.

"My family will be ruined, and brought
upon the parish," said the land-jobber.

"Charity begins at home," replied Tom;
"I must take care of myself in these hard
times."

"You have made so much money out of
me," said the speculator.

Tom lost his patience and his piety. "The
devil take me," said he, "if I have made a
farthing!"

Just then there were three loud knocks
at the street-door. He stepped out to see
who was there. A black man was holding
a black horse, which neighed and stamped
with impatience.

"Tom, you're come for," said the black
fellow, gruffly. Tom shrank back, but too
late. He had left his little Bible at the
bottom of his coat-pocket, and his big
Bible on the desk buried under the mortgage he was about to foreclose: never was
sinner taken more unawares. The black
man whisked him like a child into the
saddle, gave the horse the lash, and away
he galloped, with Tom on his back, in the
midst of the thunder-storm. The clerks
stuck their pens behind their ears, and
stared after him from the windows. Away
went Tom Walker, dashing down the
streets; his white cap bobbing up and
down; his morning-gown fluttering in the
wind, and his steed striking fire out of the
pavement at every bound. When the clerks
turned to look for the black man, he had
disappeared.

Tom Walker never returned to foreclose
the mortgage. A countryman, who lived on
the border of the swamp, reported that in
the height of the thunder-gust he had heard
a great clattering of hoofs and a howling
along the road, and running to the window

caught sight of a figure, such as I have described, on a horse that galloped like mad across the fields, over the hills, and down into the black hemlock swamp towards the old Indian fort; and that shortly after a thunder-bolt falling in that direction seemed to set the whole forest in a blaze.

The good people of Boston shook their heads and shrugged their shoulders, but had been so much accustomed to witches and goblins, and tricks of the devil, in all kinds of shapes, from the first settlement of the colony, that they were not so much horror-struck as might have been expected. Trustees were appointed to take charge of Tom's effects. There was nothing, however, to administer. On searching his coffers, all his bonds and mortgages were found reduced to cinders. In place of gold and silver, his iron chest was filled with chips and shavings; two skeletons lay in his stable instead of his half-starved horses, and the very next day his great house took fire and was burnt to the ground.

Such was the end of Tom Walker and his ill-gotten wealth. Let all griping money-brokers lay this story to heart. The truth of it is not to be doubted. The very hole under the oak-trees, whence he dug Kidd's money, is to be seen to this day; and the neighboring swamp and old Indian fort are often haunted in stormy nights by a figure on horseback, in morning-gown and white cap, which is doubtless the troubled spirit of the usurer. In fact, the story has resolved itself into a proverb, and is the origin of that popular saying, so prevalent throughout New England, of "The Devil and Tom Walker."

From
A TOUR OF THE PRAIRIES
[1835]

A SECRET EXPEDITION

ON THE following morning we were rejoined by the rangers who had remained at the last encampment, to seek for the stray horses. They had tracked them for a considerable distance through bush and brake, and across streams, until they found them cropping the herbage on the edge of a prairie. Their heads were in the direction of the fort, and they were evidently grazing their way homeward, heedless of the unbounded freedom of the prairies so suddenly laid open to them.

About noon the weather held up, and I observed a mysterious consultation going on between our half-breeds and Tonish;[1] it ended in a request that we would dispense with the services of the latter for a few hours, and permit him to join his comrades in a grand foray. We objected that Tonish was too much disabled by aches and pains for such an undertaking; but he was wild with eagerness for the mysterious enterprise, and, when permission was given him, seemed to forget all his ailments in an instant.

In a short time the trio were equipped and on horseback; with rifles on their shoulders and handkerchiefs twisted round their heads, evidently bound for a grand scamper. As they passed by the different lodges of the camp, the vainglorious little Frenchman could not help boasting to the right and left of the great things he was about to achieve; though the taciturn Beatte,[2] who rode in advance, would every now and then check his horse, and look back at him with an air of stern rebuke. It was hard, however, to make the loquacious Tonish play "Indian."

Several of the hunters, likewise, sallied forth, and the prime old woodman, Ryan, came back early in the afternoon, with ample spoil, having killed a buck and two fat does. I drew near to a group of rangers that had gathered round him as he stood by the spoil, and found they were discussing the merits of a strategem sometimes used in deer hunting. This consists in imitating, with a small instrument called

---

[1] A hunter of Irving's party.

[2] Captain of Irving's party.

a bleat, the cry of the fawn, so as to lure the doe within reach of the rifle. There are bleats of various kinds, suited to calm or windy weather, and to the age of the fawn. The poor animal, deluded by them, in its anxiety about its young, will sometimes advance close up to the hunter. "I once bleated a doe," said a young hunter, "until it came within twenty yards of me and presented a sure mark. I levelled my rifle three times, but had not the heart to shoot, for the poor doe looked so wistfully, that it in a manner made my heart yearn. I thought of my own mother, and of how anxious she used to be about me when I was a child; so to put an end to the matter, I gave a halloo, and started the doe out of rifle-shot in a moment."

"And you did right," cried honest old Ryan. "For my part, I never could bring myself to bleating deer. I've been with hunters who had bleats, and have made them throw them away. It's a rascally trick to take advantage of a mother's love for her young."

Toward evening our three worthies returned from their mysterious foray. The tongue of Tonish gave notice of their approach long before they came in sight; for he was vociferating at the top of his lungs, and rousing the attention of the whole camp. The lagging gait and reeking flanks of the horses, gave evidence of hard riding; and, on nearer approach, we found them hung round with meat like a butcher's shambles. In fact, they had been scouring an immense prairie that extended beyond the forest, and which was covered with herds of buffalo. Of this prairie, and the animals upon it, Beatte had received intelligence a few days before, in his conversation with the Osages, but had kept the information a secret from the rangers, that he and his comrades might have the first dash at the game. They had contented themselves with killing four; though, if Tonish might be believed, they might have slain them by scores.

These tidings, and the buffalo meat brought home in evidence, spread exulta-

tion through the camp, and every one looked forward with joy to a buffalo hunt on the prairies. Tonish was again the oracle of the camp, and held forth by the hour to a knot of listeners, crouched round the fire, with their shoulders up to their ears. He was now more boastful than ever of his skill as a marksman. All his want of success in the early part of our march he attributed to being "out of luck," if not "spell-bound;" and finding himself listened to with apparent credulity, gave an instance of the kind, which he declared had happened to himself, but which was evidently a tale picked up among his relations, the Osages.

According to this account, when about fourteen years of age, as he was one day hunting, he saw a white deer come out from a ravine. Crawling near to get a shot, he beheld another and another come forth, until there were seven, all as white as snow. Having crept sufficiently near, he singled one out and fired, but without effect. The deer remained unfrightened. He loaded and fired again and missed. Thus he continued firing and missing until all his ammunition was expended, and the deer remained without a wound. He returned home despairing of his skill as a marksman, but was consoled by an old Osage hunter. These white deer, said he, have a charmed life, and can only be killed by bullets of a particular kind.

The old Indian cast several balls for Tonish, but would not suffer him to be present on the occasion, nor inform him of the ingredients and mystic ceremonials.

Provided with these balls, Tonish again set out in quest of the white deer, and succeeded in finding them. He tried at first with ordinary balls, but missed as before. A magic ball, however, immediately brought a fine buck to the ground. Whereupon the rest of the herd immediately disappeared and were never seen again.

October 29th.—The morning opened gloomy and lowering; but toward eight o'clock the sun struggled forth and lighted up the forest, and the notes of the bugle gave signal to prepare for marching. Now began a scene of bustle, and clamor, and gayety. Some were scampering and brawling after their horses, some were riding in bare-backed, and driving in the horses of their comrades. Some were stripping the poles of the wet blankets that had served for shelters; others packing up with all possible dispatch, and loading the baggage horses as they arrived, while others were cracking off their damp rifles and charging them afresh, to be ready for the sport.

About ten o'clock, we began our march. I loitered in the rear of the troop as it forded the turbid brook, and defiled through the labyrinths of the forest. I always felt disposed to linger until the last straggler disappeared among the trees and the distant note of the bugle died upon the ear, that I might behold the wilderness relapsing into silence and solitude. In the present instance, the deserted scene of our late bustling encampment had a forlorn and desolate appearance. The surrounding forest had been in many places trampled into a quagmire. Trees felled and partly hewn in pieces, and scattered in huge fragments; tent-poles stripped of their covering; smouldering fires, with great morsels of roasted venison and buffalo meat, standing in wooden spits before them, hacked and slashed by the knives of hungry hunters; while around were strewed the hides, the horns, the antlers, and bones of buffaloes and deer, with uncooked joints, and unplucked turkeys, left behind with that reckless improvidence and wastefulness which young hunters are apt to indulge when in a neighborhood where game abounds. In the meantime a score or two of turkey-buzzards, or vultures, were already on the wing, wheeling their magnificent flight high in the air, and preparing for a descent upon the camp as soon as it should be abandoned.

AMUSEMENTS IN THE CAMP

On returning to the camp we found it a scene of the greatest hilarity. Some of the rangers were shooting at a mark, others were leaping, wrestling, and playing at prison bars. They were mostly young men, on their first expedition, in high health and vigor, and buoyant with anticipations; and I can conceive nothing more likely to set the youthful blood into a flow, than a wild wood life of the kind, and the range of a magnificent wilderness, abounding with game and fruitful of adventure. We send our youth abroad to grow luxurious and effeminate in Europe; it appears to me, that a previous tour on the prairies would be more likely to produce that manliness, simplicity, and self-dependence, most in unison with our political institutions.

While the young men were engaged in these boisterous amusements, a graver set, composed of the Captain, the Doctor, and other sages and leaders of the camp, were seated or stretched out on the grass, round a frontier map, holding a consultation about our position, and the course we were to pursue. . . .

Before sunset, we were summoned by little Tonish to a sumptuous repast. Blankets had been spread on the ground near to the fire, upon which we took our seats. A large dish, or bowl, made from the root of a maple tree, and which we had purchased at the Indian village, was placed on the ground before us, and into it were emptied the contents of one of the camp kettles, consisting of a wild turkey hashed, together with slices of bacon and lumps of dough. Beside it was placed another bowl of similar ware, containing an ample supply of fritters. After we had discussed the hash, two wooden spits, on which the ribs of a fat buck were broiling before the fire, were removed and planted in the ground before us, with a triumphant air, by little Tonish. Having no dishes, we had to proceed in hunter's style, cutting off strips and slices with our hunting knives, and dipping them in salt and pepper. To do justice to Tonish's cookery, however, and to the keen sauce of the prairies, never have I tasted venison so delicious. With all this, our beverage was coffee, boiled in a camp kettle, sweetened with brown sugar, and drunk out of tin cups: and such was the style of our banqueting throughout this expedition, whenever provisions were plenty, and as long as flour and coffee and sugar held out.

As the twilight thickened into night, the sentinels were marched forth to their stations around the camp; an indispensable precaution in a country infested by Indians. The encampment now presented a picturesque appearance. Camp fires were blazing and smouldering here and there among the trees, with groups of rangers round them; some seated or lying on the ground, others standing in the ruddy glare of the flames, or in shadowy relief. At some of the fires there was much boisterous mirth, where peals of laughter were mingled with loud ribald jokes and uncouth exclamations; for the group was evidently a raw, undisciplined band, levied among the wild youngsters of the frontier, who had enlisted, some for the sake of roving adventure, and some for the purpose of getting a knowledge of the country. Many of them were the neighbors of their officers, and accustomed to regard them with the familiarity of equals and companions. None of them had any idea of the restraint and decorum of a camp, or ambition to acquire a name for exactness in a profession in which they had no intention of continuing.

While this boisterous merriment prevailed at some of the fires, there suddenly rose a strain of nasal melody from another, at which a choir of "vocalists" were uniting their voices in a most lugubrious psalm tune. This was led by one of the lieutenants; a tall, spare man, who we were informed had officiated as schoolmaster, singing-master, and occasionally as Methodist preacher, in one of the villages of the frontier. The chant rose solemnly and sadly in the night air, and reminded me of the description of similar canticles in the camps of the Covenanters; and, indeed, the strange medley of figures and faces

and uncouth garbs, congregated together in our troop, would not have disgraced the banners of Praise-God Barebones.[3]

In one of the intervals of this nasal psalmody, an amateur owl, as if in competition, began his dreary hooting. Immediately there was a cry throughout the camp of "Charley's owl! Charley's owl!" It seems this "obscure bird" had visited the camp every night, and had been fired at by one of the sentinels, a half-witted lad, named Charley; who, on being called up for firing when on duty, excused himself by saying, that he understood owls made uncommonly good soup.

One of the young rangers mimicked the cry of this bird of wisdom, who, with a simplicity little consonant with his character, came hovering within sight, and alighted on the naked branch of a tree, lit up by the blaze of our fire. The young Count immediately seized his fowling-piece, took fatal aim, and in a twinkling the poor bird of ill omen came fluttering to the ground. Charley was now called upon to make and eat his dish of owl-soup, but declined, as he had not shot the bird.

In the course of the evening, I paid a visit to the Captain's fire. It was composed of huge trunks of trees, and of sufficient magnitude to roast a buffalo whole. Here were a number of the prime hunters and leaders of the camp, some sitting, some standing, and others lying on skins or blankets before the fire, telling old frontier stories about hunting and Indian warfare.

As the night advanced, we perceived above the trees to the west, a ruddy glow flushing up the sky.

"That must be a prairie set on fire by the Osage hunters," said the Captain.

"It is at the Red Fork," said Beatte, regarding the sky. "It seems but three miles distant, yet it perhaps is twenty."

About half past eight o'clock, a beautiful pale light gradually sprang up in the east,

---

[3] A Baptist preacher and member of Cromwell's "Little Parliament" of 1653. His actual name was Praisegod Barbon, or Barebone.

a precursor of the rising moon. Drawing off from the Captain's lodge, I now prepared for the night's repose. I had determined to abandon the shelter of the tent, and henceforth to bivouac like the rangers. A bear-skin spread at the foot of a tree was my bed, with a pair of saddle-bags for a pillow. Wrapping myself in blankets, I stretched myself on this hunter's couch, and soon fell into a sound and sweet sleep, from which I did not awake until the bugle sounded at daybreak.

1794 ∽ *William Cullen Bryant* ∽ 1878

WHEN in 1817 the still youthful *North American Review* published "Thanatopsis," the editor was told that he had been imposed on: "no one on this side of the Atlantic," the critic insisted, "is capable of writing such verses." The skeptic—R. H. Dana the elder—was soon to learn that William Cullen Bryant had written "Thanatopsis" not only on this side of the Atlantic, but at the age of sixteen—that he had published his first book at fourteen! Seventy fruitful years separated that juvenile volume—an imitative political satire called *The Embargo*—and Bryant's last communication to the American people, a few weeks before his death, an address on the unveiling of the statue of the Italian patriot Mazzini. The image of Bryant which is most familiar is that of the bearded patriarch of letters, full of years and honors; but it was a quiet, earnest boy in his teens and twenties, an ardent reader and walker, studying and practising law in rural villages, fighting his inward way to religious and political liberalism, who wrote the first genuine poetry of the new national literature.

His early achievement was due in no small measure to the home in which he grew up, and especially to the extraordinarily sympathetic and helpful interest of his father. Dr. Peter Bryant, widely known and loved as a physician and respected as a legislator, was a lover of books and a man of liberal sympathies in political and religious matters. He guided his son's reading and encouraged his writing. But the battles the young writer had to fight were personal ones. They marked his passage from a naive federalism to a democratic faith that made him a supporter of Andrew Jackson, and in later years one of the founders of the Republican party and one of the earliest and staunchest adherents of Abraham Lincoln in the East; and from a narrow Calvinism to Unitarianism and to even broader religious sympathies.

He spent one year at Williams College, but most of his study was private —first in preparation for college, later in reading law. He earned a living for ten years as a lawyer—and as town clerk, justice of the peace, and hog reeve—in small towns of the hill country of western Massachusetts. Here he met and married Frances Farmer, "fairest of the rural maids," matured his knowledge and love of the out-of-doors in many walking trips, and wrote steadily. He experimented unsuccessfully with fiction. But his criticism early showed extraordinary breadth of understanding and sureness of judgment; and his poetry, influenced at first by Thomson, Cowper and Southey, then by Byron and Wordsworth, soon became consistently American, and his own. While others were still only talking about a national literature, Bryant was making it.

At thirty he left rural Massachusetts for New York City, and the law for journalism. Four years later, as editor-in-chief and part owner of the *New York Evening Post,* he assumed responsibilities which he was to discharge with high distinction for almost fifty years. Bryant was one of the greatest and most consistent liberal editors in the history of American journalism. He was alive to the issues of his time, forthright in his championship of labor and his denunciation of slavery. Frequent visits to his brothers who were pioneers in Illinois kept him in touch with the development of the West. He maintained standards of journalistic dignity, courage, and good taste in a time when these qualities were rare in American newspapers.

Bryant continued to write and publish throughout his life; a verse translation of Homer was a major achievement of his later years. But most of his work which has greatest vitality had been completed before he moved to New York, and all of his best fills only a slender volume. That best wears well. It is free from obscurity either accidental or designed, from pretentiousness, from falsehood of any kind—completely integrated, simple because it is sure. It is restrained but not timid, quiet but not dull. The range of experience, both inward and outward, presented in Bryant's poetry is not wide; but it is widely accessible to readers of varying ages, backgrounds, and special tastes. In his expression of this experience Bryant challenged successfully the difficulties of the most exacting traditional poetic forms: William Ellery Leonard considers him, "with Poe, America's finest artist in verse." But the greatest virtue of his work is its integrity, its truth of form and phrase as personal utterance.

[Biographical and critical studies of Bryant are those by John Bigelow (Boston, 1890) and W. A. Bradley (New York, 1905). A good introduction is Tremaine McDowell's *Bryant* (New York, 1935) in the American Writers Series. The authorized biography is Parke Godwin's *Life of Bryant,* 2 vols. (New York, 1883). The text used in the selections is that of the collected edition, edited by Parke Godwin (New York, 1884).]

THANATOPSIS
[1821 (1817)]

TO HIM who in the love of Nature holds
Communion with her visible forms, she speaks
A various language; for his gayer hours

She has a voice of gladness, and a smile
And eloquence of beauty, and she glides 5
Into his darker musings, with a mild
And healing sympathy, that steals away
Their sharpness, ere he is aware. When thoughts
Of the last bitter hour come like a blight

Over thy spirit, and sad images   10
Of the stern agony, and shroud, and pall,
And breathless darkness, and the narrow
    house,
Make thee to shudder, and grow sick at
    heart;—
Go forth, under the open sky, and list
To Nature's teachings, while from all
    around—   15
Earth and her waters, and the depths of
    air—
Comes a still voice.[1]—

              Yet a few days, and thee
The all-beholding sun shall see no more
In all his course; nor yet in the cold
    ground,
Where thy pale form was laid, with many
    tears,   20
Nor in the embrace of ocean, shall exist
Thy image. Earth, that nourished thee,
    shall claim
Thy growth, to be resolved to earth again,
And, lost each human trace, surrendering
    up
Thine individual being, shalt thou go   25
To mix for ever with the elements,
To be a brother to the insensible rock
And to the sluggish clod, which the rude
    swain
Turns with his share, and treads upon.
    The oak
Shall send his roots abroad, and pierce thy
    mould.   30

Yet not to thine eternal resting-place
Shalt thou retire alone, nor couldst thou
    wish
Couch more magnificent. Thou shalt lie
    down
With patriarchs of the infant world—with
    kings,
The powerful of the earth—the wise, the
    good,   35
Fair forms, and hoary seers of ages past,
All in one mighty sepulchre. The hills
Rock-ribbed and ancient as the sun,—the
    vales
Stretching in pensive quietness between;
The venerable woods—rivers that move   40
In majesty, and the complaining brooks

That make the meadows green; and, poured
    round all,
Old Ocean's gray and melancholy waste,—
Are but the solemn decorations all
Of the great tomb of man. The golden
    sun,   45
The planets, all the infinite host of heaven,
Are shining on the sad abodes of death,
Through the still lapse of ages. All that
    tread
The globe are but a handful to the tribes
That slumber in its bosom.—Take the
    wings   50
Of morning, pierce the Barcan wilderness,[2]
Or lose thyself in the continuous woods
Where rolls the Oregon, and hears no
    sound,
Save his own dashings—yet the dead are
    there:
And millions in those solitudes, since
    first   55
The flight of years began, have laid them
    down
In their last sleep—the dead reign there
    alone.
So shalt thou rest, and what if thou
    withdraw
In silence from the living, and no friend
Take note of thy departure? All that
    breathe   60
Will share thy destiny. The gay will laugh
When thou art gone, the solemn brood of
    care
Plod on, and each one as before will chase
His favorite phantom; yet all these shall
    leave
Their mirth and their employments, and
    shall come   65
And make their bed with thee. As the long
    train
Of ages glides away, the sons of men,
The youth in life's fresh spring, and he
    who goes
In the full strength of years, matron and
    maid,
The speechless babe, and the gray-headed
    man—   70

---

[1] As originally printed in the *North American Review*, the poem began here.
[2] North African desert region.

Shall one by one be gathered to thy side,
By those, who in their turn shall follow
    them.

So live, that when thy summons comes to
    join
The innumerable caravan, which moves
To that mysterious realm, where each shall
    take   75
His chamber in the silent halls of death,
Thou go not, like the quarry-slave at night,
Scourged to his dungeon, but, sustained
    and soothed
By an unfaltering trust, approach thy
    grave,
Like one who wraps the drapery of his
    couch   80
About him, and lies down to pleasant
    dreams.

TO A WATERFOWL[1]
[1821 (1818)]

Whither, midst falling dew,
While glow the heavens with the last steps
    of day,
Far, through their rosy depths, dost thou
    pursue
Thy solitary way?

Vainly the fowler's eye   5
Might mark thy distant flight to do thee
    wrong,
As, darkly painted on the crimson sky,
Thy figure floats along.

Seek'st thou the plashy brink
Of weedy lake, or marge of river wide,   10
Or where the rocking billows rise and sink
On the chafed ocean-side?

There is a Power whose care
Teaches thy way along that pathless
    coast—
The desert and illimitable air—   15
Lone wandering, but not lost.

All day thy wings have fanned,
At that far height, the cold, thin atmos-
    phere,
Yet stoop not, weary, to the welcome land,
    Though the dark night is near,   20

And soon that toil shall end;
Soon shalt thou find a summer home, and
    rest,
And scream among thy fellows; reeds shall
    bend,
Soon, o'er thy sheltered nest.

Thou'rt gone, the abyss of heaven   25
Hath swallowed up thy form; yet, on my
    heart
Deeply hath sunk the lesson thou hast
    given,
And shall not soon depart.

He who, from zone to zone,
Guides through the boundless sky thy cer-
    tain flight,   30
In the long way that I must tread alone,
Will lead my steps aright.

"OH FAIREST OF THE RURAL MAIDS"
[1832 (1820)]

Oh fairest of the rural maids!
Thy birth was in the forest shades;
Green boughs, and glimpses of the sky,
Were all that met thy infant eye.

Thy sports, thy wanderings, when a child, 5
Were ever in the sylvan wild;
And all the beauty of the place
Is in thy heart and on thy face.

The twilight of the trees and rocks
Is in the light shade of thy locks;   10
Thy step is as the wind, that weaves
Its playful way among the leaves.

Thine eyes are springs, in whose serene
And silent waters heaven is seen;
Their lashes are the herbs that look   15
On their young figures in the brook.

The forest depths, by foot unpressed,
Are not more sinless than thy breast;
The holy peace that fills the air
Of those calm solitudes, is there.   20

[1] For the circumstances under which this poem was written, see Parke Godwin's *Life of Bryant* (New York, 1883), vol. I, pp. 143-44.

TO THE FRINGED GENTIAN
[1832 (1829)]

Thou blossom bright with autumn dew,
And colored with the heaven's own blue,
That openest when the quiet light
Succeeds the keen and frosty night.

Thou comest not when violets lean　　5
O'er wandering brooks and springs unseen,
Or columbines, in purple dressed,
Nod o'er the ground-bird's hidden nest.

Thou waitest late and com'st alone,
When woods are bare and birds are
　　flown,　　10
And frosts and shortening days portend
The aged year is near his end.

Then doth thy sweet and quiet eye
Look through its fringes to the sky,
Blue—blue—as if that sky let fall　　15
A flower from its cerulean wall.

I would that thus, when I shall see
The hour of death draw near to me,
Hope, blossoming within my heart,
May look to heaven as I depart.　　20

MIDSUMMER
[1832 (1826)]

A power is on the earth and in the air
　　From which the vital spirit shrinks
　　　afraid,
　　And shelters him, in nooks of deepest
　　　shade,
From the hot steam and from the fiery
　　glare.
Look forth upon the earth—her thousand
　　plants　　5
　　Are smitten; even the dark sun-loving
　　　maize
　　Faints in the field beneath the torrid
　　　blaze;
The herd beside the shaded fountain pants;
For life is driven from all the landscape
　　brown;

The bird has sought his tree, the snake
　　his den,　　10
The trout floats dead in the hot stream,
　　and men
Drop by the sun-stroke in the populous
　　town;
As if the Day of Fire had dawned, and sent
Its deadly breath into the firmament.

THE HUNTER OF THE PRAIRIES
[1836 (1834)]

Ay, this is freedom!—these pure skies
　　Were never stained with village smoke:
The fragrant wind, that through them flies,
　　Is breathed from wastes by plough un-
　　　broke.
Here, with my rifle and my steed,　　5
　　And her who left the world for me,
I plant me, where the red deer feed
　　In the green desert—and am free.

For here the fair savannas know
　　No barriers in the bloomy grass;　　10
Wherever breeze of heaven may blow,
　　Or beam of heaven may glance, I pass.
In pastures, measureless as air,
　　The bison is my noble game;
The bounding elk, whose antlers tear　　15
　　The branches, falls before my aim.

Mine are the river-fowl that scream
　　From the long stripe of waving sedge;
The bear that marks my weapon's gleam,
　　Hides vainly in the forest's edge;　　20
In vain the she-wolf stands at bay;
　　The brinded catamount, that lies
High in the boughs to watch his prey,
　　Even in the act of springing, dies.

With what free growth the elm and
　　plane　　25
　　Fling their huge arms across my way,
Grey, old, and cumbered with a train
　　Of vines, as huge, and old, and gray!
Free stray the lucid streams, and find
　　No taint in these fresh lawns and
　　　shades;　　30
Free spring the flowers that scent the wind
　　Where never scythe has swept the glades.

Alone the Fire, when frostwinds sere
  The heavy herbage of the ground,
Gathers his annual harvest here,   35
  With roaring like the battle's sound,
And hurrying flames that sweep the plain,
  And smoke-streams gushing up the sky:
I meet the flames with flames again,
  And at my door they cower and die. 40

Here, from dim woods, the aged past
  Speaks solemnly; and I behold
The boundless future in the vast
  And lonely river, seaward rolled.
Who feeds its founts with rain and dew? 45
  Who moves, I ask, its gliding mass,
And trains the bordering vines, whose blue
  Bright clusters tempt me as I pass?

Broad are these streams—my steed obeys,
  Plunges, and bears me through the
    tide.   50
Wide are these woods—I tread the maze
  Of giant stems, nor ask a guide.
I hunt till day's last glimmer dies
  O'er woody vale and grassy height;
And kind the voice and glad the eyes, 55
  That welcome my return at night.

THE BATTLE-FIELD
[1842 (1837)]

Once this soft turf, this rivulet's sands,
  Were trampled by a hurrying crowd,
And fiery hearts and armèd hands
  Encountered in the battle-cloud.

Ah! never shall the land forget   5
  How gushed the life-blood of her brave—
Gushed, warm with hope and courage yet
  Upon the soil they fought to save.

Now all is calm and fresh and still;
  Alone the chirp of flitting bird,   10
And talk of children on the hill,
  And bell of wandering kine, are heard.

No solemn host goes trailing by
  The black-mouthed gun and staggering
    wain;

Men start not at the battle cry,   15
  Oh, be it never heard again!

Soon rested those who fought; but thou,
  Who minglest in the harder strife
For truths which men receive not now,
  Thy warfare only ends with life.   20

A friendless warfare! lingering long
  Through weary day and weary year,
A wild and many-weaponed throng
  Hang on thy front, and flank, and rear.

Yet nerve thy spirit to the proof,   25
  And blench not at thy chosen lot.
The timid good may stand aloof,
  The sage may frown—yet faint thou not.

Nor heed the shaft too surely cast,
  The foul and hissing bolt of scorn; 30
For with thy side shall dwell, at last,
  The victory of endurance born.

Truth, crushed to earth, shall rise again;
  Th' eternal years of God are hers;
But Error, wounded, writhes in pain,   35
  And dies among his worshippers.

Yea, though thou lie upon the dust,
  When they who helped thee flee in fear,
Die full of hope and manly trust,
  Like those who fell in battle here. 40

Another hand thy sword shall wield,
  Another hand the standard wave,
Till from the trumpet's mouth is pealed
  The blast of triumph o'er thy grave.

THE DEATH OF LINCOLN
[1865]

Oh, slow to smite and swift to spare,
Gentle and merciful and just!
Who, in the fear of God, didst bear
The sword of power, a nation's trust!

In sorrow by thy bier we stand,   5
Amid the awe that hushes all,
And speak the anguish of a land
That shook with horror at thy fall.

Thy task is done; the bond are free:
We bear thee to an honored grave,   10
Whose proudest monument shall be
The broken fetters of the slave.

Pure was thy life; its bloody close
Hath placed thee with the sons of light,
Among the noble host of those   15
Who perished in the cause of Right.

From
AN ESSAY ON AMERICAN POETRY
[1884 (1818)]

OF THE poetry of the United States
different opinions have been entertained,
and prejudice on the one side and partiality
on the other have equally prevented a just
and rational estimate of its merits. Abroad
our literature has fallen under unmerited
contumely, from those who were but slenderly acquainted with the subject on which
they professed to decide; and at home it
must be confessed that the swaggering and
pompous pretensions of many have done
not a little to provoke and excuse the ridicule of foreigners. Either of these extremes
exerts an injurious influence on the cause
of letters in our country. To encourage
exertion and embolden merit to come forward, it is necessary that they should be
acknowledged and rewarded. Few men
have the confidence to solicit what is wan-
tonly withheld, or the courage to tread a
path which presents no prospect but the
melancholy wrecks of those who have gone
before them. National gratitude, national
pride—every high and generous feeling
that attaches us to the land of our birth, or
that exalts our characters as individuals—
ask of us that we should foster the infant
literature of our country, and that genius
and industry, employing their efforts to
hasten its perfection, should receive from
our hands that celebrity which reflects as
much honor on the nation which confers
it as on those to whom it is extended.

On the other hand, it is not necessary
for these purposes—it is even detrimental
—to bestow on mediocrity the praise due
to excellence, and still more so is the attempt to persuade ourselves and others
into an admiration of the faults of favorite
writers. We make but a contemptible figure
in the eyes of the world, and set ourselves
up as objects of pity to our posterity,
when we affect to rank the poets of our
own country with those mighty masters of
song who have flourished in Greece, Italy,
and Britain. Such extravagant admiration
may spring from a praiseworthy and patriotic motive, but it seems to us that it
defeats its own object of encouraging our
literature, by seducing those who would
aspire to the favor of the public into an
imitation of imperfect models, and leading
them to rely too much on the partiality
of their countrymen to overlook their de-
ficiencies. Were our rewards bestowed only
on what is intrinsically meritorious, merit
alone would have any apology for appearing before the public. The poetical adventurer should be taught that it is only the
production of genius, taste, and diligence
that can find favor at the bar of criticism;
that his writings are not to be applauded
merely because they are written by an
American, and are not decidedly bad; and
that he must produce some more satisfactory evidence of his claim to celebrity than
an extract from the parish register. To
show him what we expect of him, it is as
necessary to point out the faults of his
predecessors as to commend their excel-
lences. He must be taught as well what to
avoid as what to imitate. This is the only
way of diffusing and preserving a pure
taste, both among those who read and those
who write, and, in our opinion, the only
way of affording merit a proper and effectual encouragement. . . .

With respect to the style of poetry prevailing at the present day in our country,
we apprehend that it will be found, in too
many instances, tinged with a sickly and
affected imitation of the peculiar manner
of some of the late popular poets of England. We speak not of a disposition to
emulate whatever is beautiful and excel-

lent in their writings, still less would we be understood as intending to censure that sort of imitation which, exploring all the treasures of English poetry, culls from all a diction that shall form a natural and becoming dress for the conceptions of the writer—this is a course of preparation which every one ought to go through before he appears before the public—but we desire to set a mark on that servile habit of copying which adopts the vocabulary of some favorite author, and apes the fashion of his sentences, and cramps and forces the ideas into a shape which they would not naturally have taken, and of which the only recommendation is, not that it is most elegant or most striking, but that it bears some resemblance to the manner of him who is proposed as a model. This way of writing has an air of poverty and meanness; it seems to indicate a paucity of reading as well as a perversion of taste; it might almost lead us to suspect that the writer had but one or two examples of poetical composition in his hands, and was afraid of expressing himself, except according to some formula which they might contain; and it ever has been, and ever will be, the resort of those who are sensible that their works need some factitious recommendation to give them even a temporary popularity.

On the whole, there seems to be more good taste among those who read than those who write poetry in our country. . . . We know of no instance in which great poetical merit has come forward, and, finding its claims unallowed, been obliged to retire to the shade from which it emerged. Whenever splendid talents of this description shall appear, we believe that there will be found a disposition to encourage and reward them. The fondness for literature is fast increasing, and, if this were not the case, the patrons of literature have multiplied, of course, and will continue to multiply, with the mere growth of our population. The best popular English works of the day are often reprinted here—they are dispersed all over the Union—they are found in everybody's hands—they are made the subject of everybody's conversation. What should hinder our native works, if equal in merit, from meeting an equally favorable reception? . . .

THE RIGHT OF WORKMEN TO STRIKE [1]
[1884 (1836)]

SENTENCE was passed on Saturday on the twenty "men who had determined not to work." The punishment selected, on due consideration, by the judge, was that officers appointed for the purpose should immediately demand from each of the delinquents a sum of money which was named in the sentence of the court. The amount demanded would not have fallen short of the savings of many years. Either the offenders had not parted with these savings, or their brother workmen raised the ransom money for them on the spot. The fine was paid over as required. All is now well; justice has been satisfied. But if the expenses of their families had anticipated the law, and left nothing in their hands, or if friends had not been ready to buy the freedom of their comrades, they would have been sent to prison, and there they would have staid, until their wives and children, besides earning their own bread, had saved enough to redeem the captives from their cells. Such has been their punishment. What was their offence? They had committed the crime of unanimously declining to go to work at the wages offered to them by their masters. They had said to one another, "Let us come out from the meanness and misery of our caste. Let us begin to do what every order more privileged and more honoured is doing everyday. By the means which we believe to be the best let

[1] Indicted under the laws against conspiracy, 21 journeyman-tailors were tried in the New York Court of Oyer and Terminer, and convicted and heavily fined, in June, 1836. This editorial appeared in the *New York Evening Post*, June 13, 1836.

us raise ourselves and our families above the humbleness of our condition. We may be wrong, but we cannot help believing that we might do much if we were true brothers to each other, and would resolve not to sell the only thing which is our own, the cunning of our hands, for less than it is worth." What other things they may have done is nothing to the purpose: it was for this they were condemned; it is for this they are to endure the penalty of the law.

We call upon a candid and generous community to mark that the punishment inflicted upon these twenty "men who had determined not to work" is not directed against the offence of conspiring to prevent others by force from working at low wages, but expressly against the offence of settling by pre-concert the compensation which they thought they were entitled to obtain. It is certainly superfluous to repeat, that this journal would be the very last to oppose a law levelled at any attempt to molest the labourer who chooses to work for less than the prices settled by the union. We have said, and to cut off cavil, we say it now again, that a conspiracy to deter, by threats of violence, a fellow workman from arranging his own terms with his employers, is a conspiracy to commit a felony—a conspiracy which, being a crime against liberty, we should be the first to condemn—a conspiracy which no strike should, for its own sake, countenance for a moment—a conspiracy already punishable by the statute, and far easier to reach than the one of which "the twenty" stood accused; but a conspiracy, we must add, that has not a single feature in common with the base and barbarous prohibition under which the offenders were indicted and condemned.

They were condemned because they had determined not to work for the wages that were offered them! Can any thing be imagined more abhorrent to every sentiment of generosity or justice, than the law which arms the rich with the legal right to fix, by assize, the wages of the poor? If

this is not SLAVERY, we have forgotten its definition. Strike the right of associating for the sale of labour from the privileges of a freeman, and you may as well at once bind him to a master, or ascribe him to the soil. If it be not in the colour of his skin, and in the poor franchise of naming his own terms in a contract for his work, what advantage has the labourer of the north over the bondman of the south? Punish by human laws a "determination not to work," make it penal by any other penalty than idleness inflicts, and it matters little whether the task-masters be one or many, an individual or an order, the hateful scheme of slavery will have gained a foothold in the land. And then the meanness of this law, which visits with its malice those who cling to it for protection, and shelters with all its fences those who are raised above its threats. A late solicitation for its aid against employers, is treated with derision and contempt, but the moment the "masters" invoked its intervention, it came down from its high place with most indecent haste, and has now discharged its fury upon the naked heads of wretches so forlorn, that their worst faults multiply their titles to a liberty which they must learn to win from livelier sensibilities than the barren benevolence of Wealth, or the tardy magnanimity of Power.

SENSITIVENESS TO FOREIGN OPINION [1]
[1884 (1839)]

COOPER'S last work, "Home as Found," has been fiercely attacked, in more than one quarter, for its supposed tendency to convey to the people of other countries a bad idea of our national character. Without staying to examine whether all Mr. Cooper's animadversions on American manners are perfectly just, we seize

[1] This editorial appeared in the *New York Evening Post*, Jan. 11, 1839.

the occasion to protest against this excessive sensibility to the opinion of other nations. It is no matter what they think of us. We constitute a community large enough to form a great moral tribunal for the trial of any question which may arise among ourselves. There is no occasion for this perpetual appeal to the opinions of Europe. We are competent to apply the rules of right and wrong boldly and firmly, without asking in what light the superior judgment of the Old World may regard our decisions.

It has been said of Americans that they are vainglorious, boastful, fond of talking of the greatness and the advantages of their country, and of the excellence of their national character. They have this foible in common with other nations; but they have another habit which shows that, with all their national vanity, they are not so confident of their own greatness, or of their own capacity to estimate it properly, as their boasts would imply. They are perpetually asking, What do they think of us in Europe? How are we regarded abroad? If a foreigner publishes an account of his travels in this country, we are instantly on the alert to know what notion of our character he has communicated to his countrymen; if an American author publishes a book, we are eager to know how it is received abroad, that we may know how to judge it ourselves. So far has this humor been carried that we have seen an extract, from a third- or fourth-rate critical work in England, condemning some American work, copied into all our newspapers one after another, as if it determined the character of the work beyond appeal or question.

For our part, we admire and honor a fearless accuser of the faults of so thin-skinned a nation as ours, always supposing him to be sincere and well-intentioned. He may be certain that where he has sowed animadversion he will reap an abundant harvest of censure and obloquy. He will have one consolation, however, that if his book be written with ability it will be read; that the attacks which are made upon it will draw it to the public attention; and that it may thus do good even to those who recalcitrate most violently against it.

If every man who writes a book, instead of asking himself the question what good it will do at home, were first held to inquire what notions it conveys of Americans to persons abroad, we should pull the sinews out of our literature. There is much want of free-speaking as things stand at present, but this rule will abolish it altogether. It is bad enough to stand in fear of public opinion at home, but, if we are to superadd the fear of public opinion abroad, we submit to a double despotism. Great reformers, preachers of righteousness, eminent satirists in different ages of the world—did they, before entering on the work they were appointed to do, ask what other nations might think of their countrymen if they gave utterance to the voice of salutary reproof?

1789 ∽ *James Fenimore Cooper* ∽ 1851

IT IS easy to make fun of Cooper: of his stilted style, of his preposterous feminine characters, or "females," as he called them. Mark Twain, in his "Fenimore Cooper's Literary Offenses," held Cooper up to merciless ridicule; Thackeray's "The Stars and Stripes" and Bret Harte's "Muck-a-Muck" are uproarious Cooper parodies. But the reader who assumes that his laughter has taken Cooper's measure is self-deceived. There is a solid core of merit in almost every one of Cooper's fifty books. To find it one must achieve a certain immunity to, or tolerance of, his faults: his formal, pedantic sentence structure and his frequently trite and colorless vocabulary; his inveterate contentiousness and didacticism; his repeated subservience to the conventions of the bad romantic novel. For most readers of today this tolerance is not easy to attain; but it is worth the effort.

Once we can read Cooper without pain, we can read him with very real pleasure and profit, finding him amusing, entertaining, informative, even stimulating. In his pages our American world of the past, in all its diversity, becomes more picturesquely alive than in those of any other early American writer. We assemble a gallery of notable and memorable characters, sharply individualized and pungently real. We encounter many passages of external action hard to equal in any fiction. We experience also the clash of ideas, tenaciously held and vigorously set forth—ideas we may find repugnant in some instances, though candor may compel us to admit, on due reflection, that they are ideas which have great vitality today. And behind all this we come to know Cooper the man, one of the most highly individual and deeply interesting human beings in our literary history.

Much of the substance of Cooper's fiction came directly from his own life. The son of the wealthiest and most influential man of a frontier community in western New York, he had an adventurous boyhood, two stormy years at Yale, and a brief career as a naval officer before he married and settled into the life of a country squire. His first novel was a poor imitation of the currently popular British fiction of aristocratic society, but in the second he found himself as a writer. There is some justification for dating the beginning of our national literature from the publication of *The Spy* in 1821. Here was broad, just, and essentially realistic treatment of events of the Revolutionary War; here native American materials were used in fiction with unmistakable authority for the first time. The book was an immediate success, and at thirty-two Cooper found himself suddenly the most popular writer in America.

Promptly Cooper wrote again, choosing the western New York frontier of his boyhood as the new source of material. In *The Pioneers* (1823) he first sketched the character of Natty Bumppo-Hawkeye-Leatherstocking, his greatest character and a real contribution to American mythology. Less vigorous in action than its predecessor or immediate successors, *The Pioneers*, as social history, is one of the most substantial of all Cooper's novels. A third time Cooper dipped into his own past, this time into his experience at sea. *The Pilot* (1824) is the first great American sea story: strong in action, accurate in technical detail, weak as Cooper almost always is in its "heroic" and highborn characters, but fine in its delineation of Long Tom Coffin, the lonely pilot, and of the life at sea. In *The Last of the Mohicans* (1826) he greatly strengthened the dramatic figure of the man of the wilderness, and also in his trio of Indian characters—Uncas, Chingachgook and Magua—he made his second major contribution to the world-picture of the American past.

When in 1831 Cooper completed his first decade as a writer he had produced ten books, nine of them novels, eight of these American historical romances. By 1840 he was to write and publish fourteen books, but not one of them an American historical romance. In 1826 Cooper had taken his family to Paris, to give his young daughters the educational and social opportunities which he thought appropriate; he remained abroad for more than seven years, gaining perspective on both Europe and America and deriving pleasure and stimulus from association with Scott—who was generously kind—and other writers. Cooper found his romances immensely popular in England and on the continent. Only gradually did he come to realize how far were his foreign readers from interpreting these books properly and understanding contemporary America. In these years British and European travelers in steady procession were crossing the Atlantic and returning to publish books about America. To Cooper all these books were inadequate and most of them unfair. Some of the British accounts were particularly vicious, and American writers were beginning to reply in kind. Cooper was too good an American not to use his prominence and influence, and the advantage of his European residence and popularity, in this literary war. He published in 1828 a descriptive and interpretative account of his native land under the title *Notions of the Americans,* giving it the form of a series of personal letters from a cultured European traveler to the fellow members of a cosmopolitan and distinguished geographical society. Though avowedly limited in scope to the parts of the country Cooper knew at first hand, the book is scrupulously accurate in details, broad and just in general observation, and acute in analysis. But the foreign readers of Cooper were not much impressed. They preferred to believe in the picture of America in the Leatherstocking Tales—a wilderness peopled by hunters and Indians—which confirmed their prejudices. American readers, on the other hand, actively resented the adverse criticisms which Cooper's sense of truth had led him to include.

Before Cooper returned from Europe in 1832 he had written three historical novels with European settings, *The Bravo* (1831), *The Heidenmauer* (1832), and *The Headsman* (1833), designed, he declared, to reveal to American readers the inferiority of European social standards and attitudes by tracing their development. Refusing to be so edified, his American public accused him of deserting native materials. One attack in particular moved Cooper to reply, and he found himself involved in a quarrel with his own countrymen—a quarrel which deepened with the years and affected almost all his later work. Its immediate fruits were two ventures into polemics in which Cooper stated his position and defined his political philosophy, *A Letter to His Countrymen* (1834) and *The American Democrat* (1838); and *The Monikins* (1835), a satire which was much indebted to Swift's *Gulliver's Travels* and in which the brash materialism and shallow optimism of the 1830's in both America and England were caustically arraigned. Though brilliant in parts, the satire is heavy-handed and much too longwinded. The experiment of *The Monikins* having failed—the book brought only jeers and abuse—Cooper tried another: a fictional portrayal of contemporary American life with a serious critical purpose. The point of view he used (again drawing on his own experience) was that of an American returning with his family to his native land after some years abroad. Social criticism is subordinated to the excitement of a sea voyage in *Homeward Bound* (1838); but it is the chief ingredient of *Home as Found* (1838), which, for all its clumsiness and crudities, presents a caustic indictment of practices and attitudes in American society and politics conflicting with the principles Cooper laid down in the same year in *The American Democrat*. During the decade he somehow found time to put together five volumes of accounts of his European travels, and to write his admirable and unduly neglected *History of the Navy of the United States of America*.

From these years of constant controversy and almost incredible productiveness Cooper entered upon the third decade—plus two years—which would round out his career. From 1840 to his death in 1851 he wrote a series of biographies of naval officers and one of a common sailor, a play, and thirteen long novels. It is not surprising that in such a bulk of work there is much that is poor. What is surprising is that Cooper could turn from the pressures and irritations of the late 1830's to complete the Leatherstocking series with two of his best novels, *The Pathfinder* (1840) and *The Deerslayer* (1841). These books have qualities of freshness and tenderness totally absent from the work which immediately preceded them. *Satanstoe* (1845), the first of a trilogy which justifies landlords against anti-rent propaganda and includes *The Chainbearer* (1845) and *The Redskins* (1846), is also one of the best novels in all Cooper's work, perhaps the most rewarding of his books to the reader of today. In this story, written at fifty-six, Cooper achieved a mellowness both in style and in characterization which he had never attained before, nor would reach again; and the book is excellent as social history of colonial New York. Other notable novels of Cooper's last decade are *Wyandotté* (1843), which contains some of his best portrayal of Indian character, and *The Oak Openings* (1848), the fruit of a trip to the western frontier of Michigan in 1847. His last novel, *Ways of the Hour* (1850), has a certain limited interest as an attack on the jury system, and perhaps more as an ancestral example of the modern murder mystery.

The aging Cooper, playing chess with his wife in quiet evenings, long since alienated from almost all his friends and from much of his once enthusiastic popular following, is a somewhat pathetic figure. In the years following his death Bryant and others justly acknowledged his service to American letters.

But for two generations his reputation rested almost solely upon his romances of forest and sea, and only in recent years has his social criticism been fairly appraised. Today he is increasingly appreciated as a writer of lasting interest and value to the reader who will take the trouble to know him well.

[R. E. Spiller's *Fenimore Cooper, Critic of His Times* (New York, 1931) and H. W. Boynton's *James Fenimore Cooper* (New York, 1931) are the best biographies. Good introductions are to be found in Spiller's *Cooper* in the American Writers Series, in Yvor Winters' *Maule's Curse* (Norfolk, Conn., 1938), and in George Snell's *The Shapers of American Fiction* (New York, 1947).

The text of the selections from *Notions of the Americans* is that of the edition of 1828. Titles have been supplied by the present editors, and the text has been slightly abridged. The text of the selections from *The American Democrat* is that of the edition of 1838. The text of the selections from the novels is that of the collected edition, New York, 1859-61.]

From
NOTIONS OF THE AMERICANS
[1828]

THE AMERICAN SCENE

TO Sir Edward Waller, Bart:

Once for all, dear Waller, I wish you to understand that—a few peaceable and half-civilized remains of tribes, that have been permitted to reclaim small portions of land, excepted—an inhabitant of New-York is actually as far removed from a savage as an inhabitant of London. The former has to traverse many hundred leagues of territory to enjoy even the sight of an Indian, in a tolerably wild condition; and the latter may obtain a similar gratification at about the same expense of time and distance, by crossing the ocean to Labrador. A few degraded descendants of the ancient warlike possessors of this country are indeed seen wandering among the settlements, but the Indian must now be chiefly sought west of the Mississippi, to be found in any of his savage grandeur.

Cases do occur, beyond a doubt, in which luckless individuals are induced to make their settlement in some unpropitious spot where the current of emigration obsti-

nately refuses to run. These subjects of an unfortunate speculation are left to struggle for years in a condition between rude civilization, and one approaching to that of the hunter, or to abandon their possessions, and to seek a happier section of the country. Nine times in ten, the latter course is adopted. But when this tide of emigration has set steadily towards any favoured point for a reasonable time, it is absurd to seek for any vestige of a barbarous life among the people. The emigrants carry with them (I now speak of those parts of the country I have seen) the wants, the habits, and the institutions, of an advanced state of society. The shop of the artisan is reared simultaneously with the rude dwelling of the farmer. The trunks of trees, piled on each other, serve for both for a few years, and then succeed dwellings of wood, in a taste, magnitude, and comfort, that are utterly unknown to men of similar means in any other quarter of the world, which it has yet been my lot to visit. The little school-house is shortly erected at some convenient point, and a tavern, a store, (the American term for a shop of all sales,) with a few tenements occupied by mechanics, soon indicate the spot for a church, and the site of the future village. From fifty or a hundred of these centres of exertion, spread swarms that in a few years shall convert mazes of dark forests into populous, wealthy, and industrious counties. The manufactures of Europe, of the Indies, and of China, are seen exposed for sale, by the side of the coarse products of the country; and the same individual who vends the axe to fell the adjoining forest, can lay before your eyes a very tolerable specimen of Lyons silk, of English broadcloth, of Nankins, of teas, of coffees, or indeed of most of the more common luxuries of life. The number and quality of the latter increase with the growth of the establishment; and it is not too much to say, that an American village store, in a thriving part of the country, where the settlements are of twenty years' standing, can commonly supply as good an assortment of the manufactures of Europe, as a collection of shops in any European country town; and, if the general nature of their stock be considered, embracing, as it does, some of the products of all countries, one much greater.

As to wild beasts, savages, etc., etc., etc., they have no existence in these regions. A solitary bear, or panther, or even a wolf, wandering near the flocks of a country twenty years old, has an effect like that produced by an invasion. In the earlier days of the settlement, it is a task to chase the ravenous beasts from the neighbourhood. A price is offered for their heads, and for a time a mutual destruction against the flocks on one side, and the beasts on the other, is the consequence. In a year or two, this task is reduced to an occasional duty. In a few more, it is sought as an amusement: and ere the twenty years expire, the appearance of a wolf among the American farms is far less common than on the most ancient plains of certain parts of France. Every man has his rifle or his musket; and every man not only knows how, but he is fond of using them against such foes. Thus, you see, though wild beasts may be permitted, like Raphael's Seraphim, to encircle your pictures of American manners in faint relief,

they must rarely indeed be permitted to enter into the action of the piece; more especially if the scene be laid in any of the settled portions of the three States that form the subject of this letter.

We made part of this excursion in the public stages, part with hired horses, and part in steamboats. It is impossible to enter on a description of the surface of the country we saw, for it included mountains, valleys, and vast plains, intermingled in such a manner as to render the task wearisome. We had gone about fifty miles west of Albany, when my companion desired the vehicle to stop, and invited me to mount a gentle ascent on foot. On reaching the summit, he turned and pointed to a view which resembled none I had ever before witnessed.

We were travelling along the termination of a range of mountains, which, running north and south, fell gracefully away, in the former direction, into what is called the valley of the Mohawk, before they gradually rose again on the other side of that river. The descent and the ascent were very similar, the intervening country lying in broken and irregular terraces, which often had the appearance of fertile valleys, before the rich bottoms of the river are gained. Our precise position was on the very brow of one of the most projecting spurs of this broken range, and it admitted of an uninterrupted prospect to the northeast, and to the north-west, of the falling country in our front, and of the rising hills opposite, that could not have been contained in a circumference of much less than two hundred miles. The view was limited to what lay in advance of a line drawn nearly east and west, the adjacent mountains presenting obstacles to our vision, further south. It was completely an American scene, embracing all that admixture of civilization, and of the forest, of the works of man, and of the reign of nature, that one can so easily imagine to belong to this country.

There was perhaps an equal distribution of field and forest. The latter term is not, however, the best, since it was a constant succession of open land and of wood, in proportions which, without being exactly, were surprisingly equal. You have stood upon a height, and looked down upon a fertile French plain, over which agriculture has been conducted on a scale a little larger than common. You may remember the divisions formed by the hues of the grains of the vineyards, and of the grasses, which give to the whole an air so chequered and remarkable. Now, by extending the view to the size I have named, and enlarging these chequered spots to a corresponding scale, you get a tolerably accurate idea of what I would describe. The dark green shadows are produced by the foliage of a wood, reserved, perhaps, for the use of half a dozen farms, and lying in a body, (some common objection to culture influencing that number of proprietors to select adjacent ground for their reservations,) and the fields of golden yellow, or of various shades and hues, are produced by the open fields. The distance diminishes the objects to the eye, and brings the several parts so much in union, as to lend to the whole the variegated aspect of the sort of plain just mentioned. The natural river which divides this glorious panorama in nearly two equal parts, with its artificial rival,[1] and the sweet meadows that border its banks, were concealed beneath the brow of the last precipitous descent. But countless farmhouses, with their capacious out-buildings, dotted the fields, like indicated spots on a crowded map. From those in the near view, rose the light vapoury summer smoke. The fields were alive with herds, and with numberless and nearly imperceptible white atoms, which, but for their motion, it would not have been easy to imagine flocks. In the distance, though these more minute objects were lost, habitations, barns, and pyramids of hay and of grain, could be distinguished, until the power of vision failed. Immediately at our feet, at the distance of a few miles, lay a wide, rich terrace, intersected with roads, that were

bordered, as usual, by scattered farm buildings, surrounded by their granaries and barns. Near its centre, a cluster of buildings assumed the air of a hamlet. From among these roofs, rose the spire of a country church. I was told that a multitude of villages lay within the limits of the view; but as they were generally placed near some stream, for the advantage of its water-power, the uneven formation of the land hid them from our sight. The eye overlooked even the cities of Albany and Troy, and rested, in that direction, on some of the lesser spurs of the mountains of Vermont.

As I looked upon this scene, I felt it only wanted the recollections of monuments of antiquity to give it the deepest interest. The opinion might have escaped my lips, amid the expressions of a sincere delight. My companion gently touched an arm, and directed my attention from the view to himself. He was standing at my elbow with an open map of the country in his hand. As he met my eye, he gravely said, "You complain of the absence of association to give its secret, and perhaps greatest charm which such a sight is capable of inspiring. You complain unjustly. The moral feeling with which a man of sentiment and knowledge looks upon the plains of your hemisphere, is connected with his recollections; here it should be mingled with his hopes. The same effort of the mind is as equal to the one as to the other. Examine this map. You see our position, and you know the space that lies between us and the sea. Now look westward, and observe how many degrees of longitude, what broad reaches of territory must be passed before you gain the limits of our establishments, and the consequent reign of abundance and civilization." Here he dropped the map; and I fancied he even spoke with solemnity, as he continued —"Count ——," he said, "you see that I

---

[1] The great Canal, 360 miles in length. [Cooper's note. The Erie Canal, joining the Hudson River and Lake Erie. It was completed in 1825.]

am a man of middle age: listen to what even my short memory extends. Along the river which lies hid in the deep valley before us, the labours of man have existed for more than a century. There are one or two shallow streams near us, along which the enterprise of the settlers early directed itself. A few miles to the west, we shall enter a little valley, where a handfull of refugees from Ireland took up their abodes some eighty years ago; and there are other insulated spots, where solitary individuals trusted to the savage, and raised their simple dwellings before the war of the revolution. But that little plain, at our feet, could have fed, and clothed, and harboured all who were then scattered, not only over the parts of the country I have shown you here, but," sweeping his hand along the map, across states and territories larger than those governed by most of the European monarchs, "all of white colour, who then inhabited these wide regions too. I remember this country, Sir, as it existed in my childhood; and it is vain to say, it is a land without recollections. Draw a line from this spot, north and south, and all of civilization that you shall see for a thousand miles west, is what man has done since my infancy. You exclude, by this boundary, far more than you gain in the meagre exceptions. That view before you is but a fac-simile of a thousand others. I know not what honest pleasure is to be found in recollection, that cannot be excited by a knowledge of these facts. These are retrospects of the past, which, brief and familiar as they are, lead the mind insensibly to cheerful anticipations, which may penetrate into a futurity as dim and as fanciful as any fictions the warmest imaginations can conceive of the past. But the speculator on moral things can enjoy a satisfaction here, that he who wanders over the plains of Greece will seek in vain. The pleasure of the latter, if he be wise and good, is unavoidably tinged with melancholy regrets; while here all that reason allows may be hoped for in behalf of man. Every

one in mediocrity of circumstances has enjoyed some of that interest which is attendant on the advancement of those objects on which he has fastened a portion of his affections. It may be the moral or physical improvement of his child,—the embellishment of a garden, a paddock, a park, or of the conveniences of some town; but, depend on it, there is no pleasure connected with any interest of this character, that is commensurate with that we enjoy, who have seen the birth, infancy, and youth, and who are now about to become spectators of the maturity, of a whole country. We live in the excitement of a rapid and constantly progressive condition. The impetus of society is imparted to all its members and we advance because we are not accustomed to stand still. Even the sagacious and enterprising New-Englandman, gets an additional impulse in such a living current; the descendant of the Hollander is fast losing his phlegm; and men of all nations, hereditary habits and opinions, receive an onward impulse by the constant influence of such a communion. I have stood upon this identical hill, and seen nine tenths of its smiling prospect darkened by the shadows of the forest. You observe what it is to-day. He who comes a century hence, may hear the din of a city rising from that very plain, or find his faculties confused by the number and complexity of its works of art."

American Literature

TO the Abbate Giromachi:
You ask me to write freely on the subject of the literature and the arts of the United States. The subjects are so meagre as to render it a task that would require no small portion of the talents necessary to figure in either, in order to render them of interest. Still, as the request has come in so urgent a form, I shall endeavor to oblige you. . . .

As respects authorship, there is not much to be said. Compared to the books that are printed and read, those of native origin are few indeed. The principal reason of this poverty of original writers, is owing to the circumstance that men are not yet driven to their wits for bread. The United States are the first nation that possessed institutions, and, of course, distinctive opinions of its own, that was ever dependent on a foreign people for its literature. Speaking the same language as the English, and long in the habit of importing their books from the mother country, the revolution effected no immediate change in the nature of their studies, or mental amusements. The works were re-printed, it is true, for the purposes of economy, but they still continued English. Had the latter nation used this powerful engine with tolerable address, I think they would have secured such an ally in this country as would have rendered their own decline not only more secure, but as illustrious as had been their rise. There are many theories entertained as to the effect produced in this country by the falsehoods and jealous calumnies which have been undeniably uttered in the mother country, by means of the press, concerning her republican descendant. It is my own opinion that, like all other ridiculous absurdities, they have defeated themselves, and that they are now more laughed at and derided, even here, than resented. By all that I can learn, twenty years ago, the Americans were, perhaps, far too much disposed to receive the opinions and to adopt the prejudices of their relatives; whereas, I think it is very apparent that they are now beginning to receive them with singular distrust. It is not worth our while to enter further into this subject, except as it has had, or is likely to have, an influence on the national literature.

It is quite obvious, that, so far as taste and forms alone are concerned, the literature of England and that of America must be fashioned after the same models. The authors, previously to the revolution, are common property, and it is quite idle to say that the American has not just as good a right to claim Milton, and Shakspeare, and all the old masters of language, for his countrymen, as an Englishman. The Americans having continued to cultivate, and to cultivate extensively, an acquaintance with the writers of the mother country, since the separation, it is evident they must have kept pace with the trifling changes of the day. The only peculiarity that can, or ought to be expected in their literature, is that which is connected with the promulgation of their distinctive political opinions. They have not been remiss in this duty, as any one may see, who chooses to examine their books. But we will devote a few minutes to a more minute account of the actual condition of American literature. . . .

The literature of the United States has, indeed, two powerful obstacles to conquer before (to use a mercantile expression) it can ever enter the markets of its own country on terms of perfect equality with that of England. Solitary and individual works of genius may, indeed, be occasionally brought to light, under the impulses of the high feeling which has conceived them; but, I fear, a good, wholesome, profitable and continued pecuniary support, is the applause that talent most craves. The fact, that an American publisher can get an English work without money, must, for a few years longer, (unless legislative protection shall be extended to their own authors,) have a tendency to repress a national literature. No man will pay a writer for an epic, a tragedy, a sonnet, a history, or a romance, when he can get a work of equal merit for nothing. I have conversed with those who are conversant on the subject, and, I confess, I have been astonished at the information they imparted.

A capital American publisher has assured me that there are not a dozen writers in this country, whose works he should feel confidence in publishing at all, while he reprints hundreds of English books without the least hesitation. This preference is by no means so much owing to any difference in merit, as to the fact that, when the price of the original author is to be added to the uniform hazard which accompanies all literary speculations, the risk becomes too great. The general taste of the reading world in this country is better than that of England. The fact is both proved and explained by the circumstance that thousands of works that are printed and read in the mother country, are not printed and read here. The publisher on this side of the Atlantic has the advantage of seeing the reviews of every book he wishes to print, and, what is of far more importance, he knows, with the exception of books that he is sure of selling, by means of a name, the decision of the English critics before he makes his choice. Nine times in ten, popularity, which is all he looks for, is a sufficient test of general merit. Thus, while you find every English work of character, or notoriety, on the shelves of an American book-store, you may ask in vain for most of the trash that is so greedily devoured in the circulating libraries of the mother country, and which would be just as eagerly devoured here, had not a better taste been created by a compelled abstinence. That taste must now be overcome before such works could be sold at all.

When I say that books are not rejected here, from any want of talent in the writers, perhaps I ought to explain. I wish to express something a little different. Talent is sure of too many avenues to wealth and honours, in America, to seek, unnecessarily, an unknown and hazardous path. It is better paid in the ordinary pursuits of life, than it would be likely to be paid by an adventure in which an extraordinary and skilful, because practised, foreign competition is certain. Perhaps high talent does not often make the trial with the American bookseller; but it is precisely for the reason I have named.

The second obstacle against which American literature has to contend, is in the poverty of materials. There is scarcely an ore which contributes to the wealth of the author, that is found, here, in veins as rich as in Europe. There are no annals for the historian; no follies (beyond the most vulgar and commonplace) for the satirist; no manners for the dramatist; no obscure fictions for the writer of romance; no gross and hardy offences against decorum for the moralist; nor any of the rich artificial auxiliaries of poetry. The weakest hand can extract a spark from the flint, but it would baffle the strength of a giant to attempt kindling a flame with a pudding-stone. I very well know there are theorists who assume that the society and institutions of this country are, or ought to be, particularly favourable to novelties and variety. But the experience of one month, in these States, is sufficient to show any observant man the falsity of their position. The effect of a promiscuous assemblage any where, is to create a standard of deportment; and great liberty permits every one to aim at its attainment. I have never seen a nation so much alike in my life, as the people of the United States, and what is more, they are not only like each other, but they are remarkably like that which common sense tells them they ought to resemble. No doubt, traits of character that are a little peculiar, without, however, being either very poetical, or very rich, are to be found in remote districts; but they are rare, and not always happy exceptions. In short, it is not possible to conceive a state of society in which more of the attributes of plain good sense, or fewer of the artificial absurdities of life, are to be found, than here. There is no costume for the peasant, (there is scarcely a peasant at all,) no wig for the judge, no baton for the general, no diadem for the chief magistrate. The darkest ages of their history are illuminated by the light of truth; the utmost efforts of their chivalry are limited by the laws of God; and even the deeds of their sages and heroes are to be sung in a language that would differ but little from a version of the ten commandments. However useful and respectable all this may be in actual life, it indicates but one direction to the man of genius. . . .

Notwithstanding the overwhelming influence of British publications, and all the difficulties I have named, original books are getting to be numerous in the United States. The impulses of talent and intelligence are bearing down a thousand obstacles. I think the new works will increase rapidly, and that they are destined to produce a powerful influence on the world. We will pursue this subject another time. —Adieu.

From
THE AMERICAN DEMOCRAT
[1838]

AN ARISTOCRAT AND A DEMOCRAT

WE LIVE in an age, when the words aristocrat and democrat are much used, without regard to the real significations. An aristocrat is one of a few, who possess the political power of a country; a democrat, one of the many. The words are also properly applied to those who entertain notions favorable to aristocratical, or democratical forms of government. Such persons are not, necessarily, either aristocrats, or democrats in fact, but merely so in opinion. Thus a member of a democratical government may have an aristocratical bias, and *vice versa*.

To call a man who has the habits and opinions of a gentleman, an aristocrat, from that fact alone, is an abuse of terms, and betrays ignorance of the true principles of government, as well as of the world. It must be an equivocal freedom, under which every one is not the master of his own innocent acts and associations; and he is a sneaking democrat, indeed, who will submit to be dictated to, in those habits over which neither law nor morality assumes a right of control.

Some men fancy that a democrat can only be one who seeks the level, social, mental and moral, of the majority, a rule that would at once exclude all men of refinement, education and taste from the class. These persons are enemies of democracy, as they at once render it impracticable. They are usually great sticklers for their own associations and habits, too, though unable to comprehend any of a nature that are superior. They are, in truth, aristocrats in principle, though assuming a contrary pretension; the ground work of all their feelings and arguments being self. Such is not the intention of liberty, whose aim is to leave every man to be the master of his own acts; denying hereditary honors, it is true, as unjust and unnecessary, but not denying the inevitable consequences of civilization.

The law of God is the only rule of conduct, in this, as in other matters. Each man should do as he would be done by. Were the question put to the greatest advocate of indiscriminate association, whether he would submit to have his company and habits dictated to him, he would be one of the first to resist the tyranny; for they, who are the most rigid in maintaining their own claims, in such matters, are usually the loudest in decrying those whom they fancy to be better off than themselves. Indeed, it may be taken as a rule in social intercourse, that he who is the most apt to question the pretensions of others, is the most conscious of the doubtful position he himself occupies; thus establishing the very claims he affects to deny, by letting his jealousy of it be seen. Manners, education and refinement, are positive things, and they bring with them innocent tastes which are productive of high enjoyments; and it is as unjust to deny their possessors their indulgence, as it would be to insist on the less fortunate's passing the time they would rather devote to athletic amusements, in listening to operas for which they have no relish, sung in a language they do not understand.

All that democracy means, is as equal a participation in rights as is practicable; and to pretend that social equality is a condition of popular institutions, is to assume that the latter are destructive of civilization, for, as nothing is more self-evident than the impossibility of raising all men to the highest standard of tastes and refinement, the alternative would be to reduce the entire community to the lowest. The whole embarrassment on this point exists in the difficulty of making men comprehend qualities they do not themselves possess. We can all perceive the difference between ourselves and our inferiors, but when it comes to a question of the difference between us and our superiors, we fail to appreciate merits of which we have no proper conceptions. In face of this obvious difficulty, there is the safe and just governing rule, already mentioned, or that of permitting every one to be the undisturbed judge of his own habits and associations, so long as they are innocent, and do not impair the rights of others to be equally judges for themselves. It follows, that social intercourse must regulate itself, independently of institutions, with the exception that the latter, while they withhold no natural, bestow no factitious advantages beyond those which are inseparable from the rights of property, and general civilization.

In a democracy, men are just as free to aim at the highest attainable places in society, as to obtain the largest fortunes; and it would be clearly unworthy of all noble sentiment to say, that the grovelling competition for money shall alone be free, while that which enlists all the liberal acquirements and elevated sentiments of the race, is denied the democrat. Such an avowal would be at once a declaration of the inferiority of the system, since nothing but ignorance and vulgarity could be its fruits.

The democratic gentleman must differ in many essential particulars, from the aristocratical gentleman, though in their ordinary habits and tastes they are virtually identical. Their principles vary; and, to a slight degree, their deportment accordingly. The democrat, recognizing the right of all to participate in power, will be more liberal in his general sentiments, a quality of superiority in itself; but, in conceding this much to his fellow man, he will proudly maintain his own independence of vulgar domination, as indispensable to his personal habits. The same principles and manliness that would induce him to depose a royal despot, would induce him to resist a vulgar tyrant.

There is no more capital, though more common error, than to suppose him an aristocrat who maintains his independence of habits; for democracy asserts the control of the majority, only in matters of law, and not in matters of custom. The very object of the institution is the utmost practicable personal liberty, and to affirm the contrary, would be sacrificing the end to the means.

An aristocrat, therefore, is merely one who fortifies his exclusive privileges by positive institutions, and a democrat, one who is willing to admit of a free competition, in all things. To say, however, that the last supposes this competition will lead to nothing, is an assumption that means are employed without any reference to an end. He is the purest democrat who best maintains his rights, and no rights can be dearer to a man of cultivation, than exemptions from unseasonable invasions on his time, by the coarse-minded and ignorant.

ON AMERICAN EQUALITY

THE EQUALITY of the United States is no more absolute than that of any other country. There may be less inequality in this nation than in most others, but inequality exists, and, in some respects, with stronger features than it is usual to meet with in the rest of christendom.

The rights of property being an indispensable condition of civilization, and its quiet possession everywhere guaranteed, equality of condition is rendered impossible. One man must labor, while another may live luxuriously on his means; one has leisure and opportunity to cultivate his tastes, to increase his information, and to refine his habits, while another is compelled to toil, that he may live. One is reduced to serve, while another commands, and, of course, there can be no equality in their social conditions.

The justice and relative advantage of these differencies, as well as their several duties, will be elsewhere considered.

By the inequality of civil and political rights that exists in certain parts of the Union, and the great equality that exists in others, we see the necessity of referring the true character of the institutions to those of the states, without a just understanding of which, it is impossible to obtain any general and accurate ideas of the real polity of the country.

The same general exceptions to civil and political equality, that are found in other free countries, exist in this, though under laws peculiar to ourselves. Women and minors are excluded from the suffrage, and from maintaining suits at law, under the usual provisions, here as well as elsewhere. None but natives of the country can fill many of the higher offices, and paupers, felons and all those who have not fixed residences, are also excluded from the suffrage. In a few of the states property is made the test of political rights, and, in nearly half of them, a large portion of the inhabitants, who are of a different race from the original European occupants of the soil, are entirely excluded from all political, and from many of the civil rights, that are enjoyed by those who are deemed citizens. A slave can neither choose, nor be chosen to office, nor, in most of the states, can even a free man, unless a white man. A slave can neither sue nor be sued; he can not hold property, real or personal, nor can he, in many of the states, be a witness in any suit, civil or criminal.

It follows from these facts, that absolute equality of condition, of political rights, or of civil rights, does not exist in the United States, though they all exist in a much greater degree in some states than in others, and in some of the states, perhaps, to as great a degree as is practicable. In what are usually called the free

states of America, or those in which domestic slavery is abolished, there is to be found as much equality in every respect as comports with safety, civilization and the rights of property. This is also true, as respects the white population, in those states in which domestic slavery does exist; though the number of the bond is in a large proportion to that of the free.

As the tendency of the institutions of America is to the right, we learn in these truths, the power of facts, every question of politics being strictly a question of practice. They who fancy it possible to frame the institutions of a country, on the pure principles of abstract justice, as these principles exist in theories, know little of human nature, or of the restraints that are necessary to society. Abuses assail us in a thousand forms, and it is hopeless to aspire to any condition of humanity, approaching perfection. The very necessity of a government at all, arises from the impossibility of controlling the passions by any other means than that of force.

The celebrated proposition contained in the declaration of independence is not to be understood literally. All men are not "created equal," in a physical, or even in a moral sense, unless we limit the signification to one of political rights. This much is true, since human institutions are a human invention, with which nature has had no connection. Men are not born equals, physically, since one has a good constitution, another a bad; one is handsome, another ugly; one white, another black. Neither are men born equals morally, one possessing genius, or a natural aptitude, while his brother is an idiot. As regards all human institutions men are born equal, no sophistry being able to prove that nature intended one should inherit power and wealth, another slavery and want. Still artificial inequalities are the inevitable consequences of artificial ordinances, and in founding a new governing principle for the social compact, the American legislators instituted new modes of difference.

The very existence of government at all,

infers inequality. The citizen who is preferred to office becomes superior of those who are not, so long as he is the repository of power, and the child inherits the wealth of the parent as a controlling law of society. All that the great American proposition, therefore, can mean, is to set up new and juster notions of natural rights than those which existed previously, by asserting, in substance, that God has not instituted political inequalities, as was pretended by the advocates of the Jus Divinum, and that men possessed a full and natural authority to form such social institutions as best suited their necessities.

There are numerous instances in which the social inequality of America may do violence to our notions of abstract justice, but the compromise of interests under which all civilized society must exist, renders this unavoidable. Great principles seldom escape working injustice in particular things, and this so much the more, in establishing the relations of a community, for in them many great, and frequently conflicting principles enter, to maintain the more essential features of which sacrifices of parts become necessary. If we would have civilization and the exertion indispensable to its success, we must have property; if we have property, we must have its rights; if we have the rights of property, we must take those consequences of the rights of property which are inseparable from the rights themselves.

The equality of rights in America, therefore, after allowing for the striking exception of domestic slavery, is only a greater extension of the principle than common, while there is no such thing as an equality of condition. All that can be said of the first, is that it has been carried as far as a prudent discretion will at all allow, and of the last, that the inequality is the simple result of civilization, unaided by any of those factitious plans that have been elsewhere devised in order to augment the power of the strong, and to enfeeble the weak.

Equality is no where laid down as a governing principle of the institutions of the United States, neither the word, nor any inference that can be fairly deduced from its meaning, occurring in the constitution. As respects the states, themselves, the professions of an equality of rights are more clear, and slavery excepted, the intention in all their governments is to maintain it, as far as practicable, though equality of condition is no where mentioned, all political economists knowing that it is unattainable, if, indeed, it be desirable. Desirable in practice, it can hardly be, since the result would be to force all down to the level of the lowest.

All that a good government aims at, therefore, is to add no unnecessary and artificial aid to the force of its own unavoidable consequences, and to abstain from fortifying and accumulating social inequality as a means of increasing political inequalities.

From

THE SPY
[1821]

HARVEY BIRCH

IN PERSON, the pedler was a man above the middle height, spare, but full of bone and muscle. At first sight, his strength seemed unequal to manage the unwieldy burden of his pack; yet he threw it on and off with great dexterity, and with as much apparent ease as if it had been filled with feathers. His eyes were grey, sunken, restless, and, for the flitting moments that they dwelt on the countenances of those with whom he conversed, they seemed to read the very soul. They possessed, however, two distinct impressions, which, in a great measure, characterized the whole man. When engaged in traffic, the intelligence of his face appeared lively, active, and flexible, though uncommonly acute; if the conversation turned on the ordinary transactions of life, his air became abstracted and restless; but if, by chance, the revolution and the country were the topic, his whole system seemed altered—

all his faculties were concentrated: he would listen for a great length of time, without speaking, and then would break silence by some light and jocular remark, that was too much at variance with his former manner, not to be an affectation. But of the war, and of his father, he seldom spoke, and always from some very obvious necessity.

From
THE PIONEERS
[1823]

LEATHERSTOCKING

"AH! the game is becoming hard to find, indeed, Judge, with your clearings and betterments," said the old hunter, with a kind of compelled resignation. "The time has been when I have shot thirteen deer, without counting the fa'ns, standing in the door of my own hut; and for bear's meat, if one wanted a ham or so, he had only to watch a-nights, and he could shoot one by moonlight, through the cracks of the logs; nor fear of his oversleeping himself neither, for the howling of the wolves was sartin to keep his eyes open. There's old Hector"— patting with affection a tall hound of black and yellow spots, with white belly and legs, that just then came in on the scent, accompanied by the slut he had mentioned; "see where the wolves bit his throat, the night I druv them from the venison that was smoking on the chimney top— that dog is more to be trusted than many a Christian man; for he never forgets a friend, and loves the hand that gives him bread."

There was a peculiarity in the manner of the hunter that attracted the notice of the young female, who had been a close and interested observer of his appearance and equipments, from the moment he came into view. He was tall, and so meagre as to make him seem above even the six feet that he actually stood in his stockings. On his head, which was thinly covered with lank, sandy hair, he wore a cap made of foxskin, resembling in shape the one we have already described, although much inferior in finish and ornaments. His face was skinny and thin almost to emaciation; but yet it bore no signs of disease—on the contrary, it had every indication of the most robust and enduring health. The cold and exposure had, together, given it a color of uniform red. His gray eyes were glancing under a pair of shaggy brows, that overhung them in long hairs of gray mingled with their natural hue; his scraggy neck was bare, and burnt to the same tint with his face; though a small part of a shirt collar, made of the country check, was to be seen above the overdress he wore. A kind of coat, made of dressed deerskin, with the hair on, was belted close to his lank body, by a girdle of colored worsted. On his feet were deerskin moccasins, ornamented with porcupines' quills, after the manner of the Indians, and his limbs were guarded with long leggings of the same material as the moccasins, which, gartering over the knees of his tarnished buckskin breeches, had obtained for him among the settlers the nickname of Leather-Stocking. Over his left shoulder was slung a belt of deerskin, from which depended an enormous ox-horn, so thinly scraped as to discover the powder it contained. The larger end was fitted ingeniously and securely with a wooden bottom, and the other was stopped tight by a little plug. A leathern pouch hung before him, from which, as he concluded his last speech, he took a small measure, and, filling it accurately with powder, he commenced reloading the rifle, which, as its butt rested on the snow before him, reached nearly to the top of his foxskin cap.

From
THE LAST OF THE MOHICANS
[1826]

DAVID GAMUT

THE PERSON of this individual was to the last degree ungainly, without being in any particular manner deformed. He had all the bones and joints of other men, without any of their proportions. Erect, his stature surpassed that of his fellows; seated, he appeared reduced within the ordinary limits of the race. The same contrariety in his members seemed to exist throughout the whole man. His head was large; his shoulders narrow; his arms long and dangling; while his hands were small, if not delicate. His legs and thighs were thin, nearly to emaciation, but of extraordinary length; and his knees would have been considered tremendous, had they not been outdone by the broader foundations on which this false superstructure of blended human orders was so profanely reared. The ill-sorted and injudicious attire of the individual only served to render his awkwardness more conspicuous. A sky-blue coat, with short and broad skirts and low cape, exposed a long thin neck, and longer and thinner legs, to the worst animadversions of the evil-disposed. His nether garment was of yellow nankeen, closely fitted to the shape, and tied at his bunches of knees by large knots of white ribbon, a good deal sullied by use. Clouded cotton stockings, and shoes, on one of the latter of which was a plated spur, completed the costume of the lower extremity of this figure, no curve or angle of which was concealed, but, on the other hand, studiously exhibited, through the vanity or simplicity of its owner. From beneath the flap of an enormous pocket of a soiled vest of embossed silk, heavily ornamented with tarnished silver lace, projected an instrument, which, from being seen in such martial company, might have been easily mistaken for some mischievous and unknown implement of war. Small as it was, this uncommon engine [1] had excited the curiosity of most of the Europeans in the camp, though several of the provincials were seen to handle it, not only without fear, but with the utmost familiarity. A large, civil cocked hat, like those worn by clergymen within the last thirty years, surmounted the whole, furnishing dignity to a good-natured and somewhat vacant countenance, that apparently needed such artificial aid, to support the gravity of some high and extraordinary trust.

CHINGACHGOOK AND HAWKEYE

ON that day, two men were lingering on the banks of a small but rapid stream, within an hour's journey of the encampment of Webb, like those who awaited the appearance of an absent person, or the approach of some expected event. The vast canopy of woods spread itself to the margin of the river, overhanging the water, and shadowing its dark current with a deeper hue. The rays of the sun were beginning to grow less fierce, and the intense heat of the day was lessened, as the cooler vapors of the springs and fountains rose above their leafy beds, and rested in the atmosphere. Still that breathing silence, which marks the drowsy sultriness of an American landscape in July, pervaded the secluded spot, interrupted only by the low voices of the men, the occasional lazy tap of a woodpecker, the discordant cry of some gaudy jay, or a swelling on the ear, from the dull roar of a distant waterfall.

These feeble and broken sounds were, however, too familiar to the foresters, to draw their attention from the more interesting matter of their dialogue. While one of these loiterers showed the red skin and wild accoutrements of a native of the woods, the other exhibited, through the mask of his rude and nearly savage equipments, the brighter, though sunburnt and long-faded, complexion of one who might claim descent from European parentage. The former was seated on the end of a mossy log, in a posture that permitted him to heighten the effect of his earnest language, by the calm but expressive gestures of an Indian engaged in debate. His body, which was nearly naked, presented a terrific emblem of death, drawn in intermingled colors of white and black. His closely shaved head, on which no other hair than the well known and chivalrous

---

[1] David's pitch-pipe.

scalping tuft was preserved, was without ornament of any kind, with the exception of a solitary eagle's plume, that crossed his crown, and depended over the left shoulder. A tomahawk and scalping-knife, of English manufacture, were in his girdle; while a short military rifle, of that sort with which the policy of the whites armed their savage allies, lay carelessly across his bare and sinewy knee. The expanded chest, full formed limbs, and grave countenance of this warrior, would denote that he had reached the vigor of his days, though no symptoms of decay appeared to have yet weakened his manhood.

The frame of the white man, judging by such parts as were not concealed by his clothes, was like that of one who had known hardships and exertion from his earliest youth. His person, though muscular, was rather attenuated than full; but every nerve and muscle appeared strung and indurated by unremitted exposure and toil. He wore a hunting-shirt of forest green, fringed with faded yellow, and a summer cap of skins which had been shorn of their fur. He also bore a knife in a girdle of wampum, like that which confined the scanty garments of the Indian, but no tomahawk. His moccasins were ornamented after the gay fashion of the natives, while the only part of his under-dress which appeared below the hunting-frock, was a pair of buckskin leggings, that laced at the sides, and which were gartered above the knees with the sinews of a deer. A pouch and horn completed his personal accoutrements, though a rifle of great length, which the theory of the more ingenious whites had taught them was the most dangerous of all fire-arms, leaned against a neighboring sapling. The eye of the hunter, or scout, whichever he might be, was small, quick, keen, and restless, roving while he spoke, on every side of him, as if in quest of game, or distrusting the sudden approach of some lurking enemy. Notwithstanding these symptoms of habitual suspicion, his countenance was not only without guile, but at the moment at which he is introduced, it was charged with an expression of sturdy honesty.

From

THE WEPT OF WISH-TON-WISH
[1829]

THE REVEREND MEEK WOLFE

THE REVEREND Meek Wolfe was, in spirit, a rare combination of the humblest self-abasement and of fierce spiritual denunciation. Like so many others of his sacred calling in the colony he inhabited, he was not only the descendant of a line of priests, but it was his greatest earthly hope that he should also become the progenitor of a race in whom the ministry was to be perpetuated as severely as if the regulated formula of the Mosaic dispensation were still in existence. He had been educated in the infant college of Harvard, an institution that the emigrants from England had the wisdom and enterprise to found within the first five-and-twenty years of their colonial residence. Here this scion of so pious and orthodox a stock had abundantly qualified himself for the intellectual warfare of his future life, by regarding one set of opinions so steadily, as to leave little reason to apprehend he would ever abandon the most trifling outworks of his faith. No citadel ever presented a more hopeless curtain to the besieger, than did the mind of this zealot to the efforts of conviction; for on the side of his opponents, he contrived that every avenue should be closed by a wall blank as indomitable obstinacy could oppose. He appeared to think that all the minor conditions of argument and reason had been disposed of by his ancestors, and that it only remained for him to strengthen the many defences of his subject, and now and then to scatter by a fierce sortie the doctrinal skirmishers who might occasionally approach his parish. There was a remarkable singleness of mind in this religionist which, while it in some measure rendered even his bigotry respectable, greatly aided in clearing the knotty subject with which he dealt, of much embarrassing matter. In his eyes, the straight and narrow path would hold but few, besides his own flock. He admitted some fortuitous exceptions, in one or two of the nearest parishes, with whose clergymen he was in the habit of exchanging pulpits; and perhaps, here and there, in a saint of the other hemisphere, or of the more distant towns of the Colonies, the brightness of whose faith was something aided, in his eyes, by distance, as this opaque globe of ours is thought to appear a ball of light to those who inhabit its satellite. In short, there was an admixture of seeming charity with an exclusiveness of hope, an unweariness of exertion with a coolness of exterior, a disregard of self with the most complacent security, and an uncomplaining submission to temporal evils with the loftiest spiritual pretensions, that in some measure rendered him a man as difficult to comprehend as to describe.

From
HOMEWARD BOUND
[1838]

Steadfast Dodge and John Truck

THE ACCIDENTS of life could scarcely form extremes of character more remote than that of Steadfast Dodge and that of John Truck. The first never did anything beyond acts of the most ordinary kind, without first weighing its probable effect in the neighborhood; its popularity or unpopularity; how it might tally with the different public opinions that were whiffling through the country; in what manner it would influence the next election, and whether it would be likely to elevate him or depress him in the public mind. No Asiatic slave stood more in terror of a vindictive master than Mr. Dodge stood in trembling before the reproofs, comments, censures, frowns, cavillings and remarks of every man in his county, who happened to belong to the political party that just at that moment was in power. As to the minority, he was as brave as a lion, could snap his fingers at them, and was foremost in deriding and scoffing at all they said or did. This, however, was in connection with politics only; for, the instant party-drill ceased to be of value, Steadfast's valor oozed out of his composition, and in all other things he dutifully consulted every public opinion of that neighborhood. This estimable man had his weak points as well as another, and what is more, he was quite sensible of them, as was proved by a most jealous watchfulness of his besetting sins, in the way of exposure if not of indulgence. In a word, Steadfast Dodge was a man that wished to meddle with and control all things, without possessing precisely the spirit that was necessary to leave him master of himself; he had a rabid desire for the good opinion of everything human, without always taking the means necessary to preserve his own; was a stout declaimer for the rights of the community while forgetting that the community itself is but a means set up for the accomplishment of a given end; and felt an inward and profound respect for anything that was beyond his reach, which manifested itself, not in manly efforts to attain the forbidden fruit, but rather in a spirit of opposition and detraction, that only betrayed, through its jealousy, the existence of the feeling; which jealousy, however, he affected to conceal under an intense regard for popular rights, since he was apt to aver it was quite intolerable that any man should possess anything, even to qualities, in which his neighbors might not properly participate. All these, moreover, and many similar traits, Mr. Dodge encouraged in the spirit of liberty!

On the other hand, John Truck sailed his own ship; was civil to his passengers from habit as well as policy; knew that every vessel must have a captain; believed mankind to be little better than asses; took his own observations, and cared not a straw for those of his mates; was never more bent on following his own views than when all hands grumbled and opposed him; was daring by nature, decided from use and long self-reliance, and was every way a man fitted to steer his bark through the trackless ways of life, as well as those of the ocean. It was fortunate for one in his particular position, that nature had made the possessor of so much self-will and temporary authority, cool and sarcastic rather than hotheaded and violent; and for this circumstance Mr. Dodge in particular had frequent occasions for felicitation.

From
HOME AS FOUND
[1838]

ARISTABULUS BRAGG

MR. ARISTABULUS BRAGG was born in one of the western counties of Massachusetts, and emigrated to New York, after receiving his education, at the mature age of nineteen; at twenty-one he was admitted to the bar, and for the last seven years he has been a successful practitioner in all the courts of Otsego, from the justice's to the circuit. His talents are undeniable, as he commenced his education at fourteen and terminated it at twenty-one, the law course included. This man is an epitome of all that is good and all that is bad in a very large class of his fellow-citizens. He is quick-witted, prompt in action, enterprising in all things in which he has nothing to lose, but wary and cautious in all things in which he has a real stake, and ready to turn not only his hand, but his heart and his principles, to anything that offers an advantage. With him, literally, "nothing is too high to be aspired to, nothing too low to be done." He will run for Governor, or for town clerk, just as opportunities occur, is expert in all the practices of his profession, has had a quarter's dancing, with three years in the classics, and turned his attention toward medicine and divinity, before he finally settled down into the law. Such a compound of shrewdness, imprudence, common-sense, pretension, humility, cleverness, vulgarity, kind-heartedness, duplicity, selfishness, law-honesty, moral fraud and mother wit, mixed up with a smattering of learning and much penetration in practical things, can hardly be described, as any one of his prominent qualities is certain to be met by another quite as obvious that is almost its converse. Mr. Bragg, in short, is purely a creature of circumstances, his qualities pointing him out for either a member of Congress or a deputy sheriff, offices that he is equally ready to fill.

1809 ∞ *Edgar Allan Poe* ∞ *1849*

I

WALTER DE LA MARE, one of the most whimsically imaginative of modern English writers, has a short story entitled "A Revenant," to be found in his *The Wind Blows Over*. It tells how the ghost of Edgar Allan Poe revisits the glimpses of the moon for an evening in November, 1932, and attends a popular lecture on his writings by a Professor Monk. When the audience has departed, the ghost waylays the professor, puts a few modest questions, and does a bit of lecturing on his own account. The professor is soon suffering from an acute case of reduced dimensions. Among the many pointed remarks of his shadowy heckler that deflate the balloon of academic authority, the following is especially pertinent: " 'You made pretty play with the artistic temperament—with your morbid, and your moody, and your melancholy, and your misanthrope—but of the artist's *conscience* not one word.' "

The term "artistic temperament" is often used to refer to the merely eccentric or negative traits of artistically inclined people. There is warrant, of course, for applying it in this sense to the man Poe. During his bizarre career, he displayed, at one time or another and under diverse pressures, several of these traits, such as hypersensitiveness, emotional instability, intellectual arrogance, insobriety, and the like. But none of them was so central or so persistent in his many-sided personality as was a demon, a still small voice, which haunted the vortices of his brain.

This demon held up for him standards of perfection for writing both poetry and prose. It drove him ceaselessly to satisfy these standards, even at the expense of his health and the happiness prized by ordinary men. It caused him to express mournful envy of the angel Israfel, whom he imagined as singing a supreme melody in a heaven of timeless Platonic ideas and essences. It made him so unsparingly caustic toward the performances of some of the other writers of his time that George Graham, the magazine-owner for whom he worked in Philadelphia, was moved to comment: "Literature with him was religion; and he, its high-priest, with a whip of scorpions scourged the money-changers from the temple."

It was this demon of his, furthermore, that prompted him to headlong dissent from several of the prevailing literary trends in the America of the 1830's and the 1840's. New England transcendentalism, for example, became so distasteful to him that he sought to improve upon its metaphysical profundities by solving the riddle of the universe according to his own lights in his treatise or "prose poem," *Eureka*. Finally, throughout Poe's mature creative years, it was this same demon that helped keep alive in him the dream, the *ignis fatuus*, that he would some day found and edit a really first-rate magazine for a public which he thought was oversupplied with inferior ones.

For this demon of Poe's the only fitting label is "the artist's conscience." It is a useful concept to explain both the man and the writer.

II

Poe had what may be called an hereditary right to his artist's conscience, as well as to a few of the eccentricities that Philistines have exaggerated in their "pretty play" with his "artistic temperament." His English-born mother, Elizabeth Arnold, made her debut as an actress at the age of nine in Boston in 1796. When she died at the age of twenty-four in Richmond, Va., she had endeared herself to theater-goers in most of the important Atlantic seaboard cities of the United States, and had enacted 201 different rôles. These ranged from the heroines of high tragedy and melodrama through the gentlewomen of satirical and sentimental comedy to even a few hoydens of farce, and there were fourteen Shakespearean characterizations, including Ariel, Ophelia, Cordelia, Juliet, and Desdemona.

Poe's father, David Poe, Jr., of a Baltimore, Md., Irish family, abandoned study of the law and made his debut as an actor at the age of nineteen in Charleston, S. C., in 1803. He was soon playing in the same stock company with Elizabeth Arnold and her first husband, Charles Hopkins, and married her in the spring of 1806, about five months after Hopkins' death. Alcoholism, ill health, and adverse journalistic criticism of his acting drove David Poe from the stage in 1809, but his record of 137 parts, nineteen of them Shakespearean, shows that, even though he may have lacked his wife's genius, he must have been a "trouper" of no mean versatility.

Because of his parents' profession, Poe happened to be born in Boston. The day was January 19, 1809, and the only name given him was "Edgar." It was also an accident of the theatrical profession that he was left an orphan in Richmond. The day was December 8, 1811, when his mother died there on tour, and the whereabouts of his father were unknown. While his older brother, William, and his little sister, Rosalie, found other homes, he was taken into that of the wealthy Richmond tobacco merchant and shipowner, John Allan, who did not formally adopt him but stamped him permanently as his foster son by providing him with a middle name.

Thus Poe, before he was old enough to have any say in the matter, was snatched from the rootless, hard-working world of theatrical Bohemia, and established in the seemingly secure, comfortable world of the Virginia upper *bourgeoisie* and aristocracy. As he grew to manhood, however, and the security of this world proved a sham, and its comfort had too many strings attached, he preferred to make his own way in another kind of Bohemia, almost as rootless, even more hard-working than that his parents had known. This was the Bohemia of literary journalism, and as one of its harried denizens and hangers-on, he was to move, like his parents, from city to city of the Atlantic seaboard.

III

It is a mistake, however, to regard Poe's connection with the Allan family and its world as a stroke of tragic destiny. John Allan was a Scotch gentleman of considerable culture. He could write letters with a distinct literary flavor and took some interest in both philosophy and science. Poe's formal education was begun in a Richmond private school. Then, from 1815 to 1820, he had an educational experience of which no other major American writer of his time could boast. Between the highly impressionable ages of six and eleven, he traveled with the Allan family to England and Scotland and attended several schools there. During the last three years of the Allans' visit, he was a student of the Reverend John Bransby at the Manor House School at Stoke-Newington, England. Some of his reactions to this school are recorded in his story, "William Wilson."

Returning home with the Allans, he continued his formal education under several Richmond tutors. Although some of his more aristocratic schoolmates looked down on him as an outsider, he won friends and admirers by his skill at swimming, boxing, and running, his ability to quote Latin verses, and his unusual command of French.

About this time his "sentimental education" began also. When Rob Stanard, one of his young friends, took him to meet Jane Stith Craig Stanard, his beautiful mother, Poe idealized her so fervently that he was to write about her the poem, "To Helen," wherein she is associated with "the glory that was Greece," "the grandeur that was Rome," and "Holy-Land." He was deeply grieved when she died in 1824. He next fell in love with Sarah Elmira Royster, a charming Richmond girl in her middle 'teens. Although they were engaged to be married, she was soon to become the wealthy Mrs. Shelton.

The last real formal education that Poe received was the year he spent at the University of Virginia in 1826, shortly after its establishment by Thomas Jefferson. The buildings at Charlottesville were models of classic architecture, grouped in a valley through which the Rivanna River ran and beyond which, on two sides, receded mountain ridges into blue distance. By the end of the term in December, Poe ranked high in Latin, French, and Italian, and from the well-stocked library had withdrawn, among other things, several volumes of Rollins' *Ancient History* and a couple of volumes by Voltaire. But he had also piled up gambling debts on the ground that he needed, for required academic expenditures and for the maintenance of his status as a gentleman, more money than John Allan had thought fit to provide him with. Although the known facts show that Poe was in the right, Allan found his logic difficult to accept. They quarreled, and in the spring of 1827 Poe made his first attempt to break away from the world of his foster father, and of Sarah Royster, and to put the uneven but unique education he had received to the acid test of earning his own living.

The symbol of his new freedom was a thin pamphlet of verse issued by an obscure Boston printer in the early summer of that same year. The title was *Tamerlane and Other Poems*. The only indication of the author on cover and titlepage was the by-line, "By a Bostonian." There was an epigraph, from William Cowper:

"Young heads are giddy, and young hearts are warm,
And make mistakes for manhood to reform."

Today one of the rarest of Americana, this pamphlet sold then for only twelve and one-half cents. It was Poe's first book, and its title poem proclaimed the arrival of an American Byron, singing, in a strangely melodious four-stress measure, the themes of pride, love, beauty, and death.

Poe's new freedom, however, was not to be easily won. There followed several crucial years during which he seemed to be pulled by different ambitions —toward a career in the Army, toward reconciliation with John Allan, toward fame as a poet and success as a writer of magazine fiction.

After the symbolic venture in Boston, he enlisted as a private in the Army under the name of Edgar A. Perry. The artillery battery to which he belonged was sent to Fort Moultrie on Sullivan's Island, in the harbor of Charleston, S. C., and to Fortress Monroe, in Old Point, Va. From the latter station he wrote to John Allan: "Richmond & the U. States were too narrow a sphere & the world shall be my theatre."

Shortly after his promotion to the rank of regimental sergeant-major, he was partly reconciled with Allan on the occasion of Mrs. Allan's death, and through his help managed to be released from the Army and appointed to West Point. But they again quarreled, and Poe found West Point so little to his liking that he deliberately got himself court-martialed and discharged.

In Baltimore, looking up his father's people, he had found that his widowed aunt, Mrs. Maria Clemm, was eager to give him help with his clothes and sympathy for his aspirations. His second pamphlet, *Al Aaraaf, Tamerlane, and Minor Poems,* had been printed in that city in 1829. After the West Point experience and a visit to New York to see his third publication, *Poems,* through the press in 1831, he returned to Mrs. Clemm's household to add another burden to her meager budget. Baltimore was a spawning place for new periodicals. Poe hoped he could get himself out of debt by providing them and magazines elsewhere with the prose tales he was now beginning to produce in quantity, having been interested in dabbling with them ever since his college days. Then, also, there was the companionship of Mrs. Clemm's lovely child, Virginia, born in 1822, as well as the friendship of the prominent Baltimore lawyer, William Wirt, whose judgment of poetry Poe had learned to respect.

In 1831 he submitted five of his tales to a contest conducted by the *Philadelphia Saturday Courier.* He lost the contest, but the editors thought enough of his entries to accept them for publication. They appeared anonymously, and there is no proof that he was paid for them. The next year, however, he submitted six stories to a contest conducted by the *Baltimore Saturday Visiter.* With "MS. Found in a Bottle" he took the prize, and, more importantly, made the acquaintance of one of the judges, John P. Kennedy, another

Baltimore lawyer, who had already published one novel, *Swallow Barn,* who had heard of Poe from his friend, William Wirt, and who used his influence to get Poe his start in literary journalism on the *Southern Literary Messenger* back home in Richmond.

The first number of this periodical had appeared in August, 1834, several months after John Allan's death. Its owner, T. W. White, a printer, had entrusted the destinies of his fledgling to two successive editors before he asked Poe, who was becoming a standby for critical reviews and stories, to join the staff as assistant editor. Poe immediately accepted the offer and was soon editor. On January 22, 1836, he wrote thus of his success to his friend Kennedy: "Mr. White is very liberal, and besides my salary of $520 pays me liberally for extra work, so that I receive nearly $800. Next year, that is at the commencement of the second volume, I am to get $1000. Besides this I receive, from Publishers, nearly all new publications. My friends in Richmond have received me with open arms, and my reputation is extending—especially in the South. Contrast all this with those circumstances of absolute despair in which you found me, and you will see how great reason I have to be grateful to God—and to yourself."

The preceding October Poe had brought Virginia and Mrs. Clemm to Richmond to live with him at Mrs. Yarrington's boarding house. In this house, on May 16, 1836, his marriage to Virginia was performed. She was not yet fourteen, but on the marriage bond she was declared and witnessed under oath "to be of the full age of twenty-one years." Poe had finally won through, and found his world, although to make a living in it for himself and those dear to him and yet remain always true to his artist's conscience was to tax all his brilliant energies.

IV

The remaining thirteen years of his life are the story of how those energies poured themselves out prodigally in criticism, fiction, poetry, and philosophical speculation; how they continued to function despite worry over money and Virginia's illness and despite, even, the profound shock of her death; and how they were wasted by resort to drink and by transient sentimental fixations upon several emotionally susceptible literary ladies, and yet were still capable of almost their best until very near the mysterious, incredible, macabre end.

In January, 1837, Poe left the *Messenger* for a variety of reasons. White was awed by his abilities, but at the same time somewhat dissatisfied with his occasional drinking to excess and with his disinclination to accept any judgment but his own as to what should or should not be printed. Poe, for his part, was violently disillusioned with White. "The drudgery was excessive, the salary was contemptible," he wrote to one of his relatives, ". . . while my best energies were wasted in the service of an illiterate and vulgar, although well meaning man. . . ."

The Poes, with the indispensable Mrs. Clemm, moved from Richmond to New York, where Poe's fourth book and his only story approaching the length of a novel, *The Narrative of Arthur Gordon Pym*, was published by Harpers in 1838. Failing to establish himself with any periodical in New York, Poe had better luck in Philadelphia, where he lived from the summer of 1838 to the spring of 1844. Here he was co-editor of the *Gentleman's Magazine* and later on the staff of *Graham's*, to which he contributed some of his finest criticism. It was likewise in Philadelphia that he wrote many of his greatest stories and published his first story collection, *Tales of the Grotesque and Arabesque*, in two volumes in 1839 (although the title page bore the date 1840), as well as the first pamphlet in a projected serial edition of his fiction under the general title of *Prose-Romances* in 1843.

Graham, his employer, was later to say of him: "For three or four years I knew him intimately, and for eighteen months saw him almost daily; much of the time writing or conversing at the same desk; knowing all his hopes, his fears, and little annoyances of life, as well as his high-hearted struggle with adverse fate—yet he was always the same polished gentleman—the quiet, unobtrusive, thoughtful scholar—the devoted husband—frugal in his personal expenses—punctual and unwearied in his industry—*and the soul of honor,* in all his transactions."

Something of his growing reputation as a writer may be gleaned from Longfellow's tribute to him in a letter: ". . . all that I have read from your pen has inspired me with a high idea of your power; and I think you are destined to stand among the first romance-writers of the country, if such be your aim."

In 1842 Poe resigned his post on *Graham's* primarily because he hoped to found his own periodical, which was to be called *The Penn Magazine: A Monthly Literary Journal* and for which he printed an elaborate prospectus. The project fell through, however; Virginia, in singing, ruptured a blood vessel, and grew increasingly worse in health; hack work was Poe's only recourse, and how he felt about writing what others wanted him to write he had stated eloquently to a friend on whose influence he had futilely relied to obtain some government sinecure at Washington: "To coin one's brain into silver, at the nod of a master, is to my thinking, the hardest task in the world."

In 1844 the Poes moved to New York City, where Poe worked for the *Evening Mirror,* and where he was for a short time editor and proprietor of the *Broadway Journal,* although he continued to publish in such periodicals as the *Democratic Review, Godey's Lady's Book, Graham's,* and the *Southern Literary*

Messenger. "The Raven," which appeared late in January, 1845, in both the *Evening Mirror* and the *American Review,* was widely copied and commented on; it was parodied; it became, in short, the poem of the month, the poem of the year, even the poem of a generation. Poe was quick to take advantage of the furore. In that same year he published a new edition of his *Tales* and brought out the volume, *The Raven and Other Poems.* And the next spring he printed in *Graham's* his essay, "The Philosophy of Composition," explaining to an avid public how he wrote "The Raven."

While in New York City, the Poes had moved often; they now settled in the country in a cottage at Fordham. One of their visitors, Mrs. Mary Gove, a believer in mesmerism, Swedenborg, phrenology, and homeopathy, described the place as follows as it appeared to her in the summer of 1846: "There was an acre or two of greensward, fenced in about the house, as smooth as velvet and as clean as the best carpet. There were some grand old cherry-trees in the yard, that threw a massive shade around them. The house had three rooms—a kitchen, a sitting-room, and a bed-chamber over the sitting-room. There was a piazza in front of the house that was a lovely place to sit in in summer, with the shade of cherry-trees before it. There was no cultivation, no flowers—nothing but the smooth greensward and the majestic trees. . . ."

The same visitor gave thumbnail portraits of all members of the family. "Poe's voice," she wrote, "was melody itself. He always spoke low, even in a violent discussion, compelling his hearers to listen if they would know his opinion, his facts, fancies, or philosophy, or his weird imaginings."

Of Virginia, she had this vivid impression: "Mrs. Poe looked very young; she had large black eyes, and a pearly whiteness of complexion, which was a perfect pallor. Her pale face, her brilliant eyes, and her raven hair gave her an unearthly look. One felt that she was almost a disrobed spirit, and when she coughed it was made certain that she was rapidly passing away."

And Mrs. Clemm is brought to life as follows: "She was a tall, dignified old lady, with a most ladylike manner, and her black dress, though old and much worn, looked really elegant on her. She wore a widow's cap of the genuine pattern, and it suited exquisitely with her snow-white hair. Her features were large, and corresponded with her stature, and it seemed strange how such a stalwart and queenly woman could be the mother of her almost petite daughter . . . The mother seemed hale and strong, and appeared to be a sort of universal Providence for her strange children."

Virginia died of tuberculosis on January 30, 1847, and Poe suffered a severe collapse. What that death meant to him may best be seen in such of his poems as "Ulalume" (1847) and "Annabel Lee" (1849). But even more revealing than these poems is one of his letters, dated January 4, 1848, where her death is interpreted as a release from the havoc her long illness had wrought on his sensitive nature: "Six years ago, a wife, whom I loved as no man ever loved before, ruptured a blood-vessel in singing. Her life was despaired of. I took leave of her forever & underwent all the agonies of her death. She recovered partially and I again hoped. At the end of a year the vessel broke again—I went through precisely the same scene. Again in about a year afterward. Then again—again—again & even once again at varying intervals. Each time I felt all the agonies of her death—and at each accession of the disorder I loved her more dearly & clung to her life with more desperate pertinacity. But I am constitutionally sensitive—nervous in a very unusual degree. I became insane, with long intervals of horrible sanity. During these fits of absolute unconsciousness I drank, God only knows how often or how much. As a matter of course, my enemies referred the insanity to the drink rather than the drink to the insanity. I had indeed, nearly abandoned all hope of a permanent cure when I found one in the *death* of my wife. This I can & do endure as becomes a man—it was the horrible never-ending oscillation between hope & despair which I could *not* longer have endured without total loss of reason. In the death of what was my life, then, I receive a new but—oh God! how melancholy an existence."

During the period when he was recovering from the state of mind described in this letter, Poe completed his major excursion into philosophical speculation, *Eureka.* He read it as a public lecture before a small audience in New York in February, 1848; it appeared in book form the same year; he regarded it as the crowning intellectual as well as artistic achievement of his entire writing career.

He also became more and more involved in his Platonic friendships with women admirers. Virginia had encouraged the first of these, with the poetess, Mrs. Frances Sargent Osgood, the attractive thirty-four-year-old wife of an artist. Now, with Virginia gone, Poe turned to Mrs. Sarah Helen Whitman, a widow of forty-five living in Providence, R. I., who had been publishing magazine verse since 1829. Having composed "The Poetic Principle" as a possible lecture, Poe delivered it at Providence before an audience of approximately 2,000 people. Later he went to a convivial party given in his honor by some of the enthusiastic young men who had heard him. The aftermath was that his somewhat conditional engagement to be married to Mrs. Whitman was broken off by that lady and her mother. Poe found solace in chivalric devotion to the young matron, Mrs. Charles Richmond, and to Mrs. Marie Louise Shew, and, finally, to the old sweetheart of his boyhood, Mrs. Sarah Royster Shelton, now a well-to-do widow.

In 1849, when he visited Richmond to raise money for the magazine which he still dreamed of establishing and which he now desired to call *The Stylus,* Mrs. Shelton heard him deliver his lecture on "The Poetic Principle." In a letter which he persuaded her to write to Mrs. Clemm, she described the lecture as "very beautiful" and said Poe had "quite a full, and very fashionable audience. . . ." After repeating this lecture by request and concluding it as before with a reading of "The Raven," Poe intended to go to Philadelphia. He was then to proceed to New York City and to send for Mrs. Clemm to meet him there. According to Mrs. Shelton, whom it was his purpose to marry, he took leave of her on the evening of September 26. "He was very sad, and complained of being quite sick," she told Mrs. Clemm. "I felt his pulse, and found he had considerable fever, and did not think it probable he would be able to start the next morning (Thursday) as he anticipated. I felt so wretched about him all that night, that I went up early the next morning to inquire after him, when, much to my regret, he had left in the boat for Baltimore."

October 3 was election day in Baltimore. On that day one Joe Walker, a compositor on the *Baltimore Sun,* found a man lying in a semi-conscious condition outside Ryan's Fourth Ward polling place. Walker got out of him that his name was Edgar A. Poe and that he knew a Dr. Snodgrass, who lived not far away. Walker dispatched a message to the doctor, and about five o'clock that afternoon Snodgrass and one of Poe's relatives took Poe to the Washington College Hospital. He was completely unconscious, and when he recovered fell into a delirium which lasted until Saturday night. Then he began to cry out, "Reynolds! Reynolds! Reynolds!" He was apparently thinking of a J. N. Reynolds, of New York, famous in that day as an advocate and prime mover of an expedition to the South Pole.

In a review in *Graham's* in 1843 Poe had paid eloquent tribute to Reynolds and his expedition. In *Arthur Gordon Pym,* where the hero sails strange seas, he had borrowed material from Reynolds. In "MS. Found in a Bottle," the story which had launched Poe into literary journalism, he had written: "It is evident that we are hurrying onward to some exciting knowledge—some never to be imparted secret, whose attainment is destruction. Perhaps this current leads to the South Pole itself." Was that the reason Poe cried, "Reynolds! Reynolds! Reynolds!"—that night in the Baltimore hospital—before with a muttered "God help my poor soul!" he died Sunday morning, October 7, 1849?

Such, at least, is the way the poetic imagination sometimes works, as John Livingston Lowes has shown in his unusual book on Samuel Taylor Coleridge, *The Road to Xanadu.*

V

One of the values in studying Poe is that his achievement plays havoc with the pet distinctions that are often made between criticism and creation, classicism and romanticism. His critical and creative ability claim equal recognition. His criticism helps explain both his poetry and fiction, and vice versa.

In all phases of his work, imagination and reason collaborate in so curious and complex a fashion that at one moment he seems to be a classically minded romanticist, at another a romantically inclined classicist, if these terms are to be credited with any real meaning.

From his critical writing, for example, which included over 400 separate pieces, mostly book reviews and notices, may be drawn an aesthetics that combines the spirit of Aristotle with the spirit of Coleridge. In many of his poems there exists a peculiar contrast or tension between their rationally predicated structure and total effect, on the one hand, and their weirdly imaginative subject-matter and imagery, on the other, or in the clarity and economy of their wording versus the vague nadirs and zeniths of their emotive overtones, as they aspire or expire, in Walter Pater's phrase, toward "the condition of music." His arabesque tales have their moments of the Gothic sublime; his grotesque tales reflect a sometimes Voltairean sense of the ridiculous. In the resourceful personality of his detective, Dupin, as in the bewildering pages of *Eureka,* may be said to meet and blend the poet, the scientist, and the mathematician.

Today the most readable of Poe's critical pieces are those in which he formulates, as well as applies, his theory of poetry and his theory of the short story.

His conception of what a good poem should be is set forth most fully in his lecture, "The Poetic Principle." Although not written until near the end of his life and first published posthumously, this lecture contains substantially some of the same views he had expressed in his earliest discussion of poetry, the "Letter to B——," which serves as preface to the 1831 edition of his *Poems.* His views can best be understood as a reaction against vogues in poetry and poetic taste in the America of the first decades of the 19th Century.

Milton's *Paradise Lost* was widely read and admired. More recent long poems such as Joel Barlow's *The Columbiad* (1807) and Robert Pollok's *The Course of Time* (1827) commanded an audience. Criticism, both native and imported, spoke reverently of "sustained effort" as if it were one of the qualities a poem must display in order to deserve the highest praise. To Poe these were all manifestations of the same vogue. To show his detestation of it, he labeled it "the epic mania."

Sentimentalism and humanitarianism were potent forces in America, where they had become the emotional and ideological overflow and undercurrent of triumphant democracy, under the auspices of "New Light" religion. Popularized by enthusiastic advocates of progress, science was making headway in the land. Philosophy responded variously to the encroachments of science. The impact of sentimentalism, humanitarianism, science, and revitalized philosophy on the literature of the day was not by any means confined to prose. These forces invaded poetry in the form of emphasis on Duty and Truth; they led critics to insist that instruction, the communication of an inspiring moral, or "message," or "metre-making argument," was the real end and glory of a poem. To Poe, here was another vogue that needed some kind of counterblast. To convey his censure of it, he termed it "the heresy of the Didactic."

To combat "the epic mania," he advanced his striking dicta as to the proper length of a poem. To combat "the heresy of the Didactic," he developed his doctrine of the poem written to subserve but one main end—"the Human Aspiration for Supernal Beauty." The meaning of Supernal Beauty, its necessary connection with a "certain taint of sadness," the only relationship it can have to "the incitements of Passion, or the precepts of Duty, or even the lessons of Truth" in a poem's complex unity of effect—these are the matters he seeks to clarify.

Poe's "The Philosophy of Composition," telling how he wrote "The Raven," is valuable for its unorthodox version of the creative process. Instead of being inspired to communicate the nature and meaning of a compelling personal experience, Poe set out deliberately, he insists, to achieve an effect, and worked toward it as calculatingly as an engineer works out the construction of a bridge. Although Poe may have rationalized away the complexity of the actual process by which "The Raven" was written and may have underrated the rôle of his "unconscious" and its symbol-making, his analysis has the merits of debunking excessive emphasis on the inspirational passivity of the creative process and directing needed attention to the poet as an intelligent craftsman rather than an enraptured seer.

Before Poe the short story had flourished for decades in the American magazines, and most of its varieties had been either foreshadowed or actually developed. What was lacking was an adequate theory of the form that would define its end and scope and provide its practitioners with a better notion of how its artistry might be improved. In two reviews or notices of Hawthorne's *Twice-Told Tales* in *Graham's* for April and May, 1842, Poe took time out to expound such a theory. In commenting on proper length and on unity of effect in the short story, he applies to it two of the ideas that distinguish his theory of poetry, but shows wherein the range of effects in the prose tale is broader than in the poem. His other principles—originality, economy of means, and structural logic—were designed to correct the stereotyped themes and treatment, the excess verbiage, the sprawling lack of narrative symmetry which characterized the usual product of the magazines but which were so conspicuously transcended in the inimitable practice of Hawthorne.

To put a characteristic poem by Poe alongside one by Emerson or Whitman is a most illuminating exercise. Both Poe's "To Helen" and Emerson's "Each and All" are concerned with the subject of Beauty, but whereas Emerson develops the subject by presenting an interlinked set of aphoristic truths with illustrative material and ends with his personal experience of a supreme truth, Poe, from the first line to the last, is giving the reader a direct experience of

Beauty. Poe's "The City in the Sea" and Whitman's "Crossing Brooklyn Ferry" are both poems that have to do with a city and with water, with death and with immortality, but whereas Whitman is investing observed actuality with meaning, Poe conveys his meaning through suspension of our disbelief in a weird domain that lies beyond reality and is in process of symbolical convulsion.

Perspectives quite as valuable may be gained when a characteristic story by Poe is read in connection with one, say, by Hawthorne, or by Hemingway. Both Poe's "The Masque of the Red Death" and Hawthorne's "The Maypole of Merry Mount" are stories about masqueraders making merry before their doom overtakes them, but whereas Hawthorne is dramatizing an anecdote out of the history of New England for the purpose of evaluating two opposed ethical philosophies and of allegorizing life's dualism of jollity and gloom, Poe is primarily concerned with creating an effect of horror in the reader by first building up an exotic setting of ominous contrasts and then contriving a single shattering climactic episode. Poe's "The Cask of Amontillado" and Hemingway's "The Killers" are both stories of revenge, but whereas Hemingway's is "a slice of life" from the roaring 1920's, underscoring for us the decadence of a gangster-infested society, Poe's story unfolds, step by step, the execution of a perfect crime in a designed and dateless "scene" out of the Italy of melodrama with no discoverable social criticism in his mordant ironies.

It would be a mistake, however, to conclude from such comparative study that Poe is primarily a technician who makes few intellectual demands on his readers, that his art at its best was never rooted in real experience and has little to offer in the way of a criticism of life. *Eureka,* wherein he seeks to unravel the "plot of God," makes intellectual demands of the severest kind upon its readers. Some of the concepts discussed in *Eureka* are assumed or implied or explicitly present in his poems and tales. Brooding over these concepts—often under the stimulus of incidents in his actual life—constituted the very real experience in which much of his art was rooted. There is implicit criticism of life in many of his most impressionistic poems and tales in that they leave the reader speculating on some of the fundamental problems of existence and of the self. The dualism which Poe seeks to resolve in *Eureka*—the dualism of unity versus diffusion, of the One and the Many—appears in much of his poetry as a contrast between two worlds—on the one hand, the world of order, permanence, perfection, timelessness, immortality, spirit; on the other, that of disorder, change, imperfection, time, death, matter. The subtle relations of spirit and matter, of soul and body, are involved in some of his greatest stories, such as "Ligeia" and "The Fall of the House of Usher." In the preface to the first collected edition of his tales, he thus refuted the charge that he was merely an imitator of the kind of "Germanism" associated with the Gothic romance: "If in many of my productions terror has been the thesis, I maintain that terror is not of Germany but of the soul—."

VI

Three of Poe's tales of ratiocination—"The Murders in the Rue Morgue" (1841), "The Mystery of Marie Rogêt" (1842-3), and "The Purloined Letter" (1844)—had the distinction of establishing the detective story as a genre of modern fiction and anticipating the main patterns and devices which have marked its later evolution by a host of writers, from Conan Doyle and Anna Katharine Green to Agatha Christie, Dashiell Hammett, and Raymond Chandler. There had been puzzle and mystery tales long before Poe, of course, but the story making use of a "detective" had not been invented, for the simple reason that there were as yet no "detectives" in actuality. In the early 1800's the "detective" came into existence when the police systems of cities such as Paris and London developed departments of criminal investigation. Memoirs of men in these departments were soon published. Poe happened to read those of François Eugène Vidocq, of the Paris Sûreté, issued in 1829. They inspired him to create his detective, Auguste Dupin, who is the master mind of all these stories. Each has its setting in Paris, although "The Mystery of Marie Rogêt" was based on an actual New York murder case, that of Mary Cecilia Rogers, in July, 1841. One of the foremost modern connoisseurs of the detective story, Howard Haycraft, who has written its history in *Murder for Pleasure*, ranks "The Purloined Letter" as the best of Poe's three originals. There is considerable likelihood that Poe's review of Dickens' *Barnaby Rudge* in *Graham's* for February, 1842, influenced Dickens' intentions in *The Mystery of Edwin Drood,* which would undoubtedly be one of the world's great detective stories had its author lived to finish it.

Most of Poe's earliest stories—those produced at Baltimore between 1831 and 1835—were originally done in a spirit of satirical burlesque. To be entitled *Tales of the Folio Club,* they were at first eleven in number, but were probably increased to sixteen. Each was conceived as the contribution of a member of this fictitious Club and was intended to parody either a well-known author or a literary clique or fad. Mr. Snap, the president of the Folio Club, was formerly in the service of the *Down-East Review*. Messrs. Convolvulus Gondola, De Rerum Naturâ, Solomon Seadrift, Horribile Dictu, Blackwood Blackwood, Rouge-et-Noir, and Chronologos Chronology were among the narrators. As a group of satirical burlesques, however, Poe was unable to get his *Tales of the Folio Club* accepted for publication. Consequently he toned them down, offered them to magazines separately as seriously conceived tales, and scored his first successes. What is important to realize is that, from the outset, satirical burlesque was as strong a motif in his writing of fiction as was the creating of horror or terror. One is reminded of Henry Fielding, Jane Austen, and Thackeray, all of whom got interested in serious fiction after parodying the popular fiction of their day. In their case, the critical spirit, which was, so to speak, the animus of their first work, persisted in all they did. Poe, too, never lost his original motivation. From time to time he returned to the satirical sketch and strove for humor as one of the effects possible in the prose tale. Even in his most serious work, *Eureka*, the satirical and humorous Poe is very much in evidence in the opening pages. "The Literary Life of Thingum Bob, Esq." (1844) and "Some Words with a Mummy" (1845) represent the range of Poe's humor and satire while in the prime of his powers. In the latter piece, Poe's attitude toward democracy should not occasion surprise. In common with H. H. Brackenridge, James Fenimore Cooper, and many other good Americans before the Civil War, Poe feared lest the democratic principle of majority rule might lead to a tyranny of "the rascall many," under which the rights of the individual and of minorities would not be respected. Such distrust of one of the aspects of democracy is as old as Plato's *Republic*.

VII

No writer ever made a greater mistake in choosing a literary executor than did Poe. The Reverend Rufus W. Griswold, whom Poe requested to act in this capacity, was at that time the leading anthologist of American poetry. He was also an arch Philistine. He saw to it that an edition of Poe's works was ready shortly after his death, but he used Poe, in his memoir to this edition and elsewhere, as an awful object lesson to point the evils of intemperance. Not only did Griswold exaggerate Poe's vices, but he also invented some for him. Thus did the spirit of moralistic reform, one of the tendencies that Poe deplored and that was to continue running rampant in the decade after his death, seize upon him and, by distorting his character as a man, cast a shadow over his reputation as a writer.

From out that shadow, however, there was little danger that Poe would be lifted nevermore! George Graham, his former employer, and Sarah Helen Whitman, who had loved him, came forward in his defense. Charles Baudelaire, who in 1848 became the first of Poe's French translators, took Griswold to task. Modern Poe scholarship and criticism, under the leadership of Killis Campbell, James Southall Wilson, and Arthur Hobson Quinn, have gone a long way toward resurrecting the real Poe and doing justice to his mind and art.

Perhaps Professor Quinn has most effectively described the outcome: "His fame is now secure. The America in which he could find no adequate reward treasures every word he wrote, and in every city in which he lived, except the city of his birth, stands a lasting memorial to him. He has become a world artist and through the translations of his writings he speaks today to every civilized country. He has won this wide recognition by no persistent clamor of a cult, but by the royal right of preëminence. For today, nearly a hundred years since his death, he remains not only the one American, but also the one writer in the English language, who was at once foremost in criticism, supreme in fiction, and in poetry destined to be immortal."

[The most authoritative biography is Arthur Hobson Quinn's *Edgar Allan Poe: A Critical Biography* (New York, 1941). Others are Hervey Allen's *Israfel* (New York, 1926), Mary E. Phillips' *Edgar Allan Poe, the Man* (Philadelphia, 1926), James A. Harrison's *Life and Letters of Edgar Allan Poe* (New York, 1903) and George E. Woodberry's *The Life of Edgar Allan Poe* (Boston, 1909), each in two volumes, although *Israfel* is available in a one-volume edition, revised 1934. Killis Campbell's *The Mind of Poe* (Cambridge, 1933) is one of the most important contributions to Poe scholarship. Stimulating essays on various aspects of Poe's work are to be found in Paul Elmer More's *Shelburne Essays: First Series* (Boston, 1904) and *The Demon of the Absolute* (Princeton, 1928); James Southall Wilson's edition of *Tales of Edgar Allan Poe* (New York, 1927) in Modern Student's Library; Arthur Hobson Quinn's edition of *The Complete Poems and Stories of Edgar Allan Poe with Selections from His Critical Writings,* in two volumes, New York, 1946; Margaret Alterton's and Hardin Craig's *Poe* (New York, 1935) in American Writers Series; Norman Foerster's *American Criticism* (Boston, 1928); and H. W. Wells' *The American Way of Poetry* (New York, 1943). A destructive critique of Poe is included in Ivor Winters' *Maule's Curse* (Norfolk, Conn., 1938). F. O. Matthiessen's re-evaluation of Poe for the forthcoming *The Literary History of the United States* has been printed in *The Sewanee Review,* LIV (Spring, 1946) 175-205. For variations in the texts of Poe's poems, consult Killis Campbell's edition of *The Poems of Edgar Allan Poe* (Boston, 1917).]

SONNET—TO SCIENCE
[1829]

Science! true daughter of Old Time thou
    art!
Who alterest all things with thy peering
    eyes.
Why preyest thou thus upon the poet's
    heart,
Vulture, whose wings are dull realities?
How should he love thee? or how deem
    thee wise,   5
Who wouldst not leave him in his wander-
    ing
To seek for treasure in the jewelled skies,
Albeit he soared with an undaunted wing?
Hast thou not dragged Diana from her
    car?
And driven the Hamadryad from the
    wood   10
To seek a shelter in some happier star?

Hast thou not torn the Naiad from her
    flood,
The Elfin from the green grass, and from
    me
The summer dream beneath the tamarind
    tree?

TO HELEN
[1831]

Helen, thy beauty is to me
    Like those Nicéan [1] barks of yore,
That gently, o'er a perfumed sea,
    The weary, way-worn wanderer bore
    To his own native shore.   5

On desperate seas long wont to roam,
    Thy hyacinth hair, thy classic face,
Thy Naiad airs have brought me home

---

[1] This adjective, used primarily for its sound, was probably suggested by the journey of the poet Catullus to Nicasa.

To the glory that was Greece,
And the grandeur that was Rome.　10

Lo! in yon brilliant window-niche
How statue-like I see thee stand,
The agate lamp within thy hand!
Ah, Psyche, from the regions which
Are Holy-Land!　15

LENORE
[1831]

Ah, broken is the golden bowl! the spirit
　flown forever!
Let the bell toll!—a saintly soul floats on
　the Stygian river;
And, Guy De Vere, hast *thou* no tear?—
　weep now or never more!
See! on yon drear and rigid bier low lies
　thy love, Lenore!
Come! let the burial rite be read—the
　funeral song be sung!—　5
An anthem for the queenliest dead that
　ever died so young—
A dirge for her the doubly dead in that
　she died so young.

"Wretches! ye loved her for her wealth
　and hated her for her pride,
And when she fell in feeble health, ye
　blessed her—that she died!
How *shall* the ritual, then, be read—the
　requiem how be sung　10
By you—by yours, the evil eye,—by yours,
　the slanderous tongue
That did to death the innocence that died,
　and died so young?"

Peccavimus; [2] but rave not thus! and let a
　Sabbath song
Go up to God so solemnly the dead may
　feel no wrong!
The sweet Lenore hath "gone before," with
　Hope, that flew beside,　15
Leaving thee wild for the dear child that
　should have been thy bride—
For her, the fair and *debonair,* that now
　so lowly lies,
The life upon her yellow hair but not
　within her eyes—

The life still there, upon her hair—the
　death upon her eyes.

"Avaunt! to-night my heart is light. No
　dirge will I upraise,　20
But waft the angel on her flight with a
　Paean of old days!
Let *no* bell toll, then,—lest her soul, amid
　its hallowed mirth,
Should catch the note, as it doth float—
　up from the damnèd Earth!
To friends above, from fiends below, the
　indignant ghost is riven—
From Hell unto a high estate far up
　within the Heaven—　25
From grief and groan, to a golden throne,
　beside the King of Heaven."

THE CITY IN THE SEA
[1831]

Lo! Death has reared himself a throne
In a strange city lying alone
Far down within the dim West,
Where the good and the bad and the
　worst and the best
Have gone to their eternal rest.　5
There shrines and palaces and towers
(Time-eaten towers that tremble not!)
Resemble nothing that is ours.
Around, by lifting winds forgot,
Resignedly beneath the sky　10
The melancholy waters lie.

No rays from the holy heaven come down
On the long night-time of that town;
But light from out the lurid sea
Streams up the turrets silently—　15
Gleams up the pinnacles far and free—
Up domes—up spires—up kingly halls—
Up fanes—up Babylon-like walls—
Up shadowy long-forgotten bowers
Of sculptured ivy and stone flowers—　20
Up many and many a marvellous shrine
Whose wreathèd friezes intertwine
The viol, the violet, and the vine.
Resignedly beneath the sky
The melancholy waters lie.　25

---

[2] We have sinned.

So blend the turrets and shadows there
That all seem pendulous in air,
While from a proud tower in the town
Death looks gigantically down.

There open fanes and gaping graves   30
Yawn level with the luminous waves;
But not the riches there that lie
In each idol's diamond eye—
Not the gaily-jewelled dead
Tempt the waters from their bed;   35
For no ripples curl, alas!
Along that wilderness of glass—
No swellings tell that winds may be
Upon some far-off happier sea—
No heavings hint that winds have been 40
On seas less hideously serene.

But lo, a stir is in the air!
The wave—there is a movement there!
As if the towers had thrust aside,
In slightly sinking, the dull tide—   45
As if their tops had feebly given
A void within the filmy Heaven.
The waves have now a redder glow—
The hours are breathing faint and low—
And when, amid no earthly moans,   50
Down, down that town shall settle hence,
Hell, rising from a thousand thrones,
Shall do it reverence.

THE SLEEPER
[1831]

At midnight, in the month of June,
I stand beneath the mystic moon.
An opiate vapour, dewy, dim,
Exhales from out her golden rim,
And, softly dripping, drop by drop,   5
Upon the quiet mountain-top,
Steals drowsily and musically
Into the universal valley.
The rosemary nods upon the grave;
The lily lolls upon the wave;   10
Wrapping the fog about its breast,
The ruin moulders into rest;
Looking like Lethe, see! the lake
A conscious slumber seems to take,

And would not, for the world, awake.   15
All Beauty sleeps!—and lo! where lies
(Her casement open to the skies)
Irene, with her Destinies!

O lady bright! can it be right—
This window open to the night?   20
The wanton airs, from the tree-top,
Laughingly through the lattice drop—
The bodiless airs, a wizard rout,
Flit through thy chamber in and out,
And wave the curtain canopy   25
So fitfully—so fearfully—
Above the closed and fringèd lid
'Neath which thy slumb'ring soul lies hid,
That, o'er the floor and down the wall,
Like ghosts the shadows rise and fall! 30
O lady dear, hast thou no fear?
Why and what art thou dreaming here?
Sure thou art come o'er far-off seas,
A wonder to these garden trees!
Strange is thy pallor! strange thy dress! 35
Strange, above all, thy length of tress,
And this all solemn silentness!

The lady sleeps! Oh, may her sleep,
Which is enduring, so be deep!
Heaven have her in its sacred keep!   40
This chamber changed for one more holy,
This bed for one more melancholy,
I pray to God that she may lie
Forever with unopened eye,
While the dim sheeted ghosts go by!   45

My love, she sleeps! Oh, may her sleep,
As it is lasting, so be deep!
Soft may the worms about her creep!
Far in the forest, dim and old,
For her may some tall vault unfold—   50
Some vault that oft hath flung its black
And winged panels fluttering back,
Triumphant, o'er the crested palls,
Of her grand family funerals—
Some sepulchre, remote, alone,   55
Against whose portal she hath thrown,
In childhood, many an idle stone—
Some tomb from out whose sounding door
She ne'er shall force an echo more,
Thrilling to think, poor child of sin! 60
It was the dead who groaned within!

ISRAFEL
[1831]

In Heaven a spirit doth dwell
"Whose heart-strings are a lute;"
None sing so wildly well
As the angel Israfel,
And the giddy stars (so legends tell), 5
Ceasing their hymns, attend the spell
  Of his voice, all mute.[3]

Tottering above
  In her highest noon,
The enamoured moon   10
Blushes with love,
  While, to listen, the red levin
(With the rapid Pleiads, even,
  Which were seven)
Pauses in Heaven.   15

And they say (the starry choir
  And the other listening things)
That Israfeli's fire
Is owing to that lyre
  By which he sits and sings—   20
The trembling living wire
Of those unusual strings.

But the skies that angel trod,
  Where deep thoughts are a duty—
Where Love's a grown-up God—   25
  Where the Houri glances are
Imbued with all the beauty
  Which we worship in a star.

Therefore thou art not wrong,
  Israfeli, who despisest   30
An unimpassioned song;
To thee the laurels belong,
  Best bard, because the wisest!
Merrily live, and long!

The ecstasies above   35
  With thy burning measures suit—
Thy grief, thy joy, thy hate, thy love,
  With the fervour of thy lute—
Well may the stars be mute!

Yes, Heaven is thine; but this   40
  Is a world of sweets and sours;

Our flowers are merely—flowers,
And the shadow of thy perfect bliss
  Is the sunshine of ours.

If I could dwell   45
Where Israfel
  Hath dwelt, and he where I,
He might not sing so wildly well
  A mortal melody,
While a bolder note than this might
    swell   50
  From my lyre within the sky.

THE COLISEUM
[1845 (1833)]

Type of the antique Rome! Rich reliquary
Of lofty contemplation left to Time
By buried centuries of pomp and power!
At length—at length—after so many days
Of weary pilgrimage and burning thirst 5
  (Thirst for the springs of lore that in
      thee lie,)
I kneel, an altered and an humble man,
Amid thy shadows, and so drink within
My very soul thy grandeur, gloom, and
    glory!

Vastness! and Age! and Memories of
    Eld!   10
Silence! and Desolation! and dim Night!
I feel ye now—I feel ye in your strength—
O spells more sure than e'er Judaean king
Taught in the gardens of Gethsemane!
O charms more potent than the rapt
    Chaldee   15
Ever drew down from out the quiet stars![4]
Here, where a hero fell, a column falls!
Here, where the mimic eagle glared in
    gold,
A midnight vigil holds the swarthy bat!
Here, where the dames of Rome their
    gilded hair   20

---

[3] The angel Israfel is mentioned in the
Koran; the quoted line has been traced
to Thomas Moore's *Lalla Rookh* and Pierre
Jean de Béranger's "Le Refus."

[4] The references are to Christ and to
Chaldean astrology.

Waved to the wind, now wave the reed and
 thistle!
Here, where on golden throne the monarch
 lolled,
Glides, spectre-like, unto his marble home,
Lit by the wan light of the hornèd moon,
The swift and silent lizard of the stones! 25

But stay! these walls—these ivy-clad ar-
 cades—
These mouldering plinths—these sad and
 blackened shafts—
These vague entablatures—this crumbling
 frieze—
These shattered cornices—this wreck—this
 ruin—
These stones—alas! these gray stones—are
 they all—   30
All of the famed, and the colossal left
By the corrosive Hours to Fate and me?

"Not all"—the Echoes answer me—"not
 all!
Prophetic sounds and loud, arise forever
From us, and from all Ruin, unto the
 wise,   35
As melody from Memnon to the Sun.[5]
We rule the hearts of mightiest men—we
 rule
With a despotic sway all giant minds.
We are not impotent—we pallid stones.
Not all our power is gone—not all our
 fame—   40
Not all the magic of our high renown—
Not all the wonder that encircles us—
Not all the mysteries that in us lie—
Not all the memories that hang upon
And cling around about us as a garment, 45
Clothing us in a robe of more than glory."

TO ONE IN PARADISE
[1845 (1834)]

Thou wast all that to me, love,
 For which my soul did pine—
A green isle in the sea, love,
 A fountain and a shrine,
All wreathed with fairy fruits and flow-
 ers,   5

And all the flowers were mine.
Ah, dream too bright to last!

Ah, starry Hope! that didst arise
But to be overcast!
A voice from out the Future cries,   10
"On! on!"—but o'er the Past
 (Dim gulf!) my spirit hovering lies
Mute, motionless, aghast!

For, alas! alas! with me
 The light of Life is o'er!   15
No more—no more—no more—
(Such language holds the solemn sea
 To the sands upon the shore)
Shall bloom the thunder-blasted tree,
 Or the stricken eagle soar!   20

And all my days are trances,
 And all my nightly dreams
Are where thy dark eye glances,
 And where thy footstep gleams—
In what ethereal dances,   25
 By what eternal streams.

THE RAVEN
[1845]

Once upon a midnight dreary, while I
 pondered, weak and weary,
Over many a quaint and curious volume
 of forgotten lore,
While I nodded, nearly napping, suddenly
 there came a tapping,
As of some one gently rapping, rapping
 at my chamber door.
" 'Tis some visiter," I muttered, "tapping
 at my chamber door—   5
Only this, and nothing more."

Ah, distinctly I remember it was in the
 bleak December,
And each separate dying ember wrought
 its ghost upon the floor.
Eagerly I wished the morrow;—vainly I
 had sought to borrow

---

[5] At Thebes, the statue of Amenhotep
III, whom the Greeks called Memnon, was
supposed to give forth musical sounds
when touched by the sun's first rays.

From my books surcease of sorrow—sorrow for the lost Lenore—   10
For the rare and radiant maiden whom the angels name Lenore—
  Nameless here for evermore.

And the silken, sad, uncertain rustling of each purple curtain
Thrilled me—filled me with fantastic terrors never felt before;
So that now, to still the beating of my heart, I stood repeating,   15
" 'Tis some visiter entreating entrance at my chamber door—
Some late visiter entreating entrance at my chamber door;—
  This it is and nothing more."

Presently my soul grew stronger; hesitating then no longer,
"Sir," said I, "or Madam, truly your forgiveness I implore;   20
But the fact is I was napping, and so gently you came rapping,
And so faintly you came tapping, tapping at my chamber door,
That I scarce was sure I heard you"—here I opened wide the door;—
  Darkness there, and nothing more.

Deep into that darkness peering, long I stood there wondering, fearing, 25
Doubting, dreaming dreams no mortal ever dared to dream before;
But the silence was unbroken, and the stillness gave no token,
And the only word there spoken was the whispered word, "Lenore!"
This I whispered, and an echo murmured back the word, "Lenore!"
  Merely this and nothing more.

Back into the chamber turning, all my soul within me burning,
Soon I heard again a tapping somewhat louder than before.
"Surely," said I, "surely that is something at my window lattice;
Let me see, then, what thereat is, and this mystery explore—

Let my heart be still a moment and this mystery explore;—   35
  'Tis the wind and nothing more!"

Open here I flung the shutter, when, with many a flirt and flutter,
In there stepped a stately raven of the saintly days of yore;
Not the least obeisance made he; not an instant stopped or stayed he;
But, with mien of lord or lady, perched above my chamber door—   40
Perched upon a bust of Pallas just above my chamber door—
  Perched, and sat, and nothing more.

Then this ebony bird beguiling my sad fancy into smiling,
By the grave and stern decorum of the countenance it wore,
"Though thy crest be shorn and shaven, thou," I said, "art sure no craven, 45
Ghastly grim and ancient raven wandering from the Nightly shore—
Tell me what thy lordly name is on the Night's Plutonian shore!"
  Quoth the raven, "Nevermore."

Much I marveled this ungainly fowl to hear discourse so plainly,
Though its answer little meaning—little relevancy bore;   50
For we cannot help agreeing that no living human being
Ever yet was blessed with seeing bird above his chamber door—
Bird or beast upon the sculptured bust above his chamber door,
  With such name as "Nevermore."

But the raven, sitting lonely on the placid bust, spoke only   55
That one word, as if his soul in that one word he did outpour.
Nothing farther then he uttered—not a feather then he fluttered—
Till I scarcely more than muttered, "Other friends have flown before—
On the morrow *he* will leave me, as my hopes have flown before."
  Then the bird said, "Nevermore."   60

Startled at the stillness broken by reply
    so aptly spoken,
"Doubtless," said I, "what it utters is its
    only stock and store
Caught from some unhappy master whom
    unmerciful Disaster
Followed fast and followed faster till his
    songs one burden bore—
Till the dirges of his Hope that melan-
    choly burden bore   65
  Of 'Never—nevermore.' "

But the raven still beguiling all my sad
    soul into smiling,
Straight I wheeled a cushioned seat in
    front of bird and bust and door;
Then, upon the velvet sinking, I betook
    myself to linking
Fancy unto fancy, thinking what this om-
    inous bird of yore—   70
What this grim, ungainly, ghastly, gaunt,
    and ominous bird of yore
    Meant in croaking "Nevermore."

This I sat engaged in guessing, but no
    syllable expressing
To the fowl whose fiery eyes now burned
    into my bosom's core;
This and more I sat divining, with my
    head at ease reclining   75
On the cushion's velvet lining that the
    lamplight gloated o'er,
But whose velvet violet lining with the
    lamplight gloating o'er,
She shall press, ah, nevermore!

Then, methought, the air grew denser, per-
    fumed from an unseen censer
Swung by angels whose faint foot-falls
    tinkled on the tufted floor.   80
"Wretch," I cried, "thy God hath lent thee
    —by these angels he hath sent thee
Respite—respite and nepenthe from thy
    memories of Lenore!
Quaff, oh quaff this kind nepenthe and for-
    get this lost Lenore!"
  Quoth the raven, "Nevermore."

"Prophet!" said I, "thing of evil!—prophet
    still, if bird or devil!—   85

Whether Tempter sent, or whether tempest
    tossed thee here ashore,
Desolate yet all undaunted, on this desert
    land enchanted—
On this home by Horror haunted—tell me
    truly, I implore—
Is there—*is* there balm in Gilead?—tell
    me—tell me, I implore!"
  Quoth the raven, "Nevermore."   90

"Prophet!" said I, "thing of evil—prophet
    still, if bird or devil!
By that Heaven that bends above us—by
    that God we both adore—
Tell this soul with sorrow laden if, within
    the distant Aidenn,[6]
It shall clasp a sainted maiden whom the
    angels name Lenore—
Clasp a rare and radiant maiden whom
    the angels name Lenore."   95
  Quoth the raven, "Nevermore."

"Be that word our sign of parting, bird or
    fiend!" I shrieked, upstarting—
"Get thee back into the tempest and the
    Night's Plutonian shore!
Leave no black plume as a token of that
    lie thy soul hath spoken!
Leave my loneliness unbroken!—quit the
    bust above my door!   100
Take thy beak from out my heart, and take
    thy form from off my door!"
  Quoth the raven, "Nevermore."

And the raven, never flitting, still is sitting,
    still is sitting
On the pallid bust of Pallas just above my
    chamber door;
And his eyes have all the seeming of a
    demon's that is dreaming,   105
And the lamplight o'er him streaming
    throws his shadow on the floor;[7]

---

[6] Poe's spelling of Eden for the rhyme.

[7] Poe explains in one of his letters:
"*My* conception was that of the bracket
candelabrum affixed against the wall, high
up above the door and bust, as is often
seen in the English palaces, and even in
some of the better houses of New York."

And my soul from out that shadow that
  lies floating on the floor
Shall be lifted—nevermore!

ULALUME — A BALLAD
[1850 (1847)]

The skies they were ashen and sober;
  The leaves they were crispèd and sere—
  The leaves they were withering and sere;
It was night in the lonesome October
  Of my most immemorial year;   5
It was hard by the dim lake of Auber,
  In the misty mid region of Weir—
It was down by the dank tarn of Auber,
  In the ghoul-haunted woodland of Weir.[8]

Here once, through an alley Titanic,   10
  Of cypress, I roamed with my Soul—
  Of cypress, with Psyche, my Soul.
These were days when my heart was vol-
    canic
  As the scoriac rivers that roll—
  As the lavas that restlessly roll   15
Their sulphurous currents down Yaanek [9]
  In the ultimate climes of the Pole—
That groan as they roll down Mount
    Yaanek
  In the realms of the boreal pole.

Our talk had been serious and sober,   20
  But our thoughts they were palsied and
    sere—
  Our memories were treacherous and
    sere—
For we knew not the month was October,
  And we marked not the night of the
    year—
  (Ah, night of all nights in the year!) 25
We noted not the dim lake of Auber—
  (Though once we had journeyed down
    here)—
Remembered not the dank tarn of Auber,
  Nor the ghoul-haunted woodland of
    Weir.

And now, as the night was senescent   30
  And star-dials pointed to morn—
  As the star-dials hinted of morn—
At the end of our path a liquescent
  And nebulous lustre was born,

Out of which a miraculous crescent   35
  Arose with a duplicate horn—
Astarte's bediamonded crescent
  Distinct with its duplicate horn.[10]

And I said—"She is warmer than Dian:
  She rolls through an ether of sighs— 40
  She revels in a region of sighs:
She has seen that the tears are not dry on
  These cheeks, where the worm never dies,
And has come past the stars of the Lion [11]
  To point us the path to the skies— 45
  To the Lethean peace of the skies—
Come up, in despite of the Lion,
  To shine on us with her bright eyes—
Come up through the lair of the Lion,
  With love in her luminous eyes."   50

But Psyche, uplifting her finger,
  Said—"Sadly this star I mistrust—
  Her pallor I strangely mistrust:—
Oh, hasten!—oh, let us not linger!
  Oh, fly!—let us fly!—for we must." 55
In terror she spoke, letting sink her
  Wings till they trailed in the dust—
In agony sobbed, letting sink her
  Plumes till they trailed in the dust—
  Till they sorrowfully trailed in the
    dust.   60

I replied—"This is nothing but dreaming:
  Let us on by this tremulous light!
  Let us bathe in this crystalline light!
Its Sibyllic splendor is beaming
  With Hope and in Beauty to-night:— 65
  See!—it flickers up the sky through the
    night!
Ah, we safely may trust to its gleaming,
  And be sure it will lead us aright—
We safely may trust to a gleaming
  That cannot but guide us aright, 70
  Since it flickers up to Heaven through
    the night."

---

[8] Imaginary geography.

[9] More imaginary geography.

[10] Astarte, the Phrygian moon goddess, as a symbol of voluptuous passion, is placed in contrast with the Greek and Roman moon goddess, Artemis or Diana, noted for her chastity.

[11] The constellation Leo.

Thus I pacified Psyche and kissed her,
 And tempted her out of her gloom—
 And conquered her scruples and gloom;
And we passed to the end of the vista, 75
 But were stopped by the door of a
  tomb—
 By the door of a legended tomb;
And I said—"What is written, sweet sister,
 On the door of this legended tomb?"
 She replied—"Ulalume—Ulalume— 80
 'Tis the vault of thy lost Ulalume!"

Then my heart it grew ashen and sober
 As the leaves that were crispèd and
  sere—
 As the leaves that were withering and
  sere,
And I cried—"It was surely October 85
 On *this* very night of last year
 That I journeyed—I journeyed down
  here—
 That I brought a dread burden down
  here—
 On this night of all nights in the year,
 Ah, what demon has tempted me
  here? 90
Well I know, now, this dim lake of
  Auber—
 This misty mid region of Weir—
Well I know, now, this dank tarn of Auber,
 This ghoul-haunted woodland of Weir."

[Said *we*, then—the two, then—"Ah, can
  it 95
 Have been that the woodlandish ghouls,
 The pitiful, the merciful ghouls—
To bar up our way and to ban it
 From the secret that lies in these
  wolds—
 From the thing that lies hidden in these
  wolds— 100
Had drawn up the spectre of a planet
 From the limbo of lunary souls,
This sinfully scintillant planet
 From the Hell of the planetary souls?"][12]

ELDORADO
[1850 (1849)]

Gaily bedight,
A gallant knight,

In sunshine and in shadow,
 Had journeyed long,
 Singing a song, 5
In search of Eldorado.

But he grew old—
This knight so bold—
And o'er his heart a shadow
 Fell as he found 10
 No spot of ground
That looked like Eldorado.

And, as his strength
Failed him at length,
He met a pilgrim shadow— 15
 "Shadow," said he,
 "Where can it be—
This land of Eldorado?"

"Over the Mountains
 Of the Moon, 20
Down the Valley of the Shadow,
 Ride, boldly ride,"
 The shade replied,—
"If you seek for Eldorado!"

ANNABEL LEE
[1850 (1849)]

It was many and many a year ago,
 In a kingdom by the sea,
That a maiden there lived whom you may
  know
 By the name of Annabel Lee:
And this maiden she lived with no other
  thought 5
 Than to love and be loved by me.

She was a child and *I* was a child,
 In this kingdom by the sea;
But we loved with a love that was more
  than love—
 I and my Annabel Lee— 10
With a love that the wingèd seraphs of
  heaven
 Coveted her and me.

[12] In *Works*, 1850, the last stanza is
omitted; it had been included in the original publication in the *American Whig
Review*.

And this was the reason that, long ago,
  In this kingdom by the sea,
A wind blew out of a cloud, chilling   15
  My beautiful Annabel Lee—
So that her highborn kinsmen came
  And bore her away from me,
To shut her up in a sepulchre
  In this kingdom by the sea.   20

The angels, not half so happy in Heaven,
  Went envying her and me:—
Yes, that was the reason (as all men know,
  In this kingdom by the sea)
That the wind came out of the cloud by
      night   25
  Chilling and killing my Annabel Lee.

But our love it was stronger by far than
      the love
  Of those who were older than we—
  Of many far wiser than we—
And neither the angels in Heaven above, 30
  Nor the demons down under the sea,
Can ever dissever my soul from the soul
  Of the beautiful Annabel Lee:—

For the moon never beams, without bring-
      ing me dreams
  Of the beautiful Annabel Lee;   35
And the stars never rise, but I feel the
      bright eyes
  Of the beautiful Annabel Lee;
And so, all the night-tide, I lie down by
      the side
Of my darling, my darling, my life and
      my bride
  In her sepulchre there by the sea—   40
  In her tomb by the sounding sea.

THE POETIC PRINCIPLE
[1850]

IN SPEAKING of the Poetic Principle,
I have no design to be either thorough or
profound. While discussing very much at
random the essentiality of what we call
Poetry, my principal purpose will be to
cite for consideration some few of those
minor English or American poems which

best suit my own taste, or which, upon
my own fancy, have left the most definite
impression. By "minor poems" I mean,
of course, poems of little length. And here,
in the beginning, permit me to say a few
words in regard to a somewhat peculiar
principle, which, whether rightfully or
wrongfully, has always had its influence
in my own critical estimate of the poem.
I hold that a long poem does not exist. I
maintain that the phrase, "a long poem," is
simply a flat contradiction in terms.

I need scarcely observe that a poem
deserves its title only inasmuch as it excites, by elevating the soul. The value of
the poem is in the ratio of this elevating
excitement. But all excitements are,
through a psychal necessity, transient.
That degree of excitement which would
entitle a poem to be so called at all, cannot be sustained throughout a composition
of any great length. After the lapse of half
an hour, at the very utmost, it flags—fails
—a revulsion ensues—and then the poem
is, in effect, and in fact, no longer such.

There are, no doubt, many who have
found difficulty in reconciling the critical
dictum that the "Paradise Lost" is to be
devoutly admired throughout, with the absolute impossibility of maintaining for it,
during perusal, the amount of enthusiasm
which that critical dictum would demand.
This great work, in fact, is to be regarded
as poetical only when, losing sight of that
vital requisite in all works of Art, Unity,
we view it merely as a series of minor
poems. If, to preserve its Unity—its totality of effect or impression—we read it
(as would be necessary) at a single sitting,
the result is but a constant alternation of
excitement and depression. After a passage
of what we feel to be true poetry, there
follows, inevitably, a passage of platitude
which no critical pre-judgment can force
us to admire; but if, upon completing the
work, we read it again, omitting the first
book—that is to say, commencing with the
second—we shall be surprised at now finding that admirable which we before condemned—that damnable which we had pre-

viously so much admired. It follows from all this that the ultimate, aggregate, or absolute effect of even the best epic under the sun, is a nullity—and this is precisely the fact.

In regard to the Iliad, we have, if not positive proof, at least very good reason, for believing it intended as a series of lyrics; but, granting the epic intention, I can say only that the work is based in an imperfect sense of Art. The modern epic is, of the supposititious ancient model, but an inconsiderate and blindfold imitation. But the day of these artistic anomalies is over. If, at any time, any very long poem *were* popular in reality, which I doubt, it is at least clear that no very long poem will ever be popular again.

That the extent of a poetical work is, *ceteris paribus*,[1] the measure of its merit, seems undoubtedly, when we thus state it, a proposition sufficiently absurd—yet we are indebted for it to the Quarterly Reviews. Surely there can be nothing in mere *size*, abstractly considered—there can be nothing in mere *bulk*, so far as a volume is concerned, which has so continuously elicited admiration from these saturnine pamphlets! A mountain, to be sure, by the mere sentiment of physical magnitude which it conveys, *does* impress us with a sense of the sublime—but no man is impressed after *this* fashion by the material grandeur of even "The Columbiad."[2] Even the Quarterlies have not instructed us to be so impressed by it. *As yet*, they have not *insisted* on our estimating Lamartine by the cubic foot, or Pollok by the pound[3] —but what else are we to *infer* from their continued prating about "sustained effort"? If, by "sustained effort," any little gentleman has accomplished an epic, let us frankly commend him for the effort—if this indeed be a thing commendable—but let us forbear praising the epic on the effort's account. It is to be hoped that common sense, in the time to come, will prefer deciding upon a work of art rather by the impression it makes, by the effect it produces, than by the time it took to

impress the effect, or by the amount of "sustained effort" which had been found necessary in effecting the impression. The fact is, that perseverance is one thing and genius quite another—nor can all the Quarterlies in Christendom confound them. By and by, this proposition, with many which I have just been urging, will be received as self-evident. In the mean time, by being generally condemned as falsities, they will not be essentially damaged as truths.

On the other hand, it is clear that a poem may be improperly brief. Undue brevity degenerates into mere epigrammatism. A *very* short poem, while now and then producing a brilliant or vivid, never produces a profound or enduring effect. There must be the steady pressing down of the stamp upon the wax. De Béranger has wrought innumerable things, pungent and spirit-stirring; but in general they have been too imponderous to stamp themselves deeply into the public attention, and thus, as so many feathers of fancy, have been blown aloft only to be whistled down the wind.[4]

A remarkable instance of the effect of undue brevity in depressing a poem—in keeping it out of the popular view—is afforded by the following exquisite little Serenade:[5]

I arise from dreams of thee
   In the first sweet sleep of night,

---

[1] Other things being equal.

[2] Joel Barlow (1754-1812), one of "the Connecticut wits," was the author of *The Columbiad* (1807), an epic in ten books.

[3] Alphonse de Lamartine (1790-1827) was one of the French romantic poets; Robert Pollok (1798?-1827), a Scottish poet, wrote *The Course of Time*, in two volumes (1827).

[4] Pierre Jean de Béranger (1780-1857) was the author of *Chansons*, collections of songs published in 1815, 1821, 1825, 1828, and 1833.

[5] In Shelley's *Poetical Works* (1839), this poem is entitled "Lines to an Indian Air."

When the winds are breathing low,
    And the stars are shining bright;
I arise from dreams of thee,
    And a spirit in my feet
Has led me—who knows how?—
    To thy chamber-window, sweet!

The wandering airs, they faint
    On the dark, the silent stream—
The champak odors fail
    Like sweet thoughts in a dream;
The nightingale's complaint,
    It dies upon her heart,
As I must die on thine,
    O, beloved as thou art!

O, lift me from the grass!
    I die, I faint, I fail!
Let thy love in kisses rain
    On my lips and eyelids pale.
My cheek is cold and white, alas!
    My heart beats loud and fast:
Oh! press it close to thine again,
    Where it will break at last!

Very few perhaps are familiar with these lines—yet no less a poet than Shelley is their author. Their warm, yet delicate and ethereal imagination will be appreciated by all—but by none so thoroughly as by him who has himself arisen from sweet dreams of one beloved to bathe in the aromatic air of a southern midsummer night.

One of the finest poems by Willis, the very best in my opinion which he has ever written, has no doubt, through this same defect of undue brevity, been kept back from its proper position, not less in the critical than in the popular view.[6]

The shadows lay along Broadway,
    'Twas near the twilight-tide—
And slowly there a lady fair
    Was walking in her pride.
Alone walk'd she; but, viewlessly,
    Walk'd spirits at her side.

Peace charm'd the street beneath her feet,
    And Honour charm'd the air;

And all astir looked kind on her,
    And call'd her good and fair—
For all God ever gave to her
    She kept with chary care.

She kept with care her beauties rare
    From lovers warm and true—
For her heart was cold to all but gold,
    And the rich came not to woo—
But honour'd well are charms to sell,
    If priests the selling do.

Now walking there was one more fair—
    A slight girl, lily-pale;
And she had unseen company
    To make the spirit quail—
'Twixt Want and Scorn she walk'd forlorn,
    And nothing could avail.

No mercy now can clear her brow
    For this world's peace to pray;
For, as love's wild prayer dissolved in air,
    Her woman's heart gave way!—
But the sin forgiven by Christ in Heaven
    By man is cursed alway!

In this composition we find it difficult to recognize the Willis who has written so many mere "verses of society." The lines are not only richly ideal, but full of energy; while they breathe an earnestness, an evident sincerity of sentiment, for which we look in vain throughout all the other works of this author.

While the epic mania—while the idea that, to merit in poetry, prolixity is indispensable—has for some years past been gradually dying out of the public mind by mere dint of its own absurdity, we find it succeeded by a heresy too palpably false to be long tolerated, but one which, in the brief period it has already endured, may be said to have accomplished more in the

---

[6] Nathaniel Parker Willis (1806-1867) was one of Poe's friends and a popular poet and essayist. This poem is entitled "Unseen Spirits" in his *Poems* (1850). A tribute to Poe appears in his *Hurry-Graphs* (1851), pp. 240-250.

corruption of our Poetical Literature than all its other enemies combined. I allude to the heresy of *The Didactic.* It has been assumed, tacitly and avowedly, directly and indirectly, that the ultimate object of all Poetry is Truth. Every poem, it is said, should inculcate a moral, and by this moral is the poetical merit of the work to be adjudged. We Americans especially have patronized this happy idea, and we Bostonians very especially have developed it in full. We have taken it into our heads that to write a poem simply for the poem's sake, and to acknowledge such to have been our design, would be to confess ourselves radically wanting in the true Poetic dignity and force:—but the simple fact is, that would we but permit ourselves to look into our own souls, we should immediately there discover that under the sun there neither exists nor *can* exist any work more thoroughly dignified, more supremely noble than this very poem, this poem *per se,* this poem which is a poem and nothing more, this poem written solely for the poem's sake.

With as deep a reverence for the True as ever inspired the bosom of man, I would nevertheless limit, in some measure, its modes of inculcation. I would limit to enforce them. I would not enfeeble them by dissipation. The demands of Truth are severe. She has no sympathy with the myrtles. All *that* which is so indispensable in Song is precisely all *that* with which *she* has nothing whatever to do. It is but making her a flaunting paradox to wreathe her in gems and flowers. In enforcing a truth, we need severity rather than efflorescence of language. We must be simple, precise, terse. We must be cool, calm, unimpassioned. In a word, we must be in that mood which, as nearly as possible, is the exact converse of the poetical. *He* must be blind indeed who does not perceive the radical and chasmal differences between the truthful and the poetical modes of inculcation. He must be theory-mad beyond redemption who, in spite of these differences, shall still persist in attempting

to reconcile the obstinate oils and waters of Poetry and Truth.

Dividing the world of mind into its three most immediately obvious distinctions, we have the Pure Intellect, Taste, and the Moral Sense. I place Taste in the middle because it is just this position which it occupies in the mind. It holds intimate relations with either extreme, but from the Moral Sense is separated by so faint a difference that Aristotle has not hesitated to place some of its operations among the virtues themselves. Nevertheless, we find the *offices* of the trio marked with a sufficient distinction. Just as the Intellect concerns itself with Truth, so Taste informs us of the Beautiful, while the Moral Sense is regardful of Duty. Of this latter, while Conscience teaches the obligation, and Reason the expediency, Taste contents herself with displaying the charms, waging war upon Vice solely on the ground of her deformity, her disproportion, her animosity to the fitting, to the appropriate, to the harmonious, in a word, to Beauty.

An immortal instinct deep within the spirit of man is thus plainly a sense of the Beautiful. This it is which administers to his delight in the manifold forms, and sounds, and odors, and sentiments, amid which he exists. And just as the lily is repeated in the lake, or the eyes of Amaryllis in the mirror, so is the mere oral or written repetition of these forms, and sounds, and colors, and odors, and sentiments, a duplicate source of delight. But this mere repetition is not poetry. He who shall simply sing, with however glowing enthusiasm, or with however vivid a truth of description, of the sights, and sounds, and odors, and colors, and senti- ments, which greet *him* in common with all mankind—he, I say, has yet failed to prove his divine title. There is still a some- thing in the distance which he has been unable to attain. We have still a thirst unquenchable, to allay which he has not shown us the crystal springs. This thirst belongs to the immortality of Man. It is at once a consequence and an indication of his perennial existence. It is the desire of the moth for the star. It is no mere appreciation of the Beauty before us—but a wild effort to reach the Beauty above. Inspired by an ecstatic prescience of the glories beyond the grave, we struggle by multiform combinations among the things and thoughts of Time to attain a portion of that Loveliness whose very elements, perhaps, appertain to eternity alone. And thus when by Poetry—or when by Music, the most entrancing of the Poetic moods—we find ourselves melted into tears, we weep then—not as the Abbate Gravina [7] supposes—through excess of pleasure, but through a certain, petulant, impatient sorrow at our inability to grasp *now*, wholly, here on earth, at once and forever, those divine and rapturous joys, of which *through* the poem or *through* the music, we attain to but brief and indeterminate glimpses.

The struggle to apprehend the supernal Loveliness—this struggle, on the part of souls fittingly constituted—has given to the world all *that* which it (the world) has ever been enabled at once to understand and to *feel* as poetic.

The Poetic Sentiment, of course, may develop itself in various modes—in Painting, in Sculpture, in Architecture, in the Dance—very especially in Music—and very peculiarly, and with a wide field, in the composition of the Landscape Garden. Our present theme, however, has regard only to its manifestation in words. And here let me speak briefly on the topic of rhythm. Contenting myself with the certainty that Music, in its various modes of metre, rhythm, and rhyme, is of so vast a moment in Poetry as never to be wisely rejected—is so vitally important an adjunct that he is simply silly who declines its assistance—I will not now pause to maintain its absolute essentiality. It is in Music, perhaps, that the soul most nearly attains the great end for which, when inspired by the Poetic Sentiment, it struggles—the creation of supernal Beauty. It *may* be, indeed, that here this sublime end is, now

and then, attained in *fact*. We are often made to feel, with a shivering delight, that from an earthly harp are stricken notes which *cannot* have been unfamiliar to the angels. And thus there can be little doubt that in the union of Poetry with Music in its popular sense, we shall find the widest field for the Poetic development. The old Bards and Minnesingers had advantages which we do not possess—and Thomas Moore, singing his own songs, was, in the most legitimate manner, perfecting them as poems.[8]

To recapitulate, then:—I would define, in brief, the Poetry of words as *The Rhythmical Creation of Beauty*. Its sole arbiter is Taste. With the Intellect or with the Conscience, it has only collateral relations. Unless incidentally, it has no concern whatever either with Duty or with Truth.

A few words, however, in explanation. *That* pleasure which is at once the most pure, the most elevating, and the most intense, is derived, I maintain, from the contemplation of the Beautiful. In the contemplation of Beauty we alone find it possible to attain that pleasurable elevation, or excitement, *of the soul*, which we recognize as the Poetic Sentiment, and which is so easily distinguished from Truth, which is the satisfaction of the Reason, or from Passion, which is the excitement of the heart. I make Beauty, therefore,—using the word as inclusive of the sublime,—I make Beauty the province of the poem, simply because it is an obvious rule of Art that effects should be made to spring as directly as possible from their causes:—no one as yet having been weak enough to deny that the peculiar elevation in question is at least *most readily* attainable in the poem. It by no means follows, however, that the incitements of Passion,

---

[7] Ciovanna Vincenzo Gravina (1664-1718), an Italian critic, wrote *Della ragion poetica libri due* (1718), a treatise on poetry.

[8] Thomas Moore (1779-1852), the Irish poet, was very popular in the United States.

or the precepts of Duty, or even the lessons of Truth, may not be introduced into a poem, and with advantage; for they may subserve incidentally, in various ways, the general purposes of the work:—but the true artist will always contrive to tone them down in proper subjection to that *Beauty* which is the atmosphere and the real essence of the poem.

I cannot better introduce the few poems which I shall present for your consideration, than by the citation of the Proem to Mr. Longfellow's "Waif":

The day is done, and the darkness
  Falls from the wings of Night,
As a feather is wafted downward
  From an eagle in his flight.

I see the lights of the village
  Gleam through the rain and the mist,
And a feeling of sadness comes o'er me,
  That my soul cannot resist;

A feeling of sadness and longing,
  That is not akin to pain,
And resembles sorrow only
  As the mist resembles the rain.

Come, read to me some poem,
  Some simple and heartfelt lay,
That shall soothe this restless feeling,
  And banish the thoughts of day.

Not from the grand old masters,
  Not from the bards sublime,
Whose distant footsteps echo
  Through the corridors of Time.

For, like strains of martial music,
  Their mighty thoughts suggest
Life's endless toil and endeavor;
  And to-night I long for rest.

Read from some humbler poet,
  Whose songs gushed from his heart,
As showers from the clouds of summer,
  Or tears from the eyelids start;

Who through long days of labor,

And nights devoid of ease,
Still heard in his soul the music
  Of wonderful melodies.

Such songs have power to quiet
  The restless pulse of care,
And come like the benediction
  That follows after prayer.

Then read from the treasured volume
  The poem of thy choice,
And lend to the rhyme of the poet
  The beauty of thy voice.

And the night shall be filled with music,
  And the cares, that infest the day,
Shall fold their tents, like the Arabs,
  And as silently steal away.

With no great range of imagination, these lines have been justly admired for their delicacy of expression. Some of the images are very effective. Nothing can be better than

  The bards sublime
Whose distant footsteps echo
Down the corridors of Time.

The idea of the last quatrain is also very effective. The poem, on the whole, however, is chiefly to be admired for the graceful *insouciance* of its metre, so well in accordance with the character of the sentiments, and especially for the *ease* of the general manner. This "ease" or naturalness, in a literary style, it has long been the fashion to regard as ease in appearance alone—as a point of really difficult attainment. But not so:—a natural manner is difficult only to him who should never meddle with it—to the unnatural. It is but the result of writing with the understanding, or with the instinct, that *the tone,* in composition, should always be that which the mass of mankind would adopt —and must perpetually vary, of course, with the occasion. The author who, after the fashion of the "North American Review," should be upon *all* occasions merely "quiet," must necessarily upon *many* occasions be simply silly, or stupid; and has no more right to be considered "easy" or "natural" than a Cockney exquisite, or than the sleeping Beauty in the waxworks.

Among the minor poems of Bryant none has so much impressed me as the one which he entitles "June." I quote only a portion of it:

There, through the long, long summer
    hours,
  The golden light should lie,
And thick young herbs and groups of
    flowers
  Stand in their beauty by.
The oriole should build and tell
His love-tale, close beside my cell;
  The idle butterfly
Should rest him there, and there be heard
The housewife-bee and humming bird.

And what if cheerful shouts at noon
  Come, from the village sent,
Or songs of maids, beneath the moon,
  With fairy laughter blent?
And what if, in the evening light,
Betrothed lovers walk in sight
  Of my low monument?
I would the lovely scene around
Might know no sadder sight nor sound.

I know, I know I should not see
  The season's glorious show,
Nor would its brightness shine for me,
  Nor its wild music flow;
But if, around my place of sleep,
The friends I love should come to weep,
  They might not haste to go.
Soft airs, and song, and light and bloom
Should keep them lingering by my tomb.

These to their softened hearts should bear
  The thought of what has been,
And speak of one who cannot share
  The gladness of the scene;
Whose part, in all the pomp that fills
The circuit of the summer hills,
  Is—that his grave is green;

And deeply would their hearts rejoice
To hear again his living voice.

The rhythmical flow here is even voluptuous—nothing could be more melodious. The poem has always affected me in a remarkable manner. The intense melancholy which seems to well up, perforce, to the surface of all the poet's cheerful sayings about his grave, we find thrilling us to the soul—while there is the truest poetic elevation in the thrill. The impression left is one of a pleasurable sadness. And if, in the remaining compositions which I shall introduce to you, there be more or less of a similar tone always apparent, let me remind you that (how or why we know not) this certain taint of sadness is inseparably connected with all the higher manifestations of true Beauty. It is, nevertheless,

  A feeling of sadness and longing
    That is not akin to pain,
  And resembles sorrow only
    As the mist resembles the rain.[9]

The taint of which I speak is clearly perceptible even in a poem so full of brilliancy and spirit as the "Health" of Edward Coate Pinckney.[10]

I fill this cup to one made up
  Of loveliness alone,
A woman, of her gentle sex
  The seeming paragon;
To whom the better elements
  And kindly stars have given
A form so fair, that, like the air,
  'Tis less of earth than heaven.

Her every tone is music's own,
  Like those of morning birds,
And something more than melody
  Dwells ever in her words;
The coinage of her heart are they,

---

[9] See p. 462.

[10] A Maryland poet (1802-1828), who imitated Thomas Moore.

And from her lips each flows
As one may see the burden'd bee
  Forth issue from the rose.

Affections are as thoughts to her,
  The measures of her hours;
Her feelings have the fragrancy,
  The freshness of young flowers;
And lovely passions, changing oft,
  So fill her, she appears
The image of themselves by turns,—
  The idol of past years!

Of her bright face one glance will trace
  A picture on the brain,
And of her voice in echoing hearts
  A sound must long remain;
But memory, such as mine of her,
  So very much endears,
When death is nigh, my latest sigh
  Will not be life's but hers.

I fill this cup to one made up
  Of loveliness alone,
A woman, of her gentle sex
  The seeming paragon—
Her health! and would on earth there stood
  Some more of such a frame,
That life might be all poetry,
  And weariness a name.

It was the misfortune of Mr. Pinckney
to have been born too far south. Had he
been a New Englander, it is probable that
he would have been ranked as the first of
American lyrists, by that magnanimous
cabal which has so long controlled the
destinies of American Letters, in conducting the thing called "The North American
Review." The poem just cited is especially
beautiful; but the poetic elevation which it
induces, we must refer chiefly to our sympathy in the poet's enthusiasm. We pardon
his hyperboles for the evident earnestness
with which they are uttered.

It was by no means my design, however,
to expatiate upon the *merits* of what I
should read you. These will necessarily
speak for themselves. Boccalini, in his

"Advertisements from Parnassus," tells us
that Zoilus once presented Apollo a very
caustic criticism upon a very admirable
book:—whereupon the god asked him for
the beauties of the work.[11] He replied that
he only busied himself about the errors.
On hearing this, Apollo, handing him a
sack of unwinnowed wheat, bade him pick
out *all the chaff* for his reward.

Now this fable answers very well as a
hit at the critics—but I am by no means
sure that the god was in the right. I am
by no means certain that the true limits of
the critical duty are not grossly misunderstood. Excellence, in a poem especially,
may be considered in the light of an
axiom, which need only be properly *put*,
to become self-evident. It is *not* excellence
if it require to be demonstrated as such:—
and thus to point out too particularly the
merits of a work of Art, is to admit that
they are *not* merits altogether.

Among the "Melodies" of Thomas Moore
is one whose distinguished character as a
poem proper seems to have been singularly
left out of view. I allude to his lines beginning—"Come, rest in this bosom." The
intense energy of their expression is not
surpassed by anything in Byron. There
are two of the lines in which a sentiment
is conveyed that embodies the *all in all*
of the divine passion of love—a sentiment
which, perhaps, has found its echo in more,
and in more passionate, human hearts than
any other single sentiment ever embodied
in words:

Come, rest in this bosom, my own stricken
    deer,
Though the herd have fled from thee, thy
    home is still here;
Here still is the smile, that no cloud can
    o'ercast,
And a heart and a hand all thy own to
    the last.

Oh! what was love made for, if 'tis not the
    same

[11] Trajano Boccalini (1556-1613) was an
Italian satirist.

Through joy and through torment, through
    glory and shame?
I know not, I ask not, if guilt's in that
    heart,
I but know that I love thee, whatever thou
    art.

Thou hast call'd me thy Angel in moments
    of bliss,
And thy Angel I'll be, 'mid the horrors of
    this,—
Through the furnace, unshrinking, thy steps
    to pursue,
And shield thee, and save thee,—or perish
    there too!

It has been the fashion of late days to deny Moore imagination, while granting him fancy—a distinction originating with Coleridge [12]—than whom no man more fully comprehended the great powers of Moore. The fact is, that the fancy of this poet so far predominates over all his other faculties, and over the fancy of all other men, as to have induced, very naturally, the idea that he is fanciful *only*. But never was there a greater mistake. Never was a grosser wrong done the fame of a true poet. In the compass of the English language I can call to mind no poem more profoundly—more weirdly *imaginative*, in the best sense, than the lines commencing— "I would I were by that dim lake"—which are the composition of Thomas Moore. I regret that I am unable to remember them.[13]

One of the noblest—and, speaking of fancy, one of the most singularly fanciful of modern poets, was Thomas Hood.[14] His "Fair Ines" had always for me an inexpressible charm:

O saw ye not fair Ines?
  She's gone into the West,
To dazzle when the sun is down,
  And rob the world of rest:
She took our daylight with her,
  The smiles that we love best,
With morning blushes on her cheek,
  And pearls upon her breast.

O turn again, fair Ines,
  Before the fall of night,
For fear the Moon should shine alone,
  And stars unrivall'd bright;
And blessed will the lover be
  That walks beneath their light,
And breathes the love against thy cheek
  I dare not even write!

Would I had been, fair Ines,
  That gallant cavalier,
Who rode so gaily by thy side,
  And whisper'd thee so near!
Were there no bonny dames at home,
  Or no true lovers here,
That he should cross the seas to win
  The dearest of the dear?

I saw thee, lovely Ines,
  Descend along the shore,
With bands of noble gentlemen,
  And banners wav'd before;
And gentle youth and maidens gay,
  And snowy plumes they wore;
It would have been a beauteous dream,
  If it had been no more!

Alas, alas, fair Ines,
  She went away with song,
With Music waiting on her steps,
  And shoutings of the throng;
But some were sad, and felt no mirth,
  But only Music's wrong,
In sounds that sang Farewell, Farewell,
  To her you've loved so long.

Farewell, farewell, fair Ines,
  That vessel never bore
So fair a lady on its deck,
  Nor danced so light before,—
Alas for pleasure on the sea,
  And sorrow on the shore!
The smile that blest one lover's heart
  Has broken many more!

[12] This distinction is made in Coleridge's *Biographia Literaria* (1817), Ch. XIII.

[13] Poe refers to one of Moore's *Irish Melodies*, to be found in the Oxford edition of his *Poetical Works*, p. 226.

[14] This English poet (1799-1845) was noted for his humor, his sentiment, his social conscience, and his metrical facility.

"The Haunted House," by the same author, is one of the truest poems ever written, one of the *truest*, one of the most unexceptionable, one of the most thoroughly artistic, both in its theme and in its execution. It is, moreover, powerfully ideal —imaginative. I regret that its length renders it unsuitable for the purposes of this Lecture. In place of it, permit me to offer the universally appreciated "Bridge of Sighs."

One more Unfortunate,
Weary of breath,
Rashly importunate,
Gone to her death!

Take her up tenderly,
Lift her with care;—
Fashion'd so slenderly,
Young, and so fair!

Look at her garments
Clinging like cerements;
Whilst the wave constantly
Drips from her clothing;
Take her up instantly,
Loving, not loathing—

Touch her not scornfully;
Think of her mournfully,
Gently and humanly;
Not of the stains of her,
All that remains of her
Now is pure womanly.

Make no deep scrutiny
Into her mutiny
Rash and undutiful;
Past all dishonor,
Death has left on her
Only the beautiful.

Still, for all slips of hers,
One of Eve's family—
Wipe those poor lips of hers
Oozing so clammily.
Loop up her tresses
Escaped from the comb,
Her fair auburn tresses;

Whilst wonderment guesses
Where was her home?

Who was her father?
Who was her mother?
Had she a sister?
Had she a brother?
Or was there a dearer one
Still, and a nearer one
Yet, than all other?

Alas! for the rarity
Of Christian charity
Under the sun!
Oh! it was pitiful!
Near a whole city full,
Home she had none.

Sisterly, brotherly,
Fatherly, motherly
Feelings had changed:
Love, by harsh evidence,
Thrown from its eminence;
Even God's providence
Seeming estranged.

Where the lamps quiver
So far in the river,
With many a light
From window and casement,
From garret to basement,
She stood, with amazement,
Houseless by night.

The bleak wind of March
Made her tremble and shiver;
But not the dark arch,
Or the black flowing river:
Mad from life's history,
Glad to death's mystery,
Swift to be hurl'd—
Anywhere, anywhere
Out of the world!

In she plunged boldly,
No matter how coldly
The rough river ran,—
Over the brink of it,
Picture it,—think of it
Dissolute Man!

Lave in it, drink of it
Then, if you can!

Take her up tenderly,
Lift her with care,
Fashion'd so slenderly,
Young, and so fair!

Ere her limbs frigidly
Stiffen too rigidly,
Decently,—kindly,—
Smooth, and compose them;
And her eyes, close them,
Staring so blindly!

Dreadfully staring
Through muddy impurity,
As when with the daring
Last look of despairing
Fixed on futurity.

Perishing gloomily,
Spurred by contumely,
Cold inhumanity,
Burning insanity,
Into her rest,—
Cross her hands humbly,
As if praying dumbly,
Over her breast!
Owning her weakness,
Her evil behaviour,
And leaving, with meekness,
Her sins to her Savior!

The vigor of this poem is no less remarkable than its pathos. The versification, although carrying the fanciful to the very verge of the fantastic, is nevertheless admirably adapted to the wild insanity which is the thesis of the poem.

Among the minor poems of Lord Byron is one which has never received from the critics the praise which it undoubtedly deserves: [15]

Though the day of my destiny's over,
    And the star of my fate hath declined,
Thy soft heart refused to discover
    The faults which so many could find;
Though thy soul with my grief was acquainted,

It shrunk not to share it with me,
And the love which my spirit hath painted
    It never hath found but in *thee*.

Then when nature around me is smiling,
    The last smile which answers to mine,
I do not believe it beguiling,
    Because it reminds me of thine;
And when winds are at war with the ocean,
    As the breasts I believed in with me,
If their billows excite an emotion,
    It is that they bear me from *thee*.

Though the rock of my last hope is shivered,
    And its fragments are sunk in the wave,
Though I feel that my soul is delivered
    To pain—it shall not be its slave.
There is many a pang to pursue me:
    They may crush, but they shall not contemn—
They may torture, but shall not subdue me—
        'Tis of *thee* that I think—not of them.

Though human, thou didst not deceive me,
    Though woman, thou didst not forsake,
Though loved, thou forborest to grieve me,
    Though slandered, thou never couldst shake,—
Though trusted, thou didst not disclaim me,
    Though parted, it was not to fly,
Though watchful, 'twas not to defame me,
    Nor mute, that the world might belie.

Yet I blame not the world, nor despise it,
    Nor the war of the many with one—
If my soul was not fitted to prize it,
    'Twas folly not sooner to shun:
And if dearly that error hath cost me,
    And more than I once could foresee,
I have found that whatever it lost me,
    It could not deprive me of *thee*.

From the wreck of the past, which hath
        perished,

---

[15] "Stanzas to Augusta," in the *Prisoner of Chillon* volume of 1816.

Thus much I at least may recall,
It hath taught me that which I most cherished,
Deserved to be dearest of all:
In the desert a fountain is springing,
In the wide waste there still is a tree,
And a bird in the solitude singing,
Which speaks to my spirit of *thee*.

Although the rhythm here is one of the most difficult, the versification could scarcely be improved. No nobler *theme* ever engaged the pen of poet. It is the soul-elevating idea that no man can consider himself entitled to complain of Fate while, in his adversity, he still retains the unwavering love of woman.

From Alfred Tennyson—although in perfect sincerity I regard him as the noblest poet that ever lived—I have left myself time to cite only a very brief specimen. I call him, and think *him* the noblest of poets—*not* because the impressions he produces are at *all* times the most profound—*not* because the poetical excitement which he induces is at *all* times the most intense—but because it *is* at all times the most ethereal—in other words, the most elevating and most pure. What poet is so little of the earth, earthy. What I am about to read is from his last long poem, "The Princess": [16]

Tears, idle tears, I know not what they mean,
Tears from the depth of some divine despair
Rise in the heart, and gather to the eyes,
In looking on the happy Autumn-fields,
And thinking of the days that are no more.

Fresh as the first beam glittering on a sail,
That brings our friends up from the underworld,
Sad as the last which reddens over one
That sinks with all we love below the verge;
So sad, so fresh, the days that are no more.

Ah, sad and strange as in dark summer dawns
The earliest pipe of half-awaken'd birds
To dying ears, when unto dying eyes
The casement slowly grows a glimmering square;
So sad, so strange, the days that are no more.

Dear as remember'd kisses after death,
And sweet as those by hopeless fancy feign'd
On lips that are for others; deep as love,
Deep as first love, and wild with all regret;
O Death in Life, the days that are no more.

Thus, although in a very cursory and imperfect manner, I have endeavoured to convey to you my conception of the Poetic Principle. It has been my purpose to suggest that, while this Principle itself is strictly and simply the Human Aspiration for Supernal Beauty, the manifestation of the Principle is always found in *an elevating excitement of the Soul,* quite independent of that passion which is the intoxication of the Heart, or of that truth which is the satisfaction of the Reason. For in regard to Passion, alas! its tendency is to degrade rather than to elevate the Soul. Love, on the contrary—Love—the true, the divine Eros—the Uranian as distinguished from the Dionaean Venus—is unquestionably the purest and truest of all poetical themes. [17] And in regard to Truth —if, to be sure, through the attainment of a truth we are led to perceive a harmony where none was apparent before, we experience at once the true poetical effect— but this effect is referable to the harmony alone, and not in the least degree to the

---

[16] *The Princess* was published in 1847.
[17] From the foam surrounding the limbs of Uranus, the heavenly husband of Gaea or Earth, sprang Aphrodite; another myth made Aphrodite or Venus the daughter of Jupiter and Dione. Poe arbitrarily identifies the first Venus with spiritual love, the second with more earthly love. These contrasts figure in both "Ulalume" and "Ligeia."

truth which merely served to render the harmony manifest.

We shall reach, however, more immediately a distinct conception of what the true Poetry is, by mere reference to a few of the simple elements which induce in the Poet himself the true poetical effect. He recognizes the ambrosia which nourishes his soul, in the bright orbs that shine in Heaven—in the volutes of the flower—in the clustering of low shrubberies—in the waving of the grain-fields—in the slanting of tall Eastern trees—in the blue distance of mountains—in the grouping of clouds—in the twinkling of half-hidden brooks—in the gleaming of silver rivers—in the repose of sequestered lakes—in the star-mirroring depths of lonely wells. He perceives it in the songs of birds—in the harp of Aeolus—in the sighing of the night-wind—in the repining voice of the forest—in the surf that complains to the shore—in the fresh breath of the woods—in the scent of the violet—in the voluptuous perfume of the hyacinth—in the suggestive odor that comes to him at eventide from far-distant, undiscovered islands, over dim oceans, illimitable and unexplored. He owns it in all noble thoughts—in all unworldly motives—in all holy impulses—in all chivalrous, generous, and self-sacrificing deeds. He feels it in the beauty of woman—in the grace of her step—in the lustre of her eye—in the melody of her voice—in her soft laughter—in her sigh—in the harmony of the rustling of her robes. He deeply feels it in her winning endearments—in her burning enthusiasms—in her gentle charities—in her meek and devotional endurances—but above all—ah, far above all—he kneels to it, he worships it in the faith, in the purity, in the strength, in the altogether divine majesty—of her *love*.

Let me conclude by the recitation of yet another brief poem—one very different in character from any that I have before quoted. It is by Motherwell, and is called "The Song of the Cavalier." [18] With our modern and altogether rational ideas of the absurdity and impiety of warfare, we are

not precisely in that frame of mind best adapted to sympathize with the sentiments, and thus to appreciate the real excellence of the poem. To do this fully we must identify ourselves in fancy with the soul of the old cavalier.

Then mounte! then mounte, brave gallants, all,
  And don your helmes amaine:
Deathe's couriers, Fame and Honour, call
  Us to the field againe.
No shrewish tears shall fill our eye
  When the sword-hilt's in our hand,—
Heart-whole we'll part, and no whit sighe
  For the fayrest of the land;
Let piping swaine, and craven wight,
  Thus weepe and puling crye,
Our business is like men to fight,
  And hero-like to die!

HAWTHORNE'S TWICE-TOLD TALES [1]
[1842]

I

WE HAVE always regarded the *Tale* (using this word in its popular acceptation) as affording the best prose opportunity for display of the highest talent. It has peculiar advantages which the novel does not admit. It is, of course, a far finer field than the essay. It has even points of superiority over the poem. An accident has deprived us, this month, of our customary space for review; and thus nipped in the bud a design long cherished of treating this subject in detail; taking Mr. Hawthorne's volumes as a text. In May we shall endeavor to carry out our intention. At present we are forced to be brief.

With rare exception—in the case of Mr.

----

[18] William Motherwell (1797-1829) was a Scottish poet.

[1] This selection combines two notices of Hawthorne's *Twice-Told Tales* in the April and May, 1842, issues of *Graham's Magazine*.

Irving's "Tales of a Traveller" and a few other works of a like cast—we have had no American tales of high merit. We have had no skilful compositions—nothing which could bear examination as works of art. Of twattle called tale-writing we have had, perhaps, more than enough. We have had a superabundance of the Rosa-Matilda effusions—gilt-edged paper all *couleur de rose:* a full allowance of cut-and-thrust blue-blazing melodramaticisms; a nauseating surfeit of low miniature copying of low life, much in the manner, and with about half the merit, of the Dutch herrings and decayed cheeses of Van Tuyssel— of all this *eheu jam satis!* [2]

Mr. Hawthorne's volumes appear to us misnamed in two respects. In the first place they should not have been called "Twice-Told Tales"—for this is a title which will not bear *repetition*. If in the first collected edition they were twice-told, of course now they are thrice told. May we live to hear them told a hundred times! In the second place, these compositions are by no means *all* "Tales." The most of them are essays properly so called. It would have been wise in their author to have modified his title, so as to have had reference to all included. This point could have been easily arranged.

But under whatever titular blunders we receive this book, it is most cordially welcome. We have seen no prose composition by any American which can compare with *some* of these articles in the higher merits, or indeed in the lower; while there is not a single piece which would do dishonor to the best of the British essayists.

"The Rill from the Town Pump" which, through the *ad captandum* [3] nature of its title, has attracted more of public notice than any other of Mr. Hawthorne's compositions, is perhaps, the *least* meritorious. Among the best, we may briefly mention "The Hollow of the Three Hills;" "The Minister's Black Veil;" "Wakefield;" "Mr. Higginbotham's Catastrophe;" "Fancy's Show-Box;" "Dr. Heidegger's Experiment;" "David Swan;" "The Wedding Knell;" and "The White Old Maid." It is

remarkable that all these, with one exception, are from the first volume.

The style of Mr. Hawthorne is purity itself. His *tone* is singularly effective— wild, plaintive, thoughtful, and in full accordance with his themes. We have only to object that there is insufficient diversity in these themes themselves, or rather in their character. His *originality* both of incident and of reflection is very remarkable; and this trait alone would ensure him at least *our* warmest regard and commendation. We speak here chiefly of the tales; the essays are not so markedly novel. Upon the whole we look upon him as one of the few men of indisputable genius to whom our country has as yet given birth. As such, it will be our delight to do him honor; and lest, in these undigested and cursory remarks, we should appear to do him *more* honor than is his due, we postpone all farther comment until a more favorable opportunity.

II

We said a few hurried words about Mr. Hawthorne in our last number, with the design of speaking more fully in the present. We are still, however, pressed for room, and must necessarily discuss his volumes more briefly and more at random than their high merits deserve.

The book professes to be a collection of *tales,* yet is, in two respects, misnamed. These pieces are now in their third republication, and, of course, are thrice-told. Moreover, they are by no means *all* tales, either in the ordinary or in the legitimate understanding of the term. Many of them are pure essays; for example, "Sights from a Steeple," "Sunday at Home," "Little Annie's Ramble," "A Rill from the Town

---

[2] Rosa-Matilda and Van Tuyssel are satiric names invented by Poe to ridicule respectively the sentimentalism of current magazine writers and the realism of fiction and sketches suggesting the method of Dutch painting. The Latin phrase means *alas, now enough!*

[3] "Taking" or "Catchy."

Pump," "The Toll-Gatherer's Day," "The Haunted Mind," "The Sister Years," "Snow-Flakes," "Night Sketches," and "Foot-Prints on the Sea-Shore." We mention these matters chiefly on account of their discrepancy with that marked precision and finish by which the body of the work is distinguished.

Of the essays just named, we must be content to speak in brief. They are each and all beautiful, without being characterized by the polish and adaptation so visible in the tales proper. A painter would at once note their leading or predominant feature, and style it *repose*. There is no attempt at effect. All is quiet, thoughtful, subdued. Yet this repose may exist simultaneously with high originality of thought; and Mr. Hawthorne has demonstrated the fact. At every turn we meet with novel combinations; yet these combinations never surpass the limits of the quiet. We are soothed as we read; and withal is a calm astonishment that ideas so apparently obvious have never occurred or been presented to us before. Herein our author differs materially from Lamb or Hunt or Hazlitt [4]— who, with vivid originality of manner and expression, have less of the true novelty of thought than is generally supposed, and whose originality, at best, has an uneasy and meretricious quaintness, replete with startling effects unfounded in nature, and inducing trains of reflection which lead to no satisfactory result. The Essays of Hawthorne have much of the character of Irving, with more of originality, and less of finish; while, compared with the Spectator, they have a vast superiority at all points. The Spectator, Mr. Irving, and Mr. Hawthorne have in common that tranquil and subdued manner which we have chosen to denominate *repose;* but, in the case of the two former, this repose is attained rather by the absence of novel combination, or of originality, than otherwise, and consists chiefly in the calm, quiet, unostentatious expression of commonplace thoughts, in an unambitious, unadulterated Saxon. In them, by strong effort, we are made to

conceive the absence of all. In the essays before us the absence of effort is too obvious to be mistaken, and a strong undercurrent of *suggestion* runs continuously beneath the upper stream of the tranquil thesis. In short, these effusions of Mr. Hawthorne are the product of a truly imaginative intellect, restrained, and in some measure repressed, by fastidiousness of taste, by constitutional melancholy, and by indolence.

But it is of his tales that we desire principally to speak. The tale proper, in our opinion, affords unquestionably the fairest field for the exercise of the loftiest talent, which can be afforded by the wide domains of mere prose. Were we bidden to say how the highest genius could be most advantageously employed for the best display of its own powers, we should answer, without hesitation—in the composition of a rhymed poem, not to exceed in length what might be perused in an hour. Within this limit alone can the highest order of true poetry exist. We need only here say, upon this topic, that, in almost all classes of composition, the unity of effect or impression is a point of the greatest importance. It is clear, moreover, that this unity cannot be thoroughly preserved in productions whose perusal cannot be completed at one sitting. We may continue the reading of a prose composition, from the very nature of prose itself, much longer than we can persevere, to any good purpose, in the perusal of a poem. This latter, if truly fulfilling the demands of the poetic sentiment, induces an exaltation of the soul which cannot be long sustained. All high excitements are necessarily transient. Thus a long poem is a paradox. And, without unity of impression, the deepest effects cannot be brought about. Epics were the offspring of an imperfect sense of Art, and their reign is no more. A poem *too* brief may produce

---

[4] Charles Lamb (1775-1834), Leigh Hunt (1784-1859), and William Hazlitt (1778-1830) helped develop the familiar essay as an important *genre* of English literature.

a vivid, but never an intense or enduring impression. Without a certain continuity of effort—without a certain duration or repetition of purpose—the soul is never deeply moved. There must be the dropping of the water upon the rock. De Béranger has wrought brilliant things—pungent and spirit-stirring—but, like all immassive bodies, they lack *momentum,* and thus fail to satisfy the Poetic Sentiment. They sparkle and excite, but, from want of continuity, fail deeply to impress. Extreme brevity will degenerate into epigrammatism; but the sin of extreme length is even more unpardonable. *In medio tutissimus ibis.*[5]

Were we called upon, however, to designate that class of composition which, next to such a poem as we have suggested, should best fulfil the demands of high genius—should offer it the most advantageous field of exertion—we should unhesitatingly speak of the prose tale, as Mr. Hawthorne has here exemplified it. We allude to the short prose narrative, requiring from a half-hour to one or two hours in its perusal. The ordinary novel is objectionable, from its length, for reasons already stated in substance. As it cannot be read at one sitting, it deprives itself, of course, of the immense force derivable from *totality.* Worldly interests intervening during the pauses of perusal, modify, annul, or counteract, in a greater or less degree, the impressions of the book. But simple cessation in reading would, of itself, be sufficient to destroy the true unity. In the brief tale, however, the author is enabled to carry out the fulness of his intention, be it what it may. During the hour of perusal the soul of the reader is at the writer's control. There are no external or extrinsic influences—resulting from weariness or interruption.

A skilful literary artist has constructed a tale. If wise, he has not fashioned his thoughts to accommodate his incidents; but having conceived, with deliberate care, a certain unique or single *effect* to be wrought out, he then invents such incidents—he then combines such events as

may best aid him in establishing this preconceived effect. If his very initial sentence tend not to the outbringing of this effect, then he has failed in his first step. In the whole composition there should be no word written, of which the tendency, direct or indirect, is not to the one pre-established design. And by such means, with such care and skill, a picture is at length painted which leaves in the mind of him who contemplates it with a kindred art, a sense of the fullest satisfaction. The idea of the tale has been presented unblemished, because undisturbed: and this is an end unattainable by the novel. Undue brevity is just as exceptionable here as in the poem; but undue length is yet more to be avoided.

We have said that the tale has a point of superiority even over the poem. In fact, while the *rhythm* of this latter is an essential aid in the development of the poem's highest idea—the idea of the Beautiful—the artificialities of this rhythm are an inseparable bar to the development of all points of thought or expression which have their basis in *Truth.* But Truth is often, and in very great degree, the aim of the tale. Some of the finest tales are tales of ratiocination. Thus the field of this species of composition, if not in so elevated a region on the mountain of Mind, is a table-land of far vaster extent than the domain of the mere poem. Its products are never so rich, but infinitely more numerous, and more appreciable by the mass of mankind. The writer of the prose tale, in short, may bring to his theme a vast variety of modes or inflections of thought and expression—(the ratiocinative, for example, the sarcastic, or the humorous) which are not only antagonistical to the nature of the poem, but absolutely forbidden by one of its most peculiar and indispensable adjuncts; we allude, of course, to rhythm. It may be added here, *par parenthèse,* that the author who aims at the purely beautiful in a prose tale is

---

[5] You will be most safe in the middle way.

laboring at a great disadvantage. For Beauty can be better treated in the poem. Not so with terror, or passion, or horror, or a multitude of such other points. And here it will be seen how full of prejudice are the usual animadversions against those *tales of effect,* many fine examples of which were found in the earlier numbers of Blackwood. The impressions produced were wrought in a legitimate sphere of action, and constituted a legitimate although sometimes an exaggerated interest. They were relished by every man of genius: although there were found many men of genius who condemned them without just ground. The true critic will but demand that the design intended be accomplished, to the fullest extent, by the means most advantageously applicable.

We have very few American tales of real merit—we may say, indeed, none, with the exception of "The Tales of a Traveller" of Washington Irving, and these "Twice-Told Tales" of Mr. Hawthorne. Some of the pieces of Mr. John Neal abound in vigor and originality; but, in general, his compositions of this class are excessively diffuse, extravagant, and indicative of an imperfect sentiment of Art.[6] Articles at random are, now and then, met with in our periodicals which might be advantageously compared with the best effusions of the British Magazines; but, upon the whole, we are far behind our progenitors in this department of literature.

Of Mr. Hawthorne's tales we would say, emphatically, that they belong to the highest region of Art—an Art subservient to genius of a very lofty order. We had supposed, with good reason for so supposing, that he had been thrust into his present position by one of the impudent *cliques* which beset our literature, and whose pretensions it is our full purpose to expose at the earliest opportunity; but we have been most agreeably mistaken. We know of few compositions which the critic can more honestly commend than these "Twice-Told Tales." As Americans, we feel proud of the book.

Mr. Hawthorne's distinctive trait is invention, creation, imagination, originality —a trait which, in the literature of fiction, is positively worth all the rest. But the nature of the originality, so far as regards its manifestation in letters, is but imperfectly understood. The inventive or original mind as frequently displays itself in novelty of *tone* as in novelty of matter. Mr. Hawthorne is original at *all* points.

It would be a matter of some difficulty to designate the best of these tales; we repeat that, without exception, they are beautiful. "Wakefield" is remarkable for the skill with which an old idea—a well-known incident—is worked up or discussed. A man of whims conceives the purpose of quitting his wife and residing *incognito,* for twenty years, in her immediate neighborhood. Something of this kind actually happened in London. The force of Mr. Hawthorne's tale lies in the analysis of the motives which must or might have impelled the husband to such folly, in the first instance, with the possible causes of his perseverance. Upon this thesis a sketch of singular power has been constructed.

"The Wedding Knell" is full of the boldest imagination—an imagination fully controlled by taste. The most captious critic could find no flaw in this production.

"The Minister's Black Veil" is a masterly composition, of which the sole defect is that to the rabble its exquisite skill will be *caviare.* The *obvious* meaning of this article will be found to smother its insinuated one. The *moral* put into the mouth of the dying minister will be supposed to convey the *true* import of the narrative; and that a crime of dark dye (having reference to the "young lady") has been committed, is a point which only minds congenial with that of the author will perceive.

"Mr. Higginbotham's Catastrophe" is

[6] John Neal (1793-1876) was the author of *Keep Cool* (1817), *Logan* (1822), *Seventy Six* (1823), *Randolph* (1823), *Errata* (1823), *Brother Jonathan* (1825), *Rachel Dyer* (1828), *Authorship* (1830), *The Down-Easters* (1833).

vividly original, and managed most dexterously.

"Dr. Heidegger's Experiment" is exceedingly well imagined, and executed with surpassing ability. The artist breathes in every line of it.

"The White Old Maid" is objectionable even more than the "Minister's Black Veil," on the score of its mysticism. Even with the thoughtful and analytic, there will be much trouble in penetrating its entire import.

"The Hollow of the Three Hills" we would quote in full had we space;—not as evincing higher talent than any of the other pieces, but as affording an excellent example of the author's peculiar ability. The subject is commonplace. A witch subjects the Distant and the Past to the view of a mourner. It has been the fashion to describe, in such cases, a mirror in which the images of the absent appear; or a cloud of smoke is made to arise, and thence the figures are gradually unfolded. Mr. Hawthorne has wonderfully heightened his effect by making the ear, in place of the eye, the medium by which the fantasy is conveyed. The head of the mourner is enveloped in the cloak of the witch, and within its magic folds there arise sounds which have an all-sufficient intelligence. Throughout this article also, the artist is conspicuous—not more in positive than in negative merits. Not only is all done that should be done, but (what perhaps is an end with more difficulty attained) there is nothing done which should not be. Every word *tells*, and there is not a word which does *not* tell. . . .

In the way of objection we have scarcely a word to say of these tales. There is, perhaps, a somewhat too general or prevalent *tone*—a tone of melancholy and mysticism. The subjects are insufficiently varied. There is not so much of *versatility* evinced as we might well be warranted in expecting from the high powers of Mr. Hawthorne. But beyond these trivial exceptions we have really none to make. The style is purity itself. Force abounds. High imagination gleams from every page. Mr. Hawthorne is a man of the truest genius. We only regret that the limits of our Magazine will not permit us to pay him that full tribute of commendation, which, under other circumstances, we should be so eager to pay.

THE PHILOSOPHY OF COMPOSITION
[1846]

CHARLES DICKENS, in a note now lying before me, alluding to an examination I once made of the mechanism of "Barnaby Rudge," says—"By the way, are you aware that Godwin wrote his 'Caleb Williams' backwards? He first involved his hero in a web of difficulties, forming the second volume, and then, for the first, cast about him for some mode of accounting for what had been done." [1]

I cannot think this the *precise* mode of procedure on the part of Godwin—and indeed what he himself acknowledges, is not altogether in accordance with Mr. Dickens' idea—but the author of "Caleb Williams" was too good an artist not to perceive the advantage derivable from at least a somewhat similar process. Nothing is more clear than that every plot, worth the name, must be elaborated to its *dénouement* before any thing be attempted with the pen. It is only with the *dénouement* constantly in view that we can give a plot its indispensable air of consequence, or causation, by making the incidents, and especially the tone at all points, tend to the development of the intention.

There is a radical error, I think, in the

---

[1] In an article in the Philadelphia *Saturday Evening Post*, May 1, 1841, Poe forecast the outcome of *Barnaby Rudge* on the basis of its earlier installments; he reviewed the novel for *Graham's Magazine*, February, 1842. William Godwin (1756-1836) pioneered in the English sociological problem novel with *Caleb Williams* (1794), which dramatized some of the revolutionary ideas found in his *Enquiry Concerning Political Justice* (1793).

usual mode of constructing a story. Either history affords a thesis—or one is suggested by an incident of the day—or, at best, the author sets himself to work in the combination of striking events to form merely the basis of his narrative—designing, generally, to fill in with description, dialogue, or autorial comment, whatever crevices of fact, or action, may, from page to page, render themselves apparent.

I prefer commencing with the consideration of an *effect*. Keeping originality *always* in view—for he is false to himself who ventures to dispense with so obvious and so easily attainable a source of interest—I say to myself, in the first place, "Of the innumerable effects, or impressions, of which the heart, the intellect, or (more generally) the soul is susceptible, what one shall I, on the present occasion, select?" Having chosen a novel, first, and secondly a vivid effect, I consider whether it can be best wrought by incident or tone —whether by ordinary incidents and peculiar tone, or the converse, or by peculiarity both of incident and tone—afterward looking about me (or rather within) for such combinations of event, or tone, as shall best aid me in the construction of the effect.

I have often thought how interesting a magazine paper might be written by any author who would—that it to say, who could—detail, step by step, the processes by which any one of his compositions attained its ultimate point of completion. Why such a paper has never been given to the world, I am much at a loss to say—but, perhaps, the autorial vanity has had more to do with the omission than any one other cause. Most writers—poets in especial— prefer having it understood that they compose by a species of fine frenzy—an ecstatic intuition—and would positively shudder at letting the public take a peep behind the scenes, at the elaborate and vacillating crudities of thought—at the true purposes seized only at the last moment— at the innumerable glimpses of idea that arrived not at the maturity of full view— at the fully matured fancies discarded in despair as unmanageable—at the cautious selections and rejections—at the painful erasures and interpolations—in a word, at the wheels and pinions—the tackle for scene-shifting—the step-ladders and demon-traps—the cock's feathers, the red paint and the black patches, which, in ninety-nine cases out of a hundred, constitute the properties of the literary *histrio*.

I am aware, on the other hand, that the case is by no means common, in which an author is at all in condition to retrace the steps by which his conclusions have been attained. In general, suggestions, having arisen pell-mell, are pursued and forgotten in a similar manner.

For my own part, I have neither sympathy with the repugnance alluded to, nor, at any time, the least difficulty in recalling to mind the progressive steps of any of my compositions; and, since the interest of an analysis, or reconstruction, such as I have considered a *desideratum,* is quite independent of any real or fancied interest in the thing analyzed, it will not be regarded as a breach of decorum on my part to show the *modus operandi* by which some one of my own works was put together. I select "The Raven" as most generally known. It is my design to render it manifest that no one point in its composition is referrible either to accident or intuition— that the work proceeded, step by step, to its completion with the precision and rigid consequence of a mathematical problem.

Let us dismiss, as irrelevant to the poem, *per se,* the circumstance—or say the necessity—which, in the first place, gave rise to the intention of composing *a* poem that should suit at once the popular and the critical taste.

We commence, then, with this intention. The initial consideration was that of extent. If any literary work is too long to be read at one sitting, we must be content to dispense with the immensely important effect derivable from unity of impression— for, if two sittings be required, the affairs of the world interfere, and every thing like totality is at once destroyed. But since, *ceteris paribus,* no poet can afford to dispense with *any thing* that may advance his design, it but remains to be seen whether there is, in extent, any advantage to counterbalance the loss of unity which attends it. Here I say no, at once. What we term a long poem is, in fact, merely a succession of brief ones—that is to say, of brief poetical effects. It is needless to demonstrate that a poem is such, only inasmuch as it intensely excites, by elevating, the soul; and all intense excitements are, through a psychal necessity, brief. For this reason, at least one half of the "Paradise Lost" is essentially prose—a succession of poetical excitements interspersed, *inevitably,* with corresponding depressions—the whole being deprived, through the extremeness of its length, of the vastly important artistic element, totality, or unity, of effect.

It appears evident, then, that there is a distinct limit, as regards length, to all works of literary art—the limit of a single sitting—and that, although in certain classes of prose composition, such as "Robinson Crusoe," (demanding no unity,) this limit may be advantageously overpassed, it can never properly be overpassed in a poem. Within this limit, the extent of a poem may be made to bear mathematical relation to its merit—in other words, to the excitement or elevation—again, in other words, to the degree of the true poetical effect which it is capable of inducing; for it is clear that the brevity must be in direct ratio of the intensity of the intended effect:—this, with one proviso—that a certain degree of duration is absolutely requisite for the production of any effect at all.

Holding in view these considerations, as well as that degree of excitement which I deemed not above the popular, while not below the critical, taste, I reached at once what I conceived the proper *length* for my intended poem—a length of about one hundred lines. It is, in fact, a hundred and eight.

My next thought concerned the choice of an impression, or effect, to be conveyed:

and here I may as well observe that, throughout the construction, I kept steadily in view the design of rendering the work *universally* appreciable. I should be carried too far out of my immediate topic were I to demonstrate a point upon which I have repeatedly insisted, and which, with the poetical, stands not in the slightest need of demonstration—the point, I mean, that Beauty is the sole legitimate province of the poem. A few words, however, in elucidation of my real meaning, which some of my friends have evinced a disposition to misrepresent. That pleasure which is at once the most intense, the most elevating, and the most pure, is, I believe, found in the contemplation of the beautiful. When, indeed, men speak of Beauty, they mean, precisely, not a quality, as is supposed, but an effect—they refer, in short, just to that intense and pure elevation of *soul—not* of intellect, or of heart—upon which I have commented, and which is experienced in consequence of contemplating "the beautiful." Now I designate Beauty as the province of the poem, merely because it is an obvious rule of Art that effects should be made to spring from direct causes—that objects should be attained through means best adapted for their attainment—no one as yet having been weak enough to deny that the peculiar elevation alluded to, is *most readily* attained in the poem. Now the object Truth, or the satisfaction of the intellect, and the object Passion, or the excitement of the heart, are, although attainable, to a certain extent, in poetry, far more readily attainable in prose. Truth, in fact, demands a precision, and Passion a *homeliness* (the truly passionate will comprehend me) which are absolutely antagonistic to that Beauty which, I maintain, is the excitement, or pleasurable elevation, of the soul. It by no means follows from any thing here said, that passion, or even truth, may not be introduced, and even profitably introduced, into a poem—for they may serve in elucidation, or aid the general effect, as do discords in music, by contrast—but the true artist will always contrive, first, to tone them into proper subservience to the predominant aim, and, secondly, to enveil them, as far as possible, in that Beauty which is the atmosphere and the essence of the poem.

Regarding, then, Beauty as my province, my next question referred to the *tone* of its highest manifestation—and all experience has shown that this tone is one of *sadness*. Beauty of whatever kind, in its supreme development, invariably excites the sensitive soul to tears. Melancholy is thus the most legitimate of all the poetical tones.

The length, the province, and the tone, being thus determined, I betook myself to ordinary induction, with the view of obtaining some artistic piquancy which might serve me as a key-note in the construction of the poem—some pivot upon which the whole structure might turn. In carefully thinking over all the usual artistic effects— or more properly *points,* in the theatrical sense—I did not fail to perceive immediately that no one had been so universally employed as that of the *refrain.* The universality of its employment sufficed to assure me of its intrinsic value, and spared me the necessity of submitting it to analysis. I considered it, however, with regard to its susceptibility of improvement, and soon saw it to be in a primitive condition. As commonly used, the *refrain,* or burden, not only is limited to lyric verse, but depends for its impression upon the force of monotone—both in sound and thought. The pleasure is deduced solely from the sense of identity—of repetition. I resolved to diversify and so heighten, the effect, by adhering, in general, to the monotone of sound, while I continually varied that of thought: that is to say, I determined to produce continuously novel effects, by the variation *of the application* of the *refrain* —the *refrain* itself remaining, for the most part, unvaried.

These points being settled, I next bethought me of the *nature* of my *refrain.* Since its application was to be repeatedly varied, it was clear that the *refrain* itself must be brief, for there would have been an insurmountable difficulty in frequent variations of application in any sentence of length. In proportion to the brevity of the sentence, would, of course, be the facility of the variation. This led me at once to a single word as the best *refrain.*

The question now arose as to the *character* of the word. Having made up my mind to a *refrain,* the division of the poem into stanzas, was, of course, a corollary: the *refrain* forming the close to each stanza. That such a close, to have force, must be sonorous and susceptible of protracted emphasis, admitted no doubt: and these considerations inevitably led me to the long *o* as the most sonorous vowel, in connection with *r* as the most producible consonant.

The sound of the *refrain* being thus determined, it became necessary to select a word embodying this sound, and at the same time in the fullest possible keeping with that melancholy which I had predetermined as the tone of the poem. In such a search it would have been absolutely impossible to overlook the word "Nevermore." In fact, it was the very first which presented itself.

The next *desideratum* was a pretext for the continuous use of the one word "nevermore." In observing the difficulty which I at once found in inventing a sufficiently plausible reason for its continuous repetition, I did not fail to perceive that this difficulty arose solely from the pre-assumption that the word was to be so continuously or monotonously spoken by a *human* being—I did not fail to perceive, in short, that the difficulty lay in the reconciliation of this monotony with the exercise of reason on the part of the creature repeating the word. Here, then, immediately arose the idea of a *non*reasoning creature capable of speech; and, very naturally, a parrot, in the first instance, suggested itself, but was superseded forthwith by a Raven, as equally capable of speech, and infinitely more in keeping with the intended *tone.*

I had now gone so far as the conception of a Raven—the bird of ill omen—monotonously repeating the one word, "Nevermore," at the conclusion of each stanza, in a poem of melancholy tone, and in length about one hundred lines. Now, never losing sight of the object *supremeness*, or perfection, at all points, I have asked myself—"Of all melancholy topics, what, according to the *universal* understanding of mankind, is the *most* melancholy?" Death—was the obvious reply. "And when," I said, "is the most melancholy of topics most poetical?" From what I have already explained at some length, the answer, here, also, is obvious—"When it most closely allies itself to *Beauty:* the death, then, of a beautiful woman is, unquestionably, the most poetical topic in the world—and equally is it beyond doubt that the lips best suited for such topic are those of a bereaved lover."

I had now to combine the two ideas, of a lover lamenting his deceased mistress and a Raven continuously repeating the word "Nevermore."—I had to combine these, bearing in mind my design of varying, at every turn, the *application* of the word repeated; but the only intelligible mode of such combination is that of imagining the Raven employing the word in answer to the queries of the lover. And here it was that I saw at once the opportunity afforded for the effect on which I had been depending—that is to say, the effect of the *variation of application.* I saw that I could make the first query propounded by the lover—the first query to which the Raven should reply "Nevermore"—that I could make this first query a commonplace one—the second less so—the third still less, and so on—until at length the lover, startled from his original *nonchalance* by the melancholy character of the word itself—by its frequent repetition—and by a consideration of the ominous reputation of the fowl that uttered it—is at length excited to superstition, and wildly propounds queries of a far different character—queries whose solution he has passionately at heart—propounds them half in superstition and half in that species of despair which delights in self-torture—propounds them not altogether because he believes in the prophetic or demoniac character of the bird (which, reason assures him, is merely repeating a lesson learned by rote) but because he experiences a frenzied pleasure in so modeling his questions as to receive from the *expected* "Nevermore" the most delicious because the most intolerable of sorrow. Perceiving the opportunity thus afforded me—or, more strictly, thus forced upon me in the progress of the construction—I first established in mind the climax, or concluding query—that query to which "Nevermore" should be in the last place an answer—that query in reply to which this word "Nevermore" should involve the utmost conceivable amount of sorrow and despair.

Here then the poem may be said to have its beginning—at the end, where all works of art should begin—for it was here, at this point of my preconsiderations, that I first put pen to paper in the composition of the stanza:

"Prophet," said I, "thing of evil! prophet still if bird or devil!
By that heaven that bends above us—by that God we both adore,
Tell this soul with sorrow laden, if within the distant Aidenn,
It shall clasp a sainted maiden whom the angels name Lenore—
Clasp a rare and radiant maiden whom the angels name Lenore."
Quote the raven "Nevermore."

I composed this stanza, at this point, first that, by establishing the climax, I might the better vary and graduate, as regards seriousness and importance, the preceding queries of the lover—and, secondly, that I might definitely settle the rhythm, the metre, and the length and general arrangement of the stanza—as well as graduate the stanzas which were to precede, so that none of them might surpass this in rhythmical effect. Had I been able, in the subsequent composition, to construct more vigorous stanzas, I should, without scruple, have purposely enfeebled them, so as not to interfere with the climacteric effect.

And here I may as well say a few words of the versification. My first object (as usual) was originality. The extent to which this has been neglected, in versification, is one of the most unaccountable things in the world. Admitting that there is little possibility of variety in mere *rhythm*, it is still clear that the possible varieties of metre and stanza are absolutely infinite —and yet, *for centuries, no man, in verse, has ever done, or ever seemed to think of doing, an original thing.* The fact is, that originality (unless in minds of very unusual force) is by no means a matter, as some suppose, of impulse or intuition. In general, to be found, it must be elaborately sought, and although a positive merit of the highest class, demands in its attainment less of invention than negation.

Of course, I pretend to no originality in either the rhythm or metre of the "Raven." The former is trochaic—the latter is octameter acatalectic, alternating with heptameter catalectic repeated in the *refrain* of the fifth verse, and terminating with tetrameter catalectic. Less pedantically— the feet employed throughout (trochees) consist of a long syllable followed by a short: the first line of the stanza consists of eight of these feet—the second of seven and a half (in effect two-thirds)—the third of eight—the fourth of seven and a half —the fifth the same—the sixth three and a half. Now, each of these lines, taken individually, has been employed before, and what originality the "Raven" has, is in their *combination into stanza;* nothing even remotely approaching this combination has ever been attempted. The effect of this originality of combination is aided by other unusual, and some altogether novel effects, arising from an extension of the application of the principles of rhyme and alliteration.

The next point to be considered was the mode of bringing together the lover and the Raven—and the first branch of this consideration was the *locale.* For this the most natural suggestion might seem to be a forest, or the fields—but it has always appeared to me that a close *circumscription of space* is absolutely necessary to the effect of insulated incident:—it has the force of a frame to a picture. It has an indisputable moral power in keeping concentrated the attention, and, of course, must not be confounded with mere unity of place.

I determined, then, to place the lover in his chamber—in a chamber rendered sacred to him by memories of her who had frequented it. The room is represented as richly furnished—this in mere pursuance of the ideas I have already explained on the subject of Beauty, as the sole true poetical thesis.

The *locale* being thus determined, I had now to introduce the bird—and the thought of introducing him through the window, was inevitable. The idea of making the lover suppose, in the first instance, that the flapping of the wings of the bird against the shutter, is a "tapping" at the door, originated in a wish to increase, by prolonging, the reader's curiosity, and in a desire to admit the incidental effect arising from the lover's throwing open the door, finding all dark, and thence adopting the half-fancy that it was the spirit of his mistress that knocked.

I made the night tempestuous, first, to account for the Raven's seeking admission, and secondly, for the effect of contrast with the (physical) serenity within the chamber.

I made the bird alight on the bust of Pallas, also for the effect of contrast between the marble and the plumage—it being understood that the bust was absolutely *suggested* by the bird—the bust of *Pallas* being chosen, first, as most in keeping with the scholarship of the lover, and, secondly, for the sonorousness of the word, Pallas, itself.

About the middle of the poem, also, I have availed myself of the force of contrast, with a view of deepening the ultimate impression. For example, an air of the fantastic—approaching as nearly to the ludicrous as was admissible—is given to the Raven's entrance. He comes in "with many a flirt and flutter."

Not the *least obeisance made he*—not a
      moment stopped or stayed he,
But with mien of lord or lady, perched
      above my chamber door.

In the two stanzas which follow, the design is more obviously carried out:—

Then this ebony bird beguiling my sad
      fancy into smiling
By the *grave and stern decorum of the
      countenance it wore,*
"Though thy *crest be shorn and shaven,*
      thou," I said, "art sure no craven,
Ghastly grim and ancient Raven wander-
      ing from the nightly shore—
Tell me what thy lordly name is on the
      Night's Plutonian shore?"
      Quoth the Raven "Nevermore."

Much I marvelled *this ungainly fowl* to
      hear discourse so plainly,
Though its answer little meaning—little
      relevancy bore;
For we cannot help agreeing that no living
      human being
*Ever yet was blessed with seeing bird above
      his chamber door*—
*Bird or beast upon the sculptured bust
      above his chamber door,*
With such name as "Nevermore."

The effect of the *dénouement* being thus provided for, I immediately drop the fantastic for a tone of the most profound seriousness:—this tone commencing in the stanza directly following the one last quoted, with the line,

But the Raven, sitting lonely on that placid
      bust, spoke only, etc.

From this epoch the lover no longer jests —no longer sees any thing even of the fantastic in the Raven's demeanor. He speaks of him as a "grim, ungainly, ghastly, gaunt, and ominous bird of yore," and feels the "fiery eyes" burning into his "bosom's core." This revolution of thought, or fancy, on the lover's part, is intended

to induce a similar one on the part of the reader—to bring the mind into a proper frame for the *dénouement*—which is now brought about as rapidly and as *directly* as possible.

With the *dénouement* proper—with the Raven's reply, "Nevermore," to the lover's final demand if he shall meet his mistress in another world—the poem, in its obvious phase, that of a simple narrative, may be said to have its completion. So far, every thing is within the limits of the accountable —of the real. A raven, having learned by rote the single word "Nevermore," and having escaped from the custody of its owner, is driven at midnight, through the violence of a storm, to seek admission at a window from which a light still gleams— the chamber-window of a student, occupied half in poring over a volume, half in dreaming of a beloved mistress deceased. The casement being thrown open at the fluttering of the bird's wings, the bird itself perches on the most convenient seat out of the immediate reach of the student, who, amused by the incident and the oddity of the visitor's demeanor, demands of it, in jest and without looking for a reply, its name. The raven addressed, answers with its customary word, "Nevermore"—a word which finds immediate echo in the melancholy heart of the student, who, giving utterance aloud to certain thoughts suggested by the occasion, is again startled by the fowl's repetition of "Nevermore." The student now guesses the state of the case, but is impelled, as I have before explained, by the human thirst for self-torture, and in part by superstition, to propound such queries to the bird as will bring him, the lover, the most of the luxury of sorrow, through the anticipated answer "Nevermore." With the indulgence to the extreme, of this self-torture, the narration, in what I have termed its first or obvious phase, has a natural termination, and so far there has been no overstepping of the limits of the real.

But in subjects so handled, however skilfully, or with however vivid an array of incident, there is always a certain hardness or nakedness, which repels the artistical eye. Two things are invariably required— first, some amount of complexity, or more properly, adaptation; and, secondly, some amount of suggestiveness—some under current, however indefinite, of meaning. It is this latter, in especial, which imparts to a work of art so much of that *richness* (to borrow from colloquy a forcible term) which we are too fond of confounding with *the ideal*. It is the *excess* of the suggested meaning—it is the rendering this the upper instead of the under current of the theme —which turns into prose (and that of the very flattest kind) the so called poetry of the so called transcendentalists.

Holding these opinions, I added the two concluding stanzas of the poem—their suggestiveness being thus made to pervade all the narrative which has preceded them. The under-current of meaning is rendered first apparent in the lines—

"Take thy beak from out *my heart,* and
    take thy form from off my door!"
Quoth the Raven "Nevermore!"

It will be observed that the words, "from out my heart," involve the first metaphorical expression in the poem. They, with the answer, "Nevermore," dispose the mind to seek a moral in all that has been previously narrated. The reader begins now to regard the Raven as emblematical—but it is not until the very last line of the very last stanza, that the intention of making him emblematical of *Mournful and Never-ending Remembrance* is permitted distinctly to be seen:

And the Raven, never flitting, still is sitting, still is sitting,
On the pallid bust of Pallas just above my chamber door;
And his eyes have all the seeming of a demon's that is dreaming,
And the lamplight o'er him streaming throws his shadow on the floor;
And my soul *from out that shadow* that lies floating on the floor
    Shall be lifted—nevermore.

LIGEIA
[1840 (1838)]

And the will therein lieth, which dieth not. Who knoweth the mysteries of the will, with its vigor? For God is but a great will pervading all things by nature of its intentness. Man doth not yield himself to the angels, nor unto death utterly, save only through the weakness of his feeble will.

JOSEPH GLANVILL.[1]

I CANNOT, for my soul, remember how, when, or even precisely where, I first became acquainted with the Lady Ligeia. Long years have since elapsed, and my memory is feeble through much suffering. Or, perhaps, I cannot *now* bring these points to mind, because, in truth, the character of my beloved, her rare learning, her singular yet placid cast of beauty, and the thrilling and enthralling eloquence of her low, musical language, made their way into my heart by paces so steadily and stealthily progressive that they have been unnoticed and unknown. Yet I believe that I met her first and most frequently in some large, old, decaying city near the Rhine. Of her family—I have surely heard her speak—that it is of a remotely ancient date cannot be doubted. Ligeia! Buried in studies of a nature more than all else adapted to deaden impressions of the outward world, it is by that sweet word alone —by Ligeia—that I bring before mine eyes in fancy the image of her who is no more. And now, while I write, a recollection flashes upon me that I have *never known* the paternal name of her who was my friend and my betrothed, and who became the partner of my studies, and finally the wife of my bosom. Was it a playful charge on the part of my Ligeia? or was it a test of my strength of affection that I should institute no inquiries upon this point? or was it rather a caprice of my own—a

---

[1] This Cambridge Platonist, 1636-1680, may have written the passage quoted as epigraph, but it has not been located in his extant works.

wildly romantic offering on the shrine of the most passionate devotion? I but indistinctly recall the fact itself—what wonder that I have utterly forgotten the circumstances which originated or attended it? And, indeed, if ever that spirit which is entitled *Romance*—if ever she, the wan and the misty-winged *Ashtophet* of idolatrous Egypt, presided, as they tell, over marriages ill-omened, then most surely she presided over mine.[2]

There is one dear topic, however, on which my memory fails me not. It is the person of Ligeia. In stature she was tall, somewhat slender, and in her latter days, even emaciated. I would in vain attempt to portray the majesty, the quiet ease, of her demeanor, or the incomprehensible lightness and elasticity of her footfall. She came and departed like a shadow. I was never made aware of her entrance into my closed study, save by the dear music of her low sweet voice, as she placed her delicate hand upon my shoulder. In beauty of face no maiden ever equalled her. It was the radiance of an opium dream—an airy and spirit-lifting vision more wildly divine than the fantasies which hovered about the slumbering souls of the daughters of Delos.[3] Yet her features were not of that regular mould which we have been falsely taught to worship in the classical labors of the heathen. "There is no exquisite beauty," says Bacon, Lord Verulam, speaking truly of all the forms and *genera* of beauty, "without some *strangeness* in the proportions." Yet, although I saw that the features of Ligeia were not of a classic regularity, although I perceived that her loveliness was indeed "exquisite," and felt that there was much of "strangeness" pervading it, yet I have tried in vain to detect the irregularity, and to trace home my own perception of "the strange." I examined the contour of the lofty and pale forehead —it was faultless—how cold indeed that word when applied to a majesty so divine! —the skin rivalling the purest ivory, the commanding extent and repose, the gentle prominence of the regions above the tem-

ples, and then the raven-black, the glossy, the luxuriant and naturally-curling tresses, setting forth the full force of the Homeric epithet, "hyacinthine!" I looked at the delicate outlines of the nose—and nowhere but in the graceful medallions of the Hebrews had I beheld a similar perfection. There was the same luxurious smoothness of surface, the same scarcely perceptible tendency to the aquiline, the same harmoniously curved nostrils speaking the free spirit. I regarded the sweet mouth. Here was indeed the triumph of all things heavenly—the magnificent turn of the short upper lip—the soft, voluptuous slumber of the under—the dimples which sported, and the color which spoke—the teeth glancing back, with a brilliancy almost startling, every ray of the holy light which fell upon them in her serene, and placid, yet most exultingly radiant of all smiles. I scrutinized the formation of the chin—and here, too, I found the gentleness of breadth, the softness and the majesty, the fulness and the spirituality, of the Greek,—the contour which the god Apollo revealed but in a dream, to Cleomenes, the son of the Athenian.[4] And then I peered into the large eyes of Ligeia.

For eyes we have no models in the remotely antique. It might have been, too, that in these eyes of my beloved lay the secret to which Lord Verulam alludes. They were, I must believe, far larger than the ordinary eyes of our race. They were even far fuller than the fullest of the Gazelle eyes of the tribe of the valley of Nourjahad.[5] Yet it was only at intervals—in moments

---

[2] The reference is to Ashtoreth, or Ashtaroth, an oriental name for Astarte, goddess of fertility.

[3] On the island of Delos, Greek maidens brought offerings to the temple of Artemis.

[4] The Venus of Medici was ascribed to Cleomenes, son of Apollodorus, the Athenian. Poe conceives of him as inspired by Apollo.

[5] Mrs. Frances Sheridan (1724-1766) wrote the novel, *The History of Nourjahad* (1767). Poe's reference is to its exotic setting.

of intense excitement—that this peculiarity became more than slightly noticeable in Ligeia. And at such moments was her beauty—in my heated fancy thus it appeared perhaps—the beauty of beings either above or apart from the earth—the beauty of the fabulous Houri of the Turk. The color of the orbs was the most brilliant of black, and far over them hung jetty lashes of great length. The brows, slightly irregular in outline, had the same hue. The "strangeness," however, which I found in the eyes was of a nature distinct from the formation, or the color, or the brilliancy of the features, and must, after all, be referred to the *expression*. Ah, word of no meaning! behind whose vast latitude of mere sound we intrench our ignorance of so much of the spiritual. The expression of the eyes of Ligeia! How, for long hours have I pondered upon it! How have I, through the whole of a midsummer night, struggled to fathom it! What was it—that something more profound than the well of Democritus [6]—which lay far within the pupils of my beloved? What *was* it? I was possessed with a passion to discover. Those eyes! those large, those shining, those divine orbs! they became to me twin stars of Leda, and I to them devoutest of astrologers.[7] Not for a moment was the unfathomable meaning of their glance, by day or by night, absent from my soul.

There is no point, among the many incomprehensible anomalies of the science of mind, more thrillingly exciting than the fact—never, I believe, noticed in the schools—that in our endeavors to recall to memory something long forgotten we often find ourselves *upon the very verge* of remembrance without being able, in the end, to remember. And thus how frequently, in my intense scrutiny of Ligeia's eyes, have I felt approaching the full knowledge of their expression—felt it approaching—yet not quite be mine—and so at length entirely depart. And (strange, oh strangest mystery of all!) I found, in the commonest objects of the universe, a circle of analogies to that expression. I mean to say

that, subsequently to the period when Ligeia's beauty passed into my spirit, there dwelling as in a shrine, I derived, from many existences in the material world, a sentiment such as I felt always aroused within me by her large and luminous orbs. Yet not the more could I define that sentiment, or analyze, or even steadily view it. I recognized it, let me repeat, sometimes in the commonest objects of the universe. It has flashed upon me in the survey of a rapidly-growing vine—in the contemplation of a moth, a butterfly, a chrysalis, a stream of running water. I have felt it in the ocean, in the falling of a meteor. I have felt it in the glances of unusually aged people. And there are one or two stars in heaven—(one especially, a star of the sixth magnitude, double and changeable, to be found near the large star in Lyra) in a telescopic scrutiny of which I have been made aware of the feeling. I have been filled with it by certain sounds from stringed instruments, and not unfrequently by passages from books. Among innumerable other instances, I well remember something in a volume of Joseph Glanvill, which (perhaps merely from its quaintness—who shall say?) never failed to inspire me with the sentiment,—"And the will therein lieth, which dieth not. Who knoweth the mysteries of the will, with its vigor? For God is but a great will pervading all things by nature of its intentness. Man doth not yield him to the angels, nor unto death utterly, but only through the weakness of his feeble will."

Length of years, and subsequent reflection, have enabled me to trace, indeed, some remote connexion between this passage in the old English moralist and a portion of the character of Ligeia. An *intensity* in thought, action, or speech, was possibly, in her, a result, or at least an

---

[6] The Greek philosopher Democritus, fifth century B. C., said that truth lay in a deep well.

[7] Castor and Pollux, sons of Leda and Zeus, provided names for the two brightest stars in the constellation Gemini.

index, of that gigantic volition which, during our long intercourse, failed to give other and more immediate evidence of its existence. Of all the women whom I have ever known she, the outwardly calm, the ever-placid Ligeia, was the most violently a prey to the tumultuous vultures of stern passion. And of such passion I could form no estimate, save by the miraculous expansion of those eyes which at once so delighted and appalled me, by the almost magical melody, modulation, distinctness and placidity of her very low voice, and by the fierce energy (rendered doubly effective by contrast with her manner of utterance) of the words which she habitually uttered.

I have spoken of the learning of Ligeia: it was immense—such as I have never known in woman. In the classical tongues was she deeply proficient, and as far as my own acquaintance extended in regard to the modern dialects of Europe, I have never known her at fault. Indeed upon any theme of the most admired, because simply the most abstruse of the boasted erudition of the academy, have I *ever* found Ligeia at fault? How singularly, how thrillingly, this one point in the nature of my wife has forced itself, at this late period only, upon my attention! I said her knowledge was such as I had never known in woman. Where breathes the man who, like her, has traversed, and successfully, *all* the wide areas of moral, natural, and mathematical science? I saw not then what I now clearly perceive, that the acquisitions of Ligeia were gigantic, were astounding—yet I was sufficiently aware of her infinite supremacy to resign myself, with a childlike confidence, to her guidance through the chaotic world of metaphysical investigation at which I was most busily occupied during the earlier years of our marriage. With how vast a triumph—with how vivid a delight—with how much of all that is ethereal in hope—did I *feel*, as she bent over me in studies but little sought for—but less known—that delicious vista by slow but perceptible degrees expanding before me, down whose long, gorgeous, and all un-

trodden path, I might at length pass onward to the goal of a wisdom too divinely precious not to be forbidden!

How poignant, then, must have been the grief with which, after some years, I beheld my well-grounded expectations take wings to themselves and flee away! Without Ligeia I was but as a child groping benighted. Her presence, her readings alone, rendered vividly luminous the many mysteries of the transcendentalism in which we were immersed. Letters, lambent and golden, grew duller than Saturnian lead, wanting the radiant lustre of her eyes. And now those eyes shone less and less frequently upon the pages over which I pored. Ligeia grew ill. The wild eyes blazed with a too—too glorious effulgence; the pale fingers became of the transparent waxen hue of the grave—and the blue veins upon the lofty forehead swelled and sunk impetuously with the tides of the most gentle emotion. I saw that she must die—and I struggled desperately in spirit with the grim Azrael.[8] And the struggles of the passionate wife were, to my astonishment, even more energetic than my own. There had been much in her stern nature to impress me with the belief that, to her, death would have come without its terrors—but not so. Words are impotent to convey any just idea of the fierceness of resistance with which she wrestled with the dark shadow. I groaned in anguish at the pitiable spectacle. I would have soothed—I would have reasoned; but in the intensity of her wild desire for life—for life—*but* for life, solace and reason were alike the uttermost of folly. Yet not for an instant, amid the most convulsive writhings of her fierce spirit, was shaken the external placidity of her demeanor. Her voice grew more gentle—grew more low—yet I would not wish to dwell upon the wild meaning of the quietly-uttered words. My brain reeled as I hearkened entranced, to a melody more than mortal—to assumptions and aspirations which mortality had never before known.

[8] The Hebrew angel of death.

That she loved me, I should not have doubted; and I might have been easily aware that, in a bosom such as hers, love would have reigned no ordinary passion. But in death only, was I fully impressed with the strength of her affection. For long hours, detaining my hand, would she pour out before me the overflowing of a heart whose more than passionate devotion amounted to idolatry. How had I deserved to be so blessed by such confessions?—how had I deserved to be so cursed with the removal of my beloved in the hour of her making them? But upon this subject I cannot bear to dilate. Let me say only, that in Ligeia's more than womanly abandonment to a love, alas! all unmerited, all unworthily bestowed, I at length recognized the principle of her longing with so wildly earnest a desire for the life which was now fleeing so rapidly away. It is this wild longing—it is this eager vehemence of desire for life—*but* for life—that I have no power to portray—no utterance capable of expressing.

[At high noon of the night in which she departed, beckoning me, peremptorily, to her side, she bade me repeat certain verses composed by herself not many days before.[9] I obeyed her. They were these:

Lo! 'tis a gala night
Within the lonesome latter years!
An angel throng, bewinged, bedight
In veils, and drowned in tears,
Sit in a theatre, to see
A play of hopes and fears,
While the orchestra breathes fitfully
The music of the spheres.

Mimes, in the form of God on high,
Mutter and mumble low,
And hither and thither fly;
Mere puppets they, who come and go
At bidding of vast formless things
That shift the scenery to and fro,
Flapping from out their condor wings
Invisible Wo!

That motley drama!—oh, be sure
It shall not be forgot!
With its Phantom chased for evermore,
By a crowd that seize it not,
Through a circle that ever returneth in
To the self-same spot;
And much of Madness, and more of Sin
And horror, the soul of the plot!

But see, amid the mimic rout
A crawling shape intrude!
A blood-red thing that writhes from out
The scenic solitude!
It writhes!—it writhes!—with mortal pangs
The mimes become its food,
And seraphs sob at vermin fangs
In human gore imbued.

Out—out are the lights—out all!
And over each quivering form,
The curtain, a funeral pall,
Comes down with the rush of a storm—
While the angels, all pallid and wan,
Uprising, unveiling, affirm
That the play is the tragedy, "Man,"
And its hero the Conqueror Worm.

"O God!" half shrieked Ligeia, leaping to her feet and extending her arms aloft with a spasmodic movement, as I made an end of these lines—"O God! O Divine Father!—shall these things be undeviatingly so?—shall this conqueror be not once conquered? Are we not part and parcel in Thee? Who—who knoweth the mysteries of the will with its vigor? Man doth not yield him to the angels, *nor unto death utterly,* save only through the weakness of his feeble will."

And now, as if exhausted with emotion, she suffered her white arms to fall, and returned solemnly to her bed of death. And as she breathed her last sighs, there came mingled with them a low murmur from her lips. I bent to them my ear and distin-

---

[9] Poe published this poem under the title, "The Conqueror Worm," in *Graham's Magazine,* January, 1843.

guished, again, the concluding words of the passage in Glanvill:—*"Man doth not yield him to the angels, nor unto death utterly, save only through the weakness of his feeble will."*][10]

She died—and I, crushed into the very dust with sorrow, could no longer endure the lonely desolation of my dwelling in the dim and decaying city by the Rhine. I had no lack of what the world terms wealth—Ligeia had brought me far more, very far more, than ordinarily falls to the lot of mortals. After a few months, therefore, of weary and aimless wandering, I purchased, and put in some repair, an abbey, which I shall not name, in one of the wildest and least frequented portions of fair England. The gloomy and dreary grandeur of the building, the almost savage aspect of the domain, the many melancholy and time-honored memories connected with both, had much in unison with the feelings of utter abandonment which had driven me into that remote and unsocial region of the country. Yet although the external abbey, with its verdant decay hanging about it, suffered but little alteration, I gave way, with a child-like perversity, and perchance with a faint hope of alleviating my sorrows, to a display of more than regal magnificence within. For such follies even in childhood I had imbibed a taste, and now they came back to me as if in the dotage of grief. Alas, I feel how much even of incipient madness might have been discovered in the gorgeous and fantastic draperies, in the solemn carvings of Egypt, in the wild cornices and furniture, in the bedlam patterns of the carpets of tufted gold! I had become a bounden slave in the trammels of opium, and my labors and my orders had taken a coloring from my dreams. But these absurdities I must not pause to detail. Let me speak only of that one chamber, ever accursed, whither, in a moment of mental alienation, I led from the altar as my bride—as the successor of the unforgotten Ligeia—the fair-haired and blue-eyed Lady Rowena Trevanion, of Tremaine.

There is no individual portion of the architecture and decoration of that bridal chamber which is not now visibly before me. Where were the souls of the haughty family of the bride, when, through thirst of gold, they permitted to pass the threshold of an apartment *so* bedecked, a maiden and a daughter so beloved? I have said that I minutely remember the details of the chamber—yet I am sadly forgetful on topics of deep moment—and here there was no system, no keeping, in the fantastic display, to take hold upon the memory. The room lay in a high turret of the castellated abbey, was pentagonal in shape, and of capacious size. Occupying the whole southern face of the pentagon was the sole window—an immense sheet of unbroken glass from Venice—a single pane, and tinted of a leaden hue, so that the rays of either the sun or moon, passing through it, fell with a ghastly lustre upon the objects within. Over the upper portion of this huge window, extended the trellice-work of an aged vine, which clambered up the massy walls of the turret. The ceiling, of gloomy-looking oak, was excessively lofty, vaulted, and elaborately fretted with the wildest and most grotesque specimens of a semi-Gothic, semi-Druidical device. From out the most central recess of this melancholy vaulting, depended, by a single chain of gold, with long links, a huge censer of the same metal, Saracenic in pattern, and with many perforations so contrived that there writhed in and out of them, as if endued with a serpent vitality, a continual succession of parti-colored fires. Some few ottomans and golden candelabra of Eastern figure were in various stations about—and there was the couch, too, the bridal couch, of an Indian model, and low, and sculptured of solid ebony, with a canopy above. In each of the angles of the chamber, stood on end a gigantic sarcophagus of black granite, from the tombs of the kings over against Luxor, with their

---

[10] Passages enclosed in brackets did not appear in the original publication of "Ligeia" in the *American Museum.*

aged lids full of immemorial sculpture. But in the draping of the apartment lay, alas! the chief fantasy of all. The lofty walls—gigantic in height—even unproportionably so, were hung from summit to foot, in vast folds, with a heavy and massive-looking tapestry—tapestry of a material which was found alike as a carpet on the floor, as a covering for the ottomans and the ebony bed, as a canopy for the bed, and as the gorgeous volutes of the curtains which partially shaded the window. The material was the richest cloth of gold. It was spotted all over, at irregular intervals, with arabesque figures, about a foot in diameter, and wrought upon the cloth in patterns of the most jetty black. But these figures partook of the true character of the arabesque only when regarded from a single point of view. By a contrivance now common, and indeed traceable to a very remote period of antiquity, they were made changeable in aspect. To one entering the room they bore the appearance of simple monstrosities; but upon a farther advance, this appearance gradually departed; and, step by step, as the visiter moved his station in the chamber, he saw himself surrounded by an endless succession of the ghastly forms which belong to the superstition of the Northman, or arise in the guilty slumbers of the monk. The phantasmagoric effect was vastly heightened by the artificial introduction of a strong continual current of wind behind the draperies—giving a hideous and uneasy animation to the whole.

In halls such as these—in a bridal chamber such as this—I passed, with the Lady of Tremaine, the unhallowed hours of the first month of our marriage—passed them with but little disquietude. That my wife dreaded the fierce moodiness of my temper —that she shunned me, and loved me but little—I could not help perceiving—but it gave me rather pleasure than otherwise. I loathed her with a hatred belonging more to demon than to man. My memory flew back, (oh, with what intensity of regret!) to Ligeia, the beloved, the beautiful, the entombed. I revelled in recollections of her purity, of her wisdom, of her lofty, her ethereal nature, of her passionate, her idolatrous love. Now, then, did my spirit fully and freely burn with more than all the fires of her own. In the excitement of my opium dreams (for I was habitually fettered in the iron shackles of the drug) I would call aloud upon her name, during the silence of the night, or among the sheltered recesses of the glens by day, as if, through the wild eagerness, the solemn passion, the consuming ardor of my longing for the departed Ligeia I could restore her to the pathway she had abandoned upon the earth.

About the commencement of the second month of the marriage, the Lady Rowena was attacked with sudden illness from which her recovery was slow. The fever which consumed her rendered her nights uneasy, and, in her perturbed state of half-slumber, she spoke of sounds, and of motions, in and about the chamber of the turret, which had no origin save in the distemper of her fancy, or, perhaps, in the phantastic influences of the chamber itself. She became at length convalescent— finally well. Yet but a brief period elapsed, ere a second more violent disorder again threw her upon a bed of suffering—and from this attack her frame, at all times feeble, never altogether recovered. Her illnesses were, after this epoch, of alarming character, and of more alarming recurrence, defying alike the knowledge and the great exertions of her medical men. With the increase of the chronic disease, which had thus, apparently, taken too sure hold upon her constitution to be eradicated by human means, I could not fail to observe a similar increase in the nervous irritation of her temperament, and in her excitability by trivial causes of fear. Indeed reason seemed fast tottering from her throne. She spoke again, and now more frequently and pertinaciously, of the sounds, of the slight sounds, and of the unusual motions among the tapestries, to which she had formerly alluded.

One night, near the closing in of September, she pressed this distressing subject with more than usual emphasis upon my attention. She had just awakened from an unquiet slumber, and I had been watching, with feelings half of anxiety, half of vague terror, the workings of her emaciated countenance. I sat by the side of her ebony bed, upon one of the ottomans of India. She partly arose, and spoke, in an earnest low whisper, of sounds which she *then* heard, but which I could not hear, of motions which she *then* saw, but which I could not perceive. The wind was rushing hurriedly behind the tapestries, and I wished to show her (what, let me confess it, I could not *all* believe) that those faint, almost inarticulate breathings, and the very gentle variations of the figures upon the wall, were but the natural effects of that customary rushing of the wind. But a deadly pallor, overspreading her face, had proved to me that my exertions to reassure her would be fruitless. She appeared to be fainting, and no attendants were within call. I remembered where was deposited a decanter of light wine which had been ordered by her physicians, and hastened across the chamber to procure it. But, as I stepped beneath the light of the censer, two circumstances of a startling nature attracted my attention. I had felt that some palpable object had passed lightly by my person; and I saw that there lay a faint, indefinite shadow upon the golden carpet, in the very middle of the rich lustre thrown from the censer. But I was wild with the excitement of an immoderate dose of opium, and heeded these things but little, nor spoke of them to Rowena. Having found the wine, I recrossed the chamber, and poured out a gobletful, which I held to the lips of the fainting lady. She had now partially recovered, however, and took, herself, the vessel, while I sank upon an ottoman near me, with eyes riveted upon her person. It was then that I became distinctly aware of a gentle foot-fall upon the carpet, and near the couch; and, in a second thereafter, as Rowena was in the act of raising the wine to her lips, I saw, or may have dreamed that I saw, fall within the goblet, as if from some invisible spring in the atmosphere of the room, three or four large drops of a brilliant and ruby-colored fluid. If this I saw—not so Rowena. She swallowed the wine unhesitatingly, and I forbore to speak to her of a circumstance which must, after all, I considered, have been but the suggestion of a vivid imagination, rendered morbidly active by the terror of the lady, by the opium, and by the hour.

Yet—I cannot conceal it from myself—after this period, a rapid change for the worst took place in the disorder of my wife; so that, on the third subsequent night, the hands of her menials prepared her for the tomb, and on the fourth, I sat alone, with her shrouded body, in that fantastic chamber which had received her as my bride. Wild visions, opium-engendered, flitted shadow-like before me. I gazed with unquiet eye upon the sarcophagi in the angles of the room, upon the varying figures of the drapery, and upon the writhing of the parti-colored fires in the censer overhead. My eyes then fell, as I called to mind the circumstances of a former night, to the spot beneath the glare of the censer where I had seen the faint traces of the shadow. It was there, however, no longer, and breathing with greater freedom, I turned my glances to the pallid and rigid figure upon the bed. Then rushed upon me a thousand memories of Ligeia—and then came back upon my heart, with the turbulent violence of a flood, the whole of that unutterable wo with which I had regarded *her* thus enshrouded. The night waned; and still, with a bosom full of bitter thoughts of the one only and supremely beloved, I remained gazing upon the body of Rowena.

It might have been midnight, or perhaps earlier, or later, for I had taken no note of time, when a sob, low, gentle, but very distinct, startled me from my revery. I *felt* that it came from the bed of ebony—the bed of death. I listened in an agony of superstitious terror—but there was no repetition of the sound; I strained my vision to detect any motion in the corpse, but there was not the slightest perceptible. Yet I could not have been deceived. I *had* heard the noise, however faint, and my soul was awakened within me, as I resolutely and perseveringly kept my attention riveted upon the body. Many minutes elapsed before any circumstance occurred tending to throw light upon the mystery. At length it became evident that a slight, a very faint, and barely noticeable tinge of color had flushed up within the cheeks, and along the sunken small veins of the eyelids. Through a species of unutterable horror and awe, for which the language of mortality has no sufficiently energetic expression, I felt my brain reel, my heart cease to beat, my limbs grow rigid where I sat. Yet a sense of duty finally operated to restore my self-possession. I could no longer doubt that we had been precipitate in our preparations for interment—that Rowena still lived. It was necessary that some immediate exertion be made; yet the turret was altogether apart from the portion of the abbey tenanted by the servants —there were none within call,—I had no means of summoning them to my aid without leaving the room for many minutes— and this I could not venture to do. I therefore struggled alone in my endeavors to call back the spirit still hovering. In a short period it was certain, however, that a relapse had taken place; the color disappeared from both eyelid and cheek, leaving a wanness even more than that of marble; the lips became doubly shrivelled and pinched up in the ghastly expression of death; a repulsive clamminess and coldness overspread rapidly the surface of the body; and all the usual rigorous stiffness immediately supervened. I fell back with a shudder upon the couch from which I had been so startlingly aroused, and again gave myself up to passionate waking visions of Ligeia.

An hour thus elapsed when, (could it be possible?) I was a second time aware of some vague sound issuing from the region of the bed. I listened—in extremity of horror. The sound came again—it was a sigh. Rushing to the corpse, I saw— distinctly saw—a tremor upon the lips. In a minute after, they slightly relaxed, disclosing a bright line of the pearly teeth. Amazement now struggled in my bosom with the profound awe which had hitherto reigned therein alone. I felt that my vision grew dim, that my reason wandered, and it was only by a convulsive effort that I at length succeeded in nerving myself to the task which duty thus, once more, had pointed out. There was now a partial glow upon the forehead and upon the cheek and throat—a perceptible warmth pervaded the whole frame—there was even a slight pulsation at the heart. The lady lived; and with redoubled ardor I betook myself to the task of restoration. I chafed and bathed the temples and the hands, and used every exertion which experience, and no little medical reading, could suggest. But in vain. Suddenly, the color fled, the pulsation ceased, the lips resumed the expression of the dead, and, in an instant afterwards, the whole body took upon itself the icy chilliness, the livid hue, the intense rigidity, the sunken outline, and each and all of the loathsome peculiarities of that which has been, for many days, a tenant of the tomb.

And again I sunk into visions of Ligeia —and again, (what marvel that I shudder while I write?) *again* there reached my ears a low sob from the region of the ebony bed. But why shall I minutely detail the unspeakable horrors of that night? Why shall I pause to relate how, time after time, until near the period of the gray dawn, this hideous drama of revivification was repeated, and how each terrific relapse was only into a sterner and apparently more irredeemable death; [how each agony wore the aspect of a struggle with some invisible foe; and how each struggle was succeeded by I know not what of wild change in the personal appearance of the corpse?] Let me hurry to a conclusion.

The greater part of the fearful night

had worn away, and the corpse of Rowena once again stirred—and now more vigorously than hitherto, although arousing from a dissolution more appalling in its utter hopelessness than any. I had long ceased to struggle or to move, and remained sitting rigidly upon the ottoman, a helpless prey to a whirl of violent emotions, of which extreme awe was perhaps the least terrible, the least consuming. The corpse, I repeat, stirred, and now more vigorously than before. The hues of life flushed up with unwonted energy into the countenance —the limbs relaxed—and, save that the eyelids were yet pressed heavily together, and that the bandages and draperies of the grave still imparted their charnel character to the figure, I might have dreamed that Rowena had indeed shaken off, utterly, the fetters of Death. But if this idea was not, even then, altogether adopted, I could, at least, doubt no longer, when, arising from the bed, tottering, with feeble steps, with closed eyes, and with the manner of one bewildered in a dream, the Lady of Tremaine advanced boldly and palpably into the middle of the apartment.

I trembled not—I stirred not—for a crowd of unutterable fancies connected with the air, the demeanor of the figure, rushing hurriedly through my brain, had paralyzed, had chilled me into stone. I stirred not—but gazed upon the apparition. There was a mad disorder in my thoughts—a tumult unappeasable. Could it, indeed, be the *living* Rowena who confronted me? [Could it indeed be Rowena *at all*—the fair-haired, the blue-eyed Lady Rowena Trevanion of Tremaine?] Why, *why*, should I doubt it? The bandage lay heavily about the mouth—but then it was the mouth of the breathing Lady of Tremaine. And the cheeks—there were the roses as in her noon of life—yes, these were indeed the fair cheeks of the living Lady of Tremaine. And the chin, with its dimples, as in health, was it not hers?— but *had she then grown taller since her malady?* What inexpressible madness seized me with that thought? One bound,

and I had reached her feet! Shrinking from my touch, she let fall from her head, unloosened, the ghastly cerements which had confined it, and there streamed forth, into the rushing atmosphere of the chamber, huge masses of long and dishevelled hair. *It was blacker than the raven wings of the midnight!* And now the eyes opened of the figure which stood before me. "Here then, at least," I shrieked aloud, "can I never—can I never be mistaken—these are the full, and the black, and the wild eyes —of the lady—of the Lady Ligeia!"

THE FALL OF THE HOUSE OF USHER
[1840 (1839)]

Son cœur est un luth suspendu;
Sitôt qu'on le touche il résonne.[1]
DE BÉRANGER

DURING the whole of a dull, dark, and soundless day in the autumn of the year, when the clouds hung oppressively low in the heavens, I had been passing alone, on horseback, through a singularly dreary tract of country; and at length found myself, as the shades of the evening drew on, within view of the melancholy House of Usher. I know not how it was—but, with the first glimpse of the building, a sense of insufferable gloom pervaded my spirit. I say insufferable; for the feeling was unrelieved by any of that half-pleasurable, because poetic, sentiment with which the mind usually receives even the sternest natural images of the desolate or terrible. I looked upon the scene before me—upon the mere house, and the simple landscape features of the domain—upon the bleak walls—upon the vacant eye-like windows —upon a few rank sedges—and upon a few white trunks of decayed trees—with an utter depression of soul which I can compare to no earthly sensation more properly than to the after-dream of the reveller

---

[1] From "Le Refus," meaning "His heart is a suspended lute; as soon as it is touched, it resounds."

upon opium—the bitter lapse into everyday life—the hideous dropping off of the veil. There was an iciness, a sinking, a sickening of the heart—an unredeemed dreariness of thought which no goading of the imagination could torture into aught of the sublime. What was it—I paused to think—what was it that so unnerved me in the contemplation of the House of Usher? It was a mystery all insoluble; nor could I grapple with the shadowy fancies that crowded upon me as I pondered. I was forced to fall back upon the unsatisfactory conclusion, that while, beyond doubt, there *are* combinations of very simple natural objects which have the power of thus affecting us, still the analysis of this power lies among considerations beyond our depth. It was possible, I reflected, that a mere different arrangement of the particulars of the scene, of the details of the picture, would be sufficient to modify, or perhaps to annihilate its capacity for sorrowful impression; and, acting upon this idea, I reined my horse to the precipitous brink of a black and lurid tarn that lay in unruffled lustre by the dwelling, and gazed down—but with a shudder even more thrilling than before—upon the remodelled and inverted images of the gray sedge, and the ghastly tree-stems, and the vacant and eye-like windows.

Nevertheless, in this mansion of gloom I now proposed to myself a sojourn of some weeks. Its proprietor, Roderick Usher, had been one of my boon companions in boyhood; but many years had elapsed since our last meeting. A letter, however, had lately reached me in a distant part of the country—a letter from him—which, in its wildly importunate nature, had admitted of no other than a personal reply. The MS. gave evidence of nervous agitation. The writer spoke of acute bodily illness—of a mental disorder which oppressed him—and of an earnest desire to see me, as his best and indeed his only personal friend, with a view of attempting, by the cheerfulness of my society, some alleviation of his malady. It was the manner in which all this, and much more, was said—it was the apparent *heart* that went with his request—which allowed me no room for hesitation; and I accordingly obeyed forthwith what I still considered a very singular summons.

Although, as boys, we had been even intimate associates, yet I really knew little of my friend. His reserve had been always excessive and habitual. I was aware, however, that his very ancient family had been noted, time out of mind, for a peculiar sensibility of temperament, displaying itself, through long ages, in many works of exalted art, and manifested, of late, in repeated deeds of munificent yet unobtrusive charity, as well as in a passionate devotion to the intricacies, perhaps even more than to the orthodox and easily recognizable beauties, of musical science. I had learned, too, the very remarkable fact, that the stem of the Usher race, all time-honored as it was, had put forth at no period, any enduring branch; in other words, that the entire family lay in the direct line of descent, and had always, with very trifling and very temporary variation, so lain. It was this deficiency, I considered, while running over in thought the perfect keeping of the character of the premises with the accredited character of the people, and while speculating upon the possible influence which the one, in the long lapse of centuries, might have exercised upon the other—it was this deficiency, perhaps, of collateral issue, and the consequent undeviating transmission, from sire to son of the patrimony with the name, which had, at length, so identified the two as to merge the original title of the estate in the quaint and equivocal appellation of the "House of Usher"—an appellation which seemed to include, in the minds of the peasantry who used it, both the family and the family mansion.

I have said that the sole effect of my somewhat childish experiment—that of looking down within the tarn—had been to deepen the first singular impression. There can be no doubt that the consciousness of the rapid increase of my superstition—for why should I not so term it?—served mainly to accelerate the increase itself. Such, I have long known, is the paradoxical law of all sentiments having terror as a basis. And it might have been for this reason only, that, when I again uplifted my eyes to the house itself, from its image in the pool, there grew in my mind a strange fancy—a fancy so ridiculous, indeed, that I but mention it to show the vivid force of the sensations which oppressed me. I had so worked upon my imagination as really to believe that about the whole mansion and domain there hung an atmosphere peculiar to themselves and their immediate vicinity—an atmosphere which had no affinity with the air of heaven, but which had reeked up from the decayed trees, and the gray wall, and the silent tarn—a pestilent and mystic vapor, dull, sluggish, faintly discernible, and leaden-hued.

Shaking off from my spirit what *must* have been a dream, I scanned more narrowly the real aspect of the building. Its principal feature seemed to be that of an excessive antiquity. The discoloration of ages had been great. Minute fungi overspread the whole exterior, hanging in a fine tangled web-work from the eaves. Yet all this was apart from any extraordinary dilapidation. No portion of the masonry had fallen; and there appeared to be a wild inconsistency between its still perfect adaptation of parts, and the crumbling condition of the individual stones. In this there was much that reminded me of the specious totality of old wood-work which has rotted for long years in some neglected vault, with no disturbance from the breath of the external air. Beyond this indication of extensive decay, however, the fabric gave little token of instability. Perhaps the eye of a scrutinizing observer might have discovered a barely perceptible fissure, which, extending from the roof of the building in front, made its way down the wall in a zigzag direction, until it became lost in the sullen waters of the tarn.

Noticing these things, I rode over a short causeway to the house. A servant in waiting took my horse, and I entered the Gothic archway of the hall. A valet, of stealthy step, thence conducted me, in silence, through many dark and intricate passages in my progress to the *studio* of his master. Much that I encountered on the way contributed, I know not how, to heighten the vague sentiments of which I have already spoken. While the objects around me—while the carvings of the ceilings, the sombre tapestries of the walls, the ebon blackness of the floors, and the phantasmagoric armorial trophies which rattled as I strode, were but matters to which, or to such as which, I have been accustomed from my infancy—while I hesitated not to acknowledge how familiar was all this—I still wondered to find how unfamiliar were the fancies which ordinary images were stirring up. On one of the staircases, I met the physician of the family. His countenance, I thought, wore a mingled expression of low cunning and perplexity. He accosted me with trepidation and passed on. The valet now threw open a door and ushered me into the presence of his master.

The room in which I found myself was very large and lofty. The windows were long, narrow, and pointed, and at so vast a distance from the black oaken floor as to be altogether inaccessible from within. Feeble gleams of encrimsoned light made their way through the trellised panes, and served to render sufficiently distinct the more prominent objects around; the eye, however, struggled in vain to reach the remoter angles of the chamber, or the recesses of the vaulted and fretted ceiling. Dark draperies hung upon the walls. The general furniture was profuse, comfortless, antique, and tattered. Many books and musical instruments lay scattered about, but failed to give any vitality to the scene. I felt that I breathed an atmosphere of sorrow. An air of stern, deep, and irredeemable gloom hung over and pervaded all.

Upon my entrance, Usher arose from a

sofa on which he had been lying at full length, and greeted me with a vivacious warmth which had much in it, I at first thought, of an overdone cordiality—of the constrained effort of the *ennuyé* [2] man of the world. A glance, however, at his countenance, convinced me of his perfect sincerity. We sat down; and for some moments, while he spoke not, I gazed upon him with a feeling half of pity, half of awe. Surely, man had never before so terribly altered, in so brief a period, as had Roderick Usher! It was with difficulty that I could bring myself to admit the identity of the wan being before me with the companion of my early boyhood. Yet the character of his face had been at all times remarkable. A cadaverousness of complexion; an eye large, liquid, and luminous beyond comparison; lips somewhat thin and very pallid, but of a surpassingly beautiful curve; a nose of a delicate Hebrew model, but with a breadth of nostril unusual in similar formations; a finely moulded chin, speaking, in its want of prominence, of a want of moral energy; hair of a more than web-like softness and tenuity; these features, with an inordinate expansion above the regions of the temple, made up altogether a countenance not easily to be forgotten. And now in the mere exaggeration of the prevailing character of these features, and of the expression they were wont to convey, lay so much of change that I doubted to whom I spoke. The now ghastly pallor of the skin, and the now miraculous lustre of the eye, above all things startled and even awed me. The silken hair, too, had been suffered to grow all unheeded, and as, in its wild gossamer texture, it floated rather than fell about the face, I could not, even with effort, connect its Arabesque expression with any idea of simple humanity.

In the manner of my friend I was at once struck with an incoherence—an inconsistency; and I soon found this to arise from a series of feeble and futile struggles to overcome an habitual trepidancy—an excessive nervous agitation. For

something of this nature I had indeed been prepared, no less by his letter, than by reminiscences of certain boyish traits, and by conclusions deduced from his peculiar physical conformation and temperament. His action was alternately vivacious and sullen. His voice varied rapidly from a tremulous indecision (when the animal spirits seemed utterly in abeyance) to that species of energetic concision—that abrupt, weighty, unhurried, and hollow-sounding enunciation—that leaden, self-balanced and perfectly modulated guttural utterance, which may be observed in the lost drunkard, or the irreclaimable eater of opium, during the periods of his most intense excitement.

It was thus that he spoke of the object of my visit, of his earnest desire to see me, and of the solace he expected me to afford him. He entered, at some length, into what he conceived to be the nature of his malady. It was, he said, a constitutional and a family evil, and one for which he despaired to find a remedy—a mere nervous affection, he immediately added, which would undoubtedly soon pass off. It displayed itself in a host of unnatural sensations. Some of these, as he detailed them, interested and bewildered me; although, perhaps, the terms, and the general manner of the narration had their weight. He suffered much from a morbid acuteness of the senses; the most insipid food was alone endurable; he could wear only garments of certain texture; the odors of all flowers were oppressive; his eyes were tortured by even a faint light; and there were but peculiar sounds, and these from stringed instruments, which did not inspire him with horror.

To an anomalous species of terror I found him a bounden slave. "I shall perish," said he, "I *must* perish in this deplorable folly. Thus, thus, and not otherwise, shall I be lost. I dread the events of the future, not in themselves, but in their results. I shudder at the thought of any,

---

[2] Bored.

even the most trivial, incident, which may operate upon this intolerable agitation of soul. I have, indeed, no abhorrence of danger, except in its absolute effect—in terror. In this unnerved—in this pitiable condition—I feel that the period will sooner or later arrive when I must abandon life and reason together, in some struggle with the grim phantasm, FEAR."

I learned, moreover, at intervals, and through broken and equivocal hints, another singular feature of his mental condition. He was enchained by certain superstitious impressions in regard to the dwelling which he tenanted, and whence, for many years, he had never ventured forth —in regard to an influence whose supposititious force was conveyed in terms too shadowy here to be restated—an influence which some peculiarities in the mere form and substance of his family mansion, had, by dint of long sufferance, he said, obtained over his spirit—an effect which the *physique* of the gray walls and turrets, and of the dim tarn into which they all looked down, had, at length, brought about upon the *morale* of his existence.

He admitted, however, although with hesitation, that much of the peculiar gloom which thus afflicted him could be traced to a more natural and far more palpable origin—to the severe and long-continued illness—indeed to the evidently approaching dissolution—of a tenderly beloved sister —his sole companion for long years—his last and only relative on earth. "Her decease," he said, with a bitterness which I can never forget, "would leave him (him the hopeless and the frail) the last of the ancient race of the Ushers." While he spoke, the lady Madeline (for so was she called) passed slowly through a remote portion of the apartment, and, without having noticed my presence, disappeared. I regarded her with an utter astonishment not unmingled with dread—and yet I found it impossible to account for such feelings. A sensation of stupor oppressed me, as my eyes followed her retreating steps. When a door, at length, closed upon her, my glance sought instinctively and eagerly the countenance of the brother—but he had buried his face in his hands, and I could only perceive that a far more than ordinary wanness had overspread the emaciated fingers through which trickled many passionate tears.

The disease of the lady Madeline had long baffled the skill of her physicians. A settled apathy, a gradual wasting away of the person, and frequent although transient affections of a partially cataleptical character, were the unusual diagnosis. Hitherto she had steadily borne up against the pressure of her malady, and had not betaken herself finally to bed; but, on the closing in of the evening of my arrival at the house, she succumbed (as her brother told me at night with inexpressible agitation) to the prostrating power of the destroyer; and I learned that the glimpse I had obtained of her person would thus probably be the last I should obtain— that the lady, at least while living, would be seen by me no more.

For several days ensuing, her name was unmentioned by either Usher or myself: and during this period I was busied in earnest endeavors to alleviate the melancholy of my friend. We painted and read together; or I listened, as if in a dream, to the wild improvisations of his speaking guitar. And thus, as a closer and still closer intimacy admitted me more unreservedly into the recesses of his spirit, the more bitterly did I perceive the futility of all attempt at cheering a mind from which darkness, as if an inherent positive quality, poured forth upon all objects of the moral and physical universe, in one unceasing radiation of gloom.

I shall ever bear about me a memory of the many solemn hours I thus spent alone with the master of the House of Usher. Yet I should fail in any attempt to convey an idea of the exact character of the studies, or of the occupations, in which he involved me, or led me the way. An excited and highly distempered ideality threw a sulphureous lustre over all. His long improvised dirges will ring forever in my ears. Among other things, I hold painfully in mind a certain singular perversion and amplification of the wild air of the last waltz of Von Weber.[3] From the paintings over which his elaborate fancy brooded, and which grew, touch by touch, into vaguenesses at which I shuddered the more thrillingly, because I shuddered knowing not why;—from these paintings (vivid as their images now are before me) I would in vain endeavor to educe more than a small portion which should lie within the compass of merely written words. By the utter simplicity, by the nakedness of his designs, he arrested and overawed attention. If ever mortal painted an idea, that mortal was Roderick Usher. For me at least, in the circumstances then surrounding me, there arose out of the pure abstractions which the hypochondriac contrived to throw upon his canvas, an intensity of intolerable awe, no shadow of which felt I ever yet in the contemplation of the certainly glowing yet too concrete reveries of Fuseli.[4]

One of the phantasmagoric conceptions of my friend, partaking not so rigidly of the spirit of abstraction, may be shadowed forth, although feebly, in words. A small picture presented the interior of an immensely long and rectangular vault or tunnel, with low walls, smooth, white, and without interruption or device. Certain accessory points of the design served well to convey the idea that this excavation lay at an exceeding depth below the surface of the earth. No outlet was observed in any portion of its vast extent, and no torch, or other artificial source of light was discernible; yet a flood of intense rays rolled throughout, and bathed the whole in a ghastly and inappropriate splendor.

I have just spoken of that morbid condition of the auditory nerve which rendered all music intolerable to the sufferer, with the exception of certain effects of stringed instruments. It was, perhaps, the narrow limits to which he thus confined himself upon the guitar, which gave birth, in great

measure, to the fantastic character of his performances. But the fervid *facility* of his *impromptus* could not be so accounted for. They must have been, and were, in the notes, as well as in the words of his wild fantasias (for he not unfrequently accompanied himself with rhymed verbal improvisations), the result of that intense mental collectedness and concentration to which I have previously alluded as observable only in particular moments of the highest artificial excitement. The words of one of these rhapsodies I have easily remembered. I was, perhaps, the more forcibly impressed with it, as he gave it, because, in the under or mystic current of its meaning, I fancied that I perceived, and for the first time, a full consciousness on the part of Usher, of the tottering of his lofty reason upon her throne. The verses, which were entitled "The Haunted Palace," ran very nearly, if not accurately, thus:—

I

In the greenest of our valleys,
  By good angels tenanted,
Once a fair and stately palace—
  Radiant palace—reared its head.
In the monarch Thought's dominion—
  It stood there!
Never seraph spread a pinion
  Over fabric half so fair.

II

Banners yellow, glorious, golden,
  On its roof did float and flow;
(This—all this—was in the olden
  Time long ago)
And every gentle air that dallied,
  In that sweet day,
Along the ramparts plumed and pallid,
  A winged odor went away.

---

[3] Karl Maria von Weber (1786-1826), one of the great romantic musicians.

[4] J. H. Fuseli (1741-1825), painter of "The Nightmare" and Shakespearean illustrator.

III

Wanderers in that happy valley
  Through two luminous windows saw
Spirits moving musically
  To a lute's well-tunèd law,
Round about a throne, where sitting
  (Porphyrogene!)[5]
In state his glory well befitting,
  The ruler of the realm was seen.

IV

And all with pearl and ruby glowing
  Was the fair palace door,
Through which came flowing, flowing,
    flowing
  And sparkling evermore,
A troop of Echoes whose sweet duty
  Was but to sing,
In voices of surpassing beauty,
  The wit and wisdom of their king.

V

But evil things, in robes of sorrow,
  Assailed the monarch's high estate;
(Ah, let us mourn, for never morrow
  Shall dawn upon him, desolate!)
And, round about his home, the glory
  That blushed and bloomed
Is but a dim-remembered story
  Of the old time entombed.

VI

And travellers now within that valley,
  Through the red-litten windows, see
Vast forms that move fantastically
  To a discordant melody;
While, like a rapid ghastly river,
  Through the pale door,
A hideous throng rush out forever,
  And laugh—but smile no more.[6]

I well remember that suggestions arising
from this ballad, led us into a train of
thought wherein there became manifest an
opinion of Usher's which I mention not
so much on account of its novelty, (for

other men have thought thus,) as on account of the pertinacity with which he
maintained it. This opinion, in its general
form, was that of the sentience of all
vegetable things. But, in his disordered
fancy, the idea had assumed a more daring
character, and trespassed, under certain
conditions, upon the kingdom of inorgani-
zation. I lack words to express the full
extent, or the earnest *abandon* of his
persuasion. The belief, however, was connected (as I have previously hinted) with
the gray stones of the home of his forefathers. The conditions of the sentience had
been here, he imagined, fulfilled in the
method of collocation of these stones—in
the order of their arrangement, as well as
in that of the many *fungi* which overspread
them, and of the decayed trees which stood
around—above all, in the long undisturbed
endurance of this arrangement, and in its
reduplication in the still waters of the
tarn. Its evidence—the evidence of the
sentience—was to be seen, he said, (and
I here started as he spoke,) in the gradual
yet certain condensation of an atmosphere
of their own about the waters and the
walls. The result was discoverable, he
added, in that silent, yet importunate and
terrible influence which for centuries had
moulded the destinies of his family, and
which made *him* what I now saw him—
what he was. Such opinions need no comment, and I will make none.

Our books—the books which, for years,
had formed no small portion of the mental
existence of the invalid—were, as might
be supposed, in strict keeping with this
character of phantasm. We pored together
over such works as the Ververt and Chartreuse of Gresset; the Belphegor of Machiavelli; the Heaven and Hell of Swedenborg; the Subterranean Voyage of Nicholas
Klimm by Holberg; the Chiromancy of
Robert Flud, of Jean D'Indaginé, and of
De la Chambre; the Journey into the Blue

---

[5] Born to the purple.
[6] Under the title of "The Haunted
Palace," Poe contributed this poem to the
Baltimore *American Museum*, April, 1839.

Distance of Tieck; and the City of the Sun of Campanella. One favorite volume was a small octavo edition of the Directorium Inquisitorum, by the Dominican Eymeric de Gironne; and there were passages in Pomponius Mela, about the old African Satyrs and Oegipans,[7] over which Usher would sit dreaming for hours. His chief delight, however, was found in the perusal of an exceedingly rare and curious book in quarto Gothic—the manual of a forgotten church—the Vigiliae Mortuorum secundum Chorum Ecclesiae Maguntinae.[8]

I could not help thinking of the wild ritual of this work, and of its probable influence upon the hypochondriac, when, one evening, having informed me abruptly that the lady Madeline was no more, he stated his intention of preserving her corpse for a fortnight, (previously to its final interment,) in one of the numerous vaults within the main walls of the building. The worldly reason, however, assigned for this singular proceeding, was one which I did not feel at liberty to dispute. The brother had been led to his resolution (so he told me) by consideration of the unusual character of the malady of the deceased, of certain obtrusive and eager inquiries on the part of her medical men, and of the remote and exposed situation of the burial-ground of the family. I will not deny that when I called to mind the sinister countenance of the person whom I met upon the staircase, on the day of my arrival at the house, I had no desire to oppose what I regarded as at best but a harmless, and by no means an unnatural, precaution.

At the request of Usher, I personally aided him in the arrangements for the temporary entombment. The body having been encoffined, we two alone bore it to its rest. The vault in which we placed it (and which had been so long unopened that our torches, half smothered in its oppressive atmosphere, gave us little opportunity for investigation) was small, damp, and entirely without means of admission for light; lying, at great depth, immediately

beneath that portion of the building in which was my own sleeping apartment. It had been used, apparently, in remote feudal times, for the worst purposes of a donjon-keep, and, in later days as a place of deposit for powder, or some other highly combustible substance, as a portion of its floor, and the whole interior of a long archway through which we reached it, were carefully sheathed with copper. The door, of massive iron, had been, also, similarly protected. Its immense weight caused an unusually sharp grating sound, as it moved upon its hinges.

Having deposited our mournful burden upon tressels within this region of horror, we partially turned aside the yet unscrewed lid of the coffin, and looked upon the face of the tenant. A striking similitude between the brother and sister now first arrested my attention; and Usher, divining, perhaps, my thoughts, murmured out some few words from which I learned that the deceased and himself had been twins, and that sympathies of a scarcely intelligible nature had always existed between them. Our glances, however, rested not long upon the dead—for we could not regard her unawed. The disease which had thus entombed

---

[7] Men shaped like goats.

[8] The references are to *Van-vert* and *Ma Chartreuse*, poems by Jean Baptiste Gresset (1709-1777); *Belphegor*, a novel by Niccoló Macchiavelli (1469-1527); *Heaven and Hell*, originally published in Latin, by the Swedish mystic, Emanuel Swedenborg (1688-1772); *The Subterranean Voyage of Nicholas Klimm*, an imaginary voyage by Ludwig Holberg (1684-1754); the *Clavis philosophiae et alchymae Fluddanae* of Robert Fludd (1574-1637); *Chiromantia* (1522) by Joannes Indagine; *Discours sur les Principes de la Chiromancie* (1653), by Marin Cureau de la Chambre (1594-1669); an unidentified work by Ludwig Tieck (1773-1853); *The City of the Sun*, a Latin work by Thomas Campanella (1568-1639); *Directorium inquisitorum* by Nicholas Eymeric de Girone (1320-1399); the geography of Pomponius Mela (first century A. D.); and probably a manual by one Johann Schoiffer concerning the "vigils of the dead."

the lady in the maturity of youth, had left, as usual in all maladies of a strictly cataleptical character, the mockery of a faint blush upon the bosom and the face, and that suspiciously lingering smile upon the lip which is so terrible in death. We replaced and screwed down the lid, and, having secured the door of iron, made our way, with toil, into the scarcely less gloomy apartments of the upper portion of the house.

And now, some days of bitter grief having elapsed, an observable change came over the features of the mental disorder of my friend. His ordinary manner had vanished. His ordinary occupations were neglected or forgotten. He roamed from chamber to chamber with hurried, unequal, and objectless step. The pallor of his countenance had assumed, if possible, a more ghastly hue—but the luminousness of his eye had utterly gone out. The once occasional huskiness of his tone was heard no more; and a tremulous quaver, as if of extreme terror, habitually characterized his utterance. There were times, indeed, when I thought his unceasingly agitated mind was laboring with some oppressive secret, to divulge which he struggled for the necessary courage. At times, again, I was obliged to resolve all into the mere inexplicable vagaries of madness, for I beheld him gazing upon vacancy for long hours, in an attitude of the profoundest attention, as if listening to some imaginary sound. It was no wonder that his condition terrified—that it infected me. I felt creeping upon me, by slow yet certain degrees, the wild influences of his own fantastic yet impressive superstitions.

It was, especially, upon retiring to bed late in the night of the seventh or eighth day after the placing of the lady Madeline within the donjon, that I experienced the full power of such feelings. Sleep came not near my couch—while the hours waned and waned away. I struggled to reason off the nervousness which had dominion over me. I endeavored to believe that much, if not all of what I felt, was due to the bewildering influence of the gloomy furniture of the room—of the dark and tattered draperies, which, tortured into motion by the breath of a rising tempest, swayed fitfully to and fro upon the walls, and rustled uneasily about the decorations of the bed. But my efforts were fruitless. An irrepressible tremor gradually pervaded my frame; and, at length, there sat upon my very heart an incubus of utterly causeless alarm. Shaking this off with a gasp and a struggle, I uplifted myself upon the pillows, and, peering earnestly within the intense darkness of the chamber, hearkened —I know not why, except that an instinctive spirit prompted me—to certain low and indefinite sounds which came, through the pauses of the storm, at long intervals, I knew not whence. Overpowered by an intense sentiment of horror, unaccountable yet unendurable, I threw on my clothes with haste (for I felt that I should sleep no more during the night), and endeavored to arouse myself from the pitiable condition into which I had fallen, by pacing rapidly to and fro through the apartment.

I had taken but few turns in this manner, when a light step on an adjoining staircase arrested my attention. I presently recognized it as that of Usher. In an instant afterward he rapped with a gentle touch at my door, and entered, bearing a lamp. His countenance was, as usual, cadaverously wan—but, moreover, there was a species of mad hilarity in his eyes—an evidently restrained *hysteria* in his whole demeanor. His air appalled me—but anything was preferable to the solitude which I had so long endured, and I even welcomed his presence as a relief.

"And you have not seen it?" he said abruptly, after having stared about him for some moments in silence—"you have not then seen it?—but, stay! you shall." Thus speaking, and having carefully shaded his lamp, he hurried to one of the casements, and threw it freely open to the storm.

The impetuous fury of the entering gust nearly lifted us from our feet. It was, indeed, a tempestuous yet sternly beautiful night, and one wildly singular in its terror and its beauty. A whirlwind had apparently collected its force in our vicinity; for there were frequent and violent alterations in the direction of the wind; and the exceeding density of the clouds (which hung so low as to press upon the turrets of the house) did not prevent our perceiving the life-like velocity with which they flew careering from all points against each other, without passing away into the distance. I say that even their exceeding density did not prevent our perceiving this—yet we had no glimpse of the moon or stars—nor was there any flashing forth of the lightning. But the under surfaces of the huge masses of agitated vapor, as well as all terrestrial objects immediately around us, were glowing in the unnatural light of a faintly luminous and distinctly visible gaseous exhalation which hung about and enshrouded the mansion.

"You must not—you shall not behold this!" said I, shudderingly, to Usher, as I led him with a gentle violence, from the window to a seat. "These appearances, which bewilder you, are merely electrical phenomena not uncommon—or it may be that they have their ghastly origin in the rank miasma of the tarn. Let us close this casement;—the air is chilling and dangerous to your frame. Here is one of your favorite romances. I will read, and you shall listen;—and so we will pass away this terrible night together."

The antique volume which I had taken up was the "Mad Trist" of Sir Launcelot Canning; but I had called it a favorite of Usher's more in sad jest than in earnest; for, in truth, there is little in its uncouth and unimaginative prolixity which could have had interest for the lofty and spiritual ideality of my friend.[9] It was, however, the only book immediately at hand; and I indulged a vague hope that the excitement which now agitated the hypochondriac, might find relief (for the history of mental disorder is full of similar anomalies) even in the extremeness of the folly which I

should read. Could I have judged, indeed, by the wild overstrained air of vivacity with which he hearkened, or apparently hearkened, to the words of the tale, I might well have congratulated myself upon the success of my design.

I had arrived at that well-known portion of the story where Ethelred, the hero of the Trist, having sought in vain for peaceable admission into the dwelling of the hermit, proceeds to make good an entrance by force. Here, it will be remembered, the words of the narrative run thus:

"And Ethelred, who was by nature of a doughty heart, and who was now mighty withal, on account of the powerfulness of the wine which he had drunken, waited no longer to hold parley with the hermit, who, in sooth, was of an obstinate and maliceful turn, but, feeling the rain upon his shoulders, and fearing the rising of the tempest, uplifted his mace outright, and, with blows, made quickly room in the plankings of the door for his gauntleted hand; and now pulling therewith sturdily, he so cracked, and ripped, and tore all asunder, that the noise of the dry and hollow-sounding wood alarummed and reverberated throughout the forest."

At the termination of this sentence I started, and for a moment, paused; for it appeared to me (although I at once concluded that my excited fancy had deceived me)—it appeared to me that, from some very remote portion of the mansion, there came, indistinctly, to my ears, what might have been, in its exact similarity of character, the echo (but a stifled and dull one certainly) of the very cracking and ripping sound which Sir Launcelot had so particularly described. It was, beyond doubt, the coincidence alone which had arrested my attention; for, amid the rattling of the sashes of the casements, and the ordinary commingled noises of the still increasing storm, the sound, in itself, had nothing, surely, which should have interested or disturbed me. I continued the story:

---

[9] Both the book and the author are Poe's inventions.

"But the good champion Ethelred, now entering within the door, was sore enraged and amazed to perceive no signal of the maliceful hermit; but, in the stead thereof, a dragon of a scaly and prodigious demeanor, and of a fiery tongue, which sate in guard before a palace of gold, with a floor of silver; and upon the wall there hung a shield of shining brass with this legend enwritten—

Who entereth herein, a conqueror hath bin;
Who slayeth the dragon, the shield he shall win;

And Ethelred uplifted his mace, and struck upon the head of the dragon, which fell before him, and gave up his pesty breath, with a shriek so horrid and harsh, and withal so piercing, that Ethelred had fain to close his ears with his hands against the dreadful noise of it, the like whereof was never before heard."

Here again I paused abruptly, and now with a feeling of wild amazement—for there could be no doubt whatever that, in this instance, I did actually hear (although from what direction it proceeded I found it impossible to say) a low and apparently distant, but harsh, protracted, and most unusual screaming or grating sound—the exact counterpart of what my fancy had already conjured up for the dragon's unnatural shriek as described by the romancer.

Oppressed, as I certainly was, upon the occurrence of this second and most extraordinary coincidence, by a thousand conflicting sensations, in which wonder and extreme terror were predominant, I still retained sufficient presence of mind to avoid exciting, by any observation, the sensitive nervousness of my companion. I was by no means certain that he had noticed the sounds in question; although, assuredly, a strange alteration had, during the last few minutes, taken place in his demeanor. From a position fronting my own, he had gradually brought round his chair, so as to sit with his face to the door of the chamber; and thus I could but partially perceive his features, although I saw that his lips trembled as if he were mur-

muring inaudibly. His head had dropped upon his breast—yet I knew that he was not asleep, from the wide and rigid opening of the eye as I caught a glance of it in profile. The motion of his body, too, was at variance with this idea—for he rocked from side to side with a gentle yet constant and uniform sway. Having rapidly taken notice of all this, I resumed the narrative of Sir Launcelot, which thus proceeded:

"And now, the champion, having escaped from the terrible fury of the dragon, bethinking himself of the brazen shield, and of the breaking up of the enchantment which was upon it, removed the carcass from out of the way before him, and approached valorously over the silver pavement of the castle to where the shield was upon the wall; which in sooth tarried not for his full coming, but fell down at his feet upon the silver floor, with a mighty great and terrible ringing sound."

No sooner had these syllables passed my lips, than—as if a shield of brass had indeed, at the moment, fallen heavily upon a floor of silver—I became aware of a distinct, hollow, metallic, and clangorous yet apparently muffled reverberation. Completely unnerved, I leaped to my feet; but the measured rocking movement of Usher was undisturbed. I rushed to the chair in which he sat. His eyes were bent fixedly before him, and throughout his whole countenance there reigned a stony rigidity. But, as I placed my hand upon his shoulder, there came a strong shudder over his whole person; a sickly smile quivered about his lips; and I saw that he spoke in a low, hurried, and gibbering murmur, as if unconscious of my presence. Bending closely over him, I at length drank in the hideous import of his words.

"Not hear it?—yes, I hear it, and *have* heard it. Long—long—long—many minutes, many hours, many days, have I heard it—yet I dared not—oh, pity me, miserable wretch that I am!—I dared not—I *dared* not speak! *We have put her living in the tomb!* Said I not that my senses were acute? I *now* tell you that I heard her first feeble movements in the hollow coffin. I heard them—many, many days ago—yet I dared not—*I dared not speak!* And now —to-night—Ethelred—ha! ha!—the breaking of the hermit's door, and the death-cry of the dragon, and the clangor of the shield!—say, rather, the rending of her coffin, and the grating of the iron hinges of her prison, and her struggles within the coppered archway of the vault! Oh, whither shall I fly? Will she not be here anon? Is she not hurrying to upbraid me for my haste? Have I not heard her footstep on the stair? Do I not distinguish that heavy and horrible beating of her heart? Madman!"—here he sprang furiously to his feet, and shrieked out his syllables, as if in the effort he were giving up his soul —*"Madman! I tell you that she now stands without the door!"*

As if in the superhuman energy of his utterance there had been found the potency of a spell, the huge antique pannels to which the speaker pointed, threw slowly back, upon the instant, their ponderous and ebony jaws. It was the work of the rushing gust—but then without those doors there *did* stand the lofty and enshrouded figure of the Lady Madeline of Usher. There was blood upon her white robes, and the evidence of some bitter struggle upon every portion of her emaciated frame. For a moment she remained trembling and reeling to and fro upon the threshold— then, with a low moaning cry, fell heavily inward upon the person of her brother, and in her violent and now final death-agonies, bore him to the floor a corpse, and a victim to the terrors he had anticipated.

From that chamber, and from that mansion, I fled aghast. The storm was still abroad in all its wrath as I found myself crossing the old causeway. Suddenly there shot along the path a wild light, and I turned to see whence a gleam so unusual could have issued; for the vast house and its shadows were alone behind me. The radiance was that of the full, setting, and blood-red moon, which now shone vividly

through that once barely-discernible fissure, of which I have before spoken as extending from the roof of the building, in a zigzag direction, to the base. While I gazed, this fissure rapidly widened—there came a fierce breath of the whirlwind—the entire orb of the satellite burst at once upon my sight—my brain reeled as I saw the mighty walls rushing asunder—there was a long tumultuous shouting sound like the voice of a thousand waters—and the deep and dank tarn at my feet closed sullenly and silently over the fragments of the *"House of Usher."*

WILLIAM WILSON
[1840 (1839)]

What say of it? what say CONSCIENCE grim,
That spectre in my path?
—*Chamberlain's Pharronida.*[1]

LET me call myself, for the present, William Wilson. The fair page now lying before me need not be sullied with my real appellation. This has been already too much an object for the scorn—for the horror—for the detestation of my race. To the uttermost regions of the globe have not the indignant winds bruited its unparalleled infamy? Oh, outcast of all outcasts most abandoned!—to the earth art thou not for ever dead? to its honors, to its flowers, to its golden aspirations?—and a cloud, dense, dismal, and limitless, does it not hang eternally between thy hopes and heaven?

I would not, if I could, here or to-day, embody a record of my later years of unspeakable misery and unpardonable crime. This epoch—these later years—took unto themselves a sudden elevation in turpitude, whose origin alone it is my present purpose to assign. Men usually grow base by degrees. From me, in an instant, all virtue

---

[1] William Chamberlayne (1619-1689) was one of the minor Caroline poets. His *Pharonnida* was published in 1659.

dropped bodily as a mantle. From comparatively trivial wickedness I passed, with
the stride of a giant, into more than
the enormities of an Elah-Gabalus.[2] What
chance—what one event brought this evil
thing to pass, bear with me while I relate.
Death approaches; and the shadow which
foreruns him has thrown a softening influence over my spirit. I long, in passing
through the dim valley, for the sympathy—
I had nearly said for the pity—of my
fellow men. I would fain have them believe that I have been, in some measure,
the slave of circumstances beyond human
control. I would wish them to seek out
for me, in the details I am about to give,
some little oasis of *fatality* amid a wilderness of error. I would have them allow—
what they cannot refrain from allowing—
that, although temptation may have erewhile existed as great, man was never *thus*,
at least, tempted before—certainly, never
thus fell. And is it therefore that he has
never thus suffered? Have I not indeed
been living in a dream? And am I not
now dying a victim to the horror and the
mystery of the wildest of all sublunary
visions?

I am the descendant of a race whose
imaginative and easily excitable temperament has at all times rendered them remarkable; and, in my earliest infancy, I
gave evidence of having fully inherited
the family character. As I advanced in
years it was more strongly developed;
becoming, for many reasons, a cause of
serious disquietude to my friends, and of
positive injury to myself. I grew self-
willed, addicted to the wildest caprices, and
a prey to the most ungovernable passions.
Weakminded, and beset with constitutional
infirmities akin to my own, my parents
could do but little to check the evil propensities which distinguished me. Some
feeble and ill-directed efforts resulted in
complete failure on their part, and, of
course, in total triumph on mine. Thenceforward my voice was a household law; and
at an age when few children have abandoned their leading-strings, I was left to

the guidance of my own will, and became,
in all but name, the master of my own
actions.

My earliest recollections of a school-
life are connected with a large, rambling,
Elizabethan house, in a misty-looking village of England, where were a vast number
of gigantic and gnarled trees, and where
all the houses were excessively ancient.
In truth, it was a dream-like and spirit-
soothing place, that venerable old town.
At this moment, in fancy, I feel the refreshing chilliness of its deeply-shadowed
avenues, inhale the fragrance of its thousand shrubberies, and thrill anew with
undefinable delight, at the deep hollow note
of the church-bell, breaking, each hour,
with sullen and sudden roar, upon the
stillness of the dusky atmosphere in which
the fretted Gothic steeple lay imbedded
and asleep.

It gives me, perhaps, as much of pleasure
as I can now in any manner experience,
to dwell upon minute recollections of the
school and its concerns. Steeped in misery
as I am—misery, alas! only too real—I shall
be pardoned for seeking relief, however
slight and temporary, in the weakness of
a few rambling details. These, moreover,
utterly trivial, and even ridiculous in themselves, assume, to my fancy, adventitious
importance, as connected with a period and
a locality when and where I recognize the
first ambiguous monitions of the destiny
which afterward so fully overshadowed me.
Let me then remember.

The house, I have said, was old and
irregular. The grounds were extensive,
and a high and solid brick wall, topped
with a bed of mortar and broken glass,
encompassed the whole. This prison-like
rampart formed the limit of our domain;
beyond it we saw but thrice a week—once
every Saturday afternoon, when, attended
by two ushers, we were permitted to take
brief walks in a body through some of the

---

[2] Poe's variant for Heliogabalus, the
adopted name of the infamous Roman emperor Varius Avitus Bassianus (204-222
A. D.)

neighboring fields—and twice during Sunday, when we were paraded in the same formal manner to the morning and evening service in the one church of the village. Of this church the principal of our school was pastor. With how deep a spirit of wonder and perplexity was I wont to regard him from our remote pew in the gallery, as, with step solemn and slow, he ascended the pulpit! This reverend man, with countenance so demurely benign, with robes so glossy and so clerically flowing, with wig so minutely powdered, so rigid and so vast,—could this be he who, of late, with sour visage, and in snuffy habiliments, administered, ferule in hand, the Draconian Laws of the academy?[3] Oh, gigantic paradox, too utterly monstrous for solution!

At an angle of the ponderous wall frowned a more ponderous gate. It was riveted and studded with iron bolts, and surmounted with jagged iron spikes. What impressions of deep awe did it inspire! It was never opened save for the three periodical egressions and ingressions already mentioned; then, in every creak of its mighty hinges, we found a plenitude of mystery—a world of matter for solemn remark, or for more solemn meditation.

The extensive enclosure was irregular in form, having many capacious recesses. Of these, three or four of the largest constituted the playground. It was level, and covered with fine hard gravel. I well remember it had no trees, nor benches, nor any thing similar within it. Of course it was in the rear of the house. In front lay a small parterre, planted with box and other shrubs, but through this sacred division we passed only upon rare occasions indeed—such as a first advent to school or final departure thence, or perhaps, when a parent or friend having called for us, we joyfully took our way home for the Christmas or Midsummer holidays.

But the house!—how quaint an old building was this!—to me how veritable a palace of enchantment! There was really no end to its windings—to its incomprehensible subdivisions. It was difficult, at any given time, to say with certainty upon which of its two stories one happened to be. From each room to every other there were sure to be found three or four steps either in ascent or descent. Then the lateral branches were innumerable—inconceivable —and so returning in upon themselves, that our most exact ideas in regard to the whole mansion were not very far different from those with which we pondered upon infinity. During the five years of my residence here, I was never able to ascertain with precision, in what remote locality lay the little sleeping apartment assigned to myself and some eighteen or twenty other scholars.

The school-room was the largest in the house—I could not help thinking, in the world. It was very long, narrow, and dismally low, with pointed Gothic windows and a ceiling of oak. In a remote and terror-inspiring angle was a square enclosure of eight or ten feet, comprising the *sanctum,* "during hours," of our principal, the Reverend Dr. Bransby. It was a solid structure, with massy door, sooner than open which in the absence of the "Dominie," we would all have willingly perished by the *peine forte et dure.*[4] In other angles were two other similar boxes, far less reverenced, indeed, but still greatly matters of awe. One of these was the pulpit of the "classical" usher, one of the "English and mathematical." Interspersed about the room, crossing and recrossing in endless irregularity, were innumerable benches and desks, black, ancient, and time-worn, piled desperately with much bethumbed books, and so beseamed with initial letters, names at full length, grotesque figures, and other multiplied efforts of the knife, as to have entirely lost what little of original form might have been their portion in days long departed. A huge

---

[3] The Athenian archon Draco framed about 621 B. C. a code of laws prescribing the death penalty for most offenses.

[4] The worst of afflictions or violent and severe pain.

bucket with water stood at one extremity of the room, and a clock of stupendous dimensions at the other.

Encompassed by the massy walls of this venerable academy, I passed, yet not in tedium or disgust, the years of the third lustrum of my life. The teeming brain of childhood requires no external world of incident to occupy or amuse it; and the apparently dismal monotony of a school was replete with more intense excitement than my riper youth has derived from luxury, or my full manhood from crime. Yet I must believe that my first mental development had in it much of the uncommon—even much of the *outré*. Upon mankind at large the events of very early existence rarely leave in mature age any definite impression. All is gray shadow—a weak and irregular remembrance—an indistinct regathering of feeble pleasures and phantasmagoric pains. With me this is not so. In childhood I must have felt with the energy of a man what I now find stamped upon memory in lines as vivid, as deep, and as durable as the *exergues* of the Carthaginian medals.[5]

Yet in fact—in the fact of the world's view—how little was there to remember! The morning's awakening, the nightly summons to bed; the connings, the recitations; the periodical half-holidays, and perambulations; the play-ground, with its broils, its pastimes, its intrigues;—these, by a mental sorcery long forgotten, were made to involve a wilderness of sensation, a world of rich incident, an universe of varied emotion, of excitement, the most passionate and spirit-stirring. *"Oh, le bon temps, que ce siècle de fer!"*[6]

In truth, the ardor, the enthusiasm, and the imperiousness of my disposition, soon rendered me a marked character among my schoolmates, and by slow, but natural gradations, gave me an ascendancy over all not greatly older than myself;—over all with a single exception. This exception was found in the person of a scholar, who, although no relation, bore the same Christian and surname as myself;—a circum-

stance, in fact, little remarkable; for notwithstanding a noble descent, mine was one of those every-day appellations which seem, by prescriptive right, to have been, time out of mind, the common property of the mob. In this narrative I have therefore designated myself as William Wilson,—a fictitious title not very dissimilar to the real. My namesake alone, of those who in school phraseology constituted "our set," presumed to compete with me in the studies of the class—in the sports and broils of the playground—to refuse implicit belief in my assertions, and submission to my will—indeed, to interfere with my arbitrary dictation in any respect whatsoever. If there is on earth a supreme and unqualified despotism, it is the despotism of a master-mind in boyhood over the less energetic spirits of its companions.

Wilson's rebellion was to me a source of the greatest embarrassment; the more so as, in spite of the bravado with which in public I made a point of treating him and his pretensions, I secretly felt that I feared him, and could not help thinking the equality which he maintained so easily with myself, a proof of his true superiority; since not to be overcome cost me a perpetual struggle. Yet this superiority—even this equality—was in truth acknowledged by no one but myself; our associates, by some unaccountable blindness, seemed not even to suspect it. Indeed, his competition, his resistance, and especially his impertinent and dogged interference with my purposes, were not more pointed than private. He appeared to be destitute alike of the ambition which urged, and of the passionate energy of mind which enabled me to excel. In

---

[5] The reference is to the segments beneath the base lines of the subjects on these antique medals.

[6] "Oh, the good time, before this age of iron!" The source of this quotation has not been located. Unlike geologists and archaeologists, poets have often followed classical precedent in imaging a golden age long antedating the degenerate iron age.

his rivalry he might have been supposed actuated solely by a whimsical desire to thwart, astonish, or mortify myself; although there were times when I could not help observing, with a feeling made up of wonder, abasement, and pique, that he mingled with his injuries, his insults, or his contradictions, a certain most inappropriate, and assuredly most unwelcome *affectionateness* of manner. I could only conceive this singular behavior to arise from a consummate self-conceit assuming the vulgar airs of patronage and protection.

Perhaps it was this latter trait in Wilson's conduct, conjoined with our identity of name, and the mere accident of our having entered the school upon the same day, which set afloat the notion that we were brothers, among the senior classes in the academy. These do not usually inquire with much strictness into the affairs of their juniors. I have before said, or should have said, that Wilson was not, in a most remote degree, connected with my family. But assuredly if we *had* been brothers we must have been twins; for, after leaving Dr. Bransby's, I casually learned that my namesake was born on the nineteenth of January, 1813—and this is a somewhat remarkable coincidence; for the day is precisely that of my own nativity.

It may seem strange that in spite of the continual anxiety occasioned me by the rivalry of Wilson, and his intolerable spirit of contradiction, I could not bring myself to hate him altogether. We had, to be sure, nearly every day a quarrel in which, yielding me publicly the palm of victory, he, in some manner, contrived to make me feel that it was he who had deserved it; yet a sense of pride on my part, and a veritable dignity on his own, kept us always upon what are called "speaking terms," while there were many points of strong congeniality in our tempers, operating to awake in me a sentiment which our position alone, perhaps, prevented from ripening into friendship. It is difficult, indeed, to define, or even to describe, my real feelings toward him. They formed a

motley and heterogeneous admixture;— some petulant animosity, which was not yet hatred, some esteem, more respect, much fear, with a world of uneasy curiosity. To the moralist it will be necessary to say, in addition, that Wilson and myself were the most inseparable of companions.

It was no doubt the anomalous state of affairs existing between us, which turned all my attacks upon him, (and there were many, either open or covert) into the channel of banter or practical joke (giving pain while assuming the aspect of mere fun) rather than into a more serious and determined hostility. But my endeavors on this head were by no means uniformly successful, even when my plans were the most wittily concocted; for my namesake had much about him, in character, of that unassuming and quiet austerity which, while enjoying the poignancy of its own jokes, has no heel of Achilles in itself, and absolutely refuses to be laughed at. I could find, indeed, but one vulnerable point, and that, lying in a personal peculiarity, arising, perhaps, from constitutional disease, would have been spared by any antagonist less at his wit's end than myself;—my rival had a weakness in the faucial [7] or guttural organs, which precluded him from raising his voice at any time *above a very low whisper*. Of this defect I did not fail to take what poor advantage lay in my power.

Wilson's retaliations in kind were many; and there was one form of his practical wit that disturbed me beyond measure. How his sagacity first discovered at all that so petty a thing would vex me, is a question I never could solve; but having discovered, he habitually practised the annoyance. I had always felt aversion to my uncourtly patronymic, and its very common, if not plebeian prænomen. The words were venom in my ears; and when, upon the day of my arrival, a second William Wilson came also to the academy, I felt angry with him for bearing the name, and doubly disgusted

---

[7] Pertaining to the fauces or passage from the mouth to the pharynx.

with the name because a stranger bore it, who would be the cause of its twofold repetition, who would be constantly in my presence, and whose concerns, in the ordinary routine of the school business, must inevitably, on account of the detestable coincidence, be often confounded with my own.

The feeling of vexation thus engendered grew stronger with every circumstance tending to show resemblance, moral or physical, between my rival and myself. I had not then discovered the remarkable fact that we were of the same age; but I saw that we were of the same height, and I perceived that we were even singularly alike in general contour of person and outline of feature. I was galled, too, by the rumor touching a relationship, which had grown current in the upper forms. In a word, nothing could more seriously disturb me, (although I scrupulously concealed such disturbance,) than any allusion to a similarity of mind, person, or condition existing between us. But, in truth, I had no reason to believe that (with the exception of the matter of relationship, and in the case of Wilson himself,) this similarity had ever been made a subject of comment, or even observed at all by our school-fellows. That *he* observed it in all its bearings, and as fixedly as I, was apparent; but that he could discover in such circumstances so fruitful a field of annoyance, can only be attributed, as I said before, to his more than ordinary penetration.

His cue, which was to perfect an imitation of myself, lay both in words and in actions; and most admirably did he play his part. My dress it was an easy matter to copy; my gait and general manner were without difficulty appropriated; in spite of his constitutional defect, even my voice did not escape him. My louder tones were, of course, unattempted, but then the key, —it was identical; *and his singular whisper, it grew the very echo of my own.*

How greatly this most exquisite portraiture harassed me (for it could not justly be termed a caricature), I will not now

venture to describe. I had but one consolation—in the fact that the imitation, apparently, was noticed by myself alone, and that I had to endure only the knowing and strangely sarcastic smiles of my namesake himself. Satisfied with having produced in my bosom the intended effect, he seemed to chuckle in secret over the sting he had inflicted, and was characteristically disregardful of the public applause which the success of his witty endeavors might have so easily elicited. That the school, indeed, did not feel his design, perceive its accomplishment, and participate in his sneer, was, for many anxious months, a riddle I could not resolve. Perhaps the *gradation* of his copy rendered it not readily perceptible; or, more possibly, I owed my security to the masterly air of the copyist, who, disdaining the letter (which in a painting is all the obtuse can see), gave but the full spirit of his original for my individual contemplation and chagrin.

I have already more than once spoken of the disgusting air of patronage which he assumed toward me, and of his frequent officious interference with my will. This interference often took the ungracious character of advice; advice not openly given, but hinted or insinuated. I received it with a repugnance which gained strength as I grew in years. Yet, at this distant day, let me do him the simple justice to acknowledge that I can recall no occasion when the suggestions of my rival were on the side of those errors or follies so usual to his immature age and seeming inexperience; that his moral sense, at least, if not his general talents and worldly wisdom, was far keener than my own; and that I might, to-day, have been a better and thus a happier man, had I less frequently rejected the counsels embodied in those meaning whispers which I then but too cordially hated and too bitterly despised.

As it was I at length grew restive in the extreme under his distasteful supervision, and daily resented more and more openly, what I considered his intolerable arrogance. I have said that, in the first years of our connection as schoolmates, my feelings in regard to him might have been easily ripened into friendship; but, in the latter months of my residence at the academy, although the intrusion of his ordinary manner had, beyond doubt, in some measure, abated, my sentiments, in nearly similar proportion, partook very much of positive hatred. Upon one occasion he saw this, I think, and afterward avoided, or made a show of avoiding me.

It was about the same period, if I remember aright, that, in an altercation of violence with him, in which he was more than usually thrown off his guard, and spoke and acted with an openness of demeanor rather foreign to his nature, I discovered, or fancied I discovered, in his accent, in his air, and general appearance, a something which first startled, and then deeply interested me, by bringing to mind dim visions of my earliest infancy—wild, confused, and thronging memories of a time when memory herself was yet unborn. I cannot better describe the sensation which oppressed me, than by saying that I could with difficulty shake off the belief of my having been acquainted with the being who stood before me, at some epoch very long ago—some point of the past even infinitely remote. The delusion, however, faded rapidly as it came; and I mention it at all but to define the day of the last conversation I there held with my singular namesake.

The huge old house, with its countless sub-divisions, had several large chambers communicating with each other, where slept the greater number of the students. There were, however (as must necessarily happen in a building so awkwardly planned), many little nooks or recesses, the odds and ends of the structure; and these the economic ingenuity of Dr. Bransby had also fitted up as dormitories, although, being the merest closets, they were capable of accommodating but a single individual. One of these small apartments was occupied by Wilson.

One night, about the close of my fifth year at the school, and immediately after the altercation just mentioned, finding every one wrapped in sleep, I arose from bed, and, lamp in hand, stole through a wilderness of narrow passages, from my own bedroom to that of my rival. I had long been plotting one of those ill-natured pieces of practical wit at his expense in which I had hitherto been so uniformly unsuccessful. It was my intention, now, to put my scheme in operation, and I resolved to make him feel the whole extent of the malice with which I was imbued. Having reached his closet, I noiselessly entered, leaving the lamp, with a shade over it, on the outside. I advanced a step and listened to the sound of his tranquil breathing. Assured of his being asleep, I returned, took the light, and with it again approached the bed. Close curtains were around it, which, in the prosecution of my plan, I slowly and quietly withdrew, when the bright rays fell vividly upon the sleeper, and my eyes at the same moment, upon his countenance. I looked;—and a numbness, an iciness of feeling instantly pervaded my frame. My breast heaved, my knees tottered, my whole spirit became possessed with an abject yet intolerable horror. Gasping for breath, I lowered the lamp in still nearer proximity to the face. Were these—*these* the lineaments of William Wilson? I saw, indeed, that they were his, but I shook as if with a fit of the ague, in fancying they were not. What *was* there about them to confound me in this manner? I gazed;—while my brain reeled with a multitude of incoherent thoughts. Not thus he appeared—assuredly not *thus*—in the vivacity of his waking hours. The same name! the same contour of person! the same day of arrival at the academy! And then his dogged and meaningless imitation of my gait, my voice, my habits, and my manner! Was it, in truth, within the bounds of human possibility, that *what I now saw* was the result, merely, of the habitual practice of this sarcastic imitation? Awe-stricken, and with a creeping shudder, I extinguished the lamp, passed silently from the chamber, and left, at once, the halls of that old academy, never to enter them again.

After a lapse of some months, spent at home in mere idleness, I found myself a student at Eton. The brief interval had been sufficient to enfeeble my remembrance of the events at Dr. Bransby's, or at least to effect a material change in the nature of the feelings with which I remembered them. The truth—the tragedy—of the drama was no more. I could now find room to doubt the evidence of my senses; and seldom called up the subject at all but with wonder at the extent of human credulity, and a smile at the vivid force of the imagination which I hereditarily possessed. Neither was this species of skepticism likely to be diminished by the character of the life I led at Eton. The vortex of thoughtless folly into which I there so immediately and so recklessly plunged, washed away all but the froth of my past hours, engulfed at once every solid or serious impression, and left to memory only the veriest levities of a former existence.

I do not wish, however, to trace the course of my miserable profligacy here— a profligacy which set at defiance the laws, while it eluded the vigilance of the institution. Three years of folly, passed without profit, had but given me rooted habits of vice, and added, in a somewhat unusual degree, to my bodily stature, when, after a week of soulless dissipation, I invited a small party of the most dissolute students to a secret carousal in my chambers. We met at a late hour of the night; for our debaucheries were to be faithfully protracted until morning. The wine flowed freely, and there were not wanting other and perhaps more dangerous seductions; so that the gray dawn had already faintly appeared in the east while our delirious extravagance was at its height. Madly flushed with cards and intoxication, I was in the act of insisting upon a toast of more than wonted profanity, when my at-

tention was suddenly diverted by the violent, although partial, unclosing of the door of the apartment, and by the eager voice of a servant from without. He said that some person, apparently in great haste, demanded to speak with me in the hall.

Wildly excited with wine, the unexpected interruption rather delighted than surprised me. I staggered forward at once, and a few steps brought me to the vestibule of the building. In this low and small room there hung no lamp; and now no light at all was admitted, save that of the exceedingly feeble dawn which made its way through the semi-circular window. As I put my foot over the threshold, I became aware of the figure of a youth about my own height, and habited in a white kerseymere morning frock, cut in the novel fashion of the one I myself wore at the moment. This the faint light enabled me to perceive; but the features of his face I could not distinguish. Upon my entering, he strode hurriedly up to me, and, seizing me by the arm with a gesture of petulant impatience, whispered the words "William Wilson" in my ear.

I grew perfectly sober in an instant.

There was that in the manner of the stranger, and in the tremulous shake of his uplifted finger, as he held it between my eyes and the light, which filled me with unqualified amazement; but it was not this which had so violently moved me. It was the pregnancy of solemn admonition in the singular, low, hissing utterance; and, above all, it was the character, the tone, *the key*, of those few, simple, and familiar, yet *whispered* syllables, which came with a thousand thronging memories of by-gone days, and struck upon my soul with the shock of a galvanic battery. Ere I could recover the use of my senses he was gone.

Although this event failed not of a vivid effect upon my disordered imagination, yet was it evanescent as vivid. For some weeks, indeed, I busied myself in earnest enquiry, or was wrapped in a cloud of morbid speculation. I did not pretend to disguise from my perception the identity of the singular individual who thus perseveringly interfered with my affairs, and harassed me with his insinuated counsel. But who and what was this Wilson?—and whence came he?—and what were his purposes? Upon neither of these points could I be satisfied —merely ascertaining, in regard to him, that a sudden accident in his family had caused his removal from Dr. Bransby's academy on the afternoon of the day in which I myself had eloped. But in a brief period I ceased to think upon the subject, my attention being all absorbed in a contemplated departure for Oxford. Thither I soon went, the uncalculating vanity of my parents furnishing me with an outfit and annual establishment, which would enable me to indulge at will in the luxury already so dear to my heart—to vie in profuseness of expenditure with the haughtiest heirs of the wealthiest earldoms in Great Britain.

Excited by such appliances to vice, my constitutional temperament broke forth with redoubled ardor, and I spurned even the common restraints of decency in the mad infatuation of my revels. But it were absurd to pause in the detail of my extravagance. Let it suffice, that among spendthrifts I out-Heroded Herod,[8] and that, giving name to a multitude of novel follies, I added no brief appendix to the long catalogue of vices then usual in the most dissolute university of Europe.

It could hardly be credited, however, that I had, even here, so utterly fallen from the gentlemanly estate, as to seek acquaintance with the vilest arts of the gambler by profession, and, having become an adept in his despicable science, to practice it habitually as a means of increasing my already enormous income at the expense of the weak-minded among my fellow-collegians. Such, nevertheless, was the fact. And the very enormity of this offence against all manly and honorable sentiment proved, beyond doubt, the main if not the sole reason of the impunity with which it was committed. Who, indeed, among my most abandoned associates, would not rather have disputed the clearest evidence of his senses, than have suspected of such courses, the gay, the frank, the generous William Wilson—the noblest and most liberal commoner at Oxford— him whose follies (said his parasites) were but the follies of youth and unbridled fancy—whose errors but inimitable whim —whose darkest vice but a careless and dashing extravagance?

I had been now two years successfully busied in this way, when there came to the university a young *parvenu* nobleman, Glendenning—rich, said report, as Herodes Atticus[9]—his riches, too, as easily acquired. I soon found him of weak intellect, and, of course, marked him as a fitting subject for my skill. I frequently engaged him in play, and contrived, with the gambler's usual art, to let him win considerable sums, the more effectually to entangle him in my snares. At length, my schemes being ripe, I met him (with the full intention that this meeting should be final and decisive) at the chambers of a fellow-commoner (Mr. Preston), equally intimate with both, but who, to do him justice, entertained not even a remote suspicion of my design. To give to this a better coloring, I had contrived to have assembled a party of some eight or ten, and was solicitously careful that the introduction of cards should appear accidental, and originate in the proposal of my contemplated dupe himself. To be brief upon a vile topic, none of the

---

[8] This phase, meaning to exceed in violence or extravagance, owes its currency to *Hamlet*, Act I, sc. ii, where Hamlet, in his speech to the players, refers to the bombastic stock Herod of the mystery plays.

[9] The reference is probably to Herod Antipas, wealthy tetrarch of Galilee (2 B. C. — 39 A. D.), son of Herod the Great, the procurator of Judea. He acquired his wealth not only from his father but also from his marriage to an Arabian princess whom he deserted for Herodias, his brother's wife.

low finesse was omitted, so customary upon similar occasions, that it is a just matter for wonder how any are still found so besotted as to fall its victim.

We had protracted our sitting far into the night, and I had at length effected the manœuvre of getting Glendenning as my sole antagonist. The game, too, was my favorite *écarté*.[10] The rest of the company, interested in the extent of our play, had abandoned their own cards, and were standing around us as spectators. The *parvenu*, who had been induced by my artifices in the early part of the evening, to drink deeply, now shuffled, dealt, or played, with a wild nervousness of manner for which his intoxication, I thought, might partially, but could not altogether account. In a very short period he had become my debtor to a large amount, when, having taken a long draught of port, he did precisely what I had been coolly anticipating—he proposed to double our already extravagant stakes. With a well-feigned show of reluctance, and not until after my repeated refusal had seduced him into some angry words which gave a color of *pique* to my compliance, did I finally comply. The result, of course, did but prove how entirely the prey was in my toils: in less than an hour he had quadrupled his debt. For some time his countenance had been losing the florid tinge lent it by the wine; but now, to my astonishment, I perceived that it had grown to a pallor truly fearful. I say, to my astonishment. Glendenning had been represented to my eager inquiries as immeasurably wealthy; and the sums which he had as yet lost, although in themselves vast, could not, I supposed, very seriously annoy, much less so violently affect him. That he was overcome by the wine just swallowed, was the idea which most readily presented itself; and, rather with a view to the preservation of my own character in the eyes of my associates, than from any less interested motive, I was about to insist, peremptorily, upon a discontinuance of the play, when some expressions at my elbow from among the company, and an

ejaculation evincing utter despair on the part of Glendenning, gave me to understand that I had effected his total ruin under circumstances which, rendering him an object for the pity of all, should have protected him from the ill offices even of a fiend.

What now might have been my conduct it is difficult to say. The pitiable condition of my dupe had thrown an air of embarrassed gloom over all; and, for some moments, a profound silence was maintained, during which I could not help feeling my cheeks tingle with the many burning glances of scorn or reproach cast upon me by the less abandoned of the party. I will even own that an intolerable weight of anxiety was for a brief instant lifted from my bosom by the sudden and extraordinary interruption which ensued. The wide, heavy folding doors of the apartment were all at once thrown open, to their full extent, with a vigorous and rushing impetuosity that extinguished, as if by magic, every candle in the room. Their light, in dying, enabled us just to perceive that a stranger had entered, about my own height, and closely muffled in a cloak. The darkness, however, was not total; and we could only *feel* that he was standing in our midst. Before any one of us could recover from the extreme astonishment into which this rudeness had thrown all, we heard the voice of the intruder.

"Gentlemen," he said, in a low, distinct, and never-to-be-forgotten *whisper* which thrilled to the very marrow of my bones, "Gentlemen, I make an apology for this behavior, because in thus behaving, I am fulfilling a duty. You are, beyond doubt, uninformed of the true character of the person who has to-night won at *écarté* a large sum of money from Lord Glendenning. I will therefore put you upon an expeditious and decisive plan of obtaining this very necessary information. Please to examine, at your leisure, the inner linings of the cuff of his left sleeve, and the sev-

---

[10] Card-game played by two only.

eral little packages which may be found in the somewhat capacious pockets of his embroidered morning wrapper."

While he spoke, so profound was the stillness that one might have heard a pin drop upon the floor. In ceasing, he departed at once and as abruptly as he had entered. Can I—shall I describe my sensations? Must I say that I felt all the horrors of the damned? Most assuredly I had little time for reflection. Many hands roughly seized me upon the spot, and lights were immediately reproduced. A search ensued. In the lining of my sleeve were found all the court cards essential in *écarté*, and in the pockets of my wrapper, a number of packs, fac-similes of those used at our sittings, with the single exception that mine were of the species called, technically, *arrondées;* the honors being slightly convex at the ends, the lower cards slightly convex at the sides. In this disposition, the dupe who cuts, as customary, at the length of the pack, will invariably find that he cuts his antagonist an honor; while the gambler, cutting at the breadth, will, as certainly, cut nothing for his victim which may count in the records of the game.

Any burst of indignation upon this discovery would have affected me less than the silent contempt, or the sarcastic composure, with which it was received.

"Mr. Wilson," said our host, stooping to remove from beneath his feet an exceedingly luxurious cloak of rare furs, "Mr. Wilson, this is your property." (The weather was cold; and, upon quitting my own room, I had thrown a cloak over my dressing wrapper, putting it off upon reaching the scene of play.) "I presume it is supererogatory to seek here (eyeing the folds of the garment with a bitter smile) for any farther evidence of your skill. Indeed, we have had enough. You will see the necessity, I hope, of quitting Oxford —at all events, of quitting instantly my chambers."

Abased, humbled to the dust as I then was, it is probable that I should have resented this galling language by immediate personal violence, had not my whole attention been at the moment arrested by a fact of the most startling character. The cloak which I had worn was of a rare description of fur; how rare, how extravagantly costly, I shall not venture to say. Its fashion, too, was of my own fantastic invention; for I was fastidious to an absurd degree of coxcombry, in matters of this frivolous nature. When, therefore, Mr. Preston reached me that which he had picked up upon the floor, and near the folding-doors of the apartment, it was with an astonishment nearly bordering upon terror, that I perceived my own already hanging on my arm, (where I had no doubt unwittingly placed it,) and that the one presented me was but its exact counterpart in every, in even the minutest possible particular. The singular being who had so disastrously exposed me, had been muffled, I remembered, in a cloak; and none had been worn at all by any of the members of our party, with the exception of myself. Retaining some presence of mind, I took the one offered me by Preston; placed it, unnoticed, over my own; left the apartment with a resolute scowl of defiance; and, next morning ere dawn of day, commenced a hurried journey from Oxford to the continent, in a perfect agony of horror and of shame.

I fled in vain. My evil destiny pursued me as if in exultation, and proved, indeed, that the exercise of its mysterious dominion had as yet only begun. Scarcely had I set foot in Paris, ere I had fresh evidence of the detestable interest taken by this Wilson in my concerns. Years flew, while I experienced no relief. Villain!—at Rome, with how untimely, yet with how spectral an officiousness, stepped he in between me and my ambition! at Vienna, too—at Berlin—and at Moscow! Where, in truth, had I *not* bitter cause to curse him within my heart? From his inscrutable tyranny did I at length flee, panic-stricken, as from a pestilence; and to the very ends of the earth *I fled in vain.*

And again, and again, in secret communion with my own spirit, would I demand the questions "Who is he?—whence came he?—and what are his objects?" But no answer was there found. And now I scrutinized, with a minute scrutiny, the forms, and the methods, and the leading traits of his impertinent supervision. But even here there was very little upon which to base a conjecture. It was noticeable, indeed, that, in no one of the multiplied instances in which he had of late crossed my path, had he so crossed it except to frustrate those schemes, or to disturb those actions, which, if fully carried out, might have resulted in bitter mischief. Poor justification this, in truth, for an authority so imperiously assumed! Poor indemnity for natural rights of self-agency so pertinaciously, so insultingly denied!

I had also been forced to notice that my tormentor, for a very long period of time, (while scrupulously and with miraculous dexterity maintaining his whim of an identity of apparel with myself,) had so contrived it, in the execution of his varied interference with my will, that I saw not, at any moment, the features of his face. Be Wilson what he might, *this*, at least, was but the veriest of affectation, or of folly. Could he, for an instant, have supposed that, in my admonisher at Eton—in the destroyer of my honor at Oxford,—in him who thwarted my ambition at Rome, my revenge at Paris, my passionate love at Naples, or what he falsely termed my avarice in Egypt,—that in this, my arch-enemy and evil genius, I could fail to recognize the William Wilson of my school-boy days,—the name-sake, the companion, the rival—the hated and dreaded rival at Dr. Bransby's? Impossible!—But let me hasten to the last eventful scene of the drama.

Thus far I had succumbed supinely to this imperious domination. The sentiment of deep awe with which I habitually regarded the elevated character, the majestic wisdom, the apparent omnipresence and omnipotence of Wilson, added to a feeling of even terror, with which certain other traits in his nature and assumptions inspired me, had operated, hitherto, to impress me with an idea of my own utter weakness and helplessness, and to suggest an implicit, although bitterly reluctant submission to his arbitrary will. But, of late days, I had given myself up entirely to wine; and its maddening influence upon my hereditary temper rendered me more and more impatient of control. I began to murmur,—to hesitate,—to resist. And was it only fancy which induced me to believe that, with the increase of my own firmness, that of my tormentor underwent a proportional diminution? Be this as it may, I now began to feel the inspiration of a burning hope, and at length nurtured in my secret thoughts a stern and desperate resolution that I would submit no longer to be enslaved.

It was at Rome, during the Carnival of 18—, that I attended a masquerade in the palazzo of the Neapolitan Duke Di Broglio. I had indulged more freely than usual in the excesses of the wine-table; and now the suffocating atmosphere of the crowded rooms irritated me beyond endurance. The difficulty, too, of forcing my way through the mazes of the company contributed not a little to the ruffling of my temper; for I was anxiously seeking (let me not say with what unworthy motive) the young, the gay, the beautiful wife of the aged and doting Di Broglio. With a too unscrupulous confidence she had previously communicated to me the secret of the costume in which she would be habited, and now, having caught a glimpse of her person, I was hurrying to make my way into her presence. At this moment I felt a light hand placed upon my shoulder, and that ever-remembered, low, damnable *whisper* within my ear.

In an absolute frenzy of wrath, I turned at once upon him who had thus interrupted me, and seized him violently by the collar. He was attired, as I had expected, in a costume altogether similar to my own; wearing a Spanish cloak of blue velvet, begirt about the waist with a crimson belt sustaining a rapier. A mask of black silk entirely covered his face.

"Scoundrel!" I said, in a voice husky with rage, while every syllable I uttered seemed as new fuel to my fury; "scoundrel! impostor! accursed villain! you shall not—you *shall not* dog me unto death! Follow me, or I stab you where you stand!" —and I broke my way from the ballroom into a small ante-chamber adjoining, dragging him unresistingly with me as I went.

Upon entering, I thrust him furiously from me. He staggered against the wall, while I closed the door with an oath, and commanded him to draw. He hesitated but for an instant; then, with a slight sigh, drew in silence, and put himself upon his defence.

The contest was brief indeed. I was frantic with every species of wild excitement, and felt within my single arm the energy and power of a multitude. In a few seconds I forced him by sheer strength against the wainscoting, and thus, getting him at mercy, plunged my sword, with brute ferocity, repeatedly through and through his bosom.

At that instant some person tried the latch of the door. I hastened to prevent an intrusion, and then immediately returned to my dying antagonist. But what human language can adequately portray *that* astonishment, *that* horror which possessed me at the spectacle then presented to view? The brief moment in which I averted my eyes had been sufficient to produce, apparently, a material change in the arrangements of the upper or farther end of the room. A large mirror,—so at first it seemed to me in my confusion—now stood where none had been perceptible before; and as I stepped up to it in extremity of terror, mine own image, but with features all pale and dabbled in blood, advanced to meet me with a feeble and tottering gait.

Thus it appeared, I say, but was not. It was my antagonist—it was Wilson, who then stood before me in the agonies of his dissolution. His mask and cloak lay, where he had thrown them, upon the floor. Not a thread in all his raiment—not a line in all the marked and singular lineaments of his face which was not, even in the most absolute identity, *mine own!*

It was Wilson; but he spoke no longer in a whisper, and I could have fancied that I myself was speaking while he said:

"You have conquered, and I yield. Yet henceforward art thou also dead—dead to the World, to Heaven, and to Hope! In me didst thou exist—and, in my death, see by this image, which is thine own, how utterly thou hast murdered thyself."

THE MASQUE OF THE RED DEATH
[1850 (1842)]

THE "RED DEATH" had long devastated the country. No pestilence had ever been so fatal, or so hideous. Blood was its Avatar and its seal—the redness and the horror of blood. There were sharp pains, and sudden dizziness, and then profuse bleeding at the pores, with dissolution. The scarlet stains upon the body and especially upon the face of the victim, were the pest ban which shut him out from the aid and from the sympathy of his fellowmen. And the whole seizure, progress and termination of the disease, were the incidents of half an hour.

But the Prince Prospero was happy and dauntless and sagacious. When his dominions were half depopulated, he summoned to his presence a thousand hale and light-hearted friends from among the knights and dames of his court, and with these retired to the deep seclusion of one of his castellated abbeys. This was an extensive and magnificent structure, the creation of the prince's own eccentric yet august taste. A strong and lofty wall girdled it in. This wall had gates of iron. The courtiers, having entered, brought furnaces and massy hammers and welded the bolts. They resolved to leave means neither of ingress or egress to the sudden impulses of despair or of frenzy from within. The abbey was amply provisioned. With such precautions the courtiers might bid defiance to contagion. The external world could take care of itself. In the meantime it was folly to grieve, or to think. The prince had provided all the appliances of pleasure. There were buffoons, there were improvisatori, there were ballet-dancers, there were musicians, there was Beauty, there was wine. All these and security were within. Without was the "Red Death."

It was toward the close of the fifth or sixth month of his seclusion, and while the pestilence raged most furiously abroad, that the Prince Prospero entertained his thousand friends at a masked ball of the most unusual magnificence.

It was a voluptuous scene, that masquerade. But first let me tell of the rooms in which it was held. There were seven—an imperial suite. In many palaces, however, such suites form a long and straight vista, while the folding doors slide back nearly to the walls on either hand, so that the view of the whole extent is scarcely impeded. Here the case was very different; as might have been expected from the duke's love of the *bizarre*. The apartments were so irregularly disposed that the vision embraced but little more than one at a time. There was a sharp turn at every twenty or thirty yards, and at each turn a novel effect. To the right and left, in the middle of each wall, a tall and narrow Gothic window looked out upon a closed corridor which pursued the windings of the suite. These windows were of stained glass whose color varied in accordance with the prevailing hue of the decorations of the chamber into which it opened. That at the eastern extremity was hung, for example, in blue—and vividly blue were its windows. The second chamber was purple in its ornaments and tapestries, and here the panes were purple. The third was green throughout, and so were the casements. The fourth was furnished and lighted with orange—the fifth with white—the sixth with violet. The seventh apartment was closely shrouded in black velvet tapestries that hung all over the ceiling and down the walls, falling in heavy folds upon a carpet of the same material and hue. But in this chamber only, the color of the windows failed to correspond with the decorations. The panes here were scarlet— a deep blood color. Now in no one of the seven apartments was there any lamp or candelabrum, amid the profusion of golden ornaments that lay scattered to and fro or depended from the roof. There was no light of any kind emanating from lamp or candle within the suite of chambers. But in the corridors that followed the suite, there stood, opposite to each window, a heavy tripod, bearing a brazier of fire that projected its rays through the tinted glass and so glaringly illumined the room. And thus were produced a multitude of gaudy and fantastic appearances. But in the western or black chamber the effect of the firelight that streamed upon the dark hangings through the blood-tinted panes, was ghastly in the extreme, and produced so wild a look upon the countenances of those who entered, that there were few of the company bold enough to set foot within its precincts at all.

It was in this apartment, also, that there stood against the western wall, a gigantic clock of ebony. Its pendulum swung to and fro with a dull, heavy, monotonous clang; and when the minute-hand made the circuit of the face, and the hour was to be stricken, there came from the brazen lungs of the clock a sound which was clear and loud and deep and exceedingly musical, but of so peculiar a note and emphasis that, at each lapse of an hour, the musicians of the orchestra were constrained to pause, momentarily, in their performance, to hearken to the sound; and thus the waltzers perforce ceased their evolutions; and there was a brief disconcert of the whole gay company; and, while the chimes of the clock yet rang, it was observed that the giddiest grew pale, and the more aged and sedate passed their hands over their brows as if in confused revery or meditation. But when the echoes had fully ceased, a light laughter at once pervaded the assembly; the musicians looked at each other and smiled as if at their own nervousness and folly, and made whispering vows, each to the other, that the next chiming of the clock should produce in them no similar emotion; and then, after the lapse of sixty minutes (which embrace three thousand and six hundred seconds of the Time that flies,) there came yet another chiming of the clock, and then were the same disconcert and tremulousness and meditation as before.

But, in spite of these things, it was a gay and magnificent revel. The tastes of the duke were peculiar. He had a fine eye for colors and effects. He disregarded the *decora* [1] of mere fashion. His plans were bold and fiery, and his conceptions glowed with barbaric lustre. There are some who would have thought him mad. His followers felt that he was not. It was necessary to hear and see and touch him to be *sure* that he was not.

He had directed, in great part, the movable embellishments of the seven chambers, upon occasion of this great *fête*; and it was his own guiding taste which had given character to the masqueraders. Be sure they were grotesque. There were much glare and glitter and piquancy and phantasm— much of what has been since seen in "Hernani." [2] There were arabesque figures with unsuited limbs and appointments. There were delirious fancies such as the madman fashions. There was much of the beautiful, much of the wanton, much of the *bizarre*, something of the terrible, and not a little of that which might have excited disgust. To and fro in the seven chambers there stalked, in fact, a multitude of dreams. And these—the dreams— writhed in and about, taking hue from the rooms, and causing the wild music of the orchestra to seem as the echo of their steps. And, anon, there strikes the ebony clock which stands in the hall of the velvet. And then, for a moment, all is still, and all is silent save the voice of the clock.

The dreams are stiff-frozen as they stand. But the echoes of the chime die away— they have endured but an instant—and a light, half-subdued laughter floats after them as they depart. And now again the music swells, and the dreams live, and writhe to and fro more merrily than ever, taking hue from the many tinted windows through which stream the rays from the tripods. But to the chamber which lies most westwardly of the seven, there are now none of the maskers who venture; for the night is waning away; and there flows a ruddier light through the blood-colored panes; and the blackness of the sable drapery appalls; and to him whose foot falls upon the sable carpet, there comes from the near clock of ebony a muffled peal more solemnly emphatic than any which reaches *their* ears who indulge in the more remote gayeties of the other apartments.

But these other apartments were densely crowded, and in them beat feverishly the heart of life. And the revel went whirlingly on, until at length there commenced the sounding of midnight upon the clock. And then the music ceased, as I have told; and the evolutions of the waltzers were quieted; and there was an uneasy cessation of all things as before. But now there were twelve strokes to be sounded by the bell of the clock; and thus it happened, perhaps, that more of thought crept, with more of time, into the meditations of the thoughtful among those who revelled. And thus, too, it happened, perhaps, that before the last echoes of the last chime had utterly sunk into silence, there were many individuals in the crowd who had found leisure to become aware of the presence of a masked figure which had arrested the attention of no single individual before. And the rumor of this new presence having spread itself whisperingly around, there

---

[1] Decorations.

[2] Victor Hugo's *Hernani* (1830) began the vogue of romanticism in the French theater.

arose at length from the whole company, a buzz, or murmur, expressive of disapprobation and surprise—then, finally, of terror, of horror, and of disgust.

In an assembly of phantasms such as I have painted, it may well be supposed that no ordinary appearance could have excited such sensation. In truth the masquerade license of the night was nearly unlimited; but the figure in question had out-Heroded Herod,[3] and gone beyond the bounds of even the prince's indefinite decorum. There are chords in the hearts of the most reckless which cannot be touched without emotion. Even with the utterly lost, to whom life and death are equally jests, there are matters of which no jest can be made. The whole company, indeed, seemed now deeply to feel that in the costume and bearing of the stranger neither wit nor propriety existed. The figure was tall and gaunt, and shrouded from head to foot in the habiliments of the grave. The mask which concealed the visage was made so nearly to resemble the countenance of a stiffened corpse that the closest scrutiny must have had difficulty in detecting the cheat. And yet all this might have been endured, if not approved, by the mad revellers around. But the mummer had gone so far as to assume the type of the Red Death. His vesture was dabbled in *blood*—and his broad brow, with all the features of the face, was besprinkled with the scarlet horror.

When the eyes of Prince Prospero fell upon this spectral image (which with a slow and solemn movement, as if more fully to sustain its *rôle*, stalked to and fro among the waltzers) he was seen to be convulsed, in the first moment, with a strong shudder either of terror or distaste; but, in the next, his brow reddened with rage.

"Who dares?" he demanded hoarsely of the courtiers who stood near him—"who dares insult us with this blasphemous mockery? Seize him and unmask him—that we may know whom we have to hang at sunrise, from the battlements!"

It was in the eastern or blue chamber in which stood the Prince Prospero as he uttered these words. They rang throughout the seven rooms loudly and clearly—for the prince was a bold and robust man, and the music had become hushed at the waving of his hand.

It was in the blue room where stood the prince, with a group of pale courtiers by his side. At first, as he spoke, there was a slight rushing movement of this group in the direction of the intruder, who at the moment was also near at hand, and now, with deliberate and stately step, made closer approach to the speaker. But from a certain nameless awe with which the mad assumptions of the mummer had inspired the whole party, there were found none who put forth hand to seize him; so that, unimpeded, he passed within a yard of the prince's person; and, while the vast assembly, as if with one impulse, shrank from the centres of the rooms to the walls, he made his way uninterruptedly, but with the same solemn and measured step which had distinguished him from the first, through the blue chamber to the purple—through the purple to the green—through the green to the orange—through this again to the white—and even thence to the violet, ere a decided movement had been made to arrest him. It was then, however, that the Prince Prospero, maddening with rage and the shame of his own momentary cowardice, rushed hurriedly through the six chambers, while none followed him on account of a deadly terror that had seized upon all. He bore aloft a drawn dagger, and had approached, in rapid impetuosity, to within three or four feet of the retreating figure, when the latter, having attained the extremity of the velvet apartment, turned suddenly and confronted his pursuer. There was a sharp cry—and the dagger dropped gleaming upon the sable carpet, upon which, instantly afterwards, fell prostrate in death the Prince Prospero. Then, summoning the wild courage of

---

[3] See Note 8 for "William Wilson," p. 509.

despair, a throng of the revellers at once threw themselves into the black apartment, and, seizing the mummer, whose tall figure stood erect and motionless within the shadow of the ebony clock, gasped in unutterable horror at finding the grave-cerements and corpse-like mask which they handled with so violent a rudeness, untenanted by any tangible form.

And now was acknowledged the presence of the Red Death. He had come like a thief in the night. And one by one dropped the revellers in the blood-bedewed halls of their revel, and died each in the despairing posture of his fall. And the life of the ebony clock went out with that of the last of the gay. And the flames of the tripods expired. And Darkness and Decay and the Red Death held illimitable dominion over all.

THE CASK OF AMONTILLADO
[1850 (1846)]

THE THOUSAND injuries of Fortunato I had borne as I best could; but when he ventured upon insult, I vowed revenge. You, who so well know the nature of my soul, will not suppose, however, that I gave utterance to a threat. *At length* I would be avenged: this was a point definitively settled—but the very definitiveness with which it was resolved precluded the idea of risk. I must not only punish, but punish with impunity. A wrong is unredressed when retribution overtakes its redresser. It is equally unredressed when the avenger fails to make himself felt as such to him who has done the wrong.

It must be understood that neither by word nor deed had I given Fortunato cause to doubt my good will. I continued, as was my wont, to smile in his face, and he did not perceive that my smile *now* was at the thought of his immolation.

He had a weak point—this Fortunato—although in other regards he was a man to be respected and even feared. He prided himself on his connoisseurship in wine.

Few Italians have the true virtuoso spirit. For the most part their enthusiasm is adopted to suit the time and opportunity —to practice imposture upon the British and Austrian *millionaires*. In painting and gemmary, Fortunato, like his countrymen, was a quack—but in the matter of old wines he was sincere. In this respect I did not differ from him materially;—I was skilful in the Italian vintages myself, and bought largely whenever I could.

It was about dusk, one evening during the supreme madness of the carnival season, that I encountered my friend. He accosted me with excessive warmth, for he had been drinking much. The man wore motley. He had on a tight-fitting parti-striped dress, and his head was surmounted by the conical cap and bells. I was so pleased to see him that I thought I should never have done wringing his hand.

I said to him—"My dear Fortunato, you are luckily met. How remarkably well you are looking to-day. But I have received a pipe [1] of what passes for Amontillado, and I have my doubts."

"How?" said he. "Amontillado? A pipe? Impossible! And in the middle of the carnival!"

"I have my doubts," I replied; "and I was silly enough to pay the full Amontillado price without consulting you in the matter. You were not to be found, and I was fearful of losing a bargain."

"Amontillado!"

"I have my doubts."

"Amontillado!"

"And I must satisfy them."

"Amontillado!"

"As you are engaged, I am on my way to Luchresi. If any one has a critical turn, it is he. He will tell me—"

"Luchresi cannot tell Amontillado from Sherry."

"And yet some fools will have it that his taste is a match for your own."

"Come, let us go."

"Whither?"

[1] Small barrel.

"To your vaults."

"My friend, no; I will not impose upon your good nature. I perceive you have an engagement. Luchresi—"

"I have no engagement;—come."

"My friend, no. It is not the engagement, but the severe cold with which I perceive you are afflicted. The vaults are insufferably damp. They are incrusted with nitre."

"Let us go, nevertheless. The cold is merely nothing. Amontillado! You have been imposed upon. And as for Luchresi, he cannot distinguish Sherry from Amontillado."

Thus speaking, Fortunato possessed himself of my arm. Putting on a mask of black silk, and drawing a *roquelaire* [2] closely about my person, I suffered him to hurry me to my palazzo.

There were no attendants at home; they had absconded to make merry in honour of the time. I had told them that I should not return until the morning, and had given them explicit orders not to stir from the house. These orders were sufficient, I well knew, to insure their immediate disappearance, one and all, as soon as my back was turned.

I took from their sconces two flambeaus, and giving one to Fortunato, bowed him through several suites of rooms to the archway that led into the vaults. I passed down a long and winding staircase, requesting him to be cautious as he followed. We came at length to the foot of the descent, and stood together on the damp ground of the catacombs of the Montresors.

The gait of my friend was unsteady, and the bells upon his cap jingled as he strode.

"The pipe," said he.

"It is farther on," said I; "but observe the white web-work which gleams from these cavern walls."

He turned towards me, and looked into my eyes with two filmy orbs that distilled the rheum of intoxication.

"Nitre?" he asked at length.

"Nitre," I replied. "How long have you had that cough?"

"Ugh! ugh! ugh!—ugh! ugh! ugh!—ugh! ugh! ugh!—ugh! ugh! ugh!—ugh! ugh! ugh!"

My poor friend found it impossible to reply for many minutes.

"It is nothing," he said, at last.

"Come," I said, with decision, "we will go back; your health is precious. You are rich, respected, admired, beloved; you are happy, as once I was. You are a man to be missed. For me it is no matter. We will go back; you will be ill, and I cannot be responsible. Besides, there is Luchresi—"

"Enough," he said; "the cough is a mere nothing; it will not kill me. I shall not die of a cough."

"True—true," I replied; "and, indeed, I had no intention of alarming you unnecessarily—but you should use all proper caution. A draught of this Medoc will defend us from the damps."

Here I knocked off the neck of a bottle which I drew from a long row of its fellows that lay upon the mould.

"Drink," I said, presenting him the wine.

He raised it to his lips with a leer. He paused and nodded to me familiarly, while his bells jingled.

"I drink," he said, "to the buried that repose around us."

"And I to your long life."

He again took my arm, and we proceeded.

"These vaults," he said, "are extensive."

"The Montresors," I replied, "were a great and numerous family."

"I forget your arms."

"A huge human foot d'or, in a field azure; the foot crushes a serpent rampant whose fangs are embedded in the heel."

"And the motto?"

"Nemo me impune lacessit." [3]

"Good!" he said.

The wine sparkled in his eyes and the bells jingled. My own fancy grew warm with the Medoc. We had passed through long walls of piled skeletons, with casks

---

[2] Short cloak.
[3] "No one attacks me with impunity," a motto on the royal arms of Scotland.

and puncheons intermingling, into the inmost recesses of the catacombs. I paused again, and this time I made bold to seize Fortunato by an arm above the elbow.

"The nitre!" I said; "see, it increases. It hangs like moss upon the vaults. We are below the river's bed. The drops of moisture trickle among the bones. Come, we will go back ere it is too late. Your cough—"

"It is nothing," he said; "let us go on. But first, another draught of the Medoc."

I broke and reached him a flagon of De Grâve. He emptied it at a breath. His eyes flashed with a fierce light. He laughed and threw the bottle upwards with a gesticulation I did not understand.

I looked at him in surprise. He repeated the movement—a grotesque one.

"You do not comprehend?" he said.

"Not I," I replied.

"Then you are not of the brotherhood."

"How?"

"You are not of the masons."

"Yes, yes," I said; "yes, yes."

"You? Impossible! A mason?"

"A mason," I replied.

"A sign," he said, "a sign."

"It is this," I answered, producing from beneath the folds of my *roquelaire*, a trowel.

"You jest," he exclaimed, recoiling a few paces. "But let us proceed to the Amontillado."

"Be it so," I said, replacing the tool beneath the cloak, and again offering him my arm. He leaned upon it heavily. We continued our route in search of the Amontillado. We passed through a range of low arches, descended, passed on, and, descending again, arrived at a deep crypt, in which the foulness of the air caused our flambeaus rather to glow than flame.

At the most remote end of the crypt there appeared another less spacious. Its walls had been lined with human remains, piled to the vault overhead, in the fashion of the great catacombs of Paris. Three sides of this interior crypt were still ornamented in this manner. From the fourth

side the bones had been thrown down, and lay promiscuously upon the earth, forming at one point a mound of some size. Within the wall thus exposed by the displacing of the bones, we perceived a still interior crypt or recess, in depth about four feet, in width three, in height six or seven. It seemed to have been constructed for no especial use within itself, but formed merely the interval between two of the colossal supports of the roof of the catacombs, and was backed by one of their circumscribing walls of solid granite.

It was in vain that Fortunato, uplifting his dull torch, endeavoured to pry into the depth of the recess. Its termination the feeble light did not enable us to see.

"Proceed," I said; "herein is the Amontillado. As for Luchresi—"

"He is an ignoramus," interrupted my friend, as he stepped unsteadily forward, while I followed immediately at his heels. In an instant he had reached the extremity of the niche, and finding his progress arrested by the rock, stood stupidly bewildered. A moment more and I had fettered him to the granite. In its surface were two iron staples, distant from each other about two feet, horizontally. From one of these depended a short chain, from the other a padlock. Throwing the links about his waist, it was but the work of a few seconds to secure it. He was too much astounded to resist. Withdrawing the key, I stepped back from the recess.

"Pass your hand," I said, "over the wall; you cannot help feeling the nitre. Indeed it is *very* damp. Once more let me *implore* you to return. No? Then I must positively leave you. But I must first render you all the little attentions in my power."

"The Amontillado!" ejaculated my friend, not yet recovered from his astonishment.

"True," I replied; "the Amontillado."

As I said these words I busied myself among the pile of bones of which I have before spoken. Throwing them aside, I soon uncovered a quantity of building stone and mortar. With these materials and with the aid of my trowel, I began vigorously to wall up the entrance of the niche.

I had scarcely laid the first tier of the masonry when I discovered that the intoxication of Fortunato had in a great measure worn off. The earliest indication I had of this was a low moaning cry from the depth of the recess. It was *not* the cry of a drunken man. There was then a long and obstinate silence. I laid the second tier, and the third, and the fourth; and then I heard the furious vibrations of the chain. The noise lasted for several minutes, during which, that I might hearken to it with the more satisfaction, I ceased my labours and sat down upon the bones. When at last the clanking subsided, I resumed the trowel, and finished without interruption the fifth, the sixth, and the seventh tier. The wall was now nearly upon a level with my breast. I again paused, and holding the flambeaus over the mason work, threw a few feeble rays upon the figure within.

A succession of loud and shrill screams, bursting suddenly from the throat of the chained form, seemed to thrust me violently back. For a brief moment I hesitated, I trembled. Unsheathing my rapier, I began to grope with it about the recess; but the thought of an instant reassured me. I placed my hand upon the solid fabric of the catacombs, and felt satisfied. I reapproached the wall; I replied to the yells of him who clamoured. I re-echoed, I aided, I surpassed them in volume and in strength. I did this, and the clamorer grew still.

It was now midnight, and my task was drawing to a close. I had completed the eighth, the ninth, and the tenth tier. I had finished a portion of the last and the eleventh; there remained but a single stone to be fitted and plastered in. I struggled with its weight; I placed it partially in its destined position. But now there came from out the niche a low laugh that erected the hairs upon my head. It was succeeded by a sad voice, which I had difficulty in recognizing as that of the noble Fortunato. The voice said—

"Ha! ha! ha!—he! he! he!—a very good joke, indeed—an excellent jest. We will have many a rich laugh about it at the palazzo—he! he! he—over our wine—he! he! he!"

"The Amontillado!" I said.

"He! he! he!—he! he! he!—yes, the Amontillado. But is it not getting late? Will not they be awaiting us at the palazzo, the Lady Fortunato and the rest? Let us be gone."

"Yes," I said, "let us be gone."

"For the love of God, Montresor!"

"Yes," I said, "for the love of God!"

But to these words I hearkened in vain for a reply. I grew impatient. I called aloud—

"Fortunato!"

No answer. I called again—

"Fortunato!"

No answer still. I thrust a torch through the remaining aperture and let it fall within. There came forth in return only a jingling of the bells. My heart grew sick; it was the dampness of the catacombs that made it so. I hastened to make an end of my labour. I forced the last stone into its position; I plastered it up. Against the new masonry I re-erected the old rampart of bones. For the half of a century no mortal has disturbed them. *In pace requiescat.*[4]

THE PURLOINED LETTER
[1845 (1844)]

Nil sapientiae odiosius acumine nimio.
SENECA [1]

AT PARIS, just after dark one gusty evening in the autumn of 18—, I was enjoying the two-fold luxury of meditation and a meerschaum, in company with my friend C. Auguste Dupin, in his little back library, or book-closet, *au troisième, No.*

[4] May he rest in peace.
[1] The epigraph, "Nothing is more distasteful to good sense than too much subtlety," is from Lucius Annaeus Seneca (3 B. C. — 65 A. D.).

33, Rue Dunôt, Faubourg St. Germain.[2] For one hour at least we had maintained a profound silence; while each, to any casual observer, might have seemed intently and exclusively occupied with the curling eddies of smoke that oppressed the atmosphere of the chamber. For myself, however, I was mentally discussing certain topics which had formed matter for conversation between us at an earlier period of the evening; I mean the affair of the Rue Morgue, and the mystery attending the murder of Marie Rogêt.[3] I looked upon it, therefore, as something of a coincidence, when the door of our apartment was thrown open and admitted our old acquaintance, Monsieur G——, the Prefect of the Parisian police.

We gave him a hearty welcome; for there was nearly half as much of the entertaining as of the contemptible about the man, and we had not seen him for several years. We had been sitting in the dark, and Dupin now arose for the purpose of lighting a lamp, but sat down again, without doing so, upon G.'s saying that he had called to consult us, or rather to ask the opinion of my friend, about some official business which had occasioned a great deal of trouble.

"If it is any point requiring reflection," observed Dupin, as he forbore to enkindle the wick, "we shall examine it to better purpose in the dark."

"That is another of your odd notions," said the Prefect, who had a fashion of calling everything "odd" that was beyond his comprehension, and thus lived amid an absolute legion of "oddities."

"Very true," said Dupin, as he supplied his visitor with a pipe, and rolled towards him a comfortable chair.

"And what is the difficulty now?" I asked. "Nothing more in the assassination way, I hope?"

"Oh no; nothing of that nature. The fact is, the business is *very* simple indeed, and I make no doubt that we can manage it sufficiently well ourselves; but then I thought Dupin would like to hear the details of it, because it is so excessively *odd.*"

"Simple and odd," said Dupin.

"Why, yes; and not exactly that, either. The fact is, we have all been a good deal puzzled because the affair *is* so simple, and yet baffles us altogether."

"Perhaps it is the very simplicity of the thing which puts you at fault," said my friend.

"What nonsense you *do* talk!" replied the Prefect, laughing heartily.

"Perhaps the mystery is a little *too* plain," said Dupin.

"Oh, good heavens! who ever heard of such an idea?"

"A little *too* self-evident."

"Ha! ha! ha!—ha! ha! ha!—ho! ho! ho!" roared our visitor, profoundly amused, "oh, Dupin, you will be the death of me yet!"

"And what, after all, *is* the matter on hand?" I asked.

"Why, I will tell you," replied the Prefect, as he gave a long, steady, and contemplative puff, and settled himself in his chair. "I will tell you in a few words; but, before I begin, let me caution you that this is an affair demanding the greatest secrecy, and that I should most probably lose the position I now hold, were it known that I confided it to any one."

"Proceed," said I.

"Or not," said Dupin.

"Well, then; I have received personal information, from a very high quarter, that a certain document of the last importance, has been purloined from the royal apartments. The individual who purloined it is known; this beyond a doubt; he was seen to take it. It is known, also, that it still remains in his possession."

"How is this known?" asked Dupin.

"It is clearly inferred," replied the Pre-

[2] On the third floor at No. 33, Dunôt Street, in the ward of St. Germain.

[3] A reference to Poe's earlier stories of Dupin's exploits, "The Murders in the Rue Morgue" and "The Mystery of Marie Rogêt."

fect, "from the nature of the document, and from the non-appearance of certain results which would at once arise from its passing *out* of the robber's possession;—that is to say, from his employing it as he must design in the end to employ it."

"Be a little more explicit," I said.

"Well, I may venture so far as to say that the paper gives its holder a certain power in a certain quarter where such power is immensely valuable." The Prefect was fond of the cant of diplomacy.

"Still I do not quite understand," said Dupin.

"No? Well; the disclosure of the document to a third person, who shall be nameless, would bring in question the honor of a personage of most exalted station; and this fact gives the holder of the document an ascendancy over the illustrious personage whose honor and peace are so jeopardized."

"But this ascendancy," I interposed, "would depend upon the robber's knowledge of the loser's knowledge of the robber. Who would dare——"

"The thief," said G., "is the Minister D——, who dares all things, those unbecoming as well as those becoming a man. The method of the theft was not less ingenious than bold. The document in question—a letter, to be frank—had been received by the personage robbed while alone in the royal *boudoir*. During its perusal she was suddenly interrupted by the entrance of the other exalted personage from whom especially it was her wish to conceal it. After a hurried and vain endeavor to thrust it in a drawer, she was forced to place it, open as it was, upon a table. The address, however, was uppermost, and, the contents thus unexposed, the letter escaped notice.[4] At this juncture enters the Minister D—— His lynx eye immediately perceives the paper, recognizes the handwriting of the address, observes the confusion of the personage addressed, and fathoms her secret. After some business transactions, hurried through in his ordinary manner, he produces a

letter somewhat similar to the one in question, opens it, pretends to read it, and then places it in close juxtaposition to the other. Again he converses, for some fifteen minutes, upon the public affairs. At length, in taking leave, he takes also from the table the letter to which he had no claim. Its rightful owner saw, but, of course, dared not call attention to the act, in the presence of the third personage who stood at her elbow. The Minister decamped; leaving his own letter—one of no importance—upon the table."

"Here, then," said Dupin to me, "you have precisely what you demand to make the ascendancy complete—the robber's knowledge of the loser's knowledge of the robber."

"Yes," replied the Prefect; "and the power thus attained has, for some months past, been wielded, for political purposes, to a very dangerous extent. The personage robbed is more thoroughly convinced, every day, of the necessity of reclaiming her letter. But this, of course, cannot be done openly. In fine, driven to despair, she has committed the matter to me."

"Than whom," said Dupin, amid a perfect whirlwind of smoke, "no more sagacious agent could, I suppose, be desired, or even imagined."

"You flatter me," replied the Prefect; "but it is possible that some such opinion may have been entertained."

"It is clear," said I, "as you observe, that the letter is still in possession of the minister; since it is this possession, and not any employment of the letter, which bestows the power. With the employment the power departs."

"True," said G.; "and upon this conviction I proceeded. My first care was to make thorough search of the minister's hotel; and here my chief embarrassment lay in the necessity of searching without

---

[4] At this time letters were not inclosed in envelopes, but folded so they could be sealed with the blank side of the sheet left for the address.

his knowledge. Beyond all things, I have been warned of the danger which would result from giving him reason to suspect our design."

"But," said I, "you are quite *au fait* [5] in these investigations. The Parisian police have done this thing often before."

"O, yes; and for this reason I did not despair. The habits of the minister gave me, too, a great advantage. He is frequently absent from home all night. His servants are by no means numerous. They sleep at a distance from their master's apartment, and, being chiefly Neapolitans, are readily made drunk. I have keys, as you know, with which I can open any chamber or cabinet in Paris. For three months a night has not passed, during the greater part of which I have not been engaged, personally, in ransacking the D—— Hotel. My honor is interested, and, to mention a great secret, the reward is enormous. So I did not abandon the search until I had become fully satisfied that the thief is a more astute man than myself. I fancy that I have investigated every nook and corner of the premises in which it is possible that the paper can be concealed."

"But is it not possible," I suggested, "that although the letter may be in possession of the minister, as it unquestionably is, he may have concealed it elsewhere than upon his own premises?"

"This is barely possible," said Dupin. "The present peculiar condition of affairs at court, and especially of those intrigues in which D—— is known to be involved, would render the instant availability of the document—its susceptibility of being produced at a moment's notice—a point of nearly equal importance with its possession."

"Its susceptibility of being produced?" said I.

"That is to say, of being *destroyed*," said Dupin.

"True," I observed; "the paper ıs clearly then upon the premises. As for its being upon the person of the minister, we may

consider that as out of the question."

"Entirely," said the Prefect. "He has been twice waylaid, as if by footpads, and his person rigorously searched under my own inspection."

"You might have spared yourself this trouble," said Dupin. "D——, I presume, is not altogether a fool, and, if not, must have anticipated these waylayings, as a matter of course."

"Not *altogether* a fool," said G., "but then he's a poet, which I take to be only one remove from a fool."

"True," said Dupin, after a long and thoughtful whiff from his meerschaum, "although I have been guilty of certain doggerel myself."

"Suppose you detail," said I, "the particulars of your search."

"Why, the fact is, we took our time, and we searched *every where*. I have had long experience in these affairs. I took the entire building, room by room; devoting the nights of a whole week to each. We examined, first, the furniture of each apartment. We opened every possible drawer; and I presume you know that, to a properly trained police agent, such a thing as a *secret* drawer is impossible. Any man is a dolt who permits a 'secret' drawer to escape him in a search of this kind. The thing is *so* plain. There is a certain amount of bulk—of space—to be accounted for in every cabinet. Then we have accurate rules. The fiftieth part of a line could not escape us. After the cabinets we took the chairs. The cushions we probed with the fine long needles you have seen me employ. From the tables we removed the tops."

"Why so?"

"Sometimes the top of a table, or other similarly arranged piece of furniture, is removed by the person wishing to conceal an article; then the leg is excavated, the article deposited within the cavity, and the top replaced. The bottoms and tops of bed-posts are employed in the same way."

---

[5] Experienced or "in the know."

"But could not the cavity be detected by sounding?" I asked.

"By no means, if, when the article is deposited, a sufficient wadding of cotton be placed around it. Besides, in our case, we were obliged to proceed without noise."

"But you could not have removed—you could not have taken to pieces *all* articles of furniture in which it would have been possible to make a deposit in the manner you mention. A letter may be compressed into a thin spiral roll, not differing much in shape or bulk from a large knitting-needle, and in this form it might be inserted into the rung of a chair, for example. You did not take to pieces all the chairs?"

"Certainly not; but we did better—we examined the rungs of every chair in the hotel, and, indeed, the jointings of every description of furniture, by the aid of a most powerful microscope. Had there been any traces of recent disturbance we should not have failed to detect it instantly. A single grain of gimlet-dust, for example, would have been as obvious as an apple. Any disorder in the glueing—any unusual gaping in the joints—would have sufficed to insure detection."

"I presume you looked to the mirrors, between the boards and the plates, and you probed the beds and the bed-clothes, as well as the curtains and carpets."

"That of course; and when we had absolutely completed every particle of the furniture in this way, then we examined the house itself. We divided its entire surface into compartments, which we numbered, so that none might be missed; then we scrutinized each individual square inch throughout the premises, including the two houses immediately adjoining, with the microscope, as before."

"The two houses adjoining!" I exclaimed; "you must have had a great deal of trouble."

"We had; but the reward offered is prodigious."

"You include the *grounds* about the houses?"

"All the grounds are paved with brick. They gave us comparatively little trouble. We examined the moss between the bricks, and found it undisturbed."

"You looked among D——'s papers, of course, and into the books of the library?"

"Certainly; we opened every package and parcel; we not only opened every book, but we turned over every leaf in each volume, not contenting ourselves with a mere shake, according to the fashion of some of our police officers. We also measured the thickness of every book-*cover*, with the most accurate admeasurement, and applied to each the most jealous scrutiny of the microscope. Had any of the bindings been recently meddled with, it would have been utterly impossible that the fact should have escaped observation. Some five or six volumes, just from the hands of the binder, we carefully probed, longitudinally, with the needles."

"You explored the floors beneath the carpets?"

"Beyond doubt. We removed every carpet, and examined the boards with the microscope."

"And the paper on the walls?"

"Yes."

"You looked into the cellars?"

"We did."

"Then," I said, "you have been making a miscalculation, and the letter is *not* upon the premises, as you suppose."

"I fear you are right there," said the Prefect. "And now, Dupin, what would you advise me to do?"

"To make a thorough re-search of the premises."

"That is absolutely needless," replied G——. "I am not more sure that I breathe than I am that the letter is not at the Hotel."

"I have no better advice to give you," said Dupin. "You have, of course, an accurate description of the letter?"

"Oh yes!"—And here the Prefect, producing a memorandum-book, proceeded to read aloud a minute account of the internal, and especially of the external appearance of the missing document. Soon after finishing the perusal of this description, he took his departure, more entirely depressed in spirits than I had ever known the good gentleman before.

In about a month afterwards he paid us another visit, and found us occupied very nearly as before. He took a pipe and a chair and entered into some ordinary conversation. At length I said,—

"Well, but G——, what of the purloined letter? I presume you have at last made up your mind that there is no such thing as overreaching the Minister?"

"Confound him, say I—yes; I made the re-examination, however, as Dupin suggested—but it was all labor lost, as I knew it would be."

"How much was the reward offered, did you say?" asked Dupin.

"Why, a very great deal—a *very* liberal reward—I don't like to say how much, precisely; but one thing I *will* say, that I wouldn't mind giving my individual check for fifty thousand francs to any one who could obtain me that letter. The fact is, it is becoming of more and more importance every day; and the reward has been lately doubled. If it were trebled, however, I could do no more than I have done."

"Why, yes," said Dupin, drawlingly, between the whiffs of his meerschaum, "I really—think, G——, you have not exerted yourself—to the utmost in this matter. You might—do a little more, I think, eh?"

"How?—in what way?"

"Why—puff, puff—you might—puff, puff—employ counsel in the matter, eh? —puff, puff, puff. Do you remember the story they tell of Abernethy?" [6]

"No: hang Abernethy!"

"To be sure! hang him and welcome. But, once upon a time, a certain rich miser conceived the design of sponging upon this Abernethy for a medical opinion. Getting up, for this purpose, an ordinary conversation in a private company, he insinuated his case to the physician, as that of an imaginary individual.

" 'We will suppose,' said the miser, 'that his symptoms are such and such; now,

doctor, what would *you* have directed him to take?'

" 'Take!' said Abernethy, 'why, take *advice,* to be sure.' "

"But," said the Prefect, a little discomposed, "I am *perfectly* willing to take advice, and to pay for it. I would *really* give fifty thousand francs to any one who would aid me in the matter."

"In that case," replied Dupin, opening a drawer, and producing a check-book, "you may as well fill me up a check for the amount mentioned. When you have signed it, I will hand you the letter."

I was astounded. The Prefect appeared absolutely thunder-stricken. For some minutes he remained speechless and motionless, looking incredulously at my friend with open mouth, and eyes that seemed starting from their sockets; then, apparently recovering himself in some measure, he seized a pen, and after several pauses and vacant stares, finally filled up and signed a check for fifty thousand francs, and handed it across the table to Dupin. The latter examined it carefully and deposited it in his pocket-book; then, unlocking an *escritoire,*[7] took thence a letter and gave it to the Prefect. This functionary grasped it in a perfect agony of joy, opened it with a trembling hand, cast a rapid glance at its contents, and then, scrambling and struggling to the door, rushed at length unceremoniously from the room and from the house, without having uttered a syllable since Dupin had requested him to fill up the check.

When he had gone, my friend entered into some explanations.

"The Parisian police," he said, "are exceedingly able in their way. They are persevering, ingenious, cunning, and thoroughly versed in the knowledge which their duties seem chiefly to demand. Thus, when G—— detailed to us his mode of searching the premises at the Hotel D——, I felt

---

[6] Dr. John Abernethy (1764-1831), a British physician.
[7] Writing-desk.

entire confidence in his having made a satisfactory investigation—so far as his labors extended."

"So far as his labors extended?" said I.

"Yes," said Dupin. "The measures adopted were not only the best of their kind, but carried out to absolute perfection. Had the letter been deposited within the range of their search, these fellows would, beyond a question, have found it."

I merely laughed—but he seemed quite serious in all that he said.

"The measures, then," he continued, "were good in their kind, and well executed; their defect lay in their being inapplicable to the case, and to the man. A certain set of highly ingenious resources are, with the Prefect, a sort of Procrustean bed,[8] to which he forcibly adapts his designs. But he perpetually errs by being too deep or too shallow, for the matter in hand; and many a schoolboy is a better reasoner than he. I knew one about eight years of age, whose success at guessing in the game of 'even and odd' attracted universal admiration. This game is simple, and is played with marbles. One player holds in his hand a number of these toys, and demands of another whether that number is even or odd. If the guess is right, the guesser wins one; if wrong, he loses one. The boy to whom I allude won all the marbles of the school. Of course he had some principle of guessing; and this lay in mere observation and admeasurement of the astuteness of his opponents. For example, an arrant simpleton is his opponent, and, holding up his closed hand, asks, 'are they even or odd?' Our schoolboy replies, 'odd,' and loses; but upon the second trial he wins, for he then says to himself, 'the simpleton had them even upon the first trial, and his amount of cunning is just sufficient to make him have them odd upon the second; I will therefore guess odd;'—he guesses odd, and wins. Now, with a simpleton a degree above the first, he would have reasoned thus: 'This fellow finds that in the first instance I guessed odd, and, in the second, he will propose to

himself, upon the first impulse, a simple variation from even to odd, as did the first simpleton; but then a second thought will suggest that this is too simple a variation, and finally he will decide upon putting it even as before. I will therefore guess even;'—he guesses even, and wins. Now this mode of reasoning in the schoolboy, whom his fellows termed 'lucky,'—what, in its last analysis, is it?"

"It is merely," I said, "an identification of the reasoner's intellect with that of his opponent."

"It is," said Dupin; "and, upon inquiring of the boy by what means he effected the *thorough* identification in which his success consisted, I received answer as follows: 'When I wish to find out how wise, or how stupid, or how good, or how wicked is any one, or what are his thoughts at the moment, I fashion the expression of my face, as accurately as possible, in accordance with the expression of his, and then wait to see what thoughts or sentiments arise in my mind or heart, as if to match or correspond with the expression.' This response of the schoolboy lies at the bottom of all the spurious profundity which has been attributed to Rochefoucauld, to La Bougive, to Machiavelli, and to Campanella."[9]

"And the identification," I said, "of the reasoner's intellect with that of his opponent, depends, if I understand you aright, upon the accuracy with which the opponent's intellect is admeasured."

"For its practical value it depends upon this," replied Dupin; "and the Prefect

---

[8] In Greek mythology Procrustes or the Stretcher tied all travellers who stopped with him upon an iron bedstead. When they were too short to fit the bed, he stretched their limbs; when the limbs were too long for the bed, he cut them off even with it.

[9] François de la Rochefoucauld (1613-1680) wrote *Maximes* (1665); Machiavelli, *The Prince* (1513); Campanella, *The City in the Sun* (1643). La Bougive has not been identified.

and his cohort fail so frequently, first, by default of this identification, and, secondly, by ill-admeasurement, or rather through non-admeasurement, of the intellect with which they are engaged. They consider only their *own* ideas of ingenuity; and, in searching for anything hidden, advert only to the modes in which *they* would have hidden it. They are right in this much— that their own ingenuity is a faithful representative of that of *the mass*; but when the cunning of the individual felon is diverse in character from their own, the felon foils them, of course. This always happens when it is above their own, and very usually when it is below. They have no variation of principle in their investigations; at best, when urged by some unusual emergency—by some extraordinary reward —they extend or exaggerate their old modes of *practice,* without touching their principles. What, for example, in this case of D——, has been done to vary the principle of action? What is all this boring, and probing, and sounding, and scrutinizing with the microscope, and dividing the surface of the building into registered square inches—what is it all but an exaggeration *of the application* of the one principle or set of principles of search, which are based upon the one set of notions regarding human ingenuity, to which the Prefect, in the long routine of his duty, has been accustomed? Do you not see he has taken it for granted that *all* men proceed to conceal a letter,—not exactly in a gimlet-hole bored in a chair-leg—but, at least, in *some* out-of-the-way hole or corner suggested by the same tenor of thought which would urge a man to secrete a letter in a gimlet-hole bored in a chair-leg? And do you not see also, that such *recherchés* [10] nooks for concealment are adapted only for ordinary occasions, and would be adopted only by ordinary intellects; for, in all cases of concealment, a disposal of the article concealed—a disposal of it in this *recherché* manner,—is, in the very first instance, presumable and presumed; and thus its discovery depends, not at all

upon the acumen, but altogether upon the mere care, patience, and determination of the seekers; and where the case is of importance—or, what amounts to the same thing in the policial eyes, when the reward is of magnitude—the qualities in question have *never* been known to fail. You will now understand what I meant in suggesting that, had the purloined letter been hidden anywhere within the limits of the Prefect's examination—in other words, had the principle of its concealment been comprehended within the principles of the Prefect—its discovery would have been a matter altogether beyond question. This functionary however, has been thoroughly mystified; and the remote source of his defeat lies in the supposition that the Minister is a fool, because he has acquired renown as a poet. All fools are poets; this the Prefect *feels*; and he is merely guilty of a *non distributio medii* [11] in thence inferring that all poets are fools."

"But is this really the poet?" I asked. "There are two brothers, I know; and both have attained reputation in letters. The Minister I believe has written learnedly on the Differential Calculus. He is a mathematician, and no poet."

"You are mistaken; I know him well; he is both. As poet *and* mathematician, he would reason well; as mere mathematician, he could not have reasoned at all, and thus would have been at the mercy of the Prefect."

"You surprise me," I said, "by these opinions, which have been contradicted by the voice of the world. You do not mean to set at naught the well-digested idea of centuries? The mathematical reason has long been regarded as *the reason par excellence.*"

"*'Il y a à parier,'*" replied Dupin, quoting from Chamfort, "*'que toute idée publique, toute convention reçue, est une sottise, car elle a convenue au plus grand*

---

[10] Out-of-the-way or far-fetched.

[11] Undistributed middle term, a prime fallacy in syllogistic reasoning.

nombre.' [12] The mathematicians, grant you, have done their best to promulgate the popular error to which you allude, and which is none the less an error for its promulgation as truth. With an art worthy a better cause, for example, they have insinuated the term 'analysis' into application to algebra. The French are the originators of this particular deception; but if a term is of any importance—if words derive any value from applicability—then 'analysis' conveys 'algebra' about as much as, in Latin, *'ambitus'* implies 'ambition,' *'religio'* 'religion,' or *'homines honesti'* a set of *honorable* men."

"You have a quarrel on hand, I see," said I, "with some of the algebraists of Paris; but proceed."

"I dispute the availability, and thus the value, of that reason which is cultivated in any special form other than the abstractly logical. I dispute, in particular, the reason educed by mathematical study. The mathematics are the science of form and quantity; mathematical reasoning is merely logic applied to observation upon form and quantity. The great error lies in supposing that even the truths of what is called *pure* algebra, are abstract or general truths. And this error is so egregious that I am confounded at the universality with which it has been received. Mathematical axioms are *not* axioms of general truth. What is true of *relation*—of form and quantity—is often grossly false in regard to morals, for example. In this latter science it is very usually *untrue* that the aggregated parts are equal to the whole. In chemistry also the axiom fails. In the consideration of motive it fails; for two motives, each of a given value, have not, necessarily, a value when united, equal to the sum of their values apart. There are numerous other mathematical truths which are only truths within the limits of *relation*. But the mathematician argues, from his *finite truths,* through habit, as if they were of an absolutely general applicability—as the world indeed imagines them to be. Bryant, in his very learned 'Mythology,' mentions an analogous source of error, when he says that 'although the Pagan fables are not believed, yet we forget ourselves continually, and make inferences from them as existing realities.' [13] With the algebraists, however, who are Pagans themselves, the 'Pagan fables' *are* believed, and the inferences are made, not so much through lapse of memory, as through an unaccountable addling of the brains. In short, I never yet encountered the mere mathematician who could be trusted out of equal roots, or one who did not clandestinely hold it as a point of his faith that $x^2 + px$ was absolutely and unconditionally equal to q. Say to one of these gentlemen, by way of experiment, if you please, that you believe occasions may occur where $x^2 + px$ is *not* altogether equal to q, and, having made him understand what you mean, get out of his reach as speedily as convenient, for, beyond doubt, he will endeavor to knock you down.

"I mean to say," continued Dupin, while I merely laughed at his last observations, "that if the Minister had been no more than a mathematician, the Prefect would have been under no necessity of giving me this check. I knew him, however, as both mathematician and poet, and my measures were adapted to his capacity, with reference to the circumstances by which he was surrounded. I knew him as a courtier, too, and as a bold *intriguant.* Such a man, I considered, could not fail to be aware of the ordinary policial modes of action. He could not have failed to anticipate—and events have proved that he did not fail to anticipate—the waylayings to which he was subjected. He must have foreseen, I reflected, the secret investigations of his

[12] Dupin quotes from *Maximes et Pensées* by Sébastien Roch Nicolas Chamfort (1741-1794): "The odds are that every public idea, every accepted convention is a piece of folly since it is agreed to by the majority."

[13] Dupin quotes from *A New System, or, An Analysis of Ancient Mythology,* 3 vols. (1774-76), by Jacob Bryant (1715-1804).

premises. His frequent absences from home at night, which were hailed by the Prefect as certain aids to his success, I regarded only as *ruses,* to afford opportunity for thorough search to the police, and thus the sooner to impress them with the conviction to which G——, in fact, did finally arrive —the conviction that the letter was not upon the premises. I felt, also, that the whole train of thought, which I was at some pains in detailing to you just now, concerning the invariable principle of policial action in searches for articles concealed—I felt that this whole train of thought would necessarily pass through the mind of the Minister. It would imperatively lead him to despise all the ordinary *nooks* of concealment. *He* could not, I reflected, be so weak as not to see that the most intricate and remote recess of his hotel would be as open as his commonest closets to the eyes, to the probes, to the gimlets, and to the microscopes of the Prefect. I saw, in fine, that he would be driven, as a matter of course, to *simplicity,* if not deliberately induced to it as a matter of choice. You will remember, perhaps, how desperately the Prefect laughed when I suggested, upon our first interview, that it was just possible this mystery troubled him so much on account of its being so *very* self-evident."

"Yes," said I, "I remember his merriment well. I really thought he would have fallen into convulsions."

"The material world," continued Dupin, "abounds with very strict analogies to the immaterial; and thus some color of truth has been given to the rhetorical dogma, that metaphor, or simile, may be made to strengthen an argument, as well as to embellish a description. The principle of the *vis inertiae,*[14] for example, seems to be identical in physics and metaphysics. It is not more true in the former, that a large body is with more difficulty set in motion than a smaller one, and that its subsequent *momentum* is commensurate with this difficulty, than it is, in the latter, that intellects of the vaster capacity, while

more forcible, more constant, and more eventful in their movements than those of inferior grade, are yet the less readily moved, and more embarrassed and full of hesitation in the first few steps of their progress. Again: have you ever noticed which of the street signs, over the shop doors, are the most attractive of attention?"

"I have never given the matter a thought," I said.

"There is a game of puzzles," he resumed, "which is played upon a map. One party playing requires another to find a given word—the name of town, river, state or empire—any word, in short, upon the motley and perplexed surface of the chart. A novice in the game generally seeks to embarrass his opponents by giving them the most minutely lettered names; but the adept selects such words as stretch, in large characters, from one end of the chart to the other. These, like the over-largely lettered signs and placards of the street, escape observation by dint of being excessively obvious; and here the physical oversight is precisely analogous with the moral inapprehension by which the intellect suffers to pass unnoticed those considerations which are too obtrusively and too palpably self-evident. But this is a point, it appears, somewhat above or beneath the understanding of the Prefect. He never once thought it probable, or possible, that the Minister had deposited the letter immediately beneath the nose of the whole world, by way of best preventing any portion of that world from perceiving it.

"But the more I reflected upon the daring, dashing, and discriminating ingenuity of D——; upon the fact that the document must always have been *at hand,* if he intended to use it to good purpose; and upon the decisive evidence, obtained by the Prefect, that it was not hidden within the limits of that dignitary's ordinary search—the more satisfied I became that,

---

[14] Force of inertia.

to conceal this letter, the Minister had resorted to the comprehensive and sagacious expedient of not attempting to conceal it at all.

"Full of these ideas, I prepared myself with a pair of green spectacles, and called one fine morning, quite by accident, at the Ministerial hotel. I found D—— at home, yawning, lounging, and dawdling, as usual, and pretending to be in the last extremity of *ennui*. He is, perhaps, the most really energetic human being now alive—but that is only when nobody sees him.

"To be even with him, I complained of my weak eyes, and lamented the necessity of the spectacles, under cover of which I cautiously and thoroughly surveyed the apartment, while seemingly intent only upon the conversation of my host.

"I paid especial attention to a large writing-table near which he sat, and upon which lay confusedly, some miscellaneous letters and other papers, with one or two musical instruments and a few books. Here, however, after a long and very deliberate scrutiny, I saw nothing to excite particular suspicion.

"At length my eyes, in going the circuit of the room, fell upon a trumpery filigree card-rack of paste-board, that hung dangling by a dirty blue ribbon from a little brass knob just beneath the middle of the mantel-piece. In this rack, which had three or four compartments, were five or six visiting cards and a solitary letter. This last was much soiled and crumpled. It was torn nearly in two, across the middle— as if a design, in the first instance, to tear it entirely up as worthless, had been altered, or stayed, in the second. It had a large black seal, bearing the D—— cipher *very* conspicuously, and was addressed, in a diminutive female hand, to D——, the minister, himself. It was thrust carelessly, and even, as it seemed, contemptuously, into one of the upper divisions of the rack.

"No sooner had I glanced at this letter, than I concluded it to be that of which I was in search. To be sure, it was, to all appearance, radically different from the one of which the Prefect had read us so minute a description. Here the seal was large and black, with the D—— cipher; there it was small and red, with the ducal arms of the S—— family. Here, the address, to the Minister, was diminutive and feminine; there the superscription, to a certain royal personage, was markedly bold and decided; the size alone formed a point of correspondence. But, then, the *radicalness* of these differences, which was excessive; the dirt; the soiled and torn condition of the paper, so inconsistent with the *true* methodical habits of D——, and so suggestive of a design to delude the beholder into an idea of the worthlessness of the document; these things, together with the hyperobtrusive situation of this document, full in the view of every visitor, and thus exactly in accordance with the conclusions to which I had previously arrived; these things, I say, were strongly corroborative of suspicion, in one who came with the intention to suspect.

"I protracted my visit as long as possible, and, while I maintained a most animated discussion with the Minister, on a topic which I knew well had never failed to interest and excite him, I kept my attention really riveted upon the letter. In this examination, I committed to memory its external appearance and arrangement in the rack; and also fell, at length, upon a discovery which set at rest whatever trivial doubt I might have entertained. In scrutinizing the edges of the paper, I observed them to be more *chafed* than seemed necessary. They presented the *broken* appearance which is manifested when a stiff paper, having been once folded and pressed with a folder, is refolded in a reversed direction, in the same creases or edges which had formed the original fold. This discovery was sufficient. It was clear to me that the letter had been turned, as a glove, inside out, re-directed, and resealed. I bade the Minister good morning, and took my departure at once, leaving a gold snuff-box upon the table.

"The next morning I called for the snuff-box, when we resumed, quite eagerly, the conversation of the preceding day. While thus engaged, however, a loud report, as if of a pistol, was heard immediately beneath the windows of the hotel, and was succeeded by a series of fearful screams, and the shoutings of a mob. D—— rushed to a casement, threw it open, and looked out. In the meantime, I stepped to the card-rack, took the letter, put it in my pocket, and replaced it by a *fac-simile*, (so far as regards externals,) which I had carefully prepared at my lodgings; imitating the D—— cipher, very readily, by means of a seal formed of bread.

"The disturbance in the street had been occasioned by the frantic behavior of a man with a musket. He had fired it among a crowd of women and children. It proved, however, to have been without ball, and the fellow was suffered to go his way as a lunatic or a drunkard. When he had gone, D—— came from the window, whither I had followed him immediately upon securing the object in view. Soon afterwards I bade him farewell. The pretended lunatic was a man in my own pay."

"But what purpose had you," I asked, "in replacing the letter by a *fac-simile?* Would it not have been better, at the first visit, to have seized it openly, and departed?"

"D——," replied Dupin, "is a desperate man, and a man of nerve. His hotel, too, is not without attendants devoted to his interests. Had I made the wild attempt you suggest, I might never have left the Ministerial presence alive. The good people of Paris might have heard of me no more. But I had an object apart from these considerations. You know my political prepossessions. In this matter, I act as a partisan of the lady concerned. For eighteen months the Minister has had her in his power. She has now him in hers—since, being unaware that the letter is not in his

possession, he will proceed with his exactions as if it was. Thus will he inevitably commit himself, at once, to his political destruction. His downfall, too, will not be more precipitate than awkward. It is all very well to talk about the *facilis descensus Averni;* but in all kinds of climbing, as Catalani said of singing, it is far more easy to get up than to come down.[15] In the present instance I have no sympathy—at least no pity—for him who descends. He is that *monstrum horrendum,*[16] an unprincipled man of genius. I confess, however, that I should like very well to know the precise character of his thoughts, when, being defied by her whom the Prefect terms 'a certain personage,' he is reduced to opening the letter which I left for him in the card-rack."

"How? did you put anything particular in it?"

"Why—it did not seem altogether right to leave the interior blank—that would have been insulting. D——, at Vienna once, did me an evil turn, which I told him quite good-humoredly, that I should remember. So, as I knew he would feel some curiosity in regard to the identity of the person who had outwitted him, I thought it a pity not to give him a clew. He is well acquainted with my MS., and I just copied into the middle of the blank sheet the words—

'—— Un dessein si funeste,
S'il n'est digne d'Atrée, est digne de Thyeste.'

They are to be found in Crébillon's *Atrée.*"[17]

---

[15] Dupin alludes (1) to Virgil's *Aeneid,* VI, V. 125: ". . . easy [is] the descent to Avernus [Hell]" and (2) to the operatic singer, Angelica Catalani (1780-1849).

[16] Horrid monstrosity.

[17] Dupin's quotation, "A plan so fatal is worthy of Thyestes, if it is not worthy of Atreus," is from the French classical tragedy *Atrée* (1707), by Prosper Jolyot de Crébillon (1674-1762); Atreus' revenge on Thyestes was that of a villain upon a villain.

THE LITERARY LIFE OF THINGUM BOB, ESQ.

LATE EDITOR OF THE "GOOSETHERUMFOODLE"

By Himself

[1856 (1844)]

I AM now growing in years, and—since I understand that Shakespeare and Mr. Emmons [1] are deceased—it is not impossible that I may even die. It has occurred to me, therefore, that I may as well retire from the field of Letters and repose upon my laurels. But I am ambitious of signalizing my abdication of the literary sceptre by some important bequest to posterity; and, perhaps, I cannot do a better thing than just pen for it an account of my earlier career. My name, indeed, has been so long and so constantly before the public eye, that I am not only willing to admit the naturalness of the interest which it has everywhere excited, but ready to satisfy the extreme curiosity which it has inspired. In fact, it is no more than the duty of him who achieves greatness to leave behind him, in his ascent, such landmarks as may guide others to be great. I propose, therefore, in the present paper (which I had some idea of calling "Memoranda to Serve for the Literary History of America") to give a detail of those important, yet feeble and tottering, first steps, by which, at length, I attained the high road to the pinnacle of human renown.

Of one's *very* remote ancestors it is superfluous to say much. My father, Thomas Bob, Esq., stood for many years at the summit of his profession, which was that of a merchant-barber, in the city of Smug. His warehouse was the resort of all the principal people of the place, and especially of the editorial corps—a body which inspires all about it with profound veneration and awe. For my own part, I regarded them as gods, and drank in with avidity the rich wit and wisdom which continuously flowed from their august

mouths during the process of what is styled "lather." My first moment of positive inspiration must be dated from that ever-memorable epoch, when the brilliant conductor of the *Gad-Fly*, in the intervals of the important process just mentioned, recited aloud, before a conclave of our apprentices, an inimitable poem in honor of the "Only Genuine Oil-of-Bob" (so called from its talented inventor, my father), and for which effusion the editor of the *Fly* was remunerated with a regal liberality by the firm of Thomas Bob & Company, merchant-barbers.

The genius of the stanzas to the "Oil-of-Bob" first breathed into me, I say, the divine *afflatus*. I resolved at once to become a great man, and to commence by becoming a great poet. That very evening I fell upon my knees at the feet of my father.

"Father," I said, "pardon me!—but I have a soul above lather. It is my firm intention to cut the shop. I would be an editor—I would be a poet—I would pen stanzas to the 'Oil-of-Bob.' Pardon me and aid me to be great!"

"My dear Thingum," replied my father, (I had been christened Thingum after a wealthy relative so surnamed,) "My dear Thingum," he said, raising me from my knees by the ears—"Thingum, my boy, you're a trump, and take after your father in having a soul. You have an immense head, too, and it must hold a great many brains. This I have long seen, and therefore had thoughts of making you a lawyer. The business, however, has grown ungenteel, and that of politician don't pay. Upon the whole you judge wisely;—the trade of editor is best:—and if you can be a poet at the same time,—as most of the editors are, by the by,—why, you will kill two birds with one stone. To encourage you in the beginning of things, I will allow you a

---

[1] Whether Poe refers to Richard Emmons (1788-1839), author of the lengthy epic, *The Fredoniad* (1827), or to Nathanael Emmons (1745-1840), a theologian noted for his long life, is uncertain.

garret; pen, ink, and paper; a rhyming dictionary; and a copy of the *Gad-Fly*. I suppose you would scarcely demand any more."

"I would be an ungrateful villain if I did," I replied with enthusiasm. "Your generosity is boundless. I will repay it by making you the father of a genius."

Thus ended my conference with the best of men, and immediately upon its termination I betook myself with zeal to my poetical labors; as upon these, chiefly, I founded my hopes of ultimate elevation to the editorial chair.

In my first attempts at composition I found the stanzas to "The Oil-of-Bob" rather a drawback than otherwise. Their splendor more dazzled than enlightened me. The contemplation of their excellence tended, naturally, to discourage me by comparison with my own abortions; so that for a long time I labored in vain. At length there came into my head one of those exquisitely original ideas which now and then *will* permeate the brain of a man of genius. It was this:—or, rather, thus was it carried into execution. From the rubbish of an old book-stall, in a very remote corner of the town, I got together several antique and altogether unknown or forgotten volumes. The bookseller sold them to me for a song. From one of these, which purported to be a translation of one Dante's "Inferno," I copied with remarkable neatness a long passage about a man named Ugolino, who had a parcel of brats. From another, which contained a good many old plays by some person whose name I forget, I extracted in the same manner, and with the same care, a great number of lines about "angels" and "ministers saying grace," and "goblins damned," and more besides of that sort. From a third, which was the composition of some blind man or other, either a Greek or a Choctaw—I cannot be at the pains of remembering every trifle exactly,—I took about fifty verses beginning with "Achilles' wrath," and "grease," and something else. From a fourth, which I recollect was also

the work of a blind man, I selected a page or two all about "hail" and "holy light"; and, although a blind man has no business to write about light, still the verses were sufficiently good in their way.[2]

Having made fair copies of these poems, I signed every one of them "Oppodeldoc" (a fine sonorous name), and, doing each up nicely in a separate envelope, I dispatched one to each of the four principal magazines, with a request for speedy insertion and prompt pay. The result of this well-conceived plan, however, (the success of which would have saved me much trouble in after-life,) served to convince me that some editors are not to be bamboozled, and gave the *coup-de-grace* (as they say in France) to my nascent hopes (as they say in the city of the transcendentals).

The fact is, that each and every one of the magazines in question gave Mr. "Oppodeldoc" a complete using-up, in the "Monthly Notices to Correspondents." The *Hum-Drum* gave him a dressing after this fashion:

"Oppodeldoc" (whoever he is) has sent us a long *tirade* concerning a bedlamite whom he styles "Ugolino," who had a great many children that should have been all whipped and sent to bed without their suppers. The whole affair is exceedingly tame—not to say *flat*. "Oppodeldoc" (whoever he is) is entirely devoid of imagination —and imagination, in our humble opinion, is not only the soul of POESY, but also its very heart. "Oppodeldoc" (whoever he is) has the audacity to demand of us, for his twattle, a "speedy insertion and prompt pay." We neither insert nor purchase any stuff of the sort. There can be no doubt, however, that he would meet with a ready sale for all the balderdash he can scribble, at the office of either the *Rowdy-Dow*, the *Lollipop*, or the *Goosetherumfoodle*.

---

[2] Thingum Bob's cribbings are from Dante's *Inferno*, Canto XXXIII, where Count Ugolino describes how he and his sons were famished in the Tower of Pisa at the command of Archbishop Ruggieri; from Shakespeare's *Hamlet*, Act I, sc. IV; from the opening lines of Homer's *Iliad;* and from the opening lines of Book III of Milton's *Paradise Lost.*

All this, it must be acknowledged, was very severe upon "Oppodeldoc,"—but the unkindest cut was putting the word POESY in SMALL CAPS. In those five pre-eminent letters what a world of bitterness is there not involved.

But "Oppodeldoc" was punished with equal severity in the *Rowdy-Dow*, which spoke thus:

We have received a most singular and insolent communication from a person (whoever he is) signing himself "Oppodeldoc,"—thus desecrating the greatness of the illustrious Roman emperor so named. Accompanying the letter of "Oppodeldoc" (whoever he is) we find sundry lines of most disgusting and unmeaning rant about "angels and ministers of grace,"—rant such as no madman short of a Nat Lee,[3] or an "Oppodeldoc," could possibly perpetrate. And for this trash of trash, we are modestly requested to "pay promptly." No, sir—no! We pay for nothing of *that* sort. Apply to the *Hum-Drum*, the *Lollipop*, or the *Goosetherumfoodle*. These *periodicals* will undoubtedly accept any literary offal you may send them—and as undoubtedly *promise* to pay for it.

This was bitter indeed upon poor "Oppodeldoc"; but, in this instance, the weight of the satire falls upon the *Hum-Drum*, the *Lollipop*, and the *Goosetherumfoodle*, who are pungently styled "*periodicals*"—in Italics, too—a thing that must have cut them to the heart.

Scarcely less savage was the *Lollipop*, which thus discoursed:

Some *individual*, who rejoices in the appellation "Oppodeldoc," (to what low uses are the names of the illustrious dead too often applied!) has enclosed us some fifty or sixty *verses* commencing after this fashion:

'Achilles' wrath, to Greece the direful spring
Of woes unnumbered, &c., &c., &c., &c.'

"Oppodeldoc" (whoever he is) is respectfully informed that there is not a printer's devil in our office who is not in the daily habit of composing better *lines*. Those of "Oppodeldoc" will not *scan*. "Oppodeldoc" should learn to *count*. But why he should

have conceived the idea that *we* (of all others, *we!*) would disgrace our pages with his ineffable nonsense is utterly beyond comprehension. Why, the absurd twattle is scarcely good enough for the *Hum-Drum*, the *Rowdy-Dow*, the *Goosetherumfoodle*,—things that are in the practice of publishing "Mother Goose's Melodies" as original lyrics. And "Oppodeldoc" (whoever he is) has even the assurance to demand *pay* for this drivel. Does "Oppodeldoc" (whoever he is) know—is he aware that we could not be paid to insert it?

As I perused this I felt myself growing gradually smaller and smaller, and when I came to the point at which the editor sneered at the poem as "*verses*," there was little more than an ounce of me left. As for "Oppodeldoc," I began to experience *compassion* for the poor fellow. But the *Goosetherumfoodle* showed, if possible, less mercy than the *Lollipop*. It was the *Goosetherumfoodle* that said—

A wretched poetaster, who signs himself "Oppodeldoc," is silly enough to fancy that *we* will print and *pay for* a medley of incoherent and ungrammatical bombast which he has transmitted to us, and which commences with the following most *intelligible* line:

'Hail, Holy Light! Offspring of Heaven, first born.'

We say, "most *intelligible*." "Oppodeldoc" (whoever he is) will be kind enough to tell us, perhaps, how "*hail*" can be "*holy light*." We always regarded it as *frozen rain*. Will he inform us, also, how frozen rain can be, at one and the same time, both "holy light" (whatever that is) and an "offspring"?—which latter term (if we understand any thing about English) is only employed, with propriety, in reference to small babies of about six weeks old. But it is preposterous to descant upon such absurdity—although "Oppodeldoc" (whoever he is) has the unparalleled effrontery to suppose that we will not only "insert" his ignorant ravings, but (absolutely) *pay for them!*

Now this is fine—it is rich!—and we have half a mind to punish this young scribbler for his egotism by really publishing his

---

[3] The reference is to the minor English dramatist, Nathaniel Lee (1653?-1692).

effusion *verbatim et literatim,* as he has written it. We could inflict no punishment so severe, and we *would* inflict it, but for the boredom which we should cause our readers in so doing.

Let "Oppodeldoc" (whoever he is) send any future *composition* of like character to the *Hum-Drum,* the *Lollipop,* or the *Rowdy-Dow. They* will "insert" it. *They* "insert" every month just such stuff. Send it to *them.* WE are not to be insulted with impunity.

This made an end of me; and as for the *Hum-Drum,* the *Rowdy-Dow,* and the *Lollipop,* I never could comprehend how they survived it. The putting *them* in the smallest possible *minion,*[4] (that was the rub—thereby insinuating their lowness—their baseness), while WE stood looking down upon them in gigantic capitals!—oh it was *too* bitter!—it was wormwood—it was gall. Had I been either of these periodicals I would have spared no pains to have the *Goosetherumfoodle* prosecuted. It might have been done under the Act for the "Prevention of Cruelty to Animals." As for Oppodeldoc (whoever he was) I had by this time lost all patience with the fellow, and sympathized with him no longer. He was a fool, beyond doubt, (whoever he was,) and got not a kick more than he deserved.

The result of my experiment with the old books convinced me, in the first place, that "honesty is the best policy," and, in the second, that if I could not write better than Mr. Dante, and the two blind men, and the rest of the old set, it would, at least, be a difficult matter to write worse. I took heart, therefore, and determined to prosecute the "entirely original" (as they say on the covers of the magazines), at whatever cost of study and pains. I again placed before my eyes, as a model, the brilliant stanzas on "The Oil-of-Bob" by the editor of the *Gad-Fly* and resolved to construct an ode on the same sublime theme, in rivalry of what had already been done.

With my first line I had no material difficulty. It ran thus:

"*To pen an Ode upon the 'Oil-of-Bob.'*"

Having carefully looked out, however, all the legitimate rhymes to "Bob," I found it impossible to proceed. In this dilemma I had recourse to paternal aid; and, after some hours of mature thought, my father and myself thus constructed the poem:

"*To pen an Ode upon the 'Oil-of-Bob'
Is all sorts of a job.*
(Signed)   SNOB."

To be sure, this composition was of no very great length,—but I "have yet to learn," as they say in the *Edinburgh Review,* that the mere extent of a literary work has anything to do with its merit. As for the Quarterly cant about "sustained effort," it is impossible to see the sense of it. Upon the whole, therefore, I was satisfied with the success of my maiden attempt, and now the only question regarded the disposal I should make of it. My father suggested that I should send it to the *Gad-Fly,*—but there were two reasons which operated to prevent me from so doing. I dreaded the jealousy of the editor—and I had ascertained that he did not pay for original contributions. I therefore, after due deliberation, consigned the article to the more dignified pages of the *Lollipop* and waited the event in anxiety, but with resignation.

In the very next published number I had the proud satisfaction of seeing my poem printed at length, as the leading article, with the following significant words, prefixed in italics and between brackets:

[*We call the attention of our readers to the subjoined admirable stanzas on "The Oil-of-Bob." We need say nothing of their sublimity, or of their pathos:—it is impossible to peruse them without tears. Those who have been nauseated with a sad dose on the same august topic from the goose-quill of the editor of the "Gad-Fly," will do well to compare the two compositions.*

P. S.—We are consumed with anxiety to probe the mystery which envelops the

---

[4] A style of type.

*evident pseudonym "Snob." May we hope
for a personal interview?*]

All this was scarcely more than justice,
but it was, I confess, rather more than I
had expected:—I acknowledged this, be it
observed, to the everlasting disgrace of my
country and of mankind. I lost no time,
however, in calling upon the editor of the
Lollipop and had the good fortune to find
this gentleman at home. He saluted me
with an air of profound respect, slightly
blended with a fatherly and patronizing
admiration, wrought in him, no doubt, by
my appearance of extreme youth and inexperience. Begging me to be seated, he
entered at once upon the subject of my
poem;—but modesty will ever forbid me to
repeat the thousand compliments which he
lavished upon me. The eulogies of Mr.
Crab (such was the editor's name) were,
however, by no means fulsomely indiscriminate. He analyzed my composition with
much freedom and great ability—not hesitating to point out a few trivial defects—
a circumstance which elevated him highly
in my esteem. The *Gad-Fly* was, of course,
brought upon the *tapis*, and I hope never
to be subjected to a criticism so searching,
or to rebukes so withering, as were bestowed by Mr. Crab upon that unhappy
effusion. I had been accustomed to regard the editor of the *Gad-Fly* as something superhuman; but Mr. Crab soon
disabused me of that idea. He set the literary as well as the personal character of
the Fly (so Mr. C. satirically designated
the rival editor), in its true light. He,
the Fly, was very little better than he
should be. He had written infamous things.
He was a penny-a-liner, and a buffoon.
He was a villain. He had composed a
tragedy which set the whole country in a
guffaw, and a farce which deluged the
universe in tears. Besides all this, he had
the impudence to pen what he meant for a
lampoon upon himself (Mr. Crab), and
the temerity to style him "an ass." Should
I at any time wish to express my opinion
of Mr. Fly, the pages of the *Lollipop*, Mr.

Crab assured me, were at my unlimited
disposal. In the meantime, as it was very
certain that I would be attacked in the Fly
for my attempt at composing a rival poem
on the "Oil-of-Bob," he (Mr. Crab) would
take it upon himself to attend, pointedly,
to my private and personal interests. If I
were not made a man of at once, it should
not be the fault of himself (Mr. Crab).

Mr. Crab having now paused in his discourse (the latter portion of which I found
it impossible to comprehend), I ventured
to suggest something about the remuneration which I had been taught to expect for
my poem, by an announcement on the cover
of the *Lollipop*, declaring that it (the
Lollipop) "insisted upon being permitted
to pay exorbitant prices for all accepted
contributions,—frequently expending more
money for a single brief poem than the
whole annual cost of the *Hum-Drum*, the
Rowdy-Dow, and the *Goosetherumfoodle*
combined."

As I mentioned the word "remuneration,"
Mr. Crab first opened his eyes, and then
his mouth, to quite a remarkable extent,
causing his personal appearance to resemble that of a highly agitated elderly duck
in the act of quacking; and in this condition he remained (ever and anon pressing his hands tightly to his forehead, as
if in a state of desperate bewilderment)
until I had nearly made an end of what I
had to say.

Upon my conclusion, he sank back into
his seat, as if much overcome, letting his
arms fall lifelessly by his side, but keeping
his mouth still rigorously open, after the
fashion of the duck. While I remained in
speechless astonishment at behavior so
alarming, he suddenly leaped to his feet
and made a rush at the bell-rope; but just
as he reached this, he appeared to have
altered his intention, whatever it was, for
he dived under a table and immediately reappeared with a cudgel. This he was in the
act of uplifting (for what purpose I am
at a loss to imagine), when all at once,
there came a benign smile over his features,
and he sank placidly back in his chair.

"Mr. Bob," he said, (for I had sent up my card before ascending myself,) "Mr. Bob, you are a young man, I presume—*very?*"

I assented; adding that I had not yet concluded my third lustrum.

"Ah!" he replied, "very good! I see how it is—say no more! Touching this matter of compensation, what you observe is very just,—in fact it is excessively so. But ah—ah—the *first* contribution—the *first*, I say—it is never the magazine custom to pay for,—you comprehend, eh? The truth is, we are usually the *recipients* in such case." [Mr. Crab smiled blandly as he emphasized the word "recipients."] "For the most part, we are *paid* for the insertion of a maiden attempt—especially in verse. In the second place, Mr. Bob, the magazine rule is never to disburse what we term in France the *argent comptant*: [5]—I have no doubt you understand. In a quarter or two after publication of the article—or in a year or two—we make no objection to giving our note at nine months; provided, always, that we can so arrange our affairs as to be quite certain of a 'burst up' in six. I really *do* hope, Mr. Bob, that you will look upon this explanation as satisfactory." Here Mr. Crab concluded, and the tears stood in his eyes.

Grieved to the soul at having been, however innocently, the cause of pain to so eminent and so sensitive a man, I hastened to apologize, and to reassure him, by expressing my perfect coincidence with his views, as well as my entire appreciation of the delicacy of his position. Having done all this in a neat speech, I took leave.

One fine morning, very shortly afterward, "I awoke and found myself famous." [6] The extent of my renown will be best estimated by reference to the editorial opinions of the day. These opinions, it will be seen, were embodied in critical notices of the number of the *Lollipop* containing my poem, and are perfectly satisfactory, conclusive, and clear with the exception, perhaps, of the hieroglyphical marks, "*Sep.*

15—1 *t*," appended to each of the critiques. [7]

The *Owl*, a journal of profound sagacity, and well known for the deliberate gravity of its literary decisions—the *Owl*, I say, spoke as follows:

The *Lollipop!* The October number of this delicious magazine surpasses its predecessors, and sets competition at defiance. In the beauty of its typography and paper—in the number and excellence of its steel plates—as well as in the literary merit of its contributions—the *Lollipop* compares with its slow-paced rivals as Hyperion with Satyr. The *Hum-Drum*, the *Rowdy-Dow*, and the *Goosetherumfoodle*, excel, it is true, in braggadocio, but in all other points, give us the *Lollipop!* How this celebrated journal can sustain its evidently tremendous expenses, is more than we can understand. To be sure, it has a circulation of 100,000, and its subscription list has increased one fourth during the last month; but, on the other hand, the sums it disburses constantly for contributions are inconceivable. It is reported that Mr. Slyass received no less than thirty-seven and a half cents for his inimitable paper on "Pigs." With Mr. CRAB, as editor, and with such names upon the list of contributors as SNOB and Slyass, there can be no such word as "fail" for the *Lollipop*. Go and subscribe.   *Sep. 15—1 t.*

I must say that I was gratified with this high-toned notice from a paper so respectable as the *Owl*. The placing my name—that is to say, my *nom de guerre*—in priority of station to that of the great Slyass, was a compliment as happy as I felt it to be deserved.

My attention was next arrested by these paragraphs in the *Toad*—a print highly distinguished for its uprightness and independence—for its entire freedom from sycophancy and subservience to the givers of dinners:

---

[5] Cash.

[6] Lord Byron remarked, concerning the publication and reception of the first two cantos of his *Childe Harold's Pilgrimage* in 1812: "I awoke one morning and found myself famous."

[7] These instructions to the printer—to insert 1 time on September 15—mark the notices as advertisements.

The *Lollipop* for October is out in advance of all its contemporaries, and infinitely surpasses them, of course, in the splendor of its embellishments, as well as in the richness of its contents. The *Hum-Drum*, the *Rowdy-Dow*, and the *Goosetherumfoodle* excel, we admit, in braggadocio, but, in all other points, give us the *Lollipop*. How this celebrated magazine can sustain its evidently tremendous expenses is more than we can understand. To be sure, it has a circulation of 200,000, and its subscription list has increased one third during the last fortnight, but, on the other hand, the sums it disburses, monthly, for contributions, are fearfully great. We learn that Mr. Mumblethumb received no less than fifty cents for his late "Monody in a Mud-Puddle."

Among the original contributors to the present number we notice (besides the eminent editor, Mr. CRAB), such men as SNOB, Slyass, and Mumblethumb. Apart from the editorial matter, the most valuable paper, nevertheless, is, we think, a poetical gem by Snob, on the "Oil-of-Bob,"—but our readers must not suppose from the title of this incomparable *bijou*, that it bears any similitude to some balderdash on the same subject by a certain contemptible individual whose name is unmentionable to ears polite. The *present* poem "On the Oil-of-Bob," has excited universal anxiety and curiosity in respect to the owner of the evident pseudonym, "Snob,"—a curiosity which, happily, we have it in our power to satisfy. "Snob" is the *nom de plume* of Mr. Thingum Bob, of this city,—a relative of the great Mr. Thingum (after whom he is named), and otherwise connected with the most illustrious families of the State. His father, Thomas Bob, Esq., is an opulent merchant in Smug.

Sep. 15—1 *t*.

This generous approbation touched me to the heart—the more especially as it emanated from a source so avowedly—so proverbially pure as the *Toad*. The word "balderdash," as applied to the "Oil-of-Bob" of the *Fly*, I considered singularly pungent and appropriate. The words "gem" and "*bijou*," however, used in reference to my composition, struck me as being, in some degree, feeble. They seemed to me to be deficient in force. They were not sufficiently *prononcés* (as we have it in France).

I had hardly finished reading the *Toad*, when a friend placed in my hands a copy of the *Mole*, a daily, enjoying high reputation for the keenness of its perception about matters in general, and for the open, honest, above-ground style of its editorials. The *Mole* spoke of the *Lollipop* as follows:

We have just received the *Lollipop* for October, and *must* say that never before have we perused any single number of any periodical which afforded us a felicity so supreme. We speak advisedly. The *Hum-Drum*, the *Rowdy-Dow*, and the *Goosetherumfoodle* must look well to their laurels. These prints, no doubt, surpass every thing in loudness of pretension, but, in all other points, give us the *Lollipop*! How this celebrated magazine can sustain its evidently tremendous expenses, is more than we can comprehend. To be sure, it has a circulation of 300,000; and its subscription list has increased one half within the last week, but then the sum it disburses, monthly, for contributions, is astonishingly enormous. We have it upon good authority that Mr. Fatquack received no less than sixty-two cents and a half for his late domestic nouvellette, the "Dish-Clout."

The contributors to the number before us are Mr. CRAB (the eminent editor), SNOB, Mumblethumb, Fatquack, and others; but, after the inimitable compositions of the editor himself, we prefer a diamond-like effusion from the pen of a rising poet who writes over the signature "Snob"—a *nom de guerre* which we predict will one day extinguish the radiance of "Boz." [8] "SNOB," we learn, is a Mr. THINGUM BOB, Esq., sole heir of a wealthy merchant of this city, Thomas Bob, Esq., and a near relative of the distinguished Mr. Thingum. The title of Mr. B.'s admirable poem is the "Oil-of-Bob"—a somewhat unfortunate name, by-the-by, as some contemptible vagabond connected with the penny press has already disgusted the town with a great deal of drivel upon the same topic. There will be no danger, however, of confounding the compositions.

Sept. 15—1 *t*.

The generous approbation of so clear-sighted a journal as the *Mole* penetrated my soul with delight. The only objection

---

[8] The reference is to Dickens' *Sketches by Boz* (1835 and 1836).

which occurred to me was, that the terms "contemptible vagabond" might have been better written *"odious* and contemptible *wretch, villain,* and vagabond."* This would have sounded more gracefully, I think. "Diamond-like," also, was scarcely, it will be admitted, of sufficient intensity to express what the *Mole* evidently *thought* of the brilliancy of the "Oil-of-Bob."

On the same afternoon in which I saw these notices in the *Owl,* the *Toad,* and the *Mole,* I happened to meet with a copy of the *Daddy-Long-Legs,* a periodical proverbial for the extreme extent of its understanding. And it was the *Daddy-Long-Legs* which spoke thus:

The *Lollipop!!* This gorgeous magazine is already before the public for October. The question of pre-eminence is forever put to rest, and hereafter it will be excessively preposterous in the *Hum-Drum,* the *Rowdy-Dow,* or the *Goosetherumfoodle* to make any further spasmodic attempts at competition. These journals may excel the *Lollipop* in outcry, but, in all other points, give us the *Lollipop!* How this celebrated magazine can sustain its evidently tremendous expenses, is past comprehension. To be sure it has a circulation of precisely half a million, and its subscription list has increased seventy-five per cent. within the last couple of days, but then the sums it disburses, monthly, for contributions, are scarcely credible; we are cognizant of the fact, that Mademoiselle Cribalittle received no less than eighty-seven cents and a half for her late valuable Revolutionary tale, entitled "The York-Town Katy-Did, and the Bunker-Hill Katy-Didn't."

The most able papers in the present number are, of course, those furnished by the editor (the eminent Mr. CRAB), but there are numerous magnificent contributions from such names as SNOB, Mademoiselle Cribalittle, Slyass, Mrs. Fibalittle, Mumblethumb, Mrs. Squibalittle, and last, though not least, Fatquack. The world may well be challenged to produce so rich a galaxy of genius.

The poem over the signature "SNOB" is, we find, attracting universal commendation, and, we are constrained to say, deserves, if possible, even more applause than it has received. The "Oil-of-Bob" is the title of this masterpiece of eloquence and art. One or two of our readers *may* have a

very faint, although sufficiently disgusting recollection of a poem (?) similarly entitled, the perpetration of a miserable penny-a-liner, mendicant, and cut-throat, connected in the capacity of scullion, we believe, with one of the indecent prints about the purlieus of the city; we beg them, for God's sake, not to confound the compositions. The author of *the* "Oil-of-Bob," is, we hear, THINGUM BOB, Esq., a gentleman of high genius, and a scholar. "Snob" is merely a *nom de guerre.*

Sep. 15.—1 *t.*

I could scarcely restrain my indignation while I perused the concluding portions of this diatribe. It was clear to me that the yea-nay manner—not to say the gentleness, —the positive forbearance—with which the *Daddy-Long-Legs* spoke of that pig, the editor of the *Gad-Fly,*—it was evident to me, I say, that this gentleness of speech could proceed from nothing else than a partiality for the *Fly*—whom it was clearly the intention of the *Daddy-Long-Legs* to elevate into reputation at my expense. Any one, indeed, might perceive, with half an eye, that, had the real design of the *Daddy* been what it wished to appear, it (the *Daddy*) might have expressed itself in terms more direct, more pungent, and altogether more to the purpose. The words "penny-a-liner," "mendicant," "scullion," and "cut-throat," were epithets so intentionally inexpressive and equivocal, as to be worse than nothing when applied to the author of the very worst stanzas ever penned by one of the human race. We all know what is meant by "damning with faint praise," [9] and, on the other hand, who could fail seeing through the covert purpose of the *Daddy,*—that of glorifying with feeble abuse?

What the *Daddy* chose to say to the *Fly,* however, was no business of mine. What it said of myself *was.* After the noble manner in which the *Owl,* the *Toad,* the *Mole,* had expressed themselves in re-

---

[9] The phrase is based on line 201 in Pope's "Epistle to Dr. Arbuthnot" (1735): "Damn with faint praise, assent with civil leer."

spect to my ability, it was rather too much to be coolly spoken of by a thing like the *Daddy-Long-Legs*, as merely "a gentleman of high genius and a scholar." Gentleman indeed! I made up my mind at once either to get a written apology from the *Daddy-Long-Legs,* or to call it out.[10]

Full of this purpose, I looked about me to find a friend whom I could entrust with a message to his *Daddy*ship, and as the editor of the *Lollipop* had given me marked tokens of regard, I at length concluded to seek assistance upon the present occasion.

I have never yet been able to account, in a manner satisfactory to my own understanding, for the *very* peculiar countenance and demeanor with which Mr. Crab listened to me, as I unfolded to him my design. He again went through the scene of the bell-rope and cudgel, and did not omit the duck. At one period I thought he really intended to quack. His fit, nevertheless, finally subsided as before, and he began to act and speak in a rational way. He declined bearing the cartel,[11] however, and in fact, dissuaded me from sending it at all; but was candid enough to admit the *Daddy-Long-Legs* had been disgracefully in the wrong—more especially in what related to the epithets "gentleman and scholar."

Toward the end of this interview with Mr. Crab, who really appeared to take a paternal interest in my welfare, he suggested to me that I might turn an honest penny, and at the same time, advance my reputation, by occasionally playing Thomas Hawk for the *Lollipop.*

I begged Mr. Crab to inform me who was Mr. Thomas Hawk, and how it was expected that I should play him.

Here Mr. Crab again 'made great eyes" (as we say in Germany), but at length, recovering himself from a profound attack of astonishment, he assured me that he employed the words "Thomas Hawk" to avoid the colloquialism, Tommy, which was low—but that the true idea was Tommy Hawk—or tomahawk—and that by "play-

ing tomahawk" he referred to scalping, brow-beating, and otherwise using up the herd of poor-devil authors.

I assured my patron that, if this was all, I was perfectly resigned to the task of playing Thomas Hawk. Hereupon Mr. Crab desired me to use up the editor of the *Gad-Fly* forthwith, in the fiercest style within the scope of my ability, and as a specimen of my powers. This I did, upon the spot, in a review of the original "Oil-of-Bob," occupying thirty-six pages of the *Lollipop*. I found playing Thomas Hawk, indeed, a far less onerous occupation than poetizing; for I went upon *system* altogether, and thus it was easy to do the thing thoroughly well. My practice was this. I bought auction copies (cheap) of "Lord Brougham's speeches," "Cobbett's Complete Works," the "New Slang-Syllabus," the "Whole Art of Snubbing," "Prentice's Billingsgate" (folio edition), and "Lewis G. Clarke on Tongue." [12] These works I cut up thoroughly with a currycomb, and then, throwing the shreds into a sieve, sifted out carefully all that might be thought decent (a mere trifle); reserving the hard phrases, which I threw into a large tin pepper-castor with longitudinal holes, so that an entire sentence could get through without material injury. The admixture was then ready for use. When called upon to play Thomas Hawk, I anointed a sheet of foolscap with the white of a gander's egg; then, shredding the thing to be reviewed as I had previously shredded the books—only with more care, so as to get every word separate—I threw

---

[10] Challenge to a duel.

[11] A written formal challenge to a duel.

[12] Henry Brougham (1778-1868) was one of the founders of the *Edinburgh Review* and a prominent British statesman; William Cobbett (1762-1835) was a political writer in both England and America; the last two works listed were probably intended as satirical references to journalists of Poe's time—George D. Prentice (1802-1870), noted for his caustic political writing, and Lewis Gaylord Clark (1810-1873), noted for his gossip column and platitudes.

the latter shreds in with the former, screwed on the lid of the castor, gave it a shake, and so dusted out the mixture upon the egged foolscap; where it stuck. The effect was beautiful to behold. It was captivating. Indeed, the reviews I brought to pass by this simple expedient have never been approached, and were the wonder of the world. At first, through bashfulness—the result of inexperience—I was a little put out by a certain inconsistency—a certain air of the *bizarre* (as we say in France), worn by the composition as a whole. All the phrases did not *fit* (as we say in the Anglo-Saxon). Many were quite awry. Some, even, were upsidedown; and there were none of them which were not in some measure, injured in regard to effect, by this latter species of accident, when it occurred—with the exception of Mr. Lewis Clarke's paragraphs, which were so vigorous and altogether stout, that they seemed not particularly disconcerted by any extreme of position, but looked equally happy and satisfactory, whether on their heads, or on their heels.

What became of the editor of the *Gad-Fly* after the publication of my criticism on his "Oil-of-Bob," it is somewhat difficult to determine. The most reasonable conclusion is, that he wept himself to death. At all events he disappeared instantaneously from the face of the earth, and no man has seen even the ghost of him since.

This matter having been properly accomplished, and the Furies appeased, I grew at once into high favor with Mr. Crab. He took me into his confidence, gave me a permanent situation as Thomas Hawk of the *Lollipop*, and, as for the present, he could afford me no salary, allowed me to profit, at discretion, by his advice.

"My dear Thingum," said he to me one day after dinner, "I respect your abilities and love you as a son. You shall be my heir. When I die I will bequeath you the *Lollipop*. In the meantime I will make a man of you—I *will*—provided always that you follow my counsel. The first thing to do is to get rid of the old bore."

"Boar?" said I inquiringly—"pig, eh?—*aper?* (as we say in Latin)—who?—where?"

"Your father," said he.

"Precisely," I replied,—"pig."

"You have your fortune to make, Thingum," resumed Mr. Crab, "and that governor of yours is a millstone about your neck. We must cut him at once." [Here I took out my knife.] "We must cut him," continued Mr. Crab, "decidedly and forever. He won't do—he *won't*. Upon second thoughts, you had better kick him, or cane him, or something of that kind."

"What do you say," I suggested modestly, "to my kicking him in the first instance, caning him afterward, and winding up by tweaking his nose?"

Mr. Crab looked at me musingly for some moments, and then answered:

"I think, Mr. Bob, that what you propose would answer sufficiently well—indeed remarkably well—that is to say, as far as it went—but barbers are exceedingly hard to cut, and I think, upon the whole, that, having performed upon Thomas Bob the operations you suggest, it would be advisable to blacken, with your fists, both his eyes, very carefully and thoroughly, to prevent his ever seeing you again in fashionable promenades. After doing this, I really do not perceive that you can do any more. However—it might be just as well to roll him once or twice in the gutter, and then put him in charge of the police. Any time the next morning you can call at the watchhouse and swear an assault."

I was much affected by the kindness of feeling toward me personally, which was evinced in this excellent advice of Mr. Crab, and I did not fail to profit by it forthwith. The result was, that I got rid of the old bore, and began to feel a little independent and gentleman-like. The want of money, however, was, for a few weeks, a source of some discomfort; but at length, by carefully putting to use my two eyes, and observing how matters went just in front of my nose, I perceived how the thing was to be brought about. I say "thing"—be it observed—for they tell me the Latin for it is *rem*. By the way, talking of Latin, can any one tell me the meaning of *quocunque*—or what is the meaning of *modo?* [13]

My plan was exceedingly simple. I bought, for a song, a sixteenth of the *Snapping-Turtle*:—that was all. The thing was *done*, and I put money in my purse. There were some trivial arrangements afterward, to be sure; but these formed no portion of the plan. They were a consequence—a result. For example, I bought pen, ink, and paper, and put them into furious activity. Having thus completed a Magazine article, I gave it, for appellation, "FOL LOL, *by the Author of* 'THE OIL-OF-BOB,' " and enveloped it to the *Goosetherumfoodle*. That journal, however, having pronounced it "twattle" in the "Monthly Notices to Correspondents," I reheaded the paper " 'Hey-Diddle-Diddle,' by THINGUM BOB, Esq., Author of the Ode on 'The Oil-of-Bob,' *and* Editor of the *Snapping-Turtle*." With this amendment, I re-enclosed it to the *Goosetherumfoodle*, and, while I awaited a reply, published daily, in the *Turtle*, six columns of what may be termed philosophical and analytical investigation of the literary merits of the *Goosetherumfoodle*, as well as of the personal character of the editor of the *Goosetherumfoodle*. At the end of a week the *Goosetherumfoodle* discovered that it had, by some odd mistake, "confounded a stupid article, headed, 'Hey-Diddle-Diddle,' and composed by some unknown ignoramus, with a gem of resplendent lustre similarly entitled, the work of Thingum Bob, Esq., the celebrated author of 'The Oil-of-Bob.' " The *Goosetherumfoodle* deeply "regretted this very natural accident," and promised, moreover, an insertion of the *genuine* "Hey-Diddle-Diddle" in the very next number of the Magazine.

The fact is, I *thought*—I *really* thought —I thought at the time—I thought *then* —and have no reason for thinking otherwise *now*—that the *Goosetherumfoodle did* make a mistake. With the best intentions in the world, I never knew any thing that made as many singular mistakes as the *Goosetherumfoodle*. From that day I took a liking to the *Goosetherumfoodle*, and the result was I soon saw into the very depths of its literary merits, and did not fail to expatiate upon them, in the *Turtle*, whenever a fitting opportunity occurred. And it is to be regarded as a very peculiar coincidence—as one of those positively *remarkable* coincidences which set a man to serious thinking—that just such a total revolution of opinion—just such entire *bouleversement* [14] (as we say in French),— just such thorough *topsiturviness* (if I may be permitted to employ a rather forcible term of the Choctaws), as happened, *pro* and *con,* between myself on the one part, and the *Goosetherumfoodle* on the other, did actually again happen, in a brief period afterwards, and with precisely similar circumstances, in the case of myself and the *Rowdy-Dow,* and in the case of myself and the *Hum-Drum*.

Thus it was that, by a master-stroke of genius, I at length consummated my triumphs by "putting money in my purse," and thus may be said really and fairly to have commenced that brilliant and eventful career which rendered me illustrious, and which now enables me to say with Chateaubriand: "I have made history"—"*J'ai fait l'histoire.*" [15]

I have indeed "made history." From the bright epoch which I now record, my actions—my works—are the property of mankind. They are familiar to the world. It is, then, needless for me to detail how, soaring rapidly, I fell heir to the *Lollipop* —how I merged this journal in the *Hum- Drum*—how again I made purchase of the

---

[13] These are Latin adverbs, meaning respectively *whithersoever* and *only* or *but*.

[14] Overthrow or overturning.

[15] François René de Chateaubriand (1768- 1848), in an effort to discover the Northwest Passage, became a student of the American Indian; as a writer he concerned himself with Christianity, politics, and "the noble savage."

Rowdy-Dow, thus combining the three periodicals—how lastly, I effected a bargain for the sole remaining rival, and united all the literature of the country in one magnificent Magazine known everywhere as the

Rowdy-Dow, Lollipop, Hum-Drum,
and
Goosetherumfoodle.

Yes; I have made history. My fame is universal. It extends to the uttermost ends of the earth. You cannot take up a common newspaper in which you shall not see some allusion to the immortal THINGUM BOB. It is Mr. Thingum Bob said so, and Mr. Thingum Bob wrote this, and Mr. Thingum Bob did that. But I am meek and expire with an humble heart. After all, what is it?—this indescribable something which men will persist in terming "genius"? I agree with Buffon—with Hogarth—it is but *diligence* after all.[16]

Look at *me!*—how I labored—how I toiled—how I wrote! Ye Gods, did I *not* write? I knew not the word "ease." By day I adhered to my desk, and at night, a pale student, I consumed the midnight oil. You should have seen me—you *should.* I leaned to the right. I leaned to the left. I sat forward. I sat backward. I sat *tête baissée* (as they have it in the Kickapoo),[17] bowing my head close to the alabaster page. And, through all, I—*wrote.* Through joy and through sorrow, I—*wrote.* Through hunger and through thirst, I—*wrote.* Through good report and through ill report, I—*wrote.* Through sunshine and through moonshine, I—*wrote.* What I wrote it is unnecessary to say. The *style*—that *was the thing.* I caught it from Fatquack—whizz!—fizz—and I am giving you a specimen of it now.

SOME WORDS WITH A MUMMY
[1850 (1845)]

THE *symposium* of the preceding evening had been a little too much for my nerves. I had a wretched headache, and was desperately drowsy. Instead of going out, therefore, to spend the evening, as I had proposed, it occurred to me that I could not do a wiser thing than just eat a mouthful of supper and go immediately to bed.

A *light* supper, of course. I am exceedingly fond of Welsh-rabbit. More than a pound at once, however, may not at all times be advisable. Still, there can be no material objection to two. And really between two and three, there is merely a single unit of difference. I ventured, perhaps, upon four. My wife will have it five;—but, clearly, she has confounded two very distinct affairs. The abstract number, five, I am willing to admit; but, concretely, it has reference to bottles of Brown Stout, without which, in the way of condiment, Welsh-rabbit is to be eschewed.

Having thus concluded a frugal meal, and donned my nightcap, with the sincere hope of enjoying it till noon the next day, I placed my head upon the pillow, and, through the aid of a capital conscience, fell into a profound slumber forthwith.

But when were the hopes of humanity fulfilled? I could not have completed my third snore when there came a furious ringing at the street-door bell, and then an impatient thumping at the knocker, which awakened me at once. In a minute afterward, and while I was still rubbing my eyes, my wife thrust in my face a note, from my old friend, Doctor Ponnonner. It ran thus:

Come to me, by all means, my dear good friend, as soon as you receive this. Come and help us to rejoice. At last, by long persevering diplomacy, I have gained the

[16] Georges de Buffon (1707-1788) in his *Discours sur le style* (1753) expressed the view that "Genius is patience." The English painter and engraver William Hogarth (1697-1764) remarked, "Genius is nothing but labour and diligence."

[17] With bowed head; Kickapoo refers to an Indian dialect.

assent of the Directors of the City Museum, to my examination of the Mummy—you know the one I mean. I have permission to unswathe it and open it, if desirable. A few friends only will be present—you, of course. The Mummy is now at my house, and we shall begin to unroll it at eleven to-night.

Yours ever,
PONNONNER.

By the time I had reached the "Ponnonner," it struck me that I was as wide awake as a man need be. I leaped out of bed in an ecstasy, overthrowing all in my way; dressed myself with a rapidity truly marvellous; and set off, at the top of my speed, for the doctor's.

There I found a very eager company assembled. They had been awaiting me with much impatience; the Mummy was extended upon the dining-table; and the moment I entered its examination was commenced.

It was one of a pair brought, several years previously, by Captain Arthur Sabretash, a cousin of Ponnonner's, from a tomb near Eleithias, in the Lybian mountains, a considerable distance above Thebes on the Nile. The grottos at this point, although less magnificent than the Theban sepulchres, are of higher interest, on account of affording more numerous illustrations of the private life of the Egyptians. The chamber from which our specimen was taken, was said to be very rich in such illustrations—the walls being completely covered with fresco paintings and bas-reliefs, while statues, vases, and mosaic work of rich patterns, indicated the vast wealth of the deceased.

The treasure had been deposited in the museum precisely in the same condition in which Captain Sabretash had found it—that is to say, the coffin had not been disturbed. For eight years it had thus stood, subject only externally to public inspection. We had now, therefore, the complete Mummy at our disposal; and to those who are aware how very rarely the unransacked antique reaches our shores, it will be evi-

dent at once that we had great reason to congratulate ourselves upon our good fortune.

Approaching the table, I saw on it a large box, or case, nearly seven feet long, and perhaps three feet wide, by two feet and a half deep. It was oblong—not coffin-shaped. The material was at first supposed to be the wood of the sycamore (*platanus*), but, upon cutting into it, we found it to be pasteboard, or, more properly, *papier maché*, composed of papyrus. It was thickly ornamented with paintings, representing funeral scenes, and other mournful subjects—interspersed among which, in every variety of position, were certain series of hieroglyphical characters, intended, no doubt, for the name of the departed. By good luck, Mr. Gliddon formed one of our party; [1] and he had no difficulty in translating the letters, which were simply phonetic, and represented the word *Allamistakeo*.

We had some difficulty in getting this case open without injury; but, having at length accomplished the task, we came to a second, coffin-shaped, and very considerably less in size than the exterior one, but resembling it precisely in every other respect. The interval between the two was filled with resin, which had, in some degree, defaced the colors of the interior box.

Upon opening this latter (which we did quite easily), we arrived at a third case, also coffin-shaped, and varying from the second one in no particular, except in that of its material, which was cedar, and still emitted the peculiar and highly aromatic odor of that wood. Between the second and the third case there was no interval—the one fitting accurately within the other.

Removing the third case, we discovered and took out the body itself. We had expected to find it, as usual, enveloped in frequent rolls, or bandages, of linen; but, in place of these, we found a sort of sheath, made of papyrus, and coated with

---

[1] George Robins Gliddon (1809-1857), American orientalist.

a layer of plaster, thickly gilt and painted. The paintings represented subjects connected with the various supposed duties of the soul, and its presentation to different divinities, with numerous identical human figures, intended, very probably, as portraits of the persons embalmed. Extending from head to foot was a columnar, or perpendicular, inscription, in phonetic hieroglyphics, giving again his name and titles, and the names and titles of his relations.

Around the neck thus unsheathed, was a collar of cylindrical glass beads, diverse in color, and so arranged as to form images of deities, of the scarabeus, etc., with the winged globe. Around the small of the waist was a similar collar or belt.

Stripping off the papyrus, we found the flesh in excellent preservation, with no perceptible odor. The color was reddish. The skin was hard, smooth, and glossy. The teeth and hair were in good condition. The eyes (it seemed) had been removed, and glass ones substituted, which were very beautiful and wonderfully life-like, with the exception of somewhat too determined a stare. The fingers and the nails were brilliantly gilded.

Mr. Gliddon was of opinion, from the redness of the epidermis, that the embalmment had been effected altogether by asphaltum; but, on scraping the surface with a steel instrument, and throwing into the fire some of the powder thus obtained, the flavor of camphor and other sweet-scented gums became apparent.

We searched the corpse very carefully for the usual openings through which the entrails are extracted, but, to our surprise, we could discover none. No member of the party was at that period aware that entire or unopened mummies are not infrequently met. The brain it was customary to withdraw through the nose; the intestines through an incision in the side; the body was then shaved, washed, and salted; then laid aside for several weeks, when the operation of embalming, properly so called, began.

As no trace of an opening could be found, Doctor Ponnonner was preparing his instruments for dissection, when I observed that it was then past two o'clock. Hereupon it was agreed to postpone the internal examination until the next evening; and we were about to separate for the present, when some one suggested an experiment or two with the voltaic pile.

The application of electricity to a Mummy three or four thousand years old at the least, was an idea, if not very sage, still sufficiently original, and we all caught it at once. About one tenth in earnest and nine tenths in jest, we arranged a battery in the Doctor's study, and conveyed thither the Egyptian.

It was only after much trouble that we succeeded in laying bare some portions of the temporal muscle which appeared of less stony rigidity than other parts of the frame, but which, as we had anticipated, of course, gave no indication of galvanic susceptibility when brought in contact with the wire. This, the first trial, indeed, seemed decisive, and, with a hearty laugh at our own absurdity, we were bidding each other good night, when my eyes, happening to fall upon those of the Mummy, were there immediately riveted in amazement. My brief glance, in fact, had sufficed to assure me that the orbs which we had all supposed to be glass, and which were originally noticeable for a certain wild stare, were now so far covered by the lids, that only a small portion of the *tunica albuginea* [2] remained visible.

With a shout I called attention to the fact, and it became immediately obvious to all.

I cannot say that I was *alarmed* at the phenomenon, because "alarmed" is, in my case, not exactly the word. It is possible, however, that, but for the Brown Stout, I might have been a little nervous. As for the rest of the company, they really made no attempt at concealing the downright fright which possessed them. Doctor Ponnonner was a man to be pitied. Mr. Gliddon, by

[2] The white of the eye.

some peculiar process, rendered himself invisible. Mr. Silk Buckingham, I fancy, will scarcely be so bold as to deny that he made his way, upon all fours, under the table.[3]

After the first shock of astonishment, however, we resolved, as a matter of course, upon further experiment forthwith. Our operations were now directed against the great toe of the right foot. We made an incision over the outside of the exterior *os sesamoideum pollicis pedis*,[4] and thus got at the root of the *abductor* muscle. Readjusting the battery, we now applied the fluid to the bisected nerves—when, with a movement of exceeding life-likeness, the Mummy first drew up its right knee so as to bring it nearly in contact with the abdomen, and then, straightening the limb with inconceivable force, bestowed a kick upon Doctor Ponnonner, which had the effect of discharging that gentleman, like an arrow from a catapult, through a window into the street below.

We rushed out *en masse* to bring in the mangled remains of the victim, but had the happiness to meet him upon the staircase, coming up in an unaccountable hurry, brimful of the most ardent philosophy, and more than ever impressed with the necessity of prosecuting our experiment with vigor and with zeal.

It was by his advice, accordingly, that we made, upon the spot, a profound incision into the tip of the subject's nose, while the Doctor himself, laying violent hands upon it, pulled it into vehement contact with the wire.

Morally and physically—figuratively and literally—was the effect electric. In the first place, the corpse opened its eyes and winked very rapidly for several minutes, as does Mr. Barnes in the pantomime;[5] in the second place, it sneezed; in the third, it sat upon end; in the fourth, it shook its fist in Doctor Ponnonner's face; in the fifth, turning to Messieurs Gliddon and Buckingham, it addressed them, in very capital Egyptian, thus:

"I must say, gentlemen, that I am as much surprised as I am mortified at your behavior. Of Doctor Ponnonner nothing better was to be expected. He is a poor little fat fool who *knows* no better. I pity and forgive him. But you, Mr. Gliddon—and you, Silk—who have travelled and resided in Egypt until one might imagine you to the manor born—you, I say, who have been so much among us that you speak Egyptian fully as well, I think, as you write your mother-tongue—you, whom I have always been led to regard as the firm friend of the mummies—I really did anticipate more gentlemanly conduct from *you*. What am I to think of your standing quietly by and seeing me thus unhandsomely used? What am I to suppose by your permitting Tom, Dick, and Harry to strip me of my coffins, and my clothes, in this wretchedly cold climate? In what light (to come to the point) am I to regard your aiding and abetting that miserable little villain, Doctor Ponnonner, in pulling me by the nose?"

It will be taken for granted, no doubt, that upon hearing this speech under the circumstances, we all either made for the door, or fell into violent hysterics, or went off in a general swoon. One of these three things was, I say, to be expected. Indeed each and all of these lines of conduct might have been very plausibly pursued. And, upon my word, I am at a loss to know how or why it was that we pursued neither the one nor the other. But, perhaps, the true reason is to be sought in the spirit of the age, which proceeds by the rule of contraries altogether, and is now usually admitted as the solution of every thing in the way of paradox and impossibility. Or, perhaps, after all, it was only the Mummy's

---

[3] Poe probably intended this character to suggest James Silk Buckingham (1786-1855), English orientalist, who visited the United States 1838-1840.

[4] The sesamoid bone of the big toe.

[5] A reference to W. A. Barnes, a pantomimist of Poe's day on the New York stage.

exceedingly natural and matter-of-course air that divested his words of the terrible. However this may be, the facts are clear, and no member of our party betrayed any very particular trepidation, or seemed to consider that any thing had gone very especially wrong.

For my part I was convinced it was all right, and merely stepped aside, out of the range of the Egyptian's fist. Doctor Ponnonner thrust his hands into his breeches pockets, looked hard at the Mummy, and grew excessively red in the face. Mr. Gliddon stroked his whiskers and drew up the collar of his shirt. Mr. Buckingham hung down his head, and put his right thumb into the left corner of his mouth.

The Egyptian regarded him with a severe countenance for some minutes and at length, with a sneer, said:

"Why don't you speak, Mr. Buckingham? Did you hear what I asked you or not? *Do* take your thumb out of your mouth!"

Mr. Buckingham, hereupon, gave a slight start, took his right thumb out of the left corner of his mouth, and, by way of indemnification, inserted his left thumb in the right corner of the aperture abovementioned.

Not being able to get an answer from Mr. B., the figure turned peevishly to Mr. Gliddon, and, in a peremptory tone, demanded in general terms what we all meant.

Mr. Gliddon replied at great length, in phonetics; and but for the deficiency of American printing-offices in hieroglyphical type, it would afford me much pleasure to record here, in the original, the whole of his very excellent speech.

I may as well take this occasion to remark, that all the subsequent conversation in which the Mummy took a part, was carried on in primitive Egyptian, through the medium (so far as concerned myself and other untravelled members of the company) —through the medium, I say, of Messieurs Gliddon and Buckingham, as interpreters. These gentlemen spoke the mother tongue of the mummy with inimitable fluency and grace; but I could not help observing that (owing, no doubt, to the introduction of images entirely modern, and, of course, entirely novel to the stranger) the two travellers were reduced, occasionally, to the employment of sensible forms for the purpose of conveying a particular meaning. Mr. Gliddon, at one period, for example, could not make the Egyptian comprehend the term "politics," until he sketched upon the wall, with a bit of charcoal, a little carbuncle-nosed gentleman, out at elbows, standing upon a stump, with his left leg drawn back, right arm thrown forward, with his fist shut, the eyes rolled up toward Heaven, and the mouth open at an angle of ninety degrees. Just in the same way Mr. Buckingham failed to convey the absolutely modern idea "wig," until (at Doctor Ponnonner's suggestion) he grew very pale in the face, and consented to take off his own.

It will be readily understood that Mr. Gliddon's discourse turned chiefly upon the vast benefits accruing to science from the unrolling and disembowelling of mummies; apologizing, upon this score, for any disturbance that might have been occasioned *him*, in particular, the individual Mummy called Allamistakeo; and concluding with a mere hint (for it could scarcely be considered more) that, as these little matters were now explained, it might be as well to proceed with the investigation intended. Here Doctor Ponnonner made ready his instruments.

In regard to the latter suggestions of the orator, it appears that Allamistakeo had certain scruples of conscience, the nature of which I did not distinctly learn; but he expressed himself satisfied with the apologies tendered, and, getting down from the table, shook hands with the company all round.

When this ceremony was at an end, we immediately busied ourselves in repairing the damages which our subject had sustained from the scalpel. We sewed up the wound in his temple, bandaged his foot, and applied a square inch of black plaster to the tip of his nose.

It was now observed that the Count (this was the title, it seems, of Allamistakeo) had a slight fit of shivering—no doubt from the cold. The Doctor immediately repaired to his wardrobe, and soon returned with a black dress coat, made in Jennings' best manner,[6] a pair of sky-blue plaid pantaloons with straps, a pink gingham *chemise,* a flapped vest of brocade, a white sack overcoat, a walking cane with a hook, a hat with no brim, patent-leather boots, straw-colored kid gloves, an eyeglass, a pair of whiskers, and a waterfall cravat. Owing to the disparity of size between the Count and the Doctor (the proportion being as two to one), there was some little difficulty in adjusting these habiliments upon the person of the Egyptian; but when all was arranged, he might have been said to be dressed. Mr. Gliddon, therefore, gave him his arm, and led him to a comfortable chair by the fire, while the Doctor rang the bell upon the spot and ordered a supply of cigars and wine.

The conversation soon grew animated. Much curiosity was, of course, expressed in regard to the somewhat remarkable fact of Allamistakeo's still remaining alive.

"I should have thought," observed Mr. Buckingham, "that it is high time you were dead."

"Why," replied the Count, very much astonished, "I am little more than seven hundred years old! My father lived a thousand, and was by no means in his dotage when he died."

Here ensued a brisk series of questions and computations, by means of which it became evident that the antiquity of the Mummy had been grossly misjudged. It had been five thousand and fifty years and some months since he had been consigned to the catacombs at Eleithias.

"But my remark," resumed Mr. Buckingham, "had no reference to your age at the period of interment; (I am willing to grant, in fact, that you are still a young man), and my allusion was to the immensity of time during which, by your own showing, you must have been done up in asphaltum."

"In what?" said the Count.

"In asphaltum," persisted Mr. B.

"Ah, yes; I have some faint notion of what you mean; it might be made to answer, no doubt,—but in my time we employed scarcely any thing else than the Bichloride of Mercury."

"But what we are especially at a loss to understand," said Doctor Ponnonner, "is how it happens that, having been dead and buried in Egypt five thousand years ago, you are here to-day all alive and looking so delightfully well."

"Had I been, as you say, *dead*," replied the Count, "it is more than probable that dead I should still be; for I perceive you are yet in the infancy of Galvanism,[7] and cannot accomplish with it what was a common thing among us in the old days. But the fact is, I fell into catalepsy, and it was considered by my best friends that I was either dead or should be; they accordingly embalmed me at once—I presume you are aware of the chief principle of the embalming process?"

"Why, not altogether."

"Ah, I perceive;—a deplorable condition of ignorance! Well, I cannot enter into details just now: but it is necessary to explain that to embalm (properly speaking), in Egypt, was to arrest indefinitely *all* the animal functions subjected to the process. I use the word 'animal' in its widest sense, as including the physical not more than the moral and *vital* being. I repeat that the leading principle of embalmment consisted, with us, in the immediately arresting, and holding in perpetual *abeyance, all* the animal functions subjected to the process. To be brief, in whatever condition the individual was, at the period of embalmment, in that condition he remained. Now, as it is my good

---

[6] Probably a contemporary tailor.

[7] Luigi or Aloisio Galvani (1737-1798) was the founder of this science of electrical currents.

fortune to be of the blood of the Scara-bæus, I was embalmed *alive,* as you see me at present."

"The blood of the Scarabæus!" exclaimed Doctor Ponnonner.

"Yes. The Scarabæus was the *insignium,* or the 'arms,' of a very distinguished and very rare patrician family. To be 'of the blood of the Scarabæus,' is merely to be one of that family of which the Scarabæus is the *insignium.* I speak figuratively."

"But what has this to do with your being alive?"

"Why, it is the general custom in Egypt to deprive a corpse, before embalmment, of its bowels and brains; the race of the Scarabæi alone did not coincide with the custom. Had I not been a Scarabæus, therefore, I should have been without bowels and brains; and without either it is inconvenient to live."

"I perceive that," said Mr. Buckingham, "and I presume that all the *entire* mummies that come to hand are of the race of Scarabæi."

"Beyond doubt."

"I thought," said Mr. Gliddon, very meekly, "that the Scarabæus was one of the Egyptian gods."

"One of the Egyptian *what?*" exclaimed the Mummy, starting to its feet.

"Gods!" repeated the traveller.

"Mr. Gliddon, I really am astonished to hear you talk in this style," said the Count, resuming his chair. "No nation upon the face of the earth has ever acknowledged more than one *god.* The Scarabæus, the Ibis, etc., were with us (as similar creatures have been with others) the symbols, or *media,* through which we offered worship to the Creator too august to be more directly approached."

There was here a pause. At length the colloquy was renewed by Doctor Ponnonner.

"It is not improbable, then, from what you have explained," said he, "that among the catacombs near the Nile there may exist other mummies of the Scarabæus tribe, in a condition of vitality."

"There can be no question of it," replied the Count; "all the Scarabæi embalmed accidentally while alive, are alive. Even some of those *purposely* so embalmed, may have been overlooked by their executors, and still remain in the tomb."

"Will you be kind enough to explain," I said, "what you mean by 'purposely so embalmed'?"

"With great pleasure," answered the Mummy, after surveying me leisurely through his eyeglass—for it was the first time I had ventured to address him a direct question.

"With great pleasure," he said. "The usual duration of man's life, in my time, was about eight hundred years. Few men died, unless by most extraordinary accident, before the age of six hundred; few lived longer than a decade of centuries; but eight were considered the natural term. After the discovery of the embalming principle, as I have already described it to you, it occurred to our philosophers that a laudable curiosity might be gratified, and, at the same time, the interests of science much advanced, by living this natural term in instalments. In the case of history, indeed, experience demonstrated that something of this kind was indispensable. An historian, for example, having attained the age of five hundred, would write a book with great labor and then get himself carefully embalmed; leaving instructions to his executors *pro tem,* that they should cause him to be revivified after the lapse of a certain period—say five or six hundred years. Resuming existence at the expiration of this time, he would invariably find his great work converted into a species of haphazard note-book—that is to say, into a kind of literary arena for the conflicting guesses, riddles, and personal squabbles of whole herds of exasperated commentators. These guesses, etc., which passed under the name of annotations, or emendations, were found so completely to have enveloped, distorted, and overwhelmed the text, that the author had to go about with a lantern to discover his own book. When discovered, it was never worth the trouble of the search. After rewriting it throughout, it was regarded as the bounden duty of the historian to set himself to work immediately in correcting, from his own private knowledge and experience, the traditions of the day concerning the epoch at which he had originally lived. Now this process of rescription and personal rectification, pursued by various individual sages from time to time, had the effect of preventing our history from degenerating into absolute fable."

"I beg your pardon," said Doctor Ponnonner at this point, laying his hand gently upon the arm of the Egyptian—"I beg your pardon, sir, but may I presume to interrupt you for one moment?"

"By all means, *sir*," replied the Count, drawing up.

"I merely wished to ask you a question," said the Doctor. "You mentioned the historian's personal correction of *traditions* respecting his own epoch. Pray, sir, upon an average, what proportion of these Kabbala were usually found to be right?"

"The Kabbala, as you properly term them, sir, were generally discovered to be precisely on a par with the facts recorded in the un-re-written histories themselves;—that is to say, not one individual iota of either was ever known, under any circumstances, to be not totally and radically wrong."

"But since it is quite clear," resumed the Doctor, "that at least five thousand years have elapsed since your entombment, I take it for granted that your histories at that period, if not your traditions, were sufficiently explicit on that one topic of universal interest, the Creation, which took place, as I presume you are aware, only about ten centuries before."

"Sir!" said the Count Allamistakeo.

The Doctor repeated his remarks, but it was only after much additional explanation that the foreigner could be made to comprehend them. The latter at length said, hesitatingly:

"The ideas you have suggested are to me, I confess, utterly novel. During my time I never knew any one to entertain so singular a fancy as that the universe (or this world if you will have it so) ever had a beginning at all. I remember once, and once only, hearing something remotely hinted, by a man of many speculations, concerning the origin *of the human race;* and by this individual, the very word *Adam* (or Red Earth), which you make use of, was employed. He employed it, however, in a generical sense, with reference to the spontaneous germination from rank soil (just as a thousand of the lower *genera* of creatures are germinated),—the spontaneous germination, I say, of five vast hordes of men, simultaneously upspringing in five distinct and nearly equal divisions of the globe."

Here, in general, the company shrugged their shoulders, and one or two of us touched our foreheads with a very significant air. Mr. Silk Buckingham, first glancing slightly at the occiput and then at the sinciput of Allamistakeo, spoke as follows:

"The long duration of human life in your time, together with the occasional practice of passing it, as you have explained, in instalments, must have had, indeed, a strong tendency to the general development and conglomeration of knowledge. I presume, therefore, that we are to attribute the marked inferiority of the old Egyptians in all particulars of science, when compared with the moderns, and more especially with the Yankees, altogether to the superior solidity of the Egyptian skull."

"I confess again," replied the Count, with much suavity, "that I am somewhat at a loss to comprehend you; pray, to what particulars of science do you allude?"

Here our whole party, joining voices, detailed, at great length, the assumptions of phrenology and the marvels of animal magnetism.

Having heard us to an end, the Count proceeded to relate a few anecdotes, which rendered it evident that prototypes of Gall and Spurzheim had flourished and faded in Egypt so long ago as to have been nearly forgotten, and that the manœuvres of Mesmer were really very contemptible tricks when put in collation with the positive miracles of the Theban *savans,* who created lice and a great many other similar things.[8]

I here asked the Count if his people were able to calculate eclipses. He smiled rather contemptuously, and said they were.

This put me a little out, but I began to make other inquiries in regard to his astronomical knowledge, when a member of the company, who had never as yet opened his mouth, whispered in my ear, that for information on this head, I had better consult Ptolemy (whoever Ptolemy is), as well as one Plutarch *de facie lunæ.*[9]

I then questioned the Mummy about burning-glasses and lenses, and, in general, about the manufacture of glass; but I had not made an end of my inquiries before the silent member again touched me quietly on the elbow, and begged me for God's sake to take a peep at Diodorus Siculus.[10] As for the Count, he merely asked me, in the way of reply, if we moderns possessed any such microscopes as would enable us to cut cameos in the style of the Egyptians. While I was thinking how I should answer this question, little Doctor Ponnonner committed himself in a very extraordinary way.

"Look at our architecture!" he exclaimed, greatly to the indignation of both the travellers, who pinched him black and blue to no purpose.

"Look," he cried with enthusiasm, "at the Bowling-Green Fountain in New York![11] or if this be too vast a contemplation, regard for a moment the Capitol at Washington, D. C.!"—and the good little medical man went on to detail, very minutely, the proportions of the fabric to which he referred. He explained that the portico alone was adorned with no less than four and twenty columns, five feet in diameter, and ten feet apart.

The Count said that he regretted not being able to remember, just at that moment, the precise dimensions of any one

of the principal buildings of the city of Aznac, whose foundations were laid in the night of Time, but the ruins of which were still standing, at the epoch of his entombment, in a vast plain of sand to the westward of Thebes. He recollected, however, (talking of the porticos,) that one affixed to an inferior palace in a kind of suburb called Carnac, consisted of a hundred and forty-four columns, thirty-seven feet in circumference, and twenty-five feet apart. The approach to this portico, from the Nile, was through an avenue two miles long, composed of sphynxes, statues, and obelisks, twenty, sixty, and a hundred feet in height. The palace itself (as well as he could remember) was, in one direction, two miles long, and might have been altogether about seven in circuit. Its walls were richly painted all over, within and without, with hieroglyphics. He would not pretend to *assert* that even fifty or sixty of the Doctor's Capitols might have been built within these walls, but he was by no means sure that two or three hundred of them might not have been squeezed in with some trouble. That palace at Carnac was an insignificant little building after all. He (the Count), however, could not conscientiously refuse to admit the ingenuity, magnificence, and superiority of the Fountain at the Bowling Green, as described by the Doctor. Nothing like it, he was forced to allow, had ever been seen in Egypt or elsewhere.

I here asked the Count what he had to say to our railroads.

"Nothing," he replied, "in particular." They were rather slight, rather ill-con-

---

[8] The Germans Franz Joseph Gall (1758-1828) and Johann Gaspar Spurzheim (1776-1832), his disciple, who were associates at the University of Vienna, were founders of the pseudo-science of phrenology. The German Franz Anton Mesmer (1733-1815) was the originator of mesmerism.

[9] Concerning the condition of the moon.

[10] Greek historian of the first century B. C.

[11] The reference is to a fountain in a small park at the lower end of Broadway, New York City, where the Dutch of New Amsterdam played at bowls.

ceived, and clumsily put together. They
could not be compared, of course, with the
vast, level, direct, iron-grooved causeways
upon which the Egyptians conveyed entire
temples and solid obelisks of a hundred
and fifty feet in altitude.

I spoke of our gigantic mechanical
forces.

He agreed that we knew something in
that way, but inquired how I should have
gone to work in getting up the imposts on
the lintels of even the little palace of
Carnac.

This question I concluded not to hear,
and demanded if he had any idea of
Artesian wells; but he simply raised his
eyebrows; while Mr. Gliddon winked at
me very hard and said, in a low tone, that
one had been recently discovered by the
engineers employed to bore for water in
the Great Oasis.

I then mentioned our steel; but the
foreigner elevated his nose, and asked me
if our steel could have executed the sharp
carved work seen on the obelisks, and
which was wrought altogether by edge-tools
of copper.

This disconcerted us so greatly that we
thought it advisable to vary the attack to
Metaphysics. We sent for a copy of a
book called the "Dial," and read out of it
a chapter or two about something which is
not very clear, but which the Bostonians
call the Great Movement of Progress.

The Count merely said that Great Movements were awfully common things in his
day, and as for Progress, it was at one
time quite a nuisance, but it never pro-
gressed.

We then spoke of the great beauty and
importance of Democracy, and were at
much trouble in impressing the Count with
a due sense of the advantages we enjoyed
in living where there was suffrage *ad libi-
tum*, and no king.

He listened with marked interest, and in
fact seemed not a little amused. When we
had done, he said that, a great while ago,
there had occurred something of a very
similar sort. Thirteen Egyptian provinces

determined all at once to be free, and to
set a magnificent example to the rest of
mankind. They assembled their wise men,
and concocted the most ingenious constitution it is possible to conceive. For a
while they managed remarkably well; only
their habit of bragging was prodigious.
The thing ended, however, in the consolidation of the thirteen states, with some fifteen
or twenty others, in the most odious and
insupportable despotism that was ever
heard of upon the face of the Earth.

I asked what was the name of the usurping tyrant.

As well as the Count could recollect, it
was *Mob*.

Not knowing what to say to this, I
raised my voice, and deplored the Egyptian ignorance of steam.

The Count looked at me with much astonishment, but made no answer. The silent
gentleman, however, gave me a violent
nudge in the ribs with his elbows—told me
I had sufficiently exposed myself for once
—and demanded if I was really such a fool
as not to know that the modern steam-
engine is derived from the invention of
Hero, through Solomon de Caus.[12]

We were now in imminent danger of
being discomfited; but, as good luck would
have it, Doctor Ponnonner, having rallied,
returned to our rescue, and inquired if
the people of Egypt would seriously pretend to rival the moderns in the all-important particular of dress.

The Count, at this, glanced downward
to the straps of his pantaloons, and then
taking hold of the end of one of his coat-
tails, held it up close to his eyes for some
minutes. Letting it fall, at last, his mouth
extended itself very gradually from ear
to ear; but I do not remember that he said
any thing in the way of reply.

---

[12] Heron or Hero, of Alexandria, was
a Greek mathematician and mechanician
of the third century B. C. He invented a
kind of steam engine, the principle of
which was revived by the French engineer,
Salomon de Caus (1576-1626) and others
before its practical utilization by James
Watt (1736-1819) by 1769.

Hereupon we recovered our spirits, and the Doctor, approaching the Mummy with great dignity, desired it to say candidly, upon its honor as a gentleman, if the Egyptians had comprehended, at *any* period, the manufacture of either Ponnonner's lozenges or Brandreth's pills.[13]

We looked, with profound anxiety, for an answer,—but in vain. It was not forthcoming. The Egyptian blushed and hung down his head. Never was triumph more consummate; never was defeat borne with so ill a grace. Indeed, I could not endure the spectacle of the poor Mummy's mortification. I reached my hat, bowed to him stiffly, and took leave.

Upon getting home I found it past four o'clock, and went immediately to bed. It is now ten A. M. I have been up since seven, penning these memoranda for the benefit of my family and of mankind. The former I shall behold no more. My wife is a shrew. The truth is, I am heartily sick of this life and of the nineteenth century in general. I am convinced that every thing is going wrong. Besides, I am anxious to know who will be President in 2045. As soon, therefore, as I shave and swallow a cup of coffee, I shall just step over to Ponnonner's and get embalmed for a couple of hundred years.

From
EUREKA
[1848]

IF THE propositions of this Discourse are tenable, the "state of progressive collapse" is *precisely* that state in which alone we are warranted in considering All Things; and, with due humility, let me here confess that, for my part, I am at a loss to conceive how any *other* understanding of the existing condition of affairs could ever have made its way into the human brain. "The tendency to collapse," and "the attraction of gravitation are convertible phrases. In using either, we speak of the reaction of the First Act. Never was necessity less obvious than that of supposing Matter imbued with an ineradicable

equality forming part of its material nature—a quality, or instinct, *forever* inseparable from it, and by dint of which inalienable principle every atom is *perpetually* impelled to seek its fellow-atom. Never was necessity less obvious than that of entertaining this unphilosophical idea. Going boldly behind the vulgar thought, we have to conceive, metaphysically, that the gravitating principle appertains to Matter *temporarily*—only while diffused —only while existing as Many instead of as One—appertains to it by virtue of its state of irradiation alone—appertains, in a word, altogether to its *condition,* and not in the slightest degree to *itself.* In this view, when the irradiation shall have returned into its source—when the reaction shall be completed—the gravitating principle will no longer exist. And, in fact, astronomers, without at any time reaching the idea here suggested, seem to have been approximating it, in the assertion that "if there were but one body in the universe, it would be impossible to understand how the principle, Gravity, could obtain:" that is to say, from a consideration of Matter as they find it, they reach a conclusion at which I deductively arrive. That so pregnant a suggestion as the one quoted should have been permitted to remain so long unfruitful, is, nevertheless, a mystery which I find it difficult to fathom.

It is perhaps, in no little degree, however, our propensity for the continuous— for the analogical—in the present case more particularly for the symmetrical— which has been leading us astray. And, in fact, the sense of the symmetrical is an instinct which may be depended upon with an almost blindfold reliance. It is the poetical essence of the Universe—*of the Universe,* which, in the supremeness of its symmetry, is but the most sublime of poems. Now symmetry and consistency are convertible terms:—thus Poetry and Truth are one. A thing is consistent in the ratio

---

[13] Concocted by the English physician, Sir William Brandreth, these pills were a popular nostrum in Poe's day.

of its truth—true in the ratio of its consistency. *A perfect consistency, I repeat, can be nothing but an absolute truth.* We may take it for granted, then, that Man cannot long or widely err, if he suffer himself to be guided by his poetical, which I have maintained to be his truthful, in being his symmetrical, instinct. He must have a care, however, lest, in pursuing too heedlessly the superficial symmetry of forms and motions, he leave out of sight the really essential symmetry of the principles which determine and control them.

That the stellar bodies would finally be merged in one—that, at last, all would be drawn into the substance of *one stupendous central orb already existing*—is an idea which, for some time past, seems, vaguely and indeterminately, to have held possession of the fancy of mankind. It is an idea, in fact, which belongs to the class of the *excessively obvious*. It springs, instantly, from a superficial observation of the cyclic and seemingly *gyrating* or *vortical* movements of those individual portions of the Universe which come most immediately and most closely under our observation. There is not, perhaps, a human being, of ordinary education and of average reflective capacity, to whom, at some period, the fancy in question has not occurred, as if spontaneously, or intuitively, and wearing all the character of a very profound and very original conception. This conception, however, so commonly entertained, has never, within my knowledge, arisen out of any abstract considerations. Being, on the contrary, always suggested, as I say, by the vorticial movements about centres, a reason for it, also,—a *cause* for the ingathering of all the orbs into one, *imagined to be already existing*, was naturally sought in the same direction—among these cyclic movements themselves.

Thus it happened that, on announcement of the gradual and perfectly regular decrease observed in the orbit of Encke's comet,[1] at every successive revolution about our Sun, astronomers were nearly unanimous in the opinion that the cause in question was found—that a principle was discovered sufficient to account, physically, for that final, universal agglomeration which, I repeat, the analogical, symmetrical, or poetical instinct of man had predetermined to understand as something more than a simple hypothesis.

This cause—this sufficient reason for the final ingathering—was declared to exist in an exceedingly rare but still material medium pervading space; which medium, by retarding, in some degree, the progress of the comet, perpetually weakened its tangential force; thus giving a predominance to the centripetal; which, of course, drew the comet nearer and nearer at each revolution, and would eventually precipitate it upon the Sun.

All this was strictly logical—admitting the medium of ether; but this ether was assumed, most illogically, on the ground that no *other* mode than the one spoken of could be discovered, of accounting for the observed decrease in the orbit of the comet:—as if from the fact that we could *discover* no other mode of accounting for it, it followed, in any respect, that no other mode of accounting for it existed. It is clear that innumerable causes might operate, in combination, to diminish the orbit, without even a possibility of our ever becoming acquainted with one of them. In the meantime, it has never been fairly shown, perhaps, why the retardation occasioned by the skirts of the Sun's atmosphere, through which the comet passes at perihelion, is not enough to account for the phœnomenon. That Encke's comet will be absorbed into the Sun, is probable; that all the comets of the system will be absorbed, is more than merely possible; but, in such case, the principle of absorption must be referred to eccentricity of orbit—to the close approximation to the Sun, of the comets at their perihelia; and is a principle not affecting, in any degree,

---

[1] Johann Franz Encke (1791-1865), German astronomer; the comet named for him has a periodicity of 3.3 years.

the ponderous *spheres,* which are to be regarded as the true material constituents of the Universe. Touching comets in general, let me here suggest, in passing, that we cannot be far wrong in looking upon them as the *lightning-flashes of the cosmical Heaven.*

The idea of retarding ether, and, through it, of a final agglomeration of all things, seemed at one time, however, to be confirmed by the observation of a positive decrease in the orbit of the solid moon. By reference to eclipses recorded 2500 years ago, it was found that the velocity of the satellite's revolution *then* was considerably less than it is *now;* that on the hypothesis that its motion in its orbit is uniformly in accordance with Kepler's law,[2] and was accurately determined *then*—2500 years ago—it is now in advance of the position it *should* occupy, by nearly 9000 miles. The increase of velocity proved, of course, a diminution of orbit; and astronomers were fast yielding to a belief in an ether, as the sole mode of accounting for the phœnomenon, when Lagrange came to the rescue.[3] He showed that, owing to the configurations of the spheroids, the shorter axes of their ellipses are subject to variation in length; the longer axes being permanent; and that this variation is continuous and vibratory—so that every orbit is in a state of transition, either from circle to ellipse, or from ellipse to circle. In the case of the moon, where the shorter axis is *de*creasing, the orbit is passing from circle to ellipse, and, consequently, is *de*creasing too; but, after a long series of ages, the ultimate eccentricity will be attained; then the shorter axis will proceed to *in*crease, until the orbit becomes a circle; when the process of shortening will again take place;—and so on forever. In the case of the Earth, the orbit is passing from ellipse to circle. The facts thus demonstrated do away, of course, with all necessity for supposing an ether, and with all apprehension of the system's instability—on the ether's account.

It will be remembered that I have myself assumed what we may term *an ether.* I have spoken of a subtle *influence* which we know to be ever in attendance upon matter, although becoming manifest only through matter's heterogeneity. To this *influence*—without daring to touch it at all in any effort at explaining its awful *nature* —I have referred the various phœnomena of electricity, heat, light, magnetism; and more—of vitality, consciousness, and thought—in a word, of spirituality. It will be seen, at once, then, that the ether thus conceived is radically distinct from the ether of the astronomers; inasmuch as theirs is *matter* and mine *not.*

With the idea of material ether, seems, thus, to have departed altogether the thought of that universal agglomeration so long predetermined by the poetical fancy of mankind:—an agglomeration in which a sound Philosophy might have been warranted in putting faith, at least to a certain extent, if for no other reason than that by this poetical fancy it *had* been so predetermined. But so far as Astronomy —so far as mere Physics have yet spoken, the cycles of the Universe have no conceivable end. Had an end been demonstrated, however, from so purely collateral a cause as an ether, Man's instinct of the Divine *capacity to adapt,* would have rebelled against the demonstration. We should have been forced to regard the Universe with some such sense of dissatisfaction as we experience in contemplating an unnecesarily complex work of human art. Creation would have affected us as an imperfect *plot* in a romance, where the *dénouement* is awkwardly brought about by interposed incidents external and foreign to the main subject; instead of springing out of the bosom of the thesis—out of the heart of the ruling idea—instead of arising as a

[2] Johannes Kepler (1571-1630), German astronomer; Poe refers to the first of Kepler's three important laws of planetary motion—that the orbit of a planet is, with respect to the sun, an ellipse.

[3] Count Joseph Louis Lagrange (1736-1813) French geometer and astronomer.

result of the primary proposition—as in-separable and inevitable part and parcel of the fundamental conception of the book.

What I mean by the symmetry of mere surface will now be more clearly understood. It is simply by the blandishment of this symmetry that we have been beguiled into the general idea of which Mädler's[4] hypothesis is but a part—the idea of the vorticial indrawing of the orbs. Dismissing this nakedly physical conception, the symmetry of principle sees the end of all things metaphysically involved in the thought of a beginning; seeks and finds in this origin of all things the *rudiment* of this end; and perceives the impiety of supposing this end likely to be brought about less simply—less directly—less obviously—less artistically—than through *the reaction of the originating Act.*

Recurring, then, to a previous suggestion, let us understand the systems—let us understand each star, with its attendant planets—as but a Titanic atom existing in space with precisely the same inclination for Unity which characterized, in the beginning, the actual atoms after their irradiation throughout the Universal sphere. As these original atoms rushed towards each other in generally straight lines, so let us conceive as at least generally rectilinear, the paths of the system-atoms towards their respective centres of aggregation:— and in this direct drawing together of the systems into clusters, with a similar and simultaneous drawing together of the clusters themselves while undergoing consolidation, we have at length attained the great *Now*—the awful Present—the Existing Condition of the Universe.

Of the still more awful Future a not irrational analogy may guide us in framing an hypothesis. The equilibrium between the centripetal and centrifugal forces of each system, being necessarily destroyed upon attainment of a certain proximity to the nucleus of the cluster to which it belongs, there must occur, at once, a chaotic or seemingly chaotic precipitation, of the moons upon the planets, of the planets

upon the suns, and of the suns upon the nuclei; and the general result of this precipitation must be the gathering of the myriad now-existing stars of the firmament into an almost infinitely less number of almost infinitely superior spheres. In being immeasurably fewer, the worlds of that day will be immeasurably greater than our own. Then, indeed, amid unfathomable abysses, will be glaring unimaginable suns. But all this will be merely a climactic magnificence foreboding the great End. Of this End the new genesis described, can be but a very partial postponement. While undergoing consolidation, the clusters themselves, with a speed prodigiously accumulative, have been rushing towards their own general centre—and now, with a thousand-fold electric velocity, commensurate only with their material grandeur and with the spiritual passion of their appetite for oneness, the majestic remnants of the tribe of Stars flash, at length, into a common embrace. The inevitable catastrophe is at hand.

But this catastrophe—what is it? We have seen accomplished the ingathering of the orbs. Henceforward, are we not to understand *one material globe of globes* as constituting and comprehending the Universe? Such a fancy would be altogether at war with every assumption and consideration of this Discourse.

I have already alluded to that absolute *reciprocity of adaptation* which is the idiosyncrasy of the divine Art—stamping it divine. Up to this point of our reflections, we have been regarding the electrical influence as a something by dint of whose repulsion alone Matter is enabled to exist in that state of diffusion demanded for the fulfilment of its purposes:—so far, in a word, we have been considering the influence in question as ordained for Matter's sake to subserve the objects of matter. With a perfectly legitimate reciprocity, we are now permitted to look at Matter, as created *solely for the sake of this influence*

---

[4] Johann Heinrich von Mädler (1794-1874), German astronomer.

—solely to serve the objects of this spiritual Ether. Through the aid—by the means —through the agency of Matter, and by dint of its heterogeneity—is this Ether manifested—is *Spirit individualized*. It is merely in the development of this Ether, through heterogeneity, that particular masses of Matter become animate—sensitive—and in the ratio of their heterogeneity;—some reaching a degree of sensitiveness involving what we call *Thought,* and thus attaining Conscious Intelligence.

In this view, we are enabled to perceive Matter as a Means—not as an End. Its purposes are thus seen to have been comprehended in its diffusion; and with the return into Unity these purposes cease. The absolutely consolidated globe of globes would be *objectless*—therefore not for a moment could it continue to exist. Matter, created for an end, would unquestionably, on fulfilment of that end, be Matter no longer. Let us endeavor to understand that it would disappear, and that God would remain all in all.

That every work of Divine conception must coexist and coexpire with its particular design, seems to me especially obvious; and I make no doubt that, on perceiving the final globe of globes to be *objectless*, the majority of my readers will be satisfied with my *"therefore* it cannot continue to exist." Nevertheless, as the startling thought of its instantaneous disappearance is one which the most powerful intellect cannot be expected readily to entertain on grounds so decidedly abstract, let us endeavor to look at the idea from some other and more ordinary point of view:—let us see how thoroughly and beautifully it is corroborated in an *a posteriori* consideration of Matter as we actually find it.

I have before said that "Attraction and Repulsion being undeniably the sole properties by which Matter is manifested to Mind, we are justified in assuming that Matter *exists* only as Attraction and Repulsion—in other words that Attraction and Repulsion *are* Matter; there being no

conceivable case in which we may not employ the term Matter and the terms 'Attraction' and 'Repulsion' taken together, as equivalent, and therefore convertible, expressions of Logic."

Now the very definition of Attraction implies particularity—the existence of parts, particles, or atoms, for we define it as the tendency of "each atom, &c., to every other atom," &c., according to a certain law. Of course where there are *no* parts—where there is absolute Unity— where the tendency to oneness is satisfied —there can be no Attraction:—this has been fully shown, and all Philosophy admits it. When, on fulfilment of its purposes, then, Matter shall have returned into its original condition of *One*—a condition which presupposes the expulsion of the separative ether, whose province and whose capacity are limited to keeping the atoms apart until that great day when, this ether being no longer needed, the overwhelming pressure of the finally collective Attraction shall at length just sufficiently predominate and expel it:—when, I say, Matter, finally, expelling the Ether, shall have returned into absolute Unity,— it will then (to speak paradoxically for the moment) be Matter without Attraction and without Repulsion—in other words, Matter without Matter—in other words, again, *Matter no more.* In sinking into Unity, it will sink at once into that Nothingness which, to all Finite Perception, Unity must be—into that Material Nihility from which alone we can conceive it to have been evoked—to have been *created* by the Volition of God.

I repeat, then—Let us endeavor to comprehend that the final globe of globes will instantaneously disappear, and that God will remain all in all.

But are we here to pause? Not so. On the Universal agglomeration and dissolution, we can readily conceive that a new and perhaps totally different series of conditions may ensue—another creation and irradiation, returning into itself—another action and reaction of the Divine

Will. Guiding our imaginations by that omniprevalent law of laws, the law of periodicity, are we not, indeed, more than justified in entertaining a belief—let us say, rather, in indulging a hope—that the processes we have here ventured to contemplate will be renewed forever, and forever, and forever; a novel Universe swelling into existence, and then subsiding into nothingness, at every throb of the Heart Divine?

And now—this Heart Divine—what is it? *It is our own.*

Let not the merely seeming irreverence of this idea frighten our souls from that cool exercise of consciousness—from that deep tranquillity of self-inspection—through which alone we can hope to attain the presence of this, the most sublime of truths, and look it leisurely in the face.

The *phænomena* on which our conclusions must at this point depend, are merely spiritual shadows, but not the less thoroughly substantial.

We walk about, amid the destinies of our world-existence, encompassed by dim but ever present *Memories* of a Destiny more vast—very distant in the by-gone time, and infinitely awful.

We live out a Youth peculiarly haunted by such dreams; yet never mistaking them for dreams. As Memories we *know* them. *During our Youth* the distinction is too clear to deceive us even for a moment.

So long as this Youth endures, the feeling *that we exist,* is the most natural of all feelings. We understand it *thoroughly.* That there was a period at which we did *not* exist—or, that it might so have happened that we never had existed at all—are the considerations, indeed, which *during this youth,* we find difficulty in understanding. Why we should *not* exist, is, *up to the epoch of our Manhood,* of all queries the most unanswerable. Existence—self-existence—existence from all Time and to all Eternity—seems, up to the epoch of Manhood, a normal and unquestionable condition:—*seems, because it is.*

But now comes the period at which a conventional World-Reason awakens us from the truth of our dream. Doubt, Surprise and Incomprehensibility arrive at the same moment. They say:—"You live, and the time was when you lived not. You have been created. An Intelligence exists greater than your own; and it is only through this Intelligence you live at all." These things we struggle to comprehend and cannot:—*cannot,* because these things, being untrue, are thus, of necessity, incomprehensible.

No thinking being lives who, at some luminous point of his life of thought, has not felt himself lost amid the surges of futile efforts at understanding or believing, that anything exists *greater than his own soul.* The utter impossibility of any one's soul feeling itself inferior to another; the intense, overwhelming dissatisfaction and rebellion at the thought:—these, with the omniprevalent aspirations at perfection, are but the spiritual, coincident with the material, struggles towards the original Unity—are, to my mind at least, a species of proof far surpassing what Man terms demonstration, that no one soul *is* inferior to another—that nothing is, or can be, superior to any one soul—that each soul is, in part, its own God—its own Creator:—in a word, that God—the material *and* spiritual God—*now* exists solely in the diffused Matter and Spirit of the Universe; and that the regathering of this diffused Matter and Spirit will be but the reconstitution of the *purely* Spiritual and Individual God.

In this view, and in this view alone, we comprehend the riddles of Divine Injustice—or Inexorable Fate. In this view alone the existence of Evil becomes intelligible; but in this view it becomes more—it becomes endurable. Our souls no longer rebel at a *Sorrow* which we ourselves have imposed upon ourselves, in furtherance of our own purposes—with a view—if even with a futile view—to the extension of our own *Joy.*

I have spoken of *Memories* that haunt us during our youth. They sometimes pursue us even in our Manhood:—assume gradually less and less indefinite shapes:—now and then speak to us with low voices, saying:

"There was an epoch in the Night of Time, when a still-existent Being existed —one of an absolutely infinite number of similar Beings that people the absolutely infinite domains of the absolutely infinite space. It was not and is not in the power of this Being—any more than it is in your own—to extend, by actual increase, the joy of his Existence; but just as it *is* in your power to expand or to concentrate your pleasures (the absolute amount of happiness remaining always the same) so did and does a similar capability appertain to this Divine Being, who thus passes his Eternity in perpetual variation of Concentrated Self and almost Infinite Self-Diffusion. What you call The Universe is but his present expansive existence. He now feels his life through an infinity of imperfect pleasures—the partial and pain-intertangled pleasures of those inconceivably numerous things which you designate infinite individualizations of Himself. All these creatures—*all*—those which you term animate, as well as those to whom you deny life for no better reason than that

you do not behold it in operation—*all* these creatures have, in a greater or less degree, a capacity for pleasure and for pain:— *but the general sum of their sensations is precisely that amount of Happiness which appertains by right to the Divine Being when concentrated within Himself.* These creatures are all too, more or less conscious Intelligences; conscious, first, of a proper identity; conscious, secondly, and by faint indeterminate glimpses, of an identity with the Divine Being of whom we speak—of an identity with God. Of the two classes of consciousness, fancy that the former will grow weaker, the latter stronger, during the long succession of ages which must elapse before these myriads of individual Intelligences become blended—when the bright stars become blended—into One. Think that the sense of individual identity will be gradually merged in the general consciousness—that Man, for example, ceasing imperceptibly to feel himself Man, will at length attain that awfully triumphant epoch when he shall recognise his existence as that of Jehovah. In the meantime bear in mind that all is Life—Life—Life within Life—the less within the greater, and all within the *Spirit Divine.*"

1806 ∾ *William Gilmore Simms* ∾ 1870

SIMMS composed his own epitaph: "Here lies one who, after a reasonably long life, distinguished chiefly by unceasing labors, left all his better works undone." The words are not unjustified. His was the career of a man of extraordinary energy and ability, handicapped by even more extraordinary external obstacles. To some extent the adverse forces with which he contended have continued to operate since his death, with the result that not even yet is there general recognition of the quality and extent of his achievement.

When Simms was two years old his mother died. His father served under Jackson in the Creek War and remained in what was then the West—Mississippi and Alabama—leaving the infant son to the care of his maternal grandmother. Her stories of South Carolina history contributed to the boy's creative development, as did a visit to his father on the frontier at the age of eighteen. He studied and practiced law at Charleston but turned early to literature and journalism, becoming one of the first Southerners to depend on his pen for a livelihood and one of the most persistent in the attempt to establish a worthy literary magazine in the South. He was compelled, however, to look to the North for helpful literary associations and the first significant publication of his work. At Hingham, Massachusetts, in 1832, he wrote a long romantic narrative poem called *Atalantis, a Story of the Sea,* which, published in New York in that same year, was immediately successful. It was followed by his first book of fiction, *Martin Faber, the Story of a Criminal* (1833), also a popular success. Simms returned to Charleston, but not before he had become favorably known in literary circles in New York and had begun a friendship with Bryant which was to last for many years.

In *Guy Rivers* (1834) and *The Yemassee* (1835) Simms found the two fields, frontier adventure and historical romance, in which he was to do his best work. In 1836 he married the daughter of a wealthy South Carolina planter, and established the pattern which his life was to follow for twenty-five years: most of the year at "Woodlands," his father-in-law's estate, with steady writing; a few months each winter at Charleston; fairly frequent trips to New York and New England.

His production during these years was amazingly profuse and varied, and strikingly uneven. His historical romances of Revolutionary days in the South include *The Partisan* (1835), *Woodcraft* (1852), *The Forayers* (1855) and *Eutaw* (1856). Earlier history of the region was treated in *The Yemassee,* already mentioned; *Vasconselos* (1853), a story of DeSoto; and *The Cassique of Kiawah* (1859). Among the "border romances" of frontier crime and adventure, in addition to *Guy Rivers,* are *Richard Hurdis* (1838); *Beauchampe* (1842); and *Charlemont* (1856). He wrote plays and much poetry; edited a volume of Shakespeare; turned out popular biographies of Marion, Greene, and John Smith. Yet he found time to befriend and help young Southern writers. Again and again he returned to the attempt to establish a worthy Southern literary magazine. Altogether he founded or edited ten periodicals, including *The Magnolia* (1842), *The Southern and Western Monthly Magazine and Review* (1845), and—most important—*The Southern Quarterly Review* (1849-55). For these and other magazines he wrote sketches, stories, political articles, and much literary criticism, including a particularly generous and discerning estimate of Cooper, whom he was often accused of imitating in his fiction.

But the South of those decades was an unrewarding field for literary endeavor. It withheld from Simms even the social recognition that he craved. In the North many of his books were well received, and he had warm literary friendships. But as the Civil War approached and Simms inevitably became a literary protagonist of his own section, he lost his Northern audience in large part without corresponding gain in the South.

The war wrecked his life. During the war years his wife and two of his children died. Sherman's army burned "Woodlands" and with it every volume of Simms' fine library. He was a witness of the burning of Columbia. Yet, facing the Reconstruction, he found means and spirit to help other Southern writers even more unfortunate than himself. "Somehow or other you always magnetize me on to a little strength," the young poet Timrod, sick and starving, wrote to him in 1866. He set himself with full courage and characteristic industry to the task of rebuilding. In 1869 he contracted for three romances to be written concurrently. The burden was too great for even his extraordinary powers. He died at sixty-four. "Simms' genius *never had fair play!*" Paul Hamilton Hayne, his fellow-Southerner, declared. "The *man* was greater than his *works.*"

Yet the works have lasting interest; the best of them offer positive pleasure to the discerning reader of today, and in even the poorest—for example, the sensational *Charlemont*—there is felt repeatedly the play of an active and sensitive mind. It is as easy to make fun of Simms as of Cooper. There are the same stilted conversations, the same insipid women, the same clumsy artifices of plot, and the same reliance on coincidence. In treatment of the frontier Cooper was greatly superior to Simms. The "border romances" are cheap and lurid melodramas in comparison to the Leatherstocking Tales. It is in the field of historical romance that Simms' positive qualities are most apparent. In *The Yemassee* and *The Cassique of Kiawah* he shows greater knowledge and understanding of Indian life, and a far deeper sense of the tragic significance of the inevitable conflicts between red and white, than Cooper ever achieved. His writing as a whole is more sensuous than Cooper's, richer in concrete detail, especially of place; and in general his prose is more pliable and less monotonous. In the Revolutionary romances there are qualities of warmth and dignity, proceeding from Simms' devoted enthusiasm for the whole body of his material, rarely to be matched in the corresponding works of Cooper.

Finally, though many of Simms' attempts to be funny are as painful as most of Cooper's, he did achieve the creation of one fine and memorable comic character, still one of the greatest in all American fiction. Lieutenant Porgy doubtless owes much to Falstaff, and to Simms' lifelong enthusiasm for Shakespeare. But essentially he is indigenous, American and South Carolinian. In his love of certain native foods and sports he is clearly a projection of Simms' own tastes and habits in the best "Woodlands" days. Porgy appears recurringly in several of the Revolutionary romances and is central in *Woodcraft*. He deserves, with his creator, a far larger place in the knowledge and enjoyment of American readers than they have ever held.

[W. P. Trent's *William Gilmore Simms* (Boston, 1892) is still the standard biography. Alexander Cowie has a thorough critical introduction to *The Yemassee* (New York, 1937) in the American Fiction Series.]

From
THE PARTISAN [1]
[1835]

PORGY AND THE TERRAPINS

WHEN on the edge of the thicket where the horses were kept, and which skirted a long dark pond, which was fed by numerous sluices from the swamp, our forester came rather unexpectedly upon no less a person than Lieutenant Porgy.

What was the fat lieutenant doing in such a situation? What was the nature of that occupation which he pursued by the precious starlight, and when most honest men are sleeping? Davis could not divine the answer to his own questions. It was enough that the lieutenant was greatly in his way. Had Porgy been sleeping? No! He was bright enough when he found himself disturbed. But he had certainly been in a state of very profound reverie when the unconscious footstep of Davis sounded in his ears. Rifle in grasp, and crouching low upon the bankside, looking out upon the dark water which glittered in spots only beneath the starlight, the philosophic epicure was as watchful as a sentinel on duty, or a scout on trail. Davis could not say at first whether he lay flat upon the ground, or whether he was on his knees. To suppose him to be crawling upon all fours, would be a supposition scarcely consistent with the dignity of his office and the dimensions of his person. Yet there was so much that was equivocal in his attitude, that all these conjectures severally ran through the head of the woodman. He started up at the approach of Davis, disquieted by the intrusion, yet evidently desirous of avoiding all alarm. His challenge—"Who goes there?" though given in very quick, was yet delivered in very subdued accents. Our woodman gave the answer; and the tones of Porgy's voice underwent some change, but were still exceedingly soft and low. They embodied a good-natured recognition.

"Ah! Davis, my good fellow, you are just in time."

"For what, lieutenant?"

"For great service to me, to yourself, to the whole encampment. But no noise, my good fellow. Not a breath—not a word above your breath. He is a fool who suffers his tongue to spoil his supper. As quiet as possible, my boy."

"What's to do, lieutenant?" was the whispered query of Davis, much wondering at the anxiety of the speaker, who seldom showed himself so, and who usually took events, without asking for the salt or sauce to make them palatable.

"What do you see?" he continued, as the eyes of Porgy were straining across the imperfectly lighted pond.

"See!—what do I see? Oh! Blessed Jupiter, god of men as little fishes, what do I *not see?*"

And as he spoke, he motioned to Davis to sink down, crouch close, and creep towards him. Davis, much bewildered, did as he was required, Porgy meanwhile *sotto voce,* continuing to dilate after his usual fashion of eloquence—a style, by the way, that was very apt to bewilder all his hearers. Davis had never studied in the schools of euphuism; nor in any school, indeed, except that of the swamp. He fancied he knew the philosophy of the swamp as well as any other man; and that Porgy should extract from it a source of knowledge hitherto concealed from him, was a subject of very great amazement. He began, accordingly, to question the sanity of his superior, when he heard him expatiate in the following language:

"We live in a very pleasant world, Master John Davis. Nature feeds us in

[1] "Our narrative begins in South Carolina, during the summer of 1780," Simms explains in the first sentence of this novel. "The arms of the British were at that time triumphant throughout the colony." Porgy and the scout, Davis, were members of a guerilla or partisan band still maintaining resistance in swamps and forests. The title for the selection has been supplied by the editors.

all our senses, whenever we are willing and wise enough to partake. You breathe, you see, you smell, you taste, and you ought to be happy, Davis; why are you not happy?"

"Well, I don't know, lieutenant; I only know I ain't happy, and I can't be happy in this world, and I don't expect to be."

"Oh! man of little faith. It is because you won't use your senses, John Davis—your eyes. You ask me what I see! Blind mote, that thou art! Dost thou see nothing?"

"I see you, lieutenant, and the dark pond and water, and the big cypresses, and the thick vines and bushes, and just above, a little opening in the trees that shows where the stars are peeping down. I don't see nothing else."

"And what were the stars made for, John Davis, but to show you the way to other things? Look for yourself now, and let me show you the pleasantest prospect, for a dark night, that your eyes ever hungered over. Stoop, I say, and follow my finger. There! See to the lagune just beyond that old cypress, see the dead tree half rolled into the water. Look now, at the end of the fallen tree—there just where the starlight falls upon it, making a long streak in the black water. Do you see, man of little faith, and almost as little eyesight! Do you not understand now, why it is that I rejoice; why my bowels yearn, and my soul exults? Look, and feast your eyes, Jack Davis, whom they call of Goose Creek, while you anticipate better feeding still hereafter. But don't you utter a word —not a breath, lest you disturb the comely creatures, the dainty delights, our quail and manna of the swamp—sent for our blessing and enjoyment by the bountiful Heaven, which sees that we are intensely deserving, and mortal hungry at the same time. Hush! hush! not a word!"

Here he stopt himself in the utterance of his own raptures, which were growing rather more loud than prudence called for. The eye of Davis, meanwhile, had followed the guiding finger of the epicure, and the woodman nearly laughed aloud. But he dared not. Porgy was evidently too seriously bent to permit of such irreverence. The objects that so transported the other, were such as had been familiar to the eyes of both from their earliest consciousness of light. The little lagune, or bayou, on the edge of which they crouched, showed them, drowsing on the old and half-decayed tree to which Porgy had directed his own and the gaze of Davis, three enormous terrapins of that doubtful brood which the vulgar in the southern country describe as the alligator terrapin—an uncouth monster, truly, and with such well developed caudal extremities as seem to justify them in classing the animal in this connexion. The terrapins lay basking, black and shining in the starlight, their heads thrust out, and hanging over the lagune, into which the slightest alarm of an unusual nature would prompt them to plunge incontinently. Their glossy backs yet seemed to trickle with the water from which they had arisen. Their heads were up and watchful; as if preparing for that facile descent into the native home, a region black as Avernus. Porgy continued—now in a whisper—

"That's a sight, John Davis, to lift a man from a sick-bed. That's a sight to make him whole and happy again. Look how quietly they lie; that farthest one—I would it were nigher—is a superb fellow, fat as butter, and sticking full of eggs. There's soup enough in the three for a regiment; and now, my good fellow, if you will only be quiet, I will give you such a lesson of dexterity and stratagem as shall make you remember this night as long as you live. There never was a terrapin trapper that could compare with me in my youth. We shall see if my right hand hath lost its cunning. You shall see me come upon them like an Indian. I will only throw off this outer and most unnecessary covering, and put on the character of a social grunter. Ah, the hog is a noble animal—what would we do without him? It's almost a sin to mock him—but in making mock turtle, John Davis, the offence is excusable: a good dinner, I say, will sanctify a dozen sins, and here goes for one."

"But, lieutenant, them's alligator terrapins."

"Well!"

"Well, nobody eats alligator terrapins."

"Nobody's an ass, then, for his abstinence, let me tell you; an alligator terrapin is the very prince of terrapins."

"Well, he's the biggest."

"And the best! His meat is of the rarest delicacy, and with my dressing, and the cooking of my fellow, Tom, the dish is such as would tickle monstrously the palate of any prince in Europe—that is, of any prince born to a gentlemanly taste, which is not to be said of many of the tribe, I grant you. But, there's no time to be lost. Hold my rifle, and witness my exertions."

Here he forced the rifle into the hands of the Goose-Creek forester, and prepared for the proposed achievement; which we may venture to say, in this place, requires a degree of dexterity and painstaking which few can show, and which no one would attempt, not stimulated by tastes so exquisite and absorbing as those of our epicure.

Porgy's agility greatly belied his appearance. You have seen a heavy man move lightly, no doubt. It requires a certain conformation to show this anomaly. Porgy possessed this conformation. His coat was off in a jiffy. His vest followed it, and he was soon stealing away, along the edge of the hammock, and in the direction of his victims. Davis had become interested, almost to the utter forgetfulness of his own victim, Sergeant Hastings. He watched our epicure, as, almost without a sound, he pressed forward upon hands and knees, his huge form, in this attitude, appearing in the dusky light very like the animal whose outer habits he was striving to assimilate.

The terrapins were a little uneasy, and Porgy found it necessary to pause occasionally and survey them in silence. When

they appeared quiet, he renewed his progress; as he drew nearer, he boldly grunted aloud, after the porcine habit, and with such excellence of imitation that, but for his knowledge of the truth, Davis himself might have been deceived. Porgy knew the merit of his imitation, but he had some scruples at its exercise: but for the want of fresh meat in camp, and the relish with which he enjoyed his stew of terrapins, he would have been loath to make an exhibition of his peculiar powers. Even at this moment he had his reflections on his own performance, which were meant to be apologetic, though unheard.

"The Hog," he muttered as he went, "has one feature of the good aristocrat. He goes where he pleases, and grumbles as he goes. Still, I am not satisfied that it is proper for the gentleman to put on the hog, unless on occasion such as this. The pleasures of a dinner are not to be lost for a grunt. He must crawl upon his belly who would feel his way to that of a terrapin."

Thus fortifying himself with philosophy, he pressed forward to the great delight of Davis, who had become quite interested in the performance, and grunt after grunt testified to the marvellous authority which his appetite exercised over his industry. The terrapins showed themselves intelligent. Alas! the best of beasts may be taken in by man. Porgy's grunts were a sad fraud upon the unsuspecting victims. At the first sound, the largest of the three terrapins, having the greatest stake (Qu? steak) of all, betrayed a little uneasiness, and fairly wheeled himself round upon his post, prepared to plunge headlong with the approach of danger. His uneasiness was naturally due to the importance of the wealth which had been intrusted to his keeping. His bullet head, his snaky neck, were thrust out as far as possible from beneath the covers of his dwelling. Like an old soldier, he pricked his ears, and stood on the alert; but he was soon satisfied. His eye took in the forms of his drowsy companions, and he saw no sign of danger in the unbroken surface of the stagnant pond. A second grunt from the supposed porker reassured him. He had lived in intimate communion with hogs all his days. The sow had made her wallow beside his waters, and reared her brood for a hundred years along their margins. He knew that there was no sort of danger from such a presence, and he composed himself at his devotions, and prepared once more to reknit his half-unravelled slumbers.

"Beautiful creature, sleep on!" murmured Porgy to himself, in tones and words as tender as made the burden of his serenade, in the days of his youth, to the dark-eyed damsels upon the waters of the Ashley and Savannah. He made his way forward, noiselessly—the occasional grunt excepted—until he found himself fairly astride the very tree which his unconscious victims were reposing on.

You have heard, no doubt, of that curious sort of locomotion which, in the South and West, is happily styled "cooning the log?" It is the necessity, where you have to cross the torrent on the unsteady footing of a spear,—or rather, where you must needs cross on a very narrow and very slippery tree, which affords no safe footing. In plain terms, our fat friend squatted fairly upon the log, hands and knees, and slided along in a style which John Davis thought infinitely superior to anything he had seen. Telling the story long afterwards, John always did the fullest justice to the wonderful merits of the lieutenant, in some such phrase as this:—

"Lord! 'twas as slick going as down hill, with the wheels greased up to the hub!"

"Greased up to the hub!"

Porgy, you may be sure, was never suffered to hear of the villainous comparison. The anxiety of Davis, at this point of the adventure, made him fidgety and restless. It required strong resolution to keep quiet. But, though himself anxious enough, the stake was too great to suffer our epicure to peril its loss by any undue precipitation. He moved along at a snail's pace, and whenever the huge tree would vibrate

beneath his prodigious weight, the cautious trapper would pause in his journey, and send forth as good a grunt as ever echoed in Westphalian forests. The poor terrapins were completely taken in by the imitation, and lay there enjoying those insidious slumbers, which were now to be their ruin.

Nigher and nigher came the enemy. A few feet only separated the parties, and, with an extended hand, Porgy could have easily turned over the one which was nighest. But our epicure was not to be content with less than the best. His eyes had singled out the most remote, because the largest of that sweet company. He had taken in at a glance its entire dimensions, and already, in his mind, estimated, not only the quantity of rich reeking soup which could be made out of it, but the very number of eggs which it contained. Nothing short, therefore, of this particular prize would have satisfied him; and, thus extravagant in his desires, he scarcely deigned a glance to the others. At length he sat squat almost alongside of the two— the third, as they lay close together, being almost in his grasp, he had actually put out his hands for its seizure, when the long neck of his victim was again thrust forth, and, with arms still extended, Porgy remained as quiet as a mouse. But the moment the terrapin sheltered his head within the shell, the hands of the captor closed upon him with a clutch from which there was no escaping. One after another the victims were turned upon their backs; and, with a triumphant chuckle, the captor carried off his prey to the solid tussock.

"I cannot talk to you for an hour, John Davis, my boy—not for an hour—here's food for thought in all that time. Food for thought did I say! Ay, for how much thought! I am thoughtful. The body craves food, indeed, only that the mind may think, and half our earthly cares are for this material. It is falsehood and folly to speak of eating as a mere animal necessity, the love of which is vulgarly designated an animal appetite. It is not so with me. The taste of the game is nothing to the pleasure of taking it—nothing to the pleasure of preparing it in a manner worthy of the material, and of those who are to enjoy it. I am not selfish, I share with all; and, by the way, John Davis, I feel very much like whipping the fellow who shows no capacity to appreciate. I am a sort of Barmecide in that respect, though I suspect, John, you know nothing of the Barmecides."

"No; I never heard tell of them."

"So I suppose! Well, I won't vex you by talking of fine people not of your acquaintance. Now, John, tell the truth,—did I not seem to you very peculiar, very remarkable, and strange—nay, something ridiculous, John, when you saw me crawling after the terrapins?"

"Well, to say truth, lieutenant, you did seem rather ridickilous."

"Ridiculous! do you say? Well, perhaps! I forgive you, Jack Davis; though there are times when to hint such a word to me, would insure you a broken head. A man of my presence ridiculous!"

"Oh! I don't mean no offence, lieutenant."

"To be sure not! Do I not know that! But, John, think of the soup that we shall get out of these terrapins. Think of our half-starved encampment; and do you not see that the art which traps for us such admirable food, rises into absolute sublimity? Some hundreds of years from now, when our great-grandchildren think of the sort of life we led when we were fighting to secure them an inheritance, they will record this achievement of mine as worthy of Roman fame. But you don't know anything of the Romans, John."

"Not a bit, lieutenant. Is it a kind of terrapins?"

"Yes, indeed! a kind of terrapins that crawled over the whole earth, and claimed it for their own."

"You don't say so!"

"True, every syllable; but the breed's died out, John, and such as are left hav'n't marrow enough in 'em for a stew for a single squad. But, John, it was not the soup only that I thought of when I trapped these beauties. Did you ever feel the pleasure, John, of chasing a fox?"

"Yes, to be sure: a thousand times. It's prime sport, I tell you."

"But you never ate the fox, John?"

"No, indeed! the stinking creature!"

"Well, even if I shouldn't taste these terrapins, the pleasure of their capture is a feast. I have exercised my skill, my ingenuity—I feel that my right hand has not forgot its cunning. That, John, is the sort of practice that proves the true nature of the man. He is never so well satisfied as when he is contriving, inventing, scheming, planning, and showing how cunning he can be. Whether it's red-fox or red-coat, John, it's a sort of happiness to chase, and trap, and catch, run down and cut up."

"I reckon that's true, lieutenant. I feel jist so when I'm on a scout, or a hunt, or anything like it;" and John Davis was reminded of his practice with respect to Sergeant Hastings. He began to be impatient of the long speeches of Porgy; but there was no getting him out of the way, except at his own pleasure.

"Talking of cutting up, John, brings up the terrapins to-morrow. You shall see what a surprise I shall give the camp. You shall see what a thing invention is! How beautiful is art! Now I shall dress each of these beauties in a different style. Steaks and soup you shall have, and enough to satisfy, in the old fashion. But I have some inventions—I thought of them as I neared the log; and when the cunning senses of that patriarch there almost found me out, a timely grunt silenced his doubt. With that grunt came the idea of a new dish. It was a revelation. That terrapin, I said, shall be compounded with the flesh of the porker that Joe Witsell brought into camp at noon. There shall be a hash that shall make your mouth to water. There shall be such a union of the forces of hog and terrapin as shall make them irresistible; and you will then learn the great truth—great to us at short commons in the swamp—that alligator terrapin is a dish worthy to be set before a king."

John Davis looked dubiously, but said—

"Yes, I reckon, lieutenant."

"You reckon! well, but whither do you go?" he asked, as he saw the other lay down his rifle and prepare to go.

"I've got to scout for two hours, out here on the skairts of the swamp."

"Very good! But before you go—have you a handkerchief about you?"

"A mighty old one, lieutenant."

"The very one for my purposes. Mine is a new one, John, and meant for great occasions, when I am entertaining some of the big bugs in epaulettes. Let me have it, —and—but—old fellow, won't you help me home with my captives?"

"In course, lieutenant, I'll take 'em all for you." And John soon had the monsters gathered up, and on his shoulders.

"You are a good fellow, John, and must have your share of the hash as well as stew. Be sure, John, that you don't absent yourself to-morrow. I wouldn't have you miss the mess for the world. There's too much at stake; so remember. A day lost to a good stomach is a serious grievance. You not only cannot recall it, but it affects your health the day after. Don't incur any such peril."

And thus talking, Porgy led the way, and the two parties disappeared together, taking the backward route to the camp.

From
WOODCRAFT [1]
[1852]

PORGY PHILOSOPHIZES

THE MOMENT we choose for reintroducing Captain Porgy, and his late lieutenant to our readers, is one which is usually found to fulfil all the conditions of happiness to the ordinary mortal. They have dined. Crouched at ease, under the shadows of an enormous oak, they have feasted upon the simple fare provided by the hands of their excellent cook, and have done the amplest justice to the thin slices of broiled ham, "done to a turn," and the brown hoe-cake, in the proper composition of which, Tom had established in camp the most enviable reputation. These constituted the sum total of their commissariat. The sufficient potations of oily old Jamaica had followed; and with a sense of physical satisfaction which greatly brightened the prospect, Captain Porgy leaned back against the shaft of the tree, and closed his eyes in order justly to enjoy it.

That complacent sort of revery which usually occupies every mind, after the noon-day appetite has been subdued and satisfied, had already seized upon our corpulent captain. Under its present influences, the state of his affairs began to look less gloomy. The circumstances which more particularly pressed upon his thoughts at this juncture—the loss of his late employment, the involvement of his estates, the supposed abduction of all his negroes, the danger which threatened at the hands of certain creditors—sharks, in shoals, lying in wait, like tigers of the land, seeking what they may devour—these crowding and dismal figures upon his landscape which, before he dined, had rendered his thoughts a very jungle, worse than Indian, of lions, tigers, and snakes of mammoth dimensions—with the consummation of the noon-day meal, retreated from before his path, disarmed of most of their terrors, and, though still lurking and still hostile, looking so little capable of doing mischief, that our captain began to wonder at his own feebleness of soul which had, but a little while before, so greatly alarmed him on their account.

A mild and soothing languor of mood, as if by magic, changed and modified all

---

[1] This novel was first published as *The Sword and the Distaff*. The title of the selection has been supplied by the editors. Porgy and his companion have recently returned from the successful conclusion of their campaign.

the figures in his landscape: and Nature, having gained time—which is the best capital, after all, as well in morals as in war—it was surprising how grateful and agreeable became the philosophy which she had taught our captain. He actually—to the amusement of Lance Frampton, who had tried in vain to soothe his melancholy mood as they rode together before dinner—began to chuckle aloud, yet unconsciously, during his revery, and finally afforded to his young lieutenant an opportunity to twit him, good humoredly, upon his sudden change of humor, by snapping his fingers in the air, as if at the flight of some enemy, whom he had successfully combated.

"Well, I say, captain, you don't seem quite so sick of life as you said you were before dinner. I reckon you won't be shooting yourself, as you threatened, only a little while ago."

"Well, boy, what then? Is life less loathsome because one learns to laugh at it as well as hate it?"

"But you don't hate it, captain—not now."

"No, and for a good reason—because I no longer fear it. I see the worst of it. I see all that it can do, and all that it can deny, and I feel, let it do its worst, that I'm the man for it."

"And what's made you so much stronger now to bear, captain, than you were only an hour agone?" asked the youth, with an insinuating chuckle.

"Dinner, you dog, I suppose—dinner and drink. Is that what you mean? Well—I grant you. We are creatures of two lives, two principles, neither of which have perfect play at any time in the case of a man not absolutely a fanatic or a brute. The animal restrains the moral man, the moral man checks the animal. There are moments when one obtains the ascendency over the other, and our moods acknowledge this ascendency. Before dinner, my animal man was vexed and wolfish. It rendered me savage and sour. I could not think justly. I could not properly weigh and determine upon the value of the facts in my own

condition. I exaggerated all the ills of fortune, all the evils before me, my poverty, my incapacity, and the ferocious greed of my creditors. My soul was at the mercy of my stomach. But, the wolf pacified, my mind acquired freedom. The wild beast sank back into his jungle, and the man once more walked erect, having no fear. Philosophy, my boy, appears once more to comfort me, and the landscape grows bright and beautiful before my evening sun."

"Well, all's right then, captain, until you get hungry again."

"Poh, poh! boy—sufficient for the day is the evil thereof. God will provide. Vex me not with what to-morrow may bring forth, or refuse to bring forth. To-day is secure. That is enough; and the philosophy which to-day has brought, will, no doubt, reconcile me to-morrow. Hear you, Lance? It is the first policy in a time of difficulty or danger, always to know the worst—never to hide the truth from yourself—never to persuade yourself that the evil is unreal, and that things are better than they really are. When you know the worst, you know exactly what is to be done, and what is to be endured. In time of war, with the enemy before you and around you, you are required to see his whole strength, give him full credit for what he can do, and ought to do, and determine, accordingly, whether it be your policy to fight, or fly, or submit—whether you can fly—what will be your treatment if you yield, and what is the reasonable chance of safety or victory, if you resolve to fight. In time of peace the necessity is the same. Peace is only a name for civil war. Life itself is civil war; and our enemies are more or less strong and numerous, according to circumstances. One of the greatest misfortunes of men, and it has been mine until this hour, consists in the great reluctance of the mind to contemplate and review, calmly, the difficulties which surround us—to look our dangers in the face, see how they lie, where they threaten, and how we may contend against them. We are all quite too apt to refuse to look at our troubles, and prefer that they should leap on us at a bound, rather than disquiet ourselves, in advance of the conflict, by contemplating the dangers with which we think it impossible to contend. I have just succeeded in overcoming this reluctance. I have arrayed before my mind's eye all my annoyances, and the consequence is that I snap my fingers at them. As old Jerry Sanford used to cry out when he was in a fight, 'Hurrah for nothing!' Jerry was a true philosopher. His motto shall be mine. Hurrah for nothing seems to me to embody the full amount of most men's matter for rejoicing.''

"Well now, captain, it's a fine philosophy, I reckon, that'll bring a man to such a sort of feeling. But, if I may take the liberty, I'd just like to know, how such a philosophy can put a stop to the trouble, make the enemy quit the field, drive the creditors off the plantation, and fill the corn-crib when it's empty? I ask these questions with your permission, captain, seeing as how you've been good enough to talk to me upon your affairs, and your debts, and the troubles from the sheriff that you're so much afraid of.''

"Afraid of the sheriff, boy! Who dares to say that of me! Never was I afraid of a sheriff in my life. D——n him! Let him come. I have the heart, or I'm no white man, to take the whole *posse comitatus* by the snout.''

"*Posse comitatus!* Oh, I reckon you mean the deputies?''

"Ay, ay—the host of deputies—a legion of deputies if you will, from the Pee Dee to the Savannah. But you haven't caught my ideas, Lance. I must try and be more intelligible.''

"I thank you, captain.''

"You know, Lance, as well as anybody else, that I've been a d——d fool in my time.''

"Yes, captain, to be sure.''

Porgy's self-esteem was not pleased with so ready a concession.

"Well, boy, I don't mean exactly that.

How the devil do you know anything of my folly?''

"Oh, I can guess, sir.''

"Can you, indeed?'' with a sardonic grin. "You are too knowing by half, sir—presuming to know, for one so young as yourself. I mean, boy, that I've done a d——d sight too many foolish things. This don't make a man utterly a fool.''

"No, captain.''

"Unless he continues to do foolish things, mark you.''

"Yes, captain, I see.''

"Most men, the wisest, do foolish things. I don't know, indeed, but that wisdom itself requires to go through a certain probation of folly, in order to acquire the degree of knowledge, which shall teach what folly is—what shape it takes, and how it will affect us. I suppose that it was in obedience to this law of nature, that my follies were performed. But my error was that I continued my probation quite too long. I was ambitious, you see, of the highest sort of wisdom. I made too many experiments in folly, and found them too pleasant to abandon them in season. The consequence was, that I began to grow wise only as I forfeited the means for further experiment. My wisdom had its birth in my poverty, and as it was through my follies that I became poor, I suppose, logically, I am bound to say that I was wise because I had been so great a fool. Do you comprehend me?''

"A little, captain; I think I see.''

"You will understand me better as I go on. I wasted money—a great deal—ran into debt—sold negroes—mortgaged others—and when I joined the brigade, my plantation was mortgaged also—I can't tell you for how much. But, even if the British and tories had not stolen all the rest of my negroes, the sale of the whole of them would scarcely have paid the debt then, and there's some six years' interest since. A very interesting condition of affairs, you will admit, for my contemplation now.''

"Very, sir.''

"Now, to look fully these affairs in the

face requires no small degree of courage. I confess, until I had finished dinner to-day, I was scarcely the man for it. But that last draught of that blessed and blessing old Jamaica—did Millhouse and Tom get a good sup of it?"

"Pretty good, captain."

"They require good measure, both! Well Lance, boy, that last sup of the Jamaica seemed to warm up my courage, and I resolutely called up the whole case, didn't suppress any of the facts, looked at all the debts, difficulties, duns, and dangers, and said to myself, 'A fig for 'em all.' Let the lands go, and the negroes go, and still —I'm a man!—a man!"

"That's the way, captain," responded the youth, with enthusiasm, seizing the extended hand of his superior, and pressing it with a real affection.

"It was just when I had come to this conclusion, Lance, that I snapt my fingers. I couldn't help it. It was the spontaneous sign of my exultation; and as I did so, I thought I saw the d——d mealy face, blear eyes, hook nose, and utterly rascally whole, of my creditor M'Kewn, back out from before me, and take to the woods at a full run. Along with him went the sheriff and the whole swarm of deputies, all of whom have been dodging about me the whole morning, shaking their d——d writs, ca. sa's, fi. fa's,[2] and a thousand other offensive sheets of penal parchment in my face. I discomfited the wretches by that same snap of the fingers; and the adoption of old Jerry Sanford's cry of battle— 'hurrah for nothing!' has made me able to back poverty and the sheriff into the woods!"

From

VIEWS AND REVIEWS IN AMERICAN LITERATURE
[1845]

JAMES FENIMORE COOPER
THE SPY

THE SUCCESS of the "Spy" was very great, and it at once gave Mr. Cooper

reputation in Europe. It may be said to have occasioned a greater sensation in Europe than at home;—and there were good reasons for this. At that period America had no literature. Just before this time, or about this time, it was the favorite sarcasm of the British Reviewers that such a thing as an American book was never read. Mr. Irving, it is true, was writing his sweet and delicate essays; but he was not accounted in England an American writer, and he himself,—no doubt with a sufficient policy—his own fortunes alone being the subject of consideration—took no pains to assert his paternity.[1] The publication of the "Spy" may be assumed to have been the first practical reply to sarcasm, which, since that day, has found its ample refutation. It was immediately republished in England, and soon after, we believe, found its way into half the languages of Europe. Its farther and more important effect was upon the intellect of our own country. It at once opened the eyes of our people to their own resources. It was something of a wonder, to ourselves, that we should be able—(strange, self-destroying humility in a people springing directly from the Anglo-Norman stock)—to produce a writer who should so suddenly, and in his very first work ("Precaution" was not known and scarcely named in that day) rise to such an eminence—equalling most, excelling most, and second to but one, of the great historical romance writers of Britain. This itself was an important achievement —a step gained, without which, no other step could possibly have been taken. It need scarcely be said, that the efforts of a nation at performance,—particularly in letters and the arts,—must first be pre-

2 "Ca." and "fi." are customary abbreviations of legal terms, "ca." for case and "fi." for fiat or order.

1 Irving's essay, "English Writers on America," published in the *Sketch Book* and included among the selections from Irving elsewhere in this volume, shows that this charge was unjust.

ceded by a certain consciousness of the necessary resources. This consciousness, in the case of America, was wanting. Our colonial relation to Great Britain had filled us with a feeling of intellectual dependence, of which our success in shaking off her political dominion had in no respect relieved us. We had not then, and, indeed, have not entirely to this day, arrived at any just idea of the inevitable connexion between any ability to maintain ourselves in arts as well as in arms—the ability in both cases arising only from our intellectual resources, and a manly reliance upon the just origin of national strength,—Self-dependence! To Mr. Cooper the merit is due, of having first awakened us to this self-reference,—to this consciousness of mental resources, of which our provincialism dealt, not only in constant doubts, but in constant denials. The first step is half the march, as in ordinary cases, the first blow is half the battle. With what rapidity after that did the American press operate. How many new writers rose up suddenly, the moment that their neighbours had made the discovery that there were such writers —that such writers should be. Every form of fiction, the legend, tale, novel and romance—the poem, narrative and dramatic —were poured out with a prolific abundance, which proved the possession, not only of large resources of thought, but of fancy, and of an imagination equal to every department of creative fiction. It will not matter to show that a great deal of this was crude, faulty, undigested— contracted and narrow in design, and spasmodic in execution. The demand of the country called for no more. The wonder was that, so suddenly, and at such short notice, such resources could be found as had not before been imagined. The sudden rise and progress of German literature seems to have been equally surprising and sudden—equally the result of a national impulse, newly moved in a novel and unexpected direction. The wonderful birth and progress of American letters in the last twenty years—and in every depart-

ment of thought, art and science, so far from discouraging, because of its imperfections, holds forth the most signal encouragement to industry and hope—showing most clearly, that the deficiency was not in the resource but in the demand, not in the inferior quality, or limited quantity, but in the utter indifference of our people to the possession of the material.

THE PILOT AND LEATHERSTOCKING

THE VERY isolation to which, in the most successful of his stories, Mr. Cooper subjects his favourite personages, is, alone, a proof of his strength and genius. While the ordinary writer, the man of mere talent, is compelled to look around him among masses for his material, he contents himself with one man, and flings him upon the wilderness. The picture then, which follows, must be one of intense individuality. Out of this one man's nature, his moods and fortunes, he spins his story. The agencies and dependencies are few. With the self-reliance which is only found in true genius, he goes forward into the wilderness, whether of land or ocean; and the vicissitudes of either region, acting upon the natural resources of one man's mind, furnish the whole material of his work-shop. This mode of performance is highly dramatic, and thus it is that his scout, his trapper, his hunter, his pilot, all live to our eyes and thoughts, the perfect ideals of moral individuality. For this we admire them—love them we do not —they are objects not made to love—they do not appeal to our affections so much as to our minds. We admire their progress through sea and forest—their strange ingenuity, the skill with which they provide against human and savage enemies, against cold and hunger, with the same sort of admiration which we feel at watching any novel progress in arts or arms—a noble ship darting like a bird over the deep, unshivering, though the storm threatens to shiver every thing else around it—a splendid piece of machinery which works to the most consummate ends by a *modus oper-andi,* which we yet fail to detect—any curious and complex invention which dazzles our eyes, confounds our judgment, and mocks the search which would discover its secret principles. Take, for example, the character of the "Pilot," in the rapid and exciting story of that name. Here is a remarkable instance of the sort of interest which Mr. Cooper's writings are chiefly calculated to inspire. Marble could not be more inflexible than this cold, immovable pulseless personage. He says nothing, shows nothing, promises nothing. Yet we are interested in his very first appearance. Why and how? Naturally enough by the anxiety with which he is sought and looked for;—by the fact that he promises nothing, yet goes to work, without a word, in a manner that promises every thing. We feel, at a glance, that if any mortal man can save the ship, he is the man. Why is this? Simply because he goes to work, without a word, as if it was in him to do so;—as if a calm consciousness of power was his possession; as if he knew just where to lay his hands, and in what direction to expend his strength. He shows *the capacity for work,* and this constitutes the sort of manhood upon which all men rely in moments of doubt or danger. Yet he gives you no process of reasoning—he has no word save that which commands obedience, —he neither storms, implores, nor threatens —he has no books,—he deals in no declamation. He is the ideal of an abstract but innate power, which we acknowledge and perhaps fear, but cannot fathom. All is hidden within himself, and, except when at work, he is nothing—he might as well be stone. Yet, around him,—such a man—a wonderful interest gathers like a halo— bright and inscrutable,—which fills us with equal curiosity and reverence. With him, a man of whom we know nothing,—whom we see now for the first time,—whom we may never see again,—whom we cannot love—whom we should never seek; and with his ship,—timbers, tackle, ropes, spars and cordage,—a frail fabric, such as goes

to and fro along our shores, in our daily sight, without awakening a single thought or feeling;—with ship and man we grow fascinated beyond all measure of ordinary attraction. In his hands the ship becomes a being, instinct with life, beauty, sentiment—in danger, and to be saved;—and our interest in her fate, grows from our anxiety to behold the issue, in which human skill, courage and ingenuity, are to contend with storm and sea, rocks and tempest—as it were, man against omnipotence. Our interest springs from our curiosity rather than from our affections. We do not care a straw for the inmates of the vessel. They are very ordinary persons, that one man excepted—and *he* will not suffer us to love him. But *manhood,* true manhood, is a sight, always, of wondrous beauty and magnificence. The courage that looks steadily on the danger, however terrible; the composure that never swerves from its centre under the pressure of unexpected misfortune; the knowledge that can properly apply its strength, and the adroitness and energy, which, feeling the force of a manly will, flies to their task, in instant and hearty obedience; these form a picture of singular beauty, and must always rivet the admiration of the spectator. We regard Mr. Cooper's "Pilot" —breasting the storm, tried by, and finally baffling all its powers, as the Prometheus in action—inflexible, ready to endure,— isolated, but still human in a fond loyalty to all the great hopes and interests of humanity.

Hawkeye, the land sailor of Mr. Cooper, is, with certain suitable modifications, the same personage. We see and admire, in him, the qualities of hardihood and endurance, coolness, readiness of resource, keen, clear sighted observation, just reflection, and a sincere, direct, honest heart. He is more human than the other, since, naturally of gentler temperament, the life-conflict has not left upon his mind so many traces of its volcanic fires. He has had more patience, been more easily persuaded; has endured with less struggle if not more fortitude, and, in his greater pliancy, has escaped the greater force of the tempest. But he is, in all substantial respects, the same personage, and inspires us with like feelings. In the hour of danger,—at midnight,—in the green camp of the hunter,—trembling women, timid men, and weeping children, grouped together in doubt,—all eyes turn to him, as, on the sea, in storm, all eyes address themselves to the "Pilot." If any one can save them he is the man. Meanwhile, the shouts of savages are heard on every side,—the fearful whoop of slaughter;—as, on the sea, the wind howls through the ship's cordage, and the storm shrieks a requiem, in anticipation of ultimate triumph, around the shivering inmates. It is only upon true manhood that man can rely, and these are genuine men —not blocks, not feathers—neither dull, nor light of brain,—neither the stubbornly stupid, nor the frothily shallow. Now, as nothing in nature is more noble than a noble-minded, whole-souled man,—however ignorant, however poor, however deficient in imposing costume or imposing person,—so nothing, in nature, is better calculated to win the homage and command the obedience of men, than the presence of such a person in their moments of doubt and danger. It is inevitable, most usually, that such a man will save them, if they are to be saved by human agency. To Mr. Cooper we owe several specimens of this sort of moral manhood. It does not qualify our obligation to him, that they have their little defects,—that he has sometimes failed to hit the true line that divides the simplicity of nature, from the puerility of ignorance or childhood. His pictures are as perfect, of their kind, as the artist of fiction has ever given us.

THE SATIRES [2]

IT MAY be urged that Mr. Cooper had no design in "Home as Found," to make his satire general,—that his home, as found, was meant to be the small province in which his domestic gods were set up; and

that his satire was purely local, instead of general. Unhappily, then, he has so managed his work, that his censure sweeps every thing before it. This is the great danger in the preparation of such works. It is difficult to say where the line is to be drawn which limits the application of the satire. One is scarcely prepared, in the first place, to believe that a man of genius and judgment is willing to expend so much thunder on so diminutive an object. The foreigner certainly does not believe it; and for us at home, we are apprehensive that, in the hurry of Mr. Cooper's indignation, and the warmth of his anger, he confounded with his particular enemies the whole American people, and made common war against them. It is in the nature of such a mind as Mr. Cooper's to do heartily, as well as hurriedly, whatever he undertakes. He is apt to generalize too much from small beginnings. His "Travelling Bachelor" was full of proofs to this effect. That was published as "Notions of the Americans." It was very evident that the work should have been called, "Notions of the New Yorkers and New Englanders." It showed very little acquaintance with the South and West. "Homeward Bound" and "Home as Found," were no doubt true to a certain extent. We do not speak of them as such. They were truthful, so far as the satire was confined to certain classes and circles. They were false, so far as they were made to apply to the characteristics of the American people. It was Mr. Cooper's error to have written these books in a moment of great personal feeling—when the freshness of provocation was stirring in his mind,—when, suffering from injustice, his anger was naturally without measure. There was unquestionably much that deserved the keenest satire and the severest censure. The chief cities were diseased to an enormous extent. Their evil influences were spreading to the country. The rankness of trade and speculation had overrun

[2] See the introductory essay on Cooper, and the selection from *Home as Found*.

the land; its vices were fast usurping the place of virtues—fraud was a bold politician, prescribing laws for the people, and matters for government, as if the propriety of his existence were no longer matter of dispute; bankruptcy was the most profitable of all pursuits—labour was every where driven out of sight as too base for toleration; and sleight-of-hand was the great principle which determined the degrees of eminence and the rewards of service. The most dextrous was the best man, and his profits were assigned accordingly. Verily, a censor was needed; a terrible censor, dreadful in rebuke, armed with a flail of thunder, for the work of retribution. It was not in the power of an ordinary satirist to do this work. Long impunity, and constantly increasing numbers, had made the criminals bold and reckless. They laughed at ordinary reproof, they mocked at wisdom, and despised censure. Mr. Cooper would have written in vain, as others did, but that providence works out the good of man by laws, which, however natural, are not so obvious to him in the blindness of his passion, or the greedy hurry of his avarice. A terrible punishment was preparing for the excesses of our people,—unhappily, a fate which has made the innocent pay the debts of the guilty,—which has swept all with a common besom. The laws of industry, common sense and common honesty, are not to be long outraged with impunity; and the recoil came and the retribution,—and we are—what need not be said—what we are now, and—so far as mere social prosperity is concerned—what, it is feared, we must very long remain. In morals, we trust there is improvement. God works out his purposes to this end, and he does not often work in vain. We are pleased to think, and somewhat proud to say, that, touched by adversity, scourged by the just judgments of Heaven, we are an improving people. Vice is less audacious,—pride less boastful,—labour more honourable,—truth better esteemed, if not yet wholly triumphant.

Mr. Cooper committed two errors when he wrote his satires—the one much more decided than the other. He wrote them at the wrong time, and he wrote them in the wrong spirit. Vanity listens to no homily in the full sunshine of its day. Pride hears no warning, when the homage of vulgar admiration fills its ears. Trade hearkens to no admonitions of prudence, or of principle, in the full tide of a seemingly successful speculation. Mr. Cooper wrote the books which proved so offensive to the American people, at a time when an angel from heaven would have spoken to them in vain,—when, besotted with the boldest dreams of fortune that ever diseased the imagination of avarice, they seemed to have lost the usual faculties of thought, prudence and observation—when, they appeared to think, they had but to will, and *presto,* they won—to lift a finger, and, as at the wand of a magician, the waters flowed with sparkling treasures, and the sands glittered with the precious metal. The Spaniards in Peru or Mexico were never half so bedevilled with their own imaginings, as were the people of our trading cities within our recent remembrance. Our merchants assumed the port of princes, and the Merchant-Princes of the Adriatic never loomed out with a more dazzling and determined ostentation.

Was it likely, that, swollen with pride, gloating over their imaginary treasures, and swaggering with the affectations of fashion, borrowed from the old fools—and young ones—of older countries, they should listen to any censor, receive any counsel, tolerate with patience any rebuke? The attempt of Mr. Cooper was unseasonable, and only vexed them. They wished praise only,—nothing more,—praise from any quarter,—they had stomachs for no stronger aliment. They had flattered the foreigner to secure this praise. They had run with headlong speed to hail the advent of English Lord and English Lady,—had spread their dinner cloths, and thrown wide their saloons and ball-rooms and theatres—asking only for praise. That their own countryman should withhold the precious condiment—should, like the foreigner, find fault only—was an offence not to be forgiven. Nay, there was some reason for their anger. The censure of Mr. Cooper was not expressed in the right spirit. The tone of "Homeward Bound," and "Home as Found," was bad. It expressed the language of querulousness and distaste, if not disgust. It was written less in sorrow than in anger, as if the writer took a malicious delight in singling out the sore spots, which it had been the better purpose of the patriot to hide if he could not heal. He showed himself more disposed to revenge his own hurts and injuries than to amend the faults of his countrymen. Besides, as we have already said, he was unjust because too sweeping in his condemnation. This was the consequence of writing in his anger. Passion has no powers of discrimination, and the wilful mind will exercise none. But if Mr. Cooper's censure had been just in all respects, and in its entire application, it must have failed of any good result at the time of its utterance. It was unseasonable, and therefore impolitic and unwise.

1807 ∾ *Henry Wadsworth Longfellow* ∾ 1882

DURING much of his life Longfellow was the most popular living poet not only of his own country but of the world, his work known and loved in twenty languages. In America the critical attacks of Poe and a few others rather enhanced than weakened his hold on the affections and respect of the great majority of readers. The popular estimate of Longfellow, and at least part of the basis for it, was set forth by the woman journalist, Grace Greenwood, in a comment in which, after disparaging the poet who lived in a garret and starved for his art, she declared exultantly of Longfellow, "Our poet is a gentleman!" and went on to praise his taste in dress and his habit of taking his wife to the opera.

Longfellow's popularity was not limited to those whose standards followed Grace Greenwood's, of course. Scholars in the fields of both modern and classical literature, historians, critics and men of letters generally—with but few exceptions—gave him praise and honor exceeding that accorded to any other American poet of his generation. But after 1900—though people still bought his books in surprising numbers—critical estimation of Longfellow swiftly declined, to reach an excess of censure and ridicule in the decade of the 20's. Now, more than a century since he became famous, it should be possible to re-evaluate his work with some justice.

Longfellow wrote a handful of sonnets that rank close to the best in the language, and a similarly small group of lyrics perennially satisfying for their completely organic fusion of feeling and expression. Through his narrative poems he made a contribution second only to Cooper's to the formation of an American tradition. Americans needed a sense of their past in his day as now, and *Evangeline, Hiawatha,* and *The Courtship of Miles Standish* provided for

Longfellow's generation accessible and acceptable images and symbols on which that sense could feed. Finally, Longfellow's work in his translations and paraphrases, in his prose and in many of his own poems, provided the main channel, shallow but broad, through which the stream of European literature flowed into the American culture of his time.

Of Longfellow's evident limitations—limitations which must be frankly acknowledged in any attempt at just appraisal—perhaps the most decisive was his life-long and almost total separation from the real America of his times. The social and economic turmoil of his century, the rise of industrialism and the conflicts of labor and capital, the impact of immigration and the growth of the cities, struggles for reform, the great scientific and religious changes, found and left him not so much indifferent as unaware. His world was one of books, not of life; and even in that world his limitations were profound. His sense of the past was not critical or acute, but vague and sentimental. Much of the greatest in literature perplexed and embarrassed him: much he missed altogether. A major labor of his life was his verse translation of Dante, a labor of love and of many years; but there are heights and depths in Dante of which he remained wholly unaware.

Longfellow's family was old and distinguished, his father a prominent and prosperous lawyer, his boyhood home in the beautiful and thriving town of Portland, Maine, one of comfort and culture. His college career at rural Bowdoin was brilliant, but his college years were one long battle between his father's determination that he should become a lawyer and his own desire to write—a battle made more painful by the strong affection between father and son. Teaching was a compromise. Longfellow pioneered in the field of modern languages, first at Bowdoin and later at Harvard, producing in rapid succession needed textbooks in French, Spanish, and Italian, and writing scholarly articles. From reading and travel during two protracted periods of study in Europe he drew the materials of his two first books of creative prose, *Outre-Mer* (1835) and *Hyperion* (1839), rather desultory expressions of conventional Romantic attitudes. But his first volume of poems, *Voices of the Night,* also published in 1839, was immediately successful. Thereafter, except for the slight novel *Kavanagh* (1849), he recognized poetry as his medium, and advanced steadily both in its mastery and in public recognition. Though he used materials derived from his European experiences and studies in many of his books— notably in *The Spanish Student* (1843) and *The Belfry of Bruges and Other Poems* (1845), the first two decades of Longfellow's mature life as a poet were primarily devoted to poetic recreations of the American past: in *Ballads and Other Poems* (1841), in part; *Evangeline* (1847); *The Song of Hiawatha* (1855); *The Courtship of Miles Standish* (1858). Only in the slender and feeble volume of *Poems on Slavery* (1842) did he give brief attention to the national problems of these years. In 1854 he resigned his professorship at Harvard in order to devote his whole time to poetry. By 1857 his American publishers alone had sold more than 300,000 copies of his books.

Except for his unsuccessful experiments with the dramatic form in the *New England Tragedies* (1868), Longfellow's work after 1854 contained relatively little purely American material. He devoted the years to his verse translation of Dante, published in 1867, to the varied and often delightful narratives of the two series of *Tales of a Wayside Inn* (1863 and 1874), and to the more serious project of *Christus* (1872), a poetic account of the history of Christianity; and he wrote some of his finest sonnets and lyrics for the final volumes: *Keramos and Other Poems* (1874); *Ultima Thule* (1880); *In the Harbor* (1882). With wealth, leisure, honors at home and abroad, the affection of millions of readers around the world, Longfellow's last years were in harmony with his whole decorous life as a gentleman of letters.

Yet there is a genuine and appealing human being behind his Victorian gentility—glimpsed in the flashy waistcoats he affected as a young professor, reflected in the devotion of such varied friends as Charles Sumner, the abolitionist politician, Louis Agassiz, the scientist, and Charles Eliot Norton, the editor; and a real poet behind the elaborate and often artificial façade of his work, to be found by the modern reader in parts of *Evangeline* and *Hiawatha* and in a very few of his most personal poems.

[Herman S. Gorman's *A Victorian American: Henry Wadsworth Longfellow* (New York, 1926) and Lawrance Thompson's *Young Longfellow, 1807-1843* (New York, 1938) are both reliable biographies. Odell Shepard's *Longfellow* (New York, 1934) in the American Writers Series contains a good critical introduction. See also H. M. Jones' essay in *American Writers on American Literature* (New York, 1931), edited by John Macy; and W. P. Trent's *Longfellow and Other Essays* (New York, 1910).]

A PSALM OF LIFE

WHAT THE HEART OF THE YOUNG MAN
SAID TO THE PSALMIST

[1839 (1838)]

Tell me not, in mournful numbers,
  Life is but an empty dream!—
For the soul is dead that slumbers,
  And things are not what they seem.

Life is real! Life is earnest! 5
  And the grave is not its goal;
Dust thou art, to dust returnest,
  Was not spoken of the soul.

Not enjoyment, and not sorrow,
  Is our destined end or way; 10
But to act, that each to-morrow
  Find us farther than to-day.

Art is long, and Time is fleeting,
  And our hearts, though stout and brave,
Still, like muffled drums, are beating 15
  Funeral marches to the grave.

In the world's broad field of battle,
  In the bivouac of Life,
Be not like dumb, driven cattle!
  Be a hero in the strife! 20

Trust no Future, howe'er pleasant!
    Let the dead Past bury its dead!
Act,—act in the living Present!
    Heart within, and God o'erhead!

Lives of great men all remind us   25
    We can make our lives sublime,
And, departing, leave behind us
    Footprints on the sands of time;

Footprints, that perhaps another,
    Sailing o'er life's solemn main,   30
A forlorn and shipwrecked brother,
    Seeing, shall take heart again.

Let us, then, be up and doing,
    With a heart for any fate;
Still achieving, still pursuing,   35
    Learn to labor and to wait.

HYMN TO THE NIGHT
[1839]

I heard the trailing garments of the Night
    Sweep through her marble halls!
I saw her sable skirts all fringed with light
    From the celestial walls!

I felt her presence, by its spell of might, 5
    Stoop o'er me from above;
The calm, majestic presence of the Night,
    As of the one I love.

I heard the sounds of sorrow and delight,
    The manifold, soft chimes,   10
That fill the haunted chambers of the
        Night,
    Like some old poet's rhymes.

From the cool cisterns of the midnight air
    My spirit drank repose;
The fountain of perpetual peace flows
        there,—   15
    From those deep cisterns flows.

O holy Night! from thee I learn to bear
    What man has borne before!
Thou layest thy finger on the lips of Care,
    And they complain no more.   20

Peace! Peace! Orestes-like I breathe this
        prayer!
    Descend with broad-winged flight,
The welcome, the thrice-prayed for, the
        most fair,
    The best-beloved Night!

THE ARSENAL AT SPRINGFIELD
[1846 (1844)]

This is the Arsenal. From floor to ceiling,
    Like a huge organ, rise the burnished
        arms;
But from their silent pipes no anthem
        pealing
    Startles the villages with strange alarms.

Ah! what a sound will rise, how wild and
        dreary,   5
    When the death-angel touches those swift
        keys!
What loud lament and dismal Miserere
    Will mingle with their awful sympho-
        nies!

I hear even now the infinite fierce chorus,
    The cries of agony, the endless groan, 10
Which, through the ages that have gone
        before us,
    In long reverberations reach our own.

On helm and harness rings the Saxon
        hammer,
    Through Cimbric forest roars the Norse-
        man's song,
And loud, amid the universal clamor,   15
    O'er distant deserts sounds the Tartar
        gong.

I hear the Florentine, who from his palace
    Wheels out his battle-bell with dreadful
        din,
And Aztec priests upon their teocallis
    Beat the wild war-drums made of ser-
        pent's skin;   20

The tumult of each sacked and burning
        village;
    The shout that every prayer for mercy
        drowns;

The soldiers' revels in the midst of pillage;
  The wail of famine in beleaguered
    towns;

The bursting shell, the gateway wrenched
    asunder,   25
  The rattling musketry, the clashing
    blade;
And ever and anon, in tones of thunder,
  The diapason of the cannonade.

Is it, O man, with such discordant noises,
  With such accursed instruments as
    these,   30
Thou drownest Nature's sweet and kindly
    voices,
  And jarrest the celestial harmonies?

Were half the power, that fills the world
    with terror,
  Were half the wealth, bestowed on camps
    and courts,
Given to redeem the human mind from
    error,   35
  There were no need of arsenals or forts:

The warrior's name would be a name ab-
    horred!
And every nation, that should lift again
Its hand against a brother, on its forehead
  Would wear forevermore the curse of
    Cain!   40

Down the dark future, through long gen-
    erations,
  The echoing sounds grow fainter and
    then cease;
And like a bell, with solemn, sweet vibra-
    tions,
  I hear once more the voice of Christ say,
    "Peace!"

Peace! and no longer from its brazen
    portals   45
  The blast of War's great organ shakes
    the skies!
But beautiful as songs of the immortals,
  The holy melodies of love arise.

THE DAY IS DONE
[1846 (1844)]

The day is done, and the darkness
  Falls from the wings of Night,
As a feather is wafted downward
  From an eagle in his flight.

I see the lights of the village   5
  Gleam through the rain and the mist,
And a feeling of sadness comes o'er me
  That my soul cannot resist:

A feeling of sadness and longing,
  That is not akin to pain,   10
And resembles sorrow only
  As the mist resembles the rain.

Come, read to me some poem,
  Some simple and heartfelt lay,
That shall soothe this restless feeling,   15
  And banish the thoughts of day.

Not from the grand old masters,
  Not from the bards sublime,
Whose distant footsteps echo
  Through the corridors of Time.   20

For, like strains of martial music,
  Their mighty thoughts suggest
Life's endless toil and endeavor;
  And to-night I long for rest.

Read from some humbler poet,   25
  Whose songs gushed from his heart,
As showers from the clouds of summer,
  Or tears from the eyelids start;

Who, through long days of labor,
  And nights devoid of ease,   30
Still heard in his soul the music
  Of wonderful melodies.

Such songs have power to quiet
  The restless pulse of care,
And come like the benediction   35
  That follows after prayer.

Then read from the treasured volume
  The poem of thy choice,
And lend to the rhyme of the poet
  The beauty of thy voice.   40

And the night shall be filled with music,
  And the cares, that infest the day,
Shall fold their tents, like the Arabs,
  And as silently steal away.

MY LOST YOUTH
[1858]

Often I think of the beautiful town [1]
  That is seated by the sea;
Often in thought go up and down
The pleasant streets of that dear old town,
  And my youth comes back to me.   5
    And a verse of a Lapland song
    Is haunting my memory still:
  'A boy's will is the wind's will,
And the thoughts of youth are long, long
    thoughts.'

I can see the shadowy lines of its trees, 10
  And catch, in sudden gleams,
The sheen of the far-surrounding seas,
And islands that were the Hesperides
  Of all my boyish dreams.
    And the burden of that old song,   15
    It murmurs and whispers still:
  'A boy's will is the wind's will,
And the thoughts of youth are long, long
    thoughts.'

I remember the black wharves and the
    slips,
  And the sea-tides tossing free;   20
And Spanish sailors with bearded lips,
And the beauty and mystery of the ships,
  And the magic of the sea.
    And the voice of that wayward song
    Is singing and saying still: 25
  'A boy's will is the wind's will,
And the thoughts of youth are long, long
    thoughts.'

I remember the bulwarks by the shore,
  And the fort upon the hill;

The sunrise gun, with its hollow roar,   30
The drum-beat repeated o'er and o'er,
  And the bugle wild and shrill.
    And the music of that old song
    Throbs in my memory still:
  'A boy's will is the wind's will,   35
And the thoughts of youth are long, long
    thoughts.'

I remember the sea-fight [2] far away,
  How it thundered o'er the tide!
And the dead captains, as they lay
In their graves, o'erlooking the tranquil
    bay,   40
  Where they in battle died.
    And the sound of that mournful song
    Goes through me with a thrill:
  'A boy's will is the wind's will,
And the thoughts of youth are long, long
    thoughts.'   45

I can see the breezy dome of groves,
  The shadows of Deering's Woods;
And the friendships old and the early loves
Come back with a Sabbath sound, as of
    doves
  In quiet neighborhoods.   50
    And the verse of that sweet old song,
    It flutters and murmurs still:
  'A boy's will is the wind's will,
And the thoughts of youth are long, long
    thoughts.'

I remember the gleams and glooms that
    dart   55
  Across the school-boy's brain;
The song and the silence in the heart,
That in part are prophecies, and in part

---

[1] Portland, Maine, Longfellow's home
during his boyhood. For a thorough discussion of this poem and its relation to the
source from which Longfellow adapted the
refrain, see James Taft Hatfield's article,
"Longfellow's Lapland Song," *Publications of the Modern Language Association,*
XLV, 1188 ff.

[2] The *Enterprise* captured the British
brig *Boxer* and brought it into Portland
harbor in 1813. The captains of both vessels were killed in the engagement, and
Longfellow was present at their funeral.

Are longings wild and vain.
  And the voice of that fitful song   60
Sings on, and is never still:
'A boy's will is the wind's will,
And the thoughts of youth are long, long
    thoughts.'

There are things of which I may not speak;
  There are dreams that cannot die;   65
There are thoughts that make the strong
    heart weak,
And bring a pallor into the cheek,
  And a mist before the eye,
    And the words of that fatal song
    Come over me like a chill: 70
'A boy's will is the wind's will,
And the thoughts of youth are long, long
    thoughts.'

Strange to me now are the forms I meet
  When I visit the dear old town;
But the native air is pure and sweet,   75
And the trees that o'ershadow each well-
    known street,
  As they balance up and down,
    Are singing the beautiful song,
    Are sighing and whispering still:
'A boy's will is the wind's will,   80
And the thoughts of youth are long, long
    thoughts.'

And Deering's Woods are fresh and fair,
  And with joy that is almost pain
My heart goes back to wander there,
And among the dreams of the days that
    were,   85
  I find my lost youth again.
    And the strange and beautiful song,
    The groves are repeating it still:
'A boy's will is the wind's will,
And the thoughts of youth are long, long
    thoughts.'   90

HAWTHORNE
May 23, 1864
[1866 (1864)]

How beautiful it was, that one bright day
  In the long week of rain!
Though all its splendor could not chase
    away
  The omnipresent pain.

The lovely town [1] was white with apple-
    blooms,   5
  And the great elms o'erhead
Dark shadows wove on their aerial looms
  Shot through with golden thread.

Across the meadows, by the gray old
    manse,[2]
  The historic river flowed: 10
I was as one who wanders in a trance,
  Unconscious of his road.

The faces of familiar friends seemed
    strange;
  Their voices I could hear,
And yet the words they uttered seemed to
    change   15
  Their meaning to my ear.

For the one face I looked for was not
    there,
  The one low voice was mute;
Only an unseen presence filled the air,
  And baffled my pursuit.   20

Now I look back, and meadow, manse,
    and stream
  Dimly my thought defines;
I only see—a dream within a dream—
  The hill-top hearsed with pines.

I only hear above his place of rest   25
  Their tender undertone,
The infinite longings of a troubled breast,
  The voice so like his own.

There in seclusion and remote from men
  The wizard hand lies cold,   30
Which at its topmost speed let fall the pen,
  And left the tale half told.[3]

---

[1] Concord, Massachusetts, where Hawthorne's funeral was held, May 23, 1864.

[2] Hawthorne's home, 1842-46. See the
introductory essay on Hawthorne, in this
volume.

[3] Probably Longfellow refers to *The
Dolliver Romance*, serial publication of
which in the *Atlantic Monthly* was interrupted by Hawthorne's illness and death.

Ah! who shall lift that wand of magic
    power,
And the lost clew regain?
The unfinished window in Aladdin's
    tower   35
Unfinished must remain!

DIVINA COMMEDIA
[1867 (1864-1867)]

I.

Oft have I seen at some cathedral door
    A laborer, pausing in the dust and heat,
    Lay down his burden, and with reverent
        feet
    Enter, and cross himself, and on the
        floor
Kneel to repeat his paternoster o'er;
    Far off the noises of the world retreat;
    The loud vociferations of the street
Become an undistinguishable roar.
So, as I enter here from day to day,
    And leave my burden at this minster
        gate,
    Kneeling in prayer, and not ashamed
        to pray,
The tumult of the time disconsolate
    To inarticulate murmurs dies away,
    While the eternal ages watch and wait.

II.

How strange the sculptures that adorn
    these towers!
    This crowd of statues, in whose folded
        sleeves
    Birds build their nests; while canopied
        with leaves
Parvis and portal bloom like trellised
    bowers,
And the vast minster seems a cross of
    flowers!
    But fiends and dragons on the gargoyled
        eaves
    Watch the dead Christ between the living
        thieves,
And, underneath, the traitor Judas
    lowers!

Ah! from what agonies of heart and brain,
    What exultations trampling on despair,
    What tenderness, what tears, what hate
        of wrong,
What passionate outcry of a soul in pain,
    Uprose this poem of the earth and air,
    This mediæval miracle of song!

III.

I enter, and I see thee in the gloom
    Of the long aisles, O poet saturnine!
    And strive to make my steps keep pace
        with thine.
The air is filled with some unknown
    perfume;
    The congregation of the dead make room
    For thee to pass; the votive tapers
        shine;
Like rooks that haunt Ravenna's groves
    of pine
    The hovering echoes fly from tomb to
        tomb.
From the confessionals I hear arise
    Rehearsals of forgotten tragedies,
    And lamentations from the crypts be-
        low;
And then a voice celestial, that begins
    With the pathetic words, "Although
        your sins
    As scarlet be," and ends with "as the
        snow."

IV.

With snow-white veil and garments as of
    flame,
    She [1] stands before thee, who so long ago
    Filled thy young heart with passion and
        the woe
From which thy song and all its splen-
    dors came;
And while with stern rebuke she speaks
    thy name,
    The ice about thy heart melts as the
        snow

---

[1] Beatrice Portinari (1266-1290), loved
by Dante in youth. In the *Divina Commedia* he makes her his guide through
Paradise.

On mountain heights, and in swift over-
flow
Comes gushing from thy lips in sobs
of shame.
Thou makest full confession; and a gleam,
As of the dawn on some dark forest cast,
Seems on thy lifted forehead to increase;
Lethe and Eunoe [2]—the remembered dream
And the forgotten sorrow—bring at last
That perfect pardon which is perfect
peace.

V.

I lift mine eyes, and all the windows blaze
With forms of saints and holy men who
died,
Here martyred and hereafter glorified;
And the great Rose upon its leaves dis-
plays
Christ's Triumph, and the angelic rounde-
lays,
With splendor upon splendor multiplied;
And Beatrice again at Dante's side
No more rebukes, but smiles her words
of praise.
And then the organ sounds, and unseen
choirs
Sing the old Latin hymns of peace and
love,
And benedictions of the Holy Ghost;
And the melodious bells among the spires
O'er all the house-tops and through
heaven above
Proclaim the elevation of the Host!

VI.

O star of morning and of liberty!
O bringer of the light, whose splendor
shines
Above the darkness of the Apennines,
Forerunner of the day that is to be!
The voices of the city and the sea,
The voices of the mountains and the
pines,
Repeat thy song, till the familiar lines
Are footpaths for the thought of Italy!
Thy fame is blown abroad from all the
heights,

Through all the nations, and a sound
is heard,
As of a mighty wind, and men devout,
Strangers of Rome, and the new proselytes,
In their own language hear thy wondrous
word,
And many are amazed and many doubt.

A NAMELESS GRAVE
[1874]

"A soldier of the Union mustered out,"
Is the inscription on an unknown grave
At Newport News, beside the salt-sea
wave,
Nameless and dateless; sentinel or scout
Shot down in skirmish, or disastrous rout
Of battle, when the loud artillery drave
Its iron wedges through the ranks of
brave
And doomed battalions, storming the
redoubt.
Thou unknown hero sleeping by the sea
In thy forgotten grave! with secret shame
I feel my pulses beat, my forehead burn,
When I remember thou hast given for me
All that thou hadst, thy life, thy very
name,
And I can give thee nothing in return.

NATURE
[1877]

As a fond mother, when the day is o'er,
Leads by the hand her little child to bed,
Half willing, half reluctant to be led,
And leave his broken playthings on the
floor,
Still gazing at them through the open door,
Nor wholly reassured and comforted
By promises of others in their stead,
Which, though more splendid, may not
please him more;

---

[2] Rivers of the underworld. The water
of Lethe gave the drinker forgetfulness of
the past, while that of Eunoe made the
mind recall all the good deeds and experiences of life.

So Nature deals with us, and takes away
  Our playthings one by one, and by the
    hand
Leads us to rest so gently, that we go
Scarce knowing if we wish to go or stay,
  Being too full of sleep to understand
How far the unknown transcends the
    what we know.

THE HERONS OF ELMWOOD
[1878 (1877)]

Warm and still is the summer night,
  As here by the river's brink I wander;
White overhead are the stars, and white
  The glimmering lamps on the hillside
    yonder.

Silent are all the sounds of day;   5
  Nothing I hear but the chirp of crickets,
And the cry of the herons winging their
    way
  O'er the poet's house in the Elmwood [1]
    thickets.

Call to him, herons, as slowly you pass
  To your roosts in the haunts of the
    exiled thrushes,   10
Sing him the song of the green morass,
  And the tides that water the weeds and
    rushes.

Sing him the mystical Song of the Hern,
  And the secret that baffles our utmost
    seeking;
For only a sound of lament we discern, 15
  And cannot interpret the words you are
    speaking.

Sing of the air, and the wild delight
  Of wings that uplift and winds that up-
    hold you,
The joy of freedom, the rapture of flight
  Through the drift of the floating mists
    that infold you;   20

Of the landscape lying so far below,
  With its towns and rivers and desert
    places;

And the splendor of light above, and the
    glow
  Of the limitless, blue, ethereal spaces.

Ask him if songs of the Troubadours,   25
  Or of Minnesingers in old black-letter,
Sound in his ears more sweet than yours,
  And if yours are not sweeter and wilder
    and better.

Sing to him, say to him, here at his gate,
  Where the boughs of the stately elms are
    meeting,   30
Some one hath lingered to meditate,
  And send him unseen this friendly greet-
    ing;

That many another hath done the same,
  Though not by a sound was the silence
    broken;
The surest pledge of a deathless name 35
  Is the silent homage of thoughts un-
    spoken.

THE THREE SILENCES OF
MOLINOS [2]

To John Greenleaf Whittier

[1878]

Three Silences there are: the first of
    speech,
  The second of desire, the third of
    thought;
This is the lore a Spanish monk, dis-
    traught
With dreams and visions, was the first
    to teach.
These Silences, commingling each with
    each,
  Made up the perfect Silence, that he
    sought
And prayed for, and wherein at times
    he caught

---

[1] Home of James Russell Lowell.

[2] Spanish priest and mystic of the 17th
century.

Mysterious sounds from realms beyond
our reach.
O thou, whose daily life anticipates
The life to come, and in whose thought
and word
The spiritual world preponderates,
Hermit of Amesbury![3] thou too hast heard
Voices and melodies from beyond the
gates,
And speakest only when thy soul is
stirred!

AUTUMN WITHIN
[1882 (1874)]

It is autumn; not without,
But within me is the cold.
Youth and spring are all about;
It is I that have grown old.

Birds are darting through the air,
Singing, building without rest;
Life is stirring everywhere,
Save within my lonely breast.

There is silence: the dead leaves
Fall and rustle and are still;
Beats no flail upon the sheaves,
Comes no murmur from the mill.

THE CROSS OF SNOW [4]
[1886 (1879)]

In the long, sleepless watches of the night,
A gentle face—the face of one long
dead—
Looks at me from the wall, where round
its head
The night-lamp casts a halo of pale
light.
Here in this room she died; and soul more
white
Never through martyrdom of fire was
led
To its repose; nor can in books be read
The legend of a life more benedight.
There is a mountain in the distant West,
That, sun-defying, in its deep ravines
Displays a cross of snow upon its side.

Such is the cross I wear upon my breast
These eighteen years, through all the
changing scenes
And seasons, changeless since the day
she died.

From
EVANGELINE [1]
[1847]

IV

Far in the West there lies a desert land,
where the mountains
Lift, through perpetual snows, their lofty
and luminous summits.
Down from their jagged, deep ravines,
where the gorge, like a gateway,
Opens a passage rude to the wheels of the
emigrant's wagon,
Westward the Oregon flows and the Walle-
way and Owyhee.   5
Eastward, with devious course, among the
Wind-river Mountains,
Through the Sweet-water Valley precipi-
tate leaps the Nebraska;
And to the south, from the Fontaine-qui-
bout and the Spanish sierras,
Fretted with sands and rocks, and swept
by the wind of the desert,

---

[3] Massachusetts town which was Whittier's home, except for brief intervals,
from 1840 until his death in 1892. See
the introductory essay on Whittier in this
volume.

[4] Frances Appleton, Longfellow's second wife, died on July 10, 1861, from the
effects of burns caused by an accidental
fire in the library of Craigie House, the
Longfellows' home.

[1] The French inhabitants of rural Acadia
or Acadie (now known as Nova Scotia)
were expelled from their homes by the
British in 1755, as an incident of the
French and Indian War, and widely dispersed. A considerable number of them
found refuge in Louisiana. The story of
one of these exiles, Evangeline Bellefon-
taine, who was separated from her betrothed, Gabriel Lajeunesse, and sought
him for many years, was given to Longfellow by Hawthorne, who had received it
from a Boston clergyman.

Numberless torrents, with ceaseless sound,
    descend to the ocean,   10
Like the great chords of a harp, in loud
    and solemn vibrations.
Spreading between these streams are the
    wondrous, beautiful prairies,
Billowy bays of grass ever rolling in
    shadow and sunshine,
Bright with luxuriant clusters of roses and
    purple amorphas.
Over them wandered the buffalo herds, and
    the elk and the roebuck;   15
Over them wandered the wolves, and herds
    of riderless horses;
Fires that blast and blight, and winds that
    are weary with travel;
Over them wander the scattered tribes of
    Ishmael's children,
Staining the desert with blood; and above
    their terrible war-trails
Circles and sails aloft, on pinions majestic,
    the vulture,   20
Like the implacable soul of a chieftain
    slaughtered in battle,
By invisible stairs ascending and scaling
    the heavens.
Here and there rise smokes from the camps
    of these savage marauders;
Here and there rise groves from the mar-
    gins of swift-running rivers;
And the grim, taciturn bear, the anchorite
    monk of the desert,   25
Climbs down their dark ravines to dig for
    roots by the brook-side,
And over all is the sky, the clear and
    crystalline heaven,
Like the protecting hand of God inverted
    above them.

Into this wonderful land, at the base of
    the Ozark Mountains,
Gabriel far had entered, with hunters and
    trappers behind him.   30
Day after day, with their Indian guides,
    the maiden and Basil [2]
Followed his flying steps, and thought each
    day to o'ertake him.
Sometimes they saw, or thought they saw,
    the smoke of his camp-fire

Rise in the morning air from the distant
    plain; but at nightfall,
When they had reached the place, they
    found only embers and ashes.   35
And though their hearts were sad at times
    and their bodies were weary,
Hope still guided them on, as the magic
    Fata Morgana
Showed them her lakes of light, that re-
    treated and vanished before them.

    Once, as they sat by their evening fire,
    there silently entered
Into the little camp an Indian woman,
    whose features   40
Wore deep traces of sorrow, and patience
    as great as her sorrow.
She was a Shawnee woman returning home
    to her people,
From the far-off hunting-grounds of the
    cruel Comanches,
Where her Canadian husband, a coureur-
    des-bois,[3] had been murdered.
Touched were their hearts at her story, and
    warmest and friendliest welcome 45
Gave they, with words of cheer, and she
    sat and feasted among them
On the buffalo-meat and the venison cooked
    on the embers.
But when their meal was done, and Basil
    and all his companions,
Worn with the long day's march and the
    chase of the deer and the bison,
Stretched themselves on the ground, and
    slept where the quivering fire-light 50
Flashed on their swarthy cheeks, and their
    forms wrapped up in their blankets,
Then at the door of Evangeline's tent she
    sat and repeated
Slowly, with soft, low voice, and the charm
    of her Indian accent,
All the tale of her love, with its pleasures,
    and pains, and reverses.
Much Evangeline wept at the tale, and to
    know that another   55

---

[2] Gabriel's father, whom Evangeline had
found in Louisiana.

[3] French-Canadian name for a hunter
and trapper.

Hapless heart like her own had loved and
 had been disappointed.
Moved to the depths of her soul by pity
 and woman's compassion,
Yet in her sorrow pleased that one who had
 suffered was near her,
She in turn related her love and all its
 disasters.
Mute with wonder the Shawnee sat, and
 when she had ended   60
Still was mute; but at length, as if a
 mysterious horror
Passed through her brain, she spake, and
 repeated the tale of the Mowis;
Mowis, the bridegroom of snow, who won
 and wedded a maiden,
But, when the morning came, arose and
 passed from the wigwam,
Fading and melting away and dissolving
 into the sunshine,   65
Till she beheld him no more, though she
 followed far into the forest.
Then, in those sweet, low tones, that seemed
 like a weird incantation,
Told she the tale of the fair Lilinau, who
 was wooed by a phantom,
That, through the pines o'er her father's
 lodge, in the hush of the twilight,
Breathed like the evening wind, and whis-
 pered love to the maiden,   70
Till she followed his green and waving
 plume through the forest,
And nevermore returned, nor was seen
 again by her people.
Silent with wonder and strange surprise,
 Evangeline listened
To the soft flow of her magical words, till
 the region around her
Seemed like enchanted ground, and her
 swarthy guest the enchantress. 75
Slowly over the tops of the Ozark Moun-
 tains the moon rose,
Lighting the little tent, and with a mys-
 terious splendor
Touching the sombre leaves, and embrac-
 ing and filling the woodland.
With a delicious sound the brook rushed
 by, and the branches
Swayed and sighed overhead in scarcely
 audible whispers.   80

Filled with the thoughts of love was Evangeline's heart, but a secret,
Subtile sense crept in of pain and indefinite terror,
As the cold, poisonous snake creeps into
 the nest of the swallow.
It was no earthly fear. A breath from the
 region of spirits
Seemed to float in the air of night; and
 she felt for a moment   85
That, like the Indian maid, she, too, was
 pursuing a phantom.
With this thought she slept, and the fear
 and the phantom had vanished.

Early upon the morrow the march was
 resumed, and the Shawnee
Said, as they journeyed along,—"On the
 western slope of these mountains
Dwells in his little village the Black Robe
 chief of the Mission.   90
Much he teaches the people, and tells them
 of Mary and Jesus;
Loud laugh their hearts with joy, and weep
 with pain, as they hear him."
Then, with a sudden and secret emotion,
 Evangeline answered,
"Let us go to the Mission, for there good
 tidings await us!"
Thither they turned their steeds; and be-
 hind a spur of the mountains, 95
Just as the sun went down, they heard a
 murmur of voices,
And in a meadow green and broad, by the
 bank of a river,
Saw the tents of the Christians, the tents
 of the Jesuit Mission.
Under a towering oak, that stood in the
 midst of the village,
Knelt the Black Robe chief with his chil-
 dren. A crucifix fastened   100
High on the trunk of the tree, and overshadowed by grapevines,
Looked with its agonized face on the multitude kneeling beneath it.
This was their rural chapel. Aloft, through
 the intricate arches
Of its aerial roof, arose the chant of their
 vespers,
Mingling its notes with the soft susurrus

and sighs of the branches.   105
Silent, with heads uncovered, the travellers,
    nearer approaching,
Knelt on the swarded floor, and joined in
    the evening devotions.
But when the service was done, and the
    benediction had fallen
Forth from the hands of the priest, like
    seed from the hands of the sower,
Slowly the reverend man advanced to the
    strangers and bade them   110
Welcome; and when they replied, he smiled
    with benignant expression,
Hearing the homelike sounds of his mother-
    tongue in the forest,
And, with words of kindness, conducted
    them into his wigwam.
There upon mats and skins they reposed,
    and on cakes of the maize-ear
Feasted, and slaked their thirst from the
    water-gourd of the teacher.   115
Soon was their story told; and the priest
    with solemnity answered:—
"Not six suns have risen and set since
    Gabriel, seated
On this mat by my side, where now the
    maiden reposes,
Told me this same sad tale; then arose and
    continued his journey!"
Soft was the voice of the priest, and he
    spake with an accent of kind-
    ness;   120
But on Evangeline's heart fell his words as
    in winter the snow-flakes
Fall into some lone nest from which the
    birds have departed.
"Far to the north he has gone," continued
    the priest; "but in autumn,
When the chase is done, will return again
    to the Mission."
Then Evangeline said, and her voice was
    meek and submissive,   125
"Let me remain with thee, for my soul is
    sad and afflicted."
So seemed it wise and well unto all; and
    betimes on the morrow,
Mounting his Mexican steed, with his In-
    dian guides and companions,
Homeward Basil returned, and Evangeline
    stayed at the Mission.

Slowly, slowly, slowly the days succeeded
    each other,—   130
Days and weeks and months; and the
    fields of maize that were springing
Green from the ground when a stranger
    she came, now waving about her,
Lifted their slender shafts, with leaves in-
    terlacing, and forming
Cloisters for mendicant crows and gran-
    aries pillaged by squirrels.
Then in the golden weather the maize was
    husked, and the maidens   135
Blushed at each blood-red ear, for that
    betokened a lover,
But at the crooked laughed, and called it
    a thief in the corn-field.
Even the blood-red ear to Evangeline
    brought not her lover.
"Patience!" the priest would say; "have
    faith, and thy prayer will be an-
    swered!
Look at this vigorous plant that lifts its
    head from the meadow,   140
See how its leaves are turned to the north,
    as true as the magnet;
This is the compass-flower, that the finger
    of God has planted
Here in the houseless wild, to direct the
    traveller's journey
Over the sea-like, pathless, limitless waste
    of the desert.
Such in the soul of man is faith. The blos-
    soms of passion,   145
Gay and luxuriant flowers, are brighter and
    fuller of fragrance,
But they beguile us, and lead us astray,
    and their odor is deadly.
Only this humble plant can guide us here,
    and hereafter
Crown us with asphodel flowers, that are
    wet with the dews of nepenthe."

So came the autumn, and passed, and the
    winter,—yet Gabriel came not;   150
Blossomed the opening spring, and the
    notes of the robin and bluebird
Sounded sweet upon wold and in wood, yet
    Gabriel came not.
But on the breath of the summer winds a
    rumor was wafted

Sweeter than song of bird, or hue or odor
   of blossom.
Far to the north and east, it said, in the
   Michigan forests,   155
Gabriel had his lodge by the banks of the
   Saginaw River.
And, with returning guides, that sought the
   lakes of St. Lawrence,
Saying a sad farewell, Evangeline went
   from the Mission.
When over weary ways, by long and peril-
   ous marches,
She had attained at length the depths of
   the Michigan forests,   160
Found she the hunter's lodge deserted and
   fallen to ruin!

   Thus did the long sad years glide on,
      and in seasons and places
Divers and distant far was seen the wander-
   ing maiden;—
Now in the Tents of Grace of the meek
   Moravian Missions,
Now in the noisy camps and the battle-
   fields of the army,   165
Now in secluded hamlets, and towns and
   populous cities.
Like a phantom she came, and passed away
   unremembered.
Fair was she and young, when in hope
   began the long journey;
Faded was she and old, when in disap-
   pointment it ended.
Each succeeding year stole something away
   from her beauty,   170
Leaving behind it, broader and deeper, the
   gloom and the shadow.
Then there appeared and spread faint
   streaks of gray o'er her forehead,
Dawn of another life, that broke o'er her
   earthly horizon,
As in the eastern sky the first faint streaks
   of the morning.

V

   In that delightful land which is washed
      by the Delaware's waters,   175
Guarding in sylvan shades the name of
   Penn the apostle,

Stands on the banks of its beautiful stream
   the city he founded.
There all the air is balm, and the peach
   is the emblem of beauty,
And the streets still reëcho the names of
   the trees of the forest,
As if they fain would appease the Dryads
   whose haunts they molested.   180
There from the troubled sea had Evangeline landed, an exile,
Finding among the children of Penn a
   home and a country.
There old René Leblanc [4] had died; and
   when he departed,
Saw at his side only one of all his hundred
   descendants.
Something at least there was in the friendly
   streets of the city,   185
Something that spake to her heart, and
   made her no longer a stranger;
And her ear was pleased with the Thee
   and Thou of the Quakers,
For it recalled the past, the old Acadian
   country,
Where all men were equal, and all were
   brothers and sisters.
So, when the fruitless search, the disap-
   pointed endeavor,   190
Ended, to recommence no more upon earth,
   uncomplaining,
Thither, as leaves to the light, were turned
   her thoughts and her footsteps.
As from a mountain's top the rainy mists
   of the morning
Roll away, and afar we behold the landscape below us,
Sun-illumined, with shining rivers and cities
   and hamlets,   195
So fell the mists from her mind, and she
   saw the world far below her,
Dark no longer, but all illumined with love;
   and the pathway
Which she had climbed so far, lying smooth
   and fair in the distance.
Gabriel was not forgotten. Within her heart
   was his image,

---

[4] The "worthy notary" who recorded the
betrothal of Evangeline and Gabriel before
the exile.

Clothed in the beauty of love and youth,
    as last she beheld him,   200
Only more beautiful made by his deathlike
    silence and absence.
Into her thoughts of him time entered not,
    for it was not.
Over him years had no power; he was not
    changed, but transfigured;
He had become to her heart as one who is
    dead, and not absent;
Patience and abnegation of self, and devo-
    tion to others,   205
This was the lesson a life of trial and sor-
    row had taught her.
So was her love diffused, but, like to some
    odorous spices,
Suffered no waste nor loss, though filling
    the air with aroma.
Other hope had she none, nor wish in life,
    but to follow,
Meekly, with reverent steps, the sacred feet
    of her Saviour.   210
Thus many years she lived as a Sister of
    Mercy; frequenting
Lonely and wretched roofs in the crowded
    lanes of the city,
Where distress and want concealed them-
    selves from the sunlight,
Where disease and sorrow in garrets lan-
    guished neglected.
Night after night when the world was
    asleep, as the watchman repeated 215
Loud, through the gusty streets, that all
    was well in the city,
High at some lonely window he saw the
    light of her taper.
Day after day, in the gray of the dawn,
    as slow through the suburbs
Plodded the German farmer, with flowers
    and fruits for the market,
Met he that meek, pale face, returning
    home from its watchings.   220

Then it came to pass that a pestilence [5]
    fell on the city,
Presaged by wondrous signs, and mostly by
    flocks of wild pigeons,
Darkening the sun in their flight, with
    naught in their craws but an acorn.

And, as the tides of the sea arise in the
    month of September,
Flooding some silver stream, till it spreads
    to a lake in the meadow,   225
So death flooded life, and, o'erflowing its
    natural margin,
Spread to a brackish lake the silver stream
    of existence.
Wealth had no power to bribe, nor beauty
    to charm the oppressor;
But all perished alike beneath the scourge
    of his anger;—
Only, alas! the poor, who had neither
    friends nor attendants,   230
Crept away to die in the almshouse, home
    of the homeless.
Then in the suburbs it stood, in the midst
    of meadows and woodlands;—
Now the city surrounds it; but still, with
    its gateway and wicket
Meek, in the midst of splendor, its humble
    walls seem to echo
Softly the words of the Lord:—"The poor
    ye always have with you."   235
Thither, by night and by day, came the
    Sister of Mercy. The dying
Looked up into her face, and thought, in-
    deed, to behold there
Gleams of celestial light encircle her fore-
    head with splendor,
Such as the artist paints o'er the brows
    of saints and apostles,
Or such as hangs by night o'er a city seen
    at a distance.   240
Unto their eyes it seemed the lamps of the
    city celestial,
Into whose shining gates erelong their
    spirits would enter.

Thus, on a Sabbath morn, through the
    streets, deserted and silent,
Wending her quiet way, she entered the
    door of the almshouse.
Sweet on the summer air was the odor of
    flowers in the garden,   245
And she paused on her way to gather the
    fairest among them,

[5] The epidemic of yellow fever in Philadelphia, 1793.

That the dying once more might rejoice
  in their fragrance and beauty.
Then, as she mounted the stairs to the
  corridors, cooled by the east-wind,
Distant and soft on her ear fell the chimes
  from the belfry of Christ Church,
While, intermingled with these, across the
  meadows were wafted   250
Sounds of psalms, that were sung by the
  Swedes in their church at Wicaco.
Soft as descending wings fell the calm of
  the hour on her spirit;
Something within her said, "At length thy
  trials are ended;"
And, with light in her looks, she entered
  the chambers of sickness.
Noiselessly moved about the assiduous, care-
  ful attendants,   255
Moistening the feverish lip, and the aching
  brow, and in silence
Closing the sightless eyes of the dead, and
  concealing their faces,
Where on their pallets they lay, like drifts
  of snow by the roadside.
Many a languid head, upraised as Evan-
  geline entered,
Turned on its pillow of pain to gaze while
  she passed, for her presence   260
Fell on their hearts like a ray of the sun
  on the walls of a prison.
And, as she looked around, she saw how
  Death, the consoler,
Laying his hand upon many a heart, had
  healed it forever.
Many familiar forms had disappeared in
  the night time;
Vacant their places were, or filled already
  by strangers.   265

Suddenly, as if arrested by fear or a
  feeling of wonder,
Still she stood, with her colorless lips apart,
  while a shudder
Ran through her frame, and, forgotten, the
  flowerets dropped from her fingers,
And from her eyes and cheeks the light
  and bloom of the morning.
Then there escaped from her lips a cry of
  such terrible anguish,   270

That the dying heard it, and started up
  from their pillows.
On the pallet before her was stretched the
  form of an old man.
Long, and thin, and gray were the locks
  that shaded his temples;
But, as he lay in the morning light, his
  face for a moment
Seemed to assume once more the forms of
  its earlier manhood;   275
So are wont to be changed the faces of
  those who are dying.
Hot and red on his lips still burned the
  flush of the fever,
As if life, like the Hebrew, with blood had
  besprinkled its portals,
That the Angel of Death might see the
  sign, and pass over.
Motionless, senseless, dying, he lay, and
  his spirit exhausted   280
Seemed to be sinking down through infinite
  depths in the darkness,
Darkness of slumber and death, forever
  sinking and sinking.
Then through those realms of shade, in
  multiplied reverberations,
Heard he that cry of pain, and through
  the hush that succeeded
Whispered a gentle voice, in accents tender
  and saint-like,   285
"Gabriel! O my beloved!" and died away
  into silence.
Then he beheld, in a dream, once more the
  home of his childhood;
Green Acadian meadows, with sylvan rivers
  among them,
Village, and mountain, and woodlands; and,
  walking under their shadow,
As in the days of her youth, Evangeline
  rose in his vision.   290
Tears came into his eyes; and as slowly
  he lifted his eyelids,
Vanished the vision away, but Evangeline
  knelt by his bedside.
Vainly he strove to whisper her name, for
  the accents unuttered
Died on his lips, and their motion revealed
  what his tongue would have spoken.
Vainly he strove to rise; and Evangeline,
  kneeling beside him,   295

Kissed his dying lips, and laid his head
on her bosom.
Sweet was the light of his eyes; but it
suddenly sank into darkness,
As when a lamp is blown out by a gust of
wind at a casement.

All was ended now, the hope, and the
fear, and the sorrow,
All the aching of heart, the restless, unsatisfied longing,   300
All the dull, deep pain, and constant anguish of patience!
And, as she pressed once more the lifeless
head to her bosom,
Meekly she bowed her own, and murmured, "Father, I thank thee!"

Still stands the forest primeval; but far
away from its shadow,
Side by side, in their nameless graves, the
lovers are sleeping.   305
Under the humble walls of the little
Catholic churchyard,
In the heart of the city, they lie, unknown
and unnoticed.
Daily the tides of life go ebbing and flow-
ing beside them,
Thousands of throbbing hearts, where theirs
are at rest and forever,
Thousands of aching brains, where theirs
no longer are busy,   310
Thousands of toiling hands, where theirs
have ceased from their labors,
Thousands of weary feet, where theirs have
completed their journey!

Still stands the forest primeval; but
under the shade of its branches
Dwells another race, with other customs
and language.
Only along the shore of the mournful and
misty Atlantic   315
Linger a few Acadian peasants, whose
fathers from exile
Wandered back to their native land to die
in its bosom.
In the fisherman's cot the wheel and the
loom are still busy;

Maidens still wear their Norman caps and
their kirtles of homespun,
And by the evening fire repeat Evangeline's
story,   320
While from its rocky caverns the deep-
voiced, neighboring ocean
Speaks, and in accents disconsolate answers the wail of the forest.

From
THE SONG OF HIAWATHA [1]
[1855]

INTRODUCTION

Should you ask me, whence these stories?
Whence these legends and traditions,
With the odors of the forest,
With the dew and damp of meadows,
With the curling smoke of wigwams,   5
With the rushing of great rivers,
With their frequent repetitions,
And their wild reverberations,

[1] *The Song of Hiawatha*—This Indian
Edda—if I may so call it—is founded on a
tradition prevalent among the North American Indians, of a personage of miraculous
birth, who was sent among them to clear
their rivers, forests, and fishing-grounds,
and to teach them the arts of peace. He
was known among different tribes by the
several names of Michabou, Chiabo, Ma-
nabozo, Tarenyawagon, and Hiawatha. Mr.
Schoolcraft gives an account of him in his
Algic Researches, Vol. I, p. 134; and in
his *History, Condition, and Prospects of
the Indian Tribes of the United States*,
Part III, p. 314, may be found the Iroquois form of the tradition, derived from
the verbal narrations of an Onondaga
chief.
    Into this old tradition I have woven
other curious Indian legends, drawn chiefly
from the various and valuable writings
of Mr. Schoolcraft, to whom the literary
world is greatly indebted for his indefatigable zeal in rescuing from oblivion so
much of the legendary lore of the Indians.
    The scene of the poem is among the
Ojibways on the southern shore of Lake
Superior, in the region between the Pictured Rocks and the Grand Sable.—Longfellow's note.

As of thunder in the mountains?

I should answer, I should tell you,   10
"From the forests and the prairies,
From the great lakes of the Northland,
From the land of the Ojibways,
From the land of the Dacotahs,
From the mountains, moors, and fen-
    lands,   15
Where the heron, the Shuh-shuh-gah
Feeds among the reeds and rushes.
I repeat them as I heard them
From the lips of Nawadaha,
The musician, the sweet singer."   20
Should you ask where Nawadaha
Found these songs so wild and wayward,
Found these legends and traditions,
I should answer, I should tell you,
"In the bird's-nests of the forest,   25
In the lodges of the beaver,
In the hoof-prints of the bison,
In the eyry of the eagle!

"All the wild-fowl sang them to him,
In the moorlands and the fen-lands,   30
In the melancholy marshes;
Chetowaik, the plover, sang them,
Mahn, the loon, the wild goose, Wawa,
The blue heron, the Shuh-shuh-gah,
And the grouse, the Mushkodasa!"   35
If still further you should ask me,
Saying, "Who was Nawadaha?
Tell us of this Nawadaha,"
I should answer your inquiries
Straightway in such words as follow.   40
"In the Vale of Tawasentha,[2]
In the green and silent valley,
By the pleasant water-courses,
Dwelt the singer Nawadaha.
Round about the Indian village   45
Spread the meadows and the cornfields,
And beyond them stood the forest,
Stood the groves of singing pine-trees,
Green in Summer, white in Winter,
Ever sighing, ever singing.   50
"And the pleasant water-courses,
You could trace them through the valley,
By the rushing in the Spring-time,
By the alders in the Summer,
By the white fog in the Autumn,   55
By the black line in the Winter;
And beside them dwelt the singer,

In the vale of Tawasentha,
In the green and silent valley.
"There he sang of Hiawatha,   60
Sang the Song of Hiawatha,
Sang his wondrous birth and being,
How he prayed and how he fasted,
How he lived, and toiled, and suffered,
That the tribes of men might prosper,   65
That he might advance his people!"
Ye who love the haunts of Nature,
Love the sunshine of the meadow,
Love the shadow of the forest,
Love the wind among the branches,   70
And the rain-shower and the snow-storm,
And the rushing of great rivers
Through their palisades of pine-trees,
And the thunder in the mountains,
Whose innumerable echoes   75
Flap like eagles in their eyries;—
Listen to these wild traditions,
To this Song of Hiawatha!
Ye who love a nation's legends,
Love the ballads of a people,   80
That like voices from afar off
Call to us to pause and listen,
Speak in tones so plain and childlike,
Scarcely can the ear distinguish
Whether they are sung or spoken;—   85
Listen to this Indian Legend,
To this Song of Hiawatha!
Ye whose hearts are fresh and simple,
Who have faith in God and Nature,
Who believe that in all ages   90
Every human heart is human,
That in even savage bosoms
There are longings, yearnings, strivings
For the good they comprehend not,
That the feeble hands and helpless,   95
Groping blindly in the darkness,
Touch God's right hand in that darkness
And are lifted up and strengthened;—
Listen to this simple story,
To this song of Hiawatha!   100
Ye who sometimes, in your rambles
Through the green lanes of the country,
Where the tangled barberry-bushes
Hang their tufts of crimson berries

---

[2] Now known as Norman's Kill, in Albany County, New York.

Over stone walls gray with mosses,   105
Pause by some neglected graveyard,
For a while to muse, and ponder
On a half-effaced inscription,
Written with little skill of song-craft,
Homely phrases, but each letter   110
Full of hope and yet of heart-break,
Full of all the tender pathos
Of the Here and the Hereafter;—
Stay and read this rude inscription,
Read this song of Hiawatha!   115

HIAWATHA'S FASTING

You shall hear how Hiawatha
Prayed and fasted in the forest,
Not for greater skill in hunting,
Not for greater craft in fishing,
Not for triumphs in the battle,   5
And renown among the warriors,
But for profit of the people,
For advantage of the nations.
  First he built a lodge for fasting,
Built a wigwam in the forest,   10
By the shining Big-Sea-Water,
In the blithe and pleasant Spring-time,
In the Moon of Leaves he built it,
And, with dreams and visions many,
Seven whole days and nights he fasted.   15
  On the first day of his fasting
Through the leafy woods he wandered;
Saw the deer start from the thicket,
Saw the rabbit in his burrow,
Heard the pheasant, Bena, drumming,
Heard the squirrel, Adjidaumo,
Rattling in his hoard of acorns,
Saw the pigeon, the Omeme,
Building nests among the pine-trees,
And in flocks the wild goose, Wawa,   25
Flying to the fen-lands northward,
Whirring, wailing far above him.
"Master of Life!" he cried, desponding,
"Must our lives depend on these things?"
  On the next day of his fasting   30
By the river's brink he wandered,
Through the Muskoday, the meadow,
Saw the wild rice, Mahnomonee,
Saw the blueberry, Meenahga,
And the strawberry, Odahmin,   35
And the gooseberry, Shahbomin,

And the grape-vine, the Bemahgut,
Trailing o'er the alder-branches,
Filling all the air with fragrance!
"Master of Life!" he cried, desponding,   40
"Must our lives depend on these things?"
  On the third day of his fasting
By the lake he sat and pondered,
By the still, transparent water;
Saw the sturgeon, Nahma, leaping,   45
Scattering drops like beads of wampum,
Saw the yellow perch, the Sahwa,
Like a sunbeam in the water,
Saw the pike, the Maskenozha,
And the herring, Okahahwis,   50
And the Shawgashee, the craw-fish!
"Master of Life!" he cried, desponding,
"Must our lives depend on these things?"
  On the fourth day of his fasting
In his lodge he lay exhausted;   55
From his couch of leaves and branches
Gazing with half-open eyelids,
Full of shadowy dreams and visions,
On the dizzy, swimming landscape,
On the gleaming of the water,   60
On the splendor of the sunset.
  And he saw a youth approaching,
Dressed in garments green and yellow,
Coming through the purple twilight,
Through the splendor of the sunset;   65
Plumes of green bent o'er his forehead,
And his hair was soft and golden.
  Standing at the open doorway,
Long he looked at Hiawatha,
Looked with pity and compassion   70
On his wasted form and features,
And, in accents like the sighing
Of the South-Wind in the tree-tops,
Said he, "O my Hiawatha!
All your prayers are heard in heaven,   75
For you pray not like the others;
Not for greater skill in hunting,
Not for greater craft in fishing,
Not for triumph in the battle,
Nor renown among the warriors,   80
But for profit of the people,
For advantage of the nations.
  "From the Master of Life descending,
I, the friend of man, Mondamin,
Come to warn you and instruct you,   85
How by struggle and by labor

You shall gain what you have prayed for.
Rise up from your bed of branches,
Rise, O youth, and wrestle with me!"

Faint with famine, Hiawatha   90
Started from his bed of branches,
From the twilight of his wigwam
Forth into the flush of sunset
Came, and wrestled with Mondamin;
At his touch he felt new courage   95
Throbbing in his brain and bosom,
Felt new life and hope and vigor
Run through every nerve and fibre.

So they wrestled there together
In the glory of the sunset,   100
And the more they strove and struggled,
Stronger still grew Hiawatha;
Till the darkness fell around them,
And the heron, the Shuh-shuh-gah,
From her nest among the pine-trees,   105
Gave a cry of lamentation,
Gave a scream of pain and famine.

" 'Tis enough!" then said Mondamin,
Smiling upon Hiawatha,
"But to-morrow, when the sun sets,   110
I will come again to try you."
And he vanished, and was seen not;
Whether sinking as the rain sinks,
Whether rising as the mists rise,
Hiawatha saw not, knew not,   115
Only saw that he had vanished,
Leaving him alone and fainting,
With the misty lake below him,
And the reeling stars above him.

On the morrow and the next day,   120
When the sun through heaven descending,
Like a red and burning cinder
From the hearth of the Great Spirit,
Fell into the western waters,
Came Mondamin for the trial,   125
For the strife with Hiawatha;
Came as silent as the dew comes,
From the empty air appearing,
Into empty air returning,
Taking shape when earth it touches   130
But invisible to all men
In its coming and its going.

Thrice they wrestled there together
In the glory of the sunset,
Till the darkness fell around them,   135
Till the heron, the Shuh-shuh-gah,

From her nest among the pine-trees,
Uttered her loud cry of famine,
And Mondamin paused to listen.

Tall and beautiful he stood there,   140
In his garments green and yellow;
To and fro his plumes above him
Waved and nodded with his breathing,
And the sweat of the encounter
Stood like drops of dew upon him.   145

And he cried, "O Hiawatha!
Bravely have you wrestled with me,
Thrice have wrestled stoutly with me,
And the Master of Life, who sees us,
He will give to you the triumph!"   150

Then he smiled and said: "To-morrow
Is the last day of your conflict,
Is the last day of your fasting.
You will conquer and o'ercome me;
Make a bed for me to lie in,   155
Where the rain may fall upon me,
Where the sun may come and warm me;
Strip these garments, green and yellow,
Strip this nodding plumage from me,
Lay me in the earth and make it   160
Soft and loose and light above me.

"Let no hand disturb my slumber,
Let no weed nor worm molest me,
Let not Kahgahgee, the raven,
Come to haunt me and molest me,   165
Only come yourself to watch me,
Till I wake, and start, and quicken,
Till I leap into the sunshine."

And thus saying, he departed;
Peacefully slept Hiawatha,   170
But he heard the Wawonaissa,
Heard the whippoorwill complaining,
Perched upon his lonely wigwam;
Heard the rushing Sebowisha,
Heard the rivulet rippling near him, 175
Talking to the darksome forest;
Heard the sighing of the branches,
As they lifted and subsided
At the passing of the night-wind,
Heard them, as one hears in slumber   180
Far-off murmurs, dreamy whispers:
Peacefully slept Hiawatha.

On the morrow came Nokomis,[1]

---

[1] Hiawatha's grandmother and foster
parent.

On the seventh day of his fasting,
Came with food for Hiawatha,   185
Came imploring and bewailing,
Lest his hunger should o'ercome him,
Lest his fasting should be fatal.

But he tasted not, and touched not,
Only said to her, "Nokomis,   190
Wait until the sun is setting,
Till the darkness falls around us,
Till the heron, the Shuh-shuh-gah,
Crying from the desolate marshes,
Tells us that the day is ended."   195
Homeward weeping went Nokomis,
Sorrowing for her Hiawatha,
Fearing lest his strength should fail him,
Lest his fasting should be fatal.
He meanwhile sat weary waiting   200
For the coming of Mondamin,
Till the shadows, pointing eastward,
Lengthened over field and forest,
Till the sun dropped from the heaven,
Floating on the waters westward,   205
As a red leaf in the Autumn
Falls and floats upon the water,
Falls and sinks into its bosom.

And behold! the young Mondamin,
With his soft and shining tresses,   210
With his garments green and yellow,
With his long and glossy plumage,
Stood and beckoned at the doorway.
And as one in slumber walking,
Pale and haggard, but undaunted,   215
From the wigwam Hiawatha
Came and wrestled with Mondamin.

Round about him spun the landscape,
Sky and forest reeled together,
And his strong heart leaped within him, 220
As the sturgeon leaps and struggles
In a net to break its meshes.
Like a ring of fire around him
Blazed and flared the red horizon,
And a hundred suns seemed looking   225
At the combat of the wrestlers.

Suddenly upon the greensward
All alone stood Hiawatha,
Panting with his wild exertion,
Palpitating with the struggle;   230
And before him, breathless, lifeless,
Lay the youth, with hair dishevelled,
Plumage torn, and garments tattered,

Dead he lay there in the sunset.
And victorious Hiawatha   235
Made the grave as he commanded,
Stripped the garments from Mondamin,
Stripped his tattered plumage from him,
Laid him in the earth, and made it
Soft and loose and light above him; 240
And the heron, the Shuh-shuh-gah,
From the melancholy moorlands,
Gave a cry of lamentation,
Gave a cry of pain and anguish!

Homeward then went Hiawatha   245
To the lodge of old Nokomis,
And the seven days of his fasting
Were accomplished and completed.
But the place was not forgotten
Where he wrestled with Mondamin;   250
Nor forgotten nor neglected
Was the grave where lay Mondamin,
Sleeping in the rain and sunshine,
Where his scattered plumes and garments
Faded in the rain and sunshine.   255

Day by day did Hiawatha
Go to wait and watch beside it;
Kept the dark mould soft above it,
Kept it clean from weeds and insects,
Drove away, with scoffs and shoutings, 260
Kahgahgee, the king of ravens.

Till at length a small green feather
From the earth shot slowly upward,
Then another and another,
And before the Summer ended   265
Stood the maize in all its beauty,
With its shining robes about it,
And its long, soft, yellow tresses;
And in rapture Hiawatha
Cried aloud, "It is Mondamin!   270
Yes, the friend of man, Mondamin!"

Then he called to old Nokomis
And Iagoo, the great boaster,
Showed them where the maize was growing
Told them of his wondrous vision,   275
Of his wrestling and his triumph,
Of this new gift to the nations,
Which should be their food forever.

And still later, when the Autumn
Changed the long, green leaves to yel-
  low,   280
And the soft and juicy kernels
Grew like wampum hard and yellow,

Then the ripened ears he gathered,
Stripped the withered husks from off them,
As he once had stripped the wrestler, 285
Gave the first Feast of Mondamin,
And made known unto the people
This new gift of the Great Spirit.

From
TALES OF A WAYSIDE INN
[1863]

THE SICILIAN'S TALE

KING ROBERT OF SICILY

Robert of Sicily, brother of Pope Urbane
And Valmond, Emperor of Allemaine,
Appareled in magnificent attire,
With retinue of many a knight and squire,
On St. John's eve, at vespers, proudly
    sat   5
And heard the priests chant the Magnificat.
And as he listened, o'er and o'er again
Repeated, like a burden or refrain,
He caught the words, *"Deposuit potentes
De sede, et exaltavit humiles";*   10
And slowly lifting up his kingly head
He to a learned clerk beside him said,
"What mean these words?" The clerk made
    answer meet,
"He has put down the mighty from their
    seat,
And has exalted them of low degree." 15
Thereat King Robert muttered scornfully,
" 'Tis well that such seditious words are
    sung
Only by priests and in the Latin tongue;
For unto priests and people be it known,
There is no power can push me from my
    throne!"   20
And leaning back, he yawned and fell
    asleep,
Lulled by the chant monotonous and deep.

When he awoke, it was already night;
The church was empty, and there was no
    light,
Save where the lamps, that glimmered few
    and faint,   25
Lighted a little space before some saint.

He started from his seat and gazed around,
But saw no living thing and heard no
    sound.
He groped towards the door, but it was
    locked;
He cried aloud, and listened, and then
    knocked,   30
And uttered awful threatenings and com-
    plaints,
And imprecations upon men and saints.
The sounds reëchoed from the roof and
    walls
As if dead priests were laughing in their
    stalls!

At length the sexton, hearing from with-
    out   35
The tumult of the knocking and the shout,
And thinking thieves were in the house of
    prayer,
Came with his lantern, asking, "Who is
    there?"
Half choked with rage, King Robert fierce-
    ly said,
"Open: 'tis I, the King! Art thou
    afraid?"   40
The frightened sexton, muttering, with a
    curse,
"This is some drunken vagabond, or
    worse!"
Turned the great key and flung the portal
    wide;
A man rushed by him at a single stride,
Haggard, half naked, without hat or
    cloak,   45
Who neither turned, nor looked at him, nor
    spoke,
But leaped into the blackness of the night,
And vanished like a specter from his sight.

Robert of Sicily, brother of Pope Urbane
And Valmond, Emperor of Allemaine, 50
Despoiled of his magnificent attire,
Bareheaded, breathless, and besprent with
    mire,
With sense of wrong and outrage desperate,
Strode on and thundered at the palace
    gate;
Rushed through the courtyard, thrusting
    in his rage   55

To right and left each seneschal and page,
And hurried up the broad and sounding
    stair
His white face ghastly in the torches' glare.
From hall to hall he passed with breathless
    speed;
Voices and cries he heard, but did not
    heed,   60
Until at last he reached the banquet-room,
Blazing with light, and breathing with per-
    fume.

There on the dais sat another king,
Wearing his robes, his crown, his signet-
    ring,
King Robert's self in features, form, and
    height,   65
But all transfigured with angelic light!
It was an Angel; and his presence there
With a divine effulgence filled the air,
An exaltation, piercing the disguise,
Though none the hidden Angel recog-
    nize.   70

A moment speechless, motionless, amazed,
The throneless monarch on the Angel
    gazed,
Who met his looks of anger and surprise
With the divine compassion of his eyes;
Then said, "Who art thou? and why com'st
    thou here?"   75
To which King Robert answered with a
    sneer,
"I am the King, and come to claim my own
From an impostor, who usurps my throne!"
And suddenly, at these audacious words,
Up sprang the angry guests, and drew their
    swords;   80
The Angel answered, with unruffled brow,
"Nay, not the King, but the King's Jester,
    thou
Henceforth shalt wear the bells and scal-
    loped cape,
And for thy counselor shalt lead an ape;
Thou shalt obey my servants when they
    call,   85
And wait upon my henchmen in the hall!"

Deaf to King Robert's threats and cries
    and prayers,

They thrust him from the hall and down
    the stairs;
A group of tittering pages ran before,
And as they opened wide the folding-
    door,   90
His heart failed, for he heard, with strange
    alarms,
The boisterous laughter of the men-at-arms,
And all the vaulted chamber roar and ring
With the mock plaudits of "Long live the
    King!"

Next morning, waking with the day's first
    beam,   95
He said within himself, "It was a dream!"
But the straw rustled as he turned his head,
There were the cap and bells beside his bed,
Around him rose the bare, discolored walls,
Close by, the steeds were champing in their
    stalls,   100
And in the corner, a revolting shape,
Shivering and chattering sat the wretched
    ape.
It was no dream; the world he loved so
    much
Had turned to dust and ashes at his touch!

Days came and went; and now returned
    again   105
To Sicily the old Saturnian reign;
Under the Angel's governance benign
The happy island danced with corn and
    wine,
And deep within the mountain's burning
    breast
Enceladus,[1] the giant, was at rest.   110

Meanwhile King Robert yielded to his fate,
Sullen and silent and disconsolate.
Dressed in the motley garb that Jesters
    wear,
With look bewildered and a vacant stare,
Close shaven above the ears, as monks are
    shorn,   115
By courtiers mocked, by pages laughed to
    scorn,
His only friend the ape, his only food

---

[1] Leader of the giants who conspired
against Zeus, Enceladus was imprisoned
under Mount Etna, in Sicily.

What others left,—he still was unsubdued.
And when the Angel met him on his way,
And half in earnest, half in jest, would
    say, 120
Sternly, though tenderly, that he might
    feel
The velvet scabbard held a sword of steel,
"Art thou the King?" the passion of his
    woe
Burst from him in resistless overflow,
And, lifting high his forehead, he would
    fling 125
The haughty answer back, "I am, I am the
    King!"

Almost three years were ended; when there
    came
Ambassadors of great repute and name
From Valmond, Emperor of Allemaine,
Unto King Robert, saying that Pope Ur-
    bane 130
By letter summoned them forthwith to
    come
On Holy Thursday to his city of Rome.
The Angel with great joy received his
    guests,
And gave them presents of embroidered
    vests,
And velvet mantles with rich ermine
    lined, 135
And rings and jewels of the rarest kind.
Then he departed with them o'er the sea
Into the lovely land of Italy,
Whose loveliness was more resplendent
    made
By the mere passing of that cavalcade, 140
With plumes, and cloaks, and housings,
    and the stir
Of jeweled bridle and of golden spur.
And lo! among the menials, in mock state,
Upon a piebald steed, with shambling gait,
His cloak of foxtails flapping in the
    wind, 145
The solemn ape demurely perched behind,
King Robert rode, making huge merriment
In all the country towns through which
    they went.

The Pope received them with great pomp,
    and blare

Of bannered trumpets, on Saint Peter's
    square, 150
Giving his benediction and embrace,
Fervent, and full of apostolic grace.
While with congratulations and with
    prayers
He entertained the Angel unawares,
Robert, the Jester, bursting through the
    crowd, 155
Into their presence rushed, and cried aloud,
"I am the King! Look, and behold in me
Robert, your brother, King of Sicily!
This man, who wears my semblance to your
    eyes,
Is an impostor in a King's disguise. 160
Do you not know me? does no voice within
Answer my cry, and say we are akin?"
The Pope in silence, but with troubled
    mien,
Gazed at the Angel's countenance serene;
The Emperor, laughing, said, "It is strange
    sport 165
To keep a madman for thy Fool at court!"
And the poor, baffled Jester in disgrace
Was hustled back among the populace.

In solemn state the Holy Week went by,
And Easter Sunday gleamed upon the
    sky; 170
The presence of the Angel, with its light,
Before the sun rose, made the city bright,
And with new fervor filled the hearts of
    men,
Who felt that Christ indeed had risen
    again.
Even the Jester, on his bed of straw, 175
With haggard eyes the unwonted splendor
    saw,
He felt within a power unfelt before,
And, kneeling humbly on his chamber floor,
He heard the rushing garments of the
    Lord
Sweep through the silent air, ascending
    heavenward. 180

And now the visit ending, and once more
Valmond returning to the Danube's shore,
Homeward the Angel journeyed, and again
The land was made resplendent with his
    train,

Flashing along the towns of Italy 185
Unto Salerno, and from there by sea.
And when once more within Palermo's wall,
And, seated on the throne in his great hall,
He heard the Angelus from convent towers,
As if the better world conversed with
    ours, 190
He beckoned to King Robert to draw
    nigher,
And with a gesture bade the rest retire;
And when they were alone, the Angel said,
"Art thou the King?" Then bowing down
    his head,
King Robert crossed both hands upon his
    breast, 195
And meekly answered him: "Thou knowest
    best!
My sins as scarlet are; let me go hence,
And in some cloister's school of penitence,
Across those stones, that pave the way to
    heaven,
Walk barefoot, till my guilty soul be
    shriven!" 200

The Angel smiled, and from his radiant
    face
A holy light illumined all the place,
And through the open window, loud and
    clear,
They heard the monks chant in the chapel
    near,
Above the stir and tumult of the street: 205
"He has put down the mighty from their
    seat,
And has exalted them of low degree!"
And through the chant a second melody
Rose like the throbbing of a single string:
"I am an Angel, and thou art the
    King!" 210

King Robert, who was standing near the
    throne,
Lifted his eyes, and lo! he was alone!
But all appareled as in days of old,
With ermined mantle and with cloth of
    gold;
And when his courtiers came, they found
    him there 215
Kneeling upon the floor, absorbed in silent
    prayer.

From

THE MUSICIAN'S TALE

THE SAGA OF KING OLAF

THE CHALLENGE OF THOR

I am the God Thor,
I am the War God,
I am the Thunderer!
Here in my Northland,
My fastness and fortress, 5
Reign I forever!

Here amid icebergs
Rule I the nations;
This is my hammer,
Miölner the mighty; 10
Giants and sorcerers
Cannot withstand it!

These are the gauntlets
Wherewith I wield it,
And hurl it afar off; 15
This is my girdle;
Whenever I brace it,
Strength is redoubled!

The light thou beholdest
Stream through the heavens, 20
In flashes of crimson,
Is but my red beard
Blown by the night-wind,
Affrighting the nations!

Jove is my brother; 25
Mine eyes are the lightning;
The wheels of my chariot
Roll in the thunder,
The blows of my hammer
Ring in the earthquake! 30

Force rules the world still,
Has ruled it, shall rule it;
Meekness is weakness,
Strength is triumphant
Over the whole earth 35
Still is it Thor's-Day!

Thou art a God too,
O Galilean!
And thus single-handed
Unto the combat,   **40**
Gauntlet or Gospel,
Here I defy thee!

From
HYPERION
[1839]

GOETHE

WHAT most interested our travellers in
the ancient city of Frankfort was neither
the opera nor the Ariadne of Dannecker,[1]
but the house in which Goethe was born,
and the scenes he frequented in his childhood and remembered in his old age.
Such, for example, are the walks around
the city, outside the moat; the bridge over
the Maine, with the golden cock on the
cross, which the poet beheld and marvelled
at when a boy; the cloister of the Barefooted Friars, through which he stole with
mysterious awe to sit by the oilcloth-
covered table of old Rector Albrecht; and
the garden in which his grandfather walked
up and down among fruit-trees and rose-
bushes, in long morning-gown, black velvet
cap, and the antique leather gloves, which
he annually received as Mayor on Pipers
Doomsday, representing a kind of middle
personage between Alcinous and Laertes.[2]
Thus, O Genius! are thy footprints hallowed; and the star shines forever over
the place of thy nativity.

"Your English critics may rail as they
list," said the Baron,[3] while he and Flemming[4] were returning from a stroll in the
leafy gardens outside the moat; "but, after
all, Goethe was a magnificent old fellow.
Only think of his life; his youth of passion,
alternately aspiring and desponding,
stormy, impetuous, headlong;—his romantic manhood, in which passion assumes the
form of strength; assiduous, careful, toiling, without haste, without rest;—and his
sublime old age,—the age of serene and
classic repose, where he stands like Atlas,

as Claudian[5] has painted him in the Battle
of the Giants, holding the world aloft upon
his head, the ocean-streams hard frozen in
his hoary locks."

"A good illustration of what the world
calls his indifferentism."

"And do you know I rather like this indifferentism? Did you never have the misfortune to live in a community, where a
difficulty in the parish seemed to announce
the end of the world? or to know one of
the benefactors of the human race, in the
very 'storm and pressure' period of his
indiscreet enthusiasm? If you have, I think
you will see something beautiful in the
calm and dignified attitude which the old
philosopher assumes."

"It is a pity that his admirers had not a
little of this philosophic coolness. It amuses
me to read the various epithets which they
apply to him:—The Dear, dear Man! The
Life-enjoying Man! The All-sided One!
The Representative of Poetry upon Earth!
The Many-sided Master-Mind of Germany!
His enemies rush to the other extreme, and
hurl at him the fierce names of Old Humbug! and Old Heathen! which hit like
pistol-bullets."

"I confess, he was no saint."

"No; his philosophy is the old ethnic
philosophy. You will find it all in a convenient and concentrated portable form in
Horace's beautiful Ode to Thaliarcus. What
I most object to in the old gentleman is
his sensuality."

"O, nonsense! Nothing can be purer
than the Iphigenia;[6] it is as cold and pas-
sionless as a marble statue."

"Very true; but you cannot say the
same of some of the Roman Elegies, and

---

[1] Johann Heinrich von Dannecker, German sculptor. Among his most famous
works was "Ariadne on a Panther."

[2] Greek legendary heroes, respectively
friendly host and father of Odysseus.

[3][4] Characters in *Hyperion.*

[5] Late Latin classic poet.

[6] *Iphigenie auf Tauris, Iphigenia at
Taurus,* (1787), drama classical in form
but romantic in thought.

of that monstrous book, the Elective Affinities." [7]

"Ah, my friend, Goethe is an artist; and looks upon all things as objects of art merely. Why should he not be allowed to copy in words what painters and sculptors copy in colors and in marble?"

"The artist shows his character in the choice of his subject. Goethe never sculptured an Apollo, nor painted a Madonna. He gives us only sinful Magdalens and rampant Fauns. He does not so much idealize as realize."

"He only copies nature."

"So did the artists who made the bronze lamps of Pompeii. Would you hang one of those in your hall? To say that a man is an artist and copies nature is not enough. There are two great schools of art; the imitative and the imaginative. The latter is the most noble, and the most enduring; and Goethe belonged rather to the former. Have you read Mensel's attack upon him?"

"It is truly ferocious. The Silesian hews into him lustily. I hope you do not take sides with him?"

"By no means. He goes too far. He blames the poet for not being a politician. He might as well blame him for not being a missionary to the Sandwich Islands."

"And what do you think of Eckerman?" [8]

"I think he is a kind of German Boswell. Goethe knew he was drawing his portrait, and sat for it accordingly. He works very hard to make a Saint Peter out of an old Jupiter, as the Catholics did at Rome."

"Well, call him Old Humbug, or Old Heathen, or what you please; I maintain, that, with all his errors and short-comings, he was a glorious specimen of a man."

"He certainly was. Did it ever occur to you that he was in some points like Ben Franklin,—a kind of rhymed Ben Franklin? The practical tendency of his mind was the same; his love of science was the same; his benignant, philosophic spirit was the same; and a vast number of his little poetic maxims and soothsayings seem nothing more than the worldly wisdom of Poor Richard, versified."

"What most offends me is, that now every German jackass must have a kick at the dead lion."

"And every one who passes through Weimar must throw a book upon his grave, as travellers did of old a stone upon the grave of Manfredi, at Benevento. But, of all that has been said or sung, what most pleases me is Heine's Apologetic, if I may so call it; in which he says, that the minor poets, who flourished under the imperial reign of Goethe, 'resemble a young forest, where the trees first show their own magnitude after the oak of a hundred years, whose branches had towered above and overshadowed them, has fallen. There was not wanting an opposition that strove against Goethe, this majestic tree. Men of the most warring opinions united themselves for the contest. The adherents of the old faith, the orthodox, were vexed that in the trunk of the vast tree no niche with its holy image was to be found; nay, that even the naked Dryads of paganism were permitted to play their witchery there; and gladly, with consecrated axe, would they have imitated the holy Boniface,[9] and levelled the enchanted oak to the ground. The followers of the new faith, the apostles of Liberalism, were vexed, on the other hand, that the tree could not serve as a Liberty Tree, or, at any rate, as a barricade. In fact, the tree was too high; no one could plant the red cap upon its summit, or dance the Carmagnole [10] beneath its branches. The multitudes, however, venerated this tree for the very reason that it reared itself with such independent grandeur, and so

---

[7] *Die Wahlverwandschaften, The Elective Affinities* (1809), pioneer psychological novel.

[8] Johann Peter Eckermann (1792-1854), German scholar, who wrote *Gespräche mit Goethe, Conversations with Goethe* (1836-48), and edited Goethe's works.

[9] Saint Boniface (680?-755?), English monk, called "Apostle of Germany" and one of the greatest missionaries of the Church. He was zealous in destroying the rites and shrines of paganism.

[10] Revolutionary dance.

graciously filled the world with its odor, while its branches, streaming magnificently toward heaven, made it appear as if the stars were only the golden fruit of its wondrous limbs.' Do you not think that beautiful?"

"Yes, very beautiful. And I am glad to see that you can find something to admire in my favorite author, notwithstanding his frailties; or, to use an old German saying, that you can drive the hens out of the garden without trampling down the beds."

"Here is the old gentleman himself!" exclaimed Flemming.

"Where?" cried the Baron, as if for the moment he expected to see the living figure of the poet walking before them.

"Here at the window,—that full-length cast. Excellent,—is it not? He is dressed, as usual, in his long yellow nankeen surtout, with a white cravat crossed in front. What a magnificent head! and what a posture! He stands like a tower of strength. And, by heavens! he was nearly eighty years old, when that was made."

"How do you know?"

"You can see by the date on the pedestal."

"You are right. And yet how erect he stands, with his square shoulders braced back, and his hands behind him! He looks as if he were standing before the fire. I feel tempted to put a live coal in his hand, it lies so invitingly half-open. Gleim's [11] description of him, soon after he went to Weimar, is very different from this. Do you recollect it?"

"No, I do not."

"It is a story which good old father Gleim used to tell with great delight. He was one evening reading the Göttingen Musen-Almanach in a select society at Weimar, when a young man came in, dressed in a short, green shooting-jacket, booted and spurred, and having a pair of brilliant, black, Italian eyes. He, in turn, offered to read; but finding, probably, the poetry of the Musen-Almanach of that year rather too insipid for him, he soon began to improvise the wildest and most

fantastic poems imaginable, and in all possible forms and measures, pretending all the while to read from the book. 'That is either Goethe or the Devil,' said good old father Gleim to Wieland,[12] who sat near him. To which the 'Great I of Osmannstadt' replied,—'It is both, for he has the Devil in him tonight; and at such times he is like a wanton colt, that flings out before and behind, and you will do well not to go too near him!'"

"Very good!"

"And now that noble figure is but mould. Only a few months ago, those majestic eyes looked for the last time on the light of a pleasant spring morning. Calm, like a god, the old man sat; and with a smile seemed to bid farewell to the light of day, on which he had gazed for more than eighty years. Books were near him, and the pen which had just dropped, as it were, from his dying fingers. 'Open the shutters, and let in more light!' were the last words that came from those lips. Slowly stretching forth his hand, he seemed to write in the air; and, as it sank down again and was motionless, the spirit of the old man departed."

"And yet the world goes on. It is strange how soon, when a great man dies, his place is filled; and so completely, that he seems no longer wanted. But let us step in here. I wish to buy that cast."

From
KAVANAGH
[1849]

ONE EVENING as he [1] was sitting down to begin, for at least the hundredth time, the great Romance,—subject of so many resolves and so much remorse, so often determined upon but never begun,—a loud

---

[11] Johann Wilhelm Ludwig Gleim (1719-1803), German poet.
[12] Christoph Martin Wieland (1733-1813), German poet, prose writer, and editor.
[1] "Mr. Churchill," the central character of the novel.

knock at the street-door, which stood wide open, announced a visitor. Unluckily, the study-door was likewise open; and consequently, being in full view, he found it impossible to refuse himself; nor, in fact, would he have done so, had all the doors been shut and bolted,—the art of refusing one's self being at that time but imperfectly understood in Fairmeadow.[2] Accordingly, the visitor was shown in.

He announced himself as Mr. Hathaway. Passing through the village, he could not deny himself the pleasure of calling on Mr. Churchill, whom he knew by his writings in the periodicals, though not personally. He wished, moreover, to secure the coöperation of one, already so favorably known to the literary world, in a new Magazine he was about to establish, in order to raise the character of American literature, which, in his opinion, the existing reviews and magazines had entirely failed to accomplish. A daily increasing want of something better was felt by the public; and the time had come for the establishment of such a periodical as he proposed. After explaining, in rather a florid and exuberant manner, his plan and prospects, he entered more at large into the subject of American literature, which it was his design to foster and patronize.

"I think, Mr. Churchill," said he, "that we want a national literature commensurate with our mountains and rivers,—commensurate with Niagara, and the Alleghanies, and the Great Lakes!"

"Oh!"

"We want a national epic that shall correspond to the size of the country; that shall be to all other epics what Banvard's Panorama[3] of the Mississippi is to all other paintings,—the largest in the world!"

"Ah!"

"We want a national drama in which scope enough shall be given to our gigantic ideas, and to the unparalleled activity and progress of our people!"

"Of course."

"In a word, we want a national literature altogether shaggy and unshorn, that shall shake the earth, like a herd of buffaloes thundering over the prairies!"

"Precisely," interrupted Mr. Churchill; "but excuse me!—are you not confounding things that have no analogy? Great has a very different meaning when applied to a river, and when applied to a literature. Large and shallow may perhaps be applied to both. Literature is rather an image of the spiritual world, than of the physical, is it not?—of the internal, rather than the external. Mountains, lakes, and rivers are, after all, only its scenery and decorations, not its substance and essence. A man will not necessarily be a great poet because he lives near a great mountain. Nor, being a poet, will he necessarily write better poems than another, because he lives nearer Niagara."

"But, Mr. Churchill, you do not certainly mean to deny the influence of scenery on the mind?"

"No, only to deny that it can create genius. At best, it can only develop it. Switzerland has produced no extraordinary poet; nor, as far as I know, have the Andes, or the Himalaya mountains, or the Mountains of the Moon in Africa."

"But, at all events," urged Mr. Hathaway, "let us have our literature national. If it is not national, it is nothing."

"On the contrary, it may be a great deal. Nationality is a good thing to a certain extent, but universality is better. All that

[2] New England village in which the events of the novel occur.

[3] The "panorama," which may be regarded as an ancestral form of the motion picture, was a popular form of public entertainment in the mid-nineteenth century. It consisted of a series of related pictures painted on a roll of canvas, so that they could be viewed in steady succession as the canvas was unrolled. John Banvard (1815-91), American painter, made the largest and most famous of the panoramas, portraying the Mississippi River from its source to its mouth on three miles of canvas. Longfellow drew details for river scenes in *Evangeline* from Banvard's work. See also Hawthorne's story "Ethan Brand," elsewhere in this volume.

is best in the great poets of all countries is not what is national in them, but what is universal. Their roots are in their native soil; but their branches wave in the unpatriotic air, that speaks the same language unto all men, and their leaves shine with the illimitable light that pervades all lands. Let us throw all the windows open; let us admit the light and air on all sides; that we may look towards the four corners of the heavens, and not always in the same direction."

"But you admit nationality to be a good thing?"

"Yes, if not carried too far; still, I confess, it rather limits one's views of truth. I prefer what is natural. Mere nationality is often ridiculous. Every one smiles when he hears the Icelandic proverb, 'Iceland is the best land the sun shines upon.' Let us be natural, and we shall be national enough. Besides, our literature can be strictly national only so far as our character and modes of thought differ from those of other nations. Now, as we are very like the English,—are, in fact, English under a different sky,—I do not see how our literature can be very different from theirs. Westward from hand to hand we pass the lighted torch, but it was lighted at the old domestic fireside of England."

"Then you think our literature is never to be anything but an imitation of the English?"

"Not at all. It is not an imitation, but, as some one has said, a continuation."

"It seems to me that you take a very narrow view of the subject."

"On the contrary, a very broad one. No literature is complete until the language in which it is written is dead. We may well be proud of our task and of our position. Let us see if we can build in any way worthy of our forefathers."

"But I insist upon originality."

"Yes; but without spasms and convulsions. Authors must not, like Chinese soldiers, expect to win victories by turning somersets in the air."

"Well, really, the prospect from your point of view is not very brilliant. Pray, what do you think of our national literature?"

"Simply, that a national literature is not the growth of a day. Centuries must contribute their dew and sunshine to it. Our own is growing slowly but surely, striking its roots downward, and its branches upward, as is natural; and I do not wish, for the sake of what some people call originality, to invert it, and try to make it grow with its roots in the air. And as for having it so savage and wild as you want it, I have only to say, that all literature, as well as all art, is the result of culture and intellectual refinement."

"Ah! we do not want art and refinement; we want genius,—untutored, wild, original, free."

"But, if this genius is to find any expression, it must employ art, for art is the external expression of our thoughts. Many have genius, but, wanting art, are forever dumb. The two must go together to form the great poet, painter, or sculptor."

"In that sense, very well."

"I was about to say also that I thought our literature would finally not be wanting in a kind of universality. As the blood of all nations is mingling with our own, so will their thoughts and feelings finally mingle in our literature. We shall draw from the Germans, tenderness; from the Spaniards, passion; from the French, vivacity,—to mingle more and more with our English solid sense. And this will give us universality, so much to be desired."

American Literature 1800-1860

II

THE FRONTIER, WEST AND SOUTH

1785 ∽ *John James Audubon* ∽ 1851

AUDUBON was born in Haiti and educated in France; he came to America at the age of 18. In 1808 he followed the westward tide to Kentucky, keeping stores and operating a mill before he found his true vocation as student and painter of American birds. His writing was incidental to these interests, but his autobiographical sketches and his journals afford some of our clearest and most readable accounts of frontier settlements and the wilderness.

[Audubon's grand-daughter, Maria R. Audubon, edited his journals and presented these with a brief biography in *Audubon and His Journals* (2 vols., New York, 1897). Recently renewed interest in Audubon has resulted in biographies by Constance Rourke and others. Donald Culross Peattie's *Audubon's America* (Boston, 1942) presents selections from his writings with general comment.]

A WILD HORSE[1]
[1837]

WHILE residing at Henderson in Kentucky, I became acquainted with a gentleman who had returned from the country in the neighbourhood of the head waters of the Arkansas River, where he had purchased a newly caught "Wild Horse," a descendant of some of the horses originally bought from Spain, and set at liberty in the vast prairies of the Mexican lands. The animal was by no means handsome:—he had a large head, with a considerable prominence in its frontal region, his thick and unkempt mane hung along his neck to the breast, and his tail, too scanty to be called flowing, almost reached the ground. But his chest was broad, his legs clean and sinewy, and his eyes and nostrils indicated spirit, vigour, and endurance. He had never been shod, and although he had been ridden hard, and had performed a long journey, his black hoofs had suffered no damage. His colour inclined to bay, the legs of a deeper tint, and gradually darkening below until they became nearly black. I inquired what might be the value of such an animal among the Osage Indians, and was answered, that the horse being only

four years old, he had given for him, with the tree and buffalo tug fastened to his head, articles equivalent to about thirty-five dollars. The gentleman added, that he had never mounted a better horse, and had very little doubt, that if well fed, he could carry a man of ordinary weight from thirty-five to forty miles a-day, for a month, as he had travelled at that rate upon him, without giving him any food other than the grass of the prairies, or the canes of the bottom lands, until he had crossed the Mississippi at Natchez, when he fed him with corn. Having no farther use for him, now that he had ended his journey, he said he was anxious to sell him, and thought he might prove a good hunting horse for me, as his gaits were easy, and he stood fire as well as any charger he had seen. Having some need of a horse possessed of qualities similar to those represented as belonging to the one in question, I asked if I might be allowed to try him. "Try him, Sir, and welcome; nay, if you will agree

[1] This is one of the articles of a general nature introduced by Audubon into his *Ornithological Biography* (Edinburgh, 1831-39), and reprinted in *Delineations of American Scenery and Character* (New York, 1926).

to feed him and take care of him, you may keep him for a month, if you choose." So I had the horse taken to the stable and fed.

About two hours afterwards, I took my gun, mounted the prairie nag, and went to the woods. I was not long in finding him very sensible to the spur, and as I observed that he moved with great ease both to himself and his rider, I thought of leaping over a log several feet in diameter, to judge how far he might prove serviceable in deer-driving or bear-hunting. So I gave him the reins, and pressed my legs to his belly without using the spur, on which, as if aware that I wished to try his mettle, he bounded off and cleared the log as lightly as an elk. I turned him, and made him leap the same log several times, which he did with equal ease, so that I was satisfied of his ability to clear any impediment in the woods. I next determined to try his strength, for which purpose I took him to a swamp, which I knew was muddy and tough. He entered it with his nose close to the water, as if to judge of its depth, at which I was pleased, as he thus evinced due caution. I then rode through the swamp in different directions, and found him prompt, decided, and unflinching. Can he swim well? thought I;—for there are horses, which, although excellent, cannot swim at all, but will now and then lie on their side, as if contented to float with the current, when the rider must either swim and drag them to the shore, or abandon them. To the Ohio then I went, and rode into the water. He made off obliquely against the current, his head well raised above the surface, his nostrils expanded, his breathing free, and without any of the grunting noise emitted by many horses on such occasions. I turned him down the stream, then directly against it, and finding him quite to my mind, I returned to the shore, on reaching which he stopped of his own accord, spread his legs, and almost shook me off my seat. After this I put him to a gallop, and returning home through the woods, shot from the saddle a turkey-cock, which he afterwards approached as

if he had been trained to the sport, and enabled me to take it up without dismounting.

As soon as I reached the house of Dr. Rankin, where I then resided, I sent word to the owner of the horse that I should be glad to see him. When he came, I asked him what price he would take; he said, fifty dollars in silver was the lowest. So I paid the money, took a bill of sale, and became master of the horse. Then Doctor, who was an excellent judge, said smiling to me, "Mr. Audubon, when you are tired of him, I will refund you the fifty dollars, for depend upon it he is a capital horse." The mane was trimmed, but the tail left untouched; the Doctor had him shod "all round," and for several weeks he was ridden by my wife, who was highly pleased with him.

Business requiring that I should go to Philadelphia, Barro (he was so named after his former owner) was put up for ten days and well attended to. The time of my departure having arrived, I mounted him; and set off at the rate of four miles an hour;—but here I must give you the line of my journey, that you may, if you please, follow my course on some such map as that of Tanner's. From Henderson through Russellville, Nashville, and Knoxville, Abington in Virginia, the Natural Bridge, Harrisonburgh, Winchester and Harper's Ferry, Frederick and Lancaster to Philadelphia. There I remained four days, after which I returned by way of Pittsburgh, Wheeling, Zanesville, Chillicothe, Lexington, and Louisville to Henderson. But the nature of my business was such as to make me deviate considerably from the main roads, and I computed the whole distance at nearly two thousand miles, the post roads being rather more than sixteen hundred. I travelled not less than forty miles a-day, and it was allowed by the Doctor that my horse was in as good condition on my return as when I set out. Such a journey on a single horse may seem somewhat marvellous in the eyes of a European; but in those days almost every merchant had to perform the like, some from all parts of the western country, even from St. Louis on the Missouri, although the travellers not unfrequently, on their return, sold their horses at Baltimore, Philadelphia, or Pittsburgh, at which latter place they took boat. My wife rode on a single horse from Henderson to Philadelphia, travelling at the same rate. The country was then comparatively new; few coaches travelled, and in fact the roads were scarcely fit for carriages. About twenty days were considered necessary for performing a journey on horseback from Louisville to Philadelphia, whereas now the same distance may be travelled in six or seven days, or even sometimes less, this depending on the height of the water in the Ohio.

It may be not uninteresting to you to know the treatment which the horse received on these journeys. I rose every morning before day, cleaned my horse, pressed his back with my hand, to see if it had been galled, and placed on it a small blanket folded double, in such a manner that when the saddle was put on, half of the cloth was turned over it. The surcingle, beneath which the saddle-bags were placed, confined the blanket to the seat, and to the pad behind was fastened the great coat or cloak, tightly rolled up. The bridle had a snaffle bit; a breastplate was buckled in front to each skirt, to render the seat secure during an ascent; but my horse required no crupper, his shoulders being high and well-formed. On starting he trotted off at the rate of four miles an hour, which he continued. I usually travelled from fifteen to twenty miles before breakfast, and after the first hour allowed my horse to drink as much as he would. When I halted for breakfast, I generally stopped two hours, cleaned the horse, and gave him as much corn blades as he could eat. I then rode on until within half an hour of sunset, when I watered him well, poured a bucket of cold water over his back, had his skin well rubbed, his feet examined and cleaned. The rack was filled with blades,

the trough with corn, a good-sized pumpkin or some hens' eggs, whenever they could be procured, were thrown in, and if oats were to be had, half a bushel of them was given in preference to corn, which is apt to heat some horses. In the morning, the nearly empty trough and rack afforded sufficient evidence of the state of his health.

I had not ridden him many days before he became so attached to me that on coming to some limpid stream, in which I had a mind to bathe, I could leave him at liberty to graze, and he would not drink if told not to do so. He was ever sure-footed, and in such continual good spirits, that now and then, when a turkey happened to rise from a dusting place before me, the mere inclination of my body forward was enough to bring him to a smart canter, which he would continue until the bird left the road for the woods, when he never failed to resume his usual trot. On my way homewards I met at the crossings of the Juniata River a gentleman from New Orleans whose name is Vincent Nolte. He was mounted on a superb horse, for which he had paid three hundred dollars, and a servant on horseback led another as a change. I was then an utter stranger to him, and as I approached and praised his horse, he not very courteously observed that he wished I had as good a one. Finding that he was going to Bedford to spend the night, I asked him at what hour he would get there. "Just soon enough to have some trouts ready for our supper, provided you will join when you get there." I almost imagined that Barro understood our conversation; he pricked up his ears, and lengthened his pace, on which Mr. Nolte caracolled his horse, and then put him to a quick trot, but all in vain, for I reached the hotel nearly a quarter of an hour before him, ordered the trouts, saw to the putting away of my good horse, and stood at the door ready to welcome my companion. Form that day Vincent Nolte has been a friend to me. It was from him I received letters of introduction to the Rathbones of Liverpool, for which I shall ever be grateful to him. We rode together as far as Shippingport, where my worthy friend Nicholas Berthoud, Esq. resided, and on parting with me he repeated what he had many times said before, that he had never seen so serviceable a creature as Barro.

If I recollect rightly, I gave a short verbal account of this journey, and of the good qualities of my horse, to my learned friend J. Skinner, Esq. of Baltimore, who I believe has noticed them in his excellent Sporting Magazine. We agreed that the importation of horses of this kind from the Western Prairies might improve our breeds generally; and judging from those which I have seen, I am inclined to think that some of them may prove fit for the course. A few days after reaching Henderson, I parted with Barro, not without regret, for a hundred and twenty dollars.

1786 ∞ *David Crockett* ∞ 1836

NOTHING in his background or early life distinguished Crockett from many other frontiersmen of his time. He served under Andrew Jackson in the Creek War, and gradually thereafter, in the settlements of Western Tennessee, built up a reputation as a marksman and story-teller which sent him to the state legislature. His political independence and integrity, and the confidence that he was one of their own kind, led the pioneers to elect him to the federal Congress, 1827-31 and 1833-35.

Finding the frontiersman anything but subservient to his old chief, Jackson, in Washington, Whig propagandists fostered Crockett's popular reputation. His autobiography, the *Narrative of the Life of David Crockett, of the State of Tennessee* (1834), was called forth by a spurious autobiographical book published under Crockett's name the year before. Though doubtless Crockett had assistance in its writing, the *Narrative* carries conviction as a personal expression.

When his constituents failed to return him to Congress in 1836, Crockett led a small party of Tennessee hunters to the support of the new Republic of Texas in its fight for independence, and died at the Alamo. This circumstance contributed to the rapid growth of a Crockett legend, in which the real man and his actual deeds were interwoven with folk tales and fantasies of the frontier.

[The complete *Narrative* and parts of other Crockett books are available, with an introduction by Hamlin Garland, in *The Autobiography of David Crockett* (Modern Student's Library, New York, 1923). The best account of Crockett as man and writer is contained in Constance Rourke's *Davy Crockett* (New York, 1934). The background of the Crockett legend is interestingly explored in *Mike Fink, King of Mississippi Keelboatmen,* by Walter Blair and Franklin J. Meine (New York, 1933).]

From

A NARRATIVE OF THE LIFE OF DAVID CROCKETT, OF THE STATE OF TENNESSEE
[1834]

ELECTIONEERING [1]

I HAD on hand a great many skins, and so, in the month of February, I packed a horse with them, and taking my eldest son along with me, cut out for a little town called Jackson, situated about forty miles off. We got there well enough, and I sold my skins, and bought me some coffee, and sugar, powder, lead, and salt. I packed them all up in readiness for a start, which I intended to make early next morning. Morning came, but I concluded, before I started, I would go and take a horn [2] with some of my old fellow-soldiers that I had met with at Jackson.

I did so; and while we were engaged in this, I met with three candidates for the Legislature; a Doctor Butler, who was, by marriage, a nephew to General Jackson, a Major Lynn, and a Mr. McEver, all first-rate men. We all took a horn together, and some person present said to me, "Crockett, you must offer for the Legislature." I told him I lived at least forty miles from any white settlement, and had no thought of becoming a candidate at that time. So we all parted and I and my little boy went on home.

It was about a week or two after this, that a man came to my house and told me I was a candidate. I told him not so. But he took out a newspaper from his pocket, and show'd me where I was announced. I said to my wife that this was all a burlesque on me, but I was determined to make it cost the man who had put it there at least the value of the printing, and of the fun he wanted at my expense. So I hired a young man to work in my place on my farm, and turned out myself electioneering. I hadn't been out long, before I found the people began to talk very much about the bear hunter, the man from the cane; and the three gentlemen, who I have already named, soon found it necessary to enter into an agreement to have a sort of caucus at their March court, to determine which of them was the strongest, and the other two was to withdraw and support him. As the court came on, each one of them spread himself, to secure the nomination; but it fell on Dr. Butler, and the rest backed out. The doctor was a clever fellow, and I have often said he was the most talented man I ever run against for any office. His being related to Gen'l. Jackson also helped him on very much; but I was in for it, and I was determined to push ahead and go through, or stick. Their meeting was held in Madison county, which was the strongest in the representative district, which was composed of eleven counties, and they seemed bent on having the member from there.

At this time Col. Alexander [3] was a candidate for Congress, and attending one of his public meetings one day, I walked to where he was treating the people, and he gave me an introduction to several of his acquaintances, and informed them that I was out electioneering. In a little time my competitor, Doctor Butler, came along; he passed by without noticing me, and I suppose, indeed, he did not recognise me. But I hailed him, as I was for all sorts of fun; and when he turned to me, I said to him, "Well, doctor, I suppose they have weighed you out to me; but I should like to know why they fixed your election for *March* instead of *August?* This is," said I, "a branfire new way of doing business, if a caucus is to make a representative for the people!" He now discovered who I was, and cried out, "D——n it, Crockett, is that you?"—"Be sure it is," said I, "but I don't want it understood that I have come electioneering. I have just crept out of the cane, to see what discoveries I could make among the white folks." I told him that

---

[1] Title supplied by the present editors.

[2] A drink.

[3] Adam Rankin Alexander, who served in Congress, 1823-24.

when I set out electioneering, I would go prepared to put every man on as good footing when I left him as I found him on. I would therefore have me a large buckskin hunting-shirt made, with a couple of pockets holding about a peck each; and that in one I would carry a great big twist of tobacco, and in the other my bottle of liquor; for I knowed when I met a man and offered him a dram, he would throw out his quid of tobacco to take one, and after he had taken his horn, I would out with my twist and give him another chaw. And in this way he would not be worse off than when I found him; and I would be sure to leave him in a first-rate humour. He said I could beat him electioneering all hollow. I told him I would give him better evidence of that before August, notwithstanding he had many advantages over me, and particularly in the way of money; but I told him that I would go on the products of the country; that I had industrious children, and the best of coon dogs, and they would hunt every night till midnight to support my election; and when the coon fur wa'n't good, I would myself go a wolfing, and shoot down a wolf, and skin his head, and his scalp would be good to me for three dollars, in our state treasury money;[4] and in this way I would get along on the big string. He stood like he was both amused and astonished, and the whole crowd was in a roar of laughter. From this place I returned home, leaving the people in a first-rate way; and I was sure I would do a good business among them. At any rate, I was determined to stand up to my lick-log,[5] salt or no salt.

In a short time there came out two other candidates, a Mr. Shaw and a Mr. Brown. We all ran the race through; and when the election was over, it turned out that I beat them all by a majority of two hundred and forty-seven votes, and was again returned as a member of the Legislature from a new region of the country, without losing a session. This reminded me of the old saying—"A fool for luck, and a poor man for children."

I now served two years in that body from my new district, which was the years 1823 and '24. At the session of 1823, I had a small trial of my independence, and whether I would forsake principle for party, or for the purpose of following after big men.

The term of Col. John Williams had expired, who was a senator in Congress from the state of Tennessee. He was a candidate for another election, and was opposed by Pleasant M. Miller, Esq., who, it was believed, would not be able to beat the colonel. Some two or three others were spoken of, but it was at last concluded that the only man who could beat him was the present "government," General Jackson. So, a few days before the election was to come on, he was sent for to come and run for the senate. He was then in nomination for the presidency; but sure enough he came, and did run as the opponent of Colonel Williams, and beat him too, but not by my vote. The vote was, for Jackson, *thirty-five;* for Williams, *twenty-five.* I thought the colonel had honestly discharged his duty, and even the mighty name of Jackson couldn't make me vote against him.

But voting against the old chief was found a mighty uphill business to all of them except myself. I never would, nor never did, acknowledge I had voted wrong; and I am more certain now that I was right than ever.

I told the people it was the best vote I ever gave; that I had supported the public interest, and cleared my conscience in giving it, instead of gratifying the private ambition of a man.

I let the people know as early as then, that I wouldn't take a collar around my neck with the letters engraved on it,

MY DOG.

Andrew Jackson.

---

[4] The state paid a bounty on wolves killed.

[5] Cattle belonging to the settlers, which roamed at large, were given salt on logs or stumps.

1812 ∾ *William Tappan Thompson* ∾ *1882*

IN HIS early twenties Ohio-born William Tappan Thompson was associated with Augustus Baldwin Longstreet in conducting at Atlanta, Georgia, a newspaper called the *States Rights Sentinel*. Shortly he turned to magazine journalism, and wrote the first of his "Major Jones" sketches for the *Family Companion and Ladies' Mirror,* which he edited. After editing other magazines in Philadelphia and Baltimore, Thompson returned to Georgia and in 1850 established the *Savannah Morning News,* which he edited until his death, making it one of the most influential newspapers of the state.

[J. H. Nelson wrote the article about Thompson in the *Dictionary of American Biography*. Walter Blair treats some of his work in *Native American Humor (1800-1900)* (New York, 1937).]

From
MAJOR JONES'S COURTSHIP
[1843]

MAJOR JONES POPS THE QUESTION

Pineville, December 27, 1842.

TO Mr. Thompson:—*Dear Sir*—Crismus is over, and the thing is done did! You know I told you in my last letter I was gwine to bring Miss Mary up to the chalk on Crismus. Well, I done it, slick as a whistle, though it come mighty nigh bein a serious bisness. But I'll tell you all about the whole circumstance.

The fact is, I's made my mind up more'n twenty times to jest go and come right out with the whole bisness; but whenever I got whar she was, and whenever she looked at me with her witchin eyes, and kind o' blushed at me, I always felt sort o' skeered and fainty, and all what I made up to tell her was forgot, so I couldn't think of it to save me. But you's a married man, Mr. Thompson, so I couldn't tell you nothin about poppin the question, as they call it. It's a mighty grate favour to ax of a pretty gall, and to people what aint used to it, it goes monstrous hard, don't it? They say widders don't mind it no more'n nothin.

But I'm makin a transgression, as the preacher ses.

Crismus eve I put on my new suit, and shaved my face as slick as a smoothin iron, and after tea went over to old Miss Stallinses. As soon as I went into the parler whar they was all settin round the fire, Miss Carline and Miss Kesiah both laughed right out.

"There! there!" ses they, "I told you so! I know'd it would be Joseph."

"What's I done, Miss Carline?" ses I.

"You come under little sister's chicken bone, and I believe she know'd you was comin when she put it over the dore."

"No, I didn't—I didn't no such thing, now," ses Miss Mary, and her face blushed red all over.

"Oh, you needn't deny it," ses Miss Kesiah. "You belong to Joseph now, jest as sure as ther's any charm in chicken bones."

I know'd that was a first rate chance to say something, but the dear little creeter looked so sorry and kep blushin so, I couldn't say nothin zactly to the pint! so I tuck a chair and reached up and tuck down the bone and put it in my pocket.

"What are you gwine to do with that old chicken bone now, Majer?" ses Miss Mary.

"I'm gwine to keep it as long as I live," ses I, "as a Crismus present from the handsomest gall in Georgia."

When I sed that, she blushed worse and worse.

"Aint you shamed, Majer?" ses she.

"Now you ought to give her a Crismus gift, Joseph, to keep all her life," sed Miss Carline.

"Ah," ses old Miss Stallins, "when I was a gall we used to hang up our stockins——"

"Why, mother!" ses all of 'em, "to say stockins right before——"

Then I felt a little streaked too, cause they was all blushin as hard as they could.

"Highty-tity!" ses the old lady—"what monstrous 'finement to be shore! I'd like to know what harm ther is in stockins. . . . People now-a-days is gitting so mealy-mouthed they can't call nothing by its right name, and I don't see as they's any better than the old time people was. When I was a gall like you, child, I used to hang up my stockins and git 'em full of presents."

The galls kep laughin and blushin.

"Never mind," ses Miss Mary, "Majer's got to give me a Crismus gift—won't you, Majer?"

"Oh, yes," ses I, "you know I promised you one."

"But I didn't mean that," ses she.

"I've got one for you, what I want you to keep all your life, but it would take a two bushel bag to hold it," ses I.

"Oh, that's the kind," ses she.

"But will you promise to keep it as long as you live?" ses I.

"Certainly I will, Majer."

—"Monstrous 'finement now-a-days—old people don't know nothin about perliteness," said old Miss Stallins, jest gwine to sleep with her nittin in her lap.

"Now you hear that, Miss Carline," ses I. "She ses she'll keep it all her life."

"Yes, I will," ses Miss Mary—"but what is it?"

"Never mind," ses I, "you hang up a bag big enough to hold it and you'll find out what it is, when you see it in the mornin."

Miss Carline winked at Miss Kesiah, and then whispered to her—then they both laughed and looked at me as mischievous as they could. They 'spicioned something.

"You'll be shore to give it to me now, if I hang up a bag," ses Miss Mary.

"And promise to keep it," ses I.

"Well, I will, cause I know that you wouldn't give me nothing that wasn't worth keepin."

They all agreed they would hang up a bag for me to put Miss Mary's Crismus present in, on the back porch, and about ten o'clock I told 'em good evenin and went home.

I sot up till mid-night, and when they was all gone to bed I went softly into the back gate, and went up to the porch, and thar, shore enough, was a great big meal-bag hangin to the jice. It was monstrous unhandy to git to it, and I was termined not to back out. So I sot some chairs on top of a bench and got hold of the rope and let myself down into the bag; but jest as I was gittin in, it swung agin the chairs, and down they went with a terrible racket; but nobody didn't wake up but Miss Stallinses old cur dog, and here he come rippin and tearin through the yard like rath, and round and round he went tryin to find what was the matter. I scrooch'd down in the bag and didn't breathe louder nor a kitten, for fear he'd find me out, and after awhile he quit barkin.

The wind begun to blow bominable cold, and the old bag kep turnin round and swingin so it made me sea-sick as the mischief. I was afraid to move for fear the rope would break and let me fall, and thar I sot with my teeth rattlin like I had a ager. It seemed like it would never come daylight, and I do believe if I didn't love Miss Mary so powerful I would froze to death; for my heart was the only spot that felt warm, and it didn't beat more'n two licks a minit, only when I thought how she would be supprised in the mornin, and then it went in a canter. Bimeby the cussed old dog come up on the porch and begun to smell about the bag, and then he barked like he thought he'd treed something. "Bow! wow! wow!" ses he. Then he'd smell agin, and try to git up to the bag. "Git out!" ses I, very low, for fear the galls mought hear me. "Bow! wow!" ses he. "Be gone! you bominable fool," ses I, and I felt all over in spots, for I spected every minit he'd nip me, and what made it worse, I didn't know whar abouts he'd take hold. "Bow! wow! wow!" Then I tried coaxin —"Come here, good fellow," ses I, and whistled a little to him, but it wasn't no use. Thar he stood and kep up his everlastin whinin and barkin, all night. I couldn't tell when daylight was breakin, only by the chickens crowin, and I was monstrous glad to hear 'em, for if I'd had to stay thar one hour more, I don't believe I'd ever got out of that bag alive.

Old Miss Stallins come out fust, and as soon as she seed the bag, ses she,

"What upon yeath has Joseph went and put in that bag for Mary? I'll lay its a yearlin or some live animal, or Bruin wouldn't bark at it so."

She went in to call the galls, and I sot thar, shiverin all over so I couldn't hardly speak if I tried to—but I didn't say nothin. Bimeby they all come runnin out on the porch.

"My goodness! what is it?" ses Miss Mary.

"Oh, it's alive!" ses Miss Kesiah, "I seed it move."

"Call Cato, and make him cut the rope," ses Miss Carline, "and lets see what it is. Come here, Cato, and git this bag down."

"Don't hurt it for the world," ses Miss Mary.

Cato untied the rope that was round the jice, and let the bag down easy on the floor, and I tumbled out all covered with corn meal, from head to foot.

"Goodness gracious!" ses Miss Mary, "if it aint the Majer himself!"

"Yes," ses I, "and you know you promised to keep my Crismus present as long as you lived."

The galls laughed themselves almost to death, and went to brushin off the meal as fast as they could, saying they was gwine to hang that bag up every Crismus till they got husbands too. Miss Mary—bless her bright eyes—she blushed as beautiful as a morning-glory, and sed she'd stick to her word. She was right out of bed, and her hair wasn't komed, and her dress wasn't fix'd at all, but the way she looked pretty was real distractin. I do believe if I was froze stiff, one look at her sweet face, as she stood thar lookin down to the floor with her roguish eyes, and her bright curls fallin all over her snowy neck, would have fotched me to. I tell you what, it was worth hanging in a meal bag from one Crismus to another to feel as happy as I have ever sense.

I went home after we had the laugh out, and sot by the fire till I got thawed. In the forenoon all the Stallinses come over to our house and we had one of the greatest Crismus dinners that ever was seed in Georgia, and I don't believe a happier company ever sot down to the same table. Old Miss Stallins and mother settled the match, and talked over every thing that ever happened in ther families, and laughed at me and Mary, and cried about ther dead husbands, cause they wasn't alive to see ther children married.

It's all settled now, 'cept we haint sot the weddin day. I'd like to have it all over at once, but young galls always like to be engaged a while, you know, so I spose I must wait a month or so. Mary (she ses I mustn't call her Miss Mary now) has been a good deal of trouble and botheration to me; but if you could see her you wouldn't think I ought to grudge a little sufferin to git sich a sweet little wife.

You must come to the weddin if you possibly kin, I'll let you know when. No more from

Your friend, till death,
Jos. Jones.

N.B. I like to forgot to tell you about cousin Pete. He got snapt on egnog when he heard of my ingagement, and he's been as meller as hoss-apple ever sense.

From
MAJOR JONES'S SKETCHES
OF TRAVEL
[1847]

The Hoosier and the Salt Pile

IT IS very refreshin in these days of progress, after rattlin over the country for days and nights, at the rate of twenty miles a ower in a railroad car—with your mouth full of dust and smoke, and with sich a everlastin clatter in your ears that you can't hear yourself think—to git into a good, old-fashioned stage-coach. Ther's something sociable and cosey in stage-coach travellin, so different from the bustle and confusion of a railroad, whar people are whirled along "slam bang to eternal smash," like they wer so many bales and boxes of dry-goods and groceries, without so much as a chance of seein whar they're gwine, or of takin any interest in their feller sufferers. I love to hear the pop of the whip and the interestin conversation between the driver and his horses; and I like the constant variation in the motion of the stage, the rattle of the wheels over the stones, the stillness of the drag through the heavy sand, the lunging and pitching into the ruts and gullies, the slow pull up the steep hills, the rush down agin, and the splashin of the horses' feet and the wheels in the water and mud. And then one has time to see the country he's passin through, to count the rails in the panels of the fences, and the wimmen and children in the doors of the houses, to notice the appearance of the crops and the condition of the stock on the farms, and now and then to say a word to the people on the roadside. All these things is pleasant, after a long voyage on the railroad. But what's still more agreeable about stage-coach travelin, is that we have a opportunity of makin the acquaintance of our feller passengers, of conversin with 'em and studdyin their traits of character, which from the strikin contrast they often pre-

sent, never fail to amuse if they don't interest our mind.

Some years ago I had a tolerably fair specimen of a stage-coach ride from Warrenton to Milledgeville. The road wasn't the best in the world, and didn't run through the most interestin part of Georgia, but we had a good team, a good stage, and a first-rate driver, what could sing like a camp-meetin and whistle like a locomotive, and the company was jest about as good a one as could be jumped up for sich a occasion. Ther was nine of us besides the driver, and I don't believe ther ever was a crowd of the same number that presented a greater variety of characters. Ther was a old gentleman in black, with big round spectacles, and a gold headed cane; a dandy gambler, with a big diamond breast-pin and more gold chains hangin round him than would hang him; a old hardshell preacher, as they call 'em in Georgia, with the biggest mouth and the ugliest teeth I ever seed; a circus clown, whose breath smelled strong enough of whiskey to upset the stage; a cross old maid, as ugly as a tar-bucket; a butiful young school-gall, with rosy cheeks and mischievous bright eyes; a cattle-drover from Indiany, who was gwine to New Orleans to git a army contract for beef, and myself.

For a while after we started from Warrenton nobody didn't have much to say. The young lady put her green vail over her face and leaned her head back in the corner; the old maid, after a row with the driver about her band-boxes, sot up straight in her seat and looked as sharp as a steel-trap; the old gentleman with the spectacles drummed his fingers on his cane and looked out of the coach-winder; the circus-man tried to look interestin; the gambler went to sleep; the preacher looked solemn; and the hoosier stuck his head out of the winder on his side to look at the cattle what we passed every now and then.

"This aint no great stock country," ses he to the old gentleman with the specs.

"No, sir," ses the old gentleman. "There's

very little grazing here. The range in these parts is pretty much worn out."

Then ther was nothing said for some time. Bimeby the hoosier opened agin.

"It's the d——st place for 'simmon-trees and turkey-buzzards I ever did see."

The old gentleman didn't say nothin, and the preacher fetched a long groan. The young lady smiled through her vail, and the old maid snapped her eyes and looked sideways at the speaker.

"Don't make much beef down here, I reckon," ses the hoosier.

"No," ses the old gentleman.

"Well, I don't see how in the h——l they manage to live in a country whar ther aint no ranges, and they don't make no beef. A man aint considered worth a cuss in Indiany what hasn't got his brand on a hundred head or so of cattle."

"Your's is a great beef country, I believe," ses the old gentleman.

"Well, sir, it aint nothing else. A man that's got sense enough to foller his own cow-bell, with us, aint no danger of starvin. I'm gwine down to Orleans to see if I can't git a contract out of Uncle Sam, to feed the boys what's been lickin them infernal Mexicans so bad. I spose you've seed them cussed lies what's been in the newspapers about the Indiany boys at Bona Vista?" [1]

"I've read some accounts of the battle," ses the old gentleman, "that didn't give a very flattering account of the conduct of some of our troops."

With that, the Indiany man went into a full explanation of the affair, and gittin warmed up as he went along, begun to cuss and swear like he'd been through a dozen campaigns himself.

The old preacher listened to him with evident signs of displeasure, twistin and groanin every time he uttered a big oath, until he couldn't stand it no longer.

"My friend," ses he, "you must excuse me, but your conversation would be a great deal more interestin to me, and I'm sure it would please the company much better, if you wouldn't swear so terribly. It's

very wicked to swear so, and I hope you'll have respect for our religious feelins, if you hain't got no respect for your Maker."

If the hoosier had been struck with a clap of thunder and lightning he couldn't have been more completely tuck aback. He shut his mouth right in the middle of what he was sayin, and looked at the preacher, while his face got as red as fire.

"Swearin," continued the old hardshell, "is a terrible bad practise, and ther aint no use in it no how. The Bible says 'swear not at all,' and I spose you know the commandments about taking the Lord's name in vain."

The hoosier didn't open his mouth.

"I know," ses the old preacher, "a great many people swear without thinkin, and that some people don't believe in the Bible."

And then he went on to preach a regular sermon agin, and to quote the Scripture like he knowed the whole Bible by heart. In the course of his argyments he undertook to prove the Scriptures to be true, and told us all about the miracles and prophecies and their fulfillment. The old gentleman with the cane tuck a part in the conversation, and the hoosier listened without ever once openin his head.

"I've jest heard of a gentleman," sed the preacher, "what has been to the Holy Land, and went all over the Bible country. It's astonishin what wonderful things he seed thar. He was at Soddom and Gomorrow, and seed the place whar Lot's wife fell!"

"Ah?" ses the old gentleman with the specs.

"Yes," ses the preacher. "He went to the very spot, and what's the most remarkablest thing of all, he seed the pillar of salt what she was turned into."

"Is it possible?" ses the old gentleman.

The hoosier's countenance all at once brightened up, and he opened his mouth wide.

---

[1] Battle of Buena Vista, Feb. 22-23, 1847.

"Yes, sir; he seed the salt standin thar to this day."

The hoosier's curiosity was raised to a pint beyond endurance.

"What!" ses he, "real genewine good salt?"

"Yes, sir, a pillar of salt jest as it was when that wicked woman was punished for her disobedience."

All but the gambler, who was snoozin in the corner of the coach, looked at the preacher—the hoosier with an expression of countenance that plainly told that his mind was powerfully convicted of a important fact.

"Standin right out in the open air?" he axed.

"Yes, sir,—right out in the open field where she fell."

"Well," ses the hoosier, "all I've got to say is, *if she'd drap'd in Indiany, the cattle would lick'd her up long ago!*"

1815 ∾ *Thomas Bangs Thorpe* ∾ 1878

THORPE'S story "The Big Bear of Arkansas" is the most notable monument of a man of singular diversity of talent and occupation.

Thorpe was born in Massachusetts, the son of a clergyman, and showed precocious ability in painting. At sixteen he painted a picture which illustrated one of Irving's stories and was exhibited at the New York Academy of Fine Arts and later hung in Irving's home at Sunnyside. At eighteen he entered college, but left shortly to go to Louisiana because of his health.

Thorpe remained in the Southwest for twenty years, working as painter, editor, and writer. He became widely known in the region for his pictorial studies of prairie life and his portraits of such celebrated persons as Jenny Lind and Zachary Taylor. He had a share in the editing of at least five newspapers. His stories were printed in *The Spirit of the Times,* and other periodicals, praised in England, and translated in Europe. He was attached to Taylor's staff during the Mexican War, and wrote three books based on that experience. He later attempted novels, but none of his works of book length was equal in merit to some of his early short stories.

[Note F. J. Meine's article on Thorpe in *Dictionary of American Biography*, and that of A. N. De Menil in *The Literature of Louisiana Territory* (St. Louis, 1904), pp. 138-139.]

THE BIG BEAR OF ARKANSAS
[1845 (1841)]

A STEAMBOAT on the Mississippi frequently, in making her regular trips, carries between places varying from one to two thousand miles apart; and as these boats advertise to land passengers and freight at "all intermediate landings," the heterogeneous character of the passengers of one of these up-country boats can scarcely be imagined by one who has never seen it with his own eyes. Starting from New Orleans in one of these boats, you will find yourself associated with men from every state in the Union, and from every portion of the globe; and a man of observation need not lack for amusement or instruction in such a crowd, if he will take the trouble to read the great book of character so favourably opened before him. Here may be seen jostling together the wealthy Southern planter, and the pedler of tin-ware from New England—the Northern merchant, and the Southern jockey—a venerable bishop, and a desperate gambler—the land speculator, and the honest farmer—professional men of all creeds and characters — Wolvereens, Suckers, Hoosiers, Buckeyes, and Corncrackers, beside a "plentiful sprinkling" of the half-horse and half-alligator species of men, who are peculiar to "old Mississippi," and who appear to gain a livelihood simply by going up and down the river. In the pursuit of pleasure or business, I have frequently found myself in such a crowd.

On one occasion, when in New Orleans, I had occasion to take a trip of a few miles up the Mississippi, and I hurried on board the well-known "high-pressure-and-beat-every-thing" steamboat "Invincible," just as the last note of the last bell was sounding; and when the confusion and bustle that is natural to a boat's getting under way had subsided, I discovered that I was associated in as heterogeneous a crowd as was ever got together. As my trip was to be of a few hours' duration only, I made no endeavours to become acquainted with my fellow passengers, most of whom would be together many days. Instead of this, I took out of my pocket the "latest paper," and more critically than usual examined its contents; my fellow passengers at the same time disposed themselves in little groups. While I was thus busily employed in reading, and my companions were more busily still employed in discussing such subjects as suited their humours best, we were startled most unexpectedly by a loud Indian whoop, uttered in the "social hall," that part of the cabin fitted off for a bar; then was to be heard a loud crowing, which would not have continued to have interested us—such sounds being quite common in that *place of spirits*—had not the hero of these windy accomplishments stuck his head into the cabin and hallooed out, "Hurra for the Big Bar of Arkansaw!" and then might be heard a confused hum of voices, unintelligi-ble, save in such broken sentences as "horse," "screamer," "lightning is slow," &c. As might have been expected, this continued interruption attracted the attention of every one in the cabin; all conversation dropped, and in the midst of this surprise the "Big Bar" walked into the cabin, took a chair, put his feet on the stove, and looking back over his shoulder, passed the general and familiar salute of "Strangers, how are you?" He then expressed himself as much at home as if he had been at "the Forks of Cypress," and "perhaps a little more so." Some of the company at this familiarity looked a little angry, and some astonished; but in a moment every face was wreathed in a smile. There was something about the intruder that won the heart on sight. He appeared to be a man enjoying perfect health and contentment: his eyes were as sparkling as diamonds, and good-natured to simplicity. Then his perfect confidence in himself was irresistibly droll. "Perhaps," said he, "gentlemen," running on without a person speaking, "perhaps you have been to New Orleans often; I never made *the first visit before,* and I don't intend to make another in a crow's life. I am thrown away in that ar place, and useless, that ar a fact. Some of the gentlemen thar called me *green*—well, perhaps I am, said I, *but I arn't so at home;* and if I aint off my trail much, the heads of them perlite chaps themselves weren't much the hardest; for according to my notion, they were *real know-nothings,* green as a pumpkin-vine—couldn't, in farming, I'll bet, raise a crop of turnips: and as for shooting, they'd miss a barn if the door was swinging, and that, too, with the best rifle in the country. And then they talked to me 'bout hunting, and laughed at my calling the principal game in Arkansaw poker, and high-low-jack. 'Perhaps,' said I, 'you prefer chickens and rolette'; at this they laughed harder than ever, and asked me if I lived in the woods, and didn't know what *game* was? At this I rather think I laughed. 'Yes,' I roared, and says, 'Strangers, if you'd asked me *how we got our meat* in Arkansaw, I'd a told you at once, and given you a list of varmints that would make a caravan, beginning with the bar, and ending off with the cat; that's *meat* though, not game.' Game, indeed, that's what city folks call it; and with them it means chippen-birds and shite-pokes; maybe such trash live in my diggins, but I arn't noticed them yet: a bird any way is too trifling. I never did shoot at but one, and I'd never forgiven myself for that, had it weighed less than forty pounds. I wouldn't draw a rifle on any thing less than that; and when I meet with another wild turkey of the same weight I will drap him."

"A wild turkey weighing forty pounds!" exclaimed twenty voices in the cabin at once.

"Yes, strangers, and wasn't it a whopper? You see, the thing was so fat that it couldn't fly far; and when he fell out of the tree, after I shot him, on striking the ground he bust open behind, and the way the pound gobs of tallow rolled out of the opening was perfectly beautiful."

"Where did all that happen?" asked a cynical-looking Hoosier.

"Happen! happened in Arkansaw: where else could it have happened, but in the creation state, the finishing-up country— a state where the *sile* runs down to the centre of the 'arth, and government gives you a title to every inch of it? Then its airs—just breathe them, and they will make you snort like a horse. It's a state without a fault, it is."

"Excepting mosquitoes," cried the Hoosier.

"Well, stranger, except them; for it ar a fact that they are rather *enormous,* and do push themselves in somewhat troublesome. But, stranger, they never stick twice in the same place; and give them a fair chance for a few months, and you will get as much above noticing them as an alligator. They can't hurt my feelings, for they lay under the skin; and I never knew but one case of injury resulting from them, and that was to a Yankee: and they take worse to foreigners, any how, than they do

to natives. But the way they used that fellow up! first they punched him until he swelled up and busted; then he sup-per-a-ted, as the doctor called it, until he was as raw as beef; then he took the ager, owing to the warm weather, and finally he took a steamboat and left the country. He was the only man that ever took mosquitoes to heart that I know of. But mosquitoes is natur, and I never find fault with her. If they ar large, Arkansaw is large, her varmints ar large, her trees ar large, her rivers ar large, and a small mosquito would be of no more use in Arkansaw than preaching in a cane-brake."

This knock-down argument in favour of big mosquitoes used the Hoosier up, and the logician started on a new track, to explain how numerous bear were in his "diggins," where he represented them to be "about as plenty as blackberries, and a little plentifuler."

Upon the utterance of this assertion, a timid little man near me inquired if the bear in Arkansaw ever attacked the settlers in numbers.

"No," said our hero, warming with the subject, "no, stranger, for you see it ain't the natur of bar to go in droves; but the way they squander about in pairs and single ones is edifying. And then the way I hunt them—the old black rascals know the crack of my gun as well as they know a pig's squealing. They grow thin in our parts, it frightens them so, and they do take the noise dreadfully, poor things. That gun of mine is a perfect *epidemic among bar*: if not watched closely, it will go off as quick on a warm scent as my dog Bowie-knife will: and then that dog— whew! why the fellow thinks that the world is full of bar, he finds them so easy. It's lucky he don't talk as well as think; for with his natural modesty, if he should suddenly learn how much he is acknowledged to be ahead of all other dogs in the universe, he would be astonished to death in two minutes. Stranger, that dog knows a bar's way as well as a horse-jockey knows a woman's: he always barks at the right time, bites at the exact place, and whips without getting a scratch. I never could tell whether he was made expressly to hunt bar, or whether bar was made expressly for him to hunt: any way, I believe they were ordained to go together as naturally as Squire Jones says a man and woman is, when he moralizes in marrying a couple. In fact, Jones once said, said he, 'Marriage according to law is a civil contract of divine origin; it's common to all countries as well as Arkansaw, and people take to it as naturally as Jim Doggett's Bowie-knife takes to bar.'"

"What season of the year do your hunts take place?" inquired a gentlemanly foreigner, who, from some peculiarities of his baggage, I suspected to be an Englishman, on some hunting expedition, probably at the foot of the Rocky Mountains.

"The season for bar hunting, stranger," said the man of Arkansaw, "is generally all the year round, and the hunts take place about as regular. I read in history that varmints have their fat season, and their lean season. That is not the case in Arkansaw, feeding as they do upon the *spontenacious* productions of the sile, they have one continued fat season the year round; though in winter things in this way is rather more greasy than in summer, I must admit. For that reason bar with us run in warm weather, but in winter they only waddle. Fat, fat! it's an enemy to speed; it tames every thing that has plenty of it. I have seen wild turkeys, from its influence, as gentle as chickens. Run a bar in this fat condition, and the way it improves the critter for eating is amazing; it sort of mixes the ile up with the meat, until you can't tell t'other from which. I've done this often. I recollect one perty morning in particular, of putting an old he fellow on the stretch, and considering the weight he carried, he run well. But the dogs soon tired him down, and when I came up with him wasn't he in a beautiful sweat—I might say fever; and then to see his tongue sticking out of his mouth a feet, and his sides sinking and opening like a

bellows, and his cheeks so fat he couldn't look cross. In this fix I blazed at him, and pitch me naked into a briar patch if the steam didn't come out of the bullet-hole ten foot in a straight line. The fellow, I reckon, was made on the high-pressure system, and the lead sort of bust his biler."

"That column of steam was rather curious, or else the bear must have been *warm*," observed the foreigner with a laugh.

"Stranger, as you observe, that bar was WARM, and the blowing off of the steam show'd it, and also how hard the varmint had been run. I have no doubt if he had kept on two miles farther his insides would have been stewed; and I expect to meet with a varmint yet of extra bottom, who will run himself into a skinfull of bar's grease: it is possible, much onlikelier things have happened."

"Whereabouts are these bears so abundant?" inquired the foreigner, with increasing interest.

"Why, stranger, they inhabit the neighbourhood of my settlement, one of the prettiest places on old Mississippi—a perfect location, and no mistake; a place that had some defects until the river made the 'cut-off' at 'Shirt-tail bend,' and that remedied the evil, as it brought my cabin on the edge of the river—a great advantage in wet weather, I assure you, as you can now roll a barrel of whiskey into my yard in high water from a boat, as easy as falling off a log. It's a great improvement, as toting it by land in a jug, as I used to do, *evaporated* it too fast, and it became expensive. Just stop with me, stranger, a month or two, or a year if you like, and you will appreciate my place. I can give you plenty to eat; for beside hog and hominy, you can have bar-ham, and bar-sausages, and a mattrass of bar-skins to sleep on, and a wildcat-skin, pulled off hull, stuffed with corn-shucks, for a pillow. That bed would put you to sleep if you had the rheumatics in every joint in your body. I call that ar bed a *quietus*. Then look at my land—the government ain't got another such a piece to dispose of. Such timber, and such bottom land, why you can't preserve any thing natural you plant in it unless you pick it young, things thar will grow out of shape so quick. I once planted in those diggins a few potatoes and beets: they took a fine start, and after that an ox team couldn't have kept them from growing. About that time I went off to old Kentuck on bisiness, and did not hear from them things in three months, when I accidentally stumbled on a fellow who had stopped at my place, with an idea of buying me out. "How did you like things?" said I. 'Pretty well,' said he; 'the cabin is convenient, and the timber land is good; but that bottom land ain't worth the first red cent.' 'Why?' said I. ' 'Cause,' said he. ' 'Cause what?' said I. ' 'Cause it's full of cedar stumps and Indian mounds,' said he, 'and *it can't be cleared.*' 'Lord,' said I, 'them ar "cedar stumps" is beets, and them ar "Indian mounds" ar tater hills.' As I expected, the crop was overgrown and useless: the sile is too rich, *and planting in Arkansaw is dangerous.* I had a good-sized sow killed in that same bottom land. The old thief stole an ear of corn, and took it down where she slept at night to eat. Well, she left a grain or two on the ground, and lay down on them: before morning the corn shot up, and the percussion killed her dead. I don't plant any more: natur intended Arkansaw for a hunting ground, and I go according to natur."

The questioner who thus elicited the description of our hero's settlement, seemed to be perfectly satisfied, and said no more; but the "Big Bar of Arkansaw" rambled on from one thing to another with a volubility perfectly astonishing, occasionally disputing with those around him, particularly with a "live Sucker" from Illinois, who had the daring to say that our Arkansaw friend's stories "smelt rather tall."

In this manner the evening was spent; but conscious that my own association with so singular a personage would probably end before morning, I asked him if he would not give me a description of some particular bear hunt; adding, that I took

great interest in such things, though I was no sportsman. The desire seemed to please him, and he squared himself round towards me, saying, that he could give me an idea of a bar hunt that was never beat in this world, or in any other. His manner was so singular, that half of his story consisted in his excellent way of telling it, the great peculiarity of which was, the happy manner he had of emphasizing the prominent parts of his conversation. As near as I can recollect, I have italicized them, and given the story in his own words.

"Stranger," said he, "in bar hunts *I am numerous,* and which particular one, as you say, I shall tell, puzzles me. There was the old she devil I shot at the Hurricane last fall—then there was the old hog thief I popped over at the Bloody Crossing, and then—Yes, I have it! I will give you an idea of a hunt, in which the greatest bar was killed that ever lived, *none excepted;* about an old fellow that I hunted, more or less, for two or three years; and if that ain't a *particular bar hunt,* I ain't got one to tell. But in the first place, stranger, let me say, I am pleased with you, because you ain't ashamed to gain information by asking, and listening, and that's what I say to Countess's pups every day when I'm home; and I have got great hopes of them ar pups, because they are continually *nosing* about; and though they stick it sometimes in the wrong place, they gain experience any how, and may learn something useful to boot. Well, as I was saying about this big bar, you see when I and some more first settled in our region, we were driven to hunting naturally; we soon liked it, and after that we found it an easy matter to make the thing our business. One old chap who had pioneered 'afore us, gave us to understand that we had settled in the right place. He dwelt upon its merits until it was affecting, and showed us, to prove his assertions, more marks on the sassafras trees that I ever saw on a tavern door 'lection time. 'Who keeps that ar reckoning?' said I. 'The bar,' said he. 'What for?' said I. 'Can't tell,' said he; 'but so it is: the bar bite the bark and wood too, at the highest point from the ground they can reach, and you can tell, by the marks,' said he, 'the length of the bar to an inch.' 'Enough,' said I; 'I've learned something here a'ready, and I'll put it in practice.'

"Well, stranger, just one month from that time I killed a bar, and told its exact length before I measured it, by those very marks; and when I did that, I swelled up considerable—I've been a prouder man ever since. So I went on, larning something every day, until I was reckoned a buster, and allowed to be decidedly the best bar hunter in my district; and that is a reputation as much harder to earn than to be reckoned first man in Congress, as an iron ramrod is harder than a toad-stool. Did the varmints grow over-cunning by being fooled with by green-horn hunters, and by this means get troublesome; they send for me as a matter of course; and thus I do my own hunting, and most of my neighbours'. I walk into the varmints though, and it has become about as much the same to me as drinking. It is told in two sentences—a bar is started, and he is killed. The thing is somewhat monotonous now—I know just how much they will run, where they will tire, how much they will growl, and what a thundering time I will have in getting them home. I could give you this history of the chase with all the particulars at the commencement, I know the signs so well —*Stranger, I'm certain.* Once I met with a match though, and I will tell you about it; for a common hunt would not be worth relating.

"On a fine fall day, long time ago, I was trailing about for bar, and what should I see but fresh marks on the sassafras trees, about eight inches above any in the forests that I knew of. Says I, 'them marks is a hoax, or it indicates the d——t bar that was ever grown.' In fact, stranger, I couldn't believe it was real, and I went on. Again I saw the same marks, at the same height, and I *knew the thing lived.* That conviction came home to my soul like an earthquake. Says I, 'here is something

a-purpose for me: that bar is mine, or I give up the hunting business.' The very next morning what should I see but a number of buzzards hovering over my corn-field. 'The rascal has been there,' said I, 'for that sign is certain:' and, sure enough, on examining, I found the bones of what had been as beautiful a hog the day before, as was ever raised by a Buckeye. Then I tracked the critter out of the field to the woods, and all the marks he left behind, showed me that he was *the bar.*

"Well, stranger, the first fair chase I ever had with that big critter, I saw him no less than three distinct times at a distance: the dogs run him over eighteen miles and broke down, my horse gave out, and I was as nearly used up as a man can be, made on *my* principle, *which is patent.* Before this adventure, such things were unknown to me as possible; but, strange as it was, that bar got me used to it before I was done with him; for he got so at last, that he would leave me on a long chase *quite easy.* How he did it, I never could understand. That a bar runs at all, is puzzling; but how this one could tire down and bust up a pack of hounds and a horse, that were used to overhauling everything they started after in no time, was past my understanding. Well, stranger, that bar finally got so sassy, that he used to help himself to a hog off my premises whenever he wanted one; the buzzards followed after what he left, and so, between *bar and buzzard,* I rather think I was *out of pork.*

"Well, missing that bar so often took hold of my vitals, and I wasted away. The thing had been carried too far, and it reduced me in flesh faster than an ager. I would see that bar in every thing I did: *he hunted me,* and that, too, like a devil, which I began to think he was. While in this fix, I made preparations to give him a last brush, and be done with it. Having completed every thing to my satisfaction, I started at sunrise, and to my great joy, I discovered from the way the dogs run, that they were near him; finding his trail was nothing, for that had become as plain to the pack as a turnpike road. On we went, and coming to an open country, what should I see but the bar very leisurely ascending a hill, and the dogs close at his heels, either a match for him this time in speed, or else he did not care to get out of their way—I don't know which. But wasn't he a beauty, though? I loved him like a brother.

"On he went, until he came to a tree, the limbs of which formed a crotch about six feet from the ground. Into this crotch he got and seated himself, the dogs yelling all around it; and there he sat eyeing them as quiet as a pond in low water. A green-horn friend of mine, in company, reached shooting distance before me, and blazed away, hitting the critter in the centre of his forehead. The bar shook his head as the ball struck it, and then walked down from that tree as gently as a lady would from a carriage. 'Twas a beautiful sight to see him do that—he was in such a rage that he seemed to be as little afraid of the dogs as if they had been sucking pigs; and the dogs warn't slow in making a ring around him at a respectful distance, I tell you; even Bowie-knife, himself, stood off. Then the way his eyes flashed—why the fire of them would have singed a cat's hair; in fact that bar was in a *wrath all over*. Only one pup came near him, and he was brushed out so totally with the bar's left paw, that he entirely disappeared; and that made the old dogs more cautious still. In the mean time, I came up, and taking deliberate aim as a man should do, at his side, just back of his foreleg, *if my gun did not snap*, call me a coward, and I won't take it personal. Yes, stranger, *it snapped*, and I could not find a cap about my person. While in this predicament, I turned round to my fool friend—says I, 'Bill,' says I, 'you're an ass—you're a fool —you might as well have tried to kill that bar by barking the tree under his belly, as to have done it by hitting him in the head. Your shot has made a tiger of him, and blast me, if a dog gets killed or wounded when they come to blows, I will

stick my knife into your liver, I will'— my wrath was up. I had lost my caps, my gun had snapped, the fellow with me had fired at the bar's head, and I expected every moment to see him close in with the dogs, and kill a dozen of them at least. In this thing I was mistaken, for the bar leaped over the ring formed by the dogs, and giving a fierce growl, was off—the pack, of course, in full cry after him. The run this time was short, for coming to the edge of a lake the varmint jumped in, and swam to a little island in the lake, which it reached just a moment before the dogs. 'I'll have him now,' said I, for I had found my caps in the *lining of my coat*—so, rolling a log into the lake, I paddled myself across to the island, just as the dogs had cornered the bar in a thicket. I rushed up and fired—at the same time the critter leaped over the dogs and came within three feet of me, running like mad; he jumped into the lake, and tried to mount the log I had just deserted, but every time he got half his body on it, it would roll over and send him under; the dogs, too, got around him, and pulled him about, and finally Bowie-knife clenched with him, and they sunk into the lake together. Stranger, about this time I was excited, and I stripped off my coat, drew my knife, and intended to have taken a part with Bowie-knife myself, when the bar rose to the surface. But the varmint staid under—Bowie-knife came up alone, more dead than alive, and with the pack came ashore. 'Thank God,' said I, 'the old villain has got his deserts at last.' Determined to have the body, I cut a grape-vine for a rope, and dove down where I could see the bar in the water, fastened my queer rope to his leg, and fished him, with great difficulty, ashore. Stranger, may I be chawed to death by young alligators, if the thing I looked at wasn't *a she bar, and not the old critter after all*. The way matters got mixed on that island was on-accountably curious, and thinking of it made me more than ever convinced that I was hunting the devil himself. I went home that night and took to my bed—the thing was killing me. The entire team of Arkansaw in bar-hunting, acknowledged himself used up, and the fact sunk into my feelings like a snagged boat will in the Mississippi. I grew as cross as a bar with two cubs and a sore tail. The thing got out 'mong my neighbours, and I was asked how come on that individ-u-al that never lost a bar when once started? And if that same individ-u-al didn't wear telescopes when he turned a she bar, of ordinary size, into an old he one, a little larger than a horse? 'Perhaps,' said I, 'friends'—getting wrathy—'perhaps you want to call somebody a liar.' 'Oh, no,' said they, 'we only heard such things as being *rather common* of late, but we don't believe one word of it; oh, no,'—and then they would ride off and laugh like so many hyenas over a dead nigger. It was too much, and I determined to catch that bar, go to Texas, or die,—and I made my preparations accordin'. I had the pack shut up and rested. I took my rifle to pieces, and iled it. I put caps in every pocket about my person, *for fear of the lining.* I then told my neighbours, that on Monday morning—naming the day—I would start THAT BAR, and bring him home with me, or they might divide my settlement among them, the owner having disappeared. Well, stranger, on the morning previous to the great day of my hunting expedition, I went into the woods near my house, taking my gun and Bowie-knife along, just *from habit,* and there sitting down also from habit, what should I see, getting over my fence, but *the bar!* Yes, the old varmint was within a hundred yards of me, and the way he walked *over that fence*—stranger, he loomed up like a *black mist,* he seemed so large, and he walked right towards me. I raised myself, took deliberate aim, and fired. Instantly the varmint wheeled, gave a yell, and *walked through the fence* like a falling tree would through a cobweb. I started after, but was tripped up by my inexpressibles, which either from habit, or the excitement of the moment, were about my heels, and before I had really gathered myself up, I heard the old

varmint groaning in a thicket near by, like a thousand sinners, and by the time I reached him he was a corpse. Stranger, it took five niggers and myself to put that carcase on a mule's back, and old longears waddled under his load, as if he was foundered in every leg of his body, and with a common whopper of a bar, he would have trotted off, and enjoyed himself. 'Twould astonish you to know how big he was: I made a *bed-spread of his skin,* and the way it used to cover my bar mattress, and leave several feet on each side to tuck up, would have delighted you. It was in fact a creation bar, and if it had lived in Samson's time, and had met him, in a fair fight, it would have licked him in the twinkling of a dice-box. But, stranger, I never liked the way I hunted him, *and missed him.* There is something curious about it, I could never understand,—and I never was satisfied at his giving in so *easy at last.* Perhaps, he had heard of my preparations to hunt him the next day, so he jist come in, like Capt. Scott's coon, to save his wind to grunt with in dying; but that ain't likely. My private opinion is, that that bar was an *unhuntable bar, and died when his time come."*

When the story was ended, our hero sat some minutes with his auditors in a grave silence; I saw there was a mystery to him connected with the bear whose death he had just related, that had evidently made a strong impression on his mind. It was also evident that there was some superstitious awe connected with the affair,—a feeling common with all "children of the wood," when they meet with any thing out of their everyday experience. He was the first one, however, to break the silence, and jumping up, he asked all present to "liquor" before going to bed,—a thing which he did, with a number of companions, evidently to his heart's content.

Long before day, I was put ashore at my place of destination, and I can only follow with the reader, in imagination, our Arkansas friend, in his adventures at the "Forks of Cypress" on the Mississippi.

American Literature 1800-1860

III

HUMANITARIANISM IN NEW ENGLAND

1811 ∾ *Horace Greeley* ∾ 1872

A MAN who had left school at fourteen to earn his own living, after a lonely boyhood on a poverty-stricken New England farm, and who had apprenticed himself to a New York printer at twenty, for twenty-five dollars a month, was qualified to understand the social phenomena of unemployment and destitution in the metropolis in 1837. Greeley had come to New York in 1830. He spent ten years in building the modest capital and reputation which he risked in founding the *New York Tribune* in 1841. In another ten years he had attained relative wealth and wide influence with the *Tribune's* development as one of the most successful of American newspapers and a major force in national life.

Economic radicalism and leadership in many reforms marked the *Tribune's* policy. The paper was Greeley's personal organ—though he was markedly successful in choosing able associates—and it expressed the moral earnestness and passionate social concern of the man himself.

In the late 1850's the weekly edition of the *Tribune* had attained a circulation of 200,000—very large for those days—and was the political Bible of the West and upstate New York. But Greeley lost prestige during the Civil War through his vacillation in support of Lincoln and his demands for peace. The end of his life was tragic. Unfortunately persuaded by politicians and his own ambition to run for president in 1872, he was defeated by Grant in all but six states. Greeley's wife died on the eve of the election, and Greeley himself a few weeks thereafter.

[*The Autobiography of Horace Greeley, or Recollections of a Busy Life* (New York, 1868), is for the most part candid in its account of Greeley's own career, and shrewd in its comment on men and events. The general development of newspaper journalism and the part newspapers played in the controversies of the period are surveyed in Frank Luther Mott's *American Journalism* (New York, 1941). The best biography of Greeley is that by Don. C. Seitz (Indianapolis, 1926), though the more recent one by H. L. Stoddard (New York, 1946) adds some important material.]

From
THE AUTOBIOGRAPHY OF HORACE GREELEY
[1868]

SOCIALISM

THE WINTER of 1837-38, though happily mild and open till far into January, was one of pervading destitution and suffering in our city,[1] from paralysis of business and consequent dearth of employment. The liberality of those who could and would give was heavily taxed to save from famishing the tens of thousands who, being

[1] New York City.

needy and unable to find employment, first ran into debt so far as they could, and thenceforth must be helped or starve. For, in addition to all who may be said to belong here, legions of laborers, servants, etc., are annually dismissed in Autumn from the farms, country-seats, and water-ing-places of the suburban districts, and drift down to the city, whence they were mainly hired; vaguely hoping to find work here, which a small part of them do: the rest live on the good-nature of relatives, if such they have here, or on credit from boarding-houses, landlords, or grocers, so long as they can; and then make their choice between roguery and beggary, or change from this to that, or take them mixed, as chance may dictate. Since the general diffusion of railroads and the con-siderable extension of our manufacturing industry, business is far more equable than it was, even in prosperous times, thirty years ago; but Winter is still a season of privation and suffering to many thousands who live in tolerable comfort through the warmer seasons. To say that ten thousand young persons here annually take their first lessons in debauchery and crime would be to keep quite within the truth; and, while passion, ignorance, and miseducation ruin their thousands, I judge that destitution flowing from involuntary idleness sends more men and women to perdition, in this city, than any other cause, —intemperance possibly excepted.

I lived that Winter in the Sixth Ward, —then, as now, eminent for filth, squalor, rags, dissipation, want, and misery. A pub-lic meeting of its citizens was duly held early in December, and an organization formed thereat, by which committees were appointed to canvass the Ward from house to house, collect funds from those who could and would spare anything, ascertain the nature and extent of the existing desti-tution, and devise ways and means for its systematic relief. Very poor myself, I could give no money, or but a mite; so I gave time instead, and served, through several days, on one of the visiting com-mittees. I thus saw extreme destitution more closely than I had ever before ob-served it, and was enabled to scan its repulsive features intelligently. I saw two families, including six or eight children, burrowing in one cellar under a stable,— a prey to famine on the one hand, and to vermin and cutaneous maladies on the other, with sickness adding its horrors to those of a polluted atmosphere and a win-try temperature. I saw men who each, some-how, supported his family on an income of $5 per week or less, yet who cheerfully gave something to mitigate the sufferings of those who were *really* poor. I saw three widows, with as many children, living in an attic on the profits of an apple-stand which yielded less than $3 per week, and the landlord came in for a full third of that. But worst to bear of all was the pitiful plea of stout, resolute young men and young women: "We do not want alms; we are not beg-gars; we hate to sit here day by day idle and useless; help us to work,—we want no other help: why is it that we can have nothing to do?"

I pondered these scenes at intervals throughout the next two or three years, and was impelled thereby to write for *The New-Yorker*—I think, in the Winter of 1839-40—a series of articles entitled, "What shall be done for the Laborer?" I believe these attracted the attention of Mr. Albert Brisbane, a young man of liberal education and varied culture, a native of Batavia, N.Y., which he still regarded as his home, but who had travelled widely and observed thoughtfully; making the acquaintance in Paris of the school of Socialists called (after their founder) [2] St. Simonians, and that also of Charles Fourier,[3] the founder of a different school, which had been dis-tinguished by his name. Robert Owen,[4] by his experiments at New Lanark and his "New Views of Society," was the first in

[2] Claude Henri, Count de Saint-Simon, (1760-1825), French soldier and social philosopher.

[3] French socialist (1772-1837).

[4] British social reformer (1771-1858).

this century to win public attention to Socialism, though (I believe) Fourier had not only speculated, but written, before either of his co-laborers. But Owen was an extensive and successful manufacturer; St. Simon was a soldier, and the heir of a noble family; while Fourier was a poor clerk, reserved and taciturn, whose hard, dogmatic, algebraic style seemed expressly calculated to discourage readers and repel adherents; so that his disciples were few indeed, down to the date of his death in 1837. Mr. Brisbane,[5] returning not long afterward from Europe, prepared and published his first work—which was an exposition and commendation of Fourier's industrial system—in 1840. My acquaintance with the author and his work commenced soon afterward.

I sum up these three competing projects of Social Reform as follows:—

Owen.—Place human beings in proper relations, under favoring circumstances (among which I include Education and Intelligence), and they will do right rather than wrong. Hitherto, the heritage of the great majority has been filth, squalor, famine, ignorance, superstition; and these have impelled many to indolence and vice, if not to crime. Make their external conditions what they should be, and these will give place to industry, sobriety, and virtue.

St. Simon.—"Love is the fulfilling of the law." Secure to every one opportunity; let each do whatever he can do best; and the highest good of the whole will be achieved and perpetuated.

Fourier.—Society, as we find it, is organized rapacity. Half of its force is spent in repressing or resisting the jealousies and rogueries of its members. We need to organize Universal Justice based on Science. The true Eden lies before, not behind us. We may so provide that Labor, now repulsive, shall be attractive; while its efficiency in production shall be increased by the improvement of machinery and the extended use of natural forces, so as to secure abundance, education, and elegant luxury, to all. What is needed is to provide all with homes, employment, instruction, good living, the most effective implements, machinery, etc., securing to each the fair and full recompense of his achievement; and this can best be attained through the association of some four to five hundred families in a common household, and in the ownership and cultivation of a common domain, say of 2,000 acres, or about one acre to each person living thereon.

I accept, unreservedly, the views of no man, dead or living. "The master has said it," was never conclusive with me. Even though I have found him right nine times, I do not take his tenth proposition on trust; unless that also be proved sound and rational, I reject it. But I am convinced, after much study and reflection, that the Social Reformers are right on many points, even when clearly wrong on others; and I deem Fourier—though in many respects erratic, mistaken, visionary —the most suggestive and practical among them. I accept nothing on his authority; for I find many of his speculations fantastic, erroneous, and (in my view) pernicious; but on many points he commands my unreserved concurrence. Yet I prefer to set forth my own Social creed rather than his, even wherein mine was borrowed from his teachings; and mine is, briefly, as follows:—

I. I believe that there need be, and should be, no paupers who are not infantile, idiotic, or disabled; and that civilized society pays more for the support of able-bodied pauperism than the necessary cost of its extirpation.

II. I believe that they babble idly and libel Providence who talk of surplus Labor, or the inadequacy of Capital to supply employment to all who need it. Labor is often most required and best paid where

---

[5] Albert Brisbane (1809-90) published his *Social Destiny of Man* (based on the teachings of Fourier) in 1840. In the years immediately following he wrote a column for Greeley's *Tribune*.

Capital is scarcest (as was shown in California in 1849-50) ; and there is always—even in China—far more work than hands, provided the ability to devise and direct be not wanting. Where Labor stands idle, save in the presence of some great public calamity, there is a demonstrated deficiency, not of Capital, but of brains.

III. I believe that the efficiency of human effort is enormously, ruinously diminished by what I term Social Anarchy. That is to say: We spend half our energies in building fences and providing safeguards against each other's roguery, while our labor is rendered inefficient and inadequately productive by bad management, imperfect implements, a deficiency of power (animal or steam), and the inability of our producers to command and wield the most effective machinery. It is quite within the truth to estimate the annual product of our National Industry at less than one half what it might be if better applied and directed.

IV. Inefficiency in production is paralleled by waste in consumption. Insects and vermin devour at least one fourth of the farmer's harvests, which inadequate fertilizing and unskilful cultivation have already reduced far below the proper aggregate. A thousand cooks are required, and a thousand fires maintained, to prepare badly the food of a township; when a dozen fires and a hundred cooks might do it far better, and with a vast saving in quantity as well as improvement in quality. [I judge that the cooks of Paris would subsist One Million persons on the food consumed or wasted by Six Hundred Thousand in this city; feeding them better than they are now fed, and prolonging their lives by an average of five years.]

V. Youth should be a season of instruction in Industry and the Useful Arts, as well as in Letters and the Sciences mastered by their aid. Each child should be trained to skill and efficiency in productive Labor. The hours of children should be alternately devoted to Labor, Study, and Recreation, —say, two hours to each before, and a like allotment after, dinner each secular day. Thus each child would grow up an adept, not merely in letters, but in arts, —a skilful worker as well as a proficient in the lessons of the school-room,—able to do well, not one thing only, but many things—familiar with mechanical as well as agricultural processes, and acquainted with the use of steam and the direction of machinery. Not till one has achieved the fullest command, the most varied use, of all his faculties and powers, can he be properly said to be educated.

VI. Isolation is at war with efficiency and with progress. As "Iron sharpeneth iron," so are man's intellectual and inventive faculties stimulated by contact with his fellow-men. A nation of herdsmen, dwelling in movable tents, invents little or nothing, and makes no progress, or next to none. Serfdom was the general condition of the laboring class in Europe, until aggregation in cities and manufactories, diffusing intelligence, and nourishing aspiration, wrought its downfall.

VII. The poor work at perpetual disadvantage in isolation, because of the inadequacy of their means. Let us suppose that four or five hundred heads of families propose to embark in Agriculture. Each buys his little farm, his furniture, his implements, animals, seeds, fertilizers, etc., and —though he has purchased nothing that he does not urgently need—he finds his means utterly exhausted, and his farm and future exertions heavily burdened by debt. He hopes and labors to clear off the mortgage; but flood and drouth, frost and fire, work against him; his poverty compels him to do without many implements, and to plough or team with inadequate force; he runs up an account at the store, and pays twenty percent extra for his goods, because others, who buy on credit, fail to pay at all; and so he struggles on, till his strength fails, and he dies oppressed with debt. Such is the common lot.

VIII. Association would have these unite to purchase, inhabit, and cultivate a common domain,—say of two thousand acres,

—whereby these advantages over the isolated system would be realized:—

1. One fourth (at most) of the land required under the old system would be found abundant.

2. It could be far better allotted and appropriated to Grain, Grass, Fruits, Forest, Garden, etc.

3. The draught animals that were far too few, when dispersed among five hundred owners, on so many different farms, would be amply sufficient for a common domain.

4. Steam or water power could now be economically employed for a hundred purposes—cutting and sawing timber, threshing and grinding grain, ploughing the soil, and for many household uses—where the small farmer could not think of employing it.

5. Industry would find new and powerful incentives in the observation and praise or censure of the entire community; uniforms, banners, and music, with rivalry of bands of competing workers, would provoke emulation and lighten labor; while such recreations as dramas, concerts, readings, etc.,

—now utterly beyond the reach of rural workers,—would give a new zest to life. At present, our youth escape from rural industry when they can,—not that they really hate work, but that they find their leisure hours even duller and less endurable than those they give to rugged toil.

I must devote another chapter to a narration of my experiences as an advocate of the views above set forth, and a brief account of the efforts made within my knowledge to give them practical exemplification. That these efforts resulted in failures the world already knows: I will endeavor to set forth the facts dispassionately, so as to afford fair grounds for judgment as to how far these failures are due to circumstances, and how far they may be fairly charged to the system itself. I shall endeavor to lay little of the blame on well-abused Human Nature; since, if any system be ill adapted to Man as we find him, it may be excellently calculated for use on some other planet, but not on this one.

1803 ∽ *Orestes A. Brownson* ∽ 1876

LIKE Greeley left fatherless at an early age, growing up as a foster child in the household of dour and hardworking New England farmers, apprenticed as a boy of fourteen and thenceforth making his own way, Brownson too became a journalist and a reformer. While Greeley was observing the effects of the panic of 1837 in New York and preparing himself to become a great editor, Brownson was undergoing a similar tutelage in Boston. He had been active earlier in trying to establish a "workingman's party" in politics, and had edited a radical newspaper.

But Brownson's logical mind required him to look to the inner life of men for the sources of real reforms, and religious interests, which had dominated the years of his early manhood, again assumed primary importance. In Boston he became a popular minister of no denomination, and was closely associated with George Ripley, Theodore Parker, and William Ellery Channing the elder, less closely with Emerson and Bronson Alcott. His *Boston Quarterly Review*

(1838-42) was the medium for the expression of his personal views, and a markedly influential magazine.

In 1844 Brownson became a Roman Catholic. His search for a positive religious faith had previously led him from Presbyterianism to Universalism, and then through agnosticism to his own conception of the "Church of the Future," and to Unitarianism. There was no more wandering; through the medium of *Brownson's Quarterly Review,* which he edited (1844-64 and 1872-75), Brownson became the most influential Catholic layman of his generation in America.

[Brownson's own account of his religious experience, *The Convert* (1857) is his most important book. Much of Brownson's literary criticism appears in vol. XIX of *Works* (20 vols., Detroit, 1882-87), edited by his son, Henry F. Brownson. Recent belated recognition of Brownson's place in our intellectual and literary history has led to the appearance of biographical and critical studies by Arthur M. Schlesinger, Jr., *Orestes A. Brownson—A Pilgrim's Progress* (Boston, 1939); Doran Whalen, *Granite for God's House* (New York, 1943); and Theodore Maynard, *Orestes Brownson* (New York, 1944).]

THE LABORING CLASSES [1]
[1882 (1840)]

NO ONE can observe the signs of the times with much care, without perceiving that a crisis as to the relation of wealth and labor is approaching. It is useless to shut our eyes to the fact, and like the ostrich fancy ourselves secure because we have so concealed our heads that we see not the danger. We or our children will have to meet this crisis. The old war between the King and the Barons is well nigh ended, and so is that between the Barons and the Merchants and Manufacturers,—landed capital and commercial capital. The business man has become the peer of my Lord. And now commences the new struggle between the operative and his employer, between wealth and labor. Every day does this struggle extend further and wax stronger and fiercer; what or when the end will be God only knows.

In this coming contest there is a deeper question at issue than is commonly imagined; a question which is but remotely touched in your controversies about United States Banks and Sub Treasuries, chartered Banking and free Banking, free trade and corporations, although these controversies may be paving the way for it to come up. We have discovered no presentiment of it in any king's or queen's speech, nor in any president's message. It is embraced in no popular political creed of the day, whether christened Whig or Tory, *Juste-milieu* or Democratic. No popular senator, or deputy, or peer seems to have any glimpse of it; but it is working in the hearts of the million, is struggling to shape itself, and one day it will be uttered, and in thunder tones. Well will it be for him, who, on that day, shall be found ready to answer it.

What we would ask is, throughout the Christian world, the actual condition of the laboring classes, viewed simply and exclusively in their capacity of laborers? They constitute at least a moiety of the human race. We exclude the nobility, we exclude also the middle class, and include only actual laborers, who are laborers and not proprietors, owners of none of the funds of production, neither houses, shops, nor lands, nor implements of labor, being

[1] The text has been abridged from that of an article first published in the *Boston Quarterly Review.*

therefore solely dependent on their hands. We have no means of ascertaining their precise proportion to the whole number of the race; but we think we may estimate them at one half. In any contest they will be as two to one, because the large class of proprietors who are not employers, but laborers on their own lands or in their own shops will make common cause with them.

Now we will not so belie our acquaintance with political economy, as to allege that these alone perform all that is necessary to the production of wealth. We are not ignorant of the fact, that the merchant, who is literally the common carrier and exchange dealer, performs a useful service, and is therefore entitled to a portion of the proceeds of labor. But make all necessary deductions on his account, and then ask what portion of the remainder is retained, either in kind or in its equivalent, in the hands of the original producer, the workingman? All over the world this fact stares us in the face, the workingman is poor and depressed, while a large portion of the non-workingmen, in the sense we now use the term, are wealthy. It may be laid down as a general rule, with but few exceptions, that men are rewarded in an inverse ratio to the amount of actual service they perform. Under every government on earth the largest salaries are annexed to those offices, which demand of their incumbents the least amount of actual labor either mental or manual. And this is in perfect harmony with the whole system of repartition of the fruits of industry, which obtains in every department of society. Now here is the system which prevails, and here is its result. The whole class of simple laborers are poor, and in general unable to procure anything beyond the bare necessaries of life.

In regard to labor two systems obtain; one that of slave labor, the other that of free labor. Of the two, the first is, in our judgment, except so far as the feelings are concerned, decidedly the least oppressive. If the slave has never been a free man, we think, as a general rule, his sufferings are less than those of the free laborer at wages. As to actual freedom one has just about as much as the other. The laborer at wages has all the disadvantages of freedom and none of its blessings, while the slave, if denied the blessings, is freed from the disadvantages. We are no advocates of slavery, we are as heartily opposed to it as any modern abolitionist can be; but we say frankly that, if there must always be a laboring population distinct from proprietors and employers, we regard the slave system as decidedly preferable to the system at wages. It is no pleasant thing to go days without food, to lie idle for weeks, seeking work and finding none, to rise in the morning with a wife and children you love, and know not where to procure them a breakfast, and to see constantly before you no brighter prospect than the alms-house. Yet these are no unfrequent incidents in the lives of our laboring population. Even in seasons of general prosperity, when there was only the ordinary cry of "hard times," we have seen hundreds of people in a not very populous village, in a wealthy portion of our common country, suffering for want of the necessaries of life, willing to work, and yet finding no work to do. Many and many is the application of a poor man for work, merely for his food, we have seen rejected. These things are little thought of, for the applicants are poor; they fill no conspicuous place in society, and they have no biographers. But their wrongs are chronicled in heaven. It is said there is no want in this country. There may be less than in some other countries. But death by actual starvation in this country is, we apprehend, no uncommon occurrence. The sufferings of a quiet, unassuming but useful class of females in our cities, in general sempstresses, too proud to beg or to apply to the alms-house, are not easily told. They are industrious; they do all that they can find to do; but yet the little there is for them to do, and the miserable pittance they receive for it, is hardly sufficient to keep soul and body together. And yet there is a man who employs them to make shirts, trousers, etc., and grows rich on their labors. He is one of our respectable citizens, perhaps is praised in the newspapers for his liberal donations to some charitable institution. He passes among us as a pattern of morality, and is honored as a worthy Christian. And why should he not be, since our *Christian* community is made up of such as he, and since our clergy would not dare question his piety, lest they should incur the reproach of infidelity, and lose their standing, and their salaries? Nay, since our clergy are raised up, educated, fashioned, and sustained by such as he? Not a few of our churches rest on Mammon for their foundation. The basement is a trader's shop.

We pass through our manufacturing villages, most of them appear neat and flourishing. The operatives are well dressed, and we are told, well paid. They are said to be healthy, contented, and happy. This is the fair side of the picture; the side exhibited to distinguished visitors. There is a dark side, moral as well as physical. Of the common operatives, few, if any, by their wages, acquire a competence. A few of what Carlyle terms not inaptly the *body-servants* are well paid, and now and then an agent or an overseer rides in his coach. But the great mass wear out their health, spirits, and morals, without becoming one whit better off than when they commenced labor. The bills of mortality in these factory villages are not striking, we admit, for the poor girls when they can toil no longer go home to die. The average life, working life we mean, of the girls that come to Lowell, for instance, from Maine, New Hampshire, and Vermont, we have been assured, is only about three years. What becomes of them then? Few of them ever marry; fewer still ever return to their native places with reputations unimpaired. "She has worked in a Factory," is almost enough to damn to infamy the most worthy and virtuous girl. We know no sadder sight on earth than one of our factory villages

presents, when the bell at break of day, or at the hour of breakfast, or dinner, calls out its hundreds or thousands of operatives. We stand and look at these hard-working men and women hurrying in all directions, and ask ourselves, where go the proceeds of their labors? The man who employs them, and for whom they are toiling as so many slaves, is one of our city nabobs, revelling in luxury; or he is a member of our legislature, enacting laws to put money in his own pocket; or he is a member of Congress, contending for a high Tariff to tax the poor for the benefit of the rich; or in these times he is shedding crocodile tears over the deplorable condition of the poor laborer, while he docks his wages twenty-five per cent.; building miniature log cabins, shouting Harrison and "hard cider." And this man too would fain pass for a Christian and a republican. He shouts for liberty, stickles for equality, and is horrified at a Southern planter who keeps slaves.

One thing is certain; that of the amount actually produced by the operative, he retains a less proportion than it costs the master to feed, clothe, and lodge his slave. Wages is a cunning device of the devil, for the benefit of tender consciences, who would retain all the advantages of the slave system, without the expense, trouble, and odium of being slave-holders.

Messrs. Thome and Kimball, in their account of emancipation in the West Indies, establish the fact that the employer may have the same amount of labor done, twenty-five per cent. cheaper than the master. What does this fact prove, if not that wages is a more successful method of taxing labor than slavery? We really believe our Northern system of labor is more oppressive, and even more mischievous to morals, than the Southern. We, however, war against both. We have no toleration for either system. We would see the slave a man, but a free man, not a mere operative at wages. This he would not be were he now emancipated. Could the abolitionists effect all they propose, they would do the slave no service. Should emancipation work as well as they say, still it would do the slave no good. He would be a slave still, although with the title and cares of a freeman. If then we had no constitutional objections to abolitionism, we could not, for the reason here implied, be abolitionists.

The slave system, however, in name and form, is gradually disappearing from Christendom. It will not subsist much longer. But its place is taken by the system of labor at wages, and this system, we hold, is no improvement upon the one it supplants. Nevertheless the system of wages will triumph. It is the system which in name sounds honester than slavery, and in substance is more profitable to the master. It yields the wages of iniquity, without its opprobrium. It will therefore supplant slavery, and be sustained—for a time.

Now, what is the prospect of those who fall under the operation of this system? We ask, is there a reasonable chance that any considerable portion of the present generation of laborers, shall ever become owners of a sufficient portion of the funds of production, to be able to sustain themselves by laboring on their own capital, that is, as independent laborers? We need not ask this question, for everybody knows there is not. Well, is the condition of a laborer at wages the best that the great mass of the working people ought to be able to aspire to? Is it a condition,—nay can it be made a condition,—with which a man should be satisfied; in which he should be contented to live and die?

In our own country this condition has existed under its most favorable aspects, and has been made as good as it can be. It has reached all the excellence of which it is susceptible. It is now not improving but growing worse. The actual condition of the workingman to-day, viewed in all its bearings, is not so good as it was fifty years ago. If we have not been altogether misinformed, fifty years ago health and industrious habits constituted no mean stock

in trade, and with them almost any man might aspire to competence and independence. But it is so no longer. The wilderness has receded, and already the new lands are beyond the reach of the mere laborer, and the employer has him at his mercy. If the present relation subsist, we see nothing better for him in reserve than what he now possesses, but something altogether worse.

We are not ignorant of the fact that men born poor become wealthy, and that men born to wealth become poor; but this fact does not necessarily diminish the numbers of the poor, nor augment the numbers of the rich. The relative numbers of the two classes remain, or may remain, the same. But be this as it may; one fact is certain, no man born poor has ever, by his wages, as a simple operative, risen to the class of the wealthy. Rich he may have become, but it has not been by his own manual labor. He has in some way contrived to tax for his benefit the labor of others. He may have accumulated a few dollars which he has placed at usury, or invested in trade; or he may, as a master workman, obtain a premium on his journeymen; or he may have from a clerk passed to a partner, or from a workman to an overseer. The simple market wages for ordinary labor, has never been adequate to raise him from poverty to wealth. This fact is decisive of the whole controversy, and proves that the system of wages must be supplanted by some other system, or else one half of the human race must forever be the virtual slaves of the other.

Now the great work for this age and the coming, is to raise up the laborer, and to realize in our own social arrangements and in the actual condition of all men, that equality between man and man, which God has established between the rights of one and those of another. In other words, our business is to emancipate the proletaries, as the past has emancipated the slaves. This is our work. There must be no class of our fellow men doomed to toil through life as mere workmen at wages. If wages are tolerated it must be, in the case of the individual operative, only under such conditions that by the time he is of a proper age to settle in life, he shall have accumulated enough to be an independent laborer beyond the reach of the mere laborer, and on his own capital,—on his own farm or in his own shop. Here is our work. How is it to be done?

1810 ∾ *Margaret Fuller* ∾ 1850

MARGARET FULLER received an exceptional education through the perhaps excessive attention of her father, a lawyer and member of Congress, and was compelled to use it for financial ends when her father's death left her partially responsible for the support of the family. She became a protégé of Emerson's, and at his suggestion edited the magazine of the Transcendentalists, the *Dial*, 1840-42. She gave "conversations" for the women of Boston, following Bronson Alcott in this modification of the popular institution of the public lecture. In 1844 Horace Greeley hired her for his *New York Tribune*, and her best writing was done for its columns. Books based on her *Tribune* contributions were *A Summer on the Lakes* (1844), a highly readable account of a journey to Illinois and Michigan, and *Woman in the Nineteenth Century* (1845), in which she stated her arguments for increased rights and opportunities for women.

In 1846 Greeley sent his brilliant young columnist to Europe to write a series of articles on the status of women in various countries there. In Italy she met a young Italian patriot of noble family, Count Ossoli, fell in love with him, married him secretly, and participated with him in the Italian revolution of 1848. Compelled by financial distress to return to America with her husband and child on a small freighter, she was drowned off Fire Island, New York, in the great storm of July, 1850.

[Shortly after Margaret Fuller's death, Emerson and others collaborated in bringing out *Memoirs of Margaret Fuller Ossoli* (2 vols., Boston, 1852). Her brother, Arthur B. Fuller, collected many of her writings in *At Home and Abroad* (Boston, 1856) and *Life Without and Life Within* (Boston, 1869). Thomas Wentworth Higginson wrote a sympathetic biography (Boston, 1884). Modern biographies have been written by Margaret Bell, Katharine Anthony, and others.]

From
WOMAN IN THE NINETEENTH CENTURY
[1845]

THE PRINCIPLE OF LIBERTY

IT SHOULD be remarked that as the principle of liberty is better understood, and more nobly interpreted, a broader protest is made in behalf of Woman. As men become aware that few men have had a fair chance, they are inclined to say that no women have had a fair chance. The French Revolution, that strangely disguised angel, bore witness in favor of Woman, but interpreted her claims no less ignorantly than those of Man. Its idea of happiness did not rise beyond outward enjoyment, unobstructed by the tyranny of others. The title it gave was *citoyen, citoyenne;* and it is not unimportant to Woman that even this species of equality was awarded her. Before, she could be condemned to perish on the scaffold for treason, not as a citizen but as a subject. The right with which this title then invested a human being was that of bloodshed and license. The Goddess of Liberty was impure. As we read the poem addressed to her not long since by Béranger, we can scarcely refrain from tears as painful as the tears of blood that flowed when "such crimes were committed in her name." Yes! Man, born to purify and animate the unintelligent and the cold, can in his madness degrade and pollute no less the fair and the chaste. Yet truth was prophesied in the ravings of that hideous fever caused by long ignorance and abuse. Europe is conning a valued lesson from the bloodstained page. The same tendencies further unfolded will bear good fruit in this country.

Yet by men in this country, as by the Jews when Moses was leading them to the promised land, everything has been done that inherited depravity could do to hinder the promise of Heaven from its fulfillment. The cross, here as elsewhere, has been planted only to be blasphemed by cruelty and fraud. The name of the Prince of Peace has been profaned by all kinds of injustice toward the Gentile whom he said

he came to save. But I need not speak of what has been done toward the Red Man, the Black Man. Those deeds are the scoff of the world; and they have been accompanied by such pious words that the gentlest would not dare to intercede with, "Father, forgive them, for they know not what they do."

Here as elsewhere the gain of creation consists always in the growth of individual minds, which live and aspire as flowers bloom and birds sing in the midst of morasses; and in the continual development of that thought, the thought of human destiny, which it is given to eternity adequately to express, and which ages of failure only seemingly impede. Only seemingly; and whatever seems to the contrary, this country is as surely destined to elucidate a great moral law as Europe was to promote the mental culture of Man.

Though the national independence be blurred by the servility of individuals; though freedom and equality have been proclaimed only to leave room for a monstrous display of slavedealing with slavekeeping; though the free American so often feels himself free, like the Roman, only to pamper his appetites and his indolence through the misery of his fellow-beings; still it is not in vain that the verbal statement has been made, "All men are born free and equal." There it stands, a golden certainty wherewith to encourage the good, to shame the bad.

1807 ∾ *John Greenleaf Whittier* ∾ *1892*

A FOND sister and an alert editor share immediate responsibility for the initiation of the literary career of Whittier. His people had been New Englanders since 1638, and were notably devout and industrious; they were also poor and obscure. John had attended a few brief terms of a country school, worked too hard at chores and in the fields for his weak body's well-being, read such books as the household afforded—chiefly lives of prominent Quakers—

and as he could borrow. Surely many another New England youngster had discovered Burns at fourteen or so, and tried to write verses like his.

This one, however, had a sister who, believing in his talent, secretly sent his poems to the editor of a local paper; and the editor, little older than the poet, warmed generously to their meager talent, printed them, and made a horse-and-buggy journey to the Whittier farm to see the author. His name was William Lloyd Garrison.

That visit was a turning-point in Whittier's life. In from the field to meet Garrison came the tall, slender youth, barefoot, in work-stained homespun shirt and pants. He went back to the field an hour or so later—but with his father's reluctant promise that he could attend the new academy at nearby Haverhill that winter if he earned his own way, and with his feet firmly set on the road that was to bring him the love of millions of readers and the hatred of other millions, as well as a sure place at last in the history of his country's literature.

He earned the money for the academy by making shoes; and the shoemaker's trade helped at other times in the many lean years that followed, between school-teaching, more farming, and various editorial jobs. Garrison got him the jobs, at first. Very soon they came unsought, and preferment of other kinds as well. There was rare metal in the tall young Quaker with the steady eyes and quiet voice and the alert and searching mind—a quality that led his neighbors to elect him to the State Legislature at 30, and again the following year.

The second time he did not serve. He had another job, and to the prompting of his inner light a greater one. John Whittier had become an abolitionist. A majority of the most active abolitionists were Quakers; the Society of Friends had renounced slavery half a century before, under the leadership of John Woolman. The friendly influence of Garrison might not have been needed to bring Whittier into the movement of which Garrison was already the spearhead. But it was thanks in part to Garrison, surely, that his part in it became so prominent so early.

In 1833 Whittier was a delegate from Massachusetts to the history-making first convention of the American Anti-Slavery Society. He was a member of Garrison's committee that drafted the famous resolutions of that convention, and one of the signers. Thirty years later, when the objective of emancipation had been won, Whittier declared that his signature to those resolutions meant more to him than his name on the title-page of any book.

His biography for those thirty years is largely the story of the abolition movement. His first wide fame as a poet came from his contributions to Garrison's *Liberator, The National Era* (which also published *Uncle Tom's Cabin* serially), and other abolitionist periodicals; these poems were collected in 1846 under the title *Voices of Freedom.* Though Bryant, Emerson, Longfellow, and Lowell wrote anti-slavery poems during this period, Whittier surpassed them all in the volume and the vigor of his work and came to be generally recognized as the foremost literary spokesman of the movement.

Pushed aside during the three decades of his devotion to abolitionism, but never completely abandoned, was Whittier's more individual creative vision and purpose as a writer: the reflection and expression of the rural New England in which he spent all but a year or two of his long life. He struck out this field in his first volume, *Legends of New England* (1831), and cultivated it further in *Moll Pitcher* (1832) and *Mogg Megone* (1836). In the period during which his poetry was still devoted largely to the battle against slavery, this other interest found expression in prose, which has lasting interest and value and has been unduly neglected by most critics and little known to the general reader. First place in the small body of this creative prose belongs to the brief historical novel, *Margaret Smith's Journal* (1849). Rich in authentic atmosphere and sound in characterization, quiet but genuinely dramatic, this story of a young girl fresh from England in Puritan Massachusetts, in the early days of the colony, remains one of the finest of all fictional recreations of the American past. It is a not unworthy companion to Hawthorne's greater romance, *The Scarlet Letter,* published the following year. Also still vital for the modern reader is the volume of essays called *Literary Recreations and Miscellanies* (1854). A delightful individual piece is "My Summer with Dr. Singletary."

Once the battle against slavery was won, Whittier's regionalism came swiftly to its most mature expression. *Snow-Bound* (1866) is by far his most important poem. It is wholly representative of Whittier's best qualities as a writer in its simple music, homely concreteness, and warm sincerity; and it stands supreme among literary expressions of rural New England life.

For twenty-six years Whittier continued to publish occasional small volumes; the best of the poems they contain are briefer treatments of New England farm and village life. Living nearly all of his many years in small Massachusetts towns, travelling little, knowing no wide circle of friends, Whittier was the most parochial of distinguished American writers. Only two fields received his full creative effort: abolitionism, and past and present rural New England. Of his achievement in the first of these fields, the social historian may be a better judge than the literary critic. Of his achievement in the second there can be no doubt.

[Whitman Bennett's *Whittier, Bard of Freedom* (Chapel Hill, 1941) is a good biography. H. H. Clark's *Whittier* has been announced for early publication in the American Writers Series. G. R. Carpenter's *John Greenleaf Whittier* (Boston, 1903), in the American Men of Letters Series, is a readable sequence of biographical and critical essays. A more extended biographical study is that of S. T. Pickard, *The Life and Letters of John Greenleaf Whittier,* 2 vols. (Boston, 1894; revised edit., 1907).]

IN THE EVIL DAYS
[1850]

The evil days have come, the poor
  Are made a prey;
Bar up the hospitable door,
Put out the fire-lights, point no more
  The wanderer's way.   5

For Pity now is crime; the chain
  Which binds our States
Is melted at her hearth in twain,
Is rusted by her tears' soft rain:
  Close up her gates.   10

Our Union, like a glacier stirred
  By voice below,
Or bell of kine, or wing of bird,
A beggar's crust, a kindly word
  May overthrow!   15

Poor, whispering tremblers! yet we boast
  Our blood and name;
Bursting its century-bolted frost,
Each gray cairn on the Northman's coast
  Cries out for shame!   20

Oh for the open firmament,
  The prairie free,
The desert hillside, cavern-rent,
The Pawnee's lodge, the Arab's tent,
  The Bushman's tree!   25

Than web of Persian loom most rare,
  Or soft divan,
Better the rough rock, bleak and bare,
Or hollow tree, which man may share
  With suffering man.   30

I hear a voice: "Thus saith the Law,
  Let Love be dumb;
Clasping her liberal hands in awe,
Let sweet-lipped Charity withdraw
  From hearth and home."   35

I hear another voice: "The poor
  Are thine to feed;
Turn not the outcast from thy door,
Nor give to bonds and wrong once more
  Whom God hath freed."   40

Dear Lord! between that law and Thee
  No choice remains;
Yet not untrue to man's decree,
Though spurning its rewards, is he
  Who bears its pains.   45

Not mine Sedition's trumpet-blast
  And threatening word;
I read the lesson of the Past
That firm endurance wins at last
  More than the sword.   50

O clear-eyed Faith, and Patience thou
  So calm and strong!
Lend strength to weakness, teach us how
The sleepless eyes of God look through
  This night of wrong!   55

THE FAREWELL
OF A VIRGINIA SLAVE MOTHER
TO HER DAUGHTERS SOLD INTO
SOUTHERN BONDAGE
[1841 (1838)]

Gone, gone,—sold and gone,
To the rice-swamp dank and lone.
Where the slave-whip ceaseless swings,
Where the noisome insect stings,
Where the fever demon strews   5
Poison with the falling dews,
Where the sickly sunbeams glare
Through the hot and misty air;
Gone, gone,—sold and gone,
To the rice-swamp dank and lone,   10
From Virginia's hills and waters;
Woe is me, my stolen daughters!

Gone, gone,—sold and gone,
To the rice-swamp dank and lone.
There no mother's eye is near them, 15
There no mother's ear can hear them;
Never, when the torturing lash
Seams their back with many a gash,
Shall a mother's kindness bless them,

a mother's arms caress them. 20
Gone, gone,—sold and gone,
To the rice-swamp dank and lone,
From Virginia's hills and waters;
Woe is me, my stolen daughters!

Gone, gone,—sold and gone, 25
To the rice-swamp dank and lone.
Oh, when weary, sad, and slow,
From the fields at night they go,
Faint with toil, and racked with pain,
To their cheerless homes again, 30
There no brother's voice shall greet them;
There no father's welcome meet them.
Gone, gone,—sold and gone,
To the rice-swamp dank and lone,
From Virginia's hills and waters; 35
Woe is me, my stolen daughters!

Gone, gone,—sold and gone,
To the rice-swamp dank and lone.
From the tree whose shadow lay
On their childhood's place of play; 40
From the cool spring where they drank;
Rock, and hill, and rivulet bank;
From the solemn house of prayer,
And the holy counsels there;
Gone, gone,—sold and gone, 45
To the rice-swamp dank and lone,
From Virginia's hills and waters;
Woe is me, my stolen daughters!

Gone, gone,—sold and gone,
To the rice-swamp dank and lone; 50
Toiling through the weary day,
And at night the spoiler's prey.
Oh, that they had earlier died,
Sleeping calmly, side by side,
Where the tyrant's power is o'er, 55
And the fetter galls no more!
Gone, gone,—sold and gone
To the rice-swamp dank and lone;
From Virginia's hills and waters;
Woe is me, my stolen daughters! 60

Gone, gone,—sold and gone,
To the rice-swamp dank and lone.
By the holy love He beareth;
By the bruised reed He spareth;
Oh, may He, to whom alone 65

All their cruel wrongs are known,
Still their hope and refuge prove,
With a more than mother's love.
Gone, gone,—sold and gone,
To the rice-swamp dank and lone, 70
From Virginia's hills and waters;
Woe is me, my stolen daughters!

ICHABOD [1]
[1850]

So fallen! So lost! the light withdrawn
Which once he wore!
The glory from his gray hairs gone
Forevermore!

Revile him not, the Tempter hath 5
A snare for all;

---

[1] This poem was the outcome of the surprise and grief and forecast of evil consequences which I felt on reading the seventh of March speech of Daniel Webster in support of the "compromise," and the Fugitive Slave Law. No partisan or personal enmity dictated it. On the contrary my admiration of the splendid personality and intellectual power of the great Senator was never stronger than when I laid down his speech, and, in one of the saddest moments of my life, penned my protest. I saw, as I wrote, with painful clearness its sure results,— the Slave Power arrogant and defiant, strengthened and encouraged to carry out its scheme for the extension of its baleful system, or the dissolution of the Union, the guarantees of personal liberty in the free States broken down, and the whole country made the hunting-ground of slave-catchers. In the horror of such a vision, so soon fearfully fulfilled, if one spoke at all, he could only speak in tones of stern and sorrowful rebuke.

But death softens all resentments, and the consciousness of a common inheritance of frailty and weakness modifies the severity of judgment. Years after, in *The Lost Occasion*, I gave utterance to an almost universal regret that the great statesman did not live to see the flag which he loved trampled under the feet of Slavery, and, in view of this desecration, make his last days glorious in defence of "Liberty and Union, one and inseparable."—Whittier's note.

And pitying tears, not scorn and wrath,
　Befit his fall!

Oh, dumb be passion's stormy rage,
　When he who might 10
Have lighted up and led his age,
　Falls back in night.

Scorn! would the angels laugh to mark
　A bright soul driven,
Fiend-goaded, down the endless dark, 15
　From hope and heaven!

Let not the land once proud of him
　Insult him now,
Nor brand with deeper shame his dim,
　Dishonored brow.

But let its humbled sons, instead,
　From sea to lake,
A long lament, as for the dead,
　In sadness make.

Of all we loved and honored, naught 25
　Save power remains;
A fallen angel's pride of thought,
　Still strong in chains.

All else is gone; from those great eyes
　The soul has fled:
When faith is lost, when honor dies,
　The man is dead!

Then, pay the reverence of old days
　To his dead fame;
Walk backward, with averted gaze, 35
　And hide the shame!

THE RENDITION [1]
[1854]

I heard the train's shrill whistle call,
　I saw an earnest look beseech,
　And rather by that look than speech
My neighbor told me all.

And, as I thought of Liberty 5
　Marched handcuffed down that sworded
　　street,

The solid earth beneath my feet
　Reeled fluid as the sea.

I felt a sense of bitter loss,—
　Shame, tearless grief, and stifling
　　wrath, 10
　And loathing fear, as if my path
A serpent stretched across.

All love of home, all pride of place,
　All generous confidence and trust,
　Sank smothering in that deep disgust 15
And anguish of disgrace.

Down on my native hills of June,
　And home's green quiet, hiding all,
　Fell sudden darkness like the fall
Of midnight upon noon! 20

And Law, an unloosed maniac, strong,
　Blood-drunken, through the blackness
　　trod,
　Hoarse-shouting in the ear of God
The blasphemy of wrong.

"O Mother, from thy memories proud, 25
　Thy old renown, dear Commonwealth,
　Lend this dead air a breeze of health,
And smite with stars this cloud.

"Mother of Freedom, wise and brave,
　Rise awful in thy strength," I said; 30
　Ah me! I spake but to the dead;
I stood upon her grave!

[1] On the 2d of June, 1854, Anthony
Burns, a fugitive slave from Virginia, after
being under arrest for ten days in the Boston Court House, was remanded to slavery
under the Fugitive Slave Act, and taken
down State Street to a steamer chartered
by the United States Government, under
guard of United States troops and artillery, Massachusetts militia, and Boston
police. Public excitement ran high, a futile
attempt to rescue Burns having been made
during his confinement, and the streets
were crowded with tens of thousands of
people of whom many came from other
towns and cities of the State to witness
the humiliating spectacle.—Whittier's note.

SKIPPER IRESON'S RIDE[1]
[1860 (1857)]

Of all the rides since the birth of time,
Told in story or sung in rhyme,—
On Apuleius's Golden Ass,
Or one-eyed Calendar's horse of brass,
Witch astride of a human back,   5
Islam's prophet on Al-Borák,—
The strangest ride that ever was sped
Was Ireson's, out from Marblehead!
  Old Floyd Ireson, for his hard heart,
  Tarred and feathered and carried in a
    cart   10
  By the women of Marblehead!

Body of turkey, head of owl,
Wings a-droop like a rained-on fowl,
Feathered and ruffled in every part,
Skipper Ireson stood in the cart.   15
Scores of women, old and young,
Strong of muscle, and glib of tongue,
Pushed and pulled up the rocky lane,
Shouting and singing the shrill refrain:
  "Here's Flud Oirson, fur his horrd
    horrt,   20
  Torr'd an' futherr'd an' corr'd in a
    corrt
  By the women o' Morble'ead!"

Wrinkled scold with hands on hips,
Girls in bloom of cheek and lips,
Wild-eyed, free-limbed, such as chase   25
Bacchus round some antique vase,
Brief of skirt, with ankles bare,
Loose of kerchief and loose of hair,
With conch-shells blowing and fish-horns'
    twang,
Over and over the Maenads sang: 30
  "Here's Flud Oirson, for his horrd horrt,
  Torr'd an' futherr'd an' corr'd in a corrt
  By the women o' Morble'ead!"

Small pity for him—He sailed away
From a leaking ship in Chaleur Bay,—   35
Sailed away from a sinking wreck,

With his own town's-people on her deck!
"Lay by! Lay by!" they called to him.
Back he answered, "Sink or swim!
Brag of your catch of fish again!"   40
And off he sailed through the fog and
    rain!
  Old Floyd Ireson, for his hard heart,
  Tarred and feathered and carried in a
    cart
  By the women of Marblehead!

Fathoms deep in dark Chaleur   45
That wreck shall lie forevermore.
Mother and sister, wife and maid,
Looked from the rocks of Marblehead
Over the moaning and rainy sea,—
Looked for the coming that might not
    be!   50
What did the winds and the sea-birds say
Of the cruel captain who sailed away—
  Old Floyd Ireson, for his hard heart,
  Tarred and feathered and carried in a
    cart
  By the women of Marblehead!   55

Through the street, on either side,
Up flew windows, doors swung wide;
Sharp-tongued spinsters, old wives gray,
Treble lent the fish-horn's bray.
Sea-worn grandsires, cripple-bound,   60
Hulks of old sailors run aground,
Shook head, and fist, and hat, and cane,
And cracked with curses the hoarse refrain:
  "Here's Flud Oirson, fur his horrd horrt,
  Torr'd an' futherr'd an' corr'd in a
    corrt   65
  By the women o' Marble'ead!"

Sweetly along the Salem road
Bloom of orchard and lilac showed.

---

[1] Whittier based this poem on an old
Marblehead ballad, but did not adhere
fully to the facts of the incident. James
Russell Lowell, as editor of the *Atlantic
Monthly* (in which the poem was first
published) suggested the use of dialect for
the refrain.

Little the wicked skipper knew
Of the fields so green and the sky so
    blue.   70
Riding there in his sorry trim,
Like an Indian idol glum and grim,
Scarcely he seemed the sound to hear
Of voices shouting, far and near:
    "Here's Flud Oirson, fur his horrd
      horrt,   75
    Torr'd an' futherr'd an' corr'd in a
      corrt
    By the women o' Morble'ead!"

"Hear me, neighbors!" at last he cried,—
"What to me is this noisy ride?
What is the shame that clothes the skin 80
To the nameless horror that lives within?
Waking or sleeping, I see a wreck!
And hear a cry from a reeling deck!
Hate me and curse me,—I only dread
The hand of God and the face of the
    dead!"   85
    Said old Floyd Ireson, for his hard
      heart,
    Tarred and feathered and carried in a
      cart
    By the women of Marblehead!

Then the wife of the skipper lost at sea
Said, "God has touched him! Why should
    we!"   90
Said an old wife mourning her only son,
"Cut the rogue's tether and let him run!"
So with soft relentings and rude excuse,
Half scorn, half pity, they cut him loose,
And gave him a cloak to hide him in, 95
And left him alone with his shame and
    sin.
    Poor Floyd Ireson, for his hard heart,
    Tarred and feathered and carried in a
      cart
    By the women of Marblehead!

TELLING THE BEES [1]
[1860 (1858)]

Here is the place; right over the hill
Runs the path I took;

You can see the gap in the old wall still,
And the stepping-stones in the shallow
    brook.

There is the house, with the gate red-
    barred,   5
    And the poplars tall;
And the barn's brown length, and the
    cattle-yard,
    And the white horns tossing above the
      wall.

There are the beehives ranged in the sun;
    And down by the brink   10
Of the brook are her poor flowers, weed
    o'errun,
    Pansy and daffodil, rose and pink.

A year has gone, as the tortoise goes,
    Heavy and slow;
And the same rose blows, and the same
    sun glows,   15
    And the same brook sings of a year ago.

There's the same sweet clover-smell in the
    breeze:
    And the June sun warm
Tangles his wings of fire in the trees,
    Setting, as then, over Fernside farm. 20

I mind me how with a lover's care
    From my Sunday coat
I brushed off the burrs, and smoothed my
    hair,
    And cooled at the brookside my brow and
    throat.

Since we parted, a month had passed,— 25
    To love, a year;

---

[1] A remarkable custom, brought from
the Old Country, formerly prevailed in
the rural districts of New England. On
the death of a member of the family, the
bees were at once informed of the event,
and their hives dressed in mourning. This
ceremonial was supposed to be necessary
to prevent the swarms from leaving their
hives and seeking a new home.—Whittier's
note.

Down through the beeches I looked at last
On the little red gate and the well-
    sweep near.

I can see it all now,—the slantwise rain
Of light through the leaves,   30
The sundown's blaze on her window-pane,
The bloom of her roses under the eaves.

Just the same as a month before,—
The house and the trees,
The barn's brown gable, the vine by the
    door,—   35
Nothing changed but the hive of bees.

Before them, under the garden wall,
Forward and back,
Went drearily singing the chore-girl small,
Draping each hive with a shred of
    black.   40

Trembling, I listened: the summer sun
Had the chill of snow;
For I knew she was telling the bees of one
Gone on the journey we all must go!

Then I said to myself, "My Mary weeps 45
For the dead to-day:
Haply her blind old grandsire sleeps
The fret and the pain of his age away."

But her dog whined low; on the doorway
    sill,
With his cane to his chin,   50
The old man sat; and the chore-girl still
  Sung to the bees stealing out and in.

And the song she was singing ever since
In my ear sounds on:—
"Stay at home, pretty bees, fly not
    hence!   55
Mistress Mary is dead and gone!"

THE TRAILING ARBUTUS
[1881 (1879)]

I wandered lonely where the pine-trees
    made
Against the bitter East their barricade,
  And, guided by its sweet
Perfume, I found, within a narrow dell,
The trailing spring flower tinted like a
    shell   5
  Amid dry leaves and mosses at my feet.

From under dead boughs, for whose loss
    the pines
Moaned ceaseless overhead, the blossoming
    vines
  Lifted their glad surprise,
While yet the bluebird smoothed in leaf-
    less trees   10
His feathers ruffled by the chill sea-breeze,
  And snow-drifts lingered under April
    skies.

As, pausing, o'er the lonely flower I bent,
I thought of lives thus lowly, clogged and
    pent,
  Which yet find room,   15
Through care and cumber, coldness and
    decay,
To lend a sweetness to the ungenial day,
  And make the sad earth happier for their
    bloom.

SNOW-BOUND: A WINTER IDYL [1]
[1866]

TO THE MEMORY OF THE HOUSEHOLD IT
DESCRIBES, THIS POEM IS DEDICATED
BY THE AUTHOR

"As the Spirits of Darkness be stronger
in the dark, so good Spirits which be
Angels of Light are augmented not only by
the Divine light of the Sun, but also by
our common Wood Fire: and as the Celestial Fire drives away dark spirits, so
also this our Fire of Wood doth the same."
(COR. AGRIPPA, *Occult Philosophy*, book I,
chap. v.)

"Announced by all the trumpets of the sky,
    Arrives the snow; and, driving o'er the
        fields,
    Seems nowhere to alight; the whited air
    Hides hills and woods, the river and the
        heaven,
    And veils the farm-house at the garden's
        end.

The sled and traveller stopped, the cour-
        ier's feet
Delayed, all friends shut out, the house-
        mates sit
Around the radiant fireplace, inclosed
In a tumultuous privacy of storm."
            (EMERSON, *The Snow-Storm*.)

The sun that brief December day
Rose cheerless over hills of gray,
And, darkly circled, gave at noon
A sadder light than waning moon.
Slow tracing down the thickening sky 5
Its mute and ominous prophecy,
A portent seeming less than threat,
It sank from sight before it set.
A chill no coat, however stout,
Of homespun stuff could quite shut out, 10
A hard, dull bitterness of cold,
That checked, mid-vein, the circling race
Of life-blood in the sharpened face,
The coming of the snow-storm told.

---

[1] The inmates of the family at the Whittier homestead who are referred to in the
poem were my father, mother, my brother
and two sisters, and my uncle and aunt,
both unmarried. In addition, there was the
district school-master, who boarded with us.
The "not unfeared, half-welcome guest"
was Harriet Livermore, daughter of Judge
Livermore, of New Hampshire, a young
woman of fine natural ability, enthusiastic,
eccentric, with slight control over her violent temper, which sometimes made her
religious profession doubtful. She was
equally ready to exhort in school-house
prayer-meetings and dance in a Washington ball-room, while her father was a
member of Congress. She early embraced
the doctrine of the Second Advent, and
felt it her duty to proclaim the Lord's
speedy coming. With this message she
crossed the Atlantic and spent the greater
part of a long life in travelling over Europe and Asia. She lived some time with
Lady Hester Stanhope, a woman as fantastic and mentally strained as herself, on
the slope of Mt. Lebanon, but finally quar-
relled with her in regard to two white
horses with red marks on their backs which
suggested the idea of saddles, on which
her titled hostess expected to ride into
Jerusalem with the Lord. A friend of mine
found her, when quite an old woman,
wandering in Syria with a tribe of Arabs,
who with the Oriental notion that madness
is inspiration, accepted her as their prophetess and leader. At the time referred to
in *Snow-Bound* she was boarding at the
Rocks Village, about two miles from us.

In my boyhood, in our lonely farm-
house, we had scanty sources of information; few books and only a small weekly
newspaper. Our only annual was the Almanac. Under such circumstances story-
telling was a necessary resource in the
long winter evenings. My father when a
young man had traversed the wilderness
to Canada, and could tell us of his adventures with Indians and wild beasts and
of his sojourn in the French villages. My
uncle was ready with his record of hunting
and fishing and, it must be confessed, with
stories which he at least half believed, of
witchcraft and apparitions. My mother,
who was born in the Indian-haunted region of Somersworth, New Hampshire, between Dover and Portsmouth, told us of
the inroads of the savages, and the narrow
escape of her ancestors. She described
strange people who lived on the Piscataqua and Cocheco, among whom was Ban-
tam the sorcerer. I have in my possession
the wizard's "conjuring book," which he
solemnly opened when consulted. It is a
copy of Cornelius Agrippa's *Magic* printed
in 1651. . . . —Whittier's note.

The wind blew east; we heard the roar 15
Of Ocean on his wintry shore,
And felt the strong pulse throbbing there
Beat with low rhythm our inland air.
Meanwhile we did our nightly chores,—
Brought in the wood from out of doors, 20
Littered the stalls, and from the mows
Raked down the herd's-grass for the cows:
Heard the horse whinnying for his corn;
And, sharply clashing horn on horn,
Impatient down the stanchion rows 25
The cattle shake their walnut bows;
While, peering from his early perch
Upon the scaffold's pole of birch,
The cock his crested helmet bent
And down his querulous challenge sent. 30
Unwarmed by any sunset light
The gray day darkened into night,
A night made hoary with the swarm
And whirl-dance of the blinding storm,
As zigzag wavering to and fro 35
Crossed and recrossed the wingèd snow:
And ere the early bedtime came
The white drift piled the window-frame,
And through the glass the clothes-line posts
Looked in like tall and sheeted ghosts. 40

So all night long the storm roared on:
The morning broke without a sun;
In tiny spherule traced with lines
Of Nature's geometric signs,
In starry flake and pellicle 45
All day the hoary meteor fell;
And, when the second morning shone,
We looked upon a world unknown,
On nothing we could call our own.
Around the glistening wonder bent 50
The blue walls of the firmament,
No cloud above, no earth below,—
A universe of sky and snow!
The old familiar sights of ours
Took marvellous shapes; strange domes
 and towers 55
Rose up where sty or corn-crib stood,
Or garden-wall or belt of wood;
A smooth white mound the brush-pile
 showed,
A fenceless drift what once was road;
The bridle-post an old man sat 60
With loose-flung coat and high cocked hat;

The well-curb had a Chinese roof;
And even the long sweep, high aloof,
In its slant splendor, seemed to tell
Of Pisa's leaning miracle. 65

A prompt, decisive man, no breath
Our father wasted: "Boys, a path!"
Well pleased, (for when did farmer boy
Count such a summons less than joy?)
Our buskins on our feet we drew; 70
 With mittened hands, and caps drawn
 low,
 To guard our necks and ears from snow,
We cut the solid whiteness through;
And, where the drift was deepest, made
A tunnel walled and overlaid 75
With dazzling crystal: we had read
Of rare Aladdin's wondrous cave,
And to our own his name we gave,
With many a wish the luck were ours
To test his lamp's supernal powers. 80
We reached the barn with merry din,
And roused the prisoned brutes within.
The old horse thrust his long head out,
And grave with wonder gazed about;
The cock his lusty greeting said, 85
And forth his speckled harem led;
The oxen lashed their tails, and hooked,
And mild reproach of hunger looked;
The hornèd patriarch of the sheep,
Like Egypt's Amun [2] roused from sleep, 90
Shook his sage head with gesture mute,
And emphasized with stamp of foot.

All day the gusty north-wind bore
The loosening drift its breath before;
Low circling round its southern zone, 95
The sun through dazzling snow-mist shone.
No church-bell lent its Christian tone
To the savage air, no social smoke
Curled over woods of snow-hung oak.
A solitude made more intense 100
By dreary-voicèd elements,
The shrieking of the mindless wind,
The moaning tree-boughs swaying blind,
And on the glass the unmeaning beat
Of ghostly finger-tips of sleet. 105

---

[2] Amen or Amon, ram-headed deity of
life and reproduction.

Beyond the circle of our hearth
No welcome sound of toil or mirth
Unbound the spell, and testified
Of human life and thought outside.
We minded that the sharpest ear   110
The buried brooklet could not hear,
The music of whose liquid lip
Had been to us companionship,
And, in our lonely life, had grown
To have an almost human tone.   115

As night drew on, and, from the crest
Of wooded knolls that ridged the west,
The sun, a snow-blown traveller, sank
From sight beneath the smothering bank,
We piled with care our nightly stack   120
Of wood against the chimney-back,—
The oaken log, green, huge, and thick,
And on its top the stout backstick;
The knotty forestick laid apart,
And filled between with curious art   125
The ragged brush; then, hovering near,
We watched the first red blaze appear,
Heard the sharp crackle, caught the gleam
On whitewashed wall and sagging beam,
Until the old, rude-furnished room   130
Burst, flower-like, into rosy bloom;
While radiant with a mimic flame
Outside the sparkling drift became,
And through the bare-boughed lilac-tree
Our own warm hearth seemed blazing
        free.   135
The crane and pendent trammels showed,
The Turks' heads on the andirons glowed;
While childish fancy, prompt to tell
The meaning of the miracle,
Whispered the old rhyme: *"Under the
        tree*   140
When fire outdoors burns merrily,
There the witches are making tea."

The moon above the eastern wood
Shone at its full; the hill-range stood
Transfigured in the silver flood,   145
Its blown snows flashing cold and keen,
Dead white, save where some sharp ravine
Took shadow, or the sombre green
Of hemlocks turned to pitchy black
Against the whiteness at their back.   150
For such a world and such a night

Most fitting that unwarming light,
Which only seemed where'er it fell
To make the coldness visible.

Shut in from all the world without,   155
We sat the clean-winged hearth about,
Content to let the north-wind roar
In baffled rage at pane and door,
While the red logs before us beat
The frost-line back with tropic heat;   160
And ever, when a louder blast
Shook beam and rafter as it passed,
The merrier up its roaring draught
The great throat of the chimney laughed;
The house-dog on his paws outspread   165
Laid to the fire his drowsy head,
The cat's dark silhouette on the wall
A couchant tiger's seemed to fall;
And, for the winter fireside meet,
Between the andirons' straddling feet,   170
The mug of cider simmered slow,
The apples sputtered in a row,
And, close at hand, the basket stood
With nuts from brown October's wood.

What matter how the night behaved?   175
What matter how the north-wind raved?
Blow high, blow low, not all its snow
Could quench our hearth-fire's ruddy glow.
O Time and Change!—with hair as gray
As was my sire's that winter day,   180
How strange it seems, with so much gone
Of life and love, to still live on!
Ah, brother![3] only I and thou
Are left of all that circle now,—
The dear home faces whereupon   185
That fitful firelight paled and shone.
Henceforward, listen as we will,
The voices of that hearth are still;
Look where we may, the wide earth o'er,
Those lighted faces smile no more.   190
We tread the paths their feet have worn,
    We sit beneath their orchard trees,
    We hear, like them, the hum of bees
And rustle of the bladed corn;
We turn the pages that they read,   195
    Their written words we linger o'er,

---

[3] Matthew, Whittier's younger brother,
who died in 1883 at the age of 71.

But in the sun they cast no shade,
No voice is heard, no sign is made,
  No step is on the conscious floor!
Yet Love will dream and Faith will
    trust   200
(Since He who knows our need is just)
That somehow, somewhere, meet we must.
Alas for him who never sees
The stars shine through his cypress-trees!
Who, hopeless, lays his dead away,   205
Nor looks to see the breaking day
Across the mournful marbles play!
Who hath not learned, in hours of faith,
  The truth to flesh and sense unknown,
That Life is ever lord of Death,   210
  And Love can never lose its own!

We sped the time with stories old,
Wrought puzzles out, and riddles told,
Or stammered from our school-book lore
"The chief of Gambia's golden shore." [4] 215
How often since, when all the land
Was clay in Slavery's shaping hand,
As if a far-blown trumpet stirred
The languorous, sin-sick air, I heard
"Does not the voice of reason cry,   220
  Claim the first right which Nature gave,
From the red scourge of bondage fly
  Nor deign to live a burdened slave!"
Our father rode again his ride
On Memphremagog's wooded side;   225
Sat down again to moose and samp
In trapper's hut and Indian camp;
Lived o'er the old idyllic ease
Beneath St. François' hemlock trees;
Again for him the moonlight shone   230
On Norman cap and bodiced zone;
Again he heard the violin play
Which led the village dance away,
And mingled in its merry whirl
The grandam and the laughing girl.   235
Or, nearer home, our steps he led
Where Salisbury's level marshes spread
  Mile-wide as flies the laden bee;
Where merry mowers, hale and strong,
Swept, scythe on scythe, their swaths
    along   240
  The low green prairies of the sea.
We shared the fishing off Boar's Head,

And round the rocky Isles of Shoals
  The hake-broil on the driftwood coals;
The chowder on the sand-beach made, 245
Dipped by the hungry, steaming hot,
With spoons of clam-shell from the pot.
We heard the tales of witchcraft old,
And dream and sign and marvel told
To sleepy listeners as they lay   250
Stretched idly on the salted hay,
Adrift along the winding shores,
  When favoring breezes deigned to blow
The square sail of the gundalow,[5]
And idle lay the useless oars.   255

Our mother, while she turned her wheel
Or run the new-knit stocking-heel,
Told how the Indian hordes came down
At midnight on Cochecho town,
And how her own great-uncle bore   260
His cruel scalp-mark to fourscore.
Recalling, in her fitting phrase,
  So rich and picturesque and free
  (The common unrhymed poetry
Of simple life and country ways),   265
The story of her early days,—
She made us welcome to her home;
Old hearths grew wide to give us room,
We stole with her a frightened look
At the gray wizard's conjuring-book,[6] 270
The fame whereof went far and wide
Through all the simple country-side;
We heard the hawks at twilight play,
The boat-horn on Piscataqua,[7]
The loon's weird laughter far away; 275
We fished her little trout-brook, knew
What flowers in wood and meadow grew,
What sunny hillsides autumn-brown
She climbed to shake the ripe nuts down,
Saw where in sheltered cove and bay 280

---

[4] This line, and the four quoted just below, are from "The African Chief," by Sarah Wentworth Morton (1759-1846), American poetess. The poem was a favorite selection in school readers.

[5] Local name, variant of "gondola," for small craft used in New England rivers and coastal waters.

[6] See the account in Whittier's essay on "Magicians and Witch Folk," the second selection following.

[7] River of New Hampshire.

The ducks' black squadron anchored lay,
And heard the wild geese calling loud
Beneath the gray November cloud.

Then, haply, with a look more grave,
And somberer tone, some tale she gave 285
From painful Sewel's ancient tome,[8]
Beloved in every Quaker home,
Of faith fire-winged by martyrdom,
Or Chalkley's Journal,[9] old and quaint,—
Gentlest of skippers, rare sea-saint!— 290
Who, when the dreary calms prevailed,
And water-butt and bread-cask failed,
And cruel, hungry eyes pursued
His portly presence, mad for food,
With dark hints muttered under breath 295
Of casting lots for life or death,
Offered, if Heaven withheld supplies,
To be himself the sacrifice.
Then, suddenly, as if to save
The good man from his living grave, 300
A ripple on the water grew,
A school of porpoise flashed in view.
"Take, eat," he said, "and be content;
These fishes in my stead are sent
By Him who gave the tangled ram [10]   305
To spare the child of Abraham."

Our uncle, innocent of books,
Was rich in lore of fields and brooks,
The ancient teachers never dumb
Of Nature's unhoused lyceum.   310
In moons and tides and weather wise,
He read the clouds as prophecies,
And foul or fair could well divine,
By many an occult hint and sign,
Holding the cunning-warded keys   315
To all the woodcraft mysteries;
Himself to Nature's heart so near
That all her voices in his ear
Of beast or bird had meanings clear,
Like Apollonius [11] of old,   320
Who knew the tales the sparrows told,
Or Hermes,[12] who interpreted
What the sage cranes of Nilus said:
A simple, guileless, childlike man,
Content to live where life began;   325
Strong only on his native grounds,
The little world of sights and sounds
Whose girdle was the parish bounds,

Whereof his fondly partial pride
The common features magnified,   330
As Surrey hills to mountains grew
In White [13] of Selborne's loving view,—
He told how teal and loon he shot,
And how the eagle's eggs he got,
The feats on pond and river done,   335
The prodigies of rod and gun;
Till, warming with the tales he told,
Forgotten was the outside cold,
The bitter wind unheeded blew,
From ripening corn the pigeons flew, 340
The partridge drummed i' the wood, the
        mink
Went fishing down the river-brink.
In fields with bean or clover gay,
The woodchuck, like a hermit gray,

Peered from the doorway of his cell; 345
The muskrat plied the mason's trade,
And tier by tier his mud-walls laid;
And from the shagbark overhead
    The grizzled squirrel dropped his shell.

Next, the dear aunt, whose smile of
        cheer   350
And voice in dreams I see and hear,—
The sweetest woman ever Fate
Perverse denied a household mate,
Who, lonely, homeless, not the less

---

[8] William Sewel's *History of the Rise,
Increase and Progress of the People Called
Quakers*. Originally written in Low Dutch
and published at Amsterdam in 1717, it
was translated into English by the author, published at London in 1722 and at
Philadelphia in 1728, and became a Quaker
classic.

[9] Thomas Chalkley, (1675-1741), Quaker
mariner and missionary, kept a journal
of trading voyages and preaching tours,
which was published at Philadelphia in
1747. Whittier follows closely his account
of this incident.

[10] Genesis 23:13.

[11] Greek seer and wonder-worker.

[12] Hermes Trismegistus, Greek name for
the Egyptian god Thoth, master of occult
wisdom.

[13] Gilbert   White   (1720-93),   British
clergyman and naturalist, whose *Natural
History and Antiquities of Selborne* (1789)
describes the region where he spent most
of his life.

Found peace in love's unselfishness,   355
And welcome whereso'er she went,
A calm and gracious element,
Whose presence seemed the sweet income
And womanly atmosphere of home,—
Called up her girlhood memories,   360
The huskings and the apple-bees,
The sleigh-rides and the summer sails,
Weaving through all the poor details
And homespun warp of circumstance
A golden woof-thread of romance.   365
For well she kept her genial mood
And simple faith of maidenhood;
Before her still a cloud-land lay,
The mirage loomed across her way;
The morning dew, that dried so soon   370
With others, glistened at her noon;
Through years of toil and soil and care,
From glossy tress to thin gray hair,
All unprofaned she held apart
The virgin fancies of the heart.   375
Be shame to him of woman born
Who had for such but thought of scorn.

There, too, our elder sister plied
Her evening task the stand beside;
A full, rich nature, free to trust,   380
Truthful and almost sternly just,
Impulsive, earnest, prompt to act,
And make her generous thought a fact,
Keeping with many a light disguise
The secret of self-sacrifice.   385
O heart sore-tried! thou hast the best
That Heaven itself could give thee,—rest,
Rest from all bitter thoughts and things!
    How many a poor one's blessing went
    With thee beneath the low green tent 390
Whose curtain never outward swings!

As one who held herself a part
Of all she saw, and let her heart
    Against the household bosom lean,
Upon the motley-braided mat   395
Our youngest and our dearest sat,
Lifting her large, sweet, asking eyes,
Now bathed within the fadeless green
And holy peace of Paradise.[14]
Oh, looking from some heavenly hill, 400
    Or from the shade of saintly palms,
    Or silver reach of river calms,

Do those large eyes behold me still?
With me one little year ago:—
The chill weight of the winter snow   405
    For months upon her grave has lain;
And now, when summer south-winds blow
    And brier and harebell bloom again,
I tread the pleasant paths we trod,
I see the violet-sprinkled sod,   410
Whereon she leaned, too frail and weak
The hillside flowers she loved to seek,
Yet following me where'er I went
With dark eyes full of love's content.
The birds are glad; the brier-rose fills 415
The air with sweetness; all the hills
Stretch green to June's unclouded sky;
But still I wait with ear and eye
For something gone which should be nigh,
A loss in all familiar things,   420
In flower that blooms, and bird that sings.
And yet, dear heart! remembering thee,
    Am I not richer than of old?
Safe in thy immortality,
    What change can reach the wealth I
        hold?   425
    What chance can mar the pearl and gold
Thy love hath left in trust with me?
And while in life's late afternoon,
    Where cool and long the shadows grow,
I walk to meet the night that soon   430
    Shall shape and shadow overflow,
I cannot feel that thou art far,
Since near at need the angels are;
And when the sunset gates unbar,
    Shall I not see thee waiting stand, 435
And, white against the evening star,
    The welcome of thy beckoning hand?

Brisk wielder of the birch and rule,
The master of the district school
Held at the fire his favored place;   440
Its warm glow lit a laughing face
Fresh-hued and fair, where scarce appeared
The uncertain prophecy of beard.
He teased the mitten-blinded cat,
Played cross-pins on my uncle's hat,   445
Sang songs, and told us what befalls
In classic Dartmouth's college halls.

---

[14] Elizabeth, Whittier's younger sister, died in 1864, the year before *Snow-Bound* was written.

Born the wild Northern hills among,
From whence his yeoman father wrung
By patient toil subsistence scant,   450
Not competence and yet not want,
He early gained the power to pay
His cheerful, self-reliant way;
Could doff at ease his scholar's gown
To peddle wares from town to town;   455
Or through the long vacation's reach
In lonely lowland districts teach,
Where all the droll experience found
At stranger hearths in boarding round,
The moonlit skater's keen delight,   460
The sleigh-drive through the frosty night,
The rustic party, with its rough
Accompaniment of blind-man's-buff,
And whirling plate, and forfeits paid,
His winter task a pastime made.   465
Happy the snow-locked homes wherein
He tuned his merry violin,
Or played the athlete in the barn,
Or held the good dame's winding-yarn,
Or mirth-provoking versions told   470
Of classic legends rare and old,
Wherein the scenes of Greece and Rome
Had all the commonplace of home,
And little seemed at best the odds
'Twixt Yankee pedlers and old gods;   475
Where Pindus-born Arachthus [15] took
The guise of any grist-mill brook,
And dread Olympus at his will
Became a huckleberry hill.

A careless boy that night he seemed;   480
    But at his desk he had the look
And air of one who wisely schemed,
    And hostage from the future took
    In trainèd thought and lore of book.
Large-brained, clear-eyed, — of such as
        he   485
Shall Freedom's young apostles be,
Who, following in War's bloody trail,
Shall every lingering wrong assail;
All chains from limb and spirit strike,
Uplift the black and white alike;   490
Scatter before their swift advance
The darkness and the ignorance,
The pride, the lust, the squalid sloth,
Which nurtured Treason's monstrous
    growth,

Made murder pastime, and the hell   495
Of prison-torture possible;
The cruel lie of caste refute,
Old forms remould, and substitute
For Slavery's lash the freeman's will,
For blind routine, wise-handed skill;   500
A school-house plant on every hill,
Stretching in radiate nerve-lines thence
The quick wires of intelligence;
Till North and South together brought
Shall own the same electric thought,   505
In peace a common flag salute,
And, side by side in labor's free
And unresentful rivalry,
Harvest the fields wherein they fought.

Another guest that winter night   510
Flashed back from lustrous eyes the light.
Unmarked by time, and yet not young,
The honeyed music of her tongue
And words of meekness scarcely told
A nature passionate and bold,   515
Strong, self-concentred, spurning guide,
Its milder features dwarfed beside
Her unbent will's majestic pride.
She sat among us, at the best,
A not unfeared, half-welcome guest,   520
Rebuking with her cultured phrase
Our homeliness of words and ways.
A certain pard-like, treacherous grace
    Swayed the lithe limbs and dropped the
        lash,
    Lent the white teeth their dazzling
        flash;   525
    And under low brows, black with night,
    Rayed out at times a dangerous light;
The sharp heat-lightnings of her face
Presaging ill to him whom Fate
Condemned to share her love or hate.   530
A woman tropical, intense
In thought and act, in soul and sense,
She blended in a like degree
The vixen and the devotee,
Revealing with each freak or feint   535
The temper of Petruchio's Kate, [16]

---

[15] River rising in the Pindus mountains
of northwestern Greece.

[16] Heroine of Shakespeare's *The Taming
of the Shrew.*

The raptures of Siena's saint.[17]
Her tapering hand and rounded wrist
Had facile power to form a fist;
The warm, dark languish of her eyes 540
Was never safe from wrath's surprise.
Brows saintly calm and lips devout
Knew every change of scowl and pout;
And the sweet voice had notes more high
And shrill for social battle-cry.   545

Since then what old cathedral town
Has missed her pilgrim staff and gown,
What convent-gate has held its lock
Against the challenge of her knock!
Through Smyrna's plague-hushed thorough-
          fares,   550
Up sea-set Malta's rocky stairs,
Gray olive slopes of hills that hem
Thy tombs and shrines, Jerusalem,
Or startling on her desert throne
The crazy Queen of Lebanon   555
With claims fantastic as her own,
Her tireless feet have held their way;
And still, unrestful, bowed, and gray,
She watches under Eastern skies,
     With hope each day renewed and
          fresh,   560
     The Lord's quick coming in the flesh,
Whereof she dreams and prophesies!

Where'er her troubled path may be,
     The Lord's sweet pity with her go!
The outward wayward life we see,   565
     The hidden springs we may not know.
Nor is it given us to discern
     What threads the fatal sisters spun,
     Through what ancestral years has run
The sorrow with the woman born,   570
What forged her cruel chain of moods,
What set her feet in solitudes,
     And held the love within her mute,
What mingled madness in the blood,
     A lifelong discord and annoy,   575
     Water of tears with oil of joy,
And hid within the folded bud
     Perversities of flower and fruit.
It is not ours to separate
The tangled skein of will and fate,   580
To show what metes and bounds should
          stand

Upon the soul's debatable land,
And between choice and Providence
Divide the circle of events;
     But He who knows our frame is just, 585
Merciful and compassionate,
And full of sweet assurances
And hope for all the language is,
     That He remembereth we are dust!

At last the great logs, crumbling low, 590
Sent out a dull and duller glow,
The bull's-eye watch that hung in view,
Ticking its weary circuit through,
Pointed with mutely-warning sign
Its black hand to the hour of nine.   595
That sign the pleasant circle broke:
My uncle ceased his pipe to smoke,
Knocked from its bowl the refuse gray,
And laid it tenderly away,
Then roused himself to safely cover   600
The dull red brands with ashes over.
And while, with care, our mother laid
The work aside, her steps she stayed
One moment, seeking to express
Her grateful sense of happiness   605
For food and shelter, warmth and health,
And love's contentment more than wealth,
With simple wishes (not the weak,
Vain prayers which no fulfilment seek,
But such as warm the generous heart, 610
O'er-prompt to do with Heaven its part)
That none might lack, that bitter night,
For bread and clothing, warmth and light.

Within our beds awhile we heard
The wind that round the gables roared, 615
With now and then a ruder shock,
Which made our very bedsteads rock.
We heard the loosened clapboards tost,
The board-nails snapping in the frost;
And on us, through the unplastered
          wall,   620
Felt the light-sifted snow-flakes fall;
But sleep stole on, as sleep will do
When hearts are light and life is new;
Faint and more faint the murmurs grew,
Till in the summer-land of dreams   625

---

[17] Saint Catherine of Siena, famed for her gentleness.

They softened to the sound of streams,
Low stir of leaves, and dip of oars,
And lapping waves on quiet shores.

Next morn we wakened with the shout
Of merry voices high and clear;   630
And saw the teamsters drawing near
To break the drifted highways out.
Down the long hillside treading slow
We saw the half-buried oxen go,
Shaking the snow from heads uptost,   635
Their straining nostrils white with frost.
Before our door the straggling train
Drew up, an added team to gain.
The elders threshed their hands a-cold,
    Passed, with the cider-mug, their
        jokes   640
    From lip to lip; the younger folks
Down the loose snow-banks, wrestling,
        rolled,
Then toiled again the cavalcade
    O'er windy hill, through clogged ravine,
    And woodland paths that wound be-
        tween   645
Low drooping pine-boughs winter-weighed.
From every barn a team afoot,
At every house a new recruit,
Where, drawn by Nature's subtlest law,
Haply the watchful young men saw   650
Sweet doorway pictures of the curls
And curious eyes of merry girls,
Lifting their hands in mock defence
Against the snow-balls' compliments,
And reading in each missive tost   655
The charm with Eden never lost.

We heard once more the sleigh-bells' sound,
    And, following where the teamsters led,
The wise old Doctor went his round,
Just pausing at our door to say   660
In the brief autocratic way
Of one who, prompt at Duty's call,
Was free to urge her claim on all,
    That some poor neighbor sick abed
At night our mother's aid would need. 665
For, one in generous thought and deed,
    What mattered in the sufferer's sight
    The Quaker matron's inward light,
The Doctor's mail of Calvin's creed?
All hearts confess the saints elect   670

Who, twain in faith, in love agree,
And melt not in an acid sect
    The Christian pearl of charity!

So days went on: a week had passed
Since the great world was heard from
    last.   675
The Almanac we studied o'er,
Read and reread our little store
Of books and pamphlets, scarce a score;
One harmless novel, mostly hid
From younger eyes, a book forbid,   680
And poetry, (or good or bad,
A single book was all we had,)
Where Ellwood's[18] meek, drab-skirted
    Muse,
    A stranger to the heathen Nine,
Sang, with a somewhat nasal whine, 685
The wars of David and the Jews.
At last the floundering carrier bore
The village paper to our door.
Lo! broadening outward as we read,
To warmer zones the horizon spread; 690
In panoramic length unrolled
We saw the marvel that it told.[19]
Before us passed the painted Creeks,
    And daft McGregor on his raids
    In Costa Rica's everglades.   695
And up Taygetus winding slow
Rode Ypsilanti's Mainote Greeks,
A Turk's head at each saddle bow!
Welcome to us its week-old news,
Its corner for the rustic Muse,   700
    Its monthly gauge of snow and rain,
Its record, mingling in a breath
The wedding bell and dirge of death:
Jest, anecdote, and love-lorn tale,

---

[18] Thomas Ellwood (1639-1714), English
poet who became a Quaker; friend of
Milton and author of *Davideis*.

[19] The news items mentioned by Whittier
place the period of *Snow-Bound* in 1821,
the year of the removal of the Creek Indians to the Indian Territory, or in 1822,
when Sir Gregor McGregor was attempting to found a colony in Costa Rica. The
"Mainote Greeks" were pirate bands who
joined in the Greek war for independence
from Turkey, 1821-29. Demetrios Ypsilanti (1793-1832) was a leader in the revolutionary movement, which won much sympathy in the United States.

The latest culprit sent to jail; 705
Its hue and cry of stolen and lost,
Its vendue sales and goods at cost,
  And traffic calling loud for gain.
We felt the stir of hall and street,
The pulse of life that round us beat; 710
The chill embargo of the snow
Was melted in the genial glow;
Wide swung again our ice-locked door,
And all the world was ours once more!

Clasp, Angel of the backward look 715
  And folded wings of ashen gray
  And voice of echoes far away,
The brazen covers of thy book;
The weird palimpsest old and vast,
Wherein thou hid'st the spectral past; 720
Where, closely mingling, pale and glow
The characters of joy and woe;
The monographs of outlived years,
Or smile-illumed or dim with tears,
  Green hills of life that slope to death, 725
And haunts of home, whose vistaed trees
Shade off to mournful cypresses
  With the white amaranths underneath.
Even while I look, I can but heed
  The restless sands' incessant fall, 730
Importunate hours that hours succeed,
Each clamorous with its own sharp need,
  And duty keeping pace with all.
Shut down and clasp the heavy lids;
I hear again the voice that bids 735
The dreamer leave his dream midway
For larger hopes and graver fears:
Life greatens in these later years,
The century's aloe flowers to-day!

Yet, haply, in some lull of life, 740
Some Truce of God which breaks the strife,
The worldling's eyes shall gather dew,
  Dreaming in throngful city ways
Of winter joys his boyhood knew;
And dear and early friends—the few 745
Who yet remain—shall pause to view
  These Flemish pictures of old days;
Sit with me by the homestead hearth,
And stretch the hands of memory forth
  To warm them at the wood-fire's
    blaze! 750
And thanks untraced to lips unknown

Shall greet me like the odors blown
From unseen meadows newly mown,
Or lilies floating in some pond,
Wood-fringed, the wayside gaze be-
    yond; 755
The traveller owns the grateful sense
Of sweetness near, he knows not whence,
And, pausing, takes with forehead bare
The benediction of the air.

From
LITERARY RECREATIONS AND MISCELLANIES

THE LIGHTING UP
[1854 (1845)]

"He spak to the spynnsters to spynnen
it oute."
  —*Piers Ploughman*

THIS evening, the 20th of the ninth month, is the time fixed upon for lighting the mills for night labor; and I have just returned from witnessing for the first time the effect of the new illumination.

Passing over the bridge, nearly to the Dracut shore, I had a fine view of the long line of mills, the city beyond, and the broad sweep of the river from the falls. The light of a tranquil and gorgeous sunset was slowly fading from river and sky, and the shadows of the trees on the Dracut slopes were blending in dusky indistinctness with the great shadow of night. Suddenly gleams of light broke from the black masses of masonry on the Lowell bank, at first feeble and scattered, flitting from window to window, appearing and disappearing, like will-o'-wisps in a forest or fireflies in a summer's night. Anon tier after tier of windows became radiant, until the whole vast wall, stretching far up the river, from basement to roof, became checkered with light reflected with the starbeams from the still water beneath. With a little effort of fancy, one could readily transform the huge mills, thus illuminated, into palaces lighted up for festival occasions, and the figures of the workers, passing to and fro before the windows, into forms of beauty and fashion, moving in graceful dances.

Alas! this music of the shuttle and the daylong dance to it are not altogether of the kind which Milton speaks of when he invokes the "soft Lydian airs" [1] of voluptuous leisure. From this time henceforward for half a weary year, from the bell-call of morning twilight to half-past seven in the evening, with brief intermissions for two hasty meals, the operatives will be confined to their tasks. The proverbial facility of the Yankees in despatching their dinners in the least possible time seems to have been taken advantage of and reduced to a system on the Lowell corporations. Strange as it may seem to the uninitiated, the workingmen and women here contrive to repair to their lodgings, make the necessary preliminary ablutions, devour their beef and pudding, and hurry back to their looms and jacks in the brief space of half an hour. In this way the working-day in Lowell is eked out to an average throughout the year of twelve and a half hours. This is a serious evil, demanding the earnest consideration of the humane and philanthropic. Both classes—the employer and the employed—would in the end be greatly benefited by the general adoption of the "ten-hour system," although the one might suffer a slight diminution in daily wages and the other in yearly profits. Yet it is difficult to see how this most desirable change is to be effected. The stronger and healthier portion of the operatives might themselves object to it as strenuously as the distant stockholder who looks only to his semi-annual dividends. Health is too often a matter of secondary consideration. Gain is the great, all-absorbing object. Very few, comparatively, regard Lowell as their "continuing city." They look longingly back to green valleys of Vermont, to quiet farm-houses on the head-waters of the Connecticut and Merrimac, and to old familiar homes along the breezy seaboard of New England, whence

they have been urged by the knowledge that here they can earn a larger amount of money in a given time than in any other place or employment. They come here for gain, not for pleasure; for high wages, not for the comforts that cluster about home. Here are poor widows toiling to educate their children; daughters hoarding their wages to redeem mortgaged paternal homesteads or to defray the expenses of sick and infirm parents; young betrothed girls, about to add their savings to those of their country lovers. Others there are, of maturer age, lonely and poor, impelled hither by a proud unwillingness to test to its extent the charity of friends and relatives, and a strong yearning for the "glorious privilege of being independent." All honor to them! Whatever may have closed against them the gates of matrimony, whether their own obduracy or the faithlessness or indifference of others, instead of shutting themselves up in a nunnery or taxing the good nature of their friends by perpetual demands for sympathy and support, like weak vines, putting out their feelers in every direction for something to twine upon, is it not better and wiser for them to go quietly at work, to show that woman has a self-sustaining power; that she is something in and of herself; that she, too, has a part to bear in life, and, in common with the self-elected "lords of creation," has a direct relation to absolute being? To such the factory presents the opportunity of taking the first and essential step of securing, within a reasonable space of time, a comfortable competency.

There are undoubtedly many evils connected with the working of these mills; yet they are partly compensated by the fact that here, more than in any other mechanical employment, the labor of woman is placed essentially upon an equality with that of man. Here, at least, one of the many social disabilities under which woman as a distinct individual, unconnected with the other sex, has labored in all time, is

---

[1] "L'Allegro," line 136.

removed; the work of her hands is adequately rewarded; and she goes to her daily task with the consciousness that she is not "spending her strength for naught."

The *Lowell Offering*,[2] which has been for the last four years published monthly in this city, consisting entirely of articles written by females employed in the mills, has attracted much attention and obtained a wide circulation. This may be in part owing to the novel circumstances of its publication; but it is something more and better than a mere novelty. In its volumes may be found sprightly delineations of home scenes and characters, highly wrought imaginative pieces, tales of genuine pathos and humor, and pleasing fairy stories and fables. The *Offering* originated in a reading society of the mill girls, which, under the name of the Improvement Circle, was convened once in a month. At its meetings, pieces written by its members and dropped secretly into a sort of "lion's mouth," provided for the purpose of insuring the authors from detection, were read for the amusement and criticism of the company. This circle is still in existence; and I owe to my introduction to it some of the most pleasant hours I have passed in Lowell.

The manner in which the *Offering* has been generally noticed in this country has not, to my thinking, been altogether in accordance with good taste or self-respect. It is hardly excusable for men, who, whatever may be their present position, have, in common with all of us, brothers, sisters, or other relations busy in workshop and dairy, and who have scarcely washed from their own professional hands the soil of labor, to make very marked demonstrations of astonishment at the appearance of a magazine whose papers are written by factory girls. As if the compatibility of mental cultivation with bodily labor and the equality and brotherhood of the human family were still open questions, depending for their decision very much on the production of positive proof that essays may be written and carpets woven by the same set of fingers!

The truth is, our democracy lacks calmness and solidity, the repose and self-reliance which come of long habitude and settled conviction. We have not yet learned to wear its simple truths with the graceful ease and quiet air of unsolicitous assurance with which the titled European does his social fictions. As a people, we do not feel and live out our great Declaration. We lack faith in man,—confidence in simple humanity, apart from its environments.

"The age shows, to my thinking, more
    infidels to Adam,
Than directly, by profession, simple in-
    fidels to God." [3]

MAGICIANS AND WITCH FOLK
[1854 (1847)]

"FASCINATION," said Henry Cornelius Agrippa, in the fiftieth chapter of his first book on Occult Philosophy,[1] "is a binding which comes of the spirit of the witch through the eyes of him that is bewitched, entering to his heart; for the eye being opened and intent upon any one, with a strong imagination doth dart its beams, which are the vehiculum of the spirit, into the eyes of him that is opposite to her; which tender spirit strikes his eyes, stirs up and wounds his heart, and infects his spirit. Whence Apuleius saith, 'Thy eyes, sliding down through my eyes into my inmost heart, stirreth up a most vehement burning.' And when eyes are reciprocally intent upon each other, and when rays are joined to rays, and lights to lights, then the spirit of the one is joined to that of the other; so are strong ligations made and vehement loves inflamed." Taking this defi-

---

[2] Published 1840-45. See *Old South Leaflet* No. 157, Vol. VII.

[3] Elizabeth B. Browning.—Whittier's note.

[1] See quotation from this book at the beginning of *Snow-Bound*. Agrippa (1486?-1535) was a German physician, theologian, and student of the occult.

nition of witchcraft, we sadly fear it is still practised to a very great extent among us. The best we can say of it is, that the business seems latterly to have fallen into younger hands; its victims do not appear to regard themselves as especial objects of compassion; and neither church nor state seems inclined to interfere with it.

As might be expected in a shrewd community like ours, attempts are not unfrequently made to speculate in the supernatural—to "make gain of sooth-saying." In the autumn of last year a "wise woman" dreamed, or somnambulized, that a large sum of money, in gold and silver coin, lay buried in the centre of the great swamp in Poplin, New Hampshire; whereupon an immediate search was made for the precious metal. Under the bleak sky of November, in biting frost and sleet rain, some twenty or more grown men, graduates of our common schools, and liable, every mother's son of them, to be made deacons, squires, and general court members, and such other drill officers as may be requisite in the march of mind, might be seen delving in grim earnest, breaking the frozen earth, uprooting swamp-maples and hemlocks, and waking, with sledge and crowbar, unwonted echoes in a solitude which had heretofore only answered to the woodman's axe or the scream of the wild fowl. The snows of December put an end to their labors; but the yawning excavation still remains, a silent but somewhat expressive commentary upon the age of progress.

Still later, in one of our Atlantic cities, an attempt was made, partially at least successful, to form a company for the purpose of digging for money in one of the desolate sand-keys of the West Indies. It appears that some mesmerized "subject," in the course of one of those somnambulic voyages of discovery in which the traveller, like Satan in chaos [2],—

"O'er bog, o'er steep, through straight, rough, dense, or rare,
With head, hands, wings, or feet, pursues his way,

And swims, or sinks, or wades, or creeps, or flies,"—

while peering curiously into the earth's mysteries, chanced to have his eyes gladdened by the sight of a huge chest packed with Spanish coins, the spoil, doubtless, of some rich-freighted argosy, or Carthagena galleon, in the rare days of Queen Elizabeth's Christian buccaneers.

During the last quarter of a century, a colored woman in one of the villages on the southern border of New Hampshire has been consulted by hundreds of anxious inquirers into the future. Long experience in her profession has given her something of that ready estimate of character, that quick and keen appreciation of the capacity, habits, and wishes of her visitors, which so remarkably distinguished the late famous Madame Le Normand, of Paris; and if that old squalid sorceress, in her cramped Parisian attic, redolent of garlic and bestrewn with greasy implements of sorry house-wifery, was, as has been affirmed, consulted by such personages as the fair Josephine Beauharnais, and the "man of destiny," Napoleon himself, is it strange that the desire to lift the veil of the great mystery before us should overcome in some degree our peculiar and most republican prejudice against color, and reconcile us to the disagreeable necessity of looking at futurity through a black medium?

Some forty years ago, on the banks of the pleasant little creek separating Berwick, in Maine, from Somersworth, in New Hampshire, within sight of my mother's home, dwelt a plain, sedate member of the society of Friends, named Bantum. He passed throughout a circle of several miles as a conjurer and skilful adept in the art of magic. To him resorted farmers who had lost their cattle, matrons whose household gear, silver spoons, and table linen had

---

[2] Milton's *Paradise Lost*, Book II, lines 948-50.

been stolen, or young maidens whose lovers were absent; and the quiet, meek-spirited old man received them all kindly, put on his huge iron-rimmed spectacles, opened his "conjuring book," which my mother describes as a large clasped volume in strange language and black-letter type, and after due reflection and consideration gave the required answers without money and without price. The curious old volume is still in the possession of the conjurer's family. Apparently inconsistent as was this practice of the black art with the simplicity and truthfulness of his religious profession, I have not been able to learn that he was ever subjected to censure on account of it. It may be that our modern conjurer defended himself on grounds similar to those assumed by the celebrated knight of Nettesheim, in the preface to his first Book of Magic: "Some," says he, "may crie oute that I teach forbidden arts, sow the seed of heresies, offend pious ears, and scandalize excellent wits; that I am a sorcerer, superstitious and devilish, who indeed am a magician. To whom I answer, that a magician doth not among learned men signifie a sorcerer or one that is superstitious or devilish, but a wise man, a priest, a prophet, and that the sibyls prophesied most clearly of Christ; that magicians, as wise men, by the wonderful secrets of the world, knew Christ to be born, and came to worship him, first of all; and that the name of magicke is received by philosophers, commended by divines, and not unacceptable to the Gospel."

The study of astrology and occult philosophy, to which many of the finest minds of the Middle Ages devoted themselves without molestation from the Church, was never practised with impunity after the Reformation. The Puritans and Presbyterians, taking the Bible for their rule, "suffered not a witch to live;" and, not content with burning the books of those who "used curious arts" after the manner of the Ephesians, they sacrificed the students themselves on the same pile. Hence we hear little of learned and scientific wizards in New England. One remarkable character of this kind seems, however, to have escaped the vigilance of our modern Doctors of the Mosaic Law. Dr. Robert Child came to this country about the year 1644, and took up his residence in the Massachusetts colony. He was a man of wealth, and owned plantations at Nashaway, now Lancaster, and at Saco, in Maine. He was skilful in mineralogy and metallurgy, and seems to have spent a good deal of money in searching for mines. He is well known as the author of the first decided movement for liberty of conscience in Massachusetts, his name standing at the head of the famous petition of 1646 for a modification of the laws in respect to religious worship, and complaining in strong terms of the disfranchisement of persons not members of the Church. A tremendous excitement was produced by this remonstrance; clergy and magistrates joined in denouncing it; Dr. Child and his associates were arrested, tried for contempt of government, and heavily fined. The Court, in passing sentence, assured the Doctor that his crime was only equalled by that of Korah [3] and his troop, who rebelled against Moses and Aaron. He resolved to appeal to the Parliament of England, and made arrangements for his departure, but was arrested, and ordered to be kept a prisoner in his own house until the vessel in which he was to sail had left Boston. He was afterwards imprisoned for a considerable length of time, and on his release found means to return to England. The Doctor's trunks were searched by the Puritan authorities while he was in prison; but it does not appear that they detected the occult studies to which he was addicted, to which lucky circumstance it is doubtless owing that the first champion of religious liberty in the New World was not hung for a wizard.

Dr. Child was a graduate of the renowned University of Padua, and had travelled extensively in the Old World. Prob-

---

[3] Numbers, chap. 16.

ably, like Michael Scott,[4] he had

> "Learned the art of glammarye [5]
>   In Padua, beyond the sea;"

for I find in the dedication of an English translation of a Continental work on astrology and magic, printed in 1651 "at the sign of the Three Bibles," that his "sublime hermeticall and theomagicall lore" is compared to that of Hermes and Agrippa. He is complimented as a master of the mysteries of Rome and Germany, and as one who had pursued his investigations among the philosophers of the Old World and the Indians of the New, "leaving no stone unturned, the turning whereof might conduce to the discovery of what is occult."

There was still another member of the Friends' society in Vermont, of the name of Austin, who, in answer, as he supposed, to prayer and a long-cherished desire to benefit his afflicted fellow-creatures, received, as he believed, a special gift of healing. For several years applicants from nearly all parts of New England visited him with the story of their sufferings and praying for a relief, which, it is averred, was in many instances really obtained. Letters from the sick who were unable to visit him, describing their diseases, were sent him; and many are yet living who believe that they were restored miraculously at the precise period of time when Austin was engaged in reading their letters. One of my uncles was commissioned to convey to him a large number of letters from sick persons in his neighborhood. He found the old man sitting in his plain parlor in the simplest garb of his sect —grave, thoughtful, venerable—a drab-coated Prince Hohenlohe.[6] He received the letters in silence, read them slowly, casting them one after another upon a large pile of similar epistles in a corner of the apartment.

Half a century ago nearly every neighborhood in New England was favored with one or more reputed dealers in magic. Twenty years later there were two poor old sisters who used to frighten school urchins and "children of a larger growth" as they rode down from New Hampshire on their gaunt skeleton horses, strung over with baskets for the Newburyport market. They were aware of the popular notion concerning them, and not unfrequently took advantage of it to levy a sort of blackmail upon their credulous neighbors. An attendant at the funeral of one of these sisters, who when living was about as unsubstantial as Ossian's [7] ghost, through which the stars were visible, told me that her coffin was so heavy that four stout men could barely lift it.

One of my earliest recollections is that of an old woman, residing about two miles from the place of my nativity, who for many years had borne the unenviable reputation of a witch. She certainly had the look of one—a combination of form, voice, and features which would have made the fortune of an English witch finder in the days of Matthew Paris [8] or the Sir John Podgers of Dickens,[9] and insured her speedy conviction in King James's High Court of Justiciary. She was accused of divers ill-doings,—such as preventing the cream in her neighbor's churn from becoming butter, and snuffing out candles at huskings and quilting-parties.

---

[4] Michael Scot (1175?-1234?) was a mediaeval scholar who translated Aristotle and introduced the study of his work at Oxford in 1230. He was also famed for occult wisdom, and figures in this connection in Dante's *Inferno* and in Scott's *Lay of the Last Minstrel*.

[5] A Scotch variant of "grammarye," referring here to magic. Compare Scott's lines in Canto First of *Lay of the Last Minstrel:*

> "He learned the art, that none may name,
>   In Padua, far beyond the sea."

[6] Alexander Leopold, prince of Hohenlohe-Waldenburg-Schillingsfürst, (1794-1849), who became a Roman Catholic priest and monk, and gained a reputation as a miracle-worker.

[7] Legendary Irish hero and bard.

[8] English chronicler (1200?-1259), a monk of St. Albans.

[9] See *Master Humphrey's Clock*, chapter 111.

"She roamed the country far and near,
  Bewitched the children of the peasants,
Dried up the cows, and lamed the deer,
  And sucked the eggs, and killed the
    pheasants."

The poor old woman was at length so sadly annoyed by her unfortunate reputation that she took the trouble to go before a justice of the peace, and made solemn oath that she was a Christian woman, and no witch.

Not many years since a sad-visaged, middle-aged man might be seen in the streets of one of our sea-board towns at times suddenly arrested in the midst of a brisk walk and fixed motionless for some minutes in the busy thoroughfare. No effort could induce him to stir until, in his opinion, the spell was removed and his invisible tormentor suffered him to proceed. He explained his singular detention as the act of a whole family of witches whom he had unfortunately offended during a visit down East. It was rumored that the offence consisted in breaking off a matrimonial engagement with the youngest member of the family—a sorceress, perhaps, in more than one sense of the word, like that "winsome wench and walie" in Tam O'Shanter's witch-dance at Kirk Alloway. His only hope was that he should outlive his persecutors; and it is said that at the very hour in which the event took place he exultingly assured his friends that the spell was forever broken, and that the last of the family of his tormentors was no more.

When a boy, I occasionally met, at the house of a relative in an adjoining town, a stout, red-nosed old farmer of the neighborhood. A fine tableau he made of a winter's evening, in the red light of a birch-log fire, as he sat for hours watching its progress, with sleepy, half-shut eyes, changing his position only to reach the cider-mug on the shelf near him. Although he seldom opened his lips save to assent to some remark of his host or to answer a direct question, yet at times, when the cider-mug got the better of his taciturnity, he would amuse us with interesting details

of his early experiences in "the Ohio country."

There was, however, one chapter in these experiences which he usually held in reserve, and with which "the stranger intermeddled not." He was not willing to run the risk of hearing that which to him was a frightful reality turned into ridicule by scoffers and unbelievers. The substance of it, as I received it from one of his neighbors, forms as clever a tale of witchcraft as modern times have produced.

It seems that when quite a young man he left the homestead, and, strolling westward, worked his way from place to place until he found himself in one of the old French settlements on the Ohio River. Here he procured employment on the farm of a widow; and being a smart, active fellow, and proving highly serviceable in his department, he rapidly gained favor in the eyes of his employer. Ere long, contrary to the advice of the neighbors, and in spite of somewhat discouraging hints touching certain matrimonial infelicities experienced by the late husband, he resolutely stepped into the dead man's shoes: the mistress became the wife, and the servant was legally promoted to the head of the household.

For a time matters went on cosily and comfortably enough. He was now lord of the soil; and, as he laid in his crops of corn and potatoes, salted down his pork, and piled up his wood for winter's use, he naturally enough congratulated himself upon his good fortune and laughed at the sinister forebodings of his neighbors. But with the long winter months came a change over his "love's young dream." An evil and mysterious influence seemed to be at work in his affairs. Whatever he did after consulting his wife or at her suggestion resulted favorably enough; but all his own schemes and projects were unaccountably marred and defeated. If he bought a horse, it was sure to prove spavined or windbroken. His cows either refused to give down their milk, or giving it, perversely kicked it over. A fine sow which he had bargained for repaid his partiality by devouring, like Saturn, her own children. By degrees a dark thought forced its way into his mind. Comparing his repeated mischances with the ante-nuptial warnings of his neighbors, he at last came to the melancholy conclusion that his wife was a witch. The victim in Motherwell's [9] ballad of the Demon Lady, or the poor fellow in the Arabian tale who discovered that he had married a ghoul in the guise of a young and blooming princess, was scarcely in a more sorrowful predicament. He grew nervous and fretful. Old dismal nursery stories and all the witch lore of boyhood came back to his memory; and he crept to his bed like a criminal to the gallows, half afraid to fall asleep lest his mysterious companion should take a fancy to transform him into a horse, get him shod at the smithy, and ride him to a witch-meeting. And, as if to make the matter worse, his wife's affection seemed to increase just in proportion as his troubles thickened upon him. She aggravated him with all manner of caresses and endearments. This was the drop too much. The poor husband recoiled from her as from a waking nightmare. His thoughts turned to New England; he longed to see once more the old homestead, with its tall well-sweep and butternut-trees by the roadside; and he sighed amidst the rich bottom-lands of his new home for his father's rocky pasture, with its crop of stinted mulleins. So one cold November day, finding himself out of sight and hearing of his wife, he summoned courage to attempt an escape, and resolutely turning his back on the West, plunged into the wilderness towards the sunrise. After a long and hard journey he reached his birthplace, and was kindly welcomed by his old friends. Keeping a close mouth with respect to his unlucky adventure in Ohio, he soon after married one of his schoolmates, and, by dint of persevering industry and economy, in a few years found himself in possession of a comfortable home.

But his evil star still lingered above the horizon. One summer evening, on returning from the hayfield, who should meet him but his witch wife from Ohio! She came riding up the street on her old white horse, with a pillion behind the saddle. Accosting him in a kindly tone, yet not without something of gentle reproach for his unhandsome desertion of her, she informed him that she had come all the way from Ohio to take him back again.

It was in vain that he pleaded his later engagements; it was in vain that his new wife raised her shrillest remonstrances, not unmingled with expressions of vehement indignation at the revelation of her husband's real position; the witch wife was inexorable; go he must, and that speedily. Fully impressed with a belief in her supernatural power of compelling obedience, and perhaps dreading more than witchcraft itself the effects of the unlucky disclosure on the temper of his New England helpmate, he made a virtue of the necessity of the case, bade farewell to the latter amidst a perfect hurricane of reproaches, and mounted the white horse, with his old wife on the pillion behind him. Of that ride Burger [10] might have written a counterpart to his ballad:—

"Tramp, tramp, along the shore they ride,
    Splash, splash, along the sea."

Two or three years had passed away, bringing no tidings of the unfortunate husband, when he once more made his appearance in his native village. He was not disposed to be very communicative; but for one thing, at least, he seemed willing to express his gratitude. His Ohio wife, having no spell against intermittent fever, had paid the debt of nature, and had left him free; in view of which, his surviving wife, after manifesting a due degree of resentment, consented to take him back to her bed and board; and I could never learn that she had cause to regret her clemency.

---

[10] William Motherwell (1797-1835), Scottish poet, editor, and antiquary.

[11] Gottfried August Bürger (1747-1794), German romantic poet especially known for his ballads.

From
THE CONFLICT WITH SLAVERY
[1889 (1843)]

DEMOCRACY AND SLAVERY

THE great leader of American Democracy, Thomas Jefferson, was an ultra-abolitionist in theory, while from youth to age a slave-holder in practice. With a zeal which never abated, with a warmth which the frost of years could not chill, he urged the great truths, that each man should be the guardian of his own weal; that one man should never have absolute control over another. He maintained the entire equality of the race, the inherent right of self-ownership, the equal claim of all to a fair participation in the enactment of the laws by which they are governed.

He saw clearly that slavery, as it existed in the South and on his own plantation, was inconsistent with this doctrine. His early efforts for emancipation in Virginia failed of success; but he next turned his attention to the vast northwestern territory, and laid the foundation of that ordinance of 1787, which, like the flaming sword of the angel at the gates of Paradise, has effectually guarded that territory against the entrance of slavery. Nor did he stop here. He was the friend and admirer of the ultra-abolitionists of revolutionary France; he warmly urged his British friend, Dr. Price,[1] to send his anti-slavery pamphlets into Virginia; he omitted no opportunity to protest against slavery as anti-democratic, unjust, and dangerous to the common welfare; and in his letter to the territorial governor of Illinois, written in old age, he bequeathed, in earnest and affecting language, the cause of negro emancipation to the rising generation. "This enterprise," said he, "is for the young, for those who can carry it forward to its consummation. It shall have all my prayers, and these are the only weapons of an old man."

Such was Thomas Jefferson, the great founder of American Democracy, the advocate of the equality of human rights, irrespective of any conditions of birth, or climate, or color. His political doctrines, it is strange to say, found their earliest recipients and most zealous admirers in the slave states of the Union. The privileged class of slave-holders, whose rank and station "supersede the necessity of an order of nobility," became earnest advocates of equality among themselves—the democracy of aristocracy. With the misery and degradation of servitude always before them, in the condition of their own slaves, an intense love of personal independence, and a haughty impatience of any control over their actions, prepared them to adopt the democratic idea, so far as it might be applied to their own order. Of that enlarged and generous democracy, the love, not of individual freedom alone, but of the rights and liberties of all men, the unselfish desire to give to others the privileges which all men value for themselves, we are constrained to believe the great body of Thomas Jefferson's slave-holding admirers had no adequate conception. They were just such democrats as the patricians of Rome and the aristocracy of Venice; lords over their own plantations, a sort of "holy alliance" of planters, admitting and defending each other's divine right of mastership.

Still, in Virginia, Maryland, and in other sections of the slave states, truer exponents and exemplifiers of the idea of democracy, as it existed in the mind of Jefferson, were not wanting. In the debate on the memorials presented to the first Congress of the United States, praying for the abolition of slavery, the voice of the Virginia delegation in that body was unanimous in deprecation of slavery as an evil, social, moral, and political. In the Virginia constitutional convention of 1829 there were men who had the wisdom to perceive and the firmness to declare that slavery was not only incompatible with the honor and

---

[1] Richard Price (1723-1791), Welsh moral and political philosopher, and Unitarian minister in London.

prosperity of the state, but wholly indefensible on any grounds which could be consistently taken by a republican people. In the debate on the same subject in the legislature in 1832, universal and impartial democracy found utterance from eloquent lips. We might say as much of Kentucky, the child of Virginia. But it remains true that these were exceptions to the general rule. With the language of universal liberty on their lips, and moved by the most zealous spirit of democratic propagandism, the greater number of the slave-holders of the Union seem never to have understood the true meaning, or to have measured the length and breadth of that doctrine which they were the first to adopt, and of which they have claimed all along to be the peculiar and chosen advocates.

The Northern States were slow to adopt the Democratic creed. The oligarchy of New England, and the rich proprietors and landholders of the Middle States, turned with alarm and horror from the levelling doctrines urged upon them by the "liberty and equality" propagandists of the South. The doctrines of Virginia were quite as unpalatable to Massachusetts at the beginning of the present century as those of Massachusetts now are to the Old Dominion. Democracy interfered with old usages and time-honored institutions, and threatened to plough up the very foundations of the social fabric. It was zealously opposed by the representatives of New England in Congress and in the home legislatures; and in many pulpits hands were lifted to God in humble entreaty that the curse and bane of democracy, an offshoot of the rabid Jacobinism of revolutionary France, might not be permitted to take root and overshadow the goodly heritage of Puritanism. The alarmists of the South, in their most fervid pictures of the evils to be apprehended from the prevalence of anti-slavery doctrines in their midst, have drawn nothing more fearful than the visions of such "Prophets of war and harbingers of ill" as Fisher Ames in the forum and Parish [2] in the desk, when contemplating the inroads

of Jeffersonian democracy upon the politics, religion, and property of the North.

But great numbers of the free laborers of the Northern States, the mechanics and small farmers, took a very different view of the matter. The doctrines of Jefferson were received as their political gospel. It was in vain that federalism denounced with indignation the impertinent inconsistency of slave-holding interference in behalf of liberty in the free states. Come the doctrine from whom it might, the people felt it to be true. State after state revolted from the ranks of federalism, and enrolled itself on the side of democracy. The old order of things was broken up; equality before the law was established, religious tests and restrictions of the right of suffrage were abrogated. Take Massachusetts, for example. There the resistance to democratic principles was the most strenuous and longest continued. Yet, at this time, there is no state in the Union more thorough in its practical adoption of them. No property qualifications or religious tests prevail; all distinctions of sect, birth, or color, are repudiated, and suffrage is universal. The democracy, which in the South has only been held in a state of gaseous abstraction, hardened into concrete reality in the cold air of the North. The ideal became practical, for it had found lodgment among men who were accustomed to act out their convictions and test all their theories by actual experience.

While thus making a practical application of the new doctrine, the people of the free states could not but perceive the incongruity of democracy and slavery.

Selleck Osborn,[3] who narrowly escaped the honor of a Democratic martyr in Connecticut, denounced slave-holding, in com-

---

[2] Ames and Parish were prominent Federalists, the former a lawyer and member of Congress, the latter a clergyman.

[3] Selleck Osborn, editor of the Litchfield, Conn., *Witness,* was imprisoned on conviction for libel in 1806. Joel Barlow published his *Columbiad* in 1807. General William Eaton was active in freeing the Algerine captives in 1805.

mon with other forms of oppression. Barlow, fresh from communion with Gregoire, Brissot, and Robespierre, devoted to negro slavery some of the most vigorous and truthful lines of his great poem. Eaton, returning from his romantic achievements in Tunis for the deliverance of white slaves, improved the occasion to read a lecture to his countrymen on the inconsistency and guilt of holding blacks in servitude. In the Missouri struggle of 1819-20, the people of the free states, with a few ignoble exceptions, took issue with the South against the extension of slavery. Some ten years later, the present anti-slavery agitation commenced. It originated, beyond a question, in the democratic element. With the words of Jefferson on their lips, young, earnest, and enthusiastic men called the attention of the community to the moral wrong and political reproach of slavery. In the name and spirit of democracy, the moral and political powers of the people were invoked to limit, discountenance, and put an end to a system so manifestly subversive of its foundation principles. It was a revival of the language of Jefferson and Page and Randolph, an echo of the voice of him who penned the Declaration of Independence and originated the ordinance of 1787.

Meanwhile the South had wellnigh forgotten the actual significance of the teachings of its early political prophets, and their renewal in the shape of abolitionism was, as might have been expected, strange and unwelcome. Pleasant enough it had been to hold up occasionally these democratic abstractions for the purpose of challenging the world's admiration and cheaply acquiring the characters of lovers of liberty and equality. Frederick of Prussia, apostrophizing the shades of Cato and Brutus,[4]

"Vous de la liberté héros que je révère," while in the full exercise of his despotic power, was quite as consistent as these democratic slave-owners, whose admiration of liberty increased in exact ratio with its distance from their own plantations. They had not calculated upon seeing their doctrine clothed with life and power, a practical reality, pressing for application to their slaves as well as to themselves. They had not taken into account the beautiful ordination of Providence, that no man can vindicate his own rights, without directly or impliedly including in that vindication the rights of all other men. The haughty and oppressive barons who wrung from their reluctant monarch the Great Charter at Runnymede, acting only for themselves and their class, little dreamed of the universal application which has since been made of their guaranty of rights and liberties. As little did the nobles of the parliament of Paris, when strengthening themselves by limiting the kingly prerogative, dream of the emancipation of their own serfs, by a revolution to which they were blindly giving the first impulse. God's truth is universal; it cannot be monopolised by selfishness.

---

[4] "You heroes of liberty whom I revere."

1819 ∽ *James Russell Lowell* ∽ 1891

LOWELL began his career by giving up the law for literature, publishing a volume of poems (*A Year's Life*, 1841) and founding a literary magazine. How fully he was Emerson's disciple, at least in his faith in the possibilities of American literature, is revealed by the prospectus in which he and young Robert Carter, his co-editor, announced their purpose for the new magazine:

". . . . to furnish the intelligent and reflecting portion of the Reading Public with a rational substitute for the enormous quantity of thrice-diluted trash, in the shape of namby-pamby love tales and sketches, which is monthly poured out to them by many of our popular magazines,—and to offer instead thereof, a healthy and manly Periodical Literature, whose perusal will not necessarily involve a loss of time and deterioration of every moral and intellectual faculty."

The high-minded *Pioneer* expired after three issues, leaving Lowell eighteen hundred dollars in debt; but his enthusiasm was undiminished and his courage unbroken. He was in love with Maria White, herself a writer, possessed of a slender but genuine poetic talent. In 1844 they were married, and shortly both young writers were identified with abolitionism and other reform movements. Lowell wrote steadily and matured rapidly, reaching a climax of production in 1848. In that year he published four books: *Poems*, a collection of his recent serious work in verse; *A Fable for Critics*, a brilliant rhymed survey of contemporary American literature in which the promise of the founder of *The Pioneer* that "opinions of merit and demerit will be candidly and fearlessly expressed" was finally made good; *The Vision of Sir Launfal*, the Arthurian narrative which is so widely recognized as an indirect contribution to the anti-slavery cause; and the first series of *The Biglow Papers*.

The Biglow Papers were direct and outspoken in their opposition to slavery. They were written for the columns of a Boston newspaper during the Mexican war, which Lowell like many others saw as a maneuver for the extension of slavery. Ostensibly they were the work of a rural rhymester, a young farmer named Hosea Biglow, who wrote in Yankee dialect. As collected in book form, the poems were supplemented with crude letters from Hosea's father, transmitting them to the editor, and with formal and pedantic notes by the Rev. Homer Wilbur, supposedly the scholarly minister of Hosea's mythical town of Jaalam, and his poetic mentor. In *The Biglow Papers* Lowell for the first time achieved genuine originality, and corresponding impact on the thought of his times. They had immediate and powerful appeal for readers of their day, and still hold abundant intrinsic value beyond their interest as documents in social history.

In 1853 Maria White Lowell died. His writing for the time interrupted, Lowell turned to teaching, following Longfellow as Smith Professor of Modern Languages at Harvard after study in Europe. In 1857 he entered upon a second venture in literary journalism, this time under happier stars. He became the first editor of *The Atlantic Monthly,* and the extraordinary richness of its first volumes is due in large part to his skill and enthusiasm. The coming of the Civil War called forth a second series of *Biglow Papers.* In the judgment of many critics, Lowell's achievement as a poet reached its highest level in the "Commemoration Ode," which he read at Harvard University's memorial service for its Civil War dead in 1866, just midway of his career.

By this time Lowell had left *The Atlantic Monthly* for the more bookish and conservative *North American Review.* From his reviews for its pages and from the fruits of his college teaching he assembled the literary essays which made up the most popular books of his later years, *Among My Books,* two series, (1870, 1876) and *My Study Windows* (1871). He was appointed United States Minister to Spain in 1877, to England in 1880. He continued to live much in England after his appointment ended in 1885, and was widely honored on both sides of the Atlantic. A few later poems were collected in a volume called *Heartsease and Rue* in 1888, two volumes of his essays on political subjects appeared in 1887 and 1888, and other gatherings of his papers were published at intervals from the year of his death until 1920.

It has been customary to base Lowell's claim to a major position in our literature chiefly on his criticism; some modern readers will find adequate basis for the claim in his best essays. They are bright in detail and tone, witty, and usually urbane, often warmly appreciative or broadly informing. Occasionally, as in "Rousseau and the Sentimentalists," they transcend academic impressionism to anticipate the judgments and points of view of the later Neo-Humanists, Irving Babbitt and Paul Elmer More. From most of them the reader gains knowledge of literature and familiarity with it, rather than insight. In the political writing of his later years Lowell is a less integrated and forceful thinker. Of all Lowell's essays those likely to prove most satisfactory to modern taste are such personal and retrospective pieces as "Emerson the Lecturer" and "Cambridge Thirty Years Ago."

If we turn to Lowell's verse, we can hardly hold that his best achievement as a serious poet, limited to the "Commemoration Ode" and a very few other pieces, entitles him to a place of the first rank. He served well as editor and teacher, but America has had greater editors and greater teachers. We are forced back to that part of his work for which Lowell himself perhaps would least

wish to be remembered, *The Biglow Papers.* In these his achievement is individual, historically significant, and lastingly alive.

[H. E. Scudder's *James Russell Lowell* (Boston, 1901) is still the standard
biography. R. C. Beatty's study (Nashville, 1942) presents adverse critical
views. Norman Foerster and H. H. Clark have edited *Lowell* (New York,
1947) for the American Writers Series.]

STANZAS ON FREEDOM [1]
[1843]

MEN! whose boast it is that ye
Come of fathers brave and free,
If there breathe on earth a slave,
Are ye truly free and brave?
If ye do not feel the chain,   5
When it works a brother's pain,
Are ye not base slaves indeed,
Slaves unworthy to be freed?

Women! who shall one day bear
Sons to breathe New England air,   10
If ye hear, without a blush,
Deeds to make the roused blood rush
Like red lava through your veins,
For your sisters now in chains,—
Answer! are ye fit to be   15
Mothers of the brave and free?

Is true Freedom but to break
Fetters for our own dear sake,
And, with leathern hearts, forget
That we owe mankind a debt?   20
No! true freedom is to share
All the chains our brothers wear,
And, with heart and hand, to be
Earnest to make others free!

They are slaves who fear to speak   25
For the fallen and the weak;
They are slaves who will not choose
Hatred, scoffing, and abuse,
Rather than in silence shrink
From the truth they needs must think;   30
They are slaves who dare not be
In the right with two or three.

ON THE CAPTURE OF FUGITIVE
SLAVES NEAR WASHINGTON
[1848 (1845)]

Look on who will in apathy, and stifle they
    who can,

The sympathies, the hopes, the words, that
    make man truly man;
Let those whose hearts are dungeoned up
    with interest or with ease
Consent to hear with quiet pulse of loath-
    some deeds like these!

I first drew in New England's air, and from
    her hardy breast   5
Sucked in the tyrant-hating milk that will
    not let me rest;
And if my words seem treason to the dull-
    ard and the tame,
'T is but my Bay-State dialect,—our fathers
    spake the same!

Shame on the costly mockery of piling
    stone on stone
To those who won our liberty, the heroes
    dead and gone,   10
While we look coldly on and see law-
    shielded ruffians slay
The men who fain would win their own,
    the heroes of to-day!

Are we pledged to craven silence? O, fling
    it to the wind,
The parchment wall that bars us from the
    least of human kind,
That makes us cringe and temporize, and
    dumbly stand at rest,   15
While Pity's burning flood of words is
    red-hot in the breast!

Though we break our fathers' promise, we
    have nobler duties first;
The traitor to Humanity is the traitor most
    accursed;

---

[1] Written for an anti-slavery meeting on
the anniversary of West Indian emancipation, this poem was originally entitled
"Song Sung at an Anti-Slavery Picnic."

Man is more than Constitutions; better
    rot beneath the sod,
Than be true to Church and State while
    we are doubly false to God!   20

We owe allegiance to the State; but deeper,
    truer, more,
To the sympathies that God hath set within
    our spirit's core;
Our country claims our fealty; we grant
    it so, but then
Before Man made us citizens, great Nature
    made us men.

He's true to God who's true to man; wher-
    ever wrong is done,   25
To the humblest and the weakest, 'neath
    the all-beholding sun,
That wrong is also done to us; and they
    are slaves most base,
Whose love of right is for themselves, and
    not for all their race.

God works for all. Ye cannot hem the hope
    of being free
With parallels of latitude, with mountain-
    range or sea.   30
Put golden padlocks on Truth's lips, be
    callous as ye will,
From soul to soul, o'er all the world, leaps
    one electric thrill.

Chain down your slaves with ignorance, ye
    cannot keep apart,
With all your craft of tyranny, the human
    heart from heart:
When first the Pilgrims landed on the Bay
    State's iron shore,   35
The word went forth that slavery should
    one day be no more.

Out from the land of bondage 'tis decreed
    our slaves shall go,
And signs to us are offered, as erst to
    Pharaoh;
If we are blind, their exodus, like Israel's
    of yore,
Through a Red Sea is doomed to be, whose
    surges are of gore.   40

'T is ours to save our brethren, with peace
    and love to win
Their darkened hearts from error, ere
    they harden it to sin;
But if before his duty man with listless
    spirit stands,
Erelong the Great Avenger takes the work
    from out his hands.

From
THE BIGLOW PAPERS

FIRST SERIES

[1848 (1846)]

THE RECRUITING [1]

Thrash away, you'll *hev* to rattle
    On them kittle-drums o' yourn,—
'Taint a knowin' kind o' cattle
    Thet is ketched with mouldy corn;
Put in stiff, you fifer feller,   5
    Let folks see how spry you be,—
Guess you'll toot till you are yeller
    'Fore you'll git ahold o' me!
Thet air flag's a leetle rotten,
    Hope it aint your Sunday's best;—   10
Fact! it takes a sight o' cotton
    To stuff out a soger's chest:

<hr>

[1] Titles for this selection and the one
which follows have been supplied by the
present editors, and the accompanying
prose communications have been omitted.
    In introducing *The Biglow Papers:
Second Series* (1867), Lowell discussed
his purpose and method. Portions of that
introduction follow:
    . . . When, more than twenty years
ago, I wrote the first of the series, I had

no definite plan and no intention of ever
writing another. Thinking the Mexican
war, as I think it still, a national crime
committed in behoof of Slavery, our common sin, and wishing to put the feeling
of those who thought as I did in a way
that would tell, I imagined to myself such
an upcountry man as I had often seen
at antislavery gatherings, capable of dis-
trict-school English, but always instinc-

Sence we farmers hev to pay fer 't,
　　Ef you must wear humps like these,
Sposin' you should try salt hay fer 't, 15
　　It would du ez slick ez grease.

'Twould n't suit them Southun fellers,
　　They're a dreffle graspin' set,
We must ollers blow the bellers
　　Wen they want their irons het; 20
May be it's all right ez preachin',
　　But *my* narves it kind o' grates,
Wen I see the overreachin'
　　O' them nigger-drivin' States.

Them thet rule us, them slave-traders, 25
　　Haint they cut a thunderin' swarth
(Helped by Yankee renegaders),
　　Thru the vartu o' the North!

We begin to think it's nater
　　To take sarse an' not be riled;— 30
Who'd expect to see a tater
　　All on eend at bein' biled?

Ez fer war, I call it murder,—
　　There you hev it plain an' flat;
I don't want to go no furder 35
　　Than my Testyment fer that;
God hez sed so plump an' fairly,
　　It's ez long ez it is broad,
An' you've gut to git up airly
　　Ef you want to take in God. 40

'Taint your eppyletts an' feathers
　　Make the thing a grain more right;
'Taint afollerin' your bell-wethers
　　Will excuse ye in His sight;

tively falling back into the natural strong-hold of his homely dialect when heated to the point of self-forgetfulness. . . .

In choosing the Yankee dialect, I did not act without forethought. It had long seemed to me that the great vice of American writing and speaking was a studied want of simplicity, that we were in danger of coming to look on our mother-tongue as a dead language, to be sought in the grammar and dictionary rather than in the heart, and that our only chance of escape was by seeking it at its living sources among those who were, as Scottowe says of Major-General Gibbons, 'divinely illiterate.' President Lincoln, the only really great public man whom these latter days have seen, was great also in this, that he was master—witness his speech at Gettysburg—of a truly masculine English, classic because it was of no special period, and level at once to the highest and lowest of his countrymen. I learn from the highest authority that his favorite reading was in Shakespeare and Milton, to which, of course, the Bible should be added. But whoever should read the debates in Congress might fancy himself present at a meeting of the city council of some city of Southern Gaul in the decline of the Empire, where barbarians with a Latin varnish emulated each other in being more than Ciceronian. Whether it be want of culture, for the highest outcome of that is simplicity, or for whatever reason, it is certain that very few American writers or speakers wield their native language with the directness, precision, and force that are common as the day in the mother country. We use it like Scotsmen, not as if it belonged to us, but as if we wished to prove that we belonged to it, by showing our intimacy with its written rather than with its spoken dialect. And yet all the while our popular idiom is racy with life and vigor and originality, bucksome (as Milton used the word) to our new occasions, and proves itself no mere graft by sending up new suckers from the old root in spite of us. It is only from its roots in the living generations of men that a language can be reinforced with fresh vigor for its needs; what may be called a literate dialect grows ever more and more pedantic and foreign, till it becomes at last as unfitting a vehicle for living thought as monkish Latin. That we should all be made to talk like books is the danger with which we are threatened by the Universal Schoolmaster, who does his best to enslave the minds and memories of his victims to what he esteems the best models of English composition, that is to say, to the writers whose style is faultily correct and has no blood-warmth in it. No language after it has faded into *diction,* none that cannot suck up the feeding juices secreted for it in the rich mother-earth of common folk, can bring forth a sound and lusty book. True vigor and heartiness of phrase do not pass from page to page, but from man to man, where the brain is kindled and the lips suppled by downright living interests and by passion in its very throe. . . .

Ef you take a sword an' dror it,　　45
　An' go stick a feller thru,
Guv'ment aint to answer for it,
　God'll send the bill to you.

Wut's the use o' meetin'-goin'
　Every Sabbath, wet or dry,　　50
Ef it's right to go amowin'
　Feller-men like oats an' rye?
I dunno but wut it's pooty
　Trainin' round in bobtail coats,—
But it's curus Christian dooty　　55
　This 'ere cuttin' folks's throats.

They may talk o' Freedom's airy
　Tell they're pupple in the face,—
It's a grand gret cemetary
　Fer the barthrights of our race;　　60
They jest want this Californy
　So's to lug new slave-states in
To abuse ye, an' to scorn ye,
　An' to plunder ye like sin.

Aint it cute to see a Yankee　　65
　Take sech everlastin' pains,
All to git the Devil's thankee
　Helpin' on 'em weld their chains?
Wy, it's jest ez clear ez figgers,
　Clear ez one an' one make two,　　70
Chaps that make black slaves o' niggers
　Want to make wite slaves o' you.

Tell ye jest the eend I've come to
　Arter cipherin' plaguy smart,
An' it makes a handy sum, tu,　　75
　Any gump could larn by heart;
Laborin' man an laborin' woman
　Hev one glory an' one shame.
Ev'y thin' thet's done inhuman
　Injers all on 'em the same.　　80

'Taint by turnin' out to hack folks
　You're agoin' to git your right,
Nor by lookin' down on black folks
　Coz you're put upon by wite;
Slavery aint o' nary color,　　85
　'Taint the hide thet makes it wus,
All it keers fer in a feller
　'S jest to make him fill its pus.

Want to tackle *me* in, du ye?
　I expect you'll hev to wait;　　90
Wen cold lead puts daylight thru ye
　You'll begin to kal'late;
S'pose the crows wun't fall to pickin'
　All the carkiss from your bones,
Coz you helped to give a lickin'　　95
　To them poor half-Spanish drones?

Jest go home an' ask our Nancy
　Wether I'd be sech a goose
Ez to jine ye,—guess you'd fancy
　The etarnal bung wuz loose!　　100
She wants me fer home consumption,
　Let alone the hay's to mow,—
Ef you're arter folks o' gumption,
　You've a darned long row to hoe.

Take them editors thet's crowin'　　105
　Like a cockerel three months old,—
Don't ketch any on 'em goin',
　Though they *be* so blasted bold;
Aint they a prime lot o' fellers?
　'Fore they think on't guess they'll
　　　sprout　　110
(Like a peach thet's got the yellers),
　With the meanness bustin' out.

Wal, go 'long to help 'em stealin'
　Bigger pens to cram with slaves,
Help the men thet's ollers dealin'　　115
　Insults on your fathers' graves;
Help the strong to grind the feeble,
　Help the many agin the few,
Help the men thet call your people
　Witewashed slaves an' peddlin' crew!　120

Massachusetts, God forgive her,
　She's akneelin' with the rest,[2]
She, thet ough' to ha' clung ferever
　In her grand old eagle-nest;
She thet ough' to stand so fearless　　125
　Wile the wracks are round her hurled,
Holdin' up a beacon peerless
　To the oppressed of all the world!

---

[2] The governor of Massachusetts issued
a call for volunteers, May 26, 1846.

Ha'n't they sold your colored seamen?[3]
  Ha'n't they made your env'ys[4] w'iz? 130
Wut'll make ye act like freemen?
  Wut'll git your dander riz?
Come, I'll tell ye wut I'm thinkin'
  Is our dooty in this fix,
They'd ha' done 't ez quick ez winkin' 135
  In the days o' seventy-six.

Clang the bells in every steeple,
  Call all true men to disown
The tradoocers of our people,
  The enslavers o' their own;   140
Let our dear old Bay State proudly
  Put the trumpet to her mouth,
Let her ring this messidge loudly
  In the ears of all the South:—

"I'll return ye good fer evil   145
  Much ez we frail mortils can,
But I wun't go help the Devil
  Makin' man the cus o' man;
Call me coward, call me traiter,
  Jest ez suits your mean idees,—   150
Here I stand a tyrant-hater,
  An' the friend o' God an' Peace!"

Ef I'd *my* way I hed ruther
  We should go to work an' part,—
They take one way, we take t' other,— 155
  Guess it wouldn't break my heart;
Man hed ough' to put asunder
  Them thet God has noways jined;
An' I shouldn't gretly wonder
  Ef there's thousands o' my mind.   160

THE DEBATE IN THE SENATE [1]
[1848]

"Here we stan' on the Constitution, by
    thunder!
  It 's a fact o' wich ther's bushils o'
    proofs;
Fer how could we trample on 't so, I
    wonder,
  Ef 't worn't thet it's ollers under our
    hoofs?"
    Sez John C. Calhoun, sez he;   5
  "Human rights haint no more
  Right to come on this floor,
No more 'n the man in the moon,"
    sez he.

"The North haint no kind o' bisness with
    nothin',
  An' you 've no idee how much bother it
    saves;   10
We aint none riled by their frettin' an'
    frothin'
  We're *used* to layin' the string on our
    slaves,"
    Sez John C. Calhoun, sez he;—
    Sez Mister Foote,
  "I should like to shoot   15
  The holl gang, by the gret horn
    spoon!" sez he.

"Freedom's Keystone is Slavery, thet
    ther 's no doubt on,
  It's suthin' thet's—wha' d' ye call it?—
    divine,—
An' the slaves thet we ollers *make* the most
    out on
  Air them north o' Mason an' Dixon's
    line,"   20
    Sez John C. Calhoun, sez he;—
  "Fer all thet," sez Mangum,
  "'T would be better to hang 'em,
An' so git red on 'em soon," sez he.

[3] Free colored men in the naval service
of the United States had been arrested,
when visiting Southern states, and sold
as slaves.

[4] Samuel Hoar, sent to Charleston, S. C.,
to negotiate concerning legal rights of Negro citizens of Massachusetts, and George
Hubbard, sent to New Orleans on a similar mission, had been expelled from those
cities.

[1] This debate was on the resolution introduced in the United States Senate April
20, 1848, by Senator John P. Hale (N. H.),
declaring sympathy with the 77 slaves
kidnapped from Washington by Drayton
and Sayers and later recaptured. Senator
John C. Calhoun (S. C.) led the attack
on the resolution on the ground of property rights guaranteed by the Constitution. Other speakers mentioned by Lowell
are Senators Henry S. Foote (Miss.);
Willie P. Mangum (N. C.); Lewis Cass
(Ohio); Jefferson Davis (Miss., later president of the Confederacy); Edward A.
Hannegan (Ind.); Spencer Jarnagin
(Tenn.); Charles G. Atherton (N. H.);
Walter T. Colquitt (Ga.); Henry Johnson
(La.); James D. Westcott (Fla.); and
Dixon H. Lewis (Ala.).

"The mass ough' to labor an' we lay on
    soffies,   25
Thet's the reason I want to spread Free-
    dom's aree;
It puts all the cunninest on us in office,
An' reelises our Maker's orig'nal idee,"
    Sez John C. Calhoun, sez he;—
      "Thet's ez plain," sez Cass,   30
      "Ez thet some one's an ass,
    It's ez clear ez the sun is at noon," sez
he.

"Now don't go to say I'm the friend of
    oppression,
But keep all your spare breath fer coolin'
    your broth,
Fer I ollers hev strove (at least thet's my
    impression)   35
To make cussed free with the rights o'
    the North,"
    Sez John C. Calhoun, sez he;—
    "Yes," sez Davis o' Miss.,
    "The perfection o' bliss
    Is in skinnin' thet same old coon,"
    sez he.   40

"Slavery's a thing thet depends on com-
    plexion,
It's God's law thet fetters on black
    skins don't chafe;
Ef brains wuz to settle it (horrid reflec-
    tion!)
Wich of our onnable body'd be safe?"
    Sez John C. Calhoun, sez he;—   45
    Sez Mister Hannegan,
    Afore he began again,
    "Thet exception is quite opportoon," sez
he.

"Gen'nle Cass, Sir, you need n't be
    twitchin' your collar,
Your merit's quite clear by the dut on
    your knees,   50
At the North we don't make no distinc-
    tions o' color;
You can all take a lick at our shoes wen
    you please,"
    Sez John C. Calhoun, sez he;—
    Sez Mister Jarnagin,
    "They wunt hev to larn again,   55

They all on 'em know the old toon,"
    sez he.

"The slavery question aint no ways be-
    wilderin'.
North an' South hev one int'rest, it's
    plain to a glance;
No'thern men, like us patriarchs, don't sell
    their childrin,
But they *du* sell themselves, ef they git
    a good chance,"   60
    Sez John C. Calhoun, sez he;—
    Sez Atherton here,
    "This is gittin' severe,
    I wish I could live like a loon," sez he.

"It 'll break up the Union, this talk
    about freedom,   65
An' your fact'ry gals (soon ez we split)
    'll make head,
An' gittin' some Miss chief or other to
    lead 'em
'll go to work raisin' permiscoous Ned,"
    Sez John C. Calhoun, sez he;—
    "Yes, the North," sez Colquitt,   70
    "Ef we Southeners all quit,
    Would go down like a busted balloon,"
    sez he.

"Jest look wut is doin', wut annyky's
    brewin'
In the beautiful clime o' the olive an'
    vine,
All the wise aris toxy's a tumblin' to
    ruin,   75
An' the sankylots drorin' an' drinkin'
    their wine,"
    Sez John C. Calhoun, sez he;—
    "Yes," sez Johnson, "in France
    They're beginnin' to dance
    Beelzebub's own rigadoon," sez he.   80

"The South's safe enough, it don't feel
    a mite skeery,
Our slaves in their darkness an' dut air
    tu blest
Not to welcome with proud hallyluyers the
    ery
Wen our **eagle** kicks **yourn** from the
    naytional nest,"

Sez John C. Calhoun, sez he;—   85
  "O," sez Westcott o' Florida,
  "Wut treason is horrider
Then our priv'leges tryin' to proon?"
  sez he.

"It's 'coz they're so happy, thet, wen
  crazy sarpents
Stick their nose in our bizness, we git
  so darned riled;   90
We think it's our dooty to give pooty
  sharp hints,
Thet the last crumb of Edin on airth
  sha'n't be spiled,"
Sez John C. Calhoun, sez he;—
  "Ah," sez Dixon H. Lewis,
"It perfectly true is   95
Thet slavery's airth's grettest boon,"
  sez he.

From
THE BIGLOW PAPERS

SECOND SERIES
[1867 (1848)]

THE COURTIN'[1]

God makes sech nights, all white an still
  Fur 'z you can look or listen,
Moonshine an' snow on field an' hill,
  All silence an' all glisten.

Zekle crep' up quite unbeknown   5
  An' peeked in thru' the winder,
An' there sot Huldy all alone,
  'ith no one nigh to hender.

A fireplace filled the room's one side
  With half a cord o' wood in—   10
There warn't no stoves (tell comfort died)
  To bake ye to a puddin'.

The wa'nut logs shot sparkles out
  Towards the pootiest, bless her,
An' leetle flames danced all about   15
  The chiny on the dresser.

Agin the chimbley crook-necks hung,
  An' in amongst 'em rusted
The ole queen's-arm thet gran'ther Young
  Fetched back from Concord busted.   20

The very room, coz she was in,
  Seemed warm from floor to ceilin',
An' she looked full ez rosy agin
  Ez the apples she was peelin'.

'Twas kin' o' kingdom-come to look   25
  On sech a blessed cretur,
A dogrose blushin' to a brook
  Ain't modester nor sweeter.

He was six foot o' man, A 1,
  Clear grit an' human natur';   30
None could n't quicker pitch a ton,
  Nor dror a furrer straighter.

He'd sparked it with full twenty gals,
  Hed squired 'em, danced 'em, druve 'em,
Fust this one, an' then thet, by spells—   35
  All is, he could n't love 'em.

But long o' her his veins 'ould run
  All crinkly like curled maple,
The side she breshed felt full o' sun
  Ez a south slope in Ap'il.   40

She thought no v'ice hed sech a swing
  Ez hisn in the choir;
My! when he made Ole Hundred ring,
  She *knowed* the Lord was nigher.

An' she'd blush scarlit, right in prayer,   45
  When her new meetin'-bunnet
Felt somehow thru' its crown a pair
  O' blue eyes sot upon it.

Thet night, I tell ye, she looked *some!*
  She seemed to 've gut a new soul,   50
For she felt sartin-sure he'd come,
  Down to her very shoe-sole.

She heered a foot, an' knowed it tu,
  A-raspin' on the scraper,—
All ways to once her feelin's flew   55
  Like sparks in burnt-up paper.

He kin' o' l'itered on the mat,
  Some doubtfle o' the sekle,
His heart kep' goin' pity-pat,
  But hern went pity Zekle.   60

---

[1] This poem appeared in a briefer form
in the First Series of *The Biglow Papers*.

An' yit she gin her cheer a jerk
   Ez though she wished him furder,
An' on her apples kep' to work,
   Parin' away like murder.

"You want to see my Pa, I s'pose?"   65
   "Wal . . . no . . . I come designin'"—
"To see my Ma? She's sprinklin' clo'es
   Agin to-morrer's i'nin'."

To say why gals acts so or so,
   Or don't, 'ould be presumin';   70
Mebby to mean *yes* an' say *no*
   Comes nateral to women.

He stood a spell on one foot fust,
   Then stood a spell on t' other,
An' on which one he felt the wust   75
   He could n't ha' told ye nuther.

Says he, "I'd better call agin";
   Says she, "Think likely, Mister":
Thet last word pricked him like a pin,
   An' . . . Wal, he up an' kist her.   80

When Ma bimeby upon 'em slips,
   Huldy sot pale ez ashes,
All kin' o' smily roun' the lips
   An' teary roun' the lashes.

For she was jes' the quiet kind   85
   Whose naturs never vary,
Like streams that keep a summer mind
   Snowhid in Jenooary.

The blood clost roun' her heart felt glued
   Too tight for all expressin',   90
Tell mother see how metters stood,
   An' gin 'em both her blessin'.

Then her red come back like the tide
   Down to the Bay o' Fundy,
An' all I know is they was cried [2]
   In meetin' come nex' Sunday.

A NATION SAVED [1]
[1867 (1865)]

DEAR SIR,—Your letter come to han'
   Requestin' me to please be funny;

But I ain't made upon a plan
   Thet knows wut's comin', gall or honey: 5
Ther' 's times the world does look so queer,
   Odd fancies come afore I call 'em;
An' then agin, for half a year,
   No preacher 'thout a call 's more solemn.

You're 'n want o' sunthin' light an' cute, 10
   Rattlin' an' shrewd an kin' o' jingleish,
An' wish, pervidin' it 'ould suit,
   I'd take an' citify my English.
I *ken* write long-tailed, ef I please,—
   But when I'm jokin', no, I thankee;   15
Then, 'fore I know it, my idees
   Run helter-skelter into Yankee.

Sence I begun to scribble rhyme,
   I tell ye wut, I hain't ben foolin';
The parson's books, life, death, an' time 20
   Hev took some trouble with my schoolin';
Nor th' airth don't git put out with me,
   Thet love her 'z though she wuz a
      woman;
Why, th' ain't a bird upon the tree
   But half forgives my bein' human.   25

An' yit I love th' unhighschooled way
   Ol' farmers hed when I wuz younger;
Their talk was meatier, an' 'ould stay,
   While book-froth seems to whet your
      hunger;
For puttin' in a downright lick   30
   'twixt Humbug's eyes, ther' 's few can
      metch it,
An' then it helves my thoughts ez slick
   Ez stret-grained hickory doos a hetchet.

But when I can't, I can't, thet's all,
   For Natur' won't put up with gullin'; 35
Idees you hev to shove an' haul
   Like a druv pig ain't wuth a mullein:
Live thoughts ain't sent for; thru all rifts
   O' sense they pour an' resh ye onwards,
Like rivers when south-lyin' drifts   40
   Feel thet th' old airth's a-wheelin' sun-
      wards.

---

[2] Their marriage banns were announced.
[1] Title supplied by the present editors.

Time wuz, the rhymes come crowdin' thick
  Ez office-seekers arter 'lection,
An' into ary place 'ould stick
  Without no bother nor objection;   45
But sense the war my thoughts hang back
  Ez though I wanted to enlist 'em,
An' subs'tutes,—*they* don't never lack,
  But then they'll slope afore you've mist
    'em.

Nothin' don't seem like wut it wuz;   50
  I can't see wut there is to hender,
An' yit my brains jes' go buzz, buzz,
  Like bumblebees agin a winder;
'fore these times come, in all airth's row,
  Ther' wuz one quiet place, my head
    in,   55
Where I could hide an' think,—but now
  It's all one teeter, hopin', dreadin'.

Where's Peace? I start, some clear-blown
    night,
  When gaunt stone walls grow numb an'
    number,
An', creakin' 'cross the snow-crus' white, 60
  Walk the col' starlight into summer;
Up grows the moon, an' swell by swell
  Thru the pale pasturs silvers dimmer
Than the last smile thet strives to tell
  O' love gone heavenward in its shim-
    mer.   65

I hev ben gladder o' sech things
  Than cocks o' spring or bees o' clover,
They filled my heart with livin' springs,
  But now they seem to freeze 'em over;
Sights innercent ez babes on knee,   70
  Peaceful ez eyes o' pastur'd cattle,
Jes' coz they be so, seem to me
  To rile me more with thoughts o' battle.

In-doors an' out by spells I try;
  Ma'am Natur' keeps her spin-wheel
    goin',   75
But leaves my natur' stiff and dry
  Ez fiel's o' clover arter mowin';
An' her jes' keepin' on the same,
  Calmer 'n a clock, an' never carin',
An' findin' nary thing to blame,   80
  Is wus than ef she took to swearin'.

Snow-flakes come whisperin' on the pane
  The charm makes blazin' logs so pleasant,
But I can't hark to wut they 're say'n',
  With Grant or Sherman ollers pres-
    ent;   85
The chimbleys shudder in the gale,
  Thet lulls, then suddin takes to flappin'
Like a shot hawk, but all 's ez stale
  To me ez so much sperit-rappin'.[2]

Under the yaller-pines I house,   90
  When sunshine makes 'em all sweet-
    scented,
An' hear among their furry boughs
  The baskin' west-wind purr contented,
While 'way o'erhead, ez sweet an' low
  Ez distant bells thet ring for meetin' 95
The wedged wil' geese their bugles blow,
  Further an' further South retreatin'.

Or up the slippery knob I strain
  An' see a hundred hills like islan's
Lift their blue woods in broken chain 100
  Out 'o the sea o' snowy silence;
The farm-smokes, sweetes' sight on airth,
  Slow thru the winter air a-shrinkin'
Seem kin' o' sad, an' roun' the hearth
  Of empty places set me thinkin'.   105

Beaver roars hoarse with meltin' snows,
  An' rattles di'mon's from his granite;
Time wuz, he snatched away my prose,
  An' into psalms or satires ran it;
But he, nor all the rest thet once   110
  Started my blood to country-dances,
Can't set me goin' more 'n a dunce
  Thet hain't no use for dreams an' fancies.

Rat-tat-tat-tattle thru the street
  I hear the drummers makin' riot,   115
An' I set thinkin' o' the feet
  Thet follered once an' now are quiet,[3]—

---

[2] Lowell's long poem, "The Unhappy Lot of Mr. Knott," is one of the best satirical treatments of the popular interest in spiritism in the mid-nineteenth century.

[3] Three nephews of Lowell—William Lowell Putnam, James Jackson Lowell, and Charles Russell Lowell—were killed in the Civil War.

White feet ez snowdrops innercent,
  Thet never knowed the paths o' Satan,
Whose comin' step ther' 's ears thet
  won't, 120
No, nor lifelong, leave off awaitin'.

Why, hain't I held 'em on my knee?
  Didn't I love to see 'em growin',
Three likely lads as wal could be,
  Hahnsome an' brave an' not tu
  knowin'? 125
I set an' look into the blaze
  Whose natur', jes' like theirn, keeps
  climbin',
Ez long 'z it lives, in shinin' ways,
  An' half despise myself for rhymin'.

Wut's words to them whose faith an'
  truth 130
On War's red techstone rang true metal
Who ventered life an' love an' youth
  For the gret prize o' death in battle?
To him[4] who, deadly hurt, agen
  Flashed on afore the charge's thun-
  der, 135
Tippin' with fire the bolt of men
  Thet rived the Rebel line asunder?

'Tain't right to hev the young go fust,
  All throbbin' full o' gifts an' graces,
Leavin' life's paupers dry ez dust 140
  To try an' make b'lieve fill their places:
Nothin' but tells us wut we miss,
  Ther' 's gaps our lives can't never fay
  in,
An' thet world seems so fur from this
  Lef' for us loafers to grow gray in! 145

My eyes cloud up for rain; my mouth
  Will take to twitchin' roun' the corners;
I pity mothers, tu, down South,
  For all they sot among the scorners:
I'd sooner take my chance to stan' 150
  At Jedgment where your meanest slave
  is,
Than at God's bar hol' up a han'
  Ez drippin' red ez yourn, Jeff Davis!

Come, Peace! not like a mourner bowed
  For honor lost an' dear ones wasted, 155

But proud, to meet a people proud,
  With eyes thet tell o' triumph tasted!
Come, with han' grippin' on the hilt,
  An' step thet proves ye Victory's daugh-
  ter!
Longin' for you, our sperits wilt 160
  Like shipwrecked men's on raf's for
  water.

Come, while our country feels the lift
  Of a gret instinct shoutin' forwards,
An' knows thet freedom ain't a gift
  Thet tarries long in han's o' cowards! 165
Come, sech ez mothers prayed for, when
  They kissed their cross with lips thet
  quivered,
An' bring fair wages for brave men,
  A nation saved, a race delivered!

ODE RECITED AT THE HARVARD COMMEMORATION[1]

[1865]

I

Weak-winged is song,
Nor aims at that clear-ethered height
Whither the brave deed climbs for light:
  We seem to do them wrong,
Bringing our robin's-leaf to deck their
  hearse 5
Who in warm life-blood wrote their nobler
  verse,
Our trivial song to honor those who come
With ears attuned to strenuous trump and
  drum,
And shaped in squadron-strophes their
  desire,
Live battle-odes whose lines were steel and
  fire: 10

---

[4] General Charles Russell Lowell, at the Battle of Cedar Creek.
[1] Lowell wrote to Richard Watson Gilder (January 16, 1886) that this ode was "an improvisation. Two days before the Commemoration I had told my friend Child that it was impossible—that I was dull as a door-mat. But the next day something gave me a jog and the whole thing came out with a rush. I sat up all night writing it out clear. . . ."

Yet sometimes feathered words are
strong,
A gracious memory to buoy up and save
From Lethe's dreamless ooze, the common
grave
Of the unventurous throng.

II

To-day our Reverend Mother welcomes
back   15
Her wisest Scholars, those who under-
stood
The deeper teaching of her mystic tome,
And offered their fresh lives to make it
good:
No lore of Greece or Rome,
No science peddling with the names of
things,   20
Or reading stars to find inglorious fates,
Can lift our life with wings
Far from Death's idle gulf that for the
many waits,
And lengthen out our dates
With that clear fame whose memory
sings   25
In manly hearts to come, and nerves them
and dilates:
Nor such thy teaching, Mother of us all!
Not such the trumpet-call
Of thy diviner mood,
That could thy sons entice   30
From happy homes and toils, the fruitful
nest
Of those half-virtues which the world calls
best,
Into War's tumult rude;
But rather far that stern device
The sponsors chose that round thy cradle
stood   35
In the dim, unventured wood,
The VERITAS [2] that lurks beneath
The letter's unprolific sheath,
Life of whate'er makes life worth living,
Seed-grain of high emprise, immortal
food,   40
One heavenly thing whereof earth hath
the giving.

III

Many loved Truth, and lavished life's best
oil
Amid the dust of books to find her,
Content at last, for guerdon of their toil,
With the cast mantle she hath left behind
her.   45
Many in sad faith sought for her,
Many with crossed hands sighed for
her;
But these, our brothers, fought for
her;
At life's dear peril wrought for her,
So loved her that they died for her, 50
Tasting the raptured fleetness
Of her divine completeness:
Their higher instinct knew
Those love her best who to themselves are
true,
And what they dare to dream of, dare to
do;   55
They followed her and found her
Where all may hope to find,
Not in the ashes of the burnt-out mind,
But beautiful, with danger's sweetness
round her.
Where faith made whole with deed 60
Breathes its awakening breath
Into the lifeless creed,
They saw her plumed and mailed,
With sweet, stern face unveiled,
And all-repaying eyes, look proud on them
in death.   65

IV

Our slender life runs rippling by, and
glides
Into the silent hollow of the past;
What is there that abides
To make the next age better for the last?
Is earth too poor to give us   70
Something to live for here that shall
outlive us?
Some more substantial boon
Than such as flows and ebbs with Fortune's
fickle moon?
The little that we see

----
[2] Motto on the Harvard seal.

From doubt is never free; 75
The little that we do
Is but half-nobly true;
With our laborious hiving
What men call treasure, and the gods call
    dross,
Life seems a jest of Fate's contriving, 80
Only secure in every one's conniving,
A long account of nothings paid with loss,
Where we poor puppets, jerked by unseen
    wires,
After our little hour of strut and rave,
With all our pasteboard passions and de-
    sires, 85
Loves, hates, ambitions, and immortal fires,
Are tossed pell-mell together in the
    grave.
But stay! no age was e'er degenerate,
Unless men held it at too cheap a rate,
For in our likeness still we shape our
    fate. 90
Ah, there is something here
Unfathomed by the cynic's sneer,
Something that gives our feeble light
A high immunity from Night,
Something that leaps life's narrow
    bars 95
To claim its birthright with the hosts of
    heaven;
A seed of sunshine that can leaven
Our earthly dullness with the beams of
    stars,
    And glorify our clay
With light from fountains elder than
    the Day; 100
A conscience more divine than we,
A gladness fed with secret tears,
A vexing, forward-reaching sense
Of some more noble permanence;
    A light across the sea, 105
Which haunts the soul and will not let
    it be,
Still beaconing from the heights of unde-
    generate years.

V

Whither leads the path
    To ampler fates that leads?
Not down through flowery meads,

To reap an aftermath 110
Of youth's vainglorious weeds,
But up the steep, amid the wrath
And shock of deadly-hostile creeds,
Where the world's best hope and stay 115
By battle's flashes gropes a desperate way,
And every turf the fierce foot clings to
    bleeds.
Peace hath her not ignoble wreath
Ere yet the sharp, decisive word
Light the black lips of cannon, and the
    sword 120
    Dreams in its easeful sheath;
But some day the live coal behind the
    thought,
    Whether from Baäl's stone obscene,
    Or from the shrine serene
    Of God's pure altar brought, 125
Bursts up in flame; the war of tongue and
    pen
Learns with what deadly purpose it was
    fraught,
And, helpless in the fiery passion caught,
Shakes all the pillared state with shock of
    men:
Some day the soft Ideal that we wooed 130
Confronts us fiercely, foe-beset, pursued,
And cries reproachful: "Was it, then, my
    praise,
And not myself was loved? Prove now thy
    truth;
I claim of thee the promise of thy youth;
Give me thy life, or cower in empty
    phrase, 135
The victim of thy genius, not its mate!"
Life may be given in many ways,
    And loyalty to Truth be sealed
As bravely in the closet as the field,
    So bountiful is Fate; 140
    But then to stand beside her,
    When craven churls deride her,
To front a lie in arms and not to yield,
    This shows, methinks, God's plan
    And measure of a stalwart man, 145
    Limbed like the old heroic breeds,
    Who stands self-poised on manhood's
        solid earth,
Not forced to frame excuses for his birth,
Fed from within with all the strength he
    needs.

VI [3]

Such was he, our Martyr-Chief,   150
　　Whom late the Nation he had led,
　　With ashes on her head,
Wept with the passion of an angry grief:
Forgive me, if from present things I turn
To speak what in my heart will beat and
　　burn,   155
And hang my wreath on his world-honored
　　urn.
　　　Nature, they say, doth dote,
　　　And cannot make a man
　　　Save on some worn-out plan,
　　　Repeating us by rote: 160
For him her Old-World moulds aside she
　　threw,
　　And, choosing sweet clay from the
　　breast
　　Of the unexhausted West,
With stuff untainted shaped a hero new,
Wise, steadfast in the strength of God, and
　　true.   165
　　How beautiful to see
Once more a shepherd of mankind indeed,
Who loved his charge, but never loved to
　　lead;
One whose meek flock the people joyed to
　　be,
　　Not lured by any cheat of birth,   170
　　But by his clear-grained human worth,
And brave old wisdom of sincerity!
　　They knew that outward grace is dust;
　　They could not choose but trust
In that sure-footed mind's unfaltering
　　skill,   175
　　And supple-tempered will
That bent like perfect steel to spring again
　　and thrust.
　　His was no lonely mountain-peak of
　　mind,
　　Thrusting to thin air o'er our cloudy
　　bars,
　　A sea-mark now, now lost in vapors
　　blind;   180
　　Broad prairie rather, genial, level-
　　lined,
　　Fruitful and friendly for all human
　　kind,

Yet also nigh to heaven and loved of
　　loftiest stars.
　　　Nothing of Europe here,
Or, then, of Europe fronting mornward
　　still,   185
　　Ere any names of Serf and Peer
　　Could Nature's equal scheme deface
　　And thwart her genial will;
　　Here was a type of the true elder race,
And one of Plutarch's men talked with us
　　face to face.   190
I praise him not; it were too late;
And some innative weakness there must be
In him who condescends to victory
Such as the Present gives, and cannot wait,
　　Safe in himself as in a fate.   195
　　　So always firmly he:
　　　He knew to bide his time,
　　　And can his fame abide,
Still patient in his simple faith sublime,
　　　Till the wise years decide.   200
　　Great captains, with their guns and
　　drums,
　　Disturb our judgment for the hour,
　　　But at last silence comes;
These all are gone, and, standing like a
　　tower,
Our children shall behold his fame. 205
　　The kindly-earnest, brave, foreseeing
　　man,
Sagacious, patient, dreading praise, not
　　blame,
　　New birth of our new soil, the first
　　American.

VII

Long as man's hope insatiate can discern
　　Or only guess some more inspiring
　　goal   210
　　Outside of Self, enduring as the pole,
Along whose course the flying axles burn
Of spirits bravely-pitched, earth's man-
　　lier brood;
　　Long as below we cannot find
　　The meed that stills the inexorable
　　mind;   215

---

[3] This section, referring to Lincoln, was
not included in the ode as read at the
Commemoration exercises, but was added
immediately afterward.

So long this faith to some ideal Good,
Under whatever mortal names it masks,
Freedom, Law, Country, this ethereal
mood
That thanks the Fates for their severer
tasks,
Feeling its challenged pulses leap, 220
While others skulk in subterfuges cheap,
And, set in Danger's van, has all the boon
it asks,
Shall win man's praise and woman's love,
Shall be a wisdom that we set above
All other skills and gifts to culture
dear, 225
A virtue round whose forehead we in-
wreathe
Laurels that with a living passion
breathe
When other crowns grow, while we twine
them, sear.
What brings us thronging these high
rites to pay,
And seal these hours the noblest of our
year, 230
Save that our brothers found this better
way?

VIII

We sit here in the Promised Land
That flows with Freedom's honey and
milk;
But 'twas they won it, sword in hand,
Making the nettle danger soft for us as
silk. 235
We welcome back our bravest and our
best;—
Ah me! not all! some come not with the
rest,
Who went forth brave and bright as any
here!
I strive to mix some gladness with my
strain,
But the sad strings complain, 240
And will not please the ear:
I sweep them for a pæan, but they wane
Again and yet again
Into a dirge, and die away, in pain.
In these brave ranks I only see the
gaps, 245

Thinking of dear ones whom the dumb turf
wraps,
Dark to the triumph which they died to
gain:
Fitlier may others greet the living,
For me the past is unforgiving;
I with uncovered head 250
Salute the sacred dead,
Who went, and who return not.—Say not
so!
'Tis not the grapes of Canaan [4] that repay,
But the high faith that failed not by the
way;
Virtue treads paths that end not in the
grave; 255
No ban of endless night exiles the brave;
And to the saner mind
We rather seem the dead that stayed be-
hind.
Blow, trumpets, all your exultations blow!
For never shall their aureoled presence
lack: 260
I see them muster in a gleaming row,
With ever-youthful brows that nobler
show;
We find in our dull road their shining
track;
In every nobler mood
We feel the orient of their spirit glow, 265
Part of our life's unalterable good,
Of all our saintlier aspiration;
They come transfigured back,
Secure from change in their high-hearted
ways,
Beautiful evermore, and with the rays 270
Of morn on their white Shields of Expec-
tation!

IX

But is there hope to save
Even this ethereal essence from the
grave?
What ever 'scaped Oblivion's subtle
wrong
Save a few clarion names, or golden threads
of song? 275
Before my musing eye

---

[4] Numbers 13:23.

The mighty ones of old sweep by,
Disvoicëd now and insubstantial things,
As noisy once as we; poor ghosts of
  kings,
Shadows of empire wholly gone to
  dust,   280
And many races, nameless long ago,
To darkness driven by that imperious
  gust
Of ever-rushing Time that here doth
  blow:
O visionary world, condition strange,
Where naught abiding is but only
  Change,   285
Where the deep-bolted stars themselves still
  shift and range!
Shall we to more continuance make pre-
  tence?
Renown builds tombs; a life-estate is Wit;
  And, bit by bit,
The cunning years steal all from us but
  woe;   290
Leaves are we, whose decays no harvest
  sow.
      But, when we vanish hence,
Shall they lie forceless in the dark be-
  low,
Save to make green their little length of
  sods,
Or deepen pansies for a year or two, 295
Who now to us are shining-sweet as
  gods?
Was dying all they had the skill to do?
That were not fruitless: but the Soul
  resents
Such short-lived service, as if blind
  events
Ruled without her, or earth could so
  endure;   300
She claims a more divine investiture
Of longer tenure than Fame's airy rents;
Whate'er she touches doth her nature
  share;
Her inspiration haunts the ennobled air,
  Gives eyes to mountains blind, 305
Ears to the deaf earth, voices to the wind,
And her clear trump sings succor every-
  where
By lonely bivouacs to the wakeful mind;
For soul inherits all that soul could dare:

Yea, Manhood hath a wider
  span   310
And larger privilege of life than man.
The single deed, the private sacrifice,
So radiant now through proudly-hidden
  tears,
Is covered up erelong from mortal eyes
With thoughtless drift of the deciduous
  years;   315
But that high privilege that makes all
  men peers,
That leap of heart whereby a people rise
  Up to a noble anger's height,
And, flamed on by the Fates, not shrink,
  but grow more bright,
That swift validity in noble veins, 320
Of choosing danger and disdaining
  shame,
      Of being set on flame
By the pure fire that flies all contact
  base,
But wraps its chosen with angelic might,
      These are imperishable gains, 325
Sure as the sun, medicinal as light,
These hold great futures in their lusty
  reins
And certify to earth a new imperial race.

X

Who now shall sneer?
Who dare again to say we trace   330
Our lines to a plebeian race?
      Roundhead and Cavalier!
Dumb are those names erewhile in battle
  loud;
Dream-footed as the shadow of a cloud,
  They flit across the ear: 335
That is best blood that hath most iron in't,
To edge resolve with, pouring without stint
  For what makes manhood dear.
  Tell us not of Plantagenets,
Hapsburgs, and Guelfs, whose thin bloods
  crawl   340
Down from some victor in a border-brawl!
  How poor their outworn coronets,
Matched with one leaf of that plain civic
  wreath
Our brave for honor's blazon shall be-
  queath,

Through whose desert a rescued Nation
  sets   345
Her heel on treason, and the trumpet hears
Shout victory, tingling Europe's sullen ears
  With vain resentments and more vain
    regrets!

XI

  Not in anger, not in pride,
  Pure from passion's mixture rude 350
  Ever to base earth allied,
  But with far-heard gratitude,
  Still with heart and voice renewed,
To heroes living and dear martyrs dead,
The strain should close that consecrates our
  brave.   355
  Lift the heart and lift the head!
  Lofty be its mood and grave,
  Not without a martial ring,
  Not without a prouder tread
  And a peal of exultation: 360
  Little right has he to sing
  Through whose heart in such an hour
  Beats no march of conscious power,
  Sweeps no tumult of elation!
  'Tis no Man we celebrate,   365
  By his country's victories great,
A hero half, and half the whim of Fate,
  But the pith and marrow of a Nation
  Drawing force from all her men,
  Highest, humblest, weakest, all,   370
  For her time of need, and then
  Pulsing it again through them,
Till the basest can no longer cower,
Feeling his soul spring up divinely tall,
Touched but in passing by her mantle-
  hem.   375
Come back, then, noble pride, for 'tis
  her dower!
  How could poet ever tower,
  If his passions, hopes, and fears,
  If his triumphs and his tears,
  Kept not measure with his people? 380
Boom, cannon, boom to all the winds and
  waves!
Clash out, glad bells, from every rocking
  steeple!
Banners, advance with triumph, bend your
  staves!

And from every mountain-peak
Let beacon-fire to answering beacon
  speak,   385
Katahdin tell Monadnock, Whiteface [5]
  he,
And so leap on in light from sea to sea,
  Till the glad news be sent
  Across a kindling continent,
Making earth feel more firm and air
  breathe braver: 390
"Be proud! for she is saved, and all have
  helped to save her!
  She that lifts up the manhood of the
    poor,
  She of the open soul and open door,
  With room about her hearth for all
    mankind!
  The fire is dreadful in her eyes no
    more;   395
  From her bold front the helm she doth
    unbind,
  Sends all her handmaid armies back to
    spin,
  And bids her navies, that so lately
    hurled
  Their crashing battle, hold their thun-
    ders in,
  Swimming like birds of calm along the
    unharmful shore.   400
  No challenge sends she to the elder
    world,
  That looked askance and hated; a light
    scorn
  Plays o'er her mouth, as round her
    mighty knees
  She calls her children back, and waits
    the morn
Of nobler day, enthroned between her sub-
  ject seas."   405

XII

Bow down, dear Land, for thou hast found
  release!
  Thy God, in these distempered days,
  Hath taught thee the sure wisdom of His
    ways,

---

[5] Mountain peaks of Maine (Katahdin),
New Hampshire (Monadnock), and New
York (Whiteface).

And through thine enemies hath wrought
    thy peace!
    Bow down in prayer and praise!   410
No poorest in thy borders but may now
Lift to the juster skies a man's enfran-
    chised brow.
O Beautiful! my Country! ours once more!
Smoothing thy gold of war-dishevelled hair
O'er such sweet brows as never other
    wore,   415
    And letting thy set lips,
    Freed from wrath's pale eclipse,
The rosy edges of their smile lay bare,
What words divine of lover or of poet
Could tell our love and make thee
    know it,   420
Among the Nations bright beyond com-
    pare?
What were our lives without thee?
What all our lives to save thee?
We reck not what we gave thee;
    We will not dare to doubt thee,   425
But ask whatever else, and we will dare!

POETRY AND NATIONALITY [1]
[1920 (1868)]

ONE of the dreams of our earlier hor-
oscope-mongers was, that a poet should
come out of the West, fashioned on a scale
somewhat proportioned to our geographical
pretensions. Our rivers, forests, mountains,
cataracts, prairies, and inland seas were to
find in him their antitype and voice.
Shaggy he was to be, brown-fisted, careless
of proprieties, unhampered by tradition,
his Pegasus of the half-horse, half-alligator
breed. By him at last the epos of the New
World was to be fitly sung, the great tragi-
comedy of democracy put upon the stage
for all time. It was a cheap vision, for it
cost no thought; and, like all judicious
prophecy, it muffled itself from criticism
in the loose drapery of its terms. Till the
advent of this splendid apparition, who
should dare affirm positively that he would
never come? that, indeed, he was impossible? And yet his impossibility was de-
monstrable, nevertheless.

Supposing a great poet to be born in
the West, though he would naturally levy
upon what had always been familiar to his
eyes for his images and illustrations, he
would almost as certainly look for his ideal
somewhere outside of the life that lay
immediately about him. Life in its large
sense, and not as it is temporarily modified
by manners or politics, is the only subject
of the poet; and though its elements lie
always close at hand, yet in its unity it
seems always infinitely distant, and the
difference of angle at which it is seen in
India and in Minnesota is almost inap-
preciable. Moreover, a rooted discontent
seems always to underlie all great poetry,
if it be not even the motive of it. The
Iliad and the Odyssey paint manners that
are only here and there incidentally true
to the actual, but which in their larger
truth had either never existed or had long
since passed away. Had Dante's scope been
narrowed to contemporary Italy, the "Divina Commedia" would have been a pic-
turebook merely. But his theme was Man,
and the vision that inspired him was of an
Italy that never was nor could be, his
political theories as abstract as those of
Plato or Spinoza. Shakespeare shows us
less of the England that then was than any
other considerable poet of his time. The
struggle of Goethe's whole life was to
emancipate himself from Germany, and
fill his lungs for once with a more universal
air.

Yet there is always a flavor of the climate in these rare fruits, some gift of the
sun peculiar to the region that ripened
them. If we are ever to have a national
poet, let us hope that his nationality will
be of this subtile essence, something that
shall make him unspeakably nearer to us,
while it does not provincialize him for

---

[1] This selection is a portion of a review of a book of poems by John James
Piatt, published in the *North American
Review*, October, 1868. It is included in
*The Function of the Poet and Other Es-
says* (Boston and New York, 1920), edited by Albert Mordell, who made the
abridgment and supplied the present title.

the rest of mankind. The popular recipe for compounding him would give us, perhaps, the most sublimely furnished bore in human annals. The novel aspects of life under our novel conditions may give some freshness of color to our literature; but democracy itself, which many seem to regard as the necessary Lucina [2] of some new poetic birth, is altogether too abstract an influence to serve for any such purpose. If any American author may be looked on as in some sort the result of our social and political ideal, it is Emerson, who, in his emancipation from the traditional, in the irresponsible freedom of his speculation, and his faith in the absolute value of his own individuality, is certainly, to some extent, typical; but if ever author was inspired by the past, it is he, and he is as far as possible from the shaggy hero of prophecy. Of the sham-shaggy, who have tried the trick of Jacob [3] upon us, we have had quite enough, and may safely doubt whether this satyr of masquerade is to be our representative singer. Were it so, it would not be greatly to the credit of democracy as an element of aesthetics. But we may safely hope for better things.

The themes of poetry have been pretty much the same from the first; and if a man should ever be born among us with a great imagination, and the gift of the right word,—for it is these, and not sublime spaces, that make a poet,—he will be original rather in spite of democracy than in consequence of it, and will owe his inspiration quite as much to the accumulations of the Old World as to the promises of the New. But for a long while yet the proper conditions will be wanting, not, perhaps, for the birth of such a man, but for his development and culture. At present, with the largest reading population in the world, perhaps no country ever offered less encouragement to the higher forms of art or the more thorough achievements of scholarship. Even were it not so, it would be idle to expect us to produce any literature so peculiarly our own as was the natural growth of ages less communicative,

less open to every breath of foreign influence. Literature tends more and more to become a vast commonwealth, with no dividing lines of nationality. Any more Cids, or Songs of Roland, or Nibelungens, or Kalewalas are out of the question,—nay, anything at all like them; for the necessary insulation of race, of country, of religion, is impossible, even were it desirable. Journalism, translation, criticism, and facility of intercourse tend continually more and more to make the thought and turn of expression in cultivated men identical all over the world. Whether we like it or not, the costume of mind and body is gradually becoming of one cut.

EMERSON THE LECTURER [1]
[1868 (1861)]

IT IS a singular fact that Mr. Emerson is the most steadily attractive lecturer in America. Into that somewhat cold-waterish region adventurers of the sensational kind come down now and then with a splash, to become disregarded King Logs [2] before the next season. But Mr. Emerson always draws. A lecturer now for something like a third of a century, one of the pioneers of the lecturing system, the charm of his voice, his manner, and his matter has never lost its power over his earlier hearers, and continually winds new ones in its enchanting meshes. What they do not fully understand they take on trust, and listen, saying

[2] Roman goddess of childbirth.

[3] Genesis 27:16, 23. Lowell probably is referring here to Whitman.

[1] This essay appeared in the *Atlantic Monthly*, February, 1861, as a review of Emerson's *The Conduct of Life,* and was revised in 1868.

[2] A reference to Aesop's fable of the log, given by Jupiter to the frogs as a king when they asked him for a ruler, and at first accepted as wholly satisfactory, but later rejected when its true nature was discovered.

to themselves, as the old poet [3] of Sir Philip Sidney,—

"A sweet, attractive, kind of grace,
  A full assurance given by looks,
Continual comfort in a face,
  The lineaments of gospel books."

We call it a singular fact, because we Yankees are thought to be fond of the spread-eagle style, and nothing can be more remote from that than his. We are reckoned a practical folk, who would rather hear about a new airtight stove than about Plato; yet our favorite teacher's practicality is not in the least of the Poor Richard variety. If he have any Buncombe constituency, it is that unrealized commonwealth of philosophers which Plotinus proposed to establish; and if he were to make an almanac, his directions to farmers would be something like this: "OCTOBER: *Indian Summer;* now is the time to get in your early Vedas." What, then, is his secret? Is it not that he out-Yankees us all? that his range includes us all? that he is equally at home with the potato-disease and original sin, with pegging shoes and the Over-Soul? that, as we try all trades, so has he tried all cultures? and above all, that his mysticism gives us a counterpoise to our super-practicality?

There is no man living to whom, as a writer, so many of us feel and thankfully acknowledge so great an indebtedness for ennobling impulses,—none whom so many cannot abide. What does he mean? ask these last. Where is his system? What is the use of it all? What the deuce have we to do with Brahma? I do not propose to write an essay on Emerson at this time. I will only say that one may find grandeur and consolation in a starlit night without caring to ask what it means, save grandeur and consolation; one may like Montaigne, as some ten generations before us have done, without thinking him so systematic as some more eminently tedious (or shall we say tediously eminent?) authors; one may think roses as good in their way as cabbages, though the latter would make a better show in the witness-box, if cross-examined as to their usefulness; and as for Brahma, why, he can take care of himself, and won't bite us at any rate.

The bother with Mr. Emerson is, that, though he writes in prose, he is essentially a poet. If you undertake to paraphrase what he says, and to reduce it to words of one syllable for infant minds, you will make as sad work of it as the good monk with his analysis of Homer in the *Epistolæ Obscurorum Virorum.*[4] We look upon him as one of the few men of genius whom our age has produced, and there needs no better proof of it than his masculine faculty of fecundating other minds. Search for his eloquence in his books and you will perchance miss it, but meanwhile you will find that it has kindled all your thoughts. For choice and pith of language he belongs to a better age than ours, and might rub shoulders with Fuller and Browne,—though he does use that abominable word *reliable.* His eye for a fine, telling phrase that will carry true is like that of a backwoodsman for a rifle; and he will dredge you up a choice word from the mud of Cotton Mather himself. A diction at once so rich and so homely as his I know not where to match in these days of writing by the page; it is like homespun cloth-of-gold. The many cannot miss his meaning, and only the few can find it. It is the open secret of all true genius. It is wholesome to angle in those profound pools, though one be rewarded with nothing more than the leap of a fish that flashes his freckled side in the sun and as suddenly absconds in the dark and dreamy waters again. There is keen excitement, though there be no ponderable acquisition. If we carry nothing home in our baskets, there is ample gain in dilated lungs and stimulated blood. What does he mean, quotha? He means inspiring

<hr/>

[3] Matthew Roydon. His "Elegie" on Sidney, published in *The Phoenix Nest,* a poetical miscellany, in 1593, is quoted by Lowell again at the end of this essay.

[4] "Letters of Obscure Men," a sixteenth century book of uncertain authorship.

hints, a divining-rod to your deeper nature. No doubt, Emerson, like all original men, has his peculiar audience, and yet I know none that can hold a promiscuous crowd in pleased attention so long as he. As in all original men, there is something for every palate. "Would you know," says Goethe, "the ripest cherries? Ask the boys and the blackbirds."

The announcement that such a pleasure as a new course of lectures by him is coming, to people as old as I am, is something like those forebodings of spring that prepare us every year for a familiar novelty, none the less novel, when it arrives, because it is familiar. We know perfectly well what we are to expect from Mr. Emerson, and yet what he says always penetrates and stirs us, as is apt to be the case with genius, in a very unlooked-for fashion. Perhaps genius is one of the few things which we gladly allow to repeat itself,—one of the few that multiply rather than weaken the force of their impression by iteration? Perhaps some of us hear more than the mere words, are moved by something deeper than the thoughts? If it be so, we are quite right, for it is thirty years and more of "plain living and high thinking"[5] that speak to us in this altogether unique lay-preacher. We have shared in the beneficence of this varied culture, this fearless impartiality in criticism and speculation, this masculine sincerity, this sweetness of nature which rather stimulates than cloys, for a generation long. If ever there was a standing testimonial to the cumulative power and value of Character (and we need it sadly in these days), we have it in this gracious and dignified presence. What an antiseptic is a pure life! At sixty-five (or two years beyond his grand climacteric, as he would prefer to call it) he has that privilege of soul which abolishes the calendar, and presents him to us always the unwasted contemporary of his own prime. I do not know if he seem old to his younger hearers, but we who have known him so long wonder at the tenacity with which he maintains himself

even in the outposts of youth. I suppose it is not the Emerson of 1868 to whom we listen. For us the whole life of the man is distilled in the clear drop of every sentence, and behind each word we divine the force of a noble character, the weight of a large capital of thinking and being. We do not go to hear what Emerson says so much as to hear Emerson. Not that we perceive any falling-off in anything that ever was essential to the charm of Mr. Emerson's peculiar style of thought or phrase. The first lecture, to be sure, was more disjointed even than common. It was as if, after vainly trying to get his paragraphs into sequence and order, he had at last tried the desperate expedient of *shuffling* them. It was chaos come again, but it was a chaos full of shooting-stars, a jumble of creative forces. The second lecture, on "Criticism and Poetry," was quite up to the level of old times, full of that power of strangely subtle association whose indirect approaches startle the mind into almost painful attention, of those flashes of mutual understanding between speaker and hearer that are gone ere one can say it lightens. The vice of Emerson's criticism seems to be, that while no man is so sensitive to what is poetical, few men are less sensible than he of what makes a poem. He values the solid meaning of thought above the subtler meaning of style. He would prefer Donne, I suspect, to Spenser, and sometimes mistakes the queer for the original.

To be young is surely the best, if the most precarious, gift of life; yet there are some of us who would hardly consent to be young again, if it were at the cost of our recollection of Mr. Emerson's first lectures during the consulate of Van Buren. We used to walk in from the country to the Masonic Temple (I think it was), through the crisp winter night, and listen to that thrilling voice of his, so charged with subtle meaning and subtle music, as ship-

[5] From Wordsworth's sonnet, "Written in London, September, 1802."

wrecked men on a raft to the hail of a ship that came with unhoped-for food and rescue. Cynics might say what they liked. Did our own imaginations transfigure dry remainder-biscuit into ambrosia? At any rate, he brought us *life*, which, on the whole, is no bad thing. Was it all transcendentalism? magic-lantern pictures on mist? As you will. Those, then, were just what we wanted. But it was not so. The delight and the benefit were that he put us in communication with a larger style of thought, sharpened our wits with a more pungent phrase, gave us ravishing glimpses of an ideal under the dry husk of our New England; made us conscious of the supreme and everlasting originality of whatever bit of soul might be in any of us; freed us, in short, from the stocks of prose in which we had sat so long that we had grown well-nigh contented in our cramps. And who that saw the audience will ever forget it, where every one still capable of fire, or longing to renew in himself the half-forgotten sense of it, was gathered? Those faces, young and old, agleam with pale intellectual light, eager with pleased attention, flash upon me once more from the deep recesses of the years with an exquisite pathos. Ah, beautiful young eyes, brimming with love and hope, wholly vanished now in that other world we call the Past, or peering doubtfully through the pensive gloaming of memory, your light impoverishes these cheaper days! I hear again that rustle of sensation, as they turned to exchange glances over some pithier thought, some keener flash of that humor which always played about the horizon of his mind like heat-lightning, and it seems now like the sad whisper of the autumn leaves that are whirling around me. But would my picture be complete if I forgot that ample and vegete countenance of Mr. R—— of W——,—how, from its regular post at the corner of the front bench, it turned in ruddy triumph to the profaner audience as if he were the inexplicably appointed fugleman of appreciation? I was reminded of him by those hearty cherubs in Titian's Assumption that look at you as who should say, "Did you ever see a Madonna like *that*? Did you ever behold one hundred and fifty pounds of womanhood mount heavenward before like a rocket?"

To some of us that long-past experience remains as the most marvellous and fruitful we have ever had. Emerson awakened us, saved us from the body of this death. It is the sound of the trumpet that the young soul longs for, careless what breath may fill it. Sidney heard it in the ballad of "Chevy Chase," [6] and we in Emerson. Nor did it blow retreat, but called to us with assurance of victory. Did they say he was disconnected? So were the stars, that seemed larger to our eyes, still keen with that excitement, as we walked homeward with prouder stride over the creaking snow. And were *they* not knit together by a higher logic than our mere sense could master? Were we enthusiasts? I hope and believe we were, and am thankful to the man who made us worth something for once in our lives. If asked what was left? what we carried home? we should not have been careful for an answer. It would have been enough if we had said that something beautiful had passed that way. Or we might have asked in return what one brought away from a symphony of Beethoven? Enough that he had set that ferment of wholesome discontent at work in us. There is one, at least, of those old hearers, so many of whom are now in the fruition of that intellectual beauty of which Emerson gave them both the desire and the foretaste, who will always love to repeat:—

"Che in la mente m' ê fitta, ed or m'
    accuora
La cara e buona immagine paterna

---

[6] Sidney wrote of this ballad, in his *Defence of Poesie* (1598): "I never heard the old song of Percy and Douglas that I found not my heart moved more than by a trumpet."

Di voi, quando nel mondo ad ora ad ora
M' insegnavaste come l' uom s' eterna." [7]

I am unconsciously thinking, as I write, of the third lecture of the present course, in which Mr. Emerson gave some delightful reminiscences of the intellectual influences in whose movement he had shared. It was like hearing Goethe read some passages of the *Wahrheit aus seinem Leben*.[8] Not that there was not a little *Dichtung,* toc, here and there, as the lecturer built up so lofty a pedestal under certain figures as to lift them into a prominence of obscurity, and seem to masthead them there. Everybody was asking his neighbor who this or that recondite great man was, in the faint hope that somebody might once have heard of him. There are those who call Mr. Emerson cold. Let them revise their judgment in presence of this loyalty of his that can keep warm for half a century, that never forgets a friendship, or fails to pay even a fancied obligation to the uttermost farthing. This substantiation of shadows was but incidental, and pleasantly characteristic of the man to those who know and love him. The greater part of the lecture was devoted to reminiscences of things substantial in themselves. He spoke of Everett, fresh from Greece and Germany; of Channing; of the translations of Margaret Fuller, Ripley, and Dwight; of the *Dial* and Brook Farm. To what he said of the latter an undertone of good-humored irony gave special zest. But what every one of his hearers felt was that the protagonist in the drama was left out. The lecturer was no Æneas to babble the *quorum magna pars fui,*[9] and, as one of his listeners, I cannot help wishing to say how each of them was commenting the story as it went along, and filling up the necessary gaps in it from his own private store of memories. His younger hearers could not know how much they owed to the benign impersonality, the quiet scorn of everything ignoble, the never-sated hunger of self-culture, that were personified in the man before them. But the older knew how much the coun-

try's intellectual emancipation was due to the stimulus of his teaching and example, how constantly he had kept burning the beacon of an ideal life above our lower region of turmoil. To him more than to all other causes together did the young martyrs of our civil war owe the sustaining strength of thoughtful heroism that is so touching in every record of their lives. Those who are grateful to Mr. Emerson, as many of us are, for what they feel to be most valuable in their culture, or perhaps I should say their impulse, are grateful not so much for any direct teachings of his as for that inspiring lift which only genius can give, and without which all doctrine is chaff.

This was something like the *caret* which some of us older boys wished to fill up on the margin of the master's lecture. Few men have been so much to so many, and through so large a range of aptitudes and temperaments, and this simply because all of us value manhood beyond any or all other qualities of character. We may suspect in him, here and there, a certain thinness and vagueness of quality, but let the waters go over him as they list, this masculine fibre of his will keep its lively color and its toughness of texture. I have heard some great speakers and some accomplished orators, but never any that so moved and persuaded men as he. There is a kind of undertow in that rich baritone of his that sweeps our minds from their foothold into deeper waters with a drift we cannot and would not resist. And how artfully (for

---

[7] Dante's *Inferno*, XV, 82-85:
"For in my mind is fixed, and touches now
  My heart, the dear and good paternal
    image
Of you, when in the world from hour to
  hour
  You taught me how a man becomes
    eternal."
      —Longfellow's translation.

[8] Lowell refers to Goethe's famous autobiographical work, *Aus Meinem Leben, Dichtung und Wahrheit—Out of My Life, Poetry and Truth*—which was published in four parts, 1811-33.

[9] Vergil's *Aeneid*, II, 6: "Of which things I was a great part."

Emerson is a long-studied artist in these things) does the deliberate utterance, that seems waiting for the fit word, appear to admit us partners in the labor of thought and make us feel as if the glance of humor were a sudden suggestion, as if the perfect phrase lying written there on the desk were as unexpected to him as to us! In that closely filed speech of his at the Burns centenary dinner,[10] every word seemed to have just dropped down to him from the clouds. He looked far away over the heads of his hearers, with a vague kind of expectation, as into some private heaven of invention, and the winged period came at last obedient to his spell. "My dainty Ariel!"[11] he seemed murmuring to himself as he cast down his eyes as if in deprecation of the frenzy of approval and caught another sentence from the Sibylline leaves that lay before him, ambushed behind a dish of fruit and seen only by nearest neighbors. Every sentence brought down the house, as I never saw one brought down before,—and it is not so easy to hit Scotsmen with a sentiment that has no hint of native brogue in it. I watched, for it was an interesting study, how the quick sympathy ran flashing from face to face down the long tables, like an electric spark thrilling as it went, and then exploded in a thunder of plaudits. I watched till tables and faces vanished, for I, too, found myself caught up in the common enthusiasm, and my excited fancy set me under the *bema* listening to him who fulmined over Greece. I can never help applying to him what Ben Jonson said of Bacon: "There happened in my time one noble speaker, who was full of gravity in his speaking. His language was nobly censorious. No man ever spake more neatly, more pressly, more weightily, or suffered less emptiness, less idleness, in what he uttered. No member of his speech but consisted of his own graces. His hearers could not cough, or look aside from him, without loss. He commanded where he spoke." Those who heard him while their natures were yet plastic, and their mental nerves trembled

under the slightest breath of divine air, will never cease to feel and say:—

"Was never eye did see that face,
  Was never ear did hear that tongue,
Was never mind did mind his grace,
  That ever thought the travail long;
But eyes, and ears, and every thought,
Were with his sweet perfections caught."

CAMBRIDGE THIRTY YEARS AGO [1]
[1864 (1853)]

THE SEAT of the oldest college in America, it had, of course, some of that cloistered quiet which characterizes all university towns. Even now delicately-thoughtful A. H. C. [2] tells me that he finds in its intellectual atmosphere a repose which recalls that of grand old Oxford. But underlying this, it had an idiosyncrasy of its own. Boston was not yet a city, and Cambridge was still a country village, with its own habits and traditions, not yet feeling too strongly the force of suburban gravitation. Approaching it from the west by what was then called the New Road (it is called so no longer, for we change our names whenever we can, to the great detriment of all historical association), you would pause on the brow of Symonds' Hill to enjoy a view singularly soothing and placid. In front of you lay the town, tufted with elms, lindens, and horse-chestnuts, which had seen Massa-

---

[10] At Boston, January 25, 1859. Holmes wrote a poem for this celebration, at which Emerson was the chief speaker.

[11] Shakespeare's *The Tempest*, V, 1:95.

[1] This selection is an abridgement by the present editors of Lowell's essay published in 1853, descriptive of the Cambridge of his boyhood.

[2] Arthur Hugh Clough, English poet and Oxford graduate, whom Lowell met in England and who crossed the Atlantic with Lowell and Thackeray. Clough lived in Cambridge, Mass., for some months in 1852.

chusetts a colony, and were fortunately unable to emigrate with the Tories by whom, or by whose fathers, they were planted. Over it rose the noisy belfry of the College, the square, brown tower of the church, and the slim, yellow spire of the parish meeting-house, by no means ungraceful, and then an invariable characteristic of New England religious architecture. On your right, the Charles slipped smoothly through green and purple salt-meadows, darkened, here and there, with the blossoming black-grass as with a stranded cloud-shadow. Over these marshes, level as water, but without its glare, and with softer and more soothing gradations of perspective, the eye was carried to a horizon of softly-rounded hills. To your left hand, upon the Old Road, you saw some half-dozen dignified old houses of the colonial time, all comfortably fronting southward. If it were early June, the rows of horse-chestnuts along the fronts of these houses showed, through every crevice of their dark heap of foliage, and on the end of every drooping limb, a cone of pearly flowers, while the hill behind was white or rosy with the crowding blooms of various fruit-trees. There is no sound, unless a horseman clatters over the loose planks of the bridge, while his antipodal shadow glides silently over the mirrored bridge below. . . .

Such was the charmingly rural picture which he who, thirty years ago, went eastward over Symonds' Hill had given him for nothing, to hang in the Gallery of Memory. But we are a city now, and Common Councils have yet no notion of the truth (learned long ago by many a European hamlet) that picturesqueness adds to the actual money value of a town. To save a few dollars in gravel, they have cut a kind of dry ditch through the hill, where you suffocate with dust in summer, or flounder through waistdeep snow-drifts in winter, with no prospect but the crumbling earth-walls on either side. The landscape was carried away cart-load by cart-load, and, dumped down on the roads, forms a part of that unfathomable pudding, which has, I fear, driven many a teamster and pedestrian to the use of phrases not commonly found in English dictionaries.

We called it "the Village" then (I speak of Old Cambridge), and it was essentially an English village, quiet, unspeculative, without enterprise, sufficing to itself, and only showing such differences from the original type as the public school and the system of town government might superinduce. A few houses, chiefly old, stood around the bare Common, with ample elbow-room, and old women, capped and spectacled, still peered through the same windows from which they had watched Lord Percy's [3] artillery rumble by to Lexington, or caught a glimpse of the handsome Virginia General [4] who had come to wield our homespun Saxon chivalry. People were still living who regretted the late unhappy separation from the mother island, who had seen no gentry since the Vassalls [5] went, and who thought that Boston had ill kept the day of her patron saint, Botolph, on the 17th of June, 1775. The hooks were to be seen from which had swung the hammocks of Burgoyne's captive redcoats. If memory does not deceive me, women still washed clothes in the town spring, clear as that of Bandusia.[6] One coach sufficed for all the travel to the metropolis. Commencement had not ceased to be the great holiday of the Puritan Commonwealth, and a fitting one it was,— the festival of Santa Scholastica,[7] whose triumphal path one may conceive strewn with leaves of spelling-book instead of bay. The students (scholars they were called

---

[3] British commander in the Revolutionary War.

[4] Washington.

[5] Prominent colonial family, loyal to England, members of which left America after the Revolution.

[6] Fountain near Venusia, the birthplace of the Roman poet, Horace; celebrated in his poems.

[7] "Saint Scholarship."

then) wore their sober uniform, not ostentatiously distinctive or capable of rousing democratic envy, and the old lines of caste were blurred rather than rubbed out, as servitor was softened into beneficiary. The Spanish king was sure that the gesticulating student was either mad or reading Don Quixote, and if, in those days, you met a youth swinging his arms and talking to himself, you might conclude that he was either a lunatic or one who was to appear in a "part" at the next Commencement. A favorite place for the rehearsal of these orations was the retired amphitheatre of the Gravel-pit, perched unregarded on whose dizzy edge, I have heard many a burst of *plusquam Ciceronian* [8] eloquence, and (often repeated) the regular *saluto vos, præstantissimæ* [9] &c., which every year (with a glance at the gallery) causes a flutter among the fans innocent of Latin, and delights to applauses of conscious superiority the youth almost as innocent as they. It is curious, by the way, to note how plainly one can feel the pulse of self in the plaudits of an audience. At a political meeting, if the enthusiasm of the lieges hang fire, it may be exploded at once by an allusion to their intelligence or patriotism; and at a literary festival, the first Latin quotation draws the first applause, the clapping of hands being intended as a tribute to our own familiarity with that sonorous tongue, and not at all as an approval of the particular sentiment conveyed in it. For if the orator should say, "Well has Tacitus remarked, *Americani omnes quâdam vi naturæ furcâ dignissimi,*" [10] it would be all the same. But the Gravel-pit was patient, if irresponsive; nor did the declaimer always fail to bring down the house, bits of loosened earth falling now and then from the precipitous walls, their cohesion perhaps overcome by the vibrations of the voice, and happily satirizing the effect of most popular discourses, which prevail rather with the earthy than the spiritual part of the hearer. Was it possible for us in those days to conceive of a greater potentate than the President of the University, in his square doctor's cap, that still filially recalled Oxford and Cambridge? If there was a doubt, it was suggested only by the Governor, and even by him on artillery-election days alone, superbly martial with epaulets and buckskin breeches, and bestriding the war-horse, promoted to that solemn duty for his tameness and steady habits.

Thirty years ago, the town had indeed a character. Railways and omnibuses had not rolled flat all little social prominences and peculiarities, making every man as much a citizen everywhere as at home. No Charlestown boy could come to our annual festival without fighting to avenge a certain traditional porcine imputation against the inhabitants of that historic locality, and to which our youth gave vent in fanciful imitations of the dialect of the sty, or derisive shouts of "Charlestown hogs!" The penny newspaper had not yet silenced the tripod of the barber, oracle of news. Everybody knew everybody, and all about everybody, and village wit, whose high 'change was around the little market-house in the town square, had labelled every more marked individuality with nick-names that clung like burs. Things were established then, and men did not run through all the figures on the dial of society so swiftly as now, when hurry and competition seem to have quite unhung the modulating pendulum of steady thrift and competent training. Some slow-minded persons even followed their father's trade,— a humiliating spectacle, rarer every day. We had our established loafers, topers, proverb-mongers, barber, parson, nay, postmaster, whose tenure was for life. The great political engine did not then come down at regular quadrennial intervals, like a nail-cutting machine, to make all official lives of a standard length, and to generate lazy and intriguing expectancy. Life flowed in recognized channels, narrower

---

[8] "More than Ciceronian."

[9] "I salute you, most excellent ones."

[10] "All Americans are by nature most worthy to be hanged."

perhaps, but with all the more individuality and force.

There was but one white-and-yellow-washer, whose own cottage, fresh-gleaming every June through grapevine and creeper, was his only sign and advertisement. He was said to possess a secret, which died with him like that of Luca della Robbia,[11] and certainly conceived all colors but white and yellow to savor of savagery, civilizing the stems of his trees annually with liquid lime, and meditating how to extend that candent baptism even to the leaves. His *pie-plants* (the best in town), compulsory monastics, blanched under barrels, each in his little hermitage, a vegetable Certosa.[12] His fowls, his ducks, his geese, could not show so much as a gray feather among them, and he would have given a year's earnings for a white peacock. The flowers which decked his little *door-yard* were whitest China-asters and goldenest sun-flowers, which last, backsliding from their traditional Parsee faith, used to puzzle us urchins not a little by staring brazenly every way except towards the sun. Celery, too, he raised, whose virtue is its paleness, and the silvery onion, and turnip, which, though outwardly conforming to the green heresies of summer, nourish a purer faith subterraneously, like early Christians in the catacombs. In an obscure corner grew the sanguine beet, tolerated only for its usefulness in allaying the asperities of Saturday's salt-fish. He loved winter better than summer, because Nature then played the whitewasher, and challenged with her snows the scarce inferior purity of his overalls and neck-cloth. I fancy that he never rightly liked Commencement, for bringing so many black coats together. He founded no school. Others might essay his art, and were allowed to try their prentice hands on fences and the like coarse subjects, but the ceiling of every housewife waited on the leisure of Newman (*ichneumon* the students called him for his diminutiveness), nor would consent to other brush than his. There was also but one brewer,—Lewis, who made the village beer,

both spruce and ginger, a grave and amiable Ethiopian, making a discount always to the boys, and wisely, for they were his chiefest patrons. He wheeled his whole stock in a white-roofed handcart, on whose front a sign-board presented at either end an insurrectionary bottle; yet insurgent after no mad Gallic fashion, but soberly and Saxonly discharging itself into the restraining formulary of a tumbler, symbolic of orderly prescription. The artist had struggled manfully with the difficulties of his subject, but had not succeeded so well that we did not often debate in which of the twin bottles Spruce was typified, and in which Ginger. We always believed that Lewis mentally distinguished between them, but by some peculiarity occult to exoteric eyes. This ambulatory chapel of the Bacchus that gives the colic, but not inebriates, only appeared at the Commencement holidays, and the lad who bought of Lewis laid out his money well, getting respect as well as beer, three *sirs* to every glass,—"Beer, sir? yes, sir: spruce or ginger, sir?" I can yet recall the innocent pride with which I walked away after that somewhat risky ceremony, (for a bottle sometimes blew up,) dilated not alone with carbonic acid gas, but with the more ethereal fixed air of that titular flattery. Nor was Lewis proud. When he tried his fortunes in the capital on Election days, and stood amid a row of rival venders in the very flood of custom, he never forgot his small fellow-citizens, but welcomed them with an assuring smile, and served them with the first.

The barber's shop was a museum, scarce second to the larger one of Greenwood in the metropolis. The boy who was to be clipped there was always accompanied to the sacrifice by troops of friends, who thus inspected the curiosities *gratis*. While the watchful eye of R. wandered to keep in check these rather unscrupulous explorers, the unpausing shears would sometimes

---

[11] A Florentine sculptor (1399-1482), who perfected a method of applying colored enamel to terra cotta.

[12] A Carthusian monastery.

overstep the boundaries of strict tonsorial prescription, and make a notch through which the phrenological developments could be distinctly seen. As Michael Angelo's design was modified by the shape of his block, so R., rigid in artistic proprieties, would contrive to give an appearance of design to this aberration, by making it the keynote to his work, and reducing the whole head to an appearance of premature baldness. What a charming place it was,—how full of wonder and delight! The sunny little room, fronting southwest upon the Common, rang with canaries and Java sparrows, nor were the familiar notes of robin, thrush, and bobolink wanting. A large white cockatoo harangued vaguely, at intervals, in what we believed (on R.'s authority) to be the Hottentot language. He had an unveracious air, but what inventions of former grandeur he was indulging in, what sweet South-African Argos he was remembering, what tropical heats and giant trees by unconjectured rivers, known only to the wallowing hippopotamus, we could only guess at. The walls were covered with curious old Dutch prints, beaks of albatross and penguin, and whales' teeth fantastically engraved. There was Frederick the Great, with head drooped plottingly, and keen side-long glance from under the three-cornered hat. There hung Bonaparte, too, the long-haired, haggard general of Italy, his eyes sombre with prefigured destiny; and there was his island grave;—the dream and the fulfilment. Good store of sea-fights there was also; above all, Paul Jones in the Bonhomme Richard: the smoke rolling courteously to leeward, that we might see him dealing thunderous wreck to the two hostile vessels, each twice as large as his own, and the reality of the scene corroborated by streaks of red paint leaping from the mouth of every gun. Suspended over the fireplace, with the curling-tongs, were an Indian bow and arrows, and in the corners of the room stood New Zealand paddles and war-clubs, quaintly carved. The model of a ship in glass we variously estimated to be worth from a hundred to a thousand dollars, R. rather favoring the higher valuation, though never distinctly committing himself. Among these wonders, the only suspicious one was an Indian tomahawk, which had too much the peaceful look of a shingling-hatchet. Did any rarity enter the town, it gravitated naturally to these walls, to the very nail that waited to receive it, and where, the day after its accession, it seemed to have hung a lifetime. We always had a theory that R. was immensely rich, (how could he possess so much and be otherwise?) and that he pursued his calling from an amiable eccentricity. He was a conscientious artist, and never submitted it to the choice of his victim whether he would be perfumed or not. Faithfully was the bottle shaken and the odoriferous mixture rubbed in, a fact redolent to the whole school-room in the afternoon. Sometimes the persuasive tonsor would impress one of the attendant volunteers, and reduce his poll to shoe-brush crispness, at cost of the reluctant ninepence hoarded for Fresh Pond, and the next half-holiday. So purely indigenous was our population then, that R. had a certain exotic charm, a kind of game flavor, by being a Dutchman.

American Literature 1800-1860

IV
TRANSCENDENTALISM

1803 ∾ *Ralph Waldo Emerson* ∾ 1882

I

YOUNG men and women who are stirred by strong ideas must always come together in groups for discussion and argument. Collegians in their "sessions," artists and littèrateurs in the "salons" of Paris and other capitals, and those literary clubs which have often been important in the development of American writing and publishing are all results of the urge to get together and discuss stimulating new ideas. Sometimes in such informal meetings are born movements and schools in literature, art, and politics.

So it was with the New England Transcendentalists of the 1830's. Emerson speaks of the "loneliness" of these young idealists, perhaps that was one thing that drew them together. But primarily it was their common enthusiasm for the "new views" which had come upon them so suddenly, as it seemed, from certain German writers, from Coleridge, more recently from the thunder and lightning of Carlyle, and now from their own neighbor Emerson. The oldest of this New England group was A. Bronson Alcott, who was not yet forty, but who seemed a venerable sage to the others. Ralph Waldo Emerson, their leader, was thirty-three; but most of the group were in their twenties.

It was in September of 1836. Emerson's *Nature,* his first book and the manifesto of his leading ideas, was just out; Carlyle's *Sartor Resartus* was being issued by Boston publishers at Emerson's urging (not until two years later was it published in book form in England); Coleridge had died recently, and his *Literary Remains* were just coming from the press. So one day in that month Emerson, George Ripley, and Frederick H. Hedge happened to meet in Boston, and it was suggested that they and some others interested in the exciting new ideas should get together some evening and talk about them. "Come to my house," said Ripley, and an evening the following week was set. This meeting proved so satisfactory that it was repeated the next week, and an even larger group met at Emerson's house in Concord later in that same month. The club thus formed had no official name, no set programs, no officers; but it did have something to talk about, and this is what its members wanted to do. It lasted for several years and came to be called informally "The Transcendental Club."

No reporter with an eye for picturesque detail has given us an account of any of these meetings. One can imagine without difficulty, however, the tall, blonde Alcott, with his mild blue eyes and gentle manners, discoursing easily and at length, if sometimes not quite comprehensibly, in Emerson's parlor, the group about him listening respectfully. A similar dignity, almost a nobility, seemed to rest upon Emerson, the host and the newly found spokesman of these young intellectuals. "Serene" was the word for him; his disciples always felt his quiet, illuminated, masterful serenity. Then there was young Theodore Parker, big and strong in body as in intellect, just beginning a career in theology and preaching that was to make him famous. The mystical poet Jones Very was there, tall, never at ease, with eyes too bright and burning. Margaret Fuller was quite able to hold her own with all these men, and delighted to do so; ugly, perhaps (if you noticed it) and short and plump, she never troubled to conceal her frankly passionate nature, or that direct, driving mind that sometimes disconcerted Emerson. Thoreau sat in a corner, more roughly dressed than these Bostonians, his long curved nose shadowing his mouth, saying little but not unready with a caustic remark that could stop the whole conversation for a moment. The leonine Orestes Augustus Brownson, "Father" Taylor with his flowing beard, and the learned Hedge were often at these meetings.

Talk goes on and on—the doctrine of innate ideas, idealism, the highest aim, indifferentism of the churches. "These talkers who talk the sun and moon away," Emerson called them. Finally apples from the Emerson orchard are passed about on plates, and all ends with the munching of Russets and Roman-Stems.

II

Emerson's paternal ancestors for six generations back were, with one exception, clergymen. They were no men of the cloister, however; they fought the Indians and the redcoats as well as the Devil, and were the leaders that Puritan congregations expected their ministers to be in the eighteenth century. Emerson's essential Americanism, as well as his tradition of Puritanism, came to him as a natural heritage.

Ralph Waldo, the second son of the Rev. William Emerson, a brilliant and highly regarded Unitarian clergyman, was born in 1803; his father died eight years later, leaving a widow and five young sons unprovided with cash. Young Waldo learned to do his part in a family which lived frugally but cheerfully with those familiar angels—as he said many years later in his lecture on "Domestic Life"—Toil and Want, Truth and Mutual Faith. Waldo drove the family cow to pasture on Boston Common, sometimes played hooky from school and went swimming in the harbor, read and committed to memory much poetry and oratory. Education was more highly thought of in the Emerson family than food and clothes. Aunt Mary Moody, that witty and extraordinary member of the household (born in 1775, she said she was in arms at the Concord battle), contended that the Emerson boys "were born to be educated."

Waldo owed a great deal to this "aunt of genius," as he called her. She was little more than a dwarf in stature, measuring but four feet, three inches in height; but she carried herself erectly, and her blue eyes flashed with a bold spirit. A student and a wide reader, she was a great letter writer. She always had something to say and she said it remarkably well. Her very talk was challenging and inspirational: her nephew could compare it only to "the march of the mountain winds, the waving of flowers, or the flight of birds." Among the influences that made a writer of Ralph Waldo Emerson, his Aunt Mary must be ranked very high. But she probably did even more than that; her own combination of unswerving Calvinistic vigor and Yankee shrewdness and self-reliance left its impress on the nephews whom she loved as though they were her own children.

Waldo entered Harvard in 1817 at the age of fourteen—not an unusual age for matriculation—and was graduated four years later at about the middle rank in his class; he was chosen class poet only after seven others had declined the honor. There followed some years of school-teaching, study for the ministry (part of it at the Harvard Divinity School), and travel in the South for the sake of his health.

Emerson became minister of the Second Church (Unitarian) of Boston in 1829. He married that same year, but his wife died of tuberculosis less than eighteen months later. Though his pastoral work was successful, Emerson grew increasingly dissatisfied with church rituals and churchly thought. When he resigned in 1832, he gave as his chief reason his lack of sympathy with the rite of the Lord's Supper. He was not hostile to it, he said; he was merely not interested in it.

But his difficulty was more extensive than that: he felt that the church imposed upon his speculation and action bonds which he could not tolerate. Especially was he concerned with the church's hostility to science. His reading for the previous year had been largely in scientific literature. It was just before he made his decision to break with the ministry that he entered this declaration in his journal: "The Religion that is afraid of science dishonours God and commits suicide."

Partly for reasons of health and partly because he craved contact with some of the great minds with whose work he had long been familiar, Emerson traveled in Europe in 1832-33. In England he met many great men, including Landor, Coleridge, and Wordsworth; but, on the whole and in general, he was disappointed in all of them. In the home of the Carlyles at Craigenputtock, however, he made a short visit which was memorable chiefly because it was the beginning of a life-long friendship.

But he returned to Boston confirmed in his own self-reliance, convinced that the work he was to do must be done independently. He began preaching here and there, on invitation, fell in with the lecture system which was becoming important in New England, and did more writing. He married again in 1835, and moved to Concord, Massachusetts, which was to be his home for the remainder of his life. From this time forward, his energies were devoted to writing and lecturing.

His lecture tours took Emerson to many parts of the country and taught him at first hand much about the America of which he became, more than we sometimes realize, the spokesman and prophet. He crossed and recrossed the Mississippi on the ice, to speak in Iowa towns. His stage was upset in a snow-bank when he was journeying to a lecturing engagement in Maine. He escaped from a burning hotel at Niagara. His letters and journals are full of the details of these trips.

When he was seventeen years old and a junior at Harvard, Emerson had begun to keep a regular journal, as young men of a literary turn often do today. But this diary of thoughts (for it contains little of the conventionally bio-graphical) was kept up for more than fifty years and is today a fascinating record of the day-by-day activity of a great mind. Here we find jottings of ideas, analogies, figures of speech, flashes of poetry, which were later to be worked into essays, lectures, finished poems. The reader who is familiar with the great essays of Emerson is delighted to discover them in the journals in a "state of becoming"—fragmentary, thrown off in the play of an active intel-ligence, but often more stimulating by reason of their very lack of integration.

The student of the journals is amazed at the breadth of reading evident in them. If anyone is tempted to think that Emerson belongs to some neat pattern or sequence—say Kant, Novalis, Carlyle, Emerson—here is complete refutation. His constant reading in Greek philosophy, mysticism, and ethics was important—Plato, of course; Plotinus, to whom he owed a debt beyond computation; Plutarch, his frequent companion. The English philosophers and historians—Bacon, Locke, Priestley, Gibbon, Hume, and many others—he read to good purpose. Coleridge and Wordsworth were major influences upon him. The Germans he read in translation—Kant, Schelling, Fichte, Goethe, and the rest. Two of the chief gods in his literary Pantheon were Shakespeare and Montaigne. But such a short list gives little notion of the scope of Emerson's reading and study. He had a special liking for the seventeenth century English poets, and he read Scott's novels with unfailing interest.

III

Emerson's own essays are easy to read,—even for the beginner, if he ap-proaches them properly. They have an oratorical flair, and a play of fancy essentially poetical, which make them a delight to many readers. The analogies, the succinct quality, the figures of speech, the neat quotability of so many sentences help to characterize a style which successive generations of readers have found admirable. What makes Emerson hard for some is that they ap-proach him with minds so filled with the thinking of a materialistic civilization that they allow no opening for spiritual ideas. Emerson himself saw both sides, and he is continually emphasizing the two phases of existence: it was a "game" with him to see both sides. In his essay on Montaigne he wrote:

Every fact is related on one side to sensation, and on the other to morals. The game of thought is, on the appearance of one of these sides, to find the other . . . This head and tail are called, in the language of philosophy, Infinite and Finite, Relative and Absolute, Apparent and Real, and many fine names besides. Each man is born with a predisposition to one or the other of these sides of nature; and it will easily happen that men will be found devoted to one or the other. One class has the perception of difference, and is conversant with facts and surfaces, cities and persons, and the bringing of certain things to pass—men of talent and action. Another class have the perception of identity, and are men of faith and philosophy, men of genius.

Emerson belongs to the second class, but can share the point of view of the first. He sees both sides and also the whole which they make. Some philosophical critics have regarded him as a "dualist," but his dualism has a habit of dissolving into an all-inclusive monism. When he claims that his spiritual perceptions (he often calls them intuitions) are "facts" just as much as are the facts which are measurable by science, when he views the subjective and objective as two facets of the same coin and describes life as "sensations *and* states of mind" (as in his essay on "Experience"), he anticipates the Pragmatism of a later school, the philosophy which conceives experience, in William James' term, as a "double-barreled fact." If the beginning reader of Emerson will keep in mind this two-sidedness that is at the same time a perception of oneness or wholeness, and will accept the premise that a spiritual universe envelops, fuses with, and unifies the world of sense and science, he will get along well with his author.

It will be further helpful to watch for the reiterated ideas in Emerson. His paramount principles are, after all, comparatively few, though they are illuminated by countless suggestions from the streets and farms of America, from history, from poetry and philosophy. These few ideas are repeated again and again in different terms, in a hundred shapes and guises, in the essays and in the poems. This repetition is the effort of a sincere teacher to make himself understood. It may be helpful to list those ideas here. They may be groupd in various ways, and of course the list may be extended; but we shall place four in each of two classes—those dealing with Self-Reliance, and those dealing with Nature.

The foundation of the Self-Reliance group is (1) the primary Transcendental doctrine that each and every man and woman possesses a native, innate faculty for knowing called by Emerson *Intuition*. This faculty, he tells us,

is the fountain of action and of thought Here are the lungs of that inspiration which giveth man wisdom and which cannot be denied without impiety and atheism. We lie in the lap of immense intelligence, which makes us receivers of its truth and organs of its activity. When we discern justice, when we discern truth, we do nothing of ourselves but allow a passage to its beams.

Because we are the agents of this divine intelligence, (2) we have, each of us, a great importance and authority in ourselves; therefore each of us ought to be *independent,* and to stand on the knowledge of his own native worth.

A great man is coming to eat at my house. I do not wish to please him; I wish that he should wish to please me. I will stand here for humanity, and though I would make it kind, I would make it true. . . . The fact which is the upshot of all history is that there is a great responsible Thinker and Actor working wherever a man works.

Being independent, Emerson proceeds, (3) a man should not concede too much to customs and systems devised of old time. "The world is his who can see through its pretension. What deafness, what stone-blind custom, what overgrown error you behold is only there by sufferance—by your sufferance." This is a doctrine of change, of *revolution,* or at least evolution; and it is one of the ideas which make Emerson essentially a young man's writer.

Closely connected with all this insistence on the paramount importance of the individual consciousness is (4) a prevailing *optimism.* No worldly misfortune, says Emerson, is sufficient to overcome the fortified mind,

> For well the soul, if stout within,
> Can arm impregnably the skin.

After all, the whole self-reliant philosophy is optimistic: "Give me health and a day, and I will make the pomp of emperors ridiculous."

In the Nature group of ideas, (1) the Over-Soul or God as a *transcendent* power that must also be *immanent* is essentially a part of the doctrine placed first in the other group. It is expressed in this sentence from *Nature:* "There seems to be a necessity in Spirit to manifest itself in material forms; and day and night, river and storm, beast and bird, acid and alkali, preëxist in necessary Ideas in the mind of God, and are what they are by virtue of affections in the world of spirit. A Fact is the end or last issue of spirit."

If we accept that doctrine, we are more easily led to another—(2) the idea of the *microcosm.* If the same spirit runs through all natural phenomena, each particle reflects all of that spirit. "The world globes itself in a drop of dew." Emerson makes the most of this each-in-all and all-in-each conception, so common in the mysticism of the ages. "When me they fly, I am the wings," exults Brahma.

It is all a matter of (3) the *unity* of man and nature, which is also a unity with God. Our author writes:

In the woods we return to reason and faith. There I feel that nothing can befall me in life—no disgrace, no calamity, which nature cannot repair.

Standing on the bare ground, my head bathed by the blithe air, and uplifted into infinite space, all mean egotism vanishes. I become a transparent eyeball: I am nothing; I see all; the currents of the Universal Being circulate through me; I am part or particle of God.

And so God speaks through the poet or artist:

> Not from a vain or shallow thought
> His awful Jove young Phidias brought. . . .
> Himself from God he could not free,
> He builded better than he knew:
> The conscious stone to beauty grew.

Intimately connected with this concept of the art process is the idea of (4) *beauty as created by the imagination.* "Nothing is beautiful alone;" beauty is in the eye of the beholder, whether artist, critic, or amateur:

Though we travel the world over to find the beautiful, we must carry it with us, or we find it not. The best of beauty is a finer charm than skill in surfaces, in outlines, or rules of art can never teach, namely, a radiation from the work of art of human character,—a wonderful expression through stone, or canvas, or musical sound, of the deepest and simplest attributes of our nature, and therefore most intelligible at last to those souls which have these attributes.

It takes little thought to discover how closely knit together are all these ideas. They are all in and of the pattern that was Emerson. Their spiritual power, and their direct applicability to the daily life not only of the author's own day but of ours as well, give them a perennial vitality.

IV

Emerson's first small book, "the little azure-colored *Nature,*" as Carlyle called it, is an intense and often lyrical exposition of his thought. Here the ideas which have just been noted as belonging to the second group find fresh and striking expression, often lapsing into pure poetry. He takes up separately four uses of nature—four classes of the effects of nature upon the soul—discussing them in chapters entitled "Commodity," "Beauty," "Language," and "Discipline." In the first of these he talks about the utilities and comforts which nature furnishes to man. The chapter on beauty shows the lyrical essayist at his highest flight, and the reader who yields to its persuasion shares a rapture and emotional fervour which are essentially religious.

The chapter on "Language" has analogies with *Sartor Resartus.* Words, which are symbols of things, are also symbols of spirit because things themselves are symbols of spirit. Thus the use of metaphor, accompaniment of deep feeling, indicates man's instinctive idealism.

In the final chapters on "Idealism," "Spirit," and "Prospects," the author becomes more abstract. His dualism is apparent when he says of traditional idealistic philosophy:

Let it stand then, in the present state of our knowledge, merely as a useful introductory hypothesis, serving to apprise us of the eternal distinction between the soul and the world.

But this dualism quickly dissolves into an all-inclusive monism as he emphasizes the working of the Over-Soul:

We learn that the highest is present to the soul of man; that the dread universal essence, which is not wisdom, or love, or beauty, or power, but all in one, and each entirely, is that for which all things exist, and that by which they are; that spirit creates; that behind nature, throughout nature, spirit is present; one and not compound it does not act upon us from without, that is, in space and time, but spiritually, or through ourselves: therefore, that spirit, that is, the Supreme Being, does not build up nature around us, but puts it forth through us, as the life of the tree puts forth new branches and leaves through the pores of the old. As a plant upon the earth, so a man rests upon the bosom of God; he is nourished by unfailing fountains, and draws at his need inexhaustible power. Who can set bounds to the possibilities of man? Once inhale the upper air, being admitted to behold the absolute natures of justice and truth, and we learn that man has access to the entire mind of the Creator, is himself the creator in the finite.

By his creative activity man can contribute to the unification of reality:

Empirical science is apt to cloud the sight, and by the very knowledge of functions and processes to bereave the student of the manly contemplation of the whole . . . The reason why the world lacks unity, and lies broken and in heaps, is because man is disunited with himself . . . Nature is not fixed but fluid. Spirit alters, moulds, makes it . . . Build therefore your own world.

The publication of *Nature* made Emerson immediately the chief spokesman of the "new views" and won him a small but enthusiastic following, but it also marked him in the minds of many as a dangerous radical.

The next year the Phi Beta Kappa Society of Harvard asked him to deliver its annual address. The result was "The American Scholar." Years later, Lowell wrote of the occasion of its delivery:

It was an event without any former parallel in our literary annals, a scene to be always treasured in the memory for its picturesqueness and its inspiration. What crowded and breathless aisles, what windows clustering with eager heads, what enthusiasm of approval, what grim silence of foregone dissent!

Many others who sat in that crowded assembly have testified similarly to the intense interest in the address. Central in it is the emphasis on Man Thinking and the necessity for the scholar in America to be self-reliant and bold and free of bondage to tradition. "Free should the scholar be—free and brave."

The next year, invited by a committee of students, Emerson delivered before the senior class of Harvard's Divinity School an address which shocked the orthodox by its insistence on independence in religious thought. In the winter of 1838-39 he gave a series of ten lectures at the Masonic Hall in Boston, and the following winter ten more. These and other addresses were eventually worked into the essays as we have them in his works. It was Emerson's common practice to jot his reflections down in his journal, later to work the journal entries out in lectures, and finally to prepare the lectures for publication in series of essays. This was by no means an invariable literary process with him, however; and "The American Scholar," the Divinity School address, and several other early lectures to academic organizations were published separately immediately after delivery.

In 1841 in a volume called *Essays,* later entitled *Essays: First Series,* Emerson presented the work which was to form the chief basis of his fame at home and abroad. Here were twelve essays in which the author set forth the main principles of his thought. They include "Self-Reliance," "Compensation," "The Over-Soul," "History," and "Art." In his noble and challenging "Self-Reliance," Emerson wove together passages from various addresses he had been making, giving us the definitive pattern of his thinking on this, one of the major subjects which had employed his mind for many years. Its freshness, zest, and fighting challenge have moved many readers; its tonic quality has not weakened with age. "Compensation" has been scarcely less popular The application of the idea of the compensations in nature to the spiritual world made attractive speculation, and if the result was an optimistic view of life, that seemed to many readers pure gain. It brought the realistic critics down upon Emerson, however, as did the mystical metaphysics of "The Over-Soul."

Essays· Second Series appeared three years later. It began with "The Poet," one of the most enthusiastic eulogies of the poet's office ever penned, and ended with "New England Reformers," an essay containing much sound sense about classical education and a good deal of skepticism about reforms and reformers. On the whole, these nine pieces seem a little below the level of the twelve in the *First Series,* but they were better received by the public.

V

The history of Emerson's reputation in America shows a gradual increase of respect on the part of the more thoughtful, and a growing popular acceptance of the Concord philosopher. Edward Everett Hale, writing of his own early years, said that in 1837 it was considered "good form" to ridicule Emerson; and it was in the following year that the *Christian Examiner* referred to the "Divinity School Address" as "the latest form of infidelity." But steady and equable writing and living and lecturing on his own high plane gradually brought a change in the general attitude toward Emerson. This was signalized in 1844, when the *Examiner* printed a favorable review of his second series of *Essays* from the pen of that ardent Transcendentalist, F. H. Hedge. In the *Harbinger* of 1846, W. W. Story noted that "Emerson has become the fashion, or rather the fashion has become him. His admirers have gradually become the public." About the same time, the *Whig Review* pointed out that while the Transcendental movement had declined, Emerson had increased in reputation and was now writing and speaking to a larger audience than ever before. This was chiefly because his profound sympathy with basic American ideals lifted him above the position of mere spokesman for a movement.

In 1842-44 Emerson edited *The Dial,* a quarterly journal designed as the organ of the Boston Transcendental group. Margaret Fuller (assisted by George Ripley) had been editor of the first two annual volumes, and Emerson undertook the work with reluctance when Miss Fuller's health forced her to give it up. The magazine was in many ways an excellent production, though Emerson begrudged it the time and effort as well as the money he put into it. It was suspended at the end of its fourth volume.

Emerson's *Poems* were published late in 1846, though the title-page date is 1847. It was his own theory that the poet was chiefly seer. "It is not metres, but a metre-making argument, that makes a poem." Emerson's verse has been condemned for its forced rhymes, its perverse inversions, its carelessness; but the author's originality, his comparative freedom from conventional forms, his sincerity, and the force of his ideas give to many of his poems a high degree of power and beauty. They must be read in conjunction with the essays, nor is it always easy to say when the prose is poetry or the poetry prose. Certainly there are some short flights of Emerson's verse that soar very high indeed, and a surprising proportion of the *Poems* and their sequel *May-Day* (1867) is worth reading over and over, from year to year, until it becomes a part of one's own anthology of well-loved verse.

In 1847 Emerson made a second visit to Europe, lectured in London, and was stimulated by contacts with the leading men of England. He deeply enjoyed his visit to Carlyle in Chelsea. By this time his fame had spread over Europe. One admirer may be quoted: Nietzsche said of Emerson, "He simply does not know how old he is, or how young he yet will be."

The books he published in the years which followed his return to Concord —*Representative Men, English Traits, Conduct of Life*—brought a great increase in his popular following. In *Representative Men* Emerson applies the basic theories of his philosophy to six great men—Plato, Swedenborg, Montaigne, Shakespeare, Napoleon, and Goethe. The essayist's powers are nowhere better shown than in this volume, which is perhaps a more suitable "introduction" to the author than *Nature*, which stands first chronologically. Here are all the zest, incisiveness, homely sense, and soaring idealism which characterize Emerson at his best. *English Traits*, product of his second visit overseas, is one of Emerson's easiest books. Whether one agrees with its attitudes and conclusions or not, one is sure to find its admiration of English strength of character, as well as the richness and serenity of the book as a whole, interesting and enjoyable. *The Conduct of Life*, with its nine essays on such topics as fate, beauty, and illusions, might have been titled "Essays: Third Series." Close study of it will confirm the view of Professor Henry A. Pochmann that "Emerson's philosophy, far from being a haphazard affair of whim, rags and patches, and irreconcilable contrarieties, followed a course of consecutive development . . ." The same point may be made concerning *Society and Solitude* (1870) which came ten years later, shortly before the author's breakdown. The essays of this book are more informal and anecdotal—occasionally like the fireside chat of an old man. *Letters and Social Aims*, prepared for the press by a friend who was later his biographer, James Elliot Cabot, was Emerson's last book to be published during his own lifetime, though other works, including the voluminous journals, were gathered up and published later.

Emerson was reading proofs on *Society and Solitude* when his house in Concord was burned to the ground, and he suffered injuries to his health at that time that could never be repaired. He was urged to make another visit abroad in search of healing for body and mind; and he accordingly made the grand tour through England, France, Italy and Egypt, meeting many famous men and regaining something of his old energy and ambition. When he got back to Concord in May, 1873, the whole village turned out to meet him and escort him to his house, which had been rebuilt and restored in his absence by the generosity of friends and neighbors. Many of the contributors to this gracious project were readers and admirers who were quite unknown to him personally.

Emerson's last years were serene and untroubled by financial cares, but he was unable to concentrate on literary work and his mental powers declined. He died peacefully on April 27, 1882. Shortly before his death, *Harper's Weekly* declared that there was a popular "respect and affection" for him such as "few men have ever enjoyed." The writer continued, "It is a feeling which has grown constantly for more than forty years, and it is deeper, stronger, and more universal than ever."

In the seventies a cheap publishing mania invaded the book industry of the United States, brought on by economic conditions and technological changes. Among other effects of this phenomenon was the production of Emerson's *Essays* in paper-bound volumes at ten and twenty cents for popular sale. The early essays had recently emerged from copyright and were at the mercy of scores of cheap publishers. For thirty years or more following the mid-seventies, Emerson's writings, in many forms, were sold in both paper and cloth at prices under a dollar to a vast popular audience. The *Essays* and *Representative Men* enjoyed an aggregate sale which ran probably to over half a million.

Today Emerson's leading essays seem often to have a singularly contemporary meaning and force. We do not know "how young he yet will be."

[The authorized biography is James Elliot Cabot's *A Memoir of Ralph Waldo Emerson* in two volumes (Boston, 1887). Oscar W. Firkins' *Ralph Waldo Emerson* (Boston, 1915) is a stimulating critical and biographical study A short and easy biography is that of Oliver Wendell Holmes in the American Men of Letters series (Boston, 1884), while George E. Woodberry's study in the English Men of Letters series (New York, 1907) is chiefly criticism and interpretation, brilliant but scarcely sympathetic. Van Wyck Brooks' *The Life of Emerson* (New York, 1932) is a vivid and often picturesque presentation of Emerson and his circle. But perhaps the best book to read for an understanding of Emerson's personality is the book of selections from his journal edited by Bliss Perry and called *The Heart of Emerson's Journals* (Boston, 1926). Perry's own book, *Emerson Today* (Princeton, 1931) helps recreate Emerson as a human being with something to say to modern readers. *The Journals of Ralph Waldo Emerson,* in ten volumes (Boston, 1909-1914) and *The Letters of Ralph Waldo Emerson,* edited by R. L. Rusk in six volumes (New York, 1939) are indispensable sources for the scholar. Valuable essays on Emerson may be found in J. W. Beach's *The Concept of Nature in Nineteenth-Century English Poetry* (New York, 1936); W. C. Brownell's *American Prose Masters* (New York, 1909); H. S. Canby's *Classic Americans* (New York, 1931); F. I. Carpenter's *Emerson* (New York, 1934) in American Writers Series; J. J. Chapman's *Emerson and Other Essays* (New York, 1898); Norman Foerster's *American Criticism* (Boston, 1928); F. O. Matthiessen's *American Renaissance* (New York, 1941); S. P. Sherman's *Americans* (New York, 1922). H. A. Pochmann's "The Emerson Canon" in *University of Toronto Quarterly* XII (July, 1943), 476-484, is an important discussion of the state of Emerson scholarship. Kenneth Walter Cameron's *Emerson the Essayist,* in two volumes (Raleigh, N. C., 1946) is an exhaustive storehouse of materials on his development through 1836.]

CONCORD HYMN [1]
[1846 (1837)]

By the rude bridge that arched the flood,
  Their flag to April's breeze unfurled,
Here once the embattled farmers stood
  And fired the shot heard round the
    world.

The foe long since in silence slept;   5
  Alike the conqueror silent sleeps;
And Time the ruined bridge has swept
  Down the dark stream which seaward
    creeps.

---

[1] "Sung at the completion of the Battle Monument, July 4, 1837."

On this green bank, by this soft stream,
  We set to-day a votive stone;   10
That memory may their deed redeem,
  When, like our sires, our sons are gone.

Spirit, that made those heroes dare
  To die, and leave their children free,
Bid Time and Nature gently spare   15
  The shaft we raise to them and thee.

GOOD-BYE [1]
[1846 (1839)]

Good-bye, proud world! I'm going home:
Thou art not my friend, and I'm not thine.
Long through thy weary crowds I roam;
A river-ark on the ocean brine,
Long I've been tossed like the driven
    foam;   5
But now, proud world! I'm going home.

Good-bye to Flattery's fawning face;
To Grandeur with his wise grimace;
To upstart Wealth's averted eye;
To supple Office, low and high;   10
To crowded halls, to court and street;
To frozen hearts and hasting feet;
To those who go, and those who come;
Good-bye, proud world! I'm going home.

I am going to my own hearth-stone,   15
Bosomed in yon green hills alone,—
A secret nook in a pleasant land,
Whose groves the frolic fairies planned;
Where arches green, the livelong day,
Echo the blackbird's roundelay,   20
And vulgar feet have never trod
A spot that is sacred to thought and God.

O, when I am safe in my sylvan home,
I tread on the pride of Greece and Rome;
  And when I am stretched beneath the
    pines,   25
Where the evening star so holy shines,
I laugh at the lore and the pride of man,

At the sophist schools and the learned clan;
For what are they all, in their high conceit,
When man in the bush with God may
  meet?   30

EACH AND ALL
[1846 (1839)]

Little thinks, in the field, yon red-cloaked
  clown
Of thee from the hill-top looking down;
The heifer that lows in the upland farm,
Far-heard, lows not thine ear to charm;
The sexton, tolling his bell at noon,   5
Deems not that great Napoleon
Stops his horse, and lists with delight,
Whilst his files sweep round yon Alpine
    height; [2]
Nor knowest thou what argument
Thy life to thy neighbor's creed has lent. 10
All are needed by each one;
Nothing is fair or good alone.
I thought the sparrow's note from heaven,
Singing at dawn on the alder bough;
I brought him home, in his nest, at even; 15
He sings the song, but it cheers not now,
For I did not bring home the river and
  sky;—
He sang to my ear,—they sang to my eye.
The delicate shells lay on the shore;
The bubbles of the latest wave   20
Fresh pearls to their enamel gave,
And the bellowing of the savage sea
Greeted their safe escape to me.
I wiped away the weeds and foam,
I fetched my sea-born treasures home;   25

---

[1] In sending this poem to James Freeman Clarke for publication in the *Western Examiner,* of Cincinnati, the author wrote: "They were written sixteen years ago, when I kept a school in Boston, and lived in a corner of Roxbury called Canterbury. They have a slight misanthropy, a shade deeper than belongs to me. . . ."

[2] "Bonaparte was sensible to the music of bells. Hearing the bell of a parish church, he would pause, and his voice faltered as he said, 'Ah, that reminds me of the first years I spent at Brienne; I was then happy.' "—Emerson's *Journals,* 1844.

But the poor, unsightly, noisome things
Had left their beauty on the shore
With the sun and the sand and the wild
    uproar.[3]
The lover watched his graceful maid,
As 'mid the virgin train she strayed,   30
Nor knew her beauty's best attire
Was woven still by the snow-white choir.
At last she came to his hermitage,
Like the bird from the woodlands to the
    cage;—
The gay enchantment was undone,   35
A gentle wife, but fairy none.
Then I said, "I covet truth;
Beauty is unripe childhood's cheat;
I leave it behind with the games of
    youth:"—
As I spoke, beneath my feet   40
The ground-pine curled its pretty wreath,
Running over the club-moss burrs;
I inhaled the violet's breath;
Around me stood the oaks and firs;
Pine-cones and acorns lay on the
    ground;   45
Over me soared the eternal sky,
Full of light and of deity;
Again I saw, again I heard,
The rolling river, the morning bird;—
Beauty through my senses stole;   50
I yielded myself to the perfect whole.

THE RHODORA:
ON BEING ASKED, WHENCE
IS THE FLOWER?
[1846 (1839)]

In May, when sea-winds pierced our soli-
    tudes,
I found the fresh Rhodora in the woods,
Spreading its leafless blooms in a damp
    nook,
To please the desert and the sluggish brook.
The purple petals, fallen in the pool,   5
Made the black water with their beauty
    gay;
Here might the red-bird come his plumes
    to cool,
And court the flower that cheapens his
    array.

Rhodora! if the sages ask thee why
This charm is wasted on the earth and
    sky,   10
Tell them, dear, that if eyes were made for
    seeing,
Then Beauty is its own excuse for being:
Why thou wert there, O rival of the rose!
I never thought to ask, I never knew:
But, in my simple ignorance, suppose   15
The self-same Power that brought me there
    brought you.

THE HUMBLE-BEE [4]
[1846 (1839)]

Burly, dozing humble-bee,
Where thou art is clime for me.
Let them sail for Porto Rique,
Far-off heats through seas to seek;
I will follow thee alone,   5
Thou animated torrid-zone!
Zigzag steerer, desert cheerer,
Let me chase thy waving lines;
Keep me nearer, me thy hearer,
Singing over shrubs and vines.   10

Insect lover of the sun,
Joy of thy dominion!
Sailor of the atmosphere;
Swimmer through the waves of air;
Voyager of light and noon;   15
Epicurean of June;

---

[3] "I remember when I was a boy going
upon the beach and being charmed with
the colors and forms of the shells. I picked
up many and put them in my pocket.
When I got home I could find nothing
that I gathered—nothing but some dry,
ugly mussel and snail shells. Thence I
learned that Composition was more important than the beauty of individual forms
to Effect. On the shore they lay wet and
social, by the sea and under the sky."—
Emerson's *Journals*, May 16, 1834.

[4] "Yesterday in the woods I followed the
fine humble-bee with rhymes and fancies
fine. . . . The humble-bee and pine-war-
bler seem to me the proper objects of
attention in these disastrous times."—
Emerson's *Journals*, 1837. This was a year
of financial panic.

Wait, I prithee, till I come
Within earshot of thy hum,—
All without is martyrdom.

When the south wind, in May days, 20
With a net of shining haze
Silvers the horizon wall,
And with softness touching all,
Tints the human countenance
With a color of romance, 25
And infusing subtle heats,
Turns the sod to violets,
Thou, in sunny solitudes,
Rover of the underwoods,
The green silence dost displace 30
With thy mellow, breezy bass.

Hot midsummer's petted crone,
Sweet to me thy drowsy tone
Tells of countless sunny hours,
Long days, and solid banks of flowers; 35
Of gulfs of sweetness without bound
In Indian wildernesses found;
Of Syrian peace, immortal leisure,
Firmest cheer, and bird-like pleasure.
Aught unsavory or unclean 40
Hath my insect never seen;
But violets and billberry bells,
Maple-sap and daffodels,
Grass with green flag half-mast high,
Succory to match the sky, 45
Columbine with horn of honey,
Scented fern, and agrimony,
Clover, catchfly, adder's-tongue
And brier-roses, dwelt among;
All beside was unknown waste, 50
All was picture as he passed.

Wiser far than human seer,
Yellow-breeched philosopher!
Seeing only what is fair,
Sipping only what is sweet, 55
Thou dost mock at fate and care,
Leave the chaff, and take the wheat.
When the fierce northwestern blast
Cools sea and land so far and fast,
Thou already slumberest deep; 60
Woe and want thou canst outsleep;
Want and woe, which torture us,
Thy sleep makes ridiculous.

WOODNOTES I
[1846 (1840)]

1

When the pine tosses its cones
To the song of its waterfall tones,
Who speeds to the woodland walks?
To birds and trees who talks?
Cæsar of his leafy Rome, 5
There the poet is at home.
He goes to the river-side,—
Not hook nor line hath he;
He stands in the meadows wide,—
Nor gun nor scythe to see. 10
Sure some god his eye enchants:
What he knows nobody wants.
In the wood he travels glad,
Without better fortune had,
Melancholy without bad. 15
Knowledge this man prizes best
Seems fantastic to the rest:
Pondering shadows, colors, clouds,
Grass-buds and caterpillar-shrouds,
Boughs on which the wild bees settle, 20
Tints that spot the violet's petal,
Why Nature loves the number five,
And why the star-form she repeats:
Lover of all things alive,
Wonderer at all he meets, 25
Wonderer chiefly at himself,
Who can tell him what he is?
Or how meet in human elf
Coming and past eternities?

2

And such I knew, a forest seer,[1] 30
A minstrel of the natural year,
Foreteller of the vernal ides,
Wise harbinger of spheres and tides,
A lover true, who knew by heart
Each joy the mountain dales impart; 35

---

[1] Though E. W. Emerson, in his *Emerson in Concord* (Boston, 1890), p. 111, says that these lines were written before their author knew Thoreau, he admits that Thoreau "fills the portrait"; and the lines have generally been accepted as a sketch of Thoreau. Cf. Emerson's prose essay on his friend and neighbor.

It seemed that Nature could not raise
A plant in any secret place,
In quaking bog, on snowy hill,
Beneath the grass that shades the rill,
Under the snow, between the rocks,　40
In damp fields known to bird and fox,
But he would come in the very hour
It opened in its virgin bower,
As if a sunbeam showed the place,
And tell its long-descended race.　45
It seemed as if the breezes brought him,
It seemed as if the sparrows taught him;
As if by secret sight he knew
Where, in far fields, the orchis grew.
Many haps fall in the field　50
Seldom seen by wishful eyes
But all her shows did Nature yield,
To please and win this pilgrim wise.
He saw the partridge drum in the woods;
He heard the woodcock's evening hymn; 55
He found the tawny thrushes' broods;
And the shy hawk did wait for him;
What others did at distance hear,
And guessed within the thicket's gloom,
Was shown to this philosopher,　60
And at his bidding seemed to come.

3

In unploughed Maine he sought the lum-
　　berers' gang
Where from a hundred lakes young rivers
　　sprang;
He trode the unplanted forest floor,
　　whereon
The all-seeing sun for ages hath not
　　shone;　65
Where feeds the moose, and walks the
　　surly bear,
And up the tall mast runs the woodpecker.
He saw beneath dim aisles, in odorous beds,
The slight Linnæa hang its twin-born heads,
And blessed the monument of the man of
　　flowers,[2]　70
Which breathes his sweet fame through
　　the northern bowers.
He heard, when in the grove, at intervals,
With sudden roar the aged pine-tree
　　falls,—
One crash, the death-hymn of the perfect
　　tree,

Declares the close of its green century. 75
Low lies the plant to whose creation went
Sweet influence from every element;
Whose living towers the years conspired to
　　build,
Whose giddy top the morning loved to gild.
Through these green tents, by eldest Nature
　　dressed,　80
He roamed, content alike with man and
　　beast.
Where darkness found him he lay glad at
　　night;
There the red morning touched him with its
　　light.
Three moons his great heart him a hermit
　　made,
So long he roved at will the boundless
　　shade.　85
The timid it concerns to ask their way,
And fear what foe in caves and swamps
　　can stray,
To make no step until the event is known,
And ills to come as evils past bemoan.
Not so the wise; no coward watch he
　　keeps　90
To spy what danger on his pathway
　　creeps;
Go where he will, the wise man is at home,
His hearth the earth,—his hall the azure
　　dome;
Where his clear spirit leads him, there's his
　　road
By God's own light illumined and fore-
　　showed.　95

4

'T was one of the charmèd days
When the genius of God doth flow;
The wind may alter twenty ways,
A tempest cannot blow;
It may blow north, it still is warm;　100
Or south, it still is clear;
Or east, it smells like a clover-farm;
Or west, no thunder fear.
The musing peasant, lowly great,
Beside the forest water sate;　105
The rope-like pine-roots crosswise grown

---

[2] Carl von Linné (Carolus Linnaeus),
Swedish botanist (1707-1778).

Composed the network of his throne;
The wide lake, edged with sand and grass,
Was burnished to a floor of glass,
Painted with shadows green and proud 110
Of the tree and of the cloud.
He was the heart of all the scene;
On him the sun looked more serene;
To hill and cloud his face was known,—
It seemed the likeness of their own;   115
They knew by secret sympathy
The public child of earth and sky.
"You ask," he said, "what guide
Me through trackless thickets led,
Through thick-stemmed woodlands rough
    and wide.   120
I found the water's bed.
The watercourses were my guide;
I travelled grateful by their side,
Or through their channel dry;
They led me through the thicket damp, 125
Through brake and fern, the beavers' camp,
Through beds of granite cut my road,
And their resistless friendship showed:
The falling waters led me,
The foodful waters fed me,   130
And brought me to the lowest land,
Unerring to the ocean sand.
The moss upon the forest bark
Was pole-star when the night was dark;
The purple berries in the wood   135
Supplied me necessary food;
For Nature ever faithful is
To such as trust her faithfulness.
When the forest shall mislead me,
When the night and morning lie,   140
When sea and land refuse to feed me,
'T will be time enough to die;
Then will yet my mother yield
A pillow in her greenest field,
Nor the June flowers scorn to cover   145
The clay of their departed lover."

WOODNOTES II [1]
[1846 (1841)]

As sunbeams stream through liberal space
And nothing jostle or displace,
So waved the pine-tree through my thought
And fanned the dreams it never brought.

'Whether is better, the gift or the donor?
Come to me,'
Quoth the pine-tree,
'I am the giver of honor.
My garden is the cloven rock,   5
And my manure the snow;
And drifting sand-heaps feed my stock,
In summer's scorching glow.
He is great who can live by me:
The rough and bearded forester   10
Is better than the lord;
God fills the scrip and canister,
Sin piles the loaded board.
The lord is the peasant that was,
The peasant the lord that shall be;   15
The lord is hay, the peasant grass,
One dry, and one the living tree.
Who liveth by the ragged pine
Foundeth a heroic line;
Who liveth in the palace hall   20
Waneth fast and spendeth all.
He goes to my savage haunts,
With his chariot and his care;
My twilight realm he disenchants,
And finds his prison there.   25

'What prizes the town and the tower?
Only what the pine-tree yields;
Sinew that subdued the fields;
The wild-eyed boy, who in the woods
Chants his hymn to hills and floods,   30
Whom the city's poisoning spleen
Made not pale, or fat, or lean;
Whom the rain and the wind purgeth,
Whom the dawn and the day-star urgeth,
In whose cheek the rose-leaf blusheth, 35
In whose feet the lion rusheth,
Iron arms, and iron mould,
That know not fear, fatigue, or cold.
I give my rafters to his boat,
My billets to his boiler's throat,   40
And I will swim the ancient sea
To float my child to victory,

---

[1] "All my thoughts are foresters. I have scarce a day-dream on which the breath of the pines has not blown, and their shadows waved. Shall I not therefore call my little book Forest Essays?"—Emerson's *Journals*, January, 1841. But the "little book" was called simply *Essays*.

And grant to dwellers with the pine
Dominion o'er the palm and vine.
Who leaves the pine-tree, leaves his
    friend,   45
Unnerves his strength, invites his end.
Cut a bough from my parent stem,
And dip it in thy porcelain vase;
A little while each russet gem
Will swell and rise with wonted grace;   50
But when it seeks enlarged supplies,
The orphan of the forest dies.
Whoso walks in solitude
And inhabiteth the wood,
Choosing light, wave, rock and bird,   55
Before the money-loving herd,
Into that forester shall pass,
From these companions, power and grace.
Clean shall he be, without, within,
From the old adhering sin,   60
All ill dissolving in the light
Of his triumphant piercing sight:
Not vain, sour, nor frivolous;
Not mad, athirst, nor garrulous;
Grave, chaste, contented, though retired, 65
And of all other men desired.
On him the light of star and moon
Shall fall with purer radiance down;
All constellations of the sky
Shed their virtue through his eye.   70
Him Nature giveth for defence
His formidable innocence;
The mounting sap, the shells, the sea,
All spheres, all stones, his helpers be;
He shall meet the speeding year,   75
Without wailing, without fear;
He shall be happy in his love,
Like to like shall joyful prove;
He shall be happy whilst he wooes,
Muse-born, a daughter of the Muse.   80
But if with gold she bind her hair,
And deck her breast with diamond,
Take off thine eyes, thy heart forbear,
Though thou lie alone on the ground.

'Heed the old oracles,   85
Ponder my spells;
Song wakes in my pinnacles
When the wind swells.
Soundeth the prophetic wind,
The shadows shake on the rock behind,   90

And the countless leaves of the pine are
    strings
Tuned to the lay the wood-god sings.
     Hearken! Hearken!
If thou wouldst know the mystic song
Chanted when the sphere was young.   95
Aloft, abroad, the pæan swells;
O wise man! hear'st thou half it tells?
O wise man! hear'st thou the least part?
'T is the chronicle of art.
To the open ear it sings   100
Sweet the genesis of things,
Of tendency through endless ages,
Of star-dust, and star-pilgrimages,
Of rounded worlds, of space and time,
Of the old flood's subsiding slime,   105
Of chemic matter, force and form,
Of poles and powers, cold, wet, and warm:
The rushing metamorphosis
Dissolving all that fixture is,
Melts things that be to things that
    seem,   110
And solid nature to a dream.
O, listen to the undersong,
The ever old, the ever young;
And, far within those cadent pauses,
The chorus of the ancient Causes!   115
Delights the dreadful Destiny
To fling his voice into the tree,
And shock thy weak ear with a note
Breathed from the everlasting throat.
In music he repeats the pang   120
Whence the fair flock of Nature sprang.
O mortal! thy ears are stones;
These echoes are laden with tones
Which only the pure can hear;
Thou canst not catch what they recite   125
Of Fate and Will, of Want and Right,
Of man to come, of human life,
Of Death and Fortune, Growth and Strife.'

    Once again the pine-tree sung:—
'Speak not thy speech my boughs
    among: 130
Put off thy years, wash in the breeze;
My hours are peaceful centuries.
Talk no more with feeble tongue;
No more the fool of space and time,
Come weave with mine a nobler rhyme.   135
Only thy Americans

Can read thy line, can meet thy glance,
But the runes that I rehearse
Understands the universe;
The least breath my boughs which
    tossed   140
Brings again the Pentecost;
To every soul resounding clear
In a voice of solemn cheer,—
"Am I not thine? Are not these thine?"
And they reply, "Forever mine!"   145
My branches speak Italian,
English, German, Basque, Castilian,
Mountain speech to Highlanders,
Ocean tongues to islanders,
To Fin and Lap and swart Malay,   150
To each his bosom-secret say.

'Come learn with me the fatal song
Which knits the world in music strong,
Come lift thine eyes to lofty rhymes,
Of things with things, of times with
    times,   155
Primal chimes of sun and shade,
Of sound and echo, man and maid,
The land reflected in the flood,
Body with shadow still pursued.
For Nature beats in perfect tune,   160
And rounds with rhyme her every rune,
Whether she work in land or sea,
Or hide underground her alchemy.
Thou canst not wave thy staff in air,
Or dip the paddle in the lake,   165
But it carves the bow of beauty there,
And the ripples in rhymes the oar forsake.
The wood is wiser far than thou;
The wood and wave each other know
Not unrelated, unaffied,   170
But to each thought and thing allied,
Is perfect Nature's every part,
Rooted in the mighty Heart.
But thou, poor child! unbound, unrhymed,
Whence camest thou, misplaced, mis-
    timed,   175
Whence, O thou orphan and defrauded?
Is thy land peeled, thy realm marauded?
Who thee divorced, deceived and left?
Thee of thy faith who hath bereft,
And torn the ensigns from thy brow,   180
And sunk the immortal eye so low?
Thy cheek too white, thy form too slender,

Thy gait too slow, thy habits tender
For royal man;—they thee confess
An exile from the wilderness,—   185
The hills where health with health agrees,
And the wise soul expels disease.
Hark! in thy ear I will tell the sign
By which thy hurt thou may'st divine.
When thou shalt climb the mountain
    cliff,   190
Or see the wide shore from thy skiff,
To thee the horizon shall express
But emptiness on emptiness;
There lives no man of Nature's worth
In the circle of the earth;   195
And to thine eye the vast skies fall,
Dire and satirical,
On clucking hens and prating fools,
On thieves, on drudges and on dolls.
And thou shalt say to the Most High,   200
"Godhead! all this astronomy,
And fate and practice and invention,
Strong art and beautiful pretension,
This radiant pomp of sun and star,
Throes that were, and worlds that are,   205
Behold! were in vain and in vain;—
It cannot be,—I will look again.
Surely now will the curtain rise,
And earth's fit tenant me surprise;—
But the curtain does *not* rise,   210
And Nature has miscarried wholly
Into failure, into folly."

'Alas! thine is the bankruptcy,
Blessed Nature so to see.
Come, lay thee in my soothing shade,   215
And heal the hurts which sin has made.
I see thee in the crowd alone;
I will be thy companion.
Quit thy friends as the dead in doom,
And build to them a final tomb;   220
Let the starred shade that nightly falls
Still celebrate their funerals,
And the bell of beetle and bee
Knell their melodious memory.
Behind thee leave thy merchandise,   225
Thy churches and thy charities;
And leave thy peacock wit behind;
Enough for thee the primal mind
That flows in streams, that breathes in
    wind:

Leave all thy pedant lore apart;   230
God hid the whole world in thy heart.
Love shuns the sage, the child it crowns,
Gives all to them who all renounce.
The rain comes when the wind calls;
The river knows the way to the sea;   235
Without a pilot it runs and falls,
Blessing all lands with its charity;
The sea tosses and foams to find
Its way up to the cloud and wind;
The shadow sits close to the flying ball; 240
The date fails not on the palm-tree tall;
And thou,—go burn thy wormy pages,—
Shalt outsee seers, and outwit sages.
Oft didst thou thread the woods in vain
To   find   what   bird   had   piped   the
        strain:—   245
Seek not, and the little eremite
Flies gayly forth and sings in sight.

'Hearken once more!
I will tell thee the mundane lore.
Older am I than thy numbers wot,   250
Change I may, but I pass not.
Hitherto all things fast abide,
And anchored in the tempest ride.
Trenchant time behoves to hurry
All to yean and all to bury: 255
All the forms are fugitive,
But the substances survive.
Ever fresh the broad creation,
A divine improvisation,
From the heart of God proceeds,   260
A single will, a million deeds.
Once slept the world an egg of stone,
And pulse, and sound, and light was none;
And God said, "Throb!" and there was
        motion
And the vast mass became vast ocean. 265
Onward and on, the eternal Pan,
Who layeth the world's incessant plan,
Halteth never in one shape,
But forever doth escape,
Like wave or flame, into new forms   270
Of gem, and air, of plants, and worms.
I, that to-day am a pine,
Yesterday was a bundle of grass.
He is free and libertine,
Pouring of his power the wine   275
To every age, to every race;

Unto every race and age
He emptieth the beverage;
Unto each, and unto all,
Maker and original.   280
The world is the ring of his spells,
And the play of his miracles.
As he giveth to all to drink,
Thus or thus they are and think.
With one drop sheds form and feature; 285
With the next a special nature;
The third adds heat's indulgent spark;
The fourth gives light which eats the dark;
Into the fifth himself he flings,
And conscious Law is King of kings.   290
As the bee through the garden ranges,
From world to world the godhead changes;
As the sheep go feeding in the waste,
From form to form He maketh haste;
This vault which glows immense with
        light   295
Is the inn where he lodges for a night.
What recks such Traveller if the bowers
Which bloom and fade like meadow flowers
A bunch of fragrant lilies be,
Or the stars of eternity?   300
Alike to him the better, the worse,—
The glowing angel, the outcast corse.
Thou metest him by centuries,
And lo! he passes like the breeze;
Thou seek'st in globe and galaxy,   305
He hides in pure transparency;
Thou askest in fountains and in fires,
He is the essence that inquires.
He is the axis of the star;
He is the sparkle of the spar;   310
He is the heart of every creature;
He is the meaning of each feature;
And his mind is the sky,
Than all it holds more deep, more high.'

THE SNOW-STORM
[1846 (1841)]

Announced by all the trumpets of the sky,
Arrives the snow, and, driving o'er the
        fields,
Seems nowhere to alight: the whited air
Hides hills and woods, the river, and the
        heaven,

And veils the farm-house at the garden's
    end. 5
The sled and traveller stopped, the courier's
    feet
Delayed, all friends shut out, the house-
    mates sit
Around the radiant fireplace, enclosed
In a tumultuous privacy of storm.

Come see the north wind's masonry. 10
Out of an unseen quarry evermore
Furnished with tile, the fierce artificer
Curves his white bastions with projected
    roof
Round every windward stake, or tree, or
    door.
Speeding, the myriad-handed, his wild
    work 15
So fanciful, so savage, nought cares he
For number or proportion. Mockingly,
On coop or kennel he hangs Parian
    wreaths;
A swan-like form invests the hidden thorn;
Fills up the farmer's lane from wall to
    wall, 20
Maugre the farmer's sighs; and at the
    gate
A tapering turret overtops the work.
And when his hours are numbered, and the
    world
Is all his own, retiring, as he were not,
Leaves, when the sun appears, astonished
    Art 25
To mimic in slow structures, stone by stone,
Built in an age, the mad wind's nightwork,
The frolic architecture of the snow.

FORBEARANCE
[1846 (1842)]

Hast thou named all the birds without a
    gun?
Loved the wood-rose, and left it on its
    stalk?
At rich men's tables eaten bread and pulse?
Unarmed, faced danger with a heart of
    trust?
And loved so well a high behavior,

In man or maid, that thou from speech
    refrained,
Nobility more nobly to repay?
O, be my friend, and teach me to be thine!

FORERUNNERS [1]
[1846]

Long I followed happy guides,
I could never reach their sides;
Their step is forth, and, ere the day
Breaks up their leaguer, and away.
Keen my sense, my heart was young, 5
Right good-will my sinews strung,
But no speed of mine avails
To hunt upon their shining trails.
On and away, their hasting feet
Make the morning proud and sweet; 10
Flowers they strew,—I catch the scent;
Or tone of silver instrument
Leaves on the wind melodious trace;
Yet I could never see their face.
On eastern hills I see their smokes, 15
Mixed with mist by distant lochs.
I met many travellers
Who the road had surely kept;
They saw not my fine revellers,—
These had crossed them while they slept. 20
Some had heard their fair report,
In the country or the court.
Fleetest couriers alive
Never yet could once arrive,
As they went or they returned, 25
At the house where these sojourned.
Sometimes their strong speed they slacken,
Though they are not overtaken;
In sleep their jubilant troop is near,—
I tuneful voices overhear; 30
It may be in wood or waste,—
At unawares 't is come and past.
Their near camp my spirit knows
By signs gracious as rainbows.
I thenceforward and long after 35
Listen for their harp-like laughter,
And carry in my heart, for days,
Peace that hallows rudest ways.

---

[1] Cf. Whittier's "The Vanishers," Lowell's "Envoi, To the Muse," and Emerson's own treatment of this theme in the latter part of his essay on "Nature" in *Essays, Second Series.*

TO J. W.[1]
[1846]

Set not thy foot on graves;
Hear what wine and roses say;
The mountain chase, the summer waves,
The crowded town, thy feet may well delay.

Set not thy foot on graves;   5
Nor seek to unwind the shroud
Which charitable Time
And Nature have allowed
To wrap the errors of a sage sublime.

Set not thy foot on graves;   10
Care not to strip the dead
Of his sad ornament,
His myrrh, and wine, and rings,

His sheet of lead,
And trophies burièd: 15
Go, get them where he earned them when
          alive;
As resolutely dig or dive.

Life is too short to waste
In critic peep or cynic bark,
Quarrel or reprimand: 20
'T will soon be dark;
Up! mind thine own aim, and
God speed the mark!

HAMATREYA[2]
[1846]

Bulkeley, Hunt, Willard, Hosmer, Meriam,
          Flint,[3]
Possessed the land which rendered to their
          toil
Hay, corn, roots, hemp, flax, apples, wool
          and wood.
Each of these landlords walked amidst his
          farm,
Saying, " 'T is mine, my children's and my
          name's.   5
How sweet the west wind sounds in my
          own trees!
How graceful climb those shadows on my
          hill!

I fancy these pure waters and the flags
Know me, as does my dog: we sympathize;
And, I affirm, my actions smack of the
          soil."   10
Where are these men? Asleep beneath their
          grounds:
And strangers, fond as they, their furrows
          plough.
Earth laughs in flowers, to see her boastful
          boys
Earth-proud, proud of the earth which is
          not theirs;
Who steer the plough, but cannot steer
          their feet   15
Clear of the grave.
They added ridge to valley, brook to pond,
And sighed for all that bounded their do-
          main;
"This suits me for a pasture; that's my
          park;
We must have clay, lime, gravel, granite-
          ledge,   20
And misty lowland, where to go for peat.
The land is well,—lies fairly to the south.
'T is good, when you have crossed the sea
          and back,
To find the sitfast acres where you left
          them."
Ah! the hot owner sees not Death, who
          adds   25
Him to his land, a lump of mould the more.
Hear what the Earth says:—

EARTH-SONG

"Mine and yours;
Mine, not yours.
Earth endures;   30
Stars abide—
Shine down in the old sea;

---

[1] Addressed to John Weiss, scholar and
reformer, who was then pastor of a Unitarian church at Watertown, Mass. He had
recently published an attack on Goethe.

[2] This poem is based on a passage in the
dialogue between Vishnu and Maitreya in
the Hindu work known as *Vishnu Purana*.

[3] Early settlers in the town of Concord.

Old are the shores;
But where are old men?
I who have seen much,   35
Such have I never seen.

"The lawyer's deed
Ran sure,
In tail,
To them, and to their heirs   40
Who shall succeed,
Without fail,
Forevermore.

"Here is the land,
Shaggy with wood,   45
With its old valley,
Mound and flood.
But the heritors?—
Fled like the flood's foam.
The lawyer, and the laws,   50
And the kingdom,
Clean swept herefrom.

"They called me theirs,
Who so controlled me;
Yet every one   55
Wished to stay, and is gone,
How am I theirs,
If they cannot hold me,
But I hold them?"

When I heard the Earth-song,   60
I was no longer brave;
My avarice cooled
Like lust in the chill of the grave.

FABLE
[1846]

The mountain and the squirrel
Had a quarrel,
And the former called the latter "Little
     Prig;"
Bun replied,
"You are doubtless very big;   5
But all sorts of things and weather
Must be taken in together,
To make up a year
And a sphere.
And I think it no disgrace   10

To occupy my place.
If I'm not so large as you,
You are not so small as I,
And not half so spry.
I'll not deny you make   15
A very pretty squirrel track;
Talents differ; all is well and wisely put;
If I cannot carry forests on my back,
Neither can you crack a nut."

GIVE ALL TO LOVE
[1846]

Give all to love;
Obey thy heart;
Friends, kindred, days,
Estate, good-fame,
Plans, credit and the Muse,—   5
Nothing refuse.

'T is a brave master;
Let it have scope:
Follow it utterly,
Hope beyond hope: 10
High and more high
It dives into noon,
With wing unspent,
Untold intent;
But it is a god,   15
Knows its own path
And the outlets of the sky.

It was never for the mean;
It requireth courage stout.
Souls above doubt,   20
Valor unbending,
It will reward,—
They shall return
More than they were,
And ever ascending.   25

Leave all for love;
Yet, hear me, yet,
One word more thy heart behoved,
One pulse more of firm endeavor,—
Keep thee to-day,   30
To-morrow, forever,
Free as an Arab
Of thy beloved.

Cling with life to the maid;
But when the surprise,   35
First vague shadow of surmise
Flits across her bosom young,
Of a joy apart from thee,
Free be she, fancy-free;
Nor thou detain her vesture's hem,   40
Nor the palest rose she flung
From her summer diadem.

Though thou loved her as thyself,
As a self of purer clay,
Though her parting dims the day,   45
Stealing grace from all alive;
Heartily know,
When half-gods go,
The gods arrive.

THE APOLOGY
[1846]

Think me not unkind and rude
  That I walk alone in grove and glen;
I go to the god of the wood
  To fetch his word to men.

Tax not my sloth that I   5
  Fold my arms beside the brook;
Each cloud that floated in the sky
  Writes a letter in my book.

Chide me not, laborious band,
  For the idle flowers I brought;   10
Every aster in my hand
  Goes home loaded with a thought.

There was never mystery
  But 't is figured in the flowers;
Was never secret history   15
  But birds tell it in the bowers.

One harvest from thy field
  Homeward brought the oxen strong;
A second crop thine acres yield
  Which I gather in a song.   20

BRAHMA [1]
[1867 (1857)]

If the red slayer think he slays,
  Or if the slain think he is slain,
They know not well the subtle ways
  I keep, and pass, and turn again.

Far or forgot to me is near;   5
  Shadow and sunlight are the same;
The vanished gods to me appear;
  And one to me are shame and fame.

They reckon ill who leave me out;
  When me they fly, I am the wings; 10
I am the doubter and the doubt,
  And I the hymn the Brahmin sings.

The strong gods pine for my abode,
  And pine in vain the sacred Seven;
But thou, meek lover of the good!   15
  Find me, and turn thy back on heaven.

DAYS
[1867 (1857)]

Daughters of Time, the hypocritic Days,
Muffled and dumb like barefoot dervishes,
And marching single in an endless file,
Bring diadems and fagots in their hands.
To each they offer gifts after his will,
Bread, kingdoms, stars, and sky that holds
        them all.
I, in my pleached garden, watched the
        pomp,
Forgot my morning wishes, hastily
Took a few herbs and apples, and the Day
Turned and departed silent. I, too late,
Under her solemn fillet saw the scorn.

---

[1] Cf. Krishna's song in the *Bhagavat-Gîta* (Arnold's translation):

  He who shall say, "Lo, I have slain a
        man,"
  He who shall think, "Lo, I am slain!"
        those both
  Know naught! Life cannot slay. Life is
        not slain!

This was one of four poems which Emerson contributed to the first number of the *Atlantic Monthly.*

BOSTON HYMN [1]
[1867]

The word of the Lord by night
To the watching Pilgrims came,
As they sat by the seaside,
And filled their hearts with flame.

God said, I am tired of kings,   5
I suffer them no more;
Up to my ear the morning brings
The outrage of the poor.

Think ye I made this ball
A field of havoc and war,   10
Where tyrants great and tyrants small
Might harry the weak and poor?

My angel,—his name is Freedom,—
Choose him to be your king;
He shall cut pathways east and west   15
And fend you with his wing.

Lo! I uncover the land
Which I hid of old time in the West,
As the sculptor uncovers the statue
When he has wrought his best;   20

I show Columbia, of the rocks
Which dip their foot in the seas
And soar to the air-borne flocks
Of clouds and the boreal fleece.

I will divide my goods;   25
Call in the wretch and slave:
None shall rule but the humble,
And none but Toil shall have.

I will have never a noble,
No lineage counted great;   30
Fishers and choppers and ploughmen
Shall constitute a state.

Go, cut down trees in the forest
And trim the straightest boughs;
Cut down trees in the forest   35
And build me a wooden house.

Call the people together,
The young men and the sires,
The digger in the harvest field,
Hireling and him that hires;   40

And here in a pine state-house
They shall choose men to rule
In every needful faculty,
In church and state and school.

Lo, now! if these poor men   45
Can govern the land and sea
And make just laws below the sun
As planets faithful be.

And ye shall succor men;
'T is nobleness to serve;   50
Help them who cannot help again:
Beware from right to swerve.

I break your bonds and masterships,
And I unchain the slave:
Free be his heart and hand henceforth 55
As wind and wandering wave.

I cause from every creature
His proper good to flow:
As much as he is and doeth,
So much he shall bestow.   60

But, laying hands on another
To coin his labor and sweat,
He goes in pawn to his victim
For eternal years in debt.

To-day unbind the captive,   65
So only are ye unbound;
Lift up a people from the dust,
Trump of their rescue, sound!

Pay ransom to the owner
And fill the bag to the brim.   70
Who is the owner? The slave is owner,
And ever was. Pay him.

---

[1] Read in Boston Music Hall, January 1, 1863, the day on which the Emancipation Proclamation became effective.

O North! give him beauty for rags,
And honor, O South! for his shame;
Nevada! coin thy golden crags   75
With Freedom's image and name.

Up! and the dusky race
That sat in darkness long,—
Be swift their feet as antelopes,
And as behemoth strong.   80

Come, East and West and North,
By races, as snow-flakes,
And carry my purpose forth,
Which neither halts nor shakes.

My will fulfilled shall be,   85
For, in daylight or in dark,
My thunderbolt has eyes to see
His way home to the mark.

TERMINUS
[1867]

It is time to be old,
To take in sail:—
The god of bounds,
Who sets to seas a shore,
Came to me in his fatal rounds,   5
And said: "No more!
No farther shoot
Thy broad ambitious branches, and thy
          root.
Fancy departs: no more invent;
Contract thy firmament   10
To compass of a tent.
There's not enough for this and that,
Make thy option which of two;
Economize the failing river,
Not the less revere the Giver,   15
Leave the many and hold the few.
Timely wise accept the terms,
Soften the fall with wary foot;
A little while
Still plan and smile,   20
And,—fault of novel germs,—
Mature the unfallen fruit.
Curse, if thou wilt, thy sires,
Bad husbands of their fires,
Who, when they gave thee breath,   25
Failed to bequeath

The needful sinew stark as once,
The Baresark marrow to thy bones,
But left a legacy of ebbing veins,
Inconstant heat and nerveless reins,— 30
Amid the Muses, left thee deaf and dumb,
Amid the gladiators, halt and numb."

As the bird trims her to the gale,
I trim myself to the storm of time,
I man the rudder, reef the sail,   35
Obey the voice at eve obeyed at prime:
"Lowly faithful, banish fear,
Right onward drive unharmed;
The port, well worth the cruise, is near,
And every wave is charmed."   40

THE PAST
[1867]

The debt is paid,
The verdict said,
The Furies laid,
The plague is stayed,
All fortunes made;   5
Turn the key and bolt the door,
Sweet is death forevermore.
Nor haughty hope, nor swart chagrin,
Nor murdering hate, can enter in.
All is now secure and fast;   10
Not the gods can shake the Past;
Flies-to the adamantine door
Bolted down forevermore.
None can reënter there,—
No thief so politic,   15
No Satan with a royal trick
Steal in by window, chink, or hole,
To bind or unbind, add what lacked,
Insert a leaf, or forge a name,
New-face or finish what is packed,   20
Alter or mend eternal Fact.

THE AMERICAN SCHOLAR [1]
[1837]

Mr. President and Gentlemen:

I greet you on the recommencement of
our literary year. Our anniversary is one

---

[1] "An Oration delivered before the Phi
Beta Kappa Society, at Cambridge, August 31, 1837." Immediately printed, it
sold five hundred copies within a month.

of hope, and, perhaps, not enough of labor. We do not meet for games of strength or skill, for the recitation of histories, tragedies, and odes, like the ancient Greeks; for parliaments of love and poesy, like the Troubadours; nor for the advancement of science, like our contemporaries in the British and European capitals. Thus far, our holiday has been simply a friendly sign of the survival of the love of letters amongst a people too busy to give to letters any more. As such it is precious as the sign of an indestructible instinct. Perhaps the time is already come when it ought to be, and will be, something else; when the sluggard intellect of this continent will look from under its iron lids and fill the postponed expectation of the world with something better than the exertions of mechanical skill. Our day of dependence, our long apprenticeship to the learning of other lands, draws to a close. The millions that around us are rushing into life, cannot always be fed on the sere remains of foreign harvests. Events, actions arise, that must be sung, that will sing themselves. Who can doubt that poetry will revive and lead in a new age, as the star in the constellation Harp, which now flames in our zenith, astronomers announce, shall one day be the pole-star for a thousand years?

In this hope I accept the topic which not only usage but the nature of our association seem to prescribe to this day, —the AMERICAN SCHOLAR. Year by year we come up hither to read one more chapter of his biography. Let us inquire what light new days and events have thrown on his character and his hopes.

It is one of those fables which out of an unknown antiquity convey an unlooked-for wisdom, that the gods, in the beginning, divided Man into men, that he might be more helpful to himself; just as the hand was divided into fingers, the better to answer its end.

The old fable covers a doctrine ever new and sublime; that there is One Man,—present to all particular men only partially, or through one faculty; and that you must take the whole society to find the whole man. Man is not a farmer, or a professor, or an engineer, but he is all. Man is priest, and scholar, and statesman, and producer, and soldier. In the *divided* or social state these functions are parcelled out to individuals, each of whom aims to do his stint of the joint work, whilst each other performs his. The fable implies that the individual, to possess himself, must sometimes return from his own labor to embrace all the other laborers. But, unfortunately, this original unit, this fountain of power, has been so distributed to multitudes, has been so minutely subdivided and peddled out, that it is spilled into drops, and cannot be gathered. The state of society is one in which the members have suffered amputation from the trunk, and strut about so many walking monsters,—a good finger, a neck, a stomach, an elbow, but never a man.

Man is thus metamorphosed into a thing, into many things. The planter, who is Man sent out into the field to gather food, is seldom cheered by any idea of the true dignity of his ministry. He sees his bushel and his cart, and nothing beyond, and sinks into the farmer, instead of Man on the farm. The tradesman scarcely ever gives an ideal worth to his work, but is ridden by the routine of his craft, and the soul is subject to dollars. The priest becomes a form; the attorney a statute-book; the mechanic a machine; the sailor a rope of the ship.

In this distribution of functions the scholar is the delegated intellect. In the right state he is *Man Thinking*. In the degenerate state, when the victim of society, he tends to become a mere thinker, or still worse, the parrot of other men's thinking.

In this view of him, as Man Thinking, the theory of his office is contained. Him Nature solicits with all her placid, all her monitory pictures; him the past instructs; him the future invites. Is not indeed every man a student, and do not all things exist for the student's behoof? And, finally, is not the true scholar the only true master? But the old oracle said, "All things have two handles: beware of the wrong one." In life, too often, the scholar errs with mankind and forfeits his privilege. Let us see him in his school, and consider him in reference to the main influences he receives.

I. The first in time and the first in importance of the influences upon the mind is that of nature. Every day, the sun; and, after sunset, Night and her stars. Ever the winds blow; ever the grass grows. Every day, men and women, conversing—beholding and beholden. The scholar is he of all men whom this spectacle most engages. He must settle its value in his mind. What is nature to him? There is never a beginning, there is never an end, to the inexplicable continuity of this web of God, but always circular power returning into itself. Therein it resembles his own spirit, whose beginning, whose ending, he never can find,—so entire, so boundless. Far too as her splendors shine, system on system shooting like rays, upward, downward, without centre, without circumference,—in the mass and in the particle, Nature hastens to render account of herself to the mind. Classification begins. To the young mind every thing is individual, stands by itself. By and by, it finds how to join two things and see in them one nature; then three, then three thousand; and so, tyrannized over by its own unifying instinct, it goes on tying things together, diminishing anomalies, discovering roots running under ground whereby contrary and remote things cohere and flower out from one stem. It presently learns that since the dawn of history there has been a constant accumulation and classifying of facts. But what is classification but the perceiving that these objects are not chaotic, and are not foreign, but have a law which is also a law of the human mind? The astronomer discovers that geometry, a pure abstraction of the human mind, is the measure of planetary motion. The chemist finds proportions and intelligible method throughout matter; and

science is nothing but the finding of analogy, identity, in the most remote parts. The ambitious soul sits down before each refractory fact; one after another reduces all strange constitutions, all new powers, to their class and their law, and goes on forever to animate the last fibre of organization, the outskirts of nature, by insight.

Thus to him, to this schoolboy under the bending dome of day, is suggested that he and it proceed from one root; one is leaf and one is flower; relation, sympathy, stirring in every vein. And what is that root? Is not that the soul of his soul? A thought too bold; a dream too wild. Yet when this spiritual light shall have revealed the law of more earthly natures,—when he has learned to worship the soul, and to see that the natural philosophy that now is, is only the first gropings of its gigantic hand, he shall look forward to an ever expanding knowledge as to a becoming creator. He shall see that nature is the opposite of the soul, answering to it part for part. One is seal and one is print. Its beauty is the beauty of his own mind. Its laws are the laws of his own mind. Nature then becomes to him the measure of his attainments. So much of nature as he is ignorant of, so much of his own mind does he not yet possess. And, in fine, the ancient precept, "Know thyself," and the modern precept, "Study nature," become at last one maxim.

II. The next great influence into the spirit of the scholar is the mind of the Past,—in whatever form, whether of literature, of art, of institutions, that mind is inscribed. Books are the best type of the influence of the past, and perhaps we shall get at the truth,—learn the amount of this influence more conveniently,—by considering their value alone.

The theory of books is noble. The scholar of the first age received into him the world around; brooded thereon; gave it the new arrangement of his own mind, and uttered it again. It came into him life; it went out from him truth. It came to him short-lived actions; it went out from him immortal thoughts. It came to him business; it went from him poetry. It was dead fact; now, it is quick thought. It can stand, and it can go. It now endures, it now flies, it now inspires. Precisely in proportion to the depth of mind from which it issued, so high does it soar, so long does it sing.

Or, I might say, it depends on how far the process had gone, of transmuting life into truth. In proportion to the completeness of the distillation, so will the purity and imperishableness of the product be. But none is quite perfect. As no air-pump can by any means make a perfect vacuum, so neither can any artist entirely exclude the conventional, the local, the perishable from his book, or write a book of pure thought, that shall be as efficient, in all respects, to a remote posterity, as to contemporaries, or rather to the second age. Each age, it is found, must write its own books; or rather, each generation for the next succeeding. The books of an older period will not fit this.

Yet hence arises a grave mischief. The sacredness which attaches to the act of creation, the act of thought, is transferred to the record. The poet chanting was felt to be a divine man: henceforth the chant is divine also. The writer was a just and wise spirit: henceforward it is settled the book is perfect; as love of the hero corrupts into worship of his statue. Instantly the book becomes noxious: the guide is a tyrant. The sluggish and perverted mind of the multitude, slow to open to the incursions of Reason, having once so opened, having once received this book, stands upon it, and makes an outcry if it is disparaged. Colleges are built on it. Books are written on it by thinkers, not by Man Thinking; by men of talent, that is, who start wrong, who set out from accepted dogmas, not from their own sight of principles. Meek young men grow up in libraries, believing it their duty to accept the views which Cicero, which Locke, which Bacon, have given; forgetful that Cicero, Locke, and Bacon were only young

men in libraries when they wrote these books.

Hence, instead of Man Thinking, we have the bookworm. Hence the book-learned class, who value books, as such; not as related to nature and the human constitution, but as making a sort of Third Estate with the world and the soul. Hence the restorers of readings, the emendators, the bibliomaniacs of all degrees.

Books are the best of things, well used, abused, among the worst. What is the right use? What is the one end which all means go to effect? They are for nothing but to inspire. I had better never see a book than to be warped by its attraction clean out of my own orbit, and made a satellite instead of a system. The one thing in the world, of value, is the active soul. This every man is entitled to; this every man contains within him, although in almost all men obstructed and as yet unborn. The soul active sees absolute truth and utters truth, or creates. In this action it is genius; not the privilege of here and there a favorite, but the sound estate of every man. In its essence it is progressive. The book, the college, the school of art, the institution of any kind, stop with some past utterance of genius. This is good, say they,—let us hold by this. They pin me down. They look backward and not forward. But genius looks forward: the eyes of man are set in his forehead, not in his hindhead: man hopes: genius creates. Whatever talents may be, if the man create not, the pure efflux of the Deity is not his;—cinders and smoke there may be, but not yet flame. There are creative manners, there are creative actions, and creative words; manners, actions, words, that is, indicative of no custom or authority, but springing spontaneous from the mind's own sense of good and fair.

On the other part, instead of being its own seer, let it receive from another mind its truth, though it were in torrents of light, without periods of solitude, inquest, and self-recovery, and a fatal disservice is done. Genius is always sufficiently the enemy of genius by over-influence. The literature of every nation bears me witness. The English dramatic poets have Shakspearized now for two hundred years.

Undoubtedly there is a right way of reading, so it be sternly subordinated. Man Thinking must not be subdued by his instruments. Books are for the scholar's idle times. When he can read God directly, the hour is too precious to be wasted in other men's transcripts of their readings. But when the intervals of darkness come, as come they must,—when the sun is hid and the stars withdraw their shining,—we repair to the lamps which were kindled by their ray, to guide our steps to the East again, where the dawn is. We hear, that we may speak. The Arabian proverb says, "A fig tree, looking on a fig tree, becometh fruitful."

It is remarkable, the character of the pleasure we derive from the best books. They impress us with the conviction that one nature wrote and the same reads. We read the verses of one of the great English poets, of Chaucer, of Marvell, of Dryden, with the most modern joy,—with a pleasure, I mean, which is in great part caused by the abstraction of all *time* from their verses. There is some awe mixed with the joy of our surprise, when this poet, who lived in some past world, two or three hundred years ago, says that which lies close to my own soul, that which I also had well-nigh thought and said. But for the evidence thence afforded to the philosophical doctrine of the identity of all minds, we should suppose some preëstablished harmony, some foresight of souls that were to be, and some preparation of stores for their future wants, like the fact observed in insects, who lay up food before death for the young grub they shall never see.

I would not be hurried by any love of system, by any exaggeration of instincts. to underrate the Book. We all know, that as the human body can be nourished on any food, though it were boiled grass and the broth of shoes, so the human mind can be fed by any knowledge. And great and

heroic men have existed who had almost no other information than by the printed page. I only would say that it needs a strong head to bear that diet. One must be an inventor to read well. As the proverb says, "He that would bring home the wealth of the Indies, must carry out the wealth of the Indies." There is then creative reading as well as creative writing. When the mind is braced by labor and invention, the page of whatever book we read becomes luminous with manifold allusion. Every sentence is doubly significant, and the sense of our author is as broad as the world. We then see, what is always true, that as the seer's hour of vision is short and rare among heavy days and months, so is its record, perchance, the least part of his volume. The discerning will read, in his Plato or Shakspeare, only that least part, —only the authentic utterances of the oracle;—all the rest he rejects, were it never so many times Plato's and Shakspeare's.

Of course there is a portion of reading quite indispensable to a wise man. History and exact science he must learn by laborious reading. Colleges, in like manner, have their indispensable office,—to teach elements. But they can only highly serve us when they aim not to drill, but to create; when they gather from far every ray of various genius to their hospitable halls, and by the concentrated fires, set the hearts of their youth on flame. Thought and knowledge are natures in which apparatus and pretension avail nothing. Gowns and pecuniary foundations, though of towns of gold, can never countervail the least sentence or syllable of wit. Forget this, and our American colleges will recede in their public importance, whilst they grow richer every year.

III. There goes in the world a notion that the scholar should be a recluse, a valetudinarian,—as unfit for any handiwork or public labor as a penknife for an axe. The so-called "practical men" sneer at speculative men, as if, because they speculate or *see*, they could do nothing. I have heard it said that the clergy,—who are always, more universally than any other class, the scholars of their day,—are addressed as women; that the rough, spontaneous conversation of men they do not hear, but only a mincing and diluted speech. They are often virtually disfranchised; and indeed there are advocates for their celibacy. As far as this is true of the studious classes, it is not just and wise. Action is with the scholar subordinate, but it is essential. Without it he is not yet man. Without it thought can never ripen into truth. Whilst the world hangs before the eye as a cloud of beauty, we cannot even see its beauty. Inaction is cowardice, but there can be no scholar without the heroic mind. The preamble of thought, the transition through which it passes from the unconscious to the conscious, is action. Only so much do I know, as I have lived. Instantly we know whose words are loaded with life, and whose not.

The world,—this shadow of the soul, or *other me,*—lies wide around. Its attractions are the keys which unlock my thoughts and make me acquainted with myself. I run eagerly into this resounding tumult. I grasp the hands of those next me, and take my place in the ring to suffer and to work, taught by an instinct that so shall the dumb abyss be vocal with speech. I pierce its order; I dissipate its fear; I dispose of it within the circuit of my expanding life. So much only of life as I know by experience, so much of the wilderness have I vanquished and planted, or so far have I extended my being, my dominion. I do not see how any man can afford, for the sake of his nerves and his nap, to spare any action in which he can partake. It is pearls and rubies to his discourse. Drudgery, calamity, exasperation, want, are instructors in eloquence and wisdom. The true scholar grudges every opportunity of action past by, as a loss of power. It is the raw material out of which the intellect moulds her splendid products. A strange process too, this by which experience is converted into thought, as a mulberry leaf is converted into satin. The manufacture goes forward at all hours.

The actions and events of our childhood and youth are now matters of calmest observation. They lie like fair pictures in the air. Not so with our recent actions,—with the business which we now have in hand. On this we are quite unable to speculate. Our affections as yet circulate through it. We no more feel or know it than we feel the feet, or the hand, or the brain of our body. The new deed is yet a part of life, —remains for a time immersed in our unconscious life. In some contemplative hour it detaches itself from the life like a ripe fruit, to become a thought of the mind. Instantly it is raised, transfigured; the corruptible has put on incorruption. Henceforth it is an object of beauty, however base its origin and neighborhood. Observe too the impossibility of antedating this act. In its grub state, it cannot fly, it cannot shine, it is a dull grub. But suddenly, without observation, the selfsame thing unfurls beautiful wings, and is an angel of wisdom. So is there no fact, no event, in our private history, which shall not, sooner or later, lose its adhesive, inert form, and astonish us by soaring from our body into the empyrean. Cradle and infancy, school and playground, the fear of boys, and dogs, and ferules, the love of little maids and berries, and many another fact that once filled the whole sky, are gone already; friend and relative, profession and party, town and country, nation and world, must also soar and sing.

Of course, he who has put forth his total strength in fit actions has the richest return of wisdom. I will not shut myself out of this globe of action, and transplant an oak into a flower-pot, there to hunger and pine; nor trust the revenue of some single faculty, and exhaust one vein of thought, much like those Savoyards, who, getting their livelihood by carving shepherds, shepherdesses, and smoking Dutchmen, for all Europe, went out one day to the mountain to find stock, and discovered that they had whittled up the last of their pine trees. Authors we have, in numbers, who have written out their vein, and who, moved by a commendable prudence, sail for Greece or Palestine, follow the trapper into the prairie, or ramble round Algiers, to replenish their merchantable stock.

If it were only for a vocabulary, the scholar would be covetous of action. Life is our dictionary. Years are well spent in country labors; in town; in the insight into trades and manufactures; in frank intercourse with many men and women; in science; in art; to the one end of mastering in all their facts a language by which to illustrate and embody our perceptions. I learn immediately from any speaker how much he has already lived, through the poverty or the splendor of his speech. Life lies behind us as the quarry from whence we get tiles and copestones for the masonry of to-day. This is the way to learn grammar. Colleges and books only copy the language which the field and the work-yard made.

But the final value of action, like that of books, and better than books, is that it is a resource. That great principle of Undulation in nature, that shows itself in the inspiring and expiring of the breath; in desire and satiety; in the ebb and flow of the sea; in day and night; in heat and cold; and, as yet more deeply ingrained in every atom and every fluid, is known to us under the name of Polarity,—these "fits of easy transmission and reflection," as Newton called them, are the law of nature because they are the law of spirit.

The mind now thinks, now acts, and each fit reproduces the other. When the artist has exhausted his materials, when the fancy no longer paints, when thoughts are no longer apprehended and books are a weariness,—he has always the resource *to live*. Character is higher than intellect. Thinking is the function. Living is the functionary. The stream retreats to its source. A great soul will be strong to live, as well as strong to think. Does he lack organ or medium to impart his truths? He

can still fall back on this elemental force of living them. This is a total act. Thinking is a partial act. Let the grandeur of justice shine in his affairs. Let the beauty of affection cheer his lowly roof. Those "far from fame," who dwell and act with him, will feel the force of his constitution in the doings and passages of the day better than it can be measured by any public and designed display. Time shall teach him that the scholar loses no hour which the man lives. Herein he unfolds the sacred germ of his instinct, screened from influence. What is lost in seemliness is gained in strength. Not out of those on whom systems of education have exhausted their culture, comes the helpful giant to destroy the old or to build the new, but out of unhandselled savage nature; out of terrible Druids and Berserkers come at last Alfred and Shakespeare.

I hear therefore with joy whatever is beginning to be said of the dignity and necessity of labor to every citizen. There is virtue yet in the hoe and the spade, for learned as well as for unlearned hands. And labor is everywhere welcome; always we are invited to work; only be this limitation observed, that a man shall not for the sake of wider activity sacrifice any opinion to the popular judgments and modes of action.

I have now spoken of the education of the scholar by nature, by books, and by action. It remains to say somewhat of his duties.

They are such as become Man Thinking. They may all be comprised in self-trust. The office of the scholar is to cheer, to raise, and to guide men by showing them facts amidst appearances. He plies the slow, unhonored, and unpaid task of observation. Flamsteed and Herschel,[2] in their

---

[2] John Flamsteed (1646-1719) was the first Astronomer Royal of England. Sir William Herschel (1738-1822) was the discoverer of the planet Uranus; his son, Sir John (1792-1871), was attracting attention by his astronomical observations at the time Emerson wrote this essay.

glazed observatories, may catalogue the stars with the praise of all men, and the results being splendid and useful, honor is sure. But he, in his private observatory, cataloguing obscure and nebulous stars of the human mind, which as yet no man has thought of as such,—watching days and months sometimes for a few facts; correcting still his old records;—must relinquish display and immediate fame. In the long period of his preparation he must betray often an ignorance and shiftlessness in popular arts, incurring the disdain of the able who shoulder him aside. Long he must stammer in his speech; often forego the living for the dead. Worse yet, he must accept—how often!—poverty and solitude. For the ease and pleasure of treading the old road, accepting the fashions, the education, the religion of society, he takes the cross of making his own, and, of course, the self-accusation, the faint heart, the frequent uncertainty and loss of time, which are the nettles and tangling vines in the way of the self-relying and self-directed; and the state of virtual hostility in which he seems to stand to society, and especially to educated society. For all this loss and scorn, what offset? He is to find consolation in exercising the highest functions of human nature. He is one who raises himself from private considerations and breathes and lives on public and illustrious thoughts. He is the world's eye. He is the world's heart. He is to resist the vulgar prosperity that retrogrades ever to barbarism, by preserving and communicating heroic sentiments, noble biographies, melodious verse, and the conclusions of history. Whatsoever oracles the human heart, in all emergencies, in all solemn hours, has uttered as its commentary on the world of actions,—these he shall receive and impart. And whatsoever new verdict Reason from her inviolable seat pronounces on the passing men and events of to-day,—this he shall hear and promulgate.

These being his functions, it becomes him to feel all confidence in himself, and to defer never to the popular cry. He and he only knows the world. The world of any moment is the merest appearance. Some great decorum, some fetish of a government, some ephemeral trade, or war, or man, is cried up by half mankind and cried down by the other half, as if all depended on this particular up or down. The odds are that the whole question is not worth the poorest thought which the scholar has lost in listening to the controversy. Let him not quit his belief that a popgun is a popgun, though the ancient and honorable of the earth affirm it to be the crack of doom. In silence, in steadiness, in severe abstraction, let him hold by himself; add observation to observation, patient of neglect, patient of reproach, and bide his own time,—happy enough if he can satisfy himself alone that this day he has seen something truly. Success treads on every right step. For the instinct is sure, that prompts him to tell his brother what he thinks. He then learns that in going down into the secrets of his own mind he has descended into the secrets of all minds. He learns that he who has mastered any law in his private thoughts, is master to that extent of all men whose language he speaks, and of all into whose language his own can be translated. The poet, in utter solitude remembering his spontaneous thoughts and recording them, is found to have recorded that which men in crowded cities find true for them also. The orator distrusts at first the fitness of his frank confessions, his want of knowledge of the persons he addresses, until he finds that he is the complement of his hearers;—that they drink his words because he fulfils for them their own nature; the deeper he dives into his privatest, secretest presentiment, to his wonder he finds this is the most acceptable, most public, and universally true. The people delight in it; the better part of every man feels, This is my music; this is myself.

In self-trust all the virtues are comprehended. Free should the scholar be,— free and brave. Free even to the definition of freedom, "without any hindrance that

does not arise out of his own constitution."
Brave; for fear is a thing which a scholar
by his very function puts behind him.
Fear always springs from ignorance. It is
a shame to him if his tranquillity, amid
dangerous times, arise from the presumption that like children and women his is a
protected class; or if he seek a temporary
peace by the diversion of his thoughts
from politics or vexed questions, hiding his
head like an ostrich in the flowering bushes,
peeping into microscopes, and turning
rhymes, as a boy whistles to keep his
courage up. So is the danger a danger
still; so is the fear worse. Manlike let
him turn and face it. Let him look into
its eye and search its nature, inspect its
origin,—see the whelping of this lion,—
which lies no great way back; he will then
find in himself a perfect comprehension of
its nature and extent; he will have made
his hands meet on the other side, and can
henceforth defy it and pass on superior.
The world is his who can see through its
pretension. What deafness, what stone-
blind custom, what overgrown error you
behold is there only by sufferance,—by
your sufferance. See it to be a lie, and you
have already dealt it its mortal blow.

Yes, we are the cowed,—we the trust-
less. It is a mischievous notion that we
are come late into nature; that the world
was finished a long time ago. As the world
was plastic and fluid in the hands of God,
so it is ever to so much of his attributes
as we bring to it. To ignorance and sin, it
is flint. They adapt themselves to it as
they may; but in proportion as a man has
any thing in him divine, the firmament
flows before him and takes his signet and
form. Not he is great who can alter matter, but he who can alter my state of
mind. They are the kings of the world
who give the color of their present thought
to all nature and all art, and persuade
men by the cheerful serenity of their carrying the matter, that this thing which
they do is the apple which the ages have
desired to pluck, now at last ripe, and inviting nations to the harvest. The great

man makes the great thing. Wherever Mac-
donald sits, there is the head of the table.
Linnæus makes botany the most alluring
of studies, and wins it from the farmer
and the herb-woman; Davy, chemistry; and
Cuvier, fossils. The day is always his who
works in it with serenity and great aims.
The unstable estimates of men crowd to
him whose mind is filled with a truth, as
the heaped waves of the Atlantic follow
the moon.

For this self-trust, the reason is deeper
than can be fathomed,—darker than can
be enlightened. I might not carry with me
the feeling of my audience in stating my
own belief. But I have already shown the
ground of my hope, in adverting to the
doctrine that man is one. I believe man
has been wronged; he has wronged himself. He has almost lost the light that can
lead him back to his prerogatives. Men are
become of no account. Men in history,
men in the world of to-day, are bugs, are
spawn, and are called "the mass" and
"the herd." In a century, in a millennium,
one or two men; that is to say, one or
two approximations to the right state of
every man. All the rest behold in the hero
or the poet their own green and crude
being,—ripened; yes, and are content to be
less, so *that* may attain to its full stature.
What a testimony, full of grandeur, full
of pity, is borne to the demands of his
own nature, by the poor clansman, the
poor partisan, who rejoices in the glory of
his chief. The poor and the low find some
amends to their immense moral capacity,
for their acquiescence in a political and
social inferiority. They are content to be
brushed like flies from the path of a great
person, so that justice shall be done by
him to that common nature which it is
the dearest desire of all to see enlarged
and glorified. They sun themselves in the
great man's light, and feel it to be their
own element. They cast the dignity of
man from their down-trod selves upon the
shoulders of a hero, and will perish to add
one drop of blood to make that great heart
beat, those giant sinews combat and con-

quer. He lives for us, and we live in him.

Men, such as they are, very naturally seek money or power; and power because it is as good as money,—the "spoils," so called, "of office." And why not? for they aspire to the highest, and this, in their sleep-walking, they dream is highest. Wake them and they shall quit the false good and leap to the true, and leave governments to clerks and desks. This revolution is to be wrought by the gradual domestication of the idea of Culture. The main enterprise of the world for splendor, for extent, is the upbuilding of a man. Here are the materials strewn along the ground. The private life of one man shall be a more illustrious monarchy, more formidable to its enemy, more sweet and serene in its influence to its friend, than any kingdom in history. For a man, rightly viewed, comprehendeth the particular natures of all men. Each philosopher, each bard, each actor has only done for me, as by a delegate, what one day I can do for myself. The books which once we valued more than the apple of the eye, we have quite exhausted. What is that but saying that we have come up with the point of view which the universal mind took through the eyes of one scribe; we have been that man, and have passed on. First, one, then another, we drain all cisterns, and waxing greater by all these supplies, we crave a better and more abundant food. The man has never lived that can feed us ever. The human mind cannot be enshrined in a person who shall set a barrier on any one side to this unbounded, unboundable empire. It is one central fire, which, flaming now out of the lips of Etna, lightens the capes of Sicily, and now out of the throat of Vesuvius, illuminates the towers and vineyards of Naples. It is one light which beams out of a thousand stars. It is one soul which animates all men.

But I have dwelt perhaps tediously upon this abstraction of the Scholar. I ought not to delay longer to add what I have to say

of nearer reference to the time and to this country.

Historically, there is thought to be a difference in the ideas which predominate over successive epochs, and there are data for marking the genius of the Classic, of the Romantic, and now of the Reflective or Philosophical age. With the views I have intimated of the oneness or the identity of the mind through all individuals, I do not much dwell on these differences. In fact, I believe each individual passes through all three. The boy is a Greek; the youth, romantic; the adult, reflective. I deny not, however, that a revolution in the leading idea may be distinctly enough traced.

Our age is bewailed as the age of Introversion. Must that needs be evil? We, it seems, are critical; we are embarrassed with second thoughts; we cannot enjoy any thing for hankering to know whereof the pleasure consists; we are lined with eyes; we see with our feet; the time is infected with Hamlet's unhappiness,—

"Sicklied o'er with the pale cast of
        thought." [3]

It is so bad then? Sight is the last thing to be pitied. Would we be blind? Do we fear lest we should outsee nature and God, and drink truth dry? I look upon the discontent of the literary class as a mere announcement of the fact that they find themselves not in the state of mind of their fathers, and regret the coming state as untried; as a boy dreads the water before he has learned that he can swim. If there is any period one would desire to be born in, is it not the age of Revolution; when the old and the new stand side by side and admit of being compared; when the energies of all men are searched by fear and by hope; when the historic glories of the old can be compensated by the rich possibilities of the new era? This time, like all times, is a very good one, if we but know what to do with it.

I read with some joy of the auspicious

[3] *Hamlet*, Act III, scene 1.

signs of the coming days, as they glimmer already through poetry and art, through philosophy and science, through church and state.

One of these signs is the fact that the same movement which effected the elevation of what was called the lowest class in the state, assumed in literature a very marked and as benign an aspect. Instead of the sublime and beautiful, the near, the low, the common, was explored and poetized. That which had been negligently trodden under foot by those who were harnessing and provisioning themselves for long journeys into far countries, is suddenly found to be richer than all foreign parts. The literature of the poor, the feelings of the child, the philosophy of the street, the meaning of household life, are the topics of the time. It is a great stride. It is a sign—is it not?—of new vigor when the extremities are made active, when currents of warm life run into the hands and the feet. I ask not for the great, the remote, the romantic; what is doing in Italy or Arabia; what is Greek art, or Provençal minstrelsy;[4] I embrace the common, I explore and sit at the feet of the familiar, the low. Give me insight into to-day, and you may have the antique and future worlds. What would we really know the meaning of? The meal in the firkin; the milk in the pan; the ballad in the street; the news of the boat; the glance of the eye; the form and the gait of the body;—show me the ultimate reason of these matters; show me the sublime presence of the highest spiritual cause lurking, as always it does lurk, in these suburbs and extremities of nature; let me see every trifle bristling with the polarity that ranges it instantly on an eternal law; and the shop, the plough, and the ledger referred to the like cause by which light undulates and poets sing;—and the world lies no longer a dull miscellany and lumber-room, but has form and order; there is no trifle, there is no puzzle, but one design unites and animates the farthest pinnacle and the lowest trench.

This idea has inspired the genius of Goldsmith, Burns, Cowper, and, in a newer time, of Goethe, Wordsworth, and Carlyle. This idea they have differently followed and with various success. In contrast with their writing, the style of Pope, of Johnson, of Gibbon, looks cold and pedantic. This writing is blood-warm. Man is surprised to find that things near are not less beautiful and wondrous than things remote. The near explains the far. The drop is a small ocean. A man is related to all nature. This perception of the worth of the vulgar is fruitful in discoveries. Goethe, in this very thing the most modern of the moderns, has shown us, as none ever did, the genius of the ancients.

There is one man of genius who has done much for this philosophy of life, whose literary value has never yet been rightly estimated;—I mean Emanuel Swedenborg.[5] The most imaginative of men, yet writing with the precision of a mathematician, he endeavored to engraft a purely philosophical Ethics on the popular Christianity of his time. Such an attempt of course must have difficulty which no genius could surmount. But he saw and showed the connection between nature and the affections of the soul. He pierced the emblematic or spiritual character of the visible, audible, tangible world. Especially did his shade-loving muse hover over and interpret the lower parts of nature; he showed the mysterious bond that allies moral evil to the foul material forms, and has given in epical parables a theory of insanity, of beasts, of unclean and fearful things.

Another sign of our times, also marked by an analogous political movement, is the new importance given to the single person. Every thing that tends to insulate the individual,—to surround him with barriers

---

[4] The lyric poetry of southern France, in what is known as the Provençal dialect. It flourished especially in the 12th, 13th, and 14th centuries.

[5] Emerson later wrote an essay on Swedenborg, the famous Swedish mystic and theologian (1688-1772).

of natural respect, so that each man shall feel the world is his, and man shall treat with man as a sovereign state with a sovereign state,—tends to true union as well as greatness. "I learned," said the melancholy Pestalozzi,[6] "that no man in God's wide earth is either willing or able to help any other man." Help must come from the bosom alone. The scholar is that man who must take up into himself all the ability of the time, all the contributions of the past, all the hopes of the future. He must be an university of knowledges. If there be one lesson more than another which should pierce his ear, it is, The world is nothing, the man is all; in yourself is the law of all nature, and you know not yet how a globule of sap ascends; in yourself slumbers the whole of Reason; it is for you to know all; it is for you to dare all. Mr. President and Gentlemen, this confidence in the unsearched might of man belongs, by all motives, by all prophecy, by all preparation, to the American Scholar. We have listened too long to the courtly muses of Europe. The spirit of the American freeman is already suspected to be timid, imitative, tame. Public and private avarice make the air we breathe thick and fat. The scholar is decent, indolent, complaisant. See already the tragic consequence. The mind of this country, taught to aim at low objects, eats upon itself. There is no work for any but the decorous and the complaisant. Young men of the fairest promise, who begin life upon our shores, inflated by the mountain winds, shined upon by all the stars of God, find the earth below not in unison with these, but are hindered from action by the disgust which the principles on which business is managed inspire, and turn drudges, or die of disgust, some of them suicides. What is the remedy? They did not yet see, and thousands of young men as hopeful now crowding to the barriers for the career do not yet see, that if the single man plant himself indomitably on his instincts, and there abide, the huge world will come round to him. Patience,—patience; with the shades

of all the good and great for company; and for solace the perspective of your own infinite life; and for work the study and the communication of principles, the making those instincts prevalent, the conversion of the world. Is it not the chief disgrace in the world, not to be an unit;—not to be reckoned one character;—not to yield that peculiar fruit which each man was created to bear, but to be reckoned in the gross, in the hundred, or the thousand, of the party, the section, to which we belong; and our opinion predicted geographically, as the north, or the south? Not so, brothers and friends—please God, ours shall not be so. We will walk on our own feet; we will work with our own hands; we will speak our own minds. The study of letters shall be no longer a name for pity, for doubt, and for sensual indulgence. The dread of man and the love of man shall be a wall of defence and a wreath of joy around all. A nation of men will for the first time exist, because each believes himself inspired by the Divine Soul which also inspires all men.

SELF-RELIANCE
[1841]

"Ne te quæsiveris extra." [1]

"Man is his own star; and the soul that can
Render an honest and a perfect man
Commands all light, all influence, all fate;
Nothing to him falls early or too late.
Our acts our angels are, or good or ill,
Our fatal shadows that walk by us still."
—Epilogue to Beaumont and
Fletcher's *Honest Man's Fortune.*

Cast the bantling on the rocks,
Suckle him with the she-wolf's teat,
Wintered with the hawk and fox,
Power and speed be hands and feet.

---

[6] Johann Heinrich Pestalozzi (1746-1827), famous Swiss writer and educator.
[1] Seek not outside thyself.

I read the other day some verses written by an eminent painter [2] which were original and not conventional. The soul always hears an admonition in such lines, let the subject be what it may. The sentiment they instil is of more value than any thought they may contain. To believe your own thought, to believe that what is true for you in your private heart is true for all men,—that is genius. Speak your latent conviction, and it shall be the universal sense; for the inmost in due time becomes the outmost, and our first thought is rendered back to us by the trumpets of the Last Judgment. Familiar as the voice of the mind is to each, the highest merit we ascribe to Moses, Plato and Milton is that they set at naught books and traditions, and spoke not what men, but what *they* thought. A man should learn to detect and watch that gleam of light which flashes across his mind from within, more than the lustre of the firmament of bards and sages. Yet he dismisses without notice his thought, because it is his. In every work of genius we recognize our own rejected thoughts; they come back to us with a certain alienated majesty. Great works of art have no more affecting lesson for us than this. They teach us to abide by our spontaneous impression with good-humored inflexibility then most when the whole cry of voices is on the other side. Else tomorrow a stranger will say with masterly good sense precisely what we have thought and felt all the time, and we shall be forced to take with shame our own opinion from another.

There is a time in every man's education when he arrives at the conviction that envy is ignorance; that imitation is suicide; that he must take himself for better for worse as his portion; that though the wide universe is full of good, no kernel of nourishing corn can come to him but through his toil bestowed on that plot of ground which is given to him to till. The power which resides in him is new in nature, and none but he knows what that is which he can do, nor does he know until

he has tried. Not for nothing one face, one character, one fact, makes much impression on him, and another none. This sculpture in the memory is not without preëstablished harmony. The eye was placed where one ray should fall, that it might testify of that particular ray. We but half express ourselves, and are ashamed of that divine idea which each of us represents. It may be safely trusted as proportionate and of good issues, so it be faithfully imparted, but God will not have his work made manifest by cowards. A man is relieved and gay when he has put his heart into his work and done his best; but what he has said or done otherwise shall give him no peace. It is a deliverance which does not deliver. In the attempt his genius deserts him; no muse befriends; no invention, no hope.

Trust thyself: every heart vibrates to that iron string. Accept the place the divine providence has found for you, the society of your contemporaries, the connection of events. Great men have always done so, and confided themselves childlike to the genius of their age, betraying their perception that the absolutely trustworthy was seated at their heart, working through their hands, predominating in all their being. And we are now men, and must accept in the highest mind the same transcendent destiny; and not mirrors and invalids in a protected corner, not cowards fleeing before a revolution, but guides, redeemers and benefactors, obeying the Almighty effort and advancing on Chaos and the Dark.

What pretty oracles nature yields us on this text in the face and behavior of children, babes, and even brutes! That divided and rebel mind, that distrust of a sentiment because our arithmetic has computed the strength and means opposed to our purpose, these have not. Their mind being whole, their eye is as yet unconquered, and when we look in their faces we are

---

[2] Washington Allston (1779-1843), American painter and author.

disconcerted. Infancy conforms to nobody; all conform to it; so that one babe commonly makes four or five out of the adults who prattle and play to it. So God has armed youth and puberty and manhood no less with its own piquancy and charm, and made it enviable and gracious and its claims not to be put by, if it will stand by itself. Do not think the youth has no force, because he cannot speak to you and me. Hark! in the next room his voice is sufficiently clear and emphatic. It seems he knows how to speak to his contemporaries. Bashful or bold then, he will know how to make us seniors very unnecessary.

The nonchalance of boys who are sure of a dinner, and would disdain as much as a lord to do or say aught to conciliate one, is the healthy attitude of human nature. A boy is in the parlor what the pit is in the playhouse; independent, irresponsible, looking out from his corner on such people and facts as pass by, he tries and sentences them on their merits, in the swift, summary way of boys, as good, bad, interesting, silly, eloquent, troublesome. He cumbers himself never about consequences, about interests; he gives an independent, genuine verdict. You must court him; he does not court you. But the man is as it were clapped into jail by his consciousness. As soon as he has once acted or spoken with *éclat* he is a committed person, watched by the sympathy or the hatred of hundreds, whose affections must now enter into his account. There is no Lethe for this. Ah, that he could pass again into his neutrality! Who can thus avoid all pledges and, having observed, observe again from the same unaffected, unbiased, unbribable, unaffrighted innocence,—must always be formidable. He would utter opinions on all passing affairs, which being seen to be not private but necessary, would sink like darts into the ear of men and put them in fear.

These are the voices which we hear in solitude, but they grow faint and inaudible as we enter into the world. Society everywhere is in conspiracy against the manhood of every one of its members. Society is a joint-stock company, in which the members agree, for the better securing of his bread to each share-holder, to surrender the liberty and culture of the eater. The virtue in most request is conformity. Self-reliance is its aversion. It loves not realities and creators, but names and customs.

Whoso would be a man, must be a nonconformist. He who would gather immortal palms must not be hindered by the name of goodness, but must explore if it be goodness. Nothing is at last sacred but the integrity of your own mind. Absolve you to yourself, and you shall have the suffrage of the world. I remember an answer which when quite young I was prompted to make to a valued adviser who was wont to importune me with the dear old doctrines of the church. On my saying, "What have I to do with the sacredness of traditions, if I live wholly from within?" my friend suggested,—"But these impulses may be from below, not from above." I replied, "They do not seem to me to be such; but if I am the Devil's child, I will live then from the Devil." No law can be sacred to me but that of my nature. Good and bad are but names very readily transferable to that or this; the only right is what is after my constitution; the only wrong what is against it. A man is to carry himself in the presence of all opposition as if every thing were titular and ephemeral but he. I am ashamed to think how easily we capitulate to badges and names, to large societies and dead institutions. Every decent and well-spoken individual affects and sways me more than is right. I ought to go upright and vital, and speak the rude truth in all ways. If malice and vanity wear the coat of philanthropy, shall that pass? If an angry bigot assumes this bountiful cause of Abolition, and comes to me with his last news from Barbadoes,[3] why should I not say to him, "Go love thy infant; love thy wood-chopper; be good-na-

---

[3] Slavery was abolished in this island of the British West Indies in 1834.

tured and modest; have that grace; and never varnish your hard, uncharitable ambition with this incredible tenderness for black folk a thousand miles off. Thy love afar is spite at home." Rough and graceless would be such greeting, but truth is handsomer than the affectation of love. Your goodness must have some edge to it, —else it is none. The doctrine of hatred must be preached, as the counteraction of the doctrine of love, when that pules and whines. I shun father and mother and wife and brother when my genius calls me. I would write on the lintels of the doorpost, *Whim*. I hope it is somewhat better than whim at last, but we cannot spend the day in explanation. Expect me not to show cause why I seek or why I exclude company. Then again, do not tell me, as a good man did to-day, of my obligation to put all poor men in good situations. Are they *my* poor? I tell thee, thou foolish philanthropist, that I grudge the dollar, the dime, the cent I give to such men as do not belong to me and to whom I do not belong. There is a class of persons to whom by all spiritual affinity I am bought and sold; for them I will go to prison if need be; but your miscellaneous popular charities; the education at college of fools; the building of meeting-houses to the vain end to which many now stand; alms to sots, and the thousand-fold Relief Societies;—though I confess with shame I sometimes succumb and give the dollar, it is a wicked dollar, which by and by I shall have the manhood to withhold.

Virtues are, in the popular estimate, rather the exception than the rule. There is the man *and* his virtues. Men do what is called a good action, as some piece of courage or charity, much as they would pay a fine in expiation of daily non-appearance on parade. Their works are done as an apology or extenuation of their living in the world,—as invalids and the insane pay a high board. Their virtues are penances. I do not wish to expiate, but to live. My life is for itself and not for a spectacle. I much prefer that it should be of a lower strain, so it be genuine and equal, than that it should be glittering and unsteady. I wish it to be sound and sweet, and not to need diet and bleeding. I ask primary evidence that you are a man, and refuse this appeal from the man to his actions. I know that for myself it makes no difference whether I do or forbear those actions which are reckoned excellent. I cannot consent to pay for a privilege where I have intrinsic right. Few and mean as my gifts may be, I actually am, and do not need for my own assurance or the assurance of my fellows any secondary testimony.

What I must do is all that concerns me, not what the people think. This rule, equally arduous in actual and in intellectual life, may serve for the whole distinction between greatness and meanness. It is the harder because you will always find those who think they know what is your duty better than you know it. It is easy in the world to live after the world's opinion; it is easy in solitude to live after our own; but the great man is he who in the midst of the crowd keeps with perfect sweetness the independence of solitude.

The objection to conforming to usages that have become dead to you is that it scatters your force. It loses your time and blurs the impression of your character. If you maintain a dead church, contribute to a dead Bible-society, vote with a great party either for the government or against it, spread your table like base housekeepers, —under all these screens I have difficulty to detect the precise man you are: and of course so much force is withdrawn from your proper life. But do your work, and I shall know you. Do your work, and you shall reinforce yourself. A man must consider what a blind-man's-buff is this game of conformity. If I know your sect I anticipate your argument. I hear a preacher announce for his text and topic the expediency of one of the institutions of his church. Do I not know beforehand that not possibly can he say a new and spontaneous word? Do I not know that with all this ostentation of examining the grounds of the institution he will do no such thing? Do I not know that he is pledged to himself not to look but at one side, the permitted side, not as a man, but as a parish minister? He is a retained attorney, and these airs of the bench are the emptiest affectation. Well, most men have bound their eyes with one or another handkerchief, and attached themselves to some one of these communities of opinion. This conformity makes them not false in a few particulars, authors of a few lies, but false in all particulars. Their every truth is not quite true. Their two is not the real two, their four not the real four; so that every word they say chagrins us and we know not where to begin to set them right. Meantime nature is not slow to equip us in the prison-uniform of the party to which we adhere. We come to wear one cut of face and figure, and acquire by degrees the gentlest asinine expression. There is a mortifying experience in particular, which does not fail to wreak itself also in the general history; I mean "the foolish face of praise,"[4] the forced smile which we put on in company where we do not feel at ease, in answer to conversation which does not interest us. The muscles, not spontaneously moved but moved by a low usurping wilfulness, grow tight about the outline of the face, with the most disagreeable sensation.

For nonconformity the world whips you with its displeasure. And therefore a man must know how to estimate a sour face. The by-standers look askance on him in the public street or in the friend's parlor. If this aversion had its origin in contempt and resistance like his own he might well go home with a sad countenance; but the sour faces of the multitude, like their sweet faces, have no deep cause, but are put on and off as the wind blows and a newspaper directs. Yet is the discontent of the multitude more formidable than that of the senate and the college. It is easy enough for a firm man who knows the world to brook the rage of the cultivated classes. Their rage is decorous and prudent, for

they are timid, as being very vulnerable themselves. But when to their feminine rage the indignation of the people is added, when the ignorant and the poor are aroused, when the unintelligent brute force that lies at the bottom of society is made to growl and mow, it needs the habit of magnanimity and religion to treat it godlike as a trifle of no concernment.

The other terror that scares us from self-trust is our consistency; a reverence for our past act or word because the eyes of others have no other data for computing our orbit than our past acts, and we are loth to disappoint them.

But why should you keep your head over your shoulder? Why drag about this corpse of your memory, lest you contradict somewhat you have stated in this or that public place? Suppose you should contradict yourself; what then? It seems to be a rule of wisdom never to rely on your memory alone, scarcely even in acts of pure memory, but to bring the past for judgment into the thousand-eyed present, and live ever in a new day. In your metaphysics you have denied personality to the Deity, yet when the devout motions of the soul come, yield to them heart and life, though they should clothe God with shape and color. Leave your theory, as Joseph his coat in the hand of the harlot, and flee.

A foolish consistency is the hobgoblin of little minds, adored by little statesmen and philosophers and divines. With consistency a great soul has simply nothing to do. He may as well concern himself with his shadow on the wall. Speak what you think now in hard words and to-morrow speak what to-morrow thinks in hard words again, though it contradict every thing you said to-day.—"Ah, so you shall be sure to be misunderstood."—Is it so bad then to be misunderstood? Pythagoras was misunderstood, and Socrates, and Jesus, and Luther, and Copernicus, and Galileo, and Newton, and every pure and wise spirit

[4] Quoted from Alexander Pope's *Epistle to Dr. Arbuthnot*, in the satire on Addison.

that ever took flesh. To be great is to be misunderstood.

I suppose no man can violate his nature. All the sallies of his will are rounded in by the law of his being, as the inequalities of Andes and Himmaleh are insignificant in the curve of the sphere. Nor does it matter how you gauge and try him. A character is like an acrostic or Alexandrian stanza; —read it forward, backward, or across, it still spells the same thing. In this pleasing contrite wood-life which God allows me, let me record day by day my honest thought without prospect or retrospect, and, I cannot doubt, it will be found symmetrical, though I mean it not and see it not. My book should smell of pines and resound with the hum of insects. The swallow over my window should interweave that thread or straw he carries in his bill into my web also. We pass for what we are. Character teaches above our wills. Men imagine that they communicate their virtue or vice only by overt actions, and do not see that virtue or vice emit a breath every moment.

There will be an agreement in whatever variety of actions, so they be each honest and natural in their hour. For of one will, the actions will be harmonious, however unlike they seem. These varieties are lost sight of at a little distance, at a little height of thought. One tendency unites them all. The voyage of the best ship is a zigzag line of a hundred tacks. See the line from a sufficient distance, and it strengthens itself to the average tendency. Your genuine action will explain itself and will explain your other genuine actions. Your conformity explains nothing. Act singly, and what you have already done singly will justify you now. Greatness appeals to the future. If I can be firm enough to-day to do right and scorn eyes, I must have done so much right before as to defend me now. Be it how it will, do right now. Always scorn appearances and you always may. The force of character is cumulative. All the foregone days of virtue work their health into this. What makes the majesty of the heroes of the senate and the field,

which so fills the imagination? The consciousness of a train of great days and victories behind. They shed a united light on the advancing actor. He is attended as by a visible escort of angels. That is it which throws thunder into Chatham's voice, and dignity into Washington's port, and America into Adams's eye. Honor is venerable to us because it is no ephemera. It is always ancient virtue. We worship it to-day because it is not of to-day. We love it and pay it homage because it is not a trap for our love and homage, but is self-dependent, self-derived, and therefore of an old immaculate pedigree, even if shown in a young person.

I hope in these days we have heard the last of conformity and consistency. Let the words be gazetted and ridiculous henceforward. Instead of the gong for dinner, let us hear a whistle from the Spartan fife. Let us never bow and apologize more. A great man is coming to eat at my house. I do not wish to please him; I wish that he should wish to please me. I will stand here for humanity, and though I would make it kind, I would make it true. Let us affront and reprimand the smooth mediocrity and squalid contentment of the times, and hurl in the face of custom and trade and office, the fact which is the upshot of all history, that there is a great responsible Thinker and Actor working wherever a man works; that a true man belongs to no other time or place, but is the centre of things. Where he is, there is nature. He measures you and all men and all events. Ordinarily, every body in society reminds us of somewhat else, or of some other person. Character, reality, reminds you of nothing else; it takes place of the whole creation. The man must be so much that he must make all circumstances indifferent. Every true man is a cause, a country, and an age; requires infinite spaces and numbers and time fully to accomplish his design;—and posterity seem to follow his steps as a train of clients. A man Cæsar is born, and for ages after we have a Roman Empire. Christ is born, and millions of minds so grow and cleave to his genius that he is confounded with virtue and the possible of man. An institution is the lengthened shadow of one man; as, Monachism, of the Hermit Antony;[5] the Reformation, of Luther; Quakerism, of Fox; Methodism, of Wesley; Abolition, of Clarkson.[6] Scipio, Milton called "the height of Rome;" and all history resolves itself very easily into the biography of a few stout and earnest persons.

Let a man then know his worth, and keep things under his feet. Let him not peep or steal, or skulk up and down with the air of a charity-boy, a bastard, or an interloper in the world which exists for him. But the man in the street, finding no worth in himself which corresponds to the force which built a tower or sculptured a marble god, feels poor when he looks on these. To him a palace, a statue, or a costly book have an alien and forbidding air, much like a gay equipage, and seem to say like that, "Who are you, Sir?" Yet they all are his, suitors for his notice, petitioners to his faculties that they will come out and take possession. The picture waits for my verdict; it is not to command me, but I am to settle its claims to praise. That popular fable of the sot who was picked up dead-drunk in the street, carried to the duke's house, washed and dressed and laid in the duke's bed, and, on his waking, treated with all obsequious ceremony like the duke, and assured that he had been insane, owes its popularity to the fact that it symbolizes so well the state of man, who is in the world a sort of sot, but now and then wakes up, exercises his reason and finds himself a true prince.[7]

Our reading is mendicant and sycophantic. In history our imagination plays us false. Kingdom and lordship, power and estate, are a gaudier vocabulary than private John and Edward in a small house and common day's work; but the things of life are the same to both; the sum total of both is the same. Why all this deference to Alfred and Scanderbeg[8] and Gus-

tavus?[9] Suppose they were virtuous; did they wear out virtue? As great a stake depends on your private act to-day as followed their public and renowned steps. When private men shall act with original views, the lustre will be transferred from the actions of kings to those of gentlemen.

The world has been instructed by its kings, who have so magnetized the eyes of nations. It has been taught by this colossal symbol the mutual reverence that is due from man to man. The joyful loyalty with which men have everywhere suffered the king, the noble, or the great proprietor to walk among them by a law of his own, make his own scale of men and things and reverse theirs, pay for benefits not with money but with honor, and represent the law in his person, was the hieroglyphic by which they obscurely signified their consciousness of their own right and comeliness, the right of every man.

The magnetism which all original action exerts is explained when we inquire the reason of self-trust. Who is the Trustee? What is the aboriginal Self, on which a universal reliance may be grounded? What is the nature and power of that science-baffling star, without parallax, without calculable elements, which shoots a ray of beauty even into trivial and impure actions, if the least mark of independence appear? The inquiry leads us to that source, at once the essence of genius, of virtue, and of life, which we call Spontaneity or Instinct. We denote this primary

[5] St. Anthony (c. 250-350), first Christian monk.

[6] Thomas Clarkson (1760-1846), English crusader against slavery and the slave trade.

[7] See the "Induction" of Shakespeare's *The Taming of the Shrew*.

[8] Iskander Bey (1403-1468), Albanian general who led the defence of his country against the Turks.

[9] This probably refers to Gustavus Adolphus (1594-1632), Swedish king; or possibly his grandfather Gustavus Vasa (1496-1560).

wisdom as Intuition, whilst all later teachings are tuitions. In that deep force, the last fact behind which analysis cannot go, all things find their common origin. For the sense of being which in calm hours arises, we know not how, in the soul, is not diverse from things, from space, from light, from time, from man, but one with them and proceeds obviously from the same source whence their life and being also proceed. We first share the life by which things exist and afterwards see them as appearances in nature and forget that we have shared their cause. Here is the fountain of action and of thought. Here are the lungs of that inspiration which giveth man wisdom and which cannot be denied without impiety and atheism. We lie in the lap of immense intelligence, which makes us receivers of its truth and organs of its activity. When we discern justice, when we discern truth, we do nothing of ourselves, but allow a passage to its beams. If we ask whence this comes, if we seek to pry into the soul that causes, all philosophy is at fault. Its presence or its absence is all we can affirm. Every man discriminates between the voluntary acts of his mind and his involuntary perceptions, and knows that to his involuntary perceptions a perfect faith is due. He may err in the expression of them, but he knows that these things are so, like day and night, not to be disputed. My wilful actions and acquisitions are but roving;—the idlest reverie, the faintest native emotion, command my curiosity and respect. Thoughtless people contradict as readily the statement of perceptions as of opinions, or rather much more readily; for they do not distinguish between perception and notion. They fancy that I choose to see this or that thing. But perception is not whimsical, but fatal. If I see a trait, my children will see it after me, and in course of time all mankind,—although it may chance that no one has seen it before me. For my perception of it is as much a fact as the sun.

The relations of the soul to the divine spirit are so pure that it is profane to seek to interpose helps. It must be that when God speaketh he should communicate, not one thing, but all things; should fill the world with his voice; should scatter forth light, nature, time, souls, from the centre of the present thought; and new date and new create the whole. Whenever a mind is simple and receives a divine wisdom, old things pass away,—means, teachers, texts, temples fall; it lives now, and absorbs past and future into the present hour. All things are made sacred by relation to it,—one as much as another. All things are dissolved to their centre by their cause, and in the universal miracle petty and particular miracles disappear. If therefore a man claims to know and speak of God and carries you backward to the phraseology of some old mouldered nation in another country, in another world, believe him not. Is the acorn better than the oak which is its fulness and completion? Is the parent better than the child into whom he has cast his ripened being? Whence then this worship of the past? The centuries are conspirators against the sanity and authority of the soul. Time and space are but physiological colors which the eye makes, but the soul is light: where it is, is day; where it was, is night; and history is an impertinence and an injury if it be any thing more than a cheerful apologue or parable of my being and becoming.

Man is timid and apologetic; he is no longer upright; he dares not say "I think," "I am," but quotes some saint or sage. He is ashamed before the blade of grass or the blowing rose. These roses under my window make no reference to former roses or to better ones; they are for what they are; they exist with God to-day. There is no time to them. There is simply the rose; it is perfect in every moment of its existence. Before a leaf-bud has burst, its whole life acts; in the full-blown flower there is no more; in the leafless root there is no less. Its nature is satisfied and it satisfies nature in all moments alike. But man postpones or remembers; he does not live in the present, but with reverted eye laments the past, or, heedless of the riches that surround him, stands on tiptoe to foresee the future. He cannot be happy and strong until he too lives with nature in the present, above time.

This should be plain enough. Yet see what strong intellects dare not yet hear God himself unless he speak the phraseology of I know not what David, or Jeremiah, or Paul. We shall not always set so great a price on a few texts, on a few lives. We are like children who repeat by rote the sentences of grandames and tutors, and, as they grow older, of the men of talents and character they chance to see, —painfully recollecting the exact words they spoke; afterwards, when they come into the point of view which those had who uttered these sayings, they understand them and are willing to let the words go; for at any time they can use words as good when occasion comes. If we live truly, we shall see truly. It is as easy for the strong man to be strong, as it is for the weak to be weak. When we have new perception, we shall gladly disburden the memory of its hoarded treasures as old rubbish. When a man lives with God, his voice shall be as sweet as the murmur of the brook and the rustle of the corn.

And now at last the highest truth on this subject remains unsaid; probably cannot be said; for all that we say is the far-off remembering of the intuition. That thought by what I can now nearest approach to say it, is this. When good is near you, when you have life in yourself, it is not by any known or accustomed way; you shall not discern the footprints of any other; you shall not see the face of man; you shall not hear any name;—the way, the thought, the good, shall be wholly strange and new. It shall exclude example and experience. You take the way from man, not to man. All persons that ever existed are its forgotten ministers. Fear and hope are alike beneath it. There is somewhat low even in hope. In the hour

of vision there is nothing that can be called gratitude, nor properly joy. The soul raised over passion beholds identity and eternal causation, perceives the self-existence of Truth and Right, and calms itself with knowing that all things go well. Vast spaces of nature, the Atlantic Ocean, the South Sea; long intervals of time, years, centuries, are of no account. This which I think and feel underlay every former state of life and circumstances, as it does underlie my present, and what is called life and what is called death.

Life only avails, not the having lived. Power ceases in the instant of repose; it resides in the moment of transition from a past to a new state, in the shooting of the gulf, in the darting to an aim. This one fact the world hates; that the soul *becomes;* for that forever degrades the past, turns all riches to poverty, all reputation to a shame, confounds the saint with the rogue, shoves Jesus and Judas equally aside. Why then do we prate of self-reliance? Inasmuch as the soul is present there will be power not confident but agent. To talk of reliance is a poor external way of speaking. Speak rather of that which relies because it works and is. Who has more obedience than I masters me, though he should not raise his finger. Round him I must revolve by the gravitation of spirits. We fancy it rhetoric when we speak of eminent virtue. We do not yet see that virtue is Height, and that a man or a company of men, plastic and permeable to principles, by the law of nature must overpower and ride all cities, nations, kings, rich men, poets, who are not.

This is the ultimate fact which we so quickly reach on this, as on every topic, the resolution of all into the ever-blessed ONE. Self-existence is the attribute of the Supreme Cause, and it constitutes the measure of good by the degree in which it enters into all lower forms. All things real are so by so much virtue as they contain. Commerce, husbandry, hunting, whaling, war, eloquence, personal weight, are somewhat, and engage my respect as examples of its presence and impure action. I see the same law working in nature for conservation and growth. Power is, in nature, the essential measure of right. Nature suffers nothing to remain in her kingdoms which cannot help itself. The genesis and maturation of a planet, its poise and orbit, the bended tree recovering itself from the strong wind, the vital resources of every animal and vegetable, are demonstrations of the self-sufficing and therefore self-relying soul.

Thus all concentrates: let us not rove; let us sit at home with the cause. Let us stun and astonish the intruding rabble of men and books and institutions by a simple declaration of the divine fact. Bid the invaders take the shoes from off their feet, for God is here within. Let our simplicity judge them, and our docility to our own law demonstrate the poverty of nature and fortune beside our native riches.

But now we are a mob. Man does not stand in awe of man, nor is his genius admonished to stay at home, to put itself in communication with the internal ocean, but it goes abroad to beg a cup of water of the urns of other men. We must go alone. I like the silent church before the service begins, better than any preaching. How far off, how cool, how chaste the persons look, begirt each one with a precinct or sanctuary! So let us always sit. Why should we assume the faults of our friend, or wife, or father, or child, because they sit around our hearth, or are said to have the same blood? All men have my blood and I all men's. Not for that will I adopt their petulance or folly, even to the extent of being ashamed of it. But your isolation must not be mechanical, but spiritual, that is, must be elevation. At times the whole world seems to be in conspiracy to importune you with emphatic trifles. Friend, client, child, sickness, fear, want, charity, all knock at once at thy closet door and say,—"Come out unto us." But keep thy state; come not into their confusion. The power men possess to annoy me I give them by a weak curiosity. No man can come near me but through my act. "What we love that we have, but by desire we bereave ourselves of the love."

If we cannot at once rise to the sanctities of obedience and faith, let us at least resist our temptations; let us enter into the state of war and wake Thor and Woden, courage and constancy, in our Saxon breasts. This is to be done in our smooth times by speaking the truth. Check this lying hospitality and lying affection. Live no longer to the expectation of these deceived and deceiving people with whom we converse. Say to them, "O father, O mother, O wife, O brother, O friend, I have lived with you after appearances hitherto. Henceforward I am the truth's. Be it known unto you that henceforward I obey no law less than the eternal law. I will have no covenants but proximities. I shall endeavor to nourish my parents, to support my family, to be the chaste husband of one wife,—but these relations I must fill after a new and unprecedented way. I appeal from your customs. I must be myself. I cannot break myself any longer for you, or you. If you can love me for what I am, we shall be the happier. If you cannot, I will still seek to deserve that you should. I will not hide my tastes or aversions. I will so trust that what is deep is holy, that I will do strongly before the sun and moon whatever inly rejoices me and the heart appoints. If you are noble, I will love you; if you are not, I will not hurt you and myself by hypocritical attentions. If you are true, but not in the same truth with me, cleave to your companions; I will seek my own. I do this not selfishly but humbly and truly. It is alike your interest, and mine, and all men's, however long we have dwelt in lies, to live in truth. Does this sound harsh to-day? You will soon love what is dictated by your nature as well as mine, and if we follow the truth it will bring us out safe at last."—But so may you give these friends pain. Yes, but I cannot sell my liberty and my power, to save their sensibility. Besides, all persons have their moments of reason, when they look out into the region of absolute truth; then will they justify me and do the same thing.

The populace think that your rejection of popular standards is a rejection of all standard, and mere antinomianism; and the bold sensualist will use the name of philosophy to gild his crimes. But the law of consciousness abides. There are two confessionals, in one or the other of which we must be shriven. You may fulfil your round of duties by clearing yourself in the *direct,* or in the *reflex* way. Consider whether you have satisfied your relations to father, mother, cousin, neighbor, town, cat and dog—whether any of these can upbraid you. But I may also neglect this reflex standard and absolve me to myself. I have my own stern claims and perfect circle. It denies the name of duty to many offices that are called duties. But if I can discharge its debts it enables me to dispense with the popular code. If any one imagines that this law is lax, let him keep its commandment one day.

And truly it demands something godlike in him who has cast off the common motives of humanity and has ventured to trust himself for a taskmaster. High be his heart, faithful his will, clear his sight, that he may in good earnest be doctrine, society, law, to himself, that a simple purpose may be to him as strong as iron necessity is to others!

If any man consider the present aspects of what is called by distinction *society,* he will see the need of these ethics. The sinew and heart of man seem to be drawn out, and we are become timorous, desponding whimperers. We are afraid of truth, afraid of fortune, afraid of death, and afraid of each other. Our age yields no great and perfect persons. We want men and women who shall renovate life and our social state, but we see that most natures are insolvent, cannot satisfy their own wants, have an ambition out of all proportion to their practical force and do lean and beg day and night continually.

Our housekeeping is mendicant, our arts, our occupations, our marriages, our religion we have not chosen, but society has chosen for us. We are parlor soldiers. We shun the rugged battle of fate, where strength is born.

If our young men miscarry in their first enterprises they lose all heart. If the young merchant fails, men say he is *ruined.* If the finest genius studies at one of our colleges and is not installed in an office within one year afterwards in the cities or suburbs of Boston or New York, it seems to his friends and to himself that he is right in being disheartened and in complaining the rest of his life. A sturdy lad from New Hampshire or Vermont, who in turn tries all the professions, who *teams it, farms it, peddles,* keeps a school, preaches, edits a newspaper, goes to Congress, buys a township, and so forth, in successive years, and always like a cat falls on his feet, is worth a hundred of these city dolls. He walks abreast with his days and feels no shame in not "studying a profession," for he does not postpone his life, but lives already. He has not one chance, but a hundred chances. Let a Stoic open the resources of man and tell men they are not leaning willows, but can and must detach themselves; that with the exercise of self-trust, new powers shall appear; that a man is the word made flesh, born to shed healing to the nations; that he should be ashamed of our compassion, and that the moment he acts from himself, tossing the laws, the books, idolatries and customs out of the window, we pity him no more but thank and revere him;—and that teacher shall restore the life of man to splendor and make his name dear to all history.

It is easy to see that a greater self-reliance must work a revolution in all the offices and relations of men; in their religion; in their education; in their pursuits; their modes of living; their association; in their property; in their speculative views.

1. In what prayers do men allow themselves! That which they call a holy office is not so much as brave and manly. Prayer

looks abroad and asks for some foreign addition to come through some foreign virtue, and loses itself in endless mazes of natural and supernatural, and mediatorial and miraculous. Prayer that craves a particular commodity, anything less than all good, is vicious. Prayer is the contemplation of the facts of life from the highest point of view. It is the soliloquy of a beholding and jubilant soul. It is the spirit of God pronouncing his works good. But prayer as a means to effect a private end is meanness and theft. It supposes dualism and not unity in nature and consciousness. As soon as the man is at one with God, he will not beg. He will then see prayer in all action. The prayer of the farmer kneeling in his field to weed it, the prayer of the rower kneeling with the stroke of his oar, are true prayers heard throughout nature, though for cheap ends. Caratach, in Fletcher's "Bonduca," when admonished to inquire the mind of the god Andate,[10] replies,—

"His hidden meaning lies in our endeavors;
Our valors are our best gods."

Another sort of false prayers are our regrets. Discontent is the want of self-reliance: it is infirmity of will. Regret calamities if you can thereby help the sufferer; if not, attend your own work and already the evil begins to be repaired. Our sympathy is just as base. We come to them who weep foolishly and sit down and cry for company, instead of imparting to them truth and health in rough electric shocks, putting them once more in communication with their own reason. The secret of fortune is joy in our hands. Welcome evermore to gods and men is the self-helping man. For him all doors are flung wide; him all tongues greet, all honors crown, all eyes follow with desire. Our love goes out to him and embraces him because he did not need it. We solicitously and apologetically caress and celebrate him because he held on his way and scorned our disapprobation. The gods love him because men hated him. "To the persevering mortal,"

said Zoroaster, "the blessed Immortals are swift."

As men's prayers are a disease of the will, so are their creeds a disease of the intellect. They say with those foolish Israelites, "Let not God speak to us, lest we die. Speak thou, speak any man with us, and we will obey." [11] Everywhere I am hindered of meeting God in my brother, because he has shut his own temple doors and recites fables merely of his brother's, or his brother's brother's God. Every new mind is a new classification. If it prove a mind of uncommon activity and power, a Locke, a Lavoisier, a Hutton, a Bentham, a Fourier,[12] it imposes its classification on other men, and lo! a new system. In proportion to the depth of the thought, and so to the number of the objects it touches and brings within reach of the pupil, is his complacency. But chiefly is this apparent in creeds and churches, which are also classifications of some powerful mind acting on the elemental thought of duty and man's relation to the Highest. Such is Calvinism, Quakerism, Swedenborgism. The pupil takes the same delight in subordinating every thing to the new terminology as a girl who has just learned botany in seeing a new earth and new seasons thereby. It will happen for a time that the pupil will find his intellectual power has grown by the study of his master's mind. But in all unbalanced minds the classification is idolized, passes for the end and not for a

---

[10] Andate, or Andraste, a Celtic deity. The quotation from Beaumont and Fletcher's *Bonduca* actually begins: "Her hidden meaning . . ." Act III, scene 1.

[11] Deuteronomy, v. 25-27.

[12] John Locke (1632-1704), often referred to by Emerson, was the father of English empiricism; Antoine Laurent Lavoisier (1743-1794) was the father of modern chemistry; James Hutton (1726-1797), Scottish geologist, was the originator of the theory of uniformitarianism; Jeremy Bentham (1748-1832) was a leading exponent of utilitarianism; François Marie Charles Fourier (1772-1837) was the founder of a social coöperative system named after him.

speedily exhaustible means, so that the walls of the system blend to their eye in the remote horizon with the walls of the universe; the luminaries of heaven seem to them hung on the arch their master built. They cannot imagine how you aliens have any right to see,—how you can see; "It must be somehow that you stole the light from us." They do not yet perceive that light, unsystematic, indomitable, will break into any cabin, even into theirs. Let them chirp awhile and call it their own. If they are honest and do well, presently their neat new pinfold will be too strait and low, will crack, will lean, will rot and vanish, and the immortal light, all young and joyful, million-orbed, million-colored, will beam over the universe as on the first morning.

2. It is for want of self-culture that the superstition of Travelling, whose idols are Italy, England, Egypt, retains its fascination for all educated Americans. They who made England, Italy, or Greece venerable in the imagination, did so by sticking fast where they were, like an axis of the earth. In manly hours we feel that duty is our place. The soul is no traveller; the wise man stays at home, and when his necessities, his duties, on any occasion call him from his house, or into foreign lands, he is at home still and shall make men sensible by the expression of his countenance that he goes, the missionary of wisdom and virtue, and visits cities and men like a sovereign and not like an interloper or a valet.

I have no churlish objection to the circumnavigation of the globe for the purposes of art, of study, and benevolence, so that the man is first domesticated, or does not go abroad with the hope of finding somewhat greater than he knows. He who travels to be amused, or to get somewhat which he does not carry, travels away from himself, and grows old even in youth among old things. In Thebes, in Palmyra, his will and mind have become old and dilapidated as they. He carries ruins to ruins.

Travelling is a fool's paradise. Our first journeys discover to us the indifference of places. At home I dream that at Naples, at Rome, I can be intoxicated with beauty and lose my sadness. I pack my trunk, embrace my friends, embark on the sea and at last wake up in Naples, and there beside me is the stern fact, the sad self, unrelenting, identical, that I fled from. I seek the Vatican and the palaces. I affect to be intoxicated with sights and suggestions, but I am not intoxicated. My giant goes with me wherever I go.

3. But the rage of travelling is a symptom of a deeper unsoundness affecting the whole intellectual action. The intellect is vagabond, and our system of education fosters restlessness. Our minds travel when our bodies are forced to stay at home. We imitate; and what is imitation but the travelling of the mind? Our houses are built with foreign taste; our shelves are garnished with foreign ornaments; our opinions, our tastes, our faculties lean, and follow the Past and the Distant. The soul created the arts wherever they have flourished. It was in his own mind that the artist sought his model. It was an application of his own thought to the thing to be done and the conditions to be observed. And why need we copy the Doric or the Gothic model? Beauty, convenience, grandeur of thought and quaint expression are as near to us as to any, and if the American artist will study with hope and love the precise thing to be done by him, considering the climate, the soil, the length of the day, the wants of the people, the habit and form of the government, he will create a house in which all these will find themselves fitted, and taste and sentiment will be satisfied also.

Insist on yourself; never imitate. Your own gift you can present every moment with the cumulative force of a whole life's cultivation; but of the adopted talent of another you have only an extemporaneous half possession. That which each can do best, none but his Maker can teach him. No man yet knows what it is, nor can, till that person has exhibited it. Where is the master who could have taught Shakspeare? Where is the master who could have instructed Franklin, or Washington, or Bacon, or Newton? Every great man is a unique. The Scipionism of Scipio is precisely that part he could not borrow. Shakspeare will never be made by the study of Shakspeare. Do that which is assigned you, and you cannot hope too much or dare too much. There is at this moment for you an utterance brave and grand as that of the colossal chisel of Phidias, or trowel of the Egyptians, or the pen of Moses or Dante, but different from all these. Not possibly will the soul, all rich, all eloquent, with thousand-cloven tongue, deign to repeat itself; but if you can hear what these patriarchs say, surely you can reply to them in the same pitch of voice; for the ear and the tongue are two organs of one nature. Abide in the simple and noble regions of thy life, obey thy heart, and thou shalt reproduce the Foreworld again.

4. As our Religion, our Education, our Art look abroad, so does our spirit of society. All men plume themselves on the improvement of society, and no man improves.

Society never advances. It recedes as fast on one side as it gains on the other. It undergoes continual changes; it is barbarous, it is civilized, it is christianized, it is rich, it is scientific; but this change is not amelioration. For every thing that is given something is taken. Society acquires new arts and loses old instincts. What a contrast between the well-clad, reading, writing, thinking American, with a watch, a pencil and a bill of exchange in his pocket, and the naked New Zealander, whose property is a club, a spear, a mat and an undivided twentieth of a shed to sleep under! But compare the health of the two men and you shall see that the white man has lost his aboriginal strength. If the traveller tell us truly, strike the savage with a broad-axe and in a day or two the flesh shall unite and heal as if you struck the blow into soft pitch, and the same blow shall send the white to his grave.

The civilized man has built a coach, but

has lost the use of his feet. He is supported on crutches, but lacks so much support of muscle. He has a fine Geneva watch, but he fails of the skill to tell the hour by the sun. A Greenwich nautical almanac he has, and so being sure of the information when he wants it, the man in the street does not know a star in the sky. The solstice he does not observe; the equinox he knows as little; and the whole bright calendar of the year is without a dial in his mind. His notebooks impair his memory; his libraries overload his wit; the insurance-office increases the number of accidents; and it may be a question whether machinery does not encumber; whether we have not lost by refinement some energy, by a Christianity, entrenched in establishments and forms, some vigor of wild virtue. For every Stoic was a Stoic; but in Christendom where is the Christian?

There is no more deviation in the moral standard than in the standard of height or bulk. No greater men are now than ever were. A singular equality may be observed between the great men of the first and of the last ages; nor can all the science, art, religion, and philosophy of the nineteenth century avail to educate greater men than Plutarch's heroes, three or four and twenty centuries ago. Not in time is the race progressive. Phocion, Socrates, Anaxagoras, Diogenes,[13] are great men, but they leave no class. He who is really of their class will not be called by their name, but will be his own man, and in his turn the founder of a sect. The arts and inventions of each period are only its costume and do not invigorate men. The harm of the improved machinery may compensate its good. Hudson and Behring accomplished so much in their fishing-boats as to astonish Parry and Franklin,[14] whose equipment exhausted

---

[13] Named as types of Greek philosophers.

[14] Henry Hudson (d. 1611) and Vitus Bering (1680-1741) were older navigators; Sir William Edward Parry (1790-1855) and Sir John Franklin (1786-1847) were arctic explorers of Emerson's time.

the resources of science and art. Galileo, with an opera-glass, discovered a more splendid series of celestial phenomena than any one since. Columbus found the New World in an undecked boat. It is curious to see the periodical disuse and perishing of means and machinery which were introduced with loud laudation a few years or centuries before. The great genius returns to essential man. We reckoned the improvements of the art of war among the triumphs of science, and yet Napoleon conquered Europe by the bivouac, which consisted of falling back on naked valor and disencumbering it of all aids. The Emperor held it impossible to make a perfect army, says Las Cases, "without abolishing our arms, magazines, commissaries and carriages, until, in imitation of the Roman custom, the soldier should receive his supply of corn, grind it in his hand-mill and bake his bread himself." [15]

Society is a wave. The wave moves onward, but the water of which it is composed does not. The same particle does not rise from the valley to the ridge. Its unity is only phenomenal. The persons who make up a nation to-day, next year die, and their experience dies with them.

And so the reliance on Property, including the reliance on governments which protect it, is the want of self-reliance. Men have looked away from themselves and at things so long that they have come to esteem the religious, learned and civil institutions as guards of property, and they deprecate assaults on these, because they feel them to be assaults on property. They measure their esteem of each other by what each has, and not by what each is. But a cultivated man becomes ashamed of his property, out of new respect for his nature. Especially he hates what he has if he see that it is accidental,—came to him by inheritance, or gift, or crime; then he feels that it is not having; it does not belong to him, has no root in him and merely lies there because no revolution or no robber takes it away. But that which a man is, does always by necessity acquire;

and what the man acquires, is living property, which does not wait the beck of rulers, or mobs, or revolutions, or fire, or storm, or bankruptcies, but perpetually renews itself wherever the man breathes. "Thy lot or portion of life," said the Caliph Ali, "is seeking after thee; therefore be at rest from seeking after it." [16] Our dependence on these foreign goods leads us to our slavish respect for numbers. The political parties meet in numerous conventions; the greater the concourse and with each new uproar of announcement, The delegation from Essex! The Democrats from New Hampshire! The Whigs of Maine! the young patriot feels himself stronger than before by a new thousand of eyes and arms. In like manner the reformers summon conventions and vote and resolve in multitude. Not so, O friends! will the God deign to enter and inhabit you, but by a method precisely the reverse. It is only as a man puts off all foreign support and stands alone that I see him to be strong and to prevail. He is weaker by every recruit to his banner. Is not a man better than a town? Ask nothing of men, and, in the endless mutation, thou only firm column must presently appear the upholder of all that surrounds thee. He who knows that power is inborn, that he is weak because he has looked for good out of him and elsewhere, and, so perceiving, throws himself unhesitatingly on his thought, instantly rights himself, stands in the erect position, commands his limbs, works miracles; just as a man who stands on his feet is stronger than a man who stands on his head.

So use all that is called Fortune. Most men gamble with her, and gain all, and lose all, as her wheel rolls. But do thou leave as unlawful these winnings, and deal with Cause and Effect, the chancellors of God. In the Will work and acquire, and

[15] From *Mémorial de Ste. Hélène*, by Comte Emmanuel Augustin Dieudonné, Marquis de Las Cases, Napoleon's Boswell.

[16] From the *Maxims* of the Caliph Ali, son-in-law of Mohammed.

thou hast chained the wheel of Chance, and shalt sit hereafter out of fear from her rotations. A political victory, a rise of rents, the recovery of your sick or the return of your absent friend, or some other favorable event raises your spirits, and you think good days are preparing for you. Do not believe it. Nothing can bring you peace but yourself. Nothing can bring you peace but the triumph of principles.

THE POET
[1844]

A moody child and wildly wise
Pursued the game with joyful eyes,
Which chose, like meteors, their way,
And rived the dark with private ray:
They overleapt the horizon's edge,
Searched with Apollo's privilege;
Through man, and woman, and sea, and
    star
Saw the dance of nature forward far;
Through worlds, and races, and terms, and
    times
Saw musical order, and pairing rhymes.

    Olympian bards who sung
    Divine ideas below,
    Which always find us young,
    And always keep us so.[1]

Those who are esteemed umpires of taste are often persons who have acquired some knowledge of admired pictures or sculptures, and have an inclination for whatever is elegant; but if you inquire whether they are beautiful souls, and whether their own acts are like fair pictures, you learn that they are selfish and sensual. Their cultivation is local, as if you should rub a log of dry wood in one spot to produce fire, all the rest remaining cold. Their knowledge of the fine arts is some study of rules and particulars, or some limited judgment of color or form, which is exercised for amusement or for show. It is a proof of the shallowness of the doctrine of beauty as it lies in the minds of our amateurs, that

men seem to have lost the perception of the instant dependence of form upon soul. There is no doctrine of forms in our philosophy. We were put into our bodies, as fire is put into a pan to be carried about; but there is no accurate adjustment between the spirit and the organ, much less is the latter the germination of the former. So in regard to other forms, the intellectual men do not believe in any essential dependence of the material world on thought and volition. Theologians think it a pretty air-castle to talk of the spiritual meaning of a ship or a cloud, of a city or a contract, but they prefer to come again to the solid ground of historical evidence; and even the poets are contented with a civil and conformed manner of living, and to write poems from the fancy, at a safe distance from their own experience. But the highest minds of the world have never ceased to explore the double meaning, or shall I say the quadruple or the centuple or much more manifold meaning, of every sensuous fact; Orpheus, Empedocles, Heraclitus, Plato, Plutarch, Dante, Swedenborg, and the masters of sculpture, picture and poetry. For we are not pans and barrows, nor even porters of the fire and torch-bearers, but children of the fire, made of it, and only the same divinity transmuted and at two or three removes, when we know least about it. And this hidden truth, that the fountains whence all this river of Time and its creatures floweth are intrinsically ideal and beautiful, draws us to the consideration of the nature and functions of the Poet, or the man of Beauty; to the means and materials he uses, and to the general aspect of the art in the present time.

The breadth of the problem is great, for the poet is representative. He stands among partial men for the complete man, and apprises us not of his wealth, but of the common wealth. The young man reveres men of genius, because, to speak truly, they are more himself than he is. They

[1] As in this case, Emerson often wrote his own epigraphs.

receive of the soul as he also receives, but they more. Nature enhances her beauty, to the eye of loving men, from their belief that the poet is beholding her shows at the same time. He is isolated among his contemporaries by truth and by his art, but with this consolation in his pursuits, that they will draw all men sooner or later. For all men live by truth and stand in need of expression. In love, in art, in avarice, in politics, in labor, in games, we study to utter our painful secret. The man is only half himself, the other half is his expression.

Notwithstanding this necessity to be published, adequate expression is rare. I know not how it is that we need an interpreter, but the great majority of men seem to be minors, who have not yet come into possession of their own, or mutes, who cannot report the conversation they have had with nature. There is no man who does not anticipate a supersensual utility in the sun and stars, earth and water. These stand and wait to render him a peculiar service. But there is some obstruction or some excess of phlegm in our constitution, which does not suffer them to yield the due effect. Too feeble fall the impressions of nature on us to make us artists. Every touch should thrill. Every man should be so much an artist that he could report in conversation what had befallen him. Yet, in our experience, the rays or appulses have sufficient force to arrive at the senses, but not enough to reach the quick and compel the reproduction of themselves in speech. The poet is the person in whom these powers are in balance, the man without impediment, who sees and handles that which others dream of, traverses the whole scale of experience, and is representative of man, in virtue of being the largest power to receive and to impart.

For the Universe has three children, born at one time, which reappear under different names in every system of thought, whether they be called cause, operation and effect; or, more poetically, Jove, Pluto, Neptune; or, theologically, the Father, the Spirit and the Son; but which we will call here the Knower, the Doer and the Sayer. These stand respectively for the love of truth, for the love of good, and for the love of beauty. These three are equal. Each is that which he is, essentially, so that he cannot be surmounted or analyzed, and each of these three has the power of the others latent in him, and his own patent.

The poet is the sayer, the namer, and represents beauty. He is a sovereign, and stands on the centre. For the world is not painted or adorned, but is from the beginning beautiful; and God has not made some beautiful things, but Beauty is the creator of the universe. Therefore the poet is not any permissive potentate, but is emperor in his own right. Criticism is infested with a cant of materialism, which assumes that manual skill and activity is the first merit of all men, and disparages such as say and do not, overlooking the fact that some men, namely poets, are natural sayers, sent into the world to the end of expression, and confounds them with those whose province is action but who quit it to imitate the sayers. But Homer's words are as costly and admirable to Homer as Agamemnon's victories are to Agamemnon. The poet does not wait for the hero or the sage, but, as they act and think primarily, so he writes primarily what will and must be spoken, reckoning the others, though primaries also, yet, in respect to him, secondaries and servants; as sitters or models in the studio of a painter, or as assistants who bring building-materials to an architect.

For poetry was all written before time was, and whenever we are so finely organized that we can penetrate into that region where the air is music, we hear those primal warblings and attempt to write them down, but we lose ever and anon a word or a verse and substitute something of our own, and thus miswrite the poem. The men of more delicate ear write down these cadences more faithfully, and these transcripts, though imperfect, become the songs of the nations. For nature is as truly beautiful as it is good, or as it is reasonable, and must as much appear as it must be done, or be known. Words and deeds are quite indifferent modes of the divine energy. Words are also actions, and actions are a kind of words.

The sign and credentials of the poet are that he announces that which no man foretold. He is the true and only doctor; he knows and tells; he is the only teller of news, for he was present and privy to the appearance which he describes. He is a beholder of ideas and an utterer of the necessary and causal. For we do not speak now of men of poetical talents, or of industry and skill in metre, but of the true poet. I took part in a conversation the other day concerning a recent writer of lyrics, a man of subtle mind, whose head appeared to be a music-box of delicate tunes and rhythms, and whose skill and command of language we could not sufficiently praise. But when the question arose whether he was not only a lyrist but a poet, we were obliged to confess that he is plainly a contemporary, not an eternal man. He does not stand out of our low limitations, like a Chimborazo [2] under the line, running up from a torrid base through all the climates of the globe, with belts of the herbage of every latitude on its high and mottled sides; but this genius is the landscape-garden of a modern house, adorned with fountains and statues, with well-bred men and women standing and sitting in the walks and terraces. We hear, through all the varied music, the ground-tone of conventional life. Our poets are men of talents who sing, and not the children of music. The argument is secondary, the finish of the verses is primary.

For it is not metres, but a metre-making argument that makes a poem,—a thought so passionate and alive that like the spirit of a plant or an animal it has an architecture of its own, and adorns nature with a new thing. The thought and the form are equal in the order of time, but in the order of genesis the thought is prior to the form. The poet has a new thought; he

has a whole new experience to unfold; he will tell us how it was with him, and all men will be the richer in his fortune. For the experience of each new age requires a new confession, and the world seems always waiting for its poet. I remember when I was young how much I was moved one morning by tidings that genius had appeared in a youth who sat near me at table. He had left his work and gone rambling none knew whither, and had written hundreds of lines, but could not tell whether that which was in him was therein told; he could tell nothing but that all was changed,—man, beast, heaven, earth and sea. How gladly we listened! how credulous! Society seemed to be compromised. We sat in the aurora of a sunrise which was to put out all the stars. Boston seemed to be at twice the distance it had the night before, or was much farther than that. Rome,—what was Rome? Plutarch and Shakspeare were in the yellow leaf, and Homer no more should be heard of. It is much to know that poetry has been written this very day, under this very roof, by your side. What! that wonderful spirit has not expired! These stony moments are still sparkling and animated! I had fancied that the oracles were all silent, and nature had spent her fires; and behold! all night, from every pore, these fine auroras have been streaming. Every one has some interest in the advent of the poet, and no one knows how much it may concern him. We know that the secret of the world is profound, but who or what shall be our interpreter, we know not. A mountain ramble, a new style of face, a new person, may put the key into our hands. Of course the value of genius to us is in the veracity of its report. Talent may frolic and juggle; genius realizes and adds. Mankind in good earnest have availed so far in understanding themselves and their work, that the foremost watchman on the peak announces his news. It is the

[2] One of the highest mountains of the Andes, situated in Ecuador, latitude 1° 30′ S.

truest word ever spoken, and the phrase will be the fittest, most musical, and the unerring voice of the world for that time.

All that we call sacred history attests that the birth of a poet is the principal event in chronology. Man, never so often deceived, still watches for the arrival of a brother who can hold him steady to a truth until he has made it his own. With what joy I begin to read a poem which I confide in as an inspiration! And now my chains are to be broken; I shall mount above these clouds and opaque airs in which I live,—opaque, though they seem transparent,—and from the heaven of truth I shall see and comprehend my relations. That will reconcile me to life and renovate nature, to see trifles animated by a tendency, and to know what I am doing. Life will no more be a noise; now I shall see men and women, and know the signs by which they may be discerned from fools and satans. This day shall be better than my birthday: then I became an animal; now I am invited into the science of the real. Such is the hope, but the fruition is postponed. Oftener it falls that this winged man, who will carry me into the heaven, whirls me into mists, then leaps and frisks about with me as it were from cloud to cloud, still affirming that he is bound heavenward; and I, being myself a novice, am slow in perceiving that he does not know the way into the heavens, and is merely bent that I should admire his skill to rise like a fowl or a flying fish, a little way from the ground or the water; but the all-piercing, all-feeding and ocular air of heaven that man shall never inhabit. I tumble down again soon into my old nooks, and lead the life of exaggerations as before, and have lost my faith in the possibility of any guide who can lead me thither where I would be.

But, leaving these victims of vanity, let us, with new hope, observe how nature, by worthier impulses, has insured the poet's fidelity to his office of announcement and affirming, namely by the beauty of things, which becomes a new and higher beauty when expressed. Nature offers all her creatures to him as a picture-language. Being used as a type, a second wonderful value appears in the object, far better than its old value; as the carpenter's stretched cord, if you hold your ear close enough, is musical in the breeze. "Things more excellent than every image," says Jamblichus,[3] "are expressed through images." Things admit of being used as symbols because nature is a symbol, in the whole, and in every part. Every line we can draw in the sand has expression; and there is no body without its spirit or genius. All form is an effect of character; all condition, of the quality of the life; all harmony, of health; and for this reason a perception of beauty should be sympathetic, or proper only to the good. The beautiful rests on the foundations of the necessary. The soul makes the body, as the wise Spenser teaches:—

"So every spirit, as it is more pure,
  And hath in it the more of heavenly light,
  So it the fairer body doth procure
  To habit in, and it more fairly dight,
  With cheerful grace and amiable sight.
  For, of the soul, the body form doth take,
  For soul is form, and doth the body
    make."[4]

Here we find ourselves suddenly not in a critical speculation but in a holy place, and should go very warily and reverently. We stand before the secret of the world, there where Being passes into Appearance and Unity into Variety.

The Universe is the externization of the soul. Wherever the life is, that bursts into appearance around it. Our science is sensual, and therefore superficial. The earth and the heavenly bodies, physics and chemistry, we sensually treat, as if they were self-existent; but these are the retinue of that Being we have. "The mighty heaven," said Proclus, "exhibits, in its transfigura-

---

[3] Iamblichus, Greek philosopher and exponent of Syrian Neoplatonism.

[4] From Edmund Spenser's "An Hymne in Honour of Beautie."

tions, clear images of the splendor of intellectual perceptions; being moved in conjunction with the unapparent periods of intellectual natures." Therefore science always goes abreast with the just elevation of the man, keeping step with religion and metaphysics; or the state of science is an index of our self-knowledge. Since every thing in nature answers to a moral power, if any phenomenon remains brute and dark it is because the corresponding faculty in the observer is not yet active.

No wonder then, if these waters be so deep, that we hover over them with a religious regard. The beauty of the fable proves the importance of the sense; to the poet, and to all others; or, if you please, every man is so far a poet as to be susceptible of these enchantments of nature; for all men have the thoughts whereof the universe is the celebration. I find that the fascination resides in the symbol. Who loves nature? Who does not? Is it only poets, and men of leisure and cultivation, who live with her? No; but also hunters, farmers, grooms and butchers, though they express their affection in their choice of life and not in their choice of words. The writer wonders what the coachman or the hunter values in riding, in horses and dogs. It is not superficial qualities. When you talk with him he holds these at as slight a rate as you. His worship is sympathetic; he has no definitions, but he is commanded in nature by the living power which he feels to be there present. No imitation or playing of these things would content him; he loves the earnest of the north wind, of rain, of stone and wood and iron. A beauty not explicable is dearer than a beauty which we can see to the end of. It is nature the symbol, nature certifying the supernatural, body overflowed by life which he worships with coarse but sincere rites.

The inwardness and mystery of this attachment drive men of every class to the use of emblems. The schools of poets and philosophers are not more intoxicated with their symbols than the populace with theirs. In our political parties, compute the power

of badges and emblems. See the great ball which they roll from Baltimore to Bunker Hill! In the political processions, Lowell goes in a loom, and Lynn in a shoe, and Salem in a ship. Witness the cider-barrel, the log-cabin, the hickory-stick, the palmetto, and all the cognizances of party. See the power of national emblems. Some stars, lilies, leopards, a crescent, a lion, an eagle, or other figure which came into credit God knows how, on an old rag of bunting, blowing in the wind on a fort at the ends of the earth, shall make the blood tingle under the rudest or the most conventional exterior. The people fancy they hate poetry, and they are all poets and mystics!

Beyond this universality of the symbolic language, we are apprised of the divineness of this superior use of things, whereby the world is a temple whose walls are covered with emblems, pictures and commandments of the Deity,—in this, that there is no fact in nature which does not carry the whole sense of nature; and the distinctions which we make in events and in affairs, of low and high, honest and base, disappear when nature is used as a symbol. Thought makes everything fit for use. The vocabulary of an omniscient man would embrace words and images excluded from polite conversation. What would be base, or even obscene, to the obscene, becomes illustrious, spoken in a new connection of thought. The piety of the Hebrew prophets purges their grossness. The circumcision is an example of the power of poetry to raise the low and offensive. Small and mean things serve as well as great symbols. The meaner the type by which a law is expressed, the more pungent it is, and the more lasting in the memories of men; just as we choose the smallest box or case in which any needful utensil can be carried. Bare lists of words are found suggestive to an imaginative and excited mind; as it is related of Lord Chatham that he was accustomed to read in Bailey's Dictionary [5] when he was prepar-

---

[5] The fourth edition of Nathan Bailey's dictionary (1728) was long the only one in general use in England.

ing to speak in Parliament. The poorest experience is rich enough for all the purposes of expressing thought. Why covet a knowledge of new facts? Day and night, house and garden, a few books, a few actions, serve us as well as would all trades and all spectacles. We are far from having exhausted the significance of the few symbols we use. We can come to use them yet with a terrible simplicity. It does not need that a poem should be long. Every word was once a poem. Every new relation is a new word. Also we use defects and deformities to a sacred purpose, so expressing our sense that the evils of the world are such only to the evil eye. In the old mythology, mythologists observe, defects are ascribed to divine natures, as lameness to Vulcan, blindness to Cupid, and the like, —to signify exuberances.[6]

For as it is dislocation and detachment from the life of God that makes things ugly, the poet, who re-attaches things to nature and the Whole,—re-attaching even artificial things and violation of nature, to nature, by a deeper insight,—disposes very easily of the most disagreeable facts. Readers of poetry see the factory-village and the railway, and fancy that the poetry of the landscape is broken up by these; for these works of art are not yet consecrated in their reading; but the poet sees them fall within the great Order not less than the beehive or the spider's geometrical web. Nature adopts them very fast into her vital circles, and the gliding train of cars she loves like her own. Besides, in a centred mind, it signifies nothing how many mechanical inventions you exhibit. Though you add millions, and never so surprising, the fact of mechanics has not gained a grain's weight. The spiritual fact remains unaltered, by many or by few particulars; as no mountain is of any appreciable height to break the curve of the sphere. A shrewd country-boy goes to the city for the first time, and the complacent citizen is not satisfied with his little wonder. It is not that he does not see all the fine houses and know that he never saw such

before, but he disposes of them as easily as the poet finds place for the railway. The chief value of the new fact is to enhance the great and constant fact of Life, which can dwarf any and every circumstance, and to which the belt of wampum and the commerce of America are alike.

The world being thus put under the mind for verb and noun, the poet is he who can articulate it. For though life is great, and fascinates and absorbs; and though all men are intelligent of the symbols through which it is named; yet they cannot originally use them. We are symbols and inhabit symbols; workmen, work, and tools, words and things, birth and death, all are emblems; but we sympathize with the symbols, and being infatuated with the economical uses of things, we do not know that they are thoughts. The poet, by an ulterior intellectual perception, gives them a power which makes their old use forgotten, and puts eyes and a tongue into every dumb and inanimate object. He perceives the independence of the thought on the symbol, the stability of the thought, the accidency and fugacity of the symbol. As the eyes of Lynceus were said to see through the earth, so the poet turns the world to glass, and shows us all things in their right series and procession. For through that better perception he stands one step nearer to things, and sees the flowing or metamorphosis; perceives that thought is multiform; that within the form of every creature is a force impelling it to ascend into a higher form; and following with his eyes the life, uses the forms which express that life, and so his speech flows with the flowing of nature. All the facts of the animal economy, sex, nutriment, gestation, birth, growth, are symbols of the passage of the world into the soul

---

[6] The reader will find in this paragraph, as well as in other parts of the essay, a foreshadowing of the work of Walt Whitman, who freely acknowledged, in the early years of his work as a poet, the influence of Emerson.

of man, to suffer there a change and re-appear a new and higher fact. He uses forms according to the life, and not according to the form. This is true science. The poet alone knows astronomy, chemistry, vegetation and animation, for he does not stop at these facts, but employs them as signs. He knows why the plain or meadow of space was strown with these flowers we call suns and moons and stars; why the great deep is adorned with animals, with men, and gods; for in every word he speaks he rides on them as the horses of thought.

By virtue of this science the poet is the Namer or Language-maker, naming things sometimes after their appearance, sometimes after their essence, and giving to every one its own name and not another's, thereby rejoicing the intellect, which delights in detachment or boundary. The poets made all the words, and therefore language is the archives of history, and, if we must say it, a sort of tomb of the muses. For though the origin of most of our words is forgotten, each word was at first a stroke of genius, and obtained currency because for the moment it symbolized the world to the first speaker and to the hearer. The etymologist finds the deadest word to have been once a brilliant picture. Language is fossil poetry. As the limestone of the continent consists of infinite masses of the shells of animalcules, so language is made up of images or tropes, which now, in their secondary use, have long ceased to remind us of their poetic origin. But the poet names the thing because he sees it, or comes one step nearer to it than any other. This expression or naming is not art, but a second nature, grown out of the first, as a leaf out of a tree. What we call nature is a certain self-regulated motion or change; and nature does all things by her own hands, and does not leave another to baptize her but baptizes herself; and this through the metamorphosis again. I remember that a certain poet described it to me thus:—

Genius is the activity which repairs the decays of things, whether wholly or partly of a material and finite kind. Nature, through all her kingdoms, insures herself. Nobody cares for planting the poor fungus; so she shakes down from the gills of one agaric countless spores, any one of which, being preserved, transmits new billions of spores to-morrow or next day. The new agaric of this hour has a chance which the old one had not. This atom of seed is thrown into a new place, not subject to the accidents which destroyed its parent two rods off. She makes a man; and having brought him to ripe age, she will no longer run the risk of losing this wonder at a blow, but she detaches from him a new self, that the kind may be safe from accidents to which the individual is exposed. So when the soul of the poet has come to ripeness of thought, she detaches and sends away from it its poems or songs,—a fearless, sleepless, deathless progeny, which is not exposed to the accidents of the weary kingdom of time; a fearless, vivacious offspring, clad with wings (such was the virtue of the soul out of which they came) which carry them fast and far, and infix them irrecoverably into the hearts of men. These wings are the beauty of the poet's soul. The songs, thus flying immortal from their mortal parent, are pursued by clamorous flights of censures, which swarm in far greater numbers and threaten to devour them; but these last are not winged. At the end of a very short leap they fall plump down and rot, having received from the souls out of which they came no beautiful wings. But the melodies of the poet ascend and leap and pierce into the deeps of infinite time.

So far the bard taught me, using his freer speech. But nature has a higher end, in the production of new individuals, than security, namely *ascension*, or the passage of the soul into higher forms. I knew in my younger days the sculptor who made the statue of the youth which stands in the public garden. He was, as I remember, unable to tell directly what made him happy or unhappy, but by wonderful indirections he could tell. He rose one day, according to his habit, before the dawn, and saw the morning break, grand as the eternity out of which it came, and for many days after, he strove to express this tranquillity, and lo! his chisel had fashioned out of marble the form of a beautiful youth, Phosphorus, whose aspect is such that it is said all persons who look on it become silent. The poet also resigns himself to his mood, and that thought which agitated him is expressed, but *alter idem,*[7] in a manner totally new. The expression is organic, or the new type which things themselves take when liberated. As, in the sun, objects paint their images on the retina of the eye, so they, sharing the aspiration of the whole universe, tend to paint a far more delicate copy of their essence in his mind. Like the metamorphosis of things into higher organic forms is their change into melodies. Over everything stands its dæmon or soul, and, as the form of the thing is reflected by the eye, so the soul of the thing is reflected by a melody. The sea, the mountain-ridge, Niagara, and every flower-bed, pre-exist, or super-exist, in pre-cantations, which sail like odors in the air, and when any man goes by with an ear sufficiently fine, he overhears them and endeavors to write down the notes without diluting or depraving them. And herein is the legitimation of criticism, in the mind's faith that the poems are a corrupt version of some text in nature with which they ought to be made to tally. A rhyme in one of our sonnets should not be less pleasing than the iterated nodes of a seashell, or the resembling difference of a group of flowers. The pairing of the birds is an idyl, not tedious as our idyls are; a tempest is a rough ode, without falsehood or rant; a summer, with its harvest sown, reaped and stored, is an epic song, subordinating how many admirably executed parts. Why should not

the symmetry and truth that modulate these, glide into our spirits, and we participate the invention of nature?

This insight, which expresses itself by what is called Imagination, is a very high sort of seeing, which does not come by study, but by the intellect being where and what it sees; by sharing the path or circuit of things through forms, and so making them translucid to others. The path of things is silent. Will they suffer a speaker to go with them? A spy they will not suffer; a lover, a poet, is the transcendency of their own nature;—him they will suffer. The condition of true naming, on the poet's part, is his resigning himself to the divine *aura* which breathes through forms, and accompanying that.

It is a secret which every intellectual man quickly learns, that beyond the energy of his possessed and conscious intellect he is capable of a new energy (as of an intellect doubled on itself), by abandonment to the nature of things; that beside his privacy of power as an individual man, there is a great public power on which he can draw, by unlocking, at all risks, his human doors, and suffering the ethereal tides to roll and circulate through him; then he is caught up into the life of the Universe, his speech is thunder, his thought is law, and his words are universally intelligible as the plants and animals. The poet knows that he speaks adequately then only when he speaks somewhat wildly, or "with the flower of the mind;" not with the intellect used as an organ, but with the intellect released from all service and suffered to take its direction from its celestial life; or as the ancients were wont to express themselves, not with intellect alone but with the intellect inebriated by nectar. As the traveller who has lost his way throws his reins on his horse's neck and trusts to the instinct of the animal to find his road, so must we do with the divine animal who carries us through this world.

---

[7] The same thing, but different.

For if in any manner we can stimulate this instinct, new passages are opened for us into nature; the mind flows into and through things hardest and highest, and the metamorphosis is possible.

This is the reason why bards love wine, mead, narcotics, coffee, tea, opium, the fumes of sandalwood and tobacco, or whatever other procurers of animal exhilaration. All men avail themselves of such means as they can, to add this extraordinary power to their normal powers; and to this end they prize conversation, music, pictures, sculpture, dancing, theatres, travelling, war, mobs, fires, gaming, politics, or love, or science, or animal intoxication,—which are several coarser or finer *quasi*-mechanical substitutes for the true nectar, which is the ravishment of the intellect by coming nearer to the fact. These are auxiliaries to the centrifugal tendency of a man, to his passage out into free space, and they help him to escape the custody of that body in which he is pent up, and of that jail-yard of individual relations in which he is enclosed. Hence a great number of such as were professionally expressers of Beauty, as painters, poets, musicians and actors, have been more than others wont to lead a life of pleasure and indulgence; all but the few who received the true nectar; and, as it was a spurious mode of attaining freedom, as it was an emancipation not into the heavens but into the freedom of baser places, they were punished for that advantage they won, by a dissipation and deterioration. But never can any advantage be taken of nature by a trick. The spirit of the world, the great calm presence of the Creator, comes not forth to the sorceries of opium or of wine. The sublime vision comes to the pure and simple soul in a clean and chaste body. That is not an inspiration, which we owe to narcotics, but some counterfeit excitement and fury. Milton says that the lyric poet may drink wine and live generously, but the epic poet, he who shall sing of the gods and their descent unto men, must drink water out of a wooden bowl.[8] For

poetry is not "Devil's wine," but God's wine. It is with this as it is with toys. We fill the hands and nurseries of our children with all manner of dolls, drums and horses; withdrawing their eyes from the plain face and sufficing objects of nature, the sun and moon, the animals, the water and stones, which should be their toys. So the poet's habit of living should be set on a key so low that the common influences should delight him. His cheerfulness should be the gift of the sunlight; the air should suffice for his inspiration, and he should be tipsy with water. That spirit which suffices quiet hearts, which seems to come forth to such from every dry knoll of sere grass, from every pine stump and half-imbedded stone on which the dull March sun shines, comes forth to the poor and hungry, and such as are of simple taste. If thou fill thy brain with Boston and New York, with fashion and covetousness, and wilt stimulate thy jaded senses with wine and French coffee, thou shalt find no radiance of wisdom in the lonely waste of the pine woods.

If the imagination intoxicates the poet, it is not inactive in other men. The metamorphosis excites in the beholder an emotion of joy. The use of symbols has a certain power of emancipation and exhilaration for all men. We seem to be touched by a wand which makes us dance and run about happily, like children. We are like persons who come out of a cave or cellar into the open air. This is the effect on us of tropes, fables, oracles and all poetic forms. Poets are thus liberating gods. Men have really got a new sense, and found within their world another world, or nest of worlds; for, the metamorphosis once seen, we divine that it does not stop. I will not now consider how much this makes the charm of algebra and the mathematics, which also have their tropes, but it is felt in every definition; as when Aristotle defines *space* to be an immovable vessel in

8 The reference is apparently to *Elegia Sexta*, Milton's sixth Latin elegy, ll. 55-78.

which things are contained;—or when Plato defines a *line* to be a flowing point; or *figure* to be a bound of solid; and many the like. What a joyful sense of freedom we have when Vitruvius [9] announces the old opinion of artists that no architect can build any house well who does not know something of anatomy. When Socrates, in Charmides, tells us that the soul is cured of its maladies by certain incantations, and that these incantations are beautiful reasons, from which temperance is generated in souls; when Plato calls the world an animal, and Timæus [10] affirms that the plants also are animals; or affirms a man to be a heavenly tree, growing with his root, which is his head, upward; and, as George Chapman, following him, writes,

"So in our tree of man, whose nervie root
  Springs in his top;"— [11]

when Orpheus speaks of hoariness as "that white flower which marks extreme old age;" when Proclus calls the universe the statue of the intellect; when Chaucer, in his praise of "Gentilesse," compares good blood in mean condition to fire, which, though carried to the darkest house betwixt this and the mount of Caucasus, will yet hold its natural office and burn as bright as if twenty thousand men did it behold; when John saw, in the Apocalypse, the ruin of the world through evil, and the stars fall from heaven as the fig tree casteth her untimely fruit; when Æsop reports the whole catalogue of common daily relations through the masquerade of birds and beasts;—we take the cheerful hint of the immortality of our essence and its versatile habit and escapes, as when the gypsies say of themselves, "It is in vain to hang them, they cannot die."

The poets are thus liberating gods. The ancient British bards had for the title of their order, "Those who are free throughout the world." They are free, and they make free. An imaginative book renders us much more service at first, by stimulating us through its tropes, than afterward when

we arrive at the precise sense of the author. I think nothing is of any value in books excepting the transcendental and extraordinary. If a man is inflamed and carried away by his thought, to that degree that he forgets the authors and the public and heeds only this one dream which holds him like an insanity, let me read his paper, and you may have all the arguments and histories and criticism. All the value which attaches to Pythagoras, Paracelsus, Cornelius Agrippa, Cardan, Kepler, Swedenborg, Schelling, Oken, [12] or any other who introduces questionable facts into his cosmogony, as angels, devils, magic, astrology, palmistry, mesmerism, and so on, is the certificate we have of departure from routine, and that here is a new witness. That also is the best success in conversation, the magic of liberty, which puts the world like a ball in our hands. How cheap even the liberty then seems; how mean to study, when an emotion communicates to the intellect the power to sap and upheave nature; how great the perspective! nations, times, systems, enter and disappear like threads in tapestry of large figure and many colors; dream delivers us to dream, and while the drunkenness lasts we will sell our bed, our philosophy, our religion, in our opulence.

There is good reason why we should prize this liberation. The fate of the poor shepherd, who, blinded and lost in the snow-storm, perishes in a drift within a few feet of his cottage door, is an emblem

---

[9] Marcus Vitruvius Pollio, Roman architect and engineer of the first century, B.C.

[10] Charmides and Timæus participate in those Dialogues of Plato named after them respectively.

[11] From the Dedication of Chapman's Homer.

[12] Among the ancient and modern philosophers in this list are interpolated three occultists—Philippus Aureolus Paracelsus (1493?-1541), Swiss alchemist; Cornelius Heinrich Agrippa (1486?-1535), German writer on magic; and Geronimo Cardano (1501-1576) Italian astrologer.

of the state of man. On the brink of the waters of life and truth, we are miserably dying. The inaccessibleness of every thought but that we are in, is wonderful. What if you come near to it; you are as remote when you are nearest as when you are farthest. Every thought is also a prison; every heaven is also a prison. Therefore we love the poet, the inventor, who in any form, whether in an ode or in an action or in looks and behavior, has yielded us a new thought. He unlocks our chains and admits us to a new scene.

This emancipation is dear to all men, and the power to impart it, as it must come from greater depth and scope of thought, is a measure of intellect. Therefore all books of the imagination endure, all which ascend to that truth that the writer sees nature beneath him, and uses it as his exponent. Every verse or sentence possessing this virtue will take care of its own immortality. The religions of the world are the ejaculations of a few imaginative men.

But the quality of the imagination is to flow, and not to freeze. The poet did not stop at the color or the form, but read their meaning; neither may he rest in this meaning, but he makes the same objects exponents of his new thought. Here is the difference betwixt the poet and the mystic, that the last nails a symbol to one sense, which was a true sense for a moment, but soon becomes old and false. For all symbols are fluxional; all language is vehicular and transitive, and is good, as ferries and horses are, for conveyance, not as farms and houses are, for homestead. Mysticism consists in the mistake of an accidental and individual symbol for an universal one. The morning-redness happens to be the favorite meteor to the eyes of Jacob Behmen,[13] and comes to stand to him for truth and faith; and, he believes, should stand for the same realities to every reader. But the first reader prefers as naturally the symbol of a mother and child, or a gardener and his bulb, or a jeweller polishing a

gem. Either of these, or of a myriad more, are equally good to the person to whom they are significant. Only they must be held lightly, and be very willingly translated into the equivalent terms which others use. And the mystic must be steadily told, —All that you say is just as true without the tedious use of that symbol as with it. Let us have a little algebra, instead of this trite rhetoric,—universal signs, instead of these village symbols,—and we shall both be gainers. The history of hierarchies seems to show that all religious error consisted in making the symbol too stark and solid, and was at last nothing but an excess of the organ of language.

Swedenborg, of all men in the recent ages, stands eminently for the translator of nature into thought. I do not know the man in history to whom things stood so uniformly for words. Before him the metamorphosis continually plays. Everything on which his eye rests, obeys the impulses of moral nature. The figs become grapes whilst he eats them. When some of his angels affirmed a truth, the laurel twig which they held blossomed in their hands. The noise which at a distance appeared like gnashing and thumping, on coming nearer was found to be the voice of disputants. The men in one of his visions, seen in heavenly light, appeared like dragons, and seemed in darkness; but to each other they appeared as men, and when the light from heaven shone into their cabin, they complained of the darkness, and were compelled to shut the window that they might see.

There was this perception in him which makes the poet or seer an object of awe and terror, namely that the same man or society of men may wear one aspect to themselves and their companions, and a different aspect to higher intelligences. Certain priests, whom he describes as conversing very learnedly together, appeared to the children who were at some distance,

---

[13] Jakob Böhme (1575-1624), German mystic.

like dead horses; and many the like mis-appearances. And instantly the mind inquires whether these fishes under the bridge, yonder oxen in the pasture, those dogs in the yard, are immutably fishes, oxen and dogs, or only so appear to me, and perchance to themselves appear upright men; and whether I appear as a man to all eyes. The Brahmins and Pythagoras propounded the same question, and if any poet has witnessed the transformation he doubtless found it in harmony with various experiences. We have all seen changes as considerable in wheat and caterpillars. He is the poet and shall draw us with love and terror, who sees through the flowing vest the firm nature, and can declare it.

I look in vain for the poet whom I describe. We do not with sufficient plainness or sufficient profoundness address ourselves to life, nor dare we chaunt our own times and social circumstance. If we filled the day with bravery, we should not shrink from celebrating it. Time and nature yield us many gifts, but not yet the timely man, the new religion, the reconciler, whom all things await. Dante's praise is that he dared to write his autobiography in colossal cipher, or into universality. We have yet had no genius in America, with tyrannous eye, which knew the value of our incomparable materials, and saw, in the barbarism and materialism of the times, another carnival of the same gods whose picture he so much admires in Homer; then in the Middle Age; then in Calvinism. Banks and tariffs, the newspaper and caucus, Methodism and Unitarianism, are flat and dull to dull people, but rest on the same foundations of wonder as the town of Troy and the temple of Delphi, and are as swiftly passing away. Our log-rolling, our stumps and their politics, our fisheries, our Negroes and Indians, our boats and our repudiations, the wrath of rogues and the pusillanimity of honest men, the northern trade, the southern planting, the western clearing, Oregon and Texas, are yet unsung. Yet America is a poem in our

eyes; its ample geography dazzles the imagination, and it will not wait long for metres. If I have not found that excellent combination of gifts in my countrymen which I seek, neither could I aid myself to fix the idea of the poet by reading now and then in Chalmers's collection of five centuries of English poets.[14] These are wits more than poets, though there have been poets among them. But when we adhere to the ideal of the poet, we have our difficulties even with Milton and Homer. Milton is too literary, and Homer too literal and historical.

But I am not wise enough for a national criticism, and must use the old largeness a little longer, to discharge my errand from the muse to the poet concerning his art.

Art is the path of the creator to his work. The paths or methods are ideal and eternal, though few men ever see them; not the artist himself for years, or for a lifetime, unless he come into the conditions. The painter, the sculptor, the composer, the epic rhapsodist, the orator, all partake one desire, namely to express themselves symmetrically and abundantly, not dwarfishly and fragmentarily. They found or put themselves in certain conditions, as, the painter and sculptor before some impressive human figures; the orator into the assembly of the people; and the others in such scenes as each has found exciting to his intellect; and each presently feels the new desire. He hears a voice, he sees a beckoning. Then he is apprised, with wonder, what herds of dæmons hem him in. He can no more rest; he says, with the old painter, "By God, it is in me and must go forth of me." He pursues a beauty, half seen, which flies before him. The poet pours out verses in every solitude. Most of the things he says are conventional, no doubt; but by and by he says something which is original and beautiful. That charms him. He would say nothing else

---

[14] Alexander Chalmers (1759-1834) edited *Works of the English Poets from Chaucer to Cowper* in 21 volumes in 1810.

but such things. In our way of talking we say, "That is yours, this is mine;" but the poet knows well that it is not his; that it is as strange and beautiful to him as to you; he would fain hear the like eloquence at length. Once having tasted this immortal ichor, he cannot have enough of it, and as an admirable creative power exists in these intellections, it is of the last importance that these things get spoken. What a little of all we know is said! What drops of all the sea of our science are bailed up! and by what accident it is that these are exposed, when so many secrets sleep in nature! Hence the necessity of speech and song; hence these throbs and heart-beatings in the orator, at the door of the assembly, to the end namely that thought may be ejaculated as Logos, or Word.

Doubt not, O poet, but persist. Say, "It is in me, and shall out." Stand there, balked and dumb, stuttering and stammering, hissed and hooted, stand and strive, until at last rage draw out of thee that *dream*-power which every night shows thee is thine own; a power transcending all limit and privacy, and by virtue of which a man is the conductor of the whole river of electricity. Nothing walks, or creeps, or grows, or exists, which must not in turn arise and walk before him as exponent of his meaning. Comes he to that power, his genius is no longer exhaustible. All the creatures by pairs and by tribes pour into his mind as into a Noah's ark, to come forth again to people a new world. This is like the stock of air for our respiration or for the combustion of our fireplace; not a measure of gallons, but the entire atmosphere if wanted. And therefore the rich poets, as Homer, Chaucer, Shakspeare, and Raphael, have obviously no limits to their works except the limits of their lifetime, and resemble a mirror carried through the street, ready to render an image of every created thing.

O poet! a new nobility is conferred in groves and pastures, and not in castles or by the sword-blade any longer. The conditions are hard, but equal. Thou shalt leave the world, and know the muse only. Thou shalt not know any longer the times, customs, graces, politics, or opinions of men, but shalt take all from the muse. For the time of towns is tolled from the world by funereal chimes, but in nature the universal hours are counted by succeeding tribes of animals and plants, and by growth of joy on joy. God wills also that thou abdicate a manifold and duplex life, and that thou be content that others speak for thee. Others shall be thy gentlemen and shall represent all courtesy and worldly life for thee; others shall do the great and resounding actions also. Thou shalt lie close hid with nature, and canst not be afforded to the Capitol or the Exchange. The world is full of renunciations and apprenticeships, and this is thine; thou must pass for a fool and a churl for a long season. This is the screen and sheath in which Pan has protected his well-beloved flower, and thou shalt be known only to thine own, and they shall console thee with tenderest love. And thou shalt not be able to rehearse the names of thy friends in thy verse, for an old shame before the holy ideal. And this is the reward; that the ideal shall be real to thee, and the impressions of the actual world shall fall like summer rain, copious, but not troublesome to thy invulnerable essence. Thou shalt have the whole land for thy park and manor, the sea for thy bath and navigation, without tax and without envy; the woods and the rivers thou shalt own, and thou shalt possess that wherein others are only tenants and boarders. Thou true land-lord! sea-lord! air-lord! Wherever snow falls or water flows or birds fly, wherever day and night meet in twilight, wherever the blue heaven is hung by clouds or sown with stars, wherever are forms with transparent boundaries, wherever are outlets into celestial space, wherever is danger, and awe, and love,—there is Beauty, plenteous as rain, shed for thee, and though thou shouldst walk the world over, thou shalt not be able to find a condition inopportune or ignoble.

MONTAIGNE
[1850]

EVERY fact is related on one side to sensation, and, on the other, to morals. The game of thought is, on the appearance of one of these two sides, to find the other; given the upper, to find the under side. Nothing so thin, but has these two faces; and, when the observer has seen the obverse, he turns it over to see the reverse. Life is a pitching of this penny,—heads or tails. We never tire of this game, because there is still a slight shudder of astonishment at the exhibition of the other face, at the contrast of the two faces. A man is flushed with success, and bethinks himself what this good luck signifies. He drives his bargain in the street; but it occurs, that he also is bought and sold. He sees the beauty of a human face, and searches the cause of that beauty, which must be more beautiful. He builds his fortunes, maintains the laws, cherishes his children; but he asks himself, why? and whereto? This head and this tail are called, in the language of philosophy, Infinite and Finite; Relative and Absolute; Apparent and Real; and many fine names beside.

Each man is born with a predisposition to one or the other of these sides of nature; and it will easily happen that men will be found devoted to one or the other. One class has the perception of difference, and is conversant with facts and surfaces; cities and persons; and the bringing certain things to pass;—the men of talent and action. Another class have the perception of identity, and are men of faith and philosophy, men of genius.

Each of these riders drives too fast. Plotinus believes only in philosophers; Fenelon, in saints; Pindar and Byron, in poets. Read the haughty language in which Plato and the Platonists speak of all men who are not devoted to their own shining abstractions: other men are rats and mice. The literary class is usually proud and exclusive. The correspondence of Pope and Swift describes mankind around them as monsters; and that of Goethe and Schiller, in our own time, is scarcely more kind.

It is easy to see how this arrogance comes. The genius is a genius by the first look he casts on any object. Is his eye creative? Does he not rest in angles and colors, but beholds the design,—he will presently undervalue the actual object. In powerful moments, his thought has dissolved the works of art and nature into their causes, so that the works appear heavy and faulty. He has a conception of beauty, which the sculptor cannot embody. Picture, statue, temple, railroad, steam-engine, existed first in an artist's mind, without flaw, mistake, or friction, which impair the executed models. So did the church, the state, college, court, social circle, and all the institutions. It is not strange that these men, remembering what they have seen and hoped of ideas, should affirm disdainfully the superiority of ideas. Having at some time seen that the happy soul will carry all the arts in power, they say, Why cumber ourselves with superfluous realizations? and, like dreaming beggars, they assume to speak and act as if these values were already substantiated.

On the other part, the men of toil and trade and luxury,—the animal world, including the animal in the philosopher and poet also,—and the practical world, including the painful drudgeries which are never excused to philosopher or poet any more than to the rest,—weigh heavily on the other side. The trade in our streets believes in no metaphysical causes, thinks nothing of the force which necessitated traders and a trading planet to exist; no, but sticks to cotton, sugar, wool, and salt. The ward meetings, on election days, are not softened by any misgiving of the value of these ballotings. Hot life is streaming in a single direction. To the men of this world, to the animal strength and spirits, to the men of practical power, while immersed in it, the man of ideas appears out of his reason. They alone have reason.

Things always bring their own philosophy

with them, that is, prudence. No man acquires property without acquiring with it a little arithmetic, also. In England, the richest country that ever existed, property stands for more, compared with personal ability, than in any other. After dinner, a man believes less, denies more: verities have lost some charm. After dinner, arithmetic is the only science: ideas are disturbing, incendiary, follies of young men, repudiated by the solid portion of society; and a man comes to be valued by his athletic and animal qualities. Spence relates, that Mr. Pope was with Sir Godfrey Kneller, one day, when his nephew, a Guinea trader, came in. "Nephew," said Sir Godfrey, "you have the honor of seeing the two greatest men in the world." "I don't know how great men you may be," said the Guinea man, "but I don't like your looks. I have often bought a much better than both of you, all muscles and bones, for ten guineas."[1] Thus, the men of the senses revenge themselves on the professors, and repay scorn for scorn. The first had leaped to conclusions not yet ripe, and say more than is true; the others make themselves merry with the philosopher, and weigh man by the pound. They believe that mustard bites the tongue, and pepper is hot, friction-matches are incendiary, revolvers to be avoided, and suspenders hold up pantaloons; that there is much sentiment in a chest of tea; and a man will be eloquent, if you give him good wine. Are you tender and scrupulous,—you must eat more mince-pie. They hold that Luther had milk in him when he said,

"Wer nicht liebt Wein, Weib, und Gesang, Der bleibt ein Narr sein Leben lang;"[2]

and when he advised a young scholar, perplexed with foreordination and free-will, to get well drunk. "The nerves," says Cabanis,[3] "they are the man." My neighbor, a jolly farmer, in the tavern bar-room, thinks that the use of money is sure and speedy spending: "for his part," he says, "he puts his down his neck, and gets the good of it."

The inconvenience of this way of thinking is, that it runs into indifferentism, and then into disgust. Life is eating us up. We shall be fables presently. Keep cool: it will be all one a hundred years hence. Life's well enough; but we shall be glad to get out of it, and they will all be glad to have us. Why should we fret and drudge? Our meat will taste to-morrow as it did yesterday, and we may at last have had enough of it. "Ah," said my languid gentleman at Oxford, "there's nothing new or true,—and no matter."

With a little more bitterness, the cynic moans: our life is like an ass led to market by a bundle of hay being carried before him: he sees nothing but the bundle of hay. "There is so much trouble in coming into the world," said Lord Bolingbroke, "and so much more, as well as meanness, in going out of it, that 'tis hardly worth while to be here at all." I know a philosopher of this kidney,[4] who was accustomed briefly to sum up his experience of human nature in saying, "Mankind is a damned rascal:" and the natural corollary is pretty sure to follow,—'The world lives by humbug, and so will I.'

The abstractionist and the materialist thus mutually exasperating each other, and the scoffer expressing the worst of materialism, there arises a third party to occupy the middle ground between these two, the sceptic, namely. He finds both wrong by being in extremes. He labors to plant his feet, to be the beam of the balance. He will not go beyond his card. He sees the one-sidedness of these men of the street; he will not be a Gibeonite; he stands for the intellectual faculties,

---

[1] Joseph Spence (1699-1768) was a friend of Alexander Pope and a famous anecdotist. Sir Godfrey Kneller (1646-1723) was an eminent portrait painter.

[2] Who loves not wine, woman, and song Remains a fool his whole life long.

[3] Pierre Jean Georges Cabanis (1757-1809) French physician and philosopher.

[4] The reference is to a laboring man who was a neighbor of Emerson's.

a cool head, and whatever serves to keep it cool; no unadvised industry, no unrewarded self-devotion, no loss of the brains in toil. Am I an ox, or a dray?—You are both in extremes, he says. You that will have all solid, and a world of piglead, deceive yourselves grossly. You believe yourselves rooted and grounded on adamant; and yet, if we uncover the last facts of our knowledge, you are spinning like bubbles in a river, you know not whither or whence, and you are bottomed and capped and wrapped in delusions.

Neither will he be betrayed to a book, and wrapped in a gown.[5] The studious class are their own victims: they are thin and pale, their feet are cold, their heads are hot, the night is without sleep, the day a fear of interruption,—pallor, squalor, hunger, and egotism. If you come near them, and see what conceits they entertain,—they are abstractionists, and spend their days and nights in dreaming some dream; in expecting the homage of society to some precious scheme built on a truth, but destitute of proportion in its presentment, of justness in its application, and of all energy of will in the schemer to embody and vitalize it.

But I see plainly, he says, that I cannot see. I know that human strength is not in extremes, but in avoiding extremes. I, at least, will shun the weakness of philosophizing beyond my depth. What is the use of pretending to powers we have not? What is the use of pretending to assurances we have not, respecting the other life? Why exaggerate the power of virtue? Why be an angel before your time? These strings, wound up too high, will snap. If there is a wish for immortality, and no evidence, why not say just that? If there are conflicting evidences, why not state them? If there is not ground for a candid thinker to make up his mind, yea or nay,—why not suspend the judgment? I weary of these dogmatizers. I tire of these hacks of routine, who deny the dogmas. I neither affirm nor deny. I stand here to try the case. I am here to consider, σκέπτειν, to consider how it is. I will try to keep the balance true. Of what use to take the chair, and glibly rattle off theories of society, religion, and nature, when I know that practical objections lie in the way, insurmountable by me and by my mates? Why so talkative in public, when each of my neighbors can pin me to my seat by arguments I cannot refute? Why pretend that life is so simple a game, when we know how subtle and illusive the Proteus is? Why think to shut up all things in your narrow coop, when we know there are not one or two only, but ten, twenty, a thousand things, and unlike? Why fancy that you have all the truth in your keeping? There is much to say on all sides.

Who shall forbid a wise scepticism, seeing that there is no practical question on which anything more than an approximate solution can be had? Is not marriage an open question, when it is alleged, from the beginning of the world, that such as are in the institution wish to get out, and such as are out wish to get in? And the reply of Socrates, to him who asked whether he should choose a wife, still remains reasonable, "that, whether he should choose one or not, he would repent it." Is not the state a question? All society is divided in opinion on the subject of the state. Nobody loves it; great numbers dislike it, and suffer conscientious scruples to allegiance: and the only defence set up, is the fear of doing worse in disorganizing. Is it otherwise with the church? Or, to put any of the questions which touch mankind nearest,—shall the young man aim at a leading part in law, in politics, in trade? It will not be pretended that a success in either of these kinds is quite coincident with what is best and inmost in his mind. Shall he, then, cutting the stays that hold him fast to the social state, put out to sea with no guidance but his genius? There is much to say on both sides. Remember the open question

---

[5] A reference to George Herbert's poem "Affliction":

"Thou didst betray me to a lingering book,
And wrapt me in a gown."

between the present order of "competition," and the friends of "attractive and associated labor." The generous minds embrace the proposition of labor shared by all; it is the only honesty; nothing else is safe. It is from the poor man's hut alone, that strength and virtue come: and yet, on the other side, it is alleged that labor impairs the form, and breaks the spirit of man, and the laborers cry unanimously, 'We have no thoughts.' Culture, how indispensable! I cannot forgive you the want of accomplishments; and yet, culture will instantly impair that chiefest beauty of spontaneousness. Excellent is culture for a savage; but once let him read in the book, and he is no longer able not to think of Plutarch's heroes. In short, since true fortitude of understanding consists "in not letting what we know be embarrassed by what we do not know," we ought to secure those advantages which we can command, and not risk them by clutching after the airy and unattainable. Come, no chimeras! Let us go abroad; let us mix in affairs; let us learn, and get, and have, and climb. "Men are a sort of moving plants, and, like trees, receive a great part of their nourishment from the air. If they keep too much at home, they pine." Let us have a robust, manly life; let us know what we know, for certain; what we have, let it be solid, and seasonable, and our own. A world in the hand is worth two in the bush. Let us have to do with real men and women, and not with skipping ghosts.

This, then, is the right ground of the sceptic,—this of consideration, of self-containing; not at all of unbelief; not at all of universal denying, nor of universal doubting,—doubting even that he doubts; least of all, of scoffing and profligate jeering at all that is stable and good. These are no more his moods than are those of religion and philosophy. He is the considerer, the prudent, taking in sail, counting stock, husbanding his means, believing that a man has too many enemies, than that he can afford to be his own foe; that we cannot give ourselves too many advantages, in this unequal conflict, with powers so vast and unweariable ranged on one side, and this little, conceited, vulnerable popinjay that a man is, bobbing up and down into every danger, on the other. It is a position taken up for better defence, as of more safety, and one that can be maintained; and it is one of more opportunity and range: as, when we build a house, the rule is to set it not too high nor too low, under the wind, but out of the dirt.

The philosophy we want is one of fluxions and mobility. The Spartan and Stoic schemes are too stark and stiff for our occasion. A theory of Saint John, and of nonresistance, seems, on the other hand, too thin and aerial. We want some coat woven of elastic steel, stout as the first, and limber as the second. We want a ship in these billows we inhabit. An angular, dogmatic house would be rent to chips and splinters, in this storm of many elements. No, it must be tight, and fit to the form of man, to live at all; as a shell must dictate the architecture of a house founded on the sea. The soul of man must be the type of our scheme, just as the body of man is the type after which a dwelling-house is built. Adaptiveness is the peculiarity of human nature. We are golden averages, volitant stabilities, compensated or periodic errors, houses founded on the sea. The wise sceptic wishes to have a near view of the best game, and the chief players; what is best in the planet; art and nature, places and events, but mainly men. Everything that is excellent in mankind—a form of grace, an arm of iron, lips of persuasion, a brain of resources, every one skilful to play and win—he will see and judge.

The terms of admission to this spectacle, are, that he have a certain solid and intelligible way of living of his own; some method of answering the inevitable needs of human life; proof that he has played with skill and success; that he has evinced the temper, stoutness, and the range of qualities which, among his contemporaries and countrymen, entitle him to fellowship and trust. For, the secrets of life are not shown except to sympathy and likeness. Men do not confide themselves to boys, or coxcombs, or pedants, but to their peers. Some wise limitation, as the modern phrase is; some condition between the extremes, and having itself a positive quality; some stark and sufficient man, who is not salt or sugar, but sufficiently related to the world to do justice to Paris or London, and, at the same time, a vigorous and original thinker, whom cities cannot overawe, but who uses them,—is the fit person to occupy this ground of speculation.

These qualities meet in the character of Montaigne. And yet, since the personal regard which I entertain for Montaigne may be unduly great, I will, under the shield of this prince of egotists, offer, as an apology for electing him as the representative of scepticism, a word or two to explain how my love began and grew for this admirable gossip.

A single odd volume of Cotton's [6] translation of the Essays remained to me from my father's library, when a boy. It lay long neglected, until, after many years, when I was newly escaped from college, I read the book, and procured the remaining volumes. I remember the delight and wonder in which I lived with it. It seemed to me as if I had myself written the book, in some former life, so sincerely it spoke to my thought and experience. It happened, when in Paris, in 1833, that, in the cemetery of Père la Chaise, I came to a tomb of Auguste Collignon, who died in 1830, aged sixty-eight years, and who, said the monument, "lived to do right, and had formed himself to virtue on the Essays of Montaigne." Some years later, I became acquainted with an accomplished English poet, John Sterling; [7] and, in prosecuting my correspondence, I found that, from a love of Montaigne, he had made a pilgrimage to his château, still standing near Castellan, in Perigord, and, after two hundred and fifty years, had copied from the walls of his library the inscriptions which Montaigne had written there. That Journal of Mr. Sterling's, published in the

Westminster Review, Mr. Hazlitt has reprinted in the *Prolegomena* to his edition of the Essays. I heard with pleasure that one of the newly discovered autographs of William Shakspeare was in a copy of Florio's translation of Montaigne. It is the only book which we certainly know to have been in the poet's library. And, oddly enough, the duplicate copy of Florio, which the British Museum purchased, with a view of protecting the Shakspeare autograph (as I was informed in the Museum), turned out to have the autograph of Ben Jonson in the fly-leaf. Leigh Hunt relates of Lord Byron, that Montaigne was the only great writer of past times whom he read with avowed satisfaction. Other coincidences, not needful to be mentioned here, concurred to make this old Gascon still new and immortal for me.

In 1571, on the death of his father, Montaigne, then thirty-eight years old, retired from the practice of law, at Bordeaux, and settled himself on his estate. Though he had been a man of pleasure, and sometimes a courtier, his studious habits now grew on him, and he loved the compass, staidness, and independence of the country gentleman's life. He took up his economy in good earnest, and made his farms yield the most. Downright and plain dealing, and abhorring to be deceived or to deceive, he was esteemed in the country for his sense and probity. In the civil wars of the League, [8] which converted every house into a fort, Montaigne kept his gates open, and his house without defence. All parties freely came and went, his courage and honor being universally esteemed. The neighboring lords and gentry brought jew-

---

[6] Charles Cotton (1630-1687) English poet, translated Montaigne's *Essays* in 1685.

[7] This was an epistolary acquaintance. John Sterling (1806-1844) was a poet and essayist who organized a famous literary club, died young, and was celebrated in a biography by Thomas Carlyle.

[8] The Holy League, formed in 1572 under Henry of Guise to advance Catholic interests.

els and papers to him for safe-keeping. Gibbon reckons, in these bigoted times, but two men of liberality in France,—Henry IV. and Montaigne.

Montaigne is the frankest and honestest of all writers. His French freedom runs into grossness; but he has anticipated all censure by the bounty of his own confessions. In his times, books were written to one sex only, and almost all were written in Latin; so that, in a humorist, a certain nakedness of statement was permitted, which our manners, of a literature addressed equally to both sexes, do not allow. But, though a Biblical plainness, coupled with a most uncanonical levity, may shut his pages to many sensitive readers, yet the offence is superficial. He parades it: he makes the most of it: nobody can think or say worse of him than he does. He pretends to most of the vices; and, if there be any virtue in him, he says, it got in by stealth. There is no man, in his opinion, who has not deserved hanging five or six times; and he pretends no exception in his own behalf. "Five or six as ridiculous stories," too, he says, "can be told of me, as of any man living." But, with all this really superfluous frankness, the opinion of an invincible probity grows into every reader's mind.

"When I the most strictly and religiously confess myself, I find that the best virtue I have has in it some tincture of vice; and I am afraid that Plato, in his purest virtue (I, who am as sincere and perfect a lover of virtue of that stamp as any other whatever), if he had listened, and laid his ear close to himself, would have heard some jarring sound of human mixture; but faint and remote, and only to be perceived by himself."

Here is an impatience and fastidiousness at color or pretence of any kind. He has been in courts so long as to have conceived a furious disgust at appearances; he will indulge himself with a little cursing and swearing; he will talk with sailors and gypsies, use flash and street ballads: he has stayed in-doors till he is deadly sick;

he will to the open air, though it rain bullets. He has seen too much of gentlemen of the long robe, until he wishes for cannibals; and is so nervous, by factitious life, that he thinks, the more barbarous man is, the better he is. He likes his saddle. You may read theology, and grammar, and metaphysics elsewhere. Whatever you get here, shall smack of the earth and of real life, sweet, or smart, or stinging. He makes no hesitation to entertain you with the records of his disease; and his journey to Italy is quite full of that matter. He took and kept this position of equilibrium. Over his name, he drew an emblematic pair of scales, and wrote *Que sçais je?* [9] under it. As I look at his effigy opposite the title-page, I seem to hear him say, "You may play old Poz,[10] if you will; you may rail and exaggerate,—I stand here for truth, and will not, for all the states, and churches, and revenues, and personal reputations of Europe, overstate the dry fact, as I see it; I will rather mumble and prose about what I certainly know,—my house and barns; my father, my wife, and my tenants; my old lean bald pate; my knives and forks; what meats I eat, and what drinks I prefer; and a hundred straws just as ridiculous,—than I will write, with a fine crow-quill, a fine romance. I like gray days, and autumn and winter weather. I am gray and autumnal myself, and think an undress, and old shoes that do not pinch my feet, and old friends who do not constrain me, and plain topics where I do not need to strain myself and pump my brains, the most suitable. Our condition as men is risky and ticklish enough. One cannot be sure of himself and his fortune an hour, but he may be whisked off into some pitiable or ridiculous plight. Why should I vapor and play the philosopher, instead of ballasting, the best I can, this dancing balloon? So, at least, I live within compass, keep myself ready for action, and

---

[9] What do I know?

[10] To "play old Poz" is a colloquialism indicating too positive an attitude.

can shoot the gulf, at last, with decency. If there be anything farcical in such a life, the blame is not mine: let it lie at fate's and nature's door."

The Essays, therefore, are an entertaining soliloquy on every random topic that comes into his head; treating everything without ceremony, yet with masculine sense. There have been men with deeper insight; but, one would say, never a man with such abundance of thoughts: he is never dull, never insincere, and has the genius to make the reader care for all that he cares for.

The sincerity and marrow of the man reaches to his sentences. I know not anywhere the book that seems less written. It is the language of conversation transferred to a book. Cut these words and they would bleed; they are vascular and alive. One has the same pleasure in it that we have in listening to the necessary speech of men about their work, when any unusual circumstance gives momentary importance to the dialogue. For blacksmiths and teamsters do not trip in their speech; it is a shower of bullets. It is Cambridge men who correct themselves, and begin again at every half-sentence, and, moreover, will pun, and refine too much, and swerve from the matter to the expression. Montaigne talks with shrewdness, knows the world, and books, and himself, and uses the positive degree: never shrieks, or protests, or prays: no weakness, no convulsion, no superlative: does not wish to jump out of his skin, or play any antics, or annihilate space or time; but is stout and solid; tastes every moment of the day; likes pain, because it makes him feel himself, and realize things; as we pinch ourselves to know that we are awake. He keeps the plain; he rarely mounts or sinks; likes to feel solid ground, and the stones underneath. His writing has no enthusiasms, no aspiration; contented, self-respecting, and keeping the middle of the road. There is but one exception,—in his love for Socrates. In speaking of him, for once his cheek flushes, and his style rises to passion.

Montaigne died of a quinsy, at the age of sixty, in 1592. When he came to die, he caused the mass to be celebrated in his chamber. At the age of thirty-three, he had been married. "But," he says, "might I have had my own will, I would not have married Wisdom herself, if she would have had me: but 'tis to much purpose to evade it, the common custom and use of life will have it so. Most of my actions are guided by example, not choice." In the hour of death, he gave the same weight to custom. *Que sçais je?* What do I know?

This book of Montaigne the world has indorsed, by translating it into all tongues, and printing seventy-five editions of it in Europe: and that, too, a circulation somewhat chosen, namely, among courtiers, soldiers, princes, men of the world, and men of wit and generosity.

Shall we say that Montaigne has spoken wisely, and given the right and permanent expression of the human mind, on the conduct of life?

We are natural believers. Truth, or the connection between cause and effect, alone interests us. We are persuaded that a thread runs through all things: all worlds are strung on it, as beads: and men, and events, and life, come to us, only because of that thread: they pass and repass, only that we may know the direction and continuity of that line. A book or statement which goes to show that there is no line, but random and chaos, a calamity out of nothing, a prosperity and no account of it, a hero born from a fool, a fool from a hero,—dispirits us. Seen or unseen, we believe the tie exists. Talent makes counterfeit ties; genius finds the real ones. We hearken to the man of science, because we anticipate the sequence in natural phenomena which he uncovers. We love whatever affirms, connects, preserves; and dislike what scatters or pulls down. One man appears whose nature is to all men's eyes conserving and constructive: his presence supposes a well-ordered society, agriculture, trade, large institutions, and empire.

If these did not exist, they would begin to exist through his endeavors. Therefore, he cheers and comforts men, who feel all this in him very readily. The nonconformist and the rebel say all manner of unanswerable things against the existing republic, but discover to our sense no plan of house or state of their own. Therefore, though the town, and state, and way of living, which our counsellor contemplated, might be a very modest or musty prosperity, yet men rightly go for him, and reject the reformer, so long as he comes only with axe and crow-bar.

But though we are natural conservers and causationists, and reject a sour, dumpish unbelief, the sceptical class, which Montaigne represents, have reason, and every man, at some time, belongs to it. Every superior mind will pass through this domain of equilibration,—I should rather say, will know how to avail himself of the checks and balances in nature, as a natural weapon against the exaggeration and formalism of bigots and blockheads.

Scepticism is the attitude assumed by the student in relation to the particulars which society adores, but which he sees to be reverend only in their tendency and spirit. The ground occupied by the sceptic is the vestibule of the temple. Society does not like to have any breath of question blown on the existing order. But the interrogation of custom at all points is an inevitable stage in the growth of every superior mind, and is the evidence of its perception of the flowing power which remains itself in all changes.

The superior mind will find itself equally at odds with the evils of society, and with the projects that are offered to relieve them. The wise sceptic is a bad citizen; no conservative; he sees the selfishness of property, and the drowsiness of institutions. But neither is he fit to work with any democratic party that ever was constituted; for parties wish every one committed, and he penetrates the popular patriotism. His politics are those of the "Soul's Errand" of Sir Walter Raleigh;

or of Krishna, in the Bhagavat, "There is none who is worthy of my love or hatred;" whilst he sentences law, physic, divinity, commerce, and custom. He is a reformer: yet he is no better member of the philanthropic association. It turns out that he is not the champion of the operative, the pauper, the prisoner, the slave. It stands in his mind, that our life in this world is not of quite so easy interpretation as churches and school-books say. He does not wish to take ground against these benevolences, to play the part of devil's attorney, and blazon every doubt and sneer that darkens the sun for him. But he says, There are doubts.

I mean to use the occasion, and celebrate the calendar-day of our St. Michel de Montaigne, by counting and describing these doubts or negations. I wish to ferret them out of their holes, and sun them a little. We must do with them as the police do with old rogues, who are shown up to the public at the marshal's office. They will never be so formidable, when once they have been identified and registered. But I mean honestly by them,—that justice shall be done to their terrors. I shall not take Sunday objections, made up on purpose to be put down. I shall take the worst I can find, whether I can dispose of them, or they of me.

I do not press the scepticism of the materialist. I know the quadruped opinion will not prevail. 'Tis of no importance what bats and oxen think. The first dangerous symptom I report is, the levity of intellect; as if it were fatal to earnestness to know much. Knowledge is the knowing that we cannot know. The dull pray; the geniuses are light mockers. How respectable is earnestness on every platform! but intellect kills it. Nay, San Carlo,[11] my subtle and admirable friend, one of the most penetrating of men, finds that all direct ascension, even of lofty piety, leads to this ghastly insight, and sends back the votary or-

[11] Charles K. Newcomb, a mystic and a member of the Brook Farm community.

phaned. My astonishing San Carlo thought the lawgivers and saints infected. They found the ark empty; saw, and would not tell; and tried to choke off their approaching followers, by saying, 'Action, action, my dear fellows, is for you!' Bad as was to me this detection by San Carlo, this frost in July, this blow from a bride, there was still a worse, namely, the cloy or satiety of the saints. In the mount of vision, ere they have yet risen from their knees, they say, We discover that this our homage and beatitude is partial and deformed: we must fly for relief to the suspected and reviled Intellect, to the Understanding, the Mephistopheles, to the gymnastics of talent.

This is hobgoblin the first; and, though it has been the subject of much elegy, in our nineteenth century, from Byron, Goethe, and other poets of less fame, not to mention many distinguished private observers,—I confess it is not very affecting to my imagination; for it seems to concern the shattering of baby-houses and crockery-shops. What flutters the church of Rome, or of England, or of Geneva, or of Boston, may yet be very far from touching any principle of faith. I think that the intellect and moral sentiment are unanimous; and that, though philosophy extirpates bugbears, yet it supplies the natural checks of vice, and polarity to the soul. I think that the wiser a man is, the more stupendous he finds the natural and moral economy, and lifts himself to a more absolute reliance.

There is the power of moods, each setting at naught all but its own tissue of facts and beliefs. There is the power of complexions, obviously modifying the dispositions and sentiments. The beliefs and unbeliefs appear to be structural; and, as soon as each man attains the poise and vivacity which allow the whole machinery to play, he will not need extreme examples, but will rapidly alternate all opinions in his own life. Our life is March weather, savage and serene in one hour. We go forth austere, dedicated, believing in the iron links of Destiny, and will not turn on our heel to save our life: but a book or a bust, or only the sound of a name, shoots a spark through the nerves, and we suddenly believe in will: my finger-ring shall be the seal of Solomon: fate is for imbeciles: all is possible to the resolved mind. Presently, a new experience gives a new turn to our thoughts: commonsense resumes its tyranny: we say, 'Well, the army, after all, is the gate to fame, manners, and poetry: and, look you,—on the whole, selfishness plants best, prunes best, makes the best commerce, and the best citizen.' Are the opinions of a man on right and wrong, on fate and causation, at the mercy of a broken sleep or an indigestion? Is his belief in God and Duty no deeper than a stomach evidence? And what guaranty for the permanence of his opinions? I like not the French celerity,—a new church and state once a week. This is the second negation; and I shall let it pass for what it will. As far as it asserts rotation of states of mind, I suppose it suggests its own remedy, namely, in the record of larger periods. What is the mean of many states; of all the states? Does the general voice of ages affirm any principle, or is no community of sentiment discoverable in distant times and places? And when it shows the power of self-interest, I accept that as part of the divine law, and must reconcile it with aspiration the best I can.

The word Fate, or Destiny, expresses the sense of mankind, in all ages,—that the laws of the world do not always befriend, but often hurt and crush us. Fate, in the shape of *Kinde* or nature, grows over us like grass. We paint Time with a scythe; Love and Fortune, blind; and Destiny, deaf. We have too little power of resistance against this ferocity which champs us up. What front can we make against these unavoidable, victorious, maleficent forces? What can I do against the influence of Race, in my history? What can I do against hereditary and constitutional habits, against scrofula, lymph, impotence; against climate, against barbarism, in my country?

I can reason down or deny everything, except this perpetual Belly: feed he must and will, and I cannot make him respectable.

But the main resistance which the affirmative impulse finds, and one including all others, is in the doctrine of the Illusionists. There is a painful rumor in circulation, that we have been practised upon in all the principal performances of life, and free agency is the emptiest name. We have been sopped and drugged with the air, with food, with woman, with children, with sciences, with events, which leave us exactly where they found us. The mathematics, 'tis complained, leave the mind where they find it: so do all sciences; and so do all events and actions. I find a man who has passed through all the sciences, the churl he was; and through all the offices, learned, civil, and social, can detect the child. We are not the less necessitated to dedicate life to them. In fact, we may come to accept it as the fixed rule and theory of our state of education, that God is a substance, and his method is illusion. The Eastern sages owned the goddess Yoganidra, the great illusory energy of Vishnu, by whom, as utter ignorance, the whole world is beguiled.

Or, shall I state it thus?—The astonishment of life is, the absence of any appearance of reconciliation between the theory and practice of life. Reason, the prized reality, the Law, is apprehended, now and then, for a serene and profound moment, amidst the hubbub of cares and works which have no direct bearing on it;—is then lost, for months or years, and again found, for an interval, to be lost again. If we compute it in time, we may, in fifty years, have half a dozen reasonable hours. But what are these cares and works the better? A method in the world we do not see, but this parallelism of great and little, which never react on each other, nor discover the smallest tendency to converge. Experiences, fortunes, governings, readings, writings, are nothing to the purpose;

as when a man comes into the room, it does not appear whether he has been fed on yams or buffalo,—he has contrived to get so much bone and fibre as he wants, out of rice or out of snow. So vast is the disproportion between the sky of law and the pismire of performance under it, that, whether he is a man of worth or a sot, is not so great a matter as we say. Shall I add, as one juggle of this enchantment, the stunning non-intercourse law which makes coöperation impossible? The young spirit pants to enter society. But all the ways of culture and greatness lead to solitary imprisonment. He has been often balked. He did not expect a sympathy with his thought from the village, but he went with it to the chosen and intelligent, and found no entertainment for it, but mere misapprehension, distaste, and scoffing. Men are strangely mistimed and misapplied; and the excellence of each is an inflamed individualism which separates him more.

There are these, and more than these, diseases of thought, which our ordinary teachers do not attempt to remove. Now shall we, because a good nature inclines us to virtue's side, say, There are no doubts, —and lie for the right? Is life to be led in a brave or in a cowardly manner? and is not the satisfaction of the doubts essential to all manliness? Is the name of virtue to be a barrier to that which is virtue? Can you not believe that a man of earnest and burly habit may find small good in tea, essays, and catechism, and want a rougher instruction, want men, labor, trade, farming, war, hunger, plenty, love, hatred, doubt, and terror, to make things plain to him; and has not he a right to insist on being convinced in his own way? When he is convinced, he will be worth the pains.

Belief consists in accepting the affirmations of the soul; unbelief, in denying them. Some minds are incapable of scepticism. The doubts they profess to entertain are rather a civility or accommodation to the common discourse of their company. They may well give themselves leave to speculate, for they are secure of a return.

Once admitted to the heaven of thought, they see no relapse into night, but infinite invitation on the other side. Heaven is within heaven, and sky over sky, and they are encompassed with divinities. Others there are, to whom the heaven is brass, and it shuts down to the surface of the earth. It is a question of temperament, or of more or less immersion in nature. The last class must needs have a reflex or parasite faith; not a sight of realities, but an instinctive reliance on the seers and believers of realities. The manners and thoughts of believers astonish them, and convince them that these have seen something which is hid from themselves. But their sensual habit would fix the believer to his last position, whilst he as inevitably advances; and presently the unbeliever, for love of belief, burns the believer.

Great believers are always reckoned infidels, impracticable, fantastic, atheistic, and really men of no account. The spiritualist finds himself driven to express his faith by a series of scepticisms. Charitable souls come with their projects, and ask his coöperation. How can he hesitate? It is the rule of mere comity and courtesy to agree where you can, and to turn your sentence with something auspicious, and not freezing and sinister. But he is forced to say: 'O, these things will be as they must be: what can you do? These particular griefs and crimes are the foliage and fruit of such trees as we see growing. It is vain to complain of the leaf or the berry: cut it off; it will bear another just as bad. You must begin your cure lower down.' The generosities of the day prove an intractable element for him. The people's questions are not his; their methods are not his; and, against all the dictates of good-nature, he is driven to say, he has no pleasure in them.

Even the doctrines dear to the hope of man, of the divine Providence, and of the immortality of the soul, his neighbors cannot put the statement so that he shall affirm it. But he denies out of more faith, and not less. He denies out of honesty. He

had rather stand charged with the imbecility of scepticism, than with untruth. I believe, he says, in the moral design of the universe; it exists hospitably for the weal of souls; but your dogmas seem to me caricatures: why should I make believe them? Will any say, this is cold and infidel? The wise and magnanimous will not say so. They will exult in his far-sighted good-will, that can abandon to the adversary all the ground of tradition and common belief, without losing a jot of strength. It sees to the end of all transgression. George Fox saw "that there was an ocean of darkness and death; but withal, an infinite ocean of light and love which flowed over that of darkness."

The final solution in which scepticism is lost, is, in the moral sentiment, which never forfeits its supremacy. All moods may be safely tried, and their weight allowed to all objections: the moral sentiment as easily outweighs them all, as any one. This is the drop which balances the sea. I play with the miscellany of facts, and take those superficial views which we call scepticism; but I know that they will presently appear to me in that order which makes scepticism impossible. A man of thought must feel the thought that is parent of the universe: that the masses of nature do undulate and flow. This faith avails to the whole emergency of life and objects. The world is saturated with deity and with law. He is content with just and unjust, with sots and fools, with the triumph of folly and fraud. He can behold with serenity the yawning gulf between the ambition of man and his power of performance, between the demand and supply of power, which makes the tragedy of all souls.

Charles Fourier announced that "the attractions of man are proportioned to his destinies;" in other words, that every desire predicts its own satisfaction. Yet, all experience exhibits the reverse of this; the incompetency of power is the universal grief of young and ardent minds. They accuse the divine providence of a certain parsimony. It has shown the heaven and earth to every child, and filled him with a desire for the whole; a desire raging, infinite; a hunger, as of space to be filled with planets; a cry of famine, as of devils for souls. Then for the satisfaction,— to each man is administered a single drop, a bead of dew of vital power, *per day,*— a cup as large as space, and one drop of the water of life in it. Each man woke in the morning, with an appetite that could eat the solar system like a cake; a spirit for action and passion without bounds; he could lay his hand on the morning star: he could try conclusions with gravitation or chemistry; but, on the first motion to prove his strength,—hands, feet, senses, gave away, and would not serve him. He was an emperor deserted by his states, and left to whistle by himself, or thrust into a mob of emperors, all whistling: and still the sirens sang, "The attractions are proportioned to the destinies." In every house, in the heart of each maiden, and of each boy, in the soul of the soaring saint, this chasm is found,—between the largest promise of ideal power, and the shabby experience.

The expansive nature of truth comes to our succor, elastic, not to be surrounded. Man helps himself by larger generalizations. The lesson of life is practically to generalize; to believe what the years and the centuries say against the hours; to resist the usurpation of particulars; to penetrate to their catholic sense. Things seem to say one thing, and say the reverse. The appearance is immoral; the result is moral. Things seem to tend downward, to justify despondency, to promote rogues, to defeat the just; and, by knaves, as by martyrs, the just cause is carried forward. Although knaves win in every political struggle, although society seems to be delivered over from the hands of one set of criminals into the hands of another set of criminals, as fast as the government is changed, and the march of civilization is a train of felonies, yet, general ends are somehow answered. We see, now, events forced on, which seem to retard or retro-grade the civility of ages. But the world-spirit is a good swimmer, and storms and waves cannot drown him. He snaps his finger at laws: and so, throughout history, heaven seems to affect low and poor means. Through the years and the centuries, through evil agents, through toys and atoms, a great and beneficent tendency irresistibly streams.

Let a man learn to look for the permanent in the mutable and fleeting; let him learn to bear the disappearance of things he was wont to reverence, without losing his reverence; let him learn that he is here, not to work, but to be worked upon; and that, though abyss open under abyss, and opinion displace opinion, all are at last contained in the Eternal Cause.

"If my bark sink, 'tis to another sea." [12]

From
EMERSON'S "JOURNALS"
[1909-1914]

Jan. 25, 1820

THESE pages are intended at their commencement to contain a record of new thoughts (when they occur); for a receptacle of all the old ideas that partial but peculiar peepings at antiquity can furnish or furbish; for tablet to save the wear and tear of weak Memory, and, in short, for all the various purposes and utility, real or imaginary, which are usually comprehended under that comprehensive title *Common Place Book.*

June 7, 1820

Have been of late reading patches of Barrow [1] and Ben Jonson; and what the object—not curiosity? no—nor expectation of edification intellectual or moral—but merely because they are authors where

---

[12] From William Ellery Channing's poem "A Poet's Hope."

[1] Isaac Barrow (1630-1677), English theologian and mathematician.

vigorous phrases and quaint, peculiar words and expressions may be sought and found, the better 'to rattle out the battle of my thoughts.'

February, 1822

I have not much cause, I sometimes think, to wish my Alma Mater well, personally; I was not often highly flattered by success, and was every day mortified by my own ill fate or ill conduct. Still, when I went today to the ground where I had had the brightest thoughts of my life and filled up the little measure of my knowledge, and had felt sentimental for a time, and poetical for a time, and had seen many fine faces, and traversed many fine walks, and enjoyed much pleasant, learned, or friendly society,—I felt a crown of pleasant thoughts, as I went posting about from place to place, and room to chapel.

Cambridge, undated

All things are double one against another, said Solomon. The whole of what we know is a system of compensations. Every defect in one manner is made up in another. Every suffering is rewarded; every sacrifice is made up; every debt is paid.

Charleston, April 6, 1827

A new event is added to the quiet history of my life. I have connected myself by friendship to a man [2] who with as ardent a love of truth as that which animates me, with a mind surpassing mine in the variety of its research, and sharpened and strengthened to an energy for action to which I have no pretension, by advantages of birth and practical connexion with mankind beyond almost all men in the world,—is, yet, that which I had ever supposed only a creature of the imagination—a consistent Atheist,—and a disbeliever in the existence, and, of course, in the immortality of the soul. My faith in these points is strong and I trust, as I live, indestructible. Meantime I love and honour this intrepid doubter. His soul is noble, and his virtue, as the virtue of a Sadducee must always be, is sublime.

Alexandria, May 19, 1826

Mr. Adams [3] went out a swimming the other day into the Potomac, and went near to a boat which was coming down the river. Some rude blackguards were in it, who, not knowing the character of the swimmer, amused themselves with laughing at his bald head as it poppled up and down in the water, and, as they drew nearer, threatened to crack open his round pate if he came nigh them. The President of the United States was, I believe, compelled to waive the point of honour and seek a more retired bathing-place.

Concord, March 4, 1831

The Religion that is afraid of science dishonours God and commits suicide.

Boston, May 16, 1832

Shakspeare's creations indicate no sort of anxiety to be understood. There is the Cleopatra, an irregular, unfinished, glorious, sinful character; sink or swim, there she is, and not one in the thousand of his readers apprehends the noble dimensions of the heroine. Then Ariel, Hamlet, and all; all done in sport with the free, daring pencil of a master of the World. He leaves his children with God.

Florence, April 29, 1833

How like an archangel's tent is this great Cathedral of many-coloured marble set down in the midst of the city, and by its side its wondrous Campanile! I took a hasty glance at the gates of the Baptistery which Angelo said ought to be the gates of Paradise, 'digne chiudere il Paradiso,' and then at his own David, and hasted to the Tribune and to the Pitti Palace. I saw the statue that enchants the world. And truly the Venus deserves to be visited from far. It is not adequately represented by the plaster casts, as the Apollo and the Laocoön are. I must go again and see this statue. Then I went round this cabinet and

[2] Achille Murat.
[3] This refers to a much-publicized incident during the presidency of John Quincy Adams.

gallery and galleries till I was well-nigh 'dazzled and drunk with beauty.' I think no man has an idea of the powers of painting until he has come hither. Why should painters study at Rome? Here, here.

Florence, May 21, 1833

I like the sayers of No better than the sayers of Yes.

Liverpool, Sep. 1, 1833

I thank the Great God who has led me through this European scene, this last schoolroom in which he has pleased to instruct me, from Malta's isle, through Sicily, through Italy, through Switzerland, through France, through England, through Scotland, in safety and pleasure, and has now brought me to the shore and the ship that steers westward. He has shown me the men I wished to see,—Landor, Coleridge, Carlyle, Wordsworth; he has thereby comforted and confirmed me in my convictions. Many things I owe to the sight of these men. I shall judge more justly, less timidly, of wise men forevermore. To be sure not one of these is a mind of the very first class, but what the intercourse with each of these suggests is true of intercourse with better men, that they never fill the ear— fill the mind—no, it is an idealized portrait which always we draw of them. Upon an intelligent man, wholly a stranger to their names, they would make in conversation no deep impression, none of a world-filling fame,—they would be remembered as sensible, well-read, earnest men, not more. Especially are they all deficient, all these four,—in different degrees, but all deficient,—in insight into religious truth. They have no idea of that species of moral truth which I call the first philosophy. . . .

The comfort of meeting men of genius such as these is that they talk sincerely, they feel themselves to be so rich that they are above the meanness of pretending to knowledge which they have not, and they frankly tell you what puzzles them. But Carlyle—Carlyle is so amiable that I love him.

Boston, Feb. 19, 1834

A seaman in the coach told the story of an old spermwhale, which he called a white whale, which was known for many years by the whalemen as Old Tom, and who rushed upon the boats which attacked him, and crushed the boats to small chips in his jaws, the men generally escaping by jumping overboard and being picked up. A vessel was fitted out at New Bedford, he said, to take him. And he was finally taken somewhere off Payta Head by the Winslow or the Essex.[4]

Newton, June 18, 1834

Webster's speeches seem to be the utmost that the unpoetic West has accomplished or can. We all lean on England; scarce a verse, a page, a newspaper, but is writ in imitation of English forms; our very manners and conversation are traditional, and sometimes the life seems dying out of all literature, and this enormous paper currency of Words is accepted instead. I suppose the evil may be cured by this rank rabble party, the Jacksonism of the country, heedless of English and of all literature—a stone cut out of the ground without hands;—they may root out the hollow dilettantisms of our cultivation in the coarsest way, and the newborn may begin again to frame their own world with greater advantage.

Concord, Nov. 15, 1834

Hail to the quiet fields of my fathers! Not wholly unattended by supernatural friendship and favor, let me come hither. Bless my purposes as they are simple and virtuous. . . .

Henceforth I design not to utter any speech, poem or book that is not entirely and peculiarly my work. I will say at public lectures, and the like, those things which I have meditated for their own sake, and not for the first time with a view to that occasion.

[4] Cf. discussion of the origins of *Moby Dick,* under "Herman Melville," in Book I, Part 1.

Nov. 26, 1834

The shepherd or the beggar in his red cloak little knows what a charm he gives to the wide landscape that charms you on the mountaintop and whereof he makes the most agreeable feature, and I no more the part my individuality plays in the All.[5]

June 10, 1836

I gladly pay the rent of my house because I therewith get the horizon and the woods which I pay no rent for. For daybreak and evening and night, I pay no tax. I think it is a glorious bargain which I drive with the town.

June 22, 1836

Mr. Alcott has been here with his Olympian dreams. He is a world-builder. Evermore he toils to solve the problem, whence is the world? The point at which he prefers to begin is the mystery of the Birth of a child. I tell him it is idle for him to affect to feel an interest in the compositions of any one else. Particulars—particular thoughts, sentences, facts even—cannot interest him, except as for a moment they take their place as a ray from his orb. The Whole,—Nature proceeding from himself, is what he studies. But he loses, like other sovereigns, great pleasures by reason of his grandeur. I go to Shakspear, Goethe, Swift, even to Tennyson, submit myself to them, become merely an organ of hearing, and yield to the law of their being. I am paid for thus being nothing by an entire new mind, and thus, a Proteus, I enjoy the universe through the powers and organs of a hundred different men. But Alcott cannot delight in Shakspear, cannot get near him. And so with all things. What is characteristic also, he cannot recall one word or part of his own conversation or of any one's, let the expression be never so happy. He made here some majestic utterances, but so inspired me that even I forgot the words often.

April 26, 1838

Yesterday afternoon I went to the Cliff with Henry Thoreau. Warm, pleasant, misty weather, which the great mountain amphitheatre seemed to drink in with gladness. A crow's voice filled all the miles of air with sound. A bird's voice, even a piping frog, enlivens a solitude and makes world enough for us. At night I went out into the dark and saw a glimmering star and heard a frog, and Nature seemed to say, Well do not these suffice? Here is a new scene, a new experience. Ponder it, Emerson, and not like the foolish world, hanker after thunders and multitudes and vast landscapes, the sea or Niagara.

Oct. 18, 1839

Lectures.—In these golden days it behooves me once more to make my annual inventory of the world. For the five last years I have read each winter a new course of lectures in Boston, and each was my creed and confession of faith. Each told all I thought of the past, the present and the future. Once more I must renew my work, and I think only once in the same form, though I see that he who thinks he does something for the last time ought not to do it at all. Yet my objection is not to the thing, but with the form: and the concatenation of errors called society to which I still consent, until my plumes be grown, makes even a duty of this concession also. So I submit to sell tickets again.

June 24, 1840

Montaigne.—The language of the street is always strong. What can describe the folly and emptiness of scolding like the word *jawing?* I feel too the force of the double negative, though clean contrary to our grammar rules. And I confess to some pleasure from the stinging rhetoric of a rattling oath in the mouth of truckmen and teamsters. How laconic and brisk it is by the side of a page of the *North American Review.* Cut these words and they would bleed; they are vascular and alive; they walk and run. Moreover they who speak them have this elegancy, that they do not trip in their speech. It is a shower of

---

[5] See Emerson's poem "Each and All."

bullets, whilst Cambridge men and Yale men correct themselves and begin again at every half sentence.

I know nobody among my contemporaries except Carlyle who writes with any sinew and vivacity comparable to Plutarch and Montaigne. Yet always this profane swearing and bar-room wit has salt and fire in it. I cannot now read Webster's speeches. Fuller and Browne [6] and Milton are quick, but the list is soon ended. Goethe seems to be well alive, no pedant. Luther too.

October 24, 1841

I told Garrison that I thought he must be a very young man, or his time very heavy on his hands, who can afford to think much and talk much about the foibles of his neighbors, or *'denounce,'* and play 'the son of thunder' as he called it.

October, undated

Thou shalt read Homer, Æschylus, Sophocles, Euripides, Aristophanes, Plato, Proclus, Plotinus, Jamblichus, Porphyry, Aristotle, Virgil, Plutarch, Apuleius, Chaucer, Dante, Rabelais, Montaigne, Cervantes, Shakspeare, Jonson, Ford, Chapman, Beaumont and Fletcher, Bacon, Marvell, More, Milton, Moliere, Swedenborg, Goethe.

August, 1843, undated

Webster quite fills our little town, and I doubt if I shall get settled down to writing until he is well gone from the county. . . .

Elizabeth Hoar [7] says that she talked with him, as one likes to go behind the Niagara Falls, so she tried to look into those famed caverns of eyes, and see how deep they were, and the whole man was magnificent. Mr. Choate told her that he should not sleep for a week when a cause like this was pending, but that when they met in Boston on Saturday afternoon to talk over the matter, the rest of them were wide awake, but Mr. Webster went fast asleep amidst the consultation.

It seems to me the Quixotism of Criticism to quarrel with Webster because he has not this or that fine evangelical property. He is no saint, but the wild olive wood, ungrafted yet by grace, but according to his lights a very true and admirable man. His expensiveness seems to be necessary to him. Were he too prudent a Yankee it would be a sad deduction from his magnificence. I only wish he would never truckle; I do not care how much he spends.

May 24, 1847

The days come and go like muffled and veiled figures sent from a distant friendly party, but they say nothing, and if we do not use the gifts they bring, they carry them as silently away.[8]

London, June, 1848, undated

In England every man you meet is some man's son; in America, he may be some man's father.

January, undated, 1851

Tennyson's *In Memoriam* is the commonplaces of condolence among good Unitarians in the first week of mourning. The consummate skill of the versification is the sole merit.

January, undated, 1851

I found when I had finished my new lecture that it was a very good house, only the architect had unfortunately omitted the stairs.

May, 1855, undated

Jones Very, [9] who thought it an honour to wash his own face, seems to me less insane than men who hold themselves cheap.

---

[6] Thomas Fuller (1608-1661) and Sir Thomas Browne (1605-1682), English essayists.

[7] Daughter of famous Concord lawyer and legislator, Samuel Hoar. Rufus Choate (1799-1859) was U. S. Senator from Massachusetts at the time. Webster, under attack on personal and political grounds, had recently resigned as Secretary of State.

[8] Cf. Emerson's poem "Days."

[9] Transcendental poet and essayist (1813-1880).

June 24, 1863

In reading Henry Thoreau's journal, I am very sensible of the vigour of his constitution. That oaken strength which I noted whenever he walked, or worked, or surveyed wood-lots, the same unhesitating hand with which a field-labourer accosts a piece of work, which I should shun as a waste of strength, Henry shows in his literary task. He has muscle, and ventures on and performs feats which I am forced to decline. In reading him, I find the same thought, the same spirit that is in me, but he takes a step beyond, and illustrates by excellent images that which I should have conveyed in a sleepy generality. 'Tis as if I went into a gymnasium, and saw youths leap, climb, and swing with a force unapproachable,—though their feats are only continuations of my initial grapplings and jumps.

May 24, 1864

Yesterday, May 23, we buried Hawthorne in Sleepy Hollow, in a pomp of sunshine and verdure, and gentle winds. James Freeman Clarke read the service in the church and at the grave. Longfellow, Lowell, Holmes, Agassiz, Hoar, Dwight, Whipple, Norton, Alcott, Hillard, Fields, Judge Thomas, and I attended the hearse as pallbearers. Franklin Pierce was with the family. The church was copiously decorated with white flowers delicately arranged. The corpse was unwillingly shown,—only a few moments to this company of his friends. But it was noble and serene in its aspect, —nothing amiss,—a calm and powerful head. A large company filled the church and the grounds of the cemetery. All was so bright and quiet that pain or mourning was hardly suggested, and Holmes said to me that it looked like a happy meeting.

Clarke in the church said that Hawthorne had done more justice than any other to the shades of life, shown a sympathy with the crime in our nature, and, like Jesus, was the friend of sinners.

I thought there was a tragic element in the event, that might be more fully rendered,—in the painful solitude of the man, which, I suppose, could not longer be endured, and he died of it.

I have found in his death a surprise and disappointment. I thought him a greater man than any of his works betray, that there was still a great deal of work in him, and that he might one day show a purer power. Moreover, I have felt sure of him in his neighborhood, and in his necessities of sympathy and intelligence,—that I could well wait his time,—his unwillingness and caprice,—and might one day conquer a friendship. It would have been a happiness, doubtless to both of us, to have come into habits of unreserved intercourse. It was easy to talk with him,—there were no barriers,—only, he said so little, that I talked too much, and stopped only because, as he gave no indications, I feared to exceed. He showed no egotism or self-assertion, rather a humility, and, at one time, a fear that he had written himself out. One day, when I found him on the top of his hill, in the woods, he paced back the path to his house, and said, 'This path is the only remembrance of me that will remain.' Now it appears that I waited too long.

March 15, 1870

My new book sells faster, it appears, than either of its foregoers. This is not for its merit, but only shows that old age is a good advertisement. Your name has been seen so often that your book must be worth buying.

1817 ∾ *Henry David Thoreau* ∾ 1862

I

ONE evening in late July, 1846, Henry Thoreau left his little one-room house at the edge of Walden Pond and set off for the nearby village of Concord, Massachusetts. Walking was an important part of the life of this young man, and shoes are an important part of walking; his errand this evening was to pick up a shoe which he had left with the Concord cobbler a few days earlier. But he did not get the mended shoe that night, for as soon as he reached the main street of the village he was accosted by Constable Sam Staples, presented with a warrant for his arrest, and conducted, quietly and directly, to the jail.

Thoreau has made Concord and its environs memorable forever in literature, but his own standing in his home community was not very high at this time. He was commonly regarded as a shiftless and even dangerous character— a graduate of Harvard, to be sure, and a friend of Emerson and Alcott, but a ne'er-do-well. Not long before, he and a fishing companion had accidentally set fire to some woods, and much damage had been done before volunteer firemen from Concord had subdued the flames. His arrest was based not upon this escapade, however, but upon his refusal to pay his poll tax.

The Mexican War, then in progress, was regarded by many as no more than an attempt to gain more territory for the extension of the slave system. Thoreau had resolved not to "pay a tax to, or recognize the authority of, the state which buys and sells men, women, and children at the door of its senate-house." So here was the young man in jail, a martyr to the rugged individualism of his convictions, spending an interesting night in conversation with a fellow prisoner awaiting trial for barn-burning. But relatives paid his tax that night, and the next morning Thoreau was released. Sam Staples later reported he was "mad as the devil" when he walked out of the jail. He got his mended shoe and went back to his huckleberry crop on the edge of Walden Pond. His martyrdom had proved abortive.

II

This troublesome individualist was of mixed French and Scotch ancestry. His grandfather Thoreau had come to Boston from the Channel Islands just before the Revolution and had done fairly well in trade. More intellectual was the heritage from the maternal side; Grandfather Dunbar was a Harvard graduate and Congregational minister. Henry was born in Concord in 1817. By that time his father had proved a failure at shop-keeping, and for the next few years tried various shifts—farming, keeping a school in Boston, trading with the Indians at Bangor.

In 1823 the family returned to Concord, falling back upon the help of the Dunbar relatives. Here they took up pencil-making, which proved to be a moderately successful vocation and which led, many years later, to a profitable small business in the manufacture of fine graphite. But this was after Henry had reached middle age; during his youth the Thoreaus were poor, without being actually needy. Henry had a brother, to whom he was very closely attached, and two sisters. With aunts and uncles and occasional boarders, the Thoreau house was often full to overflowing. The curse of the family, as of so many New Englanders in those days, was tuberculosis, which had brought down powerful Grandfather Thoreau and which was to cause the death of Henry's sister Helen and finally of Henry himself.

The boyhood of Henry Thoreau was happy. What if his family was hard-pressed at times? Henry had the woods and swamps and river, the hills and small lakes (called ponds), of his native town to rove over. He was a hunter and fisherman, and learned the habits of the ducks, partridges, and wild pigeons, the rabbits and muskrats. In later life he was fond of telling of the pleasures of his boyhood. "My life was ecstasy," he wrote. His first schooling was in the local "academy," a private school, and at sixteen he was sent off to Harvard.

His poverty, together with his own sensitiveness and the robust independence which his Scotch blood and his outdoor life had already developed, seems to have set him apart from his fellow students. Only the scrimping and saving of his family and his own frugal habits made college possible for him at all. But one thing he did learn there, and that was how to make the most of a college library. He had become an avid reader even before he entered Harvard. For example, he had read through Chalmers' *English Poets,* which left him with a lasting affection for the verse writers of the seventeenth century and some of the Elizabethans. When Thoreau was given a leave of absence in the midst of his college course in order to earn some money with which to finish it, he was fortunate to get a school at Canton, then the home of Orestes A. Brownson. He lived at Brownson's home and was stimulated by that leonine liberal in many an evening's conversation about the new German thought and the Transcendentalists and Emerson. The two studied German together. "The morning of a new *Lebenstag*" for him, Thoreau later called this interlude in his college course.

Thoreau was graduated in 1837. His commencement oration was on "The Commercial Spirit"—object of his attack throughout life. "The order of things should be somewhat reversed," he said; "the seventh should be man's day of toil, wherein to earn his living by the sweat of his brow, and the other six his Sabbath of the affections and the Soul, in which to range this widespread garden and drink in the soft influences and sublime revelations of Nature."

III

After his graduation, Thoreau got a job teaching the town school at Concord. He announced at the start that he would spare the rod; at the end of two weeks a school-committeeman stalked in and told him to beat the scholars "or the school would spoil." That night Thoreau kept six of them after school, flogged them, and then resigned. Later he and his brother John opened a private school in the village and conducted it on more agreeable principles for three years.

Thoreau began his journal shortly after his graduation from Harvard. This daily record of his ideas, observations, reading, and inspirations he continued all his life. Published incompletely in fourteen volumes, it is Thoreau's basic literary production, both in the sense that he drew upon it for his other works, and that it furnishes a continuous record of the true, the inner Thoreau.

It was his journal that first brought our young school-teacher to the attention of Ralph Waldo Emerson, Concord's most famous resident. Mrs. Emerson's sister was a boarder at the Thoreau house; she came to share the family interest in Henry's journal and eventually showed parts of it to her brother-in-law. Henry was thereupon invited to call, and he soon became a frequent visitor at the Emerson house. "I delight much in my young friend," wrote Emerson in his own journal, "who seems to have as free and erect a mind as any I have ever met." Thoreau was accepted as a member of the informal Transcendental Club, and at its gatherings met A. Bronson Alcott, Margaret Fuller, Theodore Parker, George Ripley, and others whose names must always be connected with that extraordinary and fertile movement known as New England Transcendentalism.

Already Thoreau was spiritually a member of this group. Like many another young man, he had been deeply affected by Emerson's first book *Nature*, published during his senior year at Harvard, and had doubtless heard Emerson read "The American Scholar" as the Phi Beta Kappa address at his commencement. His brief but fruitful contact with Brownson had set him to reading the German idealists and probing the doctrine of "intuition." By this time he had fully and thoroughly accepted that doctrine, so perfectly compressed in Emerson's statement: "We lie in the lap of an immense intelligence, which makes us receivers of its truth." Again:

Meantime, whilst the doors of the temple stand open night and day before every man, and the oracles of this truth cease never, it is guarded by one stern condition; this, namely, it is an intuition. It cannot be received at second hand. Truly speaking, it is not instruction but provocation that I can receive from another soul. What he announces I must find true in me, or reject.

Thus Emerson; and thus, indeed, Thoreau.

But those who are tempted to think, as some have thought in the past, that Thoreau was merely "Emerson's man"—that he was robbing Emerson's orchard, to repeat the misjudgment of Lowell—ought to read again the above quotation from the Divinity School Address. Emerson provoked Thoreau; he did not instruct him. What Emerson announced, Thoreau either found true in himself or he rejected.

This is precisely what Emerson meant in his reference to Thoreau's "free and erect mind." The quality of individualism which had been first developed in the Middlesex woods and swamps, and which had been stiffened by his Harvard experience, found a congenial philosophy and a foundation in the Transcendental doctrine of "intuition." Further, the idea of nature as another manifestation of that "divine intelligence" which at the same time informed the mind of man, thus relating the spirit of Henry Thoreau to that of the pine tree, gave a new and necessary meaning to his woodland excursions and studies.

But the thoroughness of Thoreau's acceptance of Transcendentalism, with both its emphasis on individualism (or self-reliance) and on the polarity of idea and fact, made Thoreau difficult for his friends. He was not only "prickly," to use the adjective so often applied to him, but he was tremendously in earnest in his determination to *live* the ideology which was now making such a stir in the world. In this fierce determination we have the key to much of his life. It sets him off from those to whom Transcendentalism was only a fascinating intellectual plaything, and even from those who stopped short of practical acceptance of its implications. Let us keep this in mind as we review his adult life.

IV

For many years Thoreau seems to have been a Young Man in Search of a Career. Of course, every young man is searching for a career. Most of them are looking for a way of life increasingly rich in money and influence. Thoreau completely and sincerely rejected the money goal, asking only enough to enable him to pursue a career of observation, contemplation, and study. So far as influence (or fame) was concerned, here again he asked only enough to make him secure in a career devoted to the same three objectives. But how to get the little money, the little attention needed for such a life as he desired, without sacrificing that life itself? He could teach school, and he did for three years, but found it dull and unrewarding. "Pray, what things interest me at present? A long, soaking rain, the drops trickling down the stubble, while I lay drenched on a last year's bed of wild oats, by the side of some bare hill, ruminating. Such things are of moment." Or he could always make pencils. He could make pencils, or even do heavy farm labor, only in an emergency, however; he needed an employment that would give him six days a week to invite his soul, as he had said in his Commencement speech. This invitation to his soul was "of moment;" he must come to grips with himself. "How shall I help myself? By withdrawing into the garret and associating with spiders and mice, determining to meet myself face to face sooner or later."

What he did do when his school petered out was to become a kind of man-of-all-work at Emerson's place in Concord. Emerson was often away lecturing, and someone was needed to do the chores and help with the children, especially since Mrs. Emerson was a semi-invalid. So Henry moved into the room at the head of the stairs, and made it his home for two years (and for a briefer period later). There was talk with Emerson and with those who frequented his house. There was opportunity for an intimate acquaintance with Mrs. Emerson, for whom he came to have a deep affection. There was time for the study of Hindu literature and the writing of some articles for the *Dial*. Whatever he did, there was always time for his journal.

He had begun to study the philosophers of India while in college. Now in *The Laws of Menu* and the *Bhagavat-Gîta* he found himself stimulated anew by the knowledge that thinkers of an old race had long ago found a way of life in the search for a reality beneath the shell of surface appearances. The oriental doctrines which he now read with such passionate interest fortified a plan which he already had in mind to retire somewhere in the woods and live simply with high thoughts.

Two of the score of items which Thoreau contributed to the *Dial*, the short-lived quarterly edited by Margaret Fuller, George Ripley, and Emerson, were groups of brief selections—one from *The Laws of Menu* and the other sayings from Confucius. The *Dial* was important to Thoreau because it gave him the feeling of being a man of letters. That is what he was; and from this time forward, writing for publication seemed to open before him, not wholly as a career, but quite as much the means to a career. But he was to find the financial rewards of authorship elusive, to say the least.

Also literary was another means of earning what little he needed to live on—lecturing. The first lyceums were self-improvement groups organized in Massachusetts and Connecticut villages to study whatever was new and important, but especially geology. They were spontaneous adult education clubs. They made natural history collections, held discussions and debates, and heard papers read. Soon they began inviting scholars from neighboring villages and cities to talk to them, paying their modest traveling expense and sometimes a fee of a few dollars. Concord organized a lyceum in 1829; it admitted children of the age of twelve to membership, and Henry Thoreau joined. Shortly before his Walden experience Thoreau was secretary of the Lyceum, which by then had become a winter lecture course; he brought Emerson, Theodore Parker, and Horace Greeley, among others, before the Concord Lyceum that winter. The lectures were nearly always read, and sometimes they must have been painfully dull; but the system had prospered in New England, and had spread westward and southward over the whole country. Emerson was much in demand on the lyceum platform, though his delivery was poor and he rarely roused his audiences to any enthusiasm. But people wanted to see him because he was the great Emerson, and for many years a chief part of his income was derived from his lecturing trips.

It was plain to Thoreau that lecturing was a function of the man of letters. He could follow Emerson's pattern—piece together his journal entries for a lecture, and then make the lecture into an essay for publication. This he did, beginning with lectures in Concord, and going out to other villages and cities as invitations came. Though not a good platform man, he was sometimes effective, and his lyceum work was an important part of his later life.

Emerson, who was sometimes a little annoyed by Thoreau's failure to get ahead, to "show a performance much more manifest than that of the other grand promisers," supported him in his literary ambitions. After Thoreau had quitted the room at the head of the stairs, Emerson encouraged him to try his literary fortunes in New York, and to that end got him a position as tutor to his young nephews in the William Emerson family on Staten Island. And Henry faithfully but vainly pounded the pavement looking for a suitable opening, and then came back to Concord all ready for the Walden experience. Well he knew that his true career was that of an observer of nature and of himself, and that New York with all its publishing was no place for him. "I seem to see somewhat more of my own kith and kin in the lichens on the rocks than in any books. It does seem as if mine were a peculiarly wild nature, which so yearns toward all wildness."

V

Emerson had recently bought fourteen acres of woods and briars on the shore of the small lake known as Walden Pond. He permitted Thoreau to build a cabin there. The one-room dwelling was set a short distance from the lake and in view of the public road. It was no hermitage and Thoreau was no hermit. He had much of solitude and time for contemplation at Walden; but he also had many visitors, "whom he receives," wrote a friend, "with pleasure, and does his best to entertain."

Readers of Thoreau's matchless account of his life in this retreat have commonly failed to take it seriously enough. Perhaps its quiet humor invites too light a regard, and there is a danger of confusing it with the sentimental writing about nature which has become popular in our own time. But there are two definite (though not sharply differentiated) values in *Walden* that the student who comes to a new perusal of it must not miss. One, of course, is its fresh presentation of Transcendental idealism—its love and reverence for all the natural phenomena, regarded as Henry Thoreau's "kith and kin"—the grand ideas of Fichte and Coleridge and Emerson and the Oriental philosophers brought home to Walden Pond. The other, perhaps more important today, or more to the taste of the present, is the economic principle of the whole experiment. For Thoreau was utterly serious in his attempt to live simply and greatly—with "leisure and independence and health"—on 27 cents a week for food and about the same for clothes. Any failure of distribution in the midst of abundance, whether in the last depression or the next, invites attention to *Walden;* indeed, any revolt against over-complexity in modern civilization may find here its manifesto.

The Walden experience was good for Thoreau: he gained in self-confidence, in sound relationships with others, in his distinctively literary work. He came away from Walden (because he had "other lives to live") with the manuscript of a book ready for a publisher. It was not *Walden,* which was to be his second book, but *A Week on the Concord and Merrimack Rivers.*

The *Week* is founded upon a journey which Henry and John Thoreau had taken in September, 1839, in an interval of their school-keeping. That narrative, the descriptions of nature, and the character sketches give a certain form to the work; but the selections ("meditations" the older writers would have called them) from his long-kept journal give it body. "Virgil and White of Selborne and Izaak Walton all in one!" exulted Alcott; and many discerning readers have preferred this first book of Thoreau's to the more popular *Walden.* But publishers did not look with favor on the manuscript that came out of Walden cabin; even when Emerson and other friends urged them, they were unmoved. Thoreau then decided to have the book brought out at his own risk, but it did not sell when it was at last offered to an unappreciative public. Of the edition of 1000 copies, about 225 were sold, 75 given away, and the remainder returned, at the end of four years, to the author. "I have now," Thoreau wrote in his journal in 1853, "a library of nearly 900 volumes, 700 of which I wrote myself."

Nor was the debt to the publisher yet satisfied by that time. The financial venture, larger than any Thoreau had ever before undertaken, had made it necessary for him to earn some cash money. He thereupon gave more attention to his father's pencil business, which had now turned to the profitable line of fine graphite; Henry's inventive mind contributed to the improvement of the production processes. He also wrote and sold some articles to the magazines, aided by the advice of Horace Greeley, whose lasting friendship he had made during his visit to New York. He continued with his lecturing. And finally he became Concord's leading surveyor, marking the limits of woodlots, laying out streets and roads, drawing careful maps.

Despite all these employments, he found time to write *Walden.* Though the failure of his first book caused some delay, Thoreau eventually placed the new one with Ticknor & Fields, then well established as leading Boston publishers.

Walden appeared in 1854, and 2000 copies were sold before the author's death eight years later.

His activities as surveyor and author rehabilitated Thoreau in the eyes of his neighbors; no longer was he the shiftless woods-tramp. But any who regarded him as a transformed character were wholly mistaken. He was the same Henry Thoreau, kith and kin with the lichens: "I will take another walk to the Cliff, another row on the river, another skate on the meadow, be out in the first snow, and associate with the winter birds. Here I am at home. In the bare and bleached crust of the earth I recognize my friend." (Journal, 1858).

He was the same Henry Thoreau who had gone to jail as a protest against a government which permitted slavery. His famous essay on "Civil Disobedience," which grew out of that experience, was published two years after he left Walden. He followed it up a few years later with his defiant "Slavery in Massachusetts," delivered on the Fourth of July at Framingham. Thoreau the individualist challenged slave-holding on the highest principles: "I wish my countrymen to consider that whatever the human law may be, neither an individual nor a nation can ever commit the least act of injustice against the obscurest individual without having to pay the penalty for it."

Thoreau met John Brown of Osawatomie when he visited Concord in 1857; indeed he had the old white-bearded hero and fanatic in his own home. Two years later he heard Captain Brown speak in Concord just before he left for his tragic raid on Harper's Ferry. Thoreau was tremendously affected by the news of the raid and the imminent hanging of Old Brown. At white heat he wrote his greatest public address, "A Plea for John Brown," and delivered it with feeling to a Concord audience, and again in Worcester, and finally to a great throng in Theodore Parker's church in Boston. Emerson heard it in Concord and testified to its moving power and effect on its audience. "I plead not for his life, but for his character—his immortal life," declared Thoreau. As in his earlier political addresses, all was pitched upon the level of high principle.

In these latter years, though he was sought out by visitors and admirers and had many demands upon his time, Thoreau was still the outdoor man, still the searcher after himself in fern, tree, and wildfowl. His erect form (of medium height or under), clothed in homespun garments woven to resist thorns and brambles, and a large handkerchief about the neck, might have been seen almost any day, fair or rainy, passing through a wood opening or meadow near Concord with that long Indian stride of his, pausing now and again for examination of something on the ground or in a bush or in the air. His grey-blue eyes commonly had a downward look, as though attending the path he trod; his nose was the most prominent feature of his face, curving as it did almost low enough to touch his upper lip. Outdoors he wore a big shapeless hat with broad brim and a crown high enough to furnish storage-room for specimens he collected on his walks. Thus he still roamed the countryside, more and more intent, as he grew older, upon collection and classification.

Sometimes he went further abroad—outside of the Middlesex region. He made a trip to the Maine woods in 1846, and to Cape Cod three years later; both these visits were repeated. In 1850 he and his friend Ellery Channing spent a week in Canada—a journey which resulted in *A Yankee in Canada,* serialized in *Putnam's Magazine* a few years later. There were other trips, especially to Monadnock and the White Mountains with different friends; but he still "travelled a good deal in Concord." His last long trip—the most ambitious but least successful—was made to Minnesota in search of relief from the consumption which had then marked him for death.

Henry Thoreau died in the late spring of 1862, at the age of forty-four. In the next few years several volumes put together out of the journals and lectures appeared—*Excursions; The Maine Woods; Cape Cod; A Yankee in Canada, with Anti-Slavery and Reform Papers.* Emerson edited some of Thoreau's letters in 1865, and in the eighties H. G. O. Blake joined some of the nature descriptions of the journals in the series composed of *Early Spring in Massachusetts, Summer, Winter,* and *Autumn.* His poems were published together in 1895.

VI

Thoreau's reputation as a writer has increased rather steadily since his death. It has been hard for his critics to separate his literary performance from the eccentricities of his personality or from his positions in regard to nature, society, and politics. But the consensus now places both the *Week* and *Walden* very high among the great American masterpieces. The attentive reader may well give special consideration to Thoreau's style, noting particularly: (1) his knowing use of words, wide and varied vocabulary, employment of both archaic words and modern slang, and delight in poetic expression; (2) his mastery of the sentence, in which his most recent and perhaps ablest critic has found the chief excellency of his style; (3) his use of figures, which so often makes poetry of his prose; and (4) his quiet humor, his sarcasm, his wit sharpened into epigram. At one time Emerson thought of his friend as a poet, but he never achieved adequate mastery of the essential forms of verse.

Thoreau is, after all these years, strikingly modern. No other of the great New England group now speaks so directly to contemporary questions. This is true especially with respect to two matters. One of them is the economic retreat from the city. It is not without significance that *Walden* has been widely circulated in England as a tract for a labor-reform group representing the plan of a cheaper, simpler life outside the cities. Thoreau's other chief impact on contemporary thinking aligns him with the "rugged individualism" which protests against increasing government controls. His influence upon the philosophical anarchists, upon the Russian Tolstoy and the Indian Gandhi, has been notable and freely acknowledged. His contribution to the art and practice of political protest has been effective and world-wide.

A complicated personality, Thoreau was many things; but in all these things he was an individualist in search of the meaning of life. He lived every day to find what he tells us he sought at Walden:

I wanted to live deep and suck out all the marrow of life, to live so sturdily and Spartan-like as to put to rout all that was not life, to cut a broad swath and shave close, to drive life into a corner, and reduce it to its lowest terms, and if it proved to be mean, why then to get the whole and genuine meanness of it, and publish its meanness to the world; or if it were sublime, to know it by experience and be able to give a true account of it.

[For nearly fifty years the best existing book about Thoreau was the biography by an Englishman, H. S. Salt (London, 1890, revised 1896); but H. S. Canby's *Thoreau* (Boston, 1939), excellent both as biography and criticism, has superseded it. F. B. Sanborn wrote two books on Thoreau, the first for the American Men of Letters Series (revised edition, Boston, 1910). They are worth more as reminiscence than as ordered and careful studies. W. E. Channing's *Thoreau, the Poet-Naturalist* (Boston, 1873, revised 1902) is interesting as a Transcendental interpretation by a friend. Léon Bazalgette's *Henry Thoreau, Sauvage* (Paris, 1914), translated by Van Wyck Brooks as *Henry Thoreau, Bachelor of Nature* (New York, 1924), is a novelized biography, as soundly based on fact as could be expected—an interesting and helpful book. *The Heart of Thoreau's Journals,* edited by Odell Shepard (Boston, 1927), is a convenient source-book for the study of Thoreau's personality and ideas. Good essays on Thoreau may be found in F. O. Matthiessen's *American Renaissance* (New York, 1941), B. V. Crawford's *Thoreau* (New York, 1934) in American Writers Series; R. L. Stevenson's *Familiar Studies of Men and Books* (London, 1882); Paul Elmer More's *Shelburne Essays; First Series* (New York, 1904) and *Fifth Series* (New York, 1908). Mark Van Doren's *Henry David Thoreau, A Critical Study* (Boston, 1916) is useful.]

From
A WEEK ON THE CONCORD AND MERRIMACK RIVERS
[1849]

From
SATURDAY

"Come, come, my lovely fair, and let us try
These rural delicates."
—*Invitation to the Soul*, Quarles [1]

AT LENGTH, on Saturday, the last day of August, 1839, we two, brothers, and natives of Concord, weighed anchor in this river port; for Concord, too, lies under the sun, a port of entry and departure for the bodies as well as the souls of men; one shore at least exempted from all duties but such as an honest man will gladly discharge. A warm drizzling rain had obscured the morning, and threatened to delay our voyage, but at length the leaves and grass were

[1] Francis Quarles (1592-1644), English poet, famous for his poems in the artificial style of his times.

dried, and it came out a mild afternoon, as serene and fresh as if nature were maturing some greater scheme of her own. After this long dripping and oozing from every pore, she began to respire again more healthily than ever. So with a vigorous shove we launched our boat from the bank, while the flags and bulrushes curtseyed a God-speed, and dropped silently down the stream.

Our boat, which had cost us a week's labor in the spring, was in form like a fisherman's dory, fifteen feet long by three and a half in breadth at the widest part, painted green below, with a border of blue, with reference to the two elements in which it was to spend its existence. It had been loaded the evening before at our door, half a mile from the river, with potatoes and melons from a patch which we had cultivated, and a few utensils, and was provided with wheels in order to be rolled around falls, as well as with two sets of oars, and several slender poles for shoving in shallow places, and also two masts, one of which served for a tent-pole at night; for a buffalo skin was to be our bed, and a tent of cotton cloth our roof. It was strongly built but heavy, and hardly of better model than usual. If rightly made, a boat would be a sort of amphibious animal, a creature of two elements, related by one half its structure to some swift and shapely fish, and by the other to some strong-winged and graceful bird. The fish shows where there should be the greatest breadth of beam and depth in the hold; its fins direct where to set the oars, and the tail gives some hint for the form and position of the rudder. The bird shows how to rig and trim the sails, and what form to give to the prow that it may balance the boat and divide the air and water best. These hints we had but partially obeyed. But the eyes, though they are no sailors, will never be satisfied with any model, however fashionable, which does not answer all the requisitions of art. However, as art is all of a ship but the wood, and yet the wood alone will rudely serve the purpose of a ship,

so our boat being of wood gladly availed itself of the old law that the heavier shall float the lighter, and though a dull water fowl, proved a sufficient buoy for our purpose.

"Were it the will of Heaven, an osier bough
   Were vessel safe enough the seas to
      plow." [2]

Some village friends stood upon a promontory lower down the stream to wave us a last farewell; but we, having already performed these shore rites with excusable reserve, as befits those who are embarked on unusual enterprises, who behold but speak not, silently glided past the firm lands of Concord, both peopled cape and lonely summer meadow, with steady sweeps. And yet we did unbend so far as to let our guns speak for us, when at length we had swept out of sight, and thus left the woods to ring again with their echoes; and it may be many russet-clad children lurking in those broad meadows, with the bittern and the woodcock and the rail, though wholly concealed by brakes and hardhack and meadow-sweet, heard our salute that afternoon.

We were soon floating past the first regular battle ground of the Revolution, resting on our oars between the still visible abutments of that "North Bridge," over which in April, 1775, rolled the first faint tide of that war, which ceased not, till, as we read on the stone on our right, it "gave peace to these United States." . . .

Gradually the village murmur subsided, and we seemed to be embarked on the placid current of our dreams, floating from past to future as silently as one awakes to fresh morning or evening thoughts. We glided noiselessly down the stream, occasionally driving a pickerel from the covert of the pads, or a bream from her nest, and the smaller bittern now and then sailed away on sluggish wings from some recess in the shore, or the larger lifted itself out

---

[2] Pindar (Emerson's translation).

of the long grass at our approach, and carried its precious legs away to deposit them in a place of safety. The tortoises also rapidly dropped into the water, as our boat ruffled the surface amid the willows, breaking the reflections of the trees. The banks had passed the height of their beauty, and some of the brighter flowers showed by their faded tints that the season was verging towards the afternoon of the year; but this sombre tinge enhanced their sincerity, and in the still unabated heats they seemed like a mossy brink of some cool well. The narrow-leaved willow lay along the surface of the water in masses of light green foliage, interspersed with the large white balls of the button-bush. The rose-colored polygonum [3] raised its head proudly above the water on either hand, and, flowering at this season, and in these localities, in the midst of dense fields of the white species which skirted the sides of the stream, its little streak of red looked very rare and precious. The pure white blossoms of the arrowhead stood in the shallower parts, and a few cardinals on the margin still proudly surveyed themselves reflected in the water, though the latter, as well as the pickerel-weed, was now nearly out of blossom. The snakehead, *chelone glabra,* grew close to the shore, while a kind of coreopsis, turning its brazen face to the sun, full and rank, and a tall dull red flower, *eupatorium purpureum,* or trumpet weed, formed the rear rank of the fluvial array. The bright blue flowers of the soap-wort gentian were sprinkled here and there in the adjacent meadows, like flowers which Proserpine had dropped, and still further in the fields, or higher on the bank, were seen the Virginian rhexia, and drooping neottia or ladies'-tresses; while from the more distant waysides, which we occasionally passed, and banks where the sun had lodged, was reflected a dull yellow beam from the ranks of tansy, now in its prime. In short, nature seemed to have adorned herself for our departure with a profusion of fringes and curls, mingled with the bright tints of flowers, reflected in the water. But we

missed the white water-lily, which is the queen of river flowers, its reign being over for this season. He makes his voyage too late, perhaps, by a true water clock who delays so long. Many of this species inhabit our Concord water. I have passed down the river before sunrise on a summer morning between fields of lilies still shut in sleep; and when at length the flakes of sunlight from over the bank fell on the surface of the water, whole fields of white blossoms seemed to flash open before me, as I floated along, like the unfolding of a banner, so sensible is this flower to the influence of the sun's rays.

Late in the afternoon we passed a man on the shore fishing with a long birch pole, its silvery bark left on, and a dog at his side, rowing so near as to agitate his cork with our oars, and drive away luck for a season; and when we had rowed a mile as straight as an arrow, with our faces turned towards him, and the bubbles in our wake still visible on the tranquil surface, there stood the fisher still with his dog, like statues under the other side of the heavens, the only objects to relieve the eye in the extended meadow; and there would he stand abiding his luck, till he took his way home through the fields at evening with his fish. Thus, by one bait or another, Nature allures inhabitants into all her recesses. This man was the last of our townsmen whom we saw, and we silently through him bade adieu to our friends.

The characteristics and pursuits of various ages and races of men are always existing in epitome in every neighborhood. The pleasures of my earliest youth have become the inheritance of other men. This man is still a fisher, and belongs to an era in which I myself have lived. Perchance he is not confounded by many knowledges, and has not sought out many inventions, but how to take many fishes before the sun sets, with his slender birchen pole and flaxen line, that is invention enough for

---

[3] Water-pepper.

him. It is good even to be a fisherman in summer and in winter. Some men are judges these August days, sitting on benches, even till the court rises; they sit judging there honorably, between the seasons and between meals, leading a civil politic life, arbitrating in the case of Spaulding *versus* Cummings, it may be, from highest noon till the red vesper sinks into the west. The fisherman, meanwhile, stands in three feet of water, under the same summer's sun, arbitrating in other cases between muck-worm and shiner, amid the fragrance of water-lilies, mint, and pontederia,[4] leading his life many rods from the dry land, within a pole's length of where the larger fishes swim. Human life is to him very much like a river,

—"renning aie downward to the sea."

This was his observation. His honor made a great discovery in bailments.

I can just remember an old brown-coated man who was the Walton [5] of this stream, who had come over from New-castle, England, with his son, the latter a stout and hearty man who had lifted an anchor in his day. A straight old man he was who took his way in silence through the meadows, having passed the period of communication with his fellows; his old experienced coat hanging long and straight and brown as the yellow pine bark, glitter-ing with so much smothered sunlight, if you stood near enough, no work of art but naturalized at length. I often discovered him unexpectedly amid the pads and the gray willows when he moved, fishing in some old country method,—for youth and age then went a-fishing together,—full of incommunicable thoughts, perchance about his own Tyne and Northumberland. He was always to be seen in serene afternoons haunting the river, and almost rustling with the sedge; so many sunny hours in an old man's life, entrapping silly fish, almost grown to be the sun's familiar; what need had he of hat or raiment any, having served out his time, and seen through such

thin disguises? I have seen how his coeval fates rewarded him with the yellow perch, and yet I thought his luck was not in proportion to his years; and I have seen when, with slow steps and weighed down with aged thoughts, he disappeared with his fish under his low-roofed house on the skirts of the village. I think nobody else saw him; nobody else remembers him now, for he soon after died, and migrated to new Tyne streams. His fishing was not a sport, nor solely a means of subsistence, but a sort of solemn sacrament and withdrawal from the world, just as the aged read their Bibles. . . .

That was a long pull from Ball's Hill to Carlisle Bridge, sitting with our faces to the south, a slight breeze rising from the north; but nevertheless water still runs and grass grows, for now, having passed the bridge between Carlisle and Bedford, we see men haying far off in the meadow, their heads waving like the grass which they cut. In the distance the wind seemed to bend all alike. As the night stole over, such a freshness was wafted across the meadow that every blade of cut-grass seemed to teem with life. Faint purple clouds began to be reflected in the water, and the cow-bells tinkled louder along the banks, while, like sly water rats, we stole along nearer the shore, looking for a place to pitch our camp.

At length, when we had made about seven miles, as far as Billerica, we moored our boat on the west side of a little rising ground which in the spring forms an island in the river. Here we found huckleberries still hanging upon the bushes, where they seemed to have slowly ripened for our especial use. Bread and sugar, and cocoa boiled in river water, made our repast, and as we had drunk in the fluvial pros-pect all day, so now we took a draught of the water with our evening meal to

---

[4] *Pontederia cordata* is the pickerel-weed, referred to in the second paragraph above.

[5] Izaak Walton (1593-1683), author of *The Compleat Angler.*

propitiate the river gods, and whet our vision for the sights it was to behold. The sun was setting on the one hand, while our eminence was contributing its shadow to the night, on the other. It seemed insensibly to grow lighter as the night shut in, and a distant and solitary farm-house was revealed, which before lurked in the shadows of the noon. There was no other house in sight, nor any cultivated field. To the right and left, as far as the horizon, were straggling pine woods with their plumes against the sky, and across the river were rugged hills, covered with shrub oaks, tangled with grape vines and ivy, with here and there a gray rock jutting out from the maze. The sides of these cliffs, though a quarter of a mile distant, were almost heard to rustle while we looked at them, it was such a leafy wilderness; a place for fauns and satyrs, and where bats hung all day to the rocks, and at evening flitted over the water, and fireflies husbanded their light under the grass and leaves against the night. When we had pitched our tents on the hill-side, a few rods from the shore, we sat looking through its triangular door in the twilight at our lonely mast on the shore, just seen above the alders, and hardly yet come to a stand-still from the swaying of the stream; the first encroachment of commerce on this land. There was our port, our Ostia.[6] That straight geometrical line against the water and the sky stood for the last refinements of civilized life, and what of sublimity there is in history was there symbolized.

For the most part, there was no recognition of human life in the night, no human breathing was heard, only the breathing of the wind. As we sat up, kept awake by the novelty of our situation, we heard at intervals foxes stepping about over the dead leaves, and brushing the dewy grass close to our tent, and once a musquash fumbling among the potatoes and melons in our boat, but when we hastened to the shore we could detect only a ripple in the water ruffling the disk of a star. At intervals we

were serenaded by the song of a dreaming sparrow or the throttled cry of an owl, but after each sound which near at hand broke the stillness of the night, each crackling of the twigs, or rustling among the leaves, there was a sudden pause, and deeper and more conscious silence, as if the intruder were aware that no life was rightfully abroad at that hour. There was a fire in Lowell, as we judged, this night, and we saw the horizon blazing, and heard the distant alarm bells, as it were a faint tinkling music borne to these woods. But the most constant and memorable sound of a summer's night, which we did not fail to hear every night afterward, though at no time so incessantly and so favorably as now, was the barking of the house dogs, from the loudest and hoarsest bark to the faintest aerial palpitation under the eaves of heaven, from the patient but anxious mastiff to the timid and wakeful terrier, at first loud and rapid, then faint and slow, to be imitated only in a whisper; wow-wow-wow-wow—wo—wo—w—w. Even in a retired and uninhabited district like this, it was a sufficiency of sound for the ear of night, and more impressive than any music. I have heard the voice of a hound, just before daylight, while the stars were shining, from over the woods and river, far in the horizon, when it sounded as sweet and melodious as an instrument. The hounding of a dog pursuing a fox or other animal in the horizon, may have first suggested the notes of the hunting horn to alternate with and relieve the lungs of the dog. This natural bugle long resounded in the woods of the ancient world before the horn was invented. The very dogs that sullenly bay the moon from farmyards in these nights, excite more heroism in our breasts than all the civil exhortations or war sermons of the age. "I had rather be a dog, and bay the moon," than many a Roman that I know. The night is equally indebted to the clarion of the cock,

[6] Ancient seaport of Rome, situated at the mouth of the Tiber.

with wakeful hope, from the very setting of the sun, prematurely ushering in the dawn. All these sounds, the crowing of cocks, the baying of dogs, and the hum of insects at noon, are the evidence of nature's health or *sound* state. Such is the never failing beauty and accuracy of language, the most perfect art in the world; the chisel of a thousand years retouches it.

At length the antepenultimate and drowsy hours drew on, and all sounds were denied entrance to our ears.

From
SUNDAY

At least let us have healthy books, a stout horse-rake or a kitchen range which is not cracked. Let not the poet shed tears only for the public weal. He should be as vigorous as a sugar maple, with sap enough to maintain his own verdure, beside what runs into the troughs, and not like a vine, which being cut in the spring bears no fruit, but bleeds to death in the endeavor to heal its wounds. The poet is he that hath fat enough, like bears and marmots, to suck his claws all winter. He hibernates in this world, and feeds on his own marrow. It is pleasant to think in winter, as we walk over the snowy pastures, of those happy dreamers that lie under the sod, of dormice and all that race of dormant creatures, which have such a superfluity of life enveloped in thick folds of fur, impervious to cold. Alas, the poet too is, in one sense, a sort of dormouse gone into winter quarters of deep and serene thoughts, insensible to surrounding circumstances; his words are the relation of his oldest and finest memory, a wisdom drawn from the remotest experience. Other men lead a starved existence, meanwhile, like hawks, that would fain keep on the wing, and trust to pick up a sparrow now and then. . . .

A perfectly healthy sentence, it is true, is extremely rare. For the most part we miss the hue and fragrance of the thought; as if we could be satisfied with the dews of the morning or evening without their colors, or the heavens without their azure. The most attractive sentences are, perhaps, not the wisest, but the surest and roundest. They are spoken firmly and conclusively, as if the speaker had a right to know what he says, and if not wise, they have at least been well learned. Sir Walter Raleigh might well be studied if only for the excellence of his style, for he is remarkable in the midst of so many masters. There is a natural emphasis in his style, like a man's tread, and a breathing space between the sentences, which the best of modern writing does not furnish. His chapters are like English parks, or say rather like a western forest, where the larger growth keeps down the underwood, and one may ride on horse-back through the openings. All the distinguished writers of that period, possess a greater vigor and naturalness than the more modern,—for it is allowed to slander our own time,— and when we read a quotation from one of them in the midst of a modern author, we seem to have come suddenly upon a greener ground, a greater depth and strength of soil. It is as if a green bough were laid across the page, and we are refreshed as by the sight of fresh grass in mid-winter or early spring. You have constantly the warrant of life and experience in what you read. The little that is said is eked out by implication of the much that was done. The sentences are verduous and blooming as evergreen and flowers, because they are rooted in fact and experience, but our false and florid sentences have only the tints of flowers without their sap or roots. All men are really most attracted by the beauty of plain speech, and they even write in a florid style in imitation of this. They prefer to be misunderstood rather than to come short of its exuberance. Hussein Effendi praised the epistolary style of Ibrahim Pasha to the French traveller Botta,[7] be-

---

[7] Paul Émile Botta (1802-1870), famous for Assyrian discoveries.

cause of "the difficulty of understanding it; there was," he said, "but one person at Jidda who was capable of understanding and explaining the Pasha's correspondence." A man's whole life is taxed for the least thing well done. It is its net result. Every sentence is the result of a long probation. Where shall we look for standard English, but to the words of a standard man? The word which is best said came nearest to not being spoken at all, for it is cousin to a deed which the speaker could have better done. Nay, almost it must have taken the place of a deed by some urgent necessity, even by some misfortune, so that the truest writer will be some captive knight, after all. And perhaps the fates had such a design, when, having stored Raleigh so richly with the substance of life and experience, they made him a fast prisoner, and compelled him to make his words his deeds, and transfer to his expression the emphasis and sincerity of his action. [8]

From
TUESDAY

Early one summer morning I had left the shores of the Connecticut, and for the livelong day traveled up the bank of a river, which came in from the west; now looking down on the stream, foaming and rippling through the forest a mile off, from the hills over which the road led, and now sitting on its rocky brink and dipping my feet in its rapids, or bathing adventurously in mid-channel. The hills grew more and more frequent, and gradually swelled into mountains as I advanced, hemming in the course of the river, so that at last I could not see where it came from, and was at liberty to imagine the most wonderful meanderings and descents. At noon I slept on the grass in the shade of a maple, where the river had found a broader channel than usual, and was spread out shallow, with frequent sand-bars exposed. In the names of the towns I rec-

ognized some which I had long ago read on teamsters' wagons, that had come from far up country; quiet uplandish towns, of mountainous fame. I walked along, musing and enchanted, by rows of sugar-maples, through the small and uninquisitive villages, and sometimes was pleased with the sight of a boat drawn up on a sand-bar, where there appeared no inhabitants to use it. It seemed, however, as essential to the river as a fish, and to lend a certain dignity to it. It was like the trout of mountain streams to the fishes of the sea, or like the young of the land-crab born far in the interior, who have never yet heard the sound of the ocean's surf. The hills approached nearer and nearer to the stream, until at last they closed behind me, and I found myself just before nightfall in a romantic and retired valley, about half a mile in length, and barely wide enough for the stream at its bottom. I thought that there could be no finer site for a cottage among mountains. You could anywhere run across the stream on the rocks, and its constant murmuring would quiet the passions of mankind forever. Suddenly the road, which seemed aiming for the mountain-side, turned short to the left, and another valley opened, concealing the former, and of the same character with it. It was the most remarkable and pleasing scenery I had ever seen. I found here a few mild and hospitable inhabitants, who, as the day was not quite spent, and I was anxious to improve the light, directed me four or five miles farther on my way to the dwelling of a man whose name was Rice, who occupied the last and highest of the valleys that lay in my path, and who, they said, was a rather rude and uncivil man. But "what is a foreign country to those who have science? Who is a stranger to those who have the habit of speaking kindly?"

At length, as the sun was setting behind the mountains in a still darker and more

---

[8] Most of Raleigh's writing was done during the thirteen years he was a prisoner in the Tower of London.

solitary vale, I reached the dwelling of this man. Except for the narrowness of the plain, and that the stones were solid granite, it was the counterpart of that retreat to which Belphoebe bore the wounded Timias,—

> "In a pleasant glade,
> With mountains round about environed,
> And mighty woods, which did the valley shade,
> And like a stately theatre it made,
> Spreading itself into a spacious plain;
> And in the midst a little river played
> Amongst the pumy stones which seemed to plain,
> With gentle murmur, that his course they did restrain." [9]

I observed, as I drew near, that he was not so rude as I had anticipated, for he kept many cattle, and dogs to watch them, and I saw where he had made maple-sugar on the sides of the mountains, and above all distinguished the voices of children mingling with the murmur of the torrent before the door. As I passed his stable, I met one whom I supposed to be a hired man, attending to his cattle, and I inquired if they entertained travelers at that house. "Sometimes we do," he answered gruffly, and immediately went to the farthest stall from me, and I perceived that it was Rice himself whom I had addressed. But pardoning this incivility to the wildness of the scenery, I bent my steps to the house. There was no sign-post before it, nor any of the usual invitations to the traveler, though I saw by the road that many went and came there, but the owner's name only was fastened to the outside; a sort of implied and sullen invitation, as I thought. I passed from room to room without meeting any one, till I came to what seemed the guests' apartment, which was neat, and even had an air of refinement about it, and I was glad to find a map against the wall which would direct me on my journey on the morrow. At length I heard a step in a distant apartment, which was the first I had entered, and went to see if the landlord had come in; but it proved to be

only a child, one of those whose voices I had heard, probably his son, and between him and me stood in the doorway a large watch-dog, which growled at me, and looked as if he would presently spring, but the boy did not speak to him; and when I asked for a glass of water, he briefly said, "It runs in the corner." So I took a mug from the counter and went out of doors, and searched round the corner of the house, but could find neither well nor spring, nor any water but the stream which ran all along the front. I came back, therefore, and, setting down the mug, asked the child if the stream was good to drink; whereupon he seized the mug, and, going to the corner of the room, where a cool spring which issued from the mountain behind trickled through a pipe into the apartment, filled it, and drank, and gave it to me empty again, and, calling to the dog, rushed out of doors. Erelong some of the hired men made their appearance, and drank at the spring, and lazily washed themselves and combed their hair in silence, and some sat down as if weary, and fell asleep in their seats. But all the while I saw no women, though I sometimes heard a bustle in that part of the house from which the spring came.

At length Rice himself came in, for it was now dark, with an ox-whip in his hand, breathing hard, and he too soon settled down into his seat not far from me, as if, now that his day's work was done, he had no farther to travel, but only to digest his supper at his leisure. When I asked him if he could give me a bed, he said there was one ready, in such a tone as implied that I ought to have known it, and the less said about that the better. So far so good. And yet he continued to look at me as if he would fain have me say something further like a traveler. I remarked that it was a wild and rugged country he inhabited, and worth coming many miles to see. "Not so very rough neither," said he, and appealed to his men

---

[9] From Edmund Spenser's *Faery Queen.*

to bear witness to the breadth and smoothness of his fields, which consisted in all of one small interval, and to the size of his crops; "and if we have some hills," added he, "there's no better pasturage anywhere." I then asked if this place was the one I had heard of, calling it by a name I had seen on the map, or if it was a certain other; and he answered, gruffly, that it was neither the one nor the other; that he had settled it and cultivated it, and made it what it was, and I could know nothing about it. Observing some guns and other implements of hunting hanging on brackets around the room, and his hounds now sleeping on the floor, I took occasion to change the discourse, and inquired if there was much game in that country, and he answered this question more graciously, having some glimmering of my drift; but when I inquired if there were any bears, he answered impatiently that he was no more in danger of losing his sheep than his neighbors; he had tamed and civilized that region. After a pause, thinking of my journey on the morrow, and the few hours of daylight in that hollow and mountainous country, which would require me to be on my way betimes, I remarked that the day must be shorter by an hour there than on the neighboring plains; at which he gruffly asked what I knew about it, and affirmed that he had as much daylight as his neighbors; he ventured to say, the days were longer there than where I lived, as I should find if I stayed; that in some way, I could not be expected to understand how, the sun came over the mountains half an hour earlier, and stayed half an hour later there than on the neighboring plains. And more of like sort he said. He was, indeed, as rude as a fabled satyr. But I suffered him to pass for what he was,— for why should I quarrel with nature?— and was even pleased at the discovery of such a singular natural phenomenon. I dealt with him as if to me all manners were indifferent, and he had a sweet, wild way with him. I would not question nature, and I would rather have him as he was

than as I would have him. For I had come up here not for sympathy, or kindness, or society, but for novelty and adventure, and to see what nature had produced here. I therefore did not repel his rudeness, but quite innocently welcomed it all, and knew how to appreciate it, as if I were reading in an old drama a part well sustained. He was indeed a coarse and sensual man, and, as I have said, uncivil, but he had his just quarrel with nature and mankind, I have no doubt, only he had no artificial covering to his ill-humors. He was earthy enough, but yet there was good soil in him, and even a long-suffering Saxon probity at bottom. If you could represent the case to him, he would not let the race die out in him, like a red Indian.

At length I told him that he was a fortunate man, and I trusted that he was grateful for so much light; and, rising, said I would take a lamp, and that I would pay him then for my lodging, for I expected to recommence my journey even as early as the sun rose in his country; but he answered in haste, and this time civilly, that I should not fail to find some of his household stirring, however early, for they were no sluggards, and I could take my breakfast with them before I started, if I chose; and as he lighted the lamp I detected a gleam of true hospitality and ancient civility, a beam of pure and even gentle humanity, from his bleared and moist eyes. It was a look more intimate with me, and more explanatory, than any words of his could have been if he had tried to his dying day. It was more significant than any Rice of those parts could even comprehend, and long anticipated this man's culture,—a glance of his pure genius, which did not much enlighten him, but did impress and rule him for the moment, and faintly constrain his voice and manner. He cheerfully led the way to my apartment, stepping over the limbs of his men, who were asleep on the floor in an intervening chamber, and showed me a clean and comfortable bed. For many pleasant hours after the household was asleep I sat at the open window, for it was a sultry night, and heard the little river

"Amongst the pumy stones, which seemed to plain,
With gentle murmur, that his course they did restrain."

But I arose as usual by starlight the next morning, before my host, or his men, or even his dogs, were awake; and, having left a ninepence on the counter, was already half-way over the mountain with the sun before they had broken their fast.

From
FRIDAY

As I pass along the streets of our village of Concord on the day of our annual Cattle Show, when it usually happens that the leaves of the elms and buttonwoods begin first to strew the ground under the breath of the October wind, the lively spirits in their sap seem to mount as high as any plowboy's let loose that day; and they lead my thoughts away to the rustling woods, where the trees are preparing for their winter campaign. This autumnal festival, when men are gathered in crowds in the streets as regularly and by as natural a law as the leaves cluster and rustle by the wayside, is naturally associated in my mind with the fall of the year. The low of cattle in the streets sounds like a hoarse symphony or running base [10] to the rustling of the leaves. The wind goes hurrying down the country, gleaning every loose straw that is left in the fields, while every farmer lad too appears to scud before it,—having donned his best peajacket and pepper-and-salt waistcoat, his unbent trousers, outstanding rigging of duck, or kersymere, or corduroy, and his furry hat withal,—to country fairs and cattle shows, to that Rome among the villages where the treasures of the year are gathered. All the land over they go leaping the fences with their tough idle palms, which have never learned to hang by their sides, amid the low of calves and the bleating of sheep,—Amos, Abner, Elnathan, Elbridge,—

"From steep pine-bearing mountains to the plain."

I love these sons of earth, every mother's son of them, with their great hearty hearts rushing tumultuously in herds from spectacle to spectacle, as if fearful lest there should not be time between sun and sun to see them all, and the sun does not wait more than in haying time.

"Wise nature's darlings, they live in the world
Perplexing not themselves how it is hurled."

Running hither and thither with appetite for the coarse pastimes of the day, now with boisterous speed at the heels of the inspired negro from whose larynx the melodies of all Congo and Guinea coast have broke loose into our streets; now to see the procession of a hundred yoke of oxen, all as august and grave as Osiris, or the droves of neat cattle and milch cows as unspotted as Isis or Io. Such as had no love for Nature

"at all,
Came lovers home from this great festival." [11]

They may bring their fattest cattle and richest fruits to the fair, but they are all eclipsed by the show of men. These are stirring autumn days, when men sweep by in crowds, amid the rustle of leaves, like migrating finches; this is the true harvest of the year, when the air is but the breath

---

[10] Old form of "bass."
[11] The three quotations interpolated in this paragraph are all from poems by Christopher Marlowe.

of men, and the rustling of leaves is as the trampling of the crowd. We read now-a-days of the ancient festivals, games, and processions of the Greeks and Etruscans, with a little incredulity, or at least with little sympathy; but how natural and irrepressible in every people is some hearty and palpable greeting of Nature. The Corybantes, the Bacchantes, the rude primitive tragedians with their procession and goatsong, and the whole paraphernalia of the Panathenæa,[12] which appear so antiquated and peculiar, have their parallel now. The husbandman is always a better Greek than the scholar is prepared to appreciate, and the old custom still survives, while antiquarians and scholars grow gray in commemorating it. The farmers crowd to the fair to-day in obedience to the same ancient law which Solon or Lycurgus did not enact, as naturally as bees swarm and follow their queen.

It is worth the while to see the country's people, how they pour into the town, the sober farmer folk, now all agog, their very shirt and coat collars pointing forward,—collars so broad as if they had put their shirts on wrong end upward, for the fashions always tend to superfluity,—and with an unusual springiness in their gait, jabbering earnestly to one another. The more supple vagabond, too, is sure to appear on the least rumor of such a gathering, and the next day to disappear, and go into his hole like the seventeen-year locust, in an ever shabby coat, though finer than the farmer's best, yet never dressed; come to see the sport, and have a hand in what is going,—to know "what's the row," if there is any; to be where some men are drunk, some horses race, some cockerels fight; anxious to be shaking props under a table, and above all to see the "striped pig." He especially is the creature of the occasion. He empties both his pockets and his character into the stream, and swims in such a day. He dearly loves the social slush. There is no reserve of soberness in him.

I love to see the herd of men feeding heartily on coarse and succulent pleasures, as cattle on the husks and stalks of vegetables. Though there are many crooked and crabbed specimens of humanity among them, run all to thorn and rind, and crowded out of shape by adverse circumstances, like the third chestnut in the bur, so that you wonder to see some heads wear a whole hat, yet fear not that the race will fail or waiver in them; like the crabs which grow in hedges, they furnish the stocks of sweet and thrifty fruits still. Thus is nature recruited from age to age, while the fair and palatable varieties die out and have their period. This is that mankind. How cheap must be the material of which so many are made.

From
WALDEN
[1854]

ECONOMY

WHEN I wrote the following pages, or rather the bulk of them, I lived alone, in the woods, a mile from any neighbor, in a house which I had built myself, on the shore of Walden Pond, in Concord, Massachusetts, and earned my living by the labor of my hands only. I lived there two years and two months. At present I am a sojourner in civilized life again.

I should not obtrude my affairs so much on the notice of my readers if very particular inquiries had not been made by my townsmen concerning my mode of life, which some would call impertinent, though they do not appear to me at all impertinent, but, considering the circumstances, very natural and pertinent. Some have asked what I got to eat; if I did not feel lonesome; if I was not afraid; and the like. Others have been curious to learn what portion of my income I devoted to charitable purposes; and some, who have large families, how many poor children I main-

---

[12] The festival in honor of Athena, most important of the celebrations in ancient Athens.

tained. I will therefore ask those of my readers who feel no particular interest in me to pardon me if I undertake to answer some of these questions in this book. In most books, the *I*, or first person, is omitted; in this it will be retained; that, in respect to egotism, is the main difference. We commonly do not remember that it is, after all, always the first person that is speaking. I should not talk so much about myself if there were anybody else whom I knew as well. Unfortunately, I am confined to this theme by the narrowness of my experience. Moreover, I, on my side, require of every writer, first or last, a simple and sincere account of his own life, and not merely what he has heard of other men's lives; some such account as he would send to his kindred from a distant land; for if he has lived sincerely, it must have been in a distant land to me. Perhaps these pages are more particularly addressed to poor students. As for the rest of my readers, they will accept such portions as apply to them. I trust that none will stretch the seams in putting on the coat, for it may do good service to him whom it fits.

I would fain say something, not so much concerning the Chinese and Sandwich Islanders as you who read these pages, who are said to live in New England; something about your condition, especially your outward condition or circumstances in this world, in this town, what it is, whether it is necessary that it be as bad as it is, whether it cannot be improved as well as not. I have travelled a good deal in Concord; and everywhere, in shops, and offices, and fields, the inhabitants have appeared to me to be doing penance in a thousand remarkable ways. What I have heard of Bramins sitting exposed to four fires and looking in the face of the sun; or hanging suspended, with their heads downward, over flames; or looking at the heavens over their shoulders "until it becomes impossible for them to resume their natural position, while from the twist of the neck nothing but liquids can pass into the stomach;" or dwelling, chained for life, at the foot of a tree; or measuring with their bodies, like caterpillars, the breadth of vast empires; or standing on one leg on the tops of pillars,—even these forms of conscious penance are hardly more incredible and astonishing than the scenes which I daily witness. The twelve labors of Hercules were trifling in comparison with those which my neighbors have undertaken; for they were only twelve, and had an end; but I could never see that these men slew or captured any monster or finished any labor. They have no friend Iolaus [1] to burn with a hot iron the root of the hydra's head, but as soon as one head is crushed, two spring up.

I see young men, my townsmen, whose misfortune it is to have inherited farms, houses, barns, cattle, and farming tools; for these are more easily acquired than got rid of. Better if they had been born in the open pasture and suckled by a wolf, that they might have seen with clear eyes what field they were called to labor in. Who made them serfs of the soil? Why should they eat their sixty acres, when man is condemned to eat only his peck of dirt? Why should they begin digging their graves as soon as they are born? They have got to live a man's life, pushing all these things before them, and get on as well as they can. How many a poor immortal soul have I met well-nigh crushed and smothered under its load, creeping down the road of life, pushing before it a barn seventy-five feet by forty, its Augean stables never cleansed,[2] and one hundred acres of land, tillage, mowing, pasture, and woodlot! The portionless, who struggle with no such unnecessary inherited encumbrances, find it labor enough to subdue and cultivate a few cubic feet of flesh.

---

[1] One of the twelve labors of Hercules was the slaying of the Lernean hydra, which had nine heads. Whenever Hercules cut one off, two sprouted in its place until his charioteer Iolaus seared the stumps with a red-hot iron.

[2] The cleansing of the Augean stables was another labor of Hercules.

But men labor under a mistake. The better part of the man is soon plowed into the soil for compost. By a seeming fate, commonly called necessity, they are employed, as it says in an old book, laying up treasures which moth and rust will corrupt and thieves break through and steal. It is a fool's life, as they will find when they get to the end of it, if not before. It is said that Deucalion and Pyrrha created men by throwing stones over their heads behind them:—

Inde genus durum sumus, experiens-
que laborum,
Et documenta damus quâ simus origine
nati.[3]

Or, as Raleigh rhymes it in his sonorous way,—

"From thence our kind hard-hearted is,
      enduring pain and care,
Approving that our bodies of a stony
      nature are."

So much for a blind obedience to a blundering oracle, throwing the stones over their heads behind them, and not seeing where they fell.

Most men, even in this comparatively free country, through mere ignorance and mistake, are so occupied with the factitious cares and superfluously coarse labors of life that its finer fruits cannot be plucked by them. Their fingers, from excessive toil, are too clumsy and tremble too much for that. Actually, the laboring man has not leisure for a true integrity day by day; he cannot afford to sustain the manliest relations to men; his labor would be depreciated in the market. He has no time to be anything but a machine. How can he remember well his ignorance—which his growth requires—who has so often to use his knowledge? We should feed and clothe him gratuitously sometimes, and recruit him with our cordials, before we judge of him. The finest qualities of our nature, like the bloom on fruits, can be preserved only by the most delicate handling. Yet we do not treat ourselves nor one another thus tenderly.

Some of you, we all know, are poor, find it hard to live, are sometimes, as it were, gasping for breath. I have no doubt that some of you who read this book are unable to pay for all the dinners which you have actually eaten, or for the coats and shoes which are fast wearing or are already worn out, and have come to this page to spend borrowed or stolen time, robbing your creditors of an hour. It is very evident what mean and sneaking lives many of you live, for my sight has been whetted by experience; always on the limits, trying to-day, insolvent; seeking to curry favor, to get into business and trying to get out of debt, a very ancient slough, called by the Latins *aes alienum*, another's brass, for some of their coins were made of brass; still living, and dying, and buried by this other's brass; always promising to pay, promising to pay, to-morrow, and dying to get custom, by how many modes, only not state-prison offences; lying, flattering, voting, contracting yourselves into a nutshell of civility, or dilating into an atmosphere of thin and vaporous generosity, that you may persuade your neighbor to let you make his shoes, or his hat, or his coat, or his carriage, or import his groceries for him; making yourselves sick, that you may lay up something against a sick day, something to be tucked away in an old chest, or in a stocking behind the plastering, or, more safely, in the brick bank; no matter where, no matter how much or how little.

I sometimes wonder that we can be so frivolous, I may almost say, as to attend to the gross but somewhat foreign form of servitude called Negro Slavery, there are so many keen and subtle masters that enslave both North and South. It is hard to have a Southern overseer; it is worse to have a Northern one; but worst of all when you are the slave-driver of yourself.

---

[3] Ovid's *Metamorphoses*, I, 414-415.

Talk of a divinity in man! Look at the teamster on the highway, wending to market by day or night; does any divinity stir within him? His highest duty to fodder and water his horses! What is his destiny to him compared with the shipping interests? Does not he drive for Squire Make-a-stir? How godlike, how immortal, is he? See how he cowers and sneaks, how vaguely all the day he fears, not being immortal nor divine, but the slave and prisoner of his own opinion of himself, a fame won by his own deeds. Public opinion is a weak tyrant compared with our own private opinion. What a man thinks of himself, that it is which determines, or rather indicates, his fate. Self-emancipation even in the West Indian provinces of the fancy and imagination,—what Wilberforce [4] is there to bring that about? Think, also, of the ladies of the land weaving toilet cushions against the last day, not to betray too green an interest in their fates! As if you could kill time without injuring eternity.

The mass of men lead lives of quiet desperation. What is called resignation is confirmed desperation. From the desperate city you go into the desperate country, and have to console yourself with the bravery of minks and muskrats. A stereotyped but unconscious despair is concealed even under what are called the games and amusements of mankind. There is no play in them, for this comes after work. But it is a characteristic of wisdom not to do desperate things.

When we consider what, to use the words of the catechism, is the chief end of man, and what are the true necessaries and means of life, it appears as if men had deliberately chosen the common mode of living because they preferred it to any other. Yet they honestly think there is no choice left. But alert and healthy natures remember that the sun rose clear. It is never too late to give up our prejudices. No way of thinking or doing, however ancient, can be trusted without proof. What everybody echoes or in silence passes by as true to-day may turn out to be false-

hood to-morrow, mere smoke of opinion, which some had trusted for a cloud that would sprinkle fertilizing rain on their fields. What old people say you cannot do, you try and find that you can. Old deeds for old people, and new deeds for new. Old people did not know enough once, perchance, to fetch fresh fuel to keep the fire a-going; new people put a little dry wood under a pot, and are whirled round the globe with the speed of birds, in a way to kill old people, as the phrase is. Age is no better, hardly so well, qualified for an instructor as youth, for it has not profited so much as it has lost. One may almost doubt if the wisest man has learned anything of absolute value by living. Practically, the old have no very important advice to give the young, their own experience has been so partial, and their lives have been such miserable failures, for private reasons, as they must believe; and it may be that they have some faith left which belies that experience, and they are only less young than they were. I have lived some thirty years on this planet, and I have yet to hear the first syllable of valuable or even earnest advice from my seniors. They have told me nothing, and probably cannot tell me anything to the purpose. Here is life, an experiment to a great extent untried by me; but it does not avail me that they have tried it. If I have any experience which I think valuable, I am sure to reflect that this my Mentors said nothing about.

One farmer says to me, "You cannot live on vegetable food solely, for it furnishes nothing to make bones with;" and so he religiously devotes a part of his day to supplying his system with the raw material of bones; walking all the while he talks behind his oxen, which, with vegetable-made bones, jerk him and his lumbering plow along in spite of every obstacle. Some things are really necessaries of life in some circles, the most helpless and diseased,

[4] William Wilberforce (1759-1853), leader in the British abolition movement.

which in others are luxuries merely, and in others still are entirely unknown.

The whole round of human life seems to some to have been gone over by their predecessors, both the heights and the valleys, and all things to have been cared for. According to Evelyn,[5] "the wise Solomon prescribed ordinances for the very distances of trees; and the Roman prætors have decided how often you may go into your neighbor's land to gather the acorns which fall on it without trespass, and what share belongs to that neighbor." Hippocrates has even left directions how we should cut our nails; that is, even with the ends of the fingers, neither shorter nor longer. Undoubtedly the very tedium and ennui which presume to have exhausted the variety and the joys of life are as old as Adam. But man's capacities have never been measured; nor are we to judge of what he can do by any precedents, so little has been tried. Whatever have been thy failures hitherto, "be not afflicted, my child, for who shall assign to thee what thou hast left undone?"

We might try our lives by a thousand simple tests; as, for instance, that the same sun which ripens my beans illumines at once a system of earths like ours. If I had remembered this it would have prevented some mistakes. This was not the light in which I hoed them. The stars are the apexes of what wonderful triangles! What distant and different beings in the various mansions of the universe are contemplating the same one at the same moment! Nature and human life are as various as our several constitutions. Who shall say what prospect life offers to another? Could a greater miracle take place than for us to look through each other's eyes for an instant? We should live in all the ages of the world in an hour; ay, in all the worlds of the ages. History, Poetry, Mythology!—I know of no reading of another's experience so startling and informing as this would be.

The greater part of what my neighbors call good I believe in my soul to be bad,

and if I repent of anything, it is very likely to be my good behavior. What demon possessed me that I behaved so well? You may say the wisest thing you can, old man,—you who have lived seventy years, not without honor of a kind,—I hear an irresistible voice which invites me away from all that. One generation abandons the enterprises of another like stranded vessels.

I think that we may safely trust a good deal more than we do. We may waive just so much care of ourselves as we honestly bestow elsewhere. Nature is as well adapted to our weakness as to our strength. The incessant anxiety and strain of some is a well-nigh incurable form of disease. We are made to exaggerate the importance of what work we do; and yet how much is not done by us! or, what if we had been taken sick? How vigilant we are! determined not to live by faith if we can avoid it; all the day long on the alert, at night we unwillingly say our prayers and commit ourselves to uncertainties. So thoroughly and sincerely are we compelled to live, reverencing our life, and denying the possibility of change. This is the only way, we say; but there are as many ways as there can be drawn radii from one centre. All change is a miracle to contemplate; but it is a miracle which is taking place every instant. Confucius said, "To know that we know what we know, and that we do not know what we do not know, that is true knowledge." When one man has reduced a fact of the imagination to be a fact to his understanding, I foresee that all men will at length establish their lives on that basis.

Let us consider for a moment what most of the trouble and anxiety which I have referred to is about, and how much it is necessary that we be troubled, or at least careful. It would be some advantage to live a primitive and frontier life, though in the midst of an outward civilization, if

[5] John Evelyn (1620-1706), English diarist and writer on arboriculture, etc. His book on trees, entitled *Sylva*, is often referred to by Thoreau.

only to learn what are the gross necessaries of life and what methods have been taken to obtain them; or even to look over the old day-books of the merchants, to see what it was that men most commonly bought at the stores, what they stored, that is, what are the grossest groceries. For the improvements of ages have had but little influence on the essential laws of man's existence: as our skeletons, probably, are not to be distinguished from those of our ancestors.

By the words, *necessary of life,* I mean whatever, of all that man obtains by his own exertions, has been from the first, or from long use has become, so important to human life that few, if any, whether from savageness, or poverty, or philosophy, ever attempt to do without it. To many creatures there is in this sense but one necessary of life, Food. To the bison of the prairie it is a few inches of palatable grass, with water to drink; unless he seeks the Shelter of the forest or the mountain's shadow. None of the brute creation requires more than Food and Shelter. The necessaries of life for man in this climate may, accurately enough, be distributed under the several heads of Food, Shelter, Clothing, and Fuel; for not till we have secured these are we prepared to entertain the true problems of life with freedom and a prospect of success. Man has invented, not only houses, but clothes and cooked food; and possibly from the accidental discovery of the warmth of fire, and the consequent use of it, at first a luxury, arose the present necessity to sit by it. We observe cats and dogs acquiring the same second nature. By proper Shelter and Clothing we legitimately retain our own internal heat; but with an excess of these, or of Fuel, that is, with an external heat greater than our own internal, may not cookery properly be said to begin? Darwin, the naturalist, says of the inhabitants of Tierra del Fuego,[6] that while his own party, who were well clothed and sitting close to a fire, were far from too warm, these naked savages, who were farther off, were observed, to his great surprise, "to be streaming with perspiration at undergoing such a roasting." So, we are told, the New Hollander goes naked with impunity, while the European shivers in his clothes. Is it impossible to combine the hardiness of these savages with the intellectualness of the civilized man? According to Liebig,[7] man's body is a stove, and food the fuel which keeps up the internal combustion in the lungs. In cold weather we eat more, in warm less. The animal heat is the result of a slow combustion, and disease and death take place when this is too rapid; or for want of fuel, or from some defect in the draught, the fire goes out. Of course the vital heat is not to be confounded with fire; but so much for analogy. It appears, therefore, from the above list, that the expression *animal life,* is nearly synonymous with the expression, *animal heat;* for while Food may be regarded as the Fuel which keeps up the fire within us,—and Fuel serves only to prepare that Food or to increase the warmth of our bodies by addition from without,—Shelter and Clothing also serve only to retain the *heat* thus generated and absorbed.

The grand necessity, then, for our bodies, is to keep warm, to keep the vital heat in us. What pains we accordingly take, not only with our Food, and Clothing, and Shelter, but with our beds, which are our nightclothes, robbing the nests and breasts of birds to prepare this shelter within a shelter, as the mole has its bed of grass and leaves at the end of its burrow! The poor man is wont to complain that this is a cold world; and to cold, no less physical than social, we refer directly a great part of our ails. The summer, in some climates, makes possible to man a sort of Elysian life. Fuel, except to cook his Food, is then

---

[6] Charles Robert Darwin (1809-1882), recounts his observations on Tierra del Fuego in his *A Naturalist's Voyage Round the World,* which Thoreau had read. Darwin's more famous *On the Origin of Species* was published five years after *Walden.*

[7] Baron Justus von Liebig (1803-1873), German chemist.

unnecessary; the sun is his fire, and many of the fruits are sufficiently cooked by its rays; while Food generally is more various, and more easily obtained, and Clothing and Shelter are wholly or half unnecessary. At the present day, and in this country, as I find by my own experience, a few implements, a knife, an axe, a spade, a wheelbarrow, etc., and for the studious, lamplight, stationery, and access to a few books, rank next to necessaries, and can all be obtained at a trifling cost. Yet some, not wise, go to the other side of the globe, to barbarous and unhealthy regions, and devote themselves to trade for ten or twenty years, in order that they may live,—that is, keep comfortably warm,—and die in New England at last. The luxuriously rich are not simply kept comfortably warm, but unnaturally hot; as I implied before, they are cooked, of course *à la mode*.

Most of the luxuries, and many of the so-called comforts of life, are not only not indispensable, but positive hindrances to the elevation of mankind. With respect to luxuries and comforts, the wisest have ever lived a more simple and meagre life than the poor. The ancient philosophers, Chinese, Hindoo, Persian, and Greek, were a class than which none has been poorer in outward riches, none so rich in inward. We know not much about them. It is remarkable that *we* know so much of them as we do. The same is true of the more modern reformers and benefactors of their race. None can be an impartial or wise observer of human life but from the vantage ground of what *we* should call voluntary poverty. Of a life of luxury the fruit is luxury, whether in agriculture, or commerce, or literature, or art. There are nowadays professors of philosophy, but not philosophers. Yet it is admirable to profess because it was once admirable to live. To be a philosopher is not merely to have subtle thoughts, nor even to found a school, but so to love wisdom as to live according to its dictates, a life of simplicity, independence, magnanimity, and trust. It is to solve some of the problems of life, not only theoretically, but practically. The success of great scholars and thinkers is commonly a courtier-like success, not kingly, not manly. They make shift to live merely by conformity, practically as their fathers did, and are in no sense the progenitors of a nobler race of men. But why do men degenerate ever? What makes families run out? What is the nature of the luxury which enervates and destroys nations? Are we sure that there is none of it in our own lives? The philosopher is in advance of his age even in the outward form of his life. He is not fed, sheltered, clothed, warmed, like his contemporaries. How can a man be a philosopher and not maintain his vital heat by better methods than other men?

When a man is warmed by the several modes which I have described, what does he want next? Surely not more warmth of the same kind, as more and richer food, larger and more splendid houses, finer and more abundant clothing, more numerous, incessant, and hotter fires, and the like. When he has obtained those things which are necessary to life, there is another alternative than to obtain the superfluities; and that is, to adventure on life now, his vacation from humbler toil having commenced. The soil, it appears, is suited to the seed, for it has sent its radicle downward, and it may now send its shoot upward also with confidence. Why has man rooted himself thus firmly in the earth, but that he may rise in the same proportion into the heavens above?—for the nobler plants are valued for the fruit they bear at last in the air and light, far from the ground, and are not treated like the humbler esculents, which, though they may be biennials, are cultivated only till they have perfected their root, and often cut down at top for this purpose, so that most would not know them in their flowering season.

I do not mean to prescribe rules to strong and valiant natures, who will mind their own affairs whether in heaven or hell, and perchance build more magnificently and spend more lavishly than the richest, without ever impoverishing themselves, not knowing how they live,—if, indeed, there are any such, as has been dreamed; nor to those who find their encouragement and inspiration in precisely the present condition of things, and cherish it with the fondness and enthusiasm of lovers,—and, to some extent, I reckon myself in this number; I do not speak to those who are well employed, in whatever circumstances, and they know whether they are well employed or not;—but mainly to the mass of men who are discontented, and idly complaining of the hardness of their lot or of the times, when they might improve them. There are some who complain most energetically and inconsolably of any, because they are, as they say, doing their duty. I also have in my mind that seemingly wealthy, but most terribly impoverished class of all, who have accumulated dross, but know not how to use it, or get rid of it, and thus have forged their own golden or silver fetters.

If I should attempt to tell how I have desired to spend my life in years past, it would probably surprise those of my readers who are somewhat acquainted with its actual history; it would certainly astonish those who know nothing about it. I will only hint at some of the enterprises which I have cherished.

In any weather, at any hour of the day or night, I have been anxious to improve the nick of time, and notch it on my stick too; to stand on the meeting of two eternities, the past and future, which is precisely the present moment; to toe that line. You will pardon some obscurities, for there are more secrets in my trade than in most men's, and yet not voluntarily kept, but inseparable from its very nature. I would gladly tell all that I know about it, and never paint "No Admittance" on my gate.

I long ago lost a hound, a bay horse, and a turtledove, and am still on their trail. Many are the travellers I have spoken concerning them, describing their tracks and what calls they answered to. I have

met one or two who had heard the hound, and the tramp of the horse, and even seen the dove disappear behind a cloud, and they seemed as anxious to recover them as if they had lost them themselves. [8]

To anticipate, not the sunrise and the dawn merely, but, if possible, Nature herself! How many mornings, summer and winter, before yet any neighbor was stirring about his business, have I been about mine! No doubt, many of my townsmen have met me returning from this enterprise, farmers starting for Boston in the twilight, or woodchoppers going to their work. It is true, I never assisted the sun materially in his rising, but, doubt not, it was of the last importance only to be present at it.

So many autumn, ay, and winter days, spent outside the town, trying to hear what was in the wind, to hear and carry it express! I well-nigh sunk all my capital in it, and lost my own breath into the bargain, running in the face of it. If it had concerned either of the political parties, depend upon it, it would have appeared in the Gazette with the earliest intelligence. At other times watching from the observatory of some cliff or tree, to telegraph any new arrival; or waiting at evening on the hill-tops for the sky to fall, that I might catch something, though I never caught much, and that, manna-wise, would dissolve again in the sun.

For a long time I was reporter to a journal,[9] of no very wide circulation, whose editor has never yet seen fit to print the

[8] In the original manuscript, this paragraph, which has been the subject of much controversy, appears as a footnote in the chapter on "Winter Animals." See Van Doren's *Henry David Thoreau* and T. M. Raysor, "The Love Story of Thoreau," *Studies in Philology*, xxiii, 457-463 (October, 1926). Thoreau told Miss Ward, the aunt of Ellen Sewall, that the hound symbolized the boy Edmund Sewall; the bay horse, John Thoreau, Henry's brother; and the turtle-dove, Ellen Sewall, to whom Henry once proposed marriage.

[9] Doubtless his own journal, or diary, is here referred to. In 1906 it was published in fourteen volumes.

bulk of my contributions, and, as is too common with writers, I got only my labor for my pains. However, in this case my pains were their own reward.

For many years I was self-appointed inspector of snow-storms and rain-storms, and did my duty faithfully; surveyor, if not of highways, then of forest paths and all across-lot routes, keeping them open, and ravines bridged and passable at all seasons, where the public heel had testified to their utility.

I have looked after the wild stock of the town, which give a faithful herdsman a good deal of trouble by leaping fences; and I have had an eye to the unfrequented nooks and corners of the farm; though I did not always know whether Jonas or Solomon worked in a particular field to-day; that was none of my business. I have watered the red huckleberry, the sand cherry and the nettle-tree, the red pine and the black ash, the white grape and the yellow violet, which might have withered else in dry seasons.

In short, I went on thus for a long time (I may say it without boasting), faithfully minding my business, till it became more and more evident that my townsmen would not after all admit me into the list of town officers, nor make my place a sinecure with a moderate allowance. My accounts, which I can swear to have kept faithfully, I have, indeed, never got audited, still less accepted, still less paid and settled. However, I have not set my heart on that.

Not long since, a strolling Indian went to sell baskets at the house of a well-known lawyer in my neighborhood.[10] "Do you wish to buy any baskets?" he asked. "No, we do not want any," was the reply. "What!" exclaimed the Indian as he went out the gate, "do you mean to starve us?" Having seen his industrious white neighbors so well off,—that the lawyer had only to weave arguments, and, by some magic, wealth and standing followed,—he had said to himself: I will go into business; I will weave baskets; it is a thing which I

can do. Thinking that when he had made the baskets he would have done his part, and then it would be the white man's to buy them. He had not discovered that it was necessary for him to make it worth the other's while to buy them, or at least make him think that it was so, or to make something else which it would be worth his while to buy. I too had woven a kind of basket of a delicate texture, but I had not made it worth any one's while to buy them. Yet not the less in my case, did I think it worth my while to weave them, and instead of studying how to make it worth men's while to buy my baskets, I studied rather how to avoid the necessity of selling them. The life which men praise and regard as successful is but one kind. Why should we exaggerate any one kind at the expense of the others?

Finding that my fellow-citizens were not likely to offer me any room in the court house, or any curacy or living anywhere else, but I must shift for myself, I turned my face more exclusively than ever to the woods, where I was better known. I determined to go into business at once, and not wait to acquire the usual capital, using such slender means as I had already got. My purpose in going to Walden Pond was not to live cheaply nor to live dearly there, but to transact some private business with the fewest obstacles; to be hindered from accomplishing which for want of a little common sense, a little enterprise and business talent, appeared not so sad as foolish.

I have always endeavored to acquire strict business habits; they are indispensable to every man. If your trade is with the Celestial Empire, then some small counting house on the coast, in some Salem harbor, will be fixture enough. You will export such articles as the country affords, purely native products, much ice and pine timber and a little granite, always in native bottoms. These will be good ventures. To oversee all the details yourself in person; to be at once pilot and captain, and owner

_____

[10] Samuel Hoar.

and underwriter; to buy and sell and keep the accounts; to read every letter received, and write or read every letter sent; to superintend the discharge of imports night and day; to be upon many parts of the coast almost at the same time,—often the richest freight will be discharged upon a Jersey shore;—to be your own telegraph, unweariedly sweeping the horizon, speaking all passing vessels bound coastwise; to keep up a steady despatch of commodities, for the supply of such a distant and exorbitant market; to keep yourself informed of the state of the markets, prospects of war and peace everywhere, and anticipate the tendencies of trade and civilizations,—taking advantage of the results of all exploring expeditions, using new passages and all improvements in navigation;—charts to be studied, the position of reefs and new lights and buoys to be ascertained, and ever, and ever, the logarithmic tables to be corrected, for by the error of some calculator the vessel often splits upon a rock that should have reached a friendly pier,—there is the untold fate of La Pérouse [11];—universal science to be kept pace with, studying the lives of all great discoverers and navigators, great adventurers and merchants, from Hanno [12] and the Phœnicians down to our day; in fine, account of stock to be taken from time to time, to know how you stand. It is a labor to task the faculties of a man,—such problems of profit and loss, of interest, of tare and tret, and gauging of all kinds in it, as demand a universal knowledge.

I have thought that Walden Pond would be a good place for business, not solely on account of the railroad and the ice trade; it offers advantages which it may not be good policy to divulge; it is a good port and a good foundation. No Neva marshes to be filled; though you must everywhere build on piles of your own driving. It is said that a flood-tide, with a westerly wind, and ice in the Neva, would sweep St. Petersburg from the face of the earth.

As this business was to be entered into without the usual capital, it may not be easy to conjecture where those means, that will still be indispensable to every such undertaking, were to be obtained. As for Clothing, to come at once to the practical part of the question, perhaps we are led oftener by the love of novelty and a regard for the opinions of men, in procuring it, than by a true utility. Let him who has work to do recollect that the object of clothing is, first, to retain the vital heat, and secondly, in this state of society, to cover nakedness, and he may judge how much of any necessary or important work may be accomplished without adding to his wardrobe. Kings and queens who wear a suit but once, though made by some tailor or dressmaker to their majesties, cannot know the comfort of wearing a suit that fits. They are no better than wooden horses to hang the clean clothes on. Every day our garments become more assimilated to ourselves, receiving the impress of the wearer's character, until we hesitate to lay them aside without such delay and medical appliances and some such solemnity even as our bodies. No man ever stood the lower in my estimation for having a patch in his clothes; yet I am sure that there is greater anxiety, commonly, to have fashionable, or at least clean and unpatched clothes, than to have a sound conscience. But even if the rent is not mended, perhaps the worst vice betrayed is improvidence. I sometimes try my acquaintances by such tests as this,—Who could wear a patch, or two extra seams only, over the knee? Most behave as if they believed that their prospects for life would be ruined if they should do it. It would be easier for them to hobble to town with a broken leg than with a broken pantaloon. Often if an accident happens to a gentleman's legs, they can be mended; but if a similar accident happens to the legs of his pantaloons,

---

[11] There were no survivors to tell the story of the probable shipwreck of the two ships of the Comte de la Pérouse, explorer, in 1788.

[12] Carthaginian explorer and colonizer of the 5th Century B. C.

there is no help for it; for he considers, not what is truly respectable, but what is respected. We know but few men, a great many coats and breeches. Dress a scarecrow in your last shift, you standing shiftless by, who would not soonest salute the scarecrow? Passing a cornfield the other day, close by a hat and coat on a stake, I recognized the owner of the farm. He was only a little more weather-beaten than when I saw him last. I have heard of a dog that barked at every stranger who approached his master's premises with clothes on, but was easily quieted by a naked thief. It is an interesting question how far men would retain their relative rank if they were divested of their clothes. Could you, in such a case, tell surely of any company of civilized men which belonged to the most respected class? When Madam Pfeiffer,[13] in her adventurous travels round the world, from east to west, had got so near home as Asiatic Russia, she says that she felt the necessity of wearing other than a travelling dress, when she went to meet the authorities, for she "was now in a civilized country, where . . . people are judged of by their clothes." Even in our democratic New England towns the accidental possession of wealth, and its manifestation in dress and equipage alone, obtain for the possessor almost universal respect. But they who yield such respect, numerous as they are, are so far heathen, and need to have a missionary sent to them. Beside, clothes introduced sewing, a kind of work which you may call endless; a woman's dress, at least, is never done.

A man who has at length found something to do will not need to get a new suit to do it in; for him the old will do, that has lain dusty in the garret for an indeterminate period. Old shoes will serve a hero longer than they have served his valet,— if a hero ever has a valet,—bare feet are older than shoes, and he can make them do. Only they who go to soirées and legislative halls must have new coats, coats to change as often as the man changes in them. But if my jacket and trousers, my hat and shoes, are fit to worship God in, they will do; will they not? Who ever saw his old clothes,—his old coat, actually worn out, resolved into its primitive elements so that it was not a deed of charity to bestow it on some poor boy, by him perchance to be bestowed on some poorer still, or shall we say richer, who could do with less? I say, beware of all enterprises that require new clothes, and not rather a new wearer of clothes. If there is not a new man, how can the new clothes be made to fit? If you have any enterprise before you, try it in your old clothes. All men want, not something to *do with,* but something to *do,* or rather something to *be.* Perhaps we should never procure a new suit, however ragged or dirty the old, until we have so conducted, so enterprised or sailed in some way, that we feel like new men in the old, and that to retain it would be like keeping new wine in old bottles. Our moulting season, like that of the fowls, must be a crisis in our lives. The loon retires to solitary ponds to spend it. Thus also the snake casts its slough, and the caterpillar its wormy coat, by an internal industry and expansion; for clothes are but our outmost cuticle and mortal coil. Otherwise we shall be found sailing under false colors, and be inevitably cashiered at last by our own opinion, as well as that of mankind.

We don garment after garment, as if we grew like exogenous plants by addition without. Our outside and often thin and fanciful clothes are our epidermis, or false skin, which partakes not of our life, and may be stripped off here and there without fatal injury; our thicker garments, constantly worn, are our cellular integument, or cortex; but our shirts are our liber, or true bark, which cannot be removed without girdling and so destroying the man. I believe that all races at some seasons wear something equivalent to the shirt. It is desirable that a man be clad so simply that he can lay his hands on himself in the dark,

---

[13] Ida Laura (Reyer) Pfeiffer (1797-1858), German traveler and author.

and that he live in all respects so compactly and preparedly that, if an enemy take the town, he can, like the old philosopher,[14] walk out the gate empty-handed without anxiety. While one thick garment is, for most purposes, as good as three thin ones, and cheap clothing can be obtained at prices really to suit customers; while a thick coat can be bought for five dollars, which will last as many years, thick panta-loons for two dollars, cowhide boots for a dollar and a half a pair, a summer hat for a quarter of a dollar, and a winter cap for sixty-two and a half cents, or a better be made at home at a nominal cost, where is he so poor that, clad in such a suit, *of his own earning,* there will not be found wise men to do him reverence?

When I ask for a garment of a particu-lar form, my tailoress tells me gravely, "They do not make them so now," not emphasizing the "They" at all, as if she quoted an authority as impersonal as the Fates, and I find it difficult to get made what I want, simply because she cannot believe that I mean what I say, that I am so rash. When I hear this oracular sen-tence, I am for a moment absorbed in thought, emphasizing to myself each word separately that I may come at the meaning of it, that I may find out by what degree of consanguinity *They* are related to *me,* and what authority they may have in an affair which affects me so nearly; and, finally, I am inclined to answer her with equal mystery, and without any more emphasis of the "they,"—"It is true, they did not make them so recently, but they do now." Of what use this measuring of me if she does not measure my character, but only the breadth of my shoulders, as it were a peg to hang the coat on? We worship not the Graces, nor the Parcæ, but Fashion. She spins and weaves and cuts with full authority. The head monkey at Paris puts on a traveller's cap, and all the monkeys in America do the same. I sometimes despair of getting anything quite simple and honest done in this world by the help of men. They would have to be passed through a

powerful press first, to squeeze their old notions out of them, so that they would not soon get upon their legs again; and then there would be some one in the com-pany with a maggot in his head, hatched from an egg deposited there nobody knows when, for not even fire kills these things, and you would have lost your labor. Never-theless, we will not forget that some Egyp-tian wheat was handed down to us by a mummy.

On the whole, I think that it cannot be maintained that dressing has in this or any country risen to the dignity of an art. At present men make shift to wear what they can get. Like shipwrecked sailors, they put on what they can find on the beach, and at a little distance, whether of space or time, laugh at each other's masquerade. Every generation laughs at the old fash-ions, but follows religiously the new. We are amused at beholding the costume of Henry VIII., or Queen Elizabeth, as much as if it was that of the King and Queen of the Cannibal Islands. All costume off a man is pitiful or grotesque. It is only the serious eye peering from and the sincere life passed within it which restrain laughter and consecrate the costume of any people. Let Harlequin be taken with a fit of the colic and his trappings will have to serve that mood too. When the soldier is hit by a cannon-ball, rags are as becoming as purple.

The childish and savage taste of men and women for new patterns keeps how many shaking and squinting through kaleido-scopes that they may discover the particu-lar figure which this generation requires to-day. The manufacturers have learned that this taste is merely whimsical. Of two patterns which differ only by a few threads more or less of a particular color, the one will be sold readily, the other lie on the shelf, though it frequently happens that after the lapse of a season the latter be-comes the most fashionable. Comparatively,

---

[14] Bias (c. 6th Century B. C.). Cf. Thor-eau's *Journals,* July 12, 1840.

tattooing is not the hideous custom which it is called. It is not barbarous merely because the printing is skin-deep and unalterable.

I cannot believe that our factory system is the best mode by which men may get clothing. The condition of the operatives is becoming every day more like that of the English; and it cannot be wondered at, since, as far as I have heard or observed, the principal object is, not that mankind may be well and honestly clad, but, unquestionably, that the corporations may be enriched. In the long run men hit only what they aim at. Therefore, though they should fail immediately, they had better aim at something high.

As for a Shelter, I will not deny that this is now a necessary of life, though there are instances of men having done without it for long periods in colder countries than this. Samuel Laing [15] says that "the Laplander in his skin dress, and in a skin bag which he puts over his head and shoulders, will sleep night after night on the snow . . . in a degree of cold which would extinguish the life of one exposed to it in any woollen clothing." He had seen them asleep thus. Yet he adds, "They are not hardier than other people." But, probably, man did not live long on the earth without discovering the convenience which there is in a house, the domestic comforts, which phrase may have originally signified the satisfactions of the house more than of the family; though these must be extremely partial and occasional in those climates where the house is associated in our thoughts with winter or the rainy season chiefly, and two thirds of the year, except for a parasol, is unnecessary. In our climate, in the summer, it was formerly almost solely a covering at night. In the Indian gazettes a wigwam was the symbol of a day's march, and a row of them cut or painted on the bark of a tree signified that so many times they had camped. Man was not made so large limbed and robust but that he must seek to narrow his world, and wall in a space such as fitted him.

He was at first bare and out of doors; but though this was pleasant enough in serene and warm weather, by daylight, the rainy season and the winter, to say nothing of the torrid sun, would perhaps have nipped his race in the bud if he had not made haste to clothe himself with the shelter of a house. Adam and Eve, according to the fable, wore the bower before other clothes. Man wanted a home, a place of warmth, or comfort, first of physical warmth, then the warmth of the affections.

We may imagine a time when, in the infancy of the human race, some enterprising mortal crept into a hollow in a rock for shelter. Every child begins the world again, to some extent, and loves to stay outdoors, even in wet and cold. It plays house, as well as horse, having an instinct for it. Who does not remember the interest with which, when young, he looked at shelving rocks, or any approach to a cave? It was the natural yearning of that portion of our most primitive ancestor which still survived in us. From the cave we have advanced to roofs of palm leaves, of bark and boughs, of linen woven and stretched, of grass and straw, of boards and shingles, of stones and tiles. At last, we know not what it is to live in the open air, and our lives are domestic in more senses than we think. From the hearth the field is a great distance. It would be well, perhaps, if we were to spend more of our days and nights without any obstruction between us and the celestial bodies, if the poet did not speak so much from under a roof, or the saint dwell there so long. Birds do not sing in caves, nor do doves cherish their innocence in dovecots.

However, if one designs to construct a dwelling-house, it behooves him to exercise a little Yankee shrewdness, lest after all he find himself in a workhouse, a labyrinth without a clue, a museum, an almshouse, a prison, or a splendid mausoleum instead. Consider first how slight a shelter is abso-

[15] English writer on economic and social conditions of Scandinavia (1780-1868).

lutely necessary. I have seen Penobscot Indians, in this town, living in tents of thin cotton cloth, while the snow was nearly a foot deep around them, and I thought that they would be glad to have it deeper to keep out the wind. Formerly, when how to get my living honestly, with freedom left for my proper pursuits, was a question which vexed me even more than it does now, for unfortunately I am become somewhat callous, I used to see a large box by the railroad, six feet long by three wide, in which the laborers locked up their tools at night; and it suggested to me that every man who was hard pushed might get such a one for a dollar, and, having bored a few auger holes in it, to admit the air at least, get into it when it rained and at night, and hook down the lid, and so have freedom in his love, and in his soul be free.[16] This did not appear the worst, nor by any means a despicable alternative. You could sit up as late as you pleased, and, whenever you got up, go abroad without any landlord or house-lord dogging you for rent. Many a man is harassed to death to pay the rent of a larger and more luxurious box who would not have frozen to death in such a box as this. I am far from jesting. Economy is a subject which admits of being treated with levity, but it cannot so be disposed of. A comfortable house for a rude and hardy race, that lived mostly out of doors, was once made here almost entirely of such materials as Nature furnished ready to their hands. Gookin,[17] who was superintendent of the Indians subject to the Massachusetts Colony, writing in 1674, says, "The best of their houses are covered very neatly, tight and warm, with barks of trees, slipped from their bodies at those seasons when the sap is up, and made into great flakes, with pressure of weighty timber, when they are green. . . . The meaner sort are covered with mats which they make of a kind of bulrush, and are also indifferently tight and warm, but not so good as the former. . . . Some I have seen, sixty or a hundred feet long and thirty feet broad. . . . I have often lodged in their wigwams, and found them as warm as the best English houses." He adds that they were commonly carpeted and lined within with well-wrought embroidered mats, and were furnished with various utensils. The Indians had advanced so far as to regulate the effect of the wind by a mat suspended over the hole in the roof and moved by a string. Such a lodge was in the first instance constructed in a day or two at most, and taken down and put up in a few hours; and every family owned one, or its apartment in one.

In the savage state every family owns a shelter as good as the best, and sufficient for its coarser and simpler wants; but I think that I speak within bounds when I say that, though the birds of the air have their nests, and the foxes their holes, and the savages their wigwams, in modern civilized society not more than one half the families own a shelter. In the large towns and cities, where civilization especially prevails, the number of those who own a shelter is a very small fraction of the whole. The rest pay an annual tax for this outside garment of all, become indispensable summer and winter, which would buy a village of Indian wigwams, but now helps to keep them poor as long as they live. I do not mean to insist here on the disadvantage of hiring compared with owning, but it is evident that the savage owns his shelter because it costs so little, while the civilized man hires his commonly because he cannot afford to own it; nor can he, in the long run, any better afford to hire. But, answers one, by merely paying this tax the poor civilized man secures an abode which is a palace compared with the savage's. An annual rent of from twenty-five to a hundred dollars (these are the country rates) entitles him to the

16 "If I have freedom in my love
And in my soul am free,
Angels alone that soar above
Enjoy such liberty."
—*Richard Lovelace, "To Althea from Prison."*

17 See Daniel Gookin, Vol. I, pp. 97-101.

benefit of the improvements of centuries, spacious apartments, clean paint and paper, Rumford fireplace,[18] back plastering, Venetian blinds, copper pump, spring lock, a commodious cellar, and many other things. But how happens it that he who is said to enjoy these things is so commonly a *poor* civilized man, while the savage, who has them not, is rich as a savage? If it is asserted that civilization is a real advance in the condition of man,—and I think that it is, though only the wise improve their advantages,—it must be shown that it has produced better dwellings without making them more costly; and the cost of a thing is the amount of what I will call life which is required to be exchanged for it, immediately or in the long run. An average house in this neighborhood costs perhaps eight hundred dollars, and to lay up this sum will take from ten to fifteen years of the laborer's life, even if he is not encumbered with a family,—estimating the pecuniary value of every man's labor at one dollar a day, for if some receive more, others receive less;—so that he must have spent more than half his life commonly before *his* wigwam will be earned. If we suppose him to pay a rent instead, this is but a doubtful choice of evils. Would the savage have been wise to exchange his wigwam for a palace on these terms?

It may be guessed that I reduce almost the whole advantage of holding this superfluous property as a fund in store against the future, so far as the individual is concerned, mainly to the defraying of funeral expenses. But perhaps a man is not required to bury himself. Nevertheless this points to an important distinction between the civilized man and the savage; and, no doubt, they have designs on us for our benefit, in making the life of a civilized people an *institution*, in which the life of the individual is to a great extent absorbed, in order to preserve and perfect that of the race. But I wish to show at what a sacrifice this advantage is at present obtained, and to suggest that we may possibly so live as to secure all the advantage without suffering any of the disadvantage. What mean ye by saying that the poor ye have always with you, or that the fathers have eaten sour grapes, and the children's teeth are set on edge?

"As I live, saith the Lord God, ye shall not have occasion any more to use this proverb in Israel.

"Behold all souls are mine; as the soul of the father, so also the soul of the son is mine: the soul that sinneth, it shall die." [19]

When I consider my neighbors, the farmers of Concord, who are at least as well off as the other classes, I find that for the most part they have been toiling twenty, thirty, or forty years, that they may become the real owners of their farms, which commonly they have inherited with encumbrances, or else bought with hired money,—and we may regard one third of that toil as the cost of their houses,—but commonly they have not paid for them yet. It is true, the encumbrances sometimes outweigh the value of the farm, so that the farm itself becomes one great encumbrance, and still a man is found to inherit it, being well acquainted with it, as he says. On applying to the assessors, I am surprised to learn that they cannot at once name a dozen in the town who own their farms free and clear. If you would know the history of these homesteads, inquire at the bank where they are mortgaged. The man who has actually paid for his farm with labor on it is so rare that every neighbor can point to him. I doubt if there are three such men in Concord. What has been said of the merchants, that a very large majority, even ninety-seven in a hundred, are sure to fail, is equally true of the farmers. With regard to the merchants, however, one of them says pertinently that a great part of their failures

[18] Benjamin Thompson, Count Rumford (1753-1815), set forth the principles for the construction of chimneys and fireplaces.
[19] The quotation and part of the preceding sentence are taken from Ezekiel xviii, 2-4.

are not genuine pecuniary failures, but merely failures to fulfil their engagements, because it is inconvenient; that is, it is the moral character that breaks down. But this puts an infinitely worse face on the matter, and suggests, beside, that probably not even the other three succeed in saving their souls, but are perchance bankrupt in a worse sense than they who fail honestly. Bankruptcy and repudiation are the springboards from which much of our civilization vaults and turns its somersets, but the savage stands on the unelastic plank of famine. Yet the Middlesex Cattle Show goes off here with *éclat* annually, as if all the joints of the agricultural machine were suent.[20]

The farmer is endeavoring to solve the problem of a livelihood by a formula more complicated than the problem itself. To get his shoestrings he speculates in herds of cattle. With consummate skill he has set his trap with a hair spring to catch comfort and independence, and then, as he turned away, got his own leg into it. This is the reason he is poor; and for a similar reason we are all poor in respect to a thousand savage comforts, though surrounded by luxuries. As Chapman sings,—

"The false society of men—
　　—for earthly greatness
All heavenly comforts rarefies to air."

And when the farmer has got his house, he may not be the richer but the poorer for it, and it be the house that has got him. As I understand it, that was a valid objection urged by Momus against the house which Minerva made, that she "had not made it movable, by which means a bad neighborhood might be avoided;" and it may still be urged, for our houses are such unwieldy property that we are often imprisoned rather than housed in them; and the bad neighborhood to be avoided is our own scurvy selves. I know one or two families, at least, in this town, who, for nearly a generation, have been wishing to sell their houses in the outskirts and move

into the village, but have not been able to accomplish it, and only death will set them free.

Granted that the *majority* are able at last either to own or hire the modern house with all its improvements. While civilization has been improving our houses, it has not equally improved the men who are to inhabit them. It has created palaces, but it was not so easy to create noblemen and kings. And *if the civilized man's pursuits are no worthier than the savage's, if he is employed the greater part of his life in obtaining gross necessaries and comforts merely, why should he have a better dwelling than the former?*

But how do the poor *minority* fare? Perhaps it will be found that just in proportion as some have been placed in outward circumstances above the savage, others have been degraded below him. The luxury of one class is counterbalanced by the indigence of another. On the one side is the palace, on the other are the almshouse and "silent poor." The myriads who built the pyramids to be the tombs of the Pharaohs were fed on garlic, and it may be were not decently buried themselves. The mason who finishes the cornice of the palace returns at night perchance to a hut not so good as a wigwam. It is a mistake to suppose that, in a country where the usual evidences of civilization exist, the condition of a very large body of the inhabitants may not be as degraded as that of savages. I refer to the degraded poor, not now to the degraded rich. To know this I should not need to look farther than to the shanties which everywhere border our railroads, that last improvement in civilization; where I see in my daily walks human beings living in sties, and all winter with an open door, for the sake of light, without any visible, often imaginable, wood-pile, and the forms of both old and young are permanently contracted by the long habit of shrinking from cold and misery, and

[20] Smooth-running—a dialectal expression.

the development of all their limbs and faculties is checked. It certainly is fair to look at that class by whose labor the works which distinguish this generation are accomplished. Such too, to a greater or less extent, is the condition of the operatives of every denomination in England, which is the great workhouse of the world. Or I could refer you to Ireland, which is marked as one of the white or enlightened spots on the map. Contrast the physical condition of the Irish with that of the North American Indian, or the South Sea Islander, or any other savage race before it was degraded by contact with the civilized man. Yet I have no doubt that that people's rulers are as wise as the average of civilized rulers. Their condition only proves what squalidness may consist with civilization. I hardly need refer now to the laborers in our Southern States who produce the staple exports of this country, and are themselves a staple production of the South. But to confine myself to those who are said to be in *moderate* circumstances.

Most men appear never to have considered what a house is, and are actually though needlessly poor all their lives because they think that they must have such a one as their neighbors have. As if one were to wear any sort of coat which the tailor might cut out for him, or, gradually leaving off palm-leaf hat or cap of woodchuck skin, complain of hard times because he could not afford to buy him a crown! It is possible to invent a house still more convenient and luxurious than we have, which yet all would admit that man could not afford to pay for. Shall we always study to obtain more of these things, and not sometimes to be content with less? Shall the respectable citizen thus gravely teach, by precept and example, the necessity of the young man's providing a certain number of superfluous glow-shoes,[21] and umbrellas, and empty guest chambers for empty guests, before he dies? Why should not our furniture be as simple as the Arab's or the Indian's? When I think of the benefactors of the race, whom we have apotheosized as

messengers from heaven, bearers of divine gifts to man, I do not see in my mind any retinue at their heels, any carload of fashionable furniture. Or what if I were to allow—would it not be a singular allowance?—that our furniture should be more complex than the Arab's, in proportion as we are morally and intellectually his superiors! At present our houses are cluttered and defiled with it, and a good housewife would sweep out the greater part into the dust hole, and not leave her morning's work undone. Morning work! By the blushes of Aurora and the music of Memnon,[22] what should be man's *morning work* in this world? I had three pieces of limestone on my desk, but I was terrified to find that they required to be dusted daily, when the furniture of my mind was all undusted still, and I threw them out the window in disgust. How, then, could I have a furnished house? I would rather sit in the open air, for no dust gathers on the grass, unless where man has broken ground.

It is the luxurious and dissipated who set the fashions which the herd so diligently follow. The traveller who stops at the best houses, so called, soon discovers this, for the publicans presume him to be a Sardanapalus,[23] and if he resigned himself to their tender mercies he would soon be completely emasculated. I think that in the railroad car we are inclined to spend more on luxury than on safety and convenience, and it threatens without attaining these to become no better than a modern drawing-room, with its divans, and ottomans, and sunshades, and a hundred other oriental things, which we are taking west with us, invented for the ladies of the harem and the effeminate natives of the Celestial Empire, which Jonathan should be ashamed to know the names of. I would rather sit on a pumpkin and have it all to myself than

---

[21] Galoshes.

[22] For note on Memnon see Vol. I, p. 452.

[23] Splendid and magnificent king of Assyria 668-626 B.C.

be crowded on a velvet cushion. I would rather ride on earth in an ox cart, with a free circulation, than go to heaven in the fancy car of an excursion train and breathe a *malaria* all the way.

The very simplicity and nakedness of man's life in the primitive ages imply this advantage, at least, that they left him still but a sojourner in nature. When he was refreshed with food and sleep, he contemplated his journey again. He dwelt, as it were, in a tent in this world, and was either threading the valleys, or crossing the plains, or climbing the mountain-tops. But lo! men have become the tools of their tools. The man who independently plucked the fruits when he was hungry is become a farmer; and he who stood under a tree for shelter, a housekeeper. We now no longer camp as for a night, but have settled down on earth and forgotten heaven. We have adopted Christianity merely as an improved method of *agri*-culture. We have built for this world a family mansion, and for the next a family tomb. The best works of art are the expression of man's struggle to free himself from this condition, but the effect of our art is merely to make this low state comfortable and that higher state to be forgotten. There is actually no place in this village for a work of *fine* art, if any had come down to us, to stand, for our lives, our houses and streets, furnish no proper pedestal for it. There is not a nail to hang a picture on, nor a shelf to receive the bust of a hero or a saint. When I consider how our houses are built and paid for, or not paid for, and their internal economy managed and sustained, I wonder that the floor does not give way under the visitor while he is admiring the gew-gaws upon the mantelpiece, and let him through into the cellar, to some solid and honest though earthy foundation. I cannot but perceive that this so-called rich and refined life is a thing jumped at, and I do not get on in the enjoyment of the *fine* arts which adorn it, my attention being wholly occupied with the jump; for I remember that the greatest genuine leap, due to human

muscles alone, on record, is that of certain wandering Arabs, who are said to have cleared twenty-five feet on level ground. Without factitious support, man is sure to come to earth again beyond that distance. The first question which I am tempted to put to the proprietor of such great impropriety is, Who bolsters you? Are you one of the ninety-seven who fail, or the three who succeed? Answer me these questions, and then perhaps I may look at your bawbles and find them ornamental. The cart before the horse is neither beautiful nor useful. Before we can adorn our houses with beautiful objects the walls must be stripped, and our lives must be stripped, and beautiful housekeeping and beautiful living be laid for a foundation: now, a taste for the beautiful is most cultivated out of doors, where there is no house and no housekeeper.

Old Johnson, in his "Wonder-Working Providence," [24] speaking of the first settlers of this town, with whom he was contemporary, tells us that "they burrow themselves in the earth for their first shelter under some hillside, and, casting the soil aloft upon timber, they make a smoky fire against the earth, at the highest side." They did not "provide them houses," says he, "till the earth, by the Lord's blessing, brought forth bread to feed them," and the first year's crop was so light that "they were forced to cut their bread very thin for a long season." The secretary of the Province of New Netherland,[25] writing in Dutch, in 1650, for the information of those who wished to take up land there, states more particularly that "those in New Netherland, and especially in New England, who have no means to build farmhouses at first according to their wishes, dig a square pit in the ground, cellar fashion, six or seven feet deep, as long and

---

[24] Edward Johnson's history of New England (1654).

[25] The name was changed to New York when the British captured it in 1664. The secretary referred to was Cornelis van Tienhoven.

as broad as they think proper, case the earth inside with wood all round the wall, and line the wood with the bark of trees or something else to prevent the caving in of the earth; floor this cellar with plank, and wainscot it overhead for a ceiling, raise a roof of spars clear up, and cover the spars with bark or green sods, so that they can live dry and warm in these houses with their entire families for two, three, and four years, it being understood that partitions are run through those cellars which are adapted to the size of the family. The wealthy and principal men in New England, in the beginning of the colonies, commenced their first dwelling-houses in this fashion for two reasons: firstly, in order not to waste time in building, and not to want food the next season; secondly, in order not to discourage poor laboring people whom they brought over in numbers from Fatherland. In the course of three or four years, when the country became adapted to agriculture, they built themselves handsome houses, spending on them several thousands."

In this course which our ancestors took there was a show of prudence at least, as if their principle were to satisfy the more pressing wants first. But are the more pressing wants satisfied now? When I think of acquiring for myself one of our luxurious dwellings, I am deterred, for, so to speak, the country is not yet adapted to *human* culture, and we are still forced to cut our *spiritual* bread far thinner than our forefathers did their wheaten. Not that all architectural ornament is to be neglected even in the rudest periods; but let our houses first be lined with beauty, where they come in contact with our lives, like the tenement of the shell-fish, and not overlaid with it. But, alas! I have been inside one or two of them, and know what they are lined with.

Though we are not so degenerate but that we might possibly live in a cave or a wigwam or wear skins to-day, it certainly is better to accept the advantages, though so dearly bought, which the invention and industry of mankind offer. In such a neighborhood as this, boards and shingles, lime and bricks, are cheaper and more easily obtained than suitable caves, or whole logs, or bark in sufficient quantities, or even well-tempered clay or flat stones. I speak understandingly on this subject, for I have made myself acquainted with it both theoretically and practically. With a little more wit we might use these materials so as to become richer than the richest now are, and make our civilization a blessing. The civilized man is a more experienced and wiser savage. But to make haste to my own experiment.

Near the end of March, 1845, I borrowed an axe and went down to the woods by Walden Pond, nearest to where I intended to build my house, and began to cut down some tall, arrowy white pines, still in their youth, for timber. It is difficult to begin without borrowing, but perhaps it is the most generous course thus to permit your fellow-men to have an interest in your enterprise. The owner of the axe,[26] as he released his hold on it, said that it was the apple of his eye; but I returned it sharper than I received it. It was a pleasant hillside where I worked, covered with pine woods, through which I looked out on the pond, and a small open field in the woods where pines and hickories were springing up. The ice in the pond was not yet dissolved, though there were some open spaces, and it was all dark-colored and saturated with water. There were some slight flurries of snow during the days that I worked there; but for the most part when I came out on to the railroad, on my way home, its yellow sand-heap stretched away gleaming in the hazy atmosphere, and the rails shone in the spring sun, and I heard the lark and pewee and other birds already come to commence another year with us. They were pleasant spring days, in which the winter of man's discontent was thawing as well as the earth, and the life that had

---

[26] It was A. Bronson Alcott, famous Concord philosopher.

lain torpid began to stretch itself. One day, when my axe had come off and I had cut a green hickory for a wedge, driving it with a stone, and had placed the whole to soak in a pond-hole in order to swell the wood, I saw a striped snake run into the water, and he lay on the bottom, apparently without inconvenience, as long as I stayed there, or more than a quarter of an hour; perhaps because he had not yet fairly come out of the torpid state. It appeared to me that for a like reason men remain in their present low and primitive condition; but if they should feel the influence of the spring of springs arousing them, they would of necessity rise to a higher and more ethereal life. I had previously seen the snakes in frosty mornings in my path with portions of their bodies still numb and inflexible, waiting for the sun to thaw them. On the 1st of April it rained and melted the ice, and in the early part of the day, which was very foggy, I heard a stray goose groping about over the pond and cackling as if lost, or like the spirit of the fog.

So I went on for some days cutting and hewing timber, and also studs and rafters, all with my narrow axe, not having many communicable or scholar-like thoughts, singing to myself,—

> Men say they know many things;
> But lo! they have taken wings,—
> The arts and sciences,
> And a thousand appliances:
> The wind that blows
> Is all that anybody knows.[27]

I hewed the main timbers six inches square, most of the studs on two sides only, and the rafters and floor timbers on one side, leaving the rest of the bark on, so that they were just as straight and much stronger than sawed ones. Each stick was carefully mortised or tenoned by its stump, for I had borrowed other tools by this time. My days in the woods were not very long ones; yet I usually carried my dinner of bread and butter, and read the news-paper in which it was wrapped, at noon, sitting amid the green pine boughs which I had cut off, and to my bread was imparted some of their fragrance, for my hands were covered with a thick coat of pitch. Before I had done I was more the friend than the foe of the pine tree, though I had cut down some of them, having become better acquainted with it. Sometimes a rambler in the wood was attracted by the sound of my axe, and we chatted pleasantly over the chips which I had made.

By the middle of April, for I made no haste in my work, but rather made the most of it, my house was framed and ready for the raising. I had already bought the shanty of James Collins, an Irishman who worked on the Fitchburg Railroad, for boards. James Collins' shanty was considered an uncommonly fine one. When I called to see it he was not at home. I walked about the outside, at first unobserved from within, the window was so deep and high. It was of small dimensions, with a peaked cottage roof, and not much else to be seen, the dirt being raised five feet all around as if it were a compost heap. The roof was the soundest part, though a good deal warped and made brittle by the sun. Doorsill there was none, but a perennial passage for the hens under the door-board. Mrs. C. came to the door and asked me to view it from the inside. The hens were driven in by my approach. It was dark, and had a dirt floor for the most part, dank, clammy, and aguish, only here a board and there a board which would not bear removal. She lighted a lamp to show me the inside of the roof and the walls, and also that the board floor extended under the bed, warning me not to step into the cellar, a sort of dust hole two feet deep. In her own words, they were "good boards overhead, good boards all around, and a good window,"—of two whole squares originally, only the cat had passed out that way lately. There was a

---

[27] This is one of the four places in *Walden* in which Thoreau inserts verse of his own composition.

stove, a bed, and a place to sit, an infant in the house where it was born, a silk parasol, gilt-framed looking-glass, and a patent new coffee-mill nailed to an oak sapling, all told. The bargain was soon concluded, for James had in the meanwhile returned. I to pay four dollars and twenty-five cents to-night, he to vacate at five to-morrow morning, selling to nobody else meanwhile: I to take possession at six. It were well, he said, to be there early, and anticipate certain indistinct but wholly un-just claims on the score of ground rent and fuel. This he assured me was the only encumbrance. At six I passed him and his family on the road. One large bundle held their all,—bed, coffee-mill, looking-glass, hens,—all but the cat; she took to the woods and became a wild cat, and, as I learned afterward, trod in a trap set for woodchucks, and so became a dead cat at last.

I took down this dwelling the same morning, drawing the nails, and removed it to the pond-side by small cartloads, spreading the boards on the grass there to bleach and warp back again in the sun. One early thrush gave me a note or two as I drove along the woodland path. I was informed treacherously by a young Patrick that neighbor Seeley, an Irishman, in the intervals of the carting, transferred the still tolerable, straight, and drivable nails, staples, and spikes to his pocket, and then stood when I came back to pass the time of day, and look freshly up, unconcerned, with spring thoughts, at the devastation; there being a dearth of work, as he said. He was there to represent spectatordom, and help make this seemingly insignificant event one with the removal of the gods of Troy.

I dug my cellar in the side of a hill sloping to the south, where a woodchuck had formerly dug his burrow, down through sumach and blackberry roots, and the lowest stain of vegetation, six feet square by seven deep, to a fine sand where potatoes would not freeze in any winter. The sides were left shelving, and not stoned;

but the sun having never shone on them, the sand still keeps its place. It was but two hours' work. I took particular pleasure in this breaking of ground, for in almost all latitudes men dig into the earth for an equable temperature. Under the most splendid house in the city is still to be found the cellar where they store their roots as of old, and long after the super-structure has disappeared posterity remark its dent in the earth. The house is still but a sort of porch at the entrance of a burrow.

At length, in the beginning of May, with the help of some of my acquaintances, rather to improve so good an occasion for neighborliness than from any necessity, I set up the frame of my house. No man was ever more honored in the character of his raisers [28] than I. They are destined, I trust, to assist at the raising of loftier structures one day. I began to occupy my house on the 4th of July, as soon as it was boarded and roofed, for the boards were carefully feather-edged and lapped, so that it was perfectly impervious to rain, but before boarding I laid the foundation of a chimney at one end, bringing two cartloads of stones up the hill from the pond in my arms. I built the chimney after my hoeing in the fall, before a fire became necessary for warmth, doing my cooking in the mean-while out of doors on the ground, early in the morning: which mode I still think is in some respects more convenient and agreeable than the usual one. When it stormed before my bread was baked, I fixed a few boards over the fire, and sat under them to watch my loaf, and passed some pleasant hours in that way. In those days, when my hands were much employed, I read but little, but the least scraps of paper which lay on the ground, my holder, or tablecloth, afforded me as much enter-tainment, in fact answered the same pur-pose as the Iliad.

---

[28] They were Alcott, Emerson, Ellery Channing, George William Curtis and his brother Burrill, and Edmund Hosmer and his three sons.

It would be worth the while to build still more deliberately than I did, considering, for instance, what foundation a door, a window, a cellar, a garret, have in the nature of man, and perchance never raising any superstructure until we found a better reason for it than our temporal necessities even. There is some of the same fitness in a man's building his own house that there is in a bird's building its own nest. Who knows but if men constructed their dwellings with their own hands, and provided food for themselves and families simply and honestly enough, the poetic faculty would be universally developed, as birds universally sing when they are so engaged? But alas! we do like cowbirds and cuckoos, which lay their eggs in nests which other birds have built, and cheer no traveller with their chattering and unmusical notes. Shall we forever resign the pleasure of construction to the carpenter? What does architecture amount to in the experience of the mass of men? I never in all my walks came across a man engaged in so simple and natural an occupation as building his house. We belong to the community. It is not the tailor alone who is the ninth part of a man; it is as much the preacher, and the merchant, and the farmer. Where is this division of labor to end? and what object does it finally serve? No doubt another *may* also think for me; but it is not therefore desirable that he should do so to the exclusion of my thinking for myself.

True, there are architects so called in this country, and I have heard of one at least possessed with the idea of making architectural ornaments have a core of truth, a necessity, and hence a beauty, as if it were a revelation to him.[29] All very well perhaps from his point of view, but only a little better than the common dilettantism. A sentimental reformer in architecture, he began at the cornice, not at the foundation. It was only how to put a core of truth within the ornaments, that every sugarplum, in fact, might have an almond or caraway seed in it,—though I hold that almonds are most wholesome without the sugar,—and not how the inhabitant, the indweller, might build truly within and without, and let the ornaments take care of themselves. What reasonable man ever supposed that ornaments were something outward and in the skin merely,—that the tortoise got his spotted shell, or the shellfish its mother-o'-pearl tints, by such a contract as the inhabitants of Broadway their Trinity Church? But a man has no more to do with the style of architecture of his house than a tortoise with that of its shell: nor need the soldier be so idle as to try to paint the precise *color* of his virtue on his standard. The enemy will find it out. He may turn pale when the trial comes. This man seemed to me to lean over the cornice, and timidly whisper his half truth to the rude occupants who really knew it better than he. What of architectural beauty I now see, I know has gradually grown from within outward, out of the necessities and character of the indweller, who is the only builder,—out of some unconscious truthfulness, and nobleness, without ever a thought for the appearance; and whatever additional beauty of this kind is destined to be produced will be preceded by a like unconscious beauty of life. The most interesting dwellings in this country, as the painter knows, are the most unpretending, humble log huts and cottages of the poor commonly; it is the life of the inhabitants whose shells they are, and not any peculiarity in their surfaces merely, which makes them *picturesque;* and equally interesting will be the citizen's suburban box, when his life shall be as simple and as agreeable to the imagination, and there is as little straining after effect in the style of his dwelling. A great proportion of architectural ornaments are literally hollow, and a September gale would strip them off, like borrowed plumes, without injury to the substantials. They can do without *architecture* who have no olives nor wines in the cellar. What if

---

[29] Horatio Greenough, American sculptor (1805-1852). See Journal, Jan. 11, 1854.

an equal ado were made about the ornaments of style in literature, and the architects of our Bibles spent as much time about their cornices as the architects of our churches do? So are made the *belles-lettres* and the *beaux-arts* and their professors. Much it concerns a man, forsooth, how a few sticks are slanted over him or under him, and what colors are daubed upon his box. It would signify somewhat, if, in any earnest sense, *he* slanted them and daubed it; but the spirit having departed out of the tenant, it is of a piece with constructing his own coffin,—the architecture of the grave,—and "carpenter" is but another name for "coffin-maker." One man says, in his despair or indifference to life, take up a handful of the earth at your feet, and paint your house that color. Is he thinking of his last and narrow house? Toss up a copper for it as well. What an abundance of leisure he must have! Why do you take up a handful of dirt? Better paint your house your own complexion;

Boards	$8 03½,	mostly shanty boards.
Refuse shingles for roof and sides	4 00	
Laths	1 25	
Two second-hand windows with glass	2 43	
One thousand old brick......	4 00	
Two casks of lime...........	2 40	That was high.
Hair	0 31	More than I needed.
Mantle-tree iron	0 15	
Nails	3 90	
Hinges and screws...........	0 14	
Latch	0 10	
Chalk	0 01	
Transportation	1 40	{ I carried a good part on my back.
In all	$28 12½	

These are all the materials, excepting the timber, stones, and sand, which I claimed by squatter's right. I have also a small woodshed adjoining, made chiefly of the stuff which was left after building the house.

let it turn pale or blush for you. An enterprise to improve the style of cottage architecture! When you have got my ornaments ready, I will wear them.

Before winter I built a chimney, and shingled the sides of my house, which were already impervious to rain, with imperfect and sappy shingles made of the first slice of the log, whose edges I was obliged to straighten with a plane.

I have thus a tight shingled and plastered house, ten feet wide by fifteen long, and eight-feet posts, with a garret and a closet, a large window on each side, two trap-doors, one door at the end, and a brick fireplace opposite. The exact cost of my house, paying the usual price for such materials as I used, but not counting the work, all of which was done by myself, was as follows; and I give the details because very few are able to tell exactly what their houses cost, and fewer still, if any, the separate cost of the various materials which compose them:—

I intend to build me a house which will surpass any on the main street in Concord in grandeur and luxury, as soon as it pleases me as much and will cost me no more than my present one.

I thus found that the student who wishes

for a shelter can obtain one for a lifetime at an expense not greater than the rent which he now pays annually. If I seem to boast more than is becoming, my excuse is that I brag for humanity rather than for myself; and my shortcomings and inconsistencies do not affect the truth of my statement. Notwithstanding much cant and hypocrisy,—chaff which I find it difficult to separate from my wheat, but for which I am as sorry as any man,—I will breathe freely and stretch myself in this respect, it is such a relief to both the moral and physical system; and I am resolved that I will not through humility become the devil's attorney. I will endeavor to speak a good word for the truth. At Cambridge College the mere rent of a student's room, which is only a little larger than my own, is thirty dollars each year, though the corporation had the advantage of building thirty-two side by side and under one roof, and the occupant suffers the inconvenience of many and noisy neighbors, and perhaps a residence in the fourth story. I cannot but think that if we had more true wisdom in these respects, not only less education would be needed, because, forsooth, more would already have been acquired, but the pecuniary expense of getting an education would in a great measure vanish. Those conveniences which the student requires at Cambridge or elsewhere cost him or somebody else ten times as great a sacrifice of life as they would with proper management on both sides. Those things for which the most money is demanded are never the things which the student most wants. Tuition, for instance, is an important item in the term bill, while for the far more valuable education which he gets by associating with the most cultivated of his contemporaries no charge is made. The mode of founding a college is, commonly, to get up a subscription of dollars and cents, and then, following blindly the principles of a division of labor to its extreme, —a principle which should never be followed but with circumspection,—to call in a contractor who makes this a subject of speculation, and he employs Irishmen or other operatives actually to lay the foundations, while the students that are to be are said to be fitting themselves for it; and for these oversights successive generations have to pay. I think that it would be *better than this*, for the students, or those who desire to be benefited by it, even to lay the foundation themselves. The student who secures his coveted leisure and retirement by systematically shirking any labor necessary to man obtains but an ignoble and unprofitable leisure, defrauding himself of the experience which alone can make leisure fruitful. "But," says one, "you do not mean that the students should go to work with their hands instead of their heads?" I do not mean that exactly, but I mean something which he might think a good deal like that; I mean that they should not *play* life, or *study* it merely, while the community supports them at this expensive game, but earnestly *live* it from beginning to end. How could youths better learn to live than by at once trying the experiment of living? Methinks this would exercise their minds as much as mathematics. If I wished a boy to know something about the arts and sciences, for instance, I would not pursue the common course, which is merely to send him into the neighborhood of some professor, where anything is professed and practised but the art of life;—to survey the world through a telescope or a microscope, and never with his natural eye; to study chemistry, and not learn how his bread is made, or mechanics, and not learn how it is earned; to discover new satellites to Neptune, and not detect the motes in his eyes, or to what vagabond he is a satellite himself; or to be devoured by the monsters that swarm all around him, while contemplating the monsters in a drop of vinegar. Which would have advanced the most at the end of a month,—the boy who had made his own jackknife from the ore which he had dug and smelted, reading as much as would be necessary for this—or the boy who had attended the lectures on metallurgy at the Institute in the meanwhile, and had received a Rodgers pen-knife from his father? Which would be most likely to cut his fingers? . . . To my astonishment I was informed on leaving college that I had studied navigation!— why, if I had taken one turn down the harbor I should have known more about it. Even the *poor* student studies and is taught only *political* economy, while that economy of living which is synonymous with philosophy is not even sincerely professed in our colleges. The consequence is, that while he is reading Adam Smith, Ricardo, and Say,[30] he runs his father in debt irretrievably.

As with our colleges, so with a hundred "modern improvements;" there is an illusion about them; there is not always a positive advance. The devil goes on exacting compound interest to the last for his early share and numerous succeeding investments in them. Our inventions are wont to be pretty toys, which distract our attention from serious things. They are but improved means to an unimproved end, an end which it was already but too easy to arrive at; as railroads lead to Boston or New York. We are in great haste to construct a magnetic telegraph from Maine to Texas; but Maine and Texas, it may be, have nothing important to communicate. Either is in such a predicament as the man who was earnest to be introduced to a distinguished deaf woman,[31] but when he was presented, and one end of her ear trumpet was put into his hand, had nothing to say. As if the main object were to talk fast and not to talk sensibly. We are eager to tunnel under the Atlantic and bring the Old World some weeks nearer to the New; but perchance the first news that will leak through into the broad, flapping American ear will be that the Princess Adelaide has the whooping cough. After all, the man whose horse trots a mile a minute does not carry the most important messages; he is not an evangelist, nor does he come round eating locusts and wild honey. I doubt if Flying Childers[32] ever carried a peck of corn to mill.

One says to me, "I wonder that you do not lay up money; you love to travel; you might take the cars and go to Fitchburg to-day and see the country." But I am wiser than that. I have learned that the swiftest traveller is he that goes afoot. I say to my friend, Suppose we try who will get there first. The distance is thirty miles; the fare ninety cents. That is almost a day's wages. I remember when wages were sixty cents a day for laborers on this very road. Well, I start now on foot, and get there before night; I have travelled at that rate by the week together. You will in the meanwhile have earned your fare, and arrive there sometime to-morrow, or possibly this evening, if you are lucky enough to get a job in season. Instead of going to Fitchburg, you will be working here the greater part of the day. And so, if the railroad reached round the world, I think that I should keep ahead of you; and as for seeing the country and getting experience of that kind, I should have to cut your acquaintance altogether.

Such is the universal law, which no man can ever outwit, and with regard to the railroad even we may say it is as broad as it is long. To make a railroad round the world available to all mankind is equivalent to grading the whole surface of the planet. Men have an indistinct notion that if they keep up this activity of joint stocks and spades long enough all will at length ride somewhere, in next to no time, and for nothing; but though a crowd rushes to the depot, and the conductor shouts "All aboard!" when the smoke is blown away and the vapor condensed, it will be perceived that a few are riding, but the rest are run over,—and it will be called, and will be, "A melancholy accident." No doubt they can ride at last who

[30] Adam Smith (1723-1793), Scottish economist; David Ricardo (1772-1823), English economist; Jean Baptiste Say (1767-1832), French economist.
[31] Harriet Martineau, English novelist and economist (1802-1876), a visitor to Concord in 1836-1837.
[32] A famous English race-horse.

shall have earned their fare, that is, if they survive so long, but they will probably have lost their elasticity and desire to travel by that time. This spending of the best part of one's life earning money in order to enjoy a questionable liberty during the least valuable part of it reminds me of the Englishman who went to India to make a fortune first, in order that he might return to England and live the life of a poet. He should have gone up garret at once. "What!" exclaim a million Irishmen starting up from all the shanties in the land, "is not this railroad which we have built a good thing?" Yes, I answer, *comparatively* good, that is, you might have done worse; but I wish, as you are brothers of mine, that you could have spent your time better than digging in this dirt.

Before I finished my house, wishing to earn ten or twelve dollars by some honest and agreeable method, in order to meet my unusual expenses, I planted about two acres and a half of light and sandy soil near it chiefly with beans, but also a small part with potatoes, corn, peas, and turnips. The whole lot contains eleven acres, mostly growing up to pines and hickories, and was sold the preceding season for eight dollars and eight cents an acre. One farmer said that it was "good for nothing but to raise cheeping squirrels on." I put no manure whatever on this land, not being the owner, but merely a squatter, and not expecting to cultivate so much again, and I did not quite hoe it all once. I got out several cords of stumps in plowing, which supplied me with fuel for a long time, and left small circles of virgin mould, easily distinguishable through the summer by the greater luxuriance of the beans there. The dead and for the most part unmerchantable wood behind my house, and the driftwood from the pond, have supplied the remainder of my fuel. I was obliged to hire a team and a man for the plowing, though I held the plow myself. My farm outgoes for the first season were, for implements, seed,

work, etc., $14.72½. The seed corn was given me. This never costs anything to speak of unless you plant more than enough. I got twelve bushels of beans, and eighteen bushels of potatoes, beside some peas and sweet corn. The yellow corn and turnips were too late to come to anything. My whole income from the farm was

$23 44

Deducting the outgoes.... 14 72½

There are left........... $ 8 71½,

beside produce consumed and on hand at the time this estimate was made of the value of $4.50,—the amount on hand much more than balancing a little grass which I did not raise. All things considered, that is, considering the importance of a man's soul and of to-day, notwithstanding the short time occupied by my experiment, nay, partly even because of its transient character, I believe that that was doing better than any farmer in Concord did that year.

The next year I did better still, for I spaded up all the land which I required, about a third of an acre, and I learned from the experience of both years, not being in the least awed by many celebrated works on husbandry, Arthur Young [33] among the rest, that if one would live simply and eat only the crop which he raised, and raise no more than he ate, and not exchange it for an insufficient quantity of more luxurious and expensive things, he would need to cultivate only a few rods of ground, and that it would be cheaper to spade up that than to use oxen to plow it, and to select a fresh spot from time to time than to manure the old, and he could do all his necessary farm work as it were with his left hand at odd hours in the summer; and thus he would not be tied to an ox, or horse, or cow, or pig, as at present. I desire to speak impartially on this point, and as one not interested in the success or

---

[33] British writer on agricultural economy (1741-1820).

failure of the present economical and social arrangements. I was more independent than any farmer in Concord, for I was not anchored to a house or farm, but could follow the bent of my genius, which is a very crooked one, every moment. Beside being better off than they already, if my house had been burned or my crops had failed, I should have been nearly as well off as before.

I am wont to think that men are not so much the keepers of herds as herds are the keepers of men, the former are so much the freer. Men and oxen exchange work; but if we consider necessary work only, the oxen will be seen to have greatly the advantage, their farm is so much the larger. Man does some of his part of the exchange work in his six weeks of haying, and it is no boy's play. Certainly no nation that lived simply in all respects, that is, no nation of philosophers, would commit so great a blunder as to use the labor of animals. True, there never was and is not likely soon to be a nation of philosophers, nor am I certain it is desirable that there should be. However, *I* should never have broken a horse or bull and taken him to board for any work he might do for me, for fear I should become a horse-man or a herds-man merely; and if society seems to be the gainer by so doing, are we certain that what is one man's gain is not another's loss, and that the stable-boy has equal cause with his master to be satisfied? Granted that some public works would not have been constructed without this aid, and let man share the glory of such with the ox and horse; does it follow that he could not have accomplished works yet more worthy of himself in that case? When men begin to do, not merely unnecessary or artistic, but luxurious and idle work, with their assistance, it is inevitable that a few do all the exchange work with the oxen, or, in other words, become the slaves of the strongest. Man thus not only works for the animal within him, but, for a symbol of this, he works for the animal without him. Though we have many substantial houses

of brick or stone, the prosperity of the farmer is still measured by the degree to which the barn overshadows the house. This town is said to have the largest houses for oxen, cows, and horses hereabouts, and it is not behindhand in its public buildings; but there are very few halls for free worship or free speech in this county. It should not be by their architecture, but why not even by their power of abstract thought, that nations should seek to commemorate themselves? How much more admirable the Bhagvat-Geeta [34] than all the ruins of the East! Towers and temples are the luxury of princes. A simple and independent mind does not toil at the bidding of any prince. Genius is not a retainer to any emperor, nor is its material silver, or gold, or marble, except to a trifling extent. To what end, pray, is so much stone hammered? In Arcadia,[35] when I was there, I did not see any hammering stone. Nations are possessed with an insane ambition to perpetuate the memory of themselves by the amount of hammered stone they leave. What if equal pains were taken to smooth and polish their manners? One piece of good sense would be more memorable than a monument as high as the moon. I love better to see stones in place. The grandeur of Thebes was a vulgar grandeur. More sensible is a rod of stone wall that bounds an honest man's field than a hundred-gated Thebes that has wandered farther from the true end of life. The religion and civilization which are barbaric and heathenish build splendid temples; but what you might call Christianity does not. Most of the stone a nation hammers goes toward its tomb only. It buries itself alive. As for the Pyramids, there is nothing to wonder at in them so much as the fact that so many men could be found degraded enough to spend their lives constructing a tomb

[34] The *Bhagavat Gîta*, philosophical and mystical poem in Sanskrit, supposed to have been written in the first or second century B.C. in India.

[35] A pastoral section of ancient Greece, but used figuratively for the simple life.

for some ambitious booby, whom it would have been wiser and manlier to have drowned in the Nile, and then given his body to the dogs. I might possibly invent some excuse for them and him, but I have no time for it. As for the religion and love of art of the builders, it is much the same all the world over, whether the building be an Egyptian temple or the United States Bank. It costs more than it comes to. The mainspring is vanity, assisted by the love of garlic and bread and butter. Mr. Balcom, a promising young architect, designs it on the back of his Vitruvius,[36] with hard pencil and ruler, and the job is let out to Dobson & Sons, stonecutters. When the thirty centuries [37] begin to look down on it, mankind begin to look up at it. As for your high towers and monuments, there was a crazy fellow once in this town who undertook to dig through to China, and he got so far that, as he said,

he heard the Chinese pots and kettles rattle; but I think that I shall not go out of my way to admire the hole which he made. Many are concerned about the monuments of the West and the East,—to know who built them. For my part, I should like to know who in those days did not build them,—who were above such trifling. But to proceed with my statistics.

By surveying, carpentry, and day-labor of various other kinds in the village in the meanwhile, for I have as many trades as fingers, I had earned $13.34. The expense of food for eight months, namely, from July 4th to March 1st, the time when these estimates were made, though I lived there more than two years,—not counting potatoes, a little green corn, and some peas, which I had raised, nor considering the value of what was on hand at the last date, —was

Rice	$1 73½	
Molasses	1 73	Cheapest form of the saccharine.
Rye meal	1 04¾	
Indian meal	0 99¾	Cheaper than rye.
Pork	0 22	
Flour	0 88	Costs more than Indian meal, both money and trouble.
Sugar	0 80	
Lard	0 65	
Apples	0 25	
Dried apple	0 22	
Sweet potatoes	0 10	
One pumpkin	0 6	
One watermelon	0 2	
Salt	0 3	

All experiments which failed.

Yes, I did eat $8.74, all told; but I should not thus unblushingly publish my guilt, if I did not know that most of my readers were equally guilty with myself, and that their deeds would look no better in print. The next year I sometimes caught a mess of fish for my dinner, and once I went so far as to slaughter a woodchuck which ravaged my bean-field,—effect his transmigration, as a Tartar would say,—and

devour him, partly for experiment's sake; but though it afforded me a momentary enjoyment, notwithstanding a musky flavor, I saw that the longest use would not make

[36] Roman architect under Caesar, whose book *De Architectura* is here referred to.

[37] Napoleon, addressing his soldiers in Egypt, said: "From the summits of these monuments forty centuries look down upon you."

that a good practice, however it might seem to have your woodchucks ready dressed by the village butcher.

Clothing and some incidental expenses within the same dates, though little can be inferred from this item, amounted to

$8 40¾
Oil and some household utensils... 2 00

So that all the pecuniary outgoes, excepting for washing and mending, which for the most part were done out of the house, and their bills have not yet been received, —and these are all and more than all the ways by which money necessarily goes out in this part of the world,—were

House $28 12½
Farm one year............... 14 72½
Food eight months............ 8 74
Clothing, etc., eight months.... 8 40¾
Oil, etc., eight months........ 2 00
                              ————
In all $61 99¾

I address myself now to those of my readers who have a living to get. And to meet this I have for farm produce sold

$23 44
Earned by day-labor 13 34
                              ————
In all $36 78,

which subtracted from the sum of the outgoes leaves a balance of $25.21¾ on the one side,—this being very nearly the means with which I started, and the measure of expenses to be incurred,—and on the other, beside the leisure and independence and health thus secured, a comfortable house for me as long as I choose to occupy it.

These statistics, however accidental and therefore uninstructive they may appear, as they have a certain completeness, have a certain value also. Nothing was given me of which I have not rendered some account. It appears from the above estimate, that my food alone cost me in money about

twenty-seven cents a week. It was, for nearly two years after this, rye and Indian meal without yeast, potatoes, rice, a very little salt pork, molasses, and salt; and my drink, water. It was fit that I should live on rice, mainly, who loved so well the philosophy of India. To meet the objections of some inveterate cavillers, I may as well state, that if I dined out occasionally, as I always had done, and I trust shall have opportunities to do again, it was frequently to the detriment of my domestic arrangements. But the dining out, being, as I have stated, a constant element, does not in the least affect a comparative statement like this.

I learned from my two years' experience that it would cost incredibly little trouble to obtain one's necessary food, even in this latitude; that a man may use as simple a diet as the animals, and yet retain health and strength. I have made a satisfactory dinner, satisfactory on several accounts, simply off a dish of purslane (*Portulaca oleracea*) which I gathered in my cornfield, boiled and salted. I give the Latin on account of the savoriness of the trivial name.[38] And pray what more can a reasonable man desire, in peaceful times, in ordinary noons, than a sufficient number of ears of green sweet corn boiled, with the addition of salt? Even the little variety which I used was a yielding to the demands of appetite, and not of health. Yet men have come to such a pass that they frequently starve, not for want of necessaries, but for want of luxuries; and I know a good woman who thinks that her son lost his life because he took to drinking water only.

The reader will perceive that I am treating the subject rather from an economic than a dietetic point of view, and he will not venture to put my abstemiousness to the test unless he has a well-stocked larder.

Bread I at first made of pure Indian meal and salt, genuine hoe-cakes, which I baked before my fire out of doors on a

[38] The name of the species, *oleracea*.

shingle or the end of a stick of timber sawed off in building my house; but it was wont to get smoked and to have a piny flavor. I tried flour also; but have at last found a mixture of rye and Indian meal most convenient and agreeable. In cold weather it was no little amusement to bake several small loaves of this in succession, tending and turning them as carefully as an Egyptian his hatching eggs. They were a real cereal fruit which I ripened, and they had to my senses a fragrance like that of other noble fruits, which I kept in as long as possible by wrapping them in cloths. I made a study of the ancient and indispensable art of bread-making, consulting such authorities as offered, going back to the primitive days and first invention of the unleavened kind, when from the wildness of nuts and meats men first reached the mildness and refinement of this diet, and travelling gradually down in my studies through that accidental souring of the dough which, it is supposed, taught the leavening process, and through the various fermentations thereafter, till I came to "good, sweet, wholesome bread," the staff of life. Leaven, which some deem the soul of bread, the *spiritus* which fills its cellular tissue, which is religiously preserved like the vestal fire,—some precious bottleful, I suppose, first brought over in the Mayflower, did the business for America, and its influence is still rising, swelling, spreading, in cerealian billows over the land,—this seed I regularly and faithfully procured from the village, till at length one morning I forgot the rules, and scalded my yeast; by which accident I discovered that even this was not indispensable,—for my discoveries were not by the synthetic but analytic process,—and I have gladly omitted it since, though most housewives earnestly assured me that safe and wholesome bread without yeast might not be, and elderly people prophesied a speedy decay of the vital forces. Yet I find it not to be an essential ingredient, and after going without it for a year am still in the land of the living; and I am

glad to escape the trivialness of carrying a bottleful in my pocket, which would sometimes pop and discharge its contents to my discomfiture. It is simpler and more respectable to omit it. Man is an animal who more than any other can adapt himself to all climates and circumstances. Neither did I put any sal-soda, or other acid or alkali, into my bread. It would seem that I made it according to the recipe which Marcus Porcius Cato gave about two centuries before Christ. "Panem depsticium sic facito. Manus mortariumque bene lavato. Farinam in mortarium indito, aquae paulatim addito, subigitoque pulchre. Ubi bene subegeris, defingito, coquitoque sub testu." [39] Which I take to mean, "Make kneaded bread thus. Wash your hands and trough well. Put the meal into the trough, add water gradually, and knead it thoroughly. When you have kneaded it well, mould it, and bake it under a cover," that is, in a baking-kettle. Not a word about leaven. But I did not always use this staff of life. At one time, owing to the emptiness of my purse, I saw none of it for more than a month.

Every New Englander might easily raise all his own breadstuffs in this land of rye and Indian corn, and not depend on distant and fluctuating markets for them. Yet so far are we from simplicity and independence that, in Concord, fresh and sweet meal is rarely sold in the shops, and hominy and corn in a still coarser form are hardly used by any. For the most part the farmer gives to his cattle and hogs the grain of his own producing, and buys flour, which is at least no more wholesome, at a greater cost, at the store. I saw that I could easily raise my bushel or two of rye and Indian corn, for the former will grow on the poorest land, and the latter does not require the best, and grind them in a hand-mill, and so do without rice and pork; and if I must have some concentrated sweet, I found by experiment that I could make a very good molasses either of pump-

---

[39] Cato's *De Agri Cultura*, cap. 74.

kins or beets, and I knew that I needed only to set out a few maples to obtain it more easily still, and while these were growing I could use various substitutes beside those which I have named. "For," as the Forefathers sang,—

> "we can make liquor to sweeten
> our lips
> Of pumpkins and parsnips and walnut-
> tree chips." [40]

Finally, as for salt, the grossest of groceries, to obtain this might be a fit occasion for a visit to the seashore, or, if I did without it altogether, I should probably drink the less water. I do not learn that the Indians ever troubled themselves to go after it.

Thus I could avoid all trade and barter, so far as my food was concerned, and having a shelter already, it would only remain to get clothing and fuel. The pantaloons which I now wear were woven in a farmer's family,—thank Heaven there is so much virtue still in man; for I think the fall from the farmer to the operative as great and memorable as that from the man to the farmer;—and in a new country, fuel is an encumbrance. As for a habitat, if I were not permitted still to squat, I might purchase one acre at the same price for which the land I cultivated was sold— namely, eight dollars and eight cents. But as it was, I considered that I enhanced the value of the land by squatting on it.

There is a certain class of unbelievers who sometimes ask me such questions as, if I think that I can live on vegetable food alone; and to strike at the root of the matter at once,—for the root is faith,—I am accustomed to answer such, that I can live on board nails. If they cannot understand that, they cannot understand much that I have to say. For my part, I am glad to hear of experiments of this kind being tried; as that a young man tried for a fortnight to live on hard, raw corn on the ear, using his teeth for all mortar. The squirrel tribe tried the same and suc-

ceeded. The human race is interested in these experiments, though a few old women who are incapacitated for them, or who own their thirds in mills, may be alarmed.

My furniture, part of which I made myself,—and the rest cost me nothing of which I have not rendered an account,— consisted of a bed, a table, a desk, three chairs, a looking-glass three inche in diameter, a pair of tongs and andirons, a kettle, a skillet, and a frying-pan, a dipper, a wash-bowl, two knives and forks, three plates, one cup, one spoon, a jug for oil, a jug for molasses, and a japanned lamp. None is so poor that he need sit on a pumpkin. That is shiftlessness. There is plenty of such chairs as I like best in the village garrets to be had for taking them away. Furniture! Thank God, I can sit and I can stand without the aid of a furniture warehouse. What man but a philosopher would not be ashamed to see his furniture packed in a cart and going up country exposed to the light of heaven and the eyes of men, a beggarly account of empty boxes? That is Spaulding's furniture. I could never tell from inspecting such a load whether it belonged to a so-called rich man or a poor one; the owner always seemed poverty-stricken. Indeed, the more you have of such things the poorer you are. Each load looks as if it contained the contents of a dozen shanties; and if one shanty is poor, this is a dozen times as poor. Pray, for what do we *move* ever but to get rid of our furniture, our *exuviæ*,[41] at last to go from this world to another newly furnished, and leave this to be burned? It is the same as if all these traps were buckled to a man's belt, and he could not move over the rough country where our lines are cast without dragging them,—dragging his trap. He was a lucky fox that left his tail in the trap. The

[40] From the anonymous "New England's Annoyances."

[41] That which is stripped off, as clothing, equipment, etc.

muskrat will gnaw his third leg off to be free. No wonder man has lost his elasticity. How often he is at a dead set! "Sir, if I may be so bold, what do you mean by a dead set?" If you are a seer, whenever you meet a man you will see all that he owns, ay, and much that he pretends to disown, behind him, even to his kitchen furniture and all the trumpery which he saves and will not burn, and he will appear to be harnessed to it and making what headway he can. I think that the man is at a dead set who has got through a knot-hole or gateway where his sledge load of furniture cannot follow him. I cannot but feel compassion when I hear some trig, compact-looking man, seemingly free, all girded and ready, speak of his "furniture," as whether it is insured or not. "But what shall I do with my furniture?" My gay butterfly is entangled in a spider's web then. Even those who seem for a long while not to have any, if you inquire more narrowly you will find have some stored in some-body's barn. I look upon England to-day as an old gentleman who is travelling with a great deal of baggage, trumpery which has accumulated from long housekeeping, which he has not the courage to burn; great trunk, little trunk, bandbox, and bundle. Throw away the first three at least. It would surpass the powers of a well man nowadays to take up his bed and walk, and I should certainly advise a sick one to lay down his bed and run. When I have met an immigrant tottering under a bundle which contained his all,—looking like an enormous wen which had grown out of the nape of his neck,—I have pitied him, not because that was his all, but because he had all *that* to carry. If I have got to drag my trap, I will take care that it be a light one and do not nip me in a vital part. But perchance it would be wisest never to put one's paw into it.

I would observe, by the way, that it costs me nothing for curtains, for I have no gazers to shut out but the sun and moon, and I am willing that they should look in. The moon will not sour milk nor taint meat of mine, nor will the sun injure my furniture or fade my carpet; and if he is sometimes too warm a friend, I find it still better economy to retreat behind some curtain which nature has provided, than to add a single item to the details of housekeeping. A lady once offered me a mat, but as I had no room to spare within the house, nor time to spare within or without to shake it, I declined it, pre-ferring to wipe my feet on the sod before my door. It is best to avoid the beginnings of evil.

Not long since I was present at the auction of a deacon's effects, for his life had not been ineffectual:—

"The evil that men do lives after them." [42]

As usual, a great proportion was trumpery which had begun to accumulate in his father's day. Among the rest was a dried tapeworm. And now, after lying half a century in his garret and other dust holes, these things were not burned; instead of a *bonfire*, or purifying destruction of them, there was an *auction*, or increasing of them. The neighbors eagerly collected to view them, bought them all, and carefully transported them to their garrets and dust holes, to lie there till their estates are settled, when they will start again. When a man dies he kicks the dust.

The customs of some savage nations might, perchance, be profitably imitated by us, for they at least go through the sem-blance of casting their slough annually; they have the idea of the thing, whether they have the reality or not. Would it not be well if we were to celebrate such a "busk," or "feast of first fruits," as Bar-tram [43] describes to have been the custom of the Mucclasse Indians? "When a town cele-brates the busk," says he, "having pre-viously provided themselves with new clothes, new pots, pans, and other house-

[42] Shakespeare's *Julius Caesar*, Act. III, scene 2.
[43] For William Bartram see Vol. I, pp. 138-143.

hold utensils and furniture, they collect all their worn out clothes and other despicable things, sweep and cleanse their houses, squares, and the whole town, of their filth, which with all the remaining grain and other old provisions they cast together into one common heap, and consume it with fire. After having taken medicine, and fasted for three days, all the fire in the town is extinguished. During this fast they abstain from the gratification of every appetite and passion whatever. A general amnesty is proclaimed; all malefactors may return to their town.

"On the fourth morning, the high priest, by rubbing dry wood together, produces new fire in the public square, from whence every habitation in the town is supplied with the new and pure flame."

They then feast on the new corn and fruits, and dance and sing for three days, "and the four following days they receive visits and rejoice with their friends from neighboring towns who have in like manner purified and prepared themselves."

The Mexicans also practised a similar purification at the end of every fifty-two years, in the belief that it was time for the world to come to an end.

I have scarcely heard of a truer sacrament, that is, as the dictionary defines it, "outward and visible sign of an inward and spiritual grace," than this, and I have no doubt that they were originally inspired directly from Heaven to do thus, though they have no Biblical record of the revelation.

For more than five years I maintained myself thus solely by the labor of my hands, and I found that, by working about six weeks in a year, I could meet all the expenses of living. The whole of my winters, as well as most of my summers, I had free and clear for study. I have thoroughly tried schoolkeeping, and found that my expenses were in proportion, or rather out of proportion, to my income, for I was obliged to dress and train, not to say think and

believe, accordingly, and I lost my time into the bargain. As I did not teach for the good of my fellow-men, but simply for a livelihood, this was a failure. I have tried trade; but I found that it would take ten years to get under way in that, and that then I should probably be on my way to the devil. I was actually afraid that I might by that time be doing what is called a good business. When formerly I was looking about to see what I could do for a living, some sad experience in conforming to the wishes of friends being fresh in my mind to tax my ingenuity, I thought often and seriously of picking huckleberries; that surely I could do, and its small profits might suffice,—for my greatest skill has been to want but little,—so little capital it required, so little distraction from my wonted moods, I foolishly thought. While my acquaintances went unhesitatingly into trade or the professions, I contemplated this occupation as most like theirs; ranging the hills all summer to pick the berries which came in my way, and thereafter carelessly dispose of them; so, to keep the flocks of Admetus.[44] I also dreamed that I might gather the wild herbs, or carry evergreens to such villagers as loved to be reminded of the woods, even to the city, by hay-cart loads. But I have since learned that trade curses everything it handles; and though you trade in messages from Heaven, the whole curse of trade attaches to the business.

As I preferred some things to others, and especially valued my freedom, as I could fare hard and yet succeed well, I did not wish to spend my time in earning rich carpets or other fine furniture, or delicate cookery, or a house in the Grecian or the Gothic style just yet. If there are any to whom it is no interruption to acquire these things, and who know how to use them when acquired, I relinquish to them the pursuit. Some are "industrious," and appear to love labor for its own sake, or perhaps because it keeps them out of worse

---

[44] Apollo, banished from Olympus, kept the flocks of Admetus, king of Thessaly, for nine years.

mischief; to such I have at present nothing to say. Those who would not know what to do with more leisure than they now enjoy, I might advise to work twice as hard as they do,—work till they pay for themselves, and get their free papers. For myself I found that the occupation of a day-laborer was the most independent of any, especially as it required only thirty or forty days in a year to support one. The laborer's day ends with the going down of the sun, and he is then free to devote himself to his chosen pursuit, independent of his labor; but his employer, who speculates from month to month, has no respite from one end of the year to the other.

In short, I am convinced, both by faith and experience, that to maintain one's self on this earth is not a hardship but a pastime, if we will live simply and wisely; as the pursuits of the simpler nations are still the sports of the more artificial. It is not necessary that a man should earn his living by the sweat of his brow, unless he sweats easier than I do.

One young man of my acquaintance, who has inherited some acres, told me that he thought he should live as I did, *if he had the means.* I would not have any one adopt *my* mode of living on any account; for, beside that before he has fairly learned it I may have found out another for myself, I desire that there may be as many different persons in the world as possible; but I would have each one be very careful to find out and pursue *his own* way, and not his father's or his mother's or his neighbor's instead. The youth may build or plant or sail, only let him not be hindered from doing that which he tells me he would like to do. It is by a mathematical point only that we are wise, as the sailor or the fugitive slave keeps the polestar in his eye; but that is sufficient guidance for all our life. We may not arrive at our port within a calculable period, but we would preserve the true course.

Undoubtedly, in this case, what is true for one is truer still for a thousand, as a large house is not proportionally more ex-

pensive than a small one, since one roof may cover, one cellar underlie, and one wall separate several apartments. But for my part, I preferred the solitary dwelling. Moreover, it will commonly be cheaper to build the whole yourself than to convince another of the advantage of the common wall; and when you have done this, the common partition, to be much cheaper, must be a thin one, and that other may prove a bad neighbor, and also not keep his side in repair. The only coöperation which is commonly possible is exceedingly partial and superficial; and what little true coöperation there is, is as if it were not, being a harmony inaudible to men. If a man has faith, he will coöperate with equal faith everywhere; if he has not faith, he will continue to live like the rest of the world, whatever company he is joined to. To coöperate in the highest as well as the lowest sense, means *to get our living together.* I heard it proposed lately that two young men should travel together over the world, the one without money, earning his means as he went, before the mast and behind the plow, the other carrying a bill of exchange in his pocket. It was easy to see that they could not long be companions or coöperate, since one would not *operate* at all. They would part at the first interesting crisis in their adventures. Above all, as I have implied, the man who goes alone can start to-day; but he who travels with another must wait till that other is ready, and it may be a long time before they get off.

But all this is very selfish, I have heard some of my townsmen say. I confess that I have hitherto indulged very little in philanthropic enterprises. I have made some sacrifices to a sense of duty, and among others have sacrificed this pleasure also. There are those who have used all their arts to persuade me to undertake the support of some poor family in the town; and if I had nothing to do—for the devil finds employment for the idle—I might try my hand at some such pastime as that. However, when I have thought to indulge myself in this respect, and lay their Heaven under an obligation by maintaining certain poor persons in all respects as comfortably as I maintain myself, and have even ventured so far as to make them the offer, they have one and all unhesitatingly preferred to remain poor. While my townsmen and women are devoted in so many ways to the good of their fellows, I trust that one at least may be spared to other and less humane pursuits. You must have a genius for charity as well as for anything else. As for Doing-good, that is one of the professions which are full. Moreover, I have tried it fairly, and, strange as it may seem, am satisfied that it does not agree with my constitution. Probably I should not consciously and deliberately forsake my particular calling to do the good which society demands of me, to save the universe from annihilation; and I believe that a like but infinitely greater steadfastness elsewhere is all that now preserves it. But I would not stand between any man and his genius; and to him who does this work, which I decline, with his whole heart and soul and life, I would say, Persevere, even if the whole world call it doing evil, as it is most likely they will.

I am far from supposing that my case is a peculiar one; no doubt many of my readers would make a similar defence. At doing something,—I will not engage that my neighbors shall pronounce it good,—I do not hesitate to say that I should be a capital fellow to hire; but what that is, it is for my employer to find out. What *good* I do, in the common sense of that word, must be aside from my main path, and for the most part wholly unintended. Men say, practically, Begin where you are and such as you are, without aiming mainly to become of more worth, and with kindness aforethought go about doing good. If I were to preach at all in this strain, I should say rather, Set about being good. As if the sun should stop when he had kindled his fires up to the splendor of a moon or a star of the sixth magnitude, and go about like a Robin Goodfellow,[45] peeping in at every cottage window, inspiring lunatics, and tainting meats, and making darkness visible, instead of steadily increasing his genial heat and beneficence till he is of such brightness that no mortal can look him in the face, and then, and in the meanwhile too, going about the world in his own orbit, doing it good, or rather, as a truer philosophy has discovered, the world going about him getting good. When Phaëton, wishing to prove his heavenly birth by his beneficence, had the sun's chariot but one day, and drove out of the beaten track, he burned several blocks of houses in the lower streets of Heaven, and scorched the surface of the earth, and dried up every spring, and made the great desert of Sahara, till at length Jupiter hurled him headlong to the earth with a thunderbolt, and the sun, through grief at his death, did not shine for a year.

There is no odor so bad as that which arises from goodness tainted. It is human, it is divine, carrion. If I knew for a certainty that a man was coming to my house with the conscious design of doing me good, I should run for my life, as from that dry and parching wind of the African deserts called the simoom, which fills the mouth and nose and ears and eyes with dust till you are suffocated, for fear that I should get some of his good done to me,—some of its virus mingled with my blood. No,—in this case I would rather suffer evil the natural way. A man is not a good *man* to me because he will feed me if I should be starving, or warm me if I should be freezing, or pull me out of a ditch if I should ever fall into one. I can find you a Newfoundland dog that will do as much. Philanthropy is not love for one's fellow-man in the broadest sense. Howard [46] was no doubt an exceedingly kind and worthy man in his way, and has his reward;

---

[45] Another name for the mischievous elf Puck.

[46] John Howard (1726-1790), English philanthropist and prison reformer.

but, comparatively speaking, what are a hundred Howards to us, if their philanthropy do not help *us* in our best estate, when we are most worthy to be helped? I never heard of a philanthropic meeting in which it was sincerely proposed to do any good to me, or the like of me.

The Jesuits were quite balked by those Indians who, being burned at the stake, suggested new modes of torture to their tormentors. Being superior to physical suffering, it sometimes chanced that they were superior to any consolation which the missionaries could offer; and the law to do as you would be done by fell with less persuasiveness on the ears of those who, for their part, did not care how they were done by, who loved their enemies after a new fashion, and came very near freely forgiving them all they did.

Be sure that you give the poor the aid they most need, though it be your example which leaves them far behind. If you give money, spend yourself with it, and do not merely abandon it to them. We make curious mistakes sometimes. Often the poor man is not so cold and hungry as he is dirty and ragged and gross. It is partly his taste, and not merely his misfortune. If you give him money, he will perhaps buy more rags with it. I was wont to pity the clumsy Irish laborers who cut ice on the pond, in such mean and ragged clothes, while I shivered in my more tidy and somewhat more fashionable garments, till, one bitter cold day, one who had slipped into the water came to my house to warm him, and I saw him strip off three pairs of pants and two pairs of stockings ere he got down to the skin, though they were dirty and ragged enough, it is true, and that he could afford to refuse the *extra* garments which I offered him, he had so many *intra* ones. This ducking was the very thing he needed. Then I began to pity myself, and I saw that it would be a greater charity to bestow on me a flannel shirt than a whole slop-shop on him. There are a thousand hacking at the branches of evil to one who is striking at the root, and it may

be that he who bestows the largest amount of time and money on the needy is doing the most by his mode of life to produce that misery which he strives in vain to relieve. It is the pious slave-breeder devoting the proceeds of every tenth slave to buy a Sunday's liberty for the rest. Some show their kindness to the poor by employing them in their kitchens. Would they not be kinder if they employed themselves there? You boast of spending a tenth part of your income in charity; maybe you should spend the nine tenths so, and done with it. Society recovers only a tenth part of the property then. Is this owing to the generosity of him in whose possession it is found, or to the remissness of the officers of justice?

Philanthropy is almost the only virtue which is sufficiently appreciated by mankind. Nay, it is greatly overrated; and it is our selfishness which overrates it. A robust poor man, one sunny day here in Concord, praised a fellow-townsman to me, because, as he said, he was kind to the poor; meaning himself. The kind uncles and aunts of the race are more esteemed than its true spiritual fathers and mothers. I once heard a reverend lecturer on England, a man of learning and intelligence, after enumerating her scientific, literary, and political worthies, Shakespeare, Bacon, Cromwell, Milton, Newton, and others, speak next of her Christian heroes, whom, as if his profession required it of him, he elevated to a place far above all the rest, as the greatest of the great. They were Penn,[47] Howard, and Mrs. Fry. Every one must feel the falsehood and cant of this. The last were not England's best men and women; only, perhaps, her best philanthropists.

I would not subtract anything from the praise that is due to philanthropy, but merely demand justice for all who by their

---

[47] William Penn (1644-1718), Quaker founder of Colony of Pennsylvania. See *supra* for Howard. Elizabeth Fry (1780-1845), English Quaker philanthropist and reformer.

lives and works are a blessing to mankind. I do not value chiefly a man's uprightness and benevolence, which are, as it were, his stem and leaves. Those plants of whose greenness withered we make herb tea for the sick serve but a humble use, and are most employed by quacks. I want the flower and fruit of a man; that some fragrance be wafted over from him to me, and some ripeness flavor our intercourse. His goodness must not be a partial and transitory act, but a constant superfluity, which costs him nothing and of which he is unconscious. This is a charity that hides a multitude of sins.[48] The philanthropist too often surrounds mankind with the remembrance of his own cast-off griefs as an atmosphere, and calls it sympathy. We should impart our courage, and not our despair, our health and ease, and not our disease, and take care that this does not spread by contagion. From what southern plains comes up the voice of wailing? Under what latitudes reside the heathen to whom we would send light? Who is that intemperate and brutal man whom we would redeem? If anything ail a man, so that he does not perform his functions, if he have a pain in his bowels even,—for that is the seat of sympathy,—he forthwith sets about reforming—the world. Being a microcosm himself, he discovers—and it is a true discovery, and he is the man to make it— that the world has been eating green apples; to his eyes, in fact, the globe itself is a great green apple, which there is danger awful to think of that the children of men will nibble before it is ripe; and straightway his drastic philanthropy seeks out the Esquimau and the Patagonian, and embraces the populous Indian and Chinese villages; and thus, by a few years of philanthropic activity, the powers in the meanwhile using him for their own ends, no doubt, he cures himself of his dyspepsia, the globe acquires a faint blush on one or both of its cheeks, as if it were beginning to be ripe, and life loses its crudity and is once more sweet and wholesome to live. I never dreamed of any enormity greater than I have committed. I never knew, and never shall know, a worse man than myself.

I believe that what so saddens the reformer is not his sympathy with his fellows in distress, but, though he be the holiest son of God, is his private ail. Let this be righted, let the spring come to him, the morning rise over his couch, and he will forsake his generous companions without apology. My excuse for not lecturing against the use of tobacco is, that I never chewed it, that is a penalty which reformed tobacco-chewers have to pay; though there are things enough I have chewed which I could lecture against. If you should ever be betrayed into any of these philanthropies, do not let your left hand know what your right hand does,[49] for it is not worth knowing. Rescue the drowning and tie your shoestrings. Take your time, and set about some free labor.

Our manners have been corrupted by communication with the saints.[50] Our hymn-books resound with a melodious cursing of God and enduring Him forever.[51] One would say that even the prophets and redeemers had rather consoled the fears than confirmed the hopes of man. There is nowhere recorded a simple and irrepressible satisfaction with the gift of life, any memorable praise of God. All health and success does me good, however far off and withdrawn it may appear; all disease and failure helps to make me sad and does me evil, however much sympathy it may have with me or I with it. If, then, we would indeed restore mankind by truly Indian, botanic, magnetic, or natural means, let us first be as simple and well as Nature ourselves, dispel the clouds which hang over our own brows, and take up a little life into our

---

[48] Cf. 1 *Peter*, iv, 8.

[49] Cf. *Matthew*, vi, 3.

[50] "Evil communications corrupt good manners."—1 *Corinthians*, xv, 33.

[51] The chief end of man, according to the Westminster catechism, is to "glorify God and enjoy Him forever." See the end of the first paragraph of the following selection.

pores. Do not stay to be an overseer of the poor, but endeavor to become one of the worthies of the world.

I read in the Gulistan, or Flower Garden, of Sheik Sadi of Shiraz,[52] that "they asked a wise man, saying: Of the many celebrated trees which the Most High God has created lofty and umbrageous, they call none azad, or free, excepting the cypress, which bears no fruit; what mystery is there in this? He replied: Each has its appropriate produce, and appointed season, during the continuance of which it is fresh and blooming, and during their absence dry and withered; to neither of which states is the cypress exposed, being always flourishing; and of this nature are the azads, or religious independents.—Fix not thy heart on that which is transitory; for the Dijlah, or Tigris, will continue to flow through Bagdad after the race of caliphs is extinct: if thy hand has plenty, be liberal as the date tree; but if it affords nothing to give away, be an azad, or free man, like the cypress."

From
WHERE I LIVED, AND WHAT I LIVED FOR

I WENT to the woods because I wished to live deliberately, to front only the essential facts of life, and see if I could not learn what it had to teach, and not, when I came to die, discover that I had not lived. I did not wish to live what was not life, living is so dear; nor did I wish to practise resignation, unless it was quite necessary. I wanted to live deep and suck out all the marrow of life, to live so sturdily and Spartan-like as to put to rout all that was not life, to cut a broad swath and shave close, to drive life into a corner, and reduce it to its lowest terms, and, if it proved to be mean, why then to get the whole and genuine meanness of it, and publish its meanness to the world; or if it were sublime, to know it by experience, and be able to give a true account of it in my next excursion. For most men, it appears to me,

are in a strange uncertainty about it, whether it is of the devil or of God, and have *somewhat hastily* concluded that it is the chief end of man here to "glorify God and enjoy him forever."

Still we live meanly, like ants; though the fable tells us that we were long ago changed into men; like pygmies we fight with cranes; it is error upon error, and clout upon clout, and our best virtue has for its occasion a superfluous and evitable wretchedness. Our life is frittered away by detail. An honest man has hardly need to count more than his ten fingers, or in extreme cases he may add his ten toes, and lump the rest. Simplicity, simplicity, simplicity! I say, let your affairs be as two or three, and not a hundred or a thousand; instead of a million count half a dozen, and keep your accounts on your thumbnail. In the midst of this chopping sea of civilized life, such are the clouds and storms and quicksands and thousand-and-one items to be allowed for, that a man has to live, if he would not founder and go to the bottom and not make his port at all, by dead reckoning, and he must be a great calculator indeed who succeeds. Simplify, simplify. Instead of three meals a day, if it be necessary eat but one; instead of a hundred dishes, five; and reduce other things in proportion. Our life is like a German Confederacy, made up of petty states, with its boundary forever fluctuating, so that even a German cannot tell you how it is bounded at any moment. The nation itself, with all its so-called internal improvements, which, by the way, are all external and superficial, is just such an unwieldy and overgrown establishment, cluttered with furniture and tripped up by its own traps, ruined by luxury and heedless expense, by want of calculation and a worthy aim, as the million households in the land; and the only cure for it, as for them, is in a rigid economy, a stern and more than Spartan simplicity of life and elevation of purpose. It lives too

[52] Persian poet (1184?-1291).

fast.[1] Men think that it is essential that the *Nation* have commerce, and export ice, and talk through a telegraph, and ride thirty miles an hour, without a doubt, whether *they* do or not; but whether we should live like baboons or like men, is a little uncertain. If we do not get out sleepers, and forge rails, and devote days and nights to the work, but go to tinkering upon our *lives* to improve *them*, who will build railroads? And if railroads are not built, how shall we get to Heaven in season? But if we stay at home and mind our business, who will want railroads? We do not ride on the railroad; it rides upon us. Did you ever think what those sleepers are that underlie the railroad? Each one is a man, an Irishman, or a Yankee man. The rails are laid on them, and they are covered with sand, and the cars run smoothly over them. They are sound sleepers, I assure you. And every few years a new lot is laid down and run over; so that, if some have the pleasure of riding on a rail, others have the misfortune to be ridden upon. And when they run over a man that is walking in his sleep, a supernumerary sleeper in the wrong position, and wake him up, they suddenly stop the cars, and make a hue and cry about it, as if this were an exception. I am glad to know that it takes a gang of men for every five miles to keep the sleepers down and level in their beds as it is, for this is a sign that they may sometime get up again.

Why should we live with such hurry and waste of life? We are determined to be starved before we are hungry. Men say that a stitch in time saves nine, and so they take a thousand stitches to-day to save nine to-morrow. As for *work*, we haven't any of any consequence. We have the Saint Vitus' dance, and cannot possibly keep our heads still. If I should only give a few pulls at the parish bell-rope, as for a fire, that is, without setting the bell,[2] there is hardly a man on his farm in the outskirts of Concord, notwithstanding that press of engagements which was his excuse so many times this morning, nor a boy, nor a woman, I might almost say, but would forsake all and follow that sound, not mainly to save property from the flames, but, if we will confess the truth, much more to see it burn, since burn it must, and we, be it known, did not set it on fire,—or to see it put out, and have a hand in it, if that is done as handsomely; yes, even if it were the parish church itself. Hardly a man takes a half-hour's nap after dinner, but when he wakes he holds up his head and asks, "What's the news?" as if the rest of mankind had stood his sentinels. Some give directions to be waked every half-hour, doubtless for no other purpose; and then, to pay for it, they tell what they have dreamed. After a night's sleep the news is as indispensable as the breakfast. "Pray tell me anything new that has happened to a man anywhere on this globe,"—and he reads it over his coffee and rolls, that a man has had his eyes gouged out this morning on the Wachito River;[3] never dreaming the while that he lives in the dark unfathomed mammoth cave of this world, and has but the rudiment of an eye himself. . . .

Time is but the stream I go a-fishing in. I drink at it; but while I drink I see the sandy bottom and detect how shallow it is. Its thin current slides away, but eternity remains. I would drink deeper; fish in the sky, whose bottom is pebbly with stars. I cannot count one. I know not the first letter of the alphabet. I have always been regretting that I was not as wise as the day I was born. The intellect is a cleaver; it discerns and rifts its way into the secret of things. I do not wish to be any more busy with my hands than is necessary. My head is hands and feet. I feel all my best faculties concentrated in it. My instinct tells me that my head is an organ for burrowing, as some creatures use their snout and

---

[1] A passage in the original manuscript at this point voiced a criticism of Fourierism; it was deleted before printing.

[2] The bell is "set" when it is pulled so far over that it rests upside-down.

[3] The Ouachita, or Washita, River, then a feature of the frontier.

fore paws, and with it I would mine and burrow my way through these hills. I think that the richest vein is somewhere hereabouts; so by the divining-rod and thin rising vapors I judge; and here I will begin to mine.

From
SOUNDS

SOMETIMES, on Sundays, I heard the bells, the Lincoln, Acton, Bedford, or Concord bell, when the wind was favorable, a faint, sweet, and, as it were, natural melody, worth importing into the wilderness. At a sufficient distance over the woods this sound acquires a certain vibratory hum, as if the pine needles in the horizon were the strings of a harp which it swept. All sound heard at the greatest possible distance produces one and the same effect, a vibration of the universal lyre, just as the intervening atmosphere makes a distant ridge of earth interesting to our eyes by the azure tint it imparts to it. There came to me in this case a melody which the air had strained, and which had conversed with every leaf and needle of the wood, that portion of the sound which the elements had taken up and modulated and echoed from vale to vale. The echo is, to some extent, an original sound, and therein is the magic and charm of it. It is not merely a repetition of what was worth repeating in the bell, but partly the voice of the wood; the same trivial words and notes sung by a wood-nymph.

At evening, the distant lowing of some cow in the horizon beyond the woods sounded sweet and melodious and at first I would mistake it for the voices of certain minstrels by whom I was sometimes serenaded, who might be straying over hill and dale; but soon I was not unpleasantly disappointed when it was prolonged into the cheap and natural music of the cow. I do not mean to be satirical, but to express my appreciation of those youths' singing, when I state that I perceived

clearly that it was akin to the music of the cow, and they were at length one articulation of Nature.

Regularly at half-past seven, in one part of the summer, after the evening train had gone by, the whip-poor-wills chanted their vespers for half an hour, sitting on a stump by my door, or upon the ridge-pole of the house. They would begin to sing almost with as much precision as a clock, within five minutes of a particular time, referred to the setting of the sun, every evening. I had a rare opportunity to become acquainted with their habits. Sometimes I heard four or five at once in different parts of the wood, by accident one a bar behind another, and so near me that I distinguished not only the cluck after each note, but often that singular buzzing sound like a fly in a spider's web, only proportionally louder. Sometimes one would circle round and round me in the woods a few feet distant as if tethered by a string, when probably I was near its eggs. They sang at intervals throughout the night, and were again as musical as ever just before and about dawn.

When other birds are still, the screech owls take up the strain, like mourning women their ancient u-lu-lu. Their dismal scream is truly Ben Jonsonian.[4] Wise midnight hags! It is no honest and blunt tu-whit tu-who of the poets, but, without jesting, a most solemn graveyard ditty, the mutual consolations of suicide lovers remembering the pangs and the delights of supernal love in the infernal groves. Yet I love to hear their wailing, their doleful responses, trilled along the woodside; reminding me sometimes of music and singing birds; as if it were the dark and tearful side of music, the regrets and sighs that would fain be sung. They are the spirits, the low spirits and melancholy forebodings, of fallen souls that once in human shape night-walked the earth and did the deeds of darkness, now expiating

[4] F. H. Allen suggests the witches' scene in Jonson's *Masque of Queens* as the basis for this reference.

their sins with their wailing hymns or threnodies in the scenery of their transgressions. They give me a new sense of the variety and capacity of that nature which is our common dwelling. *Oh-o-o-o-o that I never had been bor-r-r-r-n!* sighs one on this side of the pond, and circles with the restlessness of despair to some new perch on the gray oaks. Then—*that I never had been bor-r-r-r-n!* echoes another on the farther side with tremulous sincerity, and —*bor-r-r-r-n!* comes faintly from far in the Lincoln woods.

I was also serenaded by a hooting owl. Near at hand you could fancy it the most melancholy sound in Nature, as if she meant by this to stereotype and make permanent in her choir the dying moans of a human being,—some poor weak relic of mortality who has left hope behind, and howls like an animal, yet with human sobs, on entering the dark valley, made more awful by a certain gurgling melodiousness, —I find myself beginning with the letters *gl* when I try to imitate it,—expressive of a mind which has reached the gelatinous, mildewy stage in the mortification of all healthy and courageous thought. It reminded me of ghouls and idiots and insane howlings. But now one answers from far woods in a strain made really melodious by distance,—*Hoo hoo hoo, hoorer hoo;* and indeed for the most part it suggested only pleasing associations, whether heard by day or night, summer or winter.

I rejoice that there are owls. Let them do the idiotic and maniacal hooting for men. It is a sound admirably suited to swamps and twilight woods which no day illustrates, suggesting a vast and undeveloped nature which men have not recognized. They represent the stark twilight and unsatisfied thoughts which all have. All day the sun has shone on the surface of some savage swamp, where the single spruce stands hung with usnea lichens, and small hawks circulate above, and the chickadee lisps amid the evergreens, and the partridge and rabbit skulk beneath; but now a more dismal and fitting day dawns, and a different race of creatures awakes to express the meaning of Nature there.

Late in the evening I heard the distant rumbling of wagons over bridges,—a sound heard farther than almost any other at night,—the baying of dogs, and sometimes again the lowing of some disconsolate cow in a distant barn-yard. In the meanwhile all the shore rang with the trump of bull-frogs, the sturdy spirits of ancient wine-bibbers and wassailers, still unrepentant, trying to sing a catch in their Stygian lake, —if the Walden nymphs will pardon the comparison, for though there are almost no weeds, there are frogs there,—who would fain keep up the hilarious rules of their old festal tables, though their voices have waxed hoarse and solemnly grave, mocking at mirth, and the wine has lost its flavor, and become only liquor to distend their paunches, and sweet intoxication never comes to drown the memory of the past, but mere saturation and waterloggedness and distention. The most aldermanic, with his chin upon a heart-leaf, which serves for a napkin to his drooling chops, under this northern shore quaffs a deep draught of the once scorned water, and passes round the cup with the ejaculation *tr-r-r-oonk, tr-r-r-oonk, tr-r-r-oonk!* and straightway comes over the water from some distant cove the same password repeated, where the next in seniority and girth has gulped down to his mark; and when this observance has made the circuit of the shores, then ejaculates the master of ceremonies, with satisfaction, *tr-r-r-oonk!* and each in his turn repeats the same down to the least distended, leakiest, and flabbiest paunched, that there be no mistake; and then the bowl goes round again and again, until the sun disperses the morning mist, and only the patriarch is not under the pond, but vainly bellowing *troonk* from time to time, and pausing for a reply.

I am not sure that I ever heard the sound of cock-crowing from my clearing, and I thought that it might be worth the while to keep a cockerel for his music merely, as a singing bird. The note of this once wild Indian pheasant is certainly the most remarkable of any bird's, and if they could be naturalized without being domesticated, it would soon become the most famous sound in our woods, surpassing the clangor of the goose and the hooting of the owl; and then imagine the cackling of the hens to fill the pauses when their lords' clarions rested! No wonder that man added this bird to his tame stock,— to say nothing of the eggs and drumsticks. To walk in a winter morning in a wood where these birds abounded, their native woods, and hear the wild cockerels crow on the trees, clear and shrill for miles over the resounding earth, drowning the feebler notes of other birds,—think of it! It would put nations on the alert. Who would not be early to rise, and rise earlier and earlier every successive day of his life, till he became unspeakably healthy, wealthy, and wise? This foreign bird's note is celebrated by the poets of all countries along with the notes of their native songsters. All climates agree with brave Chanticleer. He is more indigenous even than the natives. His health is ever good, his lungs are sound, his spirits never flag. Even the sailor on the Atlantic and Pacific is awakened by his voice; but its shrill sound never roused me from my slumbers. I kept neither dog, cat, cow, pig, nor hens, so that you would have said there was a deficiency of domestic sounds; neither the churn, nor the spinning-wheel, nor even the singing of the kettle, nor the hissing of the urn, nor children crying, to comfort one. An old-fashioned man would have lost his senses or died of ennui before this. Not even rats in the wall, for they were starved out, or rather were never baited in,—only squirrels on the roof and under the floor, a whippoor-will on the ridge-pole, a blue jay screaming beneath the window, a hare or woodchuck under the house, a screech owl or a cat owl behind it, a flock of wild geese or a laughing loon on the pond, and a fox to bark in the night. Not even a lark or an oriole, those mild plantation birds, ever visited my clearing. No cockerels to crow

nor hens to cackle in the yard. No yard! but unfenced nature reaching up to your very sills. A young forest growing up under your windows, and wild sumachs and blackberry vines breaking through into your cellar; sturdy pitch pines rubbing and creaking against the shingles for want of room, their roots reaching quite under the house. Instead of a scuttle or a blind blown off in the gale,—a pine tree snapped off or torn up by the roots behind your house for fuel. Instead of no path to the front-yard gate in the Great Snow,—no gate—no front-yard,—and no path to the civilized world.

THE BEAN-FIELD

MEANWHILE my beans, the length of whose rows, added together, was seven miles already planted, were impatient to be hoed, for the earliest had grown considerably before the latest were in the ground; indeed they were not easily to be put off. What was the meaning of this so steady and self-respecting, this small Herculean labor, I knew not. I came to love my rows, my beans, though so many more than I wanted. They attached me to the earth, and so I got strength like Antæus.[5] But why should I raise them? Only Heaven knows. This was my curious labor all summer,—to make this portion of the earth's surface, which had yielded only cinquefoil, blackberries, johnswort, and the like, before, sweet wild fruits and pleasant flowers, produce instead this pulse. What shall I learn of beans or beans of me? I cherish them, I hoe them, early and late I have an eye to them; and this is my day's work. It is a fine broad leaf to look on. My auxiliaries are the dews and rains which water this dry soil, and what fertility is in the soil itself, which for the most

[5] In Greek mythology, a Libyan giant who was invincible so long as he remained in contact with his mother, the earth. Hercules killed him by raising him from the ground.

part is lean and effete. My enemies are worms, cool days, and most of all wood-chucks. The last have nibbled for me a quarter of an acre clean. But what right had I to oust johnswort and the rest, and break up their ancient herb garden? Soon, however, the remaining beans will be too tough for them, and go forward to meet new foes.

When I was four years old, as I well remember, I was brought from Boston to this my native town, through these very woods and this field, to the pond. It is one of the oldest scenes stamped on my memory. And now to-night my flute has waked the echoes over that very water. The pines still stand here older than I; or, if some have fallen, I have cooked my supper with their stumps, and a new growth is rising all around, preparing another aspect for new infant eyes. Almost the same johns-wort springs from the same perennial root in this pasture, and even I have at length helped to clothe that fabulous landscape of my infant dreams, and one of the results of my presence and influence is seen in these bean leaves, corn blades, and potato vines.

I planted about two acres and a half of upland; and as it was only about fifteen years since the land was cleared, and I myself had got out two or three cords of stumps, I did not give it any manure; but in the course of the summer it appeared by the arrowheads which I turned up in hoeing, that an extinct nation had anciently dwelt here and planted corn and beans ere white men came to clear the land, and so, to some extent, had exhausted the soil for this very crop.

Before yet any woodchuck or squirrel had run across the road, or the sun had got above the shrub oaks, while all the dew was on, though the farmers warned me against it,—I would advise you to do all your work if possible while the dew is on, —I began to level the ranks of haughty weeds in my bean-field and throw dust upon their heads. Early in the morning I worked barefooted, dabbling like a plastic artist in the dewy and crumbling sand, but later in the day the sun blistered my feet. There the sun lighted me to hoe beans, pacing slowly backward and forward over that yellow gravelly upland, between the long green rows, fifteen rods, the one end terminating in a shrub oak copse where I could rest in the shade, the other in a blackberry field where the green berries deepened their tints by the time I had made another bout. Removing the weeds, putting fresh soil about the bean stems, and encouraging this weed which I had sown, making the yellow soil express its summer thought in bean leaves and blos-soms rather than in wormwood and piper and millet grass, making the earth say beans instead of grass,—this was my daily work. As I had little aid from horses or cattle, or hired men or boys, or improved implements of husbandry, I was much slower, and became much more intimate with my beans than usual. But labor of the hands, even when pursued to the verge of drudgery, is perhaps never the worst form of idleness. It has a constant and imper-ishable moral, and to the scholar it yields a classic result. A very *agricola laboriosus* [6] was I to travellers bound westward through Lincoln and Wayland to nobody knows where; they sitting at their ease in gigs, with elbows on knees, and reins loosely hanging in festoons; I the home-staying, laborious native of the soil. But soon my homestead was out of their sight and thought. It was the only open and culti-vated field for a great distance on either side of the road, so they made the most of it; and sometimes the man in the field heard more of travellers' gossip and com-ment than was meant for his ear: "Beans so late! peas so late!"—for I continued to plant when others had begun to hoe,—the ministerial husbandman had not suspected it. "Corn, my boy, for fodder; corn for fodder." "Does he *live* there?" asks the black bonnet of the gray coat; and the hard-featured farmer reins up his grateful

---

[6] Hard-working farmer.

dobbin to inquire what you are doing where he sees no manure in the furrow, and recommends a little chip dirt, or any little waste stuff, or it may be ashes or plaster. But here were two acres and a half of furrows, and only a hoe for cart and two hands to draw it,—there being an aversion to other carts and horses,—and chip dirt far away. Fellow-travellers as they rattled by compared it aloud with the fields which they had passed, so that I came to know how I stood in the agricultural world. This was one field not in Mr. Colman's report.[7] And, by the way, who estimates the value of the crop which nature yields in the still wilder fields unimproved by man? The crop of *English* hay is carefully weighed, the moisture calculated, the silicates and the potash; but in all dells and pond-holes in the woods and pastures and swamps grows a rich and various crop only unreaped by man. Mine was, as it were, the connecting link between wild and cultivated fields; as some states are civilized, and others half-civilized, and others savage or barbarous, so my field was, though not in a bad sense, a half-cultivated field. They were beans cheerfully returning to their wild and primitive state that I cultivated, and my hoe played the *Ranz des Vaches* [8] for them.

Near at hand, upon the topmost spray of a birch, sings the brown thrasher—or red mavis, as some love to call him—all the morning, glad of your society, that would find out another farmer's field if yours were not here. While you are planting the seed, he cries,—"Drop it, drop it,—cover it up, cover it up,—pull it up, pull it up, pull it up." But this was not corn, and so it was safe from such enemies as he. You may wonder what his rigmarole, his amateur Paganini [9] performances on one string or on twenty, have to do with your planting, and yet prefer it to leached ashes or plaster. It was a cheap sort of top dressing in which I had entire faith.

As I drew a still fresher soil about the rows with my hoe, I disturbed the ashes of unchronicled nations who in primeval years

lived under these heavens, and their small implements of war and hunting were brought to the light of this modern day. They lay mingled with other natural stones, some of which bore the marks of having been burned by Indian fires, and some by the sun, and also bits of pottery and glass brought hither by the recent cultivators of the soil. When my hoe tinkled against the stones, that music echoed to the woods and the sky, and was an accompaniment to my labor which yielded an instant and immeasurable crop. It was no longer beans that I hoed, nor I that hoed beans; and I remembered with as much pity as pride, if I remembered at all, my acquaintances who had gone to the city to attend the oratorios. The nighthawk circled overhead in the sunny afternoons—for I sometimes made a day of it—like a mote in the eye, or in heaven's eye, falling from time to time with a swoop and a sound as if the heavens were rent, torn at last to very rags and tatters, and yet a seamless cope remained; small imps that fill the air and lay their eggs on the ground on bare sand or rocks on the tops of hills, where few have found them; graceful and slender like ripples caught up from the pond, as leaves are raised by the wind to float in the heavens; such kindredship is in nature. The hawk is aerial brother of the wave which he sails over and surveys, those his perfect air-inflated wings answering to the elemental unfledged pinions of the sea. Or sometimes I watched a pair of hen-hawks circling high in the sky, alternately soaring and descending, approaching and leaving one another, as if they were the embodiment of my own thoughts. Or I was attracted by the passage of wild pigeons

---

[7] Henry Colman was long State Commissioner for the Agricultural Survey of Massachusetts.

[8] Song of Swiss mountain shepherds, noted by certain French observers because they made Swiss troops long for their free and wild home life.

[9] Nicolò Paganini (1782-1840), Italian violinist.

from this wood to that, with a slight quivering winnowing sound and carrier haste; or from under a rotten stump my hoe turned up a sluggish portentous and outlandish spotted salamander, a trace of Egypt and the Nile, yet our contemporary. When I paused to lean on my hoe, these sounds and sights I heard and saw anywhere in the row, a part of the inexhaustible entertainment which the country offers.

On gala days the town fires its great guns, which echo like popguns to these woods, and some waifs of martial music occasionally penetrate thus far. To me, away there in my bean-field at the other end of the town, the big guns sounded as if a puffball had burst; and when there was a military turnout [10] of which I was ignorant, I have sometimes had a vague sense all the day of some sort of itching and disease in the horizon, as if some eruption would break out there soon, either scarlatina or canker-rash, until at length some more favorable puff of wind, making haste over the fields and up the Wayland road, brought me information of the "trainers." It seemed by the distant hum as if somebody's bees had swarmed, and that the neighbors, according to Virgil's advice, by a faint *tintinnabulum* upon the most sonorous of their domestic utensils, were endeavoring to call them down into the hive again. And when the sound died quite away, and the hum had ceased, and the most favorable breezes told no tale, I knew that they had got the last drone of them all safely into the Middlesex hive, and that now their minds were bent on the honey with which it was smeared.

I felt proud to know that the liberties of Massachusetts and of our fatherland were in such safe keeping; and as I turned to my hoeing again I was filled with an inexpressible confidence, and pursued my labor cheerfully with a calm trust in the future.

When there were several bands of musicians, it sounded as if all the village was a vast bellows, and all the buildings expanded and collapsed alternately with a din. But sometimes it was a really noble and inspiring strain that reached these woods, and the trumpet that sings of fame, and I felt as if I could spit a Mexican with a good relish,—for why should we always stand for trifles?—and looked round for a woodchuck or a skunk to exercise my chivalry upon. These martial strains seemed as far away as Palestine, and reminded me of a march of crusaders in the horizon, with a slight tantivy and tremulous motion of the elm tree tops which overhang the village. This was one of the *great* days; though the sky had from my clearing only the same everlastingly great look that it wears daily, and I saw no difference in it.

It was a singular experience, that long acquaintance which I cultivated with beans, what with planting, and hoeing, and harvesting, and threshing, and picking over and selling them,—the last was the hardest of all,—I might add eating, for I did taste. I was determined to know beans. When they were growing, I used to hoe from five o'clock in the morning till noon, and commonly spent the rest of the day about other affairs. Consider the intimate and curious acquaintance one makes with various kinds of weeds,—it will bear some iteration in the account, for there was no little iteration in the labor,—disturbing their delicate organizations so ruthlessly, and making such invidious distinctions with his hoe, levelling whole ranks of one species, and sedulously cultivating another. That's Roman wormwood,—that's pigweed, —that's sorrel,—that's piper-grass,—have at him, chop him up, turn his roots upward to the sun, don't let him have a fibre in the shade, if you do he'll turn himself t'other side up and be as green as a leek in two days. A long war, not with cranes, but with weeds, those Trojans who had sun and rain and dews on their side. Daily the beans saw me come to their rescue armed with a hoe, and thin the ranks of their enemies, filling up the trenches with weedy

[10] "Training Day" for a town's militia was then an important holiday in New England.

dead. Many a lusty crest-waving Hector, that towered a whole foot above his crowding comrades, fell before my weapon and rolled in the dust.

Those summer days which some of my contemporaries devoted to the fine arts in Boston or Rome, and others to contemplation in India, and others to trade in London or New York, I thus, with the other farmers of New England, devoted to husbandry. Not that I wanted beans to eat, for I am by nature a Pythagorean,[11] so far as beans are concerned, whether they mean porridge or voting, and exchanged them for rice; but, perchance, as some must work in fields if only for the sake of tropes and expression, to serve a parable-maker one day. It was on the whole a rare amusement, which, continued too long, might have become a dissipation. Though I gave them no manure, and did not hoe them all once, I hoed them unusually well as far as I went, and was paid for it in the end, "there being in truth," as Evelyn says, "no compost or lætation whatsoever comparable to this continual motion, repastination, and turning of the mould with the spade." "The earth," he adds elsewhere, "especially if fresh, has a certain magnetism in it, by which it attracts the salt, power, or virtue (call it either) which gives it life, and is the logic of all the labor and stir we keep about it, to sustain us; all dungings and other sordid temperings being but the vicars succedaneous to this improvement." Moreover, this being one of those "worn-out and exhausted lay fields which enjoy their sabbath," had perchance, as Sir Kenelm Digby [12] thinks likely, attracted "vital spirits" from the air. I harvested twelve bushels of beans.

But to be more particular, for it is complained that Mr. Colman has reported chiefly the expensive experiments of gentlemen farmers, my outgoes were,—

For a hoe.......... $0 54
Plowing, harrowing,
  and furrowing.... 7 50   Too much.
Beans for seed..... 3 12½

Potatoes "	1 33	
Peas "	0 40	
Turnip seed.......	0 06	
White line for crow fence	0 02	
Horse cultivator and boy three hours...	1 00	
Horse and cart to get crop	0 75	
In all	$14 72½	

My income was (patremfamilias vendacen, non emacem esse oportet [13]), from

Nine bushels and twelve quarts of beans sold	$16 94
Five bushels large potatoes......	2 50
Nine " small..............	2 25
Grass	1 00
Stalks	0 75
In all	$23 44
Leaving a pecuniary profit, as I have elsewhere said, of........	$8 71½

This is the result of my experience in raising beans: Plant the common small white bush bean about the first of June, in rows three feet by eighteen inches apart, being careful to select fresh round and unmixed seed. First look out for worms, and supply vacancies by planting anew. Then look out for woodchucks, if it is an exposed place, for they will nibble off the earliest tender leaves almost clean as they go; and again, when the young tendrils make their appearance, they have notice of it, and will shear them off with both buds and young pods, sitting erect like a squirrel. But above all harvest as early as

---

[11] The cult of Pythagoras (582?-507? B.C.), Greek philosopher, forbade the eating of flesh or beans. Beans were often used in voting by ancient peoples.

[12] English author of religious and quasi-scientific works (1603-1665).

[13] The householder should be a seller, not a buyer.

possible, if you would escape frosts and have a fair and salable crop; you may save much loss by this means.

This further experience also I gained: I said to myself, I will not plant beans and corn with so much industry another summer, but such seeds, if the seed is not lost, as sincerity, truth, simplicity, faith, innocence, and the like, and see if they will not grow in this soil, even with less toil and manurance, and sustain me, for surely it has not been exhausted for these crops. Alas! I said this to myself; but now another summer is gone, and another, and another, and I am obliged to say to you, Reader, that the seeds which I planted, if indeed they *were* the seeds of those virtues, were wormeaten or had lost their vitality, and so did not come up. Commonly men will only be brave as their fathers were brave, or timid. This generation is very sure to plant corn and beans each new year precisely as the Indians did centuries ago and taught the first settlers to do, as if there were a fate in it. I saw an old man the other day, to my astonishment, making the holes with a hoe for the seventieth time at least, and not for himself to lie down in. But why should not the New Englander try new adventures, and not lay so much stress on his grain, his potato and grass crop, and his orchards,—raise other crops than these? Why concern ourselves so much about our beans for seed, and not be concerned at all about a new generation of men? We should really be fed and cheered if when we met a man we were sure to see that some of the qualities which I have named, which we all prize more than those other productions, but which are for the most part broadcast and floating in the air, had taken root and grown in him. Here comes such a subtile and ineffable quality, for instance, as truth or justice, though the slightest amount or new variety of it, along the road. Our ambassadors should be instructed to send home such seeds as these, and Congress help to distribute them over all the land. We should never stand upon ceremony with

sincerity. We should never cheat and insult and banish one another by our meanness, if there were present the kernel of worth and friendliness. We should not meet thus in haste. Most men I do not meet at all, for they seem not to have time; they are busy about their beans. We would not deal with a man thus plodding ever, leaning on a hoe or a spade as a staff between his work, not as a mushroom, but partially risen out of the earth, something more than erect, like swallows alighted and walking on the ground:—

"And as he spake, his wings would now and then
Spread, as he meant to fly, then close again,—"

so that we should suspect that we might be conversing with an angel. Bread may not always nourish us; but it always does us good, it even takes stiffness out of our joints, and makes us supple and buoyant, when we knew not what ailed us, to recognize any generosity in man or Nature, to share any unmixed and heroic joy.

Ancient poetry and mythology suggest, at least, that husbandry was once a sacred art; but it is pursued with irreverent haste and heedlessness by us, our object being to have large farms and large crops merely. We have no festival, nor procession, nor ceremony, not excepting our cattle-shows and so-called Thanksgivings, by which the farmer expresses a sense of the sacredness of his calling, or is reminded of its sacred origin. It is the premium and the feast which tempt him. He sacrifices not to Ceres and the Terrestrial Jove, but to the infernal Plutus rather.[14] By avarice and selfishness, and a grovelling habit, from which none of us is free, of regarding the soil as property, or the means of acquiring property chiefly, the landscape is deformed, husbandry is degraded with us, and the farmer

---

[14] Ceres, goddess of farming and harvest; Terrestrial Jove, supreme god of the earth, distinguished from Pluto, Jove of the under-world.

leads the meanest of lives. He knows Nature but as a robber. Cato says that the
profits of agriculture are particularly pious
or just (*maximeque pius quaestus*), and
according to Varro the old Romans "called
the same earth Mother and Ceres, and
thought that they who cultivated it led a
pious and useful life, and they alone were
left of the race of King Saturn."

We are wont to forget that the sun
looks on our cultivated fields and on the
prairies and forests without distinction.
They all reflect and absorb his rays alike,
and the former make but a small part of
the glorious picture which he beholds in
his daily course. In his view the earth is
all equally cultivated like a garden. Therefore we should receive the benefit of his
light and heat with a corresponding trust
and magnanimity. What though I value
the seeds of these beans, and harvest that
in the fall of the year? This broad field
which I have looked at so long looks not
to me as the principal cultivator, but away
from me to influences more genial to it,
which water and make it green. These beans
have results which are not harvested by me.
Do they not grow for woodchucks partly?
The ear of wheat (in Latin *spica*, obsoletely
speca, from *spe*, hope) should not be the
only hope of the husbandman; its kernel or
grain (*granum*, from *gerendo*, bearing)
is not all that it bears. How, then, can our
harvest fail? Shall I not rejoice also at
the abundance of the weeds whose seeds
are the granary of the birds? It matters
little comparatively whether the fields fill
the farmer's barns. The true husbandman
will cease from anxiety, as the squirrels
manifest no concern whether the woods will
bear chestnuts this year or not, and finish
his labor with every day, relinquishing all
claim to the produce of his fields, and sacrificing in his mind not only his first but his
last fruits also.

CONCLUSION

TO the sick the doctors wisely recommend a change of air and scenery. Thank

Heaven, here is not all the world. The
buckeye does not grow in New England,
and the mockingbird is rarely heard here.
The wild goose is more of a cosmopolite
than we; he breaks his fast in Canada,
takes a luncheon in the Ohio, and plumes
himself for the night in a southern bayou.
Even the bison, to some extent, keeps pace
with the seasons, cropping the pastures
of the Colorado only till a greener and
sweeter grass awaits him by the Yellow-
stone. Yet we think that if rail fences are
pulled down, and stone walls piled up on
our farms, bounds are henceforth set to
our lives and our fates decided. If you are
chosen town clerk, forsooth, you cannot go
to Tierra del Fuego [15] this summer: but you
may go to the land of infernal fire nevertheless. The universe is wider than our
views of it.

Yet we should oftener look over the
tafferel of our craft, like curious passengers, and not make the voyage like stupid
sailors picking oakum. The other side of
the globe is but the home of our correspondent. Our voyaging is only great-circle
sailing, and the doctors prescribe for diseases of the skin merely. One hastens to
southern Africa to chase the giraffe; but
surely that is not the game he would be
after. How long, pray, would a man hunt
giraffes if he could? Snipes and woodcocks
also may afford rare sport; but I trust it
would be nobler game to shoot one's self.—

"Direct your eye right inward, and you'll
        find
A thousand regions in your mind
Yet undiscovered. Travel them, and be
Expert in home-cosmography."

What does Africa,—what does the West
stand for? Is not our own interior white
on the chart? black though it may prove,
like the coast, when discovered. Is it the
source of the Nile, or the Niger, or the
Mississippi, or a Northwest Passage around

---

[15] The Spanish words mean "Land of
Fire."

this continent, that we would find? Are these the problems which most concern mankind? Is Franklin [16] the only man who is lost, that his wife should be so earnest to find him? Does Mr. Grinnell know where he himself is? Be rather the Mungo Park, the Lewis and Clark and Frobisher, of your own streams and oceans; explore your own higher latitudes,—with shiploads of preserved meats to support you, if they be necessary; and pile the empty cans sky-high for a sign. Were preserved meats invented to preserve meat merely? Nay, be a Columbus to whole new continents and worlds within you, opening new channels, not of trade, but of thought. Every man is the lord of a realm beside which the earthly empire of the Czar is but a petty state, a hummock left by the ice. Yet some can be patriotic who have no *self*-respect, and sacrifice the greater to the less. They love the soil which makes their graves, but have no sympathy with the spirit which may still animate their clay. Patriotism is a maggot in their heads. What was the meaning of that South-Sea Exploring Expedition, with all its parade and expense, but an indirect recognition of the fact that there are continents and seas in the moral world to which every man is an isthmus or an inlet, yet unexplored by him, but that it is easier to sail many thousand miles through cold and storm and cannibals, in a government ship, with five hundred men and boys to assist one, than it is to explore the private sea, the Atlantic and Pacific Ocean of one's being alone.—

"Erret, et extremos alter scrutetur Iberos.
  Plus habet hic vitae, plus habet ille
        viae." [17]

Let them wander and scrutinize the out-
      landish Australians.
I have more of God, they more of the road.

It is not worth the while to go round the world to count the cats in Zanzibar. Yet do this even till you can do better, and you may perhaps find some "Symmes' Hole" [18]

by which to get at the inside at last. England and France, Spain and Portugal, Gold Coast and Slave Coast, all front on this private sea; but no bark from them has ventured out of sight of land, though it is without doubt the direct way to India. If you would learn to speak all tongues and conform to the customs of all nations, if you would travel farther than all travellers, be naturalized in all climes, and cause the Sphinx to dash her head against a stone, even obey the precept of the old philosopher,[19] and Explore thyself. Herein are demanded the eye and the nerve. Only the defeated and deserters go to the wars, cowards that run away and enlist. Start now on that farthest western way, which does not pause at the Mississippi or the Pacific, nor conduct toward a worn-out China or Japan, but leads on direct, a tangent to this sphere, summer and winter, day and night, sun down, moon down, and at last earth down too.

It is said that Mirabeau [20] took to highway robbery "to ascertain what degree of resolution was necessary in order to place one's self in formal opposition to the most sacred laws of society." He declared that "a soldier who fights in the ranks does not require half so much courage as a foot-

---

[16] Sir John Franklin (1786-1847) disappeared in the Arctic, and several expeditions searched for him before he was given up as lost. Henry Grinnell (1799-1874), New York merchant, financed two of these expeditions (1850, 1853). Mungo Park (1771-1806) was a Scottish explorer in Africa. Meriwether Lewis (1774-1809) and William Clark (1770-1838) were explorers of the American Northwest, and Sir Martin Frobisher (1535?-1594) was an English mariner.

[17] Final lines of Claudian's *De Sene Veronensi*.

[18] John Cleves Symmes (1780-1829) proposed to make a hole at the North Pole to demonstrate his theory that the earth is a hollow sphere, habitable within.

[19] The advice, "Know thyself," has been given by many philosophers, and its origin as a maxim is doubtful.

[20] The Comte de Mirabeau (1749-1791), French revolutionary leader.

pad,"—"that honor and religion have never stood in the way of a well-considered and a firm resolve." This was manly, as the world goes; and yet it was idle, if not desperate. A saner man would have found himself often enough "in formal opposition" to what are deemed "the most sacred laws of society," through obedience to yet more sacred laws, and so have tested his resolution without going out of his way. It is not for a man to put himself in such an attitude to society, but to maintain himself in whatever attitude he find himself through obedience to the laws of his being, which will never be one of opposition to a just government, if he should chance to meet with such.

I left the woods for as good a reason as I went there. Perhaps it seemed to me that I had several more lives to live, and could not spare any more time for that one. It is remarkable how easily and insensibly we fall into a particular route, and make a beaten track for ourselves. I had not lived there a week before my feet wore a path from my door to the pondside; and though it is five or six years since I trod it, it is still quite distinct. It is true, I fear, that others may have fallen into it, and so helped to keep it open. The surface of the earth is soft and impressible by the feet of men; and so with the paths which the mind travels. How worn and dusty, then, must be the highways of the world, how deep the ruts of tradition and conformity! I did not wish to take a cabin passage, but rather to go before the mast and on the deck of the world, for there I could best see the moonlight amid the mountains. I do not wish to go below now.

I learned this, at least, by my experiment: that if one advances confidently in the direction of his dreams, and endeavors to live the life which he has imagined, he will meet with a success unexpected in common hours. He will put some things behind, will pass an invisible boundary; new, universal, and more liberal laws will begin to establish themselves around and within him; or the old laws be expanded, and interpreted in his favor in a more liberal sense, and he will live with the license of a higher order of beings. In proportion as he simplifies his life, the laws of the universe will appear less complex, and solitude will not be solitude, nor poverty poverty, nor weakness weakness. If you have built castles in the air, your work need not be lost; that is where they should be. Now put the foundations under them.

It is a ridiculous demand which England and America make, that you shall speak so that they can understand you. Neither men nor toadstools grow so. As if that were important, and there were not enough to understand you without them. As if Nature could support but one order of understandings, could not sustain birds as well as quadrupeds, flying as well as creeping things, and *hush* and *whoa*, which Bright [21] can understand, were the best English. As if there were safety in stupidity alone. I fear chiefly lest my expression may not be *extra-vagant* [22] enough, may not wander far enough beyond the narrow limits of my daily experience, so as to be adequate to the truth of which I have been convinced. *Extra vagance!* it depends on how you are yarded. The migrating buffalo, which seeks new pastures in another latitude, is not extravagant like the cow which kicks over the pail, leaps the cowyard fence, and runs after her calf, in milking time. I desire to speak somewhere *without* bounds; like a man in a waking moment, to men in their waking moments; for I am convinced that I cannot exaggerate enough even to lay the foundation of a true expression. Who that has heard a strain of music feared then lest he should speak extravagantly any more forever? In view of the future or possible, we should live quite laxly and undefined in front, our outlines dim and misty on that side; as our shadows reveal an insensible perspiration toward the sun. The volatile truth of

---

[21] Common name for an ox.

[22] So written to direct attention to the Latin etymology of the word from *extra*, on the outside, and *vagans*, wandering.

our words should continually betray the inadequacy of the residual statement. Their truth is instantly *translated;* its literal monument alone remains. The words which express our faith and piety are not definite; yet they are significant and fragrant like frankincense to superior natures.

Why level downward to our dullest perception always, and praise that as common sense? The commonest sense is the sense of men asleep, which they express by snoring. Sometimes we are inclined to class those who are once-and-a-half-witted with the half-witted, because we appreciate only a third part of their wit. Some would find fault with the morning red, if they ever got up early enough. "They pretend," as I hear, "that the verses of Kabir [23] have four different senses; illusion, spirit, intellect, and the exoteric doctrine of the Vedas;" but in this part of the world it is considered a ground for complaint if a man's writings admit of more than one interpretation. While England endeavors to cure the potato-rot, will not any endeavor to cure the brain-rot, which prevails so much more widely and fatally?

I do not suppose that I have attained to obscurity, but I should be proud if no more fatal fault were found with my pages on this score than was found with the Walden ice. Southern customers objected to its blue color, which is the evidence of its purity, as if it were muddy, and preferred the Cambridge ice, which is white, but tastes of weeds. The purity men love is like the mists which envelop the earth, and not like the azure ether beyond.

Some are dinning in our ears that we Americans, and moderns generally, are intellectual dwarfs compared with the ancients, or even the Elizabethan men. But what is that to the purpose? A living dog is better than a dead lion. Shall a man go and hang himself because he belongs to the race of pygmies, and not be the biggest pygmy that he can? Let every one mind his own business, and endeavor to be what he was made.

Why should we be in such desperate haste to succeed and in such desperate enterprises? If a man does not keep pace with his companions, perhaps it is because he hears a different drummer. Let him step to the music which he hears, however measured or far away. It is not important that he should mature as soon as an apple tree or an oak. Shall he turn his spring into summer? If the condition of things which we were made for is not yet, what were any reality which we can substitute? We will not be shipwrecked on a vain reality. Shall we with pains erect a heaven of blue glass over ourselves, though when it is done we shall be sure to gaze still at the true ethereal heaven far above, as if the former were not?

There was an artist in the city of Kouroo [24] who was disposed to strive after perfection. One day it came into his mind to make a staff. Having considered that in an imperfect work time is an ingredient, but into a perfect work time does not enter, he said to himself, It shall be perfect in all respects, though I should do nothing else in my life. He proceeded instantly to the forest for wood, being resolved that it should not be made of unsuitable material; and as he searched for and rejected stick after stick, his friends gradually deserted him, for they grew old in their works and died, but he grew not older by a moment. His singleness of purpose and resolution, and his elevated piety, endowed him, without his knowledge, with perennial youth. As he made no compromise with Time, Time kept out of his way, and only sighed at a distance because he could not overcome him. Before he had found a stick in all respects suitable the city of Kouroo was a hoary ruin, and he sat on one of its mounds to peel the stick. Before he had given it the proper shape the dynasty of the Candahars was at an end, and with the point of the stick he wrote the name of the last of that race in the sand, and then resumed

---

[23] Hindu mystic poet (1450?-1518).

[24] This fable is probably Thoreau's own invention, though modeled on the Hindu style.

his work. By the time he had smoothed and polished the staff Kalpa [25] was no longer the pole-star; and ere he had put on the ferule and the head adorned with precious stones, Brahma had awoke and slumbered many times. But why do I stay to mention these things? When the finishing stroke was put to his work, it suddenly expanded before the eyes of the astonished artist into the fairest of all the creations of Brahma. He had made a new system in making a staff, a world with full and fair proportions; in which, though the old cities and dynasties had passed away, fairer and more glorious ones had taken their places. And now he saw by the heap of shavings still fresh at his feet, that, for him and his work, the former lapse of time had been an illusion, and that no more time had elapsed than is required for a single scintillation from the brain of Brahma to fall on and inflame the tinder of a mortal brain. The material was pure, and his art was pure; how could the result be other than wonderful?

No face which we can give to a matter will stead us so well at last as the truth. This alone wears well. For the most part, we are not where we are, but in a false position. Through an infirmity of our natures, we suppose a case, and put ourselves into it, and hence are in two cases at the same time, and it is doubly difficult to get out. In sane moments we regard only the facts, the case that is. Say what you have to say, not what you ought. Any truth is better than make-believe. Tom Hyde, the tinker, standing on the gallows, was asked if he had anything to say. "Tell the tailors," said he, "to remember to make a knot in their thread before they take the first stitch." His companion's prayer is forgotten.

However mean your life is, meet it and live it; do not shun it and call it hard names. It is not so bad as you are. It looks poorest when you are richest. The faultfinder will find faults even in paradise. Love your life, poor as it is. You may perhaps have some pleasant, thrilling, glorious

hours, even in a poorhouse. The setting sun is reflected from the windows of the almshouse as brightly as from the rich man's abode; the snow melts before its door as early in the spring. I do not see but a quiet mind may live as contentedly there, and have as cheering thoughts, as in a palace. The town's poor seem to me often to live the most independent lives of any. Maybe they are simply great enough to receive without misgiving. Most think that they are above being supported by the town; but it oftener happens that they are not above supporting themselves by dishonest means, which should be more disreputable. Cultivate poverty like a garden herb, like sage. Do not trouble yourself much to get new things, whether clothes or friends. Turn the old; return to them. Things do not change; we change. Sell your clothes and keep your thoughts. God will see that you do not want society. If I were confined to a corner of a garret all my days, like a spider, the world would be just as large to me while I had my thoughts about me. The philosopher said: "From an army of three divisions one can take away its general, and put it in disorder; from the man the most abject and vulgar one cannot take away his thought." Do not seek so anxiously to be developed, to subject yourself to many influences to be played on; it is all dissipation. Humility like darkness reveals the heavenly lights. The shadows of poverty and meanness gather around us, "and lo! creation widens to our view." [26] We are often reminded that if there were bestowed on us the wealth of Crœsus, our aims must still be the same, and our means essentially the same. Moreover, if you are restricted in your range by poverty, if you cannot buy books and newspapers, for instance, you are but confined to the most significant and vital experiences; you are compelled to

---

[25] Sanskrit for a day of Brahma—4,320,000,000 years.

[26] From Blanco White's sonnet "To Night."

deal with the material which yields the most sugar and the most starch. It is life near the bone where it is sweetest. You are defended from being a trifler. No man loses ever on a lower level by magnanimity on a higher. Superfluous wealth can buy superfluities only. Money is not required to buy one necessary of the soul.

I live in the angle of a leaden wall, into whose composition was poured a little alloy of bell-metal. Often, in the repose of my mid-day, there reaches my ears a confused *tintinnabulum* from without. It is the noise of my contemporaries. My neighbors tell me of their adventures with famous gentlemen and ladies, what notabilities they met at the dinner-table; but I am no more interested in such things than in the contents of the Daily Times. The interest and the conversation are about costume and manners chiefly; but a goose is a goose still, dress it as you will. They tell me of California and Texas, of England and the Indies, of the Hon. Mr.—— of Georgia or of Massachusetts, all transient and fleeting phenomena, till I am ready to leap from their court-yard like the Mameluke bey.[27] I delight to come to my bearings,—not walk in procession with pomp and parade, in a conspicuous place, but to walk even with the Builder of the universe, if I may,—not to live in this restless, nervous, bustling, trivial Nineteenth Century, but stand or sit thoughtfully while it goes by. What are men celebrating? They are all on a committee of arrangements, and hourly expect a speech from somebody. God is only the president of the day, and Webster is his orator. I love to weigh, to settle, to gravitate toward that which most strongly and rightfully attracts me;—not hang by the beam of the scale and try to weigh less,—not suppose a case, but take the case that is; to travel the only path I can, and that on which no power can resist me. It affords me no satisfaction to commence to spring an arch before I have got a solid foundation. Let us not play at kittly-benders.[28] There is a solid bottom everywhere. We

read that the traveller asked the boy if the swamp before him had a hard bottom. The boy replied that it had. But presently the traveller's horse sank in up to the girths, and he observed to the boy, "I thought you said that this bog had a hard bottom." "So it has," answered the latter, "but you have not got half way to it yet." So it is with the bogs and quicksands of society; but he is an old boy that knows it. Only what is thought, said, or done at a certain rare coincidence is good. I would not be one of those who will foolishly drive a nail into mere lath and plastering; such a deed would keep me awake nights. Give me a hammer, and let me feel for the furring. Do not depend on the putty. Drive a nail home and clinch it so faithfully that you can wake up in the night and think of your work with satisfaction,—a work at which you would not be ashamed to invoke the Muse. So will help you God, and so only. Every nail driven should be as another rivet in the machine of the universe, you carrying on the work.

Rather than love, than money, than fame, give me truth. I sat at a table where were rich food and wine in abundance, and obsequious attendance, but sincerity and truth were not; and I went away hungry from the inhospitable board. The hospitality was as cold as the ices. I thought that there was no need of ice to freeze them. They talked to me of the age of the wine and the fame of the vintage; but I thought of an older, a newer, and purer wine, of a more glorious vintage, which they had not got, and could not buy. The style, the house and grounds and "entertainment" pass for nothing with me. I called on the king, but he made me wait in his hall, and conducted like a man incapacitated for hospitality. There was a man in my neighborhood who lived in a hollow tree. His

[27] At the massacre of the famous cavalry troop known as the Mamelukes by Mohammed Ali in 1811, Emin Bey is said to have escaped by leaping his horse from the fortifications.

[28] Running or skating on thin ice.

manners were truly regal. I should have done better had I called on him.

How long shall we sit in our porticoes practising idle and musty virtues, which any work would make impertinent? As if one were to begin the day with long-suffering, and hire a man to hoe his potatoes; and in the afternoon go forth to practise Christian meekness and charity with goodness aforethought! Consider the China pride and stagnant self-complacency of mankind. This generation inclines a little to congratulate itself on being the last of an illustrious line; and in Boston and London and Paris and Rome, thinking of its long descent, it speaks of its progress in art and science and literature with satisfaction. There are the Records of the Philosophical Societies, and the public Eulogies of *Great Men*! It is the good Adam contemplating his own virtue. "Yes, we have done great deeds, and sung divine songs, which shall never die,"—that is, as long as *we* can remember them. The learned societies and great men of Assyria,—where are they? What youthful philosophers and experimentalists we are! There is not one of my readers who has yet lived a whole human life. These may be but the spring months in the life of the race. If we have had the seven-years' itch, we have not seen the seventeen-year locust yet in Concord. We are acquainted with a mere pellicle of the globe on which we live. Most have not delved six feet beneath the surface, nor leaped as many above it. We know not where we are. Beside, we are sound asleep nearly half our time. Yet we esteem ourselves wise, and have an established order on the surface. Truly, we are deep thinkers, we are ambitious spirits! As I stand over the insect crawling amid the pine needles on the forest floor, and endeavoring to conceal itself from my sight, and ask myself why it will cherish those humble thoughts, and hide its head from me who might, perhaps, be its benefactor, and impart to its race some cheering information, I am reminded of the greater Benefactor and Intelligence that stands over me the human insect.

There is an incessant influx of novelty into the world and yet we tolerate incredible dulness. I need only suggest what kind of sermons are still listened to in the most enlightened countries. There are such words as joy and sorrow, but they are only the burden of a psalm, sung with a nasal twang, while we believe in the ordinary and mean. We think that we can change our clothes only. It is said that the British Empire is very large and respectable, and that the United States are a first-rate power. We do not believe that a tide rises and falls behind every man which can float the British Empire like a chip, if he should ever harbor it in his mind. Who knows what sort of seventeen-year locust will next come out of the ground? The government of the world I live in was not framed, like that of Britain, in after-dinner conversations over the wine.

The life in us is like the water in the river. It may rise this year higher than man has ever known it, and flood the parched uplands; even this may be the eventful year, which will drown out all our muskrats. It was not always dry land where we dwell. I see far inland the banks which the stream anciently washed, before science began to record its freshets. Every one has heard the story which has gone the rounds of New England, of a strong and beautiful bug which came out of the dry leaf of an old table of apple-tree wood, which had stood in a farmer's kitchen for sixty years, first in Connecticut, and afterward in Massachusetts,—from an egg deposited in the living tree many years earlier still, as appeared by counting the annual layers beyond it; which was heard gnawing out for several weeks, hatched perchance by the heat of an urn. Who does not feel his faith in a resurrection and immortality strengthened by hearing of this? Who knows what beautiful and winged life, whose egg has been buried for ages under many concentric layers of woodenness in the dead dry life of society, deposited at first in the alburnum of the green and living tree, which has been gradually converted into the semblance of its well-seasoned tomb,—heard perchance gnawing out now for years by the astonished family of man, as they sat round the festive board,—may unexpectedly come forth from amidst society's most trivial and handselled furniture, to enjoy its perfect summer life at last!

I do not say that John or Jonathan will realize all this; but such is the character of that morrow which mere lapse of time can never make to dawn. The light which puts out our eyes is darkness to us. Only that day dawns to which we are awake. There is more day to dawn. The sun is but a morning star.

CIVIL DISOBEDIENCE [1]
[1849]

I HEARTILY accept the motto,—"That government is best which governs least;" and I should like to see it acted up to more rapidly and systematically. Carried out, it finally amounts to this, which also I believe,—"That government is best which governs not at all;" and when men are prepared for it, that will be the kind of government which they will have. Government is at best but an expedient; but most governments are usually, and all governments are sometimes, inexpedient. The objections which have been brought against a standing army, and they are many and weighty, and deserve to prevail, may also at last be brought against a standing government. The standing army is only an arm of the standing government. The government itself, which is only the mode which the people have chosen to execute their will, is equally liable to be abused and perverted before the people can act through it. Witness the present Mexican war, the work of comparatively a few individuals using the standing government

as their tool; for, in the outset, the people would not have consented to this measure.

This American government,—what is it but a tradition, though a recent one, endeavoring to transmit itself unimpaired to posterity, but each instant losing some of its integrity? It has not the vitality and force of a single living man; for a single man can bend it to his will. It is a sort of wooden gun to the people themselves. But it is not the less necessary for this; for the people must have some complicated machinery or other, and hear its din, to satisfy that idea of government which they have. Governments show thus how successfully men can be imposed on, even impose on themselves, for their own advantage. It is excellent, we must all allow. Yet this government never of itself furthered any enterprise, but by the alacrity with which it got out of its way. *It* does not keep the country free. *It* does not settle the West. *It* does not educate. The character inherent in the American people has done all that has been accomplished; and it would have done somewhat more, if the government had not sometimes got in its way. For government is an expedient by which men would fain succeed in letting one another alone; and, as has been said, when it is most expedient, the governed are most let alone by it. Trade and commerce, if they were not made of India-rubber, would never manage to bounce over the obstacles which legislators are continually putting in their way; and, if one were to judge these men wholly by the effects of their actions and not partly by their intentions, they would deserve to be classed and punished with those mischievous persons who put obstructions on the railroads.

But, to speak practically and as a citizen, unlike those who call themselves no-

---

[1] The original title, when this essay was first printed in Elizabeth P. Peabody's *Aesthetic Papers* (Boston, 1849), was "Resistance to Civil Government." It was written, however, in 1847, during the War with Mexico.

government men, I ask for, not at once no government, but *at once* a better government. Let every man make known what kind of government would command his respect, and that will be one step toward obtaining it.

After all, the practical reason why, when the power is once in the hands of the people, a majority are permitted, and for a long period continue, to rule is not because they are most likely to be in the right, nor because this seems fairest to the minority, but because they are physically the strongest. But a government in which the majority rule in all cases cannot be based on justice, even as far as men understand it. Can there not be a government in which majorities do not virtually decide right and wrong, but conscience?—in which majorities decide only those questions to which the rule of expediency is applicable? Must the citizen ever for a moment, or in the least degree, resign his conscience to the legislator? Why has every man a conscience, then? I think that we should be men first, and subjects afterward. It is not desirable to cultivate a respect for the law, so much as for the right. The only obligation which I have a right to assume is to do at any time what I think right. It is truly enough said, that a corporation has no conscience; but a corporation of conscientious men is a corporation *with* a conscience. Law never made men a whit more just; and, by means of their respect for it, even the well-disposed are daily made the agents of injustice. A common and natural result of an undue respect for law is, that you may see a file of soldiers, colonel, captain, corporal, privates, powder-monkeys, and all, marching in admirable order over hill and dale to the wars, against their wills, ay, against their common sense and consciences, which makes it very steep marching indeed, and produces a palpitation of the heart. They have no doubt that it is a damnable business in which they are concerned; they are all peaceably inclined. Now, what are they? Men at all? or small movable forts and magazines, at the serv-

ice of some unscrupulous man in power? Visit the Navy-Yard, and behold a marine, such a man as an American government can make, or such as it can make a man with its black arts,—a mere shadow and reminiscence of humanity, a man laid out alive and standing, and already, as one may say, buried under arms with funeral accompaniments, though it may be,—

"Not a drum was heard, not a funeral note,
  As his corse to the rampart we hurried;
Not a soldier discharged his farewell shot
  O'er the grave where our hero we
    buried.[2]

The mass of men serve the state thus, not as men mainly, but as machines, with their bodies. They are the standing army, and the militia, jailors, constables, posse comitatus, etc. In most cases there is no free exercise whatever of the judgment or of the moral sense; but they put themselves on a level with wood and earth and stones; and wooden men can perhaps be manufactured that will serve the purpose as well. Such command no more respect than men of straw or a lump of dirt. They have the same sort of worth only as horses and dogs. Yet such as these even are commonly esteemed good citizens. Others—as most legislators, politicians, lawyers, ministers, and office-holders—serve the state chiefly with their heads; and, as they rarely make any moral distinctions, they are as likely to serve the Devil, without *intending* it, as God. A very few, as heroes, patriots, martyrs, reformers in the great sense, and *men*, serve the state with their consciences also, and so necessarily resist it for the most part; and they are commonly treated as enemies by it. A wise man will only be useful as a man, and will not submit to be "clay," and "stop a hole to keep the wind away,"[3] but leave that office to his dust at least:—

[2] From Charles Wolfe's "The Burial of Sir John Moore."

[3] Shakespeare's *Hamlet*, Act V, scene 1.

"I am too high-born to be propertied,
To be a secondary at control,
Or useful serving-man and instrument
To any sovereign state throughout the
world." [4]

He who gives himself entirely to his fellow-men appears to them useless and selfish; but he who gives himself partially to them is pronounced a benefactor and philanthropist.

How does it become a man to behave toward this American government to-day? I answer, that he cannot without disgrace be associated with it. I cannot for an instant recognize that political organization as *my* government which is the *slave's* government also.

All men recognize the right of revolution; that is, the right to refuse allegiance to, and to resist, the government, when its tyranny or its inefficiency are great and unendurable. But almost all say that such is not the case now. But such was the case, they think, in the Revolution of '75. If one were to tell me that this was a bad government because it taxed certain foreign commodities brought to its ports, it is most probable that I should not make an ado about it, for I can do without them. All machines have their friction; and possibly this does enough good to counterbalance the evil. At any rate, it is a great evil to make a stir about it. But when the friction comes to have its machine, and oppression and robbery are organized, I say, let us not have such a machine any longer. In other words, when a sixth of the population of a nation which has undertaken to be the refuge of liberty are slaves, and a whole country is unjustly overrun and conquered by a foreign army, and subjected to military law, I think that it is not too soon for honest men to rebel and revolutionize. What makes this duty the more urgent is the fact that the country so overrun is not our own, but ours is the invading army.

Paley,[5] a common authority with many on moral questions, in his chapter on the "Duty of Submission to Civil Government,"

resolves all civil obligation into expediency; and he proceeds to say, "that so long as the interest of the whole society requires it, that is, so long as the established government cannot be resisted or changed without public inconveniency, it is the will of God that the established government be obeyed, and no longer. . . . This principle being admitted, the justice of every particular case of resistance is reduced to a computation of the quantity of the danger and grievance on the one side, and of the probability and expense of redressing it on the other." Of this, he says, every man shall judge for himself. But Paley appears never to have contemplated those cases to which the rule of expediency does not apply, in which a people, as well as an individual, must do justice, cost what it may. If I have unjustly wrested a plank from a drowning man, I must restore it to him though I drown myself. This, according to Paley, would be inconvenient. But he that would save his life, in such a case, shall lose it. This people must cease to hold slaves, and to make war on Mexico, though it cost them their existence as a people.

In their practice, nations agree with Paley; but does any one think that Massachusetts does exactly what is right at the present crisis?

"A drab of state, a cloth-o'-silver slut,
  To have her train borne up, and her
    soul trail in the dirt."

Practically speaking, the opponents to a reform in Massachusetts are not a hundred thousand politicians at the South, but a hundred thousand merchants and farmers here, who are more interested in commerce and agriculture than they are in humanity, and are not prepared to do justice to the slave and to Mexico, *cost what it may*. I quarrel not with far-off foes, but with those

---

[4] Shakespeare's *King John*, Act V, scene 2.

[5] William Paley (1743-1805), English theologian and utilitarian philosopher. The work quoted is Paley's *Principles of Moral and Political Philosophy* (1785).

who, near at home, coöperate with, and do the bidding of, those far away, and without whom the latter would be harmless. We are accustomed to say, that the mass of men are unprepared; but improvement is slow, because the few are not materially wiser or better than the many. It is not so important that many should be as good as you, as that there be some absolute goodness somewhere; for that will leaven the whole lump. There are thousands who are *in opinion* opposed to slavery and to the war, who yet in effect do nothing to put an end to them; who, esteeming themselves children of Washington and Franklin, sit down with their hands in their pockets, and say that they know not what to do, and do nothing; who even postpone the question of freedom to the question of free-trade, and quietly read the prices-current along with the latest advices from Mexico, after dinner, and, it may be, fall asleep over them both. What is the price-current of an honest man and patriot to-day? They hesitate, and they regret, and sometimes they petition; but they do nothing in earnest and with effect. They will wait, well disposed, for others to remedy the evil, that they may no longer have it to regret. At most, they give only a cheap vote, and a feeble countenance and God-speed, to the right, as it goes by them. There are nine hundred and ninety-nine patrons of virtue to one virtuous man. But it is easier to deal with the real possessor of a thing than with the temporary guardian of it.

All voting is a sort of gaming, like checkers or backgammon, with a slight moral tinge to it, a playing with right and wrong, with moral questions; and betting naturally accompanies it. The character of the voters is not staked. I cast my vote, perchance, as I think right; but I am not vitally concerned that that right should prevail. I am willing to leave it to the majority. Its obligation, therefore, never exceeds that of expediency. Even voting *for the right* is *doing* nothing for it. It is only expressing to men feebly your desire that it should prevail. A wise man will not leave the right to the mercy of chance, nor wish it to prevail through the power of the majority. There is but little virtue in the action of masses of men. When the majority shall at length vote for the abolition of slavery, it will be because they are indifferent to slavery, or because there is but little slavery left to be abolished by their vote. *They* will then be the only slaves. Only *his* vote can hasten the abolition of slavery who asserts his own freedom by his vote.

I hear of a convention to be held at Baltimore, or elsewhere, for the selection of a candidate for the Presidency, made up chiefly of editors, and men who are politicians by profession; but I think, what is it to any independent, intelligent, and respectable man what decision they may come to? Shall we not have the advantage of his wisdom and honesty, nevertheless? Can we not count upon some independent votes? Are there not many individuals in the country who do not attend conventions? But no: I find that the respectable man, so called, has immediately drifted from his position, and despairs of his country, when his country has more reason to despair of him. He forthwith adopts one of the candidates thus selected as the only *available* one, thus proving that he is himself *available* for any purposes of the demagogue. His vote is of no more worth than that of any unprincipled foreigner or hireling native, who may have been bought. O for a man who is a *man,* and, as my neighbor says, has a bone in his back which you cannot pass your hand through! Our statistics are at fault: the population has been returned too large. How many *men* are there to a square thousand miles in this country? Hardly one. Does not America offer any inducement for men to settle here? The American has dwindled into an Odd Fellow,[6]—one who may be known by

---

[6] Reference is to the Independent Order of Odd Fellows, which had set up as a distinctively American organization in 1842. It originated in England in the 18th Century.

the development of his organ of gregariousness, and a manifest lack of intellect and cheerful self-reliance; whose first and chief concern, on coming into the world, is to see that the Almshouses are in good repair; and, before yet he has lawfully donned the virile garb, to collect a fund for the support of the widows and orphans that may be; who, in short, ventures to live only by the aid of the Mutual Insurance Company, which has promised to bury him decently.

It is not a man's duty, as a matter of course, to devote himself to the eradication of any, even the most enormous wrong; he may still properly have other concerns to engage him; but it is his duty, at least, to wash his hands of it, and, if he gives it no thought longer, not to give it practically his support. If I devote myself to other pursuits and contemplations, I must first see, at least, that I do not pursue them sitting upon another man's shoulders. I must get off him first, that he may pursue his contemplations too. See what gross inconsistency is tolerated. I have heard some of my townsmen say, "I should like to have them order me out to help put down an insurrection of the slaves, or to march to Mexico;—see if I would go;" and yet these very men have each, directly by their allegiance, and so indirectly, at least, by their money, furnished a substitute. The soldier is applauded who refuses to serve in an unjust war by those who do not refuse to sustain the unjust government which makes the war; is applauded by those whose own act and authority he disregards and sets at naught; as if the state were penitent to that degree that it hired one to scourge it while it sinned, but not to that degree that it left off sinning for a moment. Thus, under the name of Order and Civil Government, we are all made at last to pay homage to and support our own meanness. After the first blush of sin comes its indifference; and from immoral it becomes, as it were, *un*moral, and not quite unnecessary to that life which we have made.

The broadest and most prevalent error

requires the most disinterested virtue to sustain it. The slight reproach to which the virtue of patriotism is commonly liable, the noble are most likely to incur. Those who, while they disapprove of the character and measures of a government, yield to it their allegiance and support are undoubtedly its most conscientious supporters, and so frequently the most serious obstacles to reform. Some are petitioning the state to dissolve the Union, to disregard the requisitions of the President. Why do they not dissolve it themselves,—the union between themselves and the state,—and refuse to pay their quota into its treasury? Do not they stand in the same relation to the state that the state does to the Union? And have not the same reasons prevented the state from resisting the Union which have prevented them from resisting the state?

How can a man be satisfied to entertain an opinion merely, and enjoy *it?* Is there any enjoyment in it, if his opinion is that he is aggrieved? If you are cheated out of a single dollar by your neighbor, you do not rest satisfied with knowing that you are cheated, or with saying that you are cheated, or even with petitioning him to pay you your due; but you take effectual steps at once to obtain the full amount, and see that you are never cheated again. Action from principle, the perception and the performance of right, changes things and relations; it is essentially revolutionary, and does not consist wholly with anything which was. It not only divides states and churches, it divides families; ay, it divides the *individual,* separating the diabolical in him from the divine.

Unjust laws exist: shall we be content to obey them, or shall we endeavor to amend them, and obey them until we have succeeded, or shall we transgress them at once? Men generally, under such a government as this, think that they ought to wait until they have persuaded the majority to alter them. They think that, if they should resist, the remedy would be worse than the evil. But it is the fault of the government itself that the remedy *is* worse than the evil. *It* makes it worse. Why is it not more apt to anticipate and provide for reform? Why does it not cherish its wise minority? Why does it cry and resist before it is hurt? Why does it not encourage its citizens to be on the alert to point out its faults, and *do* better than it would have them? Why does it always crucify Christ, and excommunicate Copernicus [7] and Luther, and pronounce Washington and Franklin rebels?

One would think, that a deliberate and practical denial of its authority was the only offense never contemplated by government; else, why has it not assigned its definite, its suitable and proportionate penalty? If a man who has no property refuses but once to earn nine shillings for the state, he is put in prison for a period unlimited by any law that I know, and determined only by the discretion of those who placed him there; but if he should steal ninety times nine shillings from the state, he is soon permitted to go at large again.

If the injustice is part of the necessary friction of the machine of government, let it go, let it go: perchance it will wear smooth,—certainly the machine will wear out. If the injustice has a spring, or a pulley, or a rope, or a crank, exclusively for itself, then perhaps you may consider whether the remedy will not be worse than the evil; but if it is of such a nature that it requires you to be the agent of injustice to another, then, I say, break the law. Let your life be a counter friction to stop the machine. What I have to do is to see, at any rate, that I do not lend myself to the wrong which I condemn.

As for adopting the ways which the state has provided for remedying the evil, I know not of such ways. They take too much time, and a man's life will be gone. I have other affairs to attend to. I came into this world, not chiefly to make this a good place to live in, but to live in it, be it good or bad. A man has not everything to do, but something; and because he cannot do *everything*, it is not necessary that he should do *something* wrong. It is not my

business to be petitioning the Governor or the Legislature any more than it is theirs to petition me; and if they should not hear my petition, what should I do then? But in this case the state has provided no way: its very Constitution is the evil. This may seem to be harsh and stubborn and unconciliatory; but it is to treat with the utmost kindness and consideration the only spirit that can appreciate or deserves it. So is all change for the better, like birth and death, which convulse the body.

I do not hesitate to say, that those who call themselves Abolitionists should at once effectually withdraw their support, both in person and property, from the government of Massachusetts and not wait till they constitute a majority of one, before they suffer the right to prevail through them. I think that it is enough if they have God on their side, without waiting for that other one. Moreover, any man more right than his neighbors constitutes a majority of one already.

I meet this American government, or its representative, the state government, directly, and face to face, once a year—no more —in the person of its tax-gatherer; this is the only mode in which a man situated as I am necessarily meets it; and it then says distinctly, Recognize me; and the simplest, most effectual, and, in the present posture of affairs, the indispensablest mode of treating with it on this head, of expressing your little satisfaction with and love for it, is to deny it then. My civil neighbor, the tax-gatherer, is the very man I have to deal with,—for it is, after all, with men and not with parchment that I quarrel,—and he has voluntarily chosen to be an agent of the government. How shall he ever know well what he is and does as an officer of the government, or as a man, until he is obliged to consider whether he shall treat me, his neighbor, for whom he has respect, as a neighbor and welldisposed man, or as a maniac and disturber of the peace, and see if he can get over this obstruction to his

---

[7] Copernicus was not excommunicated.

neighborliness without a ruder and more impetuous thought or speech corresponding with his action. I know this well, that if one thousand, if one hundred, if ten men whom I could name,—if ten *honest* men only,—ay, if *one* HONEST man, in this State of Massachusetts, *ceasing to hold slaves,* were actually to withdraw from this copartnership, and be locked up in the county jail therefor, it would be the abolition of slavery in America. For it matters not how small the beginning may seem to be: what is once well done is done forever. But we love better to talk about it: that we say is our mission. Reform keeps many scores of newspapers in its service, but not one man. If my esteemed neighbor, the State's ambassador, who will devote his days to the settlement of the question of human rights in the Council Chamber, instead of being threatened with the prisons of Carolina, were to sit down the prisoner of Massachusetts, that State which is so anxious to foist the sin of slavering upon her sister,—though at present she can discover only an act of inhospitality to be the ground of a quarrel with her,—the Legislature would not wholly waive the subject the following winter.[8]

Under a government which imprisons any unjustly, the true place for a just man is also a prison. The proper place to-day, the only place which Massachusetts has provided for her freer and less desponding spirits, is in her prisons, to be put out and locked out of the State by her own act, as they have already put themselves out by their principles. It is there that the fugitive slave, and the Mexican prisoner on parole, and the Indian come to plead the wrongs of his race should find them; on that separate, but more free and honorable ground, where the State places those who are not *with* her, but *against* her,—the only house in a slave State in which a free man can abide with honor. If any think that their influence would be lost there, and their voices no longer afflict the ear of the State, that they would not be as an enemy within its walls, they do not know by how

much truth is stronger than error, nor how much more eloquently and effectively he can combat injustice who has experienced a little in his own person. Cast your whole vote, not a strip of paper merely, but your whole influence. A minority is powerless while it conforms to the majority; it is not even a minority then; but it is irresistible when it clogs by its whole weight. If the alternative is to keep all just men in prison, or give up war and slavery, the State will not hesitate which to choose. If a thousand men were not to pay their tax-bills this year, that would not be a violent and bloody measure, as it would be to pay them, and enable the State to commit violence and shed innocent blood. This is, in fact, the definition of a peaceable revolution, if any such is possible. If the tax-gatherer, or any other public officer, asks me, as one has done, "But what shall I do?" my answer is, "If you really wish to do anything, resign your office." When the subject has refused allegiance, and the officer has resigned his office, then the revolution is accomplished. But even suppose blood should flow. Is there not a sort of blood shed when the conscience is wounded? Through this wound a man's real manhood and immortality flow out, and he bleeds to an ever-lasting death. I see this blood flowing now.

I have contemplated the imprisonment of the offender, rather than the seizure of his goods—though both will serve the same purpose,—because they who assert the purest right, and consequently are most dangerous to a corrupt State, commonly have not spent much time in accumulating property. To such the State renders comparatively small service, and a slight tax is wont to appear exorbitant, particularly if they are obliged to earn it by special labor with their hands. If there were one who lived wholly without the use of money, the

---

[8] An allusion to the expulsion of Samuel Hoar from South Carolina, whither he had been sent in 1844 by the governor of Massachusetts to initiate a test case based on South Carolina slave law.

State itself would hesitate to demand it of him. But the rich man—not to make any invidious comparison—is always sold to the institution which makes him rich. Absolutely speaking, the more money, the less virtue; for money comes between a man and his objects, and obtains them for him; and it was certainly no great virtue to obtain it. It puts to rest many questions which he would otherwise be taxed to answer; while the only new question which it puts is the hard but superfluous one, how to spend it. Thus his moral ground is taken from under his feet. The opportunities of living are diminished in proportion as what are called the "means" are increased. The best thing a man can do for his culture when he is rich is to endeavor to carry out those schemes which he entertained when he was poor. Christ answered the Herodians according to their condition. "Show me the tribute-money," said he;—and one took a penny out of his pocket;—if you use money which has the image of Cæsar on it and which he has made current and valuable, that is, *if you are men of the State,* and gladly enjoy the advantages of Cæsar's government, then pay him back some of his own when he demands it. "Render therefore to Cæsar that which is Cæsar's, and to God those things which are God's" [9]— leaving them no wiser than before as to which was which; for they did not wish to know.

When I converse with the freest of my neighbors, I perceive that, whatever they may say about the magnitude and seriousness of the question, and their regard for the public tranquillity, the long and the short of the matter is, that they cannot spare the protection of the existing government, and they dread the consequences to their property and families of disobedience to it. For my own part, I should not like to think that I ever rely on the protection of the State. But, if I deny the authority of the State when it presents its tax-bill, it will soon take and waste all my property, and so harass me and my children without end. This is hard. This makes it

impossible for a man to live honestly, and at the same time comfortably, in outward respects. It will not be worth the while to accumulate property; that would be sure to go again. You must hire or squat somewhere, and raise but a small crop, and eat that soon. You must live within yourself, and depend upon yourself always tucked up and ready for a start, and not have many affairs. A man may grow rich in Turkey even, if he will be in all respects a good subject of the Turkish government. Confucius said: "If a state is governed by the principles of reason, poverty and misery are subjects of shame; if a state is not governed by the principles of reason, riches and honors are the subjects of shame." No: until I want the protection of Massachusetts to be extended to me in some distant Southern port, where my liberty is endangered, or until I am bent solely on building up an estate at home by peaceful enterprise, I can afford to refuse allegiance to Massachusetts, and her right to my property and life. It costs me less in every sense to incur the penalty of disobedience to the State than it would to obey. I should feel as if I were worth less in that case.

Some years ago, the State met me in behalf of the Church, and commanded me to pay a certain sum toward the support of a clergyman whose preaching my father attended, but never I myself. "Pay," it said, "or be locked up in the jail." I declined to pay, but, unfortunately, another man saw fit to pay it. I did not see why the schoolmaster should be taxed to support the priest, and not the priest the schoolmaster; for I was not the State's schoolmaster, but I supported myself by voluntary subscription. I did not see why the lyceum should not present its tax-bill, and have the State to back its demand, as well as the Church. However, at the request of the selectmen, I condescended to make some such statement as this in writing:—"Know all men by these presents,

---

[9] Cf. *Matthew,* xx, 19.

that I, Henry Thoreau, do not wish to be regarded as a member of any incorporated society which I have not joined." This I gave to the town clerk; and he has it. The State, having thus learned that I did not wish to be regarded as a member of that church, has never made a like demand on me since; though it said that it must adhere to its original presumption that time. If I had known how to name them, I should then have signed off in detail from all the societies which I never signed on to; but I did not know where to find a complete list.

I have paid no poll-tax for six years. I was put into a jail once on this account, for one night; and, as I stood considering the walls of solid stone, two or three feet thick, the door of wood and iron, a foot thick, and the iron grating which strained the light, I could not help being struck with the foolishness of that institution which treated me as if I were mere flesh and blood and bones, to be locked up. I wondered that it should have concluded at length that this was the best use it could put me to, and had never thought to avail itself of my services in some way. I saw that, if there was a wall of stone between me and my townsmen, there was a still more difficult one to climb or break through before they could get to be as free as I was. I did not for a moment feel confined, and the walls seemed a great waste of stone and mortar. I felt as if I alone of all my townsmen had paid my tax. They plainly did not know how to treat me, but behaved like persons who are underbred. In every threat and in every compliment there was a blunder; for they thought that my chief desire was to stand the other side of that stone wall. I could not but smile to see how industriously they locked the door on my meditations, which followed them out again without let or hindrance, and *they* were really all that was dangerous. As they could not reach me, they had resolved to punish my body; just as boys, if they cannot come at some person against whom they have a spite, will abuse his

dog. I saw that the State was half-witted, that it was timid as a lone woman with her silver spoons, and that it did not know its friends from its foes, and I lost all my remaining respect for it, and pitied it.

Thus the State never intentionally confronts a man's sense, intellectual or moral, but only his body, his senses. It is not armed with superior wit or honesty, but with superior physical strength. I was not born to be forced. I will breathe after my own fashion. Let us see who is the strongest. What force has a multitude? They only can force me who obey a higher law than I. They force me to become like themselves. I do not hear of *men* being *forced* to live this way or that by masses of men. What sort of life were that to live? When I meet a government which says to me, "Your money or your life," why should I be in haste to give it my money? It may be in a great strait, and not know what to do: I cannot help that. It must help itself; do as I do. It is not worth the while to snivel about it. I am not responsible for the successful working of the machinery of society. I am not the son of the engineer. I perceive that, when an acorn and a chestnut fall side by side, the one does not remain inert to make way for the other, but both obey their own laws, and spring and grow and flourish as best they can, till one, perchance, overshadows and destroys the other. If a plant cannot live according to its nature, it dies; and so a man.

The night in prison was novel and interesting enough. The prisoners in their shirt-sleeves were enjoying a chat and the evening air in the doorway, when I entered. But the jailer said, "Come, boys, it is time to lock up;" and so they dispersed, and I heard the sound of their steps returning into the hollow apartments. My room-mate was introduced to me by the jailer as "a first-rate fellow and a clever man." When the door was locked, he showed me where to hang my hat, and how he managed matters there. The rooms were whitewashed once a month; and this one, at least, was the whitest, most simply furnished, and probably the neatest apartment in the town. He naturally wanted to know where I came from, and what brought me there; and, when I had told him, I asked him in my turn how he came there, presuming him to be an honest man, of course; and, as the world goes, I believe he was. "Why," said he, "they accuse me of burning a barn; but I never did it." As near as I could discover, he had probably gone to bed in a barn when drunk, and smoked his pipe there; and so a barn was burnt. He had the reputation of being a clever man, had been there some three months waiting for his trial to come on, and would have to wait as much longer; but he was quite domesticated and contented, since he got his board for nothing, and thought that he was well treated.

He occupied one window, and I the other; and I saw that if one stayed there long, his principal business would be to look out the window. I had soon read all the tracts that were left there, and examined where former prisoners had broken out, and where a grate had been sawed off, and heard the history of the various occupants of that room; for I found that even here there was a history and a gossip which never circulated beyond the walls of the jail. Probably this is the only house in the town where verses are composed, which are afterward printed in a circular form, but not published. I was shown quite a long list of verses which were composed by some young men who had been detected in an attempt to escape, who avenged themselves by singing them.

I pumped my fellow-prisoner as dry as I could, for fear I should never see him again; but at length he showed me which was my bed, and left me to blow out the lamp.

It was like traveling into a far country, such as I had never expected to behold, to lie there for one night. It seemed to me that I never had heard the town-clock strike before, nor the evening sounds of the village; for we slept with the windows open, which were inside the grating. It was to see my native village in the light of the Middle Ages and our Concord was turned into a Rhine stream, and visions of knights and castles passed before me. They were the voices of old burghers that I heard in the streets. I was an involuntary spectator and auditor of whatever was done and said in the kitchen of the adjacent village-inn,—a wholly new and rare experience to me. It was a closer view of my native town. I was fairly inside of it. I never had seen its institutions before. This is one of its peculiar institutions; for it is a shire town. I began to comprehend what its inhabitants were about.

In the morning, our breakfasts were put through the hole in the door, in small oblong-square tin pans, made to fit, and holding a pint of chocolate, with brown bread, and an iron spoon. When they called for the vessels again, I was green enough to return what bread I had left; but my comrade seized it, and said that I should lay that up for lunch or dinner. Soon after he was let out to work at haying in a neighboring field, whither he went every day, and would not be back till noon; so he bade me good-day, saying that he doubted if he should see me again.

When I came out of prison,—for some one interfered, and paid that tax,—I did not perceive that great changes had taken place on the common, such as he observed who went in a youth and emerged a tottering and gray-headed man; and yet a change had to my eyes come over the scene,—the town, and State, and country,—greater than any that mere time could effect. I saw yet more distinctly the State in which I lived. I saw to what extent the people among whom I lived could be trusted as good neighbors and friends; that their friendship was for summer weather only; that they did not greatly propose to do right; that they were a distinct race from me by their prejudices and superstitions, as the Chinamen and Malays are; that in their sacrifices to humanity they ran no risks, not even to their property; that after all they were not so noble but they treated the thief as he had treated them, and hoped, by a certain outward observance and a few prayers, and by walking in a particular straight though useless path from time to time, to save their souls. This may be to judge my neighbors harshly; for I believe that many of them are not aware that they have such an institution as the jail in their village.

It was formerly the custom in our village, when a poor debtor came out of jail, for his acquaintances to salute him, looking through their fingers, which were crossed to represent the grating of a jail window, "How do ye do?" My neighbors did not thus salute me, but first looked at me, and then at one another, as if I had returned from a long journey. I was put into jail as I was going to the shoemaker's to get a shoe which was mended. When I was let out the next morning, I proceeded to finish my errand, and, having put on my mended shoe, joined a huckleberry party, who were impatient to put themselves under my conduct; and in half an hour,— for the horse was soon tackled,—was in the midst of a huckleberry field, on one of our highest hills, two miles off, and then the State was nowhere to be seen.

This is the whole history of "My Prisons." [10]

I have never declined paying the highway tax, because I am as desirous of being a good neighbor as I am of being a bad subject; and as for supporting schools, I am doing my part to educate my fellow-countrymen now. It is for no particular item in the tax-bill that I refuse to pay it. I simply wish to refuse allegiance to the State, to withdraw and stand aloof from it effectually. I do not care to trace the course of my dollar, if I could, till it buys a man, or a musket to shoot one with,—the dollar is innocent,—but I am concerned to trace the effects of my allegiance. In fact, I quietly declare war with the State, after

my fashion, though I will still make what use and get what advantage of her I can, as is usual in such cases.

If others pay the tax which is demanded of me, from a sympathy with the State, they do but what they have already done in their own case, or rather they abet injustice to a greater extent than the State requires. If they pay the tax from a mistaken interest in the individual taxed, to save his property, or prevent his going to jail, it is because they have not considered wisely how far they let their private feelings interfere with the public good.

This, then, is my position at present. But one cannot be too much on his guard in such a case, lest his action be biased by obstinacy or an undue regard for the opinions of men. Let him see that he does only what belongs to himself and to the hour.

I think sometimes, Why, this people mean well, they are only ignorant; they would do better if they knew how: why give your neighbors this pain to treat you as they are not inclined to? But I think again, This is no reason why I should do as they do, or permit others to suffer much greater pain of a different kind. Again, I sometimes say to myself, When many millions of men, without heat, without ill will, without personal feeling of any kind, demand of you a few shillings only, without the possibility, such is their constitution, of retracting or altering their present demand, and without the possibility, on your side, of appeal to any other millions, why expose yourself to this overwhelming brute force? You do not resist cold and hunger, the winds and the waves, thus obstinately; you quietly submit to a thousand similar necessities. You do not put your head into the fire. But just in proportion as I regard this as not wholly a brute force, but partly a human force, and consider that I have relations to those

---

[10] Reference is to a popular book with this title in translation—Silvio Pellico's *Le mie prigioni* (1832), dealing with the author's imprisonment by the Austrian government.

millions as to so many millions of men, and not of mere brute or inanimate things, I see that appeal is possible, first and instantaneously, from them to the Maker of them, and, secondly, from them to themselves. But if I put my head deliberately into the fire, there is no appeal to fire or to the Maker of fire, and I have only myself to blame. If I could convince myself that I have any right to be satisfied with men as they are, and to treat them accordingly, and not according, in some respects, to my requisitions and expectations of what they and I ought to be, then, like a good Mussulman and fatalist, I should endeavor to be satisfied with things as they are, and say it is the will of God. And, above all, there is this difference between resisting this and a purely brute or natural force, that I can resist this with some effect; but I cannot expect, like Orpheus, to change the nature of the rocks and trees and beasts.

I do not wish to quarrel with any man or nation. I do not wish to split hairs, to make fine distinctions, or set myself up as better than my neighbors. I seek rather, I may say, even an excuse for comforming to the laws of the land. I am but too ready to conform to them. Indeed, I have reason to suspect myself on this head; and each year, as the tax-gatherer comes round, I find myself disposed to review the acts and position of the general and State governments, and the spirit of the people, to discover a pretext for conformity.

"We must affect our country as our parents,
And if at any time we alienate
Our love or industry from doing it honor,
We must respect effects and teach the soul
Matter of conscience and religion,
And not desire of rule or benefit"

I believe that the State will soon be able to take all my work of this sort out of my hands, and then I shall be no better a patriot than my fellow-countrymen. Seen from a lower point of view, the Constitu-

tion, with all its faults, is very good; the law and the courts are very respectable; even this State and this American government are, in many respects, very admirable, and rare things, to be thankful for, such as a great many have described them; but seen from a point of view a little higher, they are what I have described them; seen from a higher still, and the highest, who shall say what they are, or that they are worth looking at or thinking of at all?

However, the government does not concern me much, and I shall bestow the fewest possible thoughts on it. It is not many moments that I live under a government, even in this world. If a man is thought-free, fancy-free, imagination-free, that which *is not* never for a long time appearing *to be* to him, unwise rulers or reformers cannot fatally interrupt him.

I know that most men think differently from myself; but those whose lives are by profession devoted to the study of these or kindred subjects content me as little as any. Statesmen and legislators, standing so completely within the institution, never distinctly and nakedly behold it. They speak of moving society, but have no resting-place without it. They may be men of a certain experience and discrimination, and have no doubt invented ingenious and even useful systems, for which we sincerely thank them; but all their wit and usefulness lie within certain not very wide limits. They are wont to forget that the world is not governed by policy and expediency. Webster never goes behind government, and so cannot speak with authority about it. His words are wisdom to those legislators who contemplate no essential reform in the existing government; but for thinkers, and those who legislate for all time, he never once glances at the subject. I know of those whose serene and wise speculations on this theme would soon reveal the limits of his mind's range and hospitality. Yet, compared with the cheap professions of most reformers, and the still cheaper wisdom and eloquence of politicians in general, his are almost the only sensible and valuable words, and we thank Heaven for him. Comparatively, he is always strong, original, and, above all, practical. Still, his quality is not wisdom, but prudence. The lawyer's truth is not Truth, but consistency or a consistent expediency. Truth is always in harmony with herself, and is not concerned chiefly to reveal the justice that may consist with wrong-doing. He well deserves to be called, as he has been called, the Defender of the Constitution. There are really no blows to be given by him but defensive ones. He is not a leader, but a follower. His leaders are the men of '87.[11] "I have never made an effort," he says, "and never propose to make an effort; I have never countenanced an effort, and never mean to countenance an effort, to disturb the arrangement as originally made, by which the various States came into the Union." Still thinking of the sanction which the Constitution gives to slavery, he says, "Because it was a part of the original compact,—let it stand."[12] Notwithstanding his special acuteness and ability, he is unable to take a fact out of its merely political relations, and behold it as it lies absolutely to be disposed of by the intellect,—what, for instance, it behooves a man to do here in America to-day with regard to slavery,—but ventures, or is driven, to make some such desperate answer as the following, while professing to speak absolutely, and as a private man,—from which what new and singular code of social duties might be inferred? "The manner," says he, "in which the governments of those States where slavery exists are to regulate it is for their own consideration, under their responsibility to their constituents, to the general laws of propriety, humanity, and justice, and to God. Associations formed elsewhere, springing from a feeling of humanity, or other cause, have nothing whatever to do with it. They have never received any encouragement from me, and they never will."[13]

They who know of no purer sources of truth, who have traced up its stream no higher, stand, and wisely stand, by the Bible and the Constitution, and drink at it there with reverence and humility; but they who behold where it comes trickling into this lake or that pool, gird up their loins once more, and continue their pilgrimage toward its fountainhead.

No man with a genius for legislation has appeared in America. They are rare in the history of the world. There are orators, politicians, and eloquent men, by the thousand; but the speaker has not yet opened his mouth to speak who is capable of settling the much-vexed questions of the day. We love eloquence for its own sake, and not for any truth which it may utter, or any heroism it may inspire. Our legislators have not yet learned the comparative value of free-trade and of freedom, of union, and of rectitude, to a nation. They have no genius or talent for comparatively humble questions of taxation and finance, commerce and manufactures and agriculture. If we were left solely to the wordy wit of legislators in Congress for our guidance, uncorrected by the seasonable experience and the effectual complaints of the people, America would not long retain her rank among the nations. For eighteen hundred years, though perchance I have no right to say it, the New Testament has been written; yet where is the legislator who has wisdom and practical talent enough to avail himself of the light which it sheds on the science of legislation?

The authority of government, even such as I am willing to submit to,—for I will cheerfully obey those who know and can do better than I, and in many things even those who neither know nor can do so well, —is still an impure one: to be strictly just, it must have the sanction and consent of the governed. It can have no pure right

[11] The authors of the Constitution.
[12] From Webster's speech on the Texas question, Dec. 22, 1845. The quotation which follows is from a speech on the bill to exclude slavery from the territories, Aug. 12, 1848.
[13] These extracts have been inserted since the lecture was read. [Thoreau's note.]

over my person and property but what I
concede to it. The progress from an absolute to a limited monarchy, from a limited
monarchy to a democracy, is a progress
toward a true respect for the individual.
Even the Chinese philosopher was wise
enough to regard the individual as the
basis of the empire. Is a democracy, such
as we know it, the last improvement possible in government? Is it not possible to
take a step further towards recognizing
and organizing the rights of man? There
will never be a really free and enlightened
State until the State comes to recognize
the individual as a higher and independent
power, from which all its own power and
authority are derived, and treats him accordingly. I please myself with imagining
a State at last which can afford to be just
to all men, and to treat the individual with
respect as a neighbor; which even would
not think it inconsistent with its own repose if a few were to live aloof from it,
not meddling with it, nor embraced by it,
who fulfilled all the duties of neighbors and
fellow-men. A State which bore this kind
of fruit, and suffered it to drop off as fast
as it ripened, would prepare the way for a
still more perfect and glorious State, which
also I have imagined, but not yet anywhere
seen.

From
WILD APPLES
[1863 (1862)]

THE FRUIT AND ITS FLAVOR

THE TIME for wild apples is the last
of October and the first of November. They
then get to be palatable, for they ripen late,
and they are still, perhaps, as beautiful as
ever. I make a great account of these fruits,
which the farmers do not think it worth
the while to gather,—wild flavors of the
Muse, vivacious and inspiriting. The farmer
thinks that he has better in his barrels;
but he is mistaken, unless he has a walker's
appetite and imagination, neither of which
can he have.

Such as grow quite wild, and are left out
till the first of November, I presume that
the owner does not mean to gather. They
belong to children as wild as themselves,
—to certain active boys that I know,—to
the wild-eyed woman of the fields, to whom
nothing comes amiss, who gleans after all
the world,—and, moreover, to us walkers.
We have met with them, and they are ours.
These rights, long enough insisted upon,
have come to be an institution in some old
countries, where they have learned how to
live. I hear that "the custom of grippling,
which may be called apple-gleaning, is, or
was formerly, practised in Herefordshire.
It consists in leaving a few apples, which
are called the gripples, on every tree,
after the general gathering, for the boys,
who go with climbing-poles and bags to
collect them."

As for those I speak of, I pluck them as
a wild fruit, native to this quarter of the
earth,—fruit of old trees that have been
dying ever since I was a boy and are not
yet dead, frequented only by the woodpecker and the squirrel, deserted now by
the owner, who has not faith enough to
look under their boughs. From the appearance of the tree-top, at a little distance, you
would expect nothing but lichens to drop
from it, but your faith is rewarded by
finding the ground strewn with spirited
fruit,—some of it, perhaps, collected at
squirrel-holes, with the marks of their
teeth by which they carried them,—some
containing a cricket or two silently feeding
within, and some, especially in damp days,
a shell-less snail. The very sticks and stones
lodged in the tree-top might have convinced
you of the savoriness of the fruit which
has been so eagerly sought after in past
years.

I have seen no account of these among
the "Fruits and Fruit-Trees of America,"
though they are more memorable to my
taste than the grafted kinds; more racy
and wild American flavors do they possess,
when October and November, when December and January, and perhaps February and March even, have assuaged them

somewhat. An old farmer in my neighborhood, who always selects the right word, says that "they have a kind of bow-arrow tang."

Apples for grafting appear to have been selected commonly, not so much for their spirited flavor, as for their mildness, their size, and bearing qualities,—not so much for their beauty, as for their fairness and soundness. Indeed, I have no faith in the selected lists of pomological gentlemen. Their "Favorites" and "Non-suches" and "Seek-no-farthers," when I have fruited them, commonly turn out very tame and forgetable. They are eaten with comparatively little zest, and have no real tang nor smack to them.

What if some of these wildings are acrid and puckery, genuine verjuice, do they not still belong to the Pomaceae,[1] which are uniformly innocent and kind to our race? I still begrudge them to the cider-mill. Perhaps they are not fairly ripe yet.

No wonder that these small and high-colored apples are thought to make the best cider. London quotes from the "Herefordshire Report," that "apples of a small size are always, if equal in quality, to be preferred to those of a larger size, in order that the rind and kernel may bear the greatest proportion to the pulp, which affords the weakest and most watery juice." And he says, that, "to prove this, Dr. Symonds, of Hereford, about the year 1800, made one hogshead of cider entirely from the rinds and cores of apples, and another from the pulp only, when the first was found of extraordinary strength and flavor, while the latter was sweet and insipid."

Evelyn [2] says that the "Red-strake" was the favorite cider-apple in his day; and he quotes one Dr. Newburg as saying, "In Jersey 't is a general observation, as I hear, that the more of red any apple has in its rind, the more proper it is for this use. Palefaced apples they exclude as much as may be from their cider-vat." This opinion still prevails.

All apples are good in November. Those which the farmer leaves out as unsalable, and unpalatable to those who frequent the markets, are choicest fruit to the walker. But it is remarkable that the wild apple, which I praise as so spirited and racy when eaten in the fields or woods, being brought into the house, has frequently a harsh and crabbed taste. The Saunterer's Apple not even the saunterer can eat in the house. The palate rejects it there, as it does haws and acorns, and demands a tamed one; for there you miss the November air, which is the sauce it is to be eaten with. Accordingly, when Tityrus, seeing the lengthening shadows, invites Meliboeus [3] to go home and pass the night with him, he promises him mild apples and soft chestnuts. I frequently pluck wild apples of so rich and spicy a flavor that I wonder all orchardists do not get a scion from that tree, and I fail not to bring home my pockets full. But perchance, when I take one out of my desk and taste it in my chamber I find it unexpectedly crude,— sour enough to set a squirrel's teeth on edge and make a jay scream.

These apples have hung in the wind and frost and rain till they have absorbed the qualities of the weather or season, and thus are highly seasoned, and they pierce and sting and permeate us with their spirit. They must be eaten in season, accordingly, —that is, out-of-doors.

To appreciate the wild and sharp flavors of these October fruits, it is necessary that you be breathing the sharp October or November air. The out-door air and exercise which the walker gets give a different tone to his palate, and he craves a fruit which the sedentary would call harsh and crabbed. They must be eaten in the fields, when your system is all aglow with exercise, when the frosty weather nips your fingers, the wind rattles the bare boughs or rustles the few remaining leaves, and the jay is heard screaming around. What is sour in the house a bracing walk makes

---

[1] The apple family, *Malaceae.*
[2] See note on Evelyn, p. 805, *Supra.*
[3] Shepherds in Vergil's first eclogue.

sweet. Some of these apples might be labelled, "To be eaten in the wind."

Of course no flavors are thrown away; they are intended for the taste that is up to them. Some apples have two distinct flavors, and perhaps one-half of them must be eaten in the house, the other outdoors. One Peter Whitney wrote from Northborough in 1782, for the Proceedings of the Boston Academy, describing an apple-tree in that town "producing fruit of opposite qualities, part of the same apple being frequently sour and the other sweet;" also some all sour, and others all sweet, and this diversity on all parts of the tree.

There is a wild apple on Nawshawtuck Hill in my town which has to me a peculiarly pleasant bitter tang, not perceived till it is three-quarters tasted. It remains on the tongue. As you eat it, it smells exactly like a squash-bug. It is a sort of triumph to eat and relish it.

I hear that the fruit of a kind of plum-tree in Provence is "called Prunes sibarelles, because it is impossible to whistle after having eaten them, from their sourness." But perhaps they were only eaten in the house and in summer, and if tried out-of-doors in a stinging atmosphere, who knows but you could whistle an octave higher and clearer?

In the fields only are the sours and bitters of Nature appreciated; just as the wood-chopper eats his meal in a sunny glade, in the middle of a winter day, with content, basks in a sunny ray there, and dreams of summer in a degree of cold which, experienced in a chamber, would make a student miserable. They who are at work abroad are not cold, but rather it is they who sit shivering in houses. As with temperatures, so with flavors; as with cold and heat, so with sour and sweet. This natural raciness, the sours and bitters which the diseased palate refuses, are the true condiments.

Let your condiments be in the condition of your senses. To appreciate the flavor of these wild apples requires vigorous and healthy senses, papillae firm and erect on the tongue and palate, not easily flattened and tamed.

From my experience with wild apples, I can understand that there may be reason for a savage's preferring many kinds of food which the civilized man rejects. The former has the palate of an out-door man. It takes a savage or wild taste to appreciate a wild fruit.

What a healthy out-of-door appetite it takes to relish the apple of life, the apple of the world, then!

"Nor is it every apple I desire,
  Nor that which pleases every palate best;
'Tis not the lasting Deuxan I require,
  Nor yet the red-cheeked Greening I request,
Nor that which first beshrewed the name of wife,
Nor that whose beauty caused the golden strife:
No, no! bring me an apple from the tree of life."

So there is one thought for the field, another for the house. I would have my thoughts, like wild apples, to be food for walkers, and will not warrant them to be palatable, if tasted in the house.

From
THOREAU'S *"JOURNALS"*
[1906]

July 21, 1851, 8 a.m.

NOW I yearn for one of those old, meandering, dry, uninhabited roads, which lead away from towns, which lead us away from temptation, which conduct to the outside of earth, over its uppermost crust; where you may forget in what country you are travelling; where no farmer can complain that you are treading down his grass, no gentleman who has recently constructed a seat in the country that you are trespassing; on which you can go off at halfcock and wave adieu to the village; along which you may travel like a pilgrim, going nowhither; where travellers are not too often to be met; where my spirit is free; where the walls and fences are not cared for; where your head is more in heaven than your feet are on earth; which have long reaches where you can see the approaching traveller half a mile off and be prepared for him; not so luxuriant a soil as to attract men; some root and stump fences which do not need attention; where travellers have no occasion to stop, but pass along and leave you to your thoughts; where it makes no odds which way you face, whether you are going or coming, whether it is morning or evening, mid-noon or midnight; where earth is cheap enough by being public; where you can walk and think with least obstruction, there being nothing to measure progress by; where you can pace when your breast is full, and cherish your moodiness; where you are not in false relations with men, are not dining nor conversing with them; by which you may go to the uttermost parts of the earth. It is wide enough, wide as the thoughts it allows to visit you. Sometimes it is some particular half-dozen rods which I wish to find myself pacing over, as where certain airs blow; then my life will come to me, methinks; like a hunter I walk in wait for it. When I am against this bare promontory of a huckleberry hill, then forsooth my thoughts will expand. Is it some influence, as a vapor which exhales from the ground, or something in the gales which blow there, or in all things there brought together agreeably to my spirit? The walls must not be too high, imprisoning me, but low, with numerous gaps. The trees must not be too numerous, nor the hills too near, bounding the view, nor the soil too rich, attracting the attention to the earth. It must simply be the way and the life,—a way that was never known to be repaired, nor to need repair, within the memory of the oldest inhabitant. I cannot walk habitually in those ways that are liable to be mended; for sure it was the devil only that wore them. Never by the heel of thinkers

(of thought) were they worn; the zephyrs could repair that damage. The saunterer wears out no road, even though he travel on it, and therefore should pay no highway, or rather *low* way, tax. He may be taxed to construct a higher way than men travel. A way which no geese defile, nor hiss along it, but only sometimes their wild brethren fly far overhead, which the kingbird and the swallow twitter over, and the song sparrow sings on its rails; where the small red butterfly is at home on the yarrow, and no boys threaten it with imprisoning hat. There I can walk and stalk and pace and plod. Which nobody but Jonas Potter travels beside me; where no cow but his is tempted to linger for the herbage by its side; where the guide-board is fallen, and now the hand points to heaven significantly,—to a Sudbury and Marlborough in the skies. That's a road I can travel, that the particular Sudbury I am bound for, six miles an hour, or two, as you please; and few there be that enter thereon. There I can walk, and recover the lost child that I am without any ringing of a bell.

There is no glory so bright but the veil of business can hide it effectually. With most men life is postponed to some trivial business, and so therefore is heaven. Men think foolishly they may abuse and misspend life as they please and when they get to heaven turn over a new leaf.

Men are very generally spoiled by being so civil and well-disposed. You can have no profitable conversation with them, they are so conciliatory, determined to agree with you. They exhibit such long-suffering and kindness in a short interview. I would meet with some provoking strangeness, so that we may be guest and host and refresh one another. It is possible for a man wholly to disappear and be merged in his manners. The thousand and one gentlemen whom I meet, I meet despairingly, and but to part from them, for I am not cheered by the hope of any rudeness from them. A cross man, a coarse man, an eccentric man, a silent, a man who does not drill well,—of him there is some hope. Your gentlemen, they are all alike.

There is always a kind of fine æolian harp music to be heard in the air. I hear now, as it were, the mellow sound of distant horns in the hollow mansions of the upper air, a sound to make all men divinely insane that hear it, far away overhead, subsiding into my ear. To ears that are expanded what a harp this world is! The occupied ear thinks that beyond the cricket no sound can be heard, but there is an immortal melody that may be heard morning, noon, and night, by ears that can attend, and from time to time this man or that hears it, having ears that were made for music. To hear this the hardhack and the meadowsweet *aspire*. They are thus beautifully painted, because they are tinged in the lower stratum of that melody.

Aug. 22, 1851

It is the fault of some excellent writers —De Quincey's [1] first impressions on seeing London suggest it to me—that they express themselves with too great fullness and detail. They give the most faithful, natural, and lifelike account of their sensations, mental and physical, but they lack moderation and sententiousness. They do not affect us by an ineffectual earnestness and a reserve of meaning, like a stutterer; they say all they mean. Their sentences are not concentrated and nutty. Sentences which suggest far more than they say, which have an atmosphere about them, which do not merely report an old, but make a new, impression; sentences which suggest as many things and are as durable as a Roman aqueduct; to frame these, that is the *art* of writing. Sentences which are expensive, towards which so many volumes, so much life, went; which lie like boulders on the page, up and down or across; which contain the seed of other sentences, not mere repetition, but creation; which a man might sell his grounds and castles to build. If De Quincey had suggested each of his pages in a sentence and passed on,

it would have been far more excellent writing. His style is nowhere kinked and knotted up into something hard and significant, which you could swallow like a diamond, without digesting.

Dec. 28, 1852

It is worth the while to apply what wisdom one has to the conduct of his life, surely. I find myself oftenest wise in little things and foolish in great ones. That I may accomplish some particular petty affair well, I live my whole life coarsely. A broad margin of leisure is as beautiful in a man's life as in a book. Haste makes waste, no less in life than in housekeeping. Keep the time, observe the hours of the universe, not of the cars. What are threescore years and ten hurriedly and coarsely lived to moments of divine leisure in which your life is coincident with the life of the universe? We live too fast and coarsely, just as we eat too fast, and do not know the true savor of our food. We consult our will and understanding and the expectation of men, not our genius. I can impose upon myself tasks which will crush me for life and prevent all expansion, and this I am but too inclined to do.

One moment of life costs many hours, hours not of business but of preparation and invitation. Yet the man who does not betake himself at once and desperately to sawing is called a loafer, though he may be knocking at the doors of heaven all the while, which shall surely be opened to him. That aim in life is highest which requires the highest and finest discipline. How much, what infinite, leisure it requires, as of a lifetime, to appreciate a single phenomenon! You must camp down beside it as for life, having reached your land of promise, and give yourself wholly to it. It must stand for the whole world to you, symbolical of all things. The least partialness is your own defect of sight and cheapens the experience fatally. Unless the

---

[1] Thomas De Quincey (1785-1859), English author, best known for *Confessions of an English Opium-Eater* (1821).

humming of a gnat is as the music of the spheres, and the music of the spheres is as the humming of a gnat, they are naught to me. It is not communications to serve for a history,—which are sciences,—but the great story itself, that cheers and satisfies us.

May 6, 1854

There is no such thing as pure *objective* observation. Your observation, to be interesting, *i.e.* to be significant, must be *subjective*. The sum of what the writer of whatever class has to report is simply some human experience, whether he be poet or philosopher or man of science. The man of most science is the man most alive, whose life is the greatest event. Senses that take cognizance of outward things merely are of no avail. It matters not where or how far you travel,—the farther commonly the worse,—but how much alive you are. If it is possible to conceive of an event outside to humanity, it is not of the slightest significance, though it were the explosion of a planet. Every important worker will report what life there is in him. It makes no odds into what seeming deserts the poet is born. Though all his neighbors pronounce it a Sahara, it will be a paradise to him; for the desert which we see is the result of the barrenness of our experience. No mere willful activity whatever, whether in writing verses or collecting statistics, will produce true poetry or science. If you are really a sick man, it is indeed to be regretted, for you cannot accomplish so much as if you were well. All that a man has to say or do that can possibly concern mankind, is in some shape or other to tell the story of his love,—to sing, and, if he is fortunate and keeps alive, he will be forever in love. This alone is to be alive to the extremities. It is a pity that this divine creature should ever suffer from cold feet; a still greater pity that the coldness so often reaches to his heart. I look over the report of the doings of a scientific association and am surprised that there is so little life to be reported; I am put off

with a parcel of dry technical terms. Anything living is easily and naturally expressed in popular language. I cannot help suspecting that the life of these learned professors has been almost as inhuman and wooden as a rain-gauge or self-registering magnetic machine. They communicate no fact which rises to the temperature of blood-heat. It doesn't all amount to one rhyme.

Dec. 1, 1856

I see the old pale-faced farmer out again on his sled now for the five-thousandth time,—Cyrus Hubbard, a man of a certain New England probity and worth, immortal and natural, like a natural product, like the sweetness of a nut, like the toughness of hickory. He, too, is a redeemer for me. How superior actually to the faith he professes! He is not an office-seeker. What an institution, what a revelation is a man! We are wont foolishly to think that the creed which a man professes is more significant than the fact he is. It matters not how hard the conditions seemed, how mean the world, for a man is a prevalent force and a new law himself. He is a system whose law is to be observed. The old farmer condescends to countenance still this nature and order of things. It is a great encouragement that an honest man makes this world his abode. . . . Moderate, natural, true, as if he were made of earth, stone, wood, snow. I thus meet in this universe kindred of mine, composed of these elements. I see men like frogs; their peeping I partially understand.

The dear wholesome color of shrub oak leaves, so clean and firm, not decaying, but which have put on a kind of immortality, not wrinkled and thin like the white oak leaves, but full-veined and plump, as nearer earth. Well-tanned leather on the one side, sun-tanned, color of colors, color of the cow and the deer, silver-downy beneath, turned toward the late bleached and russet fields. What are acanthus leaves and the rest to this? Emblem of my winter condition. I love and could embrace the shrub oak with its scanty garment of leaves rising above the snow, lowly whispering to me, akin to winter thoughts, and sunsets, and to all virtue. Covert which the hare and the partridge seek, and I too seek. What cousin of mine is the shrub oak? How can any man suffer long? For a sense of want is a prayer, and all prayers are answered. Rigid as iron, clean as the atmosphere, hardy as virtue, innocent and sweet as a maiden is the shrub oak. In proportion

as I know and love it, I am natural and sound as a partridge. I felt a positive yearning toward one bush this afternoon. There was a match found for me at last. I fell in love with a shrub oak.

No, I am a stranger in your towns. I am not at home at French's, or Lovejoy's, or Savery's. I can winter more to my mind amid the shrub oaks. I have made arrangements to stay with them.

American Literature 1800-1860

V

HUMANISM AND BEYOND

1804 ∽ *Nathaniel Hawthorne* ∽ 1864

I

TWO periods in Hawthorne's early life enabled him to achieve the kind of perspective on human existence that is necessary for the writing of philosophical romance at its best.

The first period was one of virtual invalidism between the ages of nine and twelve. As the result of a foot-injury received while playing ball, he was kept all this time away from school and from close companionship with boys and girls of his own age. His mother and two sisters lived a strange, quiet life in their three-story house in Salem, Massachusetts. Their name was "Hathorne"; Nathaniel was to change it to "Hawthorne" later. His father, also Nathaniel, had been a sea-captain and had died in far-away Surinam of yellow fever in 1808. Young Nathaniel was then four years old, having been born at Salem, July 4, 1804. Ever since his father's death, his mother, Elizabeth Manning, and his sisters, Elizabeth and Louisa, had been in mourning. Their days were a ritual of isolation from almost everyone except their relatives, the Mannings and the Forresters. Mrs. Hathorne even had her meals regularly alone, and young Nathaniel and his sisters sometimes followed her example. With his bandaged foot, there was little for him to do but read and dream.

The second period was one of self-imposed retirement from the world after he was graduated from Bowdoin College at Brunswick, Maine, in 1825. This period lasted all during his twenties and into his early thirties. For more than a decade, in fact, he spent most of his time in the same old house in Salem, in the same atmosphere of strange, quiet family living, in a dismal chamber under the eaves on the third floor. Here he continued to dream and read, but also to write—the long story, *Fanshawe*, which was published anonymously in 1828, and the short stories and sketches which appeared anonymously or pseudonymously in gift-books and magazines, and were ultimately collected in the first edition of *Twice-Told Tales* in 1837.

These periods of living apart from normal existence in a world of dreams amid an atmosphere of forlorn devotion to the past helped make of Hawthorne a modest, reticent man, with an imagination prone, like an owl, to eerie flight, but they did not transform him into a freakish recluse, nor did they give him any real morbidity of outlook. They were so happily offset by healthy contacts with nature and with worldly-tempered friends and with humdrum, robust reality that the result was a mind and personality with a balance and sanity all their own, so to speak.

At Raymond, Maine, his uncles, Richard and Robert Manning, had built houses on opposite sides of Dingley Brook. Here, to Robert's house, Elizabeth Hathorne took her children as soon as Nathaniel had recovered from his foot-injury. Legg's Hill, Rattlesnake Mountain, Thomas Pond, Sebago Lake, the deep woods everywhere—these were Nathaniel's haunts all the year round. He lived like a noble little savage, hunting, fishing, skating, swimming, walking. Although he had such companions as Robinson Cook, Jacob Dingley, and the colored boy, William Symmes, it was here, rather than in Salem, that he first got, as he was to point out later, his "cursed habits of solitude." But it was a solitude which gave him, in Wordsworth's lines,

> . . . sensations sweet,
> Felt in the blood, and felt along the heart . . .

and perhaps also

> . . . a sense sublime
> Of something far more deeply interfused . . .

Back in Salem, he worked at the ledgers in the offices of his Uncle William Manning, who was in the stagecoach business. He also studied Latin and Greek in preparation for Bowdoin, where his Uncle Richard Manning proposed to finance him for four years. The winter before he entered Bowdoin, he wrote to his mother at Raymond a somewhat playful letter in which he expressed his disapproval of studying for the ministry or the law or medicine, lamented that he wasn't rich enough to live without a profession, asked her what she thought of his becoming an author, and then dismissed even this possibility with the remark, "But authors are always poor devils, and therefore may Satan take them."

At Bowdoin, which he entered in 1821, he was a fellow student of Henry Wadsworth Longfellow; his closest friends, however, were young men who were to distinguish themselves, not in literature, but in public affairs—Franklin Pierce, who was to become President of the United States; Jonathan Cilley, who was to enter Congress under the aegis of the Democratic Party; and Horatio Bridge, who was to be one of the leading industrialists of Augusta, Maine. With these typical go-getters of a frontier college, Hawthorne played cards for modest stakes, and was fined for the misdemeanor; drilled in the campus military company; and enjoyed convivial revelry at Ward's Tavern. The studies in which he excelled were English composition and Latin, but he disliked metaphysics, mathematics, and declamation. When a cousin who visited him in his senior year at Bowdoin took back to the family a glowing account of his prospects for the future, Hawthorne deprecated such optimism in a letter to his sister Louisa: "I have thought much upon the subject, and have finally come to the conclusion that I shall never make a distinguished figure in the world, and all I hope or wish is to plod along with the multitude."

Later, when his laborious solitude in the room under the eaves proved burdensome, he could always turn to this multitude for solace. Even if he did not mingle with it, he could enjoy observing it. To do so, he would climb up into the steeple of the South Church and drink in the sights of the town. Or he would sit on the bench before the toll-gatherer's house on Beverly Bridge and watch traffic all day long. Or he would stroll on the seashore and gaze at groups of girls on holiday or groups of fishermen at work. Even better, he would take longer excursions on his uncle's stagecoaches, going all over New England, and even into New York, to Buffalo and Niagara, as ubiquitous and as curious, although never so garrulous, as his pedlar, Dominicus Pike, in "Mr. Higginbotham's Catastrophe."

II

Hawthorne's early reading contributed much to the balance and sanity of his mind and personality. Through Spenser's *The Faerie Queene,* Milton's *Paradise Lost,* and Bunyan's *The Pilgrim's Progress* he acquired a taste for allegory and absorbed the Christian Humanism of the English Renaissance. Central to that Humanism was an ethical philosophy derived from Aristotle and from the best thought of the Middle Ages and the Reformation. It was an ethical philosophy somewhat different from that held by any school of theology—by the New England Puritans of an earlier day or by the Unitarians of Hawthorne's own time. And it was different, also, from that shortly to be professed by the New England Transcendentalists. Set against any of these creeds, it was less one-sided, less pretentious, more sweetly reasonable, more chastened by the knowledge, not merely of good and evil, but of good-and-evil, to borrow a subtle but valid distinction made by the modern English novelist, E. M. Forster, in his *The Longest Journey.*

The values that were most important to this Christian Humanism may be reduced to four—introspection, or knowing oneself in the Socratic sense; measure, or avoiding extremes in anything and following always the golden mean; humility, or remembering the limitations which Providence has imposed upon one as a mortal being; and charity, or treating others with scrupulous, constant respect for whatever goodness of heart they have, for whatever grace is in them. These values were re-inforced in Hawthorne's mind by wide reading in 18th Century English literature—Swift, Pope, Addison, Goldsmith, Johnson, Thompson, and Sterne.

Through his browsing in the writings of Jean-Jacques Rousseau, William

Godwin, and Sir Walter Scott, young Hawthorne was influenced by two tendencies of the many-sided European Romantic Movement—its reverence for "the still, sad music of humanity," and its interest in *regions* as storied theaters of the past wherein the strains of this music might still be heard echoing, or as picturesque alcoves of the present where this humanity could be studied microcosmically in all its lights and shadows.

Finally, young Hawthorne steeped himself in any reading that enabled him to relive in thought and feeling and sensation the life his ancestors had known. Salem, of course, was haunted with this life, for it was a town of old houses and old wharves. From an England where Christian Humanism was in temporary decline, William Hathorne, age twenty-two, had sailed for New England on the *Arbella* as one of John Winthrop's company of Puritan emigrants. Settling first in Dorchester, he moved in 1636 to Salem. As one of Governor Endicott's lieutenants, he was a stern persecutor of the early Quakers. He defied a command of King Charles II in 1666 that he come to England as an agent to answer charges against the Massachusetts Bay Colony. He was deputy, Speaker of the House, merchant, magistrate, and father of eight children. John Hathorne, the son of William, was among the judges who presided at the witchcraft trials, in the course of which the cases of some two hundred prisoners were reviewed, nineteen of them, including women, being hanged, and one, a man, being crushed to death in accordance with the sentence meted him. Joseph Hathorne, the son of John, may have been a sailor, but turned to farming to rebuild the shattered family fortunes. Daniel Hathorne, son of Joseph, went back to the sea, captained a privateer against the British in the Revolution, and entered his son Nathaniel—Hawthorne's father—in the mercantile service.

The panorama of this ancestral life, the ghosts of the old houses and old wharves, pulsed and breathed once more for the young Hawthorne as he pored over Mather's *Magnalia* or Felt's *Annals of Salem* or the *History of Haverhill*, or tomes of travel that included Hakluyt, Turnefort, Madden, Chrishull and the like. Such experience of his family's, his town's, his region's past gave his creative imagination roots as well as wings.

"Wakefield," a twice-told tale written and first published toward the end of his long retirement from the world, was in part a half-serious, half-humorous commentary on himself. Just as Wakefield, in order to escape becoming "the Outcast of the Universe," returned to the good Mrs. Wakefield, from whom he had perversely absconded long ago, so Hawthorne decided to put his relations with mundane reality on a completely active footing, to re-assume the kind of participation in the world's life that, in some degree at least, he had been capable of during his college days. Besides, he needed a more regular income than he had yet received for any of his numerous published tales.

III

His first experience in earning such an income, in re-entering the world, was short and disillusioning. His contributions to the gift-book, *The Token*, had won him the friendship of its editor, Samuel G. Goodrich, a member of the Bewick Company of Boston, printers and engravers. Through Goodrich's influence, this firm offered Hawthorne the editorship of *The American Magazine of Useful and Entertaining Knowledge* at a salary of $500 a year. To use his own phraseology, Hawthorne proceeded to "concoct—concoct—concoct" six issues, beginning with that of March, 1836. His sister Elizabeth, laboring in Salem, assisted him in his Boston hackwork. Failing to receive his salary on time, he wrote Louisa: "The world is as full of rogues as Beelzebub is of fleas," Beelzebub being the Hawthorne family cat. Little wonder that he was soon back home in his chamber under the eaves writing more twice-told tales and looking forward to the publication of the first series of them in book form. Since Horatio Bridge, Hawthorne's old college friend, stood guarantor for the book, Goodrich got the American Stationers' Company of Boston to publish it and thus redeemed himself somewhat in Hawthorne's eyes.

Keeping a notebook had become one of Hawthorne's habits. The early entries in the one he kept from July 5, 1837, to September 24, 1838, were made at Augusta, Maine, where he had gone for a several weeks' visit with Horatio Bridge. There is abundant evidence in these entries that his interest in mundane reality is keen. Bridge himself, and his guest, the merry Mr. Schaeffer, and the successful Jonathan Cilley, whom Hawthorne saw "for the first time since we graduated," and "the only petticoat that comes within our premises . . . Nancy, the pretty, dark-eyed maid-servant of the man who keeps in the other part of the house"—these and many others drew Hawthorne out of himself.

But, paradoxically enough, it was Elizabeth Peabody, of Salem and Boston, one of the literary ladies of the new otherworldly Transcendental movement, who was to have most to do with bringing him more definitely into the world's orbit. She called at the Hawthorne home in Salem to pay homage to the new local literary celebrity, whose *Twice-Told Tales* had received a favorable notice from Longfellow in the *North American Review*. She introduced Hawthorne to her sister Sophia, who had been for years an invalid confined to her room in the Peabody home in Salem. Soon Hawthorne was squiring Sophia to Transcendentalist meetings and became engaged to marry her. Sophia spoke of Ralph Waldo Emerson as "the greatest man that ever lived," "the Attic bird," "the Word again," "Pure Tone," and the like.

In order that Sophia and Nathaniel might have enough to marry on,

Elizabeth Peabody immediately mentioned Hawthorne to George Bancroft, collector of the Port of Boston. She got results. Hawthorne was appointed to a post as measurer in the Boston Custom House and went to work there early in 1839. It was the first of several political appointments which enabled him to earn an adequate living and yet to write, on the whole, what he wanted to write, and to take time out now and then to do it.

Whereas Hawthorne, in his reading, had immersed himself so deeply in tradition, he was now to have, in his actual living, an experience of utopia. Resigning his position at the Boston Custom House with capital saved up for his marriage, he had to wait until Sophia had fully recovered her health. In the interval he was persuaded by the Reverend George Ripley to become in 1841 a full-time helper at Brook Farm, the Transcendentalist co-operative experiment at West Roxbury, Massachusetts, intended "to establish a mode of life which shall combine the enchantments of poetry with the facts of daily experience," as Ripley put it.

Hawthorne had won Bancroft's praise for his energy and industry as a Custom House measurer. At Brook Farm he was to toil conscientiously at milking, planting potatoes and peas, feeding the pigs, cutting straw and hay for the cattle, and tending the farm's "gold-mine"—the dung-heap. His zeal was eminently practical; he hoped to make a home at Brook Farm for Sophia and himself; he even went so far as to invest some of his capital in the enterprise.

There is ample evidence that he enjoyed some phases of the experience. In May, for example, he wrote to Louisa: "This is one of the most beautiful places I ever saw in my life . . . such a delectable way of life has never been seen on earth since the days of the early Christians." Yet in the late autumn he was only too glad to leave this utopia and to abandon any notion of bringing Sophia there.

He had at least two good reasons, if not more, for rejecting it as a solution to the problem of living wisely. One was the work itself, which soon became sheer drudgery, particularly certain features of it. He was moved to write to Sophia: "It is my opinion, dearest, that a man's soul may be buried and perish under a dung-heap, or in a furrow of the field, just as well as under a pile of money . . . Even my Custom House experience was not such a thralldom and weariness; my mind and heart were freer. Oh, belovedest, labor is the curse of the world, and nobody can meddle with it without becoming proportionately brutified! Dost thou think it a praiseworthy matter that I have spent five golden months in providing food for cows and horses?"

Another reason was the buzzing confusion of too many people tipsy with new doctrine. He thus described to Sophia his state of mind: "It is true, nobody intrudes into my room; but still I cannot be quiet. Nothing here is settled; everything is but beginning to arrange itself, and though thy husband would seem to have little to do with aught beside his own thoughts, still he cannot but partake of the ferment around him."

The years from 1842 through 1852 were Hawthorne's most creative. This period was auspiciously inaugurated by three events—the publication of the second edition of his *Twice-Told Tales,* in two volumes; his marriage to Sophia, July 9, 1842; and their settling down at the "Old Manse," at Concord, Massachusetts, a house where the Emersons and the Ripleys had lived since before the Revolution.

As a Christian Humanist, Hawthorne had his share of sedate pessimism. "Happiness, in this world, if it comes at all, comes incidentally," he wrote in one of his notebooks. "Make it the object of pursuit, and it leads us a wild-goose chase and is never attained. Follow some other object, and very possibly we may find that we have caught happiness without dreaming of such luck, but likely enough, it is gone the moment we say to ourselves—'Here it is!'—like the chest of gold that treasure-seekers find."

Yet happiness was surely his at the "Old Manse." Of his first summer there, he remarked: "My life, at this time, is more like that of a boy externally, than it has been since I was really a boy. It is usually supposed that the cares of life come with matrimony; but I seem to have cast off all care, and live on with as much easy trust in Providence, as Adam could possibly have felt, before he had learned that there was a world beyond his Paradise. . . . The fight with the world—the struggle of a man among men—the agony of the universal effort to wrench the means of life from a host of greedy competitors—all this seems like a dream to me."

Of this paradisical sojourn, the main literary result was *Mosses from an Old Manse,* published in 1846. In that same year Hawthorne accepted another political appointment from the Democratic Party—this time as surveyor at the Salem Custom House, a post which he held until 1849. The year after going there, he began *The Scarlet Letter,* but did not finish and publish it until 1850. In a very short time it had won for him an international reputation.

From Salem, the Hawthornes moved to the "Red House" at Lenox, Massachusetts, in 1850, and from there to the Horace Mann house in West Newton, Massachusetts, in 1851. In 1851 appeared *The House of the Seven Gables;* in 1852, *The Snow Image and Other Twice-Told Tales* and *The Blithedale Romance.* It was also in 1852 that Hawthorne purchased his permanent American home, "The Wayside," at Concord. Shortly after moving there, he accepted and discharged the commission of writing a campaign biography for his old college friend, now candidate for the Presidency of the United States—the *Life of Franklin Pierce.*

As recompense for this political pot-boiler, President Pierce, who doubtless would have been elected if it had never been written and published, appointed Hawthorne Consul at Liverpool. In 1853, with the departure for England of

Hawthorne and his family—Sophia and their three children, Una, Julian, and Rose—his most creative period was at an end. Our greatest writer of regional fiction about universal themes was to gain experience that would enable him to experiment with what Henry James later called "the international theme."

IV

Putting America behind him for approximately the next seven years, Hawthorne could look back on associations with some of the leading figures of what has been called the "American Renaissance." Among others, he had known Emerson, Ellery Channing, Margaret Fuller, Thoreau, and Melville. Although he had some enjoyable moments with Emerson, he regarded him far more critically than did Sophia. Contrasting him with the Concord yeoman, Mr. Hosmer, he remarks in his notebook: "Mr. Emerson is a great searcher for facts; but they seem to melt away and become unsubstantial in his grasp."

Of Ellery Channing he says: "He is one of those queer and clever young men whom Mr. Emerson (that everlasting rejecter of all that is, and seeker for he knows not what) is continually picking up by way of a genius."

He seems to have shied away from Margaret Fuller from the very beginning. While measurer at the Boston Custom House, he wrote to Sophia: "I was invited to dine at Mr. Bancroft's yesterday with Miss Margaret Fuller, but Providence had given me some business to do, for which I was very thankful. When . . . Sophia Hawthorne can be with me, I shall not be afraid to accept invitations to meet literary lions and lionesses because then I shall put the abovesaid redoubtable little personage in the front of the battle."

Seeing a good deal of Margaret Fuller later on, Hawthorne treats her always with a touch of irony. She leaves a book behind her, and he has to walk over to Emerson's to return it. On the way home he finds her reclining in Sleepy Hollow. He sits down beside her and they talk ". . . about Autumn— and about the pleasures of getting lost in the woods—and about the crows, whose voices Margaret had heard—and about the experiences of early childhood, whose influence remains upon the character after the recollection of them has passed away—and about the sights of mountains from a distance, and the view from the summits—and about other matters of high and low philosophy." He seems glad to abandon her to one of her kind: "In the midst of our talk, we heard footsteps above us, on the high bank; and while the intruder was still hidden among the trees, he called to Margaret, of whom he had gotten a glimpse. Then he emerged from the green shade; and behold, it was Mr. Emerson, who, in spite of his clerical consecration, had found no better way of spending the Sabbath than to ramble among the woods. He appeared to have had a pleasant time; for he said that there were Muses in the woods to-day, and whispers to be heard in the breezes. It being now nearly six o'clock, we separated, Mr. Emerson and Margaret towards his home, and I towards mine, where my little wife was very busy getting tea." One should compare such impressions of Emerson and his disciples with those in Hawthorne's essay, "The Old Manse."

Hawthorne concludes a sketch of Thoreau with this admission of praise, which carefully avoids superlatives: "On the whole, I find him a healthy and wholesome man to know." Melville, whom he saw frequently at Lenox, struck him as something of a kindred spirit. He thus describes one of their evenings: ". . . Melville and I had a talk about time and eternity, things of this world and of the next, and books, and publishers, and all possible and impossible matters, that lasted pretty deep into the night. At last, he arose, and saddled his horse (whom he had put into the barn) and rode off for his own domicile; and I hastened to make the most of what little sleeping-time remained for me."

His respect for Poe is greatly in contrast with his strictures on many of the Transcendentalists. He thus wrote to Poe in 1846: "I presume the publishers will have sent you a copy of 'Mosses from an Old Manse'—the latest (and probably the last) collection of my tales and sketches. I have read your occasional notices of my productions with great interest—not so much because your judgment was, upon the whole, favorable, as because it seemed to be given in earnest. I care for nothing but the truth; and shall always more readily accept a harsh truth, in regard to my writings, than a sugared falsehood. I confess, however, that I admire you rather as a writer of tales than as a critic upon them. I might often—and often do—dissent from your opinions in the latter capacity, but could never fail to recognize your force and originality in the former." Perhaps Hawthorne had particularly in mind Poe's interpretation of "The Minister's Black Veil." Incidentally, Poe's review of *Mosses* in *Godey's Lady's Book* for November, 1847, was most ungenerous.

V

As Hawthorne sailed for England, he could look back, too, on a considerable achievement in the writing of fiction. From the outset, he had tried, in his tales and longer pieces, to solve a technical problem such as that which confronted Samuel Taylor Coleridge in his contributions to *Lyrical Ballads* in 1798.

Whereas Wordsworth, in his poems for that volume, had proposed "to give the charm of novelty to things of every day," Coleridge's endeavors, he tells us in the *Biographia Literaria,* had been "directed to persons and characters supernatural or at least romantic; so as to transfer from our inward nature a human interest and a semblance of truth sufficient to procure for these shadows of imagination that willing suspension of disbelief for the moment, which constitutes poetic faith."

To procure this "willing suspension of disbelief" for characters and incidents in a story, it is necessary to invest them with what may be called an illusion of reality. To conjure up such an illusion is most difficult when one's urge to create characters and incidents comes from reading, from an interest in allegory, from an imagination fostered in relative removal from the world. Of this difficulty Hawthorne was acutely conscious. Concerning the first edition of his *Twice-Told Tales,* he wrote thus to Longfellow in 1837: "I have . . . great difficulty in the lack of materials, for I have seen so little of the world that I have nothing but thin air to concoct my stories of, and it is not easy to give a life-like semblance to such shadowy stuff."

To improve illusion in his fiction, Hawthorne followed two main methods. The first was to keep his notebooks. Herein, from observation of daily life, of actual people, animals, things, incidents, he jotted down vivid details to be transferred to his stories in order that their ideological skeletons might have flesh and blood. The result was a growing "realism" in his work, a steady progress in "solidity of specification"—to use a suggestive phrase from Henry James' "The Art of Fiction."

The connection between the illusion of reality in Hawthorne's stories and his careful record of everyday observations may be clearly grasped by reading "Ethan Brand" and then turning to those passages from his *American Notebooks* wherein source materials for various features of this story unquestionably appear. Or one may go through these notebooks and then read his three great American romances. The Hawthornes' first child, Una, served as a model for Pearl in *The Scarlet Letter.* The setting of *The House of the Seven Gables* is a composite transcript from actuality. Above all, in *The Blithedale Romance,* Hawthorne made use of his experiences at Brook Farm, and, in the character of Coverdale, the narrator of the story, introduced a but slightly distorted projection of himself into the Dutch painting of that utopian community. Even the discovery of Zenobia's drowned body was based on his actual participation in dredging up from the Concord River the corpse of a Miss Hunt, who had committed suicide.

The second method which Hawthorne followed to improve the illusion of reality in his fiction was to perfect its form as well as its content or "stuff." He experimented carefully with the "focus of narration" or "the point of view," as may be seen, say, in "Mr. Higginbotham's Catastrophe," or "Rappaccini's Daughter," or *The Blithedale Romance.* In both his tales and his longer romances, he strove for structure nicely adapted to the theme at hand. The structure of "Rappaccini's Daughter," for example, is worth close analysis to demonstrate how effectively it conveys Hawthorne's Humanistic critique of the scientific intellect. Dramatic structure, with "scenes" that may be regarded as the beginning, middle, and end, the attack, crisis, and resolution, of conflict involving a few characters, distinguishes each of his three great American romances. The device of "foreshadowing" or "prospect," i.e., preparing the reader in advance for later events so as to make them more credible or to create suspense or to heighten unity in the whole narrative, is brilliantly exemplified in all his best work, and may be studied particularly in such stories as "The Minister's Black Veil" and "Ethan Brand." The use of contrast in description, in "scene," in characterization, in symbol is developed to a fine point. Such tales as "The Maypole of Merry Mount" and "Endicott and the Red Cross" are rich in various kinds of contrast, as are, of course, all the longer romances.

It is no accident that one of America's greatest masters of the art of fiction, Henry James, should have written a study of Hawthorne for the *English Men of Letters* series. Nor is it surprising that one of the ablest craftsmen among English novelists, Thomas Hardy, was to learn something of his craft from reading Hawthorne, as may be understood by comparing *The Return of the Native* and *The Blithedale Romance*. Finally, it must never be forgotten that Hawthorne's practice inspired Poe to formulate his epoch-making theory of the prose tale.

In its criticism of life, Hawthorne's fiction had probed deeply. In some of his tales, such as "The Maypole of Merry Mount" and "Endicott and the Red Cross," he used episodes in the history of New England for more than one purpose—to endow ethical issues with such reality that the reader might dwell long on them, and to assess the nature and continuing value of Puritanism as a cultural force. In other tales, such as "Wakefield," "Young Goodman Brown," and "The Minister's Black Veil," he analyzed the case histories of characters who, for different reasons, became solitaries. In "Ethan Brand" and "Rappaccini's Daughter" he dealt with two protagonists of inhuman intellect, likewise immolated in their solitude. In "The Celestial Railroad" he wrote his own kind of satirical burlesque, viewing the new doctrines of the day in terms of their implications for the Christian Humanism of John Bunyan. In "Mr. Higginbotham's Catastrophe" he experimented with a mystery rather than a detective story, and, by basing it on the concept of special Providence and enriching it with "local color," anticipated such modern deviations from the Poe formula as Melville Davidsson Post's *Uncle Abner* stories.

Some of these emphases were repeated, combined, developed, and modulated as Hawthorne moved from the tale to the longer romance. As the English romancer, J. H. Shorthouse, was to point out in the 1881 preface of his *John Inglesant,* Hawthorne carried his art "to such perfection that it is only with difficulty that we perceive how absolutely every character, nay, every word and line, is subordinated to the philosophical idea of the book. . . ."

The Scarlet Letter is unified by the idea that the full acceptance of responsibility for sin is better than denying or ignoring this responsibility altogether or accepting it but half-way. *The House of the Seven Gables* is held together by the idea that, instead of being dominated by a tradition, such as

Puritanism, for example, or rejecting this tradition completely, one should conserve whatever is good in it, and build on it, and leave behind whatever is evil. *The Blithedale Romance* ironically suggests that, even among utopians—with all their nobility, their fine hopes for the future of society, their admirable faith in human brotherhood—the egotism or possessiveness associated with the passions, and the evil consequences thereof, will stalk in, sometimes assuming the mask of philanthropy or altruism, and sometimes subtly undermining the most disinterested detachment.

More truly than most fiction produced by later schools of realism and naturalism, on the one hand, or of fantasy, on the other, these three romances fulfill "the high ambition and privilege of art not to reproduce reality but without conspicuously offending against it to enlarge its confines," to quote one of the dicta of the Shakespearean critic, E. E. Stoll. In the whole range of American literature it would be difficult to find three major works of fiction by one author that are so original in conception and execution, so various in theme, felicitous in prose style, and remarkable for other technical achievements, and so rewarding in their consistent presentation of the values of a Christian Humanism through subtle contrasts of memorable characters.

VI

While Consul at Liverpool from 1853 to 1857, Hawthorne was a busy man. In his bulky *English Notebooks* he records in detail his multifarious activities— how he rambled through slum and countryside; how he visited almshouses and literary shrines—Stratford, Lichfield, Grasmere, Newstead Abbey, Dumfries; how he investigated the cases of sailors maltreated in the American merchant marine; how he attended civic banquets and literary gatherings; how he talked with James Buchanan, then American Minister and soon to be President, about politics back home; how he watched the growth of his children and worried about Sophia, who for a while had to go to Portugal for her health, taking Una and Rose along, and leaving Julian with him; and how he kept in touch with American literati abroad, such as Melville, to whom he played host, or Delia Bacon, whom he sought out and interviewed concerning her theory that Lord Bacon wrote Shakespeare's plays.

Henry Arthur Bright, whom he had first met at Concord, was one of his closest English friends; he knew Monckton Milnes well; he met such celebrities as the Brownings, Charles Reade, and Lord Macaulay; he took part in a number of conversations about Thackeray, then at the height of his popularity.

Of Browning he remarks: ". . . a younger man than I expected to see, handsome, with dark hair, a very little frosted. He is very simple and agreeable in manner, gently impulsive, talking as if his heart were uppermost. He spoke of his pleasure in meeting me, and his appreciation of my books; and (which has not often happened to me) mentioned that the Blithedale Romance was the one he admired most. I wonder why."

After praising the fine dinner he and Una and Sophia were given by Russell Sturgis, he comments: "Mr. Sturgis is a friend of Thackeray, and, speaking of the last number of the Newcomes—so touching that nobody can read it aloud without breaking down—he mentioned that Thackeray himself had read it to James Russell Lowell and William Story, in a cider cellar!" This anecdote led Hawthorne to reflect as follows: "Speaking of Thackeray, I cannot but wonder at his coolness in respect to his own pathos, and compare it with my emotions when I read the last scene of the Scarlet Letter to my wife, just after writing it—tried to read it, rather, for my voice swelled and heaved, as if I were tossed up and down on an ocean, as it subsided after a storm. But I was in a very nervous state, then, having gone through a great diversity and severity of emotion, for many months past. I think I have never overcome my own adamant in any other instance."

He has this to say of Mrs. S. C. Hall: ". . . a genuine and good woman, unspoilt by a literary career, and retaining more sentiment (for I will not call it sentimentalism) than most girls keep beyond seventeen. She told me that it had been the dream of her life to see Longfellow and myself! Good Heavens! What an object to live for!"

Resigning his consulship in 1857, Hawthorne took his family to Italy by way of Paris. At Rome, they visited the New England sculptor and writer, William Wetmore Story, whom Henry James was to regard later as the prototype of the American cosmopolitan émigré. In Florence, they saw a good deal of the Brownings and settled at the Villa Montuato on the Bellosguardo Hill. At Siena, they again called on the Storys. When they went to Rome, Una fell ill of fever, and her life hovered in the balance for months. Such distinguished Americans as ex-President Pierce, the historian John Lothrop Motley, and Charles Sumner kept the Hawthornes company.

In 1859, with Una entirely out of danger, the family left for England. In his baggage, Hawthorne carried the first draft of his romance, *The Marble Faun*. They lived at Whitby, Redcar, Leamington, Bath, and London. *The Marble Faun* was published in 1860 both in England and the United States, but the English publisher insisted on giving it the title *Transformation*, which was not by any means to its author's liking.

When the Hawthornes returned to America in 1860, to resume their life at "The Wayside," where Sophia's brother had stayed in their absence, they found that the Transcendentalist fever had developed into the Abolitionist delirium and that many of their old friends were passionate defenders of John Brown. The intimate associate of such conservative and cordially hated Democrats as Franklin Pierce and James Buchanan looked askance on such radicalism, even though he was no believer in slavery. He had written in one of his *English*

Notebooks in 1854: "If mankind were all intellect, they would be continually changing, so that one age would be entirely unlike another. The great conservative is the heart, which remains the same in all ages; so that common-places of a thousand years' standing are as effective as ever."

During the Civil War Hawthorne maintained much of his balance. While a member of the Saturday Club that dined at Parker's Hotel in Boston and included Emerson, Longfellow, Holmes, Lowell, Motley, Whittier, and Sumner among others, he reproved his friend Bright back in England for lack of sympathy with the Northern cause. Instead of deploring the War, he even looked on it somewhat optimistically: "I never imagined what a happy state of mind a civil war produces, and how it invigorates every man's whole being," he wrote to Bright. "You will live to see the Americans another people than they have hitherto been; and I truly regret that my youth was not cast in these days, instead of in a quiet time."

Because of the war, and because, too, he was getting old, Hawthorne found it difficult to do creative writing. His book on England, *Our Old Home,* was published in 1863, but he could not complete another great romance. Instead he left four torsos—*The Ancestral Footstep,* running to some 28,000 words; *Dr. Grimshawe's Secret,* running to some 85,000; *Septimus Felton,* amounting to about 60,000; and *The Dolliver Romance,* stopping at 16,000. His health began to fail fast, from some disease that seemed, in the words of Franklin Pierce, to be "in the brain or spine or both." On a trip with Pierce, Hawthorne died at Plymouth, New Hampshire, May 19, 1864.

VII

One characteristic of those men of letters who have best represented our cosmopolitan or international tradition is that in their personalities and their work two worlds have been in conflict. It has been impossible for them to abandon their Americanism and their attachment to America and in consequence there has been much in Europe which they have been unable to accept. Yet Europe has had for them an enchantment they have been powerless to shake off entirely. It has symbolized for them tradition or culture or leisure or experience or grace, and these values or essences or sheer illusions have put them out of sorts with workaday America.

There is abundant evidence of such a conflict in Hawthorne in his last years. He is distinctly critical of England's aristocratic system. In *Our Old Home* he makes the point that "there was continually a dull sound in my ears as if the old foundations of things were crumbling away. Sometime or other,— by no irreverent effort of violence, but, rather, in spite of all pious efforts to uphold a heterogeneous pile of institutions that will have outlasted their vitality, —at some unexpected moment, there must come a terrible crash." And in one of his *English Notebooks* he observes: "The public life of America is lived through the mind and heart of every man in it; here, the people feel that they have nothing to do with what is going forward, and, I suspect, care little or nothing about it. Such things they permit to be the exclusive affair of the higher classes."

Yet he writes Horatio Bridge as follows in 1854: "It sickens me to look back to America. I am sick to death of the continual fuss and tumult and excitement and bad blood we keep up about political topics." And he made these confessions to W. D. Ticknor, the first in a letter from England, the second in a letter from Rome: "To say the truth, the longer I stay away, the less I feel inclined to come back. . . . Not but what I love my country; but I can live more to my individual satisfaction elsewhere." "I wish I were a little more patriotic; but to confess the truth I had rather be a sojourner in any other country than return to my own. The United States are fit for many excellent purposes, but they are certainly not fit to live in."

As for the American literary scene, Hawthorne wrote disgustedly to Ticknor in January, 1855: "America is now wholly given over to a d——d mob of scribbling women, and I should have no chance of success while the public taste is occupied with their trash—and should be ashamed of myself if I did succeed." Yet in February he is praising one of these same "scribbling women," Sara Payson Willis, who wrote the novel, *Ruth Hall,* under her pseudonym of Fanny Fern: "In my last, I recollect, I bestowed some vituperation on female authors. I have since been reading *Ruth Hall;* and I must say I enjoyed it a good deal. The woman writes as if the Devil was in her; and that is the only condition under which a woman ever writes anything worth reading."

Hawthorne's last great romance, *The Marble Faun,* should be approached as a revelation of this conflict between America and Europe in his mind and heart. It contrasts European personality with American personality, European ethics with American ethics, in terms of their coping with the problem of evil. Although, in the end, Hawthorne seems to be telling us that the New England way of Kenyon and Hilda is superior to the way of Miriam and Donatello, the work has an ultimate ambiguity more tantalizing than the mystery of Donatello's ears. It should continue to interest readers of the 20th Century's second post-war period, when "the international theme" has come into its own as never before, not only in fiction, but in all aspects of life, and promises to develop manifold ambiguities as a challenge to our best intelligence.

[The best "modern" biographies are Newton Arvin's *Hawthorne* (Boston, 1929) and Edward Mather's *Nathaniel Hawthorne: A Modest Man* (New York, 1940). The main source-book for Hawthorne's biography is Julian Hawthorne's authorized *Nathaniel Hawthorne and His Wife* in two volumes (Boston, 1884). Other older biographical and critical studies of interest are George P. Lathrop's *A Study of Hawthorne* (Boston, 1876), Henry James' *Hawthorne* (New York,

1879) in the English Men of Letters series, and George E. Woodberry's *Nathaniel Hawthorne* (Boston, 1902) in the American Men of Letters series. Randall Stewart's editions of Hawthorne's *American Notebooks* (New Haven, 1932) and *English Notebooks* (New York, 1941) are indispensable. Stimulating critical essays on Hawthorne are to be found in Paul Elmer More's *Shelburne Essays; First Series* (Boston, 1904) and *Second Series* (Boston, 1905); Austin Warren's *Hawthorne* (New York, 1934) in American Writers Series; Yvor Winters' *Maule's Curse* (Norfolk, Conn., 1938); F. O. Matthiessen's *American Renaissance* (New York, 1941); and Newton Arvin's edition of *Hawthorne's Short Stories* (New York, 1946).]

SIGHTS FROM A STEEPLE
[1837 (1830)]

SO! I have climbed high, and my reward is small. Here I stand, with wearied knees, earth, indeed, at a dizzy depth below, but heaven far, far beyond me still. Oh that I could soar up into the very zenith, where man never breathed, nor eagle ever flew, and where the ethereal azure melts away from the eye, and appears only a deepened shade of nothingness! And yet I shiver at that cold and solitary thought. What clouds are gathering in the golden west, with direful intent against the brightness and the warmth of this summer afternoon! They are ponderous air ships, black as death, and freighted with the tempest; and at intervals their thunder, the signal guns of that unearthly squadron, rolls distant along the deep of heaven. These nearer heaps of fleecy vapor—methinks I could roll and toss upon them the whole day long!—seem scattered here and there for the repose of tired pilgrims through the sky. Perhaps—for who can tell?—beautiful spirits are disporting themselves there, and will bless my mortal eye with the brief appearance of their curly locks of golden light and laughing faces, fair and faint as the people of a rosy dream. Or, where the floating mass so imperfectly obstructs the color of the firmament, a slender foot and fairy limb, resting too heavily upon the frail support, may be thrust through, and suddenly withdrawn, while longing fancy follows them in vain. Yonder again is an airy archipelago, where the sunbeams love to linger in their journeyings through space. Every one of those little clouds has been dipped and steeped in radiance, which the slightest pressure might disengage in silvery profusion, like water wrung from a sea-maid's hair. Bright they are as a young man's visions, and, like them, would be realized in chillness, obscurity, and tears. I will look on them no more.

In three parts of the visible circle, whose centre is this spire, I discern cultivated fields, villages, white country seats, the waving lines of rivulets, little placid lakes, and here and there a rising ground, that would fain be termed a hill. On the fourth side is the sea, stretching away towards a viewless boundary, blue and calm, except where the passing anger of a shadow flits across its surface, and is gone. Hitherward, a broad inlet penetrates far into the land; on the verge of the harbor, formed by its extremity, is a town; and over it am I, a watchman, all-heeding and unheeded. Oh that the multitude of chimneys could speak, like those of Madrid, and betray, in smoky whispers, the secrets of all who, since their first foundation, have assembled at the hearths within! Oh that the Limping Devil of Le Sage would perch beside me here, extend his wand over this contiguity of roofs, uncover every chamber, and make me familiar with their inhabitants![1] The most

---

[1] Alain René Le Sage (1688-1747) wrote *Le Diable Boiteux* (1707), translated as *Asmodeus* or *The Devil on Two Sticks*, a satiric novel in which a limping devil pries into the residences of Madrid.

desirable mode of existence might be that of a spiritualized Paul Pry, hovering invisible round man and woman, witnessing their deeds, searching into their hearts, borrowing brightness from their felicity and shade from their sorrow, and retaining no emotion peculiar to himself. But none of these things are possible; and if I would know the interior of brick walls, or the mystery of human bosoms, I can but guess.

Yonder is a fair street, extending north and south. The stately mansions are placed each on its carpet of verdant grass, and a long flight of steps descends from every door to the pavement. Ornamental trees— the broad-leafed horse-chestnut, the elm so lofty and bending, the graceful but infrequent willow, and others whereof I know not the names—grow thrivingly among brick and stone. The oblique rays of the sun are intercepted by these green citizens, and by the houses, so that one side of the street is a shaded and pleasant walk. On its whole extent there is now but a single passenger, advancing from the upper end; and he, unless distance and the medium of a pocket spyglass do him more than justice, is a fine young man of twenty. He saunters slowly forward, slapping his left hand with his folded gloves, bending his eyes upon the pavement, and sometimes raising them to throw a glance before him. Certainly, he has a pensive air. Is he in doubt, or in debt? Is he, if the question be allowable, in love? Does he strive to be melancholy and gentleman-like? Or, is he merely overcome by the heat? But I bid him farewell for the present. The door of one of the houses—an aristocratic edifice, with curtains of purple and gold waving from the windows, is now opened, and down the steps come two ladies, swinging their parasols, and lightly arrayed for a summer ramble. Both are young, both are pretty, but methinks the left-hand lass is the fairer of the twain; and, though she be so serious at this moment, I could swear that there is a treasure of gentle fun within her. They stand talking a little while upon the steps, and finally proceed up the street. Mean-

time, as their faces are now turned from me, I may look elsewhere.

Upon that wharf, and down the corresponding street, is a busy contrast to the quiet scene which I have just noticed. Business evidently has its centre there, and many a man is wasting the summer afternoon in labor and anxiety, in losing riches or in gaining them, when he would be wiser to flee away to some pleasant country village, or shaded lake in the forest, or wild and cool sea-beach. I see vessels unlading at the wharf, and precious merchandise strewn upon the ground, abundantly as at the bottom of the sea, that market whence no goods return, and where there is no captain nor supercargo to render an account of sales. Here, the clerks are diligent with their paper and pencils, and sailors ply the block and tackle that hang over the hold, accompany-- ing their toil with cries, long drawn and roughly melodious, till the bales and puncheons ascend to upper air. At a little dis- tance a group of gentlemen are assembled round the door of a warehouse. Grave seniors be they, and I would wager—if it were safe in these times to be responsible for any one—that the least eminent among them might vie with old Vicentio, that incomparable trafficker of Pisa.[2] I can even select the wealthiest of the company. It is the elderly personage, in somewhat rusty black, with powdered hair, the superfluous whiteness of which is visible upon the cape of his coat. His twenty ships are wafted on some of their many courses by every breeze that blows, and his name—I will venture to say, though I know it not—is a familiar sound among the far separated merchants of Europe and the Indies.

But I bestow too much of my attention in this quarter. On looking again to the long and shady walk, I perceive that the two fair girls have encountered the young man. After a sort of shyness in the recognition, he turns back with them. Moreover,

---

[2] An allusion to a character in Shakespeare's *The Taming of the Shrew*.

he has sanctioned my taste in regard to his companions by placing himself on the inner side of the pavement, nearest the Venus to whom I—enacting, on a steeple top, the part of Paris on the top of Ida— adjudged the golden apple.

In two streets, converging at right angles towards my watchtower, I distinguish three different processions. One is a proud array of voluntary soldiers, in bright uniform, resembling, from the height whence I look down, the painted veterans that garrison the windows of a toyshop. And yet, it stirs my heart; their regular advance, their nodding plumes, the sunflash on their bayonets and musket barrels, the roll of their drums ascending past me, and the fife ever and anon piercing through— these things have wakened a warlike fire, peaceful though I be. Close to their rear marches a battalion of school-boys, ranged in crooked and irregular platoons, shouldering sticks, thumping a harsh and unripe clatter from an instrument of tin, and ridiculously aping the intricate manœuvres of the foremost band. Nevertheless, as slight differences are scarcely perceptible from a church spire, one might be tempted to ask, "Which are the boys?"—or rather, "Which the men?" But, leaving these, let us turn to the third procession, which, though sadder in outward show, may excite identical reflections in the thoughtful mind. It is a funeral. A hearse, drawn by a black and bony steed, and covered by a dusty pall; two or three coaches rumbling over the stones, their drivers half asleep; a dozen couple of careless mourners in their every-day attire; such was not the fashion of our fathers, when they carried a friend to his grave. There is now no doleful clang of the bell to proclaim sorrow to the town. Was the King of Terrors more awful in those days than in our own, that wisdom and philosophy have been able to produce this change? Not so. Here is a proof that he retains his proper majesty. The military men and the military boys are wheeling round the corner, and meet the funeral full in the face. Immediately the drum is

silent, all but the tap that regulates each simultaneous footfall. The soldiers yield the path to the dusty hearse and unpretending train, and the children quit their ranks, and cluster on the sidewalks, with timorous and instinctive curiosity. The mourners enter the churchyard at the base of the steeple, and pause by an open grave among the burial stones; the lightning glimmers on them as they lower down the coffin, and the thunder rattles heavily while they throw the earth upon its lid. Verily, the shower is near, and I tremble for the young man and the girls, who have now disappeared from the long and shady street.

How various are the situations of the people covered by the roofs beneath me, and how diversified are the events at this moment befalling them! The new born, the aged, the dying, the strong in life, and the recent dead, are in the chambers of these many mansions. The full of hope, the happy, the miserable, and the desperate, dwell together within the circle of my glance. In some of the houses over which my eyes roam so coldly, guilt is entering into hearts that are still tenanted by a debased and trodden virtue,—guilt is on the very edge of commission, and the impending deed might be averted; guilt is done, and the criminal wonders if it be irrevocable. There are broad thoughts struggling in my mind, and, were I able to give them distinctness, they would make their way in eloquence. Lo! the raindrops are descending.

The clouds, within a little time, have gathered over all the sky, hanging heavily, as if about to drop in one unbroken mass upon the earth. At intervals, the lightning flashes from their brooding hearts, quivers, disappears, and then comes the thunder, travelling slowly after its twin-born flame. A strong wind has sprung up, howls through the darkened streets, and raises the dust in dense bodies, to rebel against the approaching storm. The disbanded soldiers fly, the funeral has already vanished like its dead, and all people hurry homeward—all that have a home; while a few lounge by the corners, or trudge on desperately, at their leisure. In a narrow lane, which comunicates with the shady street, I discern the rich old merchant, putting himself to the top of his speed, lest the rain should convert his hair powder to a paste. Unhappy gentleman! By the slow vehemence and painful moderation wherewith he journeys, it is but too evident that Podagra [3] has left its thrilling tenderness in his great toe. But yonder, at a far more rapid pace, come three other of my acquaintance, the two pretty girls and the young man, unseasonably interrupted in their walk. Their footsteps are supported by the risen dust,—the wind lends them its velocity,—they fly like three sea-birds driven landward by the tempestuous breeze. The ladies would not thus rival Atalanta if they but knew that any one were at leisure to observe them. Ah! as they hasten onward, laughing in the angry face of nature, a sudden catastrophe has chanced. At the corner where the narrow lane enters into the street, they come plump against the old merchant, whose tortoise motion has just brought him to that point. He likes not the sweet encounter; the darkness of the whole air gathers speedily upon his visage, and there is a pause on both sides. Finally, he thrusts aside the youth with little courtesy, seizes an arm of each of the two girls, and plods onward, like a magician with a prize of captive fairies. All this is easy to be understood. How disconsolate the poor lover stands! regardless of the rain that threatens an exceeding damage to his well-fashioned habiliments, till he catches a backward glance of mirth from a bright eye, and turns away with whatever comfort it conveys.

The old man and his daughters are safely housed, and now the storm lets loose its fury. In every dwelling I perceive the faces of the chambermaids as they shut down the windows, excluding the impetuous shower, and shrinking away from the quick fiery glare. The large drops descend with force upon the slated roofs, and rise again in smoke. There is a rush and roar, as of a river through the air, and muddy streams bubble majestically along the pavement, whirl their dusky foam into the kennel, and disappear beneath iron grates. Thus did Arethusa sink.[4] I love not my station here aloft, in the midst of the tumult which I am powerless to direct or quell, with the blue lightning wrinkling on my brow, and the thunder muttering its first awful syllables in my ear. I will descend. Yet let me give another glance to the sea, where the foam breaks out in long white lines upon a broad expanse of blackness, or boils up in far distant points, like snowy mountain tops in the eddies of a flood; and let me look once more at the green plain, and little hills of the country, over which the giant of the storm is striding in robes of mist, and at the town, whose obscured and desolate streets might beseem a city of the dead; and turning a single moment to the sky, now gloomy as an author's prospects, I prepare to resume my station on lower earth. But stay! A little speck of azure has widened in the western heavens; the sunbeams find a passage, and go rejoicing through the tempest; and on yonder darkest cloud, born, like hallowed hopes, of the glory of another world and the trouble and tears of this, brightens forth the Rainbow!

MR. HIGGINBOTHAM'S CATASTROPHE
[1837 (1834)]

A YOUNG fellow, a tobacco pedlar by trade, was on his way from Morristown, where he had dealt largely with the Deacon of the Shaker settlement, to the village of Parker's Falls, on Salmon River. He had a neat little cart, painted green, with a box of cigars depicted on each side panel, and an Indian chief, holding a pipe and

---

[3] The gout.

[4] A wood nymph who, to escape her pursuer, the river god Alpheus, was changed to a stream running under the sea.

a golden tobacco stalk, on the rear. The pedlar drove a smart little mare, and was a young man of excellent character, keen at a bargain, but none the worse liked by the Yankees; who, as I have heard them say, would rather be shaved with a sharp razor than a dull one. Especially was he beloved by the pretty girls along the Connecticut, whose favor he used to court by presents of the best smoking tobacco in his stock; knowing well that the country lasses of New England are generally great performers on pipes. Moreover, as will be seen in the course of my story, the pedlar was inquisitive, and something of a tattler, always itching to hear the news and anxious to tell it again.

After an early breakfast at Morristown, the tobacco pedlar, whose name was Dominicus Pike, had travelled seven miles through a solitary piece of woods, without speaking a word to anybody but himself and his little gray mare. It being nearly seven o'clock, he was as eager to hold a morning gossip as a city shop-keeper to read the morning paper. An opportunity seemed at hand when, after lighting a cigar with a sun-glass, he looked up, and perceived a man coming over the brow of the hill, at the foot of which the pedlar had stopped his green cart. Dominicus watched him as he descended, and noticed that he carried a bundle over his shoulder on the end of a stick, and travelled with a weary, yet determined pace. He did not look as if he had started in the freshness of the morning, but had footed it all night, and meant to do the same all day.

"Good morning, mister," said Dominicus, when within speaking distance. "You go a pretty good jog. What's the latest news at Parker's Falls?"

The man pulled the broad brim of a gray hat over his eyes, and answered, rather suddenly, that he did not come from Parker's Falls, which, as being the limit of his own day's journey, the pedlar had naturally mentioned in his inquiry.

"Well then," rejoined Dominicus Pike,

"let's have the latest news where you did come from. I'm not particular about Parker's Falls. Any place will answer."

Being thus importuned, the traveller—who was as ill looking a fellow as one would desire to meet in a solitary piece of woods—appeared to hesitate a little, as if he was either searching his memory for news, or weighing the expediency of telling it. At last, mounting on the step of the cart, he whispered in the ear of Dominicus, though he might have shouted aloud and no other mortal would have heard him.

"I do remember one little trifle of news," said he. "Old Mr. Higginbotham, of Kimballton, was murdered in his orchard, at eight o'clock last night, by an Irishman and a nigger. They strung him up to the branch of a St. Michael's pear-tree, where nobody would find him till the morning."

As soon as this horrible intelligence was communicated, the stranger betook himself to his journey again, with more speed than ever, not even turning his head when Dominicus invited him to smoke a Spanish cigar and relate all the particulars. The pedlar whistled to his mare and went up the hill, pondering on the doleful fate of Mr. Higginbotham, whom he had known in the way of trade, having sold him many a bunch of long nines, and a great deal of pigtail, lady's twist, and fig tobacco. He was rather astonished at the rapidity with which the news had spread. Kimballton was nearly sixty miles distant in a straight line; the murder had been perpetrated only at eight o'clock the preceding night; yet Dominicus had heard of it at seven in the morning, when, in all probability, poor Mr. Higginbotham's own family had but just discovered his corpse, hanging on the St. Michael's pear-tree. The stranger on foot must have worn seven-league boots to travel at such a rate.

"Ill news flies fast, they say," thought Dominicus Pike; "but this beats railroads. The fellow ought to be hired to go express with the President's Message."

The difficulty was solved by supposing

that the narrator had made a mistake of one day in the date of the occurrence; so that our friend did not hesitate to introduce the story at every tavern and country store along the road, expending a whole bunch of Spanish wrappers among at least twenty horrified audiences. He found himself invariably the first bearer of the intelligence, and was so pestered with questions that he could not avoid filling up the outline, till it became quite a respectable narrative. He met with one piece of corroborative evidence. Mr. Higginbotham was a trader; and a former clerk of his, to whom Dominicus related the facts, testified that the old gentleman was accustomed to return home through the orchard about nightfall, with the money and valuable papers of the store in his pocket. The clerk manifested but little grief at Mr. Higginbotham's catastrophe, hinting, what the pedlar had discovered in his own dealings with him, that he was a crusty old fellow, as close as a vice. His property would descend to a pretty niece who was now keeping school in Kimballton.

What with telling the news for the public good, and driving bargains for his own, Dominicus was so much delayed on the road that he chose to put up at a tavern, about five miles short of Parker's Falls. After supper, lighting one of his prime cigars, he seated himself in the bar-room, and went through the story of the murder, which had grown so fast that it took him half an hour to tell. There were as many as twenty people in the room, nineteen of whom received it all for gospel. But the twentieth was an elderly farmer, who had arrived on horseback a short time before, and was now seated in a corner smoking his pipe. When the story was concluded, he rose up very deliberately, brought his chair right in front of Dominicus, and stared him full in the face, puffing out the vilest tobacco smoke the pedlar had ever smelt.

"Will you make affidavit," demanded he, in the tone of a country justice taking an examination, "that old Squire Higgin-

botham of Kimballton was murdered in his orchard the night before last, and found hanging on his great pear-tree yesterday morning?"

"I tell the story as I heard it, mister," answered Dominicus, dropping his half-burnt cigar; "I don't say that I saw the thing done. So I can't take my oath that he was murdered exactly in that way."

"But I can take mine," said the farmer, "that if Squire Higginbotham was murdered night before last, I drank a glass of bitters with his ghost this morning. Being a neighbor of mine, he called me into his store, as I was riding by, and treated me, and then asked me to do a little business for him on the road. He didn't seem to know any more about his own murder than I did."

"Why, then, it can't be a fact!" exclaimed Dominicus Pike.

"I guess he'd have mentioned, if it was," said the old farmer; and he removed his chair back to the corner, leaving Dominicus quite down in the mouth.

Here was a sad resurrection of old Mr. Higginbotham! The pedlar had no heart to mingle in the conversation any more, but comforted himself with a glass of gin and water, and went to bed where, all night long, he dreamed of hanging on the St. Michael's pear-tree. To avoid the old farmer (whom he so detested that his suspension would have pleased him better than Mr. Higginbotham's), Dominicus rose in the gray of the morning, put the little mare into the green cart, and trotted swiftly away towards Parker's Falls. The fresh breeze, the dewy road, and the pleasant summer dawn, revived his spirits, and might have encouraged him to repeat the old story had there been anybody awake to hear it. But he met neither ox team, light wagon chaise, horseman, nor foot traveller, till, just as he crossed Salmon River, a man came trudging down to the bridge with a bundle over his shoulder, on the end of a stick.

"Good morning, mister," said the pedlar,

reining in his mare. "If you come from Kimballton or that neighborhood, may be you can tell me the real fact about this affair of old Mr. Higginbotham. Was the old fellow actually murdered two or three nights ago, by an Irishman and a nigger?"

Dominicus had spoken in too great a hurry to observe, at first, that the stranger himself had a deep tinge of negro blood. On hearing this sudden question, the Ethiopian appeared to change his skin, its yellow hue becoming a ghastly white, while, shaking and stammering, he thus replied:—

"No! no! There was no colored man! It was an Irishman that hanged him last night, at eight o'clock. I came away at seven! His folks can't have looked for him in the orchard yet."

Scarcely had the yellow man spoken, when he interrupted himself, and though he seemed weary enough before, continued his journey at a pace which would have kept the pedlar's mare on a smart trot. Dominicus stared after him in great perplexity. If the murder had not been committed till Tuesday night, who was the prophet that had foretold it, in all its circumstances, on Tuesday morning? If Mr. Higginbotham's corpse were not yet discovered by his own family, how came the mulatto, at above thirty miles' distance, to know that he was hanging in the orchard, especially as he had left Kimballton before the unfortunate man was hanged at all? These ambiguous circumstances, with the stranger's surprise and terror, made Dominicus think of raising a hue and cry after him, as an accomplice in the murder; since a murder, it seemed, had really been perpetrated.

"But let the poor devil go," thought the pedlar. "I don't want his black blood on my head; and hanging the nigger wouldn't unhang Mr. Higginbotham. Unhang the old gentleman! It's a sin, I know; but I should hate to have him come to life a second time, and give me the lie!"

With these meditations, Dominicus Pike drove into the street of Parker's Falls, which, as everybody knows, is as thriving a village as three cotton factories and a slitting mill can make it. The machinery was not in motion, and but a few of the shop doors unbarred, when he alighted in the stable yard of the tavern, and made it his first business to order the mare four quarts of oats. His second duty, of course, was to impart Mr. Higginbotham's catastrophe to the hostler. He deemed it advisable, however, not to be too positive as to the date of the direful fact, and also to be uncertain whether it were perpetrated by an Irishman and a mulatto, or by the son of Erin alone. Neither did he profess to relate it on his own authority, or that of any one person; but mentioned it as a report generally diffused.

The story ran through the town like fire among girdled trees, and became so much the universal talk that nobody could tell whence it had originated. Mr. Higginbotham was as well known at Parker's Falls as any citizen of the place, being part owner of the slitting mill, and a considerable stockholder in the cotton factories. The inhabitants felt their own prosperity interested in his fate. Such was the excitement, that the Parker's Falls Gazette anticipated its regular day of publication, and came out with half a form of blank paper and a column of double pica emphasized with capitals, and headed HORRID MURDER OF MR. HIGGINBOTHAM! Among other dreadful details, the printed account described the mark of the cord round the dead man's neck, and stated the number of thousand dollars of which he had been robbed; there was much pathos also about the affliction of his niece, who had gone from one fainting fit to another, ever since her uncle was found hanging on the St. Michael's pear-tree with his pockets inside out. The village poet likewise commemorated the young girl's grief in seventeen stanzas of a ballad. The selectmen held a meeting, and, in consideration of Mr. Higginbotham's claims on the town, determined to issue handbills, offering a reward of five hundred dollars for the apprehension of his murderers, and the recovery of the stolen property.

Meanwhile the whole population of Parker's Falls, consisting of shopkeepers, mistresses of boarding-houses, factory girls, millmen, and school boys, rushed into the street and kept up such a terrible loquacity as more than compensated for the silence of the cotton machines, which refrained from their usual din out of respect to the deceased. Had Mr. Higginbotham cared about posthumous renown, his untimely ghost would have exulted in this tumult. Our friend Dominicus, in his vanity of heart, forgot his intended precautions, and mounting on the town pump, announced himself as the bearer of the authentic intelligence which had caused so wonderful a sensation. He immediately became the great man of the moment, and had just begun a new edition of the narrative, with a voice like a field preacher, when the mail stage drove into the village street. It had travelled all night, and must have shifted horses at Kimballton, at three in the morning.

"Now we shall hear all the particulars," shouted the crowd.

The coach rumbled up to the piazza of the tavern, followed by a thousand people; for if any man had been minding his own business till then, he now left it at sixes and sevens, to hear the news. The pedlar, foremost in the race, discovered two passengers, both of whom had been startled from a comfortable nap to find themselves in the centre of a mob. Every man assailing them with separate questions, all propounded at once, the couple were struck speechless, though one was a lawyer and the other a young lady.

"Mr. Higginbotham! Mr. Higginbotham! Tell us the particulars about old Mr. Higginbotham!" bawled the mob. "What is the coroner's verdict? Are the murderers apprehended? Is Mr. Higginbotham's niece come out of her fainting fits? Mr. Higginbotham! Mr. Higginbotham!!"

The coachman said not a word, except to swear awfully at the hostler for not bringing him a fresh team of horses. The lawyer inside had generally his wits about him even when asleep; the first thing he did, after learning the cause of the excitement, was to produce a large, red pocket-book. Meantime Dominicus Pike, being an extremely polite young man, and also suspecting that a female tongue would tell the story as glibly as a lawyer's, had handed the lady out of the coach. She was a fine, smart girl, now wide awake and bright as a button, and had such a sweet pretty mouth, that Dominicus would almost as lief have heard a love tale from it as a tale of murder.

"Gentlemen and ladies," said the lawyer to the shopkeepers, the millmen, and the factory girls, "I can assure you that some unaccountable mistake, or, more probably, a wilful falsehood, maliciously contrived to injure Mr. Higginbotham's credit, has excited this singular uproar. We passed through Kimballton at three o'clock this morning, and most certainly should have been informed of the murder had any been perpetrated. But I have proof nearly as strong as Mr. Higginbotham's own oral testimony, in the negative. Here is a note relating to a suit of his in the Connecticut courts, which was delivered me from that gentleman himself. I find it dated at ten o'clock last evening."

So saying, the lawyer exhibited the date and signature of the note, which irrefragably proved, either that this perverse Mr. Higginbotham was alive when he wrote it, or—as some deemed the more probable case, of two doubtful ones—that he was so absorbed in worldly business as to continue to transact it even after his death. But unexpected evidence was forthcoming. The young lady, after listening to the pedlar's explanation, merely seized a moment to smooth her gown and put her curls in order, and then appeared at the tavern door, making a modest signal to be heard.

"Good people," said she, "I am Mr. Higginbotham's niece."

A wondering murmur passed through the crowd on beholding her so rosy and bright; that same unhappy niece, whom they had supposed, on the authority of the Parker's Falls Gazette, to be lying at death's door in a fainting fit. But some shrewd fellows had doubted, all along, whether a young lady would be quite so desperate at the hanging of a rich old uncle.

"You see," continued Miss Higginbotham, with a smile, "that this strange story is quite unfounded as to myself; and I believe I may affirm it to be equally so in regard to my dear uncle Higginbotham. He has the kindness to give me a home in his house, though I contribute to my own support by teaching a school. I left Kimballton this morning to spend the vacation of commencement week with a friend, about five miles from Parker's Falls. My generous uncle, when he heard me on the stairs, called me to his bedside, and gave me two dollars and fifty cents to pay my stage fare, and another dollar for my extra expenses. He then laid his pocket-book under his pillow, shook hands with me, and advised me to take some biscuit in my bag, instead of breakfasting on the road. I feel confident, therefore, that I left my beloved relative alive, and trust that I shall find him so on my return."

The young lady courtesied at the close of her speech, which was so sensible and well worded, and delivered with such grace and propriety, that everybody thought her fit to be preceptress of the best academy in the State. But a stranger would have supposed that Mr. Higginbotham was an object of abhorrence at Parker's Falls, and that a thanksgiving had been proclaimed for his murder; so excessive was the wrath of the inhabitants on learning their mistake. The millmen resolved to bestow public honors on Dominicus Pike, only hesitating whether to tar and feather him, ride him on a rail, or refresh him with an ablution at the town pump, on the top of which he had declared himself the bearer of the news. The selectmen, by advice of the lawyer, spoke of prosecuting him for a misdemeanor, in circulating unfounded reports, to the great disturbance of the peace of the Commonwealth. Nothing saved Dominicus, either from mob law or a court of justice, but an eloquent appeal made by the young lady in his behalf. Addressing a few words of heartfelt gratitude to his benefactress, he mounted the green cart and rode out of town, under a discharge of artillery from the school boys, who found plenty of ammunition in the neighboring clay-pits and mud holes. As he turned his head to exchange a farewell glance with Mr. Higginbotham's niece, a ball, of the consistence of hasty pudding, hit him slap in the mouth, giving him a most grim aspect. His whole person was so bespattered with the like filthy missiles, that he had almost a mind to ride back, and supplicate for the threatened ablution at the town pump; for, though not meant in kindness, it would now have been a deed of charity.

However, the sun shone bright on poor Dominicus, and the mud, an emblem of all stains of undeserved opprobrium, was easily brushed off when dry. Being a funny rogue, his heart soon cheered up; nor could he refrain from a hearty laugh at the uproar which his story had excited. The handbills of the selectmen would cause the commitment of all the vagabonds in the State; the paragraph in the Parker's Falls Gazette would be reprinted from Maine to Florida, and perhaps form an item in the London newspapers; and many a miser would tremble for his money bags and life, on learning the catastrophe of Mr. Higginbotham. The pedlar meditated with much fervor on the charms of the young schoolmistress, and swore that Daniel Webster never spoke nor looked so like an angel as Miss Higginbotham, while defending him from the wrathful populace at Parker's Falls.

Dominicus was now on the Kimballton turnpike, having all along determined to visit that place, though business had drawn him out of the most direct road from Morristown. As he approached the scene of the supposed murder, he continued to revolve the circumstances in his mind, and was astonished at the aspect which the whole case assumed. Had nothing occurred to corroborate the story of the first traveller, it might now have been considered as a hoax; but the yellow man was evidently acquainted either with the report or the fact; and there was a mystery in his dismayed and guilty look on being abruptly questioned. When, to this singular combination of incidents, it was added that the rumor tallied exactly with Mr. Higginbotham's character and habits of life; and that he had an orchard, and a St. Michael's pear-tree, near which he always passed at nightfall: the circumstantial evidence appeared so strong that Dominicus doubted whether the autograph produced by the lawyer, or even the niece's direct testimony, ought to be equivalent. Making cautious inquiries along the road, the pedlar further learned that Mr. Higginbotham had in his service an Irishman of doubtful character, whom he had hired without a recommendation, on the score of economy.

"May I be hanged myself," exclaimed Dominicus Pike aloud, on reaching the top of a lonely hill, "if I'll believe old Higginbotham is unhanged till I see him with my own eyes, and hear it from his own mouth! And as he's a real shaver, I'll have the minister or some other responsible man for an indorser."

It was growing dusk when he reached the toll-house on Kimballton turnpike, about a quarter of a mile from the village of this name. His little mare was fast bringing him up with a man on horseback, who trotted through the gate a few rods in advance of him, nodded to the toll-gatherer, and kept on towards the village. Dominicus was acquainted with the toll-man, and, while making change, the usual remarks on the weather passed between them.

"I suppose," said the pedlar, throwing back his whiplash, to bring it down like a feather on the mare's flank, "you have not seen anything of old Mr. Higginbotham within a day or two?"

"Yes," answered the toll-gatherer. "He passed the gate just before you drove up,

and yonder he rides now, if you can see him through the dusk. He's been to Woodfield this afternoon, attending a sheriff's sale there. The old man generally shakes hands and has a little chat with me; but to-night, he nodded,—as if to say, 'Charge my toll,' and jogged on; for wherever he goes, he must always be home by eight o'clock."

"So they tell me," said Dominicus.

"I never saw a man look so yellow and thin as the squire does," continued the toll-gatherer. "Says I to myself, to-night, he's more like a ghost or an old mummy than good flesh and blood."

The pedlar strained his eyes through the twilight, and could just discern the horseman now far ahead on the village road. He seemed to recognize the rear of Mr. Higginbotham; but through the evening shadows, and amid the dust from the horse's feet, the figure appeared dim and unsubstantial; as if the shape of the mysterious old man were faintly moulded of darkness and gray light. Dominicus shivered.

"Mr. Higginbotham has come back from the other world, by way of the Kimballton turnpike," thought he.

He shook the reins and rode forward, keeping about the same distance in the rear of the gray old shadow, till the latter was concealed by a bend of the road. On reaching this point, the pedlar no longer saw the man on horseback, but found himself at the head of the village street, not far from a number of stores and two taverns, clustered round the meeting-house steeple. On his left were a stone wall and a gate, the boundary of a wood-lot, beyond which lay an orchard, farther still, a mowing field, and last of all, a house. These were the premises of Mr. Higginbotham, whose dwelling stood beside the old highway, but had been left in the background by the Kimballton turnpike. Dominicus knew the place; and the little mare stopped short by instinct; for he was not conscious of tightening the reins.

"For the soul of me, I cannot get by this gate!" said he, trembling. "I never shall be my own man again, till I see whether Mr. Higginbotham is hanging on the St. Michael's pear-tree!"

He leaped from the cart, gave the rein a turn round the gate post, and ran along the green path of the wood-lot as if Old Nick were chasing behind. Just then the village clock tolled eight, and as each deep stroke fell, Dominicus gave a fresh bound and flew faster than before, till, dim in the solitary centre of the orchard, he saw the fated pear-tree. One great branch stretched from the old contorted trunk across the path, and threw the darkest shadow on that one spot. But something seemed to struggle beneath the branch!

The pedlar had never pretended to more courage than befits a man of peaceable occupation, nor could he account for his valor on this awful emergency. Certain it is, however, that he rushed forward, prostrated a sturdy Irishman with the butt end of his whip, and found—not indeed hanging on the St. Michael's pear-tree, but trembling beneath it, with a halter round his neck—the old, identical Mr. Higginbotham!

"Mr. Higginbotham," said Dominicus tremulously, "you're an honest man, and I'll take your word for it. Have you been hanged or not?"

If the riddle be not already guessed, a few words will explain the simple machinery by which this "coming event" was made to "cast its shadow before." Three men had plotted the robbery and murder of Mr. Higginbotham; two of them, successively, lost courage and fled, each delaying the crime one night by their disappearance; the third was in the act of perpetration, when a champion, blindly obeying the call of fate, like the heroes of old romance, appeared in the person of Dominicus Pike.

It only remains to say, that Mr. Higginbotham took the pedlar into high favor, sanctioned his addresses to the pretty schoolmistress, and settled his whole property on their children, allowing themselves the interest. In due time, the old gentleman capped the climax of his favors, by dying a Christian death, in bed, since which

melancholy event Dominicus Pike has removed from Kimballton, and established a large tobacco manufactory in my native village.

YOUNG GOODMAN BROWN
[1846 (1835)]

YOUNG Goodman Brown came forth at sunset into the street at Salem village; but put his head back, after crossing the threshold, to exchange a parting kiss with his young wife. And Faith, as the wife was aptly named, thrust her own pretty head into the street, letting the wind play with the pink ribbons of her cap while she called to Goodman Brown.

"Dearest heart," whispered she, softly and rather sadly, when her lips were close to his ear, "prithee put off your journey until sunrise and sleep in your own bed to-night. A lone woman is troubled with such dreams and such thoughts that she's afeared of herself sometimes. Pray tarry with me this night, dear husband, of all nights in the year."

"My love and my Faith," replied young Goodman Brown, "of all nights in the year, this one night must I tarry away from thee. My journey, as thou callest it, forth and back again, must needs be done 'twixt now and sunrise. What, my sweet, pretty wife, dost thou doubt me already, and we but three months married?"

"Then God bless you!" said Faith, with the pink ribbons; "and may you find all well when you come back."

"Amen!" cried Goodman Brown. "Say thy prayers, dear Faith, and go to bed at dusk, and no harm will come to thee."

So they parted; and the young man pursued his way until, being about to turn the corner by the meeting-house, he looked back and saw the head of Faith still peeping after him with a melancholy air, in spite of her pink ribbons.

"Poor little Faith!" thought he, for his heart smote him. "What a wretch am I to leave her on such an errand! She talks of dreams, too. Methought as she spoke there was trouble in her face, as if a dream had warned her what work is to be done to-night. But no, no; 't would kill her to think it. Well, she's a blessed angel on earth; and after this one night I'll cling to her skirts and follow her to heaven."

With this excellent resolve for the future, Goodman Brown felt himself justified in making more haste on his present evil purpose. He had taken a dreary road, darkened by all the gloomiest trees of the forest, which barely stood aside to let the narrow path creep through, and closed immediately behind. It was all as lonely as could be; and there is this peculiarity in such a solitude, that the traveller knows not who may be concealed by the innumerable trunks and the thick boughs overhead; so that with lonely footsteps he may yet be passing through an unseen multitude.

"There may be a devilish Indian behind every tree," said Goodman Brown to himself; and he glanced fearfully behind him as he added, "What if the devil himself should be at my very elbow!"

His head being turned back, he passed a crook of the road, and, looking forward again, beheld the figure of a man, in grave and decent attire, seated at the foot of an old tree. He arose at Goodman Brown's approach and walked onward side by side with him.

"You are late, Goodman Brown," said he. "The clock of the Old South was striking as I came through Boston, and that is full fifteen minutes agone." [1]

"Faith kept me back a while," replied the young man, with a tremor in his voice, caused by the sudden appearance of his companion, though not wholly unexpected.

It was now deep dusk in the forest, and deepest in that part of it where these two were journeying. As nearly as could be discerned, the second traveller was about fifty years old, apparently in the same rank of life as Goodman Brown, and bearing a considerable resemblance to him, though perhaps more in expression than in features. Still they might have been taken for father and son. And yet, though the elder person was as simply clad as the younger, and as simple in manner too, he had an indescribable air of one who knew the world, and who would not have felt abashed at the governor's dinner table or in King William's court, were it possible that his affairs should call him thither. [2] But the only thing about him that could be fixed upon as remarkable was his staff, which bore the likeness of a great black snake, so curiously wrought that it might almost be seen to twist and wriggle itself like a living serpent. This, of course, must have been an ocular deception, assisted by the uncertain light.

"Come, Goodman Brown," cried his fellow-traveller, "this is a dull pace for the beginning of a journey. Take my staff, if you are so soon weary."

"Friend," said the other, exchanging his slow pace for a full stop, "having kept covenant by meeting thee here, it is my purpose now to return whence I came. I have scruples touching the matter thou wot'st of."

"Sayest thou so?" replied he of the serpent, smiling apart. "Let us walk on, nevertheless, reasoning as we go; and if I convince thee not thou shalt turn back. We are but a little way in the forest yet."

"Too far! too far!" exclaimed the goodman, unconsciously resuming his walk. "My father never went into the woods on such an errand, nor his father before him. We have been a race of honest men and good Christians since the days of the martyrs; and shall I be the first of the name of Brown that ever took this path and kept"—

"Such company, thou wouldst say," observed the elder person, interpreting his pause. "Well said, Goodman Brown! I have been as well acquainted with your family as with ever a one among the Puritans; and that's no trifle to say. I helped

---

[1] The Old South Church in Boston was built in 1730.

[2] The reference is to William III (1650-1702), England's King 1689-1702.

your grandfather, the constable, when he lashed the Quaker woman so smartly through the streets of Salem; and it was I that brought your father a pitch-pine knot, kindled at my own hearth, to set fire to an Indian village, in King Philip's war. They were my good friends, both; and many a pleasant walk have we had along this path, and returned merrily after midnight. I would fain be friends with you for their sake."

"If it be as thou sayest," replied Goodman Brown, "I marvel they never spoke of these matters; or, verily, I marvel not, seeing that the least rumor of the sort would have driven them from New England. We are a people of prayer, and good works to boot, and abide no such wickedness."

"Wickedness or not," said the traveller with the twisted staff, "I have a very general acquaintance here in New England. The deacons of many a church have drunk the communion wine with me; the selectmen of divers towns make me their chairman; and a majority of the Great and General Court are firm supporters of my interest. The governor and I, too— But these are state secrets."

"Can this be so?" cried Goodman Brown, with a stare of amazement at his undisturbed companion. "Howbeit, I have nothing to do with the governor and council; they have their own ways, and are no rule for a simple husbandman like me. But, were I to go on with thee, how should I meet the eye of that good old man, our minister, at Salem village? Oh, his voice would make me tremble both Sabbath day and lecture day."

Thus far the elder traveller had listened with due gravity; but now burst into a fit of irrepressible mirth, shaking himself so violently that his snake-like staff actually seemed to wriggle in sympathy.

"Ha! ha! ha!" shouted he again and again; then composing himself, "Well, go on, Goodman Brown, go on; but, prithee, don't kill me with laughing."

"Well, then, to end the matter at once," said Goodman Brown, considerably nettled, "there is my wife, Faith. It would break her dear little heart; and I'd rather break my own."

"Nay, if that be the case," answered the other, "e'en go thy ways, Goodman Brown. I would not for twenty old women like the one hobbling before us that Faith should come to any harm."

As he spoke he pointed his staff at a female figure on the path, in whom Goodman Brown recognized a very pious and exemplary dame, who had taught him his catechism in youth, and was still his moral and spiritual adviser, jointly with the minister and Deacon Gookin.

"A marvel, truly, that Goody Cloyse should be so far in the wilderness at nightfall," said he. "But with your leave, friend, I shall take a cut through the woods until we have left this Christian woman behind. Being a stranger to you, she might ask whom I was consorting with and whither I was going."

"Be it so," said his fellow-traveller. "Betake you to the woods, and let me keep the path."

Accordingly the young man turned aside, but took care to watch his companion, who advanced softly along the road until he had come within a staff's length of the old dame. She, meanwhile, was making the best of her way, with singular speed for so aged a woman, and mumbling some indistinct words—a prayer, doubtless—as she went. The traveller put forth his staff and touched her withered neck with what seemed the serpent's tail.

"The devil!" screamed the pious old lady.

"Then Goody Cloyse knows her old friend?" observed the traveller, confronting her and leaning on his writhing stick.

"Ah, forsooth, and is it your worship indeed?" cried the good dame. "Yea, truly is it, and in the very image of my old gossip, Goodman Brown, the grandfather of the silly fellow that now is. But—would your worship believe it?—my broomstick hath strangely disappeared, stolen, as I suspect, by that unhanged witch, Goody

Cory, and that, too, when I was all anointed with the juice of smallage, and cinquefoil, and wolf's bane"—

"Mingled with fine wheat and the fat of a new-born babe," said the shape of old Goodman Brown.

"Ah, your worship knows the recipe," cried the old lady, cackling aloud. "So, as I was saying, being all ready for the meeting, and no horse to ride on, I made up my mind to foot it; for they tell me there is a nice young man to be taken into communion to-night. But now your good worship will lend me your arm, and we shall be there in a twinkling."

"That can hardly be," answered her friend. "I may not spare you my arm, Goody Cloyse; but here is my staff, if you will."

So saying, he threw it down at her feet, where, perhaps, it assumed life, being one of the rods which its owner had formerly lent to the Egyptian magi. Of this fact, however, Goodman Brown could not take cognizance. He had cast up his eyes in astonishment, and, looking down again, beheld neither Goody Cloyse nor the serpentine staff, but his fellow-traveller alone, who waited for him as calmly as if nothing had happened.

"That old woman taught me my catechism," said the young man; and there was a world of meaning in this simple comment.

They continued to walk onward, while the elder traveller exhorted his companion to make good speed and persevere in the path, discoursing so aptly that his arguments seemed rather to spring up in the bosom of his auditor than to be suggested by himself. As they went, he plucked a branch of maple to serve for a walking stick, and began to strip it of the twigs and little boughs, which were wet with evening dew. The moment his fingers touched them they became strangely withered and dried up as with a week's sunshine. Thus the pair proceeded, at a good free pace, until suddenly, in a gloomy hollow of the road, Goodman Brown sat

himself down on the stump of a tree and refused to go any farther.

"Friend," said he, stubbornly, "my mind is made up. Not another step will I budge on this errand. What if a wretched old woman do choose to go to the devil when I thought she was going to heaven: is that any reason why I should quit my dear Faith and go after her?"

"You will think better of this by and by," said his acquaintance, composedly. "Sit here and rest yourself a while; and when you feel like moving again, there is my staff to help you along."

Without more words, he threw his companion the maple stick, and was as speedily out of sight as if he had vanished into the deepening gloom. The young man sat a few moments by the roadside, applauding himself greatly, and thinking with how clear a conscience he should meet the minister in his morning walk, nor shrink from the eye of good old Deacon Gookin. And what calm sleep would be his that very night, which was to have been spent so wickedly, but so purely and sweetly now, in the arms of Faith! Amidst these pleasant and praiseworthy meditations, Goodman Brown heard the tramp of horses along the road, and deemed it advisable to conceal himself within the verge of the forest, conscious of the guilty purpose that had brought him thither, though now so happily turned from it.

On came the hoof tramps and the voices of the riders, two grave old voices, conversing soberly as they drew near. These mingled sounds appeared to pass along the road, within a few yards of the young man's hiding-place; but, owing doubtless to the depth of the gloom at that particular spot, neither the travellers nor their steeds were visible. Though their figures brushed the small boughs by the wayside, it could not be seen that they intercepted, even for a moment, the faint gleam from the strip of bright sky athwart which they must have passed. Goodman Brown alternately crouched and stood on tiptoe, pulling aside the branches and thrusting forth his head as far as he durst without discerning so much as a shadow. It vexed him the more, because he could have sworn, were such a thing possible, that he recognized the voices of the minister and Deacon Gookin, jogging along quietly, as they were wont to do, when bound to some ordination or ecclesiastical council. While yet within hearing, one of the riders stopped to pluck a switch.

"Of the two, reverend sir," said the voice like the deacon's, "I had rather miss an ordination dinner than to-night's meeting. They tell me that some of our community are to be here from Falmouth and beyond, and others from Connecticut and Rhode Island, besides several of the Indian powwows, who, after their fashion, know almost as much deviltry as the best of us. Moreover, there is a goodly young woman to be taken into communion."

"Mighty well, Deacon Gookin!" replied the solemn old tones of the minister. "Spur up, or we shall be late. Nothing can be done, you know, until I get on the ground."

The hoofs clattered again; and the voices, talking so strangely in the empty air, passed on through the forest, where no church had ever been gathered or solitary Christian prayed. Whither, then, could these holy men be journeying so deep into the heathen wilderness? Young Goodman Brown caught hold of a tree for support, being ready to sink down on the ground, faint and overburdened with the heavy sickness of his heart. He looked up to the sky, doubting whether there really was a heaven above him. Yet there was the blue arch, and the stars brightening in it.

"With heaven above and Faith below, I will yet stand firm against the devil!" cried Goodman Brown.

While he still gazed upward into the deep arch of the firmament and had lifted his hands to pray, a cloud, though no wind was stirring, hurried across the zenith and hid the brightening stars. The blue sky was still visible, except directly overhead, where this black mass of cloud was sweeping swiftly northward. Aloft in the air, as if from the depths of the cloud, came a confused and doubtful sound of voices. Once the listener fancied that he could distinguish the accents of towns-people of his own, men and women, both pious and ungodly, many of whom he had met at the communion table, and had seen others rioting at the tavern. The next moment, so indistinct were the sounds, he doubted whether he had heard aught but the murmur of the old forest, whispering without a wind. Then came a stronger swell of those familiar tones, heard daily in the sunshine at Salem village, but never until now from a cloud of night. There was one voice, of a young woman, uttering lamentations, yet with an uncertain sorrow, and entreating for some favor, which, perhaps, it would grieve her to obtain; and all the unseen multitude, both saints and sinners, seemed to encourage her onward.

"Faith!" shouted Goodman Brown, in a voice of agony and desperation; and the echoes of the forest mocked him, crying, "Faith! Faith!" as if bewildered wretches were seeking her all through the wilderness.

The cry of grief, rage, and terror was yet piercing the night, when the unhappy husband held his breath for a response. There was a scream, drowned immediately in a louder murmur of voices, fading into far-off laughter, as the dark cloud swept away, leaving the clear and silent sky above Goodman Brown. But something fluttered lightly down through the air and caught on the branch of a tree. The young man seized it, and beheld a pink ribbon.

"My Faith is gone!" cried he, after one stupefied moment. "There is no good on earth; and sin is but a name. Come, devil; for to thee is this world given."

And, maddened with despair, so that he laughed loud and long, did Goodman Brown grasp his staff and set forth again, at such a rate that he seemed to fly along the forest path rather than to walk or run. The road grew wilder and drearier and more faintly traced, and vanished at length, leaving him in the heart of the dark wilderness, still rushing onward with the instinct that guides mortal man to evil. The whole forest was peopled with frightful sounds—the creaking of the trees, the howling of wild beasts, and the yell of Indians; while sometimes the wind tolled like a distant church bell, and sometimes gave a broad roar around the traveller, as if all Nature were laughing him to scorn. But he was himself the chief horror of the scene, and shrank not from its other horrors.

"Ha! ha! ha!" roared Goodman Brown when the wind laughed at him. "Let us hear which will laugh loudest. Think not to frighten me with your deviltry. Come witch, come wizard, come Indian powwow, come devil himself, and here comes Goodman Brown. You may as well fear him as he fear you."

In truth, all through the haunted forest there could be nothing more frightful than the figure of Goodman Brown. On he flew among the black pines, brandishing his staff with frenzied gestures, now giving vent to an inspiration of horrid blasphemy, and now shouting forth such laughter as set all the echoes of the forest laughing like demons around him. The fiend in his own shape is less hideous than when he rages in the breast of man. Thus sped the demoniac on his course, until, quivering among the trees, he saw a red light before him, as when the felled trunks and branches of a clearing have been set on fire, and throw up their lurid blaze against the sky, at the hour of midnight. He paused, in a lull of the tempest that had driven him onward, and heard the swell of what seemed a hymn, rolling solemnly from a distance with the weight of many voices. He knew the tune; it was a familiar one in the choir of the village meeting-house. The verse died heavily away, and was lengthened by a chorus, not of human voices, but of all the sounds of the benighted wilderness pealing in awful harmony together. Goodman Brown cried out, and his cry was lost to his own ear by its unison with the cry of the desert.

In the interval of silence he stole forward until the light glared full upon his eyes. At one extremity of an open space, hemmed in by the dark wall of the forest, arose a rock, bearing some rude, natural resemblance either to an altar or a pulpit, and surrounded by four blazing pines, their tops aflame, their stems untouched, like candles at an evening meeting. The mass of foliage that had overgrown the summit of the rock was all on fire, blazing high into the night and fitfully illuminating the whole field. Each pendent twig and leafy festoon was in a blaze. As the red light arose and fell, a numerous congregation alternately shone forth, then disappeared in shadow, and again grew, as it were, out of the darkness, peopling the heart of the solitary woods at once.

"A grave and dark-clad company," quoth Goodman Brown.

In truth they were such. Among them, quivering to and fro between gloom and splendor, appeared faces that would be seen next day at the council board of the province, and others which, Sabbath after Sabbath, looked devoutly heavenward, and benignantly over the crowded pews, from the holiest pulpits in the land. Some affirm that the lady of the governor was there. At least there were high dames well known to her, and wives of honored husbands, and widows, a great multitude, and ancient maidens, all of excellent repute, and fair young girls, who trembled lest their mothers should espy them. Either the sudden gleams of light flashing over the obscure field bedazzled Goodman Brown, or he recognized a score of the church members of Salem village famous for their especial sanctity. Good old Deacon Gookin had arrived, and waited at the skirts of that venerable saint, his revered pastor. But, irreverently consorting with these grave, reputable, and pious people, these elders of the church, these chaste dames and dewy virgins, there were men of dissolute lives and women of spotted fame, wretches given over to all mean and filthy vice, and suspected even of horrid crimes. It was strange to see that the good shrank not from the wicked, nor were the sinners abashed by the saints.

Scattered also among their pale-faced enemies were the Indian priests, or powwows, who had often scared their native forest with more hideous incantations than any known to English witchcraft.

"But where is Faith?" thought Goodman Brown; and, as hope came into his heart, he trembled.

Another verse of the hymn arose, a slow and mournful strain, such as the pious love, but joined to words which expressed all that our nature can conceive of sin, and darkly hinted at far more. Unfathomable to mere mortals is the lore of fiends. Verse after verse was sung; and still the chorus of the desert swelled between like the deepest tone of a mighty organ; and with the final peal of that dreadful anthem there came a sound, as if the roaring wind, the rushing streams, the howling beasts, and every other voice of the unconcerted wilderness were mingling and according with the voice of guilty man in homage to the prince of all. The four blazing pines threw up a loftier flame, and obscurely discovered shapes and visages of horror on the smoke wreaths above the impious assembly. At the same moment the fire on the rock shot redly forth and formed a glowing arch above its base, where now appeared a figure. With reverence be it spoken, the figure bore no slight similitude, both in garb and manner, to some grave divine of the New England churches.

"Bring forth the converts!" cried a voice that echoed through the field and rolled into the forest.

At the word, Goodman Brown stepped forth from the shadow of the trees and approached the congregation, with whom he felt a loathful brotherhood by the sympathy of all that was wicked in his heart. He could have well-nigh sworn that the shape of his own dead father beckoned him to advance, looking downward from a smoke wreath, while a woman, with dim features of despair, threw out her hand to warn him back. Was it his mother? But he had no power to retreat one step, nor to resist, even in thought, when the minister

and good old Deacon Gookin seized his arms and led him to the blazing rock. Thither came also the slender form of a veiled female, led between Goody Cloyse, that pious teacher of the catechism, and Martha Carrier, who had received the devil's promise to be queen of hell.[3] A rampant hag was she. And there stood the proselytes beneath the canopy of fire.

"Welcome, my children," said the dark figure, "to the communion of your race. Ye have found thus young your nature and your destiny. My children, look behind you!"

They turned; and flashing forth, as it were, in a sheet of flame, the fiend worshippers were seen; the smile of welcome gleamed darkly on every visage.

"There," resumed the sable form, "are all whom ye have reverenced from youth. Ye deemed them holier than yourselves and shrank from your own sin, contrasting it with their lives of righteousness and prayerful aspirations heavenward. Yet here are they all in my worshipping assembly. This night it shall be granted you to know their secret deeds; how hoary-bearded elders of the church have whispered wanton words to the young maids of their households; how many a woman, eager for widows' weeds, has given her husband a drink at bedtime and let him sleep his last sleep in her bosom; how beardless youths have made haste to inherit their fathers' wealth; and how fair damsels—blush not, sweet ones —have dug little graves in the garden, and bidden me, the sole guest, to an infant's funeral. By the sympathy of your human hearts for sin ye shall scent out all the places—whether in church, bedchamber, street, field, or forest—where crime has been committed, and shall exult to behold the whole earth one stain of guilt, one mighty blood spot. Far more than this. It shall be yours to penetrate, in every bosom,

---

[3] Martha Carrier, Goody Cloyse, and Goody Cory were the names of witches sentenced to death by Hawthorne's great-great-grandfather in 1692.

the deep mystery of sin, the fountain of all wicked arts, and which inexhaustibly supplies more evil impulses than human power—than my power at its utmost—can make manifest in deeds. And now, my children, look upon each other."

They did so; and, by the blaze of the hell-kindled torches, the wretched man beheld his Faith, and the wife her husband, trembling before that unhallowed altar.

"Lo, there ye stand, my children," said the figure, in a deep and solemn tone, almost sad with its despairing awfulness, as if his once angelic nature could yet mourn for our miserable race. "Depending upon one another's hearts, ye had still hoped that virtue were not all a dream. Now are ye undeceived. Evil is the nature of mankind. Evil must be your only happiness. Welcome again, my children, to the communion of your race."

"Welcome," repeated the fiend worshippers, in one cry of despair and triumph.

And there they stood, the only pair, as it seemed, who were yet hesitating on the verge of wickedness in this dark world. A basin was hollowed, naturally, in the rock. Did it contain water, reddened by the lurid light? or was it blood? or, perchance, a liquid flame? Herein did the shape of evil dip his hand and prepare to lay the mark of baptism upon their foreheads, that they might be partakers of the mystery of sin, more conscious of the secret guilt of others, both in deed and thought, than they could now be of their own. The husband cast one look at his pale wife, and Faith at him. What polluted wretches would the next glance show them to each other, shuddering alike at what they disclosed and what they saw!

"Faith! Faith!" cried the husband, "look up to heaven, and resist the wicked one."

Whether Faith obeyed he knew not. Hardly had he spoken when he found himself amid calm night and solitude, listening to a roar of the wind which died heavily away through the forest. He staggered against the rock, and felt it chill and damp; while a hanging twig, that had been all on

fire, besprinkled his cheek with the coldest dew.

The next morning young Goodman Brown came slowly into the street of Salem village, staring around him like a bewildered man. The good old minister was taking a walk along the graveyard to get an appetite for breakfast and meditate his sermon, and bestowed a blessing, as he passed, on Goodman Brown. He shrank from the venerable saint as if to avoid an anathema. Old Deacon Gookin was at domestic worship, and the holy words of his prayer were heard through the open window. "What God doth the wizard pray to?" quoth Goodman Brown. Goody Cloyse, that excellent old Christian, stood in the early sunshine at her own lattice, catechizing a little girl who had brought her a pint of morning's milk. Goodman Brown snatched away the child as from the grasp of the fiend himself. Turning the corner by the meeting-house, he spied the head of Faith, with the pink ribbons, gazing anxiously forth, and bursting into such joy at sight of him that she skipped along the street and almost kissed her husband before the whole village. But Goodman Brown looked sternly and sadly into her face, and passed on without a greeting.

Had Goodman Brown fallen asleep in the forest and only dreamed a wild dream of a witch-meeting?

Be it so if you will; but, alas! it was a dream of evil omen for young Goodman Brown. A stern, a sad, a darkly meditative, a distrustful, if not a desperate man did he become from the night of that fearful dream. On the Sabbath day, when the congregation were singing a holy psalm, he could not listen because an anthem of sin rushed loudly upon his ear and drowned all the blessed strain. When the minister spoke from the pulpit with power and fervid eloquence, and, with his hand on the open Bible, of the sacred truths of our religion, and of saint-like lives and triumphant deaths, and of future bliss or misery unutterable, then did Goodman Brown turn pale, dreading lest the roof should thunder down upon the gray blasphemer and his hearers. Often, awaking suddenly at midnight, he shrank from the bosom of Faith; and at morning or eventide, when the family knelt down at prayer, he scowled and muttered to himself, and gazed sternly at his wife, and turned away. And when he had lived long, and was borne to his grave a hoary corpse, followed by Faith, an aged woman, and children and grandchildren, a goodly procession, besides neighbors not a few, they carved no hopeful verse upon his tombstone, for his dying hour was gloom.

WAKEFIELD
[1837 (1835)]

IN some old magazine or newspaper I recollect a story, told as truth, of a man —let us call him Wakefield—who absented himself for a long time from his wife. The fact, thus abstractedly stated, is not very uncommon, nor—without a proper distinction of circumstances—to be condemned either as naughty or nonsensical. Howbeit, this, though far from the most aggravated, is perhaps the strangest, instance on record, of marital delinquency; and, moreover, as remarkable a freak as may be found in the whole list of human oddities. The wedded couple lived in London. The man, under pretence of going a journey, took lodgings in the next street to his own house, and there, unheard of by his wife or friends, and without the shadow of a reason for such self-banishment, dwelt upwards of twenty years. During that period, he beheld his home every day, and frequently the forlorn Mrs. Wakefield. And after so great a gap in his matrimonial felicity—when his death was reckoned certain, his estate settled, his name dismissed from memory, and his wife, long, long ago, resigned to her autumnal widowhood—he entered the door one evening, quietly, as from a day's absence, and became a loving spouse till death.

This outline is all that I remember. But the incident, though of the purest original-

ity, unexampled, and probably never to be repeated, is one, I think, which appeals to the generous sympathies of mankind. We know, each for himself, that none of us would perpetrate such a folly, yet feel as if some other might. To my own contemplations, at least, it has often recurred, always exciting wonder, but with a sense that the story must be true, and a conception of its hero's character. Whenever any subject so forcibly affects the mind, time is well spent in thinking of it. If the reader choose, let him do his own meditation; or if he prefer to ramble with me through the twenty years of Wakefield's vagary, I bid him welcome; trusting that there will be a pervading spirit and a moral, even should we fail to find them, done up neatly, and condensed into the final sentence. Thought has always its efficacy, and every striking incident its moral.

What sort of a man was Wakefield? We are free to shape out our own idea, and call it by his name. He was now in the meridian of life; his matrimonial affections, never violent, were sobered into a calm, habitual sentiment; of all husbands, he was likely to be the most constant, because a certain sluggishness would keep his heart at rest, wherever it might be placed. He was intellectual, but not actively so; his mind occupied itself in long and lazy musings, that ended to no purpose, or had not vigor to attain it; his thoughts were seldom so energetic as to seize hold of words. Imagination, in the proper meaning of the term, made no part of Wakefield's gifts. With a cold but not depraved nor wandering heart, and a mind never feverish with riotous thoughts, nor perplexed with originality, who could have anticipated that our friend would entitle himself to a foremost place among the doers of eccentric deeds? Had his acquaintances been asked, who was the man in London the surest to perform nothing today which should be remembered on the morrow, they would have thought of Wakefield. Only the wife of his bosom might have hesitated. She, without having analyzed his character, was partly aware of a quiet selfishness, that had rusted into his inactive mind; of a peculiar sort of vanity, the most uneasy attribute about him; of a disposition to craft, which had seldom produced more positive effects than the keeping of petty secrets, hardly worth revealing; and, lastly, of what she called a little strangeness, sometimes, in the good man. This latter quality is indefinable, and perhaps non-existent.

Let us now imagine Wakefield bidding adieu to his wife. It is the dusk of an October evening. His equipment is a drab great-coat, a hat covered with an oilcloth, top-boots, an umbrella in one hand and a small portmanteau in the other. He has informed Mrs. Wakefield that he is to take the night coach into the country. She would fain inquire the length of his journey, its object, and the probable time of his return; but, indulgent to his harmless love of mystery, interrogates him only by a look. He tells her not to expect him positively by the return coach, nor to be alarmed should he tarry three or four days; but, at all events, to look for him at supper on Friday evening. Wakefield himself, be it considered, has no suspicion of what is before him. He holds out his hand, she gives her own, and meets his parting kiss in the matter-of-course way of a ten years' matrimony; and forth goes the middle-aged Mr. Wakefield, almost resolved to perplex his good lady by a whole week's absence. After the door has closed behind him, she perceives it thrust partly open, and a vision of her husband's face, through the aperture, smiling on her, and gone in a moment. For the time, this little incident is dismissed without a thought. But, long afterwards, when she has been more years a widow than a wife, that smile recurs, and flickers across all her reminiscences of Wakefield's visage. In her many musings, she surrounds the original smile with a multitude of fantasies, which make it strange and awful: as, for instance, if she imagines him in a coffin, that parting look is frozen on his pale features; or, if she dreams of him in heaven, still his blessed spirit wears a quiet and crafty smile. Yet, for its sake, when all others have given him up for dead, she sometimes doubts whether she is a widow.

But our business is with the husband. We must hurry after him along the street, ere he lose his individuality, and melt into the great mass of London life. It would be vain searching for him there. Let us follow close at his heels, therefore, until, after several superfluous turns and doublings, we find him comfortably established by the fireside of a small apartment, previously bespoken. He is in the next street to his own, and at his journey's end. He can scarcely trust his good fortune, in having got thither unperceived—recollecting that, at one time, he was delayed by the throng, in the very focus of a lighted lantern; and, again, there were footsteps that seemed to tread behind his own, distinct from the multitudinous tramp around him; and, anon, he heard a voice shouting afar, and fancied that it called his name. Doubtless, a dozen busybodies had been watching him, and told his wife the whole affair. Poor Wakefield! Little knowest thou thine own insignificance in this great world! No mortal eye but mine has traced thee. Go quietly to thy bed, foolish man; and, on the morrow, if thou wilt be wise, get thee home to good Mrs. Wakefield, and tell her the truth. Remove not thyself, even for a little week, from thy place in her chaste bosom. Were she, for a single moment, to deem thee dead, or lost, or lastingly divided from her, thou wouldst be wofully conscious of a change in thy true wife forever after. It is perilous to make a chasm in human affections; not that they gape so long and wide—but so quickly close again!

Almost repenting of his frolic, or whatever it may be termed, Wakefield lies down betimes, and starting from his first nap, spreads forth his arms into the wide and solitary waste of the unaccustomed bed. "No,"—thinks he, gathering the bedclothes about him,—"I will not sleep alone another night."

In the morning he rises earlier than usual, and sets himself to consider what he really means to do. Such are his loose and rambling modes of thought that he has taken this very singular step with the consciousness of a purpose, indeed, but without being able to define it sufficiently for his own contemplation. The vagueness of the project, and the convulsive effort with which he plunges into the execution of it, are equally characteristic of a feeble-minded man. Wakefield sifts his ideas, however, as minutely as he may, and finds himself curious to know the progress of matters at home—how his exemplary wife will endure her widowhood of a week; and, briefly, how the little sphere of creatures and circumstances, in which he was a central object, will be affected by his removal. A morbid vanity, therefore, lies nearest the bottom of the affair. But, how is he to attain his ends? Not, certainly, by keeping close in this comfortable lodging, where, though he slept and awoke in the next street to his home, he is as effectually abroad as if the stagecoach had been whirling him away all night. Yet, should he reappear, the whole project is knocked in the head. His poor brains being hopelessly puzzled with this dilemma, he at length ventures out, partly resolving to cross the head of the street, and send one hasty glance towards his forsaken domicile. Habit—for he is a man of habits—takes him by the hand, and guides him, wholly unaware, to his own door, where, just at the critical moment, he is aroused by the scraping of his foot upon the step. Wakefield! whither are you going?

At that instant his fate was turning on the pivot. Little dreaming of the doom to which his first backward step devotes him, he hurries away, breathless with agitation hitherto unfelt, and hardly dares turn his head at the distant corner. Can it be that nobody caught sight of him? Will not the whole household—the decent Mrs. Wakefield, the smart maid servant, and the dirty little footboy—raise a hue and cry, through London streets, in pursuit of their fugitive lord and master? Wonderful escape! He gathers courage to pause and look homeward, but is perplexed with a sense of change about the familiar edifice, such as affects us all, when, after a separation of months or years, we again see some hill or lake, or work of art, with which we were friends of old. In ordinary cases, this indescribable impression is caused by the comparison and contrast between our imperfect reminiscences and the reality. In Wakefield, the magic of a single night has wrought a similar transformation, because, in that brief period, a great moral change has been effected. But this is a secret from himself. Before leaving the spot, he catches a far and momentary glimpse of his wife, passing athwart the front window, with her face turned towards the head of the street. The crafty nincompoop takes to his heels, scared with the idea that, among a thousand such atoms of mortality, her eye must have detected him. Right glad is his heart, though his brain be somewhat dizzy, when he finds himself by the coal fire of his lodgings.

So much for the commencement of this long whimwham. After the initial conception, and the stirring up of the man's sluggish temperament to put it in practice, the whole matter evolves itself in a natural train. We may suppose him, as the result of deep deliberation, buying a new wig, of reddish hair, and selecting sundry garments, in a fashion unlike his customary suit of brown, from a Jew's old-clothes bag. It is accomplished. Wakefield is another man. The new system being now established, a retrograde movement to the old would be almost as difficult as the step that placed him in his unparalleled position. Furthermore, he is rendered obstinate by a sulkiness occasionally incident to his temper, and brought on at present by the inadequate sensation which he conceives to have been produced in the bosom of Mrs. Wakefield. He will not go back until she be frightened half to death. Well; twice or thrice has she passed before his sight, each time with a heavier step, a paler cheek, and more anxious brow; and in the third week of his non-appearance he detects a portent of evil entering the house, in the guise of an apothecary. Next day the knocker is muffled. Towards nightfall comes the chariot of a physician, and deposits its big-wigged and solemn burden at Wakefield's door, whence, after a quarter of an hour's visit, he emerges, perchance the herald of a funeral. Dear woman! Will she die? By this time, Wakefield is excited to something like energy of feeling, but still lingers away from his wife's bedside, pleading with his conscience that she must not be disturbed at such a juncture. If aught else restrains him, he does not know it. In the course of a few weeks she gradually recovers; the crisis is over; her heart is sad, perhaps, but quiet; and, let him return soon or late, it will never be feverish for him again. Such ideas glimmer through the mist of Wakefield's mind, and render him indistinctly conscious that an almost impassable gulf divides his hired apartment from his former home. "It is but in the next street!" he sometimes says. Fool! it is in another world. Hitherto, he has put off his return from one particular day to another; henceforward, he leaves the precise time undetermined. Not to-morrow—probably next week—pretty soon. Poor man! The dead have nearly as much chance of revisiting their earthly homes as the self-banished Wakefield.

Would that I had a folio to write, instead of an article of a dozen pages! Then might I exemplify how an influence beyond our control lays its strong hand on every deed which we do, and weaves its consequences into an iron tissue of necessity. Wakefield is spell-bound. We must leave him, for ten years or so, to haunt around his house, without once crossing the threshold, and to be faithful to his wife, with all the affection of which his heart is capable, while he is slowly fading out of hers. Long since, it must be remarked, he had lost the perception of singularity in his conduct.

Now for a scene! Amid the throng of a London street we distinguish a man, now waxing elderly, with few characteristics to attract careless observers, yet bearing, in his whole aspect, the handwriting of no common fate, for such as have the skill to read it. He is meagre; his low and narrow forehead is deeply wrinkled; his eyes, small and lustreless, sometimes wander apprehensively about him, but oftener seem to look inward. He bends his head, and moves with an indescribable obliquity of gait, as if unwilling to display his full front to the world. Watch him long enough to see what we have described, and you will allow that circumstances—which often produce remarkable men from nature's ordinary handiwork—have produced one such here. Next, leaving him to sidle along the footwalk, cast your eyes in the opposite direction, where a portly female, considerably in the wane of life, with a prayer-book in her hand, is proceeding to yonder church. She has the placid mien of settled widowhood. Her regrets have either died away, or have become so essential to her heart, that they would be poorly exchanged for joy. Just as the lean man and well-conditioned woman are passing, a slight obstruction occurs, and brings these two figures directly in contact. Their hands touch; the pressure of the crowd forces her bosom against his shoulder; they stand, face to face, staring into each other's eyes. After a ten years' separation, thus Wakefield meets his wife!

The throng eddies away, and carries them asunder. The sober widow, resuming her former pace, proceeds to church, but pauses in the portal, and throws a perplexed glance along the street. She passes in, however, opening her prayer-book as she goes. And the man! with so wild a face that busy and selfish London stands to gaze after him, he hurries to his lodgings, bolts the door, and throws himself upon the bed. The latent feelings of years break out; his feeble mind acquires a brief energy from their strength; all the miserable strangeness of his life is revealed to him at a glance: and he cries out, passionately, "Wakefield! Wakefield! You are mad!"

Perhaps he was so. The singularity of his situation must have so moulded him to himself, that, considered in regard to his fellow-creatures and the business of life, he could not be said to possess his right mind. He had contrived, or rather he had happened, to dissever himself from the world—to vanish—to give up his place and privileges with living men, without being admitted among the dead. The life of a hermit is nowise parallel to his. He was in the bustle of the city, as of old; but the crowd swept by and saw him not; he was, we may figuratively say, always beside his wife and at his hearth, yet must never feel the warmth of the one nor the affection of the other. It was Wakefield's unprecedented fate to retain his original share of human sympathies, and to be still involved in human interests, while he had lost his reciprocal influence on them. It would be a most curious speculation to trace out the effect of such circumstances on his heart and intellect, separately, and in unison. Yet, changed as he was, he would seldom be conscious of it, but deem himself the same man as ever; glimpses of the truth, indeed, would come, but only for the moment; and still he would keep saying, "I shall soon go back!"—nor reflect that he had been saying so for twenty years.

I conceive, also, that these twenty years would appear, in the retrospect, scarcely longer than the week to which Wakefield had at first limited his absence. He would look on the affair as no more than an interlude in the main business of his life. When, after a little while more, he should deem it time to reënter his parlor, his wife would clap her hands for joy, on beholding the middle-aged Mr. Wakefield. Alas, what a mistake! Would Time but await the close of our favorite follies, we should be young men, all of us, and till Doomsday.

One evening, in the twentieth year since he vanished, Wakefield is taking his customary walk towards the dwelling which he still calls his own. It is a gusty night of autumn, with frequent showers that patter down upon the pavement, and are gone before a man can put up his umbrella. Pausing near the house, Wakefield discerns, through the parlor windows of the second floor, the red glow and the glimmer and fitful flash of a comfortable fire. On the ceiling appears a grotesque shadow of good Mrs. Wakefield. The cap, the nose and chin, and the broad waist, form an admirable caricature, which dances, moreover, with the up-flickering and down-sinking blaze, almost too merrily for the shade of an elderly widow. At this instant a shower chances to fall, and is driven, by the unmannerly gust, full into Wakefield's face and bosom. He is quite penetrated with its autumnal chill. Shall he stand, wet and shivering here, when his own hearth has a good fire to warm him, and his own wife will run to fetch the gray coat and small-clothes, which, doubtless, she has kept carefully in the closet of their bed chamber? No! Wakefield is no such fool. He ascends the steps—heavily!—for twenty years have stiffened his legs since he came down—but he knows it not. Stay, Wakefield! Would you go to the sole home that is left you? Then step into your grave! The door opens. As he passes in, we have a parting glimpse of his visage, and recognize the crafty smile, which was the precursor of the little joke that he has ever since been playing off at his wife's expense. How unmercifully has he quizzed the poor woman! Well, a good night's rest to Wakefield!

This happy event—supposing it to be such—could only have occurred at an unpremeditated moment. We will not follow our friend across the threshold. He has left us much food for thought, a portion of which shall lend its wisdom to a moral, and be shaped into a figure. Amid the seeming confusion of our mysterious world, individuals are so nicely adjusted to a system, and systems to one another and to a whole, that, by stepping aside for a moment, a man exposes himself to a fearful risk of losing his place forever. Like Wakefield, he may become, as it were, the Outcast of the Universe.

THE MINISTER'S BLACK VEIL
A Parable
[1837 (1835)]

Another clergyman in New England, Mr. Joseph Moody, of York, Maine, who died about eighty years since, made himself remarkable by the same eccentricity that is here related of the Reverend Mr. Hooper. In his case, however, the symbol had a different import. In early life he had accidentally killed a beloved friend; and from that day till the hour of his own death, he hid his face from men.—Hawthorne's note.

THE SEXTON stood in the porch of Milford meeting-house, pulling busily at the bell-rope. The old people of the village came stooping along the street. Children, with bright faces, tripped merrily beside their parents, or mimicked a graver gait, in the conscious dignity of their Sunday clothes. Spruce bachelors looked sidelong at the pretty maidens, and fancied that the Sabbath sunshine made them prettier than on week days. When the throng had mostly streamed into the porch, the sexton began to toll the bell, keeping his eye on the Reverend Mr. Hooper's door. The first glimpse of the clergyman's figure was the signal for the bell to cease its summons.

"But what has good Parson Hooper got upon his face?" cried the sexton in astonishment.

All within hearing immediately turned about, and beheld the semblance of Mr. Hooper, pacing slowly his meditative way towards the meeting-house. With one accord they started, expressing more wonder than if some strange minister were coming to dust the cushions of Mr. Hooper's pulpit.

"Are you sure it is our parson?" inquired Goodman Gray of the sexton.

"Of a certainty it is good Mr. Hooper," replied the sexton. "He was to have exchanged pulpits with Parson Shute, of Westbury; but Parson Shute sent to excuse himself yesterday, being to preach a funeral sermon."

The cause of so much amazement may appear sufficiently slight. Mr. Hooper, a gentlemanly person, of about thirty, though still a bachelor, was dressed with due clerical neatness, as if a careful wife had starched his band, and brushed the weekly dust from his Sunday's garb. There was but one thing remarkable in his appearance. Swathed about his forehead, and hanging down over his face, so low as to be shaken by his breath, Mr. Hooper had on a black veil. On a nearer view it seemed to consist of two folds of crape, which entirely concealed his features, except the mouth and chin, but probably did not intercept his sight, further than to give a darkened aspect to all living and inanimate things. With this gloomy shade before him, good Mr. Hooper walked onward, at a slow and quiet pace, stooping somewhat, and looking on the ground, as is customary with abstracted men, yet nodding kindly to those of his parishioners who still waited on the meeting-house steps. But so wonder-struck were they that his greeting hardly met with a return.

"I can't really feel as if good Mr. Hooper's face was behind that piece of crape," said the sexton.

"I don't like it," muttered an old woman, as she hobbled into the meeting-house. "He has changed himself into something awful, only by hiding his face."

"Our parson has gone mad!" cried Goodman Gray, following him across the threshold.

A rumor of some unaccountable phenomenon had preceded Mr. Hooper into the meeting-house, and set all the congregation astir. Few could refrain from twisting their heads towards the door; many stood upright, and turned directly about; while several little boys clambered upon the seats, and came down again with a terrible racket. There was a general bustle, a rustling of the women's gowns and shuffling of the men's feet, greatly at variance with that hushed repose which should attend the entrance of the minister. But Mr. Hooper appeared not to notice the perturbation of his people. He entered with an almost noiseless step, bent his head mildly to the pews on each side, and bowed as he passed his oldest parishioner, a white-haired great-grandsire, who occupied an arm-chair in the centre of the aisle. It was strange to observe how slowly this venerable man became conscious of something singular in the appearance of his pastor. He seemed not fully to partake of the prevailing wonder, till Mr. Hooper had ascended the stairs, and showed himself in the pulpit, face to face with his congregation, except for the black veil. That mysterious emblem was never once withdrawn. It shook with his measured breath, as he gave out the psalm; it threw its obscurity between him and the holy page, as he read the Scriptures; and while he prayed, the veil lay heavily on his uplifted countenance. Did he seek to hide it from the dread Being whom he was addressing?

Such was the effect of this simple piece of crape, that more than one woman of delicate nerves was forced to leave the meeting-house. Yet perhaps the pale-faced congregation was almost as fearful a sight to the minister, as his black veil to them.

Mr. Hooper had the reputation of a good preacher, but not an energetic one: he strove to win his people heavenward by mild, persuasive influences, rather than to drive them thither by the thunders of the Word. The sermon which he now delivered was marked by the same characteristics of style and manner as the general series of his pulpit oratory. But there was something, either in the sentiment of the discourse itself, or in the imagination of the auditors, which made it greatly the most powerful effort that they had ever heard from their pastor's lips. It was tinged, rather more darkly than usual, with the gentle gloom of Mr. Hooper's temperament. The subject had reference to secret sin, and those sad mysteries which we hide from our nearest and dearest, and would fain conceal from our own consciousness, even forgetting that the Omniscient can detect them. A subtle power was breathed into his words. Each member of the con-gregation, the most innocent girl, and the man of hardened breast, felt as if the preacher had crept upon them, behind his awful veil, and discovered their hoarded iniquity of deed or thought. Many spread their clasped hands on their bosoms. There was nothing terrible in what Mr. Hooper said, at least, no violence; and yet, with every tremor of his melancholy voice, the hearers quaked. An unsought pathos came hand in hand with awe. So sensible were the audience of some unwonted attribute in their minister, that they longed for a breath of wind to blow aside the veil, almost believing that a stranger's visage would be discovered, though the form, gesture, and voice were those of Mr. Hooper.

At the close of the services, the people hurried out with indecorous confusion, eager to communicate their pent-up amazement, and conscious of lighter spirits the moment they lost sight of the black veil. Some gathered in little circles, huddled closely together, with their mouths all whispering in the centre; some went homeward alone, wrapt in silent meditation; some talked loudly, and profaned the Sabbath day with ostentatious laughter. A few shook their sagacious heads, intimating that they could penetrate the mystery; while one or two affirmed that there was no mystery at all, but only that Mr. Hooper's eyes were so weakened by the midnight lamp, as to require a shade. After a brief interval, forth came good Mr. Hooper also, in the rear of his flock. Turning his veiled face from one group to another, he paid due reverence to the hoary heads, saluted the middle aged with kind dignity as their friend and spiritual guide, greeted the young with mingled authority and love, and laid his hands on the little chidlren's heads to bless them. Such was always his custom on the Sabbath day. Strange and bewildered looks repaid him for his courtesy. None, as on former occasions, aspired to the honor of walking by their pastor's side. Old Squire Saunders, doubtless by an accidental lapse of memory, neglected to invite Mr. Hooper to his table, where the good clergyman had been wont to bless the food, almost every Sunday since his settlement. He returned, therefore, to the parsonage, and, at the moment of closing the door, was observed to look back upon the people, all of whom had their eyes fixed upon the minister. A sad smile gleamed faintly from beneath the black veil, and flickered about his mouth, glimmering as he disappeared.

"How strange," said a lady, "that a simple black veil, such as any woman might wear on her bonnet, should become such a terrible thing on Mr. Hooper's face!"

"Something must surely be amiss with Mr. Hooper's intellects," observed her husband, the physician of the village. "But the strangest part of the affair is the effect of this vagary, even on a sober-minded man like myself. The black veil, though it covers only our pastor's face, throws its influence over his whole person, and makes him ghostlike from head to foot. Do you not feel it so?"

"Truly do I," replied the lady; "and I would not be alone with him for the world. I wonder he is not afraid to be alone with himself!"

"Men sometimes are so," said her husband.

The afternoon service was attended with similar circumstances. At its conclusion, the bell tolled for the funeral of a young lady. The relatives and friends were assembled in the house, and the more distant acquaintances stood about the door, speaking of the good qualities of the deceased, when their talk was interrupted by the appearance of Mr. Hooper, still covered with his black veil. It was now an appropriate emblem. The clergyman stepped into the room where the corpse was laid, and bent over the coffin, to take a last farewell of his deceased parishioner. As he stooped, the veil hung straight down from his forehead, so that, if her eyelids had not been closed forever, the dead maiden might have seen his face. Could Mr. Hooper be fearful of her glance, that he so hastily caught

back the black veil? A person who watched the interview between the dead and living, scrupled not to affirm, that, at the instant when the clergyman's features were disclosed, the corpse had slightly shuddered, rustling the shroud and muslin cap, though the countenance retained the composure of death. A superstitious old woman was the only witness of this prodigy. From the coffin Mr. Hooper passed into the chamber of the mourners, and thence to the head of the staircase, to make the funeral prayer. It was a tender and heart-dissolving prayer, full of sorrow, yet so imbued with celestial hopes, that the music of a heavenly harp, swept by the fingers of the dead, seemed faintly to be heard among the saddest accents of the minister. The people trembled, though they but darkly understood him when he prayed that they, and himself, and all of mortal race, might be ready, as he trusted this young maiden had been, for the dreadful hour that should snatch the veil from their faces. The bearers went heavily forth, and the mourners followed, saddening all the street, with the dead before them, and Mr. Hooper in his black veil behind.

"Why do you look back?" said one in the procession to his partner.

"I had a fancy," replied she, "that the minister and the maiden's spirit were walking hand in hand."

"And so had I, at the same moment," said the other.

That night, the handsomest couple in Milford village were to be joined in wedlock. Though reckoned a melancholy man, Mr. Hooper had a placid cheerfulness for such occasions, which often excited a sympathetic smile where livelier merriment would have been thrown away. There was no quality of his disposition which made him more beloved than this. The company at the wedding awaited his arrival with impatience, trusting that the strange awe, which had gathered over him throughout the day, would now be dispelled. But such was not the result. When Mr. Hooper came, the first thing that their eyes rested on was the same horrible black veil, which had added deeper gloom to the funeral, and could portend nothing but evil to the wedding. Such was its immediate effect on the guests that a cloud seemed to have rolled duskily from beneath the black crape, and dimmed the light of the candles. The bridal pair stood up before the minister. But the bride's cold fingers quivered in the tremulous hand of the bridegroom, and her deathlike paleness caused a whisper that the maiden who had been buried a few hours before was come from her grave to be married. If ever another wedding were so dismal, it was that famous one where they tolled the wedding knell.[1] After performing the ceremony, Mr. Hooper raised a glass of wine to his lips, wishing happiness to the new-married couple in a strain of mild pleasantry that ought to have brightened the features of the guests, like a cheerful gleam from the hearth. At that instant, catching a glimpse of his figure in the looking-glass, the black veil involved his own spirit in the horror with which it overwhelmed all others. His frame shuddered, his lips grew white, he spilt the untasted wine upon the carpet, and rushed forth into the darkness. For the Earth, too, had on her Black Veil.

The next day, the whole village of Milford talked of little else than Parson Hooper's black veil. That, and the mystery concealed behind it, supplied a topic for discussion between acquaintances meeting in the street, and good women gossiping at their open windows. It was the first item of news that the tavern-keeper told to his guests. The children babbled of it on their way to school. One imitative little imp covered his face with an old black handkerchief, thereby so affrighting his playmates that the panic seized himself, and he well-nigh lost his wits by his own waggery.

It was remarkable that of all the busybodies and impertinent people in the parish, not one ventured to put the plain question to Mr. Hooper, wherefore he did this thing. Hitherto, whenever there appeared the slightest call for such interference, he had never lacked advisers, nor shown himself averse to be guided by their judgment. If he erred at all, it was by so painful a degree of self-distrust, that even the mildest censure would lead him to consider an indifferent action as a crime. Yet, though so well acquainted with this amiable weakness, no individual among his parishioners chose to make the black veil a subject of friendly remonstrance. There was a feeling of dread, neither plainly confessed nor carefully concealed, which caused each to shift the responsibility upon another, till at length it was found expedient to send a deputation of the church, in order to deal with Mr. Hooper about the mystery, before it should grow into a scandal. Never did an embassy so ill discharge its duties. The minister received them with friendly courtesy, but became silent, after they were seated, leaving to his visitors the whole burden of introducing their important business. The topic, it might be supposed, was obvious enough. There was the black veil swathed round Mr. Hooper's forehead, and concealing every feature above his placid mouth, on which, at times, they could perceive the glimmering of a melancholy smile. But that piece of crape, to their imagination, seemed to hang down before his heart, the symbol of a fearful secret between him and them. Were the veil but cast aside, they might speak freely of it, but not till then. Thus they sat a considerable time, speechless, confused, and shrinking uneasily from Mr. Hooper's eye, which they felt to be fixed upon them with an invisible glance. Finally, the deputies returned abashed to their constituents, pronouncing the matter too weighty to be handled, except by a council of the churches, if, indeed, it might not require a general synod.

But there was one person in the village unappalled by the awe with which the black veil had impressed all beside herself. When the deputies returned without an explana-

---

[1] The reference is to an incident in another of Hawthorne's *Twice-Told Tales*, "The Wedding Knell."

tion, or even venturing to demand one, she, with the calm energy of her character, determined to chase away the strange cloud that appeared to be settling round Mr. Hooper, every moment more darkly than before. As his plighted wife, it should be her privilege to know what the black veil concealed. At the minister's first visit, therefore, she entered upon the subject with a direct simplicity, which made the task easier both for him and her. After he had seated himself, she fixed her eyes steadfastly upon the veil, but could discern nothing of the dreadful gloom that had so overawed the multitude: it was but a double fold of crape, hanging down from his forehead to his mouth, and slightly stirring with his breath.

"No," said she aloud, and smiling, "there is nothing terrible in this piece of crape, except that it hides a face which I am always glad to look upon. Come, good sir, let the sun shine from behind the cloud. First lay aside your black veil: then tell me why you put it on."

Mr. Hooper's smile glimmered faintly.

"There is an hour to come," said he, "when all of us shall cast aside our veils. Take it not amiss, beloved friend, if I wear this piece of crape till then."

"Your words are a mystery, too," returned the young lady. "Take away the veil from them, at least."

"Elizabeth, I will," said he, "so far as my vow may suffer me. Know, then, this veil is a type and a symbol, and I am bound to wear it ever, both in light and darkness, in solitude and before the gaze of multitudes, and as with strangers, so with my familiar friends. No mortal eye will see it withdrawn. This dismal shade must separate me from the world: even you, Elizabeth, can never come behind it!"

"What grievous affliction hath befallen you," she earnestly inquired, "that you should thus darken your eyes forever?"

"If it be a sign of mourning," replied Mr. Hooper, "I, perhaps, like most other mortals, have sorrows dark enough to be typified by a black veil."

"But what if the world will not believe that it is the type of an innocent sorrow?" urged Elizabeth. "Beloved and respected as you are, there may be whispers that you hide your face under the consciousness of secret sin. For the sake of your holy office, do away this scandal!"

The color rose into her cheeks as she intimated the nature of the rumors that were already abroad in the village. But Mr. Hooper's mildness did not forsake him. He even smiled again—that same sad smile, which always appeared like a faint glimmering of light, proceeding from the obscurity beneath the veil.

"If I hide my face for sorrow, there is cause enough," he merely replied; "and if I cover it for secret sin, what mortal might not do the same?"

And with this gentle, but unconquerable obstinacy did he resist all her entreaties. At length Elizabeth sat silent. For a few moments she appeared lost in thought, considering, probably, what new methods might be tried to withdraw her lover from so dark a fantasy, which, if it had no other meaning, was perhaps a symptom of mental disease. Though of a firmer character than his own, the tears rolled down her cheeks. But, in an instant, as it were, a new feeling took the place of sorrow: her eyes were fixed insensibly on the black veil, when, like a sudden twilight in the air, its terrors fell around her. She arose, and stood trembling before him.

"And do you feel it then, at last?" said he mournfully.

She made no reply, but covered her eyes with her hand, and turned to leave the room. He rushed forward and caught her arm.

"Have patience with me, Elizabeth!" cried he, passionately. "Do not desert me, though this veil must be between us here on earth. Be mine, and hereafter there shall be no veil over my face, no darkness between our souls! It is but a mortal veil—it is not for eternity! O! you know not how lonely I am, and how frightened, to be alone behind my black veil. Do not leave me in this miserable obscurity forever!"

"Lift the veil but once, and look me in the face," said she.

"Never! It cannot be!" replied Mr. Hooper.

"Then farewell!" said Elizabeth.

She withdrew her arm from his grasp, and slowly departed, pausing at the door, to give one long shuddering gaze, that seemed almost to penetrate the mystery of the black veil. But, even amid his grief, Mr. Hooper smiled to think that only a material emblem had separated him from happiness, though the horrors, which it shadowed forth, must be drawn darkly between the fondest of lovers.

From that time no attempts were made to remove Mr. Hooper's black veil, or, by a direct appeal, to discover the secret which it was supposed to hide. By persons who claimed a superiority to popular prejudice, it was reckoned merely an eccentric whim, such as often mingles with the sober actions of men otherwise rational, and tinges them all with its own semblance of insanity. But with the multitude, good Mr. Hooper was irreparably a bugbear. He could not walk the street with any peace of mind, so conscious was he that the gentle and timid would turn aside to avoid him, and that others would make it a point of hardihood to throw themselves in his way. The impertinence of the latter class compelled him to give up his customary walk at sunset to the burial ground; for when he leaned pensively over the gate, there would always be faces behind the gravestones, peeping at his black veil. A fable went the rounds that the stare of the dead people drove him thence. It grieved him, to the very depth of his kind heart, to observe how the children fled from his approach, breaking up their merriest sports, while his melancholy figure was yet afar off. Their instinctive dread caused him to feel more strongly than aught else, that a preternatural horror was interwoven with the threads of the black crape. In truth, his own antipathy to the veil was known to be so great, that he

never willingly passed before a mirror, nor stooped to drink at a still fountain, lest, in its peaceful bosom, he should be affrighted by himself. This was what gave plausibility to the whispers, that Mr. Hooper's conscience tortured him for some great crime too horrible to be entirely concealed, or otherwise than so obscurely intimated. Thus, from beneath the black veil, there rolled a cloud into the sunshine, an ambiguity of sin or sorrow, which enveloped the poor minister, so that love or sympathy could never reach him. It was said that ghost and fiend consorted with him there. With self-shudderings and outward terrors, he walked continually in its shadow, groping darkly within his own soul, or gazing through a medium that saddened the whole world. Even the lawless wind, it was believed, respected his dreadful secret, and never blew aside the veil. But still good Mr. Hooper sadly smiled at the pale visages of the worldly throng as he passed by.

Among all its bad influences, the black veil had the one desirable effect, of making its wearer a very efficient clergyman. By the aid of his mysterious emblem—for there was no other apparent cause—he became a man of awful power over souls that were in agony for sin. His converts always regarded him with a dread peculiar to themselves, affirming, though but figuratively, that, before he brought them to celestial light, they had been with him behind the black veil. Its gloom, indeed, enabled him to sympathize with all dark affections. Dying sinners cried aloud for Mr. Hooper, and would not yield their breath till he appeared; though ever, as he stooped to whisper consolation, they shuddered at the veiled face so near their own. Such were the terrors of the black veil, even when Death had bared his visage! Strangers came long distances to attend service at his church, with the mere idle purpose of gazing at his figure, because it was forbidden them to behold his face. But many were made to quake ere they departed!

Once, during Governor Belcher's administration,[2] Mr. Hooper was appointed to preach the election sermon. Covered with his black veil, he stood before the chief magistrate, the council, and the representatives, and wrought so deep an impression, that the legislative measures of that year were characterized by all the gloom and piety of our earliest ancestral sway.

In this manner Mr. Hooper spent a long life, irreproachable in outward act, yet shrouded in dismal suspicions; kind and loving, though unloved, and dimly feared; a man apart from men, shunned in their health and joy, but ever summoned to their aid in mortal anguish. As years wore on, shedding their snows above his sable veil, he acquired a name throughout the New England churches, and they called him Father Hooper. Nearly all his parishioners, who were of mature age when he was settled, had been borne away by many a funeral: he had one congregation in the church, and a more crowded one in the churchyard; and having wrought so late into the evening, and done his work so well, it was now good Father Hooper's turn to rest.

Several persons were visible by the shaded candle-light, in the death chamber of the old clergyman. Natural connections he had none. But there was the decorously grave, though unmoved physician, seeking only to mitigate the last pangs of the patient whom he could not save. There were the deacons, and other eminently pious members of his church. There, also, was the Reverend Mr. Clark, of Westbury, a young and zealous divine, who had ridden in haste to pray by the bedside of the expiring minister. There was the nurse, no hired handmaiden of death, but one whose calm affection had endured thus long in secrecy, in solitude, amid the chill of age, and would not perish, even at the dying hour. Who, but Elizabeth! And there lay the hoary head of good Father Hooper upon the death pillow, with the black veil still swathed about his brow, and reaching down over his face, so that each more difficult gasp of his faint breath caused it to stir. All through life that piece of crape had hung between him and the world: it had separated him from cheerful brotherhood and woman's love, and kept him in that saddest of all prisons, his own heart: and still it lay upon his face, as if to deepen the gloom of his darksome chamber, and shade him from the sunshine of eternity.

For some time previous, his mind had been confused, wavering doubtfully between the past and the present, and hovering forward, as it were, at intervals, into the indistinctness of the world to come. There had been feverish turns, which tossed him from side to side, and wore away what little strength he had. But in his most convulsive struggles, and in the wildest vagaries of his intellect, when no other thought retained its sober influence, he still showed an awful solicitude lest the black veil should slip aside. Even if his bewildered soul could have forgotten, there was a faithful woman at his pillow, who, with averted eyes, would have covered that aged face, which she had last beheld in the comeliness of manhood. At length the death-stricken old man lay quietly in the torpor of mental and bodily exhaustion, with an imperceptible pulse, and breath that grew fainter and fainter, except when a long, deep, and irregular inspiration seemed to prelude the flight of his spirit.

The minister of Westbury approached the bedside.

"Venerable Father Hooper," said he, "the moment of your release is at hand. Are you ready for the lifting of the veil that shuts in time from eternity?"

Father Hooper at first replied merely by a feeble motion of his head; then, apprehensive, perhaps, that his meaning might be doubtful, he exerted himself to speak.

"Yea," said he, in faint accents, "my

<hr />

[2] Jonathan Belcher (1681-1757) was governor of Massachusetts and New Hampshire 1730-41.

soul hath a patient weariness until that veil be lifted."

"And is it fitting," resumed the Reverend Mr. Clark, "that a man so given to prayer, of such a blameless example, holy in deed and thought, so far as mortal judgment may pronounce; is it fitting that a father in the church should leave a shadow on his memory, that may seem to blacken a life so pure? I pray you, my venerable brother, let not this thing be! Suffer us to be gladdened by your triumphant aspect as you go to your reward. Before the veil of eternity be lifted, let me cast aside this black veil from your face!"

And thus speaking, the Reverend Mr. Clark bent forward to reveal the mystery of so many years. But, exerting a sudden energy, that made all the beholders stand aghast, Father Hooper snatched both his hands from beneath the bedclothes, and pressed them strongly on the black veil, resolute to struggle, if the minister of Westbury would contend with a dying man.

"Never!" cried the veiled clergyman. "On earth, never!"

"Dark old man!" exclaimed the affrighted minister, "with what horrible crime upon your soul are you now passing to the judgment?"

Father Hooper's breath heaved; it rattled in his throat; but, with a mighty effort, grasping forward with his hands, he caught hold of life, and held it back till he should speak. He even raised himself in bed; and there he sat, shivering with the arms of death around him, while the black veil hung down, awful, at that last moment, in the gathered terrors of a lifetime. And yet the faint, sad smile, so often there, now seemed to glimmer from its obscurity, and linger on Father Hooper's lips.

"Why do you tremble at me alone?" cried he, turning his veiled face round the circle of pale spectators. "Tremble also at each other! Have men avoided me, and women shown no pity, and children screamed and fled, only for my black veil? What, but the mystery which it obscurely typifies, has made this piece of crape so

awful? When the friend shows his inmost heart to his friend; the lover to his best beloved; when man does not vainly shrink from the eye of his Creator, loathsomely treasuring up the secret of his sin; then deem me a monster, for the symbol beneath which I have lived, and die! I look around me, and, lo! on every visage a Black Veil!"

While his auditors shrank from one another, in mutual affright, Father Hooper fell back upon his pillow, a veiled corpse, with a faint smile lingering on the lips. Still veiled, they laid him in his coffin, and a veiled corpse they bore him to the grave. The grass of many years has sprung up and withered on that grave, the burial stone is moss-grown, and good Mr. Hooper's face is dust; but awful is still the thought that it mouldered beneath the Black Veil!

THE MAYPOLE OF MERRY MOUNT
[1837 (1835)]

There is an admirable foundation for a philosophic romance in the curious history of the early settlement of Mount Wollaston, or Merry Mount. In the slight sketch here attempted, the facts, recorded on the grave pages of our New England annalists, have wrought themselves, almost spontaneously, into a sort of allegory. The masques, mummeries, and festive customs, described in the text, are in accordance with the manners of the age. Authority on these points may be found in Strutt's Book of English Sports and Pastimes.—Hawthorne's note.

BRIGHT were the days at Merry Mount, when the Maypole was the banner staff of that gay colony! They who reared it, should their banner be triumphant, were to pour sunshine over New England's rugged hills, and scatter flower seeds throughout the soil. Jollity and gloom were contending for an empire. Midsummer eve had come, bringing deep verdure to the forest, and roses in her lap, of a more vivid hue than the tender buds of Spring. But May, or her mirthful spirit, dwelt all the year round at Merry Mount, sporting with the Summer months, and revelling with Autumn, and basking in the glow of Winter's fireside. Through a world of toil and care she flitted with a dreamlike smile, and came hither to find a home among the lightsome hearts of Merry Mount.

Never had the Maypole been so gayly decked as at sunset on midsummer eve. This venerated emblem was a pine-tree, which had preserved the slender grace of youth, while it equalled the loftiest height of the old wood monarchs. From its top streamed a silken banner, colored like the rainbow. Down nearly to the ground the pole was dressed with birchen boughs, and others of the liveliest green, and some with silvery leaves, fastened by ribbons that fluttered in fantastic knots of twenty different colors, but no sad ones. Garden flowers, and blossoms of the wilderness, laughed gladly forth amid the verdure, so fresh and dewy that they must have grown by magic on that happy pine-tree. Where this green and flowery splendor terminated, the shaft of the Maypole was stained with the seven brilliant hues of the banner at its top. On the lowest green bough hung an abundant wreath of roses, some that had been gathered in the sunniest spots of the forest, and others, of still richer blush, which the colonists had reared from English seed. O, people of the Golden Age, the chief of your husbandry was to raise flowers!

But what was the wild throng that stood hand in hand about the Maypole? It could not be that the fauns and nymphs, when driven from their classic groves and homes of ancient fable, had sought refuge, as all the persecuted did, in the fresh woods of the West. These were Gothic monsters, though perhaps of Grecian ancestry. On the shoulders of a comely youth uprose the head and branching antlers of a stag; a second, human in all other points, had the grim visage of a wolf; a third, still with the trunk and limbs of a mortal man, showed the beard and horns of a venerable

he-goat. There was the likeness of a bear erect, brute in all but his hind legs, which were adorned with pink silk stockings. And here again, almost as wondrous, stood a real bear of the dark forest, lending each of his fore paws to the grasp of a human hand, and as ready for the dance as any in that circle. His inferior nature rose half way, to meet his companions as they stooped. Other faces wore the similitude of man or woman, but distorted or extravagant, with red noses pendulous before their mouths, which seemed of awful depth, and stretched from ear to ear in an eternal fit of laughter. Here might be seen the Salvage Man, well known in heraldry, hairy as a baboon, and girdled with green leaves. By his side, a noble figure, but still a counterfeit, appeared an Indian hunter, with feathery crest and wampum belt. Many of this strange company wore foolscaps, and had little bells appended to their garments, tinkling with a silvery sound, responsive to the inaudible music of their gleesome spirits. Some youths and maidens were of soberer garb, yet well maintained their places in the irregular throng by the expression of wild revelry upon their features. Such were the colonists of Merry Mount, as they stood in the broad smile of sunset round their venerated Maypole.

Had a wanderer, bewildered in the melancholy forest, heard their mirth, and stolen a half-affrighted glance, he might have fancied them the crew of Comus,[1] some already transformed to brutes, some midway between man and beast, and the others rioting in the flow of tipsy jollity that foreran the change. But a band of Puritans, who watched the scene, invisible themselves, compared the masques to those devils and ruined souls with whom their superstition peopled the black wilderness.

Within the ring of monsters appeared the two airiest forms that had ever trodden on any more solid footing than a purple and golden cloud. One was a youth in

[1] The reference is to Milton's *Comus*, lines 92 ff.

glistening apparel, with a scarf of the rainbow pattern crosswise on his breast. His right hand held a gilded staff, the ensign of high dignity among the revellers, and his left grasped the slender fingers of a fair maiden, not less gayly decorated than himself. Bright roses glowed in contrast with the dark and glossy curls of each, and were scattered round their feet, or had sprung up spontaneously there. Behind this lightsome couple, so close to the Maypole that its boughs shaded his jovial face, stood the figure of an English priest, canonically dressed, yet decked with flowers, in heathen fashion, and wearing a chaplet of the native vine leaves. By the riot of his rolling eye, and the pagan decorations of his holy garb, he seemed the wildest monster there, and the very Comus of the crew.

"Votaries of the Maypole," cried the flower-decked priest, "merrily, all day long, have the woods echoed to your mirth. But be this your merriest hour, my hearts! Lo, here stand the Lord and Lady of the May, whom I, a clerk of Oxford, and high priest of Merry Mount, am presently to join in holy matrimony. Up with your nimble spirits, ye morris-dancers, green men, and glee maidens, bears and wolves, and horned gentlemen! Come; a chorus now, rich with the old mirth of Merry England, and the wilder glee of this fresh forest; and then a dance, to show the youthful pair what life is made of, and how airily they should go through it! All ye that love the Maypole, lend your voices to the nuptial song of the Lord and Lady of the May!"

This wedlock was more serious than most affairs of Merry Mount, where jest and delusion, trick and fantasy, kept up a continual carnival. The Lord and Lady of the May, though their titles must be laid down at sunset, were really and truly to be partners for the dance of life, beginning the measure that same bright eve. The wreath of roses, that hung from the lowest green bough of the Maypole, had been twined for them, and would be thrown over both their heads, in symbol of their flowery

union. When the priest had spoken, therefore, a riotous uproar burst from the rout of monstrous figures.

"Begin you the stave, reverend Sir," cried they all; "and never did the woods ring to such a merry peal as we of the Maypole shall send up!"

Immediately a prelude of pipe, cithern, and viol, touched with practised minstrelsy, began to play from a neighboring thicket, in such a mirthful cadence that the boughs of the Maypole quivered to the sound. But the May Lord, he of the gilded staff, chancing to look into his Lady's eyes, was wonder struck at the almost pensive glance that met his own.

"Edith, sweet Lady of the May," whispered he reproachfully, "is yon wreath of roses a garland to hang above our graves, that you look so sad? O, Edith, this is our golden time! Tarnish it not by any pensive shadow of the mind; for it may be that nothing of futurity will be brighter than the mere remembrance of what is now passing."

"That was the very thought that saddened me! How came it in your mind too?" said Edith, in a still lower tone than he, for it was high treason to be sad at Merry Mount. "Therefore do I sigh amid this festive music. And besides, dear Edgar, I struggle as with a dream, and fancy that these shapes of our jovial friends are visionary, and their mirth unreal, and that we are no true Lord and Lady of the May. What is the mystery in my heart?"

Just then, as if a spell had loosened them, down came a little shower of withering rose leaves from the Maypole. Alas, for the young lovers! No sooner had their hearts glowed with real passion than they were sensible of something vague and unsubstantial in their former pleasures, and felt a dreary presentiment of inevitable change. From the moment that they truly loved, they had subjected themselves to earth's doom of care and sorrow, and troubled joy, and had no more a home at Merry Mount. That was Edith's mystery. Now leave we the priest to marry them,

and the masquers to sport round the Maypole, till the last sunbeam be withdrawn
from its summit, and the shadows of the
forest mingle gloomily in the dance. Meanwhile, we may discover who these gay people were.

Two hundred years ago, and more, the
old world and its inhabitants became mutually weary of each other. Men voyaged
by thousands to the West: some to barter
glass beads, and such like jewels, for the
furs of the Indian hunter; some to conquer virgin empires; and one stern band to
pray. But none of these motives had much
weight with the colonists of Merry Mount.
Their leaders were men who had sported
so long with life, that when Thought and
Wisdom came, even these unwelcome guests
were led astray by the crowd of vanities
which they should have put to flight. Erring Thought and perverted Wisdom were
made to put on masques, and play the
fool. The men of whom we speak, after
losing the heart's fresh gayety, imagined
a wild philosophy of pleasure, and came
hither to act out their latest day-dream.
They gathered followers from all that
giddy tribe whose whole life is like the
festal days of soberer men. In their train
were minstrels, not unknown in London
streets; wandering players, whose theatres
had been the halls of noblemen; mummers,
rope-dancers, and mountebanks, who would
long be missed at wakes, church ales, and
fairs; in a word, mirth makers of every
sort, such as abounded in that age, but now
began to be discountenanced by the rapid
growth of Puritanism. Light had their
footsteps been on land, and as lightly
they came across the sea. Many had been
maddened by their previous troubles into
a gay despair; others were as madly gay
in the flush of youth, like the May Lord
and his Lady; but whatever might be the
quality of their mirth, old and young were
gay at Merry Mount. The young deemed
themselves happy. The elder spirits, if they
knew that mirth was but the counterfeit
of happiness, yet followed the false shadow
wilfully, because at least her garments
glittered brightest. Sworn triflers of a
lifetime, they would not venture among the
sober truths of life not even to be truly
blest.

All the hereditary pastimes of Old England were transplanted hither. The King
of Christmas was duly crowned, and the
Lord of Misrule bore potent sway. On
the Eve of St. John, they felled whole
acres of the forest to make bonfires, and
danced by the blaze all night, crowned with
garlands, and throwing flowers into the
flame. At harvest time, though their crop
was of the smallest, they made an image
with the sheaves of Indian corn, and
wreathed it with autumnal garlands, and
bore it home triumphantly. But what chiefly
characterized the colonists of Merry Mount
was their veneration for the Maypole. It
has made their true history a poet's tale.
Spring decked the hallowed emblem with
young blossoms and fresh green boughs;
Summer brought roses of the deepest blush,
and the perfected foliage of the forest;
Autumn enriched it with that red and
yellow gorgeousness which converts each
wildwood leaf into a painted flower; and
Winter silvered it with sleet, and hung it
round with icicles, till it flashed in the
cold sunshine, itself a frozen sunbeam.
Thus each alternate season did homage to
the Maypole, and paid it a tribute of its
own richest splendor. Its votaries danced
round it, once, at least, in every month;
sometimes they called it their religion, or
their altar; but always, it was the banner
staff of Merry Mount.

Unfortunately, there were men in the
new world of a sterner faith than these
Maypole worshippers. Not far from Merry
Mount was a settlement of Puritans, most
dismal wretches, who said their prayers before daylight, and then wrought in the
forest or the cornfield till evening made
it prayer time again. Their weapons were
always at hand to shoot down the straggling savage. When they met in conclave,
it was never to keep up the old English
mirth, but to hear sermons three hours
long, or to proclaim bounties on the heads

of wolves and the scalps of Indians. Their festivals were fast days, and their chief pastime the singing of psalms. Woe to the youth or maiden who did but dream of a dance! The selectman nodded to the constable; and there sat the light-heeled reprobate in the stocks; or if he danced, it was round the whipping-post, which might be termed the Puritan Maypole.

A party of these grim Puritans, toiling through the difficult woods, each with a horseload of iron armor to burden his footsteps, would sometimes draw near the sunny precincts of Merry Mount. There were the silken colonists, sporting round their Maypole; perhaps teaching a bear to dance, or striving to communicate their mirth to the grave Indians; or masquerading in the skins of deer and wolves, which they had hunted for that especial purpose. Often, the whole colony were playing at blindman's buff, magistrates and all, with their eyes bandaged, except a single scapegoat, whom the blinded sinners pursued by the tinkling of the bells at his garments. Once, it is said, they were seen following a flower-decked corpse, with merriment and festive music, to his grave. But did the dead man laugh? In their quietest times, they sang ballads and told tales, for the edification of their pious visitors; or perplexed them with juggling tricks; or grinned at them through horse collars; and when sport itself grew wearisome, they made game of their own stupidity, and began a yawning match. At the very least of these enormities, the men of iron shook their heads and frowned so darkly that the revellers looked up, imagining that a momentary cloud had overcast the sunshine, which was to be perpetual there. On the other hand, the Puritans affirmed that, when a psalm was pealing from their place of worship, the echo which the forest sent them back seemed often like the chorus of a jolly catch, closing with a roar of laughter. Who but the fiend, and his bond slaves, the crew of Merry Mount, had thus disturbed them? In due time, a feud arose, stern and bitter on one side, and as serious

on the other as anything could be among such light spirits as had sworn allegiance to the Maypole. The future complexion of New England was involved in this important quarrel. Should the grizzly saints establish their jurisdiction over the gay sinners, then would their spirits darken all the clime and make it a land of clouded visages, of hard toil, of sermon and psalm forever. But should the banner staff of Merry Mount be fortunate, sunshine would break upon the hills, and flowers would beautify the forest, and late posterity do homage to the Maypole.

After these authentic passages from history, we return to the nuptials of the Lord and Lady of the May. Alas! we have delayed too long, and must darken our tale too suddenly. As we glance again at the Maypole, a solitary sunbeam is fading from the summit, and leaves only a faint, golden tinge blended with the hues of the rainbow banner. Even that dim light is now withdrawn, relinquishing the whole domain of Merry Mount to the evening gloom, which has rushed so instantaneously from the black surrounding woods. But some of these black shadows have rushed forth in human shape.

Yes, with the setting sun, the last day of mirth had passed from Merry Mount. The ring of gay masquers was disordered and broken; the stag lowered his antlers in dismay; the wolf grew weaker than a lamb; the bells of the morris-dancers tinkled with tremulous affright. The Puritans had played a characteristic part in the Maypole mummeries. Their darksome figures were intermixed with the wild shapes of their foes, and made the scene a picture of the moment, when waking thoughts start up amid the scattered fantasies of a dream. The leader of the hostile party stood in the centre of the circle, while the route of monsters cowered around him, like evil spirits in the presence of a dread magician. No fantastic foolery could look him in the face. So stern was the energy of his aspect, that the whole man, visage, frame, and soul, seemed wrought of iron, gifted with life and thought, yet all of one substance with his headpiece and breastplate. It was the Puritan of Puritans; it was Endicott himself! [2]

"Stand off, priest of Baal!" said he, with a grim frown, and laying no reverent hand upon the surplice. "I know thee, Blackstone! [3] Thou art the man who couldst not abide the rule even of thine own corrupted church, and hast come hither to preach iniquity, and to give example of it in thy life. But now shall it be seen that the Lord hath sanctified this wilderness for his peculiar people. Woe unto them that would defile it! And first, for this flower-decked abomination, the altar of thy worship!"

And with his keen sword Endicott assaulted the hallowed Maypole. Nor long did it resist his arm. It groaned with a dismal sound; it showered leaves and rosebuds upon the remorseless enthusiast; and finally, with all its green boughs and ribbons and flowers, symbolic of departed pleasures, down fell the banner staff of Merry Mount. As it sank, tradition says, the evening sky grew darker, and the woods threw forth a more sombre shadow.

"There," cried Endicott, looking triumphantly on his work, "there lies the only Maypole in New England! The thought is strong within me that, by its fall, is shadowed forth the fate of light and idle mirth makers, amongst us and our posterity. Amen, saith John Endicott."

"Amen!" echoed his followers.

But the votaries of the Maypole gave one groan for their idol. At the sound, the Puritan leader glanced at the crew of Comus, each a figure of broad mirth, yet, at this moment, strangely expressive of sorrow and dismay.

"Valiant captain," quoth Peter Palfrey, the Ancient of the band, "what order shall be taken with the prisoners?"

"I thought not to repent me of cutting down a Maypole," replied Endicott, "yet now I could find in my heart to plant it again, and give each of these bestial pagans one other dance round their idol. It would

have served rarely for a whipping-post!"

"But there are pine-trees enow," suggested the lieutenant.

"True, good Ancient," said the leader. "Wherefore, bind the heathen crew, and bestow on them a small matter of stripes apiece, as earnest of our future justice. Set some of the rogues in the stocks to rest themselves, so soon as Providence shall bring us to one of our own well-ordered settlements, where such accommodations may be found. Further penalties, such as branding and cropping of ears, shall be thought of hereafter."

"How many stripes for the priest?" inquired Ancient Palfrey.

"None as yet," answered Endicott, bending his iron frown upon the culprit. "It must be for the Great and General Court to determine, whether stripes and long imprisonment, and other grievous penalty, may atone for his transgressions. Let him look to himself! For such as violate our civil order, it may be permitted us to show mercy. But woe to the wretch that troubleth our religion!"

"And this dancing bear," resumed the officer. "Must he share the stripes of his fellows?"

"Shoot him through the head!" said the energetic Puritan. "I suspect witchcraft in the beast."

"Here be a couple of shining ones," continued Peter Palfrey, pointing his weapon at the Lord and Lady of the May. "They seem to be of high station among these misdoers. Methinks their dignity will not be fitted with less than a double share of stripes."

Endicott rested on his sword, and closely surveyed the dress and aspect of the hap-

---

[2] John Endicott (c. 1588-1665), governor of Massachusetts Bay after 1644.

[3] Did Governor Endicott speak less positively, we should suspect a mistake here. The Rev. Mr. Blackstone, though an eccentric, is not known to have been an immoral man. We rather doubt his identity with the priest of Merry Mount.—Hawthorne's note.

less pair. There they stood, pale, downcast, and apprehensive. Yet there was an air of mutual support, and of pure affection, seeking aid and giving it, that showed them to be man and wife, with the sanction of a priest upon their love. The youth, in the peril of the moment, had dropped his gilded staff, and thrown his arm about the Lady of the May, who leaned against his breast, too lightly to burden him, but with weight enough to express that their destinies were linked together, for good or evil. They looked first at each other, and then into the grim captain's face. There they stood, in the first hour of wedlock, while the idle pleasures, of which their companions were the emblems, had given place to the sternest cares of life, personified by the dark Puritans. But never had their youthful beauty seemed so pure and high as when its glow was chastened by adversity.

"Youth," said Endicott, "ye stand in an evil case, thou and thy maiden wife. Make ready presently, for I am minded that ye shall both have a token to remember your wedding day!"

"Stern man," cried the May Lord, "how can I move thee? Were the means at hand, I would resist to the death. Being powerless, I entreat! Do with me as thou wilt, but let Edith go untouched!"

"Not so," replied the immitigable zealot. "We are not wont to show an idle courtesy to that sex, which requireth the stricter discipline. What sayest thou, maid? Shall thy silken bridegroom suffer thy share of the penalty, besides his own?"

"Be it death," said Edith, "and lay it all on me!"

Truly, as Endicott had said, the poor lovers stood in a woful case. Their foes were triumphant, their friends captive and abased, their home desolate, the benighted wilderness around them, and a rigorous destiny, in the shape of the Puritan leader, their only guide. Yet the deepening twilight could not altogether conceal that the iron man was softened: he smiled at the fair spectacle of early love; he almost sighed for the inevitable blight of early hopes.

"The troubles of life have come hastily on this young couple," observed Endicott. "We will see how they comport themselves under their present trials ere we burden them with greater. If, among the spoil, there be any garments of a more decent fashion, let them be put upon this May Lord and his Lady, instead of their glistening vanities. Look to it, some of you."

"And shall not the youth's hair be cut?" asked Peter Palfrey, looking with abhorrence at the lovelock and long glossy curls of the young man.

"Crop it forthwith, and that in the true pumpkinshell fashion," answered the captain. "Then bring them along with us, but more gently than their fellows. There be qualities in the youth, which may make him valiant to fight, and sober to toil, and pious to pray; and in the maiden, that may fit her to become a mother in our Israel, bringing up babes in better nurture than her own hath been. Nor think ye, young ones, that they are the happiest, even in our lifetime of a moment, who misspend it in dancing round a Maypole!"

And Endicott, the severest Puritan of all who laid the rock foundation of New England, lifted the wreath of roses from the ruin of the Maypole, and threw it, with his own gauntleted hand, over the heads of the Lord and Lady of the May. It was a deed of prophecy. As the moral gloom of the world overpowers all systematic gayety, even so was their home of wild mirth made desolate amid the sad forest. They returned to it no more. But as their flowery garland was wreathed of the brightest roses that had grown there, so, in the tie that united them, were intertwined all the purest and best of their early joys. They went heavenward, supporting each other along the difficult path which it was their lot to tread, and never wasted one regretful thought on the vanities of Merry Mount.

ENDICOTT AND THE RED CROSS
[1842 (1837)]

AT NOON of an autumnal day, more than two centuries ago, the English colors were displayed by the standard-bearer of the Salem trainband, which had mustered for martial exercise under the orders of John Endicott. It was a period when the religious exiles were accustomed often to buckle on their armor, and practise the handling of their weapons of war. Since the first settlement of New England, its prospects had never been so dismal. The dissensions between Charles the First and his subjects were then, and for several years afterwards, confined to the floor of Parliament. The measures of the King and ministry were rendered more tyrannically violent by an opposition, which had not yet acquired sufficient confidence in its own strength to resist royal injustice with the sword. The bigoted and haughty primate, Laud, Archbishop of Canterbury, controlled the religious affairs of the realm, and was consequently invested with powers which might have wrought the utter ruin of the two Puritan colonies, Plymouth and Massachusetts.[1] There is evidence on record that our forefathers perceived their danger, but were resolved that their infant country should not fall without a struggle, even beneath the giant strength of the King's right arm.

Such was the aspect of the times when the folds of the English banner, with the Red Cross in its field, were flung out over a company of Puritans. Their leader, the famous Endicott, was a man of stern and resolute countenance, the effect of which was heightened by a grizzled beard that swept the upper portion of his breastplate. This piece of armor was so highly polished that the whole surrounding scene had its image in the glittering steel. The central object in the mirrored picture was an edifice of humble architecture with neither steeple nor bell to proclaim it—what nevertheless it was—the house of prayer. A token of the perils of the wilderness was seen in the grim head of a wolf, which had just been slain within the precincts of the town, and according to the regular mode of claiming the bounty, was nailed on the porch of the meeting-house. The blood was still plashing on the doorstep. There happened to be visible, at the same noontide hour, so many other characteristics of the times and manners of the Puritans, that we must endeavor to represent them in a sketch, though far less vividly than they were reflected in the polished breastplate of John Endicott.

In close vicinity to the sacred edifice appeared that important engine of Puritanic authority, the whipping-post—with the soil around it well trodden by the feet of evil doers, who had there been disciplined. At one corner of the meeting-house was the pillory, and at the other the stocks; and, by a singular good fortune for our sketch, the head of an Episcopalian and suspected Catholic was grotesquely incased in the former machine; while a fellow-criminal, who had boisterously quaffed a health to the king, was confined by the legs in the latter. Side by side, on the meeting-house steps, stood a male and female figure. The man was a tall, lean, haggard personification of fanaticism, bearing on his breast this label,—A WANTON GOSPELLER,—which betokened that he had dared to give interpretations of Holy Writ unsanctioned by the infallible judgment of the civil and religious rulers. His aspect showed no lack of zeal to maintain his heterodoxies, even at the stake. The woman wore a cleft stick on her tongue, in appropriate retribution for having wagged that unruly member against the elders of the church; and her countenance and gestures gave much cause to apprehend that, the moment the stick should be removed, a repetition of the offence would demand new ingenuity in chastising it.

---

[1] William Laud (1573-1645), archbishop of Canterbury, 1633-45.

The above-mentioned individuals had been sentenced to undergo their various modes of ignominy, for the space of one hour at noonday. But among the crowd were several whose punishment would be life-long; some, whose ears had been cropped, like those of puppy dogs; others, whose cheeks had been branded with the initials of their misdemeanors; one, with his nostrils slit and seared; and another, with a halter about his neck, which he was forbidden ever to take off, or to conceal beneath his garments. Methinks he must have been grievously tempted to affix the other end of the rope to some convenient beam or bough. There was likewise a young woman, with no mean share of beauty, whose doom it was to wear the letter A on the breast of her gown, in the eyes of all the world and her own children. And even her own children knew what that initial signified. Sporting with her infamy, the lost and desperate creature had embroidered the fatal token in scarlet cloth, with golden thread and the nicest art of needlework; so that the capital A might have been thought to mean Admirable, or anything rather than Adulteress.

Let not the reader argue, from any of these evidences of iniquity, that the times of the Puritans were more vicious than our own, when, as we pass along the very street of this sketch, we discern no badge of infamy on man or woman. It was the policy of our ancestors to search out even the most secret sins, and expose them to shame, without fear or favor, in the broadest light of the noonday sun. Were such the custom now, perchance we might find materials for a no less piquant sketch than the above.

Except the malefactors whom we have described, and the diseased or infirm persons, the whole male population of the town, between sixteen years and sixty, were seen in the ranks of the trainband. A few stately savages, in all the pomp and dignity of the primeval Indian, stood gazing at the spectacle. Their flint-headed arrows were but childish weapons compared with the matchlocks of the Puritans, and would have rattled harmlessly against the steel caps and hammered iron breastplates which inclosed each soldier in an individual fortress. The valiant John Endicott glanced with an eye of pride at his sturdy followers, and prepared to renew the martial toils of the day.

"Come, my stout hearts!" quoth he, drawing his sword. "Let us show these poor heathen that we can handle our weapons like men of might. Well for them, if they put us not to prove it in earnest!"

The iron-breasted company straightened their line, and each man drew the heavy butt of his matchlock close to his left foot, thus awaiting the orders of the captain. But, as Endicott glanced right and left along the front, he discovered a personage at some little distance with whom it behooved him to hold a parley. It was an elderly gentleman, wearing a black cloak and band, and a high-crowned hat, beneath which was a velvet skull-cap, the whole being the garb of a Puritan minister. This reverend person bore a staff which seemed to have been recently cut in the forest, and his shoes were bemired as if he had been travelling on foot through the swamps of the wilderness. His aspect was perfectly that of a pilgrim, heightened also by an apostolic dignity. Just as Endicott perceived him, he laid aside his staff, and stooped to drink at a bubbling fountain which gushed into the sunshine about a score of yards from the corner of the meeting-house. But, ere the good man drank, he turned his face heavenward in thankfulness, and then, holding back his gray beard with one hand, he scooped up his simple draught in the hollow of the other.

"What, ho! good Mr. Williams," shouted Endicott. "You are welcome back again to our town of peace. How does our worthy Governor Winthrop? And what news from Boston?"

"The Governor hath his health, worshipful Sir," answered Roger Williams, now resuming his staff, and drawing near. "And for the news, here is a letter, which, knowing I was to travel hitherward to-day, his Excellency committed to my charge. Belike it contains tidings of much import; for a ship arrived yesterday from England."

Mr. Williams, the minister of Salem and of course known to all the spectators, had now reached the spot where Endicott was standing under the banner of his company, and put the Governor's epistle into his hand. The broad seal was impressed with Winthrop's coat of arms. Endicott hastily unclosed the letter and began to read, while, as his eye passed down the page, a wrathful change came over his manly countenance. The blood glowed through it, till it seemed to be kindling with an internal heat; nor was it unnatural to suppose that his breastplate would likewise become red-hot with the angry fire of the bosom which it covered. Arriving at the conclusion, he shook the letter fiercely in his hand, so that it rustled as loud as the flag above his head.

"Black tidings these, Mr. Williams," said he; "blacker never came to New England. Doubtless you know their purport?"

"Yea, truly," replied Roger Williams; "for the Governor consulted, respecting this matter, with my brethren in the ministry at Boston; and my opinion was likewise asked. And his Excellency entreats you by me, that the news be not suddenly noised abroad, lest the people be stirred up unto some outbreak, and thereby give the King and the Archbishop a handle against us."

"The Governor is a wise man—a wise man, and a meek and moderate," said Endicott, setting his teeth grimly. "Nevertheless, I must do according to my own best judgment. There is neither man, woman, nor child in New England, but has a concern as dear as life in these tidings; and if John Endicott's voice be loud enough, man, woman, and child shall hear them. Soldiers, wheel into a hollow square! Ho, good people! Here are news for one and all of you."

The soldiers closed in around their captain; and he and Roger Williams stood together under the banner of the Red Cross; while the women and the aged men pressed forward, and the mothers held up their children to look Endicott in the face. A few taps of the drum gave signal for silence and attention.

"Fellow-soldiers,—fellow-exiles," began Endicott, speaking under strong excitement, yet powerfully restraining it, "wherefore did ye leave your native country? Wherefore, I say, have we left the green and fertile fields, the cottages, or, perchance, the old gray halls, where we were born and bred, the churchyards where our forefathers lie buried? Wherefore have we come hither to set up our own tombstones in a wilderness? A howling wilderness it is! The wolf and the bear meet us within halloo of our dwellings. The savage lieth in wait for us in the dismal shadow of the woods. The stubborn roots of the trees break our ploughshares, when we would till the earth. Our children cry for bread, and we must dig in the sands of the seashore to satisfy them. Wherefore, I say again, have we sought this country of a rugged soil and wintry sky? Was it not for the enjoyment of our civil rights? Was it not for liberty to worship God according to our conscience?"

"Call you this liberty of conscience?" interrupted a voice on the steps of the meeting-house.

It was the Wanton Gospeller. A sad and quiet smile flitted across the mild visage of Roger Williams. But Endicott, in the excitement of the moment, shook his sword wrathfully at the culprit—an ominous gesture from a man like him.

"What hast thou to do with conscience, thou knave?" cried he. "I said liberty to worship God, not license to profane and ridicule him. Break not in upon my speech, or I will lay thee neck and heels till this time to-morrow! Hearken to me, friends, nor heed that accursed rhapsodist. As I was saying, we have sacrificed all things, and have come to a land whereof the old world hath scarcely heard, that we might make a new world unto ourselves, and painfully seek a path from hence to heaven. But what think ye now? This son of a Scotch tyrant—this grandson of a Papistical and adulterous Scotch woman, whose death proved that a golden crown doth not always save an anointed head from the block"—

"Nay, brother, nay," interposed Mr. Williams; "thy words are not meet for a secret chamber, far less for a public street."

"Hold thy peace, Roger Williams!" answered Endicott, imperiously. "My spirit is wiser than thine, for the business now in hand. I tell ye, fellow-exiles, that Charles of England, and Laud, our bitterest persecutor, arch-priest of Canterbury, are resolute to pursue us even hither. They are taking counsel, saith this letter, to send over a governor-general, in whose breast shall be deposited all the law and equity of the land. They are minded, also, to establish the idolatrous forms of English Episcopacy; so that, when Laud shall kiss the Pope's toe, as cardinal of Rome, he may deliver New England, bound hand and foot, into the power of his master!"

A deep groan from the auditors,—a sound of wrath, as well as fear and sorrow, —responded to this intelligence.

"Look ye to it, brethren," resumed Endicott, with increasing energy. "If this king and this arch-prelate have their will, we shall briefly behold a cross on the spire of this tabernacle which we have builded, and a high altar within its walls, with wax tapers burning round it at noonday. We shall hear the sacring bell, and the voices of the Romish priests saying the mass. But think ye, Christian men, that these abominations may be suffered without a sword drawn? without a shot fired? without blood spilt, yea, on the very stairs of the pulpit? No,—be ye strong of hand and stout of heart! Here we stand on our own soil, which we have bought with our goods, which we have won with our swords, which we have cleared with our axes, which we have tilled with the sweat of our brows, which we have sanctified with our prayers

to the God that brought us hither! Who shall enslave us here? What have we to do with this mitred prelate,—with this crowned king? What have we to do with England?"

Endicott gazed round at the excited countenances of the people, now full of his own spirit, and then turned suddenly to the standard-bearer, who stood close behind him.

"Officer, lower your banner!" said he.

The officer obeyed; and, brandishing his sword, Endicott thrust it through the cloth, and, with his left hand, rent the Red Cross completely out of the banner. He then waved the tattered ensign above his head.

"Sacrilegious wretch!" cried the high-churchman in the pillory, unable longer to restrain himself, "thou hast rejected the symbol of our holy religion!"

"Treason, treason!" roared the royalist in the stocks. "He hath defaced the King's banner!"

"Before God and man, I will avouch the deed," answered Endicott. "Beat a flourish, drummer!—shout, soldiers and people!—in honor of the ensign of New England. Neither Pope nor Tyrant hath part in it now!"

With a cry of triumph, the people gave their sanction to one of the boldest exploits which our history records. And forever honored be the name of Endicott! We look back through the mist of ages, and recognize in the rending of the Red Cross from New England's banner the first omen of that deliverance which our fathers consummated after the bones of the stern Puritan had lain more than a century in the dust.

THE CELESTIAL RAILROAD
[1846 (1843)]

NOT a great while ago, passing through the gate of dreams, I visited that region of the earth in which lies the famous City of Destruction. It interested me much to learn that by the public spirit of some of the inhabitants a railroad has recently been established between this populous and flourishing town and the Celestial City. Having a little time upon my hands, I resolved to gratify a liberal curiosity by making a trip thither. Accordingly, one fine morning after paying my bill at the hotel, and directing the porter to stow my luggage behind a coach, I took my seat in the vehicle and set out for the station-house. It was my good fortune to enjoy the company of a gentleman—one Mr. Smooth-it-away [1]—who, though he had never actually visited the Celestial City, yet seemed as well acquainted with its laws, customs, policy, and statistics, as with those of the City of Destruction, of which he was a native townsman. Being, moreover, a director of the railroad corporation and one of its largest stockholders, he had it in his power to give me all desirable information respecting that praiseworthy enterprise.

Our coach rattled out of the city, and at a short distance from its outskirts passed over a bridge of elegant construction, but somewhat too slight, as I imagined, to sustain any considerable weight. On both sides lay an extensive quagmire, which could not have been more disagreeable, either to sight or smell, had all the kennels of the earth emptied their pollution there.

"This," remarked Mr. Smooth-it-away, "is the famous Slough of Despond—a disgrace to all the neighborhood; and the greater that it might so easily be converted into firm ground."

"I have understood," said I, "that efforts have been made for that purpose from time immemorial. Bunyan mentions that above twenty thousand cartloads of wholesome instructions had been thrown in here without effect."

"Very probably! And what effect could be anticipated from such unsubstantial stuff?" cried Mr. Smooth-it-away. "You observe this convenient bridge. We obtained a sufficient foundation for it by throwing into the slough some editions of books of morality; volumes of French philosophy and German rationalism; tracts, sermons,

and essays of modern clergymen; extracts from Plato, Confucius, and various Hindoo sages, together with a few ingenious commentaries upon texts of Scripture,—all of which by some scientific process, have been converted into a mass like granite. The whole bog might be filled up with similar matter."

It really seemed to me, however, that the bridge vibrated and heaved up and down in a very formidable manner; and, in spite of Mr. Smooth-it-away's testimony to the solidity of its foundation, I should be loath to cross it in a crowded omnibus, especially if each passenger were encumbered with as heavy luggage as that gentleman and myself. Nevertheless we got over without accident, and soon found ourselves at the station-house. This very neat and spacious edifice is erected on the site of the little wicket gate, which formerly, as all old pilgrims will recollect, stood directly across the highway, and, by its inconvenient narrowness, was a great obstruction to the traveller of liberal mind and expansive stomach. The reader of John Bunyan will be glad to know that Christian's old friend Evangelist, who was accustomed to supply each pilgrim with a mystic roll, now presides at the ticket office. Some malicious persons, it is true, deny the identity of this reputable character with the Evangelist of old times, and even pretend to bring competent evidence of an imposture. Without involving myself in a dispute I shall merely observe that, so far as my experience goes, the square pieces of pasteboard now delivered to passengers are much more convenient and useful along the road than the antique roll of parchment. Whether they will be as readily received at the gate of the Celestial City I decline giving an opinion.

A large number of passengers were already at the station-house awaiting the departure of the cars. By the aspect and demeanor of these persons it was easy to

---

[1] Mr. Smooth-man was a citizen of Vanity Fair in Bunyan's *Pilgrim's Progress*.

judge that the feelings of the community had undergone a very favorable change in reference to the celestial pilgrimage. It would have done Bunyan's heart good to see it. Instead of a lonely and ragged man with a huge burden on his back, plodding along sorrowfully on foot while the whole city hooted after him, here were parties of the first gentry and most respectable people in the neighborhood setting forth towards the Celestial City as cheerfully as if the pilgrimage were merely a summer tour. Among the gentlemen were characters of deserved eminence—magistrates, politicians, and men of wealth, by whose example religion could not but be greatly recommended to their meaner brethren. In the ladies' apartment, too, I rejoiced to distinguish some of those flowers of fashionable society who are so well fitted to adorn the most elevated circles of the Celestial City. There was much pleasant conversation about the news of the day, topics of business and politics, or the lighter matters of amusement; while religion, though indubitably the main thing at heart, was thrown tastefully into the background. Even an infidel would have heard little or nothing to shock his sensibility.

One great convenience of the new method of going on pilgrimage I must not forget to mention. Our enormous burdens, instead of being carried on our shoulders as had been the custom of old, were all snugly deposited in the baggage car, and, as I was assured, would be delivered to their respective owners at the journey's end. Another thing, likewise, the benevolent reader will be delighted to understand. It may be remembered that there was an ancient feud between Prince Beelzebub and the keeper of the wicket gate, and that the adherents of the former distinguished personage were accustomed to shoot deadly arrows at honest pilgrims while knocking at the door. This dispute, much to the credit as well of the illustrious potentate above mentioned as of the worthy and enlightened directors of the railroad, has been pacifically arranged on the principle of mutual com-

promise. The prince's subjects are now pretty numerously employed about the station-house, some in taking care of the baggage, others in collecting fuel, feeding the engines, and such congenial occupations; and I can conscientiously affirm that persons more attentive to their business, more willing to accommodate, or more generally agreeable to the passengers, are not to be found on any railroad. Every good heart must surely exult at so satisfactory an arrangement of an immemorial difficulty.

"Where is Mr. Greatheart?" inquired I. "Beyond a doubt the directors have engaged that famous old champion to be chief conductor on the railroad?" [2]

"Why, no," said Mr. Smooth-it-away, with a dry cough. "He was offered the situation of brakeman; but, to tell you the truth, our friend Greatheart has grown preposterously stiff and narrow in his old age. He has so often guided pilgrims over the road on foot that he considers it a sin to travel in any other fashion. Besides, the old fellow had entered so heartily into the ancient feud with Prince Beelzebub that he would have been perpetually at blows or ill language with some of the prince's subjects, and thus have embroiled us anew. So, on the whole, we were not sorry when honest Greatheart went off to the Celestial City in a huff and left us at liberty to choose a more suitable and accommodating man. Yonder comes the engineer of the train. You will probably recognize him at once."

The engine at this moment took its station in advance of the cars, looking, I must confess, much more like a sort of mechanical demon that would hurry us to the infernal regions than a laudable contrivance for smoothing our way to the Celestial City. On its top sat a personage almost enveloped in smoke and flame, which, not to startle the reader, appeared to gush from his own mouth and stomach

---

[2] Mr. Greatheart is a character in the second part of Bunyan's *Pilgrim's Progress*,

as well as from the engine's brazen abdomen.

"Do my eyes deceive me?" cried I. "What on earth is this! A living creature? If so, he is own brother to the engine he rides upon!"

"Poh, poh, you are obtuse!" said Mr. Smooth-it-away, with a hearty laugh. "Don't you know Apollyon, Christian's old enemy, with whom he fought so fierce a battle in the Valley of Humiliation?[3] He was the very fellow to manage the engine; and so we have reconciled him to the custom of going on pilgrimage, and engaged him as chief engineer."

"Bravo, bravo!" exclaimed I, with irrepressible enthusiasm; "this shows the liberality of the age; this proves, if anything can, that all musty prejudices are in a fair way to be obliterated. And how will Christian rejoice to hear of this happy transformation of his old antagonist! I promise myself great pleasure in informing him of it when we reach the Celestial City."

The passengers being all comfortably seated, we now rattled away merrily, accomplishing a greater distance in ten minutes than Christian probably trudged over in a day. It was laughable, while we glanced along, as it were, at the tail of a thunderbolt, to observe two dusty foot travellers in the old pilgrim guise, with cockle shell and staff, their mystic rolls of parchment in their hands and their intolerable burdens on their backs. The preposterous obstinacy of these honest people in persisting to groan and stumble along the difficult pathway rather than take advantage of modern improvements, excited great mirth among our wiser brotherhood. We greeted the two pilgrims with many pleasant gibes and a roar of laughter; whereupon they gazed at us with such woful and absurdly compassionate visages that our merriment grew tenfold more obstreperous. Apollyon also entered heartily into the fun, and contrived to flirt the smoke and flame of the engine, or of his own breath, into their faces, and envelop them in an atmosphere of scalding steam. These little practical

jokes amused us mightily, and doubtless afforded the pilgrims the gratification of considering themselves martyrs.

At some distance from the railroad Mr. Smooth-it-away pointed to a large antique edifice, which, he observed, was a tavern of long standing, and had formerly been a noted stopping-place for pilgrims. In Bunyan's road-book it is mentioned as the Interpreter's House.

"I have long had a curiosity to visit that old mansion," remarked I.

"It is not one of our stations, as you perceive," said my companion. "The keeper was violently opposed to the railroad; and well he might be, as the track left his house of entertainment on one side, and thus was pretty certain to deprive him of all his reputable customers. But the footpath still passes his door, and the old gentleman now and then receives a call from some simple traveller, and entertains him with fare as old-fashioned as himself."

Before our talk on this subject came to a conclusion we were rushing by the place where Christian's burden fell from his shoulders at the sight of the Cross. This served as a theme for Mr. Smooth-it-away, Mr. Live-for-the-world, Mr. Hide-sin-in-the-heart, Mr. Scaly-conscience, and a knot of gentlemen from the town of Shun-repentance, to descant upon the inestimable advantages resulting from the safety of our baggage. Myself, and all the passengers indeed, joined with great unanimity in this view of the matter; for our burdens were rich in many things esteemed precious throughout the world; and, especially, we each of us possessed a great variety of favorite Habits, which we trusted would not be out of fashion even in the polite circles of the Celestial City. It would have been a sad spectacle to see such an assortment of valuable articles tumbling into the sepulchre. Thus pleasantly conversing on the favorable circumstances of our position as compared with those of past pilgrims

---

[3] The reference is to an incident in Bunyan's *Pilgrim's Progress*.

and of narrow-minded ones at the present day, we soon found ourselves at the foot of the Hill Difficulty. Through the very heart of this rocky mountain a tunnel has been constructed of most admirable architecture, with a lofty arch and a spacious double track; so that, unless the earth and rocks should chance to crumble down, it will remain an eternal monument of the builder's skill and enterprise. It is a great though incidental advantage that the materials from the heart of the Hill Difficulty have been employed in filling up the Valley of Humiliation, thus obviating the necessity of descending into that disagreeable and unwholesome hollow.

"This is a wonderful improvement, indeed," said I. "Yet I should have been glad of an opportunity to visit the Palace Beautiful and be introduced to the charming young ladies—Miss Prudence, Miss Piety, Miss Charity, and the rest—who have the kindness to entertain pilgrims there."

"Young ladies!" cried Mr. Smooth-it-away, as soon as he could speak for laughing. "And charming young ladies! Why, my dear fellow, they are old maids, every soul of them—prim, starched, dry, and angular; and not one of them, I will venture to say, has altered so much as the fashion of her gown since the days of Christian's pilgrimage."

"Ah, well," said I, much comforted, "then I can very readily dispense with their acquaintance."

The respectable Apollyon was now putting on the steam at a prodigious rate, anxious, perhaps, to get rid of the unpleasant reminiscences connected with the spot where he had so disastrously encountered Christian. Consulting Mr. Bunyan's road-book, I perceived that we must now be within a few miles of the Valley of the Shadow of Death, into which doleful region, at our present speed, we should plunge much sooner than seemed at all desirable. In truth, I expected nothing better than to find myself in the ditch on one side or the quag on the other; but on communicating my apprehensions to Mr. Smooth-it-away, he assured me that the difficulties of this passage, even in its worst condition, had been vastly exaggerated, and that, in its present state of improvement, I might consider myself as safe as on any railroad in Christendom.

Even while we were speaking the train shot into the entrance of this dreaded Valley. Though I plead guilty to some foolish palpitations of the heart during our headlong rush over the causeway here constructed, yet it were unjust to withhold the highest encomiums on the boldness of its original conception and the ingenuity of those who executed it. It was gratifying, likewise, to observe how much care had been taken to dispel the everlasting gloom and supply the defect of cheerful sunshine, not a ray of which has ever penetrated among these awful shadows. For this purpose, the inflammable gas which exudes plentifully from the soil is collected by means of pipes, and thence communicated to a quadruple row of lamps along the whole extent of the passage. Thus a radiance has been created even out of the fiery and sulphurous curse that rests forever upon the valley—a radiance hurtful, however, to the eyes, and somewhat bewildering, as I discovered by the changes which it wrought in the visages of my companions. In this respect, as compared with natural daylight, there is the same difference as between truth and falsehood; but if the reader have ever travelled through the dark Valley, he will have learned to be thankful for any light that he could get —if not from the sky above, then from the blasted soil beneath. Such was the red brilliancy of these lamps that they appeared to build walls of fire on both sides of the track, between which we held our course at lightning speed, while a reverberating thunder filled the Valley with its echoes. Had the engine run off the track,—a catastrophe, it is whispered, by no means unprecedented,—the bottomless pit, if there be any such place, would undoubtedly have received us. Just as some dismal fooleries of this nature had made my heart quake there came a tremendous shriek, careering along the valley as if a thousand devils had burst their lungs to utter it, but which proved to be merely the whistle of the engine on arriving at a stopping-place.

The spot where we had now paused is the same that our friend Bunyan—a truthful man, but infected with many fantastic notions—has designated, in terms plainer than I like to repeat, as the mouth of the infernal region. This, however, must be a mistake, inasmuch as Mr. Smooth-it-away, while we remained in the smoky and lurid cavern, took occasion to prove that Tophet has not even a metaphorical existence. The place, he assured us, is no other than the crater of a half-extinct volcano, in which the directors had caused forges to be set up for the manufacture of railroad iron. Hence, also, is obtained a plentiful supply of fuel for the use of the engines. Whoever had gazed into the dismal obscurity of the broad cavern mouth, whence ever and anon darted huge tongues of dusky flame, and had seen the strange, half-shaped monsters, and visions of faces horribly grotesque, into which the smoke seemed to wreathe itself, and had heard the awful murmurs, and shrieks, and deep shuddering whispers of the blast, sometimes forming themselves into words almost articulate, would have seized upon Mr. Smooth-it-away's comfortable explanation as greedily as we did. The inhabitants of the cavern, moreover, were unlovely personages, dark, smoke-begrimed, generally deformed, with misshapen feet, and a glow of dusky redness in their eyes as if their hearts had caught fire and were blazing out of the upper windows. It struck me as a peculiarity that the laborers at the forge and those who brought fuel to the engine, when they began to draw short breath, positively emitted smoke from their mouth and nostrils.

Among the idlers about the train, most of whom were puffing cigars which they had lighted at the flame of the crater, I was perplexed to notice several who, to my certain knowledge, had heretofore set forth by railroad for the Celestial City. They looked dark, wild, and smoky, with a singular resemblance, indeed, to the native inhabitants, like whom, also, they had a disagreeable propensity to ill-natured gibes and sneers, the habit of which had wrought a settled contortion of their visages. Having been on speaking terms with one of these persons,—an indolent, good-for-nothing fellow, who went by the name of Take-it-easy,—I called him, and inquired what was his business there.

"Did you not start," said I, "for the Celestial City?"

"That's a fact," said Mr. Take-it-easy, carelessly puffing some smoke into my eyes. "But I heard such bad accounts that I never took pains to climb the hill on which the city stands. No business doing, no fun going on, nothing to drink, and no smoking allowed, and a thrumming of church music from morning till night. I would not stay in such a place if they offered me house room and living free."

"But, my good Mr. Take-it-easy," cried I, "why take up your residence here, of all places in the world?"

"Oh," said the loafer, with a grin, "it is very warm hereabouts, and I meet with plenty of old acquaintances, and altogether the place suits me. I hope to see you back again some day soon. A pleasant journey to you."

While he was speaking the bell of the engine rang, and we dashed away after dropping a few passengers, but receiving no new ones. Rattling onward through the Valley, we were dazzled with the fiercely gleaming gas lamps, as before. But sometimes, in the dark of intense brightness, grim faces, that bore the aspect and expression of individual sins, or evil passions, seemed to thrust themselves through the veil of light, glaring upon us, and stretching forth a great, dusky hand, as if to impede our progress. I almost thought that they were my own sins that appalled me there. These were freaks of imagination —nothing more, certainly—mere delusions,

which I ought to be heartily ashamed of;
but all through the Dark Valley I was
tormented, and pestered, and dolefully bewildered with the same kind of waking
dreams. The mephitic gases of that region
intoxicate the brain. As the light of natural
day, however, began to struggle with the
glow of the lanterns, these vain imaginations lost their vividness, and finally vanished with the first ray of sunshine that
greeted our escape from the Valley of the
Shadow of Death. Ere we had gone a mile
beyond it I could well-nigh have taken my
oath that this whole gloomy passage was a
dream.

At the end of the valley, as John Bunyan
mentions, is a cavern, where, in his days,
dwelt two cruel giants, Pope and Pagan,
who had strown the ground about their
residence with the bones of slaughtered
pilgrims. These vile old troglodytes are no
longer there; but into their deserted cave
another terrible giant has thrust himself,
and makes it his business to seize upon
honest travellers and fatten them for his
table with plentiful meals of smoke, mist,
moonshine, raw potatoes, and sawdust. He
is a German by birth, and is called Giant
Transcendentalist; but as to his form, his
features, his substance, and his nature
generally, it is the chief peculiarity of
this huge miscreant that neither he for
himself, nor anybody for him, has ever
been able to describe them. As we rushed
by the cavern's mouth we caught a hasty
glimpse of him, looking somewhat like an
ill-proportioned figure, but considerably
more like a heap of fog and duskiness.
He shouted after us, but in so strange a
phraseology that we knew not what he
meant, nor whether to be encouraged or
affrighted.

It was late in the day when the train
thundered into the ancient city of Vanity,
where Vanity Fair is still at the height of
prosperity, and exhibits an epitome of
whatever is brilliant, gay, and fascinating
beneath the sun. As I purposed to make a
considerable stay here, it gratified me to
learn that there is no longer the want of
harmony between the town's-people and
pilgrims, which impelled the former to
such lamentably mistaken measures as the
persecution of Christian and the fiery martyrdom of Faithful. On the contrary, as
the new railroad brings with it great trade
and a constant influx of strangers, the lord
of Vanity Fair is its chief patron, and the
capitalists of the city are among the largest
stockholders. Many passengers stop to take
their pleasure or make their profit in the
Fair, instead of going onward to the
Celestial City. Indeed, such are the charms
of the place that people often affirm it to
be the true and only heaven; stoutly contending that there is no other, that those
who seek further are mere dreamers, and
that, if the fabled brightness of the Celestial City lay but a bare mile beyond the
gates of Vanity, they would not be fools
enough to go thither. Without subscribing
to these perhaps exaggerated encomiums,
I can truly say that my abode in the city
was mainly agreeable, and my intercourse
with the inhabitants productive of much
amusement and instruction.

Being naturally of a serious turn, my
attention was directed to the solid advantages derivable from a residence here,
rather than to the effervescent pleasures
which are the grand object with too many
visitants. The Christian reader, if he have
had no accounts of the city later than
Bunyan's time, will be surprised to hear
that almost every street has its church,
and that the reverend clergy are nowhere
held in higher respect than at Vanity Fair.
And well do they deserve such honorable
estimation; for the maxims of wisdom and
virtue which fall from their lips come from
as deep a spiritual source, and tend to as
lofty a religious aim, as those of the
sagest philosophers of old. In justification
of this high praise I need only mention the
names of the Rev. Mr. Shallow-deep, the
Rev. Mr. Stumble-at-truth, that fine old
clerical character the Rev. Mr. This-to-day,
who expects shortly to resign his pulpit to
the Rev. Mr. That-to-morrow; together
with the Rev. Mr. Bewilderment, the Rev.

Mr. Clog-the-spirit, and, last and greatest, the Rev. Dr. Wind-of-doctrine. The labors of these eminent divines are aided by those of innumerable lecturers, who diffuse such a various profundity, in all subjects of human or celestial science, that any man may acquire an omnigenous erudition without the trouble of even learning to read. Thus literature is etherealized by assuming for its medium the human voice; and knowledge, depositing all its heavier particles, except, doubtless, its gold, becomes exhaled into a sound, which forthwith steals into the ever-open ear of the community. These ingenious methods constitute a sort of machinery, by which thought and study are done to every person's hand without his putting himself to the slightest inconvenience in the matter. There is another species of machine for the wholesale manufacture of individual morality. This excellent result is effected by societies for all manner of virtuous purposes, with which a man has merely to connect himself, throwing, as it were, his quota of virtue into the common stock, and the president and directors will take care that the aggregate amount be well applied. All these, and other wonderful improvements in ethics, religion, and literature, being made plain to my comprehension by the ingenious Mr. Smooth-it-away, inspired me with a vast admiration of Vanity Fair.

It would fill a volume, in an age of pamphlets, were I to record all my observations in this great capital of human business and pleasure. There was an unlimited range of society—the powerful, the wise, the witty, and the famous in every walk of life; princes, presidents, poets, generals, artists, actors, and philanthropists,—all making their own market at the fair, and deeming no price too exorbitant for such commodities as hit their fancy. It was well worth one's while, even if he had no idea of buying or selling, to loiter through the bazaars and observe the various sorts of traffic that were going forward.

Some of the purchasers, I thought, made very foolish bargains. For instance, a young man having inherited a splendid fortune, laid out a considerable portion of it in the purchase of diseases, and finally spent all the rest for a heavy lot of repentance and a suit of rags. A very pretty girl bartered a heart as clear as crystal, and which seemed her most valuable possession, for another jewel of the same kind, but so worn and defaced as to be utterly worthless. In one shop there were a great many crowns of laurel and myrtle, which soldiers, authors, statesmen, and various other people pressed eagerly to buy; some purchased these paltry wreaths with their lives, others by a toilsome servitude of years, and many sacrificed whatever was most valuable, yet finally slunk away without the crown. There was a sort of stock of scrip, called Conscience, which seemed to be in great demand, and would purchase almost anything. Indeed, few rich commodities were to be obtained without paying a heavy sum in this particular stock, and a man's business was seldom very lucrative unless he knew precisely when and how to throw his hoard of conscience into the market. Yet as this stock was the only thing of permanent value, whoever parted with it was sure to find himself a loser in the long run. Several of the speculations were of a questionable character. Occasionally a member of Congress recruited his pocket by the sale of his constituents; and I was assured that public officers have often sold their country at very moderate prices. Thousands sold their happiness for a whim. Gilded chains were in great demand, and purchased with almost any sacrifice. In truth, those who desired, according to the old adage, to sell anything valuable for a song, might find customers all over the Fair; and there were innumerable messes of pottage, piping hot, for such as chose to buy them with their birthrights. A few articles, however, could not be found genuine at Vanity Fair. If a customer wished to renew his stock of youth the dealers offered him a set of false teeth and an auburn wig; if he demanded peace of mind, they recommended opium or a brandy bottle.

Tracts of land and golden mansions, situate in the Celestial City, were often exchanged, at very disadvantageous rates, for a few years' lease of small, dismal, inconvenient tenements in Vanity Fair. Prince Beelzebub himself took great interest in this sort of traffic, and sometimes condescended to meddle with smaller matters. I once had the pleasure to see him bargaining with a miser for his soul, which, after much ingenious skirmishing on both sides, his highness succeeded in obtaining at about the value of sixpence. The prince remarked with a smile, that he was a loser by the transaction.

Day after day, as I walked the streets of Vanity, my manners and deportment became more and more like those of the inhabitants. The place began to seem like home; the idea of pursuing my travels to the Celestial City was almost obliterated from my mind. I was reminded of it, however, by the sight of the same pair of simple pilgrims at whom we had laughed so heartily when Apollyon puffed smoke and steam into their faces at the commencement of our journey. There they stood amidst the densest bustle of Vanity; the dealers offering them their purple and fine linen and jewels, the men of wit and humor gibing at them, a pair of buxom ladies ogling them askance, while the benevolent Mr. Smooth-it-away whispered some of his wisdom at their elbows, and pointed to a newly-erected temple; but there were these worthy simpletons, making the scene look wild and monstrous, merely by their sturdy repudiation of all part in its business or pleasures.

One of them—his name was Stick-to-the-right—perceived in my face, I suppose, a species of sympathy and almost admiration, which, to my own great surprise, I could not help feeling for this pragmatic couple. It prompted him to address me.

"Sir," inquired he, with a sad, yet mild and kindly voice, "do you call yourself a pilgrim?"

"Yes," I replied, "my right to that appellation is indubitable. I am merely a sojourner here in Vanity Fair, being bound to the Celestial City by the new railroad."

"Alas, friend," rejoined Mr. Stick-to-the-right, "I do assure you, and beseech you to receive the truth of my words, that that whole concern is a bubble. You may travel on it all your lifetime, were you to live thousands of years, and yet never get beyond the limits of Vanity Fair. Yea, though you should deem yourself entering the gates of the blessed city, it will be nothing but a miserable delusion."

"The Lord of the Celestial City," began the other pilgrim, whose name was Mr. Foot-it-to-heaven, "has refused, and will ever refuse, to grant an act of incorporation for this railroad; and unless that be obtained, no passenger can ever hope to enter his dominions. Wherefore every man who buys a ticket must lay his account with losing the purchase money, which is the value of his own soul."

"Poh, nonsense!" said Mr. Smooth-it-away, taking my arm and leading me off, "these fellows ought to be indicted for a libel. If the law stood as it once did in Vanity Fair we should see them grinning through the iron bars of the prison window."

This incident made a considerable impression on my mind, and contributed with other circumstances to indispose me to a permanent residence in the city of Vanity; although, of course, I was not simple enough to give up my original plan of gliding along easily and commodiously by railroad. Still, I grew anxious to be gone. There was one strange thing that troubled me. Amid the occupations or amusements of the Fair, nothing was more common than for a person—whether at feast, theatre, or church, or trafficking for wealth and honors, or whatever he might be doing, and however unseasonable the interruption—suddenly to vanish like a soap bubble, and be never more seen of his fellows; and so accustomed were the latter to such little accidents that they went on with their business as quietly as if nothing had happened. But it was otherwise with me.

Finally, after a pretty long residence at the Fair, I resumed my journey towards the Celestial City, still with Mr. Smooth-it-away at my side. At a short distance beyond the suburbs of Vanity we passed the ancient silver mine, of which Demas was the first discoverer, and which is now wrought to great advantage, supplying nearly all the coined currency of the world. A little further onward was the spot where Lot's wife had stood forever under the semblance of a pillar of salt. Curious travellers have long since carried it away piecemeal. Had all regrets been punished as rigorously as this poor dame's were, my yearning for the relinquished delights of Vanity Fair might have produced a similar change in my own corporeal substance, and left me a warning to future pilgrims.

The next remarkable object was a large edifice, constructed of mossgrown stone, but in a modern and airy style of architecture. The engine came to a pause in its vicinity, with the usual tremendous shriek.

"This was formerly the castle of the redoubted giant Despair," observed Mr. Smooth-it-away; "but since his death Mr. Flimsy-faith has repaired it, and keeps an excellent house of entertainment here. It is one of our stopping-places."

"It seems but slightly put together," remarked I, looking at the frail yet ponderous walls. "I do not envy Mr. Flimsy-faith his habitation. Some day it will thunder down upon the heads of the occupants."

"We shall escape at all events," said Mr. Smooth-it-away, "for Apollyon is putting on the steam again."

The road now plunged into a gorge of the Delectable Mountains, and traversed the field where in former ages the blind men wandered and stumbled among the tombs. One of these ancient tombstones had been thrust across the track by some malicious person, and gave the train of cars a terrible jolt. Far up the rugged side of a mountain I perceived a rusty iron door, half overgrown with bushes and creeping plants, but with smoke issuing from its crevices.

"Is that," inquired I, "the very door in the hill-side which the shepherds assured Christian was a by-way to hell?"

"That was a joke on the part of the shepherds," said Mr. Smooth-it-away, with a smile. "It is neither more nor less than the door of a cavern which they use as a smoke-house for the preparation of mutton hams."

My recollections of the journey are now, for a little space, dim and confused, inasmuch as a singular drowsiness here overcame me, owing to the fact that we were passing over the enchanted ground, the air of which encourages a disposition to sleep. I awoke, however, as soon as we crossed the borders of the pleasant land of Beulah. All the passengers were rubbing their eyes, comparing watches, and congratulating one another on the prospect of arriving so seasonably at the journey's end. The sweet breezes of this happy clime came refreshingly to our nostrils; we beheld the glimmering gush of silver fountains, overhung by trees of beautiful foliage and delicious fruit, which were propagated by grafts from the celestial gardens. Once, as we dashed onward like a hurricane, there was a flutter of wings and the bright appearance of an angel in the air, speeding forth on some heavenly mission. The engine now announced the close vicinity of the final station-house by one last and horrible scream, in which there seemed to be distinguishable every kind of wailing and woe, and bitter fierceness of wrath, all mixed up with the wild laughter of a devil or a madman. Throughout our journey, at every stopping-place, Apollyon had exercised his ingenuity in screwing the most abominable sounds out of the whistle of the steam-engine; but in this closing effort he outdid himself and created an infernal uproar, which, besides disturbing the peaceful inhabitants of Beulah, must have sent its discord even through the celestial gates.

While the horrid clamor was still ringing

in our ears we heard an exulting strain, as if a thousand instruments of music, with height and depth and sweetness in their tones, at once tender and triumphant, were struck in unison, to greet the approach of some illustrious hero, who had fought the good fight and won a glorious victory, and was come to lay aside his battered arms forever. Looking to ascertain what might be the occasion of this glad harmony, I perceived, on alighting from the cars, that a multitude of shining ones had assembled on the other side of the river, to welcome two poor pilgrims, who were just emerging from its depths. They were the same whom Apollyon and ourselves had persecuted with taunts, and gibes, and scalding steam, at the commencement of our journey—the same whose unworldly aspect and impressive words had stirred my conscience amid the wild revellers of Vanity Fair.

"How amazingly well those men have got on," cried I to Mr. Smooth-it-away. "I wish we were secure of as good a reception."

"Never fear, never fear!" answered my friend. "Come, make haste; the ferry boat will be off directly, and in three minutes you will be on the other side of the river. No doubt you will find coaches to carry you up to the city gates."

A steam ferry boat, the last improvement on this important route, lay at the river side, puffing, snorting, and emitting all those other disagreeable utterances which betoken the departure to be immediate. I hurried on board with the rest of the passengers, most of whom were in great perturbation: some bawling out for their baggage; some tearing their hair and exclaiming that the boat would explode or sink; some already pale with the heaving of the stream; some gazing affrighted at the ugly aspect of the steersman; and some still dizzy with the slumberous influences of the Enchanted Ground. Looking back to the shore, I was amazed to discern Mr. Smooth-it-away waving his hand in token of farewell.

"Don't you go over to the Celestial City?" exclaimed I.

"Oh, no!" answered he with a queer smile, and that same disagreeable contortion of visage which I had remarked in the inhabitants of the Dark Valley. "Oh, no! I have come thus far only for the sake of your pleasant company. Good-by! We shall meet again."

And then did my excellent friend Mr. Smooth-it-away laugh outright, in the midst of which cachinnation a smoke-wreath issued from his mouth and nostrils, while a twinkle of lurid flame darted out of either eye, proving indubitably that his heart was all of a red blaze. The impudent fiend! To deny the existence of Tophet, when he felt its fiery tortures raging within his breast. I rushed to the side of the boat, intending to fling myself on shore; but the wheels, as they began their revolutions, threw a dash of spray over me so cold—so deadly cold, with the chill that will never leave those waters until Death be drowned in his own river—that with a shiver and a heartquake I awoke. Thank Heaven it was a Dream!

RAPPACCINI'S DAUGHTER [1]
[1846 (1844)]

A YOUNG man, named Giovanni Guasconti, came, very long ago, from the more southern region of Italy, to pursue his studies at the University of Padua. Giovanni, who had but a scanty supply of gold ducats in his pocket, took lodgings in a high and gloomy chamber of an old edifice which looked not unworthy to have been the palace of a Paduan noble, and which, in fact, exhibited over its entrance the armorial bearings of a family long since extinct. The young stranger, who

[1] Hawthorne's facetious prefatory note to this story in the *Democratic Review* for December, 1844, has been omitted; it is reprinted in the American Writers Series *Hawthorne*, ed. Austin Warren, pp. 20 f.

was not unstudied in the great poem of his country, recollected that one of the ancestors of this family, and perhaps an occupant of this very mansion, had been pictured by Dante as a partaker of the immortal agonies of his Inferno. These reminiscences and associations, together with the tendency to heartbreak natural to a young man for the first time out of his native sphere, caused Giovanni to sigh heavily as he looked around the desolate and ill-furnished apartment.

"Holy Virgin, signor!" cried old Dame Lisabetta, who, won by the youth's remarkable beauty of person, was kindly endeavoring to give the chamber a habitable air, "what a sigh was that to come out of a young man's heart! Do you find this old mansion gloomy? For the love of Heaven, then, put your head out of the window, and you will see as bright sunshine as you have left in Naples."

Guasconti mechanically did as the old woman advised, but could not quite agree with her that the Paduan sunshine was as cheerful as that of southern Italy. Such as it was, however, it fell upon a garden beneath the window and expended its fostering influences on a variety of plants, which seemed to have been cultivated with exceeding care.

"Does this garden belong to the house?" asked Giovanni.

"Heaven forbid, signor, unless it were fruitful of better pot herbs than any that grow there now," answered old Lisabetta. "No; that garden is cultivated by the own hands of Signor Giacomo Rappaccini, the famous doctor, who, I warrant him, has been heard of as far as Naples. It is said that he distils these plants into medicines that are as potent as a charm. Oftentimes you may see the signor doctor at work, and perchance the signora, his daughter, too, gathering the strange flowers that grow in the garden."

The old woman had now done what she could for the aspect of the chamber; and, commending the young man to the protection of the saints, took her departure.

Giovanni still found no better occupation than to look down into the garden beneath his window. From its appearance, he judged it to be one of those botanic gardens which were of earlier date in Padua than elsewhere in Italy or in the world. Or, not improbably, it might once have been the pleasure-place of an opulent family; for there was the ruin of a marble fountain, in the centre, sculptured with rare art, but so wofully shattered that it was impossible to trace the original design from the chaos of remaining fragments. The water, however, continued to gush and sparkle into the sunbeams as cheerfully as ever. A little gurgling sound ascended to the young man's window, and made him feel as if the fountain were an immortal spirit that sung its song unceasingly and without heeding the vicissitudes around it, while one century imbodied it in marble and another scattered the perishable garniture on the soil. All about the pool into which the water subsided grew various plants, that seemed to require a plentiful supply of moisture for the nourishment of gigantic leaves, and, in some instances, flowers gorgeously magnificent. There was one shrub in particular, set in a marble vase in the midst of the pool, that bore a profusion of purple blossoms, each of which had the lustre and richness of a gem; and the whole together made a show so resplendent that it seemed enough to illuminate the garden, even had there been no sunshine. Every portion of the soil was peopled with plants and herbs, which, if less beautiful, still bore tokens of assiduous care, as if all had their individual virtues, known to the scientific mind that fostered them. Some were placed in urns, rich with old carving, and others in common garden pots; some crept serpent-like along the ground or climbed on high, using whatever means of ascent was offered them. One plant had wreathed itself round a statue of Vertumnus,[2] which was thus

---

[2] Roman god of the seasons.

quite veiled and shrouded in a drapery of hanging foliage, so happily arranged that it might have served a sculptor for a study.

While Giovanni stood at the window he heard a rustling behind a screen of leaves, and became aware that a person was at work in the garden. His figure soon emerged into view, and showed itself to be that of no common laborer, but a tall, emaciated, sallow, and sickly-looking man, dressed in a scholar's garb of black. He was beyond the middle term of life, with gray hair, a thin, gray beard, and a face singularly marked with intellect and cultivation, but which could never, even in his more youthful days, have expressed much warmth of heart.

Nothing could exceed the intentness with which this scientific gardener examined every shrub which grew in his path: it seemed as if he was looking into their inmost nature, making observations in regard to their creative essence, and discovering why one leaf grew in this shape and another in that, and wherefore such and such flowers differed among themselves in hue and perfume. Nevertheless, in spite of this deep intelligence on his part, there was no approach to intimacy between himself and these vegetable existences. On the contrary, he avoided their actual touch or the direct inhaling of their odors with a caution that impressed Giovanni most disagreeably; for the man's demeanor was that of one walking among malignant influences, such as savage beasts, or deadly snakes, or evil spirits, which, should he allow them one moment of license, would wreak upon him some terrible fatality. It was strangely frightful to the young man's imagination to see this air of insecurity in a person cultivating a garden, that most simple and innocent of human toils, and which had been alike the joy and labor of the unfallen parents of the race. Was this garden, then, the Eden of the present world? And this man, with such a perception of harm in what his own hands caused to grow,—was he the Adam?

The distrustful gardener, while plucking away the dead leaves or pruning the too luxuriant growth of the shrubs, defended his hands with a pair of thick gloves. Nor were these his only armor. When, in his walk through the garden, he came to the magnificent plant that hung its purple gems beside the marble fountain, he placed a kind of mask over his mouth and nostrils, as if all this beauty did but conceal a deadlier malice; but, finding his task still too dangerous, he drew back, removed the mask, and called loudly, but in the infirm voice of a person affected with inward disease,—

"Beatrice! Beatrice!"

"Here am I, my father. What would you?" cried a rich and youthful voice from the window of the opposite house—a voice as rich as a tropical sunset, and which made Giovanni, though he knew not why, think of deep hues of purple or crimson and of perfumes heavily delectable. "Are you in the garden?"

"Yes, Beatrice," answered the gardener, "and I need your help."

Soon there emerged from under a sculptured portal the figure of a young girl, arrayed with as much richness of taste as the most splendid of the flowers, beautiful as the day, and with a bloom so deep and vivid that one shade more would have been too much. She looked redundant with life, health, and energy; all of which attributes were bound down and compressed, as it were, and girdled tensely, in their luxuriance, by her virgin zone. Yet Giovanni's fancy must have grown morbid while he looked down into the garden; for the impression which the fair stranger made upon him was as if here were another flower, the human sister of those vegetable ones, as beautiful as they, more beautiful than the richest of them, but still to be touched only with a glove, nor to be approached without a mask. As Beatrice came down the garden path, it was observable that she handled and inhaled the odor of several of the plants which her father had most sedulously avoided.

"Here, Beatrice," said the latter, "see how many needful offices require to be done to our chief treasure. Yet, shattered as I am, my life might pay the penalty of approaching it so closely as circumstances demand. Henceforth, I fear, this plant must be consigned to your sole charge."

"And gladly will I undertake it," cried again the rich tones of the young lady, as she bent towards the magnificent plant and opened her arms as if to embrace it. "Yes, my sister, my splendor, it shall be Beatrice's task to nurse and serve thee; and thou shalt reward her with thy kisses and perfumed breath, which to her is as the breath of life."

Then, with all the tenderness in her manner that was so strikingly expressed in her words, she busied herself with such attentions as the plant seemed to require; and Giovanni, at his lofty window, rubbed his eyes and almost doubted whether it were a girl tending her favorite flower, or one sister performing the duties of affection to another. The scene soon terminated. Whether Dr. Rappaccini had finished his labors in the garden, or that his watchful eye had caught the stranger's face, he now took his daughter's arm and retired. Night was already closing in; oppressive exhalations seemed to proceed from the plants and steal upward past the open window; and Giovanni, closing the lattice, went to his couch and dreamed of a rich flower and beautiful girl. Flower and maiden were different, and yet the same, and fraught with some strange peril in either shape.

But there is an influence in the light of morning that tends to rectify whatever errors of fancy, or even of judgment, we may have incurred during the sun's decline, or among the shadows of the night, or in the less wholesome glow of moonshine. Giovanni's first movement, on starting from sleep, was to throw open the window and gaze down into the garden which his dreams had made so fertile of mysteries. He was surprised and a little ashamed to find how real and matter-of-fact an affair it proved to be, in the first rays of the sun which gilded the dewdrops that hung upon leaf and blossom, and, while giving a brighter beauty to each rare flower, brought everything within the limits of ordinary experience. The young man rejoiced that, in the heart of the barren city, he had the privilege of overlooking this spot of lovely and luxuriant vegetation. It would serve, he said to himself, as a symbolic language to keep him in communion with Nature. Neither the sickly and thoughtworn Dr. Giacomo Rappaccini, it is true, nor his brilliant daughter, were now visible; so that Giovanni could not determine how much of the singularity which he attributed to both was due to their own qualities and how much to his wonder-working fancy; but he was inclined to take a most rational view of the whole matter.

In the course of the day he paid his respects to Signor Pietro Baglioni, professor of medicine in the university, a physician of eminent repute, to whom Giovanni had brought a letter of introduction. The professor was an elderly personage, apparently of genial nature, and habits that might almost be called jovial. He kept the young man to dinner, and made himself very agreeable by the freedom and liveliness of his conversation, especially when warmed by a flask or two of Tuscan wine. Giovanni, conceiving that men of science, inhabitants of the same city, must needs be on familiar terms with one another, took an opportunity to mention the name of Dr. Rappaccini. But the professor did not respond with so much cordiality as he had anticipated.

"Ill would it become a teacher of the divine art of medicine," said Professor Pietro Baglioni, in answer to a question of Giovanni, "to withhold due and well-considered praise of a physician so eminently skilled as Rappaccini; but, on the other hand, I should answer it but scantily to my conscience were I to permit a worthy youth like yourself, Signor Giovanni, the son of an ancient friend, to imbibe erroneous ideas respecting a man who might hereafter chance to hold your life and death in his hands. The truth is, our worshipful Dr. Rappaccini has as much science as any member of the faculty—with perhaps one single exception—in Padua, or all Italy; but there are certain grave objections to his professional character."

"And what are they?" asked the young man.

"Has my friend Giovanni any disease of body or heart, that he is so inquisitive about physicians?" said the professor, with a smile. "But as for Rappaccini, it is said of him—and I, who know the man well, can answer for its truth—that he cares infinitely more for science than for mankind. His patients are interesting to him only as subjects for some new experiment. He would sacrifice human life, his own among the rest, or whatever else was dearest to him, for the sake of adding so much as a grain of mustard seed to the great heap of his accumulated knowledge."

"Methinks he is an awful man indeed," remarked Guasconti, mentally recalling the cold and purely intellectual aspect of Rappaccini. "And yet, worshipful professor, is it not a noble spirit? Are there many men capable of so spiritual a love of science?"

"God forbid," answered the professor, somewhat testily; "at least, unless they take sounder views of the healing art than those adopted by Rappaccini. It is his theory that all medicinal virtues are comprised within those substances which we term vegetable poisons. These he cultivates with his own hands, and is said even to have produced new varieties of poison, more horribly deleterious than Nature, without the assistance of this learned person, would ever have plagued the world withal. That the signor doctor does less mischief than might be expected with such dangerous substances is undeniable. Now and then, it must be owned, he has effected, or seemed to effect, a marvellous cure; but, to tell you my private mind, Signor Giovanni, he should receive little credit for such instances of success,—they being probably the work of chance,—but should be held strictly accountable for his failures, which may justly be considered his own work."

The youth might have taken Baglioni's opinions with many grains of allowance had he known that there was a professional warfare of long continuance between him and Dr. Rappaccini, in which the latter was generally thought to have gained the advantage. If the reader be inclined to judge for himself, we refer him to certain black-letter tracts on both sides, preserved in the medical department of the University of Padua.

"I know not, most learned professor," returned Giovanni, after musing on what had been said of Rappaccini's exclusive zeal for science,—"I know not how dearly this physician may love his art; but surely there is one object more dear to him. He has a daughter."

"Aha!" cried the professor, with a laugh. "So now our friend Giovanni's secret is out. You have heard of this daughter, whom all the young men in Padua are wild about, though not half a dozen have ever had the good hap to see her face. I know little of the Signora Beatrice save that Rappaccini is said to have instructed her deeply in his science, and that, young and beautiful as fame reports her, she is already qualified to fill a professor's chair. Perchance her father destines her for mine! Other absurd rumors there be, not worth talking about or listening to. So now, Signor Giovanni, drink off your glass of lachryma."

Guasconti returned to his lodgings somewhat heated with the wine he had quaffed, and which caused his brain to swim with strange fantasies in reference to Dr. Rappaccini and the beautiful Beatrice. On his way, happening to pass by a florist's, he bought a fresh bouquet of flowers.

Ascending to his chamber, he seated himself near the window, but within the shadow thrown by the depth of the wall, so that he could look down into the garden with little risk of being discovered. All beneath his eye was a solitude. The strange plants were basking in the sunshine, and now and then nodding gently to one another, as if in acknowledgment of sympathy and kindred. In the midst, by the shattered fountain, grew the magnificent shrub, with its purple gems clustering all over it; they glowed in the air, and gleamed back again out of the depths of the pool, which thus seemed to overflow with colored radiance from the rich reflection that was steeped in it. At first, as we have said, the garden was a solitude. Soon, however,—as Giovanni had half hoped, half feared, would be the case,—a figure appeared beneath the antique sculptured portal, and came down between the rows of plants, inhaling their various perfumes as if she were one of those beings of old classic fable that lived upon sweet odors. On again beholding Beatrice, the young man was even startled to perceive how much her beauty exceeded his recollection of it; so brilliant, so vivid, was its character, that she glowed amid the sunlight, and, as Giovanni whispered to himself, positively illuminated the more shadowy intervals of the garden path. Her face being now more revealed than on the former occasion, he was struck by its expression of simplicity and sweetness,—qualities that had not entered into his idea of her character, and which made him ask anew what manner of mortal she might be. Nor did he fail again to observe, or imagine, an analogy between the beautiful girl and the gorgeous shrub that hung its gemlike flowers over the fountain,—a resemblance which Beatrice seemed to have indulged a fantastic humor in heightening, both by the arrangement of her dress and the selection of its hues.

Approaching the shrub, she threw open her arms, as with a passionate ardor, and drew its branches into an intimate embrace —so intimate that her features were hidden in its leafy bosom and her glistening ringlets all intermingled with the flowers.

"Give me thy breath, my sister," exclaimed Beatrice; "for I am faint with common air. And give me this flower of thine, which I separate with gentlest fingers from the stem and place it close beside my heart."

With these words the beautiful daughter of Rappaccini plucked one of the richest blossoms of the shrub, and was about to fasten it in her bosom. But now, unless Giovanni's draughts of wine had bewildered his senses, a singular incident occurred. A small orange-colored reptile, of the lizard or chameleon species, chanced to be creeping along the path, just at the feet of Beatrice. It appeared to Giovanni,—but, at the distance from which he gazed, he could scarcely have seen anything so minute,—it appeared to him, however, that a drop or two of moisture from the broken stem of the flower descended upon the lizard's head. For an instant the reptile contorted itself violently, and then lay motionless in the sunshine. Beatrice observed this remarkable phenomenon, and crossed herself, sadly, but without surprise; nor did she therefore hesitate to arrange the fatal flower in her bosom. There it blushed, and almost glimmered with the dazzling effect of a precious stone, adding to her dress and aspect the one appropriate charm which nothing else in the world could have supplied. But Giovanni, out of the shadow of his window, bent forward and shrank back, and murmured and trembled.

"Am I awake? Have I my senses?" said he to himself. "What is this being? Beautiful shall I call her, or inexpressibly terrible?"

Beatrice now strayed carelessly through the garden, approaching closer beneath Giovanni's window, so that he was compelled to thrust his head quite out of its concealment in order to gratify the intense and painful curiosity which she excited. At this moment there came a beautiful insect over the garden wall; it had, perhaps, wandered through the city, and found no flowers or verdure among those antique haunts of men until the heavy perfumes of Dr. Rappaccini's shrubs had lured it from afar. Without alighting on the flowers, this winged brightness seemed to be attracted by Beatrice, and lingered in the air and fluttered about her head. Now, here it could not be but that Giovanni Guasconti's eyes deceived him. Be that as it might, he fancied that, while Beatrice was gazing at the insect with childish delight, it grew faint and fell at her feet; its bright wings shivered; it was dead—from no cause that he could discern, unless it were the atmosphere of her breath. Again Beatrice crossed herself and sighed heavily as she bent over the dead insect.

An impulsive movement of Giovanni drew her eyes to the window. There she beheld the beautiful head of the young man—rather a Grecian than an Italian head, with fair, regular features, and a glistening of gold among his ringlets— gazing down upon her like a being that hovered in mid air. Scarcely knowing what he did, Giovanni threw down the bouquet which he had hitherto held in his hand.

"Signora," said he, "there are pure and healthful flowers. Wear them for the sake of Giovanni Guasconti."

"Thanks, signor," replied Beatrice, with her rich voice, that came forth as it were like a gush of music, and with a mirthful expression half childish and half womanlike. "I accept your gift, and would fain recompense it with this precious purple flower; but if I toss it into the air it will not reach you. So Signor Guasconti must even content himself with my thanks."

She lifted the bouquet from the ground, and then, as if inwardly ashamed at having stepped aside from her maidenly reserve to respond to a stranger's greeting, passed swiftly homeward through the garden. But few as the moments were, it seemed to Giovanni, when she was on the point of vanishing beneath the sculptured portal, that his beautiful bouquet was already beginning to wither in her grasp. It was an idle thought; there could be no possibility of distinguishing a faded flower from a fresh one at so great a distance.

For many days after this incident the young man avoided the window that looked into Dr. Rappaccini's garden, as if something ugly and monstrous would have blasted his eyesight had he been betrayed into a glance. He felt conscious of having put himself, to a certain extent, within the influence of an unintelligible power by the communication which he had opened with Beatrice. The wisest course would have been, if his heart were in any real danger, to quit his lodgings and Padua itself at once; the next wiser, to have accustomed himself, as far as possible, to the familiar and daylight view of Beatrice—thus bringing her rigidly and systematically within the limits of ordinary experience. Least of all, while avoiding her sight, ought Giovanni to have remained so near this extraordinary being that the proximity and possibility even of intercourse should give a kind of substance and reality to the wild vagaries which his imagination ran riot continually in producing. Guasconti had not a deep heart—or, at all events, its depths were not sounded now; but he had a quick fancy, and an ardent southern temperament, which rose every instant to a higher fever pitch. Whether or no Beatrice possessed those terrible attributes, that fatal breath, the affinity with those so beautiful and deadly flowers which were indicated by what Giovanni had witnessed, she had at least instilled a fierce and subtle poison into his system. It was not love, although her rich beauty was a madness to him; nor horror, even while he fancied her spirit to be imbued with the same baneful essence that seemed to pervade her physical frame; but a wild offspring of both love and horror that had each parent in it, and burned like one and shivered like the other. Giovanni knew not what to dread; still less did he know what to hope; yet hope and dread kept a continual warfare in his breast, alternately vanquishing one another and starting up afresh to renew the contest. Blessed are all simple emotions, be they dark or bright! it is the lurid intermixture of the two that produces the illuminating blaze of the infernal regions. Sometimes he endeavored to assuage the fever of his spirit by a rapid walk through the streets of Padua or beyond its gates: his footsteps kept time with the throbbings of his brain, so that the walk was apt to accelerate itself to a race. One day he found himself arrested; his arm was seized by a portly personage, who had turned back on recognizing the young man and expended much breath in overtaking him.

"Signor Giovanni! Stay, my young friend!" cried he. "Have you forgotten me? That might well be the case if I were as much altered as yourself."

It was Baglioni, whom Giovanni had avoided ever since their first meeting, from a doubt that the professor's sagacity would look too deeply into his secrets. Endeavoring to recover himself, he stared forth wildly from his inner world into the outer one and spoke like a man in a dream.

"Yes; I am Giovanni Guasconti. You are Professor Pietro Baglioni. Now let me pass!"

"Not yet, not yet, Signor Giovanni Guasconti," said the professor, smiling, but at the same time scrutinizing the youth with an earnest glance. "What! did I grow up side by side with your father? and shall his son pass me like a stranger in these old streets of Padua? Stand still, Signor Giovanni; for we must have a word or two before we part."

"Speedily, then, most worshipful professor, speedily," said Giovanni, with feverish impatience. "Does not your worship see that I am in haste?"

Now, while he was speaking there came a man in black along the street, stooping and moving feebly like a person in inferior health. His face was all overspread with a most sickly and sallow hue, but yet so pervaded with an expression of piercing and active intellect that an observer might easily have overlooked the merely physical attributes and have seen only this wonderful energy. As he passed, this person exchanged a cold and distant salutation with Baglioni, but fixed his eyes upon Giovanni with an intentness that seemed to bring out whatever was within him

worthy of notice. Nevertheless, there was a peculiar quietness in the look, as if taking merely a speculative, not a human, interest in the young man.

"It is Dr. Rappaccini!" whispered the professor when the stranger had passed. "Has he ever seen your face before?"

"Not that I know," answered Giovanni, starting at the name.

"He *has* seen you! he must have seen you!" said Baglioni, hastily. "For some purpose or other, this man of science is making a study of you. I know that look of his! It is the same that coldly illuminates his face as he bends over a bird, a mouse, or a butterfly, which, in pursuance of some experiment, he has killed by the perfume of a flower; a look as deep as Nature itself, but without Nature's warmth of love. Signor Giovanni, I will stake my life upon it, you are the subject of one of Rappaccini's experiments!"

"Will you make a fool of me?" cried Giovanni, passionately. "*That,* signor professor, were an untoward experiment."

"Patience! patience!" replied the imperturbable professor. "I tell thee, my poor Giovanni, that Rappaccini has a scientific interest in thee. Thou hast fallen into fearful hands! And the Signora Beatrice,—what part does she act in this mystery?"

But Guasconti, finding Baglioni's pertinacity intolerable, here broke away, and was gone before the professor could again seize his arm. He looked after the young man intently and shook his head.

"This must not be," said Baglioni to himself. "The youth is the son of my old friend, and shall not come to any harm from which the arcana of medical science can preserve him. Besides, it is too insufferable an impertinence in Rappaccini, thus to snatch the lad out of my own hands, as I may say, and make use of him for his infernal experiments. This daughter of his! It shall be looked to. Perchance, most learned Rappaccini, I may foil you where you little dream of it!"

Meanwhile Giovanni had pursued a circuitous route, and at length found himself at the door of his lodgings. As he crossed the threshold he was met by old Lisabetta, who smirked and smiled, and was evidently desirous to attract his attention; vainly, however, as the ebullition of his feelings had momentarily subsided into a cold and dull vacuity. He turned his eyes full upon the withered face that was puckering itself into a smile, but seemed to behold it not. The old dame, therefore, laid her grasp upon his cloak.

"Signor! signor!" whispered she, still with a smile over the whole breadth of her visage, so that it looked not unlike a grotesque carving in wood, darkened by centuries. "Listen, signor! There is a private entrance into the garden!"

"What do you say?" exclaimed Giovanni, turning quickly about, as if an inanimate thing should start into feverish life. "A private entrance into Dr. Rappaccini's garden?"

"Hush! hush! not so loud!" whispered Lisabetta, putting her hand over his mouth. "Yes; into the worshipful doctor's garden, where you may see all his fine shrubbery. Many a young man in Padua would give gold to be admitted among those flowers."

Giovanni put a piece of gold into her hand.

"Show me the way," said he.

A surmise, probably excited by his conversation with Baglioni, crossed his mind, that this interposition of old Lisabetta might perchance be connected with the intrigue, whatever were its nature, in which the professor seemed to suppose that Dr. Rappaccini was involving him. But such a suspicion, though it disturbed Giovanni, was inadequate to restrain him. The instant that he was aware of the possibility of approaching Beatrice, it seemed an absolute necessity of his existence to do so. It mattered not whether she were angel or demon; he was irrevocably within her sphere, and must obey the law that whirled him onward, in ever-lessening circles, towards a result which he did not attempt

to foreshadow; and yet, strange to say, there came across him a sudden doubt whether this intense interest on his part were not delusory; whether it were really of so deep and positive a nature as to justify him in now thrusting himself into an incalculable position; whether it were not merely the fantasy of a young man's brain, only slightly or not at all connected with his heart.

He paused, hesitated, turned half about, but again went on. His withered guide led him along several obscure passages, and finally undid a door, through which, as it was opened, there came the sight and sound of rustling leaves, with the broken sunshine glimmering among them. Giovanni stepped forth, and, forcing himself through the entanglement of a shrub that wreathed its tendrils over the hidden entrance, stood beneath his own window in the open area of Dr. Rappaccini's garden.

How often is it the case that, when impossibilities have come to pass and dreams have condensed their misty substance into tangible realities, we find ourselves calm, and even coldly self-possessed, amid circumstances which it would have been a delirium of joy or agony to anticipate! Fate delights to thwart us thus. Passion will choose his own time to rush upon the scene, and lingers sluggishly behind when an appropriate adjustment of events would seem to summon his appearance. So was it now with Giovanni. Day after day his pulses had throbbed with feverish blood at the improbable idea of an interview with Beatrice, and of standing with her, face to face, in this very garden, basking in the Oriental sunshine of her beauty, and snatching from her full gaze the mystery which he deemed the riddle of his own existence. But now there was a singular and untimely equanimity within his breast. He threw a glance around the garden to discover if Beatrice or her father were present, and, perceiving that he was alone, began a critical observation of the plants.

The aspect of one and all of them dissatisfied him; their gorgeousness seemed fierce, passionate, and even unnatural. There was hardly an individual shrub which a wanderer, straying by himself through a forest, would not have been startled to find growing wild, as if an unearthly face had glared at him out of the thicket. Several also would have shocked a delicate instinct by an appearance of artificialness indicating that there had been such commixture, and, as it were, adultery, of various vegetable species, that the production was no longer of God's making, but the monstrous offspring of man's depraved fancy, glowing with only an evil mockery of beauty. They were probably the result of experiment, which in one or two cases had succeeded in mingling plants individually lovely into a compound possessing the questionable and ominous character that distinguished the whole growth of the garden. In fine, Giovanni recognized but two or three plants in the collection, and those of a kind that he well knew to be poisonous. While busy with these contemplations he heard the rustling of a silken garment, and, turning, beheld Beatrice emerging from beneath the sculptured portal.

Giovanni had not considered with himself what should be his deportment; whether he should apologize for his intrusion into the garden, or assume that he was there with the privity at least, if not by the desire, of Dr. Rappaccini or his daughter; but Beatrice's manner placed him at his ease, though leaving him still in doubt by what agency he had gained admittance. She came lightly along the path and met him near the broken fountain. There was surprise in her face, but brightened by a simple and kind expression of pleasure.

"You are a connoisseur in flowers, signor," said Beatrice, with a smile, alluding to the bouquet which he had flung her from the window. "It is no marvel, therefore, if the sight of my father's rare collection has tempted you to take a nearer view. If he were here, he could tell you many strange and interesting facts as to the nature and habits of these shrubs; for he has spent a lifetime in such studies, and this garden is his world."

"And yourself, lady," observed Giovanni, "if fame says true,—you likewise are deeply skilled in the virtues indicated by these rich blossoms and these spicy perfumes. Would you deign to be my instructress, I should prove an apter scholar than if taught by Signor Rappaccini himself."

"Are there such idle rumors?" asked Beatrice, with the music of a pleasant laugh. "Do people say that I am skilled in my father's science of plants? What a jest is there! No; though I have grown up among these flowers, I know no more of them than their hues and perfume; and sometimes methinks I would fain rid myself of even that small knowledge. There are many flowers here, and those not the least brilliant, that shock and offend me when they meet my eye. But pray, signor, do not believe these stories about my science. Believe nothing of me save what you see with your own eyes."

"And must I believe all that I have seen with my own eyes?" asked Giovanni, pointedly, while the recollection of former scenes made him shrink. "No, signora; you demand too little of me. Bid me believe nothing save what comes from your own lips."

It would appear that Beatrice understood him. There came a deep flush to her cheek; but she looked full into Giovanni's eyes, and responded to his gaze of uneasy suspicion with a queenlike haughtiness.

"I do so bid you, signor," she replied. "Forget whatever you may have fancied in regard to me. If true to the outward senses, still it may be false in its essence; but the words of Beatrice Rappaccini's lips are true from the depths of the heart outward. Those you may believe."

A fervor glowed in her whole aspect and beamed upon Giovanni's consciousness like the light of truth itself; but while she spoke there was a fragrance in the atmosphere around her, rich and delightful, though evanescent, yet which the young man, from an indefinable reluctance, scarcely dared to draw into his lungs. It might be the odor of the flowers. Could it be Beatrice's breath which thus embalmed her words with a strange richness, as if by steeping them in her heart? A faintness passed like a shadow over Giovanni and flitted away; he seemed to gaze through the beautiful girl's eyes into her transparent soul, and felt no more doubt or fear.

The tinge of passion that had colored Beatrice's manner vanished; she became gay, and appeared to derive a pure delight from her communion with the youth not unlike what the maiden of a lonely island might have felt conversing with a voyager from the civilized world. Evidently her experience of life had been confined within the limits of that garden. She talked now about matters as simple as the daylight or summer clouds, and now asked questions in reference to the city, or Giovanni's distant home, his friends, his mother, and his sisters—questions indicating such seclusion, and such lack of familiarity with modes and forms, that Giovanni responded as if to an infant. Her spirit gushed out before him like a fresh rill that was just catching its first glimpse of the sunlight and wondering at the reflections of earth and sky which were flung into its bosom. There came thoughts, too, from a deep source, and fantasies of a gemlike brilliancy, as if diamonds and rubies sparkled upward among the bubbles of the fountain. Ever and anon there gleamed across the young man's mind a sense of wonder that he should be walking side by side with the being who had so wrought upon his imagination, whom he had idealized in such hues of terror, in whom he had positively witnessed such manifestations of dreadful attributes,—that he should be conversing with Beatrice like a brother, and should find her so human and so maidenlike. But such reflections were only momentary; the

effect of her character was too real not to make itself familiar at once.

In this free intercourse they had strayed through the garden, and now, after many turns among its avenues, were come to the shattered fountain, beside which grew the magnificent shrub, with its treasury of glowing blossoms. A fragrance was diffused from it which Giovanni recognized as identical with that which he had attributed to Beatrice's breath, but incomparably more powerful. As her eyes fell upon it, Giovanni beheld her press her hand to her bosom as if her heart were throbbing suddenly and painfully.

"For the first time in my life," murmured she, addressing the shrub, "I had forgotten thee."

"I remember, signora," said Giovanni, "that you once promised to reward me with one of these living gems for the bouquet which I had the happy boldness to fling to your feet. Permit me now to pluck it as a memorial of this interview."

He made a step towards the shrub with extended hand; but Beatrice darted forward, uttering a shriek that went through his heart like a dagger. She caught his hand and drew it back with the whole force of her slender figure. Giovanni felt her touch thrilling through his fibres.

"Touch it not!" exclaimed she, in a voice of agony. "Not for thy life! It is fatal!"

Then, hiding her face, she fled from him and vanished beneath the sculptured portal. As Giovanni followed her with his eyes, he beheld the emaciated figure and pale intelligence of Dr. Rappaccini, who had been watching the scene, he knew not how long, within the shadow of the entrance.

No sooner was Guasconti alone in his chamber than the image of Beatrice came back to his passionate musings, invested with all the witchery that had been gathering around it ever since his first glimpse of her, and now likewise imbued with a tender warmth of girlish womanhood. She was human; her nature was endowed with all gentle and feminine qualities; she was worthiest to be worshipped; she was capable, surely, on her part, of the height and heroism of love. Those tokens which he had hitherto considered as proofs of a frightful peculiarity in her physical and moral system were now either forgotten, or, by the subtle sophistry of passion transmitted into a golden crown of enchantment, rendering Beatrice the more admirable by so much as she was the more unique. Whatever had looked ugly was now beautiful; or, if incapable of such a change, it stole away and hid itself among those shapeless half ideas which throng the dim region beyond the daylight of our perfect consciousness. Thus did he spend the night, nor fell asleep until the dawn had begun to awake the slumbering flowers in Dr. Rappaccini's garden, whither Giovanni's dreams doubtless led him. Up rose the sun in his due season, and, flinging his beams upon the young man's eyelids, awoke him to a sense of pain. When thoroughly aroused, he became sensible of a burning and tingling agony in his hand—in his right hand—the very hand which Beatrice had grasped in her own when he was on the point of plucking one of the gemlike flowers. On the back of that hand there was now a purple print like that of four small fingers, and the likeness of a slender thumb upon his wrist.

Oh, how stubbornly does love,—or even that cunning semblance of love which flourishes in the imagination, but strikes no depth of root into the heart,—how stubbornly does it hold its faith until the moment comes when it is doomed to vanish into thin mist! Giovanni wrapped a handkerchief about his hand and wondered what evil thing had stung him, and soon forgot his pain in a reverie of Beatrice.

After the first interview, a second was in the inevitable course of what we call fate. A third; a fourth; and a meeting with Beatrice in the garden was no longer an incident in Giovanni's daily life, but the whole space in which he might be said to live; for the anticipation and memory of that ecstatic hour made up the remainder. Nor was it otherwise with the daughter of Rappaccini. She watched for the youth's appearance, and flew to his side with confidence as unreserved as if they had been playmates from early infancy—as if they were such playmates still. If, by any unwonted chance, he failed to come at the appointed moment, she stood beneath the window and sent up the rich sweetness of her tones to float around him in his chamber and echo and reverberate throughout his heart: "Giovanni! Giovanni! Why tarriest thou? Come down!" And down he hastened into that Eden of poisonous flowers.

But, with all this intimate familiarity, there was still a reserve in Beatrice's demeanor, so rigidly and invariably sustained that the idea of infringing it scarcely occurred to his imagination. By all appreciable signs, they loved; they had looked love with eyes that conveyed the holy secret from the depths of one soul into the depths of the other, as if it were too sacred to be whispered by the way; they had even spoken love in those gushes of passion when their spirits darted forth in articulated breath like tongues of long-hidden flame; and yet there had been no seal of lips, no clasp of hands, nor any slightest caress such as love claims and hallows. He had never touched one of the gleaming ringlets of her hair; her garment—so marked was the physical barrier between them—had never been waved against him by a breeze. On the few occasions when Giovanni had seemed tempted to overstep the limit, Beatrice grew so sad, so stern, and withal wore such a look of desolate separation, shuddering at itself, that not a spoken word was requisite to repel him. At such times he was startled at the horrible suspicions that rose, monster-like, out of the caverns of his heart and stared him in the face; his love grew thin and faint as the morning mist, his doubts alone had substance. But, when Beatrice's face brightened again after the momentary shadow, she was transformed at once from the mysterious, questionable being whom he had watched with so much awe and horror; she was now the beautiful and unsophisticated girl whom he felt his spirit knew with a certainty beyond all other knowledge.

A considerable time had now passed since Giovanni's last meeting with Baglioni. One morning, however, he was disagreeably surprised by a visit from the professor, whom he had scarcely thought of for whole weeks, and would willingly have forgotten still longer. Given up as he had long been to a pervading excitement, he could tolerate no companions except upon condition of their perfect sympathy with his present state of feeling. Such sympathy was not to be expected from Professor Baglioni.

The visitor chatted carelessly for a few moments about the gossip of the city and the university, and then took up another topic.

"I have been reading an old classic author lately," said he, "and met with a story that strangely interested me. Possibly you may remember it. It is of an Indian prince, who sent a beautiful woman as a present to Alexander the Great. She was as lovely as the dawn and gorgeous as the sunset; but what especially distinguished her was a certain rich perfume in her breath—richer than a garden of Persian roses. Alexander, as was natural to a youthful conqueror, fell in love at first sight with this magnificent stranger; but a certain sage physician, happening to be present, discovered a terrible secret in regard to her."

"And what was that?" asked Giovanni, turning his eyes downward to avoid those of the professor.

"That this lovely woman," continued Baglioni, with emphasis, "had been nourished with poisons from her birth upward, until her whole nature was so imbued with them that she herself had become the deadliest poison in existence. Poison was her element of life. With that rich perfume of her breath she blasted the very air. Her love would have been poison—her embrace death. Is not this a marvellous tale?"

"A childish fable," answered Giovanni, nervously starting from his chair. "I marvel how your worship finds time to read such nonsense among your graver studies."

"By the by," said the professor, looking uneasily about him, "what singular fragrance is this in your apartment? Is it the perfume of your gloves? It is faint, but delicious; and yet, after all, by no means agreeable. Were I to breathe it long, methinks it would make me ill. It is like the breath of a flower; but I see no flowers in the chamber."

"Nor are there any," replied Giovanni, who had turned pale as the professor spoke; "nor, I think, is there any fragrance except in your worship's imagination. Odors, being a sort of element combined of the sensual and the spiritual, are apt to deceive us in this manner. The recollection of a perfume, the bare idea of it, may easily be mistaken for a present reality."

"Ay; but my sober imagination does not often play such tricks," said Baglioni; "and, were I to fancy any kind of odor, it would be that of some vile apothecary drug, wherewith my fingers are likely enough to be imbued. Our worshipful friend Rappaccini, as I have heard, tinctures his medicaments with odors richer than those of Araby. Doubtless, likewise, the fair and learned Signora Beatrice would minister to her patients with draughts as sweet as a maiden's breath; but woe to him that sips them!"

Giovanni's face evinced many contending emotions. The tone in which the professor alluded to the pure and lovely daughter of Rappaccini was a torture to his soul; and yet the intimation of a view of her character, opposite to his own, gave instantaneous distinctness to a thousand dim suspicions, which now grinned at him like so many demons. But he strove hard to quell them and to respond to Baglioni with a true lover's perfect faith.

"Signor professor," said he, "you were

my father's friend; perchance, too, it is your purpose to act a friendly part towards his son. I would fain feel nothing towards you save respect and deference; but I pray you to observe, signor, that there is one subject on which we must not speak. You know not the Signora Beatrice. You cannot, therefore, estimate the wrong—the blasphemy, I may even say—that is offered to her character by a light or injurious word."

"Giovanni! my poor Giovanni!" answered the professor, with a calm expression of pity, "I know this wretched girl far better than yourself. You shall hear the truth in respect to the poisoner Rappaccini and his poisonous daughter; yes, poisonous as she is beautiful. Listen; for, even should you do violence to my gray hairs, it shall not silence me. That old fable of the Indian woman has become a truth by the deep and deadly science of Rappaccini and in the person of the lovely Beatrice."

Giovanni groaned and hid his face.

"Her father," continued Baglioni, "was not restrained by natural affection from offering up his child in this horrible manner as the victim of his insane zeal for science; for, let us do him justice, he is as true a man of science as ever distilled his own heart in an alembic. What, then, will be your fate? Beyond a doubt you are selected as the material of some new experiment. Perhaps the result is to be death; perhaps a fate more awful still. Rappaccini, with what he calls the interest of science before his eyes, will hesitate at nothing."

"It is a dream," muttered Giovanni to himself; "surely it is a dream."

"But," resumed the professor, "be of good cheer, son of my friend. It is not yet too late for the rescue. Possibly we may even succeed in bringing back this miserable child within the limits of ordinary nature, from which her father's madness has estranged her. Behold this little silver vase! It was wrought by the hands of the renowned Benvenuto Cellini,[3] and is well worthy to be a love gift to the fairest dame in Italy. But its contents are invaluable. One little sip of this antidote would have rendered the most virulent poisons of the Borgias innocuous. Doubt not that it will be as efficacious against those of Rappaccini. Bestow the vase, and the precious liquid within it, on your Beatrice, and hopefully await the result."

Baglioni laid a small, exquisitely wrought silver vial on the table and withdrew, leaving what he had said to produce its effect upon the young man's mind.

"We will thwart Rappaccini yet," thought he, chuckling to himself, as he descended the stairs; "but, let us confess the truth of him, he is a wonderful man— a wonderful man indeed; a vile empiric, however, in his practice, and therefore not to be tolerated by those who respect the good old rules of the medical profession."

Throughout Giovanni's whole acquaintance with Beatrice, he had occasionally, as we have said, been haunted by dark surmises as to her character; yet so thoroughly had she made herself felt by him as a simple, natural, most affectionate, and guileless creature, that the image now held up by Professor Baglioni looked as strange and incredible as if it were not in accordance with his own original conception. True, there were ugly recollections connected with his first glimpses of the beautiful girl; he could not quite forget the bouquet that withered in her grasp, and the insect that perished amid the sunny air, by no ostensible agency save the fragrance of her breath. These incidents, however, dissolving in the pure light of her character, had no longer the efficacy of facts, but were acknowledged as mistaken fantasies, by whatever testimony of the senses they might appear to be substantiated. There is something truer and more real than what we can see with the eyes and touch with the finger. On such better evidence had Giovanni founded his confidence in Beatrice,

[3] Renaissance artist (1500-1571), whose *Autobiography* is one of the world's classics.

though rather by the necessary force of her high attributes than by any deep and generous faith on his part. But now his spirit was incapable of sustaining itself at the height to which the early enthusiasm of passion had exalted it; he fell down, grovelling among earthly doubts, and defiled therewith the pure whiteness of Beatrice's image. Not that he gave her up; he did but distrust. He resolved to institute some decisive test that should satisfy him, once for all, whether there were those dreadful peculiarities in her physical nature which could not be supposed to exist without some corresponding monstrosity of soul. His eyes, gazing down afar, might have deceived him as to the lizard, the insect, and the flowers; but if he could witness, at the distance of a few paces, the sudden blight of one fresh and healthful flower in Beatrice's hand, there would be room for no further question. With this idea he hastened to the florist's and purchased a bouquet that was still gemmed with the morning dew-drops.

It was now the customary hour of his daily interview with Beatrice. Before descending into the garden, Giovanni failed not to look at his figure in the mirror,— a vanity to be expected in a beautiful young man, yet, as displaying itself at that troubled and feverish moment, the token of a certain shallowness of feeling and insincerity of character. He did gaze, however, and said to himself that his features had never before possessed so rich a grace, nor his eyes such vivacity, nor his cheeks so warm a hue of superabundant life.

"At least," thought he, "her poison has not yet insinuated itself into my system. I am no flower to perish in her grasp."

With that thought he turned his eyes on the bouquet, which he had never once laid aside from his hand. A thrill of indefinable horror shot through his frame on perceiving that those dewy flowers were already beginning to droop; they wore the aspect of things that had been fresh and lovely yesterday. Giovanni grew white as marble, and stood motionless before the

mirror, staring at his own reflection there as at the likeness of something frightful. He remembered Baglioni's remark about the fragrance that seemed to pervade the chamber. It must have been the poison in his breath! Then he shuddered—shuddered at himself. Recovering from his stupor, he began to watch with curious eye a spider that was busily at work hanging its web from the antique cornice of the apartment, crossing and recrossing the artful system of interwoven lines—as vigorous and active a spider as ever dangled from an old ceiling. Giovanni bent towards the insect, and emitted a deep, long breath. The spider suddenly ceased its toil; the web vibrated with a tremor originating in the body of the small artisan. Again Giovanni sent forth a breath, deeper, longer, and imbued with a venomous feeling out of his heart: he knew not whether he were wicked, or only desperate. The spider made a convulsive gripe with his limbs and hung dead across the window.

"Accursed! accursed!" muttered Giovanni, addressing himself. "Hast thou grown so poisonous that this deadly insect perishes by thy breath?"

At that moment a rich, sweet voice came floating up from the garden.

"Giovanni! Giovanni! It is past the hour! Why tarriest thou? Come down!"

"Yes," muttered Giovanni again. "She is the only being whom my breath may not slay! Would that it might!"

He rushed down, and in an instant was standing before the bright and loving eyes of Beatrice. A moment ago his wrath and despair had been so fierce that he could have desired nothing so much as to wither her by a glance; but with her actual presence there came influences which had too real an existence to be at once shaken off: recollections of the delicate and benign power of her feminine nature, which had so often enveloped him in a religious calm; recollections of many a holy and passionate outgush of her heart, when the pure fountain had been unsealed from its depths and made visible in its transparency to his mental eye; recollections which, had Giovanni known how to estimate them, would have assured him that all this ugly mystery was but an earthly illusion, and that, whatever mist of evil might seem to have gathered over her, the real Beatrice was a heavenly angel. Incapable as he was of such high faith, still her presence had not utterly lost its magic. Giovanni's rage was quelled into an aspect of sullen insensibility. Beatrice, with a quick spiritual sense, immediately felt that there was a gulf of blackness between them which neither he nor she could pass. They walked on together, sad and silent, and came thus to the marble fountain and to its pool of water on the ground, in the midst of which grew the shrub that bore gem-like blossoms. Giovanni was affrighted at the eager enjoyment—the appetite, as it were—with which he found himself inhaling the fragrance of the flowers.

"Beatrice," asked he, abruptly, "whence came this shrub?"

"My father created it," answered she, with simplicity.

"Created it! created it!" repeated Giovanni. "What mean you, Beatrice?"

"He is a man fearfully acquainted with the secrets of Nature," replied Beatrice; "and, at the hour when I first drew breath, this plant sprang from the soil, the offspring of his science, of his intellect, while I was but his earthly child. Approach it not!" continued she, observing with terror that Giovanni was drawing nearer to the shrub. "It has qualities that you little dream of. But I, dearest Giovanni,—I grew up and blossomed with the plant and was nourished with its breath. It was my sister, and I loved it with a human affection; for, alas!—hast thou not suspected it?—there was an awful doom."

Here Giovanni frowned so darkly upon her that Beatrice paused and trembled. But her faith in his tenderness reassured her, and made her blush that she had doubted for an instant.

"There was an awful doom," she continued, "the effect of my father's fatal love of science, which estranged me from all society of my kind. Until Heaven sent thee, dearest Giovanni, oh, how lonely was thy poor Beatrice!"

"Was it a hard doom?" asked Giovanni, fixing his eyes upon her.

"Only of late have I known how hard it was," answered she, tenderly. "Oh, yes; but my heart was torpid, and therefore quiet."

Giovanni's rage broke forth from his sullen gloom like a lightning flash out of a dark cloud.

"Accursed one!" cried he, with venomous scorn and anger. "And, finding thy solitude wearisome, thou hast severed me likewise from all the warmth of life and enticed me into thy region of unspeakable horror!"

"Giovanni!" exclaimed Beatrice, turning her large bright eyes upon his face. The force of his words had not found its way into her mind; she was merely thunderstruck.

"Yes, poisonous thing!" repeated Giovanni, beside himself with passion. "Thou hast done it! Thou hast blasted me! Thou hast filled my veins with poison! Thou hast made me as hateful, as ugly, as loathsome and deadly a creature as thyself— a world's wonder of hideous monstrosity! Now, if our breath be happily as fatal to ourselves as to all others, let us join our lips in one kiss of unutterable hatred, and so die!"

"What has befallen me?" murmured Beatrice, with a low moan out of her heart. "Holy Virgin, pity me, a poor heartbroken child!"

"Thou,—dost thou pray?" cried Giovanni, still with the same fiendish scorn. "Thy very prayers, as they come from thy lips, taint the atmosphere with death. Yes, yes; let us pray! Let us to church and dip our fingers in the holy water at the portal! They that come after us will perish as by a pestilence! Let us sign crosses in the air! It will be scattering curses abroad in the likeness of holy symbols!"

"Giovanni," said Beatrice, calmly, for her grief was beyond passion, "why dost thou join thyself with me thus in those terrible words? I, it is true, am the horrible thing thou namest me. But thou,— what hast thou to do, save with one other shudder at my hideous misery to go forth out of the garden and mingle with thy race, and forget that there ever crawled on earth such a monster as poor Beatrice?"

"Dost thou pretend ignorance?" asked Giovanni, scowling upon her. "Behold! this power have I gained from the pure daughter of Rappaccini."

There was a swarm of summer insects flitting through the air in search of the food promised by the flower odors of the fatal garden. They circled round Giovanni's head, and were evidently attracted towards him by the same influence which had drawn them for an instant within the sphere of several of the shrubs. He sent forth a breath among them, and smiled bitterly at Beatrice as at least a score of the insects fell dead upon the ground.

"I see it! I see it!" shrieked Beatrice. "It is my father's fatal science! No, no, Giovanni; it was not I! Never! never! I dreamed only to love thee and be with thee a little time, and so to let thee pass away, leaving but thine image in mine heart; for, Giovanni, believe it, though my body be nourished with poison, my spirit is God's creature, and craves love as its daily food. But my father,—he has united us in this fearful sympathy. Yes; spurn me, tread upon me, kill me! Oh, what is death after such words as thine? But it was not I. Not for a world of bliss would I have done it."

Giovanni's passion had exhausted itself in its outburst from his lips. There now came across him a sense, mournful, and not without tenderness, of the intimate and peculiar relationship between Beatrice and himself. They stood, as it were, in an utter solitude, which would be made none the less solitary by the densest throng of human life. Ought not, then, the desert of humanity around them to press this in-

sulated pair closer together? If they should be cruel to one another, who was there to be kind to them? Besides, thought Giovanni, might there not still be a hope of his returning within the limits of ordinary nature, and leading Beatrice, the redeemed Beatrice, by the hand? O, weak, and selfish, and unworthy spirit, that could dream of an earthly union and earthly happiness as possible, after such deep love had been so bitterly wronged as was Beatrice's love by Giovanni's blighting words! No, no; there could be no such hope. She must pass heavily, with that broken heart, across the borders of Time—she must bathe her hurts in some fount of paradise, and forget her grief in the light of immortality, and *there* be well.

But Giovanni did not know it.

"Dear Beatrice," said he, approaching her, while she shrank away as always at his approach, but now with a different impulse, "dearest Beatrice, our fate is not yet so desperate. Behold! there is a medicine, potent, as a wise physician has assured me, and almost divine in its efficacy. It is composed of ingredients the most opposite to those by which thy awful father has brought this calamity upon thee and me. It is distilled of blessed herbs. Shall we not quaff it together, and thus be purified from evil?"

"Give it me!" said Beatrice, extending her hand to receive the little silver vial which Giovanni took from his bosom. She added, with a peculiar emphasis, "I will drink; but do thou await the result."

She put Baglioni's antidote to her lips; and, at the same moment, the figure of Rappaccini emerged from the portal and came slowly towards the marble fountain. As he drew near, the pale man of science seemed to gaze with a triumphant expression at the beautiful youth and maiden, as might an artist who should spend his life in achieving a picture or a group of statuary and finally be satisfied with his success. He paused; his bent form grew erect with conscious power; he spread out his hands over them in the attitude of a father imploring a blessing upon his children; but those were the same hands that had thrown poison into the stream of their lives. Giovanni trembled. Beatrice shuddered nervously, and pressed her hand upon her heart.

"My daughter," said Rappaccini, "thou art no longer lonely in the world. Pluck one of those precious gems from thy sister shrub and bid thy bridegroom wear it in his bosom. It will not harm him now. My science and the sympathy between thee and him have so wrought within his system that he now stands from common men, as thou dost, daughter of my pride and triumph, from ordinary women. Pass on, then, through the world, most dear to one another and dreadful to all besides!"

"My father," said Beatrice, feebly,—and still as she spoke she kept her hand upon her heart,—"wherefore didst thou inflict this miserable doom upon thy child?"

"Miserable!" exclaimed Rappaccini. "What mean you, foolish girl? Dost thou deem it misery to be endowed with marvellous gifts against which no power nor strength could avail an enemy—misery, to be able to quell the mightiest with a breath—misery, to be as terrible as thou art beautiful? Wouldst thou, then, have preferred the condition of a weak woman, exposed to all evil and capable of none?"

"I would fain have been loved, not feared," murmured Beatrice, sinking down upon the ground. "But now it matters not. I am going, father, where the evil which thou hast striven to mingle with my being will pass away like a dream—like the fragrance of these poisonous flowers, which will no longer taint my breath among the flowers of Eden. Farewell, Giovanni! Thy words of hatred are like lead within my heart; but they, too, will fall away as I ascend. Oh, was there not, from the first, more poison in thy nature than in mine?"

To Beatrice,—so radically had her earthly part been wrought upon by Rappaccini's skill,—as poison had been life, so the powerful antidote was death; and thus the poor victim of man's ingenuity and of thwarted nature, and of the fatality that attends all such efforts of perverted wisdom, perished there, at the feet of her father and Giovanni. Just at that moment Professor Pietro Baglioni looked forth from the window, and called loudly, in a tone of triumph mixed with horror, to the thunderstricken man of science,—

"Rappaccini! Rappaccini! and is *this* the upshot of your experiment!"

THE OLD MANSE
THE AUTHOR MAKES THE READER ACQUAINTED WITH HIS ABODE
[1846]

BETWEEN two tall gateposts of rough-hewn stone (the gate itself having fallen from its hinges at some unknown epoch) we beheld the gray front of the old parsonage terminating the vista of an avenue of black ash-trees. It was now a twelve-month since the funeral procession of the venerable clergyman, its last inhabitant, had turned from that gateway towards the village burying-ground. The wheel-track leading to the door, as well as the whole breadth of the avenue, was almost overgrown with grass, affording dainty mouthfuls to two or three vagrant cows and an old white horse who had his own living to pick up along the roadside. The glimmering shadows that lay half asleep between the door of the house and the public highway were a kind of spiritual medium, seen through which the edifice had not quite the aspect of belonging to the material world. Certainly it had little in common with those ordinary abodes which stand so imminent upon the road that every passer-by can thrust his head, as it were, into the domestic circle. From these quiet windows the figures of passing travellers looked too remote and dim to disturb the sense of privacy. In its near retirement and accessible seclusion it was the very spot for the residence of a clergyman,—a man not estranged from human life, yet enveloped in the midst of it with a veil woven of intermingled gloom and brightness. It was worthy to have been one of the time-honored parsonages of England in which, through many generations, a succession of holy occupants pass from youth to age, and bequeath each an inheritance of sanctity to pervade the house and hover over it as with an atmosphere.

Nor, in truth, had the Old Manse ever been profaned by a lay occupant until that memorable summer afternoon when I entered it as my home. A priest had built it; a priest had succeeded to it; other priestly men from time to time had dwelt in it; and children born in its chambers had grown up to assume the priestly character. It was awful to reflect how many sermons must have been written there. The latest inhabitant alone—he by whose translation to paradise the dwelling was left vacant —had penned nearly three thousand discourses, besides the better, if not the greater, number that gushed living from his lips. How often, no doubt, had he paced to and fro along the avenue, attuning his meditations to the sighs and gentle murmurs, and deep and solemn peals of the wind among the lofty tops of the trees! In that variety of natural utterances he could find something accordant with every passage of his sermon, were it of tenderness or reverential fear. The boughs over my head seemed shadowy with solemn thoughts as well as with rustling leaves. I took shame to myself for having been so long a writer of idle stories, and ventured to hope that wisdom would descend upon me with the falling leaves of the avenue, and that I should light upon an intellectual treasure in the Old Manse well worth those hoards of long-hidden gold which people seek for in moss-grown houses. Profound treatises of morality; a layman's unprofessional and therefore unprejudiced views of religion; histories (such as Bancroft [1] might have written had he taken up his abode here as he once purposed) bright with picture, gleaming over a depth of philosophic thought,— these were the works that might fitly have

flowed from such a retirement. In the humblest event I resolved at least to achieve a novel that should evolve some deep lesson and should possess physical substance enough to stand alone.

In furtherance of my design, and as if to leave me no pretext for not fulfilling it, there was in the rear of the house the most delightful little nook of a study that ever afforded its snug seclusion to a scholar. It was here that Emerson wrote Nature; for he was then an inhabitant of the Manse, and used to watch the Assyrian dawn and Paphian sunset and moonrise from the summit of our eastern hill. When I first saw the room its walls were blackened with the smoke of unnumbered years, and made still blacker by the grim prints of Puritan ministers that hung around. These worthies looked strangely like bad angels, or at least like men who had wrestled so continually and so sternly with the devil that somewhat of his sooty fierceness had been imparted to their own visages. They had all vanished now; a cheerful coat of paint and golden-tinted paper-hangings lighted up the small apartment; while the shadow of a willow-tree that swept against the overhanging eaves attempered the cheery western sunshine. In place of the grim prints there was the sweet and lovely head of one of Raphael's Madonnas and two pleasant little pictures of the Lake of Como. The only other decorations were a purple vase of flowers, always fresh, and a bronze one containing graceful ferns. My books (few, and by no means choice; for they were chiefly such waifs as chance had thrown in my way) stood in order about the room, seldom to be disturbed.

The study had three windows, set with little, old-fashioned panes of glass, each with a crack across it. The two on the western side looked, or rather peeped, between the willow branches down into the orchard, with glimpses of the river through the trees. The third, facing northward,

[1] George Bancroft (1800-1891), author of History of the United States (1834-74).

commanded a broader view of the river at a spot where its hitherto obscure waters gleam forth into the light of history. It was at this window that the clergyman who then dwelt in the Manse stood watching the outbreak of a long and deadly struggle between two nations; he saw the irregular array of his parishioners on the farther side of the river and the glittering line of the British on the hither bank. He awaited in an agony of suspense the rattle of the musketry. It came, and there needed but a gentle wind to sweep the battle smoke around this quiet house.

Perhaps the reader, whom I cannot help considering as my guest in the Old Manse and entitled to all courtesy in the way of sight-showing,—perhaps he will choose to take a nearer view of the memorable spot. We stand now on the river's brink. It may well be called the Concord, the river of peace and quietness; for it is certainly the most unexcitable and sluggish stream that ever loitered imperceptibly towards its eternity—the sea. Positively, I had lived three weeks beside it before it grew quite clear to my perception which way the current flowed. It never has a vivacious aspect except when a northwestern breeze is vexing its surface on a sunshiny day. From the incurable indolence of its nature, the stream is happily incapable of becoming the slave of human ingenuity, as is the fate of so many a wild, free mountain torrent. While all things else are compelled to subserve some useful purpose, it idles its sluggish life away in lazy liberty, without turning a solitary spindle or affording even water-power enough to grind the corn that grows upon its banks. The torpor of its movement allows it nowhere a bright, pebbly shore, nor so much as a narrow strip of glistening sand, in any part of its course. It slumbers between broad prairies, kissing the long meadow grass, and bathes the overhanging boughs of elder bushes and willows or the roots of elms and ash-trees and clumps of maples. Flags and rushes grow along its plashy shore; the yellow water-lily spreads its broad, flat

leaves on the margin; and the fragrant white pond-lily abounds, generally selecting a position just so far from the river's brink that it cannot be grasped save at the hazard of plunging in.

It is a marvel whence this perfect flower derives its loveliness and perfume, springing as it does from the black mud over which the river sleeps, and where lurk the slimy eel and speckled frog and the mud turtle, whom continual washing cannot cleanse. It is the very same black mud out of which the yellow lily sucks its obscene life and noisome odor. Thus we see, too, in the world that some persons assimilate only what is ugly and evil from the same moral circumstances which supply good and beautiful results—the fragrance of celestial flowers—to the daily life of others.

The reader must not, from any testimony of mine, contract a dislike towards our slumberous stream. In the light of a calm and golden sunset it becomes lovely beyond expression; the more lovely for the quietude that so well accords with the hour, when even the wind, after blustering all day long, usually hushes itself to rest. Each tree and rock, and every blade of grass, is distinctly imaged, and, however unsightly in reality, assumes ideal beauty in the reflection. The minutest things of earth and the broad aspect of the firmament are pictured equally without effort and with the same felicity of success. All the sky glows downward at our feet; the rich clouds float through the unruffled bosom of the stream like heavenly thoughts through a peaceful heart. We will not, then, malign our river as gross and impure while it can glorify itself with so adequate a picture of the heaven that broods above it; or, if we remember its tawny hue and the muddiness of its bed, let it be a symbol that the earthliest human soul has an infinite spiritual capacity and may contain the better world within its depths. But, indeed, the same lesson might be drawn out of any mud puddle in the streets of a city; and, being taught us everywhere, it must be true.

Come, we have pursued a somewhat devious track in our walk to the battle-ground. Here we are, at the point where the river was crossed by the old bridge, the possession of which was the immediate object of the contest. On the hither side grow two or three elms, throwing a wide circumference of shade, but which must have been planted at some period within the threescore years and ten that have passed since the battle day. On the farther shore, overhung by a clump of elder bushes, we discern the stone abutment of the bridge. Looking down into the river, I once discovered some heavy fragments of the timbers, all green with half a century's growth of water moss; for during that length of time the tramp of horses and human footsteps had ceased along this ancient highway. The stream has here about the breadth of twenty strokes of a swimmer's arm,—a space not too wide when the bullets were whistling across. Old people who dwell hereabouts will point out the very spots on the western bank where our countrymen fell down and died; and on this side of the river an obelisk of granite has grown up from the soil that was fertilized with British blood. The monument, not more than twenty feet in height, is such as it befitted the inhabitants of a village to erect in illustration of a matter of local interest rather than what was suitable to commemorate an epoch of national history. Still, by the fathers of the village this famous deed was done; and their descendants might rightfully claim the privilege of building a memorial.

A humbler token of the fight, yet a more interesting one than the granite obelisk, may be seen close under the stone-wall which separates the battle-ground from the precincts of the parsonage. It is the grave—marked by a small, mossgrown fragment of stone at the head and another at the foot—the grave of two British soldiers who were slain in the skirmish, and have ever since slept peacefully where Zechariah Brown and Thomas Davis buried them. Soon was their warfare ended; a weary night march from Boston, a rattling volley of musketry across the river, and then these many years of rest. In the long procession of slain invaders who passed into eternity from the battle-fields of the revolution, these two nameless soldiers led the way.

Lowell, the poet, as we were once standing over this grave, told me a tradition in reference to one of the inhabitants below. The story has something deeply impressive, though its circumstances cannot altogether be reconciled with probability. A youth in the service of the clergyman happened to be chopping wood, that April morning, at the back door of the Manse, and when the noise of battle rang from side to side of the bridge he hastened across the intervening field to see what might be going forward. It is rather strange, by the way, that this lad should have been so diligently at work when the whole population of town and country were startled out of their customary business by the advance of the British troops. Be that as it might, the tradition says that the lad now left his task and hurried to the battle-field with the axe still in his hand. The British had by this time retreated, the Americans were in pursuit; and the late scene of strife was thus deserted by both parties. Two soldiers lay on the ground—one was a corpse; but, as the young New Englander drew nigh, the other Briton raised himself painfully upon his hands and knees and gave a ghastly stare into his face. The boy,—it must have been a nervous impulse, without purpose, without thought, and betokening a sensitive and impressible nature rather than a hardened one,—the boy uplifted his axe and dealt the wounded soldier a fierce and fatal blow upon the head.

I could wish that the grave might be opened; for I would fain know whether either of the skeleton soldiers has the mark of an axe in his skull. The story comes home to me like truth. Oftentimes, as an intellectual and moral exercise, I have sought to follow that poor youth through his subsequent career, and observe how his soul was tortured by the blood stain, contracted as it had been before the long custom of war had robbed human life of its sanctity, and while it still seemed murderous to slay a brother man. This one circumstance has borne more fruit for me than all that history tells us of the fight.[2]

Many strangers come in the summer time to view the battle-ground. For my own part, I have never found my imagination much excited by this or any other scene of historic celebrity; nor would the placid margin of the river have lost any of its charm for me had men never fought and died there. There is a wilder interest in the tract of land—perhaps a hundred yards in breadth—which extends between the battlefield and the northern face of our Old Manse, with its contiguous avenue and orchard. Here, in some unknown age, before the white man came, stood an Indian village, convenient to the river, whence its inhabitants must have drawn so large a part of their subsistence. The site is identified by the spear and arrowheads, the chisels, and other implements of war, labor, and the chase, which the plough turns up from the soil. You see a splinter of stone, half hidden beneath a sod; it looks like nothing worthy of note; but, if you have faith enough to pick it up, behold a relic! Thoreau, who has a strange faculty of finding what the Indians have left behind them, first set me on the search; and I afterwards enriched myself with some very perfect specimens, so rudely wrought that it seemed almost as if chance had fashioned them. Their great charm consists in this rudeness and in the individuality of each article, so different from the productions of civilized machinery, which shapes everything on one pattern. There is exquisite delight, too, in picking up for one's self an arrowhead that was dropped centuries ago and has never been handled since, and which we thus receive directly from the hand of the red hunter, who purposed to shoot it at his game or at an enemy. Such an incident builds up again the Indian village and its encircling

forest, and recalls to life the painted chiefs and warriors, the squaws at their household toil, and the children sporting among the wigwams, while the little wind-rocked papoose swings from the branch of the tree. It can hardly be told whether it is a joy or a pain, after such a momentary vision, to gaze around in the broad daylight of reality and see stone fences, white houses, potato fields, and men doggedly hoeing in their shirt-sleeves and homespun pantaloons. But this is nonsense. The Old Manse is better than a thousand wigwams.

The Old Manse! We had almost forgotten it, but will return thither through the orchard. This was set out by the last clergyman, in the decline of his life, when the neighbors laughed at the hoary-headed man for planting trees from which he could have no prospect of gathering fruit. Even had that been the case, there was only so much the better motive for planting them, in the pure and unselfish hope of benefiting his successors,—an end so seldom achieved by more ambitious efforts. But the old minister, before reaching his patriarchal age of ninety, ate the apples from this orchard during many years, and added silver and gold to his annual stipend by disposing of the superfluity. It is pleasant to think of him walking among the trees in the quiet afternoons of early autumn and picking up here and there a windfall, while he observes how heavily the branches are weighed down, and computes the number of empty flour barrels that will be filled by their burden. He loved each tree, doubtless, as if it had been his own child. An orchard has a relation to mankind, and readily connects itself with matters of the heart. The trees possess a domestic character; they have lost the wild nature of their forest kindred, and have grown humanized by receiving the care of man as well as by contributing to his wants. There is so much individuality of character, too, among apple-trees that it gives them an

_____

[2] Hawthorne's unfinished *Septimus Felton* may be regarded in part as fruit of this circumstance.

additional claim to be the objects of human interest. One is harsh and crabbed in its manifestations; another gives us fruit as mild as charity. One is churlish and illiberal, evidently grudging the few apples that it bears; another exhausts itself in free-hearted benevolence. The variety of grotesque shapes into which apple-trees contort themselves has its effect on those who get acquainted with them: they stretch out their crooked branches, and take such hold of the imagination that we remember them as humorists and odd-fellows. And what is more melancholy than the old apple-trees that linger about the spot where once stood a homestead, but where there is now only a ruined chimney rising out of a grassy and weed-grown cellar? They offer their fruit to every wayfarer,—apples that are bitter sweet with the moral of Time's vicissitude.

I have met with no other such pleasant trouble in the world as that of finding myself, with only the two or three mouths which it was my privilege to feed, the sole inheritor of the old clergyman's wealth of fruits. Throughout the summer there were cherries and currants; and then came autumn, with his immense burden of apples, dropping them continually from his overladen shoulders as he trudged along. In the stillest afternoon, if I listened, the thump of a great apple was audible, falling without a breath of wind, from the mere necessity of perfect ripeness. And, besides, there were pear-trees, that flung down bushels upon bushels of heavy pears; and peach-trees, which, in a good year, tormented me with peaches, neither to be eaten nor kept, nor, without labor and perplexity, to be given away. The idea of an infinite generosity and exhaustless bounty on the part of our Mother Nature was well worth obtaining through such cares as these. That feeling can be enjoyed in perfection only by the natives of summer islands, where the bread-fruit, the cocoa, the palm, and the orange grow spontaneously and hold forth the ever-ready meal; but likewise almost as well

by a man long habituated to city life, who plunges into such a solitude as that of the Old Manse, where he plucks the fruit of trees that he did not plant, and which therefore, to my heterodox taste, bear the closest resemblance to those that grew in Eden. It has been an apothegm these five thousand years, that toil sweetens the bread it earns. For my part (speaking from hard experience, acquired while belaboring the rugged furrows of Brook Farm), I relish best the free gifts of Providence.

Not that it can be disputed that the light toil requisite to cultivate a moderately-sized garden imparts such zest to kitchen vegetables as is never found in those of the market gardener. Childless men, if they would know something of the bliss of paternity, should plant a seed,—be it squash, bean, Indian corn, or perhaps a mere flower or worthless weed,—should plant it with their own hands, and nurse it from infancy to maturity altogether by their own care. If there be not too many of them, each individual plant becomes an object of separate interest. My garden, that skirted the avenue of the Manse, was of precisely the right extent. An hour or two of morning labor was all that it required. But I used to visit and revisit it a dozen times a day, and stand in deep contemplation over my vegetable progeny with a love that nobody could share or conceive of who had never taken part in the process of creation. It was one of the most bewitching sights in the world to observe a hill of beans thrusting aside the soil, or a row of early peas just peeping forth sufficiently to trace a line of delicate green. Later in the season the humming-birds were attracted by the blossoms of a peculiar variety of bean; and they were a joy to me, those little spiritual visitants, for deigning to sip airy food out of my nectar cups. Multitudes of bees used to bury themselves in the yellow blossoms of the summer squashes. This, too, was a deep satisfaction; although when they had laden themselves with sweets they flew away to some unknown hive, which would give back nothing in requital of what my garden had contributed. But I was glad thus to fling a benefaction upon the passing breeze with the certainty that somebody must profit by it, and that there would be a little more honey in the world to allay the sourness and bitterness which mankind is always complaining of. Yes, indeed; my life was the sweeter for that honey.

Speaking of summer squashes, I must say a word of their beautiful and varied forms. They presented an endless diversity of urns and vases, shallow or deep, scalloped or plain, moulded in patterns which a sculptor would do well to copy, since Art has never invented anything more graceful. A hundred squashes in the garden were worthy, in my eyes at least, of being rendered indestructible in marble. If ever Providence (but I know it never will) should assign me a superfluity of gold, part of it shall be expended for a service of plate, or most delicate porcelain, to be wrought into the shapes of summer squashes gathered from vines which I will plant with my own hands. As dishes for containing vegetables they would be peculiarly appropriate.

But not merely the squeamish love of the beautiful was gratified by my toil in the kitchen garden. There was a hearty enjoyment, likewise, in observing the growth of the crook-necked winter squashes, from the first little bulb, with the withered blossom adhering to it, until they lay strewn upon the soil, big, round fellows, hiding their heads beneath the leaves, but turning up their great yellow rotundities to the noontide sun. Gazing at them, I felt that by my agency something worth living for had been done. A new substance was born into the world. They were real and tangible existences, which the mind could seize hold of and rejoice in. A cabbage, too,—especially the early Dutch cabbage, which swells to a monstrous circumference, until its ambitious heart often bursts asunder,—is a matter to be proud of when we can claim a share with the earth and sky in

producing it. But, after all, the hugest pleasure is reserved until these vegetable children of ours are smoking on the table, and we, like Saturn, make a meal of them.

What with the river, the battle-field, the orchard and the garden, the reader begins to despair of finding his way back into the Old Manse. But in agreeable weather it is the truest hospitality to keep him out-of-doors. I never grew quite acquainted with my habitation till a long spell of sulky rain had confined me beneath its roof. There could not be a more sombre aspect of external Nature than as then seen from the windows of my study. The great willow-tree had caught and retained among its leaves a whole cataract of water, to be shaken down at intervals by the frequent gusts of wind. All day long, and for a week together, the rain was drip-drip-dripping and splash-splash-splashing from the eaves, and bubbling and foaming into the tubs beneath the spouts. The old, unpainted shingles of the house and out-buildings were black with moisture; and the mosses of ancient growth upon the walls looked green and fresh, as if they were the newest things and afterthought of Time. The usually mirrored surface of the river was blurred by an infinity of raindrops; the whole landscape had a completely water-soaked appearance, conveying the impression that the earth was wet through like a sponge; while the summit of a wooded hill, about a mile distant, was enveloped in a dense mist, where the demon of the tempest seemed to have his abiding-place and to be plotting still direr inclemencies.

Nature has no kindness, no hospitality, during a rain. In the fiercest heat of sunny days she retains a secret mercy, and welcomes the wayfarer to shady nooks of the woods whither the sun cannot penetrate; but she provides no shelter against her storms. It makes us shiver to think of those deep, umbrageous recesses, those overshadowing banks, where we found such enjoyment during the sultry afternoons. Not a twig of foliage there but would dash a little shower into our faces. Looking reproachfully towards the impenetrable sky,—if sky there be above that dismal uniformity of cloud,—we are apt to murmur against the whole system of the universe, since it involves the extinction of so many summer days in so short a life by the hissing and spluttering rain. In such spells of weather—and it is to be supposed such weather came—Eve's bower in paradise must have been but a cheerless and aguish kind of shelter, nowise comparable to the old parsonage, which had resources of its own to beguile the week's imprisonment. The idea of sleeping on a couch of wet roses!

Happy the man who in a rainy day can betake himself to a huge garret, stored, like that of the Manse, with lumber that each generation has left behind it from a period before the revolution. Our garret was an arched hall, dimly illuminated through small and dusty windows. It was but a twilight at the best; and there were nooks, or rather caverns, of deep obscurity, the secrets of which I never learned, being too reverent of their dust and cobwebs. The beams and rafters, roughly hewn and with strips of bark still on them, and the rude masonry of the chimneys, made the garret look wild and uncivilized,—an aspect unlike what was seen elsewhere in the quiet and decorous old house. But on one side there was a little whitewashed apartment which bore the traditionary title of the Saint's Chamber, because holy men in their youth had slept and studied and prayed there. With its elevated retirement, its one window, its small fireplace, and its closet, convenient for an oratory, it was the very spot where a young man might inspire himself with solemn enthusiasm and cherish saintly dreams. The occupants, at various epochs, had left brief records and ejaculations inscribed upon the walls. There, too, hung a tattered and shrivelled roll of canvas, which on inspection proved to be the forcibly wrought picture of a clergyman, in wig, band, and gown, holding a Bible in his hand. As I turned his face towards the light he eyed me with an air of authority such as men of his profession seldom assume in our days. The original had been pastor of the parish more than a century ago, a friend of Whitefield, and almost his equal in fervid eloquence.[3] I bowed before the effigy of the dignified divine, and felt as if I had now met face to face with the ghost by whom, as there was reason to apprehend, the Manse was haunted.

Houses of any antiquity in New England are so invariably possessed with spirits that the matter seems hardly worth alluding to. Our ghost used to heave deep sighs in a particular corner of the parlor, and sometimes rustled paper, as if he were turning over a sermon in the long upper entry,—where nevertheless he was invisible in spite of the bright moonshine that fell through the eastern window. Not improbably he wished me to edit and publish a selection from a chest full of manuscript discourses that stood in the garret. Once, while Hillard[4] and other friends sat talking with us in the twilight, there came a rustling noise as of a minister's silk gown, sweeping through the very midst of the company so closely as almost to brush against the chairs. Still there was nothing visible. A yet stranger business was that of a ghostly servant maid, who used to be heard in the kitchen at deepest midnight, grinding coffee, cooking, ironing,—performing, in short, all kinds of domestic labor,—although no traces of anything accomplished could be detected the next morning. Some neglected duty of her servitude —some ill-starched ministerial band—disturbed the poor damsel in her grave and kept her at work without any wages.

But to return from this digression. A part of my predecessor's library was stored in the garret,—no unfit receptacle indeed for such dreary trash as comprised the

---

[3] George Whitefield (1714-1770), Methodist evangelist from England, preached at Concord at the invitation of the Rev. Daniel Bliss, an ancestor of Emerson.

[4] George Stillman Hillard (1808-1879), author and lawyer.

greater number of volumes. The old books would have been worth nothing at an auction. In this venerable garret, however, they possessed an interest, quite apart from their literary value, as heirlooms, many of which had been transmitted down through a series of consecrated hands from the days of the mighty Puritan divines. Autographs of famous names were to be seen in faded ink on some of their flyleaves; and there were marginal observations or interpolated pages closely covered with manuscript in illegible shorthand, perhaps concealing matter of profound truth and wisdom. The world will never be the better for it. A few of the books were Latin folios, written by Catholic authors; others demolished Papistry, as with a sledge-hammer, in plain English. A dissertation on the book of Job—which only Job himself could have had patience to read—filled at least a score of small, thickset quartos, at the rate of two or three volumes to a chapter. Then there was a vast folio body of divinity—too corpulent a body, it might be feared, to comprehend the spiritual element of religion. Volumes of this form dated back two hundred years or more, and were generally bound in black leather, exhibiting precisely such an appearance as we should attribute to books of enchantment. Others equally antique were of a size proper to be carried in the large waistcoat pockets of old times,—diminutive, but as black as their bulkier brethren, and abundantly interfused with Greek and Latin quotations. These little old volumes impressed me as if they had been intended for very large ones, but had been unfortunately blighted at an early stage of their growth.

The rain pattered upon the roof and the sky gloomed through the dusty garret windows, while I burrowed among these venerable books in search of any living thought which should burn like a coal of fire, or glow like an inextinguishable gem, beneath the dead trumpery that had long hidden it. But I found no such treasure; all was dead alike; and I could not but muse deeply and

wonderingly upon the humiliating fact that the works of man's intellect decay like those of his hands. Thought grows mouldy. What was good and nourishing food for the spirits of one generation affords no sustenance for the next. Books of religion, however, cannot be considered a fair test of the enduring and vivacious properties of human thought, because such books so seldom really touch upon their ostensible subject, and have, therefore, so little business to be written at all. So long as an unlettered soul can attain to saving grace, there would seem to be no deadly error in holding theological libraries to be accumulations of, for the most part, stupendous impertinence.

Many of the books had accrued in the latter years of the last clergyman's lifetime. These threatened to be of even less interest than the elder works, a century hence, to any curious inquirer who should then rummage them as I was doing now. Volumes of the "Liberal Preacher" and "Christian Examiner," [5] occasional sermons, controversial pamphlets, tracts, and other productions of a like fugitive nature took the place of the thick and heavy volumes of past time. In a physical point of view there was much the same difference as between a feather and a lump of lead; but, intellectually regarded, the specific gravity of old and new was about upon a par. Both also were alike frigid. The elder books, nevertheless, seemed to have been earnestly written, and might be conceived to have possessed warmth at some former period; although, with the lapse of time, the heated masses had cooled down even to the freezing point. The frigidity of the modern productions, on the other hand, was characteristic and inherent, and evidently had little to do with the writer's qualities of mind and heart. In fine, of this whole dusty heap of literature I tossed aside all the sacred part, and felt myself none the less a Christian for eschewing it.

[5] The first of these religious periodicals was published 1827-30 and 1831-36; the second 1824-69.

There appeared no hope of either mounting to the better world on a Gothic staircase of ancient folios or of flying thither on the wings of a modern tract.

Nothing, strange to say, retained any sap except what had been written for the passing day and year without the remotest pretension or idea of permanence. There were a few old newspapers, and still older almanacs, which reproduced to my mental eye the epochs when they had issued from the press with a distinctness that was altogether unaccountable. It was as if I had found bits of magic looking-glass among the books, with the images of a vanished century in them. I turned my eyes towards the tattered picture above mentioned, and asked of the austere divine wherefore it was that he and his brethren, after the most painful rummaging and groping into their minds, had been able to produce nothing half so real as these newspaper scribblers and almanac makers had thrown off in the effervescence of a moment. The portrait responded not; so I sought an answer for myself. It is the age itself that writes newspapers and almanacs, which, therefore, have a distinct purpose and meaning at the time, and a kind of intelligible truth for all times; whereas most other works—being written by men who, in the very act, set themselves apart from their age—are likely to possess little significance when new, and none at all when old. Genius, indeed, melts many ages into one, and thus effects something permanent, yet still with a similarity of office to that of the more ephemeral writer. A work of genius is but the newspaper of a century, or perchance of a hundred centuries.

Lightly as I have spoken of these old books, there yet lingers with me a superstitious reverence for literature of all kinds. A bound volume has a charm in my eyes similar to what scraps of manuscript possess for the good Mussulman. He imagines that those wind-wafted records are perhaps hallowed by some sacred verse; and I, that every new book or antique one may contain the "open sesame,"—the spell to disclose treasures hidden in some unsuspected cave of Truth. Thus it was not without sadness that I turned away from the library of the Old Manse.

Blessed was the sunshine when it came again at the close of another stormy day, beaming from the edge of the western horizon; while the massive firmament of clouds threw down all the gloom it could, but served only to kindle the golden light into a more brilliant glow by the strongly contrasted shadows. Heaven smiled at the earth, so long unseen, from beneath its heavy eyelid. To-morrow for the hill-tops and the wood paths.

Or it might be that Ellery Channing [6] came up the avenue to join me in a fishing excursion on the river. Strange and happy times were those when we cast aside all irksome forms and strait-laced habitudes, and delivered ourselves up to the free air, to live like the Indians or any less conventional race during one bright semicircle of the sun. Rowing our boat against the current, between wide meadows, we turned aside into the Assabeth. A more lovely stream than this, for a mile above its junction with the Concord, has never flowed on earth,—nowhere, indeed, except to lave the interior regions of a poet's imagination. It is sheltered from the breeze by woods and a hill-side; so that elsewhere there might be a hurricane, and here scarcely a ripple across the shaded water. The current lingers along so gently that the mere force of the boatman's will seems sufficient to propel his craft against it. It comes flowing softly through the midmost privacy and deepest heart of a wood which whispers it to be quiet; while the stream whispers back again from its sedgy borders, as if river and wood were hushing one another to sleep. Yes; the river sleeps along its course and dreams of the sky and of the clustering foliage, amid which fall showers of broken sunlight, im-

---

[6] William Ellery Channing the younger (1818-1901), one of the Transcendentalist poets and nephew of the Unitarian clergyman of the same name.

parting specks of vivid cheerfulness, in contrast with the quiet depth of the prevailing tint. Of all this scene, the slumbering river has a dream picture in its bosom. Which, after all, was the most real—the picture, or the original?—the objects palpable to our grosser senses, or their apotheosis in the stream beneath? Surely the disembodied images stand in closer relation to the soul. But both the original and the reflection had here an ideal charm; and, had it been a thought more wild, I could have fancied that this river had strayed forth out of the rich scenery of my companion's inner world; only the vegetation along its banks should then have had an Oriental character.

Gentle and unobtrusive as the river is, yet the tranquil woods seem hardly satisfied to allow it passage. The trees are rooted on the very verge of the water, and dip their pendent branches into it. At one spot there is a lofty bank, on the slope of which grow some hemlocks, declining across the stream with outstretched arms, as if resolute to take the plunge. In other places the banks are almost on a level with the water; so that the quiet congregation of trees set their feet in the flood, and are fringed with foliage down to the surface. Cardinal flowers kindle their spiral flames and illuminate the dark nooks among the shrubbery. The pond-lily grows abundantly along the margin—that delicious flower, which, as Thoreau tells me, opens its virgin bosom to the first sunlight and perfects its being through the magic of that genial kiss. He has beheld beds of them unfolding in due succession as the sunrise stole gradually from flower to flower—a sight not to be hoped for unless when a poet adjusts his inward eye to a proper focus with the outward organ. Grape-vines here and there twine themselves around shrub and tree and hang their clusters over the water within reach of the boatman's hand. Oftentimes they unite two trees of alien race in an inextricable twine, marrying the hemlock and the maple against their will, and enriching them with a purple offspring of

which neither is the parent. One of these ambitious parasites has climbed into the upper branches of a tall, white pine, and is still ascending from bough to bough, unsatisfied till it shall crown the tree's airy summit with a wreath of its broad foliage and a cluster of its grapes.

The winding course of the stream continually shut out the scene behind us, and revealed as calm and lovely a one before. We glided from depth to depth, and breathed new seclusion at every turn. The shy kingfisher flew from the withered branch close at hand to another at a distance, uttering a shrill cry of anger or alarm. Ducks that had been floating there since the preceding eve were startled at our approach, and skimmed along the glassy river, breaking its dark surface with a bright streak. The pickerel leaped from among the lilypads. The turtle, sunning itself upon a rock or at the root of a tree, slid suddenly into the water with a plunge. The painted Indian who paddled his canoe along the Assabeth three hundred years ago could hardly have seen a wilder gentleness displayed upon its banks and reflected in its bosom than we did. Nor could the same Indian have prepared his noontide meal with more simplicity. We drew up our skiff at some point where the overarching shade formed a natural bower, and there kindled a fire with the pine cones and decayed branches that lay strewn plentifully around. Soon the smoke ascended among the trees, impregnated with a savory incense, not heavy, dull, and surfeiting, like the steam of cookery within doors, but sprightly and piquant. The smell of our feast was akin to the woodland odors with which it mingled: there was no sacrilege committed by our intrusion there: the sacred solitude was hospitable, and granted us free leave to cook and eat in the recess that was at once our kitchen and banqueting hall. It is strange what humble offices may be performed in a beautiful scene without destroying its poetry. Our fire, red gleaming among the trees, and we beside it, busied with culinary rites and spreading out our meal on a mossgrown log, all seemed in unison with the river gliding by and the foliage rustling over us. And, what was strangest, neither did our mirth seem to disturb the propriety of the solemn woods; although the hobgoblins of the old wilderness and the will-of-the-wisps that glimmered in the marshy places might have come trooping to share our table talk, and have added their shrill laughter to our merriment. It was the very spot in which to utter the extremest nonsense or the profoundest wisdom, or that ethereal product of the mind which partakes of both, and may become one or the other, in correspondence with the faith and insight of the auditor.

So amid sunshine and shadow, rustling leaves and sighing waters, up gushed our talk like the babble of a fountain. The evanescent spray was Ellery's; and his, too, the lumps of golden thought that lay glimmering in the fountain's bed and brightened both our faces by the reflection. Could he have drawn out that virgin gold and stamped it with the mint mark that alone gives currency, the world might have had the profit, and he the fame. My mind was the richer merely by the knowledge that it was there. But the chief profit of those wild days to him and me lay, not in any definite idea, not in any angular or rounded truth, which we dug out of the shapeless mass of problematical stuff, but in the freedom which we thereby won from all custom and conventionalism and fettering influences of man on man. We were so free to-day that it was impossible to be slaves again to-morrow. When we crossed the threshold of the house or trod the thronged pavements of a city, still the leaves of the trees that overhang the Assabeth were whispering to us, "Be free! be free!" Therefore along that shady riverbank there are spots, marked with a heap of ashes and half-consumed brands, only less sacred in my remembrance than the hearth of a household fire.

And yet how sweet, as we floated homeward adown the golden river at sunset,—

how sweet was it to return within the system of human society, not as to a dungeon and a chain, but as to a stately edifice, whence we could go forth at will into statelier simplicity! How gently, too, did the sight of the Old Manse, best seen from the river, overshadowed with its willow and all environed about with the foliage of its orchard and avenue,—how gently did its gray, homely aspect rebuke the speculative extravagances of the day! It had grown sacred in connection with the artificial life against which we inveighed; it had been a home for many years in spite of all; it was my home too; and, with these thoughts, it seemed to me that all the artifice and conventionalism of life was but an impalpable thinness upon its surface, and that the depth below was none the worse for it. Once, as we turned our boat to the bank, there was a cloud, in the shape of an immensely gigantic figure of a hound, couched above the house, as if keeping guard over it. Gazing at this symbol, I prayed that the upper influences might long protect the institutions that had grown out of the heart of mankind.

If ever my readers should decide to give up civilized life, cities, houses, and whatever moral or material enormities in addition to these the perverted ingenuity of our race has contrived, let it be in the early autumn. Then Nature will love him better than at any other season, and will take him to her bosom with a more motherly tenderness. I could scarcely endure the roof of the old house above me in those first autumnal days. How early in the summer, too, the prophecy of autumn comes! Earlier in some years than in others; sometimes even in the first weeks of July. There is no other feeling like what is caused by this faint, doubtful, yet real perception—if it be not rather a foreboding—of the year's decay, so blessedly sweet and sad in the same breath.

Did I say that there was no feeling like it? Ah, but there is a half-acknowledged melancholy like to this when we stand in the perfected vigor of our life and feel that Time has now given us all his flowers, and that the next work of his never idle fingers must be to steal them one by one away.

I have forgotten whether the song of the cricket be not as early a token of autumn's approach as any other,—that song which may be called an audible stillness; for though very loud and heard afar, yet the mind does not take note of it as a sound, so completely is its individual existence merged among the accompanying characteristics of the season. Alas for the pleasant summer time! In August the grass is still verdant on the hills and in the valleys; the foliage of the trees is as dense as ever, and as green; the flowers gleam forth in richer abundance along the margin of the river, and by the stone walls, and deep among the woods; the days, too, are as fervid now as they were a month ago; and yet in every breath of wind and in every beam of sunshine we hear the whispered farewell and behold the parting smile of a dear friend. There is a coolness amid all the heat, a mildness in the blazing noon. Not a breeze can stir but it thrills us with the breath of autumn. A pensive glory is seen in the far golden gleams, among the shadows of the trees. The flowers—even the brightest of them, and they are the most gorgeous of the year—have this gentle sadness wedded to their pomp, and typify the character of the delicious time each within itself. The brilliant cardinal flower has never seemed gay to me.

Still later in the season Nature's tenderness waxes stronger. It is impossible not to be fond of our mother now; for she is so fond of us! At other periods she does not make this impression on me, or only at rare intervals; but in those genial days of autumn, when she has perfected her harvests and accomplished every needful thing that was given her to do, then she overflows with a blessed superfluity of love. She has leisure to caress her children now. It is good to be alive at such times. Thank Heaven for breath—yes, for mere breath

—when it is made up of a heavenly breeze like this! It comes with a real kiss upon our cheeks; it would linger fondly around us if it might; but, since it must be gone, it embraces us with its whole kindly heart and passes onward to embrace likewise the next thing that it meets. A blessing is flung abroad and scattered far and wide over the earth, to be gathered up by all who choose. I recline upon the still unwithered grass and whisper to myself, "O perfect day! O beautiful world! O beneficent God!" And it is the promise of a blessed eternity; for our Creator would never have made such lovely days and have given us the deep hearts to enjoy them, above and beyond all thought, unless we were meant to be immortal. This sunshine is the golden pledge thereof. It beams through the gates of paradise and shows us glimpses far inward.

By and by, in a little time, the outward world puts on a drear austerity. On some October morning there is a heavy hoarfrost on the grass and along the tops of the fences; and at sunrise the leaves fall from the trees of our avenue without a breath of wind, quietly descending by their own weight. All summer long they have murmured like the noise of waters; they have roared loudly while the branches were wrestling with the thunder gust; they have made music both glad and solemn; they have attuned my thoughts by their quiet sound as I paced to and fro beneath the arch of intermingling boughs. Now they can only rustle under my feet. Henceforth the gray parsonage begins to assume a larger importance, and draws to its fireside,—for the abomination of the air-tight stove is reserved till wintry weather,—draws closer and closer to its fireside the vagrant impulses that had gone wandering about through the summer.

When summer was dead and buried the Old Manse became as lonely as a hermitage. Not that ever—in my time at least—it had been thronged with company; but, at no rare intervals, we welcomed some friend out of the dusty glare and tumult of the world, and rejoiced to share with him the transparent obscurity that was floating over us. In one respect our precincts were like the Enchanted Ground through which the pilgrim travelled on his way to the Celestial City! The guests, each and all, felt a slumberous influence upon them; they fell asleep in chairs, or took a more deliberate siesta on the sofa, or were seen stretched among the shadows of the orchard, looking up dreamily through the boughs. They could not have paid a more acceptable compliment to my abode, nor to my own qualities as a host. I held it as a proof that they left their cares behind them as they passed between the stone gate-posts at the entrance of our avenue, and that the so powerful opiate was the abundance of peace and quiet within and all around us. Others could give them pleasure and amusement or instruction—these could be picked up anywhere; but it was for me to give them rest—rest in a life of trouble. What better could be done for those weary and world-worn spirits? [7]— for him whose career of perpetual action was impeded and harassed by the rarest of his powers and the richest of his acquirements?—for another who had thrown his ardent heart from earliest youth into the strife of politics, and now, perchance, began to suspect that one lifetime is too brief for the accomplishment of any lofty aim—for her on whose feminine nature had been imposed the heavy gift of intellectual power, such as a strong man might have staggered under, and with it the necessity to act upon the world?—in a word, not to multiply instances, what better could be done for anybody who came within our magic circle than to throw the spell of a tranquil spirit over him? And when it had wrought its full effect, then we dismissed him, with but misty reminiscences, as if he had been dreaming of us.

Were I to adopt a pet idea, as so many people do, and fondle it in my embraces to the exclusion of all others, it would be, that the great want which mankind labors under at this present period is sleep. The world should recline its vast head on the first convenient pillow and take an age-long nap. It has gone distracted through a morbid activity, and, while preternaturally wide awake, is nevertheless tormented by visions that seem real to it now, but would assume their true aspect and character were all things once set right by an interval of sound repose. This is the only method of getting rid of old delusions and avoiding new ones; of regenerating our race, so that it might in due time awake as an infant out of dewy slumber; of restoring to us the simple perception of what is right, and the single-hearted desire to achieve it, both of which have long been lost in consequence of this weary activity of brain and torpor or passion of the heart that now afflict the universe. Stimulants, the only mode of treatment hitherto attempted, cannot quell the disease; they do but heighten the delirium.

Let not the above paragraph ever be quoted against the author; for, though tinctured with its modicum of truth, it is the result and expression of what he knew, while he was writing, to be but a distorted survey of the state and prospects of mankind. There were circumstances around me which made it difficult to view the world precisely as it exists; for, severe and sober as was the Old Manse, it was necessary to go but a little way beyond its threshold before meeting with stranger moral shapes of men than might have been encountered elsewhere in a circuit of a thousand miles.

These hobgoblins of flesh and blood were attracted thither by the wide-spreading influence of a great original thinker, who had his earthly abode at the opposite extremity of our village. His mind acted upon other minds of a certain constitution with wonderful magnetism, and drew many men upon long pilgrimages to speak with him face to face. Young visionaries—to whom just so much of insight had been imparted

---

[7] These are probably Horatio Bridge (1806-1893), Franklin Pierce (1804-1869), and Margaret Fuller (1810-1850).

as to make life all a labyrinth around them —came to seek the clew that should guide them out of their self-involved bewilderment. Grayheaded theorists—whose systems, at first air, had finally imprisoned them in an iron frame-work—travelled painfully to his door, not to ask deliverance, but to invite the free spirit into their own thraldom. People that had lighted on a new thought, or a thought that they fancied new, came to Emerson, as the finder of a glittering gem hastens to a lapidary, to ascertain its quality and value. Uncertain, troubled, earnest wanderers through the midnight of the moral world beheld his intellectual fire as a beacon burning on a hill-top, and, climbing the difficult ascent, looked forth into the surrounding obscurity more hopefully than hitherto. The light revealed objects unseen before,—mountains, gleaming lakes, glimpses of a creation among the chaos; but, also, as was unavoidable, it attracted bats and owls and the whole host of night birds, which flapped their dusky wings against the gazer's eyes, and sometimes were mistaken for fowls of angelic feather. Such delusions always hover nigh whenever a beacon fire of truth is kindled.

For myself, there had been epochs of my life when I, too, might have asked of this prophet the master word that should solve me the riddle of the universe; but now, being happy, I felt as if there were no question to be put, and therefore admired Emerson as a poet of deep beauty and austere tenderness, but sought nothing from him as a philosopher. It was good, nevertheless, to meet him in the woodpaths, or sometimes in our avenue, with that pure intellectual gleam diffused about his presence like the garment of a shining one; and he so quiet, so simple, so without pretension, encountering each man alive as if expecting to receive more than he could impart. And, in truth, the heart of many an ordinary man had, perchance, inscriptions which he could not read. But it was impossible to dwell in his vicinity without inhaling more or less the mountain atmosphere of his lofty thought, which, in the brains of some people, wrought a singular giddiness,—new truth being as heady as new wine. Never was a poor little country village infested with such a variety of queer, strangely-dressed, oddly-behaved mortals, most of whom took upon themselves to be important agents of the world's destiny, yet were simply bores of a very intense water. Such, I imagine, is the invariable character of persons who crowd so closely about an original thinker as to draw in his unuttered breath and thus become imbued with a false originality. This triteness of novelty is enough to make any man of common sense blaspheme at all ideas of less than a century's standing, and pray that the world may be petrified and rendered immovable in precisely the worst moral and physical state that it ever yet arrived at, rather than be benefited by such schemes of such philosophers.

And now I begin to feel—and perhaps should have sooner felt—that we have talked enough of the Old Manse. Mine honored reader, it may be, will vilify the poor author as an egotist for babbling through so many pages about a mossgrown country parsonage, and his life within its walls and on the river and in the woods, and the influences that wrought upon him from all these sources. My conscience, however, does not reproach me with betraying anything too sacredly individual to be revealed by a human spirit to its brother or sister spirit. How narrow—how shallow and scanty too—is the stream of thought that has been flowing from my pen, compared with the broad tide of dim emotions, ideas, and associations which swell around me from that portion of my existence! How little have I told! and of that little, how almost nothing is even tinctured with any quality that makes it exclusively my own! Has the reader gone wandering, hand in hand with me, through the inner passages of my being? and have we groped together into all its chambers and examined their treasures or their rubbish? Not so. We have been standing on the greensward, but just within the cavern's mouth, where the common sunshine is free to penetrate, and where every footstep is therefore free to come. I have appealed to no sentiment or sensibilities save such as are diffused among us all. So far as I am a man of really individual attributes I veil my face; nor am I, nor have I ever been, one of those supremely hospitable people who serve up their own hearts, delicately fried, with brain sauce, as a tidbit for their beloved public.

Glancing back over what I have written, it seems but the scattered reminiscences of a single summer. In fairyland there is no measurement of time; and, in a spot so sheltered from the turmoil of life's ocean, three years hastened away with a noiseless flight, as the breezy sunshine chases the cloud shadows across the depths of a still valley. Now came hints, growing more and more distinct, that the owner of the old house was pining for his native air. Carpenters next appeared, making a tremendous racket among the out-buildings, strewing the green grass with pine shavings and chips of chestnut joists, and vexing the whole antiquity of the place with their discordant renovations. Soon, moreover, they divested our abode of the veil of woodbine which had crept over a large portion of its southern face. All the aged mosses were cleared unsparingly away; and there were horrible whispers about brushing up the external walls with a coat of paint—a purpose as little to my taste as might be that of rouging the venerable cheeks of one's grandmother. But the hand that renovates is always more sacrilegious than that which destroys. In fine, we gathered up our household goods, drank a farewell cup of tea in our pleasant little breakfast room,—delicately fragrant tea, an unpurchasable luxury, one of the many angel gifts that had fallen like dew upon us,—and passed forth between the tall stone gateposts as uncertain as the wandering Arabs where our tent might next be pitched. Providence took me by the hand,

and—an oddity of dispensation which, I trust, there is no irreverence in smiling at —has led me, as the newspapers announce while I am writing, from the Old Manse into a custom house. As a story teller, I have often contrived strange vicissitudes for my imaginary personages, but none like this.

The treasure of intellectual good which I hoped to find in our secluded dwelling had never come to light. No profound treatise of ethics, no philosophic history, no novel even, that could stand unsupported on its edges. All that I had to show, as a man of letters, were these few tales and essays, which had blossomed out like flowers in the calm summer of my heart and mind. Save editing (an easy task) the journal of my friend of many years, the African Cruiser, I had done nothing else.[8] With these idle weeds and withering blossoms I have intermixed some that were produced long ago,—old, faded things, reminding me of flowers pressed between the leaves of a book,—and now offer the bouquet, such as it is, to any whom it may please. These fitful sketches, with so little of external life about them, yet claiming no profundity of purpose,— so reserved, even while they sometimes seem so frank,—often but half in earnest, and never, even when most so, expressing satisfactorily the thoughts which they profess to image,—such trifles, I truly feel, afford no solid basis for a literary reputation. Nevertheless, the public—if my limited number of readers, whom I venture to regard rather as a circle of friends, may be termed a public—will receive them the more kindly, as the last offering, the last collection, of this nature which it is my purpose ever to put forth. Unless I could do better, I have done enough in this kind. For myself the book will always retain one charm—as reminding me of the river, with its delightful solitudes, and of the avenue, the garden, and the orchard, and

[8] Hawthorne edited Horatio Bridge's *The Journal of an African Cruiser* (1845).

especially the dear old Manse, with the little study on its western side, and the sunshine glimmering through the willow branches while I wrote.

Let the reader, if he will do me so much honor, imagine himself my guest, and that, having seen whatever may be worthy of notice within and about the Old Manse, he has finally been ushered into my study. There, after seating him in an antique elbow chair, an heirloom of the house, I take forth a roll of manuscript and entreat his attention to the following tales—an act of personal inhospitality, however, which I never was guilty of, nor ever will be, even to my worst enemy.

SOURCE MATERIAL FOR "ETHAN BRAND"
FROM

THE AMERICAN NOTEBOOKS
[1932 (1868)]

JULY 26, 1838: This morning an under-witted old man met me on a walk, and held a pretty long conversation, insisting upon shaking hands (to which I was averse, lest his hand should not be clean), and insisting on his right to do so, as being a "friend of mankind." He was an old gray, bald-headed, wrinkled-visaged figure, decently dressed, with cowhide shoes, a coat on one arm, and an umbrella on the other; and said that he was going to see a widow in the neighborhood. Finding that I was not provided with a wife, he recommended a certain "maid" of forty years, who had 300 acres of land. He spoke of his children, who are proprietors of a circus establishment, and have taken a granddaughter to bring up in their way of life; and he gave me a message to tell them, in case we should meet. While this old man is wandering among the hills, his children are in the gaze of multitudes. He told me the place where he was born, directing me to it by pointing to a wreath of mist which lay on the side of a moun-

tain ridge, which he termed the "smoke yonder." Speaking of the widow, he said, "My wife has been dead these seven years, and why should not I enjoy myself a little." His manner was full of quirks and quips and eccentricities, waving his umbrella and gesticulating strangely, with a great deal of action. I suppose, to help his natural foolishness, he had been drinking. We parted, he exhorting me not to forget his message to his sons, and I shouting after him a request to be remembered to the widow. Conceive something tragical to be talked about; and much might be made of this interview, in a wild road among the hills; with Graylock at no great distance, looking sombre and angry by reason of the gray, heavy mist upon his head.

July 29, 1838: Remarkable characters: —a disagreeable figure, waning from middle-age, clad in a pair of tow homespun pantaloons and very dirty shirt, bare-foot, and with one of his feet maimed by an axe; also, an arm amputated two or three inches below the elbow. His beard of a week's growth, grim and grisly, with a general effect of black;—altogether a filthy and disgusting object. Yet he has signs of having been a handsome man in his idea; though now such a beastly figure that, probably, no living thing but his great dog would touch him without an effort. Coming to the stoop, where several persons were sitting,—"Good morning, gentlemen," said the wretch. Nobody answered for a time, till at last one said, "I don't know who you speak to;—not me, I'm sure;" meaning that he did not claim to be a gentleman. "Why, I thought you'd all speak at once," replied the figure laughing. So he sat himself down on the lower step of the stoop, and began to talk; and the conversation being turned upon his bare feet, by one of the company, he related the story of his losing his toes by the glancing aside of an axe, and with what grim fortitude he bore it. Then he made a transition to the loss of his arm; and setting his teeth and drawing in his breath, said that the pain was dreadful; but this, too, he seems to have borne like an Indian; and a person testified to his fortitude by saying that he did not suppose that there was any feeling in him, from observing how he bore it. The man spoke of the pain of cutting the muscles, and the particular agony at one moment, while the bone was being sawed asunder; and there was a strange expression of remembered agony, as he shrugged his half-limb, and described the matter. Afterwards, in a reply to a question of mine whether he still seemed to feel the hand that had been amputated, he answered that he did, always—and baring the stump, he moved the severed muscles, saying, "There is the thumb, there the forefinger" &c. Then he talked to me about phrenology, of which he seems a firm believer and skilful practitioner, telling how he had hit upon the true characters of many people. There was a great deal of sense and acuteness in his talk, and something of elevation in his expression; perhaps a studied elevation—and a sort of courtesy in his manner; but his sense had something out of the way in it; something wild, and ruined, and desperate, in his talk, though I can hardly say what it was. There was something of the gentleman and man of intellect in his deep degradation; and a pleasure in intellectual pursuits, and an acuteness and trained judgment, which bespoke a mind once strong and cultivated. "My study is man," said he. And looking at me "I do not know your name," said he, "but there is something of the hawk-eye about you too." This man was formerly a lawyer in good practice, but taking to drinking, was reduced to this lowest state. Yet not the lowest; for, after the amputation of his arm, being advised by divers persons to throw himself upon the public for support, he told them that, even if he should lose his other arm, he would still be able to support himself and a waiter. Certainly he is a strong minded and iron-constitutioned man; but, looking at the stump of his arm, he said "that the pain

of the mind was a thousand times greater than the pain of the body—That hand could make the pen go fast," said he. Among people in general, he does not seem to have any greater consideration in his ruin, for the sake of his former standing in society. He supports himself by making soap; and on account of the offals used in that business, there is probably rather an evil smell in his domicile. Talking about a dead horse, near his house, he said that he could not bear the scent of it. "I should not think you could smell carrion in that house," said a stage-agent. Whereupon the soap-maker dropped his head, with a little snort, as it were, of wounded feeling; but immediately said that he took all in good part. There was an old squire of the village, a lawyer probably, whose demeanor was different—with a distance, yet a kindliness; for he remembered the times when they met on equal terms. "You and I," said the squire, alluding to their respective troubles and sicknesses, "would have died long ago, if we had not had the courage to live." The poor devil kept talking to me long after everybody else had left the stoop, giving vent to much practical philosophy and just observation on the ways of men, mingled with rather more assumption of literature and cultivation, than belonged to the present condition of his mind. Meantime his great dog—a cleanly looking, and not ill-bred dog, being the only decent attribute appertaining to his master—a well natured dog, too, and receiving civilly any demonstration of courtesy from other people, though preserving a certain distance of deportment—this great dog grew weary of his master's lengthy talk, and expressed his impatience to be gone, by thrusting himself between his legs, rolling over on his back, seizing his ragged trowsers, or playfully taking his maimed bare foot into his mouth—using, in short, the kindly and humorous freedom of a friend, with a wretch to whom all are free enough, but none other kind. His master rebuked him, but with kindness too, and not so that the dog felt himself bound to desist, though he seemed willing to allow his master all the time that could possibly be spared. And, at last, having said many times that he must go and shave and dress himself—and as his beard had been at least a week growing, it might have seemed almost a week's work to get rid of it—he rose from the stoop, and went his way, a forlorn and miserable thing in the light of the cheerful summer Sabbath morning. Yet he seems to keep his spirits up, and still preserves himself a man among men, asking nothing from them—nor is it clearly perceptible what right they have to scorn him, though he seems to acquiesce, in a sort, in their doing so. And yet he cannot wholly have lost his self-respect; and doubtless there were persons on the stoop more grovelling than himself.

July 30, 1838: A little boy, named Joe, who haunts about the bar-room and the stoop, about four years old, in a thin short jacket, and full-breeched trowsers, and bare feet. The men plague him, and put quids of tobacco in his mouth, under pretence of giving him a fig, and he gets enraged, and utters a peculiar sharp, spiteful cry, and strikes at them with a stick, to their great mirth. He is always in trouble, yet will not keep away. They dispatch him with two or three cents to buy candy, and nuts and raisins. They set him down in a niche of the door, and tell him to remain there a day and a half; he sits down very demurely, as if he really meant to fulfil his penance;—but, a moment after, behold there is little Joe, capering across the street to join two or three boys who are playing in a wagon. Take this boy as the germ of a tavern-haunter, a country roué, to spend a wild and brutal youth, ten years of his prime in the State-Prison, and his age in the poor-house.

July 31, 1838: A steam engine in a factory to be supposed to possess a malignant spirit; it catches one man's arm, and pulls it off; seizes another by the

coat-tails, and almost grapples him bodily; —catches a girl by the hair, and scalps her;—and finally draws a man, and crushes him to death.

The one-armed soap-maker, lawyer Haynes, wears an iron hook, which serves him instead of a hand for the purposes of holding on. They nickname him Black Hawk.

Doctors walk about the village with their saddle-bags on their arms. One always with a pipe in his mouth.

August 11, 1838: A doctor, a stout, tall, round-paunched, red-faced, brutal looking old fellow, who gets drunk daily. He sat down on the step of our stoop, looking surly, and speaking to nobody; then got up and walked homeward, with a surly swagger, and a slight unevenness of track, attended by a fine Newfoundland dog.

August 31, 1838: A ride, on Tuesday, to Shelburne Falls—twenty-two miles, or thereabouts, distant. Started at about eight o'clock in a wagon with Mr. Leach and Mr. Buck. Our road lay over the Green Mountain; the long ridge of which was made awful by a dark, heavy, threatening cloud, apparently rolled and condensed along the whole summit. As we ascended the zig-zig road, we looked behind, at every opening through the forest, and beheld a wide landscape of mountain-swells, and valleys intermixt, and old Graylock, and the whole of Saddle-back. Over this wide scene, there was a general gloom; but there was a continual vicissitude of bright sunshine flitting over it; now resting for a brief space on portions of the heights, now flooding the valleys with green brightness, now marking out distinctly each dwelling, and the hotels, and then two small brick churches of the distant village—denoting its prosperity, while all around seemed under adverse fortunes. But we, who stood so elevated above mortal things, and saw so wide and far, could see the sunshine of prosperity departing from one spot and rolling toward another; so that we could not think it much matter which spot were sunny or gloomy at any one moment.

The top of this Green Mountain is a long ridge, marked on the county map as 2160 ft. above the sea; the summit is occupied by a valley, not very deep, but one or two miles wide, composing the town of Lebrida. Here there are respectable farmers, though it is a rough, and must be a bleak place. The first house, after reaching the summit, is a small, homely tavern, kept by P. Witt. We left our horse in the shed; and entering the little unpainted bar-room, we heard a voice, in a strange outlandish accent, explaining a diorama. It was an old man, with a full, gray-bearded countenance; and Mr. Leach exclaimed "Ah here's the old Dutchman again!" And he answered "Yes, Captain, here's the old Dutchman,"—tho' by the way, he is a German, and travels the country with this diorama, in a wagon; and had recently been at South Adams, and was now returning from Saratoga Springs. We looked through the glass orifice of his machine, while he exhibited a succession of the very worst scratchings and daubings that can be imagined—worn out, too, and full of cracks and wrinkles, besmeared with tobacco smoke, and every otherwise dilapidated. There were none in a later fashion than thirty years since, except some figures that had been cut from tailors' show-bills. There were views of cities and edifices in Europe, and ruins,—and of Napoleon's battles and Nelson's sea-fights; in the midst of which would be seen a gigantic, brown, hairy hand—the Hand of Destiny—pointing at the principal points of the conflict, while the old Dutchman explained. He gave considerable dramatic effect to his descriptions, but his accent and intonation cannot be written. He seemed to take an interest and pride in his exhibition; yet when the utter and ludicrous miserability thereof made us laugh, he joined in the joke very readily. When the last picture had been exhibited, he caused a country boor, who stood gaping beside the machine.

to put his head within it, and thrust his tongue out. The head becoming gigantic, a singular effect was produced.

The old Dutchman's exhibition over, a great dog—apparently an elderly dog—suddenly made himself the object of notice, evidently in rivalship of the Dutchman. He had seemed to be a good-natured, quiet kind of dog, offering his head to be patted by those kindly disposed towards him. This great, old dog, suddenly and of his own motion, began to run round after his own not very long tail, with the utmost eagerness; and catching hold of it, he growled furiously at it, and still continued to circle round, growling and snarling, with increasing rage, as if one half of his body were at deadly enmity with the other. Faster and faster went he round and round-about, growling still fiercer, till at last he ceased in a state of utter exhaustion; but no sooner had his exhibition finished, than he became the same mild, quiet, sensible old dog as before; and no one could have suspected him of such nonsense as getting enraged with his own tail. He was first taught this trick by attaching a bell to the end of his tail; but he now commences entirely of his own accord, and I really believe feels vain at the attention he excites.

It was chill and bleak on the mountain-top, and a fire was burning in the bar-room. The old Dutchman bestowed on everybody the title of Captain—perhaps because such a title has a great chance of suiting an American.

September 7, 1838: Mr. Leach and I took a walk by moonlight, last evening, on the road that leads over the mountain. Remote from houses, far up on the hill side, we found a lime kiln burning near the road side; and approaching it, a watcher started from the ground, where he had been lying at his length. There are several of these lime-kilns in this vicinity; they are built circular with stones, like a round tower, eighteen or twenty feet high; having a hillock heaped around a considerable of their circumference, so that the marble may be brought and thrown in by cart loads at the top. At the bottom there is a doorway large enough to admit a man in a stooping posture. Thus an edifice of great solidity is composed, which will endure for centuries, unless needless pains are taken to tear it down. There is one on the hill side close to the village, wherein weeds grow at the bottom, and grass, and shrubs too are rooted in the interstices of the stones; and its low doorway had a dungeonlike aspect; and we look down from the top as into a roofless tower. It apparently has not been used for many years; and the lime, and weather-stained fragments of marble are scattered about.

But in the one we saw last night, a hard wood fire was burning merrily beneath the superincumbent marble—the kiln being heaped full; and shortly after we came, the man (a dark, black-bearded figure in shirt-sleeves) opened the iron door, through the chinks of which the fire was gleaming, and thrust in huge logs of wood, and stirred the immense coals with a long pole; and showed us the glowing lime-stone,—the lower layer of it. The glow of the fire was powerful, at the distance of several yards from the open door. He talked very sociably with us,— being doubtless glad to have two visitors to vary his solitary night-watch; for it would not do for him to get asleep; since the fire should be refreshed as often as every twenty minutes. We ascended the hillock to the top of the kiln; and the marble was red-hot and burning with a bluish lambent flame, quivering up, sometimes, nearly a yard high, and resembling the flame of anthracite coal—only, the marble being in larger fragments, the flame was higher. The kiln was perhaps six or eight feet across. Four hundred bushels of marble were then in a state of combustion. The expense of converting this quantity into lime is about fifty dollars; and it sells for 25 cts per bushel at the kiln. We talked with the man about whether he would run across the top of the intensely burning kiln for a thousand

dollars, barefooted; and he said he would for ten;—he said that the lime had been burning 48 hours, and would be finished in 36 more, and cooled sufficiently to handle in 12 more. He liked the business of watching it better by night than day; because the days were often hot; but such a mild and beautiful night as the last was just right. Here a poet might make verses, with moonlight in them—and a gleam of fierce firelight flickering through them. It is a shame to use this brilliant, white, almost transparent marble, in this way. A man said of it, the other day, that into some pieces of it, when polished, one could see a considerable distance; and instanced a certain gravestone.

Mr. Leach told me how a girl, to whom he was once paying attention, with some idea of marrying her, made a confession of having forfeited her chastity. He had heard rumors of her having been indiscreet, with reference to a man who was formerly attentive to her—but had no idea of anything more than a merely pardonable indiscretion, in having trusted herself in long and solitary walk with this man. He began to talk with her on this subject, intending gently to reprehend her; but she became greatly agitated, and fell aweeping bitterly—her thoughts flying immediately to her guilt, and probably thinking that he was aware or suspicious of the full extent of it. She told so much, or betrayed so much, that he besought her to say no more. "That was the only time, Mr. Leach," sobbed she, "that I ever strayed from the path of virtue." Much might be made of such a scene—the lover's astoundment, at discovering so much more than he expected. Mr. Leach spoke to me as if one deviation from chastity might not be an altogether insuperable objection to making a girl his wife!!

(1844): The search of an investigator for the Unpardonable Sin;—he at last finds it in his own heart and practice.

·   ·   ·   ·   ·   ·

The Unpardonable Sin might consist in a want of love and reverence for the

Human Soul; in consequence of which, the investigator pried into its dark depths, not with a hope or purpose of making it better, but from a cold philosophical curiosity,—content that it should be wicked in whatever kind or degree, and only desiring to study it out. Would not this, in other words, be the separation of the intellect from the heart?

July 29, 1849: Una makes infinite complaint, and whining, and teazing about her hair, which has not been combed and put in order this morning—everybody being busy with grandmamma. At last comes in Dora, and takes her into the little room, where I hear her busily prattling about various matters, while Dora combs her hair. Julian, who, I think, has remarkable sensibility to musical sounds, sits on the floor, playing a sort of tune, by pulling a string across a bar of iron. Soon, he gets up and runs into the little room to talk with Dora and Una. His mother making a momentary and flitting appearance, he requests to go up to see grandmamma with her; being refused, he asks for a kiss, and, while receiving it, still offers up a gentle and mournful petition to be allowed to go with his mother. As this cannot be, he remains behind, with a most woeful countenance and some few quiet tears; the shower, however, is averted by Dora's telling him a story, while she continues to fix Una's hair. Julian has too much tenderness, love, and sensibility in his nature; he needs to be hardened and tempered. I would not take a particle of the love out of him; but methinks it is highly desirable that some sterner quality should be interfused throughout the softness of his heart; else, in course of time, the hard intercourse of the world, and the many knocks and bruises he will receive, will cause a morbid crust of callousness to grow over his heart; so that, for at least a portion of his life, he will have less sympathy and love for his fellow-beings than those who began life with a much smaller portion. After a lapse of years, indeed, if he have native vigor

enough, there may be a second growth of love and benevolence; but the first crop, with its wild luxuriance, stands a good chance of being blighted.

September 5, 1849: After breakfast, it being cloudy and damp, with a south-east wind, the children did not run out-of-doors, but went up on the front-stairs, and absolutely filled the house with their shouting and hallooing. I went up to dress, and on coming down again, found them enacting the parts of Mr. and Mrs. Mann,—Una holding a baby in her arms, which was the subject of conversation. Julian has now just taken out the box of blocks, and, I suppose, is about to erect an edifice.

September 6, 1849: "Are you a good little boy?" quoth I to Julian. "Yes," said he.—"What are you good for?" asked I.—"Because I love all people," answered he. His mother will be in raptures with this response—a heavenly infant, powerless to do anything, but diffusing the richness of his pure love throughout the moral atmosphere, to make all mankind happier and better!!!!! Or perhaps he understood the question to be for what reason he was good,—and meant to reply, that good deeds gushed forth from his heart of love, as the natural stream of such a fountain.

ETHAN BRAND

A CHAPTER FROM AN ABORTIVE ROMANCE
[1851 (1850)]

Bartram the lime-burner, a rough, heavy-looking man, begrimed with charcoal, sat watching his kiln, at nightfall, while his little son played at building houses with the scattered fragments of marble, when, on the hillside below them, they heard a roar of laughter, not mirthful, but slow, and even solemn, like a wind shaking the boughs of the forest.

"Father, what is that?" asked the little boy, leaving his play, and pressing betwixt his father's knees.

"Oh, some drunken man, I suppose," answered the lime-burner; "some merry fellow from the bar-room in the village, who dared not laugh loud enough within doors lest he should blow the roof of the house off. So here he is, shaking his jolly sides at the foot of Graylock."

"But, father," said the child, more sensitive than the obtuse, middle-aged clown, "he does not laugh like a man that is glad. So the noise frightens me!"

"Don't be a fool, child!" cried his father, gruffly. "You will never make a man, I do believe; there is too much of your mother in you. I have known the rustling of a leaf startle you. Hark! Here comes the merry fellow now. You shall see that there is no harm in him."

Bartram and his little son, while they were talking thus, sat watching the same lime-kiln that had been the scene of Ethan Brand's solitary and meditative life, before he began his search for the Unpardonable Sin. Many years, as we have seen, had now elapsed, since that portentous night when the IDEA was first developed. The kiln, however, on the mountain-side, stood unimpaired, and was in nothing changed since he had thrown his dark thoughts into the intense glow of its furnace, and melted them, as it were, into the one thought that took possession of his life. It was a rude, round, tower-like structure about twenty feet high, heavily built of rough stones, and with a hillock of earth heaped about the larger part of its circumference; so that the blocks and fragments of marble might be drawn by cart-loads, and thrown in at the top. There was an opening at the bottom of the tower, like an oven-mouth, but large enough to admit a man in a stooping posture, and provided with a massive iron door. With the smoke and jets of flame issuing from the chinks and crevices of this door, which seemed to give admittance into the hillside, it resembled nothing so much as the private entrance to the infernal regions, which the shepherds of the Delectable Mountains were accustomed to show to pilgrims.[1]

There are many such lime-kilns in that tract of country, for the purpose of burning the white marble which composes a large part of the substance of the hills. Some of them, built years ago, and long deserted, with weeds growing in the vacant round of the interior, which is open to the sky, and grass and wild-flowers rooting themselves into the chinks of the stones, look already like relics of antiquity, and may yet be overspread with the lichens of centuries to come. Others, where the lime-burner still feeds his daily and night-long fire, afford points of interest to the wanderer among the hills, who seats himself on a log of wood or a fragment of marble, to hold a chat with the solitary man. It is a lonesome, and, when the character is inclined to thought, may be an intensely thoughtful occupation; as it proved in the case of Ethan Brand, who had mused to such strange purpose, in days gone by, while the fire in this very kiln was burning.

The man who now watched the fire was of a different order, and troubled himself with no thoughts save the very few that were requisite to his business. At frequent intervals, he flung back the clashing weight of the iron door, and, turning his face from the insufferable glare, thrust in huge logs of oak, or stirred the immense brands with a long pole. Within the furnace were seen the curling and riotous flames, and the burning marble, almost molten with the intensity of heat; while without, the reflection of the fire quivered on the dark intricacy of the surrounding forest, and showed in the foreground a bright and ruddy little picture of the hut, the spring beside its door, the athletic and coal-begrimed figure of the lime-burner, and the half-frightened child, shrinking into the protection of his father's shadow. And when again the iron door was closed, then reappeared the tender light of the half-full moon, which vainly strove to trace out the indistinct shapes of the neighboring

---

[1] A reference to an incident in Bunyan's *Pilgrim's Progress*.

mountains; and, in the upper sky, there was a flitting congregation of clouds, still faintly tinged with the rosy sunset, though thus far down into the valley the sunshine had vanished long and long ago.

The little boy now crept still closer to his father, as footsteps were heard ascending the hillside, and a human form thrust aside the bushes that clustered beneath the trees.

"Halloo! who is it?" cried the lime-burner, vexed at his son's timidity, yet half infected by it. "Come forward, and show yourself, like a man, or I'll fling this chunk of marble at your head!"

"You offer me a rough welcome," said a gloomy voice, as the unknown man drew nigh. "Yet I neither claim nor desire a kinder one, even at my own fireside."

To obtain a distincter view, Bartram threw open the iron door of the kiln, whence immediately issued a gush of fierce light, that smote full upon the stranger's face and figure. To a careless eye there appeared nothing very remarkable in his aspect, which was that of a man in a coarse, brown, country-made suit of clothes, tall and thin, with the staff and heavy shoes of a wayfarer. As he advanced, he fixed his eyes—which were very bright—intently upon the brightness of the furnace, as if he beheld, or expected to behold, some object worthy of note within it.

"Good evening, stranger," said the lime-burner; "whence come you, so late in the day?"

"I come from my search," answered the wayfarer; "for, at last, it is finished."

"Drunk!—or crazy!" muttered Bartram to himself. "I shall have trouble with the fellow. The sooner I drive him away, the better."

The little boy, all in a tremble, whispered to his father, and begged him to shut the door of the kiln, so that there might not be so much light; for that there was something in the man's face which he was afraid to look at, yet could not look away from. And, indeed, even the lime-burner's dull and torpid sense began to be impressed by an indescribable something in that thin, rugged, thoughtful visage, with the grizzled hair hanging wildly about it, and those deeply sunken eyes, which gleamed like fires within the entrance of a mysterious cavern. But, as he closed the door, the stranger turned towards him, and spoke in a quiet, familiar way, that made Bartram feel as if he were a sane and sensible man, after all.

"Your task draws to an end, I see," said he. "This marble has already been burning three days. A few hours more will convert the stone to lime."

"Why, who are you?" exclaimed the lime-burner. "You seem as well acquainted with my business as I am myself."

"And well I may be," said the stranger; "for I followed the same craft many a long year, and here, too, on this very spot. But you are a new-comer in these parts. Did you never hear of Ethan Brand?"

"The man that went in search of the Unpardonable Sin?" asked Bartram, with a laugh.

"The same," answered the stranger. "He has found what he sought, and therefore he comes back again."

"What! then you are Ethan Brand himself?" cried the lime-burner, in amazement. "I am a new-comer here, as you say, and they call it eighteen years since you left the foot of Graylock. But, I can tell you, the good folks still talk about Ethan Brand, in the village yonder, and what a strange errand took him away from his lime-kiln. Well, and so you have found the Unpardonable Sin?"

"Even so!" said the stranger, calmly.

"If the question is a fair one," proceeded Bartram, "where might it be?"

Ethan Brand laid his finger on his own heart.

"Here!" replied he.

And then, without mirth in his countenance, but as if moved by an involuntary recognition of the infinite absurdity of seeking throughout the world for what was the closest of all things to himself, and looking into every heart, save his own, for what was hidden in no other breast, he broke into a laugh of scorn. It was the same slow, heavy laugh, that had almost appalled the lime-burner when it heralded the wayfarer's approach.

The solitary mountain-side was made dismal by it. Laughter, when out of place, mistimed, or bursting forth from a disordered state of feeling, may be the most terrible modulation of the human voice. The laughter of one asleep, even if it be a little child,—the madman's laugh,—the wild, screaming laugh of a born idiot,—are sounds that we sometimes tremble to hear, and would always willingly forget. Poets have imagined no utterance of fiends or hobgoblins so fearfully appropriate as a laugh. And even the obtuse lime-burner felt his nerves shaken, as this strange man looked inward at his own heart, and burst into laughter that rolled away into the night, and was indistinctly reverberated among the hills.

"Joe," said he to his little son, "scamper down to the tavern in the village, and tell the jolly fellows there that Ethan Brand has come back, and that he has found the Unpardonable Sin!"

The boy darted away on his errand, to which Ethan Brand made no objection, nor seemed hardly to notice it. He sat on a log of wood, looking steadfastly at the iron door of the kiln. When the child was out of sight, and his swift and light footsteps ceased to be heard treading first on the fallen leaves and then on the rocky mountain-path, the lime-burner began to regret his departure. He felt that the little fellow's presence had been a barrier between his guest and himself, and that he must now deal, heart to heart, with a man who, on his own confession, had committed the one only crime for which Heaven could afford no mercy. That crime, in its indistinct blackness, seemed to overshadow him. The lime-burner's own sins rose up within him, and made his memory riotous with a throng of evil shapes that asserted their kindred with the Master Sin, whatever it might be, which it was within the scope of

man's corrupted nature to conceive and cherish. They were all of one family; they went to and fro between his breast and Ethan Brand's, and carried dark greetings from one to the other.

Then Bartram remembered the stories which had grown traditionary in reference to this strange man, who had come upon him like a shadow of the night, and was making himself at home in his old place, after so long absence that the dead people, dead and buried for years, would have had more right to be at home, in any familiar spot, than he. Ethan Brand, it was said, had conversed with Satan himself in the lurid blaze of this very kiln. The legend had been matter of mirth heretofore, but looked grisly now. According to this tale, before Ethan Brand departed on his search, he had been accustomed to evoke a fiend from the hot furnace of the lime-kiln, night after night, in order to confer with him about the Unpardonable Sin; the man and the fiend each laboring to frame the image of some mode of guilt which could neither be atoned for nor forgiven. And, with the first gleam of light upon the mountain-top, the fiend crept in at the iron door, there to abide the intensest element of fire, until again summoned forth to share in the dreadful task of extending man's possible guilt beyond the scope of Heaven's else infinite mercy.

While the lime-burner was struggling with the horror of these thoughts, Ethan Brand rose from the log, and flung open the door of the kiln. The action was in such accordance with the idea in Bartram's mind, that he almost expected to see the Evil One issue forth, red-hot, from the raging furnace.

"Hold! hold!" cried he, with a tremulous attempt to laugh; for he was ashamed of his fears, although they overmastered him. "Don't, for mercy's sake, bring out your Devil now!"

"Man!" sternly replied Ethan Brand, "what need have I of the Devil? I have left him behind me, on my track. It is with such half-way sinners as you that he busies himself. Fear not, because I open the door. I do but act by old custom, and am going to trim your fire, like a lime-burner, as I was once."

He stirred the vast coals, thrust in more wood, and bent forward to gaze into the hollow prison-house of the fire, regardless of the fierce glow that reddened upon his face. The lime-burner sat watching him, and half suspected this strange guest of a purpose, if not to evoke a fiend, at least to plunge bodily into the flames, and thus vanish from the sight of man. Ethan Brand, however, drew quietly back, and closed the door of the kiln.

"I have looked," said he, "into many a human heart that was seven times hotter with sinful passions than yonder furnace is with fire. But I found not there what I sought. No, not the Unpardonable Sin!"

"What is the Unpardonable Sin?" asked the lime-burner; and then he shrank farther from his companion, trembling lest his question should be answered.

"It is a sin that grew within my own breast," replied Ethan Brand, standing erect, with a pride that distinguishes all enthusiasts of his stamp. "A sin that grew nowhere else! The sin of an intellect that triumphed over the sense of brotherhood with man and reverence for God, and sacrificed everything to its own mighty claims! The only sin that deserves a recompense of immortal agony! Freely, were it to do again, would I incur the guilt. Unshrinkingly I accept the retribution!"

"The man's head is turned," muttered the lime-burner to himself. "He may be a sinner like the rest of us,—nothing more likely,—but, I'll be sworn, he is a madman too."

Nevertheless, he felt uncomfortable at his situation, alone with Ethan Brand on the wild mountain-side, and was right glad to hear the rough murmur of tongues, and the footsteps of what seemed a pretty numerous party, stumbling over the stones and rustling through the underbrush. Soon appeared the whole lazy regiment that was

wont to infest the village tavern, comprehending three or four individuals who had drunk flip beside the bar-room fire through all the winters, and smoked their pipes beneath the stoop through all the summers, since Ethan Brand's departure. Laughing boisterously, and mingling all their voices together in unceremonious talk, they now burst into the moonshine and narrow streaks of firelight that illuminated the open space before the lime-kiln. Bartram set the door ajar again, flooding the spot with light, that the whole company might get a fair view of Ethan Brand, and he of them.

There, among other old acquaintances, was a once ubiquitous man, now almost extinct, but whom we were formerly sure to encounter at the hotel of every thriving village throughout the country. It was the stage-agent. The present specimen of the genus was a wilted and smoke-dried man, wrinkled and red-nosed, in a smartly cut, brown, bob-tailed coat, with brass buttons, who, for a length of time unknown, had kept his desk and corner in the bar-room, and was still puffing what seemed to be the same cigar that he had lighted twenty years before. He had great fame as a dry joker, though, perhaps, less on account of any intrinsic humor than from a certain flavor of brandy-toddy and tobacco-smoke, which impregnated all his ideas and expressions, as well as his person. Another well-remembered, though strangely altered, face was that of Lawyer Giles, as people still called him in courtesy; an elderly ragamuffin, in his soiled shirt-sleeves and tow-cloth trousers. This poor fellow had been an attorney, in what he called his better days, a sharp practitioner, and in great vogue among the village litigants; but flip, and sling, and toddy, and cocktails, imbibed at all hours, morning, noon, and night, had caused him to slide from intellectual to various kinds and degrees of bodily labor, till at last, to adopt his own phrase, he slid into a soap-vat. In other words, Giles was now a soap-boiler, in a small way. He had come to be but the fragment of a human being, a part of one foot having been chopped off by an axe, and an entire hand torn away by the devilish grip of a steam-engine. Yet, though the corporeal hand was gone, a spiritual member remained; for, stretching forth the stump, Giles stead-fastly averred that he felt an invisible thumb and fingers with as vivid a sensation as before the real ones were amputated. A maimed and miserable wretch he was; but one, nevertheless, whom the world could not trample on, and had no right to scorn, either in this or any previous stage of his misfortunes, since he had still kept up the courage and spirit of a man, asked nothing in charity, and with his one hand —and that the left one—fought a stern battle against want and hostile circum-stances.

Among the throng, too, came another personage, who, with certain points of sim-ilarity to Lawyer Giles, had many more of difference. It was the village doctor; a man of some fifty years, whom, at an earlier period of his life, we introduced as paying a professional visit to Ethan Brand during the latter's supposed insanity. He was now a purple-visaged, rude, and brutal, yet half-gentlemanly figure, with something wild, ruined, and desperate in his talk, and in all the details of his gesture and man-ners. Brandy possessed this man like an evil spirit, and made him as surly and savage as a wild beast, and as miserable as a lost soul; but there was supposed to be in him such wonderful skill, such native gifts of healing, beyond any which medical science could impart, that society caught hold of him, and would not let him sink out of its reach. So, swaying to and fro upon his horse, and grumbling thick ac-cents at the bedside, he visited all the sick-chambers for miles about among the moun-tain towns, and sometimes raised a dying man, as it were, by miracle, or quite as often, no doubt, sent his patient to a grave that was dug many a year too soon. The doctor had an everlasting pipe in his

mouth, and, as somebody said, in allusion to his habit of swearing, it was always alight with hell-fire.

These three worthies pressed forward, and greeted Ethan Brand each after his own fashion, earnestly inviting him to partake of the contents of a certain black bottle, in which, as they averred, he would find something far better worth seeking for than the Unpardonable Sin. No mind, which has wrought itself by intense and solitary meditation into a high state of enthusiasm, can endure the kind of con-tact with low and vulgar modes of thought and feeling to which Ethan Brand was now subjected. It made him doubt—and, strange to say, it was a painful doubt— whether he had indeed found the Unpar-donable Sin, and found it within himself. The whole question on which he had ex-hausted life, and more than life, looked like a delusion.

"Leave me," he said bitterly, "ye brute beasts, that have made yourselves so, shriv-elling up your souls with fiery liquors! I have done with you. Years and years ago, I groped into your hearts, and found noth-ing there for my purpose. Get ye gone!"

"Why, you uncivil scoundrel," cried the fierce doctor, "is that the way you respond to the kindness of your best friends? Then let me tell you the truth. You have no more found the Unpardonable Sin than yonder boy Joe has. You are but a crazy fellow,— I told you so twenty years ago,—neither better nor worse than a crazy fellow, and the fit companion of old Humphrey, here!"

He pointed to an old man, shabbily dressed, with long white hair, thin visage, and unsteady eyes. For some years past this aged person had been wandering about among the hills, inquiring of all travellers whom he met for his daughter. The girl, it seemed, had gone off with a company of circus-performers; and occasionally tidings of her came to the village, and fine stories were told of her glittering appearance as she rode on horseback in the ring, or per-formed marvellous feats on the tight-rope.

The white-haired father now approached Ethan Brand, and gazed unsteadily into his face.

"They tell me you have been all over the earth," said he, wringing his hands with earnestness. "You must have seen my daughter, for she makes a grand figure in the world, and everybody goes to see her. Did she send any word to her old father, or say when she was coming back?"

Ethan Brand's eye quailed beneath the old man's. That daughter, from whom he so earnestly desired a word of greeting, was the Esther of our tale, the very girl whom, with such cold and remorseless purpose, Ethan Brand had made the subject of a psychological experiment, and wasted, absorbed, and perhaps annihilated her soul, in the process.

"Yes," murmured he, turning away from the hoary wanderer; "it is no delusion. There is an Unpardonable Sin!"

While these things were passing, a merry scene was going forward in the area of cheerful light, beside the spring and before the door of the hut. A number of the youth of the village, young men and girls, had hurried up the hillside, impelled by curiosity to see Ethan Brand, the hero of so many a legend familiar to their childhood. Finding nothing, however, very remarkable in his aspect,—nothing but a sunburnt wayfarer, in plain garb and dusty shoes, who sat looking into the fire as if he fancied pictures among the coals, —these young people speedily grew tired of observing him. As it happened, there was other amusement at hand. An old German Jew, travelling with a diorama on his back, was passing down the mountain-road towards the village just as the party turned aside from it, and, in hopes of eking out the profits of the day, the showman had kept them company to the lime-kiln.

"Come, old Dutchman," cried one of the young men, "let us see your pictures, if you can swear they are worth looking at!"

"Oh, yes, Captain," answered the Jew, —whether as a matter of courtesy or craft, he styled everybody Captain,—"I shall show you, indeed, some very superb pictures!"

So, placing his box in a proper position, he invited the young men and girls to look through the glass orifices of the machine, and proceeded to exhibit a series of the most outrageous scratchings and daubings, as specimens of the fine arts, that ever an itinerant showman had the face to impose upon his circle of spectators. The pictures were worn out, moreover, tattered, full of cracks and wrinkles, dingy with tobacco-smoke, and otherwise in a most pitiable condition. Some purported to be cities, public edifices, and ruined castles in Europe; others represented Napoleon's battles and Nelson's sea-fights; and in the midst of these would be seen a gigantic, brown, hairy hand,—which might have been mistaken for the Hand of Destiny, though, in truth, it was only the showman's,—pointing its forefinger to various scenes of the conflict, while its owner gave historical illustrations. When, with much merriment at its abominable deficiency of merit, the exhibition was concluded, the German bade little Joe put his head into the box. Viewed through the magnifying-glasses, the boy's round, rosy visage assumed the strangest imaginable aspect of an immense Titanic child, the mouth grinning broadly, and the eyes and every other feature overflowing with fun at the joke. Suddenly, however, that merry face turned pale, and its expression changed to horror, for this easily impressed and excitable child had become sensible that the eye of Ethan Brand was fixed upon him through the glass.

"You make the little man to be afraid, Captain," said the German Jew, turning up the dark and strong outline of his visage, from his stooping posture. "But look again, and, by chance, I shall cause you to see somewhat that is very fine, upon my word!"

Ethan Brand gazed into the box for an instant, and then starting back, looked fixedly at the German. What had he seen? Nothing, apparently; for a curious youth, who had peeped in almost at the same moment, beheld only a vacant space of canvas.

"I remember you now," muttered Ethan Brand to the showman.

"Ah, Captain," whispered the Jew of Nuremberg, with a dark smile, "I find it to be a heavy matter in my show-box,—this Unpardonable Sin! By my faith, Captain, it has wearied my shoulders, this long day, to carry it over the mountain."

"Peace," answered Ethan Brand, sternly, "or get thee into the furnace yonder!"

The Jew's exhibition had scarcely concluded, when a great, elderly dog—who seemed to be his own master, as no person in the company laid claim to him—saw fit to render himself the object of public notice. Hitherto, he had shown himself a very quiet, well-disposed old dog, going round from one to another, and, by way of being sociable, offering his rough head to be patted by any kindly hand that would take so much trouble. But now, all of a sudden, this grave and venerable quadruped, of his own mere motion, and without the slightest suggestion from anybody else, began to run round after his tail, which, to heighten the absurdity of the proceeding, was a great deal shorter than it should have been. Never was seen such headlong eagerness in pursuit of an object that could not possibly be attained; never was heard such a tremendous outbreak of growling, snarling, barking, and snapping,—as if one end of the ridiculous brute's body were at deadly and most unforgivable enmity with the other. Faster and faster, round about went the cur; and faster and still faster fled the unapproachable brevity of his tail; and louder and fiercer grew his yells of rage and animosity; until, utterly exhausted, and as far from the goal as ever, the foolish old dog ceased his performance as suddenly as he had begun it. The next moment he was as mild, quiet, sensible, and respectable in his deportment, as when he first scraped acquaintance with the company.

As may be supposed, the exhibition was greeted with universal laughter, clapping of hands, and shouts of encore, to which the canine performer responded by wagging all that there was to wag of his tail, but appeared totally unable to repeat his very successful effort to amuse the spectators.

Meanwhile, Ethan Brand had resumed his seat upon the log, and moved, it might be, by a perception of some remote analogy between his own case and that of this self-pursuing cur, he broke into the awful laugh, which, more than any other token, expressed the condition of his inward being. From that moment, the merriment of the party was at an end; they stood aghast, dreading lest the inauspicious sound should be reverberated around the horizon, and that mountain would thunder it to mountain, and so the horror be prolonged upon their ears. Then, whispering one to another that it was late,—that the moon was almost down,—that the August night was growing chill,—they hurried homewards, leaving the lime-burner and little Joe to deal as they might with their unwelcome guest. Save for these three human beings, the open space on the hillside was a solitude, set in a vast gloom of forest. Beyond that darksome verge, the firelight glimmered on the stately trunks and almost black foliage of pines, intermixed with the lighter verdure of sapling oaks, maples, and poplars, while here and there lay the gigantic corpses of dead trees, decaying on the leaf-strewn soil. And it seemed to little Joe—a timorous and imaginative child—that the silent forest was holding its breath until some fearful thing should happen.

Ethan Brand thrust more wood into the fire, and closed the door of the kiln; then looking over his shoulder at the lime-burner and his son, he bade, rather than advised, them to retire to rest.

"For myself, I cannot sleep," said he. "I have matters that it concerns me to meditate upon. I will watch the fire, as I used to do in the old time."

"And call the Devil out of the furnace

to keep you company, I suppose," muttered Bartram, who had been making intimate acquaintance with the black bottle above mentioned. "But watch, if you like, and call as many devils as you like! For my part, I shall be all the better for a snooze. Come, Joe!"

As the boy followed his father into the hut, he looked back at the wayfarer, and the tears came into his eyes, for his tender spirit had an intuition of the bleak and terrible loneliness in which this man had enveloped himself.

When they had gone, Ethan Brand sat listening to the crackling of the kindled wood, and looking at the little spirts of fire that issued through the chinks of the door. These trifles, however, once so familiar, had but the slightest hold of his attention, while deep within his mind he was reviewing the gradual but marvellous change that had been wrought upon him by the search to which he had devoted himself. He remembered how the night dew had fallen upon him,—how the dark forest had whispered to him,—how the stars had gleamed upon him,—a simple and loving man, watching his fire in the years gone by, and ever musing as it burned. He remembered with what tenderness, with what love and sympathy for mankind, and what pity for human guilt and woe, he had first begun to contemplate those ideas which afterwards became the inspiration of his life; with what reverence he had then looked into the heart of man, viewing it as a temple originally divine, and, however desecrated, still to be held sacred by a brother; with what awful fear he had deprecated the success of his pursuit, and prayed that the Unpardonable Sin might never be revealed to him. Then ensued that vast intellectual development, which, in its progress, disturbed the counterpoise between his mind and heart. The Idea that possessed his life had operated as a means of education; it had gone on cultivating his powers to the highest point of which they were susceptible; it had raised him from the level of an unlettered laborer to stand on a star-lit eminence, whither the philosophers of the earth, laden with the lore of universities, might vainly strive to clamber after him. So much for the intellect! But where was the heart? That, indeed, had withered,—had contracted,—had hardened, —had perished! It had ceased to partake of the universal throb. He had lost his hold of the magnetic chain of humanity. He was no longer a brother-man, opening the chambers or the dungeons of our common nature by the key of holy sympathy, which gave him a right to share in all its secrets; he was now a cold observer, looking on mankind as the subject of his experiment, and, at length, converting man and woman to be his puppets, and pulling the wires that moved them to such degrees of crime as were demanded for his study.

Thus Ethan Brand became a fiend. He began to be so from the moment that his moral nature had ceased to keep the pace of improvement with his intellect. And now, as his highest effort and inevitable development,—as the bright and gorgeous flower, and rich, delicious fruit of his life's labor,—he had produced the Unpardonable Sin!

"What more have I to seek? what more to achieve?" said Ethan Brand to himself. "My task is done, and well done!"

Starting from the log with a certain alacrity in his gait and ascending the hillock of earth that was raised against the stone circumference of the lime-kiln, he thus reached the top of the structure. It was a space of perhaps ten feet across, from edge to edge, presenting a view of the upper surface of the immense mass of broken marble with which the kiln was heaped. All these innumerable blocks and fragments of marble were red-hot and vividly on fire, sending up great spouts of blue flame, which quivered aloft and danced madly, as within a magic circle, and sank and rose again, with continual and multitudinous activity. As the lonely man bent forward over this terrible body of fire, the blasting heat smote up against his person with a breath that, it might be supposed, would have scorched and shrivelled him up in a moment.

Ethan Brand stood erect, and raised his arms on high. The blue flames played upon his face, and imparted the wild and ghastly light which alone could have suited its expression; it was that of a fiend on the verge of plunging into his gulf of intensest torment.

"O Mother Earth," cried he, "who art no more my Mother, and into whose bosom this frame shall never be resolved! O mankind, whose brotherhood I have cast off, and trampled thy great heart beneath my feet! O stars of heaven, that shone on me of old, as if to light me onward and upward!—farewell all, and forever. Come, deadly element of Fire,—henceforth my familiar frame! Embrace me, as I do thee!"

That night the sound of a fearful peal of laughter rolled heavily through the sleep of the lime-burner and his little son; dim shapes of horror and anguish haunted their dreams, and seemed still present in the rude hovel, when they opened their eyes to the daylight.

"Up, boy, up!" cried the lime-burner, staring about him. "Thank Heaven, the night is gone, at last; and rather than pass such another, I would watch my lime-kiln, wide awake, for a twelvemonth. This Ethan Brand, with his humbug of an Unpardonable Sin, has done me no such mighty favor, in taking my place!"

He issued from the hut, followed by little Joe, who kept fast hold of his father's hand. The early sunshine was already pouring its gold upon the mountain-tops, and though the valleys were still in shadow, they smiled cheerfully in the promise of the bright day that was hastening onward. The village, completely shut in by hills, which swelled away gently about it, looked as if it had rested peacefully in the hollow of the great hand of Providence. Every dwelling was distinctly visible; the little spires of the two churches pointed upwards, and caught a foreglimmering of brightness from the sun-gilt skies upon their gilded weathercocks. The tavern was astir, and the figure of the old, smoke-dried stage-agent, cigar in mouth, was seen beneath the stoop. Old Graylock was glorified with a golden cloud upon his head. Scattered likewise over the breasts of the surrounding mountains, there were heaps of hoary mist, in fantastic shapes, some of them far down into the valley, others high up towards the summits, and still others, of the same family of mist or cloud, hovering in the gold radiance of the upper atmosphere. Stepping from one to another of the clouds that rested on the hills, and thence to the loftier brotherhood that sailed in air, it seemed almost as if a mortal man might thus ascend into the heavenly regions. Earth was so mingled with sky that it was a day-dream to look at it.

To supply that charm of the familiar and homely, which Nature so readily adopts into a scene like this, the stage coach was rattling down the mountain-road, and the driver sounded his horn, while Echo caught up the notes, and intertwined them into a rich and varied and elaborate harmony, of which the original performer could lay claim to little share. The great hills played a concert among themselves, each contributing a strain of airy sweetness.

Little Joe's face brightened at once.

"Dear father," cried he, skipping cheerily to and fro, "that strange man is gone, and the sky and the mountains all seem glad of it!"

"Yes," growled the lime-burner, with an oath, "but he has let the fire go down, and no thanks to him if five hundred bushels of lime are not spoiled. If I catch the fellow hereabouts again, I shall feel like tossing him into the furnace!"

With his long pole in his hand, he ascended to the top of the kiln. After a moment's pause, he called to his son.

"Come up here, Joe!" said he.

So little Joe ran up the hillock, and stood by his father's side. The marble was all burnt into perfect, snow-white lime. But on its surface, in the midst of the circle, —snow-white too, and thoroughly converted into lime,—lay a human skeleton, in the attitude of a person who, after long toil, lies down to long repose. Within the ribs—strange to say—was the shape of a human heart.

"Was the fellow's heart made of marble?" cried Bartram, in some perplexity at this phenomenon. "At any rate, it is burnt into what looks like special good lime; and, taking all the bones together, my kiln is half a bushel the richer for him."

So saying, the rude lime-burner lifted his pole, and, letting it fall upon the skeleton, the relics of Ethan Brand were crumbled into fragments.

1819 ∾ *Herman Melville* ∾ 1891

I

HERMAN MELVILLE brought to his work as a writer richer and more adventurous external experience than did any other American of his literary generation. When he published his first novel at the age of twenty-seven, he had earned a living as farmhand, bank clerk, school-teacher, and retail salesman; he had crossed the Atlantic as a cabin boy on a freighter and had rounded Cape Horn as a maintopman on a man-of-war; he had pulled an oar and cooked blubber with the crews of three whaling vessels; he had lived among savages and had been imprisoned as a mutineer.

This wealth of experience was the fruit of Herman Melville's native courage and curiosity. Though the circumstances of his youth were neither happy nor easy, he was under no evident compulsion to follow the adventurous course he chose. The decisive event of his early years was his father's death, when Herman, the third of eight children, was thirteen. Allan Melville had been a decorously urbane gentleman of business, a lover of good food and of polite society, a collector of objects of art, vain in his famous Scottish name and ancestors and in his own good looks. He had enjoyed the opportunities given by his occupation—that of an importer of fashionable garments and fine fabrics—for frequent journeyings to Liverpool, London, and Paris, where he had admired the right things and cultivated the right people. When the effects of the War of 1812 began to destroy his business, he cheerfully poured into it the portion of his father's estate which should have been inherited by his own children, and borrowed from members of his own and his wife's families. But his personal philosophy—expressly stated in his declaration that "money is the only solid substratum on which man can safely build in this world"— contained little provision against adversity and none against disaster. When his New York firm definitely failed and an effort to reëstablish himself in Albany proved fruitless, he surrendered the struggle; he died in 1832, mentally deranged.

Maria Gansevoort Melville, the widow who succeeded to the headship of the household, had shared many of her husband's tastes. She had been proud of her fine New York house, managed with traditional Dutch thoroughness and effectiveness; of her handsome face and figure, which so worthily displayed her husband's finest importations; of the Gansevoort family, famous and influential in New Netherland and New York, and in her own time in the nation. A devout and active member of the Dutch Reformed church throughout her long life, she had subjected her children to a rigorously pious denominational training. With her older sons, she set about a practical and determined effort to rebuild the family fortune. For Herman there were dull and undistinguished years at an academy in Albany, a job at fifteen in the bank of which his mother's brother was the president, a job in the store which his mother and his brother Gansevoort had started, a job on another uncle's farm in Massachusetts. At eighteen he started out to find and to make his own way.

II

To the American youth of the 1830's and '40's there were two chief roads to adventure and independence, the West and the sea. The westward movement was replacing the forests of the Ohio valley with farms and cities, sweeping across the Mississippi and the Missouri, venturing into the vast lands beyond. In these same years the American merchant marine, swiftly expanding since the War of 1812, was becoming the greatest in the world, and Yankee clippers were already the queens of all the oceans.

Herman Melville's choice of the sea was a natural one. One of his uncles was a retired sea captain, and a cousin—only a few years his senior, and a frequent companion during Herman's stay at Albany—was an officer in the United States Navy. But no intercession of influential relatives softened the experience of his first voyage. The ship on which he sailed was the *Highlander*, a freighter bound for Liverpool. His job was menial. The new boy was hazed by the brutal crew and abused or neglected by the officers. But he was husky and determined, and in the thirty days of the voyage he learned to be resourceful and self-sufficient.

Herman Melville had crossed the Atlantic with high expectation to find the England of his father's admiring stories—historic shrines, gracious people, the fine flower of civilization. What he saw, while the *Highlander* lay at Liverpool for many weeks awaiting a cargo, was the dockside slum: abject poverty, filth, drunkenness, vice. The experience was decisive for his whole life. When at last the ship returned to New York, Herman was glad to escape from it, and ready to spend three years ashore—school-teaching, reading, trying to write— before he tried the sea again at twenty-two: this time as a common sailor on a whaling vessel which took him from New Bedford to the South Pacific and to his most exciting adventures.

The *Acushnet* was one of the new additions to the rapidly growing American whaling fleet. But her crew was badly fed and ill-treated; only half of the original group of twenty-six made the full voyage of four years. When the *Acushnet* reached the Marquesas after eighteen months at sea, Melville and a companion decided they had had enough of blows and bad biscuit. They deserted.

The natives of the Marquesas group had been as yet little influenced by contact with white men. Their easy, joyous life in a place of sunlight and flowers and bright water seemed to Melville as beautiful as that of the Liverpool slums was ugly. In person they were beautiful, and Melville found them virtuous as well—generous, trustworthy, and compassionate. He recognized something of the richness of their social system, though he was far from understanding it fully, and of their traditional wisdom and poetry. But when after a few weeks another whaler touched at the Marquesas, he joined her crew.

This ship, a small one from Australia, proved even less agreeable than the *Acushnet*. The captain was so grossly incompetent that part of the crew, Melville among them, ultimately took over control of the ship at Tahiti, refusing to sail farther. They were thrown into prison as mutineers. Melville escaped, and after a few weeks in which he observed the life of the Tahitian natives, much more influenced by white traders and missionaries than that of the Marquesans, he shipped on yet a third whaler.

On shore again in the Sandwich Islands (as the Hawaiian group was then called), he obtained a job in a store in Honolulu. Here he had opportunity to assess the full effect of white commerce and settlement on the native population. When an American naval vessel, the frigate *United States,* touched at Honolulu, Melville enlisted as an ordinary seaman, on August 17, 1843, for the voyage home.

III

Books of travel were in great popular demand at this time both in England and America, especially those dealing with the South Seas. Herman's older brothers—Allan, now established in a law practice in New York, and Gansevoort, in business in London—encouraged the returned sailor to write the story of his adventures in the Pacific, and helped him to find his first publishers, in both London and New York.

No reader of *Typee* (1846), the lively book Melville made out of his weeks on the Marquesas, can doubt that he enjoyed writing it. He wrote with easy naturalness, and with a pervasive good humor only occasionally ruffled when he touched on the mistreatment of the natives by the whites. The book was immediately successful. For the first time in his life Herman Melville knew the feeling of being well paid for enjoyable work. Small wonder that he decided to go on writing.

He was encouraged in this decision by a new friend, the editor directly responsible for the publication of *Typee* in America. This was Evert Duyckinck, son of a respected New York publisher and an active and influential figure in American literary life for a generation. Duyckinck knew Irving, Poe, Simms, Hawthorne, and many lesser figures, and saw to it that Melville met these men and became known in their circles. Duyckinck had a large private library, and loaned his books to Melville freely. Rabelais, Tegnér, Sir Thomas Browne, John Donne, William Blake and Shakespeare were among the writers he read eagerly and with matured understanding, and discussed with Duyckinck and his group in long convivial evenings at Duyckinck's home—or in letters whenever the friends were separated for a few days. Public affairs were exciting as well, in these years of the Mexican War and the boundary controversy with Great Britain. Melville caught something of Duyckinck's active interest in politics, and wrote a series of sketches about Zachary Taylor for *Yankee Doodle,* a humorous magazine edited by members of the Duyckinck group. He followed the current books, and contributed many reviews—including a long and appreciative discussion of Hawthorne's *Mosses from an Old Manse*—to *The Literary World,* edited by Duyckinck. He went to the theatre, looked at pictures and sculpture, listened to music.

Meanwhile he had written a second long narrative based on the Tahitian episodes of his South Seas experience. *Omoo* (1847), though less idyllic than its predecessor, is even more adventurous and was equally popular. With prospects so bright, Melville married. His bride, Elizabeth Shaw, was the daughter of Chief Justice Lemuel Shaw of Boston, an old friend of the Melville family and one of the most distinguished American judges of his time. Allan Melville was newly married also, and late in 1847 the two couples set up housekeeping together at 103 Fourth Avenue, New York, to be joined soon by Maria Gansevoort Melville and the two unmarried Melville sisters. It was in this menage that Herman Melville wrote three novels and began a fourth in the next three years.

Mardi (1849), published just a month after Melville's first child was born, begins as though it were a sequel to *Omoo,* with the departure of a whaler from Tahiti, but changes suddenly to satirical fantasy, and blossoms into poetic allegory. The result is a literary mixture which the critics sampled gingerly and the public rejected outright. Rebuked—and pressed for money—Melville returned to the proved pattern. Writing with increased power and control of his materials, he produced in rapid succession *Redburn* (1849), based on his first sea voyage on the freighter to Liverpool, and *Whitejacket* (1850), in which he used the experience of his months on a man-of-war.

But even such productiveness could not meet the financial demands of the New York establishment. Early in 1850 Melville acquired, with the help of his father-in-law, a farm in the Berkshire Hills near Pittsfield, Massachusetts, and moved there with his family. No doubt he hoped to reduce living costs, to secure retired leisure for writing, and to simplify his life in other ways. He found the farm work demanding and exhausting, and the frequent visitors from New York—though welcome—equally so. Yet somehow he completed, for publication late in 1851, his greatest book, *Moby-Dick*.

The months at Pittsfield had been greatly enriched for Melville by a swiftly maturing friendship with Hawthorne and his wife, who had come to the region at about the same time. Melville admired Hawthorne's work profoundly, and had expressed in his review of *Mosses from an Old Manse* the opinion that Hawthorne was the first really great American writer. Now he turned eagerly for understanding to the man he was willing, in his fully achieved knowledge of his own powers, to call master. His forthrightness and exuberance may have embarrassed the older and colder man. But Melville was happy in what he found of response; and he was a frequent visitor, warmly welcomed, at the Hawthorne home.

We owe to the discerning eyes of Sophia Peabody, the wife of Hawthorne, our clearest contemporary portrait of Melville, in a long letter to her mother, almost wholly devoted to him:

I am not sure that I do not think him a very great man. . . . A man with a true, warm heart, and a soul and an intellect,—with life to his finger-tips; earnest, sincere and reverent; very tender and modest. . . . Once in a while, his animation gives place to a singularly quiet expression . . . an indrawn, dim look, but which at the same time makes you feel that he is at that moment taking deepest note of what is before him. It is a strange, lazy glance, but with a power in it quite unique.

Julian Hawthorne recounts a childhood memory of an evening visit in the course of which Melville, spinning a South Sea yarn for the entertainment of the Hawthornes, acted out a war dance so convincingly that after he had gone home the whole family searched for the war club—wholly imaginary—which he had supposedly forgotten.

To Hawthorne, then, Melville dedicated *Moby-Dick;* and he rejoiced in Hawthorne's characteristically measured praise of the book. A few critics, also, both in England and America, appreciated its quality and importance in some degree. But in general the reviews were unfavorable; and sales were poor.

Disappointed and resentful, baffled by his poverty and harassed by debts, saddened by the removal of the Hawthornes to Concord, Melville plunged at once into the writing of another novel. *Pierre* (1852) is externally a romantic melodrama; internally it is a passionate outpouring of the dark and troubled mind of Herman Melville at thirty-two, a desperate attempt to read the riddle of good and evil, of human motive and human fate. If Melville expected favor for the book from any quarter, he was disappointed.

Perhaps Melville faced at this time a crisis somewhat like that to which his father had surrendered twenty years before. His wife wrote later of these months that "after the writing of *Pierre* his health was much despaired of." He survived, and went on writing, but on a less ambitious scale and in a changed tone.

Israel Potter (1855), Melville's first novel after *Pierre,* was avowedly a fictional retelling of an obscure fragment of autobiography from an old book Melville had picked up. "Benito Cereno," a long story which most fully illustrates the height of technical mastery Melville had attained at this time, likewise uses old material. Only in a few unpretentious personal essays which he contributed to magazines, and in "The Encantadas," a series of related sketches of the Galapagos Islands—which he had twice visited in his Pacific journey—did he touch at all his personal experience. With the partial completion of *The Confidence Man* (1857)—a satirical and didactic panorama of people on a Mississippi River steamboat—he abruptly stopped writing prose fiction.

In 1856-7 Melville made a journey to Italy and the Holy Land, visiting Hawthorne at his consulate at Liverpool on the way. Again in 1860 he was on the sea, this time as a passenger to San Francisco on a clipper-ship commanded by his brother Thomas Melville. In these years he attempted rather unsuccessfully to make some money by lecturing—which was proving so remunerative to Emerson and other writers of the time—and tried repeatedly to obtain a government appointment which would assure an income. At last he gave up the Massachusetts farm and returned to New York.

He was still writing, but poetry rather than fiction. A volume of his poems occasioned by events and impressions of the Civil War appeared in 1866, *Battle-Pieces and Aspects of the War,* with a notable prose "Supplement" urging the same attitude toward the defeated South as that expressed by Lincoln in the "Second Inaugural Address." In the same year he finally obtained a government appointment, but one of no honor or comfort and with a meagre salary: that of District Inspector of Customs in the New York Harbor. Melville held this position for nineteen years.

The last thirty years of Melville's life were neither so unproductive nor so isolated as some biographers have suggested. In 1872 he published (with the financial assistance of his uncle, Peter Gansevoort) the long narrative poem *Clarel.* In this work he repeated the essential method of *Moby-Dick,* using a fictional framework and details from his own personal experience—of his visit to the Holy Land—to project philosophical and religious problems. Though in no way did Melville participate in the literary life of New York at this time as he had in earlier years, his friendship with Duyckinck was renewed in regular association until Duyckinck's death. Occasionally, though rarely, an admirer of his work sought him out. Most of his not abundant leisure was given to reading and study. Poems accumulated to make up two small volumes, *John Marr and Other Sailors* (1888) and *Timoleon* (1891), which he published privately in editions of twenty-five copies each; and a third left in manuscript at his death. At the very end of his life he returned to fiction, to produce one of the finest of all his works, the long story *Billy Budd,* not published until 1924. He died in 1891, his death little noticed by the literary world.

IV

Long neglected by critics and literary historians—though ordinary people went on reading and enjoying *Typee, Omoo* and *Moby-Dick,* in both England and America—Melville's work was suddenly rediscovered in the early 1920's, arousing a degree of interest unparalleled by that in any other American writer of his century. Skepticism and negation were prominent aspects of thought and of literary expression in the 1920's. It is not surprising that the newly enthusiastic criticism of Melville tended to read into him its own dominant attitudes. In more recent years much careful research has clarified many events in Melville's life, and broader study of his work as a whole has made possible a better understanding of his major books.

Typee is one of these, primarily in its own right as entertainment. Such are the freshness, the vitality, the abundant humor and active movement of this story that it is hard to imagine a reader who would find nothing to enjoy in it. Melville's delight in the unspoiled, childlike people of whom he wrote is matched by his exuberant pleasure in his own power to recall and share that delight. The lovely figure of Fayaway, the Marquesan girl, at once strange and exotic and very real and human, is hardly to be equalled in all the extensive literature in which men of the complex modern world have sought to record their discovery of beauty and value in primitive characters. Toby Greene is as engaging a companion in adventure as one could ask for. In his writing of *Typee* Melville found a style amazingly easy, spontaneous, vivid—truly amazing if one remembers his extremely limited experience in writing, and if one examines the stolidly factual or falsely rhetorical narration of most other books of travel of the time. Yet this style is already characteristic in its occasional swift modulations to fit Melville's barbed commentary on the conduct of white men in the South Seas, or his candid examination of his own actions and motives.

It is in these ethical considerations that *Typee* is linked with its successors. Already in this first novel questions of right and wrong are troubling Melville, and he is not satisfied by conventional and easy answers. The contrast between

Liverpool slum and Marquesan valley, terribly real in his own experience, lies behind his questioning—and it is the value of civilization itself that he is moved to question. The conduct of the Typees is contrary to a thousand rules of civilized behaviour; but they are happy, kind, good—until white men teach them to be civilized!

In *Omoo* the ethical problems are intensified. The novel has no lack of the flavor and charm of its predecessor: the Tahitian landscape is as vividly presented as the Marquesan; the movement of the story is lively and absorbing. Melville's increasing ability to delineate character is apparent in Doctor Long Ghost, much more complete and arresting as the narrator's companion than Toby Greene. The other important characters are more or less directly related to the statement of ethical questions. The Tahitians had suffered longer than the Marquesans the effects of white supremacy, and the corresponding probings of critical commentary are more numerous and more prominent.

In *Mardi* Melville surrendered (after 150 pages of brilliant "straight" narration) to the impulse to play with words and, especially, with ideas. Ship and whales—real whales in a real ocean—are alike abandoned, for symbolic voyages in a world of fantasy. Fayaway is transmuted into Yillah, embodiment of pure delight briefly enjoyed and then lost forever. In the quest for her—doomed to frustration seemingly because his first possession of her has resulted from a crime of violence—the hero of the tale encounters Queen Hautia, whose dusky handmaidens afford a strange, recurring chorus of evil omen as they offer—vainly—earthly love and the pleasures of the senses as a substitute for the lost Yillah. The remaining bulk of *Mardi,* inexpert and vague in narrative structure, consists of satirical fantasy. In company with a poet and a philosopher the hero visits many lands, seeking news of Yillah, but pausing to question the inhabitants and observe their life. Into these episodes Melville poured the hodgepodge of his reading and thinking of the moment, his excited discovery of the world of ideas and affairs in which he was living and writing in those crowded years in New York. It is not hard to recognize satirical comments on the South and slavery, on the North and industrialism, on Britain and France and Russia. And in this totally different context and method, ethical inconsistencies and contradictions are noted as sharply as in *Typee* and *Omoo,* but —as was not true of the earlier novels—their philosophical and religious implications are approached, though somewhat clumsily and tentatively.

When, disappointed by the critics' harsh reception of *Mardi* and sobered by the refusal of the public to buy it, Melville returned to worlds wholly recognizable as actual, it was with a deepened sense of his calling as a writer and with rapidly maturing powers. He himself referred to *Redburn* as a potboiler, written hastily for money. But in both *Redburn* and *Whitejacket* he made experiments and gained experience necessary in preparation for *Moby-Dick.* For one thing, he developed in these novels the technique of embodying great amounts of factual information in an adventurous narrative. This was the technique he was to use so extensively in the "encyclopedia of whales and whaling" which forms such a large and important part of *Moby-Dick*. When one has read *Redburn* he knows the life of the common sailors on a typical ocean freighter of Melville's time intimately and thoroughly. When he has read *Whitejacket* he knows even more completely the actual texture and movement of life on a man-of-war in the last days of the navy of sails. Growth in power of characterization is likewise noteworthy in these novels. Jackson, the venomous and degenerate sailor who becomes young Redburn's chief tormentor, is a more strongly portrayed character than any Melville had achieved before, masterly in pitiful ugliness. Similarly Jack Chase, of *Whitejacket,* is Melville's first full projection of human excellence in a man of courage and nobility. Perhaps even more significantly, these novels, and especially *Whitejacket,* show advance in the treatment of inner experience. Melville had never before written with such penetration and such sureness as he displayed in the incident of Whitejacket's fall from the mast-head and his near approach to death by drowning.

But it is in their ethical bearings that *Redburn* and *Whitejacket* are most interesting. Melville's quarrel with his own society has now become overt, aggressive. No longer proceeding by indirection or allegory, he attacks directly specific evils of his time. *Redburn* is marked by the powerful pictures of human misery and degradation seen by the young sailor in the Liverpool slums, and by the bitter contrast between the sufferings of the immigrants in the steerage and the callousness of the cabin passengers on the return voyage. Among *Whitejacket's* chief targets was the system of flogging in the Navy, and Melville's revelation of its inhumanity gave added force to a current demand for reform, shortly effective. In these aspects of his work Melville is the humanitarian reformer, in full harmony with his time.

But Melville's thinking was reaching to deeper levels in these years than that of most reformers of his time ever attained. He was not satisfied with movements and organizations; nor did he think that men can be saved by anything they make or do, by anything but what they are. It is in this emphasis on individual responsibility—confirmed in the novel's final paragraph: "From the last ills no being can save another; therein each man must be his own saviour"—that *Whitejacket* is the true predecessor of *Moby-Dick*.

V

In the five years that preceded the writing of *Moby-Dick* Melville had completed five novels. He had married, and his first child had been born. He had tasted fame and financial success and had encountered adversity. He had entered actively into the literary and political life of his times. He had read widely and enthusiastically.

Though the fruits of what he had lived, emotionally and intellectually, in these and earlier years are the chief elements of substance in *Moby-Dick,* the effects of his reading are perhaps most immediately apparent. To Richard Burton and Sir Thomas Browne *Moby-Dick* must owe something of its wealth of allusion and recondite lore, and something of the rolling music of its prose. To Blake it may owe something of its symbolism, to Rabelais something of its massiveness and discursiveness, its gusto and broad humor. To Shakespeare Melville's indebtedness is much more important. From the greatest of masters— whose plays he discussed eagerly with Duyckinck in letters and conversations of these years—he learned much of the actual technique he employed in *Moby-Dick.* Whole chapters of the novel are in dramatic form, and other passages not so denoted are actually Shakespearian soliloquies in the strictest sense. Even more significantly the thought of Shakespeare, especially of *King Lear,* entered into the conceptions of man and the world which Melville was to project in his greatest novel.

Moby-Dick is closely linked with its predecessors, however. Its narrative core is the actual experience of a whaling voyage, the richest portion of his life at sea, which Melville had left untouched—except for a few pages in *Mardi*— in the earlier books. And so brilliantly is this story told, as story, that *Moby-Dick* has been read with delight by many thousands for the story alone, and is to be obtained in some bookstores even today only in the juvenile department!

Also, as in the earlier novels, we have in *Moby-Dick* great quantities of factual information: the natural history of whales, the literature of whaling, the actual processes of chasing and capturing the whale, stripping the blubber, refining and storing the oil. A once great industry, today all but extinct, receives here its fullest and most illuminating history.

The richness of this history may make *Moby-Dick* seem, on first reading, a sprawling and amorphous book. The reader may find himself skipping chapters of detail to get on with the story. Only gradually does he come to see that both the narrative of action and the lore of whaling are subordinate to the real purpose of the novel. That purpose is revealed through the characters, and only by degrees.

Apart from the always shadowy narrator, Ishmael, the most important figure of the opening chapters of *Moby-Dick* is the savage harpooner Queequeg, who becomes Ishmael's friend: a person fully kin to the people of *Typee* and *Omoo,* though far richer than any of the earlier figures in human appeal and meaning. A savage, he is a rare demonstration of the potentials of human dignity and goodness—epitomized in his saving of the life of one who has insulted him—and with this a very real and likable person.

Not until many chapters have established a firm background of detail and emotion does Melville let us see, with Ishmael and Queequeg, the major character of the novel, and learn with them his purpose which affords its theme. He bears the name of that proud and blasphemous Old Testament king who "did more to provoke the Lord God of Israel to anger than all the kings of Israel that were before him." Ahab's intention is not the ordinary harvest of whale-bone and oil, but a personal revenge on the giant white whale that in an earlier encounter has "reaped his right leg" and left the strong man a cripple. To support of this purpose he wins the crew by the seduction of gold and by the magnetism of his own hatred. The first mate, Starbuck, pleads with him, but in vain. Ahab acknowledges that his course is impious, even blasphemous. He feels remorse for those he is endangering and regret for the lost happiness of his own life. But he persists. He has identified the great whale with all the obscure, ineluctable evil of life; and his pursuit is a considered and purposeful defiance of a universe in which unexplained and uncontrollable evil exists.

The great theme of *Moby-Dick* is stated clearly in its ninth chapter, in Father Mapple's sermon on the blessedness of harmony with the will of God. Ahab's real adversary is within himself—his pride, and the selfishness with which he ruthlessly uses and destroys the lives of other men for his own purposes. He refuses to see that he could gain wholeness of mind and spirit by acceptance of his bodily mutilation, and mastery of life by submission to its conditions. The meaning of *Moby-Dick* is essentially religious. The novel is a mighty parable, of sinful pride and its self-imposed destruction. About this central theme Melville has projected the intricate and yet organic tissue of the novel, with no character unnecessary, no incident digressive or superfluous, no detail without meaning. And as he wrote he became one of the great masters of English prose. No other American novel of its century approaches *Moby-Dick* in variety and forcefulness of images, in sureness and resourcefulness of word choices, in subtleness and suppleness of rhythm.

VI

How far the general failure of his contemporaries to recognize the full merits of *Moby-Dick*—in spite of a few discerning comments—may have affected Melville's next novel can be only conjectured; what persuaded him to write *Pierre*—after the authentic and original beauties of *Moby-Dick*—in a style which often seems compounded from those of the traditional Gothic tale and the conventional sentimental romance it is impossible to guess. If he hoped to beguile the public by a superficial resemblance to such current best sellers as George Lippard's *The Quaker City* (1844) and Susan B. Warner's *The Wide, Wide World* (1850), he was self-defeated. For the material that he clothed in this largely conventional and artificial style was in the highest degree inflammable and explosive.

It was, in fact, the old ethical confusion first noted in *Typee*: the relation between good and evil in a world of inconsistencies and contradictions. The central character, Pierre, does what he believes to be right, and believes that he does it unselfishly. His action has the ultimate effect of destroying the happiness and the lives of all he loves; and in the end he is not sure of his own first motives. In *Pierre* as in *Mardi*, an evil action for good ends is not thereby made good. In this novel as in all its predecessors, and more intensely, with more scorn and bitterness, Melville indicts false conventions and moral hypocrisies and all that was most odious in the society of Victorian America. In part *Pierre* continues and to some degree espouses Ahab's quarrel with the universe as it is. But there are deeper elements than all these in *Pierre*, personal elements of pain and protest, sometimes open and easily understood as in the sharply detailed account of Pierre's experiences as a writer, sometimes veiled beyond hope of assured interpretation. Surely the last of the major novels of Melville for the student to read, as it was the last in composition, *Pierre* will as surely prove first in ability to tease the mind with suppositions and surmises.

In *Israel Potter* (1855) Melville turned with almost obvious relief from the agonized inner questioning of *Pierre* to the outer world again. Only briefly in its pages is a window opened on the turmoil which still raged in his heart. The prevailing mood of its wonderfully simple and lucid prose is tenderness, a quiet compassion. Comparable objectiveness and restraint characterize most of Melville's prose after *Pierre;* though *The Confidence Man,* carelessly written and left incomplete—seemingly given up as a bad job—carries the theme of ethical confusions and contradictions as its whole reason for being.

The poetry to which Melville gave most of his creative strength in the last thirty years of his life makes few concessions to popular taste, shows little effort to gain or hold an audience. But to the reader to whom unmistakable sincerity is the first of literary virtues, *Clarel* and many of the shorter poems have positive value. In *Clarel* the ethical problems which still tortured Melville are stated in specifically religious terms, in the experiences of a pilgrim in the Holy Land and his conversations with widely differing acquaintances of the journey. Its atmosphere is one of outward calm; the travellers and the poem proceed at a sedate pace. But there is a desperate tension, a deep earnestness at the heart of the narrative. Its slender but genuine dramatic core is a tragedy as unrelieved as that of *Pierre;* the tortured yearning for understanding which it expresses is no less profound. *Clarel* is written in a poetic form no longer fashionable, with almost harsh classic simplicity, a rigorous rejection of all artifice and ornament. But it is a far greater book, of far deeper meaning both in its revelation of Melville's problems and in relation to those of the reader of today, than most commentators on Melville's work have realized. Like *Moby-Dick, Clarel* is a major document of the religious experience of the 19th Century, of the cleavage between fact and faith, the conflict between traditional religion and widening knowledge of the world as it is. In *Clarel* the dilemma is resolved, in the epilogue, by an act of faith. In *Billy Budd,* written by Melville with death at his elbow, the understanding reader may find a restatement of that faith, not merely acquiescent but triumphant.

When Melville's life and work are viewed in their entirety, it is seen that he never ceased to be the adventurer. His journeyings turned inward in his later years, but the oceans of the mind he then explored were no less vast and perilous than those he sailed in the *Highlander* and the *Acushnet* and reported in *Redburn, Typee, Omoo* and *Whitejacket.* In his humanitarianism, his outright criticism of social wrongs, his earnest searching after causes and relationships in the world about him, he was the true child of the 19th Century, a major spokesman of his time. But in the most significant expressions of his thought he was much more than a Victorian American. His search for truth was more courageous and more persistent, his record of it more candid and complete, than that of any of his contemporaries. He rejected the easy bypass offered by Transcendentalism, as he rejected the static Calvinism of his inheritance. In *Moby-Dick,* in *Pierre,* in *Clarel,* in *Billy Budd,* he faced the greatest of all the questions of men's thinking: faced them forthrightly, and embodied them in creative expressions unsurpassed in power, in depth, in lasting meaning, by any other writings of his place and time.

[The discussion of Melville's life and work during his lifetime has little but historical interest, but the student will find rewarding of examination the passages relating to Melville in Rose Hawthorne Lathrop's *Memories of Hawthorne* (Boston, 1897) and Julian Hawthorne's *Nathaniel Hawthorne and His Wife* (2 vols., Boston, 1884). A number of very interesting letters are included in *Family Correspondence of Herman Melville,* 1830-1904 (New York, 1929), edited by V. H. Paltsits. Books about Melville since the revival of interest in him during the 1920's are, with few exceptions, both biographical and critical. The pioneer work is R. M. Weaver's *Herman Melville, Mariner and Mystic* (New York, 1921). It is markedly inadequate in treatment of Melville's later life and work. Lewis Mumford's *Herman Melville* (New York, 1929) is appreciative and admirably written, not always dependable in interpretation. John Freeman's *Herman Melville* (London, 1926), a briefer study, is incomplete in some respects but generally sound in judgments. Of more recent works, Charles Roberts Anderson's *Melville in the South Seas* (New York, 1939) offers the first definitive study of both the actual events of the period treated and the relevant literature. William Braswell's *Melville's Religious Thought* (Durham, 1943) is more valuable for the factual study of Melville's work which it contains than for critical analysis. William Ellery Sedgwick's *Herman Melville: The Tragedy of Mind* (Cambridge, 1944) gives the best discussion thus far presented of *Clarel* and the later work in general. A most penetrating and illuminating essay on Melville is that by F. O. Matthiessen in *American*

Renaissance (New York, 1941). Of brief discussions of Melville, this and that of Willard Thorp in *Herman Melville* (New York, 1938), in American Writers Series, are the most valuable.

The texts used in the selections are those of *The Works of Herman Melville,* Standard edition (London, 1924), with slight alterations. *Collected Poems of Herman Melville* (Chicago, 1947), edited by Howard P. Vincent, has appeared as Vol. XIV of *Complete Works of Herman Melville.* A revised and corrected text of *Billy Budd,* edited by F. Barron Freeman, has been announced.]

From
"HAWTHORNE AND HIS MOSSES"
[1922 (1850)]

BUT it is the least part of genius that attracts admiration. Where Hawthorne is known, he seems to be deemed a pleasant writer, with a pleasant style—a sequestered, harmless man, from whom any deep and weighty thing would hardly be anticipated—a man who means no meanings. But there is no man, in whom humor and love, like mountain peaks, soar to such a rapt height as to receive the irradiations of the upper skies;—there is no man in whom humor and love are developed in that high form called genius; no such man can exist without also possessing, as the indispensable complement of these, a great, deep intellect, which drops down into the universe like a plummet. Or, love and humor are only the eyes through which such an intellect views this world. The great beauty in such a mind is but the product of its strength. What, to all readers, can be more charming than the piece entitled *Monsieur du Miroir;* and to a reader at all capable of fully fathoming it, what, at the same time, can possess more mystical depth of meaning?—yes, there he sits and looks at me, this "shape of mystery," this "identical MONSIEUR DU MIROIR!" "Methinks I should tremble now were his wizard power of gliding through all impediments in search of me to place him suddenly before my eyes."

How profound, nay, appalling, is the moral evolved by the *Earth's Holocaust;*

where—beginning with the hollow follies and affectations of the world,—all vanities and empty theories and forms are, one after another, and by an admirably graduated, growing comprehensiveness, thrown into the allegorical fire, till, at length, nothing is left but the all-engendering heart of man; which remaining still unconsumed, the great conflagration is naught.

Of a piece with this, is the *Intelligence Office,* a wondrous symbolizing of the secret workings in men's souls. There are other sketches still more charged with ponderous import.

The Christmas Banquet, and *The Bosom Serpent,* would be fine subjects for a curious and elaborate analysis, touching the conjectural parts of the mind that produced them. For spite of all the Indian-summer sunlight on the hither side of Hawthorne's soul, the other side—like the dark half of the physical sphere—is shrouded in a blackness, ten times black. But this darkness but gives more effect to the ever-moving dawn, that forever advances through it, and circumnavigates his world. Whether Hawthorne has simply availed himself of this mystical blackness as a means to the wondrous effects he makes it to produce in his lights and shades; or whether there really lurks in him, perhaps unknown to himself, a touch of Puritanic gloom,—this, I cannot altogether tell. Certain it is, however, that this great power of blackness in him derives its force from its appeals to that Calvinistic sense of Innate Depravity and Original Sin, from whose visitations, in some shape or other, no deeply thinking mind is always and wholly free. For, in certain moods, no man can weigh this world without throwing in something, some-how like Original Sin, to strike the uneven balance. At all events, perhaps no writer has ever wielded this terrific thought with greater terror than this same harmless Hawthorne. Still more: this black conceit pervades him through and through. You may be witched by his sunlight, transported by the bright gildings in the skies he builds over you; but there is the blackness of darkness beyond; and even his bright gildings but fringe and play upon the edges of thunder-clouds. In one word, the world is mistaken in this Nathaniel Haw-thorne. He himself must often have smiled at its absurd misconception of him. He is immeasurably deeper than the plummet of the mere critic. For it is not the brain that can test such a man; it is only the heart. You cannot come to know greatness by inspecting it; there is no glimpse to be caught of it, except by intuition; you need not ring it, you but touch it, and you find it is gold.

Now, it is that blackness in Hawthorne, of which I have spoken, that so fixes and fascinates me. It may be, nevertheless, that it is too largely developed in him. Perhaps he does not give us a ray of light for every shade of his dark. But however this may be, this blackness it is that furnishes the infinite obscure of his background—that background, against which Shakespeare plays his grandest conceits, the things that have made for Shakespeare his loftiest but most circumscribed renown, as the pro-foundest of thinkers. For by philosophers Shakespeare is not adored, as the great man of tragedy and comedy: "Off with his head; so much for Buckingham!" This sort of rant interlined by another hand, brings down the house—those mistaken souls, who dream of Shakespeare as a mere man of Richard the Third humps and Macbeth daggers. But it is those deep far-away things in him; those occasional flash-ings-forth of the intuitive Truth in him;

those short, quick probings at the very axis of reality; these are the things that make Shakespeare, Shakespeare. Through the mouths of the dark characters of Ham-let, Timon, Lear, and Iago, he craftily says, or sometimes insinuates the things which we feel to be so terrifically true, that it were all but madness for any good man, in his own proper character, to utter, or even hint of them. Tormented into desperation, Lear, the frantic king, tears off the mask and speaks the same madness of vital truth. But, as I before said, it is the least part of genius that attracts admiration. And so, much of the blind, unbridled admira-tion that has been heaped upon Shake-speare, has been lavished upon the least part of him. And few of his endless com-mentators and critics seem to have remem-bered, or even perceived, that the immedi-ate products of a great mind are not so great as that undeveloped and sometimes undevelopable yet dimly-discernible great-ness, to which those immediate products are but the infallible indices. In Shakespeare's tomb lies infinitely more than Shakespeare ever wrote. And if I magnify Shakespeare, it is not so much for what he did do as for what he did not do, or refrained from doing. For in this world of lies, Truth is forced to fly like a scared white doe in the woodlands; and only by cunning glimpses will she reveal herself, as in Shakespeare and other masters of the great Art of Telling the Truth,—even though it be covertly and by snatches.

But if this view of the all-popular Shakespeare be seldom taken by his readers, and if very few who extol him have ever read him deeply, or perhaps, only have seen him on the tricky stage (which alone made, and is still making him his mere mob renown)—if few men have time, or patience, or palate, for the spiritual truth as it is in that great genius—it is then no matter of surprise, that in a contempo-raneous age, Nathaniel Hawthorne is a man as yet almost utterly mistaken among men. Here and there, in some quiet arm-chair in the noisy town, or some deep nook among the noiseless mountains, he may be appreciated for something of what he is. But unlike Shakespeare, who was forced to the contrary course by circumstances, Hawthorne (either from simple disinclination, or else from inaptitude) refrains from all the popularizing noise and show of broad farce and blood-besmeared tragedy; content with the still, rich utterance of a great intellect in repose, and which sends few thoughts into circulation, except they be arterialized at his large warm lungs, and expanded in his honest heart.

Nor need you fix upon that blackness in him, if it suit you not. Nor, indeed, will all readers discern it; for it is, mostly, insinuated to those who may best understand it, and account for it; it is not obtruded upon every one alike.

Some may start to read of Shakespeare and Hawthorne on the same page. They may say, that if an illustration were needed, a lesser light might have sufficed to elucidate this Hawthorne, this small man of yesterday. But I am not willingly one of those who, as touching Shakespeare at least, exemplify the maxim of Rochefoucauld,[1] that "we exalt the reputation of some, in order to depress that of others"; who, to teach all noble-souled aspirants that there is no hope for them, pronounce Shakespeare absolutely unapproachable. But Shakespeare has been approached. There are minds that have gone as far as Shakespeare into the universe. And hardly a mortal man, who, at some time or other, has not felt as great thoughts in him as any you will find in Hamlet. We must not inferentially malign mankind for the sake of any one man, whoever he may be. This is too cheap a purchase of contentment for conscious mediocrity to make. Besides, this absolute and unconditional adoration of Shakespeare has grown to be a part of our Anglo-Saxon superstitions. The Thirty-Nine Articles are now Forty. Intolerance has come to exist in this matter. You must believe in Shakespeare's unapproachability, or quit the country. But what sort of a belief is this for an American, a man who is

bound to carry republican progressiveness into Literature as well as into Life? Believe me, my friends, that men, not very much inferior to Shakespeare, are this day being born on the banks of the Ohio. And the day will come when you shall say, Who reads a book by an Englishman that is a modern? The great mistake seems to be, that even with those Americans who look forward to the coming of a great literary genius among us, they somehow fancy he will come in the costume of Queen Elizabeth's day; be a writer of dramas founded upon old English history or the tales of Boccaccio. Whereas, great geniuses are parts of the times, they themselves are the times, and possess a corresponding coloring. It is of a piece with the Jews, who, while their Shiloh was meekly walking in their streets, were still praying for his magnificent coming; looking for him in a chariot, who was already among them on an ass. Nor must we forget that, in his own lifetime, Shakespeare was not Shakespeare, but only Master William Shakespeare of the shrewd, thriving, business firm of Condell,[2] Shakespeare and Co., proprietors of the Globe Theatre in London; and by a courtly author, of the name of Chettle, was looked at as an "upstart crow," beautified "with other birds' feathers." For, mark it well, imitation is often the first charge brought against originality. Why this is so, there is not space to set forth here. You must have plenty of sea-room to tell the Truth in; especially when it seems to have an aspect of newness, as America did in 1492, though it was then just as old, and perhaps older than Asia, only those sagacious philosophers, the common sailors, had never seen it before, swearing it was all water and moonshine there.

Now I do not say that Nathaniel of Salem is a greater man than William of Avon, or as great. But the difference be-

---

[1] Duc François de La Rochefoucauld (1613-1680), French writer.

[2] Henry Condell or Cundell (d. 1627), English actor and editor, friend and associate of Shakespeare.

tween the two men is by no means immeasurable. Not a very great deal more, and Nathaniel were verily William.

This, too, I mean, that if Shakespeare has not been equalled, give the world time, and he is sure to be surpassed in one hemisphere or the other. Nor will it at all do to say that the world is getting grey and grizzled now, and has lost that fresh charm which she wore of old, and by virtue of which the great poets of past times made themselves what we esteem them to be. Not so. The world is as young to-day as when it was created; and this Vermont morning dew is as wet to my feet, as Eden's dew to Adam's. Nor has nature been all over ransacked by our progenitors, so that no new charms and mysteries remain for this latter generation to find. Far from it. The trillionth part has not yet been said; and all that has been said, but multiplies the avenues to what remains to be said. It is not so much paucity as superabundance of material that seems to incapacitate modern authors.

Let America, then, prize and cherish her writers; yea, let her glorify them. They are not so many in number as to exhaust her goodwill. And while she has good kith and kin of her own, to take to her bosom, let her not lavish her embraces upon the household of an alien. For believe it or not, England after all, is in many things an alien to us. China has more bonds of real love for us than she. But even were there no strong literary individualities among us, as there are some dozens at least, nevertheless, let America first praise mediocrity even, in her children, before she praises (for everywhere, merit demands acknowledgement from every one) the best excellence in the children of any other land. Let her own authors, I say, have the priority of appreciation. I was much pleased with a hot-headed Carolina cousin of mine, who once said,—"If there were no other American to stand by, in literature, why, then, I would stand by Pop Emmons[3] and his *Fredoniad*, and till a better epic came along, swear it was not very far

behind the *Iliad*." Take away the words, and in spirit he was sound.

Not that American genius needs patronage in order to expand. For that explosive sort of stuff will expand though screwed up in a vice, and burst it, though it were triple steel. It is for the nation's sake, and not for her authors' sake, that I would have America be heedful of the increasing greatness among her writers. For how great the shame, if other nations should be before her, in crowning her heroes of the pen! But this is almost the case now. American authors have received more just and discriminating praise (however loftily and ridiculously given, in certain cases) even from some Englishmen, than from their own countrymen. There are hardly five critics in America; and several of them are asleep. As for patronage, it is the American author who now patronizes his country, and not his country him. And if at times some among them appeal to the people for more recognition, it is not always with selfish motives, but patriotic ones.

It is true, that but few of them as yet have evinced that decided originality which merits great praise. But that graceful writer, who perhaps of all Americans has received the most plaudits from his own country for his productions,—that very popular and amiable writer, however good and self-reliant in many things, perhaps owes his chief reputation to the self-acknowledged imitation of a foreign model, and to the studied avoidance of all topics but smooth ones.[4] But it is better to fail in originality, than to succeed in imitation. He who has never failed somewhere, that man cannot be great. Failure is the true test of greatness. And if it be said, that continual success is a proof that a man wisely knows his powers,—it is only to be added, that, in that case, he knows them to

---

[3] See the first footnote to Poe's "The Literary Life of Thingum Bob, Esq.," p. 532.

[4] Some critics have suggested that this sentence refers to Washington Irving.

be small. Let us believe, it, then, once for all, that there is no hope for us in these smooth, pleasing writers that know their powers. Without malice, but to speak the plain fact, they but furnish an appendix to Goldsmith, and other English authors. And we want no American Goldsmiths, nay, we want no American Miltons. It were the vilest thing you could say of a true American author, that he were an American Tompkins. Call him an American and have done, for you cannot say a nobler thing of him. But it is not meant that all American writers should studiously cleave to nationality in their writings; only this, no American writer should write like an Englishman or a Frenchman; let him write like a man, for then he will be sure to write like an American. Let us away with this leaven of literary flunkeyism towards England. If either must play the flunkey in this thing, let England do it, not us. While we are rapidly preparing for that political supremacy among the nations which prophetically awaits us at the close of the present century, in a literary point of view, we are deplorably unprepared for it; and we seem studious to remain so. Hitherto, reasons might have existed why this should be; but no good reason exists now. And all that is requisite to amendment in this matter, is simply this: that while fully acknowledging all excellence everywhere, we should refrain from unduly lauding foreign writers, and, at the same time, duly recognize the meritorious writers that are our own; those writers who breathe that unshackled, democratic spirit of Christianity in all things, which now takes the practical lead in this world, though at the same time led by ourselves—us Americans. Let us boldly condemn all imitation, though it comes to us graceful and fragrant as the morning; and foster all originality though at first it be crabbed and ugly as our own pine knots. And if any of our authors fail, or seem to fail, then, in the words of my Carolina cousin, let us clap him on the shoulder and back him against all Europe for his second round. The truth is, that in one point of view this matter of a national literature has come to such a pass with us, that in some sense we must turn bullies, else the day is lost, or superiority so far beyond us, that we can hardly say it will ever be ours.

And now, my countrymen, as an excellent author of your own flesh and blood—an unimitating, and, perhaps, in his way, an inimitable man—whom better can I commend to you, in the first place, than Nathaniel Hawthorne. He is one of the new, and far better generation of your writers. The smell of young beeches and hemlocks is upon him; your own broad prairies are in his soul; and if you travel away inland into his deep and noble nature, you will hear the far roar of his Niagara. Give not over to future generations the glad duty of acknowledging him for what he is. Take that joy to yourself, in your own generation; and so shall he feel those grateful impulses on him, that may possibly prompt him to the full flower of some still greater achievement in your eyes. And by confessing him you thereby confess others; you brace the whole brotherhood. For genius, all over the world, stands hand in hand, and one shock of recognition runs the whole circle round.

BENITO CERENO
[1856 (1855)]

IN the year 1799, Captain Amasa Delano, of Duxbury, in Massachusetts, commanding a large sealer and general trader, lay at anchor, with a valuable cargo, in the harbour of St. Maria—a small, desert, uninhabited island towards the southern extremity of the long coast of Chili. There he had touched for water.

On the second day, not long after dawn, while lying in his berth, his mate came below, informing him that a strange sail was coming into the bay. Ships were then not so plenty in those waters as now. He rose, dressed, and went on deck.

The morning was one peculiar to that coast. Everything was mute and calm; everything grey. The sea, though undulated into long roods of swells, seemed fixed, and was sleeked at the surface like waved lead that has cooled and set in the smelter's mould. The sky seemed a grey mantle. Flights of troubled grey fowl, kith and kin with flights of troubled grey vapours among which they were mixed, skimmed low and fitfully over the waters, as swallows over meadows before storms. Shadows present, foreshadowing deeper shadows to come.

To Captain Delano's surprise, the stranger, viewed through the glass, showed no colours; though to do so upon entering a haven, however uninhabited in its shores, where but a single other ship might be lying, was the custom among peaceful seamen of all nations. Considering the lawlessness and loneliness of the spot, and the sort of stories, at that day, associated with those seas, Captain Delano's surprise might have deepened into some uneasiness had he not been a person of a singularly undistrustful good nature, not liable, except on extraordinary and repeated excitement, and hardly then, to indulge in personal alarms, any way involving the imputation of malign evil in man. Whether, in view of what humanity is capable, such a trait implies, along with a benevolent heart, more than ordinary quickness and accuracy of intellectual perception, may be left to the wise to determine.

But whatever misgivings might have obtruded on first seeing the stranger, would almost, in any seaman's mind, have been dissipated by observing that the ship, in navigating into the harbour, was drawing too near the land, for her own safety's sake, owing to a sunken reef making out off her bow. This seemed to prove her a stranger, indeed, not only to the sealer, but the island; consequently, she could be no wonted freebooter on that ocean. With no small interest, Captain Delano continued to watch her—a proceeding not much facilitated by the vapours partly mantling

the hull, through which the far matin light from her cabin streamed equivocally enough; much like the sun—by this time crescented on the rim of the horizon, and apparently, in company with the strange ship, entering the harbour—which, wimpled by the same low, creeping clouds, showed not unlike a Lima intriguante's [1] one sinister eye peering across the Plaza from the Indian loop-hole of her dusk *saya-y-manta*. [2]

It might have been but a deception of the vapours, but, the longer the stranger was watched, the more singular appeared her manœuvres. Ere long it seemed hard to decide whether she meant to come in or no—what she wanted, or what she was about. The wind, which had breezed up a little during the night, was now extremely light and baffling, which the more increased the apparent uncertainty of her movements.

Surmising, at last, that it might be a ship in distress, Captain Delano ordered his whale-boat to be dropped, and, much to the wary opposition of his mate, prepared to board her, and, at the least, pilot her in. On the night previous, a fishing-party of the seamen had gone a long distance to some detached rocks out of sight from the sealer, and, an hour or two before day-break, had returned, having met with no small success. Presuming that the stranger might have been long off soundings, the good captain put several baskets of the fish, for presents, into his boat, and so pulled away. From her continuing too near the sunken reef, deeming her in danger, calling to his men, he made all haste to apprise those on board of their situation. But, some time ere the boat came up, the wind, light though it was, having shifted, had headed the vessel off, as well as partly broken the vapours from about her.

Upon gaining a less remote view, the ship, when made signally visible on the

[1] Flirt or siren.
[2] An enveloping type of cloak, or "skirt and shawl."

verge of the leaden-hued swells, with the shreds of fog here and there raggedly furring her, appeared like a white-washed monastery after a thunder-storm, seen perched upon some dun cliff among the Pyrenees. But it was no purely fanciful resemblance which now, for a moment, almost led Captain Delano to think that nothing less than a ship-load of monks was before him. Peering over the bulwarks were what really seemed, in the hazy distance, throngs of dark cowls; while, fitfully revealed through the open port-holes, other dark moving figures were dimly descried, as of Black Friars pacing the cloisters.

Upon a still nigher approach, this appearance was modified, and the true character of the vessel was plain—a Spanish merchantman of the first class; carrying negro slaves, amongst other valuable freight, from one colonial port to another. A very large, and, in its time, a very fine vessel, such as in those days were at intervals encountered along that main; sometimes superseded Acapulco [3] treasure-ships, or retired frigates of the Spanish king's navy, which, like superannuated Italian palaces, still, under a decline of masters, preserved signs of former state.

As the whale-boat drew more and more nigh, the cause of the peculiar pipe-clayed aspect of the stranger was seen in the slovenly neglect pervading her. The spars, ropes, and great part of the bulwarks, looked woolly, from long unacquaintance with the scraper, tar, and the brush. Her keel seemed laid, her ribs put together, and she launched, from Ezekiel's Valley of Dry Bones.[4]

In the present business in which she was engaged, the ship's general model and rig appeared to have undergone no material change from their original warlike and Froissart[5] pattern. However, no guns were seen.

The tops were large, and were railed about with what had once been octagonal net-work, all now in sad disrepair. These tops hung overhead like three ruinous aviaries, in one of which was seen perched, on a ratlin, a white noddy, a strange fowl, so called from its lethargic somnambulistic character, being frequently caught by hand at sea. Battered and mouldy, the castellated forecastle seemed some ancient turret, long ago taken by assault, and then left to decay. Towards the stern, two high-raised quarter galleries—the balustrades here and there covered with dry, tindery sea-moss—opening out from the unoccupied state-cabin, whose dead lights, for all the mild weather, were hermetically closed and caulked—these tenantless balconies hung over the sea as if it were the grand Venetian canal. But the principal relic of faded grandeur was the ample oval of the shield-like stern-piece, intricately carved with the arms of Castile and Leon,[6] medallioned about by groups of mythological or symbolical devices; uppermost and central of which was a dark satyr in a mask, holding his foot on the prostrate neck of a writhing figure, likewise masked.

Whether the ship had a figure-head, or only a plain beak, was not quite certain, owing to canvas wrapped about that part, either to protect it while undergoing a refurbishing, or else decently to hide its decay. Rudely painted or chalked, as in a sailor freak, along the forward side of a sort of pedestal below the canvas, was the sentence, *"Seguid vuestro jefe,"* (follow your leader); while upon the tarnished head-boards, near by, appeared, in stately capitals, once gilt, the ship's name, "SAN DOMINICK," each letter streakingly corroded with tricklings of copper-spike rust; while, like mourning weeds, dark festoons of sea-grass slimily swept to and fro over

---

[3] Mexico's chief Pacific port, long a leading port-of-call for Spanish ships plying between South America and the Spanish possessions in the Orient.

[4] Ezekiel 37:1-10.

[5] Jean Froissart (1333?-1400?), French chronicler of the age of chivalry in England.

[6] Ancient kingdoms, later provinces, of Spain.

the name, with every hearse-like roll of the hull.

As at last the boat was hooked from the bow along toward the gangway amidship, its keel, while yet some inches separated from the hull, harshly grated as on a sunken coral reef. It proved a huge bunch of conglobated barnacles adhering below the water to the side like a wen; a token of baffling airs and long calms passed somewhere in those seas.

Climbing the side, the visitor was at once surrounded by a clamorous throng of whites and blacks, but the latter out-numbering the former more than could have been expected, negro transportation-ship as the stranger in port was. But, in one language, and as with one voice, all poured out a common tale of suffering; in which the negresses, of whom there were not a few, exceeded the others in their dolorous vehemence. The scurvy, together with a fever, had swept off a great part of their number, more especially the Span-iards. Off Cape Horn, they had narrowly escaped shipwreck; then, for days to-gether, they had lain tranced without wind; their provisions were low; their water next to none; their lips that moment were baked.

While Captain Delano was thus made the mark of all eager tongues, his one eager glance took in all the faces, with every other object about him.

Always upon first boarding a large and populous ship at sea, especially a foreign one, with a nondescript crew such as Las-cars or Manilla men, the impression varies in a peculiar way from that produced by first entering a strange house with strange inmates in a strange land. Both house and ship, the one by its walls and blinds, the other by its high bulwarks like ramparts, hoard from view their interiors till the last moment; but in the case of the ship there is this addition: that the living spectacle it contains, upon its sudden and complete dis-closure, has, in contrast with the blank ocean which zones it, something of the effect of enchantment. The ship seems un-real; these strange costumes, gestures, and faces, but a shadowy tableau just emerged from the deep, which directly must receive back what it gave.

Perhaps it was some such influence as above is attempted to be described which, in Captain Delano's mind, heightened what-ever, upon a staid scrutiny, might have seemed unusual; especially the conspicuous figures of four elderly grizzled negroes, their heads like black, doddered willow tops, who, in venerable contrast to the tumult below them, were couched sphynx-like, one on the starboard cat-head, another on the larboard, and the remaining pair face to face on the opposite bulwarks above the main-chains. They each had bits of unstranded old junk in their hands, and, with a sort of stoical self-content, were picking the junk into oakum, a small heap of which lay by their sides. They accom-panied the task with a continuous, low, monotonous chant; droning and drooling away like so many grey-headed bag-pipers playing a funeral march.

The quarter-deck rose into an ample elevated poop, upon the forward verge of which, lifted, like the oakum-pickers, some eight feet above the general throng, sat along in a row, separated by regular spaces, the cross-legged figures of six other blacks; each with a rusty hatchet in his hand, which, with a bit of brick and a rag, he was engaged like a scullion in scouring; while between each two was a small stack of hatchets, their rusted edges turned for-ward awaiting a like operation. Though occasionally the four oakum-pickers would briefly address some person or persons in the crowd below, yet the six hatchet-polish-ers neither spoke to others, nor breathed a whisper among themselves, but sat in-tent upon their task, except at intervals, when, with the peculiar love in negroes of uniting industry with pastime, two-and-two they sideways clashed their hatchets together, like cymbals, with a barbarous din. All six, unlike the generality, had the raw aspect of unsophisticated Africans.

But that first comprehensive glance which

took in those ten figures, with scores less conspicuous, rested but an instant upon them, as, impatient of the hubbub of voices, the visitor turned in quest of whomsoever it might be that commanded the ship.

But as if not unwilling to let nature make known her own case among his suffering charge, or else in despair of restraining it for the time, the Spanish captain, a gentlemanly, reserved-looking, and rather young man to a stranger's eye, dressed with singular richness, but bearing plain traces of recent sleepless cares and disquietudes, stood passively by, leaning against the main-mast, at one moment casting a dreary, spiritless look upon his excited people, at the next an unhappy glance toward his visitor. By his side stood a black of small stature, in whose rude face, as occasionally, like a shepherd's dog, he mutely turned it up into the Spaniard's, sorrow and affection were equally blended.

Struggling through the throng, the American advanced to the Spaniard, assuring him of his sympathies, and offering to render whatever assistance might be in his power. To which the Spaniard returned, for the present, but grave and ceremonious acknowledgments, his national formality dusked by the saturnine mood of ill health.

But losing no time in mere compliments, Captain Delano returning to the gangway, had his baskets of fish brought up, and as the wind still continued light, so that some hours at least must elapse ere the ship could be brought to the anchorage, he bade his men return to the sealer, and fetch back as much water as the whale-boat could carry, with whatever soft bread the steward might have, all the remaining pumpkins on board, with a box of sugar, and a dozen of his private bottles of cider.

Not many minutes after the boat's pushing off, to the vexation of all, the wind entirely died away, and the tide turning, began drifting back the ship helplessly seaward. But trusting this would not long last, Captain Delano sought with good hopes to cheer up the strangers, feeling no

small satisfaction that, with persons in their condition he could—thanks to his frequent voyages along the Spanish main—converse with some freedom in their native tongue.

While left alone with them, he was not long in observing some things tending to heighten his first impressions; but surprise was lost in pity, both for the Spaniards and blacks, alike evidently reduced from scarcity of water and provisions; while long-continued suffering seemed to have brought out the less good-natured qualities of the negroes, besides, at the same time, impairing the Spaniard's authority over them. But, under the circumstances, precisely this condition of things was to have been anticipated. In armies, navies, cities, or families—in nature herself—nothing more relaxes good order than misery. Still, Captain Delano was not without the idea, that had Benito Cereno been a man of greater energy, misrule would hardly have come to the present pass. But the debility, constitutional or induced by the hardships, bodily and mental, of the Spanish captain, was too obvious to be overlooked. A prey to settled dejection, as if long mocked with hope he would not now indulge it, even when it had ceased to be a mock, the prospect of that day or evening at furthest, lying at anchor, with plenty of water for his people, and a brother captain to counsel and befriend, seemed in no perceptible degree to encourage him. His mind appeared unstrung, if not still more seriously affected. Shut up in these oaken walls, chained to one dull round of command, whose unconditionality cloyed him, like some hypochondriac abbot he moved slowly about, at times suddenly pausing, starting, or staring, biting his lip, biting his finger-nail, flushing, paling, twitching his beard, with other symptoms of an absent or moody mind. This distempered spirit was lodged, as before hinted, in as distempered a frame. He was rather tall, but seemed never to have been robust, and now with nervous suffering was almost worn to a skeleton. A tendency to some pulmonary complaint appeared to have been lately confirmed. His voice was like that of one with lungs half gone, hoarsely suppressed, a husky whisper. No wonder that, as in this state he tottered about, his private servant apprehensively followed him. Sometimes the negro gave his master his arm, or took his handkerchief out of his pocket for him; performing these and similar offices with that affectionate zeal which transmutes into something filial or fraternal acts in themselves but menial; and which has gained for the negro the repute of making the most pleasing body servant in the world; one, too, whom a master need be on no stiffly superior terms with, but may treat with familiar trust; less a servant than a devoted companion.

Marking the noisy indocility of the blacks in general, as well as what seemed the sullen inefficiency of the whites, it was not without humane satisfaction that Captain Delano witnessed the steady good conduct of Babo.

But the good conduct of Babo, hardly more than the ill-behaviour of others, seemed to withdraw the half-lunatic Don Benito from his cloudy languor. Not that such precisely was the impression made by the Spaniard on the mind of his visitor. The Spaniard's individual unrest was, for the present, but noted as a conspicuous feature in the ship's general affliction. Still, Captain Delano was not a little concerned at what he could not help taking for the time to be Don Benito's unfriendly indifference toward himself. The Spaniard's manner, too, conveyed a sort of sour and gloomy disdain, which he seemed at no pains to disguise. But this the American in charity ascribed to the harassing effects of sickness, since, in former instances, he had noted that there are peculiar natures on whom prolonged physical suffering seems to cancel every social instinct of kindness; as if forced to black bread themselves, they deemed it but equity that each person coming nigh them should, indirectly, by some slight or affront, be made to partake of their fare.

But ere long Captain Delano bethought him that, indulgent as he was at the first, in judging the Spaniard, he might not, after all, have exercised charity enough. At bottom it was Don Benito's reserve which displeased him; but the same reserve was shown toward all but his personal attendant. Even the formal reports which, according to sea-usage, were at stated times made to him by some petty underling (either a white, mulatto or black), he hardly had patience enough to listen to, without betraying contemptuous aversion. His manner upon such occasions was, in its degree, not unlike that which might be supposed to have been his imperial countryman's, Charles V.,[7] just previous to the anchoritish retirement of that monarch from the throne.

This splenetic disrelish of his place was evinced in almost every function pertaining to it. Proud as he was moody, he condescended to no personal mandate. Whatever special orders were necessary, their delivery was delegated to his body-servant, who in turn transferred them to their ultimate destination, through runners, alert Spanish boys or slave boys, like pages or pilot-fish within easy call continually hovering round Don Benito. So that to have beheld this undemonstrative invalid gliding about, apathetic and mute, no landsman could have dreamed that in him was lodged a dictatorship beyond which, while at sea, there was no earthly appeal.

Thus, the Spaniard, regarded in his reserve, seemed as the involuntary victim of mental disorder. But, in fact, his reserve might, in some degree, have proceeded from design. If so, then in Don Benito was evinced the unhealthy climax of that icy though conscientious policy, more or less adopted by all commanders of large ships, which, except in signal emergencies, obliterates alike the manifestation of sway with every trace of sociality; transforming the

---

[7] Holy Roman emperor and king of Spain as Charles I (1500-58), who retired to a monastery the year before his death.

man into a block, or rather into a loaded cannon, which, until there is call for thunder, has nothing to say.

Viewing him in this light, it seemed but a natural token of the perverse habit induced by a long course of such hard self-restraint, that, notwithstanding the present condition of his ship, the Spaniard should still persist in a demeanour, which, however harmless—or it may be, appropriate—in a well-appointed vessel, such as the *San Dominick* might have been at the outset of the voyage, was anything but judicious now. But the Spaniard perhaps thought that it was with captains as with gods: reserve, under all events, must still be their cue. But more probably this appearance of slumbering dominion might have been but an attempted disguise to conscious imbecility—not deep policy, but shallow device. But be all this as it might, whether Don Benito's manner was designed or not, the more Captain Delano noted its pervading reserve, the less he felt uneasiness at any particular manifestation of that reserve toward himself.

Neither were his thoughts taken up by the captain alone. Wonted to the quiet orderliness of the sealer's comfortable family of a crew, the noisy confusion of the *San Dominick's* suffering host repeatedly challenged his eye. Some prominent breaches not only of discipline but of decency were observed. These Captain Delano could not but ascribe, in the main, to the absence of those subordinate deck-officers to whom, along with higher duties, is entrusted what may be styled the police department of a populous ship. True, the old oakum-pickers appeared at times to act the part of monitorial constables to their countrymen, the blacks; but though occasionally succeeding in allaying trifling outbreaks now and then between man and man, they could do little or nothing toward establishing general quiet. The *San Dominick* was in the condition of a transatlantic emigrant ship, among whose multitude of living freight are some individuals, doubtless, as little troublesome as crates and

bales; but the friendly remonstrances of such with their ruder companions are of not so much avail as the unfriendly arm of the mate. What the *San Dominick* wanted was, what the emigrant ship has, stern superior officers. But on these decks not so much as a fourth mate was to be seen.

The visitor's curiosity was roused to learn the particulars of those mishaps which had brought about such absenteeism, with its consequences; because, though deriving some inkling of the voyage from the wails which at the first moment had greeted him, yet of the details no clear understanding had been had. The best account would, doubtless, be given by the captain. Yet at first the visitor was loth to ask it, unwilling to provoke some distant rebuff. But plucking up courage, he at last accosted Don Benito, renewing the expression of his benevolent interest, adding, that did he (Captain Delano) but know the particulars of the ship's misfortunes, he would, perhaps, be better able in the end to relieve them. Would Don Benito favour him with the whole story?

Don Benito faltered; then, like some somnambulist suddenly interfered with, vacantly stared at his visitor, and ended by looking down on the deck. He maintained this posture so long, that Captain Delano, almost equally disconcerted, and involuntarily almost as rude, turned suddenly from him, walking forward to accost one of the Spanish seamen for the desired information. But he had hardly gone five paces, when with a sort of eagerness Don Benito invited him back, regretting his momentary absence of mind, and professing readiness to gratify him.

While most part of the story was being given, the two captains stood on the after part of the main-deck, a privileged spot, no one being near but the servant.

"It is now a hundred and ninety days," began the Spaniard, in his husky whisper, "that this ship, well officered and well manned, with several cabin passengers—some fifty Spaniards in all—sailed from

Buenos Ayres bound to Lima, with a general cargo, Paraguay tea and the like—and," pointing forward, "that parcel of negroes, now not more than a hundred and fifty, as you see, but then numbering over three hundred souls. Off Cape Horn we had heavy gales. In one moment, by night, three of my best officers, with fifteen sailors, were lost, with the main-yard; the spar snapping under them in the slings, as they sought, with heavers, to beat down the icy sail. To lighten the hull, the heavier sacks of mata[8] were thrown into the sea, with most of the water-pipes lashed on deck at the time. And this last necessity it was, combined with the prolonged detentions afterwards experienced, which eventually brought about our chief causes of suffering. When—"

Here there was a sudden fainting attack of his cough, brought on, no doubt, by his mental distress. His servant sustained him, and drawing a cordial from his pocket placed it to his lips. He a little revived. But unwilling to leave him unsupported while yet imperfectly restored, the black with one arm still encircled his master, at the same time keeping his eye fixed on his face, as if to watch for the first sign of complete restoration, or relapse, as the event might prove.

The Spaniard proceeded, but brokenly and obscurely, as one in a dream.

—"Oh, my God! rather than pass through what I have, with joy I would have hailed the most terrible gales; but—"

His cough returned and with increased violence; this subsiding, with reddened lips and closed eyes he fell heavily against his supporter.

"His mind wanders. He was thinking of the plague that followed the gales," plaintively sighed the servant; "my poor, poor master!" wringing one hand, and with the other wiping the mouth. "But be patient, Señor," again turning to Captain Delano, "these fits do not last long; master will soon be himself."

Don Benito reviving, went on; but as this portion of the story was very brokenly delivered, the substance only will here be set down.

It appeared that after the ship had been many days tossed in storms off the Cape, the scurvy broke out, carrying off numbers of the whites and blacks. When at last they had worked round into the Pacific, their spars and sails were so damaged, and so inadequately handled by the surviving mariners, most of whom were become invalids, that, unable to lay her northerly course by the wind, which was powerful, the unmanageable ship for successive days and nights was blown northwestward, where the breeze suddenly deserted her, in unknown waters, to sultry calms. The absence of the water-pipes now proved as fatal to life as before their presence had menaced it. Induced, or at least aggravated, by the more than scanty allowance of water, a malignant fever followed the scurvy; with the excessive heat of the lengthened calm, making such short work of it as to sweep away, as by billows, whole families of the Africans, and a yet larger number, proportionably, of the Spaniards, including, by a luckless fatality, every officer on board. Consequently, in the smart west winds eventually following the calm, the already rent sails having to be simply dropped, not furled, at need, had been gradually reduced to the beggar's rags they were now. To procure substitutes for his lost sailors, as well as supplies of water and sails, the captain at the earliest opportunity had made for Baldivia, the southernmost civilized port of Chili and South America; but upon nearing the coast the thick weather had prevented him from so much as sighting that harbour. Since which period, almost without a crew, and almost without canvas and almost without water, and at intervals giving its added dead to the sea, the *San Dominick* had been battledored about by contrary winds, inveigled by currents, or grown weedy in calms. Like

[8] Mate or Paraguay tea; leaves of a South American plant used in preparing a beverage.

a man lost in woods, more than once she had doubled upon her own track.

"But throughout these calamities," huskily continued Don Benito, painfully turning in the half embrace of his servant, "I have to thank those negroes you see, who, though to your inexperienced eyes appearing unruly, have, indeed, conducted themselves with less of restlessness than even their owner could have thought possible under such circumstances."

Here he again fell faintly back. Again his mind wandered: but he rallied, and less obscurely proceeded.

"Yes, their owner was quite right in assuring me that no fetters would be needed with his blacks; so that while, as is wont in this transportation, those negroes have always remained upon deck—not thrust below, as in the Guineamen [9]—they have, also, from the beginning, been freely permitted to range within given bounds at their pleasure."

Once more the faintness returned—his mind roved—but, recovering, he resumed:

"But it is Babo here to whom, under God, I owe not only my own preservation, but likewise to him, chiefly, the merit is due, of pacifying his more ignorant brethren, when at intervals tempted to murmurings."

"Ah, master," sighed the black, bowing his face, "don't speak of me; Babo is nothing; what Babo has done was but duty."

"Faithful fellow!" cried Captain Delano. "Don Benito, I envy you such a friend; slave I cannot call him."

As master and man stood before him, the black upholding the white, Captain Delano could not but bethink him of the beauty of that relationship which could present such a spectacle of fidelity on the one hand and confidence on the other. The scene was heightened by the contrast in dress, denoting their relative positions. The Spaniard wore a loose Chili jacket of dark velvet; white small clothes and stockings, with silver buckles at the knee and instep; a high-crowned sombrero, of fine grass; a

slender sword, silver mounted, hung from a knot in his sash; the last being an almost invariable adjunct, more for utility than ornament, of a South American gentleman's dress to this hour. Excepting when his occasional nervous contortions brought about disarray, there was a certain precision in his attire, curiously at variance with the unsightly disorder around; especially in the belittered Ghetto, forward of the main-mast, wholly occupied by the blacks.

The servant wore nothing but wide trousers, apparently, from their coarseness and patches, made out of some old topsail; they were clean, and confined at the waist by a bit of unstranded rope, which, with his composed, deprecatory air at times, made him look something like a begging friar of St. Francis.

However unsuitable for the time and place, at least in the blunt-thinking American's eyes, and however strangely surviving in the midst of all his afflictions, the toilette of Don Benito might not, in fashion at least, have gone beyond the style of the day among South Americans of his class. Though on the present voyage sailing from Buenos Ayres, he had avowed himself a native and resident of Chili, whose inhabitants had not so generally adopted the plain coat and once plebeian pantaloons; but, with a becoming modification, adhered to their provincial costume, picturesque as any in the world. Still, relatively to the pale history of the voyage, and his own pale face, there seemed something so incongruous in the Spaniard's apparel, as almost to suggest the image of an invalid courtier tottering about London streets in the time of the plague.

The portion of the narrative which, perhaps, most excited interest, as well as some surprise, considering the latitudes in question, was the long calms spoken of, and more particularly the ship's so long drifting about. Without communicating the opinion,

---

[9] Vessels engaged in the African slave trade.

of course, the American could not but impute at least part of the detentions both to clumsy seamanship and faulty navigation. Eyeing Don Benito's small, yellow hands, he easily inferred that the young captain had not got into command at the hawsehole but the cabin-window, and if so, why wonder at incompetence, in youth, sickness, and aristocracy united? Such was his democratic conclusion.

But drowning criticism in compassion, after a fresh repetition of his sympathies, Captain Delano having heard out his story, not only engaged, as in the first place, to see Don Benito and his people supplied in their immediate bodily needs, but, also, now further promised to assist him in procuring a large permanent supply of water, as well as some sails and rigging; and, though it would involve no small embarrassment to himself, yet he would spare three of his best seamen for temporary deck officers; so that without delay the ship might proceed to Concepción, there fully to refit for Lima, her destined port.

Such generosity was not without its effect, even upon the invalid. His face lighted up; eager and hectic, he met the honest glance of his visitor. With gratitude he seemed overcome.

"This excitement is bad for master," whispered the servant, taking his arm, and with soothing words gently drawing him aside.

When Don Benito returned, the American was pained to observe that his hopefulness, like the sudden kindling in his cheek, was but febrile and transient.

Ere long, with a joyless mien, looking up toward the poop, the host invited his guest to accompany him there, for the benefit of what little breath of wind might be stirring.

As during the telling of the story, Captain Delano had once or twice started at the occasional cymballing of the hatchet-polishers, wondering why such an interruption should be allowed, especially in that part of the ship, and in the ears of

an invalid; and, moreover, as the hatchets had anything but an attractive look, and the handlers of them still less so, it was, therefore, to tell the truth, not without some lurking reluctance, or even shrinking, it may be, that Captain Delano, with apparent complaisance, acquiesced in his host's invitation. The more so, since with an untimely caprice of punctilio, rendered distressing by his cadaverous aspect, Don Benito, with Castilian bows, solemnly insisted upon his guest's preceding him up the ladder leading to the elevation; where, one on each side of the last step, sat four armorial supporters and sentries, two of the ominous file. Gingerly enough stepped good Captain Delano between them, and in the instant of leaving them behind, like one running the gauntlet, he felt an apprehensive twitch in the calves of his legs.

But when, facing about, he saw the whole file, like so many organ-grinders, still stupidly intent on their work, unmindful of everything beside, he could not but smile at his late fidgeting panic.

Presently, while standing with Don Benito, looking forward upon the decks below, he was struck by one of those instances of insubordination previously alluded to. Three black boys, with two Spanish boys, were sitting together on the hatchets, scraping a rude wooden platter, in which some scanty mess had recently been cooked. Suddenly, one of the black boys, enraged at a word dropped by one of his white companions, seized a knife, and though called to forbear by one of the oakum-pickers, struck the lad over the head, inflicting a gash from which blood flowed.

In amazement, Captain Delano inquired what this meant. To which the pale Benito dully muttered, that it was merely the sport of the lad.

"Pretty serious sport, truly," rejoined Captain Delano. "Had such a thing happened on board the *Bachelor's Delight*, instant punishment would have followed."

At these words the Spaniard turned upon the American one of his sudden, staring, half-lunatic looks; then, relapsing into his torpor, answered, "Doubtless, doubtless, Señor."

Is it, thought Captain Delano, that this helpless man is one of those paper captains I've known, who by policy wink at what by power they cannot put down? I know no sadder sight than a commander who has little of command but the name.

"I should think, Don Benito," he now said, glancing toward the oakum-picker who had sought to interfere with the boys, "that you would find it advantageous to keep all your blacks employed, especially the younger ones, no matter at what useless task, and no matter what happens to the ship. Why, even with my little band, I find such a course indispensable. I once kept a crew on my quarter-deck thrumming mats for my cabin, when, for three days, I had given up my ship—mats, men, and all—for a speedy loss, owing to the violence of a gale in which we could do nothing but helplessly drive before it."

"Doubtless, doubtless," muttered Don Benito.

"But," continued Captain Delano, again glancing upon the oakum-pickers and then at the hatchet-polishers, near by, "I see you keep some at least of your host employed."

"Yes," was again the vacant response.

"Those old men there, shaking their pows from their pulpits," continued Captain Delano, pointing to the oakum-pickers, "seem to act the part of old dominies to the rest, little heeded as their admonitions are at times. Is this voluntary on their part, Don Benito, or have you appointed them shepherds to your flock of black sheep?"

"What posts they fill, I appointed them," rejoined the Spaniard in an acrid tone, as if resenting some supposed satiric reflection.

"And these others, these Ashantee conjurors here," continued Captain Delano, rather uneasily eyeing the brandished steel of the hatchet-polishers, where in spots it

had been brought to a shine, "this seems a curious business they are at, Don Benito?"

"In the gales we met," answered the Spaniard, "what of our general cargo was not thrown overboard was much damaged by the brine. Since coming into calm weather, I have had several cases of knives and hatchets daily brought up for overhauling and cleaning."

"A prudent idea, Don Benito. You are part owner of ship and cargo, I presume; but not of the slaves, perhaps?"

"I am owner of all you see," impatiently returned Don Benito, "except the main company of blacks, who belonged to my late friend, Alexandro Aranda."

As he mentioned this name, his air was heart-broken, his knees shook; his servant supported him.

Thinking he divined the cause of such unusual emotion, to confirm his surmise, Captain Delano, after a pause, said, "And may I ask, Don Benito, whether—since awhile ago you spoke of some cabin passengers—the friend, whose loss so afflicts you, at the outset of the voyage accompanied his blacks?"

"Yes."

"But died of the fever?"

"Died of the fever.—Oh, could I but—"

Again quivering, the Spaniard paused.

"Pardon me," said Captain Delano slowly, "but I think that, by a sympathetic experience, I conjecture, Don Benito, what it is that gives the keener edge to your grief. It was once my hard fortune to lose at sea a dear friend, my own brother, then supercargo. Assured of the welfare of his spirit, its departure I could have borne like a man; but that honest eye, that honest hand—both of which had so often met mine—and that warm heart; all, all—like scraps to the dogs—to throw all to the sharks! It was then I vowed never to have for fellow-voyager a man I loved, unless, unbeknown to him, I had provided every requisite, in case of a fatality, for embalming his mortal part for interment on shore. Were your friend's remains now on board this ship, Don Benito, not thus strangely would the mention of his name affect you."

"On board this ship?" echoed the Spaniard. Then, with horrified gestures, as directed against some spectre, he unconsciously fell into the ready arms of his attendant, who, with a silent appeal toward Captain Delano, seemed beseeching him not again to broach a theme so unspeakably distressing to his master.

This poor fellow now, thought the pained American, is the victim of that sad superstition which associates goblins with the deserted body of man, as ghosts with an abandoned house. How unlike are we made! What to me, in like case, would have been a solemn satisfaction, the bare suggestion, even, terrifies the Spaniard into this trance. Poor Alexandro Aranda! what would you say could you here see your friend—who, on former voyages, when you for months were left behind, has, I dare say, often longed, and longed, for one peep at you—now transported with terror at the least thought of having you anyway nigh him.

At this moment, with a dreary graveyard toll, betokening a flaw, the ship's forecastle bell, smote by one of the grizzled oakum-pickers, proclaimed ten o'clock through the leaden calm; when Captain Delano's attention was caught by the moving figure of a gigantic black, emerging from the general crowd below, and slowly advancing toward the elevated poop. An iron collar was about his neck, from which depended a chain, thrice wound round his body; the terminating links padlocked together at a broad band of iron, his girdle.

"How like a mute Atufal moves," murmured the servant.

The black mounted the steps of the poop, and, like a brave prisoner, brought up to receive sentence, stood in unquailing muteness before Don Benito, now recovered from his attack.

At the first glimpse of his approach, Don Benito had started, a resentful shadow swept over his face; and, as with the sudden memory of bootless rage, his white lips glued together.

This is some mulish mutineer, thought Captain Delano, surveying, not without a mixture of admiration, the colossal form of the negro.

"See, he waits your question, master," said the servant.

Thus reminded, Don Benito, nervously averting his glance, as if shunning, by anticipation, some rebellious response, in a disconcerted voice, thus spoke:

"Atufal, will you ask my pardon now?"

The black was silent.

"Again, master," murmured the servant, with bitter upbraiding eyeing his countryman; "Again, master; he will bend to master yet."

"Answer," said Don Benito, still averting his glance, "say but the one word *pardon*, and your chains shall be off."

Upon this, the black, slowly raising both arms, let them lifelessly fall, his links clanking, his head bowed; as much as to say, "No, I am content."

"Go," said Don Benito, with inkept and unknown emotion.

Deliberately as he had come, the black obeyed.

"Excuse me, Don Benito," said Captain Delano, "but this scene surprises me; what means it, pray?"

"It means that that negro alone, of all the band, has given me peculiar cause of offence. I have put him in chains; I—"

Here he paused; his hand to his head, as if there were a swimming there, or a sudden bewilderment of memory had come over him; but meeting his servant's kindly glance seemed reassured, and proceeded:

"I could not scourge such a form. But I told him he must ask my pardon. As yet he has not. At my command, every two hours he stands before me."

"And how long has this been?"

"Some sixty days."

"And obedient in all else? And respectful?"

"Yes."

"Upon my conscience, then," exclaimed

Captain Delano, impulsively, "he has a royal spirit in him, this fellow."

"He may have some right to it," bitterly returned Don Benito; "he says he was king in his own land."

"Yes," said the servant, entering a word, "those slits in Atufal's ears once held wedges of gold; but poor Babo here, in his own land, was only a poor slave; a black man's slave was Babo, who now is the white's."

Somewhat annoyed by these conversational familiarities, Captain Delano turned curiously upon the attendant, then glanced inquiringly at his master; but, as if long wonted to these little informalities, neither master nor man seemed to understand him.

"What, pray, was Atufal's offence, Don Benito?" asked Captain Delano; "if it was not something very serious, take a fool's advice, and, in view of his general docility, as well as in some natural respect for his spirit, remit his penalty."

"No, no, master never will do that," here murmured the servant to himself, "proud Atufal must first ask master's pardon. The slave there carries the padlock, but master here carries the key."

His attention thus directed, Captain Delano now noticed for the first time that, suspended by a slender silken cord, from Don Benito's neck hung a key. At once, from the servant's muttered syllables divining the key's purpose, he smiled and said: "So, Don Benito—padlock and key—significant symbols, truly."

Biting his lip, Don Benito faltered.

Though the remark of Captain Delano, a man of such native simplicity as to be incapable of satire or irony, had been dropped in playful allusion to the Spaniard's singularly evidenced lordship over the black; yet the hypochondriac seemed in some way to have taken it as a malicious reflection upon his confessed inability thus far to break down, at least, on a verbal summons, the entrenched will of the slave. Deploring this supposed misconception, yet despairing of correcting it, Captain

Delano shifted the subject; but finding his companion more than ever withdrawn, as if still slowly digesting the lees of the presumed affront above-mentioned, by-and-by Captain Delano likewise became less talkative, oppressed, against his own will, by what seemed the secret vindictiveness of the morbidly sensitive Spaniard. But the good sailor himself, of a quite contrary disposition, refrained, on his part, alike from the appearance as from the feeling of resentment, and if silent, was only so from contagion.

Presently the Spaniard, assisted by his servant, somewhat discourteously crossed over from Captain Delano; a procedure which, sensibly enough, might have been allowed to pass for idle caprice of ill-humour, had not master and man, lingering round the corner of the elevated skylight, begun whispering together in low voices. This was unpleasing. And more: the moody air of the Spaniard, which at times had not been without a sort of valetudinarian stateliness, now seemed anything but dignified; while the menial familiarity of the servant lost its original charm of simple-hearted attachment.

In his embarrassment, the visitor turned his face to the other side of the ship. By so doing, his glance accidentally fell on a young Spanish sailor, a coil of rope in his hand, just stepped from the deck to the first round of the mizzen-rigging. Perhaps the man would not have been particularly noticed, were it not that, during his ascent to one of the yards, he, with a sort of covert intentness, kept his eye fixed on Captain Delano, from whom, presently, it passed, as if by a natural sequence, to the two whisperers.

His own attention thus redirected to that quarter, Captain Delano gave a slight start. From something in Don Benito's manner just then, it seemed as if the visitor had, at least partly, been the subject of the withdrawn consultation going on—a conjecture as little agreeable to the guest as it was little flattering to the host.

The singular alternations of courtesy and

ill-breeding in the Spanish captain were unaccountable, except on one of two suppositions—innocent lunacy, or wicked imposture.

But the first idea, though it might naturally have occurred to an indifferent observer, and, in some respects, had not hitherto been wholly a stranger to Captain Delano's mind, yet, now that, in an incipient way, he began to regard the stranger's conduct something in the light of an intentional affront, of course the idea of lunacy was virtually vacated. But if not a lunatic, what then? Under the circumstances, would a gentleman, nay, any honest boor, act the part now acted by his host? The man was an impostor. Some lowborn adventurer, masquerading as an oceanic grandee; yet so ignorant of the first requisites of mere gentlemanhood as to be betrayed into the present remarkable indecorum. That strange ceremoniousness, too, at other times evinced, seemed not uncharacteristic of one playing a part above his real level. Benito Cereno—Don Benito Cereno—a sounding name. One, too, at that period, not unknown, in the surname, to supercargoes and sea captains trading along the Spanish Main, as belonging to one of the most enterprising and extensive mercantile families in all those provinces; several members of it having titles; a sort of Castilian Rothschild,[10] with a noble brother, or cousin, in every great trading town of South America. The alleged Don Benito was in early manhood, about twenty-nine or thirty. To assume a sort of roving cadetship in the maritime affairs of such a house, what more likely scheme for a young knave of talent and spirit? But the Spaniard was a pale invalid. Never mind. For even to the degree of simulating mortal disease, the craft of some tricksters had been known to attain. To think that, under the aspect of infantile weakness, the most savage energies might be couched—those velvets of the Spaniard but the velvet paw to his fangs.

From no train of thought did these fancies come; not from within, but from without; suddenly, too, and in one throng, like hoar frost; yet as soon to vanish as the mild sun of Captain Delano's good-nature regained its meridian.

Glancing over once again toward Don Benito—whose side-face, revealed above the skylight, was now turned toward him— Captain Delano was struck by the profile, whose clearness of cut was refined by the thinness incident to ill-health, as well as ennobled about the chin by the beard. Away with suspicion. He was a true off-shoot of a true hidalgo Cereno.

Relieved by these and other better thoughts, the visitor, lightly humming a tune, now began indifferently pacing the poop, so as not to betray to Don Benito that he had at all mistrusted incivility, much less duplicity; for such mistrust would yet be proved illusory, and by the event; though, for the present, the circumstance which had provoked that distrust remained unexplained. But when that little mystery should have been cleared up, Captain Delano thought he might extremely regret it, did he allow Don Benito to become aware that he had indulged in ungenerous surmises. In short, to the Spaniard's black-letter text, it was best, for a while, to leave open margin.

Presently, his pale face twitching and overcast, the Spaniard, still supported by his attendant, moved over toward his guest, when, with even more than his usual embarrassment, and a strange sort of intriguing intonation in his husky whisper, the following conversation began:

"Señor, may I ask how long you have lain at this isle?"

"Oh, but a day or two, Don Benito."

"And from what port are you last?"

"Canton."

"And there, Señor, you exchanged your seal-skins for teas and silks, I think you said?"

---

[10] Family of Jewish financiers powerful throughout Europe; founded late in the 18th Century by Meyer A. Rothschild, who trained his five sons as bankers.

"Yes. Silks, mostly."

"And the balance you took in specie, perhaps?"

Captain Delano, fidgeting a little, answered—

"Yes; some silver; not a very great deal, though."

"Ah—well. May I ask how many men have you on board, Señor?"

Captain Delano slightly started, but answered:

"About five-and-twenty, all told."

"And at present, Señor, all on board, I suppose?"

"All on board, Don Benito," replied the captain now with satisfaction.

"And will be to-night, Señor?"

At this last question, following so many pertinacious ones, for the soul of him Captain Delano could not but look very earnestly at the questioner, who, instead of meeting the glance, with every token of craven discomposure dropped his eyes to the deck; presenting an unworthy contrast to his servant, who, just then, was kneeling at his feet adjusting a loose shoe-buckle; his disengaged face meantime, with humble curiosity, turned openly up into his master's downcast one.

The Spaniard, still with a guilty shuffle, repeated his question:

"And—and will be to-night, Señor?"

"Yes, for aught I know," returned Captain Delano,—"but nay," rallying himself into fearless truth, "some of them talked of going off on another fishing party about midnight."

"Your ships generally go—go more or less armed, I believe, Señor?"

"Oh, a six-pounder or two, in case of emergency," was the intrepidly indifferent reply, "with a small stock of muskets, sealing-spears, and cutlasses, you know."

As he thus responded, Captain Delano again glanced at Don Benito, but the latter's eyes were averted; while abruptly and awkwardly shifting the subject, he made some peevish allusion to the calm, and then, without apology, once more, with his attendant, withdrew to the opposite

bulwarks, where the whispering was resumed.

At this moment, and ere Captain Delano could cast a cool thought upon what had just passed, the young Spanish sailor before mentioned was seen descending from the rigging. In act of stooping over to spring inboard to the deck, his voluminous, unconfined frock, or shirt, of coarse woollen, much spotted with tar, opened out far down the chest, revealing a soiled under-garment of what seemed the finest linen, edged, about the neck, with a narrow blue ribbon, sadly faded and worn. At this moment the young sailor's eye was again fixed on the whisperers, and Captain Delano thought he observed a lurking significance in it, as if silent signs of some freemason sort had that instant been interchanged.

This once more impelled his own glance in the direction of Don Benito, and, as before, he could not but infer that himself formed the subject of the conference. He paused. The sound of the hatchet-polishing fell on his ears. He cast another swift side-look at the two. They had the air of conspirators. In connection with the late questionings, and the incident of the young sailor, these things now begat such return of involuntary suspicion, that the singular guilelessness of the American could not endure it. Plucking up a gay and humorous expression, he crossed over to the two rapidly, saying: "Ha, Don Benito, your black here seems high in your trust; a sort of privy-counsellor, in fact."

Upon this, the servant looked up with a good-natured grin, but the master started as from a venomous bite. It was a moment or two before the Spaniard sufficiently recovered himself to reply; which he did, at last, with cold constraint: "Yes, Señor, I have trust in Babo."

Here Babo, changing his previous grin of mere animal humour into an intelligent smile, not ungratefully eyed his master.

Finding that the Spaniard now stood silent and reserved, as if involuntarily, or purposely giving hint that his guest's proximity was inconvenient just then, Captain

Delano, unwilling to appear uncivil even to incivility itself, made some trivial remark and moved off; again and again turning over in his mind the mysterious demeanour of Don Benito Cereno.

He had descended from the poop, and, wrapped in thought, was passing near a dark hatchway, leading down into the steerage, when, perceiving motion there, he looked to see what moved. The same instant there was a sparkle in the shadowy hatchway, and he saw one of the Spanish sailors, prowling there, hurriedly placing his hand in the bosom of his frock, as if hiding something. Before the man could have been certain who it was that was passing, he slunk below out of sight. But enough was seen of him to make it sure that he was the same young sailor before noticed in the rigging.

What was that which so sparkled? thought Captain Delano. It was no lamp—no match—no live coal. Could it have been a jewel? But how come sailors with jewels?—or with silk-trimmed under-shirts either? Has he been robbing the trunks of the dead cabin passengers? But if so, he would hardly wear one of the stolen articles on board ship here. Ah,—if now that was, indeed, a secret sign I saw passing between this suspicious fellow and his captain awhile since; if I could only be certain that in my uneasiness my senses did not deceive me, then—

Here, passing from one suspicious thing to another, his mind revolved the point of the strange questions put to him concerning his ship.

By a curious coincidence, as each point was recalled, the black wizards of Ashantee would strike up with their hatchets, as in ominous comment on the white stranger's thoughts. Pressed by such enigmas and portents, it would have been almost against nature, had not, even into the least distrustful heart, some ugly misgivings obtruded.

Observing the ship now helplessly fallen into a current, with enchanted sails, drifting with increased rapidity seaward; and noting that, from a lately intercepted projection of the land, the sealer was hidden, the stout mariner began to quake at thoughts which he barely durst confess to himself. Above all, he began to feel a ghostly dread of Don Benito. And yet when he roused himself, dilated his chest, felt himself strong on his legs, and coolly considered it—what did all these phantoms amount to?

Had the Spaniard any sinister scheme, it must have reference not so much to him (Captain Delano) as to his ship (the *Bachelor's Delight*). Hence the present drifting away of the one ship from the other, instead of favouring any such possible scheme, was, for the time at least, opposed to it. Clearly any suspicion, combining such contradictions, must need be delusive. Beside, was it not absurd to think of a vessel in distress—a vessel by sickness almost dismanned of her crew—a vessel whose inmates were parched for water—was it not a thousand times absurd that such a craft should, at present, be of a piratical character; or her commander, either for himself or those under him, cherish any desire but for speedy relief and refreshment? But then, might not general distress, and thirst in particular, be affected? And might not that same undiminished Spanish crew, alleged to have perished off to a remnant, be at that very moment lurking in the hold? On heartbroken pretence of entreating a cup of cold water, fiends in human form had got into lonely dwellings, nor retired until a dark deed had been done. And among the Malay pirates, it was no unusual thing to lure ships after them into their treacherous harbours, or entice boarders from a declared enemy at sea, by the spectacle of thinly manned or vacant decks, beneath which prowled a hundred spears with yellow arms ready to upthrust them through the mats. Not that Captain Delano had entirely credited such things. He had heard of them—and now, as stories, they recurred. The present destination of the ship was the anchorage. There she would be near his own vessel. Upon gaining that vicinity, might not the *San Dominick*, like a slumbering volcano, suddenly let loose energies now hid?

He recalled the Spaniard's manner while telling his story. There was a gloomy hesitancy and subterfuge about it. It was just the manner of one making up his tale for evil purposes, as he goes. But if that story was not true, what was the truth? That the ship had unlawfully come into the Spaniard's possession? But in many of its details, especially in reference to the more calamitous parts, such as the fatalities among the seamen, the consequent prolonged beating about, the past sufferings from obstinate calms, and still continued suffering from thirst; in all these points, as well as others, Don Benito's story had corroborated not only the wailing ejaculations of the indiscriminate multitude, white and black, but likewise—what seemed impossible to be counterfeit—by the very expression and play of every human feature, which Captain Delano saw. If Don Benito's story was throughout an invention, then every soul on board, down to the youngest negress, was his carefully drilled recruit in the plot: an incredible inference. And yet, if there was ground for mistrusting the Spanish captain's veracity, that inference was a legitimate one.

In short, scarce an uneasiness entered the honest sailor's mind but, by a subsequent spontaneous act of good sense, it was ejected. At last he began to laugh at these forebodings; and laugh at the strange ship for, in its aspect someway siding with them, as it were; and laugh, too, at the odd-looking blacks, particularly those old scissors-grinders, the Ashantees; and those bed-ridden old knitting-women, the oakum-pickers; and, in a human way, he almost began to laugh at the dark Spaniard himself, the central hobgoblin of all.

For the rest, whatever in a serious way seemed enigmatical, was now good-naturedly explained away by the thought that, for the most part, the poor invalid scarcely knew what he was about; either sulking in black vapours, or putting random questions without sense or object. Evidently, for the present, the man was not fit to be entrusted with the ship. On some benevolent plea withdrawing the command from him, Captain Delano would yet have to send her to Concepción in charge of his second mate, a worthy person and good navigator—a plan which would prove no wiser for the *San Dominick* than for Don Benito; for —relieved from all anxiety, keeping wholly to his cabin—the sick man, under the good nursing of his servant, would probably, by the end of the passage, be in a measure restored to health and with that he should also be restored to authority.

Such were the American's thoughts. They were tranquillizing. There was a difference between the idea of Don Benito's darkly pre-ordaining Captain Delano's fate, and Captain Delano's lightly arranging Don Benito's. Nevertheless, it was not without something of relief that the good seaman presently perceived his whale-boat in the distance. Its absence had been prolonged by unexpected detention at the sealer's side, as well as its returning trip lengthened by the continual recession of the goal.

The advancing speck was observed by the blacks. Their shouts attracted the attention of Don Benito, who, with a return of courtesy, approaching Captain Delano, expressed satisfaction at the coming of some supplies, slight and temporary as they must necessarily prove.

Captain Delano responded; but while doing so, his attention was drawn to something passing on the deck below: among the crowd climbing the landward bulwarks, anxiously watching the coming boat, two blacks, to all appearances accidentally incommoded by one of the sailors, flew out against him with horrible curses, which the sailor someway resenting, the two blacks dashed him to the deck and jumped upon him, despite the earnest cries of the oakum-pickers.

"Don Benito," said Captain Delano quickly, "do you see what is going on there? Look!"

But, seized by his cough, the Spaniard staggered, with both hands to his face, on the point of falling. Captain Delano would have supported him, but the servant was more alert, who, with one hand sustaining his master, with the other applied the cordial. Don Benito restored, the black withdrew his support, slipping aside a little, but dutifully remaining within call of a whisper. Such discretion was here evinced as quite wiped away, in the visitor's eyes, any blemish of impropriety which might have attached to the attendant, from the indecorous conferences before mentioned; showing, too, that if the servant were to blame, it might be more the master's fault than his own, since when left to himself he could conduct thus well.

His glance thus called away from the spectacle of disorder to the more pleasing one before him, Captain Delano could not avoid again congratulating Don Benito upon possessing such a servant, who, though perhaps a little too forward now and then, must upon the whole be invaluable to one in the invalid's situation.

"Tell me, Don Benito," he added, with a smile—"I should like to have your man here myself—what will you take for him? Would fifty doubloons be any object?"

"Master wouldn't part with Babo for a thousand doubloons," murmured the black, overhearing the offer, and taking it in earnest, and, with the strange vanity of a faithful slave appreciated by his master, scorning to hear so paltry a valuation put upon him by a stranger. But Don Benito, apparently hardly yet completely restored, and again interrupted by his cough, made but some broken reply.

Soon his physical distress became so great, affecting his mind, too, apparently, that, as if to screen the sad spectacle, the servant gently conducted his master below.

Left to himself, the American, to while away the time till his boat should arrive, would have pleasantly accosted some one of the few Spanish seamen he saw; but recalling something that Don Benito had said touching their ill conduct, he refrained, as a ship-master indisposed to countenance cowardice or unfaithfulness in seamen.

While, with these thoughts, standing with eye directed forward toward that handful of sailors—suddenly he thought that some of them returned the glance and with a sort of meaning. He rubbed his eyes, and looked again; but again seemed to see the same thing. Under a new form, but more obscure than any previous one, the old suspicions recurred, but, in the absence of Don Benito, with less of panic than before. Despite the bad account given of the sailors, Captain Delano resolved forthwith to accost one of them. Descending the poop, he made his way through the blacks, his movement drawing a queer cry from the oakum-pickers, prompted by whom the negroes, twitching each other aside, divided before him; but, as if curious to see what was the object of this deliberate visit to their Ghetto, closing in behind, in tolerable order, followed the white stranger up. His progress thus proclaimed as by mounted kings-at-arms, and escorted as by a Caffre [11] guard of honour, Captain Delano, assuming a good-humoured, off-hand air, continued to advance; now and then saying a blithe word to the negroes, and his eye curiously surveying the white faces, here and there sparsely mixed in with the blacks, like stray white pawns venturously involved in the ranks of the chessmen opposed.

While thinking which of them to select for his purpose, he chanced to observe a sailor seated on the deck engaged in tarring the strap of a large block, with a circle of blacks squatted round him inquisitively eyeing the process.

The mean employment of the man was in contrast with something superior in his

---

[11] South African tribe of the Bantu family, notable for fine physiques and warlike qualities; commonly spelled Kaffir.

figure. His hand, black with continually thrusting it into the tar-pot held for him by a negro, seemed not naturally allied to his face, a face which would have been a very fine one but for its haggardness. Whether this haggardness had aught to do with criminality, could not be determined; since, as intense heat and cold, though unlike, produce like sensations, so innocence and guilt, when, through casual association with mental pain, stamping any visible impress, use one seal—a hacked one.

Not again that this reflection occurred to Captain Delano at the time, charitable man as he was. Rather another idea. Because observing so singular a haggardness to be combined with a dark eye, averted as in trouble and shame, and then, however illogically, uniting in his mind his own private suspicions of the crew with the confessed ill-opinion on the part of their captain, he was insensibly operated upon by certain general notions, which, while disconnecting pain and abashment from virtue, as invariably link them with vice.

If, indeed, there be any wickedness on board this ship, thought Captain Delano, be sure that man there has fouled his hand in it, even as now he fouls it in the pitch. I don't like to accost him. I will speak to this other, this old Jack here on the windlass.

He advanced to an old Barcelona tar, in ragged red breeches and dirty night-cap, cheeks trenched and bronzed, whiskers dense as thorn hedges. Seated between two sleepy-looking Africans, this mariner, like his younger shipmate, was employed upon some rigging—splicing a cable—the sleepy-looking blacks performing the inferior function of holding the outer parts of the ropes for him.

Upon Captain Delano's approach, the man at once hung his head below its previous level; the one necessary for business. It appeared as if he desired to be thought absorbed, with more than common fidelity, in his task. Being addressed, he glanced up, but with what seemed a furtive, diffident

air, which sat strangely enough on his weather-beaten visage, much as if a grizzly bear, instead of growling and biting, should simper and cast sheep's eyes. He was asked several questions concerning the voyage—questions purposely referring to several particulars in Don Benito's narrative—not previously corroborated by those impulsive cries greeting the visitor on first coming on board. The questions were briefly answered, confirming all that remained to be confirmed of the story. The negroes about the windlass joined in with the old sailor, but, as they became talkative, he by degrees became mute, and at length quite glum, seemed morosely unwilling to answer more questions, and yet, all the while, this ursine air was somehow mixed with his sheepish one.

Despairing of getting into unembarrassed talk with such a centaur, Captain Delano, after glancing round for a more promising countenance, but seeing none, spoke pleasantly to the blacks to make way for him; and so, amid various grins and grimaces, returned to the poop, feeling a little strange at first, he could hardly tell why, but upon the whole with regained confidence in Benito Cereno.

How plainly, thought he, did that old whiskerando [12] yonder betray a consciousness of ill-desert. No doubt, when he saw me coming, he dreaded lest I, apprised by his captain of the crew's general misbehaviour, came with sharp words for him, and so down with his head. And yet—and yet, now that I think of it, that very old fellow, if I err not, was one of those who seemed so earnestly eyeing me here awhile since. Ah, these currents spin one's head round almost as much as they do the ship. Ha, there now's a pleasant sort of sunny sight; quite sociable, too.

His attention had been drawn to a slumbering negress, partly disclosed through the lace-work of some rigging, lying, with youthful limbs carelessly disposed, under

---

[12] A heavily whiskered man—from the character Whiskerandos in Sheridan's play, *The Critic.*

the lee of the bulwarks, like a doe in the shade of a woodland rock. Sprawling at her lapped breasts was her wide-awake fawn, stark naked, its black little body half lifted from the deck, crosswise with its dam's; its hands, like two paws, clambering upon her; its mouth and nose ineffectually rooting to get at the mark; and meantime giving a vexatious half-grunt, blending with the composed snore of the negress.

The uncommon vigour of the child at length roused the mother. She started up, at distance facing Captain Delano. But, as if not at all concerned at the attitude in which she had been caught, delightedly she caught the child up, with maternal transports, covering it with kisses.

There's naked nature, now; pure tenderness and love, thought Captain Delano, well pleased.

This incident prompted him to remark the other negresses more particularly than before. He was gratified with their manners; like most uncivilized women, they seemed at once tender of heart and tough of constitution; equally ready to die for their infants or fight for them. Unsophisticated as leopardesses; loving as doves. Ah! thought Captain Delano, these perhaps are some of the very women whom Mungo Park [13] saw in Africa, and gave such a noble account of.

These natural sights somehow insensibly deepened his confidence and ease. At last he looked to see how his boat was getting on; but it was still pretty remote. He turned to see if Don Benito had returned; but he had not.

To change the scene, as well as to please himself with a leisurely observation of the coming boat, stepping over into the mizzen-chains he clambered his way into the starboard quarter-gallery; one of those abandoned Venetian-looking water-balconies previously mentioned; retreats cut off from the deck. As his foot pressed the half-damp, half-dry sea-mosses matting the place, and a chance phantom cats-paw—an islet of breeze, unheralded, unfollowed—as this ghostly cats-paw came fanning his cheek, as his glance fell upon the row of small, round dead-lights, all closed like coppered eyes of the coffined, and the state-cabin door, once connecting with the gallery, even as the dead-lights had once looked out upon it, but now caulked fast like a sarcophagus lid, to a purple-black, tarred-over panel, threshold, and post; and he bethought him of the time, when that state-cabin and this state-balcony had heard the voices of the Spanish king's officers, and the forms of the Lima viceroy's daughters had perhaps leaned where he stood—as these and other images flitted through his mind, as the cats-paw through the calm, gradually he felt rising a dreamy inquietude, like that of one who alone on the prairie feels unrest from the repose of the noon.

He leaned against the carved balustrade, again looking off toward his boat; but found his eye falling upon the ribboned grass, trailing along the ship's water-line, straight as a border of green box; and parterres of sea-weed, broad ovals and crescents, floating nigh and far, with what seemed long formal alleys between, crossing the terraces of swells, and sweeping round as if leading to the grottoes below. And overhanging all was the balustrade by his arm, which, partly stained with pitch and partly embossed with moss, seemed the charred ruin of some summer-house in a grand garden long running to waste.

Trying to break one charm, he was but becharmed anew. Though upon the wide sea, he seemed in some far inland country; prisoner in some deserted château, left to stare at empty grounds, and peer out at vague roads, where never wagon or wayfarer passed.

But these enchantments were a little disenchanted as his eye fell on the corroded main-chains. Of an ancient style, massy and rusty in link, shackle and bolt, they seemed even more fit for the ship's present business than the one for which probably she had been built.

---

[13] Scottish explorer of Africa (1771-1806).

Presently he thought something moved nigh the chains. He rubbed his eyes, and looked hard. Groves of rigging were about the chains; and there, peering from behind a great stay, like an Indian from behind a hemlock, a Spanish sailor, a marlingspike in his hand, was seen, who made what seemed an imperfect gesture toward the balcony—but immediately, as if alarmed by some advancing step along the deck within, vanished into the recesses of the hempen forest, like a poacher.

What meant this? Something the man had sought to communicate, unbeknown to any one, even to his captain. Did the secret involve aught unfavourable to his captain? Were those previous misgivings of Captain Delano's about to be verified? Or, in his haunted mood at the moment, had some random, unintentional motion of the man, while busy with the stay, as if repairing it, been mistaken for a significant beckoning?

Not unbewildered, again he gazed off for his boat. But it was temporarily hidden by a rocky spur of the isle. As with some eagerness he bent forward, watching for the first shooting view of its beak, the balustrade gave way before him like charcoal. Had he not clutched an outreaching rope he would have fallen into the sea. The crash, though feeble, and the fall, though hollow, of the rotten fragments, must have been overheard. He glanced up. With sober curiosity peering down upon him was one of the old oakum-pickers, slipped from his perch to an outside boom; while below the old negro—and, invisible to him, reconnoitring from a port-hole like a fox from the mouth of its den—crouched the Spanish sailor again. From something suddenly suggested by the man's air, the mad idea now darted into Captain Delano's mind; that Don Benito's plea of indisposition, in withdrawing below, was but a pretence: that he was engaged there maturing some plot, of which the sailor, by some means gaining an inkling, had a mind to warn the stranger against; incited, it may be, by gratitude for a kind word on first boarding the ship. Was it from foreseeing some possible interference like this, that Don Benito had, beforehand, given such a bad character of his sailors, while praising the negroes; though, indeed, the former seemed as docile as the latter the contrary? The whites, too, by nature, were the shrewder race. A man with some evil design, would not he be likely to speak well of that stupidity which was blind to his depravity, and malign that intelligence from which it might not be hidden? Not unlikely, perhaps. But if the whites had dark secrets concerning Don Benito, could then Don Benito be any way in complicity with the blacks? But they were too stupid. Besides, who ever heard of a white so far a renegade as to apostatize from his very species almost, by leaguing in against it with negroes? These difficulties recalled former ones. Lost in their mazes, Captain Delano, who had now regained the deck, was uneasily advancing along it, when he observed a new face: an aged sailor seated cross-legged near the main hatchway. His skin was shrunk up with wrinkles like a pelican's empty pouch; his hair frosted; his countenance grave and composed. His hands were full of ropes, which he was working into a large knot. Some blacks were about him obligingly dipping the strands for him, here and there, as the exigencies of the operation demanded.

Captain Delano crossed over to him, and stood in silence surveying the knot; his mind, by a not uncongenial transition, passing from its own entanglements to those of the hemp. For intricacy such a knot he had never seen in an American ship, or indeed any other. The old man looked like an Egyptian priest, making gordian knots for the temple of Ammon. The knot seemed a combination of double-bowline-knot, treble-crown-knot, back-handed-well-knot, knot-in-and-out-knot, and jamming-knot.

At last, puzzled to comprehend the meaning of such a knot, Captain Delano, addressed the knotter:—

"What are you knotting there, my man?"

"The knot," was the brief reply, without looking up.

"So it seems; but what is it for?"

"For some one else to undo," muttered back the old man, plying his fingers harder than ever, the knot being now nearly completed.

While Captain Delano stood watching him, suddenly the old man threw the knot toward him, and said in broken English, —the first heard in the ship,—something to this effect—"Undo it, cut it, quick." It was said lowly, but with such condensation of rapidity, that the long, slow words in Spanish, which had preceded and followed, almost operated as covers to the brief English between.

For a moment, knot in hand, and knot in head, Captain Delano stood mute; while, without further heeding him, the old man was now intent upon other ropes. Presently there was a slight stir behind Captain Delano. Turning, he saw the chained negro, Atufal, standing quietly there. The next moment the old sailor rose, muttering, and, followed by his subordinate negroes, removed to the forward part of the ship, where in the crowd he disappeared.

An elderly negro, in a clout like an infant's, and with a pepper and salt head, and a kind of attorney air, now approached Captain Delano. In tolerable Spanish, and with a good-natured, knowing wink, he informed him that the old knotter was simple-witted, but harmless; often playing his old tricks. The negro concluded by begging the knot, for of course the stranger would not care to be troubled with it. Unconsciously, it was handed to him. With a sort of congé, the negro received it, and turning his back ferreted into it like a detective Custom House officer after smuggled laces. Soon, with some African word, equivalent to pshaw, he tossed the knot overboard.

All this is very queer now, thought Captain Delano, with a qualmish sort of emotion; but as one feeling incipient seasickness, he strove, by ignoring the symptoms, to get rid of the malady. Once more he looked off for his boat. To his delight, it was now again in view, leaving the rocky spur astern.

The sensation here experienced, after at first relieving his uneasiness, with unforeseen efficiency, soon began to remove it. The less distant sight of that well-known boat—showing it, not as before, half blended with the haze, but with outline defined, so that its individuality, like a man's, was manifest; that boat, *Rover* by name, which, though now in strange seas, had often pressed the beach of Captain Delano's home, and, brought to its threshold for repairs, had familiarly lain there, as a Newfoundland dog; the sight of that household boat evoked a thousand trustful associations, which, contrasted with previous suspicions, filled him not only with lightsome confidence, but somehow with half humorous self-reproaches at his former lack of it.

"What, I, Amasa Delano—Jack of the Beach, as they called me when a lad—I, Amasa; the same that, duck-satchel in hand, used to paddle along the waterside to the schoolhouse made from the old hulk;—I, little Jack of the Beach, that used to go berrying with cousin Nat and the rest; I to be murdered here at the ends of the earth, on board a haunted pirate-ship by a horrible Spaniard?—Too nonsensical to think of! Who would murder Amasa Delano? His conscience is clean. There is some one above. Fie, fie, Jack of the Beach! you are a child indeed; a child of the second childhood, old boy; you are beginning to dote and drule, I'm afraid."

Light of heart and foot, he stepped aft, and there was met by Don Benito's servant, who, with a pleasing expression, responsive to his own present feelings, informed him that his master had recovered from the effects of his coughing fit, and had just ordered him to go present his compliments to his good guest, Don Amasa, and say that he (Don Benito) would soon have the happiness to rejoin him.

There now, do you mark that? again thought Captain Delano, walking the poop.

What a donkey I was. This kind gentle-man who here sends me his kind compli-ments, he, but ten minutes ago, dark-lantern in hand, was dodging round some old grind-stone in the hold, sharpening a hatchet for me, I thought. Well, well; these long calms have a morbid effect on the mind, I've often heard, though I never believed it before. Ha! glancing toward the boat; there's *Rover*; a good dog; a white bone in her mouth. A pretty big bone though, seems to me.—What? Yes, she has fallen afoul of the bubbling tide-rip there. It sets her the other way, too, for the time. Patience.

It was now about noon, though, from the greyness of everything, it seemed to be getting toward dusk.

The calm was confirmed. In the far distance, away from the influence of land, the leaden ocean seemed laid out and leaded up, its course finished, soul gone, defunct. But the current from landward, where the ship was, increased; silently sweeping her further and further toward the tranced waters beyond.

Still, from his knowledge of those lati-tudes, cherishing hopes of a breeze, and a fair and fresh one, at any moment, Cap-tain Delano, despite present prospects, buoyantly counted upon bringing the *San Dominick* safely to anchor ere night. The distance swept over was nothing; since, with a good wind, ten minutes' sailing would retrace more than sixty minutes' drifting. Meantime, one moment turning to mark *Rover* fighting the tide-rip, and the next to see Don Benito approaching, he continued walking the poop.

Gradually he felt a vexation arising from the delay of his boat; this soon merged into uneasiness; and at last, his eye falling continually, as from a stage-box into the pit, upon the strange crowd before and below him, and by-and-by rec-ognizing there the face—now composed to indifference—of the Spanish sailor who had seemed to beckon from the main chains, something of his old trepidations returned.

Ah, thought he—gravely enough—this is like the ague: because it went off, it follows not that it won't come back.

Though ashamed of the relapse, he could not altogether subdue it; and so, exerting his good nature to the utmost, insensibly he came to a compromise.

Yes, this is a strange craft; a strange history, too, and strange folks on board. But—nothing more.

By way of keeping his mind out of mischief till the boat should arrive, he tried to occupy it with turning over and over, in a purely speculative sort of way, some lesser peculiarities of the captain and crew. Among others, four curious points recurred.

First, the affair of the Spanish lad assailed with a knife by the slave boy; an act winked at by Don Benito. Second, the tyranny in Don Benito's treatment of Atufal, the black; as if a child should lead a bull of the Nile by the ring in his nose. Third, the trampling of the sailor by the two negroes; a piece of insolence passed over without so much as a reprimand. Fourth, the cringing submission to their master of all the ship's underlings, mostly blacks; as if by the least inadvertance they feared to draw down his despotic dis-pleasure.

Coupling these points, they seemed some-what contradictory. But what then, thought Captain Delano, glancing toward his now nearing boat,—what then? Why, this Don Benito is a very capricious commander. But he is not the first of the sort I have seen; though it's true he rather exceeds any other. But as a nation—continued he in his reveries—these Spaniards are all an odd set; the very word Spaniard has a curious, conspirator, Guy-Fawkish [14] twang to it. And yet, I dare say, Spaniards in the main are as good folks as any in Dux-bury, Massachusetts. Ah, good! At last "Rover" has come.

As, with its welcome freight, the boat

---

[14] Guy Fawkes (1570-1606) conspired to blow up the Houses of Parliament (1605).

touched the side, the oakum-pickers, with venerable gestures, sought to restrain the blacks, who, at the sight of three gurried [15] water-casks in its bottom, and a pile of wilted pumpkins in its bow, hung over the bulwarks in disorderly raptures.

Don Benito with his servant now appeared; his coming, perhaps, hastened by hearing the noise. Of him Captain Delano sought permission to serve out the water, so that all might share alike, and none injure themselves by unfair excess. But sensible, and, on Don Benito's account, kind as this offer was, it was received with what seemed impatience; as if aware that he lacked energy as a commander, Don Benito, with the true jealousy of weakness, resented as an affront any interference. So, at least, Captain Delano inferred.

In another moment the casks were being hoisted in, when some of the eager negroes accidentally jostled Captain Delano, where he stood by the gangway; so that, unmindful of Don Benito, yielding to the impulse of the moment, with good-natured authority he bade the blacks stand back; to enforce his words making use of a half-mirthful, half-menacing gesture. Instantly the blacks paused, just where they were, each negro and negress suspended in his or her posture, exactly as the word had found them —for a few seconds continuing so—while, as between the responsive posts of a telegraph, an unknown syllable ran from man to man among the perched oakum-pickers. While Captain Delano's attention was fixed by this scene, suddenly the hatchet-polishers half rose, and a rapid cry came from Don Benito.

Thinking that at the signal of the Spaniard he was about to be massacred, Captain Delano would have sprung for his boat, but paused, as the oakum-pickers, dropping down into the crowd with earnest exclamations, forced every white and every negro back, at the same moment, with gestures friendly and familiar, almost jocose, bidding him, in substance, not be a fool. Simultaneously the hatchet-polishers

resumed their seats, quietly as so many tailors, and at once, as if nothing had happened, the work of hoisting in the casks was resumed, whites and blacks singing at the tackle.

Captain Delano glanced toward Don Benito. As he saw his meagre form in the act of recovering itself from reclining in the servant's arms, into which the agitated invalid had fallen, he could not but marvel at the panic by which himself had been surprised on the darting supposition that such a commander, who upon a legitimate occasion, so trivial, too, as it now appeared, could lose all self-command, was, with energetic iniquity, going to bring about his murder.

The casks being on deck, Captain Delano was handed a number of jars and cups by one of the steward's aides, who, in the name of Don Benito, entreated him to do as he had proposed: dole out the water. He complied, with republican impartiality as to this republican element, which always seeks one level, serving the oldest white no better than the youngest black; excepting, indeed, poor Don Benito, whose condition, if not rank, demanded an extra allowance. To him, in the first place, Captain Delano presented a fair pitcher of the fluid; but, thirsting as he was for fresh water, Don Benito quaffed not a drop until after several grave bows and salutes: a reciprocation of courtesies which the sight-loving Africans hailed with clapping of hands.

Two of the less wilted pumpkins being reserved for the cabin table, the residue were minced up on the spot for the general regalement. But the soft bread, sugar, and bottled cider, Captain Delano would have given the Spaniards alone, and in chief Don Benito; but the latter objected; which disinterestedness, on his part, not a little pleased the American; and so mouthfuls all around were given alike to whites and blacks; excepting one bottle of cider, which

---

[15] Soiled with the offal of fish or other animals.

Babo insisted upon setting aside for his master.

Here it may be observed that as, on the first visit of the boat, the American had not permitted his men to board the ship, neither did he now; being unwilling to add to the confusion of the decks.

Not uninfluenced by the peculiar good humour at present prevailing, and for the time oblivious of any but benevolent thoughts, Captain Delano, who from recent indications counted upon a breeze within an hour or two at furthest, despatched the boat back to the sealer with orders for all the hands that could be spared immediately to set about rafting casks to the watering-place and filling them. Likewise he bade word be carried to his chief officer, that if against present expectation the ship was not brought to anchor by sunset, he need be under no concern, for as there was to be a full moon that night, he (Captain Delano) would remain on board ready to play the pilot, should the wind come soon or late.

As the two captains stood together, observing the departing boat—the servant as it happened having just spied a spot on his master's velvet sleeve, and silently engaged rubbing it out—the American expressed his regrets that the *San Dominick* had no boats; none, at least, but the unseaworthy old hulk of the long-boat, which, warped as a camel's skeleton in the desert, and almost as bleached, lay pot-wise inverted amidships, one side a little tipped, furnishing a subterraneous sort of den for family groups of the blacks, mostly women and small children; who, squatting on old mats below, or perched above in the dark dome, on the elevated seats, were descried, some distance within, like a social circle of bats, sheltering in some friendly cave; at intervals, ebon flights of naked boys and girls, three or four years old, darting in and out of the den's mouth.

"Had you three or four boats now, Don Benito," said Captain Delano, "I think that, by tugging at the oars, your negroes here might help along matters some.—Did you sail from port without boats, Don Benito?"

"They were stove in the gales, Señor."

"That was bad. Many men, too, you lost then. Boats and men.—Those must have been hard gales, Don Benito."

"Past all speech," cringed the Spaniard.

"Tell me, Don Benito," continued his companion with increased interest, "tell me, were these gales immediately off the pitch of Cape Horn?"

"Cape Horn?—who spoke of Cape Horn?"

"Yourself did, when giving me an account of your voyage," answered Captain Delano with almost equal astonishment at this eating of his own words, even as he ever seemed eating his own heart, on the part of the Spaniard. "You yourself, Don Benito, spoke of Cape Horn," he emphatically repeated.

The Spaniard turned, in a sort of stooping posture, pausing an instant, as one about to make a plunging exchange of elements, as from air to water.

At this moment a messenger-boy, a white, hurried by, in the regular performance of his function carrying the last expired half-hour forward to the forecastle, from the cabin time-piece, to have it struck at the ship's large bell.

"Master," said the servant, discontinuing his work on the coat sleeve, and addressing the rapt Spaniard with a sort of timid apprehensiveness, as one charged with a duty, the discharge of which, it was foreseen, would prove irksome to the very person who had imposed it, and for whose benefit it was intended, "master told me never mind where he was, or how engaged, always to remind him, to a minute, when shaving-time comes. Miguel has gone to strike the half-hour afternoon. It is *now*, master. Will master go into the cuddy?"

"Ah—yes," answered the Spaniard, starting, somewhat as from dreams into realities; then turning upon Captain Delano, he said that ere long he would resume the conversation.

"Then if master means to talk more to

Don Amasa," said the servant, "why not let Don Amasa sit by master in the cuddy, and master can talk, and Don Amasa can listen, while Babo here lathers and strops."

"Yes," said Captain Delano, not unpleased with this sociable plan, "yes, Don Benito, unless you had rather not, I will go with you."

"Be it so, Señor."

As the three passed aft, the American could not but think it another strange instance of his host's capriciousness, this being shaved with such uncommon punctuality in the middle of the day. But he deemed it more than likely that the servant's anxious fidelity had something to do with the matter; inasmuch as the timely interruption served to rally his master from the mood which had evidently been coming upon him.

The place called the cuddy was a light deck-cabin formed by the poop, a sort of attic to the large cabin below. Part of it had formerly been the quarters of the officers; but since their death all the partitionings had been thrown down, and the whole interior converted into one spacious and airy marine hall; for absence of fine furniture and picturesque disarray, of odd appurtenances, somewhat answering to the wide, cluttered hall of some eccentric bachelor-squire in the country, who hangs his shooting-jacket and tobacco-pouch on deer antlers, and keeps his fishing-rod, tongs, and walking-stick in the same corner.

The similitude was heightened, if not originally suggested, by glimpses of the surrounding sea; since, in one aspect, the country and the ocean seem cousins-german.

The floor of the cuddy was matted. Overhead, four or five old muskets were stuck into horizontal holes along the beams. On one side was a claw-footed old table lashed to the deck; a thumbed missal on it, and over it a small, meagre crucifix attached to the bulkhead. Under the table lay a dented cutlass or two, with a hacked harpoon, among some melancholy old rigging, like a heap of poor friar's girdles.

There were also two long, sharp-ribbed settees of malacca cane, black with age, and uncomfortable to look at as inquisitors' racks, with a large, misshapen arm-chair, which, furnished with a rude barber's crutch at the back, working with a screw, seemed some grotesque Middle Age engine of torment. A flag locker was in one corner, exposing various coloured bunting, some rolled up, others half unrolled, still others tumbled. Opposite was a cumbrous washstand, of black mahogany, all of one block, with a pedestal, like a font, and over it a railed shelf, containing combs, brushes, and other implements of the toilet. A torn hammock of stained grass swung near; the sheets tossed, and the pillow wrinkled up like a brow, as if whoever slept here slept but illy, with alternate visitations of sad thoughts and bad dreams.

The further extremity of the cuddy, overhanging the ship's stern, was pierced with three openings, windows or port holes, according as men or cannon might peer, socially or unsocially, out of them. At present neither men nor cannon were seen, though huge ring-bolts and other rusty iron fixtures of the wood-work hinted of twenty-four-pounders.

Glancing toward the hammock as he entered, Captain Delano said, "You sleep here, Don Benito?"

"Yes, Señor, since we got into mild weather."

"This seems a sort of dormitory, sitting-room, sail-loft, chapel, armoury, and private closet together, Don Benito," added Captain Delano, looking round.

"Yes, Señor; events have not been favourable to much order in my arrangements."

Here the servant, napkin on arm, made a motion as if waiting his master's good pleasure. Don Benito signified his readiness, when, seating him in the malacca arm-chair, and for the guest's convenience drawing opposite it one of the settees, the servant commenced operations by throwing back his master's collar and loosening his cravat.

There is something in the negro which, in a peculiar way, fits him for avocations about one's person. Most negroes are natural valets and hair-dressers; taking to the comb and brush congenially as to the castanets, and flourishing them apparently with almost equal satisfaction. There is, too, a smooth tact about them in this employment, with a marvellous, noiseless, gliding briskness, not ungraceful in its way, singularly pleasing to behold, and still more so to be the manipulated subject of. And above all is the great gift of good humour. Not the mere grin or laugh is here meant. Those were unsuitable. But a certain easy cheerfulness, harmonious in every glance and gesture; as though God had set the whole negro to some pleasant tune.

When to all this is added the docility arising from the unaspiring contentment of a limited mind, and that susceptibility of blind attachment sometimes inhering in indisputable inferiors, one readily perceives why those hypochondriacs, Johnson and Byron—it may be something like the hypochondriac, Benito Cereno—took to their hearts, almost to the exclusion of the entire white race, their serving men, the negroes, Barber and Fletcher. But if there be that in the negro which exempts him from the inflicted sourness of the morbid or cynical mind, how, in his most prepossessing aspects, must he appear to a benevolent one? When at ease with respect to exterior things, Captain Delano's nature was not only benign, but familiarly and humorously so. At home, he had often taken rare satisfaction in sitting in his door, watching some free man of colour at his work or play. If on a voyage he chanced to have a black sailor, invariably he was on chatty, and half-gamesome terms with him. In fact, like most men of a good, blithe heart, Captain Delano took to negroes, not philanthropically, but genially, just as other men to Newfoundland dogs.

Hitherto the circumstances in which he found the *San Dominick* had repressed the tendency. But in the cuddy, relieved from his former uneasiness, and, for various reasons, more sociably inclined than at any previous period of the day, and seeing the coloured servant, napkin on arm, so debonair about his master, in a business so familiar as that of shaving, too, all his old weakness for negroes returned.

Among other things, he was amused with an odd instance of the African love of bright colours and fine shows, in the black's informally taking from the flag-locker a great piece of bunting of all hues, and lavishly tucking it under his master's chin for an apron.

The mode of shaving among the Spaniards is a little different from what it is with other nations. They have a basin, specially called a barber's basin, which on one side is scooped out, so as accurately to receive the chin, against which it is closely held in lathering; which is done, not with a brush, but with soap dipped in the water of the basin and rubbed on the face.

In the present instance salt-water was used for lack of better; and the parts lathered were only the upper lip, and low down under the throat, all the rest being cultivated beard.

These preliminaries being somewhat novel to Captain Delano he sat curiously eyeing them, so that no conversation took place, nor for the present did Don Benito appear disposed to renew any.

Setting down his basin, the negro searched among the razors, as for the sharpest, and having found it, gave it an additional edge by expertly stropping it on the firm, smooth, oily skin of his open palm; he then made a gesture as if to begin, but midway stood suspended for an instant, one hand elevating the razor, the other professionally dabbling among the bubbling suds on the Spaniard's lank neck. Not unaffected by the close sight of the gleaming steel, Don Benito nervously shuddered; his usual ghastliness was heightened by the lather, which lather, again, was intensified in its hue by the contrasting sootiness of the negro's body. Altogether the scene was somewhat peculiar, at least to Captain Delano, nor, as he saw the two thus postured, could he resist the vagary, that in the black he saw a headsman, and in the white, a man at the block. But this was one of those antic conceits, appearing and vanishing in a breath, from which, perhaps, the best regulated mind is not free.

Meantime the agitation of the Spaniard had a little loosened the bunting from around him, so that one broad fold swept curtain-like over the chair-arm to the floor, revealing, amid a profusion of armorial bars and ground-colours—black, blue and yellow—a closed castle in a blood-red field diagonal with a lion rampant in a white.

"The castle and the lion," exclaimed Captain Delano—"why, Don Benito, this is the flag of Spain you use here. It's well it's only I, and not the King, that sees this," he added with a smile, "but"—turning toward the black,—"it's all one, I suppose, so the colours be gay," which playful remark did not fail somewhat to tickle the negro.

"Now, master," he said, readjusting the flag, and pressing the head gently further back into the crotch of the chair; "now master," and the steel glanced nigh the throat.

Again Don Benito faintly shuddered.

"You must not shake so, master.—See, Don Amasa, master always shakes when I shave him. And yet master knows I never yet have drawn blood, though it's true, if master will shake so, I may some of these times. Now, master," he continued. "And now, Don Amasa, please go on with your talk about the gale, and all that, master can hear, and between times master can answer."

"Ah yes, these gales," said Captain Delano; "but the more I think of your voyage, Don Benito, the more I wonder, not at the gales, terrible as they must have been, but at the disastrous interval following them. For here, by your account, have you been these two months and more getting from Cape Horn to St. Maria, a distance which I myself, with a good wind, have sailed in a few days. True, you had calms, and long

ones, but to be becalmed for two months, that is, at least, unusual. Why, Don Benito, had almost any other gentleman told me such a story, I should have been half disposed to a little incredulity."

Here an involuntary expression came over the Spaniard, similar to that just before on the deck, and whether it was the start he gave, or a sudden gawky roll of the hull in the calm, or a momentary unsteadiness of the servant's hand; however it was, just then the razor drew blood, spots of which stained the creamy lather under the throat; immediately the black barber drew back his steel, and remaining in his professional attitude, back to Captain Delano, and face to Don Benito, held up the trickling razor, saying, with a sort of half humorous sorrow, "See, master,— you shook so—here's Babo's first blood."

No sword drawn before James the First of England, no assassination in that timid King's presence, could have produced a more terrified aspect than was now presented by Don Benito.

Poor fellow, thought Captain Delano, so nervous he can't even bear the sight of barber's blood; and this unstrung, sick man, is it credible that I should have imagined he meant to spill all my blood, who can't endure the sight of one little drop of his own? Surely, Amasa Delano, you have been beside yourself this day. Tell it not when you get home, sappy Amasa. Well, well, he looks like a murderer, doesn't he? More like as if himself were to be done for. Well, well, this day's experience shall be a good lesson.

Meantime, while these things were running through the honest seaman's mind, the servant had taken the napkin from his arm, and to Don Benito had said: "But answer Don Amasa, please, master, while I wipe this ugly stuff off the razor, and strop it again."

As he said the words, his face was turned half round, so as to be alike visible to the Spaniard and the American, and seemed by its expression to hint, that he was desirous, by getting his master to go on with the conversation, considerably to with-draw his attention from the recent annoy-ing accident. As if glad to snatch the of-fered relief, Don Benito resumed, rehears-ing to Captain Delano, that not only were the calms of unusual duration, but the ship had fallen in with obstinate currents; and other things he added, some of which were but repetitions of former statements, to explain how it came to pass that the passage from Cape Horn to St. Maria had been so exceedingly long, now and then mingling with his words, incidental praises, less qualified than before, to the blacks, for their general good conduct.

These particulars were not given con-secutively, the servant now and then using his razor, and so, between the intervals of shaving, the story and panegyric went on with more than usual huskiness.

To Captain Delano's imagination, now again not wholly at rest, there was some-thing so hollow in the Spaniard's manner, with apparently some reciprocal hollowness in the servant's dusky comment of silence, that the idea flashed across him, that pos-sibly master and man, for some unknown purpose, were acting out, both in word and deed, nay, to the very tremor of Don Benito's limbs, some juggling play before him. Neither did the suspicion of collusion lack apparent support, from the fact of those whispered conferences before men-tioned. But then, what could be the object of enacting this play of the barber before him? At last, regarding the notion as a whimsy, insensibly suggested, perhaps, by the theatrical aspect of Don Benito in his harlequin ensign, Captain Delano speedily banished it.

The shaving over, the servant bestirred himself with a small bottle of scented waters, pouring a few drops on the head, and then diligently rubbing; the vehemence of the exercise causing the muscles of his face to twitch rather strangely.

His next operation was with comb, scis-sors and brush; going round and round, smoothing a curl here, clipping an unruly whisker-hair there, giving a graceful sweep to the temple-lock, with other impromptu touches evincing the hand of a master; while, like any resigned gentleman in barber's hands, Don Benito bore all, much less uneasily, at least, than he had done the razoring; indeed, he sat so pale and rigid now, that the negro seemed a Nubian sculptor finishing off a white statue-head.

All being over at last, the standard of Spain removed, tumbled up, and tossed back into the flag-locker, the negro's warm breath blowing away any stray hair which might have lodged down his master's neck; collar and cravat readjusted; a speck of lint whisked off the velvet lapel; all this being done; backing off a little space, and pausing with an expression of subdued self-complacency, the servant for a mo-ment surveyed his master, as, in toilet at least, the creature of his own tasteful hands.

Captain Delano playfully complimented him upon his achievement; at the same time congratulating Don Benito.

But neither sweet waters, nor shampoo-ing, nor fidelity, nor sociality, delighted the Spaniard. Seeing him relapsing into forbidding gloom, and still remaining seated, Captain Delano, thinking that his presence was undesired just then, with-drew, on pretence of seeing whether, as he had prophesied, any signs of a breeze were visible.

Walking forward to the mainmast, he stood awhile thinking over the scene, and not without some undefined misgivings, when he heard a noise near the cuddy, and turning, saw the negro, his hand to his cheek. Advancing, Captain Delano per-ceived that the cheek was bleeding. He was about to ask the cause, when the negro's wailing soliloquy enlightened him.

"Ah, when will master get better from his sickness; only the sour heart that sour sickness breeds made him serve Babo so; cutting Babo with the razor, because, only by accident, Babo had given master one little scratch; and for the first time in so many a day, too. Ah, ah, ah," holding his hand to his face.

Is it possible, thought Captain Delano; was it to wreak in private his Spanish spite against this poor friend of his, that Don Benito, by his sullen manner, impelled me to withdraw? Ah, this slavery breeds ugly passions in man! Poor fellow!

He was about to speak in sympathy to the negro, but with a timid reluctance he now re-entered the cuddy.

Presently master and man came forth; Don Benito leaning on his servant as if nothing had happened.

But a sort of love-quarrel, after all, thought Captain Delano.

He accosted Don Benito, and they slowly walked together. They had gone but a few paces, when the steward—a tall, rajah-looking mulatto, orientally set off with a pagoda turban formed by three or four Madras handkerchiefs wound about his head, tier on tier—approaching with a salaam, announced lunch in the cabin.

On their way thither, the two captains were preceded by the mulatto, who, turning round as he advanced, with continual smiles and bows, ushered them in, a display of elegance which quite completed the insignificance of the small bare-headed Babo, who, as if not unconscious of inferiority, eyed askance the graceful steward. But in part, Captain Delano imputed his jealous watchfulness to that peculiar feeling which the full-blooded African entertains for the adulterated one. As for the steward, his manner, if not bespeaking much dignity of self-respect, yet evidenced his extreme desire to please; which is doubly meritorious, as at once Christian and Chesterfieldian.[16]

Captain Delano observed with interest that while the complexion of the mulatto was hybrid, his physiognomy was European; classically so.

"Don Benito," whispered he, "I am glad to see this usher-of-the-golden-rod of yours; the sight refutes an ugly remark once made to me by a Barbados planter that when a mulatto has a regular European face, look out for him; he is a devil. But see, your steward here has features more

regular than King George's of England; and yet there he nods, and bows, and smiles; a king, indeed—the king of kind hearts and polite fellows. What a pleasant voice he has, too?"

"He has, Señor."

"But, tell me, has he not, so far as you have known him, always proved a good, worthy fellow?" said Captain Delano, pausing, while with a final genuflexion the steward disappeared into the cabin; "come, for the reason just mentioned, I am curious to know."

"Francesco is a good man," rather sluggishly responded Don Benito, like a phlegmatic appreciator, who would neither find fault nor flatter.

"Ah, I thought so. For it were strange indeed, and not very creditable to us white-skins, if a little of our blood mixed with the African's, should, far from improving the latter's quality, have the sad effect of pouring vitriolic acid into black broth; improving the hue, perhaps, but not the wholesomeness."

"Doubtless, doubtless, Señor, but"—glancing at Babo—"not to speak of negroes, your planter's remark I have heard applied to the Spanish and Indian intermixtures in our provinces. But I know nothing about the matter," he listlessly added.

And here they entered the cabin.

The lunch was a frugal one. Some of Captain Delano's fresh fish and pumpkins, biscuit and salt beef, the reserved bottle of cider, and the *San Dominick's* last bottle of Canary.

As they entered, Francesco, with two or three coloured aids, was hovering over the table giving the last adjustments. Upon perceiving their master they withdrew, Francesco making a smiling congé, and the Spaniard, without condescending to notice it, fastidiously remarking to his compan-

---

[16] The reference is to Philip Stanhope, 4th Earl of Chesterfield (1694-1773), British statesman and writer, famed for his *Letters to his Son* on matters of politic conduct and worldly wisdom.

ion that he relished not superfluous attendance.

Without companions, host and guest sat down, like a childless married couple, at opposite ends of the table, Don Benito waving Captain Delano to his place, and, weak as he was, insisting upon that gentleman being seated before himself.

The negro placed a rug under Don Benito's feet, and a cushion behind his back, and then stood behind, not his master's chair, but Captain Delano's. At first, this a little surprised the latter. But it was soon evident that, in taking his position, the black was still true to his master; since by facing him he could the more readily anticipate his slightest want.

"This is an uncommonly intelligent fellow of yours, Don Benito," whispered Captain Delano across the table.

"You say true, Señor."

During the repast, the guest again reverted to parts of Don Benito's story, begging further particulars here and there. He inquired how it was that the scurvy and fever should have committed such wholesale havoc upon the whites, while destroying less than half of the blacks. As if this question reproduced the whole scene of plague before the Spaniard's eyes, miserably reminding him of his solitude in a cabin where before he had had so many friends and officers round him, his hand shook, his face became hueless, broken words escaped; but directly the same memory of the past seemed replaced by insane terrors of the present. With starting eyes he stared before him at vacancy. For nothing was to be seen but the hand of his servant pushing the Canary over towards him. At length a few sips served partially to restore him. He made random reference to the different constitutions of races, enabling one to offer more resistance to certain maladies than another. The thought was new to his companion.

Presently Captain Delano, intending to say something to his host concerning the pecuniary part of the business he had undertaken for him, especially—since he was strictly accountable to his owners—with reference to the new suit of sails, and other things of that sort; and naturally preferring to conduct such affairs in private, was desirous that the servant should withdraw; imagining that Don Benito for a few minutes could dispense with his attendance. He, however, waited awhile; thinking that, as the conversation proceeded, Don Benito, without being prompted, would perceive the propriety of the step.

But it was otherwise. At last catching his host's eye, Captain Delano, with a slight backward gesture of his thumb, whispered, "Don Benito, pardon me, but there is an interference with the full expression of what I have to say to you."

Upon this the Spaniard changed countenance; which was imputed to his resenting the hint, as in some way a reflection upon his servant. After a moment's pause, he assured his guest that the black's remaining with them could be of no disservice; because since losing his officers he had made Babo (whose original office, it now appeared, had been captain of the slaves) not only his constant attendant and companion, but in all things his confidant.

After this, nothing more could be said; though, indeed, Captain Delano could hardly avoid some little tinge of irritation upon being left ungratified in so inconsiderable a wish, by one, too, for whom he intended such solid services. But it is only his querulousness, thought he; and so filling his glass he proceeded to business.

The price of the sails and other matters was fixed upon. But while this was being done, the American observed that, though his original offer of assistance had been hailed with hectic animation, yet now when it was reduced to a business transaction, indifference and apathy were betrayed. Don Benito, in fact, appeared to submit to hearing the details more out of regard to common propriety, than from any impression that weighty benefit to himself and his voyage was involved.

Soon, this manner became still more reserved. The effort was vain to seek to draw him into social talk. Gnawed by his splenetic mood, he sat twitching his beard, while to little purpose the hand of his servant, mute as that on the wall, slowly pushed over the Canary.

Lunch being over, they sat down on the cushioned transom; the servant placing a pillow behind his master. The long continuance of the calm had now affected the atmosphere. Don Benito sighed heavily, as if for breath.

"Why not adjourn to the cuddy," said Captain Delano; "there is more air there." But the host sat silent and motionless.

Meantime his servant knelt before him, with a large fan of feathers. And Francesco, coming in on tiptoes, handed the negro a little cup of aromatic waters, with which at intervals he chafed his master's brow, smoothing the hair along the temples as a nurse does a child's. He spoke no word. He only rested his eye on his master's, as if, amid all Don Benito's distress, a little to refresh his spirit by the silent sight of fidelity.

Presently the ship's bell sounded two o'clock; and through the cabin-windows a slight rippling of the sea was discerned; and from the desired direction.

"There," exclaimed Captain Delano, "I told you so, Don Benito, look!"

He had risen to his feet, speaking in a very animated tone, with a view the more to rouse his companion. But though the crimson curtain of the stern-window near him that moment fluttered against his pale cheek, Don Benito seemed to have even less welcome for the breeze than the calm.

Poor fellow, thought Captain Delano, bitter experience has taught him that one ripple does not make a wind, any more than one swallow a summer. But he is mistaken for once. I will get his ship in for him, and prove it.

Briefly alluding to his weak condition, he urged his host to remain quietly where he was, since he (Captain Delano) would with pleasure take upon himself the responsibility of making the best use of the wind.

Upon gaining the deck, Captain Delano started at the unexpected figure of Atufal, monumentally fixed at the threshold, like one of those sculptured porters of black marble guarding the porches of Egyptian tombs.

But this time the start was, perhaps, purely physical. Atufal's presence, singularly attesting docility even in sullenness, was contrasted with that of the hatchet-polishers, who in patience evinced their industry; while both spectacles showed, that lax as Don Benito's general authority might be, still, whenever he chose to exert it, no man so savage or colossal but must, more or less, bow.

Snatching a trumpet which hung from the bulwarks, with a free step Captain Delano advanced to the forward edge of the poop, issuing his orders in his best Spanish. The few sailors and many negroes, all equally pleased, obediently set about heading the ship toward the harbour.

While giving some directions about setting a lower stu'n'-sail, suddenly Captain Delano heard a voice faithfully repeating his orders. Turning, he saw Babo, now for the time acting, under the pilot, his original part of captain of the slaves. This assistance proved valuable. Tattered sails and warped yards were soon brought into some trim. And no brace or halyard was pulled but to the blithe songs of the inspirited negroes.

Good fellows, thought Captain Delano, a little training would make fine sailors of them. Why see, the very women pull and sing, too. These must be some of those Ashantee negresses that make such capital soldiers, I've heard. But who's at the helm? I must have a good hand there.

He went to see.

The *San Dominick* steered with a cumbrous tiller, with large horizontal pullies attached. At each pulley-end stood a subordinate black, and between them, at the tiller-head, the responsible post, a Spanish seaman, whose countenance evinced his due share in the general hopefulness and confidence at the coming of the breeze.

He proved the same man who had behaved with so shamefaced an air on the windlass.

"Ah,—it is you, my man," exclaimed Captain Delano—"well, no more sheep's-eyes now;—look straightforward and keep the ship so. Good hand, I trust? And want to get into the harbour, don't you?"

"Sí Señor," assented the man with an inward chuckle, grasping the tiller-head firmly. Upon this, unperceived by the American, the two blacks eyed the sailor askance.

Finding all right at the helm, the pilot went forward to the forecastle, to see how matters stood there.

The ship now had way enough to breast the current. With the approach of evening, the breeze would be sure to freshen.

Having done all that was needed for the present, Captain Delano, giving his last orders to the sailors, turned aft to report affairs to Don Benito in the cabin; perhaps additionally incited to rejoin him by the hope of snatching a moment's private chat while his servant was engaged upon deck.

From opposite sides, there were, beneath the poop, two approaches to the cabin; one further forward than the other, and consequently communicating with a longer passage. Marking the servant still above, Captain Delano, taking the nighest entrance—the one last named, and at whose porch Atufal still stood—hurried on his way, till, arrived at the cabin threshold, he paused an instant, a little to recover from his eagerness. Then, with the words of his intended business upon his lips, he entered. As he advanced toward the Spaniard, on the transom, he heard another footstep, keeping time with his. From the opposite door, a salver in hand, the servant was likewise advancing.

"Confound the faithful fellow," thought Captain Delano; "what a vexatious coincidence."

Possibly, the vexation might have been something different, were it not for the buoyant confidence inspired by the breeze. But even as it was, he felt a slight twinge, from a sudden involuntary association in his mind of Babo with Atufal.

"Don Benito," said he, "I give you joy; the breeze will hold, and will increase. By the way, your tall man and time-piece, Atufal, stands without. By your order, of course?"

Don Benito recoiled, as if at some bland satirical touch, delivered with such adroit garnish of apparent good-breeding as to present no handle for retort.

He is like one flayed alive, thought Captain Delano; where may one touch him without causing a shrink?

The servant moved before his master, adjusting a cushion; recalled to civility, the Spaniard stiffly replied: "You are right. The slave appears where you saw him, according to my command; which is, that if at the given hour I am below, he must take his stand and abide my coming."

"Ah now, pardon me, but that is treating the poor fellow like an ex-king denied. Ah, Don Benito," smiling, "for all the license you permit in some things, I fear lest, at bottom, you are a bitter hard master."

Again Don Benito shrank; and this time, as the good sailor thought, from a genuine twinge of his conscience.

Conversation now became constrained. In vain Captain Delano called attention to the now perceptible motion of the keel gently cleaving the sea; with lack-lustre eye, Don Benito returned words few and reserved.

By-and-by, the wind having steadily risen, and still blowing right into the harbour, bore the *San Dominick* swiftly on. Rounding a point of land, the sealer at distance came into open view.

Meantime Captain Delano had again repaired to the deck, remaining there some time. Having at last altered the ship's course, so as to give the reef a wide berth, he returned for a few moments below.

I will cheer up my poor friend, this time, thought he.

"Better and better, Don Benito," he cried as he blithely re-entered; "there will soon be an end to your cares, at least for awhile. For when, after a long, sad voyage, you know, the anchor drops into the haven, all its vast weight seems lifted from the captain's heart. We are getting on famously, Don Benito. My ship is in sight. Look through this side-light here; there she is; all a-taunt-o! The *Bachelor's Delight,* my good friend. Ah, how this wind braces one up. Come, you must take a cup of coffee with me this evening. My old steward will give you as fine a cup as ever any sultan tasted. What say you, Don Benito, will you?"

At first, the Spaniard glanced feverishly up, casting a longing look toward the sealer, while with mute concern his servant gazed into his face. Suddenly the old ague of coldness returned, and dropping back to his cushions he was silent.

"You do not answer. Come, all day you have been my host; would you have hospitality all on one side?"

"I cannot go," was the response.

"What? it will not fatigue you. The ships will lie together as near as they can, without swinging foul. It will be little more than stepping from deck to deck; which is but as from room to room. Come, come, you must not refuse me."

"I cannot go," decisively and repulsively repeated Don Benito.

Renouncing all but the last appearance of courtesy, with a sort of cadaverous sullenness, and biting his thin nails to the quick, he glanced, almost glared, at his guest; as if impatient that a stranger's presence should interfere with the full indulgence of his morbid hour. Meantime the sound of the parted waters came more and more gurglingly and merrily in at the windows; as reproaching him for his dark

spleen; as telling him that, sulk as he might, and go mad with it, nature cared not a jot; since, whose fault was it, pray?

But the foul mood was now at its depth as the fair wind at its height.

There was something in the man so far beyond any mere unsociality or sourness previously evinced, that even the forbearing good-nature of his guest could no longer endure it. Wholly at a loss to account for such demeanour, and deeming sickness with eccentricity, however extreme, no adequate excuse, well satisfied, too, that nothing in his own conduct could justify it, Captain Delano's pride began to be roused. Himself became reserved. But all seemed one to the Spaniard. Quitting him, therefore, Captain Delano once more went to the deck.

The ship was now within less than two miles of the sealer. The whale-boat was seen darting over the interval.

To be brief, the two vessels, thanks to the pilot's skill, ere long in neighbourly style lay anchored together.

Before returning to his own vessel, Captain Delano had intended communicating to Don Benito the practical details of the proposed services to be rendered. But, as it was, unwilling anew to subject himself to rebuffs, he resolved, now that he had seen the *San Dominick* safely moored, immediately to quit her, without further allusion to hospitality or business. Indefinitely postponing his ulterior plans, he would regulate his future actions according to future circumstances. His boat was ready to receive him; but his host still tarried below. Well, thought Captain Delano, if he has little breeding, the more need to show mine. He descended to the cabin to bid a ceremonious, and, it may be, tacitly rebukeful adieu. But to his great satisfaction, Don Benito, as if he began to feel the weight of that treatment with which his slighted guest had, not indecorously, retaliated upon him, now supported by his servant, rose to his feet, and grasping Captain Delano's hand, stood tremulous;

too much agitated to speak. But the good augury hence drawn was suddenly dashed, by his resuming all his previous reserve, with augmented gloom, as, with half-averted eyes, he silently reseated himself on his cushions. With a corresponding return of his own chilled feelings, Captain Delano bowed and withdrew.

He was hardly midway in the narrow corridor, dim as a tunnel, leading from the cabin to the stairs, when a sound, as of the tolling for execution in some jail-yard, fell on his ears. It was the echo of the ships' flawed bell, striking the hour, drearily reverberated in this subterranean vault. Instantly, by a fatality not to be withstood, his mind, responsive to the portent, swarmed with superstitious suspicions. He paused. In images far swifter than these sentences, the minutest details of all his former distrusts swept through him.

Hitherto, credulous good-nature had been too ready to furnish excuses for reasonable fears. Why was the Spaniard, so superfluously punctilious at times, now heedless of common propriety in not accompanying to the side his departing guest? Did indisposition forbid? Indisposition had not forbidden more irksome exertion that day. His last equivocal demeanour recurred. He had risen to his feet, grasped his guest's hand, motioned toward his hat; then, in an instant, all was eclipsed in sinister muteness and gloom. Did this imply one brief, repentant relenting at the final moment, from some iniquitous plot, followed by remorseless return to it? His last glance seemed to express a calamitous, yet acquiescent farewell to Captain Delano for ever. Why decline the invitation to visit the sealer that evening? Or was the Spaniard less hardened than the Jew, who refrained not from supping at the board of him whom the same night he meant to betray? What imported all those day-long enigmas and contradictions, except they were intended to mystify, preliminary to some stealthy blow? Atufal, the pretended rebel, but punctual shadow, that moment lurked by the threshold without. He seemed a

sentry, and more. Who, by his own confession, had stationed him there? Was the negro now lying in wait?

The Spaniard behind—his creature before: to rush from darkness to light was the involuntary choice.

The next moment, with clenched jaw and hand, he passed Atufal, and stood unharmed in the light. As he saw his trim ship lying peacefully at her anchor, and almost within ordinary call; as he saw his household boat, with familiar faces in it, patiently rising and falling on the short waves by the *San Dominick's* side; and then, glancing about the decks where he stood, saw the oakum-pickers still gravely plying their fingers; and heard the low, buzzing whistle and industrious hum of the hatchet-polishers, still bestirring themselves over their endless occupation; and more than all, as he saw the benign aspect of Nature, taking her innocent repose in the evening; the screened sun in the quiet camp of the west shining out like the mild light from Abraham's tent; as his charmed eye and ear took in all these, with the chained figure of the black, the clenched jaw and hand relaxed. Once again he smiled at the phantoms which had mocked him, and felt something like a tinge of remorse, that, by indulging them even for a moment, he should, by implication, have betrayed an almost atheist doubt of the ever-watchful Providence above.

There was a few minutes' delay, while, in obedience to his orders, the boat was being hooked along to the gangway. During this interval, a sort of saddened satisfaction stole over Captain Delano, at thinking of the kindly offices he had that day discharged for a stranger. Ah, thought he, after good actions one's conscience is never ungrateful, however much so the benefited party may be.

Presently, his foot, in the first act of descent into the boat, pressed the first round of the side-ladder, his face presented inward upon the deck. In the same moment, he heard his name courteously sounded; and, to his pleased surprise, saw Don

Benito advancing—an unwonted energy in his air, as if, at the last moment, intent upon making amends for his recent discourtesy. With instinctive good feeling, Captain Delano, revoking his foot, turned and reciprocally advanced. As he did so, the Spaniard's nervous eagerness increased, but his vital energy failed; so that, the better to support him, the servant, placing his master's hand on his naked shoulder, and gently holding it there, formed himself into a sort of crutch.

When the two captains met, the Spaniard again fervently took the hand of the American, at the same time casting an earnest glance into his eyes, but, as before, too much overcome to speak.

I have done him wrong, self-reproachfully thought Captain Delano; his apparent coldness has deceived me; in no instance has he meant to offend.

Meantime, as if fearful that the continuance of the scene might too much unstring his master, the servant seemed anxious to terminate it. And so, still presenting himself as a crutch, and walking between the two captains, he advanced with them toward the gangway; while still, as if full of kindly contrition, Don Benito would not let go the hand of Captain Delano, but retained it in his, across the black's body.

Soon they were standing by the side, looking over into the boat, whose crew turned up their curious eyes. Waiting a moment for the Spaniard to relinquish his hold, the now embarrassed Captain Delano lifted his foot, to overstep the threshold of the open gangway; but still Don Benito would not let go his hand. And yet, with an agitated tone, he said, "I can go no further; here I must bid you adieu. Adieu, my dear, dear Don Amasa. Go—go!" suddenly tearing his hand loose, "go, and God guard you better than me, my best friend."

Not unaffected, Captain Delano would now have lingered; but catching the meekly admonitory eye of the servant, with a hasty farewell he descended into his boat, followed by the continual adieus of Don Benito, standing rooted in the gangway.

Seating himself in the stern, Captain Delano, making a last salute, ordered the boat shoved off. The crew had their oars on end. The bowsman pushed the boat a sufficient distance for the oars to be lengthwise dropped. The instant that was done, Don Benito sprang over the bulwarks, falling at the feet of Captain Delano; at the same time, calling towards his ship, but in tones so frenzied, that none in the boat could understand him. But, as if not equally obtuse, three Spanish sailors, from three different and distant parts of the ship, splashed into the sea, swimming after their captain, as if intent upon his rescue.

The dismayed officer of the boat eagerly asked what this meant. To which, Captain Delano, turning a disdainful smile upon the unaccountable Benito Cereno, answered that, for his part, he neither knew nor cared; but it seemed as if the Spaniard had taken it into his head to produce the impression among his people that the boat wanted to kidnap him. "Or else—give way for your lives," he wildly added, starting at a clattering hubbub in the ship, above which rang the tocsin of the hatchet-polishers; and seizing Don Benito by the throat he added, "this plotting pirate means murder!" Here, in apparent verification of the words, the servant, a dagger in his hand, was seen on the rail overhead, poised, in the act of leaping, as if with desperate fidelity to befriend his master to the last; while, seemingly to aid the black, the three Spanish sailors were trying to clamber into the hampered bow. Meantime, the whole host of negroes, as if inflamed at the sight of their jeopardized captain, impended in one sooty avalanche over the bulwarks.

All this, with what preceded, and what followed, occurred with such involutions of rapidity, that past, present, and future seemed one.

Seeing the negro coming, Captain Delano

had flung the Spaniard aside, almost in the very act of clutching him, and, by the unconscious recoil, shifting his place, with arms thrown up, so promptly grappled the servant in his descent, that with dagger presented at Captain Delano's heart, the black seemed of purpose to have leaped there as to his mark. But the weapon was wrenched away, and the assailant dashed down into the bottom of the boat, which now, with disentangled oars, began to speed through the sea.

At this juncture, the left hand of Captain Delano, on one side, again clutched the half-reclined Don Benito, heedless that he was in a speechless faint, while his right foot, on the other side, ground the prostrate negro; and his right arm pressed for added speed on the after oar, his eye bent forward, encouraging his men to their utmost.

But here, the officer of the boat, who had at last succeeded in beating off the towing Spanish sailors, and was now, with face turned aft, assisting the bowsman at his oar, suddenly called to Captain Delano, to see what the black was about; while a Portuguese oarsman shouted to him to give heed to what the Spaniard was saying.

Glancing down at his feet, Captain Delano saw the freed hand of the servant aiming with a second dagger—a small one, before concealed in his wool—with this he was snakishly writhing up from the boat's bottom, at the heart of his master, his countenance lividly vindictive, expressing the centred purpose of his soul; while the Spaniard, half-choked, was vainly shrinking away, with husky words, incoherent to all but the Portuguese.

That moment, across the long benighted mind of Captain Delano, a flash of revelation swept, illuminating in unanticipated clearness Benito Cereno's whole mysterious demeanour, with every enigmatic event of the day, as well as the entire past voyage of the San Dominick. He smote Babo's hand down. but his own heart smote him harder. With infinite pity he withdrew his hold from Don Benito. Not Captain Delano, but Don Benito, the black, in leaping into the boat, had intended to stab.

Both the black's hands were held, as, glancing up toward the San Dominick, Captain Delano, now with the scales dropped from his eyes, saw the negroes, not in misrule, not in tumult, not as if frantically concerned for Don Benito, but with mask torn away, flourishing hatchets and knives, in ferocious piratical revolt. Like delirious black dervishes, the six Ashantees danced on the poop. Prevented by their foes from springing into the water, the Spanish boys were hurrying up to the topmost spars, while such of the few Spanish sailors, not already in the sea, less alert, were descried, helplessly mixed in, on deck, with the blacks.

Meantime Captain Delano hailed his own vessel, ordering the ports up, and the guns run out. But by this time the cable of the San Dominick had been cut; and the fag-end, in lashing out, whipped away the canvas shroud about the beak, suddenly revealing, as the bleached hull swung round toward the open ocean, death for the figurehead, in a human skeleton; chalky comment on the chalked words below, "Follow your leader."

At the sight, Don Benito, covering his face, wailed out: "'Tis he, Aranda! my murdered, unburied friend!"

Upon reaching the sealer, calling for ropes, Captain Delano bound the negro, who made no resistance, and had him hoisted to the deck. He would then have assisted the now almost helpless Don Benito up the side; but Don Benito, wan as he was, refused to move, or be moved, until the negro should have been first put below out of view. When, presently assured that it was done, he no more shrank from the ascent.

The boat was immediately despatched back to pick up the three swimming sailors. Meantime, the guns were in readiness, though, owing to the San Dominick having glided somewhat astern of the sealer, only the aftermost one could be brought to bear. With this, they fired six times; thinking to cripple the fugitive ship by bringing down her spars. But only a few inconsiderable ropes were shot away. Soon the ship was beyond the guns' range, steering broad out of the bay; the blacks thickly clustering round the bowsprit, one moment with taunting cries toward the whites, the next with upthrown gestures hailing the now dusky expanse of ocean —cawing crows escaped from the hand of the fowler.

The first impulse was to slip the cables and give chase. But, upon second thought, to pursue with whale-boat and yawl seemed more promising.

Upon inquiring of Don Benito what firearms they had on board the *San Dominick*, Captain Delano was answered that they had none that could be used; because, in the earlier stages of the mutiny, a cabin-passenger, since dead, had secretly put out of order the locks of what few muskets there were. But with all his remaining strength, Don Benito entreated the American not to give chase, either with ship or boat; for the negroes had already proved themselves such desperadoes, that, in case of a present assault, nothing but a total massacre of the whites could be looked for. But, regarding this warning as coming from one whose spirit had been crushed by misery, the American did not give up his design.

The boats were got ready and armed. Captain Delano ordered twenty-five men into them. He was going himself when Don Benito grasped his arm.

"What! have you saved my life, Señor, and are you now going to throw away your own?"

The officers also, for reasons connected with their interests and those of the voyage, and a duty owing to the owners, strongly objected against their commander's going. Weighing their remonstrances a moment, Captain Delano felt bound to remain; appointing his chief mate—an athletic and resolute man, who had been a privateer's man, and, as his enemies whispered, a pirate—to head the party. The more to encourage the sailors, they were told that the Spanish captain considered his ship as good as lost; that she and her cargo, including some gold and silver, were worth upwards of ten thousand doubloons. Take her, and no small part should be theirs. The sailors replied with a shout.

The fugitives had now almost gained an offing. It was nearly night; but the moon was rising. After hard, prolonged pulling, the boats came up on the ship's quarters, at a suitable distance laying upon their oars to discharge their muskets. Having no bullets to return, the negroes sent their yells. But, upon the second volley, Indian-like, they hurtled their hatchets. One took off a sailor's fingers. Another struck the whale-boat's bow, cutting off the rope there, and remaining stuck in the gunwale, like a woodman's axe. Snatching it, quivering from its lodgment, the mate hurled it back. The returned gauntlet now stuck in the ship's broken quarter-gallery, and so remained.

The negroes giving too hot a reception, the whites kept a more respectful distance. Hovering now just out of reach of the hurtling hatchets, they, with a view to the close encounter which must soon come, sought to decoy the blacks into entirely disarming themselves of their most murderous weapons in a hand-to-hand fight, by foolishly flinging them, as missiles, short of the mark, into the sea. But ere long perceiving the stratagem, the negroes desisted, though not before many of them had to replace their lost hatchets with handspikes; an exchange which, as counted upon, proved in the end favourable to the assailants.

Meantime, with a strong wind, the ship still clove the water; the boats alternately falling behind, and pulling up, to discharge fresh volleys.

The fire was mostly directed toward the stern, since there, chiefly, the negroes, at present, were clustering. But to kill or maim the negroes was not the object. To take them, with the ship, was the object. To do it, the ship must be boarded; which could not be done by boats while she was sailing so fast.

A thought now struck the mate. Observing the Spanish boys still aloft, high as they could get, he called to them to descend to the yards, and cut adrift the sails. It was done. About this time, owing to causes hereafter to be shown, two Spaniards, in the dress of sailors and conspicuously showing themselves, were killed; not by volleys, but by deliberate marksman's shots; while, as it afterwards appeared, during one of the general discharges, Atufal, the black, and the Spaniard at the helm likewise were killed. What now, with the loss of the sails, and loss of leaders, the ship became unmanageable to the negroes.

With creaking masts she came heavily round to the wind; the prow slowly swinging into view of the boats, its skeleton gleaming in the horizontal moonlight, and casting a gigantic ribbed shadow upon the water. One extended arm of the ghost seemed beckoning the whites to avenge it.

"Follow your leader!" cried the mate; and, one on each bow, the boats boarded. Scaling-spears and cutlasses crossed hatchets and handspikes. Huddled upon the long-boat amidships, the negresses raised a wailing chant, whose chorus was the clash of the steel.

For a time, the attack wavered; the negroes wedging themselves to beat it back; the half-repelled sailors, as yet unable to gain a footing, fighting as troopers in the saddle, one leg sideways flung over the bulwarks, and one without, plying their cutlasses like carters' whips. But in vain. They were almost overborne, when, rallying themselves into a squad as one man, with a huzza, they sprang inboard; where, entangled, they involuntarily separated again. For a few breaths' space there was a vague, muffled, inner sound as of submerged sword-fish rushing hither and thither through shoals of black-fish. Soon, in a reunited band, and joined by the Spanish seamen, the whites came to the surface, irresistibly driving the negroes toward the stern. But a barricade of casks and sacks, from side to side, had been thrown up by the mainmast. Here the negroes faced about, and though scorning peace or truce, yet fain would have had a respite. But, without pause, overleaping the barrier, the unflagging sailors again closed. Exhausted, the blacks now fought in despair. Their red tongues lolled, wolf-like, from their black mouths. But the pale sailors' teeth were set; not a word was spoken; and, in five minutes more, the ship was won.

Nearly a score of the negroes were killed. Exclusive of those by the balls, many were mangled; their wounds— mostly inflicted by the long-edged scaling-spears—resembling those shaven ones of the English at Preston Pans,[17] made by the poled scythes of the Highlanders. On the other side, none were killed, though several were wounded; some severely, including the mate. The surviving negroes were temporarily secured, and the ship, towed back into the harbour at midnight, once more lay anchored.

Omitting the incidents and arrangements ensuing, suffice it that, after two days spent in refitting, the two ships sailed in company for Concepcion in Chili, and thence for Lima in Peru; where, before the vice-regal courts, the whole affair, from the beginning, underwent investigation.

Though, midway on the passage, the ill-fated Spaniard, relaxed from constraint, showed some signs of regaining health with free-will; yet, agreeably to his own foreboding, shortly before arriving at Lima, he relapsed, finally becoming so reduced as to be carried ashore in arms. Hearing of his story and plight, one of

---

[17] Town near Edinburgh, scene of defeat of British army on Sept. 21, 1745, by Highland Jacobites under Prince Charles Edward.

the many religious institutions of the City of Kings [18] opened an hospitable refuge to him, where both physician and priest were his nurses, and a member of the order volunteered to be his one special guardian and consoler, by night and by day.

The following extracts, translated from one of the official Spanish documents, will, it is hoped, shed light on the preceding narrative, as well as, in the first place, reveal the true port of departure and true history of the *San Dominick's* voyage, down to the time of her touching at the island of Santa Maria.

But, ere the extracts come, it may be well to preface them with a remark.

The document selected, from among many others, for partial translation, contains the deposition of Benito Cereno; the first taken in the case. Some disclosures therein were, at the time, held dubious for both learned and natural reasons. The tribunal inclined to the opinion that the deponent, not undisturbed in his mind by recent events, raved of some things which could never have happened. But subsequent depositions of the surviving sailors, bearing out the revelations of their captain in several of the strangest particulars, gave credence to the rest. So that the tribunal, in its final decision, rested its capital sentences upon statements which, had they lacked confirmation, it would have deemed it but duty to reject.

. . . .

I, Don José de Abos and Padilla, His Majesty's Notary for the Royal Revenue, and Register of this Province, and Notary Public of the Holy Crusade of this Bishopric, etc.

Do certify and declare, as much as is requisite in law, that, in the criminal cause commenced the twenty-fourth of the month of September, in the year seventeen hundred and ninety-nine, against the Senegal negroes of the ship *San Dominick*, the following declaration before me was made.

Declaration of the first witness,
Don Benito Cereno.

The same day, and month, and year, His Honour, Doctor Juan Martinez de Dozas, Councillor of the Royal Audience of this Kingdom, and learned in the law of this Intendancy, ordered the captain of the ship *San Dominick*, Don Benito Cereno, to appear; which he did in his litter, attended by the monk Infelez; of whom he received, before Don José de Abos and Padilla, Notary Public of the Holy Crusade, the oath, which he took by God, our Lord, and a sign of the Cross; under which he promised to tell the truth of whatever he should know and should be asked;—and being interrogated agreeably to the tenor of the act commencing the process, he said, that on the twentieth of May last, he set sail with his ship from the port of Valparaiso, bound to that of Callao; loaded with the produce of the country and one hundred and sixty blacks, of both sexes, mostly belonging to Don Alexandro Aranda, gentleman, of the city of Mendoza; that the crew of the ship consisted of thirty-six men, beside the persons who went as passengers; that the negroes were in part as follows:

[*Here, in the original, follows a list of some fifty names, descriptions, and ages, compiled from certain recovered documents of Aranda's, and also from recollections of the deponent, from which portions only are extracted.*]

—One, from about eighteen to nineteen years, named José, and this was the man that waited upon his master, Don Alexandro, and who speaks well the Spanish, having served him four or five years; . . . a mulatto, named Francesco, the cabin

[18] So called because Lima was founded on January 6, the feast-day of the Wise Men, or the Three Kings. Pizarro was the founder, in 1535.

steward, of a good person and voice, having sung in the Valparaiso churches, native of the province of Buenos Ayres, aged about thirty-five years. . . . A smart negro, named Dago, who had been for many years a grave-digger among the Spaniards, aged forty-six years. . . . Four old negroes, born in Africa, from sixty to seventy, but sound, caulkers by trade, whose names are as follows:—the first was named Muri, and he was killed (as was also his son named Diamelo); the second, Nacta; the third, Yola, likewise killed; the fourth, Ghofan; and six full-grown negroes, aged from thirty to forty-five, all raw, and born among the Ashantees—Martinqui, Yan, Lecbe, Mapenda, Yambaio, Akim; four of whom were killed; . . . a powerful negro named Atufal, who, being supposed to have been a chief in Africa, his owners set great store by him. . . . And a small negro of Senegal, but some years among the Spaniards, aged about thirty, which negro's name was Babo; . . . that he does not remember the names of the others, but that still expecting the residue of Don Alexandro's papers will be found, will then take due account of them all, and remit to the court; . . . and thirty-nine women and children of all ages.

[*After the catalogue, the deposition goes on as follows:*]

. . . That all the negroes slept upon deck, as is customary in this navigation, and none wore fetters, because the owner, his friend Aranda, told him that they were all tractable; . . . that on the seventh day after leaving port, at three o'clock in the morning, all the Spaniards being asleep except the two officers on the watch, who were the boatswain, Juan Robles, and the carpenter, Juan Bautista Gayete, and the helmsman and his boy, the negroes revolted suddenly, wounded dangerously the boatswain and the carpenter, and successively killed eighteen men of those who were sleeping upon deck, some with handspikes

and hatchets, and others by throwing them alive overboard, after tying them; that of the Spaniards upon deck, they left about seven, as he thinks, alive and tied, to manœuvre the ship and three or four more who hid themselves, remained also alive. Although in the act of revolt the negroes made themselves masters of the hatchway, six or seven wounded went through it to the cockpit, without any hindrance on their part; that in the act of revolt, the mate and another person, whose name he does not recollect, attempted to come up through the hatchway, but having been wounded at the onset, they were obliged to return to the cabin; that the deponent resolved at break of day to come up the companion-way, where the negro Babo was, being the ringleader, and Atufal, who assisted him, and having spoken to them, exhorted them to cease committing such atrocities, asking them, at the same time, what they wanted and intended to do, offering, himself, to obey their commands; that, notwithstanding this, they threw, in his presence, three men, alive and tied, overboard; that they told the deponent to come up, and that they would not kill him; which having done, the negro Babo asked him whether there were in those seas any negro countries where they might be carried, and he answered them, No; that the negro Babo afterwards told him to carry them to Senegal, or to the neighbouring islands of St. Nicholas; and he answered, that this was impossible, on account of the great distance, the necessity involved of rounding Cape Horn, the bad condition of the vessel, the want of provisions, sails, and water; but that the negro Babo replied to him he must carry them in any way; that they would do and conform themselves to everything the deponent should require as to eating and drinking; that after a long conference, being absolutely compelled to please them, for they threatened him to kill all the whites if they were not, at all events, carried to Senegal, he told them that what was most wanting for the voyage was water; that they would go near the coast to take it, and hence they would proceed on their course; that the negro Babo agreed to it; and the deponent steered toward the intermediate ports, hoping to meet some Spanish or foreign vessel that would save them; that within ten or eleven days they saw the land, and continued their course by it in the vicinity of Nasca; that the deponent observed that the negroes were now restless and mutinous, because he did not effect the taking in of water, the negro Babo having required, with threats, that it should be done, without fail, the following day; he told him he saw plainly that the coast was steep, and the rivers designated in the maps were not to be found, with other reasons suitable to the circumstances; that the best way would be to go to the island of Santa Maria, where they might water and victual easily, it being a desert island, as the foreigners did; that the deponent did not go to Pisco, that was near, nor make any other port of the coast, because the negro Babo had intimated to him several times, that he would kill all the whites the very moment he should perceive any city, town, or settlement of any kind on the shores to which they should be carried: that having determined to go to the island of Santa Maria, as the deponent had planned, for the purpose of trying whether, in the passage or in the island itself, they could find any vessel that should favour them, or whether he could escape from it in a boat to the neighbouring coast of Arruco; to adopt the necessary means he immediately changed his course, steering for the island; that the negroes Babo and Atufal held daily conferences, in which they discussed what was necessary for their design of returning to Senegal, whether they were to kill all the Spaniards, and particularly the deponent; that eight days after parting from the coast of Nasca, the deponent being on the watch a little after day-break, and soon after the negroes had their meeting, the negro Babo came to the place where the deponent was, and told him that he had determined to kill his master, Don Alexandro Aranda, both because he and his companions could not otherwise be sure of their liberty, and that, to keep the seamen in subjection, he wanted to prepare a warning of what road they should be made to take did they or any of them oppose him; and that, by means of the death of Don Alexandro, that warning would best be given; but, that what this last meant, the deponent did not at the time comprehend, nor could not, further than that the death of Don Alexandro was intended; and moreover, the negro Babo proposed to the deponent to call the mate Raneds, who was sleeping in the cabin, before the thing was done, for fear, as the deponent understood it, that the mate, who was a good navigator, should be killed with Don Alexandro and the rest; that the deponent, who was the friend from youth of Don Alexandro, prayed and conjured, but all was useless; for the negro Babo answered him that the thing could not be prevented, and that all the Spaniards risked their death if they should attempt to frustrate his will in this matter, or any other; that, in this conflict, the deponent called the mate, Raneds, who was forced to go apart, and immediately the negro Babo commanded the Ashantee Martinqui and the Ashantee Lecbe to go and commit the murder; that those two went down with hatchets to the berth of Don Alexandro; that, yet half alive and mangled, they dragged him on deck; that they were going to throw him overboard in that state, but the negro Babo stopped them, bidding the murder be completed on the deck before him, which was done, when, by his orders, the body was carried below, forward; that nothing more was seen of it by the deponent for three days; . . . that Don Alonzo Sidonia, an old man, long resident at Valparaiso, and lately appointed to a civil office in Peru, whither he had taken passage, was at the time sleeping in the berth opposite Don Alexandro's; that, awakening at his cries, surprised by them, and at the sight of the negroes with their bloody hatchets in their hands, he threw himself into the sea through a window which was near him, and was drowned, without it being in the power of the deponent to assist or take him up; . . . that, a short time after killing Aranda, they brought upon deck his german-cousin, of middle-age, Don Francisco Masa, of Mendoza, and the young Don Joaquin, Marques de Aramboalaza, then lately from Spain, with his Spanish servant Ponce, and the three young clerks of Aranda, José Mozairi, Lorenzo Bargas, and Hermenegildo Gandix, all of Cadiz; that Don Joaquin and Hermenegildo Gandix, the negro Babo for purposes hereafter to appear, preserved alive; but Don Francisco Masa, José Mozairi, and Lorenzo Bargas, with Ponce, the servant, beside the boatswain, Juan Robles, the boatswain's mates, Manuel Viscaya and Roderigo Hurta, and four of the sailors, the negro Babo ordered to be thrown alive into the sea, although they made no resistance, nor begged for anything else but mercy; that the boatswain, Juan Robles, who knew how to swim, kept the longest above water, making acts of contrition, and, in the last words he uttered, charged this deponent to cause mass to be said for his soul to our Lady of Succour: . . . that, during the three days which followed, the deponent, uncertain what fate had befallen the remains of Don Alexandro, frequently asked the negro Babo where they were, and, if still on board, whether they were to be preserved for interment ashore, entreating him so to order it; that the negro Babo answered nothing till the fourth day, when at sunrise, the deponent coming on deck, the negro Babo showed him a skeleton, which had been substituted for the ship's proper figure-head, the image of Christopher Colon, the discoverer of the New World; that the negro Babo asked him whose skeleton that was, and whether, from its whiteness, he should not think it a

white's; that, upon his covering his face, the negro Babo, coming close, said words to this effect: "Keep faith with the blacks from here to Senegal, or you shall in spirit, as now in body, follow your leader," pointing to the prow; . . . that the same morning the negro Babo took by succession each Spaniard forward, and asked him whose skeleton that was, and whether, from its whiteness, he should not think it a white's; that each Spaniard covered his face; that then to each the negro Babo repeated the words in the first place said to the deponent; . . . that they (the Spaniards), being then assembled aft, the negro Babo harangued them, saying that he had now done all; that the deponent (as navigator for the negroes) might pursue his course, warning him and all of them that they should, soul and body, go the way of Don Alexandro if he saw them (the Spaniards) speak or plot anything against them (the negroes)—a threat which was repeated every day; that, before the events last mentioned, they had tied the cook to throw him overboard, for it is not known what thing they heard him speak, but finally the negro Babo spared his life, at the request of the deponent; that a few days after, the deponent, endeavouring not to omit any means to preserve the lives of the remaining whites, spoke to the negroes peace and tranquillity, and agreed to draw up a paper, signed by the deponent and the sailors who could write, as also by the negro Babo, for himself and all the blacks, in which the deponent obliged himself to carry them to Senegal, and they not to kill any more, and he formally to make over to them the ship, with the cargo, with which they were for that time satisfied and quieted. . . . But the next day, the more surely to guard against the sailors' escape, the negro Babo commanded all the boats to be destroyed but the long-boat, which was unseaworthy, and another, a cutter in good condition, which, knowing it would yet be wanted for lowering the water casks, he had it lowered down into the hold.

[Various particulars of the prolonged and perplexed navigation ensuing here follow, with incidents of a calamitous calm, from which portion one passage is extracted, to wit:]

—That on the fifth day of the calm, all on board suffering much from the heat, and want of water, and five having died in fits, and mad, the negroes became irritable, and for a chance gesture, which they deemed suspicious—though it was harmless—made by the mate, Raneds, to the deponent, in the act of handing a quadrant, they killed him; but that for this they afterwards were sorry, the mate being the only remaining navigator on board, except the deponent.

—That omitting other events, which daily happened, and which can only serve uselessly to recall past misfortunes and conflicts, after seventy-three days' navigation, reckoned from the time they sailed from Nasca, during which they navigated under a scanty allowance of water, and were afflicted with the calms before mentioned, they at last arrived at the island of Santa Maria, on the seventeenth of the month of August, at about six o'clock in the afternoon, at which hour they cast anchor very near the American ship, *Bachelor's Delight,* which lay in the same bay, commanded by the generous Captain Amasa Delano; but at six o'clock in the morning, they had already descried the port, and the negroes became uneasy, as soon as at distance they saw the ship, not having expected to see one there; that the negro Babo pacified them, assuring them that no fear need be had; that straightway he ordered the figure on the bow to be covered with canvas, as for repairs, and had the decks a little set in order; that for a time the negro Babo and the negro Atufal conferred; that the negro Atufal was for sailing away, but the negro Babo would not, and, by himself, cast about what to do; that at last he came to the deponent, proposing to him to say and do all that the deponent

declares to have said and done to the American captain; . . . that the negro Babo warned him that if he varied in the least, or uttered any word, or gave any look that should give the least intimation of the past events or present state, he would instantly kill him, with all his companions, showing a dagger, which he carried hid, saying something which, as he understood it, meant that that dagger would be alert as his eye; that the negro Babo then announced the plan to all his companions, which pleased them; that he then, the better to disguise the truth, devised many expedients, in some of them uniting deceit and defence; that of this sort was the device of the six Ashantees before named, who were his bravos; that them he stationed on the break of the poop, as if to clean certain hatchets (in cases, which were part of the cargo), but in reality to use them, and distribute them at need, and at a given word he told them; that, among other devices, was the device of presenting Atufal, his right-hand man, as chained, though in a moment the chains could be dropped; that in every particular he informed the deponent what part he was expected to enact in every device, and what story he was to tell on every occasion, always threatening him with instant death if he varied in the least: that, conscious that many of the negroes would be turbulent, the negro Babo appointed the four aged negroes, who were caulkers, to keep what domestic order they could on the decks; that again and again he harangued the Spaniards and his companions, informing them of his intent, and of his devices, and of the invented story that this deponent was to tell, charging them lest any of them varied from that story; that these arrangements were made and matured during the interval of two or three hours, between their first sighting the ship and the arrival on board of Captain Amasa Delano; that this happened at about half-past seven in the morning, Captain Amasa Delano coming in his boat, and all gladly receiving him; that the deponent, as well as he could force himself, acting then the part of principal owner, and a free captain of the ship, told Captain Amasa Delano, when called upon, that he came from Buenos Ayres, bound to Lima, with three hundred negroes; that off Cape Horn, and in a subsequent fever, many negroes had died; that also, by similar casualties, all the sea officers and the greatest part of the crew had died.

[*And so the deposition goes on, circumstantially recounting the fictitious story dictated to the deponent by Babo, and through the deponent imposed upon Captain Delano; and also recounting the friendly offers of Captain Delano, with other things, but all of which is here omitted. After the fictitious, strange story, etc., the deposition proceeds:*]

—That the generous Captain Amasa Delano remained on board all the day, till he left the ship anchored at six o'clock in the evening, deponent speaking to him always of his pretended misfortunes, under the fore-mentioned principles, without having had it in his power to tell a single word, or give him the least hint, that he might know the truth and state of things; because the negro Babo, performing the office of an officious servant with all the appearance of submission of the humble slave, did not leave the deponent one moment; that this was in order to observe the deponent's actions and words, for the negro Babo understands well the Spanish; and besides, there were thereabout some others who were constantly on the watch, and likewise understood the Spanish; . . . that upon one occasion, while deponent was standing on the deck conversing with Amasa Delano, by a secret sign the negro Babo drew him (the deponent) aside, the act appearing as if originating with the deponent; that then, he being drawn aside, the negro Babo proposed to him to gain from Amasa Delano full particulars about his ship, and crew, and arms; that the deponent asked "For what?" that the negro

Babo answered he might conceive; that, grieved at the prospect of what might overtake the generous Captain Amasa Delano, the deponent at first refused to ask the desired questions, and used every argument to induce the negro Babo to give up this new design; that the negro Babo showed the point of his dagger; that, after the information had been obtained, the negro Babo again drew him aside, telling him that that very night he (the deponent) would be captain of two ships instead of one, for that, great part of the American's ship's crew being to be absent fishing, the six Ashantees, without any one else, would easily take it; that at this time he said other things to the same purpose; that no entreaties availed; that before Amasa Delano's coming on board, no hint had been given touching the capture of the American ship: that to prevent this project the deponent was powerless; . . . — that in some things his memory is confused, he cannot distinctly recall every event; . . . —that as soon as they had cast anchor at six of the clock in the evening, as has before been stated, the American captain took leave to return to his vessel; that upon a sudden impulse, which the deponent believes to have come from God and his angels, he, after the farewell had been said, followed the generous Captain Amasa Delano as far as the gunwale, where he stayed, under the pretence of taking leave, until Amasa Delano should have been seated in his boat; that on shoving off, the deponent sprang from the gunwale, into the boat, and fell into it, he knows not how, God guarding him; that—

[*Here, in the original, follows the account of what further happened at the escape, and how the "San Dominick" was retaken, and of the passage to the coast; including in the recital many expressions of "eternal gratitude" to the "generous Captain Amasa Delano." The deposition then proceeds with recapitulatory remarks, and a partial renumeration of the negroes, making record of their individual part in*] *the past events, with a view to furnishing, according to command of the court, the data whereon to found the criminal sentences to be pronounced. From this portion is the following:*]

—That he believes that all the negroes, though not in the first place knowing to the design of revolt, when it was accomplished, approved it. . . . That the negro, José, eighteen years old, and in the personal service of Don Alexandro, was the one who communicated the information to the negro Babo, about the state of things in the cabin, before the revolt; that this is known, because, in the preceding midnight, he used to come from his berth, which was under his master's, in the cabin, to the deck where the ringleader and his associates were, and had secret conversations with the negro Babo, in which he was several times seen by the mate; that, one night, the mate drove him away twice; . . . that this same negro José, was the one who, without being commanded to do so by the negro Babo, as Lecbe and Martinqui were, stabbed his master, Don Alexandro, after he had been dragged half-lifeless to the deck; . . . that the mulatto steward, Francesco, was of the first band of revolters, that he was, in all things, the creature and tool of the negro Babo; that, to make his court, he, just before a repast in the cabin, proposed, to the negro Babo, poisoning a dish for the generous Captain Amasa Delano; this is known and believed, because the negroes have said it; but that the negro Babo, having another design, forbade Francesco; . . . that the Ashantee Lecbe was one of the worst of them; for that, on the day the ship was retaken, he assisted in the defence of her, with a hatchet in each hand, with one of which he wounded, in the breast, the chief mate of Amasa Delano, in the first act of boarding; this all knew; that, in sight of the deponent, Lecbe struck, with a hatchet, Don Francisco Masa when, by the negro Babo's orders, he was carrying him to throw him overboard, alive; beside partici-

pating in the murder, before mentioned, of Don Alexandro Aranda, and others of the cabin-passengers; that, owing to the fury with which the Ashantees fought in the engagement with the boats, but this Lecbe and Yan survived; that Yan was bad as Lecbe; that Yan was the man who, by Babo's command, willingly prepared the skeleton of Don Alexandro, in a way the negroes afterwards told the deponent, but which he, so long as reason is left him, can never divulge; that Yan and Lecbe were the two who, in a calm by night, riveted the skeleton to the bow; this also the negroes told him; that the negro Babo was he who traced the inscription below it; that the negro Babo was the plotter from first to last; he ordered every murder, and was the helm and keel of the revolt; that Atufal was his lieutenant in all; but Atufal, with his own hand, committed no murder; nor did the negro Babo; . . . that Atufal was shot, being killed in the fight with the boats, ere boarding; . . . that the negresses, of age, were knowing to the revolt, and testified themselves satisfied at the death of their master, Don Alexandro; that, had the negroes not restrained them, they would have tortured to death, instead of simply killing, the Spaniards slain by command of the negro Babo; that the negresses used their utmost influence to have the deponent made away with; that, in the various acts of murder, they sang songs and danced—not gaily, but solemnly; and before the engagement with the boats, as well as during the action, they sang melancholy songs to the negroes, and that this melancholy tone was more inflaming than a different one would have been, and was so intended; that all this is believed, because the negroes have said it.

—That of the thirty-six men of the crew—exclusive of the passengers (all of whom are now dead), which the deponent had knowledge of—six only remained alive, with four cabin-boys and ship-boys, not included with the crew; . . . —that the negroes broke an arm of one of the cabin-boys and gave him strokes with hatchets.

[Then follow various random disclosures referring to various periods of time. The following are extracted:]

—That during the presence of Captain Amasa Delano on board, some attempts were made by the sailors, and one by Hermenegildo Gandix, to convey hints to him of the true state of affairs; but that these attempts were ineffectual, owing to fear of incurring death, and furthermore owing to the devices which offered contradictions to the true state of affairs; as well as owing to the generosity and piety of Amasa Delano, incapable of sounding such wickedness; . . . that Luys Galgo, a sailor about sixty years of age, and formerly of the king's navy, was one of those who sought to convey tokens to Captain Amasa Delano; but his intent, though undiscovered, being suspected, he was, on a pretence, made to retire out of sight, and at last into the hold, and there was made away with. This the negroes have since said; . . . that one of the ship-boys feeling, from Captain Amasa Delano's presence, some hopes of release, and not having enough prudence, dropped some chance-word respecting his expectations, which being overheard and understood by a slave-boy with whom he was eating at the time, the latter struck him on the head with a knife, inflicting a bad wound, but of which the boy is now healing; that likewise, not long before the ship was brought to anchor, one of the seamen, steering at the time, endangered himself by letting the blacks remark a certain unconscious hopeful expression in his countenance, arising from some cause similar to the above; but this sailor, by his heedful after conduct, escaped; . . . that these statements are made to show the court that from the beginning to the end of the revolt, it was impossible for the deponent and his men to act otherwise than they did; . . . —that the third clerk, Hermenegildo Gandix, who before had been forced to live among the seamen, wearing a seaman's habit, and in all respects appearing to be one for the time;

he, Gandix, was killed by a musket-ball fired through a mistake from the American boats before boarding; having in his fright ran up the mizzen-rigging, calling to the boats—"don't board," lest upon their boarding the negroes should kill him; that this inducing the Americans to believe he some way favoured the cause of the negroes, they fired two balls at him, so that he fell wounded from the rigging, and was drowned in the sea; . . . —that the young Don Joaquin, Marques de Arambaolaza, like Hermenegildo Gandix, the third clerk, was degraded to the office and appearance of a common seaman; that upon one occasion, when Don Joaquin shrank, the negro Babo commanded the Ashantee Lecbe to take tar and heat it, and pour it upon Don Joaquin's hands; . . . —that Don Joaquin was killed owing to another mistake of the Americans, but one impossible to be avoided, as upon the approach of the boats, Don Joaquin, with a hatchet tied edge out and upright to his hand, was made by the negroes to appear on the bulwarks; whereupon, seen with arms in his hands and in a questionable attitude, he was shot for a renegade seaman; . . . —that on the person of Don Joaquin was found secreted a jewel, which, by papers that were discovered, proved to have been meant for the shrine of our Lady of Mercy in Lima; a votive offering, beforehand prepared and guarded, to attest his gratitude, when he should have landed in Peru, his last destination, for the safe conclusion of his entire voyage from Spain; . . . —that the jewel, with the other effects of the late Don Joaquin, is in the custody of the brethren of the Hospital de Sacerdotes, awaiting the decision of the honourable court; . . . — that, owing to the condition of the deponent, as well as the haste in which the boats departed for the attack, the Americans were not forewarned that there were, among the apparent crew, a passenger and one of the clerks disguised by the negro Babo; . . . —that, beside the negroes killed in the action, some were killed after the

1054 HERMAN MELVILLE

capture and re-anchoring at night, when shackled to the ring-bolts on deck; that these deaths were committed by the sailors, ere they could be prevented. That so soon as informed of it, Captain Amasa Delano used all his authority, and, in particular with his own hand, struck down Martinez Gola, who, having found a razor in the pocket of an old jacket of his, which one of the shackled negroes had on, was aiming it at the negro's throat; that the noble Captain Amasa Delano also wrenched from the hand of Bartholomew Barlo, a dagger secreted at the time of the massacre of the whites, with which he was in the act of stabbing a shackled negro, who, the same day, with another negro, had thrown him down and jumped upon him; . . . —that, for all the events, befalling through so long a time, during which the ship was in the hands of the negro Babo, he cannot here give account; but that, what he has said is the most substantial of what occurs to him at present, and is the truth under the oath which he has taken; which declaration he affirmed and ratified, after hearing it read to him.

He said that he is twenty-nine years of age, and broken in body and mind; that when finally dismissed by the court, he shall not return home to Chili, but betake himself to the monastery on Mount Agonia without; and signed with his honour, and crossed himself, and, for the time, departed as he came, in his litter, with the monk Infelez, to the Hospital de Sacerdotes.

BENITO CERENO.
DOCTOR ROZAS.

If the deposition of Benito Cereno has served as the key to fit into the lock of the complications which preceded it, then, as a vault whose door has been flung back, the *San Dominick's* hull lies open to-day.

Hitherto the nature of this narrative, besides rendering the intricacies in the beginning unavoidable, has more or less required that many things, instead of being set down in the order of occurrence, should be retrospectively, or irregularly given; this last is the case with the following passages, which will conclude the account:

During the long, mild voyage to Lima, there was, as before hinted, a period during which Don Benito a little recovered his health, or, at least in some degree, his tranquillity. Ere the decided relapse which came, the two captains had many cordial conversations—their fraternal unreserve in singular contrast with former withdrawments.

Again and again, it was repeated, how hard it had been to enact the part forced on the Spaniard by Babo.

"Ah, my dear Don Amasa," Don Benito once said, "at those very times when you thought me so morose and ungrateful—nay when, as you now admit, you half thought me plotting your murder—at those very times my heart was frozen; I could not look at you, thinking of what, both on board this ship and your own, hung, from other hands, over my kind benefactor. And as God lives, Don Amasa, I know not whether desire for my own safety alone could have nerved me to that leap into your boat, had it not been for the thought that, did you, unenlightened, return to your ship, you, my best friend, with all who might be with you, stolen upon, that night, in your hammocks, would never in this world have wakened again. Do but think how you walked this deck, how you sat in this cabin, every inch of ground mined into honey-combs under you. Had I dropped the least hint, made the least advance toward an understanding between us, death, explosive death—yours as mine—would have ended the scene."

"True, true," cried Captain Delano, starting, "you saved my life, Don Benito, more than I yours; saved it, too, against my knowledge and will."

"Nay, my friend," rejoined the Spaniard, courteous even to the point of religion, "God charmed your life, but you saved mine. To think of some things you did—those smilings and chattings, rash pointings and gesturings. For less than these, they slew my mate, Raneds; but you had the Prince of Heaven's safe conduct through all ambuscades."

"Yes, all is owing to Providence, I know; but the temper of my mind that morning was more than commonly pleasant, while the sight of so much suffering— more apparent than real—added to my good nature, compassion, and charity, happily interweaving the three. Had it been otherwise, doubtless, as you hint, some of my interferences with the blacks might have ended unhappily enough. Besides that, those feelings I spoke of enabled me to get the better of momentary distrust, at times when acuteness might have cost me my life, without saving another's. Only at the end did my suspicions get the better of me, and you know how wide of the mark they then proved."

"Wide, indeed," said Don Benito, sadly; "you were with me all day; stood with me, sat with me, talked with me, looked at me, ate with me, drank with me; and yet, your last act was to clutch for a villain, not only an innocent man, but the most pitiable of all men. To such degree may malign machinations and deceptions impose. So far may even the best men err, in judging the conduct of one with the recesses of whose condition he is not acquainted. But you were forced to it; and you were in time undeceived. Would that, in both respects, it was so ever, and with all men."

"I think I understand you; you generalize, Don Benito; and mournfully enough. But the past is passed; why moralize upon it? Forget it. See, yon bright sun has forgotten it all, and the blue sea, and the blue sky; these have turned over new leaves."

"Because they have no memory," he dejectedly replied; "because they are not human."

"But these mild trades that now fan your cheek, Don Benito, do they not come with a human-like healing to you? Warm friends, steadfast friends are the trades."

"With their steadfastness they but waft me to my tomb, Señor," was the foreboding response.

"You are saved, Don Benito," cried Captain Delano, more and more astonished and pained; "you are saved; what has cast such a shadow upon you?"

"The negro."

There was silence, while the moody man sat, slowly and unconsciously gathering his mantle about him, as if it were a pall.

There was no more conversation that day.

But if the Spaniard's melancholy sometimes ended in muteness upon topics like the above, there were others upon which he never spoke at all; on which, indeed, all his old reserves were piled. Pass over the worst and, only to elucidate, let an item or two of these be cited. The dress so precise and costly, worn by him on the day whose events have been narrated, had not willingly been put on. And that silver-mounted sword, apparent symbol of despotic command, was not, indeed, a sword, but the ghost of one. The scabbard, artificially stiffened, was empty.

As for the black—whose brain, not body, had schemed and led the revolt, with the plot—his slight frame, inadequate to that which it held, had at once yielded to the superior muscular strength of his captor, in the boat. Seeing all was over, he uttered no sound, and could not be forced to. His aspect seemed to say: since I cannot do deeds, I will not speak words. Put in irons in the hold, with the rest, he was carried to Lima. During the passage Don Benito did not visit him. Nor then, nor at any time after, would he look at him. Before the tribunal he refused. When pressed by the judges he fainted. On the testimony of the sailors alone rested the legal identity of Babo. And yet the Spaniard would, upon occasion, verbally refer to the negro, as has been shown; but look on him he would not, or could not.

Some months after, dragged to the gibbet at the tail of a mule, the black met his voiceless end. The body was burned to ashes; but for many days, the head,

that hive of subtlety, fixed on a pole in
the Plaza, met, unabashed, the gaze of
the whites; and across the Plaza looked
toward St. Bartholomew's church, in whose
vaults slept then, as now, the recovered
bones of Aranda; and across the Rimac
bridge looked toward the monastery, on
Mount Agonia without; where, three
months after being dismissed by the court,
Benito Cereno, borne on the bier, did, indeed, follow his leader.

THE PORTENT
[1866]

Hanging from the beam,
  Slowly swaying (such the law),
Gaunt the shadow on your green,
  Shenandoah! [1]
The cut is on the crown
  (Lo, John Brown),
And the stabs shall heal no more.

Hidden in the cap
  Is the anguish none can draw;
So your future veils its face,
  Shenandoah!
But the streaming beard is shown
  (Weird John Brown),
The meteor of the war.

MALVERN HILL
[1866]

Ye elms that wave on Malvern Hill
  In prime of morn and May,
Recall ye how McClellan's men
  Here stood at bay?
While deep within yon forest dim   5
  Our rigid comrades lay—
Some with the cartridge in their mouth,
Others with fixed arms lifted South—
  Invoking so
The cypress glades? Ah wilds of woe!   10

The spires of Richmond, late beheld
  Through rifts in musket-haze,

Were closed from view in clouds of dust
  On leaf-walled ways,
Where streamed our wagons in
    caravan;   15
  And the Seven Nights and Days
Of march and fast, retreat and fight,
Pinched our grimed faces to ghastly
    plight—
  Does the elm wood
Recall the haggard beards of blood?   20

The battle-smoked flag, with stars eclipsed,
  We followed (it never fell!)—
In silence husbanded our strength—
  Received their yell;
Till on this slope we patient turned   25
  With cannon ordered well;
Reverse we proved was not defeat;
But ah, the sod what thousands meet!—
  Does Malvern Wood
Bethink itself, and muse and brood?   30

    We elms of Malvern Hill
      Remember everything;
    But sap the twig will fill:
    Wag the world how it will,
      Leaves must be green in Spring. 35

SHERIDAN AT CEDAR CREEK
[1866]

Shoe the steed with silver
  That bore him to the fray,
When he heard the guns at dawning—
  Miles away;
When he heard them calling, calling—   5
  Mount! nor stay:
    Quick, or all is lost;
    They've surprised and stormed the
      post,
    They push your routed host—
Gallop! retrieve the day.   10

House the horse in ermine—
  For the foam-flake blew
White through the red October;
  He thundered into view;

---

[1] Charles Town, W. Va., where Brown
was hanged, is in the Shenandoah Valley.

They cheered him in the looming, 15
  Horseman and horse they knew.
    The turn of the tide began,
    The rally of bugles ran,
    He swung his hat in the van;
  The electric hoof-spark flew. 20

Wreathe the steed and lead him—
  For the charge he led
Touched and turned the cypress
  Into amaranths for the head
Of Philip,[2] king of riders, 25
  Who raised them from the dead.
    The camp (at dawning lost),
    By eve, recovered—forced,
    Rang with laughter of the host
  At belated Early[3] fled. 30

Shroud the horse in sable—
  For the mounds they heap!
There is firing in the Valley,
  And yet no strife they keep;
It is the parting volley,
  It is the pathos deep.
    There is glory for the brave
    Who lead, and nobly save,
    But no knowledge in the grave
  Where the nameless followers sleep. 40

THE COLLEGE COLONEL
[1866]

He rides at their head;
  A crutch by his saddle just slants in
    view,
One slung arm is in splints, you see,
  Yet he guides his strong steed—how
    coldly too.

He brings his regiment home— 5
  Not as they filed two years before,
But a remnant half-tattered, and battered,
    and worn,
  Like castaway sailors, who—stunned
    by the surf's loud roar,
    Their mates dragged back and seen no
      more— 10
Again and again breast the surge,
  And at last crawl, spent, to shore.

A still rigidity and pale—
  An Indian aloofness lones his brow;
He has lived a thousand years 15
Compressed in battle's pains and prayers,
  Marches and watches slow.

There are welcoming shouts, and flags;
  Old men off hat to the Boy,
Wreaths from gay balconies fall at his
    feet, 20
  But to *him*—there comes alloy.

It is not that a leg is lost,
  It is not that an arm is maimed,
It is not that the fever has racked—
  Self he has long disclaimed. 25

But all through the Seven Days' Fight,
  And deep in the Wilderness grim,
And in the field-hospital tent,
  And Petersburg crater, and dim
Lean brooding in Libby, there came— 30
  Ah heaven!—what *truth* to him.

SUPPLEMENT to "BATTLE PIECES"
[1866]

WERE I fastidiously anxious for the symmetry of this book, it would close with the notes. But the times are such that patriotism—not free from solicitude—urges a claim overriding all literary scruples.

It is more than a year since the memorable surrender, but events have not yet rounded themselves into completion. Not justly can we complain of this. There has been an upheaval affecting the basis of things; to altered circumstances complicated adaptations are to be made; there are difficulties great and novel. But is Reason still waiting for Passion to spend itself? We have sung of the soldiers and sailors, but who shall hymn the politicians?

---

[2] Gen. Philip Henry Sheridan (1831-88), hero of "Sheridan's Ride," Oct. 19, 1864.

[3] Gen. Jubal A. Early (1816-94), defeated by Sheridan at Winchester.

In view of the infinite desirableness of Re-establishment, and considering that, so far as feeling is concerned, it depends not mainly on the temper in which the South regards the North, but rather conversely; one who never was a blind adherent feels constrained to submit some thoughts, counting on the indulgence of his countrymen.

And, first, it may be said that, if among the feelings and opinions growing immediately out of a great civil convulsion, there are any which time shall modify or do away, they are presumably those of a less temperate and charitable cast.

There seems no reason why patriotism and narrowness should go together, or why intellectual impartiality should be confounded with political trimming, or why serviceable truth should keep cloistered because not partisan. Yet the work of Reconstruction, if admitted to be feasible at all, demands little but common sense and Christian charity. Little but these? These are much.

Some of us are concerned because as yet the South shows no penitence. But what exactly do we mean by this? Since down to the close of the war she never confessed any for braving it, the only penitence now left her is that which springs solely from the sense of discomfiture; and since this evidently would be a contrition hypocritical, it would be unworthy in us to demand it. Certain it is that penitence, in the sense of voluntary humiliation, will never be displayed. Nor does this afford just ground for unreserved condemnation. It is enough, for all practical purposes, if the South have been taught by the terrors of civil war to feel that Secession, like Slavery, is against Destiny; that both now lie buried in one grave; that her fate is linked with ours; and that together we comprise the Nation.

The clouds of heroes who battled for the Union it is needless to eulogize here. But how of the soldiers on the other side? And when of a free community we name the soldiers, we thereby name the people. It was in subserviency to the slave-interest that Secession was plotted; but it was under the plea, plausibly urged, that certain inestimable rights guaranteed by the Constitution were directly menaced, that the people of the South were cajoled into revolution. Through the arts of the conspirators and the perversity of fortune, the most sensitive love of liberty was entrapped into the support of a war whose implied end was the erecting in our advanced century of an Anglo-American empire based upon the systematic degradation of man.

Spite this clinging reproach, however, signal military virtues and achievements have conferred upon the Confederate arms historic fame, and upon certain of the commanders a renown extending beyond the sea—a renown which we of the North could not suppress, even if we would. In personal character, also, not a few of the military leaders of the South enforce forbearance; the memory of others the North refrains from disparaging; and some, with more or less of reluctance, she can respect. Posterity, sympathising with our convictions, but removed from our passions, may perhaps go farther here. If George IV could, out of the graceful instinct of a gentleman, raise an honorable monument in the great fane of Christendom over the remains of the enemy of his dynasty, Charles Edward,[1] the invader of England and victor in the rout of Prestonpans—upon whose head the king's ancestor but one reign removed had set a price—is it probable that the grandchildren of General Grant will pursue with rancor, or slur by sour neglect, the memory of Stonewall Jackson?

But the South herself is not wanting in recent histories and biographies which record the deeds of her chieftains—writings freely published at the North by loyal

[1] Charles Edward Stuart (1720-88), called "Bonnie Prince Charlie," leading the Scottish Jacobite uprising against England in the time of George II (1745), defeated the English at the Scottish town of Prestonpans. He was buried in St. Peter's at Rome.

houses, widely read here, and with a deep though saddened interest. By students of the war such works are hailed as welcome accessories, and tending to the completeness of the record.

Supposing a happy issue out of present perplexities, then, in the generation next to come, Southerners there will be yielding allegiance to the Union, feeling all their interests bound up in it, and yet cherishing unrebuked that kind of feeling for the memory of the soldiers of the fallen Confederacy that Burns, Scott, and the Ettrick Shepherd [2] felt for the memory of the gallant clansmen ruined through their fidelity to the Stuarts—a feeling whose passion was tempered by the poetry imbuing it, and which in no wise affected their loyalty to the Georges, and which, it may be added, indirectly contributed excellent things to literature. But, setting this view aside, dishonorable would it be in the South were she willing to abandon to shame the memory of brave men who with signal personal disinterestedness warred in her behalf, though from motives, as we believe, so deplorably astray.

Patriotism is not baseness, neither is it inhumanity. The mourners who this summer bear flowers to the mounds of the Virginian and Georgian dead are, in their domestic bereavement and proud affection, as sacred in the eye of Heaven as are those who go with similar offerings of tender grief and love into the cemeteries of our Northern martyrs. And yet, in one aspect, how needless to point the contrast.

Cherishing such sentiments, it will hardly occasion surprise that, in looking over the battle-pieces in the foregoing collection, I have been tempted to withdraw or modify some of them, fearful lest in presenting, though but dramatically and by way of a poetic record, the passions and epithets of civil war, I might be contributing to a bitterness which every sensible American must wish at an end. So, too, with the emotion of victory as reproduced on some pages, and particularly toward the close. It should not be construed into an exultation

misapplied—an exultation as ungenerous as unwise, and made to minister, however indirectly, to that kind of censoriousness too apt to be produced in certain natures by success after trying reverses. Zeal is not of necessity religion, neither is it always of the same essence with poetry or patriotism.

There are excesses which marked the conflict, most of which are perhaps inseparable from a civil strife so intense and prolonged, and involving warfare in some border countries new and imperfectly civilized. Barbarities also there were, for which the Southern people collectively can hardly be held responsible, though perpetrated by ruffians in their name. But surely other qualities—exalted ones—courage and fortitude matchless, were likewise displayed, and largely; and justly may these be held the characteristic traits, and not the former.

In this view, what Northern writer, however patriotic, but must revolt from acting on paper a part any way akin to that of the live dog to the dead lion; and yet it is right to rejoice for our triumph, so far as it may justly imply an advance for our whole country and for humanity.

Let it be held no reproach to any one that he pleads for reasonable consideration for our late enemies, now stricken down and unavoidably debarred, for the time, from speaking through authorized agencies for themselves. Nothing has been urged here in the foolish hope of conciliating those men—few in number, we trust—who have resolved never to be reconciled to the Union. On such hearts everything is thrown away except it be religious commiseration, and the sincerest. Yet let them call to mind that unhappy Secessionist,[3] not a military man, who with impious alacrity

---

[2] James Hogg (1770-1835), author who dealt with Scottish legend and history.

[3] The reference is to Edmund Ruffin (1794-1865), planter and writer on agricultural subjects, prominent and irreconcilable Secessionist.

fired the first shot of the Civil War at Sumter, and a little more than four years afterward fired the last one into his own heart at Richmond.

Noble was the gesture into which patriotic passion surprised the people in a utilitarian time and country; yet the glory of the war falls short of its pathos—a pathos which now at last ought to disarm all animosity.

How many and earnest thoughts still rise, and how hard to repress them. We feel what past years have been, and years, unretarded years, shall come. May we all have moderation; may we all show candor. Though, perhaps, nothing could ultimately have averted the strife, and though to treat of human actions is to deal wholly with second causes, nevertheless, let us not cover up or try to extenuate what, humanly speaking, is the truth—namely, that those unfraternal denunciations, continued through years, and which at last inflamed to deeds that ended in bloodshed, were reciprocal; and that, had the preponderating strength and the prospect of its unlimited increase lain on the other side, on ours might have lain those actions which now in our late opponents we stigmatize under the name of Rebellion. As frankly let us own—what it would be unbecoming to parade were foreigners concerned—that our triumph was won not more by skill and bravery than by superior resources and crushing numbers; that it was a triumph, too, over a people for years politically misled by designing men, and also by some honestly-erring men, who from their position could not have been otherwise than broadly influential; a people who, though, indeed, they sought to perpetuate the curse of slavery, and even extend it, were not the authors of it, but (less fortunate, not less righteous than we) were the fated inheritors; a people who, having a like origin with ourselves, share essentially in whatever worthy qualities we may possess. No one can add to the lasting reproach which hopeless defeat has now

cast upon Secession by withholding the recognition of these verities.

Surely we ought to take it to heart that that kind of pacification, based upon principles operating equally all over the land, which lovers of their country yearn for, and which our arms, though signally triumphant, did not bring about, and which lawmaking, however anxious, or energetic, or repressive, never by itself can achieve, may yet be largely aided by generosity of sentiment public and private. Some revisionary legislation and adaptive is indispensable; but with this should harmoniously work another kind of prudence, not unallied with entire magnanimity. Benevolence and policy—Christianity and Machiavelli—dissuade from penal severities toward the subdued. Abstinence here is as obligatory as considerate care for our unfortunate fellow-men late in bonds, and, if observed, would equally prove to be wise forecast. The great qualities of the South, those attested in the War, we can perilously alienate, or we may make them nationally available at need.

The blacks, in their infant pupilage to freedom, appeal to the sympathies of every humane mind. The paternal guardianship which for the interval Government exercises over them was prompted equally by duty and benevolence. Yet such kindliness should not be allowed to exclude kindliness to communities who stand nearer to us in nature. For the future of the freed slaves we may well be concerned; but the future of the whole country, involving the future of the blacks, urges a paramount claim upon our anxiety. Effective benignity, like the Nile, is not narrow in its bounty, and true policy is always broad. To be sure, it is vain to seek to glide, with moulded words, over the difficulties of the situation. And for them who are neither partisans, nor enthusiasts, nor theorists, nor cynics, there are some doubts not readily to be solved. And there are fears. Why is not the cessation of war now at length attended with the settled calm of peace? Wherefore in a clear sky do we still turn our eyes toward the South as the Neopolitan, months after the eruption, turns his toward Vesuvius? Do we dread lest the repose may be deceptive? In the recent convulsion has the crater but shifted? Let us revere that sacred uncertainty which forever impends over men and nations. Those of us who always abhorred slavery as an atheistical iniquity, gladly we join in the exulting chorus of humanity over its downfall. But we should remember that emancipation was accomplished not by deliberate legislation; only through agonized violence could so mighty a result be effected. In our natural solicitude to confirm the benefit of liberty to the blacks, let us forbear from measures of dubious constitutional rightfulness toward our white countrymen —measures of a nature to provoke, among other of the last evils, exterminating hatred of race toward race. In imagination let us place ourselves in the unprecedented position of the Southerners—their position as regards the millions of ignorant manumitted slaves in their midst, for whom some of us now claim the suffrage. Let us be Christians toward our fellow-whites, as well as philanthropists toward the blacks, our fellow-men. In all things, and toward all, we are enjoined to do as we would be done by. Nor should we forget that benevolent desires, after passing a certain point, can not undertake their own fulfillment without incurring the risk of evils beyond those sought to be remedied. Something may well be left to the graduated care of future legislation, and to heaven. In one point of view the co-existence of the two races in the South—whether the negro be bond or free—seems (even as it did to Abraham Lincoln) a grave evil. Emancipation has ridded the country of the reproach, but not wholly of the calamity. Especially in the present transition period for both races in the South, more or less of trouble may not unreasonably be anticipated; but let us not hereafter be too swift to charge the blame exclusively in any one

quarter. With certain evils men must be more or less patient. Our institutions have a potent digestion, and may in time convert and assimilate to good all elements thrown in, however originally alien.

But, so far as immediate measures looking toward permanent Re-establishment are concerned, no consideration should tempt us to pervert the national victory into oppression for the vanquished. Should plausible promise of eventual good, or a deceptive or spurious sense of duty, lead us to essay this, count we must on serious consequences, not the least of which would be divisions among the Northern adherents of the Union. Assuredly, if any honest Catos [4] there be who thus far have gone with us, no longer will they do so, but oppose us, and as resolutely as hitherto they have supported. But this path of thought leads toward those waters of bitterness from which one can only turn aside and be silent.

But supposing Re-establishment so far advanced that the Southern seats in Congress are occupied, and by men qualified in accordance with those cardinal principles of representative government which hitherto have prevailed in the land—what then? Why, the Congressmen elected by the people of the South will—represent the people of the South. This may seem a flat conclusion; but, in view of the last five years, may there not be latent significance in it? What will be the temper of those Southern members? And, confronted by them, what will be the mood of our own representatives? In private life true reconciliation seldom follows a violent quarrel; but, if subsequent intercourse be unavoidable, nice observances and mutual are indispensable to the prevention of a new rupture. Amity itself can only be maintained by reciprocal respect, and true friends are punctilious equals. On the floor

---

[4] A reference to the honest and uncompromising character of Marcus Porcius Cato (96-46 B.C.), who stabbed himself rather than surrender to Caesar.

of Congress North and South are to come together after a passionate duel, in which the South, though proving her valor, has been made to bite the dust. Upon differences in debate shall acrimonious recriminations be exchanged? Shall censorious superiority assumed by one section provoke defiant self-assertion on the other? Shall Manassas and Chickamauga be retorted for Chattanooga and Richmond?[5] Under the supposition that the full Congress will be composed of gentlemen, all this is impossible. Yet, if otherwise, it needs no prophet of Israel to foretell the end. The maintenance of Congressional decency in the future will rest mainly with the North. Rightly will more forbearance be required from the North than the South, for the North is victor.

But some there are who may deem these latter thoughts inapplicable, and for this reason: Since the test-oath operatively excludes from Congress all who in any way participated in Secession, therefore none but Southerners wholly in harmony with the North are eligible to seats. This is true for the time being. But the oath is alterable; and in the wonted fluctuations of parties not improbably it will undergo alteration, assuming such a form, perhaps, as not to bar the admission into the National Legislature of men who represent the populations lately in revolt. Such a result would involve no violation of the principles of democratic government. Not readily can one perceive how the political existence of the millions of late Secessionists can permanently be ignored by this Republic. The years of the war tried our devotion to the Union; the time of peace may test the sincerity of our faith in democracy.

In no spirit of opposition, not by way of challenge, is anything here thrown out. These thoughts are sincere ones; they seem natural—inevitable. Here and there they must have suggested themselves to many thoughtful patriots. And, if they be just thoughts, ere long they must have that weight with the public which already they have had with individuals.

For that heroic band—those children of the furnace who, in regions like Texas and Tennessee, maintained their fidelity through terrible trials—we of the North felt for them, and profoundly we honor them. Yet passionate sympathy, with resentments so close as to be almost domestic in their bitterness, would hardly in the present juncture tend to discreet legislation. Were the Unionists and Secessionists but as Guelphs and Ghibellines?[6] If not, then far be it from a great nation now to act in the spirit that animated a triumphant town-faction in the Middle Ages. But crowding thoughts must at last be checked; and, in times like the present, one who desires to be impartially just in the expression of his views, moves as among sword-points presented on every side.

Let us pray that the terrible historic tragedy of our time may not have been enacted without instructing our whole beloved country through terror and pity; and may fulfillment verify in the end those expectations which kindle the bards of Progress and Humanity.

EPILOGUE from "CLAREL"
[1876]

If Luther's day expand to Darwin's year,
Shall that exclude the hope — foreclose the fear?

Unmoved by all the claims our times avow,
The ancient Sphinx still keeps the porch of shade;
And comes Despair, whom not her calm may cow,
And coldly on that adamantine brow
Scrawls undeterred his bitter pasquinade.

---

[5] That is, Confederate for Union victories.

[6] The struggle between these Italian factions throughout the Middle Ages constitutes much of the history of Italy and neighboring countries for over 500 years.

But Faith (who from the scrawl indignant
turns)   6
With blood warm oozing from her wounded
trust,
Inscribes even on her shards of broken
urns
The sign o' the cross—*the spirit above the
dust!*

    Yea, ape and angel, strife and old
debate—
The harps of heaven and dreary gongs of
hell;   10
Science the feud can only aggravate—
No umpire she betwixt the chimes and
knell:
The running battle of the star and clod
Shall run forever—if there be no God.

    Degrees we know, unknown in days be-
fore;   15
The light is greater, hence the shadow
more;
And tantalized and apprehensive Man
Appealing—Wherefore ripen us to pain?
Seems there the spokesman of dumb Na-
ture's train.

    But through such strange illusions have
they passed   20
Who in life's pilgrimage have baffled
striven—
Even death may prove unreal at the last,
And stoics be astounded into heaven.

    Then keep thy heart, though yet but
ill-resigned—
Clarel, thy heart, the issues there but
mind;   25
That like the crocus budding through the
snow—
That like a swimmer rising from the
deep—
That like a burning secret which doth go
Even from the bosom that would hoard and
keep;
Emerge thou mayst from the last whelming
sea,   30
And prove that death but routs life into
victory.

JOHN MARR
[1888]

Since as in night's deck-watch ye show,
Why, lads, so silent here to me,
Your watchmate of times long ago?

Once, for all the darkling sea,
You your voices raised how clearly,   5
Striking in when tempest sung;
Hoisting up the storm-sail cheerly,
Life is storm—let storm! you rung.
Taking things as fated merely,
Child-like though the world ye spanned;10
Nor holding unto life too dearly,
Ye who held your lives in hand—
Skimmers, who on oceans four
Petrels were, and larks ashore.

O, not from memory lightly flung,   15
Forgot, like strains no more availing,
The heart to music haughtier strung;
Nay, frequent near me, never staling,
Whose good feeling kept ye young.
Like tides that enter creek or stream,   20
Ye come, ye visit me, or seem
Swimming out from seas of faces,
Alien myriads memory traces,
To enfold me in a dream!

I yearn as ye. But rafts that strain,   25
Parted, shall they lock again?
Twined we were, entwined, then riven,
Ever to new embracements driven,
Shifting gulf-weed of the main!
And how if one here shift no more,   30
Lodged by the flinging surge ashore?
Nor less, as now, in eve's decline,
Your shadowy fellowship is mine.
Ye float around me, form and feature:—
Tattooings, ear-rings, love-locks curled;35
Barbarians of man's simpler nature,
Unworldly servers of the world.
Yea, present all, and dear to me,
Though shades, or scouring China's sea.

Whither, whither, merchant-sailors,   40
Whitherward now in roaring gales?
Competing still, ye huntsman-whalers,

In leviathan's wake what boat prevails?
And man-of-war's men, whereaway?
If now no dinned drum beat to quarters 45
On the wilds of midnight waters—
Foemen looming through the spray;
Do yet your gangway lanterns, streaming,
Vainly strive to pierce below,
When, tilted from the slant plank gleam-
    ing,   50
A brother you see to darkness go?

But, gunmates lashed in shotted canvas,
If where long watch-below ye keep,
Never the shrill *"All hands up hammocks!"*
Breaks the spell that charms your sleep, 55
And summoning trumps might vainly call,
And booming guns implore—
A beat, a heart-beat musters all,
One heart-beat at heart-core.
It musters. But to clasp, retain;   60
To see you at the halyards main—
To hear your chorus once again!

FAR OFF-SHORE
[1888]

Look, the raft, a signal flying,
  Thin—a shred;
None upon the lashed spars lying,
  Quick or dead.

Cries the sea-fowl, hovering over,
  "Crew, the crew?"
And the billow, reckless rover,
  Sweeps anew!

TO NED
[1888]

Where is the world we roved, Ned Bunn?
  Hollows thereof lay rich in shade
By voyagers old inviolate thrown
  Ere Paul Pry cruised with Pelf and
    Trade.
To us old lads some thoughts come home 5
Who roamed a world young lads no more
  shall roam.

Nor less the satiate year impends
  When, wearying of routine-resorts,

The pleasure-hunter shall break loose,
  Ned, for our Pantheistic ports:—   10
Marquesas and glenned isles that be
Authentic Edens in a Pagan sea.

The charm of scenes untried shall lure,
  And, Ned, a legend urge the flight—
The Typee-truants under stars   15
  Unknown to Shakespeare's *Midsummer-
    Night;*
And man, if lost to Saturn's Age,[1]
Yet feeling life no Syrian pilgrimage.[2]

But, tell, shall he, the tourist, find
  Our isles the same in violet-glow   20
Enamoring us what years and years—
  Ah, Ned, what years and years ago!
Well, Adam advances, smart in pace,
But scarce by violets that advance you
  trace.

But we, in anchor-watches calm,   25
  The Indian Psyche's languor won,
And, musing, breathed primeval balm
  From Edens ere yet overrun;
Marvelling mild if mortal twice,
Here and hereafter, touch a Paradise. 30

THE ENVIABLE ISLES
[1888]

Through storms you reach them and from
  storms are free.
  Afar descried, the foremost drear in hue,
But, nearer, green; and, on the marge, the
  sea
  Makes thunder low and mist of rain-
  bowed dew.

But, inland, where the sleep that folds the
  hills   5
A dreamier sleep, the trance of God, in-
  stills—
  On uplands hazed, in wandering airs
  aswoon,
Slow-swaying palms salute love's cypress
  tree

---

[1] Golden Age.
[2] Desert pilgrimage.

Adown in vale where pebbly runlets
croon
A song to lull all sorrow and all glee.   10

Sweet-fern and moss in many a glade are
here,
Where, strown in flocks, what cheek-
flushed myriads lie
Dimpling in dream—unconscious slumberers mere,
While billows endless round the beaches
die.

THE RAVAGED VILLA
[1891]

In shards the sylvan vases lie,
  Their links of dance undone,
And brambles wither by thy brim,
  Choked fountain of the sun!
The spider in the laurel spins,   5
  The weed exiles the flower;
And, flung to kiln, Apollo's bust
  Makes lime for Mammon's tower.

MONODY
[1891]

To have known him, to have loved him
  After loneness long;
And then to be estranged in life,
  And neither in the wrong;
And now for death to set his seal—   5
  Ease me, a little ease, my song!

By wintry hills his hermit-mound
  The sheeted snow-drifts drape,
And houseless there the snow-bird flits
  Beneath the fir-trees' crape: 10
Glazed now with ice the cloistral vine
  That hid the shyest grape.

THE ENTHUSIAST
[1891]
*"Though He slay me yet will I
trust in Him."*

Shall hearts that beat no base retreat
  In youth's magnanimous years—
Ignoble hold it, if discreet

When interest tames to fears;
Shall spirits that worship light   5
  Perfidious deem its sacred glow,
  Recant, and trudge where worldlings go,
Conform and own them right?

Shall Time with creeping influence cold
  Unnerve and cow? the heart   10
Pine for the heartless ones enrolled
  With palterers of the mart?
Shall faith abjure her skies,
  Or pale probation blench her down
  To shrink from Truth so still, so lone   15
Mid loud gregarious lies?

Each burning boat in Caesar's rear,
  Flames—No return through me!
So put the torch to ties though dear,
  If ties but tempters be.   20
Nor cringe if come the night:
  Walk through the cloud to meet the pall,
  Though light forsake thee, never fall
From fealty to light.

BILLY BUDD, FORETOPMAN

WHAT BEFELL HIM IN THE YEAR OF
THE GREAT MUTINY

[1924]

Dedicated
to
JACK CHASE
Englishman
Wherever That Great Heart May Now Be
Here on Earth or Harboured in Paradise
Captain of the Maintop
in the Year 1843
in the U. S. Frigate
"United States"

PREFACE

The year 1797, the year of this narrative, belongs to a period which, as every
thinker now feels, involved a crisis for
Christendom not exceeded in its undetermined momentousness at the time by any
other era whereof there is record. The

opening proposition made by the Spirit of that Age involved rectification of the Old World's hereditary wrongs. In France, to some extent, this was bloodily effected. But what then? Straightway the Revolution itself became a wrongdoer, one more oppressive than the kings. Under Napoleon it enthroned upstart kings, and initiated that prolonged agony of continual war whose final throe was Waterloo. During those years not the wisest could have foreseen that the outcome of all would be what to some thinkers apparently it has since turned out to be—a political advance along nearly the whole line for Europeans.

Now, as elsewhere hinted, it was something caught from the Revolutionary Spirit that at Spithead [1] emboldened the man-of-war's men to rise against real abuses, long-standing ones, and afterwards at the Nore [2] to make inordinate and aggressive demands —successful resistance to which was confirmed only when the ringleaders were hung for an admonitory spectacle to the anchored fleet. Yet in a way analogous to the operation of the Revolution at large— the Great Mutiny, though by Englishmen naturally deemed monstrous at the time, doubtless gave the first latent prompting to most important reforms in the British navy.

CHAPTER I

(An Inside Narrative)

IN THE TIME before steamships, or then more frequently than now, a stroller along the docks of any considerable seaport would occasionally have his attention arrested by a group of bronzed marines, man-of-war's men or merchant-sailors in holiday attire ashore on liberty. In certain instances they would flank, or, like a body-guard, quite surround some superior figure of their own class, moving along with them like Aldebaran among the lesser lights of his constellation. That signal object was the "Handsome Sailor" of the less prosaic time, alike of the military and merchant

navies. With no perceptible trace of the vainglorious about him, rather with the off-hand unaffectedness of natural regality, he seemed to accept the spontaneous homage of his shipmates. A somewhat remarkable instance recurs to me. In Liverpool, now half a century ago I saw under the shadow of the great dingy street-wall of Prince's Dock (an obstruction long since removed) a common sailor, so intensely black that he must needs have been a native African of the unadulterated blood of Ham. A symmetric figure, much above the average in height. The two ends of a gay silk handkerchief thrown loose about the neck danced upon the displayed ebony of his chest; in his ears were big hoops of gold, and a Scotch Highland bonnet with a tartan band set off his shapely head.

It was a hot noon in July, and his face, lustrous with perspiration, beamed with barbaric good-humour. In jovial sallies right and left, his white teeth flashing into view, he rollicked along, the centre of a company of his shipmates. These were made up of such an assortment of tribes and complexions as would have well fitted them to be marched up by Anacharsis Cloots [3] before the bar of the first French Assembly as Representatives of the Human Race. At each spontaneous tribute rendered by the wayfarers to this black pagod of a fellow—the tribute of a pause and stare, and less frequent an exclamation—the motley retinue showed that they took that sort of pride in the evoker of it which the Assyrian priests doubtless showed for their grand sculptured Bull when the faithful prostrated themselves. To return—

If in some cases a bit of a nautical

---

[1] Roadstead in the English Channel between Portsmouth and the Isle of Wight.

[2] Sandbank at the mouth of the Thames, scene of the famous mutiny of 1797.

[3] Jean Baptiste du Val, Baron von Cloots (1755-94), for his "Declaration of the Rights of Man" before the French Assembly called "the orator of the human race."

Murat [4] in setting forth his person ashore, the Handsome Sailor of the period in question evinced nothing of the dandified Billy-be-Damn—an amusing character all but extinct now, but occasionally to be encountered, and in a form yet more amusing than the original, at the tiller of the boats on the tempestuous Erie Canal or, more likely, vapouring in the groggeries along the towpath. Invariably a proficient in his perilous calling, he was also more or less of a mighty boxer or wrestler. It was strength and beauty. Tales of his prowess were recited. Ashore he was the champion; afloat the spokesman; on every suitable occasion always foremost. Close-reefing topsails in a gale, there he was—astride the weather yard-arm-end, foot in "stirrup," both hands tugging at the "ear-ring" as at a bridle, in very much the attitude of the young Alexander curbing the fiery Bucephalus. A superb figure, tossed up as by the horns of Taurus against the thunderous sky, cheerily hallooing to the strenuous file along the spar.

The moral nature was seldom out of keeping with the physical make. Indeed, except as toned by the former, the comeliness and power, always attractive in masculine perfection, hardly could have drawn the sort of homage the Handsome Sailor, in some examples, received from his less gifted associates.

Such a cynosure, at least in aspect, and something such too in nature, though with important variations made apparent as the story proceeds, was welkin-eyed Billy Budd, or Baby Budd—as more familiarly, under circumstances hereafter to be given, he at last came to be called—aged twenty-one, a foretopman of the fleet towards the close of the last decade of the eighteenth century. It was not very long prior to the time of the narration that follows, that he had entered the King's Service, having been impressed on the Narrow Seas from a homeward-bound English merchantman into a seventy-four outward-bound, H.M.S. *Indomitable*; which ship, as was not unusual in those hurried days, had been obliged to put to sea short of her proper complement of men. Plump upon Billy at first sight in the gangway the boarding officer, Lieutenant Ratcliffe, pounced, even before the merchantman's crew formally was mustered on the quarter-deck for his deliberate inspection. And him only he elected. For whether it was because the other men when ranged before him showed to ill advantage after Billy, or whether he had some scruples in view of the merchantman being rather short-handed; however it might be, the officer contented himself with his first spontaneous choice. To the surprise of the ship's company, though much to the Lieutenant's satisfaction, Billy made no demur. But indeed any demur would have been as idle as the protest of a goldfinch popped into a cage.

Noting this uncomplaining acquiescence, all but cheerful one might say, the shipmates turned a surprised glance of silent reproach at the sailor. The shipmaster was one of those worthy mortals found in every vocation,—even the humbler ones,—the sort of person whom everybody agrees in calling "a respectable man." And—nor so strange to report as it may appear to be—though a ploughman of the troubled waters, life-long contending with the intractable elements, there was nothing this honest soul at heart loved better than simple peace and quiet. For the rest, he was fifty or thereabouts, a little inclined to corpulence, a prepossessing face, unwhiskered, and of an agreeable colour—a rather full face, humanely intelligent in expression. On a fair day with a fair wind and all going well, a certain musical chime in his voice seemed to be the veritable unobstructed outcome of the innermost man. He had much prudence, much conscientiousness, and there were occasions when these virtues were the cause of overmuch disquietude in him. On a passage, so long as his craft was in any proximity to land, there was no sleep for Captain Graveling.

---

[4] Joachim Murat (1767-1815), one of Napoleon's leading generals, later king of Naples.

He took to heart those serious responsibilities not so heavily borne by some shipmasters.

Now, while Billy Budd was down in the forecastle, getting his kit together, the *Indomitable's* Lieutenant—burly and bluff, nowise disconcerted by Captain Graveling's omitting to proffer the customary hospitalities on an occasion so unwelcome to him; an omission simply caused by preoccupation of thought—unceremoniously invited himself into the cabin, and also to a flask from the spirit locker, a receptacle which his experienced eye instantly discovered. In fact, he was one of those sea-dogs in whom all the hardship and peril of naval life in the great prolonged wars of his time never impaired the natural instinct for sensuous enjoyment. His duty he always faithfully did; but duty is sometimes a dry obligation, and he was for irrigating its aridity whensoever possible with a fertilizing decoction of strong waters. For the cabin's proprietor there was nothing left but to play the part of the enforced host with whatever grace and alacrity were practicable. As necessary adjuncts to the flask he silently placed tumbler and water-jug before the irrepressible guest. But excusing himself from partaking just then, he dismally watched the unembarrassed officer deliberately diluting his grog a little, then tossing it off in three swallows, pushing the empty tumbler away, yet not so far as to be beyond easy reach, at the same time settling himself in his seat and smacking his lips with high satisfaction, looking straight at the host.

These proceedings over, the Master broke the silence; and there lurked a rueful reproach in the tone of his voice: "Lieutenant, you are going to take my best man from me, the jewel of 'em."

"Yes, I know," rejoined the other, immediately drawing back the tumbler preliminary to a replenishing. "Yes, I know. Sorry."

"Beg pardon, but you don't understand, Lieutenant. See here now. Before I shipped that young fellow, my forecastle was a rat-pit of quarrels. It was black times, I tell you, aboard the *'Rights'* here. I was worried to that degree my pipe had no comfort for me. But Billy came; and it was like a Catholic priest striking peace in an Irish shindy. Not that he preached to them or said or did anything in particular; but a virtue went out of him, sugaring the sour ones. They took to him like hornets to treacle; all but the bluffer of the gang, the big shaggy chap with the fire-red whiskers. He, indeed, out of envy perhaps of the newcomer, and thinking such a "sweet and pleasant fellow," as he mockingly designated him to the others, could hardly have the spirit of a game-cock, must needs bestir himself in trying to get up an ugly row with him. Billy forbore with him and reasoned with him in a pleasant way—he is something like myself, Lieutenant, to whom aught like a quarrel is hateful—but nothing served. So, in the second dog-watch one day the Red-Whiskers, in the presence of the others, under pretence of showing Billy just whence a sirloin steak was cut—for the fellow had once been a butcher—insultingly gave him a dig under the ribs. Quick as lightning Billy let fly his arm. I dare say he never meant to do quite as much as he did, but anyhow he gave the burly fool a terrible drubbing. It took about half a minute, I should think. And, Lord bless you, the lubber was astonished at the celerity. And will you believe it, Lieutenant, the Red-Whiskers now really loves Billy—loves him, or is the biggest hypocrite that ever I heard of. But they all love him. Some of 'em do his washing, darn old trousers for him; the carpenter is at odd times making a pretty little chest of drawers for him. Anybody will do anything for Billy Budd; and it's the happy family here. Now, Lieutenant, if that young fellow goes—I know how it will be aboard the *'Rights.'* Not again very soon shall I, coming up from dinner, lean over the capstan smoking a quiet pipe—no, not very soon again, I think. Ay, Lieutenant, you are going to take away the jewel of 'em; you are going to take away my peacemaker." And with that the good soul had really some ado in checking a rising sob.

"Well," answered the Lieutenant, who had listened with amused interest to all this, and now waxing merry with his tipple, "Well, blessed are the peacemakers, especially the fighting peacemakers! And such are the seventy-four beauties, some of which you see poking their noses out of the portholes of yonder warship lying-to there for me," pointing through the cabin window at the *Indomitable*. "But courage! don't look so down-hearted, man. Why, I pledge you in advance the royal approbation. Rest assured that His Majesty will be delighted to know that in a time when his hard-tack is not sought for by sailors with such avidity as should be; a time also when some shipmasters privily resent the borrowing from them of a tar or two for the service; His Majesty, I say, will be delighted to learn that *one* shipmaster, at least, cheerfully surrenders to the King the flower of his flock: a sailor who with equal loyalty makes no dissent.—But where's my beauty? Ah," looking through the cabin's open door. "Here he comes; and, by jove —lugging along his chest—Apollo with his portmanteau! My man," stepping out to him, "you can't take that big box on board a warship. The boxes there are mostly shot-boxes. Put up your duds in a bag, lad. Boot and saddle for the cavalryman, bag and hammock for the man-of-war's man."

The transfer from chest to bag was made. And, after seeing his man into the cutter, and then following him down, the Lieutenant pushed off from the *Rights-of-Man*. That was the merchant ship's name; though by her master and crew abbreviated in sailor fashion into the *"Rights."* The hard-headed Dundee owner was a staunch admirer of Thomas Paine, whose book in rejoinder to Burke's arraignment of the French Revolution had then been published for some time and had gone everywhere. In christening his vessel after the title of Paine's volume,[5] the man of Dundee was

something like his contemporary shipowner, Stephen Girard of Philadelphia, whose sympathies alike with his native land and its liberal philosophies he evinced by naming his ships after Voltaire, Diderot, and so forth.

But now, when the boat swept under the merchantman's stern, and officer and oarsmen were noting,—some bitterly and others with a grin,—the name emblazoned there; just then it was that the new recruit jumped up from the bow where the coxswain had directed him to sit, waving his hat to his silent shipmates sorrowfully looking over at him from the taffrail, and bade the lads a genial good-bye. Then making a salutation as to the ship herself, "And good-bye to you too, old *Rights-of-Man!*"

"Down, Sir," roared the Lieutenant, instantly assuming all the rigour of his rank, though with difficulty repressing a smile.

To be sure, Billy's action was a terrible breach of naval decorum. But in that decorum he had never been instructed; in consideration of which the Lieutenant would hardly have been so energetic in reproof but for the concluding farewell to the ship. This he rather took as meant to convey a covert sally on the new recruit's part—a sly slur at impressment in general, and that of himself in especial. And yet, more likely, if satire it was in effect, it was hardly so by intention, for Billy (though happily endowed with the gaiety of high health, youth and a free heart) was yet by no means of a satirical turn. The will to it and the sinister dexterity were alike wanting. To deal in double meaning and insinuations of any sort was quite foreign to his nature.

As to his enforced enlistment—that he seemed to take pretty much as he was wont to take any vicissitude of weather. Like the animals, though no philosopher, he was, without knowing it, practically a fatalist. And, it may be, that he rather liked this adventurous turn in his affairs which promised an opening into novel scenes and martial excitements.

Aboard the *Indomitable* our merchant-sailor was forthwith rated as an able seaman, and assigned to the starboard watch of the foretop. He was soon at home in the service, not at all disliked for his unpretentious good looks and his rather genial happy-go-lucky air. No merrier man in his mess; in marked contrast to certain other individuals included like himself among the impressed portions of the ship's company; for these when not actively employed were sometimes—and more particularly in the last dog-watch, when the drawing near of twilight induced revery—apt to fall into a saddish mood which in some partook of sullenness. But they were not so young as our foretopman, and no few of them must have known a hearth of some sort, others may have had wives and children left, too probably, in uncertain circumstances, and hardly any but must have acknowledged kith and kin; while for Billy, as will shortly be seen, his entire family was practically invested in himself.

Chapter II

Though our new-made foretopman was well received in the top and on the gundecks, hardly here was he that cynosure he had previously been among those minor ship's companies of the merchant marine, with which companies only had he hitherto consorted.

He was young; and despite his all but fully developed frame, in aspect looked even younger than he really was. This was owing to a lingering adolescent expression in the as yet smooth face, all but feminine in purity of natural complexion, but where, thanks to his seagoing, the lily was quite suppressed and the rose had some ado visibly to flush through the tan.

To one essentially such a novice in the complexities of factitious life, the abrupt transition from his former and simpler sphere to the ampler and more knowing world of a great war-ship—this might well

have abashed him had there been any conceit or vanity in his composition. Among her miscellaneous multitude, the *Indomitable* mustered several individuals who, however inferior in grade, were of no common natural stamp: sailors more signally susceptive of that air which continuous martial discipline and repeated presence in battle can in some degree impart even to the average man. As the "Handsome Sailor" Billy Budd's position aboard the seventy-four was something analogous to that of a rustic beauty transplanted from the provinces and brought into competition with the high-born dames of the court. But this change of circumstances he scarce noted. As little did he observe that something about him provoked an ambiguous smile in one or two harder faces among the blue-jackets. Nor less unaware was he of the peculiar favourable effect his person and demeanour had upon the more intelligent gentlemen of the quarter-deck. Nor could this well have been otherwise. Cast in a mould peculiar to the finest physical examples of those Englishmen in whom the Saxon strain would seem not at all to partake of any Norman or other admixture, he showed in face that humane look of reposeful good nature which the Greek sculptor in some instances gave to his heroic strong man, Hercules. But this again was subtly modified by another and pervasive quality. The ear, small and shapely, the arch of the foot, the curve in mouth and nostril, even the indurated hand dyed to the orange-tawny of the toucan's bill, a hand telling of the halyards and tar-buckets; but, above all, something in the mobile expression, and every chance attitude and movement, something suggestive of a mother eminently favoured by Love and the Graces; all this strangely indicated a lineage in direct contradiction to his lot. The mysteriousness here became less mysterious through a matter of fact elicited when Billy at the capstan was being formally mustered into the service. Asked by the officer, a small, brisk little gentleman as it chanced, among other questions, his place of birth, he replied, "Please, Sir, I don't know."

"Don't know where you were born? Who was your father?"

"God knows, Sir."

Struck by the straightforward simplicity of these replies, the officer next asked, "Do you know anything about your beginning?"

"No, Sir. But I have heard that I was found in a pretty silk-lined basket hanging one morning from the knocker of a good man's door in Bristol."

" 'Found,' say you? Well," throwing back his head and looking up and down the new recruit; "well, it turns out to have been a pretty good find. Hope they'll find some more like you, my man; the fleet sadly needs them."

Yes, Billy Budd was a foundling, a presumable by-blow, and, evidently, no ignoble one. Noble descent was as evident in him as in a blood horse.

For the rest, with little or no sharpness of faculty or any trace of the wisdom of the serpent, nor yet quite a dove, he possessed that kind and degree of intelligence which goes along with the unconventional rectitude of a sound human creature—one to whom not as yet had been proffered the questionable apple of knowledge. He was illiterate. He could not read, but he could sing, and like the illiterate nightingale was sometimes the composer of his own song.

Of self-consciousness he seemed to have little or none, or about as much as we may reasonably impute to a dog of St. Bernard's breed.

Habitually being with the elements, and knowing little more of the land than as a beach, or, rather, that portion of the terraqueous globe providentially set apart for dance-houses, doxies and tapsters, in short what sailors call a "fiddlers' green," his simple nature remained unsophisticated by those moral obliquities which are not in every case incomparable with that manufacturable thing known as respectability. But are sailors, frequenters of fiddlers' greens, without vices? No; but less often

than with landsmen do their vices, so called, partake of crookedness of heart, seeming less to proceed from viciousness than from exuberance of vitality after long restraint, frank manifestations in accordance with natural law. By his original constitution aided by the coöperating influences of his lot, Billy in many respects was little more than a sort of upright barbarian, much such perhaps as Adam presumably might have been ere the urbane Serpent wriggled himself into his company.

And here be it submitted that, apparently going to corroborate the doctrine of man's fall—a doctrine now popularly ignored—it is observable that where certain virtues pristine and unadulterate peculiarly characterize anybody in the external uniform of civilization, they will upon scrutiny seem not to be derived from custom or convention but rather to be out of keeping with these, as if indeed exceptionally transmitted from a period prior to Cain's City and citified man. The character marked by such qualities has to an unvitiated taste an untampered-with flavour like that of berries, while the man thoroughly civilized, even in a fair specimen of the breed, has to the same moral palate a questionable smack as of a compounded wine. To any stray inheritor of these primitive qualities found, like Caspar Hauser,[6] wandering dazed in any Christian capital of our time, the poet's famous invocation, near two thousand years ago, of the good rustic out of his latitude in the Rome of the Cæsars, still appropriately holds:—

"Faithful in word and thought,
What has Thee, Fabian, to the city
brought?" [7]

Though our Handsome Sailor had as

---

[6] A youth found in Nuremberg in 1828, dressed as a peasant but seemingly wholly unaccustomed to human society. He was befriended by Earl Stanhope, and later mysteriously assassinated. His story is the subject of a novel by the German writer, Jakob Wassermann, and of other works.

[7] Martial. bk. IV. 5.

much of masculine beauty as one can expect anywhere to see; nevertheless, like the beautiful woman in one of Hawthorne's minor tales,[8] there was just one thing amiss in him. No visible blemish, indeed, as with the lady; no, but an occasional liability to a vocal defect. Though in the hour of elemental uproar or peril, he was everything that a sailor should be, yet under sudden provocation of strong heart-feeling his voice, otherwise singularly musical, as if expressive of the harmony within, was apt to develop an organic hesitancy,—in fact more or less of a stutter or even worse. In this particular Billy was a striking instance that the arch interpreter, the envious marplot of Eden, still has more or less to do with every human consignment to this planet of earth. In every case, one way or another, he is sure to slip in his little card, as much as to remind us—I too have a hand here.

The avowal of such an imperfection in the Handsome Sailor should be evidence not alone that he is not presented as a conventional hero, but also that the story in which he is the main figure is no romance.

CHAPTER III

At the time of Billy Budd's arbitrary enlistment into the *Indomitable* that ship was on her way to join the Mediterranean fleet. No long time elapsed before the junction was effected. As one of that fleet the seventy-four participated in its movements: though at times on account of her superior sailing qualities, in the absence of frigates, despatched on separate duty as a scout—and at times on less temporary service. But with all this the story has little concernment, restricted as it is to the inner life of one particular ship and the career of an individual sailor.

It was the summer of 1797. In April of that year had occurred the commotion at Spithead followed in May by a second and yet more serious outbreak in the fleet at the Nore. The latter is known, and without

exaggeration in the epithet, as the Great Mutiny. It was indeed a demonstration more menacing to England than the contemporary manifestoes and conquering and proselyting armies of the French Directory.

To the Empire, the Nore Mutiny was what a strike in the fire-brigade would be to London threatened by general arson. In a crisis when the Kingdom might well have anticipated the famous signal that some years later published along the naval line of battle what it was that upon occasion England expected of Englishmen; *that* was the time when at the mast-heads of the three-deckers and seventy-fours moored in our own roadstead—a fleet, the right arm of a Power then all but the sole free conservative one of the Old World, the blue-jackets, to be numbered by thousands, ran up with hurras the British colours with the union and cross wiped out; by that cancellation transmuting the flag of founded law and freedom defined, into the enemy's red meteor of unbridled and unbounded revolt. Reasonable discontent growing out of practical grievances in the fleet had been ignited into irrational combustion as by live cinders blown across the Channel from France in flames.

The event converted into irony for a time those spirited strains of Dibdin [9]—as a song-writer no mean auxiliary to the English Government—at this European conjuncture, strains celebrating, among other things, the patriotic devotion of the British tar:

"And as for my life, 'tis the King's!"

Such an episode in the Island's grand naval story her naval historians naturally abridge; one of them (G. P. R. James [10]) candidly acknowledging that fain would

---

[8] "The Birthmark."

[9] Charles Dibdin (1745-1814), writer of plays and sea-songs.

[10] Historical novelist and historian (1799-1860).

he pass it over did not "impartiality forbid fastidiousness." And yet his mention is less a narration than a reference, having to do hardly at all with details. Nor are these readily to be found in the libraries. Like some other events in every age befalling states everywhere, including America, the Great Mutiny was of such character that national pride along with views of policy would fain shade it off into the historical background. Such events cannot be ignored, but there is a considerate way of historically treating them. If a well-constituted individual refrains from blazoning aught amiss or calamitous in his family, a nation in the like circumstance may without reproach be equally discreet.

Though after parleyings between Government and the ring-leaders, and concessions by the former as to some glaring abuses, the first uprising—that at Spithead —with difficulty was put down, or matters for a time pacified; yet at the Nore the unforeseen renewal of insurrection on a yet larger scale, and emphasized in the conferences that ensued by demands deemed by the authorities not only inadmissible but aggressively insolent, indicated, if the red flag did not sufficiently do so, what was the spirit animating the men. Final suppression, however, there was, but only made possible perhaps by the unswerving loyalty of the marine corps, and a voluntary resumption of loyalty among influential sections of the crews. To some extent the Nore Mutiny may be regarded as analogous to the distempering *irruption* of contagious fever in a frame constitutionally sound, and which anon throws it off.

At all events, of these thousands of mutineers were some of the tars who not so very long afterwards—whether wholly prompted thereto by patriotism, or pugnacious instinct, or by both,—helped to win a coronet for Nelson at the Nile,[11] and the naval crown of crowns for him at Trafalgar. To the mutineers those battles, and especially Trafalgar, were a plenary absolution; and a grand one; for all that goes to make up scenic naval display is heroic

magnificence in arms. Those battles, especially Trafalgar, stand unmatched in human annals.

Chapter IV

Concerning
"The greatest sailor since the world began."
—Tennyson.

In this matter of writing, resolve as one may to keep to the main road, some by-paths have an enticement not readily to be withstood. Beckoned by the genius of Nelson, I am going to err into such a by-path. If the reader will keep me company I shall be glad. At the least we can promise ourselves that pleasure which is wickedly said to be in sinning, for a literary sin the divergence will be.

Very likely it is no new remark that the inventions of our time have at last brought about a change in sea warfare in degree corresponding to the revolution in all warfare effected by the original introduction from China into Europe of gunpowder. The first European firearm, a clumsy contrivance, was, as is well known, scouted by no few of the knights as a base implement, good enough peradventure for weavers too craven to stand up crossing steel with steel in frank fight. But as ashore knightly valour, though shorn of its blazonry, did not cease with the knights, neither on the seas, though nowadays in encounters there a certain kind of displayed gallantry be fallen out of date as hardly applicable under changed circumstances, did the nobler qualities of such naval magnates as Don John of Austria, Doria, Van Tromp, Jean Bart, the long line of British admirals and the American Decaturs of 1812 be-

---

[11] Horatio Nelson (1758-1805), leading British naval hero. He defeated the French fleet at Aboukir Bay, Aug. 1798, and was for that feat created Baron Nelson of the Nile; but his greatest victory was that over the allied fleets of France and Spain off Trafalgar in 1805, in which he was wounded and died on his own quarter-deck

come obsolete with their wooden walls.[12]

Nevertheless, to anybody who can hold the Present at its worth without being inappreciative of the Past, it may be forgiven, if to such an one the solitary old hulk at Portsmouth, Nelson's *Victory,* seems to float there, not alone as the decaying monument of a fame incorruptible, but also as a poetic reproach, softened by its picturesqueness, to the *Monitors* and yet mightier hulls of the European ironsides. And this not altogether because such craft are unsightly, unavoidably lacking the symmetry and grand lines of the old battleships, but equally for other reasons.

There are some, perhaps, who while not altogether inaccessible to that poetic reproach just alluded to, may yet on behalf of the new order be disposed to parry it; and this to the extent of iconoclasm, if need be. For example, prompted by the sight of the star inserted in the *Victory's* deck designating the spot where the Great Sailor fell, these martial utilitarians may suggest considerations implying that Nelson's ornate publication of his person in battle was not only unnecessary, but not military, nay, savoured of foolhardiness and vanity. They may add, too, that at Trafalgar it was in effect nothing less than a challenge to death: and death came; and that but for his bravado the victorious admiral might possibly have survived the battle, and so, instead of having his sagacious dying injunction overruled by his immediate successor in command, he himself when the contest was decided might have brought his shattered fleet to anchor, a proceeding which might have averted the deplorable loss of life by shipwreck in the elemental tempest that followed the martial one.

Well, should we set aside the more disputable point whether for various reasons it was possible to anchor the fleet, then plausibly enough the Benthamites[13] of war may urge the above.

But it *might have been* is but boggy ground to build on. And certainly in foresight as to the larger issue of an encounter, and anxious preparation for it—buoying the deadly way and mapping it out, as at Copenhagen[14]—few commanders have been so painstakingly circumspect as this reckless declarer of his person in fight.

Personal prudence, even when dictated by quite other than selfish considerations, is surely no special virtue in a military man; while an excessive love of glory, exercising to the uttermost a heartfelt sense of duty, is the first. If the name of *Wellington* is not so much a trumpet to the blood as the simpler name of *Nelson,* the reason for this may be inferred from the above. Alfred in his funeral ode on the victor of Waterloo ventures not to call him the greatest soldier of all time, though in the same ode he invokes Nelson as "the greatest sailor since the world began."[15]

At Trafalgar, Nelson, on the brink of opening the fight, sat down and wrote his last brief will and testament. If under the presentiment of the most magnificent of all victories, to be crowned by his own glorious death, a sort of priestly motive led him to dress his person in the jewelled vouchers of his own shining deeds; if thus

---

[12] John of Austria (1547-78), statesman and naval commander; Andrea Doria (1468?-1560), Genoese admiral; Maarten H. Tromp, (1597-1653), Dutch admiral; Jean Bart (1651?-1702), French admiral and naval hero; Stephen Decatur (1779-1820), American naval commander in the wars with the Algerine pirates and the War of 1812.

[13] Followers of Jeremy Bentham (1748-1832), famous British jurist and philosopher; chief advocate of utilitarianism.

[14] Reference to the naval battle of Copenhagen, 1801, in which Nelson was second in command to Sir Hyde Parker.

[15] Melville is inaccurate in this reference to Alfred Tennyson's "Ode on the Death of the Duke of Wellington." Tennyson wrote:

. . . Mighty Seaman, this is he
Was great by land as thou by sea.
Thine island loves thee well, thou famous
   man,
The greatest sailor since our world began.
Now, to the roll of muffled drums,
To thee the greatest soldier comes; . . .

to have adorned himself for the altar and the sacrifice were indeed vainglory, then affectation and fustian is each truly heroic line in the great epics and dramas, since in such lines the poet but embodies in verse those exaltations of sentiment that a nature like Nelson, the opportunity being given, vitalizes into acts.

CHAPTER V

The outbreak at the Nore was put down. But not every grievance was redressed. If the contractors, for example, were no longer permitted to ply some practices peculiar to their tribe everywhere, such as providing shoddy cloth, rations not sound, or false in the measure; not the less impressment, for one thing, went on. By custom sanctioned for centuries, and judicially maintained by a Lord Chancellor as late as Mansfield,[16] that mode of manning the fleet, a mode now fallen into a sort of abeyance but never formally renounced, it was not practicable to give up in those years. Its abrogation would have crippled the indispensable fleet, one wholly under canvas, no steam-power, its innumerable sails and thousands of cannon, everything, in short, worked by muscle alone; a fleet the more insatiate in demand for men, because then multiplying its ships of all grades against contingencies present and to come of the convulsed Continent.

Discontent foreran the Two Mutinies, and more or less it lurkingly survived them. Hence it was not unreasonable to apprehend some return of trouble, sporadic or general. One instance of such apprehensions: In the same year with this story, Nelson, then Vice-Admiral Sir Horatio, being with the fleet off the Spanish coast, was directed by the Admiral in command to shift his pennant from the *Captain* to the *Theseus*; and for this reason: that the latter ship having newly arrived in the station from home where it had taken part in the Great Mutiny, danger was apprehended from the temper of the men; and it was thought that an officer like Nelson was

the one, not indeed to terrorize the crew into base subjection, but to win them by force of his mere presence back to an allegiance, if not as enthusiastic as his own, yet as true. So it was that for a time on more than one quarter-deck anxiety did exist. At sea precautionary vigilance was strained against relapse. At short notice an engagement might come on. When it did, the lieutenants assigned to batteries felt it incumbent on them in some instances to stand with drawn swords behind the men working the guns.

But on board the seventy-four in which Billy now swung his hammock, very little in the manner of the men and nothing obvious in the demeanour of the officers would have suggested to an ordinary observer that the Great Mutiny was a recent event. In their general bearing and conduct the commissioned officers of a warship naturally take their tone from the commander, that is if he has that ascendency of character that ought to be his.

Captain the Honourable Edward Fairfax Vere, to give his full title, was a bachelor of forty or thereabouts, a sailor of distinction, even in a time prolific of renowned seamen. Though allied to the higher nobility, his advancement had not been altogether owing to influences connected with that circumstance. He had seen much service, been in various engagements, always acquitting himself as an officer mindful of the welfare of his men, but never tolerating an infraction of discipline; thoroughly versed in the science of his profession, and intrepid to the verge of temerity, though never injudiciously so. For his gallantry in the West Indian waters as flag-lieutenant under Rodney[17] in that Admiral's crowning victory, over De Grasse, he was made a post-captain.

---

[16] William Murray, Earl of Mansfield (1705-1793).

[17] George Brydges Rodney (1719-1792), defeated the combined French and Spanish squadrons under the French admiral De Grasse off Martinique.

Ashore in the garb of a civilian, scarce any one would have taken him for a sailor, more especially that he never garnished unprofessional talk with nautical terms, and grave in his bearing, evinced little appreciation of mere humour. It was not out of keeping with these traits that on a passage when nothing demanded his paramount action, he was the most undemonstrative of men. Any landsman observing this gentleman not conspicuous by his stature and wearing no pronounced insignia, emerging from his retreat to the open deck, and noting the silent deference of the officers retiring to leeward, might have taken him for the King's guest, a civilian aboard the King's ship, some highly honourable discreet envoy on his way to an important post. But, in fact, this unobtrusiveness of demeanour may have proceeded from a certain unaffected modesty of manhood sometimes accompanying a resolute nature, a modesty evinced at all times not calling for pronounced action, and which shown in any rank of life suggests a virtue aristocratic in kind.

As with some others engaged in various departments of the world's more heroic activities, Captain Vere, though practical enough upon occasion, would at times betray a certain dreaminess of mood. Standing alone on the weather-side of the greater deck, one hand holding by the rigging, he would absently gaze off at the black sea. At the presentation to him then of some minor matter interrupting the current of his thoughts, he would show more or less irascibility; but instantly he would control it.

In the navy he was popularly known by the appellation—Starry Vere. How such a designation happened to fall upon one who, whatever his sturdy qualities, was without any brilliant ones, was in this wise: a favourite kinsman, Lord Denton, a free-handed fellow, had been the first to meet and congratulate him upon his return to England from the West Indian cruise; and but the day previous turning over a copy of Andrew Marvell's [18] poems

had lighted, not for the first time, however, upon the lines entitled "Appleton House," the name of one of the seats of their common ancestor, a hero in the German wars of the seventeenth century, in which poem occur the lines,

> *"This 'tis to have been from the first*
> *In a domestic heaven nursed,*
> *Under the discipline severe*
> *Of Fairfax and the starry Vere."*

And so, upon embracing his cousin fresh from Rodney's victory, wherein he had played so gallant a part, brimming over with just family pride in the sailor of their house, he exuberantly exclaimed, "Give ye joy, Ed; give ye joy, my starry Vere!" This got currency, and the novel prefix serving in familiar parlance readily to distinguish the *Indomitable's* Captain from another Vere, his senior, a distant relative, an officer of like rank in the navy, it remained permanently attached to the surname.

CHAPTER VI

In view of the part that the commander of the *Indomitable* plays in scenes shortly to follow, it may be well to fill out that sketch of him outlined in the previous chapter. Aside from his qualities as a sea-officer Captain Vere was an exceptional character. Unlike no few of England's renowned sailors, long and arduous service with signal devotion to it, had not resulted in absorbing and *salting* the entire man. He had a marked leaning towards everything intellectual. He loved books, never going to sea without a newly replenished library, compact but of the best. The isolated leisure, in some cases so wearisome, falling at intervals to commanders even during a war-cruise, never was tedious to Captain Vere. With nothing of that literary taste which less heeds the

---

[18] British poet, 1621-1678.

thing conveyed than the vehicle, his bias was towards those books to which every serious mind of superior order occupying any active post of authority in the world, naturally inclines; books treating of actual men and events, no matter of what era— history, biography and unconventional writers, who, free from cant and convention, like Montaigne, honestly, and in the spirit of common sense, philosophize upon realities.

In this love of reading he found confirmation of his own more reserved thoughts —confirmation which he had vainly sought in social converse, so that as touching most fundamental topics, there had got to be established in him some positive convictions which he forefelt would abide in him essentially unmodified so long as his intelligent part remained unimpaired. In view of the humbled position in which his lot was cast, this was well for him. His settled convictions were as a dyke against those invading waters of novel opinion, social, political, and otherwise, which carried away as in a torrent no few minds in those days, minds by nature not inferior to his own. While other members of that aristocracy to which by birth he belonged were incensed at the innovators mainly because their theories were inimical to the privileged classes, Captain Vere disinterestedly opposed them because they seemed to him incapable of embodiment in lasting institutions, but at war with the peace of the world and the good of mankind.

With minds less stored than his and less earnest, some officers of his rank, with whom at times he would necessarily consort, found him lacking in the companionable quality, a dry and bookish gentleman as they deemed. Upon any chance withdrawal from their company one would be apt to say to another something like this: "Vere is a noble fellow, Starry Vere. 'Spite the gazettes, Sir Horatio is at bottom scarce a better seaman or fighter. But between you and me now, don't you think there is a queer streak of the pedantic running

through him? Yes, like the King's yarn in a coil of navy-rope?"

Some apparent ground there was for this sort of confidential criticism; since not only did the Captain's discourse never fall into the jocosely familiar, but in illustrating any point touching the stirring personages and events of the time, he would cite some historic character or incident of antiquity with the same easy air that he would cite from the moderns. He seemed unmindful of the circumstance that to his bluff company such remote allusions, however pertinent they might really be, were altogether alien to men whose reading was mainly confined to the journals. But considerateness in such matters is not easy to natures constituted like Captain Vere's. Their honesty prescribes to them directness, sometimes far-reaching, like that of a migratory fowl that in its flight never heeds when it crosses a frontier.

CHAPTER VII

The lieutenants and other commissioned gentlemen forming Captain Vere's staff it is not necessary here to particularize nor needs it to make mention of any of the warrant-officers. But among the petty officers was one who, having much to do with the story, may as well be forthwith introduced. This portrait I essay, but shall never hit it.

This was John Claggart, the master-at-arms. But that sea-title may to landsmen seem somewhat equivocal. Originally, doubtless, that petty-officer's function was the instruction of the men in the use of arms, sword, or cutlass. But very long ago, owing to the advance in gunnery making hand-to-hand encounters less frequent— and giving to nitre and sulphur the pre-eminence over steel—that function ceased; the master-at-arms of a great war-ship becoming a sort of Chief of Police charged, among other matters, with the duty of preserving order on the populous lower gun-decks.

Claggart was a man of about five-and-thirty, somewhat spare and tall yet of no ill figure upon the whole. His hand was too small and shapely to have been accustomed to hard toil. The face was a notable one; the features, all except the chin, cleanly cut as those on a Greek medallion; yet the chin, beardless as Tecumseh's,[19] had something of the strange protuberant heaviness in its make that recalled the prints of the Rev. Dr. Titus Oates,[20] the historical deponent with the clerical drawl in the time of Charles II, and the fraud of the alleged Popish Plot. It served Claggart in his office that his eye could cast a tutoring glance. His brow was of the sort phrenologically associated with more than average intellect; silken jet curls partly clustering over it, making a foil to the pallor below, a pallor tinged with a faint shade of amber akin to the hue of time-tinted marbles of old.

This complexion singularly contrasting with the red or deeply bronzed visages of the sailors, and in part the result of his official seclusion from the sunlight, though it was not exactly displeasing, nevertheless seemed to hint of something defective or abnormal in the constitution and blood. But his general aspect and manner were so suggestive of an education and career incongruous with his naval function, that when not actively engaged in it he looked like a man of high quality, social and moral, who for reasons of his own was keeping incog. Nothing was known of his former life. It might be that he was an Englishman; and yet there lurked a bit of accent in his speech suggesting that possibly he was not such by birth, but through naturalization in early childhood. Among certain grizzled sea-gossips of the gun-decks and forecastle went a rumour perdue that the master-at-arms was a chevalier who had volunteered into the King's navy by way of compounding for some mysterious swindle whereof he had been arraigned at the King's bench. The fact that nobody could substantiate this report was, of course, nothing against its

secret currency. Such a rumour once started on the gun-decks in reference to almost any one below the rank of a commissioned officer would, during the period assigned to this narrative, have seemed not altogether wanting in credibility to the tarry old wiseacres of a man-of-war crew. And indeed a man of Claggart's accomplishments, without prior nautical experience entering the navy at mature life, as he did, and necessarily allotted at the start to the lowest grade in it; a man, too, who never made allusion to his previous life ashore; these were circumstances which in the dearth of exact knowledge as to his true antecedents opened to the invidious a vague field for unfavourable surmise.

But the sailors' dog-watch gossip concerning him derived a vague plausibility from the fact that now, for some period, the British Navy could so little afford to be squeamish in the matter of keeping up the muster-rolls, that not only were press-gangs notoriously abroad both afloat and ashore, but there was little or no secret about another matter, namely, that the London police were at liberty to capture any able-bodied suspect, and any questionable fellow at large, and summarily ship him to the dock-yard or fleet. Furthermore, even among voluntary enlistments, there were instances where the motive thereto partook neither of patriotic impulse nor yet of a random desire to experience a bit of sea-life and martial adventure. Insolvent debtors of minor grade, together with the promiscuous lame ducks of morality, found in the navy a convenient and secure refuge. Secure, because once enlisted aboard a King'sship, they were as much in sanctuary, as the transgressor of the middle ages harbouring himself under the shadow of the altar. Such sanctioned irregularities, which for obvious reasons

[19] Indian chief and leader of a confederation against the whites, 1768?-1813.
[20] Forger of the story of the plot to massacre the Protestants and burn London, in 1687 (1649-1795).

the Government would hardly think to parade at the time—and which consequently, and as affecting the least influential class of mankind, have all but dropped into oblivion—lend colour to something for the truth whereof I do not vouch, and hence have some scruple in stating; something I remember having seen in print, though the book I cannot recall; but the same thing was personally communicated to me now more than forty years ago by an old pensioner in a cocked hat, with whom I had a most interesting talk on the terrace at Greenwich, a Baltimore negro, a Trafalgar man. It was to this effect: In the case of a war-ship short of hands, whose speedy sailing was imperative, the deficient quota, in lack of any other way of making it good, would be eked out by drafts called direct from the jails. For reasons previously suggested it would not perhaps be very easy at the present day directly to prove or disprove the allegation. But allowed as a verity, how significant would it be of England's straits at the time, confronted by those wars which, like a flight of harpies, rose shrieking from the din and dust of the fallen Bastille. That era appears measurably clear to us who look back at it, and but read of it. But to the grandfathers of us greybeards, the thoughtful of them, the genius of it presented an aspect like that of Camoëns' [21] "Spirit of the Cape," an eclipsing menace, mysterious and prodigious. Not America even was exempt from apprehension. At the height of Napoleon's unexampled conquests, there were Americans who had fought at Bunker Hill, who looked forward to the possibility that the Atlantic might prove no barrier against the ultimate schemes of this portentous upstart from the revolutionary chaos, who seemed in act of fulfilling the judgment prefigured in the Apocalypse.

But the less credence was to be given to the gun-deck talk touching Claggart, seeing that no man holding his office in a man-of-war can ever hope to be popular with the crew. Besides, in derogatory comments upon any one against whom they have a grudge, or for any reason or no reason mislike, sailors are much like landsmen: they are apt to exaggerate or romance.

About as much was really known to the *Indomitable's* tars of the Master-at-arms' career before entering the service as an astronomer knows about a comet's travels prior to its first observable appearance in the sky. The verdict of the sea *quidnuncs* has been cited only by way of showing what sort of moral impression the man made upon rude uncultivated natures whose conceptions of human wickedness were necessarily of the narrowest, limited to ideas of vulgar rascality,—a thief among the swinging hammocks during a night-watch, or the man-brokers and land-sharks of the seaports.

It was no gossip, however, but fact, that though, as before hinted, Claggart upon his entrance into the navy was, as a novice, assigned to the least honourable section of a man-of-war's crew, embracing the drudges, he did not long remain there. The superior capacity he immediately evinced, his constitutional sobriety, his ingratiating deference to superiors, together with a peculiar ferreting genius manifested on a singular occasion, all this capped by a certain austere patriotism, abruptly advanced him to the position of Master-at-arms.

Of this maritime Chief of Police the ship's-corporals, so called, were the immediate subordinates, and compliant ones; and this—as is to be noted in some business departments ashore—almost to a degree inconsistent with entire moral volition. His place put various converging wires of underground influence under the Chief's control, capable when astutely worked through his understrappers of operating to the mysterious discomfort, if nothing worse, of any of the sea-commonalty.

[21] Luiz Vaz de Camões, English spelling Camoëns (1524-80), Portuguese poet.

CHAPTER VIII

Life in the foretop well agreed with Billy Budd. There, when not actually engaged on the yards yet higher aloft, the topmen, who as such had been picked out for youth and activity, constituted an aerial club, lounging at ease against the smaller stun'sails rolled up into cushions, spinning yarns like the lazy gods, and frequently amused with what was going on in the busy world of the decks below. No wonder then that a young fellow of Billy's disposition was well content in such society. Giving no cause of offence to anybody, he was always alert at a call. So in the merchant service it had been with him. But now such punctiliousness in duty was shown that his topmates would sometimes good-naturedly laugh at him for it. This heightened alacrity had its cause, namely, the impression made upon him by the first formal gangway-punishment he had ever witnessed, which befell the day following his impressment. It had been incurred by a little fellow, young, a novice, an afterguardsman absent from his assigned post when the ship was being put about, a dereliction resulting in a rather serious hitch to that manœuvre, one demanding instantaneous promptitude in letting go and making fast. When Billy saw the culprit's naked back under the scourge gridironed with red welts, and worse; when he marked the dire expression in the liberated man's face, as with his woolen shirt flung over him by the executioner, he rushed forward from the spot to bury himself in the crowd, Billy was horrified. He resolved that never through remissness would he make himself liable to such a visitation, or do or omit aught that might merit even verbal reproof. What then was his surprise and concern when ultimately he found himself getting into petty trouble occasionally about such matters as the stowage of his bag, or something amiss in his hammock, matters under the police oversight of the ship's-corporals of the lower decks, and which brought down on

him a vague threat from one of them.

So heedful in all things as he was, how could this be? He could not understand it, and it more than vexed him. When he spoke to his young topmates about it, they were either lightly incredulous, or found something comical in his unconcealed anxiety. "Is it your bag, Billy?" said one; "well, sew yourself up in it, Billy boy, and then you'll be sure to know if anybody meddles with it."

Now there was a veteran aboard who, because his years began to disqualify him for more active work, had been recently assigned duty as mainmast-man in his watch, looking to the gear belayed at the rail round about that great spar near the deck. At off-times the foretopman had picked up some acquaintance with him, and now in his trouble it occurred to him that he might be the sort of person to go to for wise council. He was an old Dansker long anglicized in the service, of few words, many wrinkles and some honourable scars. His wizened face, time-tinted and weather-stormed to the complexion of an antique parchment, was here and there peppered blue by the chance explosion of a gun-cartridge in action. He was an *Agamemnon*-man; some two years prior to the time of this story having served under Nelson, when but Sir Horatio, in that ship immortal in naval memory, and which, dismantled and in part broken up to her bare ribs, is seen a grand skeleton in Haydon's [22] etching. As one of a boarding-party from the *Agamemnon* he had received a cut slantwise along one temple and cheek, leaving a long pale scar like a streak of dawn's light falling athwart the dark visage. It was on account of that scar and the affair in which it was known that he had received it, as well as from his blue-peppered complexion, that the Dansker went among the *Indomitable's* crew by the name of "Board-her-in-the-smoke."

Now the first time that his small weazel-

---

[22] Benjamin Robert Haydon (1786-1846), British historical painter.

eyes happened to light on Billy Budd, a certain grim internal merriment set all his ancient wrinkles into antic play. Was it that his eccentric unsentimental old sapience, primitive in its kind, saw, or thought it saw, something which in contrast with the war-ship's environment looked oddly incongruous in the Handsome Sailor? But after slyly studying him at intervals, the old Merlin's equivocal merriment was modified. For now when the twain would meet, it would start in his face a quizzing sort of look, but it would be but momentary, and sometimes replaced by an expression of speculative query as to what might eventually befall a nature like that, dropped into a world not without some man-traps and against whose subtleties simple courage lacking experience and address and without any touch of defensive ugliness, is of little avail; and where such innocence as man is capable of does yet, in a moral emergency, not always sharpen the faculties or enlighten the will.

However it was, the Dansker in his ascetic way rather took to Billy. Nor was this only because of a certain philosophic interest in such a character. There was another cause. While the old man's eccentricities, sometimes bordering on the ursine, repelled the juniors, Billy, undeterred thereby, would make advances, never passing the old *Agamemnon*-man without a salutation marked by that respect which is seldom lost on the aged, however crabbed at times, or whatever their station in life. There was a vein of dry humour, or what not, in the mast-man; and whether in freak of patriarchal irony touching Billy's youth and athletic frame, or for some other and more recondite reason, from the first in addressing him he always substituted Baby for Billy. The Dansker, in fact, being the originator of the name by which the foretopman eventually became known aboard ship.

Well then, in his mysterious little difficulty going in quest of the wrinkled one, Billy found him off duty in a dog-watch ruminating by himself, seated on a shot-box of the upper gun-deck, now and then surveying with a somewhat cynical regard certain of the more swaggering promenaders there. Billy recounted his trouble, again wondering how it all happened. The salt seer attentively listened, accompanying the foretopman's recitals with queer twitchings of his wrinkles and problematical little sparkles of his small ferret eyes. Making an end of his story, the foretopman asked, "And now, Dansker, do tell me what you think of it."

The old man, shoving up the front of his tarpaulin and deliberately rubbing the long slant scar at the point where it entered the thin hair, laconically said, "Baby Budd, *Jimmy Legs*" (meaning the master-at-arms) "is down on you."

"*Jimmy Legs!*" ejaculated Billy, his welkin eyes expanding; "what for? Why he calls me *the sweet and pleasant young fellow*, they tell me."

"Does he so?" grinned the grizzled one; then said, "Ay, Baby Lad, a sweet voice has *Jimmy Legs*."

"No, not always. But to me he has. I seldom pass him but there comes a pleasant word."

"And that's because he's down upon you, Baby Budd."

Such reiteration, along with the manner of it (incomprehensible to a novice), disturbed Billy almost as much as the mystery for which he had sought explanation. Something less unpleasingly oracular he tried to extract. But the old sea-Chiron,[23] thinking perhaps that for the nonce he had sufficiently instructed his young Achilles, pursed his lips, gathered all his wrinkles together, and would commit himself to nothing further.

Years, and those experiences which befall certain shrewder men subordinated lifelong to the will of superiors, all this had developed in the Dansker the pithy guarded cynicism that was his leading characteristic.

[23] One of the Centaurs, teacher of Achilles.

CHAPTER IX

The next day an incident served to confirm Billy Budd in his incredulity as to the Dansker's strange summing up of the case submitted.

The ship at noon going large before the wind was rolling on her course, and he, below at dinner and engaged in some sportful talk with the members of his mess, chanced in a sudden lurch to spill the entire contents of his soup-pan upon the new scrubbed deck. Claggart, the Master-at-arms, official rattan in hand, happened to be passing along the battery, in a bay of which the mess was lodged, and the greasy liquid streamed just across his path. Stepping over it, he was proceeding on his way without comment, since the matter was nothing to take notice of under the circumstances, when he happened to observe who it was that had done the spilling. His countenance changed. Pausing, he was about to ejaculate something hasty at the sailor, but checked himself, and pointing down to the streaming soup, playfully tapped him from behind with his rattan, saying, in a low musical voice, peculiar to him at times, "Handsomely done, my lad! And handsome is as handsome did it, too!" and with that passed on. Not noted by Billy as not coming within his view was the involuntary smile, or rather grimace, that accompanied Claggart's equivocal words. Aridly it drew down the thin corners of his shapely mouth. But everybody taking his remark as meant for humorous, and at which therefore as coming from a superior they were bound to laugh, "with counterfeited glee" acted accordingly; and Billy tickled, it may be, by the allusion to his being the handsome sailor, merrily joined in; then addressing his messmates exclaimed, "There now, who says that Jimmy Legs is down on me!"

"And who said he was, Beauty?" demanded one Donald with some surprise. Whereat the foretopman looked a little foolish, recalling that it was only one person, Board-her-in-the-smoke, who had suggested what to him was the smoky idea that this master-at-arms was in any peculiar way hostile to him. Meantime that functionary resuming his path must have momentarily worn some expression less guarded than that of the bitter smile and, usurping the face from the heart, some distorting expression perhaps—for a drummer-boy, heedlessly frolicking along from the opposite direction, and chancing to come into light collision with his person was strangely disconcerted by his aspect. Nor was the impression lessened when the official, impulsively giving him a sharp cut with the rattan, vehemently exclaimed, "Look where you go!"

CHAPTER X

What was the matter with the Master-at-arms? And, be the matter what it might, how could it have direct relation to Billy Budd, with whom prior to the affair of the spilled soup he had never come into any special contact, official or otherwise? What indeed could the trouble have to do with one so little inclined to give offence as the merchantship's *peacemaker*, even him who in Claggart's own phrase was "The sweet and pleasant young fellow"? Yes, why should *Jimmy Legs,* to borrow the Dansker's expression, be *down* on the Handsome Sailor?

But at heart and not for nothing, as the late chance encounter may indicate to the discerning, down on him, secretly down on him, he assuredly was.

Now to invent something touching the more private career of Claggart—something involving Billy Budd, of which something the latter should be wholly ignorant, some romantic incident implying that Claggart's knowledge of the young blue-jacket began at some period anterior to catching sight of him on board the seventy-four—all this, not so difficult to do, might avail in a more or less interesting way to account for whatever enigma may appear to lurk in the case. But, in fact, there was nothing of the sort. And yet the cause, necessarily to be assumed as the sole one assignable, is in its very realism as much charged with that prime element of Radcliffian [24] romance, *the mysterious,* as any that the ingenuity of the author of the "Mysteries of Udolpho" could devise. For what can more partake of the mysterious than an antipathy spontaneous and profound such as is evoked in certain exceptional mortals by the mere aspect of some other mortal, however harmless he may be?—if not called forth by that very harmlessness itself.

Now there can exist no irritating juxtaposition of dissimilar personalities comparable to that which is possible aboard a great war-ship fully manned and at sea. There, every day, among all ranks, almost every man comes into more or less of contact with almost every other man. Wholly there to avoid even the sight of an aggravating object one must needs give it Jonah's toss, or jump overboard himself. Imagine how all this might eventually operate on some peculiar human creature the direct reverse of a saint?

But for the adequate comprehending of Claggart by a normal nature, these hints are insufficient. To pass from a normal nature to him one must cross "The deadly space between," and this is best done by indirection.

Long ago an honest scholar, my senior, said to me in reference to one who like himself is now no more, a man so unimpeachably respectable that against him nothing was ever openly said, though among the few something was whispered, "Yes, X—— is a nut not to be cracked by the tap of a lady's fan. You are aware that I am the adherent of no organized religion, much less of any philosophy built into a system. Well, for all that, I think that to try and get into X——, enter his labyrinth and get out again, without a clue derived from some source other than what is known as *knowledge of the world*—that were hardly possible, at least for me."

"Why," said I, "X——, however singular a study to some, is yet human, and knowledge of the world assuredly implies the knowledge of human nature, and in most of its varieties."

"Yes, but a superficial knowledge of it, serving ordinary purposes. But for anything deeper, I am not certain whether to know the world and to know human nature be not two distinct branches of knowledge, which while they may co-exist in the same heart, yet either may exist with little or nothing of the other. Nay, in an average man of the world, his constant rubbing with it blunts that fine spiritual insight indispensable to the understanding of the essential in certain exceptional characters, whether evil ones or good. In a matter of some importance I have seen a girl wind an old lawyer about her little finger. Nor was it the dotage of senile love. Nothing of the sort. But he knew law better than he knew the girl's heart. Coke and Blackstone hardly shed so much light into obscure spiritual places as the Hebrew prophets. And who were they? Mostly recluses."

At the time my inexperience was such that I did not quite see the drift of all this. It may be that I see it now. And, indeed, if that lexicon which is based on Holy Writ were any longer popular, one might with less difficulty define and denominate certain phenomenal men. . . . As it is, one must turn to some authority not liable to the charge of being tinctured with the Biblical element.

In a list of definitions included in the authentic translation of Plato, a list attributed to him, occurs this: "Natural Depravity: a depravity according to nature." A definition which though savouring of Calvinism by no means involves Calvin's dogma as to total mankind. Evidently its intent makes it applicable but to individuals. Not many are the examples of this depravity which the gallows and jail supply. At any rate, for notable instances,—since these have no vulgar alloy of the brute in them, but invariably are dominated by intellectuality,—one must go elsewhere. Civilization,

[24] Ann Radcliffe (1764-1823) was a British author of Gothic romances, including *The Mysteries of Udolpho* (1794).

especially if of the austerer sort, is auspicious to it. It folds itself in the mantle of respectability. It has its certain negative virtues serving as silent auxiliaries. It never allows wine to get within its guard. It is not going too far to say that it is without vices or small sins. There is a phenomenal pride in it that excludes them from anything. Never mercenary or avaricious. In short, the depravity here meant partakes nothing of the sordid or sensual. It is serious, but free from acerbity. Though no flatterer of mankind it never speaks ill of it.

But the thing which in eminent instances signalizes so exceptional a nature is this: though the man's even temper and discreet bearing would seem to intimate a mind peculiarly subject to the law of reason, not the less in his soul's recesses he would seem to riot in complete exemption from that law, having apparently little to do with reason further than to employ it as an ambidexter implement for effecting the irrational. That is to say: towards the accomplishment of an aim which in wantonness of malignity would seem to partake of the insane, he will direct a cool judgment sagacious and sound.

These men are true madmen, and of the most dangerous sort, for their lunacy is not continuous, but occasional; evoked by some special object; it is secretive and self-contained: so that when most active it is, to the average mind, not distinguished from sanity, and for the reason above suggested that whatever its aims may be (and the aim is never disclosed) the method and the outward proceeding is always perfectly rational.

Now something such was Claggart, in whom was the mania of an evil nature, not engendered by vicious training or corrupting books or licentious living, but born with him and innate, in short, "a depravity according to nature."

Can it be this phenomenon, disowned or not acknowledged, that in some criminal cases puzzles the courts? For this cause have our juries at times not only to endure the prolonged contentions of lawyers with their fees, but also the yet more perplexing strife of the medical experts with theirs? And why leave it to them? Why not subpoena as well the clerical proficients? Their vocation bringing them into peculiar contact with so many human beings, and sometimes in their least guarded hour, in interviews very much more confidential than those of physician and patient; this would seem to qualify them to know something about those intricacies involved in the question of moral responsibility; whether in a given case, say, the crime proceeded from mania in the brain or rabies of the heart. As to any differences among themselves which clerical proficients might develop on the stand, these could hardly be greater than the direct contradictions exchanged between the remunerated medical experts.

Dark sayings are these, some will say. But why? It is because they somewhat savour of Holy Writ in its phrase "mysteries of iniquity."

The point of the story turning on the hidden nature of the Master-at-arms has necessitated this chapter. With an added hint or two in connection with the incident at the mess, the resumed narrative must be left to vindicate as it may its own credibility.

Chapter XI

Pale ire, envy and despair.[25]

That Claggart's figure was not amiss, and his face, save the chin, well moulded, has already been said. Of these favourable points he seemed not insensible, for he was not only neat but careful in his dress. But the form of Billy Budd was heroic; and if his face was without the intellectual look of the pallid Claggart's, not the less was it lit, like his, from within, though from a different source. The bonfire in his heart

[25] The line is from Milton's *Paradise Lost*, Bk. IV, l. 115, descriptive of Satan approaching Eden.

made luminous the rose-tan in his cheek.

In view of the marked contrast between the persons of the twain, it is more than probable that when the Master-at-arms in the scene last given applied to the sailor the proverb *Handsome is as handsome does* he there let escape an ironic inkling, not caught by the young sailors who heard it, as to what it was that had first moved him against Billy, namely, his significant personal beauty.

Now envy and antipathy, passions irreconcilable in reason, nevertheless in fact may spring conjoined like Chang and Eng [26] in one birth. Is Envy then such a monster? Well, though many an arraigned mortal has in hopes of mitigated penalty pleaded guilty to horrible actions, did ever anybody seriously confess to envy? Something there is in it universally felt to be more shameful than even felonious crime. And not only does everybody disown it, but the better sort are inclined to incredulity when it is in earnest imputed to an intelligent man. But since its lodgment is in the heart, not the brain, no degree of intellect supplies a guarantee against it. But Claggart's was no vulgar form of the passion. Nor, as directed toward Billy Budd, did it partake of that streak of apprehensive jealousy which marred Saul's visage perturbedly brooding on the comely young David. Claggart's envy struck deeper. If askance he eyed the good looks, cheery health and frank enjoyment of young life in Billy Budd, it was because these happened to go along with a nature that, as Claggart magnetically felt, had in its simplicity never willed malice or experienced the reactionary bite of that serpent. To him, the spirit lodged within Billy, and looking out from his welkin eyes as from windows—that ineffability it was which made the dimple in his dyed cheeks, suppled his joints, and dancing in his yellow curls made him pre-eminently the Handsome Sailor. One person excepted, the Master-at-arms was perhaps the only man in the ship intellectually capable of adequately appreciating the moral phe-nomenon presented in Billy Budd, and the insight but intensified his passion, which, assuming various secret forms within him, at times assumed that of cynic disdain—disdain of innocence. To be nothing more than innocent! Yet in an æsthetic way he saw the charm of it, the courageous free-and-easy temper of it, and fain would have shared it, but he despaired of it.

With no power to annul the elemental evil in himself, though readily enough he could hide it; apprehending the good, but powerless to be it; a nature like Claggart's, surcharged with energy as such natures almost invariably are, what recourse is left to it but to recoil upon itself and like the scorpion for which the Creator alone is responsible, act out to the end the part allotted it.

Passion, and passion in its profoundest, is not a thing demanding a palatial stage whereon to play its part. Down among the groundlings, among the beggars and rakers of the garbage, profound passion is enacted. And the circumstances that provoke it, however trivial or mean, are no measure of its power. In the present instance the stage is a scrubbed gun-deck, and one of the external provocations a man-of-war's man's spilled soup.

Now when the Master-at-arms noticed whence came that greasy fluid streaming before his feet, he must have taken it—to some extent wilfully perhaps—not for the mere accident it assuredly was, but for the sly escape of a spontaneous feeling on Billy's part more or less answering to the antipathy on his own. In effect a foolish demonstration he must have thought, and very harmless, like the futile kick of a heifer, which yet were the heifer a shod stallion would not be so harmless. Even so was it that into the gall of envy Claggart infused the vitriol of his contempt. But the incident confirmed to him certain tell-tale reports purveyed to his ear by *Squeak,* one of his more cunning corporals, a grizzled little man, so nicknamed by the sailors on

---

[26] The famous Siamese twins (1811-74).

account of his squeaky voice and sharp visage ferreting about the dark corners of the lower decks after interlopers, satirically suggesting to them the idea of a rat in a cellar.

Now his chief's employing him as an implicit tool in laying little traps for the worriment of the foretopman—for it was from the Master-at-arms that the petty persecutions heretofore adverted to had proceeded—the corporal, having naturally enough concluded that his master could have no love for the sailor, made it his business, faithful understrapper that he was, to ferment the ill blood by perverting to his chief certain innocent frolics of the good-natured foretopman, besides inventing for his master sundry contumelious epithets he claimed to have overheard him let fall. The Master-at-arms never suspected the veracity of these reports, more especially as to the epithets, for he well knew how secretly unpopular may become a Master-at-arms—at least a Master-at-arms of those days, zealous in his function—how the blue-jackets shot at him in private their raillery and wit; the nickname by which he goes among them (*Jimmy Legs*) implying under the form of merriment their cherished disrespect and dislike.

But in view of the greediness of hate for provocation, it hardly needed a purveyor to feed Claggart's passion. An uncommon prudence is habitual with the subtler depravity, for it has everything to hide. And in case of any merely suspected injury its secretiveness voluntarily cuts it off from enlightenment or disillusion; and not unreluctantly, action is taken upon surmise as upon certainty. And the retaliation is apt to be in monstrous disproportion to the supposed offence; for when in anybody was revenge in its exactions aught else but an inordinate usurer? But how with Claggart's conscience? For though consciences are unlike as foreheads, every intelligence, not including the Scriptural devils who "believe and tremble," has one. But Claggart's conscience being but the lawyer to his will, made ogres of trifles,

probably arguing that the motive imputed to Billy in spilling the soup just when he did, together with the epithets alleged—these, if nothing more, made a strong case against him; nay, justified animosity into a sort of retributive righteousness. The Pharisee is the Guy Fawkes [27] prowling in the hid chambers underlying some natures like Claggart's. And they can really form no conception of an unreciprocated malice. Probably, the Master-at-arms' clandestine persecutions of Billy were started to try the temper of the man; but they had not developed any quality in him that enmity could make official use of, or ever pervert into even plausible self-justification; so that the occurrence at the mess, petty if it were, was a welcome one to that peculiar conscience assigned to be the private mentor of Claggart; and for the rest, not improbably it put him upon new experiments.

CHAPTER XII

Not many days after the last incident narrated, something befell Billy Budd that more gravelled him than aught that had previously occurred.

It was a warm night for the latitude; and the foretopman, whose watch at the time was properly below, was dozing on the uppermost deck whither he had ascended from his hot hammock—one of hundreds suspended so closely wedged together over a lower gun-deck that there was little or no swing to them. He lay as in the shadow of a hill-side stretched under the lee of the *booms,* a piled ridge of spare spars, and among which the ship's largest boat, the launch, was stowed. Alongside of three other slumberers from below, he lay near one end of the booms which approached from the foremast; his station aloft on duty as a foretopman being just over the deck station of the forecastlemen entitling him according to usage to make himself more or less at home in that neighbourhood.

[27] See note 14 on "Benito Cereno."

Presently he was stirred into semi-consciousness by somebody, who must have previously sounded the sleep of the others, touching his shoulder, and then as the foretopman raised his head, breathing into his ear in a quick whisper, "Slip into the lee fore-chains, Billy; there is something in the wind—don't speak. Quick. I will meet you there;" and disappeared.

Now Billy—like sundry other essentially good-natured ones—had some of the weakness inseparable from essential good nature; and among these was a reluctance, almost an incapacity of plumply saying *no* to an abrupt proposition not obviously absurd, on the face of it, nor obviously unfriendly, nor iniquitous. And being of warm blood he had not the phlegm to negative any proposition by unresponsive inaction. Like his sense of fear, his apprehension as to aught outside of the honest and natural was seldom very quick. Besides, upon the present occasion, the drowse from his sleep still hung upon him.

However it was, he mechanically rose and, sleepily wondering what could be *in the wind,* betook himself to the designated place, a narrow platform, one of six, outside of the high bulwarks and screened by the great dead-eyes and multiple columned lanyards of the shrouds and back-stays; and, in a great war-ship of that time, of dimensions commensurate to the ample hull's magnitude; a tarry balcony, in short, overhanging the sea, and so secluded that one mariner of the *Indomitable,* a nonconformist old tar of serious turn, made it even in daytime his private oratory.

In this retired nook the stranger soon joined Billy Budd. There was no moon as yet; a haze obscured the star-light. He could not distinctly see the stranger's face. Yet from something in the outline and carriage, Billy took him to be, and correctly, one of the afterguard.

"Hist Billy!" said the man, in the same quick cautionary whisper as before; "You were impressed, weren't you? Well, so was I;" and he paused as to mark the effect. But Billy, not knowing exactly what to make of this, said nothing. Then the other: "We are not the only impressed ones, Billy. There's a gang of us. Couldn't you —help—at a pinch?"

"What do you mean?" demanded Billy, here shaking off his drowse.

"Hist, hist!" the hurried whisper now growing husky, "see here;" and the man held up two small objects faintly twinkling in the night light; "See, they are yours, Bill, if you'll only——"

But Billy here broke in, and in his resentful eagerness to deliver himself his vocal infirmity somewhat intruded; "D-D-Damme, I don't know what you are d-driving at, or what you mean, but you had better g-g-go where you belong!" For the moment the fellow, as confounded, did not stir; and Billy, springing to his feet, said, "If you d-don't start, I'll t-t-toss you back over the r-rail!" There was no mistaking this, and the mysterious emissary decamped, disappearing in the direction of the mainmast in the shadow of the booms.

"Hallo, what's the matter?" here came growling from a forecastleman awakened from his deck-doze by Billy's raised voice. And as the foretopman reappeared and was recognized by him; "Ah, *Beauty,* is it you? Well, something must have been the matter for you st-st-stuttered."

"Oh," rejoined Billy, now mastering the impediment; "I found an afterguardsman in our part of the ship here and I bid him be off where he belongs."

"And is that all you did about it, foretopman?" gruffly demanded another, an irascible old fellow of brick-coloured visage and hair, and who was known to his associate forecastlemen as *Red Pepper.*

"Such sneaks I should like to marry to the gunner's daughter!" by that expression meaning that he would like to subject them to disciplinary castigation over a gun.

However, Billy's rendering of the matter satisfactorily accounted to these inquirers for the brief commotion, since of all the sections of a ship's company the forecastlemen, veterans for the most part, and bigoted in their sea-prejudices, are the most jealous in resenting territorial encroachments, especially on the part of any of the after guard, of whom they have but a sorry opinion, chiefly landsmen, never going aloft except to reef or furl the mainsail, and in no wise competent to handle a marlingspike or turn in a *deadeye,* say.

Chapter XIII

This incident sorely puzzled Billy Budd. It was an entirely new experience—the first time in his life that he had ever been personally approached in underhanded intriguing fashion. Prior to this encounter he had known nothing of the afterguardsman, the two men being stationed wide apart, one forward and aloft during his watch, the other on deck and aft.

What could it mean? And could they really be guineas, those two glittering objects the interloper had held up to his (Billy's) eyes? Where could the fellow get guineas? Why, even buttons, spare buttons, are not so plentiful at sea. The more he turned the matter over, the more he was nonplussed, and made uneasy and discomfited. In his disgustful recoil from an overture which, though he but ill comprehended, he instinctively knew must involve evil of some sort—Billy Budd was like a young horse fresh from the pasture suddenly inhaling a vile whiff from some chemical factory and by repeated snortings trying to get it out of his nostrils and lungs. This frame of mind barred all desire of holding further parley with the fellow, even were it but for the purpose of gaining some enlightenment as to his design in approaching him. And yet he was not without natural curiosity to see how such a visitor in the dark would look in broad day.

He espied him the following afternoon in his first dog-watch below, one of the smokers on that forward part of the upper gun-deck allotted to the pipe. He recognized him by his general cut and build, more than by his round freckled face and glassy eyes of pale blue, veiled with lashes all but white. And yet Billy was a bit uncertain whether indeed it were he—yonder chap about his own age, chatting and laughing in a free-hearted way, leaning against a gun,—a genial young fellow enough to look at, and something of a rattle-brain, to all appearance. Rather chubby, too, for a sailor, even an afterguardsman. In short the last man in the world—one would think—to be overburthened with thoughts, especially those perilous thoughts that must needs belong to a conspirator in any serious project, or even to the underling of such a conspirator.

Although Billy was not aware of it, the fellow, with one sidelong watchful glance had perceived Billy first, and then noting that Billy was looking at him, thereupon nodded a familiar sort of friendly recognition as to an old acquaintance, without interrupting the talk he was engaged in with the group of smokers. A day or two afterwards, chancing in the evening promenade on a gun-deck, to pass Billy, he offered a flying word of good-fellowship, as it were, which by its unexpectedness, and equivocalness under the circumstances, so embarrassed Billy that he knew not how to respond to it, and let it go unnoticed.

Billy was now left more at a loss than before. The ineffectual speculations into which he was led were so disturbingly alien to him that he did his best to smother them. It never entered his mind that here was a matter, which, from its extreme questionableness, it was his duty as a loyal bluejacket to report in the proper quarter. And, probably, had such a step been suggested to him, he would have been deterred from taking it by the thought—one of novice-magnanimity—that it would savour overmuch of the dirty work of a tell-tale. He kept the thing to himself. Yet upon one occasion he could not forbear a little disburthening himself to the old Dansker, tempted thereto perhaps by the influence of a balmy night when the ship lay becalmed; the twain, silent for the most part, sitting together on deck, their heads propped against the bulwarks. But it was only a partial and anonymous account that Billy gave—the unfounded scruples above referred to preventing full disclosure to anybody. Upon hearing Billy's version, the sage Dansker seemed to divine more than he was told; and after a little meditation, during which his wrinkles were pursed as into a point—quite effacing for the time that quizzing expression his face sometimes wore—answered: "Didn't I say so, Baby Budd?"

"Say what?" demanded Billy.

"Why, *Jimmy Legs* is *down* on you."

"And what," rejoined Billy in amazement, "has *Jimmy Legs* to do with that cracked afterguardsman?"

"Ho, it was an afterguardsman, then: a cat's-paw, only a cat's-paw!" And with that exclamation, which, whether it had reference to a light puff of air just then coming over the calm sea, or subtler relation to the afterguardsman, there is no telling. The old Merlin gave a twisting wrench with his black teeth at his plug of tobacco—vouchsafing no reply to Billy's impetuous question, though now repeated, for it was his wont to relapse into grim silence when interrogated in sceptical sort as to any of his sententious oracles, not always very clear ones, but rather partaking of that obscurity which invests most Delphic deliverances from any quarter.

CHAPTER XIV

Long experience had very likely brought this old man to that bitter prudence which never interferes in aught, and never gives advice.

Yes, despite the Dansker's pithy insistence as to the Master-at-arms being at the bottom of these strange experiences of Billy on board the *Indomitable,* the young sailor was ready to ascribe them to almost anybody but the man who, to use Billy's own expression, "always had a pleasant word for him." This is to be wondered at. Yet not so much to be wondered at. In certain matters, some sailors even in ma-

ture life, remain unsophisticated enough. But a young seafarer of the disposition of our athletic foretopman is yet very much of a child-man. And yet a child's utter innocence is but its blank ignorance, and the innocence more or less wanes as intelligence waxes. But in Billy Budd intelligence, such as it was, had advanced, while yet his simple-mindedness remained for the most part unaffected. Experience is a teacher indeed; yet did Billy's years make his experience small. Besides, he had none of that intuitive knowledge of the bad which in natures not good or incompletely so, foreruns experience, and therefore may pertain, as in some instances it too clearly does pertain, even to youth.

And what could Billy know of man except of man as a mere sailor? And the old-fashioned sailor, the veritable man-before-the-mast—the sailor from boyhood up—he, though indeed of the same species as a landsman, is in some respects singularly distinct from him. The sailor is frankness, the landsman is finesse. Life is not a game with the sailor, demanding the long head; no intricate game of chess where few moves are made in straightforwardness, and ends are attained by indirection; an oblique, tedious, barren game hardly worth that poor candle burnt out in playing it.

Yes, as a class, sailors are in character a juvenile race. Even their deviations are marked by juvenility. And this more especially holding true with the sailors of Billy's time. Then, too, certain things which apply to all sailors, do more pointedly operate here and there upon the junior one. Every sailor, too, is accustomed to obey orders without debating them; his life afloat is externally ruled for him; he is not brought into that promiscuous commerce with mankind where unobstructed free agency on equal terms—equal superficially, at least—soon teaches one that unless upon occasion he exercises a distrust keen in proportion to the fairness of the appearance, some foul turn may be served him. A ruled, undemonstrative distrustfulness is so habitual, not with business-men so much, as with men who know their kind in less shallow relations than business, namely certain men-of-the-world: that they come at last to employ it all but unconsciously; and some of them would very likely feel real surprise at being charged with it as one of their general characteristics.

CHAPTER XV

But after the little matter at the mess Billy Budd no more found himself in strange trouble at times about his hammock or his clothes-bag, or what not. While, as to that smile that occasionally sunned him, and the pleasant passing word: these were, if not more frequent, yet if anything more pronounced than before.

But for all that, there were certain other demonstrations now. When Claggart's unobserved glance happened to light on belted Billy rolling along the upper gun-deck in the leisure of the second dog-watch, exchanging passing broadsides of fun with other young promenaders in the crowd; that glance would follow the cheerful Sea Hyperion [28] with a settled meditative and melancholy expression—his eyes strangely suffused with incipient feverish tears. Then would Claggart look like the man of sorrows. Yes, and sometimes the melancholy expression would have in it a touch of soft yearning, as if Claggart could even have loved Billy but for fate and ban. But this was an evanescence, and quickly repented of, as it were, by an immitigable look, pinching and shrivelling the visage into the momentary semblance of a wrinkled walnut. But sometimes, catching sight in advance of the foretopman coming in his direction, he would, upon their nearing, step aside a little to let him pass, dwelling upon Billy for the moment with the glittering dental satire of a Guise.[29] Yet, upon an abrupt unforeseen encounter, a red light would flash forth from his eye, like a spark from an anvil in a dusky smithy. That quick fierce light was a strange one, darted from orbs which in repose were of a colour nearest approaching a deeper violet, the softest of shades.

Though some of these caprices of the pit could not but be observed by their object, yet were they beyond the construing of such a nature. And the thews of Billy were hardly comparable with that sort of sensitive spiritual organization which in some cases instinctively conveys to ignorant innocence an admonition of the proximity of the malign. He thought the Master-at-arms acted in a manner rather queer at times. That was all. But the occasional frank air and pleasant word went for what they purported to be—the young sailor never having heard as yet of the "too fair-spoken man."

Had the foretopman been conscious of having done or said anything to provoke the ill will of the official, it would have been different with him, and his sight might have been purged if not sharpened. So was it with him in yet another matter. Two minor officers, the Armourer, and Captain of the Hold, with whom he had never exchanged a word, his position on the ship not bringing him into contact with them; these men now for the first began to cast upon Billy—when they chanced to encounter him—that peculiar glance which evidences that the man from whom it comes has been some way tampered with, and to the prejudice of him upon whom the glance lights. Never did it occur to Billy as a thing to be noted, or a thing suspicious—though he well knew the fact that the Armourer and Captain of the Hold, with the ship's yeoman, apothecary, and others of that grade, were by naval usage, messmates of the Master-at-arms; men with ears convenient to his confidential tongue.

[28] Name applied by poets to Apollo, god of manly youth and beauty.

[29] French family of Lorraine, 16th and 17th Centuries, notable for sardonic attitudes, and for activity in plots and conspiracies. One of the Guises was portrayed as a "grinning villain" by Dumas.

But the general popularity of our Handsome Sailor's manly forwardness upon occasion, and irresistible good nature, indicating no mental superiority tending to excite an invidious feeling; this good will on the part of most of his ship-mates made him the less to concern himself about such mute aspects toward him as those whereto allusion has just been made.

As to the afterguardsman, though Billy for reasons already given, necessarily saw little of him, yet when the two did happen to meet, invariably came the fellow's offhand cheerful recognition, sometimes accompanied by a passing pleasant word or two. Whatever that equivocal young person's original design may really have been, or the design of which he might have been the deputy, certain it was from his manner upon these occasions, that he had wholly dropped it.

It was as if his precocity of crookedness (and every vulgar villain is precocious) had for once deceived him, and the man he had sought to entrap as a simpleton had, through his very simplicity, baffled him.

But shrewd ones may opine that it was hardly possible for Billy to refrain from going up to the afterguardsman and bluntly demanding to know his purpose in the initial interview, so abruptly closed in the fore-chains. Shrewd ones may also think it but natural in Billy to set about sounding some of the other impressed men of the ship in order to discover what basis, if any, there was for the emissary's obscure suggestions as to plotting disaffection aboard. The shrewd may so think. But something more, or rather, something else than mere shrewdness is perhaps needful for the due understanding of such a character as Billy Budd's.

As to Claggart, the monomania in the man—if that indeed it were—as involuntarily disclosed by starts in the manifestations detailed, yet in general covered over by his self-contained and rational demeanour; this, like a subterranean fire was eating its way deeper and deeper in him. Something decisive must come of it.

CHAPTER XVI

After the mysterious interview in the fore-chains—the one so abruptly ended there by Billy—nothing especially germane to the story occurred until the events now about to be narrated.

Elsewhere it has been said that owing to the lack of frigates (of course better sailors than line-of-battle ships) in the English squadron up the Straits at that period, the *Indomitable* was occasionally employed not only as an available substitute for a scout, but at times on detached service of more important kind. This was not alone because of her sailing qualities, not common in a ship of her rate, but quite as much, probably, that the character of her commander—it was thought—specially adapted him for any duty where, under unforeseen difficulties, a prompt initiative might have to be taken in some matter demanding knowledge and ability in addition to those qualities employed in good seamanship. It was on an expedition of the latter sort, a somewhat distant one, and when the *Indomitable* was almost at her furthest remove from the fleet, that in the latter part of an afternoon-watch she unexpectedly came in sight of a ship of the enemy. It proved to be a frigate. The latter—perceiving through the glass that the weight of men and metal would be heavily against her—invoking her light heels, crowded on sail to get away. After a chase urged almost against hope—and lasting until about the middle of the first dog-watch—she signally succeeded in effecting her escape.

Not long after the pursuit had been given up, and ere the excitement incident thereto had altogether waned away, the Master-at-arms, ascending from his cavernous sphere, made his appearance (cap in hand) by the mainmast: respectfully awaiting the notice of Captain Vere—then solitary walking the weather-side of the quarter-deck—doubtless somewhat chafed at the failure of the pursuit. The spot where Claggart stood was the place allotted to the men of lesser grades when seeking some more particular interview either with the officer-of-the-deck or the Captain himself. But from the latter it was not often that a sailor or petty-officer of those days would seek a hearing; only some exceptional cause, would, according to established custom, have warranted that.

Presently, just as the Commander, absorbed in his reflections, was on the point of turning aft in his promenade, he became sensible of Claggart's presence, and saw the doffed cap held in deferential expectancy. Here be it said that Captain Vere's personal knowledge of this petty-officer had only begun at the time of the ship's last sailing from home, Claggart then for the first, in transfer from a ship detained for repairs, supplying on board the *Indomitable* the place of a previous Master-at-arms disabled and ashore.

No sooner did the Commander observe who it was that now so deferentially stood awaiting his notice, than a peculiar expression came over him. It was not unlike that which uncontrollably will flit across the countenance of one at unawares encountering a person, who, though known to him, indeed, has hardly been long enough known for thorough knowledge, but something in whose aspect nevertheless now, for the first time, provokes a vaguely repellent distaste. Coming to a stand and resuming much of his wonted official manner, save that a sort of impatience lurked in the intonation of the opening word, he said, "Well? what is it, Master-at-arms?"

With the air of a subordinate grieved at the necessity of being a messenger of ill tidings, and while conscientiously determined to be frank, yet equally resolved upon shunning overstatement, Claggart at this invitation, or rather summons to disburthen, spoke up. What he said, conveyed in the language of no uneducated man, was to the effect following if not altogether in these words, namely, that during the chase and preparations for the possible encounter he had seen enough to convince him that at least one sailor aboard was a dangerous character in a ship mustering some who

not only had taken a guilty part in the late serious trouble, but others also who, like the man in question, had entered His Majesty's service under another form than enlistment.

At this point Captain Vere, with some impatience, interrupted him:

"Be direct, man; say impressed men."

Claggart made a gesture of subservience and proceeded. Quite lately he (Claggart) had begun to suspect that some sort of movement prompted by the sailor in question was covertly going on, but he had not thought himself warranted in reporting the suspicion so long as it remained indistinct. But from what he had that afternoon observed in the man referred to, the suspicion of something clandestine going on had advanced to a point less removed from certainty. He deeply felt—he added —the serious responsibility assumed in making a report involving such possible consequences to the individual mainly concerned, besides tending to augment those natural anxieties which every naval commander must feel in view of the extraordinary outbreak so recent as those which, he sorrowfully said it, it needed not to name.

Now at the first broaching of the matter Captain Vere, taken by surprise, could not wholly dissemble his disquietude, but as Claggart went on, the former's aspect changed into restiveness under something in the testifier's manner in giving his testimony. However, he refrained from interrupting him. And Claggart, continuing, concluded with this:

"God forbid, your honour, that the *Indomitable's* should be the experience of the—"

"Never mind that!" here peremptorily broke in the superior, his face altering with anger instantly, divining the ship that the other was about to name, one in which the Nore Mutiny had assumed a singularly tragical character that for a time jeopardized the life of its Commander. Under the circumstances he was indignant at the purposed allusion. When the commissioned officers themselves were on all occasions very heedful how they referred to the recent events,—for a petty-officer unnecessarily to allude to them in the presence of his Captain, this struck him as a most immodest presumption. Besides, to his quick sense of self-respect, it even looked under the circumstances something like an attempt to alarm him. Nor at that was he without some surprise that one who, so far as he had hitherto come under his notice, had shown considerable tact in his function, should in this particular evince such lack of it.

But these thoughts and kindred dubious ones flitting across his mind were suddenly replaced by an intuitional surmise, which though as yet obscure in form, served practically to affect his reception of the ill tidings. Certain it is that, long versed in everything pertaining to the complicated gun-deck life (which like every other form of life has its secret mines and dubious side; the side popularly disclaimed), Captain Vere did not permit himself to be unduly disturbed by the general tenor of his subordinate's report. Furthermore, if in view of recent events prompt action should be taken at the first palpable sign of recurring insubordination—for all that, not judicious would it be, he thought, to keep the idea of lingering disaffection alive by undue forwardness in crediting an informer, even if his own subordinate, and charged with police surveillance of the crew. This feeling would not perhaps have so prevailed with him were it not that upon a prior occasion the patriotic zeal officially evinced by Claggart had somewhat irritated him as appearing rather supersensible and strained. Furthermore, something even in the official's self-possessed and somewhat ostentatious manner in making his specifications strangely reminded him of a bandsman, a perjured witness in a capital case before a court-martial ashore of which when a lieutenant he, Captain Vere, had been a member.

Now the peremptory check given to Claggart in the matter of the arrested allusion was quickly followed up by this: "You say that there is at least one dangerous man aboard. Name him."

"William Budd, a foretopman, your honour—"

"William Budd," repeated Captain Vere with unfeigned astonishment, "and mean you the man our Lieutenant Ratcliffe took from the merchantman not very long ago—the young fellow who seems to be so popular with the men—Billy, the Handsome Sailor, as they call him?"

"The same, your honour; but for all his youth and good looks, a deep one. Not for nothing does he insinuate himself into the good will of his shipmates, since at the least they will at a pinch say a good word for him at all hazards. Did Lieutenant Ratcliffe happen to tell your honour of that adroit fling of Budd's jumping up in the Cutter's bow under the merchantman's stern when he was being taken off? It is even masqued by that sort of good-humoured air that at heart he resents his impressment. You have but noted his fair cheek. A man-trap may be under his fine ruddy-tipped daisies."

Now the *Handsome Sailor,* as a signal figure among the crew, had naturally enough attracted the Captain's attention from the first. Though in general not very demonstrative to his officers, he had congratulated Lieutenant Ratcliffe upon his good fortune in lighting on such a fine specimen of the *genus homo* who, in the nude, might have posed for a statue of young Adam before the fall.

As to Billy's adieu to the ship *Rights-of-Man,* which the boarding lieutenant had indeed reported to him, but in a deferential way—more as a good story than aught else, though mistakenly understanding it as a satiric sally—Captain Vere had but thought so much the better of the impressed man for it; as a military sailor, admiring the spirit that could take an arbitrary enlistment so merrily and sensibly. The foretopman's conduct, too, so far as it had fallen under the Captain's notice had confirmed the first happy augury, while the new recruit's qualities as a *sailor-man* seemed to be such that he had thought of recommending him to the executive officer for promotion to a place that would more frequently bring him under his own observation, namely, the captaincy of the mizzen-top, replacing there in the starboard watch a man not so young whom partly for that reason he deemed less fitted for the post. Be it parenthesized here that since the mizzen-top-men have not to handle such breadths of heavy canvas as the lower sailors on the main-mast and fore-mast, a young man if of the right stuff not only seems best adapted to duty there, but, in fact, is generally selected for the captaincy of that top, and the company under him are light hands, and often but striplings. In sum, Captain Vere had from the beginning deemed Billy Budd to be what in the naval parlance of the times was called a *"King's bargain,"* that is to say, for His Britannic Majesty's navy a capital investment at small outlay or none at all.

After a brief pause—during which the reminiscences above mentioned passed vividly through his mind—he weighed the import of Claggart's last suggestion, conveyed in the phrase, "pitfall under the clover," and the more he weighed it the less reliance he felt in the informer's good faith. Suddenly he turned upon him: "Do you come to me, Master-at-arms, with so foggy a tale? As to Budd, cite me an act or spoken word of his confirmatory of what you here in general charge against him. Stay," drawing nearer to him, "heed what you speak. Just now and in a case like this, there is a yard-arm-end for the false-witness."

"Ah, your honour!" sighed Claggart mildly shaking his shapely head as in sad deprecation of such unmerited severity of tone. Then bridling—erecting himself as in virtuous self-assertion, he circumstantially alleged certain words and acts, which collectively if credited, led to presumptions mortally inculpating Budd, and for

some of these averments, he added, substantiating proof was not far.

With grey eyes now impatient and distrustful, essaying to fathom to the bottom Claggart's calm violet ones, Captain Vere again heard him out; then for the moment stood ruminating. The mood he evinced, Claggart—himself for the time liberated from the other's scrutiny—steadily regarded with a look difficult to render:—a look curious of the operation of his tactics, a look such as might have been that of the spokesman of the envious children of Jacob deceptively imposing upon the troubled patriarch the blood-dyed coat of young Joseph.

Though something exceptional in the moral quality of Captain Vere made him, in earnest encounter with a fellow-man, a veritable touchstone of that man's essential nature, yet now as to Claggart and what was really going on in him his feeling partook less of intuitional conviction than of strong suspicion clogged by strange dubieties. The perplexity he evinced proceeded less from aught touching the man informed against—as Claggart doubtless opined—than from considerations how best to act in regard to the informer. At first, indeed, he was naturally for summoning that substantiation of his allegations which Claggart said was at hand. But such a proceeding would result in the matter at once getting abroad—which—in the present stage of it, he thought, might undesirably affect the ship's company. If Claggart was a false witness,—that closed the affair. And therefore, before trying the accusation, he would first practically test the accuser; and he thought this could be done in a quiet undemonstrative way.

The measure he determined upon involved a shifting of the scene—a transfer to a place less exposed to observation than the broad quarter-deck. For although the few gun-room officers there at the time had, in due observance of naval etiquette, withdrawn to leeward the moment Captain Vere had begun his promenade on the deck's weather-side; and though during the colloquy with Claggart they of course ventured not to diminish the distance; and though throughout the interview Captain Vere's voice was far from high, and Claggart's silvery and low; and the wind in the cordage and the wash of the sea helped the more to put them beyond ear-shot; nevertheless, the interview's continuance already had attracted observation from some topmen aloft, and other sailors in the waist or further forward.

Having now determined upon his measures, Captain Vere forthwith took action. Abruptly turning to Claggart he asked, "Master-at-arms, is it now Budd's watch aloft?"

"No, your honour." Whereupon—"Mr. Wilkes," summoning the nearest midshipman, "tell Albert to come to me." Albert was the Captain's hammock-boy, a sort of sea-valet in whose discretion and fidelity his master had much confidence. The lad appeared. "You know Budd the foretopman?"

"I do, Sir."

"Go find him. It is his watch off. Manage to tell him out of ear-shot that he is wanted aft. Contrive it that he speaks to nobody. Keep him in talk yourself. And not till you get well aft here, not till then, let him know that the place where he is wanted is my cabin. You understand. Go. —Master-at-arms, show yourself on the decks below, and when you think it time for Albert to be coming with his man, stand by quietly to follow the sailor in."

CHAPTER XVII

Now when the foretopman found himself closeted, as it were, in the cabin with the Captain and Claggart, he was surprised enough. But it was a surprise unaccompanied by apprehension or distrust. To an immature nature, essentially honest and humane, forewarning intimations of subtler danger from one's kind come tardily, if at all. The only thing that took shape in the

young sailor's mind was this: "Yes, the Captain, I have always thought, looks kindly upon me. I wonder if he's going to make me his coxswain. I should like that. And maybe now he is going to ask the Master-at-arms about me."

"Shut the door there, sentry," said the commander. "Stand without and let nobody come in.—Now, Master-at-arms, tell this man to his face what you told of him to me;" and stood prepared to scrutinize the mutually confronting visages.

With the measured step and calm collected air of an asylum physician approaching in the public hall some patient beginning to show indications of a coming paroxysm, Claggart deliberately advanced within short range of Billy, and mesmerically looking him in the eye, briefly recapitulated the accusation.

Not at first did Billy take it in. When he did the rose-tan of his cheek looked struck as by white leprosy. He stood like one impaled and gagged. Meanwhile the accuser's eyes, removing not as yet from the blue, dilated ones, underwent a phenomenal change, their wonted rich violet colour blurring into a muddy purple. Those lights of human intelligence losing human expression, gelidly protruding like the alien eyes of certain uncatalogued creatures of the deep.

The first mesmeric glance was one of surprised fascination; the last was the hungry lurch of the torpedo-fish.

"Speak, man!" said Captain Vere to the transfixed one, struck by his aspect even more than by Claggart's, "Speak! defend yourself." Which appeal caused but a strange, dumb gesturing and gurgling in Billy; amazement at such an accusation so suddenly sprung on inexperienced nonage; this, and it may be horror at the accuser, serving to bring out his lurking defect, and in this instance for the time intensifying it into a convulsed tongue-tie; while the intent head and entire form straining forward in an agony of ineffectual eagerness to obey the injunction to speak and defend himself, gave an expression to the face like that of a condemned vestal priestess in the moment of her being buried alive, and in the first struggle against suffocation.

Though at the time Captain Vere was quite ignorant of Billy's liability to vocal impediment, he now immediately divined it, since vividly Billy's aspect recalled to him that of a bright young schoolmate of his whom he had seen struck by much the same startling impotence in the act of eagerly rising in the class to be foremost in response to a testing question put to it by the master. Going close up to the young sailor, and laying a soothing hand on his shoulder, he said, "There is no hurry, my boy. Take your time, take your time." Contrary to the effect intended, these words, so fatherly in tone, doubtless touching Billy's heart to the quick, prompted yet more violent efforts at utterance—efforts soon ending for the time in confirming the paralysis, and bringing to the face an expression which was as a crucifixion to behold. The next instant, quick as the flame from a discharged cannon at night—his right arm shot out and Claggart dropped to the deck. Whether intentionally, or but owing to the young athlete's superior height, the blow had taken effect full upon the forehead, so shapely and intellectual-looking a feature in the Master-at-arms; so that the body fell over lengthwise, like a heavy plank tilted from erectness. A gasp or two and he lay motionless.

"Fated boy," breathed Captain Vere in a tone so low as to be almost a whisper, "what have you done! But here, help me."

The twain raised the felled one from the loins up into a sitting position. The spare form flexibly acquiesced, but inertly. It was like handling a dead snake. They lowered it back. Regaining erectness, Captain Vere with one hand covering his face stood to all appearance as impassive as to the object at his feet. Was he absorbed in taking in all the bearings of the event, and what was best not only now at once to be done, but also in the sequel? Slowly he

uncovered his face; forthwith the effect was as if the moon, emerging from eclipse, should reappear with quite another aspect than that which had gone into hiding. The father in him, manifested towards Billy thus far in the scene, was replaced by the military disciplinarian. In his official tone he bade the foretopman retire to a state-room aft, (pointing it out), and there remain till thence summoned. This order Billy in silence mechanically obeyed. Then, going to the cabin door where it opened on the quarter-deck, Captain Vere said to the sentry without, "Tell somebody to send Albert here." When the lad appeared his master so contrived it that he should not catch sight of the prone one. "Albert," he said to him, "tell the surgeon I wish to see him. You need not come back till called."

When the surgeon entered—a self-poised character of that grave sense and experience that hardly anything could take him aback—Captain Vere advanced to meet him, thus unconsciously interrupting his view of Claggart and, interrupting the other's wonted ceremonious salutation, said, "Nay, tell me how it is with yonder man," directing his attention to the prostrate one.

The surgeon looked, and for all his self-command, somewhat started at the abrupt revelation. On Claggart's always pallid complexion, thick black blood was now oozing from mouth and ear. To the gazer's professional eyes it was unmistakably no living man that he saw.

"Is it so, then?" said Captain Vere intently watching him. "I thought it. But verify it." Whereupon the customary tests confirmed the surgeon's first glance, who now looking up in unfeigned concern, cast a look of intense inquisitiveness upon his superior. But Captain Vere, with one hand to his brow, was standing motionless. Suddenly, catching the surgeon's arm convulsively, he exclaimed, pointing down to the body,—"It is the divine judgment of Ananias! [30] Look!"

Disturbed by the excited manner he had

---

[30] Acts 5:5.

never before observed in the *Indomitable's* Captain, and as yet wholly ignorant of the affair, the prudent surgeon nevertheless held his peace, only again looking an earnest interrogation as to what it was that had resulted in such a tragedy.

But Captain Vere was now again motionless, standing absorbed in thought. Once again starting, he vehemently exclaimed—"Struck dead by an angel of God. Yet the angel must hang!"

At these interjections, incoherences to the listener as yet unapprised of the antecedent events, the surgeon was profoundly discomfited. But now, as recollecting himself, Captain Vere in less harsh tone briefly related the circumstances leading up to the event.

"But come; we must despatch," he added, "help me to remove him (meaning the body) to yonder compartment"—designating one opposite where the foretopman remained immured. Anew disturbed by a request that, as implying a desire for secrecy, seemed unaccountably strange to him, there was nothing for the subordinate to do but comply.

"Go now," said Captain Vere, with something of his wonted manner, "Go now. I shall presently call a drum-head court. Tell the lieutenants what has happened, and tell Mr. Morton"—meaning the captain of marines. "And charge them to keep the matter to themselves."

Full of disquietude and misgivings, the surgeon left the cabin. Was Captain Vere suddenly affected in his mind, or was it but a transient excitement brought about by so strange and extraordinary a happening? As to the drum-head court, it struck the surgeon as impolitic, if nothing more. The thing to do, he thought, was to place Billy Budd in confinement, and in a way dictated by usage, and postpone further action in so extraordinary a case to such time as they should again join the squadron, and then transfer it to the Admiral. He recalled the unwonted agitation of Captain Vere and his exciting exclamations so at variance with his normal

manner. Was he unhinged? But assuming that he was, it were not so susceptible of proof. What then could he do? No worse trying situation is conceivable than that of an officer subordinated under a Captain whom he suspects to be, not mad indeed, but yet not quite unaffected in his intellect. To argue his order to him would be insolence. To resist him would be mutiny. In obedience to Captain Vere he communicated to the lieutenants and captain of marines what had happened; saying nothing as to the Captain's state. They stared at him in surprise and concern. Like him they seemed to think that such a matter should be reported to the Admiral.

Who in the rainbow can draw the line where the violet tint ends and the orange tint begins? Distinctly we see the difference of the colour, but where exactly does the first one visibly enter into the other? So with sanity and insanity. In pronounced cases there is no question about them. But in some cases, in various degrees supposedly less pronounced, to draw the line of demarkation few will undertake, though for a fee some professional experts will. There is nothing namable but that some men will undertake to do for pay. In other words, there are instances where it is next to impossible to determine whether a man is sane or beginning to be otherwise.

Whether Captain Vere, as the surgeon professionally surmised, was really the sudden victim of any degree of aberration, one must determine for himself by such light as this narrative may afford.

CHAPTER XVIII

The unhappy event which has been narrated could not have happened at a worse juncture. For it was close on the heel of the suppressed insurrections, an after-time very critical to naval authority, demanding from every English sea-commander two qualities not readily interfusable—prudence and rigour. Moreover, there was something crucial in the case.

In the jugglery of circumstances preceding and attending the event on board the *Indomitable* and in the light of that martial code whereby it was formally to be judged, innocence and guilt, personified in Claggart and Budd, in effect changed places.

In the legal view the apparent victim of the tragedy was he who had sought to victimize a man blameless; and the indisputable deed of the latter, navally regarded, constituted the most heinous of military crimes. Yet more. The essential right and wrong involved in the matter, the clearer that might be, so much the worse for the responsibility of a loyal sea-commander, inasmuch as he was authorized to determine the matter on that primitive legal basis.

Small wonder then that the *Indomitable's* Captain, though in general a man of rigid decision, felt that circumspectness not less than promptitude was necessary. Until he could decide upon his course, and in each detail; and not only so, but until the concluding measure was upon the point of being enacted he deemed it advisable, in view of all the circumstances, to guard as much as possible against publicity. Here he may or may not have erred. Certain it is, however, that subsequently in the confidential talk of more than one or two gun-rooms and cabins he was not a little criticized by some officers, a fact imputed by his friends, and vehemently by his cousin Jack Denton, to professional jealousy of Starry Vere. Some imaginative ground for invidious comment there was. The maintenance of secrecy in the matter, the confining all knowledge of it for a time to the place where the homicide occurred —the quarter-deck cabin; in these particulars lurked some resemblance to the policy adopted in those tragedies of the palace which have occurred more than once in the capital founded by Peter [31] the Barbarian, great chiefly by his crimes.

The case was such that fain would the *Indomitable's* Captain have deferred taking any action whatever respecting it further than to keep the foretopman a close pris-

oner till the ship rejoined the squadron, and then submitting the matter to the judgment of his Admiral.

But a true military officer is, in one particular, like a true monk. Not with more of self-abnegation will the latter keep his vows of monastic obedience than the former his vows of allegiance to martial duty.

Feeling that unless quick action were taken on it, the deed of the foretopman, as soon as it should be known on the gundecks, would tend to awaken any slumbering embers of the Nore among the crews —a sense of the urgency of the case overruled in Captain Vere all other considerations. But though a conscientious disciplinarian, he was no lover of authority for mere authority's sake. Very far was he from embracing opportunities for monopolizing to himself the perils of moral responsibility, none at least that could properly be referred to an official superior, or shared with him by his official equals or even subordinates. So thinking, he was glad it would not be at variance with usage to turn the matter over to a summary court of his own officers, reserving to himself, as the one on whom the ultimate accountability would rest, the right of maintaining a supervision of it, or formally or informally interposing at need. Accordingly a drum-head court was summarily convened, he electing the individuals composing it, the First Lieutenant, the Captain of Marines, and the Sailing Master.

In associating an officer of marines with the sea-lieutenants in a case having to do with a sailor, the Commander perhaps deviated from general custom. He was prompted thereto by the circumstances that he took that soldier to be a judicious person, thoughtful and not altogether incapable of gripping with a difficult case unprecedented in his prior experience. Yet even as to him he was not without some

---

[31] Peter I of Russia (1672-1725), called Peter the Great; founder of St. Petersburg (now Leningrad).

latent misgiving, for withal he was an extremely good-natured man, an enjoyer of his dinner, a sound sleeper, and inclined to obesity. The sort of man who, though he would always maintain his manhood in battle, might not prove altogether reliable in a moral dilemma involving aught of the tragic. As to the First Lieutenant and the Sailing Master, Captain Vere could not but be aware that though honest natures, of approved gallantry upon occasion, their intelligence was mostly confined to the matter of active seamanship, and the fighting demands of their profession. The court was held in the same cabin where the unfortunate affair had taken place. This cabin, the Commander's, embraced the entire area under the poop-deck. Aft, and on either side, was a small state-room—the one room temporarily a jail, and the other a dead-house—and a yet smaller compartment leaving a space between, expanding forward into a goodly oblong of length coinciding with the ship's beam. A sky-light of moderate dimension was overhead, and at each end of the oblong space were two sashed port-hole windows, easily convertible back into embrasures for short cannonades.

All being quickly in readiness, Billy Budd was arraigned, Captain Vere necessarily appearing as the sole witness in the case, and as such temporarily sinking his rank, though singularly maintaining it in a matter apparently trivial, namely, that he testified from the ship's weather-side, with that object having caused the court to sit on the lee-side. Concisely he narrated all that had led up to the catastrophe, omitting nothing in Claggart's accusation and deposing as to the manner in which the prisoner had received it. At this testimony the three officers glanced with no little surprise at Billy Budd, the last man they would have suspected, either of mutinous design alleged by Claggart, or of the undeniable deed he himself had done. The First Lieutenant, taking judicial primacy and turning towards the prisoner, said, "Captain Vere has spoken. Is it or is it not as Captain Vere says?" In response came syllables not so much impeded in the utterance as might have been anticipated. They were these:

"Captain Vere tells the truth. It is just as Captain Vere says, but it is not as the Master-at-arms said. I have eaten the King's bread and I am true to the King."

"I believe you, my man," said the witness, his voice indicating a suppressed emotion not otherwise betrayed.

"God will bless you for that, your honour!" not without stammering said Billy, and all but broke down. But immediately was recalled to self-control by another question, with which the same emotional difficulty of utterance came: "No, there was no malice between us. I never bore malice against the Master-at-arms. I am sorry that he is dead. I did not mean to kill him. Could I have used my tongue I would not have struck him. But he foully lied to my face, and in the presence of my Captain, and I had to say something, and I could only say it with a blow. God help me!"

In the impulsive above-board manner of the frank one the court saw confirmed all that was implied in words which just previously had perplexed them, coming as they did from the testifier to the tragedy, and promptly following Billy's impassioned disclaimer of mutinous intent—Captain Vere's words, "I believe you, my man."

Next it was asked of him whether he knew of or suspected aught savouring of incipient trouble (meaning a mutiny, though the explicit term was avoided) going on in any section of the ship's company.

The reply lingered. This was naturally imputed by the court to the same vocal embarrassment which had retarded or obstructed previous answers. But in main it was otherwise here; the question immediately recalling to Billy's mind the interview with the afterguardsman in the fore-chains. But an innate repugnance to playing a part at all approaching that of an informer against one's own shipmates—

the same erring sense of uninstructed honour which had stood in the way of his reporting the matter at the time; though as a loyal man-of-war's man it was incumbent on him, and failure so to do, charged against him and proven, would have subjected him to the heaviest of penalties: this, with the blind feeling now his, that nothing really was being hatched, prevailed with him. When the answer came it was a negative.

"One question more," said the officer of marines now first speaking and with a troubled earnestness. "You tell us that what the Master-at-arms said against you was a lie. Now why should he have so lied, so maliciously lied, since you declare there was no malice between you?"

At that question unintentionally touching on a spiritual sphere wholly obscure to Billy's thoughts, he was nonplussed, evincing a confusion indeed that some observers, such as can be imagined, would have construed into involuntary evidence of hidden guilt. Nevertheless he strove some way to answer, but all at once relinquished the vain endeavour, at the same time turning an appealing glance towards Captain Vere as deeming him his best helper and friend. Captain Vere, who had been seated for a time, rose to his feet, addressing the interrogator. "The question you put to him comes naturally enough. But can he rightly answer it?—or anybody else? unless indeed it be he who lies within there," designating the compartment where lay the corpse. "But the prone one there will not rise to our summons. In effect though, as it seems to me, the point you make is hardly material. Quite aside from any conceivable motive actuating the Master-at-arms, and irrespective of the provocation of the blow, a martial court must needs in the present case confine its attention to the blow's consequence, which consequence is to be deemed not otherwise than as the striker's deed!"

This utterance, the full significance of which it was not at all likely that Billy took in, nevertheless caused him to turn a wistful, interrogative look towards the speaker, a look in its dumb expressiveness not unlike that which a dog of generous breed might turn upon his master, seeking in his face some elucidation of a previous gesture ambiguous to the canine intelligence. Nor was the same utterance without marked effect upon the three officers, more especially the soldier. Couched in it seemed to them a meaning unanticipated, involving a prejudgment on the speaker's part. It served to augment a mental disturbance previously evident enough.

The soldier once more spoke, in a tone of suggestive dubiety addressing at once his associates and Captain Vere: "Nobody is present—none of the ship's company, I mean, who might shed lateral light, if any is to be had, upon what remains mysterious in this matter."

"That is thoughtfully put," said Captain Vere; "I see your drift. Ay, there is a mystery; but to use a Scriptural phrase, it is 'a mystery of iniquity,' a matter for only psychologic theologians to discuss. But what has a military court to do with it? Not to add that for us any possible investigation of it is cut off by the lasting tongue-tie of him in yonder," again designating the mortuary state-room. "The prisoner's deed. With that alone we have to do."

To this, and particularly the closing reiteration, the marine soldier, knowing not how aptly to reply, sadly abstained from saying aught. The First Lieutenant, who at the outset had not unnaturally assumed primacy in the court, now overrulingly instructed by a glance from Captain Vere (a glance more effective than words), resumed that primacy. Turning to the prisoner: "Budd," he said, and scarce in equable tones, "Budd, if you have aught further to say for yourself, say it now."

Upon this the young sailor turned another quick glance towards Captain Vere; then, as taking a hint from that aspect, a hint confirming his own instinct that silence was now best, replied to the Lieutenant, "I have said all, Sir."

The marine—the same who had been the sentinel without the cabin-door at the time that the foretopman, followed by the Master-at-arms, entered it—he, standing by the sailor throughout their judicial proceedings, was now directed to take him back to the after compartment originally assigned to the prisoner and his custodian. As the twain disappeared from view, the three officers, as partially liberated from some inward constraint associated with Billy's mere presence—simultaneously stirred in their seats. They exchanged looks of troubled indecision, yet feeling that decide they must, and without long delay; for Captain Vere was for the time sitting unconsciously with his back towards them, apparently in one of his absent fits, gazing out from a sashed port-hole to windward upon the monotonous blank of the twilight sea. But the court's silence continuing, broken only at moments by brief consultations in low earnest tones, this seemed to assure him and encourage him. Turning, he to-and-fro paced the cabin athwart; in the returning ascent to windward, climbing the slant deck in the ship's lee roll; without knowing it symbolizing thus in his action a mind resolute to surmount difficulties even if against primitive instincts strong as the wind and the sea. Presently he came to a stand before the three. After scanning their faces he stood less as mustering his thoughts for expression, than as one in deliberating how best to put them to well-meaning men not intellectually mature—men with whom it was necessary to demonstrate certain principles that were axioms to himself. Similar impatience as to talking is perhaps one reason that deters some minds from addressing any popular assemblies; under which head is to be classed most legislatures in a Democracy.

When speak he did, something both in the substance of what he said and his manner of saying it, showed the influence of unshared studies, modifying and tempering the practical training of an active career. This, along with his phraseology now and then, was suggestive of the grounds whereon rested that imputation of a certain pedantry socially alleged against him by certain naval men of wholly practical cast, captains who nevertheless would frankly concede that His Majesty's Navy mustered no more efficient officers of their grade than "Starry Vere."

What he said was to this effect: "Hitherto I have been but the witness, little more; and I should hardly think now to take another tone, that of your coadjutor, for the time, did I not perceive in you—at the crisis too—a troubled hesitancy, proceeding, I doubt not, from the clashing of military duty with moral scruple—scruple vitalized by compassion. For the compassion, how can I otherwise but share it? But, mindful of paramount obligation, I strive against scruples that may tend to enervate decision. Not, gentlemen, that I hide from myself that the case is an exceptional one. Speculatively regarded, it well might be referred to a jury of casuists. But for us here, acting not as casuists or moralists, it is a case practical and under martial law practically to be dealt with.

"But your scruples! Do they move as in a dusk? Challenge them. Make them advance and declare themselves. Come now—do they import something like this: If, mindless of palliating circumstances, we are bound to regard the death of the Master-at-arms as the prisoner's deed, then does that deed constitute a capital crime whereof the penalty is a mortal one? But in natural justice is nothing but the prisoner's overt act to be considered? How can we adjudge to summary and shameful death a fellow-creature innocent before God, and whom we feel to be so?—Does that state it aright? You sign sad assent. Well, I, too, feel that, the full force of that. It is Nature. But do these buttons that we wear attest that our allegiance is to Nature? No, to the King. Though the ocean, which is inviolate Nature primeval, though this be the element where we move and have our being as sailors, yet as the King's officers lies our duty in a sphere correspondingly natural? So little is that true, that in receiving our commissions we in the most important regards ceased to be natural free-agents. When war is declared, are we, the commissioned fighters, previously consulted? We fight at command. If our judgments approve the war, that is but coincidence. So in other particulars. So now, would it be so much we ourselves that would condemn as it would be martial law operating through us? For that law and the rigour of it, we are not responsible. Our vowed responsibility is in this: That however pitilessly that law may operate, we nevertheless adhere to it and administer it.

"But the exceptional in the matter moves the heart within you. Even so, too, is mine moved. But let not warm hearts betray heads that should be cool. Ashore in a criminal case will an upright judge allow himself when off the bench to be waylaid by some tender kinswoman of the accused seeking to touch him with her tearful plea? Well, the heart here is as that piteous woman. The heart is the feminine in man, and hard though it be, she must here be ruled out."

He paused, earnestly studying them for a moment; then resumed.

"But something in your aspect seems to urge that it is not solely that heart that moves in you, but also the conscience, the private conscience. Then, tell me whether or not, occupying the position we do, private conscience should not yield to that imperial one formulated in the code under which alone we officially proceed?"

Here the three men moved in their seats, less convinced than agitated by the course of an argument troubling but the more the spontaneous conflict within. Perceiving which, the speaker paused for a moment; then abruptly changing his tone, went on:

"To steady us a bit, let us recur to the facts.—In war-time at sea a man-of-war's man strikes his superior in grade, and the blow kills. Apart from its effect, the blow

itself is, according to the Articles of War, a capital crime. Furthermore—"

"Ay, Sir," emotionally broke in the officer of marines, "in one sense it was. But surely Budd purposed neither mutiny nor homicide."

"Surely not, my good man. And before a court less arbitrary and more merciful than a martial one that plea would largely extenuate. At the Last Assizes it shall acquit. But how here? We proceed under the law of the Mutiny Act. In feature no child can resemble his father more than that Act resembles in spirit the thing from which it derives—War. In His Majesty's service—in this ship indeed—there are Englishmen forced to fight for the King against their will. Against their conscience, for aught we know. Though as their fellow-creatures some of us may appreciate their position, yet as Navy officers, what reck we of it? Still less recks the enemy. Our impressed men he would fain cut down in the same swath with our volunteers. As regards the enemy's naval conscripts, some of whom may even share our own abhorrence of the regicidal French Directory,[32] it is the same on our side. War looks but to the frontage, the appearance. And the Mutiny Act, War's child, takes after the father. Budd's intent or non-intent is nothing to the purpose.

"But while, put to it by those anxieties in you which I cannot but respect, I only repeat myself—while thus strangely we prolong proceedings that should be summary, the enemy may be sighted and an engagement result. We must do; and one of two things must we do—condemn or let go."

"Can we not convict and yet mitigate the penalty?" asked the junior Lieutenant here speaking, and falteringly, for the first time.

"Lieutenant, were that clearly lawful for us under the circumstances, consider the

---

[32] The French government, regarded as responsible for the execution of Louis XVI.

consequences of such clemency. The people" (meaning the ship's company) "have native sense; most of them are familiar with our naval usage and tradition; and how would they take it? Even could you explain to them—which our official position forbids—they, long moulded by arbitrary discipline, have not that kind of intelligent responsiveness that might qualify them to comprehend and discriminate. No, to the people the foretopman's deed, however it be worded in the announcement, will be plain homicide committed in a flagrant act of mutiny. What penalty for that should follow, they know. But it does not follow. *Why?* they will ruminate. You know what sailors are. Will they not revert to the recent outbreak at the Nore? Ay, they know the well-founded alarm—the panic it struck throughout England. Your clement sentence they would account pusillanimous. They would think that we flinch, that we are afraid of them—afraid of practising a lawful rigour singularly demanded at this juncture lest it should provoke new troubles. What shame to us such a conjecture on their part, and how deadly to discipline. You see then whither, prompted by duty and the law, I steadfastly drive. But I beseech you, my friends, do not take me amiss. I feel as you do for this unfortunate boy. But did he know our hearts, I take him to be of that generous nature that he would feel even for us on whom in this military necessity so heavy a compulsion is laid."

With that, crossing the deck, he resumed his place by the sashed port-hole, tacitly leaving the three to come to a decision. On the cabin's opposite side the troubled court sat silent. Loyal lieges, plain and practical, though at bottom they dissented from some points Captain Vere had put to them, they were without the faculty, hardly had the inclination to gainsay one whom they felt to be an earnest man—one, too, not less their superior in mind than in naval rank. But it is not improbable that even such of his words as

were not without influence over them, less came home to them than his closing appeal to their instinct as sea-officers, in the forethought he threw out as to the practical consequences to discipline (considering the unconfirmed tone of the fleet at the time) —should a man-of-war's man's violent killing at sea of a superior in grade be allowed to pass for aught else than a capital crime, demanding prompt infliction of the penalty?

Not unlikely they were brought to something more or less akin to that harassed frame of mind which in the year 1842 actuated the commander of the U.S. brig-of-war *Somers* to resolve (under the so-called Articles of War—Articles modelled upon the English Mutiny Act) to resolve upon the execution at sea of a midshipman and two petty-officers as mutineers designing the seizure of the brig. Which resolution was carried out, though in a time of peace and within not many days' sail of home. An act vindicated by a naval court of inquiry subsequently convened ashore —history, and here cited without comment. True, the circumstances on board the *Somers* were different from those on board the *Indomitable*. But the urgency felt, well-warranted or otherwise, was much the same.

Says a writer whom few know, "Forty years after a battle it is easy for a non-combatant to reason about how it ought to have been fought. It is another thing personally and under fire to direct the fighting while involved in the obscuring smoke of it. Much so with respect to other emergencies involving considerations both practical and moral, and when it is imperative promptly to act. The greater the fog, the more it imperils the steamer, and speed is put on though at the hazard of running somebody down. Little ween the snug card-players in the cabin of the responsibilities of the sleepless man on the bridge."

In brief, Billy Budd was formally convicted and sentenced to be hung at the yard-arm in the early morning-watch, it being now night. Otherwise, as is customary in such cases, the sentence would forthwith have been carried out. In war-time on the field or in the fleet, a mortal punishment decreed by a drum-head court—on the field sometimes decreed by but a nod from the General—follows without a delay on the heel of conviction without appeal.

CHAPTER XIX

It was Captain Vere himself who, of his own motion, communicated the finding of the court to the prisoner; for that purpose going to the compartment where he was in custody, and bidding the marine there to withdraw for the time.

Beyond the communication of the sentence, what took place at this interview was never known. But, in view of the character of the twain briefly closeted in that state-room, each radically sharing in the rarer qualities of one nature—so rare, indeed, as to be all but incredible to average minds however much cultivated—some conjectures may be ventured.

It would have been in consonance with the spirit of our Captain Vere should he on this occasion have concealed nothing from the condemned one—should he indeed have frankly disclosed to him the part he himself had played in bringing about the decision, at the same time revealing his actuating motives. On Billy's side it is not improbable that such a confession would have been received in much the same spirit that prompted it. Not without a sort of joy indeed he might have appreciated the brave opinion of him implied in his Captain making such a confidant of him. Nor as to the sentence itself could he have been insensible that it was imparted to him as to one not afraid to die. Even more may have been. Captain Vere in the end may have developed the passion sometimes latent under an exterior stoical or indifferent. He was old enough to have been Billy's father. The austere devoteé of military duty, letting himself melt back into what remains primeval in our formalized humanity, may in the end have caught Billy to heart, even as Abraham may have caught young Isaac on the brink of resolutely offering him up in obedience to the exacting behest. But there is no telling the sacrament—seldom if in any case revealed to the gadding world—wherever under circumstances at all akin to those here attempted to be set forth, two of great Nature's nobler order embrace. There is privacy at the time, inviolable to the survivor, and holy oblivion (the sequel to each diviner magnanimity) providentially covers all at last.

The first to encounter Captain Vere in the act of leaving the compartment was the senior Lieutenant. The face he beheld, for the moment one expressive of the agony of the strong, was to that officer, though a man of fifty, a startling revelation. That the condemned one suffered less than he who mainly had effected the condemnation, was apparently indicated by the former's exclamation in the scene soon perforce to be touched upon.

Of a series of incidents within a brief term rapidly following each other, the adequate narration may take up a term less brief, especially if explanation or comment here and there seem requisite to the better understanding of such incidents. Between the entrance into the cabin of him who never left it alive, and him who when he did leave it left it as one condemned to die; between this and the closeted interview just given, less than an hour and a half had elapsed. It was an interval long enough, however, to awaken speculations among no few of the ship's company as to what it was that could be detaining in the cabin the Master-at-arms and the sailor, for it was rumoured that both of them had been seen to enter it and neither of them had been seen to emerge. This rumour had got abroad upon the gundecks and in the tops; the people of a great war-ship being in one respect like villagers, taking microscopic note of every untoward movement or non-movement going on. When therefore in weather not at all tempestuous all hands were called in the second dog-watch, a summons under such circumstances not usual in those hours, the crew were not wholly unprepared for some announcement extraordinary, one having connection, too, with the continued absence of the two men from their wonted haunts.

There was a moderate sea at the time; and the moon, newly risen and near to being at its full, silvered the white spardeck wherever not blotted by the clear-cut shadows horizontally thrown of fixtures and moving men. On either side of the quarter-deck the marine guard under arms was drawn up; and Captain Vere, standing up in his place surrounded by all the ward-room officers, addressed his men. In so doing his manner showed neither more nor less than that properly pertaining to his supreme position aboard his own ship. In clear terms and concise he told them what had taken place in the cabin; that the Master-at-arms was dead; that he who had killed him had been already tried by a summary court and condemned to death; and that the execution would take place in the early morning watch. The word *mutiny* was not named in what he said. He refrained, too, from making the occasion an opportunity for any preachment as to the maintenance of discipline, thinking, perhaps, that under existing circumstances in the navy the consequence of violating discipline should be made to speak for itself.

Their Captain's announcement was listened to by the throng of standing sailors in a dumbness like that of a seated congregation of believers in Hell listening to the clergyman's announcement of his Calvinistic text.

At the close, however, a confused murmur went up. It began to wax all but instantly, then, at a sign, was pierced and suppressed by shrill whistles of the Boatswain and his mates piping "Down one watch."

To be prepared for burial Claggart's body was delivered to certain petty-officers of his mess. And here, not to clog the sequel with lateral matters, it may be added that at a suitable hour, the Master-at-arms was committed to the sea with every funeral honour properly belonging to his naval grade.

In this proceeding, as in every public one growing out of the tragedy, strict adherence to usage was observed. Nor in any point could it have been at all deviated from, either with respect to Claggart or Billy Budd, without begetting undesirable speculations in the ship's company, the sailors, and more particularly the men-of-war's men, being of all men the greatest sticklers for usage.

For similar cause all communication between Captain Vere and the condemned one ended with the closeted interview already given, the latter being now surrendered to the ordinary routine preliminary to the end. This transfer under guard from the Captain's quarters was effected without unusual precautions—at least no visible ones.

If possible, not to let the men so much as surmise that their officers anticipate aught amiss from them, is the tacit rule in a military ship. And the more that some sort of trouble should really be apprehended, the more do the officers keep that apprehension to themselves; though not the less unostentatious vigilance may be augmented.

In the present instance the sentry placed over the prisoner had strict orders to let no one have communication with him but the Chaplain. And certain unobtrusive measures were taken absolutely to insure this point.

CHAPTER XX

In a seventy-four of the old order the deck known as the upper gun-deck was the one covered over by the spar-deck, which last, though not without its armament, was for the most part exposed to the weather. In general it was at all hours free from hammocks; those of the crew swinging on the lower gun-deck and berth-deck, the latter being not only a dormitory but also the place for the stowing of the sailors' bags, and on both sides lined with the large chests or movable pantries of the many messes of the men.

On the starboard side of the *Indomitable's* upper gun-deck, behold Billy Budd under sentry lying prone in irons in one of the bays formed by the regular spacing of the guns comprising the batteries on either side. All these pieces were of the heavier calibre of that period. Mounted on lumbering wooden carriages, they were hampered with cumbersome harness of breeching and strong side-tackles for running them out. Guns and carriages, together with the long rammers and shorter lintstocks lodged in loops overhead—all these, as customary, were painted black; and the heavy hempen breechings, tarred to the same tint, wore the like livery of the undertakers. In contrast with the funereal tone of these surroundings the prone sailor's exterior apparel, white *jumper* and white duck trousers, each more or less soiled, dimly glimmered in the obscure light of the bay like a patch of discoloured snow in early April lingering at some upland cave's black mouth. In effect he is already in his shroud or the garments that shall serve him in lieu of one. Over him, but scarce illuminating him, two battle-lanterns swing from two massive beams of the deck above. Fed with the oil supplied by the war-contractors (whose gains, honest or otherwise, are in every land an anticipated portion of the harvest of death), with flickering splashes of dirty yellow light they pollute the pale moonshine all but ineffectually struggling in obstructed flecks through the open ports from which the tompioned cannon protrude. Other lanterns at intervals serve but to bring out somewhat the obscurer bays which, like small confessionals or side-chapels in a cathedral, branch from the long, dim-vasted, broad aisle between the two batteries of that covered tier.

Such was the deck where now lay the Handsome Sailor. Through the rose-tan of his complexion, no pallor could have shown. It would have taken days of sequestration from the winds and the sun to have brought about the effacement of that young sea-bloom. But the skeleton in the cheek-bone at the point of its angle was just beginning delicately to be defined under the warm-tinted skin. In fervid hearts self-contained some brief experiences devour our human tissue as secret fire in a ship's hold consumes cotton in the bale.

But now, lying between the two guns, as nipped in the vice of fate, Billy's agony, mainly proceeding from a generous young heart's virgin experience of the diabolical incarnate and effective in some men—the tension of that agony was over now. It survived not the something healing in the closeted interview with Captain Vere. Without movement, he lay as in a trance, that adolescent expression previously noted as his taking on something akin to the look of a slumbering child in the cradle when the warm hearth-glow of the still chamber of night plays on the dimples that at whiles mysteriously form in the cheek, silently coming and going there. For now and then in the gyved one's trance, a serene happy light born of some wandering reminiscence or dream would diffuse itself over his face, and then wane away only anew to return.

The Chaplain coming to see him and finding him thus, and perceiving no sign that he was conscious of his presence, attentively regarded him for a space, then slipping aside, withdrew for the time, peradventure feeling that even he, the minister of Christ, though receiving his stipend from wars, had no consolation to proffer which could result in a peace transcending that which he beheld. But in the small hours he came again. And the prisoner, now awake to his surroundings, noticed his approach, and civilly, all but cheerfully, welcomed him. But it was to little purpose that in the interview following the good man sought to bring Billy Budd to some Godly understanding that he must die, and at dawn. True, Billy himself freely referred to his death as a thing close at hand; but it was something in the way that children will refer to death in general, who yet among their other sports will play a funeral with hearse and mourners. Not that like children Billy was incapable of conceiving what death really is. No, but he was wholly without irrational fear of it, a fear more prevalent in highly civilized communities than those so-called barbarous ones which in all respects stand nearer to unadulterate Nature. And, as elsewhere said, a barbarian Billy radically was; as much so, for all the costume, as his countrymen the British captives, living trophies made to march in the Roman triumph of Germanicus.[33] Quite as much so as those later barbarians, young men probably, and picked specimens among the earlier British converts to Christianity, at least nominally such, and taken to Rome (as to-day converts from lesser isles of the sea may be taken to London), of whom the Pope of that time, admiring the strangeness of their personal beauty—so unlike the Italian stamp, their clear, ruddy complexions and curled flaxen locks, exclaimed, "Angles" (meaning *English,* the modern derivative) —"Angles do you call them? And is it because they look so like *Angels?*" Had it been later in time one would think that the Pope had in mind Fra Angelico's [34] seraphs, some of whom, plucking apples in gardens of Hesperides, have the faint rose-bud complexion of the more beautiful English girls.

CHAPTER XXI

If in vain the kind Chaplain sought to impress the young barbarian with ideas of death akin to those conveyed in the skull, dial and cross-bones on old tombstones; equally futile to all appearances were his efforts to bring home to him the thought of salvation and a Saviour. Billy listened, but less out of awe or reverence, perhaps, than from a certain natural politeness; doubtless at bottom regarding all that in

much the same way which most mariners of his class take any discourse abstract or out of the common tone of the workaday world. And this sailor way of taking clerical discourse is not wholly unlike the way in which the pioneer of Christianity—full of transcendant miracles—was received long ago on tropic isles by any superior *savage* so called: a Tahitian say of Captain Cook's [35] time or shortly after that time. Out of natural courtesy he received but did not appreciate. It was like a gift placed in the palm of an out-stretched hand upon which the fingers do not close.

But the *Indomitable's* Chaplain was a discreet man possessing the good sense of a good heart. So he insisted not in his vocation here. At the instance of Captain Vere, a lieutenant had apprised him of pretty much of everything as to Billy; and since he felt that innocence was even a better thing than religion wherewith to go to judgment, he reluctantly withdrew; but in his emotion not without performing an act strange enough in an Englishman, and under the circumstances yet more so in any regular priest. Stooping over, he kissed on the fair cheek his fellow man, a felon in martial law, one who, though in the confines of death, he felt he could never convert to a dogma; nor for all that he did fear for his future.

Marvel not that, having been made acquainted with the young sailor's essential innocence, the worthy man lifted not a finger to avert the doom of such a martyr to martial discipline. So to do would not only have been as idle as invoking the desert, but would also have been an audacious transgression of the bounds of his function—one as exactly prescribed to him

[33] Roman general, whose victory over the Germans was celebrated at Rome in a formal triumph, 17 A.D.

[34] Italian painter of religious subjects, 1387-1455.

[35] Captain James Cook, British explorer and mariner (1728-79). He visited Tahiti in the course of his famous exploring voyage around the earth, 1772-75.

by military law as that of any other naval officer. Bluntly put, a chaplain is the minister of the Prince of Peace serving in the host of the God of War—Mars. As such, he is as incongruous as a musket would be on the altar at Christmas. Why then is he there? Because he indirectly subserves the purpose attested by the cannon; because, too, he lends the sanction of the religion of the meek to that which practically is the abrogation of everything but force.[36]

Chapter XXII

The night so luminous on the spar-deck, but otherwise on the cavernous ones below —levels so very like the tiered galleries in a coal-mine—the luminous night passed away. Like the prophet in the chariot disappearing in heaven and dropping his mantle to Elisha, the withdrawing night transferred its pale robe to the peeping day. A meek shy light appeared in the East, where stretched a diaphanous fleece of white furrowed vapour. That light slowly waxed. Suddenly eight bells was struck aft, responded to by eight louder metallic strokes from forward. It was four o'clock in the morning. Instantly the silver whistles were heard summoning all hands to witness punishment. Up through the great hatchway rimmed with racks of heavy shot, the watch below came pouring, overspreading with the watch already on deck the space between the mainmast and foremast, including that occupied by the capacious *launch* and the black booms tiered on either side of it—boat and booms making a summit of observation for the powder boys and younger tars. A different group comprising one watch of topmen leaned over the side of the rail of that sea-balcony, no small one in a seventy-four, looking down on the crowd below. Man or boy, none spake but in whisper, and few spake at all. Captain Vere—as before, the central figure among the assembled commissioned officers—stood nigh the break of the poop-deck, facing forward. Just below

him on the quarter-deck the marines in full equipment were drawn up much as at the scene of the promulgated sentence.

At sea in the old time, the execution by halter of a military sailor was generally from the fore-yard. In the present instance —for special reasons—the main-yard was assigned. Under an arm of that yard the prisoner was presently brought up, the Chaplain attending him. It was noted at the time, and remarked upon afterwards, that in this final scene the good man evinced little or nothing of the perfunctory. Brief speech indeed he had with the condemned one, but the genuine gospel was less on his tongue than in his aspect and manner towards him. The final preparations personal to the latter being speedily brought to an end by two boatswain's-mates, the consummation impended. Billy stood facing aft. At the penultimate moment, his words, his only ones, words wholly unobstructed in the utterance, were these—"God bless Captain Vere!" Syllables so unanticipated coming from one with the ignominious hemp about his neck—a conventional felon's benediction directed aft towards the quarters of honour; syllables, too, delivered in the clear melody of a singing-bird on the point of launching from the twig, had a phenomenal effect, not unenhanced by the rare personal beauty of the young sailor, spiritualized now through late experiences so poignantly profound.

Without volition, as it were, as if indeed the ship's populace were the vehicles of some vocal electric current, with one voice, from alow and aloft, came a resonant echo —"God bless Captain Vere!" And yet, at that instant, Billy alone must have been in their hearts, even as he was in their eyes.

At the pronounced words and the spontaneous echo that voluminously rebounded them, Captain Vere, either through stoic self-control or a sort of momentary paralysis induced by emotional shock, stood

---

[36] An irruption of heretic thought hard to suppress.—Melville's note.

erectly rigid as a musket in the ship-armour's rack.

The hull, deliberately recovering from the periodic roll to leeward, was just regaining an even keel—when the last signal, the preconcerted dumb one, was given. At the same moment it chanced that the vapoury fleece hanging low in the East, was shot through with a soft glory as of the fleece of the Lamb of God seen in mystical vision; and simultaneously therewith, watched by the wedged mass of upturned faces, Billy ascended; and ascending, took the full rose of the dawn.

In the pinioned figure, arrived at the yard-end, to the wonder of all no motion was apparent save that created by the slow roll of the hull, in moderate weather so majestic in a great ship heavy-cannoned.

A DIGRESSION

When, some days afterwards, in reference to the singularity just mentioned, the Purser (a rather ruddy, rotund person, more accurate as an accountant than profound as a philosopher) said at mess to the Surgeon, "What testimony to the force lodged in will-power," the latter, spare and tall, one in whom a discreet causticity went along with a manner less genial than polite, replied, "Your pardon, Mr. Purser. In a hanging so scientifically conducted—and, under special orders, I myself directed how Budd's was to be effected—any movement following the completed suspension and originating in the body suspended, such movement indicates mechanical spasm in the muscular system. Hence the absence of that is no more attributable to will-power, as you call it, than to horse-power—begging your pardon."

"But this muscular spasm you speak of —is not that, in a degree, more or less invariable in these cases?"

"Assuredly so, Mr. Purser."

"How then, my good sir, do you account for its absence in this instance?"

"Mr. Purser, it is clear that your sense of the singularity in this matter equals not mine. You account for it by what you call will-power, a term not yet included in the lexicon of science. As for me, I do not with my present knowledge pretend to account for it at all. Even should one assume the hypothesis that, at the first touch of the halyards, the action of Budd's heart, intensified by extraordinary emotion at its climax, abruptly stopped—much like a watch when in carelessly winding it up you strain at the finish, thus snapping the spring—even under that hypothesis, how account for the phenomenon that followed?"

"You admit, then, that the absence of spasmodic movement was phenomenal?"

"It was phenomenal, Mr. Purser, in the sense that it was an appearance, the cause of which is not immediately to be assigned."

"But tell me, my dear Sir," pertinaciously continued the other, "was the man's death effected by the halter, or was it a species of euthanasia?"

"*Euthanasia,* Mr. Purser, is something like your will-power; I doubt its authenticity as a scientific term—begging your pardon again. It is at once imaginative and metaphysical; in short, Greek. But," abruptly changing his tone, "there is a case in the sick-bay which I do not care to leave to my assistants. Begging your pardon, but excuse me." And rising from the mess he formally withdrew.

CHAPTER XXIII

The silence at the moment of execution, and for a moment or two continuing thereafter (but emphasized by the regular wash of the sea against the hull, or the flutter of a sail caused by the helmsman's eyes being tempted astray), this emphasized silence was gradually disturbed by a sound not easily to be here verbally rendered. Whoever has heard the freshet-wave of a torrent suddenly swelled by pouring showers in tropical mountains, showers not shared by the plain; whoever has heard the first muffled murmur of its sloping advance through precipitous woods, may form some conception of the sound now heard. The seeming remoteness of its source was because of its murmurous indistinctness, since it came from close by, even from the men massed on the ship's open deck. Being inarticulate, it was dubious in significance further in that it seemed to indicate some capricious revulsion of thought or feeling such as mobs ashore are liable to —in the present instance possibly implying a sullen revocation on the men's part of their involuntary echoing of Billy's benediction. But ere the murmur had time to wax into clamour it was met by a strategic command, the more telling that it came with abrupt unexpectedness.

"Pipe down the starboard watch, Boatswain, and see that they go."

Shrill as the shriek of the sea-hawk the whistles of the Boatswain and his Mates pierced that ominous low sound, dissipating it; and yielding to the mechanism of discipline the throng was thinned by one half. For the remainder most of them were set to temporary employments connected with trimming the yards and so forth, business readily to be found upon occasion by any officer-of-the-deck.

Now each proceeding that follows a mortal sentence pronounced at sea by a drum-head court is characterized by a promptitude not perceptibly merging into hurry, though bordering that. The hammock—the one which had been Billy's bed when alive, having already been ballasted with shot and otherwise prepared to serve for his canvas coffin—the last offices of the sea-undertakers, the Sail-maker's Mates, were now speedily completed. When everything was in readiness, a second call for all hands, made necessary by the strategic movement before mentioned, was sounded: and now to witness burial.

The details of this closing formality it needs not to give. But when the tilted plank let slide its freight into the sea, a second strange human murmur was heard —blended now with another inarticulate sound proceeding from certain larger sea-fowl, whose attention having been attracted by the peculiar commotion in the water resulting from the heavy sloped dive of the shotted hammock into the sea, flew screaming to the spot. So near the hull did they come, that the stridor or bony creak of their gaunt double-jointed pinions was audible. As the ship under light airs passed on, leaving the burial spot astern, they still kept circling it low down with the moving shadow of their outstretched wings and the cracked requiem of their cries.

Upon sailors as superstitious as those of the age preceding ours—all men-of-war's men, too, who had just beheld the prodigy of repose in the form suspended in air and now foundering in the deeps; to such mariners the action of the sea-fowl, though dictated by a mere animal greed for prey, was big with no prosaic significance. An uncertain movement began among them, in which some encroachment was made. It was tolerated but for a moment. For suddenly the drum beat to quarters—which familiar sound, happening at least twice every day, had upon the present occasion some signal peremptoriness in it. True martial discipline long continued superinduces in an average man a sort of impulse of docility, whose operation at the official tone of command much resembles in its promptitude the effect of an instinct.

The drum-beat dissolved the multitude, distributing most of them along the batteries of the two covered gun-decks. There, as wont, the gun crews stood by their respective cannon erect and silent. In due course the First officer, sword under arm and standing in his place on the quarter-deck, formally received the successive reports of the sworded Lieutenants commanding the sections of batteries below; the last of which reports being made, the summed report he delivered with the customary salute to the Commander. All of this occupied time, which, in the present case, was the object of beating to quarters at an hour prior to the customary one. That such variance from usage was authorized by an officer like Captain Vere (a martinet as some deemed him), was evidence of the necessity for unusual action implied in what he deemed to be temporarily the mood of his men. "With mankind," he would say, "forms, measured forms, are everything; and that is the import couched in the story of Orpheus, with his lyre, spell-binding the wild denizens of the woods." And this he once applied to the disruption of forms going on across the Channel and the consequence thereof.

At this unwonted muster at quarters, all proceeded as at the regular hour. The band on the quarter-deck played a sacred air. After which the Chaplain went through with the customary morning service. That done, the drum beat the retreat, and toned by music and religious rites subserving the discipline and purpose of war, the men in their wonted, orderly manner dispersed to the places allotted them when not at the guns.

And now it was full day. The fleece of low-hanging vapour had vanished, licked up by the sun that late had so glorified it. And the circumambient air in the clearness of its serenity was like smooth white marble in the polished block not yet removed from the marble-dealer's yard.

Chapter XXIV

The symmetry of form attainable in pure fiction cannot so readily be achieved in a narration essentially having less to do with fable than with fact. Truth uncompromisingly told will always have its ragged edges; hence the conclusion of such a narration is apt to be less finished than an architectural finial.

How it fared with the Handsome Sailor during the year of the great mutiny has been faithfully given. But though properly the story ends with his life, something in way of a sequel will not be amiss. Three brief chapters will suffice.

In the general re-christening under the Directory of the craft originally forming the navy of the French Monarchy, the *St. Louis* line-of-battle ship was named the *Athéiste*. Such a name, like some other substituted ones in the Revolutionary fleet, while proclaiming the infidel audacity of the ruling power, was yet (though not so intended to be) the aptest name, if one consider it, ever given to a war-ship; far more so, indeed, than the *Devastation* or the *Eritus* (the Hell) and similar names bestowed upon fighting ships.

On the return passage to the full English fleet from the detached cruise during which occurred the events already recorded, the *Indomitable* fell in with the *Athéiste*. An engagement ensued; during which Captain Vere, in the act of putting his ship alongside the enemy with a view of throwing his boarders across the bulwarks, was hit by a musket-ball from a port-hole of the enemy's main cabin. More than disabled, he dropped to the deck and was carried below to the same cock-pit where some of his men already lay. The senior Lieutenant took command. Under him the enemy was finally captured, and though much crippled, was by rare good fortune successfully taken into Gibraltar, an English fort not very distant from the scene of the fight. There Captain Vere with the rest of the wounded was put ashore. He lingered for some days, but the end came. Unhappily he was cut off too early for the Nile and Trafalgar. The spirit that, in spite of its philosophic austerity, may yet have indulged in the most secret of all passions—ambition—never attained to the fulness of fame.

Not long before death, while lying under the influence of that magical drug which, in soothing the physical frame, mysteriously operates on the subtler element in man, he was heard to murmur words inexplicable to his attendant—"Billy Budd, Billy Budd." That these were not the accents of remorse, would seem clear from what the attendant said to the *Indomitable's* senior officer of marines, who, as the most reluctant to condemn of the members of the drum-head court, too well knew (though here he kept the knowledge to himself) who Billy Budd was.

Chapter XXV

Some few weeks after the execution, among other matters under the main head of *News from the Mediterranean,* there appeared in one naval chronicle of the time, an authorized weekly publication, an account of the affair. It was doubtless for the most part written in good faith, though the medium, partly rumour, through which the facts must have reached the writer, served to deflect and in part to falsify them. The account was as follows:—

"On the tenth of the last month a deplorable occurrence took place on board *H.M.S. Indomitable.* John Claggart, the ship's Master-at-arms, discovering that some sort of plot was incipient among an inferior section of the ship's company, and that the ringleader was one William Budd, he, Claggart, in the act of arraigning the man before the Captain was vindictively stabbed to the heart by the suddenly drawn sheath-knife of Budd.

"The deed and the implement employed sufficiently suggest that, though mustered into the service under an English name, the assassin was no Englishman but one of those aliens adopting English cognomen whom the present extraordinary necessities of the Service have caused to be admitted into it in considerable numbers.

"The enormity of the crime and the extreme depravity of the criminal, appear the greater in view of the character of the victim—a middle-aged man, respectable and discreet, belonging to that minor official grade, the petty-officers, upon whom, as none know better than the commissioned gentlemen, the efficiency of His Majesty's navy so largely depends. His function was a responsible one—at once onerous and thankless—and his fidelity in it the greater because of his strong patriotic impulse. In this instance, as in so many other instances in these days, the character of the unfortunate man signally refutes, if refutation were needed, that peevish saying attributed to the late Dr. Johnson, that patriotism is the last refuge of a scoundrel.

"The criminal paid the penalty of his crime. The promptitude of the punishment has proved salutary. Nothing amiss is now apprehended aboard the *H.M.S. Indomitable.*"

The above item, appearing in a publication now long ago superannuated and forgotten, is all that hitherto has stood in human record, to attest what manner of men respectively were John Claggart and Billy Budd.

Chapter XXVI

Everything is for a season remarkable in navies. Any tangible object associated with some striking incident of the service is converted into a monument. The spar from which the foretopman was suspended was for some few years kept trace of by the blue-jackets. Then knowledge followed it from ship to dock-yard, and again from dock-yard to ship, still pursuing it even when at last reduced to a mere dock-yard boom. To them a chip of it was as a piece of the Cross. Ignorant though they were of the real facts of the happening, and not thinking but that the penalty was unavoidably inflicted from the naval point of view, for all that they instinctively felt that Billy was a sort of man as incapable of mutiny as of wilful murder. They recalled the fresh young image of the Handsome Sailor, that face never deformed by a sneer or subtler vile freak of the heart within! This impression of him was doubtless deepened by the fact that he was gone, and in a measure mysteriously gone. On the gun-decks of the *Indomitable* the general estimate of his nature and its unconscious simplicity eventually found rude utterance from another foretopman, one of his own watch, gifted as some sailors are with an artless poetic temperament. Those tarry hands made some lines which, after circulating among the ship-board crew for a while, finally were rudely printed at Portsmouth as a ballad. The title given to it was the sailor's own:

BILLY IN THE DARBIES [37]

Good of the Chaplain to enter Lone Bay
And down on his marrow-bones here and
    pray
For the likes just o' me, Billy Budd.—But
    look:
Through the port comes the moon-shine
    astray!
It tips the guard's cutlass and silvers this
    nook;
But 'twill die in the dawning of Billy's
    last day.
A jewel-block they'll make of me to-mor-
    row,
Pendant pearl from the yard-arm-end
Like the ear-drop I gave to Bristol Molly—
O, 'tis me, not the sentence, they'll suspend.
Ay, Ay, all is up; and I must up too
Early in the morning, aloft from alow.
On an empty stomach, now, never it would
    do.
They'll give me a nibble—bit o' biscuit ere
    I go.
Sure, a messmate will reach me the last
    parting cup;
But, turning heads away from the hoist
    and the belay,
Heaven knows who will have the running
    of me up!

No pipe to those halyards—but aren't it
    all sham?
A blur's in my eyes, it is dreaming that
    I am.
A hatchet to my hawser? all adrift to
    go?
The drum roll to grog, and Billy never
    know?
But Donald he has promised to stand by
    the plank;
So I'll shake a friendly hand ere I sink.
But—no! It is dead then I'll be, come to
    think.—
I remember Taff the Welshman when he
    sank.
And his cheek it was like the budding pink.
But me, they'll lash me in hammock, drop
    me deep
Fathoms down, fathoms down, how I'll
    dream fast asleep.
I feel it stealing now. Sentry, are you
    there?
Just ease these darbies at the wrist.
And roll me over fair.
I am sleepy, and the oozy weeds about me
    twist.

---

[37] Handcuffs; also, fetters.

INDEX OF AUTHORS AND TITLES